D1384512

INSTRUCTOR'S EDITION

Fourth Edition

FINANCIAL ACCOUNTING

BELVERD E. NEEDLES, JR.

Ph.D., C.P.A., C.M.A.
Arthur Andersen & Co. Alumni
Distinguished Professor of Accounting
DePaul University

HOUGHTON MIFFLIN COMPANY BOSTON TORONTO
Dallas Geneva, Illinois Palo Alto Princeton, New Jersey

To my wife, Marian,
To my mother, Mrs. Belverd E. Needles, Sr., and
In memory of my father, Mr. Belverd E. Needles, Sr.,
and my grandparents, Mr. and Mrs. Benjamin E. Needles

Senior Sponsoring Editor: Donald Golini
Senior Development Editor: Jane Sherman
Senior Project Editor: Joanne Dauksewicz
Electronic Project Supervisor: John Robbins
Assistant Design Manager: Anthony Saizon
Production Coordinator: Renée Le Verrier
Manufacturing Specialist: Holly Schuster
Marketing Manager: Karen Natale

This book is written to provide accurate and authoritative information concerning the covered topics. It is not meant to take the place of professional advice.

Coin photograph by Keller/Peet Associates.

Printed in the U.S.A.

Library of Congress Catalog Card Number: 91-71970

Student Edition ISBN: 0-395-47301-2
Instructor's Edition ISBN: 0-395-59404-9

ABCDEFGHIJ-VH-954321

Contents
Instructor's Edition

Using the Text As a Teaching/Learning Tool

Financial Accounting, Fourth Edition, is written and designed to meet the teaching, learning, and student skill objectives for a first course in accounting. The learning objectives, figures, exhibits, and assignments provide a wealth of material that may be used to organize the course, structure classroom presentations, emphasize key concepts, and provide examples for use in class. The following examples highlight these elements and describe their function in the fourth edition.

Planning and Organizing the Course

For Instructors:
Learning objectives assist instructors in making reading assignments, and allow instructors to select specific topics to emphasize or cover in a chapter. They also provide teachers with the ability to select assignments based on content, level of difficulty, and desired student output.

> ***LEARNING OBJECTIVES***
>
> 1. *Describe the statement of cash flows, and define cash and cash equivalents.*
> 2. *State the principal purposes and uses of the statement of cash flows.*
> 3. *Identify the principal components of the classifications of cash flows, and state the significance of noncash investing and financing transactions.*
> 4. *Determine cash flows from operating activ-*
>
> **CHAPTER 14**
>
> The Statement of Cash Flows
>
> Earlier in this book you studied the balance sheet, the income statement, and the statement of stockholders' equity. In this chapter you will learn to prepare a fourth major financial statement, the statement of cash flows. After studying this chapter, you should be able to meet the learning objectives listed on the left.

Developing and Organizing Accounting Information

For Students:
Learning objectives support the text presentation and assignment material. They help students find material in the text, review chapter contents, and complete homework assignments.

> **Restrictions on Retained Earnings**
>
> *OBJECTIVE 4 Describe the disclosure of restrictions on retained earnings*
>
> A corporation may wish or be required to restrict all or a portion of retained earnings. A **restriction on retained earnings** means that dividends may be declared only to the extent of the *unrestricted* retained earnings. The following are several reasons why a corporation might do this:
>
> 1. *A contractual agreement.* For example, bond indentures may place a limitation on the dividends to be paid by the company.
> 2. *State law.* Many states will not allow dividends or the purchase of treasury stock if doing so impairs the legal capital of a company.
> 3. *Voluntary action by the board of directors.* Many times a board will decide to retain assets in the business for future needs. For example, the company may be planning to build a new plant and may wish to show that

Illustrations help students organize information and understand accounting relationships.

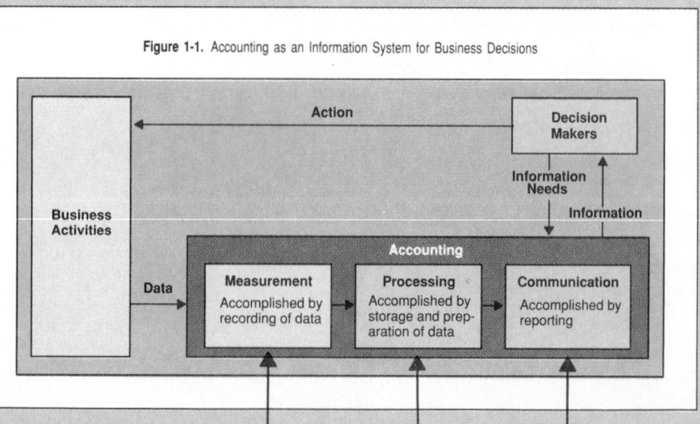

Figure 1-1. Accounting as an Information System for Business Decisions

Where pedagogically appropriate, the same colors are used in the illustrations as in the source documents (light red), working papers (light green), and financial statements (tan).

Recall and Comprehension

Important terms are defined in the text and restated in the end-of-chapter Review of Concepts and Terminology, which appears in the Chapter Review.

Nature of Bonds

OBJECTIVE 1 *Identify and contrast the major characteristics of bonds*

A **bond** is a security, usually long-term, representing money borrowed by a corporation from the investing public. (Other kinds of bonds are issued by the United States government, state and local governments, and foreign companies and countries to raise money.) Bonds must be repaid at a certain time and require periodic payments of interest. Interest is usually paid semiannually, or twice a year. Bonds must not be confused with stocks. Because stocks are shares of ownership, stockholders are owners. Bondholders, however, are creditors. Bonds are promises to repay the

Review of Concepts and Terminology

The following concepts and terms were introduced in this chapter:

(L.O. 1) **Bond:** A security, usually long-term, representing money borrowed by a corporation from the investing public.

(L.O. 1) **Bond certificate:** Evidence of a company's debt to the bondholder.

(L.O. 1) **Bond indenture:** A supplementary agreement to a bond issue that defines the rights, privileges, and limitations of bondholders.

(L.O. 1) **Bond issue:** The total number of bonds that are issued at one time.

(L.O. 6) **Callable bonds:** Bonds that a corporation may buy back and retire at a given

The extensive use of real-world data in many figures is key to student understanding of important concepts.

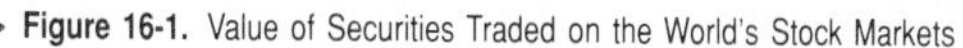

Figure 16-1. Value of Securities Traded on the World's Stock Markets

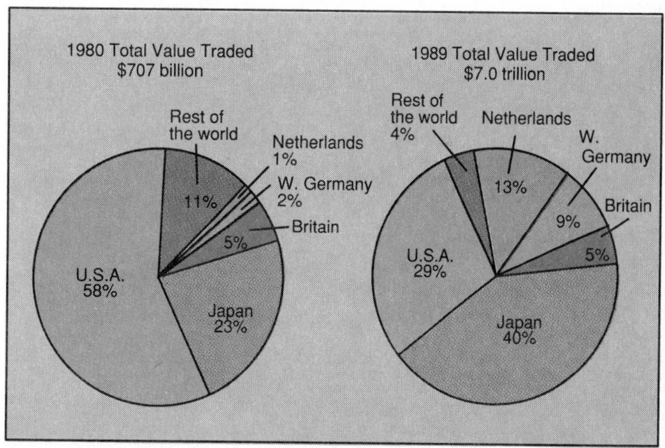

Source: Emerging Markets Fact Book (Washington, D.C.: International Finance Corporation, 1990).

Comprehensive Chapter Reviews help students remember the most important information in each chapter.

Chapter Review

Review of Learning Objectives

1. **Identify and contrast the major characteristics of bonds.** When bonds are issued, the corporation enters into a contract with the bondholders, called a bond indenture. The bond indenture identifies the major conditions of the bonds. A corporation may issue several types of bonds, each having different characteristics. For example, a bond issue may or may not require security (secured versus unsecured). It may be payable at a single time (term) or at several times (serial). The holder may receive interest automatically (registered) or may have to return coupons to receive interest (coupon bond). The bond may be callable or convertible into other

The Review Problem models important strategies and techniques for completing chapter problems.

Review Problem
Interest and Amortization of Bond Discount, Bond Retirement, and Bond Conversion

(L.O. 2, 4, 6) When the Merrill Manufacturing Company was expanding its metal window division in Utah, the company did not have enough capital to finance the expansion. Thus, management sought and received approval from the board of directors to issue bonds for the activity. The company planned to issue $5,000,000 of 8 percent, five-year bonds in 19x1. Interest would be paid on December 31 and June 30 of each year. The bonds would be callable at 104, and each $1,000 bond would be convertible into 30 shares of $10 par value common stock.

The bonds were sold at 96 on January 1, 19x1 because the market rate for similar investments was 9 percent. The company decided to amortize the bond discount by using the effective interest method. On July 1, 19x3, management called and retired half the bonds, and investors converted the other half into common stock.

Required

1. Prepare an interest and amortization schedule for the first five interest payment dates.

Applying Accounting Information

Working papers, including journals and ledgers, shown in green throughout the text, clearly depict the accounting process and teach students how to classify and evaluate information.

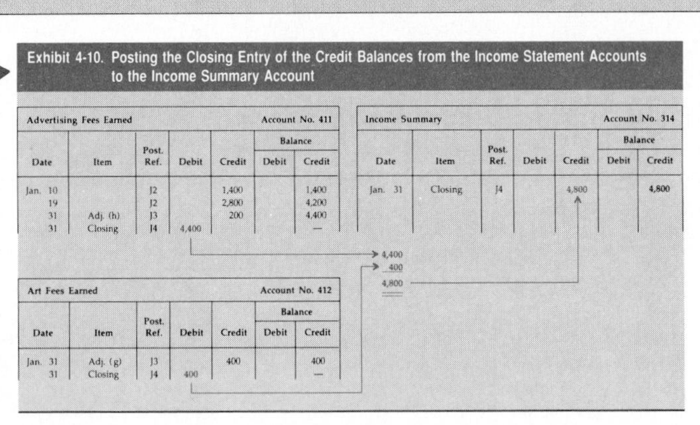

Exhibit 4-10. Posting the Closing Entry of the Credit Balances from the Income Statement Accounts to the Income Summary Account

Advertising Fees Earned — Account No. 411

Date	Item	Post. Ref.	Debit	Credit	Balance Debit	Balance Credit
Jan. 10		J2		1,400		1,400
19		J2		2,800		4,200
31	Adj. (h)	J3		200		4,400
31	Closing	J4	4,400			—

Art Fees Earned — Account No. 412

Date	Item	Post. Ref.	Debit	Credit	Balance Debit	Balance Credit
Jan. 31	Adj. (g)	J3		400		400
31	Closing	J4	400			—

4,400
400
4,800

Income Summary — Account No. 314

Date	Item	Post. Ref.	Debit	Credit	Balance Debit	Balance Credit
Jan. 31	Closing	J4		4,800		4,800

Applications used by real companies are stressed in the many illustrations throughout the text.

Figure 9-4. Depreciation Methods Used by 600 Large Companies

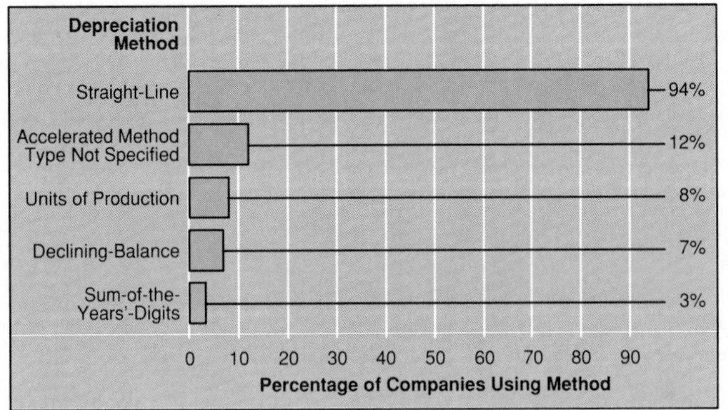

Total percentage exceeds 100 because some companies used different methods for different types of depreciable assets.

Source: American Institute of Certified Public Accountants, *Accounting Trends and Techniques* (New York: AICPA, 1990), p. 261

Differences among industries are obvious in a series of charts beginning in Chapter 6.

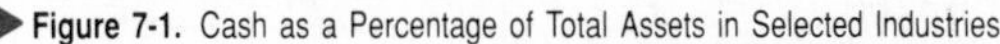

Figure 7-1. Cash as a Percentage of Total Assets in Selected Industries

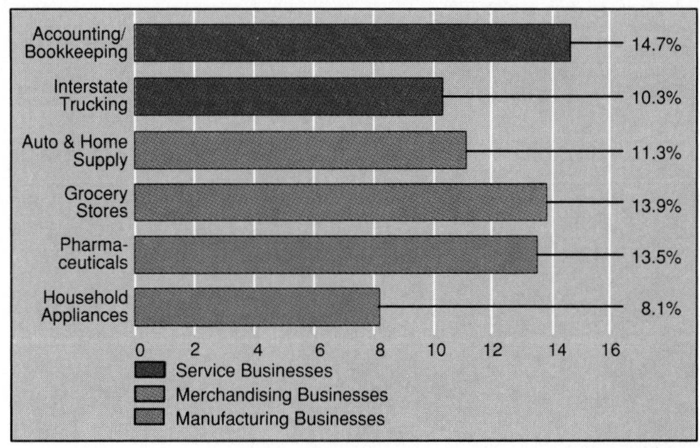

Source: Data from Dun and Bradstreet, *Industry Norms and Ratios*, 1990–91.

Analysis and Decision Making

Decision Points teach students how real companies use accounting information to make decisions that affect organizational success.

DECISION POINT
Marriott Corporation

Marriott Corporation is a world leader in lodging and contract services. The company's annual report provides an excellent picture of management's philosophy and performance. The company's balance sheet—like that of any company—shows, at a point in time, how management has invested the company's assets, and how those assets are financed by liabilities and stockholders' equity. The income statement shows how much the company earned on its assets during the year. The statement of stockholders' equity shows changes in the ownership of the business, including

Financial statements, shown in tan, help students see the statements' importance in the decision-making process.

Exhibit 6-1. Classified Balance Sheet for Shafer Auto Parts Corporation

Shafer Auto Parts Corporation
Balance Sheet
December 31, 19xx

Assets			
Current Assets			
Cash		$10,360	
Short-Term Investments		2,000	
Notes Receivable		8,000	
Accounts Receivable		35,300	
Merchandise Inventory		60,400	
Prepaid Insurance		6,600	
Store Supplies		1,060	
Office Supplies		636	
Total Current Assets			$124,356
Investments			
Land Held for Future Use			5,000
Property, Plant, and Equipment			
Land		$ 4,500	
Building	$20,650		
Less Accumulated Depreciation	8,640	12,010	
Delivery Equipment	$18,400		
Less Accumulated Depreciation	9,450	8,950	
Office Equipment	$ 8,600		
Less Accumulated Depreciation	5,000	3,600	
Total Property, Plant, and Equipment			29,060
Intangible Assets			
Trademark			500
Total Assets			$158,916

Assessing Student Progress

Each type of chapter assignment corresponds to a specific level of student knowledge and reinforces skills development on six different levels.

Recall and Comprehension:

Using the Discussion Questions and most of the Classroom Exercises in class ensures that students recall and understand basic concepts from the chapter.

> ## Chapter Assignments
>
> ### Discussion Questions
>
> 1. What is the difference between a bond certificate, a bond issue, and a bond indenture? What are some examples of items found in a bond indenture?
> 2. What are the essential differences between (a) secured versus debenture bonds, (b) term versus serial bonds, and (c) registered versus coupon bonds?
> 3. Napier Corporation sold $500,000 of 5 percent bonds on the interest payment date. What would the proceeds from the sale be if the bonds were issued at 95, at 100, and at 102?
> 4. If you were buying a bond on which the face interest rate was less than the market interest rate, would you expect to pay more or less than par value for the bonds? Why?
> 5. Why does the amortization of a bond discount increase interest expense to an amount greater than interest paid? Why does a premium have the opposite effect?
> 6. When the effective interest rate method of amortizing a bond discount or premium is used, why does the amount of interest expense change from

Communication Skills:

Communication Skills Exercises address real accounting issues and are based on real companies. Students learn to organize and evaluate information while they expand their ability to communicate accounting information and perform basic research tasks.

> ### Communication Skills Exercises
>
> **Communication 11-1. Bond Interest Rates and Market Prices** *(L.O. 1)*
>
> *RJR Nabisco*'s debt restructuring was the subject of the decision point that appeared at the beginning of this chapter. The following statement relates to this plan:
>
> The refinancing plan's chief objective is to purge away most of the reset bonds of 2007 and 2009. These bonds have proved to be an immense headache for RJR. . . . That's because the bonds' interest rate must be reset so that they trade at full face value. The bonds had sunk to a deep discount earlier this year, raising the prospect that RJR might have to accept a painfully high reset rate of 20% or more to meet its reset obligations.[9]
>
> What is a "deep discount," and what causes bonds to sell at a deep discount? Who loses when they do? What does "the bonds' interest rate must be reset so that they trade at full value" mean? Why would this provision in the covenant be "an immense headache" to RJR Nabisco?
>
> **Communication 14-3. Basic Research Skills** *(L.O. 7)*
>
> In your library, select the annual reports of three corporations. You may choose them from the same industry or at random, at the direction of your instructor. (If you did a related exercise in a previous chapter, use the same three companies.) Prepare a table with a column for each corporation. Then, for any year covered by the statement of cash flows, answer the following questions: Does the company use the direct or the indirect approach? Is net income more or less than net cash flows from operating activities? What are the major causes of differences between net income and net cash flows from operating activities? Compare net cash flows from operating activities to dividends paid. Does the dividend appear secure? Did the company make signifi-

Application Skills:

Classroom Exercises give students a brief experience in applying accounting information and procedures and prepare students for the problems.

> ### Classroom Exercises
>
> **Exercise 14-1. Classification of Cash Flow Transactions** *(L.O. 3)*
>
> Horizon Corporation engaged in the following transactions. Identify each as (1) an operating activity, (2) an investing activity, (3) a financing activity, (4) a noncash transaction, or (5) none of the above.
>
> a. Declared and paid a cash dividend.
> b. Purchased an investment.
> c. Received cash from customers.
> d. Paid interest.
> e. Sold equipment at a loss.
> f. Issued long-term bonds for plant assets.
> g. Received dividends on securities held.
> h. Issued common stock.
> i. Declared and issued a stock dividend.
> j. Repaid notes payable.
> k. Paid employees for wages.
> l. Purchased a sixty-day Treasury bill.
> m. Purchased land.
>
> **Exercise 14-2. Cash Receipts from Sales** *(L.O. 4a)*
>
> During 19x2, Union Chemical Company, a distributor of farm fertilizers and herbicides, had sales of $6,500,000. The ending balances of Accounts Receivable were $850,000 in 19x1 and $1,200,000 in 19x2. Calculate cash receipts from sales in 19x2.

Analysis and Decision-making Skills:

Interpretation Cases from Business give students experience in analyzing published financial information.

Interpretation Cases from Business

ICB 14-2.
Airborne Freight Corporation[8]
(L.O. 7)

Airborne Freight Corporation, which is known as Airborne Express, is an air express transportation company, providing next-day, morning delivery of small packages and documents throughout the United States. Airborne Express is one of three major participants, along with Federal Express and United Parcel Service, in the air express industry. The following statement appears in "Management's discussion and analysis of results of operations and financial condition" from the company's 1990 annual report: "Capital expenditures and financing associated with those expenditures continued to be the primary factor affecting the financial condition of the company." The company's statements of cash flows for 1990, 1989, and 1988 are presented below.

Extensions of the Application Skills

A matched set of A and B Problems requires students to perform basic accounting procedures. They are graduated in difficulty from easier to more complex.

Problem Set A

Problem 14A-4.
The Statement of Cash Flows—Direct Method
(L.O. 6a, 7)

Meridian Corporation's 19x2 income statement and its comparative balance sheets as of December 31, 19x2 and 19x1 appear as follows:

Meridian Corporation
Income Statement
For the Year Ended December 31, 19x2

Sales		$804,500
Cost of Goods Sold		563,900
Gross Margin from Sales		$240,600
Operating Expenses (including Depreciation Expense of $23,400)		224,700
Income from Operations		$ 15,900
Other Income (Expenses)		
Gain on Disposal of Furniture and Fixtures	$ 3,500	
Interest Expense	(11,600)	(8,100)
Income Before Income Taxes		$ 7,800
Income Taxes		2,300
Net Income		$ 5,500

Financial Decision Cases give students the opportunity to extend chapter content and make decision analyses.

Financial Decision Cases

9-1.
Hyde Computer Company
(L.O. 4)

The Hyde Computer Company manufactures computers for sale or rent. On January 2, 19x1, the company completed the manufacture of a computer for a total cost of $190,000. A customer leased the computer on the same day for a five-year period at a monthly rental of $5,000. Although the computer will last longer than five years, it is likely but not certain that it will be technologically obsolete by the end of the five-year period. Hyde's management estimates that if the computer is obsolete, it can be sold for $20,000 at the end of the lease, and if it is not obsolete, it can be sold for $40,000 because it would probably last for another two years. On the basis of its experience in leasing many computers, management estimates that the expenses associated with the lease of this computer will be as follows:

	Insurance and Property Taxes	Repairs and Maintenance
19x1	$7,000	$3,000
19x2	6,400	4,500
19x3	5,800	6,000
19x4	5,200	7,500
19x5	4,600	9,000

Required

1. What estimated useful life and estimated residual value do you recommend that Hyde use for the computer? Explain.
2. Prepare two schedules that show for each year the lease revenue, expenses, and income before income taxes. Also, show on each schedule for each year the carrying value of the computer at the end of the year, and compute the ratio of income before income taxes to carrying value (return on assets). Round components to one decimal place. The first schedule should compute depreciation using the straight-line method, and the second schedule should use the sum-of-the-years'-digits method.
3. Compare the two schedules in **2**, and discuss the results. Which of the methods do you feel produces the most realistic pattern of income before taxes, and why?

1 Accounting as an Information System

Learning Objectives Chart

Learning Objectives	Questions	Exercises	Cases	A & B Problems	New Concepts and Terminology
1. Define *accounting* and describe its role in making informed decisions.	1, 2, 3	CSE 1, CSE 5 Ex. 1	ICB 1		accounting, bookkeeping, computer, control, evaluation, management information system (MIS), planning
2. Identify the many users of accounting information in society.	4, 5, 6, 7	CSE 2, CSE 5 Ex. 1	ICB 1		liquidity, management, profitability
3. Distinguish between financial and management accounting, define generally accepted accounting principles (GAAP), and identify the organizations that influence GAAP.	8, 9, 10, 11	CSE 1, CSE 15			American Institute of Certified Public Accountants (AICPA), audit, certified public accountant (CPA), financial accounting, Financial Accounting Standards Board (FASB), generally accepted accounting principles, (GAAP), Governmental Accounting Standards Board (GASB), independence, Internal Revenue Service (IRS), management accounting, Securities and Exchange Commission (SEC)
4. Explain the importance of business transactions, money measure, and separate entity to accounting measurement.	12	Ex. 2, Ex. 3			business transactions, exchange rate, money measure, separate entity
5. Describe the corporate form of business organization.	13, 14				articles of incorporation, audit committee, corporation, management partnership, share of stock, sole proprietorship
6. Define *financial position* and show how it is affected by simple transactions.	15, 16, 17, 18	CSE 4 Ex. 4, Ex. 5, Ex. 6, Ex. 7, Ex. 8, Ex. 9	ICB 2, ICB 3 FDC 1	1, 2, 3, 5	accounting equation, accounts, assets, contributed capital, dividends, equity, expenses, financial position, liabilities, net assets, net income (loss), owners' equity, retained earnings, revenues, stockholders' equity
7. Identify the four basic financial statements.	19, 20, 21, 22	CSE 8 Ex. 9, Ex. 10, Ex. 11, Ex. 12, Ex. 13, Ex. 14, Ex. 15	FDC 1	4, 5	balance sheet, financial statements, income statement, statement of cash flows, statement of retained earnings
8. Describe accounting as a profession with ethical responsibilities and a wide career choice.	23, 24, 25, 26, 27, 28				attest function, certified internal auditor (CIA), certified management accountant (CMA), due care, ethics, independence, integrity, management accounting, management advisory services, objectivity, professional ethics, public accounting, tax services

Teaching Strategies

1. Begin with the AICPA's modern definition of accounting.
2. Set up an example of a business decision to be made. Refer to Figure 1.2 to discuss the steps in making a business decision.
3. Point out the differences in business organization between a sole proprietorship, a partnership, and a corporation. Use Table 1.1 to illustrate the concepts of separate legal entities and separate accounting entities.
4. Stress the importance of understanding the exact effect of each transaction on the components of the balance sheet.

Suggested Readings from the Study Guide

Gary John Previts, "The Accountant in Our History: A Bicentennial Overview," *Journal of Accountancy*

Larry L. Axline, "The Bottom Line on Ethics," *Journal of Accountancy*

Text Examples and Illustrations

Real Company Examples

Decision Point	Financial goals of a corporation	Gerber Products Company
Table 1-1	Partial listing of foreign exchange rates	
Fig. 1-4	Number and receipts of U.S. proprietorships, partnerships, and corporations	
Decision Point	Organizing as a corporation	Santini Tours Company*
p. 33	Management accountants who become company officers	American Airlines (AMR Corp.), General Foods, and others
Table 1-2	Large international CPA firms	
CSE 1-2	Users of accounting information	Commonwealth Power Company
CSE 1-4	Concept of an asset	Foote, Cone & Belding
ICB 1-1	Public utility rate increase	Newark, New Jersey Public Service Electric & Gas Co.
ICB 1-2	Evaluation of annual report	Merrill Lynch & Co., Inc.
ICB 1-3	Financial statements, evaluation	Ponderosa, Inc.

Professional Ethics Issues

CSE 1-3	Ethical choices

International Business Issues

Table 1-1	Partial listing of foreign exchange rates
Ex. 1-3	Money measure

*Indicates the real company has been disguised.

2 Measuring and Recording Business Transactions

Learning Objectives Chart

Learning Objectives	Questions	Exercises	Cases	A & B Problems	New Concepts and Terminology
1. Explain in simple terms the generally accepted ways of solving the measurement issues of recognition, valuation, and classification.	1, 2, 3, 4, 5	CSE 1, CSE 2, CSE 3 Ex. 1, Ex. 3	ICB 2 FDC 1		classification, cost, cost principle, recognition, recognition point, valuation
2. Define and use the terms *account* and *general ledger*.	6, 20				account, chart of accounts, general ledger, ledger
3. Recognize commonly used asset, liability, and stockholders' equity accounts.	14, 23	Ex. 2	ICB 1 FDC 1, FDC 2		
4. Define *double-entry system* and state the rules for debit and credit.	7, 8, 9, 10, 11, 12, 15, 20, 23	CSE 4 Ex. 2	FDC 2		balance (account balance), credit, debit, double-entry system, footing, T account
5. Apply the procedure for transaction analysis to simple transactions.	13	CSE 4 Ex. 4, Ex. 5, Ex. 7, Ex. 8, Ex. 9	ICB 1, ICB 3 FDC 1	1, 2, 3, 4	
6. Record transactions in the general journal.	15, 18, 20	Ex. 11	FDC 2	2, 3, 4, 5	compound entry, general journal, journal, journal entry, journalizing, ledger account form
7. Explain the relationship of the general journal to the general ledger.	15, 19, 20, 21, 22	Ex. 10, Ex. 11		5	posting
8. Prepare a trial balance and recognize its value and limitations.	15, 16, 17	Ex. 2, Ex. 6, Ex. 12, Ex. 13, Ex. 14, Ex. 15	FDC 1	1, 2, 3, 4, 5	normal balance, trial balance

Teaching Strategies

1. Discuss different ways to approach the recognition, valuation, and classification issues. The text example illustrates that the recognition problem is not always easily solved; the valuation text example illustrates exceptions to the historical cost principle.
2. Tell students to think of debit and credit as being directions, with debit meaning left and credit meaning right.
3. Discuss the process called posting.

Suggested Readings from the Study Guide

Lee Berton, "Some Computer Software Makers' Earnings Likely to Slide: Blame it on the Accountants," *Wall Street Journal*

Jill Andresky, "Setting the Date," *Forbes*

Text Examples and Illustrations

Real Company Examples

Decision Point	Measuring and recording business transactions	UAL Corporation, The Boeing Company
Decision Point	Improper recording practices	American Collegiate Sales
CSE 2-1	Communication valuation issues	Foxboro Company
CSE 2-2	Recognition point issues	Paramount Communications
CSE 2-3	Recognition point, ethics issues	Penn Office Supplies Corporation*
ICB 2-1	Transaction analysis	First Chicago Corporation
ICB 2-2	Recognition, valuation, classification issues	Stauffer Chemical Company
ICB 2-3	Transaction analysis	Yellow Freight System, Inc.
FDC 2-2	General journal entries	Shelley Corporation*

Professional Ethics Issues

Decision Point	Improper recording practices	
CSE 2-3	Recognition point, ethical issues	Penn Office Supplies Corp.*

*Indicates the real company has been disguised.

3 Business Income and Adjusting Entries

Learning Objectives Chart

Learning Objectives	Questions	Exercises	Cases	A & B Problems	New Concepts and Terminology
1. Define *net income* and its two major components, *revenues* and *expenses*.	1, 2, 3		ICB 2 FDC 1		expenses, net income, net loss, permanent (real) accounts, profit, revenues, temporary (nominal) accounts
2. Explain the difficulties of income measurement caused by (a) the accounting period issue, (b) the continuity issue, and (c) the matching issue.	4, 5, 6, 18	CSE 1, CSE 2, CSE 4	ICB 1, ICB 3		accounting period issue, cash basis of accounting, continuity issue, fiscal year, going concern (continuity), matching rule, periodicity
3. Define *accrual accounting* and explain two broad ways of accomplishing it.	7, 8	CSE 1, CSE 2, CSE 3, CSE 4 Ex.1	ICB 3	5	accrual accounting, revenue recognition
4. State the four principal situations that require adjusting entries.	9, 10, 11	CSE 1, CSE 2, CSE 3, CSE 4, CSE 5, Ex. 1			accrual, adjusting entries, deferral
5. Prepare typical adjusting entries.	12, 13, 14, 15, 16, 17, 19, 20	Ex. 2, Ex. 3, Ex. 4, Ex. 5, Ex. 6, Ex. 7, Ex. 8, Ex. 9, Ex. 10, Ex. 11, Ex. 12, Ex. 13, Ex. 14, Ex. 15	ICB 1, ICB 2 FDC 1, FDC 2	1, 2, 3, 4, 5	accrued expenses, accumulated depreciation, carrying value, contra account, depreciation (depreciation expense), prepaid expenses, unearned revenues, unrecorded (accrued) revenues
6. Prepare financial statements from an adjusted trial balance.	21		FDC 2	3, 4, 5	adjusted trial balance
7. State all the steps in the accounting cycle.	23	Ex. 11	FDC 2		accounting system (accounting cycle)

Teaching Strategies

1. Explain and discuss accruals by drawing on students' personal experiences.
2. Discuss how schedules, tables, and other supporting information that may be kept with accounting records are used.

Suggested Reading from the Study Guide

Laura Jereski, "Soft Numbers," *Forbes*

Text Examples and Illustrations

Real Company Examples

Decision Point	Accrual accounting and the matching rule	Never Flake, Inc.*
CSE 3-1	Account identification	Takashimaya Company, Ltd.
CSE 3-2	Importance of adjustments	Central Appliance Service Co., Inc.*
CSE 3-3	Accrual accounting	Lyric Opera of Chicago
CSE 3-4	Nature of depreciation	Exxon Corporation
ICB 3-1	Matching rules, adjusting entries	Orion Pictures Corporation
ICB 3-2	Adjusting entries	Sperry & Hutchinson Co., Inc.
ICB 3-3	Income measurement	The City of Chicago

International Business Issues

CSE 3-1	Account identification	Takashimaya Company, Ltd.

*Indicates the real company has been disguised.

4 Completing the Accounting Cycle

Learning Objectives Chart

Learning Objectives	Questions	Exercises	Cases	A & B Problems	New Concepts and Terminology
1. Prepare a work sheet.	1, 2, 3, 5, 6, 7, 8, 9, 10	CSE 1 Ex. 1, Ex. 5		2, 3, 4, 5	crossfooting, working papers, work sheet
2. Identify the three principal uses of a work sheet.		CSE 1			
3. Prepare financial statements from a work sheet.		CSE 1, CSE 3 Ex. 2, Ex. 6	ICB 2 FDC 1	1, 2, 3, 4, 5	
4. Record the adjusting entries from a work sheet.	4, 12, 13	CSE 1, CSE 2, CSE 3 Ex. 3, Ex. 6	ICB 1, ICB 2	2, 3, 4, 5	
5. Explain the purposes of closing entries.	11, 13, 14	CSE 1, CSE 2, CSE 3	ICB 1		closing entries, income summary
6. Prepare the required closing entries.	15	CSE 1, CSE 3		1, 2, 3, 4	
7. Prepare the post-closing trial balance.	16, 17	CSE 1, CSE 3		4	post-closing trial balance
8. Prepare reversing entries as appropriate.	18, 19	CSE 1, CSE 2, CSE 3 Ex. 3, Ex. 7		1, 2, 3	reversing entry

Teaching Strategies

1. Show students that adjustment columns are a preliminary "scratch sheet" for organizing adjustment entries in the general journal. Confirm that the work sheet is a "working paper," not a formal statement.
2. Emphasize that the information for closing entries has been organized on the work sheet. Refer to illustrations in the text that present closing entries.
3. Point out that the income summary is an account used only at the end of a period when closing entries are made.

Suggested Reading from the Study Guide

George H. Sorter, "Accounting for Baseball," *Journal of Accountancy*

Text Examples and Illustrations

Real Company Examples

Decision Point	Interim financial statements	Maintenance Management, Inc.*
CSE 4-1	Interim financial statements	Ocean Oil Services Corp.*
CSE 4-2	Accounting efficiency	Way Heaters, Inc.*
ICB 4-1	Adjusting and closing entries	H&R Block, Inc.
ICB 4-2	Closing entries	Halliburton Company

*Indicates the real company has been disguised.

5 Accounting for Merchandising Operations

Learning Objectives Chart

Learning Objectives	Questions	Exercises	Cases	A & B Problems	New Concepts and Terminology
1. Compare the income statements for service and merchandising concerns.	1, 2, 3	CSE 1	ICB 1, ICB 2		cost of goods sold, gross margin from sales (gross profit), income before income taxes, net income, operating expenses, operating income (income from operations), revenues from sales
2. Record transactions involving revenues for merchandising concerns.	6, 7, 8, 9, 10	Ex. 1, Ex. 2, Ex. 3, Ex. 5		1, 2	gross sales; net sales; sales discounts; sales returns and allowances; trade discounts; 2/10, n/30
3. Calculate cost of goods sold.	4, 5	Ex. 2, Ex. 3, Ex. 4	FDC 1		goods available for sale, merchandise inventory
4. Record transactions involving purchases of merchandise.	11, 12, 13, 14, 15	Ex. 3, Ex. 5, Ex. 6, Ex. 7		2	FOB destination, FOB shipping point, freight in (transportation in), gross method, net method, net purchases, purchases, purchases discounts, purchases returns and allowances
5. Differentiate the perpetual inventory system from the periodic inventory system.	16, 17, 18, 19	CSE 2			beginning inventory, ending inventory, periodic inventory system, perpetual inventory system, taking a physical inventory
6. Prepare a worksheet statement for a merchandising concern.		CSE 1 Ex. 8, Ex. 9	ICB 2	3, 5, 6	
7. Explain the objectives of handling merchandise inventory at the end of the accounting period and how they are achieved.			ICB 3		
8. Prepare a work sheet and adjusting and closing entries for a merchandising concern.	20	Ex. 10, Ex. 11		5, 6	
9. Define *internal control* and identify the three elements of the internal control structure, including seven examples of control procedures.	21, 22, 23, 24, 27	CSE 3, CSE 4 Ex. 12, Ex. 13, Ex. 14, Ex. 15		4	
10. Describe the inherent limitations of internal control.	25		FDC 2	4	accounting system, bonding, control environment, control procedures, internal control, internal control structure
11. Apply control procedures to certain merchandising transactions.	26	Ex. 16	FDC 2		check, check authorization, invoice, purchase order, purchase requisition, receiving report

Teaching Strategies

1. Identify the flow of information and calculations for cost of goods sold on an income statement.
2. Explain the merchandising firm's sales as a revenue category.
3. Illustrate how the sales revenue account is used only for sales of merchandise.
4. Explain that the purchases account is used only for purposes of merchandise for resale. Purchases of any other assets are recorded in the corresponding asset account.
5. Emphasize that under the periodic system, it is necessary to calculate the cost of goods sold because no record of the inventory sold is maintained. Students should understand the formula for cost of goods sold.
6. Explain how the auditor needs to evaluate a business's internal control to determine how extensive the testing of accounting records should be.

Suggested Reading from the Study Guide

Julie L. Nicklin, "Many Colleges Learn the Hard Way That They Are Vulnerable to Embezzlement by Employees and Need Strict Procedures," *The Chronicle of Higher Education*

Text Examples and Illustrations

Real Company Examples

Decision Point	Merchandising operations	Target Stores
Decision Point (pt. 1)	Perpetual inventory system	High Country, Inc.*
Decision Point (pt. 2)	Internal control structure	High Country, Inc.*
CSE 5-1	Merchandising income statement	Village TV*, TV Warehouse*
CSE 5-2	Periodic vs. perpetual inventory system	The Book Nook*
CSE 5-3	Basic control procedures	The Book Nook*
ICB 5-1	Income statements	Wal-Mart Stores, Inc.; Kmart Corp.
ICB 5-2	Merchandise inventory	Best Products, Inc.
ICB 5-3	Adjusting, closing entries	J. Walter Thompson Co.

*Indicates the real company has been disguised.

6 Accounting Concepts and Classified Financial Statements

Learning Objectives Chart

Learning Objectives	Questions	Exercises	Cases	A & B Problems	New Concepts and Terminology
1. State the objectives of financial reporting.	1	Ex. 2			general-purpose external financial statements
2. State the qualitative characteristics of accounting information, and describe their interrelationships.	2	Ex. 2			qualitative characteristics, relevance, reliability
3. Define and describe the use of the conventions of *comparability* and *consistency, materiality, conservatism, full disclosure*, and *cost-benefit*.	3	CSE 1, CSE 2 Ex. 1, Ex. 2		1	comparability, conservatism, consistency, cost-benefit, full disclosure, materiality
4. Summarize the concepts underlying financial accounting and their relationship to ethical financial reporting.	4	CSE 3, CSE 4 Ex. 2			fraudulent financial reporting
5. Identify and describe the basic components of a classified balance sheet.	5, 6, 7, 8, 9, 10, 11, 12, 13	Ex. 3, Ex. 5	ICB 1, ICB 4	3, 5	classified financial statements; current assets; current liabilities; intangible assets; investments; long-term liabilities; other assets; property, plant, and equipment
6. Prepare the multistep and single-step types of classified income statements.	14, 15, 21, 22	Ex. 4, Ex. 6, Ex. 7	ICB 1, ICB 3	2, 5	condensed financial statements, earnings per share (net income per share, net earnings per share), income from operations, income taxes (income taxes expense, provision for income taxes), multistep form, other revenues and expenses, single-step form
7. Use classified financial statements for the simple evaluation of liquidity and profitability.	16, 17, 18, 19, 20	CSE 5 Ex. 8, Ex. 9, Ex. 10, Ex. 11, Ex. 12	ICB 1, ICB 2, ICB 3, ICB 4 FDC 1, FDC 2	4, 5	asset turnover, current ratio, debt to equity ratio, liquidity, profitability, profit margin, return on assets, return on equity, working capital
8. Identify the major components of a corporate annual report.	23, 24	CSE 5	ICB 1		accountants' (auditors') report, annual report, comparative financial statements, consolidated (financial statements), earnings per share (net income per share, net earnings per share), income taxes, (income taxes expense, provision for income taxes), interim financial statements, notes to the financial statements, opinion section, scope section, summary of significant accounting policies

Teaching Strategies

1. Discuss the concept of estimation of amounts on financial statements using depreciation as an example. The term depreciation should be defined at this time; methods will be described later.
2. Students enjoy the discussion on ethics, especially anecdotes on fraud.
3. Annual reports are effective teaching aids for this chapter.

Suggested Readings from the Study Guide

M. Frank Barton and L. Mason Rockwell, "Who's Responsible For The Content of Financial Statements?" *Management Accounting*

"How Do CFO's Evaluate the Annual Report?" *FE; the magazine for financial executives*

Barbara Donnelly, "Wiping Away Cosmetics in Corporate Earnings Reports," *Wall Street Journal*

Coca Cola Company's *Annual Report* (in the back of the Study Guide)

Text Examples and Illustrations

Real Company Examples

Decision Point	Accounting concepts and classified financial statements	The Gap, Inc.
Fig. 6-4	Average current ratio	Dun and Bradstreet, survey of selected industries
Fig. 6-5	Average profit margin, asset turnover, and return on assets	Dun and Bradstreet, survey of selected industries
Fig. 6-6	Average debt to equity	Dun and Bradstreet, survey of selected industries
Fig. 6-7	Average return on equity	Dun and Bradstreet, survey of selected industries
pp. 356–66	Study of annual report	Toys "R" Us, Inc.
Fig. 6-8	Financial highlights	Toys "R" Us, Inc.
Fig. 6-9	Statements of consolidated earnings	Toys "R" Us, Inc.
Fig. 6-10	Consolidated balance sheets	Toys "R" Us, Inc.
Fig. 6-11	Statements of consolidated cash flows	Toys "R" Us, Inc.
Fig. 6-12	Auditors' report	Toys "R" Us, Inc.
CSE 6-1	Materiality	Mackey Electronics*
CSE 6-2	Accounting conventions	Mason Parking*
CSE 6-3	Ethics and financial reporting	Salem Software*
CSE 6-4	Ethics and financial reporting	Treon Microsystems, Inc.*
ICB 6-1	Classified financial statement	Toys "R" Us, Inc.
ICB 6-2	Ratio analysis: liquidity, profitability	Albertson's, Inc.; A & P; and American Stores Company
ICB 6-3	Income statement, ratio analysis	Toys "R" Us, Inc.
ICB 6-4	Classified balance sheet, ratio analysis	Wellcome plc

Professional Ethics Issues

Ex. 6-1	Accounting concepts and conventions	
CSE 6-3	Ethics and financial reporting	Salem Software*
CSE 6-4	Ethics and financial reporting	Treon Microsystems, Inc.*

International Business Issues

ICB 6-4	Classified balance sheet, ratio analysis	Wellcome plc

7 Short-Term Liquid Assets

Learning Objectives Chart

Learning Objectives	Questions	Exercises	Cases	A & B Problems	New Concepts and Terminology
1. Account for cash and short-term investments.	1, 2	CSE 1, CSE 4 Ex. 1, Ex. 2	ICB 3 FDC 1, FDC 2		cash, cash equivalent, compensating balance, short-term investments (marketable accounts), short-term liquid assets
2. Define *accounts receivable*, and explain its relationships among credit policies, sales, and uncollectible accounts.	3, 4, 5, 6, 7, 8, 11	CSE 2	ICB 2, ICB 3 FDC 2		accounts receivable, allowance for uncollectible accounts, trade credit, uncollectible accounts
3. Apply the allowance method of accounting for uncollectible accounts, including using the percentage of net sales method and the accounts receivable aging method to estimate uncollectible accounts.	9, 10, 12	Ex. 3, Ex. 4, Ex. 5, Ex. 6, Ex. 7	ICB 1, ICB 2	1, 2	accounts receivable aging method, aging of accounts receivable, controlling (or control) account, percentage of net sales method, subsidiary ledger
4. Identify methods of financing accounts receivable and other issues related to accounts receivable.	13, 14, 15	CSE 3 Ex. 8			direct charge-off method, factor, factoring, installment accounts receivable
5. Define and describe a *promissory note*, and make calculations involving promissory notes.	16, 17, 18, 19	Ex. 9, Ex. 10	ICB 2	3, 4, 5	discount, duration of note, interest, maturity date, maturity value, notes payable, notes receivable, proceeds from discounting, promissory note
6. Journalize entries involving notes receivable.		CSE 3 Ex. 11, Ex. 12, Ex. 13		3, 4, 5	contingent liability, dishonored note, notice of protest, protest fee
7. Demonstrate control of cash by preparing a bank reconciliation.	20, 21	Ex. 14, Ex. 15, Ex. 16		6, 7	book reconciliation, book statement
8. Demonstrate the use of a simple imprest system.	22, 23, 24	Ex. 17, Ex. 18			imprest system, petty cash fund, petty cash voucher

Teaching Strategies

1. Distinguish between short-term and long-term marketable securities, and explain that the definition and category for each investment are determined by the company's intentions.
2. Discuss government securities to help students understand marketable securities.
3. To clarify how credit policies fit into the overall accounting system, discuss students' experience with credit policies of companies with which they have dealt.
4. Refer to the text illustration to explain the use of an uncollectible account to more accurately present the value of Accounts Receivable.

Suggested Readings from the Study Guide

Alan G. Seidner, "Investing excess corporate cash," *Financial Executive*

Current Asset Section, Coca Cola Company's *Annual Report* (in the back of the Study Guide)

Text Examples and Illustrations

Real Company Examples

Decision Point	Short-term liquid assets	Bell Atlantic Corporation
Fig. 7-1	Cash as a percentage of total assets	Dun and Bradstreet, survey of large corporations
p. 396	Credit sales to customers	Sears, Roebuck and Co.
Fig. 7-2	Accounts receivable as a percentage of total assets	Dun and Bradstreet, survey of large corporations
Decision Point	Sale of receivables	Fleetwood Enterprises, Inc.
p. 406	Financial companies owned by large corporations	Ford Motor Credit Company and others
p. 407	Installment accounts receivable	J. C. Penney, Sears, Roebuck
p. 407	Credit card sales	VISA, MasterCard, American Express
Decision Point	Sale of notes receivable from affiliates	Marriott Corporation
CSE 7-1	Management of cash	University Publishing Company*
CSE 7-2	Role of credit sales	Mitsubishi Corporation
CSE 7-3	Asset financing	Siegel Appliances, Inc.*
ICB 7-1	Accounting for uncollectible accounts	Winton Sharrer Company*
ICB 7-2	Consumer and commercial loans	AmeriBank*
ICB 7-3	Accounts receivable	Chrysler Corporation

International Business Issues

CSE 7-1	Role of credit sales	Mitsubishi Corporation

*Indicates the real company has been disguised.

8 Inventories

Learning Objectives Chart

Learning Objectives	Questions	Exercises	Cases	A & B Problems	New Concepts and Terminology
1. Define *merchandise inventory*, and show how inventory measurement affects income determination.	1, 2, 3, 4, 5	CSE 1 Ex. 1	ICB 1		consignment, merchandise inventory
2. Define *inventory cost*, and relate it to goods flow and cost flow.	6	CSE 4	ICB 2		cost flow, goods flow, inventory cost
3. Calculate the pricing of inventory, using the cost basis according to the (a) specific identification method; (b) average-cost method; (c) first-in, first-out (FIFO) method; (d) last-in, first-out (LIFO) method.	9, 10, 11	Ex. 2, Ex. 3, Ex. 5, Ex. 6, Ex. 8, Ex. 9	FDC 1	1, 3, 4	average-cost method; first-in, first-out (FIFO) method; last-in, first-out (LIFO) method; specific identification method
4. State the effects of each method on income determination and income taxes in periods of changing prices.	7, 8, 16	CSE 2 Ex. 4, Ex. 5, Ex. 8	ICB 2, ICB 3 FDC 1, FDC 2		LIFO liquidation
5. Apply the perpetual inventory system to accounting for inventories and cost of goods sold.	12, 13, 19	CSE 3, CSE 4 Ex. 6, Ex. 7, Ex. 9		4	periodic inventory system, perpetual inventory system
6. Apply the lower-of-cost-or-market rule to inventory valuation.	14, 15	Ex. 10		2	item-by-item method, lower-of-cost-or-market (LCM) rule, major category method, market, total inventory method
7. Estimate the cost of ending inventory using (a) the retail inventory method and (b) the gross profit method.	17, 18, 19	Ex. 11, Ex. 12		5, 6	gross profit method, retail method

Teaching Strategies

1. Refer to examples 1, 2, and 3 to explain that mistakes in inventory do self-correct, as long as the next inventory valuation is done without error.
2. A discussion of LIFO is the most effective means for distinguishing the flow of goods from the flow of costs. Compare details between FIFO and LIFO.
3. Point out that the perpetual inventory system is not a substitute for making a physical count of inventory.

Suggested Readings from the Study Guide

Stuart Weiss, "How Inventories Could Bury 1985 Computer Profits", *Business Week*

Inventories and related notes, Coca Cola Company's *Annual Report* (in the back of the Study Guide)

Text Examples and Illustrations

Real Company Examples

Decision Point (pt. 1)	Inventory measurement	Amoco Corporation
Fig. 8-1	Inventory as a percentage of total assets	Dun and Bradstreet, survey of selected industries
Fig. 8-2	Inventory cost methods used by 600 large corporations	American Institute of Certified Public Accountants, survey
Decision Point (pt. 2)	Methods of pricing inventory	Amoco Corporation
CSE 8-1	Inventories, income determination, ethics	Flare, Inc.*
CSE 8-2	LIFO inventory method	paper and electronic equipment industries
CSE 8-3	Periodic vs. perpetual inventory systems	The Foot Joint, Inc.*
ICB 8-1	Inventory measurement	Crazy Eddie, Inc.
ICB 8-2	Inventory cost and goods flow	Hershey Foods Corporation
ICB 8-3	Income determination and income taxes	General Motors Corporation

Professional Ethics Issues

CSE 8-1	Inventories, income determination, ethics	Flare, Inc.*
ICB 8-1	Inventory measurement	Crazy Eddie, Inc.

*Indicates the real company has been disguised.

9 Long-Term Assets: Acquisition and Depreciation

Learning Objectives Chart

Learning Objectives	Questions	Exercises	Cases	A & B Problems	New Concepts and Terminology
1. Describe the nature, types, and problems of long-term assets.	1, 2, 3, 4		ICB 3		amortization, depletion, depreciation, fixed assets, intangible assets, long-term assets, natural resources, tangible assets
2. Account for the cost of property, plant, and equipment.	5, 6, 7	Ex. 1, Ex. 2, Ex. 3		1, 4	
3. Define *depreciation*, state the factors that affect its computation, and show how to record it.	8, 9, 10, 11, 12	CSE 1 Ex. 2, Ex. 4		1, 2, 4	depreciable cost, estimated useful life, obsolescence, physical deterioration, residual value (salvage value, disposal value)
4. Compute periodic depreciation under (a) the straight-line method, (b) the production method, and (c) accelerated methods, including (1) the sum-of-the-years'-digits method and (2) the declining-balance method.	13, 14, 15	CSE 2 Ex. 2, Ex. 4, Ex. 5, Ex. 6, Ex. 7, Ex. 8	FDC 1, FDC 2	1, 2, 3, 4	accelerated methods, declining-balance method, double-declining-balance method, production method, straight-line method, sum-of-the-years'-digits method
5. Apply depreciation methods to problems of partial years, revised rates, items of low unit cost, groups of similar items, and accelerated cost recovery.	16, 17, 18, 19, 20	CSE 3 Ex. 5, Ex. 7, Ex. 8, Ex. 9	ICB 1	1, 3, 4	Accelerated Cost Recovery System (ACRS), group depreciation, Modified Accelerated Cost Recovery System (MACRS), Tax Reform Act of 1986
6. Apply the matching rule to the allocation of expired costs for capital expenditures and revenue expenditures.	21, 22, 23, 24	Ex. 10, Ex. 11		5	additions, betterments, capital expenditure, expenditure, extraordinary repairs, ordinary repairs, revenue expenditure
7. Account for disposal of depreciable assets not involving exchanges.	25	CSE 5 Ex. 12, Ex. 13, Ex. 14	ICB 2	5, 6	
8. Account for disposal of depreciable assets involving exchanges.	26, 27	Ex. 12, Ex. 13, Ex. 14	FDC 2	6	
9. Identify natural resource accounting issues and compute depletion.	28, 29	CSE 4 Ex. 15, Ex. 16			depletion, full-costing, successful efforts accounting, wasting assets
10. Apply the matching rule to intangible asset accounting issues.	30, 31, 32, 33, 34, 35	CSE 4 Ex. 17	FDC 3	7	copyright, franchise, goodwill, leasehold, leasehold improvement, license, patent, trademark

Teaching Strategies

1. Use references to deterioration, obsolescence, and the allocation of costs under the matching rule. These concepts become more complex as students are required to apply the underlying principles. Stress the understanding of the relationship between cost and expense categories.
2. Stress that depreciation and valuation are not the same.
3. Define *capital expenditures*. Review the concept of materiality and the matching rule.
4. Begin a demonstration in which the same asset, with corresponding accumulated depreciation, is disposed of by each of the possible disposal methods.

Suggested Readings from the Study Guide

Penelope Wang, "High Dudgeon in the Ivory Tower," *Forbes*

Subrata N. Chakravarty and Rita Koselka, "When Does Life Really Begin?" *Forbes*

Dana Wechsler, "Earnings Helper," *Forbes*

Property, Plant, and Equipment section and related notes, Coca Cola Company's *Annual Report* (in the back of the Study Guide)

Text Examples and Illustrations

Real Company Examples

Decision Point	Long-term assets: acquisition and depreciation	H. J. Heinz Company
Fig. 9-1	Long-term assets as a percentage of total assets	Dun and Bradstreet, survey of selected industries
p. 510	Group depreciation and plant assets	Survey of large firms from the *National Public Accountant*
Decision Point Fig. 9-4	Choice of depreciation methods and income taxes	American Institute of Certified Public Accountants, survey of 600 large companies
CSE 9-1	Depreciation and amortization and estimated useful lives	General Motors Corporation
CSE 9-2	Choice of depreciation methods	Ford Motor Company
CSE 9-3	Depreciation method and income taxes	The Goodyear Tire & Rubber Company
CSE 9-4	Trademarks	The Quaker Oats Company
ICB 9-1	Depreciation method and income taxes	Century Steelworks Company*
ICB 9-2	Disposal of depreciable assets not involving exchanges	Pan American World Airways, Inc.
ICB 9-3	Accounting for long-term assets	Ocean Drilling & Exploration Company (ODECO)

*Indicates the real company has been disguised.

10 Current Liabilities and the Time Value of Money

Learning Objectives Chart

Learning Objectives	Questions	Exercises	Cases	A & B Problems	New Concepts and Terminology
1. Explain how the issues of recognition, valuation, and classification apply to liabilities.	1, 2, 3, 4, 5, 6		ICB 1 FDC 1		current liabilities, financial instruments, off-balance-sheet liabilities, liabilities, long-term liabilities
2. Identify, compute, and record definitely determinable and estimated current liabilities.	7, 8, 9, 10, 11, 12, 13, 14	CSE 1, CSE 2, CSE 3 Ex. 1, Ex. 2, Ex. 3, Ex. 4, Ex. 5, Ex. 6	ICB 1 FDC 1	1, 2, 3, 4, 5	commercial paper, definitely determinable liabilities, estimated liabilities, line of credit, unearned or deferred revenues
3. Define a *contingent liability*.	15, 16		ICB 2		contingent liability
4. Distinguish simple from compound interest.	17	CSE 5			compound interest, interest, simple interest, future value, ordinary annuity, present value
5. Use compound interest tables to compute the future value of a single invested sum at compound interest and of an ordinary annuity.	19	Ex. 7, Ex. 8, Ex. 10, Ex. 11, Ex. 12, Ex. 13, Ex. 18		6	
6. Use compound interest tables to compute the present value of a single sum due in the future and of an ordinary annuity.	18, 20	Ex. 9, Ex. 14, Ex. 15	ICB 3 FDC 2	5, 6	
7. Apply the concept of present value to simple accounting situations.	21	CSE 4 Ex. 16, Ex. 17, Ex. 19, Ex. 20, Ex. 21, Ex. 22	FDC 2	6	

Teaching Strategies

1. Remind students of the definition of a *liability* and the definition of *current period.* This will be helpful in defining the *classification of liabilities.*
2. Point out the difficulty in determining when an obligation occurs while discussing the recognition of liabilities.
3. Explain the difference between definitely determinable accounts and estimated accounts while discussing the valuation of liabilities.

Suggested Readings from the Study Guide

Current Liabilities and related notes, Coca Cola Company's *Annual Report* (in the back of the Study Guide)

Text Examples and Illustrations

Real Company Examples

Decision Point	Current liabilities	USAir Group, Inc.
Fig. 10-1	Current liabilities as a percentage of total assets	Dun and Bradstreet, survey of selected industries
p. 471	Contingent liabilities	Humana, Inc.
Decision Point	Projection of annual cash flows	Safety-Net Corporation*
CSE 10-1	Identification of current liabilities	several businesses
CSE 10-2	Identification of current liabilities	Stanhome, Inc.
CSE 10-3	Estimated liabilities	American South Airways*
CSE 10-4	Renegotiation of contracts	The St. Louis Browns*
ICB 10-1	Definitely determinable and estimated current liabilities	Trans World Airlines, Inc.
ICB 10-2	Contingent liabilities	Texaco, Inc.
ICB 10-3	Present value calculations	Internal Revenue Service

*Indicates the real company has been disguised.

11 Long-Term Liabilities

Learning Objectives Chart

Learning Objectives	Questions	Exercises	Cases	A & B Problems	New Concepts and Terminology
1. Identify and contrast the major characteristics of bonds.	1, 2	CSE 1			bond, bond certificate, bond indenture, bond issue, coupon bonds, junk bonds, registered bonds, secured bonds, serial bonds, term bonds, unsecured bonds (debentures)
2. Record the issuance of bonds at face value and at a discount or premium.	3, 4	CSE 2, CSE 5 Ex. 1, Ex. 2, Ex. 3, Ex. 4, Ex. 10, Ex. 12	ICB 1, ICB 2 FDC 1, FDC 2	1, 2, 3, 4, 5, 6	discount, face interest rate, market interest rate, premium
3. Determine the value of bonds using present values.		Ex. 6, Ex. 7, Ex. 8, Ex. 9	ICB 2		
4. Amortize (a) bond discounts and (b) bond premiums by using the straight-line and effective interest methods.	5, 6	Ex. 1, Ex. 2, Ex. 3, Ex. 4, Ex. 5, Ex. 12	ICB 1, ICB 2 FDC 2	1, 2, 3, 4, 5, 6	effective interest method, effective rate, straight-line method, zero coupon bonds
5. Account for bonds issued between interest dates and make year-end adjustments.	7	Ex. 10, Ex. 11, Ex. 12		1, 2, 3, 4, 6	
6. Account for the retirement of bonds and the conversion of bonds into stock.	8, 9	Ex. 9, Ex. 13, Ex. 14	ICB 3	5, 6	callable bonds, convertible bonds, early extinguishment of debt
7. Explain the basic features of mortgages payable, installment notes payable, long-term leases, pensions, and postretirement benefits as long-term liabilities.	10, 11, 12, 13, 14	CSE 3, CSE 4 Ex. 9, Ex. 15, Ex. 16, Ex. 17, Ex. 18	FDC 2	4	capital lease installment notes payable, mortgage, operating lease, other postretirement benefits, pension fund, pension plan

Teaching Strategies

1. Review the features of bonds with the students. Then have students contrast each of the features with the corresponding features of common stock.
2. Show how the effective interest method of amortization is comparable to declining-balance depreciation.
3. Review the way corporations pay interest to whoever owns the bonds on the payment date and why they do it.
4. Compare the retirement of bonds to the sale of a long-term asset with accumulated depreciation.

Suggested Readings from the Study Guide

Christopher Farrell, Leah Nathans, and Leslie Helm, "Bondholders are mad as hell—and they're not going to take it anymore," *Business Week*

Long-Term debt, Deferred income taxes, and related notes, Coca Cola Company's *Annual Report* (in the back of the Study Guide)

Text Examples and Illustrations

Real Company Examples

Decision Point	Long-term liabilities	RJR Nabisco
Fig. 11-1	Average long-term debt as a percentage of total assets	Dun and Bradstreet, survey of selected industries
Decision Point	Issuance of convertible bonds	Inco Limited
p. 537	Deferred pension plan costs	The Goodyear Tire & Rubber Company
p. 538	Postretirement benefits	IBM Corporation
CSE 11-1	Bond interest rates and market prices	RJR Nabisco
CSE 11-2	Convertible bonds	Sumitomo Corporation
CSE 11-3	Lease financing	Federal Express Corporation
CSE 11-4	Effects of taxes on business decisions	Midstates Financial Corporation
ICB 11-1	Interest expense for long-term notes issues	The Times Mirror Company
ICB 11-2	Issuance of bonds	Franklin Savings Association
ICB 11-3	Operating leases, capital leases	UAL Corporation
FDC 11-1	Issuance of bonds	J. C. Penney Company, Inc.

International Business Issues

CSE 11-2	Convertible bonds	Sumitomo Corporation

12 Contributed Capital

Learning Objectives Chart

Learning Objectives	Questions	Exercises	Cases	A & B Problems	New Concepts and Terminology
1. Define a *corporation* and state the advantages and disadvantages of the corporate form of business.	1, 2, 3, 4, 5	CSE 1, CSE 2			articles of incorporation, audit committee, corporation, double taxation, proxy, share of stock
2. Account for organization costs.	6, 7	Ex. 1		1, 4, 5	organization costs
3. Identify the components of stockholders' equity.	8	Ex. 2, Ex. 3, Ex. 4	ICB 1, ICB 3 FDC 1	1, 2, 4, 5	authorized stock, common stock, issued stock, legal capital, outstanding stock, par value, residual equity, stock certificate
4. Account for cash dividends.	10, 11	Ex. 5, Ex. 6	ICB 2	1, 4, 5	dividend, ex-dividend, liquidating dividend, preferred stock
5. Calculate the division of dividends between common and preferred stockholders.	13, 14	CSE 4 Ex. 2, Ex. 7, Ex. 8	ICB 2	3	callable preferred stock, convertible preferred stock, cumulative stock, dividends in arrears, noncumulative
6. Account for the issuance of common and preferred stock for cash and other assets.	9, 15	CSE 2, CSE 3, CSE 4 Ex. 3, Ex. 9, Ex. 10, Ex. 11, Ex. 12	ICB 1, ICB 3	1, 2, 4, 5	no-par stock, stated value
7. Account for stock subscriptions.	12	Ex. 13		2, 4, 5	stock subscription
8. Account for the exercise of stock options.	16	CSE 4 Ex. 14, Ex. 15	ICB 3, ICB 4	5	stock option plan

Teaching Strategies

1. Write "Advantages" and "Disadvantages" on the board, and ask the students to give examples of each for corporations.
2. Explain preferred stock as stock that has preference over common stock in some way; also note that preferred stock has no voting rights.
3. Explain what a stock subscription is, and compare it to "lay-away" at a retail store. Emphasize that Subscriptions Receivable is a current asset and that Stock Subscribed is an equity account.

Suggested Readings from the Study Guide

"It Can Pay Off to Turn Common into Preferred," *Business Week*

Stockholders' Equity Section and related notes, Coca Cola Company's *Annual Report* (in the back of the Study Guide)

Text Examples and Illustrations

Real Company Examples

Decision Point	Contributed capital	Gensia Pharmaceuticals, Inc.
Fig. 12-1	Sources of capital raised by corporations in the U.S.	Data from *Securities Industry Handbook*
Decision Point	Preferred stock issues	J. C. Penney Company, Inc.
CSE 12-1	The corporate form of business and ethical issues for accounting	The accounting profession
CSE 12-2	Reasons for stock issue	UAL Corporation
CSE 12-3	Omission of preferred dividend	Tucson Electric Company
ICB 12-1	Journal entries, stockholders' equity	UAL Corporation
ICB 12-2	Cash dividends and common stockholders	Navistar International Corporation
ICB 12-3	Callable, convertible, cumulative preferred stock outstanding	Navistar International Corporation
ICB 12-4	Exercise of stock options	The Limited, Inc.

Professional Ethics Issues

CSE 12-1	The corporate form of business and ethical issues for accounting	The accounting profession

13 Retained Earnings and Corporate Income Statements

Learning Objectives Chart

Learning Objectives	Questions	Exercises	Cases	A & B Problems	New Concepts and Terminology
1. Define *retained earnings*, and prepare a statement of retained earnings.	1, 2, 3	Ex. 1		3, 5	deficit, prior period adjustments, retained earnings
2. Account for stock dividends and stock splits.	4, 5	CSE 1, CSE 4 Ex. 2, Ex. 3, Ex. 4, Ex. 5	ICB 4 FDC 2	2, 3, 5	stock dividend, stock split
3. Account for treasury stock transactions.	7	CSE 2, CSE 4 Ex. 6	ICB 4 FDC 2	1, 2, 5	treasury stock
4. Describe the disclosure of restrictions on retained earnings.	6	Ex. 8	ICB 2	3, 5	restriction on retained earnings
5. Prepare a statement of stockholders' equity.	8	CSE 4 Ex. 9		2, 3, 5	statement of stockholders' equity
6. Calculate book value per share, and distinguish it from market value.	9	CSE 4 Ex. 10	FDC 2		book value, market value
7. Prepare a corporate income statement.		CSE 3, CSE 4 Ex. 7, Ex. 11, Ex. 15	ICB 1, ICB 3 FDC 1	4	comprehensive income
8. Show the relationships among income taxes expense, deferred income taxes, and net of taxes.	10, 11	CSE 4 Ex. 12, Ex. 13, Ex. 15	FDC 1	4	deferred income taxes, income tax allocation, net of taxes
9. Describe the disclosure on the income statement of discontinued operations, extraordinary items, and accounting changes.	12, 14	CSE 3, CSE 4 Ex. 15	ICB 1 FDC 1	4	cumulative effect of an accounting change, discontinued operations, extraordinary items
10. Compute earnings per share.	13, 15, 16	Ex. 14, Ex. 15		4	common stock equivalents, complex capital structure, fully diluted earnings per share, potentially dilutive securities, primary earnings per share, simple capital structure

Teaching Strategies

1. Begin the discussion of stock dividends by asking students to compare and contrast cash dividends and stock dividends; ask the students what a stock split is and why it is done, and refer to the illustration in the text to show the memo entry and the "before" and "after" effect.
2. Explain what treasury stock is and why a company purchases its own stock. Then refer to paragraph 3 in the Chapter Review for a summary of journal entries.
3. Ask students to name as many values of common stock as they can: par value, stated value, book value, market value.
4. Use Exhibit 13-3 to introduce the income statement. Exhibit 13-3 can be used for the rest of the objectives in this chapter.

Suggested Readings from the Study Guide

Subrata N. Chakravarty, "Unreal Accounting," *Forbes*

Ben Weberman, "Rumpelstilzchen Accounting," *Forbes*

Consolidated Statement of Stockholders' Equity, Coca Cola Company's *Annual Report* (in the back of the Study Guide)

Text Examples and Illustrations

Real Company Examples

Decision Point	Retained earnings and corporate income statements	International Business Machines Corporation (IBM)
Decision Point	Corporate earnings reports	Eastman Kodak Company
CSE 13-1	Motivation for stock dividends	Athey Products Corporation
CSE 13-2	Purpose of treasury stock	Atlantic Richfield Company
CSE 13-3	Interpretation of earnings reports	McDonnell Douglas Corporation
ICB 13-1	Interpretation of earnings reports	Lockheed Corporation
ICB 13-2	Disclosure of restrictions on retained earnings	Jackson Electronics, Inc.*
ICB 13-3	Corporate income statement	Sara Lee Corporation
ICB 13-4	Stock dividends, stock splits, treasury stock transactions	Ford Motor Company

*Indicates the real company has been disguised.

14 The Statement of Cash Flows

Learning Objectives Chart

Learning Objectives	Questions	Exercises	Cases	A & B Problems	New Concepts and Terminology
1. Describe the statement of cash flows and define *cash* and *cash equivalents*.	1, 2				Cash, cash equivalents, statement of cash flows
2. State the principal purposes and uses of the statement of cash flows.	3, 4				
3. Identify the principal components of the classifications of cash flows, and state the significance of noncash investing and financing transactions.	5, 6	CSE 1 Ex. 1		1	financing activities, investing activities, noncash investing and financing transactions, operating activities
4. Determine cash flows from operating activities using the (a) direct and (b) indirect methods.	7, 8, 9, 10, 11, 12	Ex. 2, Ex. 3, Ex. 4, Ex. 5, Ex. 6, Ex. 7, Ex. 8, Ex. 9, Ex. 10		2, 3	direct method, indirect method
5. Determine cash flows from (a) investing activities and (b) financing activities.	13	Ex. 11, Ex. 12, Ex. 13			
6. Prepare a statement of cash flows using the (a) direct and (b) indirect methods.	14	Ex. 14, Ex. 15	ICB 1 FDC 1, FDC 2	4, 5, 6	
7. Interpret the statement of cash flows.		CSE 2, CSE 3	ICB 1, ICB 2 FDC 1, FDC 2	4, 6	
8. Prepare a work sheet for the statement of cash flows.	15	Ex. 15		5, 6	

Teaching Strategies

1. List the primary and secondary purposes of the statement of cash flows. Ask students to suggest a list of management uses as well as investors' and creditors' uses.
2. Use part 2 of the solution to the review problem as an illustration of a statement of cash flows. Distinguish between cash equivalents and short-term investments/marketable securities.
3. While teaching each formula and component of the statement of cash flows, stress the reason why a formula is the way it is. Students will attempt to memorize formulas rather than learning the underlying substance.

Suggested Readings from the Study Guide

Jeffrey M. Laderman, "The Savviest Investors Are Going With the Flow," *Business Week*

Tatiana Pouschine, "Now You See It. . . ," *Forbes*

Consolidated Statements of Cash Flows, Coca Cola Company's *Annual Report* (in the back of the Study Guide)

Text Examples and Illustrations

Real Company Examples

Decision Point	Statement of cash flows	Marriott Corporation
Decision Point	The direct and indirect methods of determining cash flows from operating activities	American Institute of Public Accountants, survey of 600 large companies
CSE 14-1	Direct vs. indirect method of determining cash flows	United States Surgical Corporation
CSE 14-2	Definitions and interpretations of cash flows	Tandy Corporation
ICB 14-1	Statement of cash flows	National Communications, Inc.
ICB 14-2	Statement of cash flows	Airborne Express, Inc.

15 Financial Statement Analysis

Learning Objectives Chart

Learning Objectives	Questions	Exercises	Cases	A & B Problems	New Concepts and Terminology
1. Describe and discuss the objectives of financial statement analysis.	1, 2				financial statement analysis, portfolio
2. Describe and discuss the standards for financial statement analysis.	3, 4	CSE 1	FDC 2		diversified companies (conglomerates)
3. State the sources of information for financial statement analysis.	5	CSE 4			interim financial statements
4. Identify the issues related to the evaluation of the quality of a company's earnings.		CSE 2 Ex. 1, Ex. 2	ICB 1 FDC 1	1	
5. Apply horizontal analysis, trend analysis, and vertical analysis to financial statements.	6, 7, 8	CSE 3 Ex. 3, Ex. 4, Ex. 5	FDC 2	2	base year, common-size statement, horizontal analysis, index number, trend analysis, vertical analysis
6. Apply ratio analysis to financial statements in the study of an enterprise's liquidity, profitability, long-term solvency, and market tests.	9, 10, 11, 12, 13, 14, 15, 16, 17	CSE 3 Ex. 2, Ex. 6, Ex. 7, Ex. 8, Ex. 9, Ex. 10	ICB 2, ICB 3	1, 3, 4, 5	asset turnover, average days' sales uncollected, beta (β), current ratio, debt to equity ratio, dividends yield, earnings per share, interest coverage ratio, inventory turnover, leverage, market risk, price/earnings (P/E) ratio, profit margin, quick ratio, ratio analysis, receivable turnover, return on assets, return on equity

Teaching Strategies

1. Distribute copies of a financial statement of a local company to each student in the class, and ask them what they would look at if they were thinking of buying the stock or bonds of the corporation.
2. Use paragraph 6 in the chapter review to discuss each of the ratios. Simplify the chore of memorizing the ratios by pointing out the following:
   The liquidity ratios involve only current balance sheet accounts; there are three turnover ratios, and the only reason the asset turnover ratio is not a liquidity ratio is that it includes noncurrent balance sheet accounts; all the "return on" ratios have net income as the numerator; profit margin may be thought of as "return on" sales.

Suggested Readings from the Study Guide

Holly A. Clemente, "What Wall Street sees when it looks at your P/E ratio," *Financial Executive*

Charles H. Gibson, "How Industry Perceives Financial Ratios," *Management Accounting*

Financial Statements and notes, Coca Cola Company's *Annual Report* (in the back of the Study Guide)

Text Examples and Illustrations

Real Company Examples

Decision Point	Financial statement analysis	Moody's Investors Service
Exhibit 15-1	Segment information	Eastman Kodak Company
Decision Point	Effect of diversification on financial performance	Eastman Kodak Company
Exhibit 15-2	Comparative balance sheets with horizontal analysis	Eastman Kodak Company
Exhibit 15-3	Comparative income statements with horizontal analysis	Eastman Kodak Company
Exhibit 15-4	Trend analysis	Eastman Kodak Company
Fig. 15-1	Trend analysis presented graphically	Eastman Kodak Company
Fig. 15-2	Common-size balance sheets presented graphically	Eastman Kodak Company
Fig. 15-3	Common-size income statements presented graphically	Eastman Kodak Company
Exhibit 15-5	Common-size balance sheets	Eastman Kodak Company
Exhibit 15-6	Common-size income statements	Eastman Kodak Company
p. 817	Market risk or beta (β)	U. S. Steel, Bethlehem Steel, and other companies
CSE 15-1	Communication standards for financial analysis	Helene Curtis
CSE 15-2	Quality of earnings	International Business Machines Corporation (IBM)
CSE 15-3	Financial analysis and interpretation	Businessland, Inc.
ICB 15-1	Quality of earnings	The Walt Disney Company
ICB 15-2	Ratio analysis	Ford Motor Company

16 International Accounting and Intercompany Investments

Learning Objectives Chart

Learning Objectives	Questions	Exercises	Cases	A & B Problems	New Concepts and Terminology
1. Define *exchange rate* and record transactions that are affected by changes in foreign exchange rates.	1, 2	CSE 1, CSE 2, CSE 4 Ex. 1, Ex. 2		1	exchange gains or losses, exchange rate, multinational (transnational) corporation
2. Describe the restatement of a foreign subsidiary's financial statements in U.S. dollars.	3, 4				functional currency, reporting currency, restatement
3. Describe progress toward international accounting standards.	5		ICB 1		
4. Apply the cost method and the equity method to the appropriate situations in accounting for long-term investments.	6, 7, 8, 11	CSE 3 Ex. 3, Ex. 4, Ex. 5, Ex. 6	FDC 1	2, 3	consolidated financial statements, control, cost method, equity method, parent company, significant influence, subsidiary
5. Explain when to prepare consolidated financial statements and describe their uses.	9, 10, 12	CSE 3 Ex. 3	FDC 2	5	eliminations, purchase method
6. Prepare consolidated balance sheets at acquisition date for purchase at (a) book value and (b) other than book value.	13, 14, 15, 16	Ex. 7, Ex. 8, Ex. 9, Ex. 10	ICB 2, ICB 3		
7. Prepare consolidated income statements for intercompany transactions.	17	Ex. 11		4, 5	goodwill (goodwill from consolidation), minority interest

Teaching Strategies

1. After explaining the need for international accounting standards for what is becoming a global economy, show and discuss the following:

   The Accountants International Study Group, 1986—Surveys and reports

   International Accounting Standards Committee (IASC), 1973—Develop/adopt balanced, relevant, comparable accounting principles and financial statement presentations.

   International Federation of Accountants (IFAC), 1977—Develop guidelines for auditing, ethics, education, and management accounting.

   Ask students to state the situations where the cost, equity, and consolidation methods are used and ask them to discuss why different methods are necessary.

2. Compare and contrast the cost and equity methods by using a table similar to the following:

Event	**Effect**	
	Cost Method	**Equity Method**

Acquiring the asset	Long-Term Investment
	  Cash
		Investment in (?)
		  Cash

Receiving dividends	Cash
	  Dividend Income
		Cash
		  Investment in (?)

Investee profits	No entry	Investment in (?) Income, (?) Investment
Investee losses	No entry	Investment in (?) Income, (?) Investment
Adjusting entry	Allowance account Unrealized Loss	No entry
	or	
	Unrealized Loss Allowance account	No entry

In the above entries, (?) refers to the name of the company whose stock we own.

Suggested Readings from the Study Guide

Roger K. Doost and Karen M. Ligon, "How U. S. and European Accounting Practices Differ," *Management Accounting*

Valuing Global Securities, *Arthur Andersen*

Dana Wechsler, "Mishmash Accounting," *Forbes*

Investments in Affiliates, and related notes, Coca Cola Company's *Annual Report* (in the back of the Study Guide)

Text Examples and Illustrations

Real Company Examples

Decision Point (pt. 1)	Hostile takeovers of U.S. firms by foreign companies	Schneider S.A., Square Deal Company
Table 16-1	Extent of foreign business	selected companies
Fig. 16-1	Value of securities traded on the world's stock markets	
Table 16-1	Partial listing of foreign exchange rates	
Decision Point (pt. 2)	Hostile takeover of U.S. firm	Schneider S.A., Square Deal Company
CSE 16-1	Effect of change in exchange rates	Compagnie Générale des Establissements Michelin
CSE 16-2	Effects of changes in exchange rates	Japan Air Lines
CSE 16-3	Effects of accounting treatments of long-term investments	Masco Corporation
ICB 16-1	Progress toward international accounting standards	Maxwell Communications Corporation plc
ICB 16-2	Consolidated balance sheets	General Electric Company, RCA Corporation
ICB 16-3	Consolidated balance sheets	U. S. Steel Corporation, Marathon Oil Company
FDC 16-2	Consolidated balance sheets, consolidated income statements	Metropolitan Stores Corporation*

*Fictitious companies based on information gained from real companies

International Business Issues

Decision Point (pt. 1)	Hostile takeover of a U.S. firm by a foreign company	Schneider S.A., Square Deal Company
Table 16-1	Extent of foreign business	selected companies
Fig. 16-1	Value of securities traded on the world's stock markets	
Table 16-1	Partial listing of foreign exchange rates	
Decision Point (pt. 2)	Hostile takeover of a U.S. firm by a foreign company	Schneider S.A., Square Deal Company
CSE 16-1	Effect of change in exchange rates	Compagnie Générale des Establissements Michelin
CSE 16-2	Effects of change in exchange rates	Japan Air Lines
Ex. 16-1	Recording international transactions	States Corporation**
Ex. 16-2	Recording international transactions	U.S. Corporation**
Prob. 16A-1	Recording international transactions	Tsin Import/Export Company**
Prob. 16B-1	Recording international transactions	Mountain States Company**
ICB 16-1	Progress toward international accounting standards	Maxwell Communications Corporation plc

**fictitious companies

A Accounting for Unincorporated Businesses

Learning Objectives Chart

Learning Objectives	Questions	Exercises	Problems	New Concepts and Terminology
1. Record the basic transactions affecting the owner's equity of a sole proprietorship.	1	1		sole proprietorship
2. Identify the major characteristics of a partnership.	2, 3, 4			partnership, partnership agreement, limited life, mutual agency, unlimited liability, limited partnership
3. Identify the advantages and disadvantages of a partnership, and compare it to other forms of business.	6, 7			
4. Record investments of cash and of other assets by the partners in forming a partnership.		2	1	partners' equity
5. Compute the profit or loss that partners share, based on a stated ratio, a capital investment ratio, and salaries and interest to partners.	5, 10	3, 4	1, 2	
6. Record the admission of a new partner.		5	3	dissolution
7. Describe the implications of the withdrawal or death of a partner and of the liquidation of a partnership.	8, 9		3	liquidation

B Overview of Governmental and Not-for-Profit Accounting

Learning Objectives Chart

Learning Objectives	Questions	Exercises	Problems	New Concepts and Terminology
1. Explain and differentiate some basic concepts related to governmental and not-for-profit accounting.	1, 2			fund, modified accrual accounting
2. Describe the types of funds used in governmental accounting.	4	1		governmental funds, proprietary funds, fiduciary funds, account groups
3. Explain the modified accrual basis of accounting used by state and local governments.	3, 5, 6, 7	1, 2	1	revenues, expenditures, encumbrance accounting
4. Describe the financial reporting system used in governmental accounting.				
5. Provide a brief introduction to other types of not-for-profit accounting.	8, 9, 10	1		

C Special-Purpose Journals

Learning Objectives Chart

Learning Objectives	Questions	Exercises	Problems	New Concepts and Terminology
1. Explain the objectives and uses of special-purpose journals.	1	1, 2		special-purpose journal
2. Construct and use the following types of special-purpose journals: sales journal, purchases journal, cash receipts journal, cash payments journal, and others as needed.	2, 4	3, 4, 5, 6	1, 2, 3, 4	sales journal, purchases journal, cash receipts journal, cash payments journal
3. Explain the purposes and relationships of controlling accounts and subsidiary ledgers.	3, 5	4, 5	1, 3, 4	subsidiary ledger, controlling or control account

D Introduction to Payroll Accounting

Learning Objectives Chart

Learning Objectives	Questions	Exercises	Problems	New Concepts and Terminology
1. Identify and compute the liabilities associated with payroll accounting.	1, 2, 3, 4, 5, 6	1, 2, 3	1, 2, 3, 4	wages, salaries
2. Record transactions associated with payroll accounting.	7, 8	2, 3	1, 2, 3, 4	employee earnings record, payroll register

E Accounting for Bond Investments

Learning Objectives Chart

Learning Objectives	Questions	Exercises	Problems
1. Account for the purchase of bonds between interest dates.	1, 2	1	1, 2
2. Amortize the premium or discount of a bond.		1	1, 2
3. Account for the sale of bonds.		1	1, 2

FINANCIAL ACCOUNTING

Note to Students:

For business majors, this may be the **only** accounting textbook you purchase during your college career.

The author and the publisher want you to be aware that your copy of *Financial Accounting*, **Fourth Edition**, is a valuable investment toward your success in this **and** other business courses. Financial accounting is the foundation of the business curriculum; you will find that other business courses require you to use information learned from this text. You will enhance your success as a business major if, after completing this course, you retain this textbook as a reference. The following list, while not exhaustive, indicates those courses for which this book will be an asset:

Economics: *Financial Accounting* is useful in understanding microeconomic topics such as costs of doing business, marginal cost analysis, profitability analysis, profit maximization, and foreign exchange rates; and macroeconomic topics such as money and banking, national income accounting, and foreign exchange transactions.

Finance: *Financial Accounting* is useful in understanding the topics of financial statement analysis; cash flow analysis; capital budgeting; the time value of money; credit and banking transactions; working capital management (including cash, investments, receivables, and inventories); short- and long-term financing using notes, bonds, leases, and capital stocks; and mergers and acquisitions.

Information Systems: *Financial Accounting* is useful in understanding accounting and computer systems, system documentation, internal control, and purchasing and payroll systems.

Management: *Financial Accounting* is useful in understanding forms of business organizations, characteristics of corporations, and performance measurement.

Marketing: *Financial Accounting* is useful in understanding pricing policies, the relationship of sales to profitability, and incentive plans.

We are very proud of *Financial Accounting*, **Fourth Edition.** We encourage you to keep it and to refer to it often throughout your college and professional career.

Elizabeth L. Hacking
Director
College Division
Houghton Mifflin Company

Belverd E. Needles, Jr.
Professor of Accounting
DePaul University
Chicago, IL

Fourth Edition

FINANCIAL ACCOUNTING

BELVERD E. NEEDLES, JR.

Ph.D., C.P.A., C.M.A.
Arthur Andersen & Co. Alumni
Distinguished Professor of Accounting
DePaul University

HOUGHTON MIFFLIN COMPANY BOSTON TORONTO

Dallas Geneva, Illinois Palo Alto Princeton, New Jersey

To my wife, Marian,
To my mother, Mrs. Belverd E. Needles, Sr., and
In memory of my father, Mr. Belverd E. Needles, Sr.,
and my grandparents, Mr. and Mrs. Benjamin E. Needles

Senior Sponsoring Editor: Donald Golini
Senior Development Editor: Jane Sherman
Senior Project Editor: Joanne Dauksewicz
Electronic Project Supervisor: John Robbins
Assistant Design Manager: Anthony Saizon
Production Coordinator: Renée Le Verrier
Manufacturing Specialist: Holly Schuster
Marketing Manager: Karen Natale

This book is written to provide accurate and authoritative information concerning the covered topics. It is not meant to take the place of professional advice.

Coin photograph by Keller/Peet Associates.

Printed in the U.S.A.

Library of Congress Catalog Card Number: 91-71970

ISBN: 0-395-47301-2

ABCDEFGHIJ-VH-954321

Contents in Brief

Contents

Notes:
The topic of income tax is integrated throughout the book. It is covered at those points where it is relevant to the discussion.
Each chapter concludes with a Chapter Review consisting of Review of Learning Objectives, Review of Concepts and Terminology, and Review Problem with Answer. Each set of Chapter Assignments includes Discussion Questions, Communication Skills Exercises, Classroom Exercises, Interpretation Cases from Business, 'A' and 'B' Problem Sets and one or more Financial Decision Case.

4 Completing the Accounting Cycle 164

5 Accounting for Merchandising Operations 209

Preface

FINANCIAL ACCOUNTING, Fourth Edition, is intended for students who are taking their first course in financial accounting and who have no previous training in accounting or business. Designed for both business and accounting majors at the undergraduate or graduate level, this textbook is part of a well-integrated package for students and instructors that includes several manual and computer ancillaries not found in previous editions. It has proven successful in a traditional one-quarter or one-semester course and has been used equally well in a two-quarter course in financial accounting.

Fundamental Approach

I wrote this book believing that the use of integrated learning objectives can significantly improve the teaching and learning of accounting. This system of learning by objectives enhances the role of the overall package, and particularly that of the textbook, by achieving complete and thorough communication between instructor and student.

The success of the first three editions of this book has justified my confidence in the fundamental approach that has guided me in developing and writing FINANCIAL ACCOUNTING. Basic to this approach are the following objectives: (1) to write for business and management students as well as accounting majors; (2) to emphasize the role of accounting in decision making; (3) to use the learning-by-objectives approach throughout the text, assignment material, and ancillaries; (4) to make the content authoritative, practical, and contemporary; (5) to adhere to a strict system of quality control; and (6) to develop the most complete and flexible teaching/learning system available.

Written for Business and Management Students as Well as Accounting Majors

An important requirement of financial accounting courses is that they meet the needs of both business and management majors, who will read, analyze, and interpret financial statements throughout their careers, and of accounting majors, who must have a solid foundation for their intermediate and advanced accounting courses. When writing FINANCIAL ACCOUNTING, I focused on the needs of this dual audience. For example, emphasis is placed on the interrelationships between concepts and practice and between information and decision making that will be useful to students in their business or accounting careers. The use and interpretation of accounting information are more easily understood in the real-world context presented in this textbook.

Emphasis on Decision Making

Another goal is to present the contemporary business world and the real-life complexities of accounting in a clear, concise, easy-to-understand manner. Throughout the text, I have vigorously combined clear presentation with a consistent reading level and a uniform use of terminology. Accounting is treated as an information system that helps managers, investors, and creditors make economic decisions. In addition to questions, exercises, and problems, the chapter assignments include two decision-oriented features: Interpretation Cases from Business, in which students are asked to interpret and analyze facts from actual annual reports or business periodicals, and Financial Decision Cases, from which students must extract information and make a decision or recommendation. A new feature in this edition is the Decision Point, a short vignette based on real companies that shows how accounting is used by managers, creditors, and investors to make crucial business decisions.

Learning by Objectives

I have taken a definite pedagogical approach to writing the Fourth Edition of FINANCIAL ACCOUNTING, by extensively using learning objectives and learning theory. Learning objectives have been integrated throughout the text and package from the chapter previews and presentations to the chapter reviews, the assignment material, student study guide, and testing and evaluation material.

Authoritative, Practical, and Contemporary

This book presents accounting as it is practiced and carefully explains the concepts underlying the practices. Accounting terms and concepts are defined according to the pronouncements of the AICPA, APB, and FASB. The Statements of Financial Accounting Concepts and the FASB's Conceptual Framework study form the theoretical underpinning of the book and are used to assess various accounting situations and controversies. In addition, steps have been taken to ensure that, to the extent possible within the framework of introductory accounting, the material reflects realistically the way that accounting is carried out today.

Quality Control

Together with my publisher, I have developed a system of quality control for all parts of the package to ensure the most technically and conceptually accurate textbook and ancillaries possible. This system involves many steps, including thorough reviews by users, visits to and discussions with users by the author, extensive in-house editorial review and accuracy checking, and class testing.

Complete and Flexible Learning System

I believe that FINANCIAL ACCOUNTING, Fourth Edition, represents the most complete and flexible package available for a financial accounting course. All of its elements fit within the pedagogical system of learning by objectives established by the author. This comprehensive system is described in the following sections.

Flexible Organization of the Fourth Edition

The three-part organization of the book is designed for and has been used successfully in three distinct formats: (1) a traditional one-quarter or one-semester course; (2) a more conceptual one-quarter or one-semester course; and (3) a comprehensive two-course sequence.

Traditional Sequence

For the traditional one-quarter or one-semester course, illustrated below, the first two parts, consisting of thirteen chapters, can be considered a basic course in financial accounting. The chapters in Part Three (14, 15, and 16) and all of the appendices are optional. Obviously, the number of chapters and appendices that can be covered depends on whether the course length is one quarter or one semester and on the specific objectives of the course. For example, at certain schools the statement of cash flows and financial statement analysis are covered in a managerial accounting course.

Traditional Sequence

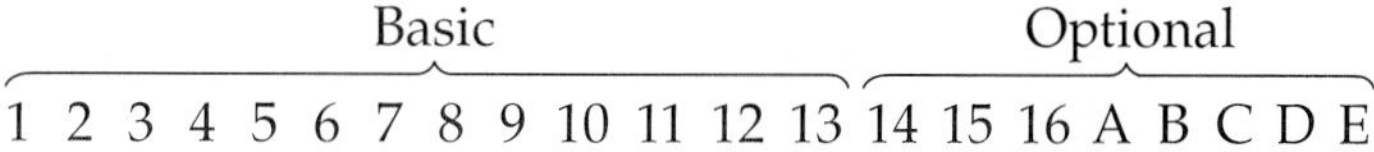

The appendices may be inserted wherever the professor finds it convenient to teach them. Suggested placements are: Appendix A after Chapter 11, Appendix B after Chapter 16, Appendix C after Chapter 5, Appendix D after Chapter 10, and Appendix E after Chapter 16. If a manual or computer practice set is used with this text, Appendix C must be covered.

Conceptual Approaches

Two strategies, which may be used separately or in conjunction with one another, are recommended for those professors desiring a more conceptual approach to financial accounting. Under Strategy A, Chapter 4, "Completing the Accounting Cycle," and Learning Objective number 11 (on the worksheet, adjusting, and closing entries) from Chapter 5 are deleted. The book has been designed so that the work sheet and closing entries do not have to be covered. Under this approach, more subjects among the optional topics may be chosen. This organization is as follows:

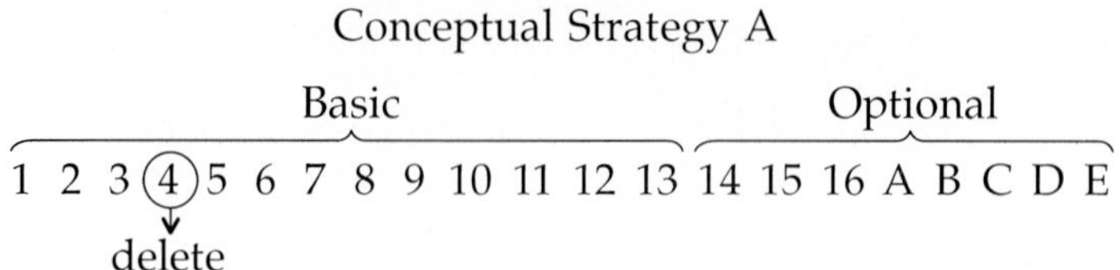

Under Strategy B, financial statement analysis may be emphasized through adjusting the schedule under Strategy A by inserting either Chapter 14 ("Statement of Cash Flows"), Chapter 15 ("Financial Statement Analysis"), or both, after Chapter 6 ("Accounting Concepts and the Use of Classified Financial Statements"), as follows:

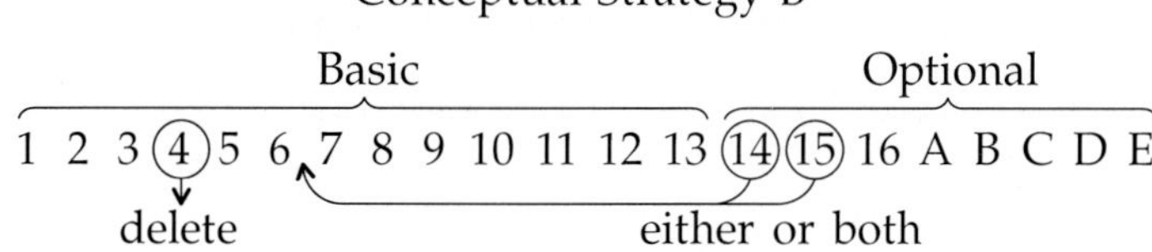

This organization of chapters allows for the introduction and analysis of more complex financial statements early in the course. In using Strategy B, it is best to stress the direct method in the preparation of the statement of cash flows. This strategy has been used very effectively by the author and has facilitated the use of financial analysis cases, HEARTLAND AIRWAYS, INC., Third Edition, and RICHLAND HOME CENTERS, INC., Second Edition, that accompany FINANCIAL ACCOUNTING, Fourth Edition.

If either Strategy A or B is used, more emphasis should be placed on the Communication Skills Exercises (described later), the Interpretation Cases from Business, and the Financial Decision Cases in the text. The topical readings from business periodicals and the Coca-Cola Specimen Financial Statements in the Study Guide provide additional practice.

Comprehensive Two-Quarter Sequence

For those schools that have a comprehensive two-quarter sequence in financial accounting, the book contains ample material to fill both terms. Professors at these schools may wish to cover all 16 chapters and six appendices. Most of the appendices are self-contained learning units with learning objectives, questions, exercises, and problems. A sample chapter organization for these courses is as follows:

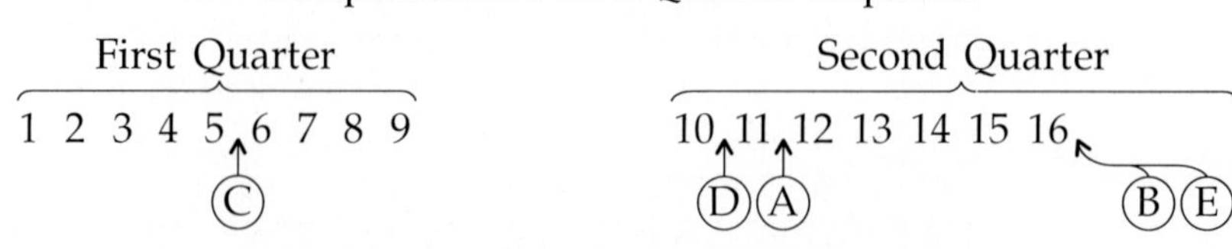

Objectives of the Fourth Edition

In addition to the objectives encompassed by the fundamental approach that we have already described, the fourth edition was written with the following objectives in mind: (1) to enhance the clarity of presentation and ease of use whenever possible; (2) to increase the real-world emphasis of the text and chapter assignments; (3) to provide an abundant variety and depth of chapter assignment materials; and (4) to introduce more coverage, examples, and opportunities for discussion of international business, ethical considerations, governmental not-for-profit organizations, and communication situations. How each of these objectives was accomplished is discussed in turn.

To Enhance Clarity and Ease of Use

Revision of Chapter Assignments. All retained exercises and problems have been thoroughly examined and appropriately revised. To avoid confusion on the part of the students, special attention was paid to the wording of transactions and of "Required" statements.

Enhanced Pedagogical Use of Color. The text uses a four-color design consistently throughout the text and illustration program to enhance student's understanding of the accounting process. The chart below displays the value of this pedagogical approach to color. Pedagogical features such as learning objectives, key terms, and emphasized material in the text are printed in red, as are all source documents. Green is used to represent accounting forms and working papers, which are part of the ongoing process of accounting, and to emphasize the major headings in the chapter. Light brown highlights the actual financial statements, the final product of the accounting process. Gray and various shades of brown also appear on selected tables and illustrations to heighten the contrasts and enhance student understanding.

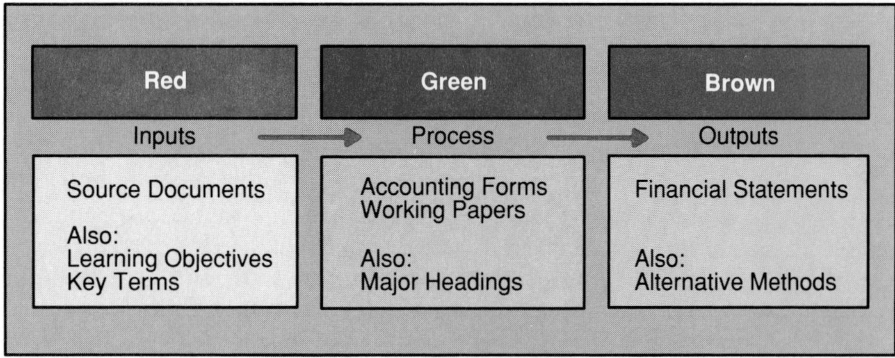

Revised Learning Objectives. All learning objectives were carefully reviewed and revised as necessary for clarity. These action-oriented objectives at the beginning of each chapter indicate in precise terms what students should be able to do when they complete the chapter. The learning objective is restated in the margin beside pertinent text. All end-of-chapter components—Review of Learning Objectives, Review of Concepts and Terminology, and Review Problem—are clearly referenced to learning objectives, and end-of-chapter assignments are keyed to specific objectives.

Expanded Key Terms. Throughout the book, key accounting terms are emphasized in bold red type and are clearly defined in context. All these terms are now listed alphabetically with definitions and learning objective references in each Chapter Review.

New Transaction Index. A new feature of the Fourth Edition, the index of transactions, appears inside the front cover of the text. This unique index allows students to look up any transaction and find the page number on which it is discussed and illustrated. The transaction index is especially useful to students when solving homework problems.

New Guide to Accounting Formats and Financial Statements. Inside the back cover of the text, another student aid is provided. This guide illustrates the proper formats for financial statements and references pages on which common accounting forms and financial statements can be found.

Expanded Chapter Review. A unique feature of each chapter is a special review section. The Review of Learning Objectives summarizes the chapter's main points in relation to the objectives. The Review of Concepts and Terminology presents all key terms from the chapter with definitions and learning objective references. The Review Problem with a complete solution demonstrates the chapter's major procedures before students work the exercises and problems.

Real-World Emphasis

New Decision Points. A new feature of the fourth edition, Decision Points are short vignettes based on real companies that show how accounting is used in decision making by management or by investors and creditors. Most chapters have at least two Decision Points: one at the beginning of the chapter shows the relevance of the material in the chapter to decision makers, and one or more later in the chapter illustrate key concepts.

Citations of Real Companies. Information from annual reports of real companies and from articles about them in business journals, like *Business Week*, *Forbes*, and the *Wall Street Journal*, have been used to enhance students' appreciation for the usefulness and relevance of accounting information. In total, more than one hundred publicly held companies have been used in the text as examples or chapter assignments. In addition, Chapter 6 contains the annotated financial statements of Toys "R" Us,

Inc., and Chapter 15 demonstrates financial statement analysis using the financial statements of Eastman Kodak Company.

Real-World Examples and Illustrations. Graphs or tables illustrating how the actual business practices relate to chapter topics are presented in most chapters. Many of these illustrations are based on data from studies of 600 annual reports published in *Accounting Trends and Techniques.* Beginning in Chapter 6 most chapters have one or more original graphics that show relevant ratios for six selected industries based on Dun & Bradstreet data. Service industries are (1) accounting and bookkeeping and (2) interstate trucking companies. Merchandising industries are (3) auto and home supply and (4) grocery store companies. Manufacturing industries are (5) pharmaceuticals and (6) appliance companies. Most Interpretation Cases from Business are based on the published financial reports of real companies.

Business Practice Interviews. Periodically, the author interviews businesspeople to ascertain current business practices. For example, revisions of Chapter 7, "Short-Term Liquid Assets," and Chapter 10, "Current Liabilities and the Time Value of Money," are based on interviews with loan officers of banks.

Abundant Variety and Depth of Chapter Assignment Materials

Discussion Questions. Discussion questions, which begin the assignment material at the end of each chapter, focus on major concepts and terms and provide thought-provoking questions.

Communication Skills Exercises. Communication Skills Exercises, a new feature to this edition, address *real accounting issues and are based on real companies and situations.* They are designed so that a written solution is appropriate, but most may be used in other kinds of communication modes. For instance, they may be used for class discussion, as small group activities, or as the basis for presentations by students. The last Communication Skills Exercise in all but a few chapters focuses on *basic research skills.* These exercises are designed to acquaint students with business periodicals, use of annual reports and business references, and use of the library. Field activities at actual businesses improve students' interviewing and observation skills.

Classroom Exercises. Classroom exercises provide practice in applying concepts and procedures taught in the chapter and are effective in illustrating lecture points. Each exercise is keyed to one or more learning objectives. *The number of exercises have been expanded by 25 percent in this edition.* In addition, solution transparencies are available for all exercise solutions.

Interpretation Cases from Business. This feature asks the student to interpret published financial information. Such reports and information are based on excerpts from actual reports or on published articles about well-known corporations and organizations. Among the companies included are Kmart, H & R Block, Hershey Foods Corporation, Toys "R" Us, General Motors, and UAL (United Airlines). Each exercise requires students to analyze published information by extracting data and making computations and interpretations.

A and B Problems. We have included two sets of problems to provide maximum flexibility in homework assignments. Generally, the problems are arranged in order of difficulty, with problems A-1 and B-1 for each chapter being the simplest. A and B problems also have been matched by topic, thus A-1 and B-1 are equivalent in content and level of difficulty. In addition, all problems are keyed to the learning objectives. For each problem, ratings of difficulty, time estimates, and solutions are available to the instructor, as are transparencies of all solutions.

Financial Decision Cases. Most chapters contain two cases that emphasize the usefulness of accounting information in decision making. The business background and financial information for each case are presented in the context of the decision. The decision maker may be a manager, an investor, an analyst, or a creditor. In the role of decision maker, the student is asked to extract relevant data from the case, make computations as necessary, and arrive at a decision.

Comprehensive Problem. A comprehensive problem covering chapters 12 and 13 has been added after Chapter 13. Comprehensive stockholders' equity transactions for Sundial Corporation are recorded and a statement of stockholders' equity is prepared.

More Coverage of International Accounting, Ethical Considerations, Governmental and Not-for-Profit Organizations, and Communication Situations

International Accounting. In recognition of the global economy in which all businesses operate today, international accounting and related examples are introduced in Chapter 1 and integrated throughout the text. Some examples of foreign companies mentioned in the text and assignments are Wellcome (British), Mitsubishi (Japanese), and Compagnie Générale des Etablissements Michelin (French).

Ethical Considerations. In recognition of the need for accounting and business students to be exposed in all their courses to ethical considerations, ethical situations are introduced in the text and assignments in Chapter 1 and at appropriate other points in the text, not only as they apply to auditors but also as they apply to financial and managerial accountants and to business professionals.

Governmental and Not-for-Profit Organizations. Because of the importance of governmental and not-for-profit organizations in our society, discussion and examples using these types of organizations are included at appropriate points. Among the organizations cited are the City of Chicago and the Lyric Opera. Appendix B provides an introduction to accounting for governmental and not-for-profit organizations.

Communication. In recognition of the fact that our students need to be better prepared in writing and other communication skills, ample assignments provide abundant opportunities for students to practice communication skills. All sections of the end-of-chapter material now contain written assignments. Discussion Questions, Communication Skills Exercises, Interpretation Cases from Business, and Financial Decision Cases require written answers. In addition, selected classroom exercises and A and B problems in each chapter contain writing components. The Interpretation Cases from Business and Financial Decision Cases are excellent vehicles for improving communication skills through small group discussion and oral reports. Communication Skills Exercises can provide a structure for oral presentations and promote students' research skills. Appropriately structured, these activities take far less time than might be thought and are valuable to the students.

Summary of Changes in the Fourth Edition

This new edition benefited from suggestions offered by the many users and reviewers who corresponded with us. Major changes have been listed below:

1. *The text has been shortened by one chapter from seventeen chapters to sixteen chapters.* A new appendix on bond investments has been added.
2. *International accounting and ethical considerations are introduced in Chapter 1.* Ethical situations and international companies and currencies are used appropriately throughout the text and chapter assignments. Further coverage of international accounting is included with intercompany investments in Chapter 16.
3. *Decision Points, based on real companies or situations, show the use of accounting information in decision making.* These vignettes introduce every chapter and occur at appropriate points in each chapter. More than 100 real companies are cited in the text and assignment material.
4. *Beginning in Chapter 6 most chapters have new charts that show pertinent ratios for six selected industries based on Dun & Bradstreet data.*
5. *All retained exercises and problems were painstakingly analyzed and appropriately revised with special attention to the wording of transactions and of "Required" statements.*
6. *The number of classroom exercises has been expanded by 25 percent.*

7. *Communication Skills Exercises, more than fifty in total, have been added to the chapter assignments of every chapter.* Included in each chapter is a basic research skills exercise.
8. *All learning objectives have been reviewed and modified as necessary.* Many small changes to increase clarity have been made in every chapter as a result of reviewers' comments.
9. *Alternative methods and procedures are clearly identified in the text so that students can focus on the method preferred by their instructor.*
10. *The inside front and back covers contain student reference aids.* Inside the front of the book, the Transaction Index allows students to look up any transaction and find the page on which it is presented. Inside the back of the book, the Guide to Accounting Formats and Financial Statements provides model formats for and page references to essential accounting forms and financial statements.
11. *The Review of Concepts and Terminology at the end of each chapter has been expanded to include all key terms introduced in the chapter.*
12. *The text has been updated to reflect recent data and changes in authoritative pronouncements including the concept of internal control structure and requirements concerning the disclosure of information about the market value of financial instruments.*
13. *Quality control procedures have been applied to the text, assignment material, and solutions.*

Changes in the specific chapters are described below.

Chapter 1 Accounting as an Information System. A section on ethical considerations in accounting has been added with appropriate coverage in the chapter assignments. Also added were sections on the applicability of accounting to government and not-for-profit organizations and on the relation of the independent CPA to the organizations they audit. The discussion of monetary units has been expanded to include foreign currencies and foreign exchange.

Chapter 2 Measuring and Recording Business Transactions. Recognition, valuation, and classification are presented as accounting issues.

Chapter 3 Business Income and Adjusting Entries. The preparation of the adjusted trial balance using the initial columns of the work sheet at the end of the chapter has been deleted so that the entire coverage of the work sheet can be found in Chapter 4.

Chapter 4 Completing the Accounting Cycle. This chapter now includes the entire coverage of the worksheet and may be regarded as optional by teachers who prefer not to cover the worksheet.

Chapter 5 Merchandising Operations and Internal Control. The presentation of internal control has been extensively revised to represent current concepts and components of the internal control structure. The section on inventory losses has been moved to provide a more linear presentation.

Chapter 6 Accounting Concepts and Classified Financial Statements. A section on ethics and financial reporting has been added to this chapter. The discussion of qualitative characteristics at the beginning of the chapter has been greatly simplified. An illustration of the financial accounting concepts presented thus far in the text assists the student in seeing the interrelationships of these concepts. To add realism, this chapter and subsequent chapters present charts showing pertinent ratios for selected industries from data published by Dun & Bradstreet. Service industries are accounting and bookkeeping and interstate trucking companies. Merchandising industries are auto and home supply and grocery store companies. Manufacturing industries are pharmaceuticals and appliance companies. The ratios for Shafer Auto Parts, the example company in the chapter, are compared with the auto and home supply industry figures. The annotated Toys "R" Us financial statements are updated. The new standard three-paragraph audit report is presented with the financial statements of Toys "R" Us and discussed.

Chapter 7 Short-Term Liquid Assets. The term *cash equivalents* is now defined and discussed. A chart showing cash as a percentage of total assets for selected industries is presented. A section on financing accounts receivable has been introduced. The more common practice of selling notes receivable has been added to the presentation of discounting notes receivable. An annotated illustration of a note receivable has been added. Many new illustrative journal entries provide further clarity.

Chapter 8 Inventories. A chart showing inventories as a percentage of total assets for selected industries is presented. An improved table showing the effects of errors in inventory measurement on net income is included.

Chapter 9 Long-Term Assets. A chart showing long-term assets as a percentage of total assets for selected industries is presented. The section on cost recovery for federal tax purposes has been revised. A new learning objective concerning accounting for disposals of depreciable assets involving exchanges has been inserted, and the material under this objective also has been revised. A short section on development and exploration costs in the oil and gas industries and on accounting for goodwill has been added under intangible assets.

Chapter 10 Current Liabilities and the Time Value of Money. This chapter has been extensively revised, including a new introduction to short- and long-term liabilities. A chart showing current liabilities as a percentage of total assets for selected industries is presented, and the section on disclosure of liabilities has been revised to include disclosure of off-balance-sheet liabilities and disclosure of information about the market value of financial instruments. A new section on bank loans and commercial paper is added. The section on the time value of money has been significantly expanded to include more applications of present and future value concepts to accounting.

Chapter 11 Long-Term Liabilities. This chapter has been completely reorganized and extensively revised. A chart showing long-term liabilities as a percentage of total assets for selected industries is presented. The issuance of bonds at a premium and the issuance of bonds at a discount are now explained together. Both the straight-line and effective interest methods of amortization are presented as alternative methods. New illustrations show the relationships of carrying value and interest expense for bonds issued at a discount and at a premium. The section on bond sinking funds has been deleted. New sections on installment notes receivable and other postretirement benefits are added. A new summary table of bonds issued at a discount and at a premium is presented in the Chapter Review.

Chapter 12 Contributed Capital. Two new illustrations are presented in this chapter. One shows the sources of capital raised by corporations and the other shows new U.S. common stock, preferred stock, and bond issues over the years 1985 through 1989.

Chapter 13 Retained Earnings and Corporate Income Statements. The section on appropriation of retained earnings has been shortened and rewritten to focus on the disclosure of restrictions on retained earnings instead of journal entries. Reissuance of treasury stock is now regarded as a sale of treasury stock. An objective to prepare a corporate income statement was added.

Chapter 14 Statement of Cash Flows. The introduction is rewritten.

Chapter 15 Financial Statement Analysis. The illustrated analysis of Eastman Kodak Company has been updated.

Chapter 16 International Accounting and Intercompany Investments. This is a new chapter created from parts of Chapters 16 and 17 in the previous edition. International accounting is covered first to reflect the growing importance of the international sphere on society and business. The section on the search for comparability of international accounting standards reflects new developments in the establishment of such standards. This chapter has been revised to reflect the FASB *Statement No. 94* on consolidation of all majority-owned subsidiaries. The section on bond investments has been moved to an appendix.

Appendix D Introduction to Payroll Accounting. This appendix has been updated for changes in payroll laws and rates.

Appendix E Accounting for Bond Investments. This is a new appendix; it was formerly part of Chapter 16.

Supplementary Learning Aids

The supplementary learning aids form a variety of useful resources for students. They consist of the following:

Study Guide and Selected Readings organized around learning objectives, and including relevant, current readings from the business press as well as the financial statements of Coca-Cola Company

Working Papers for Exercises and A Problems, Blank Working Papers for Use with A and B Problems

Check List of Key Figures

Soft-Tec, Inc., 4/e, a traditional practice set

Financial Analysis Cases, including:
- Richland Home Centers, Inc., 2/e
- Heartland Airways, Inc., 3/e
- General Mills, Inc.

Computer-assisted practice sets, decision case, and spreadsheet workbook
- Parks Computer Company
- Matthew Sports Company
- Cook's Solar Energy Systems, 2/e
- Sounds Abound, 2/e
- Heartland Airways, Inc., 3/e, with financial analysis software
- Lotus® Problems for Accounting: A Working Papers Approach
- Correlation Chart for Lotus® Problems for Accounting to accompany *Financial Accounting*, 4/e

Student Resource Videos

Instructor's Support Materials

Instructor's Edition

Instructor's Handbook

Instructor's Solutions Manual

A.S.S.E.T.: Accounting Software System for Enhanced Teaching (presentation software for microcomputers)

Test Bank

Computerized Test Bank

Achievement Test Masters with Solutions

Teaching Transparencies

Solutions Transparencies
- Box 1: Exercises, A Problems, Cases, and Lecture Outlines
- Box 2: B Problems

Guide to Student Resource Videos

Instructor's Solutions Manual for Heartland Airways, Inc., 3/e

Instructor's Solutions Manual for Richland Home Centers, Inc., 2/e

Instructor's Solutions Manual for Soft-Tec, Inc., 4/e

Instructor's Solutions Manuals for Computer-Assisted Practice Sets

Additional information regarding any of these materials may be found in the Instructor's Handbook.

Special Acknowledgment

I express my thanks and admiration to my two colleagues, Henry R. Anderson of the University of Central Florida and James C. Caldwell of Andersen Consulting, Dallas, Texas, for their support and contribution to this textbook. The learning by objectives system in this text is based on the one developed by the three of us and used in all of our texts.

Acknowledgments

Preparing a financial accounting text is a long and demanding project that cannot really succeed without the help of one's colleagues. I am grateful to a large number of professors, other professional colleagues, and students for their many constructive comments on the text. Unfortunately, any attempt to list those who have helped means that some who have contributed would be slighted by omission. Some attempt, however, must be made to mention those who have been so helpful.

I wish to express my deep appreciation to my colleagues at DePaul University, who have been extremely supportive and encouraging.

The thoughtful and meticulous work of Edward Julius (California Lutheran University) is reflected not only in the Study Guide, Test Bank, and Instructor's Handbook, but also in many other ways.

I also wish to express my appreciation to William P. Stevens of DePaul University for his assistance in the preparation of Appendix B: Overview of Governmental and Not-for-Profit Accounting.

Very important to the quality of this book are the supportive collaboration of my sponsoring editor, Donald Golini, and the efficiency and patience of my developmental editor, Jane Sherman. I further benefited from the ideas and guidance of Peggy Monahan, Special Projects Editor. Also very helpful were Fred Shafer and Tari Szatkowski, who assisted with the preparation of the manuscript.

Others who have been supportive and have had an impact on this book through their willingness to supply the author with content and accuracy reviews, suggestions, and class testing are listed below:

Joseph H. Anthony
Michigan State University

Martin E. Batross
Franklin University

David M. Bukovinsky
University of Kentucky

Neil Dale
Mt. Hood Community College

Diane Davis
Indiana University–Purdue University at Fort Wayne

Edward Goodhart
Shippensburg University

Marcia L. Halvorsen
University of Cincinnati

Dick Houser
Northern Arizona University

Jay G. LaGregs
Tyler Junior College

Johanna D. Lyle
Kansas State University

Cheryl Matsumoto
University of Hawaii–Manoa

Catherine J. Pitts
Highline Community College

Marian Powers
University of Illinois at Chicago

Grace J. Selby
Elgin Community College

Donald Shannon
DePaul University

S. Murray Simons
Northeastern University

Ralph S. Spanswick
California State University, Los Angeles

John Sperry
Virginia Commonwealth University

Marion Taube
University of Pittsburgh

T. Sterling Wetzel
Oklahoma State University

Without the help of these and others, this book would not have been possible.

B.E.N.

FINANCIAL ACCOUNTING

Part One
The Basic Accounting Model

Accounting is an information system for measuring, processing, and communicating information that is useful in making economic decisions. Part One presents the fundamental concepts and techniques of the basic accounting system, including accounting for service and merchandising enterprises.

Chapter 1 explores the nature and environment of accounting, with special emphasis on the users of accounting information, the roles of accountants in society, and the organizations that influence accounting practice. It also introduces the four basic financial statements, the concept of accounting measurement, and the effects of business transactions on financial position.

Chapter 2 continues the discussion of accounting measurement by focusing on the problems of recognition, valuation, and classification and how they are solved in the recording of business transactions.

Chapter 3 defines the accounting concept of business income, discusses the role of adjusting entries in its measurement, and demonstrates the preparation of financial statements.

Chapter 4 focuses on the preparation of the work sheet and closing entries.

Chapter 5 introduces the merchandising business and the merchandising income statement. The periodic and perpetual inventory methods are discussed as are closing and adjusting entries and the work sheet for merchandising concerns. Internal control for merchandising transactions is the final topic of the chapter.

LEARNING OBJECTIVES

1. *Define accounting and describe its role in making informed decisions.*
2. *Identify the many users of accounting information in society.*
3. *Distinguish between financial and management accounting, define generally accepted accounting principles (GAAP), and identify the organizations that influence GAAP.*
4. *Explain the importance of business transactions, money measure, and separate entity to accounting measurement.*
5. *Describe the corporate form of business organization.*
6. *Define financial position and show how it is affected by simple transactions.*
7. *Identify the four basic financial statements.*
8. *Describe accounting as a profession with ethical responsibilities and a wide career choice.*

CHAPTER 1

Accounting as an Information System

Your first accounting course begins with a general view of the accounting discipline and profession. In this chapter, you will begin the study of accounting measurement of business transactions and communication through financial statements. You will also learn about the important roles that accountants play in society and about the organizations where accountants work. After studying this chapter, you should be able to meet the learning objectives listed on the left.

DECISION POINT

Gerber Products Company[1]

Top management of Gerber Products Company, a leader in baby and toddler food products, children's clothes, and other markets, has set the following financial goals in its 1989 annual report to the company's stockholders.

1. Seek real earnings growth of 6 to 8 percent annually.
2. Sustain a return on equity of at least 22 percent.
3. Maintain cash flow from operations (earnings before interest, taxes, and depreciation) at a minimum of 15 percent of revenues.
4. Increase dividends commensurate with earnings growth.

Management views these goals as essential to building the long-term wealth of the company's owners. What financial knowledge will the company's managers need in order to contribute to achieving these goals?

Each of these goals is stated in terms of financial results. Successful managers for Gerber must have a thorough knowledge of accounting in order to understand how the operations for which they are responsible contribute to the firm's overall financial health as reflected by these goals. This requires knowledge of the terminology and concepts

1. Excerpts from 1989 Annual Report used by permission of Gerber Products Company.

that underlie financial information, of the way in which that information is generated, and of how to interpret and analyze that information. The purpose of this textbook is to provide that knowledge. ■

Accounting Defined

OBJECTIVE 1
Define accounting and describe its role in making informed decisions

Early definitions of accounting generally focused on the traditional recordkeeping functions of the accountant. In 1941, the American Institute of Certified Public Accountants (AICPA) defined accounting as "the art of recording, classifying, and summarizing in a significant manner and in terms of money, transactions and events which are, in part at least, of a financial character, and interpreting the results thereof."[2] The modern definition of accounting, however, is much broader.

In 1970, the AICPA stated that the function of accounting is "to provide quantitative information, primarily financial in nature, about economic entities that is intended to be useful in making economic decisions."[3] (An economic entity is a unit such as a business that has an independent existence.)

The modern accountant, therefore, is concerned not only with recordkeeping but also with a whole range of activities involving planning and problem solving; control and attention directing; and evaluation, review, and auditing. Today's accountant focuses on the ultimate needs of those who use accounting information, whether these users are inside or outside the business itself. So **accounting** "is not an end in itself."[4] Instead it is defined as **an information system that measures, processes, and communicates financial information about an identifiable economic entity**. This information allows users to make "reasoned choices among alternative uses of scarce resources in the conduct of business and economic activities."[5]

This modern view of accounting is shown in Figure 1-1. In this view, accounting is seen as a service activity. It is a link between business activities and decision makers. First, accounting measures business activities by recording data about them for future use. Second, through data processing, the data are stored until needed, then processed in such a way as to become useful information. Third, the information is communicated, through reports, to those who can use it in making decisions. One might say that data about business activities are the input to the accounting system, and useful information for decision makers is the output.

2. Committee on Accounting Terminology, *Accounting Terminology Bulletin No. 1* (New York: American Institute of Certified Public Accountants, 1953), par. 9.
3. *Statement of the Accounting Principles Board No. 4,* "Basic Concepts and Accounting Principles Underlying Financial Statements of Business Enterprises" (New York: American Institute of Certified Public Accountants, 1970), par. 40.
4. *Statement of Financial Accounting Concepts No. 1,* "Objectives of Financial Reporting by Business Enterprises" (Stamford, Conn.: Financial Accounting Standards Board, 1978), par. 9.
5. Ibid.

Figure 1-1. Accounting as an Information System for Business Decisions

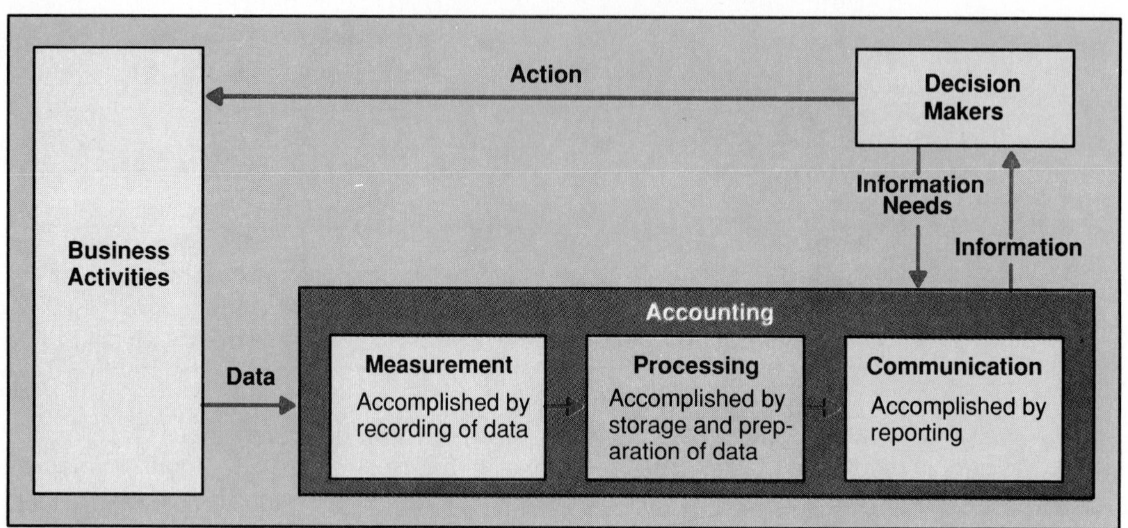

To avoid certain misunderstandings about accounting, it is important to clarify its relationship with bookkeeping, the computer, and management information systems.

People often fail to understand the difference between accounting and bookkeeping. **Bookkeeping**, which is a process of accounting, is the means of recording transactions and keeping records. Mechanical and repetitive, bookkeeping is only a small, simple but important part of accounting. Accounting, on the other hand, includes the design of an information system that meets user needs. The major goal of accounting is the analysis, interpretation, and use of information. Accountants look for important relationships in the information they produce. They are interested in finding trends and studying the effects of different alternatives. Accounting includes systems design, budgeting, cost analysis, auditing, and income tax preparation or planning.

The **computer** is an electronic tool that is used to collect, organize, and communicate vast amounts of information with great speed. Accountants were among the earliest and most enthusiastic users of computers, and today they use microcomputers in all aspects of their work. It may appear that the computer is doing the accountant's job, but in fact the computer is only a tool that is instructed to do the routine bookkeeping and to perform complex calculations for decision-making purposes in a more time-efficient way. It is important that the user of accounting information and the new accountant understand the processes underlying accounting. For this reason, most examples in this book are treated from the standpoint of manual accounting. You should remember, however, that most accounting operations are now computerized.

Most businesses also use a large amount of nonfinancial information. Their marketing departments, for example, are interested in the style or packaging of competitors' products. Personnel departments keep health and employment records of employees. Manufacturing departments must operate in the new environment of automation. With the widespread use of the computer today, many of these varied information needs are being organized into what might be called a **management information system (MIS)**. The management information system consists of the interconnected subsystems that provide the information needed to run a business. The accounting information system is the most important subsystem because it plays the primary role of managing the flow of economic data to all parts of a business and to interested parties outside the business. Accounting is the financial hub of the management information system. It gives both management and outsiders a complete view of the business organization.

Accounting Information and Decision Making

The major reason for studying accounting is to acquire the knowledge and skills to participate in important economic decisions. The information that accounting provides is the basis for such decisions both inside and outside the business enterprise.

Thus accounting information

> is a tool and, like most tools, cannot be of much direct help to those who are unable or unwilling to use it or who misuse it. Its use can be learned, however, and [accounting] should provide information that can be used by all—nonprofessionals as well as professionals—who are willing to use it properly.[6]

The first step in this learning process is to understand how decisions are made and how accountants can contribute to the process.

To make a wise decision and carry it out effectively, the decision maker must answer the following questions:

What is the goal to be achieved? (Step 1)

What different means are available to reach the goal? (Step 2)

Which alternative provides the best way to achieve the goal? (Step 3)

What action should be taken? (Step 4)

Was the goal achieved? (Step 5)

Figure 1-2 shows the steps that an individual or an institution follows in making a decision.

When the decision involves business and economic questions, accounting information is essential to the decision-making system. It provides quantitative information for three functions: planning, control, and evaluation.

Planning is the process of formulating a course of action. It includes setting a goal, finding alternative ways of accomplishing the goal, and deciding which alternative is the best. In this stage, the accountant should be

6. Ibid., par. 36.

Figure 1-2. A Decision System

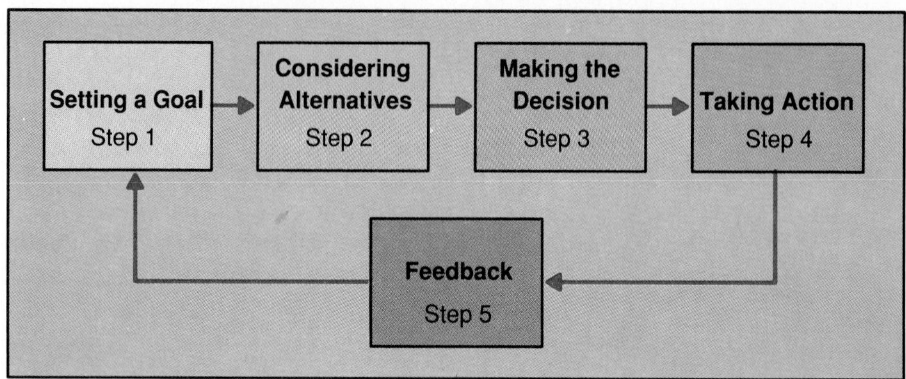

able to present a clear statement of financial alternatives. Accounting information dealing with projections of income and budgets of cash requirements is also important in planning for the future.

Control is the process of seeing that plans are, in fact, carried out. In other words, do actions agree with plans? At this point, the accountant might be expected to present information that compares actual costs and revenues with those planned earlier.

Evaluation, which involves the whole decision system, is the process of studying the system to improve it. It asks the question: Was the original goal satisfactorily met (feedback)? If not, the reason could have been poor planning or control, or perhaps the wrong goal was chosen. An evaluation based on accounting information may be given in annual reports and other financial statements.

Decision Makers: The Users of Accounting Information

OBJECTIVE 2
Identify the many users of accounting information in society

Accounting and accounting information are used more than is commonly realized. The users of accounting information can be divided roughly into three groups: (1) those who manage a business; (2) those outside a business enterprise who have a direct financial interest in the business; and (3) those persons, groups, or agencies that have an indirect financial interest in the business. These groups are shown in Figure 1-3.

Management

Management is the group of people in a business who have overall responsibility for operating the business and for achieving the company's goals. In a small business, management may include the owners of the business. In a large business, management more often consists of hired managers. Business enterprises have numerous, varied, and often complex objectives. These goals include achieving an acceptable level of earnings,

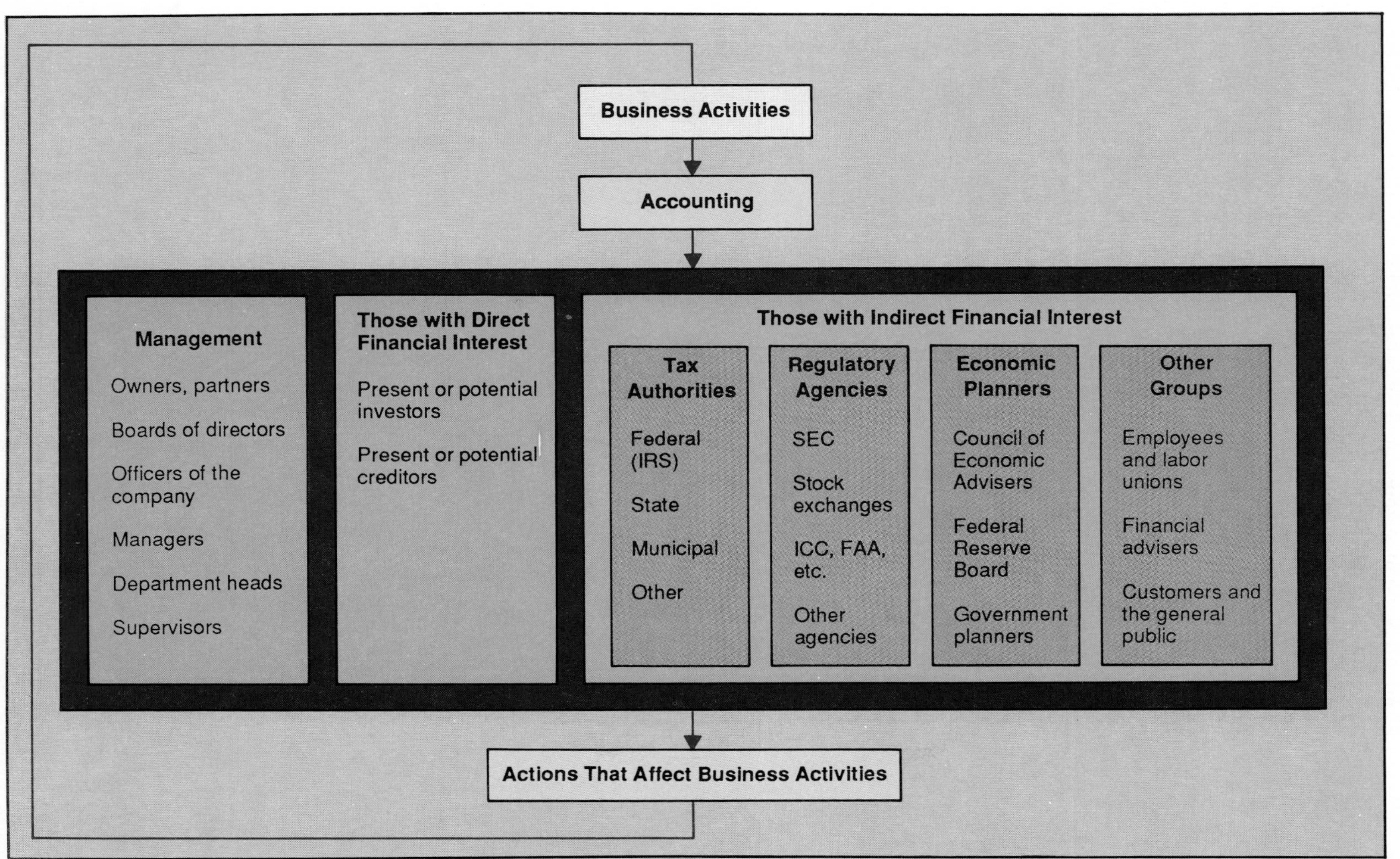
Business Activities
Accounting
Management
Owners, partners
Boards of directors
Officers of the company
Managers
Department heads
Supervisors
Those with Direct Financial Interest
Present or potential investors
Present or potential creditors
Those with Indirect Financial Interest
Tax Authorities
Federal (IRS)
State
Municipal
Other
Regulatory Agencies
SEC
Stock exchanges
ICC, FAA, etc.
Other agencies
Economic Planners
Council of Economic Advisers
Federal Reserve Board
Government planners
Other Groups
Employees and labor unions
Financial advisers
Customers and the general public
Actions That Affect Business Activities

providing quality goods and services at low cost, creating new and improved products, increasing the number of jobs available, improving the environment, and accomplishing many other tasks. To achieve these general goals, of course, the company must be successful. Success and survival in a competitive business environment require that management concentrate much of its effort on two important goals: profitability and liquidity. **Profitability** is the ability to earn enough income to attract and hold investment capital. **Liquidity** means having enough funds on hand to pay debts when they fall due.

Managers must constantly decide what to do, how to do it, and whether the results match the original plans. Successful managers consistently make the right decisions on the basis of timely and valid information. Many of these decisions are based on the flow of accounting data and their analysis. For this reason, management is one of the most important users of accounting information, and a major function of accounting is to provide management with relevant and useful information. For example, some typical questions that a manager might ask include: What was the company's net income during the past quarter? Is the rate of return to the owners adequate? Does the company have enough cash? What products are most profitable? What is the cost of manufacturing each product?

Users with a Direct Financial Interest

Another major function of accounting is to measure and report information about how a business has performed. Most businesses periodically publish a set of general-purpose financial statements that report on their success in meeting the objectives of profitability and liquidity. These statements show what has happened in the past and are important guides to future success. Today there are many people outside the company who carefully study these financial reports.

Present or Potential Investors. Those who are thinking of investing in a company and those who advise investors, such as financial analysts, are interested in the past success of the business and its potential earnings in the future. A thorough study of the company's financial statements will help potential investors judge the prospects for a profitable investment. After investing in a company, investors must continually review their commitment.

Present or Potential Creditors. Most companies must borrow money for both long- and short-term operating needs. The creditors, who lend money or deliver goods and services before being paid, are interested mainly in whether the company will have the cash to pay the interest charges and repay the debt at the appropriate time. They will study the company's liquidity and cash flow as well as its profitability. Banks, finance companies, mortgage companies, securities firms, insurance firms, suppliers, individuals, and others who lend money expect to analyze a company's financial position before making a loan to the company.

Users with an Indirect Financial Interest

Society as a whole, through its government officials and public groups, has in recent years become one of the biggest and most important users of accounting information. Some of the users who need accounting information to make decisions on public issues include (1) tax authorities, (2) regulatory agencies, (3) economic planners, and (4) other groups.

Tax Authorities. Our governments are financed through the collection of taxes. Under federal, state, and local laws, companies and individuals pay many kinds of taxes. Among these levies are federal, state, and city income taxes; social security and other payroll taxes; excise taxes; and sales taxes. Each tax requires special tax returns and often a complex set of records as well. Proper reporting is generally a matter of law and can be very complicated. The Internal Revenue Code of the federal government, for instance, contains thousands of rules governing preparation of the accounting information used in computing federal income taxes.

Regulatory Agencies. Most companies must report to one or more regulatory agencies at the federal, state, and local levels. All public corporations must report periodically to the Securities and Exchange Commission (SEC). This body was set up by Congress to protect the public and regulates the issuing, buying, and selling of stocks in the United States. Companies that are listed on stock exchanges, such as the New York Stock Exchange, must also meet the special reporting requirements of their exchange. The Interstate Commerce Commission (ICC) regulates industries such as trucking and railroads, and the Federal Aviation Administration (FAA) regulates airlines. Most public utilities, such as electric and gas companies, are regulated and must defend their rates with accounting reports. Accounting is also involved in new and broader regulations like those of the Environmental Protection Agency, which is concerned with, among other things, the cost and speed of reducing environmental pollution.

Economic Planners. Since the 1930s, the federal government's wish to take a more active part in planning and forecasting economic activity has led to greater use of accounting and accounting information. A system of accounting for the whole economy called national income accounting has been developed. It deals with the total production, inventories, income, dividends, taxes, and so forth of our economy. Planners who are members of the President's Council of Economic Advisers or are connected with the Federal Reserve System use this information to set economic policies and judge economic programs.

Other Groups. Labor unions study the financial statements of corporations as part of their preparation for important contract negotiations. The amount and computation of income and costs are often important in these negotiations. Those who advise investors and creditors also have an indirect interest in the financial performance and prospects of a business. In this group are financial analysts and advisers, brokers, underwriters, lawyers, economists, and the financial press. Consumers' groups, customers, and the general public have become more concerned about the financing and earnings of corporations as well as about the effects that corporations have on inflation, the environment, social problems, and the quality of life.

Applicability to Government and Not-for-Profit Organizations

More than 30 percent of the U.S. economy is generated by government and not-for-profit organizations such as hospitals, universities, professional organizations, and charities. The managers of these diverse entities have a need for accounting information that approximates that of managers of business entities. Like the heads of private firms, these managers need to raise funds and deploy scarce resources. They need to plan for paying for operations and repaying creditors on a timely basis. Moreover, they have an obligation to report on their financial performance to legislators, boards, and contributors. Although most of the examples in this text focus on business enterprises, the same basic principles apply to government and not-for-profit organizations. An appendix to the textbook is devoted to accounting for these types of organizations.

Financial and Management Accounting

OBJECTIVE 3 *Distinguish between financial and management accounting, define generally accepted accounting principles (GAAP), and identify the organizations that influence GAAP*

Accounting was defined earlier as an information system that measures, processes, and communicates information that is useful for decision making. A distinction is commonly made between the concepts of management accounting and financial accounting. **Management accounting** refers to all types of accounting information that are measured, processed, and communicated for the internal use of management. **Financial accounting** refers to accounting information that, in addition to being used internally by management, is communicated to those outside the organization. This book focuses on financial accounting.

Generally Accepted Accounting Principles

Because it is important that all who receive accounting reports be able to interpret them, a set of practices has developed that provides guidelines for financial accounting. The term used to describe these practices is **generally accepted accounting principles (GAAP)**. Although the term has several meanings in the literature, perhaps the best definition is the following: "Generally accepted accounting principles encompass the conventions, rules, and procedures necessary to define accepted accounting practice at a particular time."[7] In other words, GAAP arise from wide

7. *Statement of the Accounting Principles Board No. 4*, par. 138.

agreement on the theory and practice of accounting at a particular time. These "principles" are not like the unchangeable laws of nature found in chemistry or physics. They are developed by accountants and businesses to serve the needs of decision makers, and they can be altered as better methods are developed or as circumstances change.

In this book, we present accounting practice, or GAAP, as it is today. We also try to explain the reasons or theory on which the practice is based. The two—theory and practice—are part and parcel of the study of accounting. However, you should realize that accounting is a discipline that is always growing, changing, and improving. Just as years of research may be necessary before a new surgical method or lifesaving drug can be introduced into medical practice, research and new discoveries in accounting frequently take years to become common practice. As a result, you may sometimes hear of practices that seem inconsistent. In some cases, we have pointed toward new directions in accounting. Your instructor may also mention certain weaknesses in current theory or practice.

GAAP and the Independent CPA's Report

Because financial statements are prepared by the management of the company and are therefore subject to falsification for personal gain, all companies that sell ownership to the public and many companies that apply for sizable loans have their financial statements audited by an independent certified public accountant. **Certified Public Accountants (CPAs)** are licensed by all states for the same reason that lawyers and doctors are—to protect the public by ensuring a high quality of professional service. An important attribute of CPAs is **independence**. They are independent in that they have no financial or other compromising ties with the companies they audit. This gives the public confidence in their work. When reporting on a company's financial statements, an independent CPA makes an **audit** or examination of the financial statements and the accounting systems, controls, and records that produced them. The purpose of the audit is to ascertain that the financial statements have been properly prepared in accordance with generally accepted accounting principles. If the independent accountant is satisfied that this standard has been met, the resulting report will contain the following language:

> In our opinion, the financial statements . . . present fairly, in all material respects . . . in conformity with generally accepted accounting principles.

This wording emphasizes the fact that accounting and auditing are not an exact science. Since the framework of GAAP provides room for interpretation and its application necessitates the making of estimates, the auditor can only render an opinion or judgment that the financial statements *present fairly* or conform *in all material respects* to GAAP. The accountant's report does not preclude minor or immaterial errors in the financial statements. However, it does imply that, on the whole, investors and creditors can rely on those statements. Historically, the reputation of auditors for competence and independence has been highly regarded. As a result, banks, investors, and creditors have been willing to rely on the auditor's opinion when deciding to invest in companies and make loans to firms that have been audited. The independent audit is an important factor in the worldwide growth of financial markets.

Organizations That Influence Current Practice

Many organizations directly or indirectly influence GAAP and thus influence much of what is in this book. The most important of these organizations are the Financial Accounting Standards Board, the American Institute of Certified Public Accountants, the Securities and Exchange Commission, the Internal Revenue Service, and the Government Accounting Standards Board. There are international and other groups as well.

Financial Accounting Standards Board. Founded in 1973, the **Financial Accounting Standards Board (FASB)** has the primary responsibility for developing and issuing rules on accounting practice. This independent body issues Statements of Financial Accounting Standards. Departures from these statements must be justified and reported in a company's financial statements. The FASB is governed by the Financial Accounting Foundation.

American Institute of Certified Public Accountants. The **American Institute of Certified Public Accountants (AICPA)** has been concerned with accounting practice longer than most other groups. From 1938 to 1958 the AICPA's Committee on Accounting Procedures issued a series of pronouncements dealing with accounting principles, procedures, and terms. In 1959 the AICPA organized the Accounting Principles Board (APB) to replace the Committee on Accounting Procedures. The board published a number of APB Opinions on accounting practice, many of which are still in effect even though the APB was ended in 1973 when the FASB took over the standard-setting authority. The AICPA still influences accounting practice through the activities of its senior technical committees.

Securities and Exchange Commission. The **Securities and Exchange Commission (SEC)** is an agency of the U.S. government that has the legal power to set and enforce accounting practices for companies whose securities are offered for sale to the general public. As such, it has great influence on accounting practice. Because the APB failed to solve some of the major problems and abuses in accounting practice, the SEC began to play a larger and more aggressive part in deciding rules of accounting. The FASB represents a major effort on the part of accountants to keep control over their profession and to limit the SEC to its traditional role of allowing the accounting profession to regulate itself. It appears certain that during the coming years the SEC will keep putting pressure on the accounting profession to regulate itself. The success or failure of the FASB will be important in determining how much future influence the SEC will have on accounting.

Internal Revenue Service. The U.S. tax laws govern the assessment and collection of revenue for operating the government. Because a major source of the government's revenue is the income tax, the law specifies the rules for determining taxable income. These rules are interpreted and enforced by the **Internal Revenue Service (IRS).** In some cases, these rules may be in conflict with good accounting practice, but they are an important influence on practice. Businesses must use certain accounting practices simply because they are required by the tax law. Sometimes companies follow an accounting practice specified in the tax law to take advantage of rules that will help them financially. Cases where the tax law may affect accounting practice are noted throughout this book.

Governmental Accounting Standards Board. Concern over the financial reporting of government units has resulted in increased attention to the development of accounting principles for these units. The **Governmental Accounting Standards Board (GASB),** which was established in 1984 under the same governing body as the Financial Accounting Standards Board, is responsible for issuing accounting standards for state and local governments. The GASB will undoubtedly have a great influence on financial reporting by these units.

International Organizations. With the growth of financial markets throughout the world, the need for financial statements that are understandable by investors and auditors in different countries has increased. As a result, worldwide cooperation in the development of accounting principles has become a priority. The International Accounting Standards Committee (IASC) has approved more than twenty international standards; these have been translated into six languages. In 1977, the International Federation of Accountants (IFAC), made up of professional accounting bodies from more than sixty countries, was founded to promote international agreement on accounting questions.

Other Organizations Concerned with Accounting. The Institute of Management Accountants (IMA) is composed mainly of management accountants. This organization is engaged in education and research, with an emphasis on management accounting and accounting for management decisions. The Financial Executives Institute (FEI) is made up of persons who hold the highest financial positions in large businesses. It is most interested in standards and research in financial accounting.

The American Accounting Association (AAA) was founded in 1935, succeeding the American Association of University Instructors in Accounting, which was started in 1916. This group has an academic and theoretical point of view. Its members have contributed greatly to the development of accounting theory.

Accounting Measurement

OBJECTIVE 4
Explain the importance of business transactions, money measure, and separate entity to accounting measurement

Accounting has been defined thus far as an information system that measures, processes, and communicates financial information. This section begins the study of the measurement aspects of accounting. You will learn what accounting actually measures and study the effects of certain transactions on a company's financial position.

The accountant must answer four basic questions to make an accounting measurement:

1. What is to be measured?
2. When should the measurement occur?
3. What value should be placed on what is measured?
4. How is what is measured to be classified?

All the questions deal with basic underlying assumptions and generally accepted accounting principles, and their answers establish what accounting is and what it is not. Accountants in industry, professional associations, public accounting, government, and academic circles debate the answers to these questions constantly. As explained earlier, the answers change as new knowledge and practice require, but the basis of today's accounting practice rests on a number of widely accepted concepts and conventions, which are described in this book. The answers to questions **2**, **3**, and **4** are reserved for the chapter on measuring and recording business transactions.

What Is to Be Measured?

The world contains an unlimited number of things that can be measured. For example, consider a machine that makes bottle caps. How many measurements of this machine could be made? They might include size, location, weight, cost, and many others. Some attributes of this machine are relevant to accounting; some are not. Every system must define what it measures, and accounting is no exception. Basically, **financial accounting is concerned with measuring the impact of business transactions on specific business entities in terms of money measures.** The concepts of business transactions, money measure, and separate entity are discussed in the next sections.

Business Transactions as the Object of Measurement

Business transactions are economic events that affect the financial position of a business entity. Business entities may have hundreds or even thousands of transactions every day. These transactions are the raw material of accounting reports.

A transaction may involve an exchange of value (such as a purchase, sale, payment, collection, or borrowing) between two or more independent parties. A transaction may also involve a nonexchange economic event that has the same effect as an exchange transaction. Some examples of nonexchange transactions are losses from fire, flood, explosion, and theft; physical wear and tear on machinery and equipment; and the day-by-day accumulation of interest.

In any case, to be recorded, the transaction must relate directly to the business entity. For example, a customer buys a shovel from Ace Hardware but must buy a hoe from a competing store because Ace is sold out of hoes. The transaction of selling the shovel is recorded in Ace's records. However, the purchase of the hoe from a competitor is not recorded in Ace's records because, even though it indirectly affects Ace economically, it does not directly involve an exchange of value between Ace and the customer.

Money Measure

All business transactions are recorded in terms of money. This concept is termed the **money measure**. Of course, information of a nonfinancial nature may be recorded, but it is through the recording of dollar amounts that the diverse transactions and activities of a business are measured. Money is the only factor common to all business transactions, and thus it is the only practical unit of measure that can produce financial data that are alike and can be compared.

The monetary unit used by a business depends on the country in which it resides. For example, in the United States, the basic unit of money is the dollar. In Japan, it is the yen; in France, the franc; in Germany, the mark; and in the United Kingdom, the pound. If there are transactions between countries, the units must be translated from one currency to another, using exchange rates. An **exchange rate** is the value of one currency in terms of another. For example, an English person purchasing goods from a U.S. company and paying in U.S. dollars must exchange British pounds for U.S. dollars before making payment. In effect, the currencies are goods that can be bought and sold. Table 1-1 illustrates the exchange rates for several currencies in terms of dollars. It shows the exchange rate for British pounds as $1.79 per pound on a particular date. Like the price of any good or service, these prices change daily according to supply and demand for the currencies. For example, a few years earlier the exchange rate for British pounds was $1.20. Although our discussion in this book focuses on dollars, selected examples and assignments will be in foreign currencies.

The Concept of Separate Entity

For accounting purposes, a business is treated as a **separate entity** that is distinct not only from its creditors and customers but also from its owner or owners. It should have a completely separate set of records. Its financial records and reports refer only to its own financial affairs. The business owns assets and owes creditors and owners in the amount of their claims.

Table 1-1. Partial Listing of Foreign Exchange Rates

Country	Price in $ U.S.	Country	Price in $ U.S.
Britain (pound)	1.79	Italy (lira)	.0008
Canada (dollar)	.87	Japan (yen)	.0073
France (franc)	.18	Mexico (peso)	.0003
Germany (mark)	.60	Philippines (peso)	.037
Hong Kong (dollar)	.13	Taiwan (dollar)	.037

Source: The Wall Street Journal, April 10, 1991. Reprinted by permission of *The Wall Street Journal*,

For example, the Jones Florist Company should have a bank account that is separate from the account of Kay Jones, the owner. Kay Jones may own a home, a car, and other property, and she may have personal debts, but these are not the Jones Florist Company's assets or debts. Kay Jones may also own another business, such as a stationery shop. If she does own another business, she should have a completely separate set of records for each business.

OBJECTIVE 5 *Describe the corporate form of business organization*

There are three basic forms of business enterprise. Besides the corporate form, there are the sole proprietorship form and the partnership form. Whichever form is used, the business should be viewed for accounting purposes as a separate entity, and all its records and reports should be developed separate and apart from those of its owners.

Corporations Differentiated from Sole Proprietorships and Partnerships

A **sole proprietorship** is a business owned by one person. The individual receives all profits or losses and is liable for all obligations of the business. Proprietorships represent the largest number of businesses in the United States, but typically they are the smallest in size. A **partnership** is like a proprietorship in most ways except that it has two or more co-owners who carry on the business for a profit. The partners share profits and losses of the partnership according to an agreed-upon formula. Generally, any partner can bind the partnership to another party and, if necessary, the personal resources of each partner can be called on to pay obligations of the partnership. A partnership must be dissolved if the ownership changes, as when a partner leaves or dies. If the business is to continue as a partnership after this occurs, a new partnership must be formed. For both the sole proprietorship and the partnership, the business organization is a convenient way of separating the business activities of the owners from their personal activities. But legally there is no economic separation between the owners and the businesses.[8]

A **corporation**, on the other hand, is a business unit that is legally separate from its owners (the stockholders). The owners, whose ownership is represented by shares of stock in the corporation, do not directly control the operations of the corporation. Instead they elect a board of directors to run the corporation for the benefit of the stockholders. In exchange for limited involvement in the corporation's actual operations, stockholders enjoy limited liability. That is, their risk of loss is limited to the amount paid for their shares. If they wish, stockholders can sell their shares to other persons without affecting corporate operations. Because of this limited liability, stockholders are often willing to invest in riskier, but potentially more profitable, activities. Also, because ownership can be transferred without dissolving the corporation, the life of the corporation is unlimited and not subject to the whims or health of a proprietor or a partner.

The characteristics of corporations make them very efficient in amassing capital for the formation and growth of very large companies. Even though corporations are fewer in number than sole proprietorships and partnerships, they contribute much more to the U.S. economy in monetary terms (see Figure 1-4). For example, in 1990, General Motors generated more revenues than all but thirteen of the world's countries. Because of the economic significance of corporations, this book will emphasize accounting for the corporate form of business.

DECISION POINT
Santini Tours Company

Carlos Santos, an owner of a successful travel agency that operates in Chicago as a sole proprietorship, has just merged his company with Tiniger Tours Agency of Detroit, which is operated by three brothers as a partnership. Santos and the Tiniger brothers hope to make the new Santini Tours Company the Midwest's largest provider of specialized tours. To achieve this objective, they will need to raise money from investors and creditors. They are talking about organizing the new company as a corporation. Considering the differences between a sole proprietorship, a partnership, and a corporation, should they organize as a corporation?

Because Santini Tours Company has multiple owners and expects future growth, organizing as a corporation has advantages for the company. The corporate structure allows the transfer of ownership among multiple owners with a minimum of difficulty. In addition, it is often easier for a corporation to raise investment funds and secure loans from outside parties than it is for a sole proprietorship or a partnership. ■

8. Accounting for sole proprietorships and partnerships is discussed in an appendix to this book.

Figure 1-4. Number and Receipts of U.S. Proprietorships, Partnerships, and Corporations, 1988

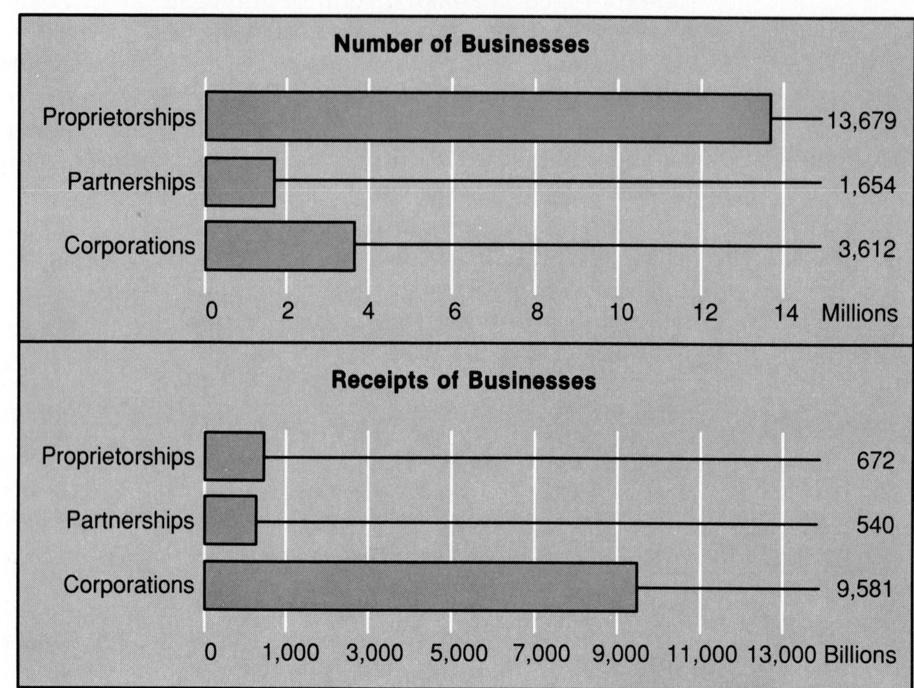

Source: U.S. Treasury Department, Internal Revenue Service, *Statistics of Income Bulletin,* Winter 1990–1991, pp. 79–80.

Formation of a Corporation

To form a corporation, most states require individuals, called incorporators, to sign an application and file it with the proper state official. This application contains the **articles of incorporation**. If approved by the state, these articles become, in effect, a contract between the state and the incorporators, called the company charter. The company is then authorized to do business.

Organization of a Corporation

The authority to manage the corporation is delegated by the stockholders to the board of directors and by the board of directors to the corporate officers (see Figure 1-5). That is, the stockholders elect the board of directors, which sets company policies and chooses the corporate officers, who in turn carry out the corporate policies by managing the business.

Stockholders. A unit of ownership in a corporation is called a **share of stock**. The articles of incorporation state the maximum or authorized number of shares of a stock that the corporation will be allowed to issue. The number of shares held by stockholders is the outstanding capital stock, and it may be less than the number authorized in the articles of incorporation. To invest in a corporation, a stockholder transfers cash or other resources to the corporation. In return, the stockholder receives shares of stock representing a proportionate share of ownership in the corporation. Afterward, the stockholder may transfer the shares at will. Corporations may have more than one kind of capital stock, but the first part of this book will refer only to common stock.

Board of Directors. As noted, the stockholders elect the board of directors, which in turn decides on the major business policies of the corporation. Among the specific duties of the board are authorizing contracts, deciding on executive salaries, and arranging major loans with banks. The declaration of dividends is also an important function of the board of directors. Only the board has the authority to declare dividends. Dividends are distributions of resources, generally in the form of cash, to the stockholders. Paying dividends is one way of rewarding stockholders for their investment in the corporation when it has been successful in earning a profit. (The other way is a rise in the market value of the stock.) Although there is usually a delay of two or three weeks between the time when the board declares a dividend and the date of the actual payment, we shall assume in the early chapters of this book that declaration and payment are made on the same day.

The composition of the board of directors will vary from company to company, but in most cases it will contain several officers of the corporation and several outsiders. Today, the formation of an **audit committee** with several outside directors is encouraged to make sure that the board will be objective in evaluating management's performance. One function of the audit committee is to engage the company's independent auditors and review their work. Another is to make sure the company has put in place the proper systems to safeguard the company's resources and to ensure that reliable accounting records are kept.

Management. The board of directors appoints the managers of a corporation to carry out the company's policies and to run the day-to-day operations. The management consists of the operating officers, who are generally the president, vice presidents, controller, treasurer, and secretary. Besides being responsible for running the business, management has the duty of reporting the financial results of its administration to the board of directors and to the stockholders. Though management may and gener-

Figure 1-5. The Corporate Form of Business

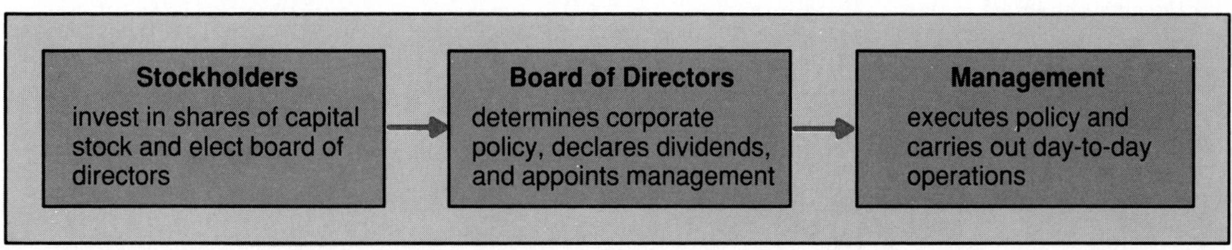
Stockholders
invest in shares of capital stock and elect board of directors
Board of Directors
determines corporate policy, declares dividends, and appoints management
Management
executes policy and carries out day-to-day operations

ally does report more often, it must report at least once a year. For large public corporations, these annual reports are available to the public. Excerpts from many of them will be used throughout this book.

Financial Position and the Accounting Equation

OBJECTIVE 6
Define financial position and show how it is affected by simple transactions

Financial position refers to the economic resources belonging to a company and the claims against those resources at a point in time. Another term for claims is equities. Thus, a company can be viewed as economic resources and equities:

Economic resources = equities

Every company has two types of equity, creditors' equity and owners' equity. Thus,

Economic resources = creditors' equity + owners' equity

Since, in accounting terminology, economic resources are referred to as assets and creditors' equities are referred to as liabilities, this equation may be presented as follows:

Assets = liabilities + owners' equity

This equation is known as the **accounting equation**. The two sides of the equation must always be equal or "in balance." The components of this equation will now be defined.

Assets

Assets are "probable future economic benefits obtained or controlled by a particular entity as a result of past transactions or events."[9] In other words, they are economic resources owned by a business that are expected to benefit future operations. Certain kinds of assets are monetary items, such as cash and money owed to the company from customers (called *Accounts Receivable*). Other assets are nonmonetary physical things, such as inventories (goods held for sale), land, buildings, and equipment. Still other assets are nonphysical rights, such as those granted by patent, trademark, or copyright.

Liabilities

Liabilities are "probable future sacrifices of economic benefits arising from present obligations of a particular entity to transfer assets or provide services to other entities in the future as a result of past transactions or events."[10] Among these are debts of the business, amounts owed to creditors for goods or services bought on credit (called *Accounts Payable*), bor-

9. *Statement of Financial Accounting Concepts No. 6,* "Elements of Financial Statements" (Stamford, Conn.: Financial Accounting Standards Board, December 1985), par. 25.
10. Ibid., par. 35.

rowed money (such as that owed on loans payable to banks), salaries and wages owed to employees, taxes owed to the government, and services to be performed.

As debts, liabilities are claims recognized by law. That is, the law gives creditors the right to force the sale of a company's assets if the company fails to pay the debts. Creditors have rights over owners and must be paid in full before the owners may receive anything, even if payment of the debts uses up all assets of the business.

Owners' Equity

Equity is "the residual interest in the assets of an entity that remains after deducting its liabilities."[11] In a business, the equity is called the ownership interest or **owners' equity**. Owners' equity is the resources invested in the business by the owners or stockholders. Owners' equity is also known as the residual equity because, theoretically, it is what would be left over if all the liabilities were paid. Transposing the accounting equation, we can state owners' equity as follows:

Owners' equity = assets – liabilities

Because it equals the assets after deducting the liabilities, owners' equity is sometimes said to equal **net assets**.

The owners' equity of a corporation is called **stockholders' equity** and has two parts: **contributed capital** and **retained earnings**. Contributed capital is the amount invested by the stockholders in the business. The ownership in the business is represented by shares of capital stock. An example of a stock certificate, which represents this ownership, is shown in Figure 1-6. Typically, contributed capital is divided between par value and additional paid-in capital. Par value is an amount per share that is entered in the corporation's capital stock account and is the minimum amount that can be reported as contributed capital. Additional paid-in capital results when the stock is issued at an amount greater than par value. In the initial chapters of this book, contributed capital will be shown as common stock that has been issued at par value. Retained earnings represent the equity of the stockholders in the assets generated from the income-producing activities of the business and kept for use in the business. As you will see in Figure 1-7, retained earnings are affected by three kinds of transactions.

Two types of transactions that affect retained earnings are revenues and expenses. Simply stated, **revenues** and **expenses** are the increases and decreases in retained earnings that result from operating the business. For example, if a customer pays cash to Shannon Realty, Inc. in return for a service provided by the company, a revenue results. The assets (cash) of Shannon Realty, Inc. have increased, and the retained earnings in those assets have also increased. On the other hand, if Shannon Realty, Inc. pays out cash in the process of providing the service, an expense results and is represented by a decrease in assets (cash) and in retained earnings. Gen-

11. Ibid., par. 49.

Figure 1-6. A Stock Certificate

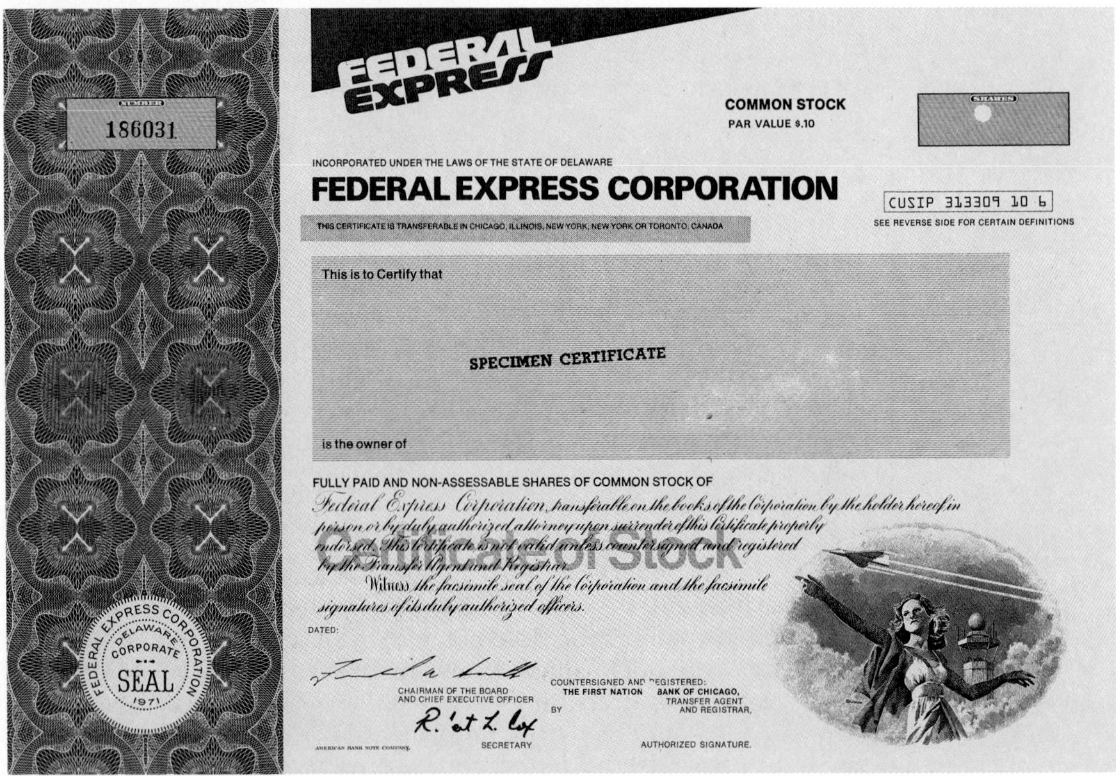

Source: Courtesy of Federal Express Corporation.

erally speaking, a company is successful if its revenues exceed its expenses. When revenues exceed expenses, the difference is called **net income**, and when expenses exceed revenues, the difference is called **net loss**. If the company is successful in earning a net income, it may then pay out dividends, the third type of transaction that affects retained earnings. **Dividends** are distributions to stockholders of assets (usually cash) generated by past earnings. It is important not to confuse expenses and dividends, both of which reduce retained earnings.

Some Illustrative Transactions

Let us now examine the effect of some of the most common business transactions on the accounting equation. Suppose that James and John Shannon open a real estate agency called Shannon Realty, Inc. on December 1. During December, their business engages in the transactions described in the following paragraphs.

Owners' Investments. James and John Shannon file articles of incorporation with the state and receive their charter. To begin their new business, they invest $50,000 in Shannon Realty, Inc., in exchange for 5,000 shares of

$10 par value stock. The first balance sheet of the new company would show the asset cash as well as contributed capital (Common Stock) of the owners:

	Assets	=	Stockholders' Equity	
	Cash		Common Stock	Type of SE Transaction
1.	$50,000		$50,000	Owners' Investments

At this point, the company has no liabilities, and assets equal stockholders' equity. The labels Cash and Common Stock are called **accounts** and are used by accountants to accumulate amounts that result from similar transactions. Transactions that affect stockholders' equity are identified by type so that similar types may later be grouped together on accounting reports.

Purchase of Assets with Cash. After a good location is found, the company purchases with cash a lot for $10,000 and a small building on the lot for $25,000. This transaction does not change the total assets, liabilities, or stockholders' equity of Shannon Realty, Inc., but it does change the composition of the assets—decreasing Cash and increasing Land and Building:

	Assets			=	Stockholders' Equity	
	Cash	Land	Building		Common Stock	Type of SE Transaction
bal.	$50,000				$50,000	
2.	−35,000	+$10,000	+$25,000			
bal.	$15,000	$10,000	$25,000		$50,000	
		$50,000				

Figure 1-7. Three Types of Transactions That Affect Retained Earnings

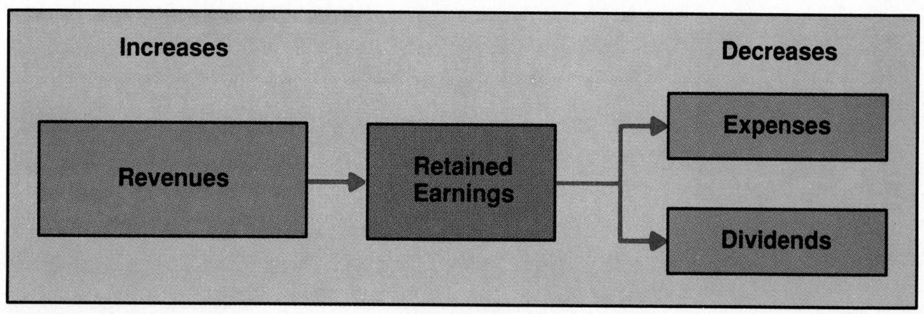

Purchase of Assets by Incurring a Liability. Assets do not always have to be purchased with cash. They may also be purchased on credit, that is, on the basis of an agreement to pay for them later. Suppose the company buys some office supplies for $500 on credit. This transaction increases the assets (Supplies) and increases the liabilities of Shannon Realty, Inc. This liability is designated by an account called Accounts Payable:

	Assets				= **Liabilities** +	**Stockholders' Equity**	
	Cash	**Supplies**	**Land**	**Building**	**Accounts Payable**	**Common Stock**	**Type of SE Transaction**
bal.	$15,000		$10,000	$25,000		$50,000	
3.		+$500			+$500		
bal.	$15,000	$500	$10,000	$25,000	$500	$50,000	
	$50,500				$50,500		

Note that this transaction increases both sides of the accounting equation to $50,500.

Payment of a Liability. If John later pays $200 of the $500 owed for the supplies, both assets (Cash) and liabilities (Accounts Payable) will decrease, but Supplies will be unaffected:

	Assets				= **Liabilities** +	**Stockholders' Equity**	
	Cash	**Supplies**	**Land**	**Building**	**Accounts Payable**	**Common Stock**	**Type of SE Transaction**
bal.	$15,000	$500	$10,000	$25,000	$500	$50,000	
4.	–200				–200		
bal.	$14,800	$500	$10,000	$25,000	$300	$50,000	
	$50,300				$50,300		

Note that the accounting equation is still equal on both sides of the equation, although now at a total of $50,300.

Revenues. Shannon Realty, Inc. earns revenues in the form of commissions received from selling houses for clients. Sometimes these commissions are paid to Shannon Realty, Inc. immediately in the form of cash, and sometimes the client agrees to pay the commission later. In either case, the commission is recorded when it is earned, and Shannon Realty,

Inc. has a right to a current or future receipt of cash. First, assume that Shannon Realty, Inc. sells a house and receives a commission in cash of $1,500. This transaction increases both assets (Cash) and stockholders' equity (Retained Earnings):

	Assets				= Liabilities +	Stockholders' Equity		
	Cash	Supplies	Land	Building	Accounts Payable	Common Stock	Retained Earnings	Type of SE Transaction
bal.	$14,800	$500	$10,000	$25,000	$300	$50,000		
5.	+1,500						+1,500	Commissions Earned
bal.	$16,300	$500	$10,000	$25,000	$300	$50,000	$1,500	
	$51,800				$51,800			

Now assume that Shannon Realty, Inc. sells a house calling for a commission of $2,000, for which the company agrees to wait for payment. Since the commission is earned now, a bill or invoice is sent to the client and the transaction is recorded now. This revenue transaction increases both assets and stockholders' equity as before, but a new asset account, Accounts Receivable, shows that Shannon Realty, Inc. is awaiting receipt of the commission:

	Assets					= Liabilities +	Stockholders' Equity		
	Cash	Accounts Receivable	Supplies	Land	Building	Accounts Payable	Common Stock	Retained Earnings	Type of SE Transaction
bal.	$16,300		$500	$10,000	$25,000	$300	$50,000	$1,500	
6.		+$2,000						+ 2,000	Commissions Earned
bal.	$16,300	$2,000	$500	$10,000	$25,000	$300	$50,000	$3,500	
	$53,800					$53,800			

The use of separate accounts for revenue accounts, like Commissions Earned, will be introduced in the chapter on measuring and recording business transactions.

Collection of Accounts Receivable. If it is assumed that a few days later Shannon Realty, Inc. receives $1,000 from the client in transaction **6**, the asset Cash is increased and the asset Accounts Receivable is decreased:

	Assets					= Liabilities +	Stockholders' Equity		
	Cash	Accounts Receiv-able	Supplies	Land	Building	Accounts Payable	Common Stock	Retained Earnings	Type of SE Transaction
bal.	$16,300	$2,000	$500	$10,000	$25,000	$300	$50,000	$3,500	
7.	+1,000	−1,000							
bal.	$17,300	$1,000	$500	$10,000	$25,000	$300	$50,000	$3,500	
	$53,800					$53,800			

Note that this transaction does not affect stockholders' equity because the commission revenue has already been recorded in transaction **6**. Also, note that the balance of Accounts Receivable is $1,000, indicating that $1,000 is still to be collected.

Expenses. Just as revenues are recorded when they are earned, expenses are recorded when they are incurred. Expenses may be paid in cash when they occur; or if payment is to be made later, a liability such as Accounts Payable or Wages Payable is increased. In both cases, stockholders' equity is decreased. Assume that Shannon Realty, Inc. pays $1,000 to rent some equipment for the office and $400 in wages to a part-time helper. These transactions reduce assets (Cash) and stockholders' equity (Retained Earnings):

	Assets					= Liabilities +	Stockholders' Equity		
	Cash	Accounts Receiv-able	Supplies	Land	Building	Accounts Payable	Common Stock	Retained Earnings	Type of SE Transaction
bal.	$17,300	$1,000	$500	$10,000	$25,000	$300	$50,000	$3,500	
8.	−1,000							−1,000	Equipment Rental Expense
9.	−400							−400	Wages Expense
bal.	$15,900	$1,000	$500	$10,000	$25,000	$300	$50,000	$2,100	
	$52,400					$52,400			

Also, Shannon Realty, Inc. has not paid the bill for utility expense of $300 that was incurred for December. In this case, the effect on stockholders' equity is the same as when the expense is paid in cash, but instead of a reduction in assets, there is an increase in liabilities (Accounts Payable), as follows:

	Assets					= Liabilities +	Stockholders' Equity		
	Cash	Accounts Receiv-able	Supplies	Land	Building	Accounts Payable	Common Stock	Retained Earnings	Type of SE Transaction
bal.	$15,900	$1,000	$500	$10,000	$25,000	$300	$50,000	$2,100	
10.						+300		−300	Utility Expense
bal.	$15,900	$1,000	$500	$10,000	$25,000	$600	$50,000	$1,800	
	$52,400					$52,400			

The use of separate accounts for expenses will be introduced in the chapter on measuring and recording business transactions.

Dividends. A dividend of $600 is declared, and it is paid by taking $600 out of the company's bank account and paying it to the stockholders for deposit in their personal bank accounts. The payment of dividends reduces assets (Cash) and stockholders' equity (Retained Earnings). Note that although these dividends reduce retained earnings in the same way as the expenses in transactions **8**, **9**, and **10**, they perform a different function. They are distributions of assets (Cash) to the stockholders, whereas the function of the expenses is to pay for services that helped produce the revenues in transactions **5** and **6**.

	Assets					= Liabilities +	Stockholders' Equity		
	Cash	Accounts Receiv-able	Supplies	Land	Building	Accounts Payable	Common Stock	Retained Earnings	Type of SE Transaction
bal.	$15,900	$1,000	$500	$10,000	$25,000	$600	$50,000	$1,800	
11.	−600							−600	Dividends
bal.	$15,300	$1,000	$500	$10,000	$25,000	$600	$50,000	$1,200	
	$51,800					$51,800			

Summary. A summary of these eleven illustrative transactions is presented in Exhibit 1-1 (on page 28).

Exhibit 1-1. Summary of Effects of Illustrative Transactions on Financial Position

	Assets					= Liabilities +	Stockholders' Equity		
	Cash	Accounts Receiv-able	Supplies	Land	Building	Accounts Payable	Common Stock	Retained Earnings	Type of Stockholders' Equity Transaction
1.	$50,000						$50,000		Owners' Investments
2.	−35,000			+$10,000	+$25,000				
bal.	$15,000			$10,000	$25,000		$50,000		
3.			+$500			+$500			
bal.	$15,000		$500	$10,000	$25,000	$500	$50,000		
4.	−200					−200			
bal.	$14,800		$500	$10,000	$25,000	$300	$50,000		
5.	+1,500							+$1,500	Commissions Earned
bal.	$16,300		$500	$10,000	$25,000	$300	$50,000	$1,500	
6.		+$2,000						+2,000	Commissions Earned
bal.	$16,300	$2,000	$500	$10,000	$25,000	$300	$50,000	$3,500	
7.	+1,000	−1,000							
bal.	$17,300	$1,000	$500	$10,000	$25,000	$300	$50,000	$3,500	
8.	−1,000							−1,000	Equipment Rental Expense
9.	−400							−400	Wages Expense
bal.	$15,900	$1,000	$500	$10,000	$25,000	$300	$50,000	$2,100	
10.						+300		−300	Utility Expense
bal.	$15,900	$1,000	$500	$10,000	$25,000	$600	$50,000	$1,800	
11.	−600							−600	Dividends
	$15,300	$1,000	$500	$10,000	$25,000	$600	$50,000	$1,200	
			$51,800				$51,800		

Accounting Communication Through Financial Statements

OBJECTIVE 7
Identify the four basic financial statements

Financial statements are a central feature of accounting because they are the primary means of communicating important accounting information to users. It is helpful to think of these statements as models of the business enterprise, because they are attempts to show the business in financial terms. As is true of all models, however, financial statements are not perfect pictures of the real thing, but rather the accountant's best effort to represent what is real.

Four major financial statements are used to communicate the required accounting information about a business. One is the income statement, which reports the income-generating activities or earnings of a business during the period. A second statement, called the statement of retained earnings, shows the changes in the retained earnings portion of stockholders' equity. These statements are prepared from the three types of transactions that affect retained earnings. This is why in Exhibit 1-1 and prior examples, these transactions were identified by type.

A third financial statement is the balance sheet. The balance sheet shows the financial position of the business at a particular date, such as at the end of the accounting period. A fourth statement, called the statement of cash flows, is used to summarize all the changes in cash that result from operating activities, investing activities, and financing activities. Exhibit 1-2 illustrates the relationships of the first three statements by showing how they would appear for Shannon Realty, Inc. after the eleven illustrative transactions shown in Exhibit 1-1. It is assumed that these transactions took place during the month of December, 19xx.

Note that each statement is headed in a similar way. Each heading identifies the company and the kind of statement. The balance sheet gives the specific date to which it applies, and the income statement and statement of retained earnings give the time period to which they apply. These statements are typical ones for corporations.

The Income Statement

The **income statement** is a financial statement that summarizes the amount of revenues earned and expenses incurred by a business over a period of time. Many people consider it the most important financial report because its purpose is to measure whether the business achieved or failed to achieve its primary objective of earning an acceptable income. In Exhibit 1-2, Shannon Realty, Inc. had revenues in the form of commissions earned of $3,500. From this amount, total expenses of $1,700 were deducted, consisting of equipment rental expense of $1,000, wages expense of $400, and utility expense of $300, to arrive at a net income of $1,800. To show that it applies to a period of time, the statement is dated, "For the Month Ended December 31, 19xx."

Exhibit 1-2. Income Statement, Statement of Retained Earnings, and Balance Sheet for Shannon Realty, Inc.

Shannon Realty, Inc.
Income Statement
For the Month Ended December 31, 19xx

Revenues		
Commissions Earned		$3,500
Expenses		
Equipment Rental Expense	$1,000	
Wages Expense	400	
Utility Expense	300	
Total Expenses		1,700
Net Income		**$1,800**

Shannon Realty, Inc.
Statement of Retained Earnings
For the Month Ended December 31, 19xx

Retained Earnings, December 1, 19xx	$ 0
Net Income for the Month	**1,800**
Subtotal	$1,800
Less Dividends	600
Retained Earnings, December 31, 19xx	**$1,200**

Shannon Realty, Inc.
Balance Sheet
December 31, 19xx

Assets		**Liabilities**		
Cash	$15,300	Accounts Payable		$ 600
Accounts Receivable	1,000			
Supplies	500	**Stockholders' Equity**		
Land	10,000			
Building	25,000	Common Stock	$50,000	
		Retained Earnings	**1,200**	
		Total Stockholders' Equity		51,200
Total Assets	$51,800	Total Liabilities and Stockholders' Equity		$51,800

The Statement of Retained Earnings

The **statement of retained earnings** shows the changes in retained earnings over a period of time. In Exhibit 1-2, the beginning retained earnings is zero because the company was started in this accounting period. During the month, the company earned an income (as shown in the income statement) of $1,800. Deducted from this amount are the dividends for the month of $600, leaving an ending balance of $1,200 of earnings retained in the business.

The Balance Sheet

The purpose of the **balance sheet** is to show the financial position of a business on a certain date. For this reason, it is often called the statement of financial position and is dated as of a certain date. The balance sheet presents a view of the business as the holder of resources or assets that are equal to the sources of or claims against those assets. The sources or claims consist of the company's liabilities and the stockholders' equity in the company. In Exhibit 1-2, Shannon Realty, Inc. has several categories of assets, which total $51,800. These assets equal the total liabilities of $600 (Accounts Payable) plus the ending balance of stockholders' equity of $51,200. Note that the Retained Earnings account on the balance sheet comes from the ending balance shown on the statement of retained earnings.

The Statement of Cash Flows

During the past three decades it has become clear that the income statement has a major deficiency. It shows only the changes in financial position caused by those operations that produced a net income or loss. Many important events, especially those related to investing and financing activities, can take place during an accounting period and not appear on the income statement. For example, the stockholders may put more money into the business or cash dividends may be paid. Buildings, equipment, or other assets may be bought or sold. New liabilities can be incurred or old ones paid off. For this reason, the **statement of cash flows** is now widely used to show the cash produced by operating the business as well as important investing and financing transactions that take place during an accounting period.

Exhibit 1-3 is an example of the statement of cash flows for Shannon Realty, Inc. Note that the name of the company, the title of the statement, and the period covered by the statement are identified. Also note that the statement explains how the Cash account changed during the period. Cash increased by $15,300. Operating activities produced net cash flows of $900, and financing activities produced net cash flows of $49,400. Investment activities used cash flows of $35,000.

This statement is directly related to the other three statements. Notice that Net Income comes from the income statement and that Dividends comes from the statement of retained earnings. The other items in the statement represent changes in the balance sheet accounts of Accounts

Receivable, Supplies, Accounts Payable, Land, Buildings, and Common Stock. The reader should focus here on the importance and overall structure of the statement. Its construction and use are discussed in detail in the chapter on the statement of cash flows.

Relationships Among the Four Statements

At this stage, you are not expected to understand all the fine points and terminology of these four statements. They are presented to show that accounting tries to sum up in a meaningful and useful way the financial history of a business, no matter how large and complex, in four relatively simple financial statements—an amazing feat. Two of the statements—the income statement and the statement of cash flows—deal with the activities of the business over time. One statement—the balance sheet—shows the financial position of the business at a particular point in time. Another statement—the statement of retained earnings—ties the balance sheet and income statement together over a period of time. Much of the rest of this book deals with how to develop, use, and interpret these four statements.

Exhibit 1-3. Statement of Cash Flows for Shannon Realty, Inc.

Shannon Realty, Inc.
Statement of Cash Flows
For the Month Ended December 31, 19xx

Cash Flows from Operating Activities		
Net Income		$ 1,800
Noncash Expenses and Revenues Included in Income		
Increase in Accounts Receivable	$ (1,000)	
Increase in Supplies	(500)	
Increase in Accounts Payable	600	(900)
Net Cash Flows from Operating Activities		$ 900
Cash Flows from Investing Activities		
Purchase of Land	$(10,000)	
Purchase of Building	(25,000)	
Net Cash Flows from Investing Activities		(35,000)
Cash Flows from Financing Activities		
Investment by Owners (Common Stock)	$ 50,000	
Dividends	(600)	
Net Cash Flows from Financing Activities		49,400
Net Increase (Decrease) in Cash		**$15,300**
Cash at Beginning of Month		0
Cash at End of Month		$15,300

Professional Ethics and the Accounting Profession

OBJECTIVE 8
Describe accounting as a profession with ethical responsibilities and a wide career choice

Ethics is the application of a code of conduct to everyday life. It addresses the question of whether actions are good or bad, right or wrong. Ethical actions are the results of individual decisions, and you are faced with many ethical situations every day. Some may be potentially illegal, such as the temptation to take office supplies from your employer to use when you do homework. Others are not illegal, but are equally unethical, such as knowingly failing to tell a fellow student who missed class that a test has been announced for the next class period. When an organization is said to act ethically or unethically, it means individuals within the organization have made a decision to act ethically or unethically. When a company uses false advertising, cheats a customer, pollutes the environment, treats employees poorly, or misleads investors by presenting false financial statements, members of management and other employees of the company have consciously made decisions to lead the company in these directions. Likewise, in a company that subscribes to ethical practices, that ethical behavior is a direct result of the actions and decisions of employees in the company.

Professional ethics is the application of a code of conduct to the practice of a profession. Like the ethical conduct of a company, the ethical actions of a profession are a collection of individual actions. As members of a profession, accountants have a responsibility, not only to their employers and clients but to society as a whole, to uphold the highest ethical standards. A recent survey of over 1,000 prominent people in business, education, and government ranked the accounting profession second only to the clergy as having the highest ethical standards.[12]

The accounting function is as old as the need to exchange things of value and keep track of the wealth. The commercial and trading revolution of the Renaissance was a great impetus to accounting, as was the Industrial Revolution. The enormous growth of industry and government in the twentieth century has expanded the need for accountants even further. Today, the accounting profession offers interesting, challenging, well-paying, and satisfying careers. It is the responsibility of every person who becomes an accountant to uphold the high standards of the profession regardless of the field of accounting in which the individual engages.

Management Accounting

An accountant who is employed by a business is said to be in **management accounting**. A small business may have only one person doing this work; a medium-size or large company may have hundreds of accountants working under a chief accounting officer called a controller, treasurer, or financial vice president. Other positions that may be held by accountants at lower managerial levels are assistant controller, chief accountant,

12. Touche Ross & Co., "Ethics in American Business" (New York: Touche Ross & Co., 1988), p. 7.

accounting manager, internal auditor, plant accountant, systems analyst, financial accountant, and cost accountant.

Because of their broad and intimate view of all aspects of a company's operations, management accountants often have an important effect on management decision making. According to most recent surveys, more top-level business executives have backgrounds in accounting and finance than in any other field. Just a few of the well-known companies whose presidents or chairmen of the board are (or have been) accountants are American Airlines (AMR Corporation), General Foods, International Business Machines, Caterpillar, General Motors, Kennecott Copper, Ford, General Electric, GTE, Consolidated Edison, International Telephone and Telegraph, and Minnesota Mining and Manufacturing.

The main task of management accountants is to give management the information it needs to make wise decisions. Management accountants also set up a system of internal control to increase efficiency and prevent fraud. They aid in profit planning, budgeting, and cost control. It is their duty to see that a company has good records, prepares proper financial reports, and complies with tax laws and government regulations. Management accountants also need to keep up with the latest developments in the use of computers and in computer systems design.

Management accountants may certify their professional competence and training by qualifying for the status of **Certified Management Accountant (CMA)**, which is awarded to qualified accountants by the Institute of Certified Management Accountants of the Institute of Management Accountants. Under the CMA program, candidates must pass an examination consisting of several parts and meet educational and professional standards.

The National Association of Accountants (now the IMA) adopted a Code of Professional Conduct for Management Accountants. This ethical code emphasizes that management accountants have a responsibility to achieve the competence necessary to do their jobs, to keep information confidential except when they are authorized or legally required to disclose it, to maintain integrity and avoid conflicts of interest, and to communicate information objectively and without bias.[13]

Public Accounting

The field of **public accounting**, which is practiced by certified public accountants (CPAs), offers auditing, tax, and management consulting services to the public for a fee. In the short time since about 1900, public accounting has gained a stature in this country similar to that of the older professions of law and medicine.

Requirements. To become a CPA, the applicant must meet rigorous requirements. These requirements vary from state to state but have certain characteristics in common. An applicant must be a person of integrity and

13. *Statement Number 1C*, "Standards of Ethical Conduct for Management Accountants" (Montvale, N.J.: National Association of Accountants, June 1, 1983).

have at least a high school education. Most states require four years of college (a few require five years) with the equivalent of a major in accounting, and the AICPA has voted to make 150 college-level semester hours of education (i.e., five years) a requirement for membership after the year 2000. Further, the applicant must pass a difficult and comprehensive two-and-one-half-day examination in accounting practice, accounting theory, auditing, and business law. Although the examination is uniform in all states, some states also require an examination in such areas as economics or professional ethics. The examination is prepared by the American Institute of Certified Public Accountants and is given twice a year. Most states also require from one to five years' experience in the office of a certified public accountant or acceptable equivalent experience. In some cases, additional education can be substituted for one or more years of accounting experience. Less than 20 percent of the accountants in the United States are CPAs.

Professional Ethics. The profession can be divided into four broad fields: (1) management accounting, (2) public accounting, (3) government and not-for-profit accounting, and (4) accounting education. To ensure that its members understand the responsibilities of being professional accountants, the AICPA and each state have adopted Codes of Professional Conduct as guides to action. Fundamental to these codes is responsibility to the public, including clients, creditors, investors, and anyone else who relies on the accountant's work. In resolving conflicts among these various groups, the accountant must act with integrity even at the sacrifice of personal benefit. **Integrity** means that the accountant is honest and candid and subordinates personal gain to service and the public trust. The accountant must also be objective. **Objectivity** means that he or she is impartial and intellectually honest. Furthermore, the accountant must be independent. **Independence** is the avoidance of all relationships that impair or appear to impair the objectivity of the accountant. One way in which an auditor of a company upholds independence is by having no direct financial interest in that company and not being an employee of the company. The accountant must exercise **due care** in all activities, carrying out professional responsibilities with competence and diligence. For example, an accountant must not accept a job for which he or she is not qualified, even at the risk of losing a client to another firm; and careless work is not acceptable. These broad principles are supported by more specific rules that accountants must follow (for instance, with certain exceptions, client information must be kept confidential). Accountants who violate the rules may be disciplined or suspended from the practice of accounting.

Accounting Firms. Certified public accountants offer their services to the public for a fee, just as doctors or lawyers do. Accounting firms are made up of partners, who must be CPAs, and staff accountants, many of whom are CPAs and hope to become partners someday. Accounting firms vary in size from large international firms with hundreds of partners and thou-

Table 1-2. Accounting's Large International Certified Public Accounting Firms

Firm	Home Office	Some Major Clients
Arthur Andersen & Co.	Chicago	ITT, Texaco, United Airlines
Coopers & Lybrand	New York	AT&T, Ford
Deloitte & Touche	New York	General Motors, Procter & Gamble, Sears
Ernst & Young	New York	Mobil, McDonald's, Coca-Cola
KPMG Peat Marwick	New York	General Electric, Xerox
Price Waterhouse	New York	IBM, Exxon, Du Pont
Grant Thornton	Chicago	Fretter, Grainger, Home Shopping Network

sands of employees (see Table 1-2) to small one- or two-person firms. The firms listed in Table 1-2 employ about 25 percent of all CPAs.

The work of the public accountant is varied, complex, and interesting. Most accounting firms organize themselves into several principal areas of specialization, which may include (1) auditing, (2) tax services, (3) management advisory services, and (4) small business services.

Auditing. The most important and distinctive function of a certified public accountant is auditing (also called the **attest function**), which is the examination and testing of financial statements for the purpose of rendering an opinion on the fair presentation of the statements in accordance with GAAP.

Tax Services. In the area of **tax services**, public accountants assist businesses and individuals in preparing tax returns and complying with tax laws. They also help plan business decisions to reduce taxes in the future. Tax accounting work calls for specific knowledge and skill regardless of the size of a business. Few business decisions are without tax effects.

Management Advisory Services. An increasingly important part of most public accounting firms' practice is **management advisory services**, or consulting. With their intimate knowledge of a business's operations, auditors can make important suggestions for improvements and, as a matter of course, usually do. In the past, these recommendations have dealt mainly with accounting records, budgeting, and cost accounting. But in the last five to ten years they have expanded into marketing, organizational planning, personnel and recruiting, production, and many other business areas. The wide use of computers has led to services in systems design and control and to the use of mathematical and statistical decision models. All these different services combined make up management advisory services.

Small Business Services. Many small businesses look to their CPAs for advice on operating their businesses and keeping their accounting records. Although small CPA firms have traditionally performed these functions, large firms are also establishing small business practice units. Among the types of services a CPA might provide are setting up or revising an accounting system, compiling monthly financial statements, preparing a budget of cash needs over the coming year, and assisting the client in obtaining a bank loan.

Government and Other Not-for-Profit Accounting

Agencies and departments at all levels of government hire accountants to prepare reports so that officials can responsibly carry out their duties. Millions of income, payroll, and sales tax returns must be checked and audited. The Federal Bureau of Investigation and the Internal Revenue Service use thousands of accountants. The General Accounting Office audits government activities for Congress, using many auditors and other accounting specialists all over the world. Federal agencies such as the Securities and Exchange Commission, Interstate Commerce Commission, and Federal Communications Commission hire accountants. State agencies such as those dealing with public utilities regulation or tax collection also use the services of accountants.

Many other not-for-profit enterprises employ accountants. Some of these organizations are hospitals, colleges, universities, and foundations. These institutions, like the government, are interested in compliance with the law and efficient use of public resources. They account for over 25 percent of the gross output of our economy. Clearly, the role of accountants in helping these organizations use their resources wisely is important to our society.

Accounting Education

Training new accountants is a challenging and rewarding career, and today instructors of accounting are in great demand. Accounting instructors at the secondary level must have a college degree with a major in accounting and must meet state teacher certification requirements. One entry-level requirement for teaching at the smaller and two-year college level is the master's degree. Faculty members at most larger universities must have a Ph.D. degree and engage in research. In many schools, holding the CPA, CMA, or **CIA (Certified Internal Auditor)** certificate will help an instructor to advance professionally.

Chapter Review

Review of Learning Objectives

1. **Define accounting and describe its role in making informed decisions.**
Accounting is an information system that measures, processes, and communicates information, primarily financial in nature, about an identifiable entity for the purpose of making economic decisions. It is not an end in itself but is a tool to be used in providing information that is useful in making reasoned choices among alternative uses of scarce resources in the conduct of business and economic activities.

2. **Identify the many users of accounting information in society.**
Accounting plays a significant role in society by providing information to managers of all institutions and to individuals with a direct financial interest in those institutions, such as present or potential investors or creditors. Accounting information is also important to those with an indirect financial interest in the business, such as tax authorities, regulatory agencies, economic planners, and other groups.

3. **Distinguish between financial and management accounting, define generally accepted accounting principles (GAAP), and identify the organizations that influence GAAP.**
Financial accounting refers to the development and use of accounting reports that are communicated to those external to the business organization as well as to management, whereas management accounting refers to the preparation of information primarily for internal use by management. Acceptable accounting practice at a particular time consists of those conventions, rules, and procedures that make up generally accepted accounting principles. GAAP are essential to the preparation and interpretation of financial accounting reports. Among the organizations that influence the formulation of GAAP are the American Institute of Certified Public Accountants, the Financial Accounting Standards Board, the Securities and Exchange Commission, and the Internal Revenue Service. Other organizations with an interest in accounting are the Institute of Management Accountants, the Financial Executives Institute, and the American Accounting Association.

4. **Explain the importance of business transactions, money measure, and separate entity to accounting measurement.**
To make an accounting measurement, the accountant must determine what is to be measured, when the measurement should occur, what value should be placed on what is measured, and how what is measured should be classified. Generally accepted accounting principles define the objects of accounting measurement as business transactions, money measure, and separate entities. Relating these three concepts, financial accounting measures the business transactions of separate entities in terms of money measures.

5. **Describe the corporate form of business organization.**
Corporations, whose ownership is represented by shares of stocks, are separate entities for both legal and accounting purposes. The stockholders own the corporation and elect the board of directors, whose duty it is to determine corporate policy. The corporate officers or management of the corporation are appointed by the board of directors and are responsible for the operation of the business in accordance with the board's policies.

6. **Define financial position and show how it is affected by simple transactions.**
   Financial position is the economic resources belonging to a company and the claims against those resources at a point in time. Business transactions affect financial position by decreasing or increasing assets, liabilities, and/or owners' equity in such a way that the basic accounting equation (assets = liabilities + owners' equity) is always in balance.

7. **Identify the four basic financial statements.**
   Financial statements are the means by which accountants communicate the financial condition and activities of a business to those who have an interest in the business. The four basic financial statements are the balance sheet, the income statement, the statement of retained earnings, and the statement of cash flows.

8. **Describe accounting as a profession with ethical responsibilities and a wide career choice.**
   The people who provide accounting information to users make up the accounting profession. They may be management accountants, public accountants, or government or other not-for-profit accountants. All accountants are required to follow a code of professional ethics, the foundation of which is responsibility to the public. Accountants must act with integrity, objectivity, and independence, and they must exercise due care in all activities. Another career choice open to accountants is that of being accounting educators. Each type of accounting work is an important specialization and represents a challenging career.

Review of Concepts and Terminology

The following concepts and terms were introduced in this chapter:

(L.O. 1) **Accounting:** An information system that measures, processes, and communicates financial information about an identifiable economic entity.

(L.O. 6) **Accounting equation:** Assets = liabilities + owners' equity, or, Owners' equity = assets − liabilities.

(L.O. 6) **Accounts:** Labels used by accountants to accumulate amounts from similar transactions.

(L.O. 3) **American Institute of Certified Public Accountants (AICPA):** The professional association of CPAs.

(L.O. 5) **Articles of incorporation:** An official document filed with and approved by a state that authorizes a business to do business as a corporation.

(L.O. 6) **Assets:** Probable future economic benefits obtained or controlled by a particular entity as a result of past transactions or events.

(L.O. 8) **Attest function:** The examination and testing of financial statements by a certified public accountant. (Also called auditing.)

(L.O. 3) **Audit:** An examination of the financial statements of a company in order to render an independent professional opinion as to the fairness of their presentation in accordance with generally accepted accounting principles. (Also called the attest function.)

(L.O. 5) **Audit committee:** A committee of the board of directors of a corporation that engages the company's independent auditors and reviews their work.

(L.O. 7) **Balance sheet:** The financial statement that shows the assets, liabilities, and owners' equity of a business at a point in time.

(L.O. 1) **Bookkeeping:** The means by which transactions are recorded and records are kept.

(L.O. 4) **Business transactions:** Economic events that affect the financial position of the business entity.

(L.O. 8) **Certified internal auditor (CIA):** Professional certification for auditors who carry out their work from within a company.

(L.O. 8) **Certified management accountant (CMA):** Professional certification awarded qualified management accountants by the Institute of Certified Management Accountants.

(L.O. 3) **Certified public accountant (CPA):** Public accountant who has met stringent licensing requirements as set by the individual states.

(L.O. 1) **Computer:** An electronic tool for the rapid collection, organization, and communication of large amounts of information.

(L.O. 6) **Contributed capital:** The part of stockholders' equity that represents the amount invested in the business by owners (stockholders).

(L.O. 1) **Control:** The process of seeing that plans are carried out.

(L.O. 5) **Corporation:** A body of persons granted a charter legally recognizing it as a separate entity having its own rights, privileges, and liabilities distinct from those of its owners.

(L.O. 6) **Dividends:** Distributions to stockholders of assets (usually cash) generated by past earnings.

(L.O. 8) **Due care:** The act of carrying out professional responsibilities with competence and diligence.

(L.O. 6) **Equity:** The residual interest in the assets of an entity that remains after deducting its liabilities; called stockholders' equity in a corporation.

(L.O. 8) **Ethics:** The application of a code of conduct, addressing whether actions are good or bad, right or wrong, to everyday life.

(L.O. 1) **Evaluation:** The examination of the entire decision system with a view to improving it.

(L.O. 4) **Exchange rate:** The value of one currency in terms of another.

(L.O. 6) **Expenses:** Decreases in retained earnings that result from operating the business.

(L.O. 3) **Financial accounting:** Accounting information that is communicated to those outside the organization for their use in evaluating the entity as well as being used internally.

(L.O. 3) **Financial Accounting Standards Board (FASB):** Body that has responsibility for developing and issuing rules on accounting practice; issues Statements of Financial Accounting Standards.

(L.O. 6) **Financial position:** The economic resources belonging to a company and the claims against those resources at a point in time.

(L.O. 7) **Financial statements:** The primary means of communicating important accounting information to users.

(L.O. 3) **Generally accepted accounting principles (GAAP):** The conventions, rules, and procedures necessary to define accepted accounting practice at a particular time.

(L.O. 3) **Government Accounting Standards Board (GASB):** Board established in 1984 under the same governing body as FASB with responsibility for issuing accounting standards for state and local governments.

(L.O. 7) **Income statement:** The financial statement that summarizes the amount of revenues earned and expenses incurred by a business entity over a period of time.

(L.O. 3, 8) **Independence:** The avoidance of all relationships that impair or appear to impair the objectivity of the accountant.

(L.O. 8) **Integrity:** An accountant exhibits integrity when he or she is honest and candid and subordinates personal gain to service and the public trust.

(L.O. 3) **Internal Revenue Service (IRS):** Federal agency that interprets and enforces the U.S. tax laws governing the assessment and collection of revenue for operating the government.

(L.O. 6) **Liabilities:** Probable future sacrifices of economic benefits arising from present obligations of a particular entity to transfer assets or provide services to other entities in the future as a result of past transactions or events.

(L.O. 2) **Liquidity:** Having enough funds on hand to pay debts when they are due.

(L.O. 2, 5) **Management:** The group of people in a business who have overall responsibility for operating the business and for achieving the company's goals.

(L.O. 3, 8) **Management accounting:** Accounting information for the internal use of a company's management.

(L.O. 8) **Management advisory services:** Consulting services offered by public accountants.

(L.O. 1) **Management information system (MIS):** The interconnected subsystems that provide the information necessary to operate a business.

(L.O. 4) **Money measure:** The recording of all business transactions in the form of money.

(L.O. 6) **Net assets:** Owners' equity, or assets minus liabilities.

(L.O. 6) **Net income (loss):** Revenues minus expenses.

(L.O. 8) **Objectivity:** The act of being impartial and intellectually honest.

(L.O. 6) **Owners' equity:** The claims by the owners against the assets of the business.

(L.O. 5) **Partnership:** An association of two or more persons to carry on as co-owners of a business for profit.

(L.O. 1) **Planning:** The process of formulating a course of action.

(L.O. 8) **Professional ethics:** The application of a code of conduct to the practice of a profession.

(L.O. 2) **Profitability:** The ability to earn enough income to attract and hold investment capital.

(L.O. 8) **Public accounting:** The field of accounting that offers services in auditing, taxes, and management advising to the public for a fee.

(L.O. 6) **Retained earnings:** The part of stockholders' equity that represents the assets generated from the income-producing activities of the business and kept for use in the business.

(L.O. 6) **Revenues:** Increases in retained earnings that result from operating the business.

(L.O. 3) **Securities and Exchange Commission (SEC):** An agency of the federal government that has the legal power to set and enforce accounting practices for firms reporting to it.

(L.O. 4) **Separate entity:** The concept that treats a business as distinct and apart from its creditors, customers, and owners.

(L.O. 5) **Share of stock:** A unit of ownership in a corporation.

(L.O. 5) **Sole proprietorship:** A business owned by one person.

(L.O. 7) **Statement of cash flows:** The financial statement that shows the inflows and outflows of cash from operating activities, investing activities, and financing activities over a period of time.

(L.O. 7) **Statement of retained earnings:** The financial statement that shows the changes in retained earnings over a period of time.

(L.O. 6) **Stockholders' equity:** The owners' equity of a corporation, consisting of contributed capital and retained earnings.

(L.O. 8) **Tax services:** Services offered by public accountants in tax planning, compliance, and reporting.

Review Problem
Effect of Transactions on the Accounting Equation

(L.O. 6) Charlene Rudek finished law school in June and immediately set up her own law practice. During the first month of operation she completed the following transactions:

a. Invested in the practice by placing $2,000 in a bank account established for the business, in exchange for 1,000 shares of $2 par value common stock of the corporation.
b. Purchased a law library for $900 cash.
c. Purchased office supplies for $400 on credit.
d. Accepted $500 in cash for completing a contract.
e. Billed clients $1,950 for services rendered during the month.
f. Paid $200 of the amount owed for office supplies.
g. Received $1,250 in cash from one client who had been previously billed for services rendered.
h. Paid rent expense for the month in the amount of $1,200.
i. Declared and paid a dividend of $400.

Required Show the effect of each of these transactions on the balance sheet equation by completing a table similar to Exhibit 1-1 (page 28). Identify each owners' equity transaction.

Answer to Review Problem

	Assets				= Liabilities +	Stockholders' Equity		
	Cash	Accounts Receiv-able	Office Supplies	Law Library	Accounts Payable	Common Stock	Retained Earnings	Type of SE Transaction
a.	$2,000					$2,000		Owners' Investment
b.	-900			+$900				
bal.	$1,100			$900		$2,000		
c.			+$400		+$400			
bal.	$1,100		$400	$900	$400	$2,000		
d.	+500						+$ 500	Service Revenue
bal.	$1,600		$400	$900	$400	$2,000	$ 500	
e.		+$1,950					+1,950	Service Revenue
bal.	$1,600	$1,950	$400	$900	$400	$2,000	$2,450	
f.	-200				-200			
bal.	$1,400	$1,950	$400	$900	$200	$2,000	$2,450	
g.	+1,250	-1,250						
bal.	$2,650	$ 700	$400	$900	$200	$2,000	$2,450	
h.	-1,200						-1,200	Expenses
bal.	$1,450	$ 700	$400	$900	$200	$2,000	$1,250	
i.	-400						-400	Dividends
bal.	$1,050	$ 700	$400	$900	$200	$2,000	$ 850	
		$3,050			=	$3,050		

Chapter Assignments

Discussion Questions

1. Why is accounting considered an information system?
2. Distinguish among these terms: accounting, bookkeeping, and management information systems.
3. How are decisions made, and what is the role of accounting in the decision system?
4. What decision makers use accounting information?
5. What broad management objectives are facilitated by using accounting information?
6. Why are investors and creditors interested in the financial statements of a company?
7. Why has society as a whole become one of the biggest users of accounting information? What groups besides business managers, investors, and creditors use accounting information?
8. Distinguish financial accounting from management accounting.
9. What are GAAP, and why are they important to readers of financial statements?

10. What does the auditor mean by the phrase "in all material respects" when stating in the independent accountant's report that the financial statements "present fairly, in all material respects . . . in conformity with generally accepted accounting principles"?
11. What organization has the most influence on GAAP?
12. Use the terms *business transaction, money measure,* and *separate entity* in a single sentence that demonstrates their relevance to financial accounting.
13. What are the functions in a corporation of stockholders, the board of directors, and management?
14. How do sole proprietorships, partnerships, and corporations differ?
15. Define assets, liabilities, and owners' equity.
16. What three items affect retained earnings, and how?
17. Arnold Smith's company has assets of $22,000 and liabilities of $10,000. What is the amount of his owners' equity?
18. Give examples of the types of transactions that will (a) increase assets and (b) increase liabilities.
19. Why is the balance sheet sometimes called the statement of financial position?
20. Contrast the purposes of the balance sheet with those of the income statement.
21. How does the income statement differ from the statement of cash flows?
22. A statement for an accounting period that ends in June may have either (1) June 30, 19xx, or (2) For the Year Ended June 30, 19xx, as part of its identification. State which heading would be appropriate with (a) a balance sheet, and (b) an income statement.
23. What are some of the fields encompassed by the accounting profession?
24. What are some activities in which the management accountant might participate?
25. How is a public accountant different from a management accountant?
26. Describe in general terms the requirements that an individual must meet to become a CPA and the four major activities of CPAs.
27. Accounting can be viewed as (a) an intellectual discipline, (b) a profession, or (c) a social force. In what sense is it each of these?
28. Compare and contrast the professional ethics of public accountants and management accountants as reflected by their respective codes of professional conduct.

Communication Skills Exercises

Communication Skills Exercises are *real accounting issues* designed so that they allow you to improve your communication skills as future managers and accountants. Most of these exercises may be completed as written assignments, but your instructor may also want to use them as discussion cases, group exercises, or presentation assignments.

Communication 1-1. Role of Computer, Bookkeeper, and Accountant *(L.O. 1)*

Jane, Judy, and Jud opened a clothing store earlier this year called The 3 Js. They began by opening a checking account in the name of the business, renting a store, and buying some clothes to sell. They paid for the purchases and expenses out of the checking account and deposited cash in the account when they sold the clothes. At this point, they are arguing over how their business is doing and how much each of them should be paid. They also realize that they are supposed to make certain tax reports and payments, but they know very little about them. The following statements are excerpts from their conversation:

Jane: If we just had a computer, we wouldn't have had this argument.
Judy: No, what we need is a bookkeeper.
Jud: I don't know, but maybe we need an accountant.

Distinguish among a computer, a bookkeeper, and an accountant, and comment on how each might help the operations of The 3 Js.

Communication 1-2. Users of Accounting Information *(L.O. 2)*

Public companies report annually on their success or failure in making a net income or net loss. Suppose that the following item appeared in the newspaper:

New York. Commonwealth Power Company, a major electric utility, reported yesterday that its net income for the year just ended represented a 50 percent increase over the previous year. . . .

Explain why each of the following individuals or groups may be interested in seeing the accounting reports that support this statement.

1. The management of Commonwealth Power
2. The stockholders of Commonwealth Power
3. The creditors of Commonwealth Power
4. Potential stockholders of Commonwealth Power
5. The Internal Revenue Service
6. The Securities and Exchange Commission
7. The electrical workers' union
8. A consumers' group called the Public Cause
9. An economic adviser to the president

Communication 1-3. Professional Ethics *(L.O. 8)*

Discuss the ethical choices you would face in the situations below. In each case, determine the alternative courses of action, describe the ethical dilemmas, and tell what you would do.

a. You are the payroll accountant for a small business. A friend asks you how much the hourly pay of another employee in the business is.
b. As an accountant for the branch office of a wholesale supplier, you become aware of several instances when the branch manager has submitted the receipts from "nights out" with his spouse for reimbursement as selling expense by the home office.
c. You are an accountant in the purchasing department of a construction company. Upon arriving home from work on December 22, you find a large ham in a box marked "Happy Holidays—It's a pleasure to work with you." You note that the gift is from a supplier who has bid on a contract to be awarded by your employer next week.
d. As an auditor with one year's experience at a local CPA firm, you are expected to complete a certain part of an audit in 20 hours. Because of your lack of experience, you cannot finish the job within this timeframe. Rather than admit this, you are thinking of working late to finish the job, but not telling anyone about it.

e. You are a tax accountant at a local CPA firm. You assist your neighbor in filling out her tax return. She pays you $200 in cash. Since there is no record of this transaction, you are considering not reporting it on your tax return.
f. The accounting firm for which you work as a CPA has just gained a new client in which you own 200 shares of stock that you received as an inheritance from your grandmother. Since it is only a small number of shares and you think the company will be very successful, you are thinking of not disclosing the investment.

Communication 1-4. Concept of an Asset *(L.O. 6)*

Foote, Cone & Belding Communications, Inc. is one of the largest and most successful advertising agencies in the world. Its 1989 annual report carries the following statement: "Our principal asset is our people. Our success depends in large part on our ability to attract and retain personnel who are competent in the various aspects of our business."[14] Are personnel considered assets in the financial statements? In what sense does Foote, Cone & Belding consider its employees its principal asset?

Communication 1-5. Basic Research Skills *(L.O. 1, 2)*

Clip an article about a company from the business section of your local paper or of a nearby metropolitan daily. List all the financial and accounting terms used in the article. Bring the article to class and be prepared to discuss how a knowledge of accounting would help a reader to understand the content of the article.

Classroom Exercises

Exercise 1-1. The Nature of Accounting *(L.O. 1, 2, 3)*

Match the terms on the left with the descriptions on the right.

____ 1. Bookkeeping	A. A function of accounting
____ 2. Creditor	B. Often confused with accounting
____ 3. Measurement	C. User of accounting information
____ 4. Financial Accounting Standards Board (FASB)	D. Organization that influences current practice
____ 5. Tax authorities	
____ 6. Computer	
____ 7. Communication	
____ 8. Securities and Exchange Commission (SEC)	
____ 9. Investors	
____ 10. Processing	
____ 11. Management	
____ 12. Management information system	

Exercise 1-2. Separate Entity *(L.O. 4)*

Jason owns and operates a local mini-mart. State which of the transactions that follow are properly accounted for as an expense of the business. Explain why the others are not regarded as transactions.

14. Excerpts from 1989 Annual Report used by permission of Foote, Cone & Belding Communications, Inc. All rights reserved.

a. Jason takes a loaf of bread and a gallon of milk from the mini-mart's shelves for use at home over the weekend.
b. Jason pays a high school student cash for cleaning up the drive behind the mini-mart.
c. Jason fills his son's car with gasoline in payment for restocking the vending machines and the snack food shelves.
d. Jason pays interest to himself on a loan he made three years ago to the business.

Exercise 1-3. Money Measure *(L.O. 4)*

You have been asked to compare four companies that make computer chips on the basis of sales and assets in order to determine which company is the largest in each category. You have gathered the following data, but they do not offer grounds for direct comparison because each company's sales and assets are in its own currency:

Company (Currency)	Sales	Assets
Inchip (U.S. dollar)	20,000,000	13,000,000
Wong (Taiwan dollar)	50,000,000	24,000,000
Mitzu (Japanese yen)	3,500,000,000	2,500,000,000
Works (German mark)	35,000,000	39,000,000

Assuming that the exchange rates in Table 1-1 are current and appropriate, convert all the figures to U.S. dollars and determine which company is the largest in each category.

Exercise 1-4. The Accounting Equation *(L.O. 6)*

Use the accounting equation to answer each question below. Show any calculations you make.

1. The assets of Newport Company are $650,000, and the owners' equity is $360,000. What is the amount of the liabilities?
2. The liabilities and owners' equity of Fitzgerald Company are $95,000 and $32,000, respectively. What is the amount of the assets?
3. The liabilities of Emerald Co. equal one-third of the total assets, and owners' equity is $120,000. What is the amount of the liabilities?
4. At the beginning of the year, Sherman Company's assets were $220,000, and its owners' equity was $100,000. During the year, assets increased $60,000, and liabilities decreased $10,000. What was the owners' equity at the end of the year?

Exercise 1-5. Owners' Equity Transactions *(L.O. 6)*

Identify the following transactions by type of owners' equity transaction by marking each as either an owners' investment (I), dividend (D), revenue (R), expense (E), or not an owners' equity transaction (NOE).

a. Received cash for providing a service.
b. Took assets out of business as a dividend.
c. Received cash from a customer previously billed for a service.
d. Transferred assets to the business in exchange for common stock.
e. Paid service station for gasoline.

f. Performed a service and received a promise of payment.
g. Paid cash to purchase equipment.
h. Paid cash to employee for services performed.

Exercise 1-6. Effect of Transactions on Accounting Equation *(L.O. 6)*

During the month of April, Grissom Co. had the following transactions:

a. Paid salaries for April, $1,800.
b. Purchased equipment on credit, $3,000.
c. Purchased supplies with cash, $100.
d. Additional investment by stockholder, $4,000.
e. Received payment for services performed, $600.
f. Paid for part of equipment previously purchased on credit, $1,000.
g. Billed customers for services performed, $1,600.
h. Received payment from customers billed previously, $300.
i. Received utility bill, $70.
j. Declared and paid dividends of $1,500.

On a sheet of paper, list the letters a through j, with columns for Assets, Liabilities, and Owners' Equity. In the columns, indicate whether each transaction caused an increase (+), a decrease (–), or no change (NC) in assets, liabilities, and owners' equity.

Exercise 1-7. Examples of Transactions *(L.O. 6)*

For each of the following categories, describe a transaction that will have the required effect on the elements of the accounting equation.

1. Increase one asset and decrease another asset.
2. Decrease an asset and decrease a liability.
3. Increase an asset and increase a liability.
4. Increase an asset and increase owners' equity.
5. Decrease an asset and decrease owners' equity.

Exercise 1-8. Effect of Transactions on Accounting Equation *(L.O. 6)*

The total assets and liabilities at the beginning and end of the year for Pizarro Company are listed below.

	Assets	Liabilities
Beginning of the year	$110,000	$ 45,000
End of the year	200,000	120,000

Determine Pizarro Company's net income for the year under each of the following alternatives:

1. There were no investments in the business and no dividends during the year.
2. There were no investments in the business, but dividends of $22,000 were paid during the year.
3. There was an investment of $13,000, but no dividends were paid during the year.
4. There was an investment of $10,000 in the business, and dividends of $22,000 were paid during the year.

Exercise 1-9. Identification of Accounts *(L.O. 6, 7)*

Indicate below whether each account is an asset (A), a liability (L), or a part of stockholders' equity (SE):

_____ a. Cash
_____ b. Salaries Payable
_____ c. Accounts Receivable
_____ d. Common Stock
_____ e. Land
_____ f. Accounts Payable
_____ g. Supplies

Indicate below whether each account would be shown on the income statement (IS), the statement of retained earnings (RE), or the balance sheet (BS):

_____ h. Repair Revenue
_____ i. Automobile
_____ j. Fuel Expense
_____ k. Cash
_____ l. Rent Expense
_____ m. Accounts Payable
_____ n. Dividends

Exercise 1-10. Preparation of Balance Sheet *(L.O. 7)*

Appearing in random order below are the balances for balance sheet items for Herron Company as of December 31, 19xx.

Accounts Payable	$ 40,000	Accounts Receivable	$50,000
Building	90,000	Cash	20,000
Common Stock	100,000	Equipment	40,000
Supplies	10,000	Retained Earnings	70,000

Sort the balances and prepare a balance sheet similar to the one in Exhibit 1-2.

Exercise 1-11. Completion of Financial Statements *(L.O. 7)*

Determine the amounts corresponding to the letters by completing the following independent sets of financial statements:

Income Statement	**Set A**	**Set B**	**Set C**
Revenues	$ 550	$ g	$120
Expenses	a	2,600	m
Net Income	$ b	$ h	$ 40
Statement of Retained Earnings			
Beginning Balance	$1,450	$ 7,700	$100
Net Income	c	800	n
Dividends	(100)	i	o
Ending Balance	$1,500	$ j	$ p
Balance Sheet			
Total Assets	$ d	$15,500	$ q
Liabilities	$ 800	$ 2,500	$ r
Stockholders' Equity			
Capital Stock	1,000	5,000	50
Retained Earnings	e	k	140
Total Liabilities and Stockholders' Equity	$ f	$ l	$290

Exercise 1-12. Preparation of Financial Statements
(L.O. 7)

Kingsley Corporation engaged in the following activities during 19x1: Service Revenues, $26,400; Rent Expense, $2,400; Wages Expense, $16,540; Advertising Expense, $2,700; Utility Expense, $1,800; and Dividends, $1,400. In addition, the year-end balances of selected accounts were as follows: Cash, $3,100; Accounts Receivable, $1,500; Supplies, $200; Land, $2,000; Accounts Payable, $900; and Common Stock, $2,000.

Prepare in good form the income statement, statement of retained earnings, and balance sheet for Kingsley Corporation for 19x1 (assume December 31 year end). **Hint:** You must solve for the year-end balances of retained earnings for 19x0 and 19x1.

Exercise 1-13. Revenues, Expenses, and Cash Flows
(L.O. 7)

Abigail, an attorney, bills her clients at a rate of $50 per hour. During April, she worked 150 hours for clients and billed them appropriately. By the end of April, 80 of these hours remained unpaid. At the beginning of the month, clients owed Abigail $4,000, of which $2,800 was paid during April.

Abigail has one employee, a secretary who is paid $10 per hour. During April, the secretary worked 170 hours, of which 16 hours were to be paid in May. The rest were paid in April. Further, Abigail paid the secretary for 8 hours worked in March.

Determine the amount of revenue from clients, wages expense for secretary, cash received from customers, and cash paid for secretary for the month of April.

Exercise 1-14. Statement of Cash Flows
(L.O. 7)

Cirro Corporation began the year 19x1 with cash of $43,000. In addition to earning a net income of $25,000 and paying a cash dividend of $15,000, Cirro borrowed $60,000 from the bank and purchased equipment for $90,000 with cash. Also, Accounts Receivable increased by $6,000 and Accounts Payable increased by $9,000.

Determine the amount of cash on hand at the end of the year (December 31) by preparing in good form a statement of cash flows similar to the one in Exhibit 1-3.

Exercise 1-15. Accounting Abbreviations
(L.O. 3, 8)

Identify the accounting meaning of each of the following abbreviations: AICPA, SEC, GAAP, FASB, IRS, GASB, IASC, IFAC, IMA, FEI, AAA, CMA, CPA, and CIA.

Interpretation Cases from Business

ICB 1-1. Public Service Electric & Gas Company
(L.O. 1, 2)

The *Wall Street Journal* is the leading daily financial newspaper in the United States. The following excerpts from an article entitled "Public Service E & G Asks $464.5 Million Annual Rates Rise" appeared in the *Wall Street Journal* on January 10, 1983:

> *Newark, N.J.* Public Service Electric & Gas Co. said it asked the New Jersey Board of Public Utilities to authorize increases in gas and electric rates that would add $464.5 million to annual revenue, an 11.5% jump.
>
> The utility said that more than half of the added revenue would go to paying federal income taxes, and the state gross receipts and franchise tax.
>
> The request asks for a 15.6% increase in electric rates, amounting to added revenue of $398 million a year, and a 4.5% increase in gas rates, which would bring added annual revenue of $67 million. . . .

Explaining its need for expanded revenue, the utility said it has suffered a decline in electricity demand as a result of the recession. Kilowatt-hour sales fell 2.7% in 1982, and gas sales dropped 2%, the utility said. . . .[15]

Required

1. Assume that you are a member of the New Jersey Board of Public Utilities and are faced with the above request for a rate increase. What five factors would you consider most important or relevant to making an informed decision? Be as specific as possible.
2. What do you suppose would be the best source or sources of information about each of the factors you listed in **1**?

ICB 1-2. Merrill Lynch & Co., Inc.[16] *(L.O. 6)*

Merrill Lynch & Co., Inc. is a U.S.-based global financial services firm. Condensed and adapted balance sheets for 1990 and 1989 from the company's annual report are presented below. (All numbers are in thousands.) The owners' equity section has been adapted for use in this case.

Merrill Lynch & Co., Inc.
Condensed Balance Sheets
December 31, 1990 and 1989

	1990	1989
Assets		
Cash	$ 1,786,779	$ 2,051,347
Marketable Securities	17,283,836	15,721,216
Accounts Receivable	32,260,458	31,644,718
Property and Equipment	1,646,276	1,669,406
Other Assets	15,152,178	12,855,576
Total Assets	$68,129,527	$63,942,263
Liabilities		
Short-Term Liabilities	$58,562,538	$53,893,811
Long-Term Liabilities	6,341,559	6,897,109
Total Liabilities	$64,904,097	$60,790,920
Stockholders' Equity		
Common Stock	$ 996,709	$ 986,841
Retained Earnings	2,228,721	2,164,502
Total Liabilities and Stockholders' Equity	$68,129,527	$63,942,263

15. Source: *The Wall Street Journal,* January 10, 1983. Reprinted by permission of the *Wall Street Journal,* © 1983 Dow Jones and Company, Inc. All Rights Reserved Worldwide.
16. Excerpts from the 1990 Annual Report used by permission of Merrill Lynch & Co., Inc. Copyright © 1990.

Three students who were looking at Merrill Lynch's annual report were overheard to make the following comments:

Student A: What a superb year Merrill Lynch & Co., Inc. had in 1990! The company earned a net income of $4,187,264, because total assets increased by that amount ($68,129,527 – $63,942,263).

Student B: But the change in total assets is not the same as net income! The company had a net loss of $264,568, because cash decreased by that amount ($2,051,347 – $1,786,779).

Student C: I see from the annual report that Merrill Lynch paid cash dividends of $127,637 in 1990. Don't you have to take this fact into consideration when analyzing the company's performance?

Required

1. Comment on the interpretation of students A and B and answer student C's question.
2. Calculate the 1990 net income for Merrill Lynch & Co., Inc.

ICB 1-3.
Ponderosa, Inc.[17]
(L.O. 6)

Ponderosa, Inc. is the well-known operator of Ponderosa Steakhouses located throughout the United States. Selected amounts from the company's condensed financial statements for 1985 and 1986 are presented below, with several amounts missing (all figures are in thousands). The 1984 end-of-year balance of retained earnings is $82,883.

Required

1. Determine the missing amounts indicated by the letters.
2. Given the data presented, did the company's profitability improve from 1985 to 1986? Would you characterize the company as a "growth" company? Why or why not?

Income Statement	**1986**	**1985**
Revenues	$490,304	$ a
Costs and Expenses	h	(501,295)
Income Taxes	(853)	(3,603)
Net Income	$ i	$ b
Statement of Retained Earnings		
Beginning-of-year Balance	$ j	$ c
Net Income	3,747	d
Dividends	k	(3,845)
End-of-year Balance	$ l	$ e
Balance Sheet		
Total Assets	$ m	$ 246,481
Total Liabilities	110,192	102,239
Common Stock	57,968	56,800
Retained Earnings	n	f
Total Liabilities and Stockholders' Equity	$255,473	$ g

17. Excerpts from the 1985 and 1986 annual reports used by permission of Ponderosa, Inc. Copyright © 1985 and 1986.

Problem Set A

Problem 1A-1. Effect of Transactions on the Balance Sheet Equation
(L.O. 6)

Selected transactions for the Redmond Transport Corporation, begun on June 1 by Henry Redmond, are as follows:

a. Henry Redmond deposits $66,000 in cash in the name of Redmond Transport Corporation, in exchange for 6,600 shares of $10 par value stock of the corporation.
b. A truck is purchased by the business for $43,000 cash.
c. Equipment is purchased on credit for $9,000.
d. A fee of $1,200 for hauling goods is billed to a customer.
e. A fee of $2,300 for hauling goods is received in cash.
f. Cash of $600 is received from the customer who was billed in **d**.
g. A payment of $5,000 is made on the equipment purchased in **c**.
h. Expenses of $1,700 are paid in cash.
i. Dividends of $1,200 are declared and paid.

Required

1. Arrange the asset, liability, and stockholders' equity accounts in an equation similar to Exhibit 1-1, using the following account titles: Cash, Accounts Receivable, Truck, Equipment, Accounts Payable, Common Stock, and Retained Earnings.
2. Show by addition and subtraction, as in Exhibit 1-1, the effects of the transactions on the balance sheet equation. Show new balances after each transaction, and identify each stockholders' equity transaction by type.

Problem 1A-2. Effect of Transactions on the Balance Sheet Equation
(L.O. 6)

Carmen Vega, after receiving her degree in computer science, began her own business, called Custom Systems Corporation. She completed the following transactions soon after starting the business:

a. Carmen began her business by investing $9,000 in cash and a systems library, which cost $920, in exchange for 992 shares of $10 par value stock in the corporation.
b. Paid one month's rent on an office for her business. The rent is $360 per month.
c. Purchased a minicomputer for $7,000 cash.
d. Purchased computer supplies on credit, $600.
e. Collected revenue from a client, $800.
f. Billed a client $710 upon completion of a short project.
g. Paid expenses of $400.
h. Received $80 from the client billed previously.
i. Paid $200 of amount owed on computer supplies purchased in **d**.
j. Declared and paid dividends of $250.

Required

1. Arrange the asset, liability, and stockholders' equity accounts in an equation similar to Exhibit 1-1, using the following account titles: Cash, Accounts Receivable, Supplies, Equipment, Systems Library, Accounts Payable, Common Stock, and Retained Earnings.
2. Show by addition and subtraction, as in Exhibit 1-1, the effects of the transactions on the balance sheet equation. Show new totals after each transaction, and identify each stockholders' equity transaction by type.

Problem 1A-3. Effect of Transactions on the Balance Sheet Equation *(L.O. 6)*

Dr. Paul Rosello, psychologist, moved from his home town to set up an office in Cincinnati. After one month, the business had the following assets: Cash, $2,800; Accounts Receivable, $680; Office Supplies, $300; and Office Equipment, $7,500. Stockholders' Equity consisted of $8,000 of Common Stock and $680 of Retained Earnings. The Accounts Payable were $2,600 for purchases of office equipment on credit. During a short period of time, the following transactions were completed:

a. Paid one month's rent, $350.
b. Billed patient $60 for services rendered.
c. Made payment on accounts owed, $300.
d. Paid for office supplies, $100.
e. Paid secretary's salary, $300.
f. Received $800 from patients not previously billed.
g. Made payment on accounts owed, $360.
h. Paid telephone bill for current month, $70.
i Received $290 from patients previously billed.
j. Purchased additional office equipment on credit, $300.
k. Declared and paid dividends of $500.

Required

1. Arrange the asset, liability, and stockholders' equity accounts in an equation similar to Exhibit 1-1, using the following account titles: Cash, Accounts Receivable, Office Supplies, Office Equipment, Accounts Payable, Common Stock, and Retained Earnings.
2. Enter the beginning balances of the assets, liabilities, and stockholders' equity into your equation.
3. Show by addition and subtraction, as in Exhibit 1-1, the effects of the transactions on the balance sheet equation. Show new totals after each transaction, and identify each stockholders' equity transaction by type.

Problem 1A-4. Preparation of Financial Statements *(L.O. 7)*

At the end of October, 19xx, the Common Stock account of Sunnydale Riding Club, Inc. had a balance of $30,000, and Retained Earnings totaled $7,300. After operating during November, the riding club had the following account balances:

Cash	$ 8,700	Building	$30,000
Accounts Receivable	1,200	Horses	10,000
Supplies	1,000	Accounts Payable	17,800
Land	21,000		

In addition, the following transactions affected stockholders' equity:

Owners' Investment in Common Stock	$16,000	Feed Expense	$1,000
Riding Lesson Revenue	6,200	Utility Expense	600
Locker Rental Revenue	1,700	Dividends	3,200
Salaries Expense	2,300		

Required

Using Exhibit 1-2 as a model, prepare an income statement, a statement of retained earnings, and a balance sheet for Sunnydale Riding Club, Inc. (**Hint:** The final balance of Stockholders' Equity is $54,100.)

Problem 1A-5. Effect of Transactions on the Balance Sheet Equation and Preparation of Financial Statements *(L.O. 6, 7)*

On April 1, 19xx, Dependable Taxi Service, Inc. began operation. It engaged in the following transactions during April:

a. Madeline Curry deposited $42,000 in a bank account in the name of the corporation, in exchange for 4,200 shares of $10 par value stock in the corporation.
b. Purchase of taxi for cash, $19,000.
c. Purchase of uniforms on credit, $400.
d. Taxi fares received in cash, $3,200.
e. Paid wages to part-time drivers, $500.
f. Purchased gasoline during month for cash, $800.
g. Purchased car washes during month on credit, $120.
h. Further investment by owner in exchange for stock, $5,000.
i. Paid part of the amount owed for the uniforms purchased on credit in **c**, $200.
j. Billed major client for fares, $900.
k. Paid for automobile repairs, $250.
l. Declared and paid dividends of $1,000.

Required

1. Arrange the asset, liability, and stockholders' equity accounts in an equation similar to Exhibit 1-1, using these account titles: Cash, Accounts Receivable, Uniforms, Taxi, Accounts Payable, Common Stock, and Retained Earnings.
2. Show by addition and subtraction, as in Exhibit 1-1, the effects of the transactions on the balance sheet equation. Show new balances after each transaction, and identify each stockholders' equity transaction by type.
3. Using Exhibit 1-2 as a guide, prepare an income statement, a statement of retained earnings, and a balance sheet for Dependable Taxi Service, Inc.

Problem Set B

Problem 1B-1. Effect of Transactions on the Balance Sheet Equation *(L.O. 6)*

The Jiffy Messenger Corporation was founded by Hector Moreno on December 1 and engaged in the following transactions:

a. Hector Moreno began the business by placing $9,000 cash in a bank account established in the name of Jiffy Messenger Corporation, in exchange for 9,000 shares of $1 par value stock of the corporation.
b. Purchased a motor bike on credit, $3,100.
c. Purchased delivery supplies for cash, $200.
d. Billed customer for delivery fee, $100.
e. Received delivery fees in cash, $300.
f. Made payment on motor bike, $700.
g. Paid expenses, $120.
h. Received payment from customer billed in **d**, $50.
i. Declared and paid dividends of $150.

Required

1. Arrange the following asset, liability, and stockholders' equity accounts in an equation similar to Exhibit 1-1: Cash, Accounts Receivable, Delivery Supplies, Motor Bike, Accounts Payable, Common Stock, and Retained Earnings.
2. Show by addition and subtraction, as in Exhibit 1-1, the effects of the transactions on the balance sheet equation. Show new balances after each transaction, and identify each stockholders' equity transaction by type.

Problem 1B-2. Effect of Transactions on the Balance Sheet Equation *(L.O. 6)*

Frame-It Center, Inc. was started by Brenda Kuzma in a small shopping center. In the first weeks, she completed the following transactions:

a. Deposited $7,000 in a bank account in the name of the corporation in exchange for 700 shares of $10 par value stock of the corporation.
b. Paid current month's rent, $500.
c. Purchased store equipment on credit, $3,600.
d. Purchased framing supplies for cash, $1,700.
e. Received framing revenues, $800.
f. Billed customers for framing services, $700.
g. Paid utility expenses, $250.
h. Received payment from customers in **f**, $200.
i. Made payment on store equipment purchased in transaction **c**, $1,800.
j. Declared and paid dividends of $400.

Required

1. Arrange the following asset, liability, and stockholders' equity accounts in an equation similar to Exhibit 1-1: Cash, Accounts Receivable, Framing Supplies, Store Equipment, Accounts Payable, Common Stock, and Retained Earnings.
2. Show by addition and subtraction, as in Exhibit 1-1, the effects of the transactions on the balance sheet equation. Show new balances after each transaction, and identify each stockholders' equity transaction by type.

Problem 1B-3. Effect of Transactions on the Balance Sheet Equation *(L.O. 6)*

After completing her Ph.D. in management, Delia Chan set up a consulting practice. At the end of her first month of operation, Dr. Chan had the following account balances: Cash, $2,930; Accounts Receivable, $1,400; Office Supplies, $270; Office Equipment, $4,200; Accounts Payable, $1,900; Common Stock, $6,000; and Retained Earnings, $900. Soon thereafter the following transactions were completed:

a. Paid current month's rent, $400.
b. Made payment toward accounts payable, $450.
c. Billed clients for services performed, $800.
d. Received amount from clients billed last month, $1,000.
e. Purchased office supplies, $80.
f. Paid secretary's salary, $850.
g. Paid utility expense, $90.
h. Paid telephone expense, $50.
i. Purchased additional office equipment for cash, $400.
j. Received cash from clients for services performed, $1,200.
k. Declared and paid dividends of $500.

Required

1. Arrange the following asset, liability, and stockholders' equity accounts in an equation similar to Exhibit 1-1: Cash, Accounts Receivable, Office Supplies, Office Equipment, Accounts Payable, Common Stock, and Retained Earnings.
2. Enter the beginning balances of the assets, liabilities, and stockholders' equity.
3. Show by addition and subtraction, as in Exhibit 1-1, the effects of the transactions on the balance sheet equation. Show new balances after each transaction, and identify each stockholders' equity transaction by type.

Problem 1B-4. Preparation of Financial Statements *(L.O. 7)*

At the end of its first month of operation, June, 19xx, Lerner Plumbing Corporation had the following account balances:

Cash	$29,300	Tools	$3,800
Accounts Receivable	5,400	Accounts Payable	4,300
Delivery Truck	19,000		

In addition, during the month of June, the following transactions affected stockholders' equity:

Investment by M. Lerner	$20,000	Salaries Expense	$8,300
Further investment by M. Lerner	30,000	Rent Expense	700
Contract Revenue	11,600	Fuel Expense	200
Repair Revenue	2,800	Dividends	2,000

Required

Using Exhibit 1-2 as a model, prepare an income statement, a statement of retained earnings, and a balance sheet for Lerner Plumbing Corporation. (**Hint:** The final total of Stockholders' Equity is $53,200.)

Problem 1B-5. Effect of Transactions on the Balance Sheet Equation and Preparation of Financial Statements *(L.O. 6, 7)*

Royal Copying Service, Inc. began operation and engaged in the following transactions during July, 19xx:

a. Linda Friedman deposited $5,000 in a bank account in the name of the corporation, in exchange for 500 shares of $10 par value stock of the corporation.
b. Paid current month's rent, $450.
c. Purchased copier, $2,500.
d. Copying jobs payments received in cash, $890.
e. Copying job billed to major customer, $680.
f. Paid cash for paper and other copier supplies, $190.
g. Paid wages to part-time employees, $280.
h. Purchased additional copier supplies on credit, $140.
i. Received partial payment from customer in **e**, $300.
j. Paid current month's utility bill, $90.
k. Made partial payment on supplies purchased in **h**, $70.
l. Declared and paid dividends of $700.

Required

1. Arrange the asset, liability, and stockholders' equity accounts in an equation similar to Exhibit 1-1, using these account titles: Cash, Accounts Receivable, Supplies, Copier, Accounts Payable, Common Stock, and Retained Earnings.
2. Show by addition and subtraction, as in Exhibit 1-1, the effects of the transactions on the balance sheet equation. Show new balances after each transaction, and identify each stockholders' equity transaction by type.
3. Using Exhibit 1-2 as a guide, prepare an income statement, a statement of retained earnings, and a balance sheet for Royal Copying Service, Inc.

Financial Decision Case

1-1. Murphy Lawn Services, Inc. *(L.O. 6, 7)*

Instead of hunting for a summer job after finishing her junior year in college, Beth Murphy organized a lawn service company in her neighborhood. To start her business on June 1, she deposited $2,700 in a new bank account in the name of her corporation. The $2,700 consisted of a $1,000 loan from her father and $1,700 of her own money. (Assume for this case that Beth issued 1,700 shares of $1 par value common stock to herself.)

Using the money in this checking account, she rented lawn equipment, purchased supplies, and hired neighborhood high school students to mow and trim the lawns of neighbors who had agreed to pay her for the service.

At the end of each month, she mailed bills to her customers. On September 30, Beth was ready to dissolve her business and go back to school for the fall quarter. Because she had been so busy, she had not kept any records other than her checkbook and a list of amounts owed to her by customers.

Her checkbook had a balance of $3,520, and the amount owed to her by the customers totaled $875. She expected these customers to pay her during October. She remembered that she could return unused supplies to the Lawn Care Center for a full credit of $50. When she brought back the rented lawn equipment, the Lawn Care Center would also return a deposit of $200 she had made in June. She owed the Lawn Care Center $525 for equipment rentals and supplies. In addition, she owed the students who had worked for her $100, and she still owed her father $700. Though Beth feels she did quite well, she is not sure just how successful she was.

Required

1. Prepare a balance sheet dated June 1 and one dated September 30 for Murphy Lawn Services, Inc.
2. Comment on the performance of Murphy Lawn Services, Inc. by comparing the two balance sheets. Did the company have a profit or loss? (Assume that Beth used none of the company's assets for personal purposes.)
3. If Beth is to continue her business next summer, what kind of information from her recordkeeping system would help make it easier to tell whether she is earning a profit or losing money?

LEARNING OBJECTIVES

1. *Explain in simple terms the generally accepted ways of solving the measurement issues of recognition, valuation, and classification.*
2. *Define and use the terms* account *and* general ledger.
3. *Recognize commonly used asset, liability, and stockholders' equity accounts.*
4. *Define* double-entry system *and state the rules for debit and credit.*
5. *Apply the procedure for transaction analysis to simple transactions.*
6. *Record transactions in the general journal.*
7. *Explain the relationship of the general journal to the general ledger.*
8. *Prepare a trial balance and recognize its value and limitations.*

CHAPTER 2

Measuring and Recording Business Transactions

In the chapter on accounting as an information system, you learned the answer to the question: What is to be measured? Chapter 2 opens with a discussion of these questions: When should the measurement occur? What value should be placed on the measurement? and How is the measurement to be classified? Then, as the focus shifts from accounting concepts to actual practice, you begin working with the double-entry system and applying it to the analysis and recording of business transactions. After studying this chapter, you should be able to meet the learning objectives listed on the left.

DECISION POINT

UAL Corporation and The Boeing Company[1]

In October, 1990, UAL Corporation, United Airlines' parent company, announced that it had ordered up to 128 Boeing wide-body jets, including 68 of the long-awaited 777 models and 60 747-400 models. This order, which is estimated to come to more than $22 billion, was the largest order ever placed for commercial aircraft. The agreement included firm orders for half the aircraft and options to buy the other half. Boeing will make the aircraft for UAL, and the new planes will be delivered beginning in 1995. Some financial terms remained to be worked out. How should this important announcement be recorded, if at all, in the records of UAL and of Boeing? When should the forthcoming purchase and sale be recorded in the companies' records?

This order of aircraft is obviously an important event carrying long-term consequences for both companies. It is not, however, as will be shown in this chapter, an event that is recorded in the accounting records of either company. At the time of the order, the aircraft are yet to be manufactured and will not begin to be delivered for five years. For half

1. Information from the *Wall Street Journal*, October 16, 1990, p. 83. Excerpts from the 1989 Annual Report of The Boeing Co. are used with permission.

the aircraft, UAL has been allowed an option that may be accepted or refused. Even for the "firm" orders, Boeing cautions in its 1989 annual report that "An economic downturn could result in airline equipment requirements less than currently anticipated resulting in requests to negotiate the rescheduling or possible cancellation of firm orders." The aircraft are not assets of UAL, and no liability would be recorded because no aircraft has been delivered or even built and UAL is not obligated to pay at this point. Also, no sales will be recorded as revenue for Boeing until the aircraft are manufactured and delivered to UAL, at which time the title, or ownership, of the aircraft shifts from Boeing to UAL. To understand and use financial statements, it is important to know how to analyze events in order to determine the extent of their impact on the financial statements. ■

Measurement Issues

OBJECTIVE 1 *Explain in simple terms the generally accepted ways of solving the measurement issues of recognition, valuation, and classification*

Business transactions were defined earlier as economic events that affect the financial position of a business entity. To measure a business transaction, the accountant must decide when the transaction occurred (the recognition issue), what value should be placed on the transaction (the valuation issue), and how the components of the transaction should be categorized (the classification issue).

These three issues—recognition, valuation, and classification—are the basis of almost every major issue in financial accounting today. They lie at the heart of such complex issues as accounting for pension plans, mergers of giant companies, international transactions, and the effects of inflation. In discussing the three basic issues, we follow generally accepted accounting principles and use an approach that promotes the understanding of the basic ideas of accounting. Keep in mind, however, that controversy does exist; and some solutions to these problems are not as cut and dried as they may appear.

The Recognition Issue

The **recognition** issue refers to the difficulty of deciding when a business transaction should be recorded. Often the facts of a situation are known, but there is disagreement as to *when* the events should be recorded. For instance, consider when to recognize or first record a simple purchase. A company orders, receives, and pays for an office desk. Which of the following actions constitutes a recordable event?

1. An employee sends a purchase requisition to the purchasing department.
2. The purchasing department sends a purchase order to the supplier.
3. The supplier ships the desk.
4. The company receives the desk.
5. The company receives the bill from the supplier.
6. The company pays the bill.

The answer to this question is important because the amounts in the financial statements are affected by the date on which the purchase is recorded. Accounting tradition provides for the transaction to be recorded when title to the desk passes from supplier to purchaser and an obligation to pay results. Thus, depending on the details of the shipping agreement, the transaction is recognized at the time of either action **3** or action **4**. This is the guideline that we will generally use in this book. However, in many small businesses that have simple accounting systems, the initial recording of the transaction occurs when the bill is received (action **5**) or when the transfer of cash occurs (action **6**) because these are the implied points of title transfer. The predetermined time at which a transaction is to be recorded is the **recognition point**.

The recognition problem is not always solved easily. Consider the case of an advertising agency that is asked by a client to prepare a major advertising campaign. People may work on the campaign several hours per day for a number of weeks. Value is added to the plan as the employees develop it. Should the amount of value added be recognized as the campaign is being produced or at the time it is completed? Normally, the increase in value is recorded at the time the plan is finished and the client is billed for it. However, if the plan will take a long period to develop, the agency and the client may agree that the client will be billed at key points during its development.

The Valuation Issue

The **valuation** issue is perhaps the most controversial issue in accounting. It concerns the difficulty of assigning a monetary value to a business transaction. Generally accepted accounting principles state that the appropriate valuation to assign to all business transactions, and therefore to all assets, liabilities, owners' equity, revenues, and expenses acquired by a business, is the original cost (often called historical cost). **Cost** is defined here as the exchange price associated with a business transaction at the point of recognition. According to this guideline, the purpose of accounting is not to account for "value," which may change after a transaction occurs, but to account for the cost or value at the time of the transaction. For example, the cost of assets is recorded when they are acquired, and their "value" is held at that level until they are sold, expire, or are consumed. In this context, value in accounting means the cost at the time of the transaction. This practice is referred to by accountants as the **cost principle**.

Suppose that a person offers a building for sale at $120,000. It may be valued for real estate taxes at $75,000, and it may be insured for $90,000. One prospective buyer may offer $100,000 for the building, and another may offer $105,000. At this point, several different, unverifiable opinions of value have been expressed. Finally, the seller and a buyer may settle on a price and complete a sale for $110,000. All these figures are values of one kind or another, but only the last figure is sufficiently reliable to be used in the records. The market value of this building may vary over the years, but it will remain on the new buyer's records at $110,000 until it is sold again. At that point, the accountant would record the new transaction at the new exchange price, and a profit or loss would be recognized.

The cost principle is used because it meets the standard of verifiability. Cost is verifiable because it results from the actions of independent buyers and sellers who come to an agreement about price. This exchange price is an objective price that can be verified by evidence created at the time of the transaction. Both the buyer and the seller may have thought they got the better deal, but their opinions are irrelevant in recording cost. The final price of $110,000, verified by agreement of the two parties, is the price at which the transaction is recorded.

The Classification Issue

The **classification** issue is that of assigning all the transactions in which a business engages to appropriate categories, called accounts. For example, a company's ability to borrow money may be affected by the way in which some of its debts are categorized. Or a company's income may be affected by whether purchases of small items such as tools are considered repair expenses or equipment (assets). Proper classification depends not only on the correct analysis of the effect of each transaction on the business enterprise but also on the maintenance of a system of accounts that will reflect that effect. The rest of this chapter explains the classification of accounts and the analysis and recording of transactions.

Accounts

OBJECTIVE 2
Define and use the terms account *and* general ledger

When large amounts of data are gathered in the measurement of business transactions, a method of storage is required. Business people should be able to retrieve transaction data quickly and in the form desired. In other words, there should be a filing system to sort out or classify all the transactions that occur in a business. Only in this way can financial statements and other reports be prepared quickly and easily. This filing system consists of accounts. An **account** is the basic storage unit for accounting data. An accounting system has separate accounts for each asset, each liability, and each component of owners' equity, including revenues and expenses. Whether a company keeps records by hand or by computer, management must be able to refer to these accounts so that it can study the company's financial history and plan for the future. A very small company may need only a few dozen accounts, whereas a multinational corporation will have thousands.

In a manual accounting system, each account is kept on a separate page or card. These pages or cards are placed together in a book or file. This book or file containing the company's accounts is called the **general ledger**. In a computer system, which most companies have today, the accounts are maintained on magnetic tapes or disks. However, as a matter of convenience, the accountant still refers to the group of company accounts as the general ledger, or simply the **ledger**.

To be able to find an account in the ledger easily and to identify accounts, an accountant often numbers them. A list of these numbers with the corresponding account names is called a **chart of accounts**. A very simple chart of accounts appears in Exhibit 2-1. Note that the first digit refers to the major financial statement classifications. An account number beginning with the digit 1 is an asset, an account number beginning with a 2 is a liability, and so forth.

You will be introduced to these accounts in the following section and over the next two-and-a-half chapters through the illustrative case of the Joan Miller Advertising Agency, Inc. At this time, notice the gaps in the sequence of numbers. These gaps allow for expansion in the number of accounts. Of course, every company develops a chart of accounts for its

Exhibit 2-1. Chart of Accounts for a Small Business

Assets		Liabilities	
Cash	111	Notes Payable	211
Notes Receivable	112	Accounts Payable	212
Accounts Receivable	113	Unearned Art Fees	213
Fees Receivable	114	Wages Payable	214
Art Supplies	115	Mortgage Payable	221
Office Supplies	116		
Prepaid Rent	117	**Stockholders' Equity**	
Prepaid Insurance	118		
Land	141	Common Stock	311
Buildings	142	Retained Earnings	312
Accumulated Depreciation, Buildings	143	Dividends	313
Art Equipment	144	Income Summary	314
Accumulated Depreciation, Art Equipment	145	**Revenues**	
Office Equipment	146	Advertising Fees Earned	411
Accumulated Depreciation, Office Equipment	147	Art Fees Earned	412
		Expenses	
		Office Wages Expense	511
		Utility Expense	512
		Telephone Expense	513
		Rent Expense	514
		Insurance Expense	515
		Art Supplies Expense	516
		Office Supplies Expense	517
		Depreciation Expense, Buildings	518
		Depreciation Expense, Art Equipment	519
		Depreciation Expense, Office Equipment	520

own needs. Seldom will two companies have exactly the same chart of accounts, and larger companies will require more digits to accommodate all of their accounts. In keeping its records, each company should follow a consistent framework for its own chart of accounts.

Types of Commonly Used Accounts

OBJECTIVE 3
Recognize commonly used asset, liability, and stockholders' equity accounts

The specific accounts used by a company depend on the nature of the company's business. A steel company will have many equipment and inventory accounts, whereas an advertising agency may have only a few. Each company must design its accounts in a way that reflects the nature of its business and the needs of its management. There are, however, accounts that are common to most businesses. Some important ones are described in the following paragraphs.

Asset Accounts. A company must keep records of the increases and decreases in each asset that it owns. Some of the more common asset accounts are as follows:

Cash "Cash" is the title of the account used to record increases and decreases in cash. Cash consists of money or any medium of exchange that a bank will accept at face value for deposit. Included are coins, currency, checks, postal and express money orders, and money deposited in a bank or banks. The Cash account also includes cash on hand, such as that in a cash register or a safe.

Notes Receivable A promissory note is a written promise to pay a definite sum of money at a fixed future date. Amounts due from others in the form of promissory notes are recorded in an account called Notes Receivable.

Accounts Receivable Companies often sell goods and services to customers on the basis of the customers' oral or implied promises to pay in the future, such as in thirty days or at the first of the month. These sales are called Credit Sales, or Sales on Account, and the promises to pay are known as Accounts Receivable. Credit sales increase Accounts Receivable, and collections from customers decrease Accounts Receivable. Of course, it is necessary to keep a record of how much each customer owes the company. How these records are kept is explained in the chapter on short-term liquid assets.

Prepaid Expenses Companies often pay for goods and services before they receive or use them. These prepaid expenses are considered assets until they are used, or expire, at which time they become expenses. There should be a separate account for each prepaid expense. An example of a prepaid expense is Prepaid Insurance (or Unexpired Insurance). Insurance protection against fire, theft, and other hazards is usually paid in advance for a period of one to five years. When the premiums are paid, the Prepaid Insurance account is increased. These premiums expire day by day and month by month. Therefore, at intervals, usually at the end of the accounting period, Prepaid Insurance must be reduced by the amount of insurance that has expired. Another common type of prepaid expense is

Office Supplies. Stamps, stationery, pencils, pens, paper, and other office supplies are assets when they are purchased and are recorded as an increase in Office Supplies. As the office supplies are used, the account is reduced. Other typical prepaid expenses that are assets when they are purchased and become expenses through use or the passage of time are prepaid rent (rent paid for more than one month in advance), store supplies, and prepaid taxes.

Land An account called Land is used to record purchases of property to be used in the ordinary operations of the business.

Buildings Purchases of structures to be used in the business are recorded in an account called Buildings. Although a building cannot be separated from the land it occupies, it is important to maintain separate accounts for the land and the building. The reason for doing so is that the building is subject to wear and tear, but the land is not. Later in the book the subject of depreciation will be introduced. Wear and tear is an important aspect of depreciation.

Equipment A company may own many different types of equipment. Usually there is a separate account for each type. Transactions involving desks, chairs, office machines, filing cabinets, and typewriters are recorded in an account called Office Equipment. Increases and decreases in cash registers, counters, showcases, shelves, and similar items are recorded in the Store Equipment account. When a company has a factory, it may own lathes, drill presses, and other equipment and would record changes in such items in an account titled Machinery and Equipment. Some companies may have use for a Trucks and Automobiles account.

Liability Accounts. Another word for *liability* is *debt.* Most companies have fewer liability accounts than asset accounts. But it is just as important to keep records of what the company owes as of what it owns (assets). There are two types of liabilities: short-term and long-term. The distinction between them is introduced in the chapter on current liabilities. The following accounts are classified as liabilities:

Notes Payable The account called Notes Payable is the opposite of Notes Receivable. It is used to record increases and decreases in promissory note amounts owed to creditors within the next year or operating cycle.

Accounts Payable Similarly, Accounts Payable is the opposite of Accounts Receivable. It represents amounts owed to creditors on the basis of an oral or implied promise to pay. Accounts payable usually arise as the result of the purchase of merchandise, services, supplies, or equipment on credit. When Company A buys an item from Company B and promises to pay at the beginning of the month, the amount of the transaction is an Account Payable on Company A's books and an Account Receivable on Company B's books. As with Accounts Receivable, records of amounts owed to individual creditors must be known. The chapter on current liabilities covers the method of accomplishing this task.

Other Short-Term Liabilities A few other liability accounts are Wages Payable, Taxes Payable, Rent Payable, and Interest Payable. Often customers make deposits on, or pay in advance for, goods and services to be delivered in the future. Such customers' deposits are also recorded as liabilities. They are liabilities because they represent claims by the customers for goods to be delivered or services to be performed. These kinds of liability accounts are often called Unearned Fees, Customer Deposits, Advances from Customers, or, more commonly, Unearned Revenues.

Long-Term Liabilities The most common types of long-term liabilities are notes due in more than one year, bonds, and property mortgages. Because a wide variety of bonds and mortgages have been developed for special financing needs, it is difficult to classify them. They may or may not require the backing of certain of the company's assets for security. For example, a mortgage holder may have the right to force the sale of certain assets if the mortgage debt is not paid when due.

Stockholders' Equity Accounts. In the chapter on accounting as an information system, several transactions affected owners' equity. The effects of all these transactions were shown by the increases or decreases in the stockholders' columns representing equity accounts (see the exhibit "Summary of Effects of Illustrative Transactions" in the chapter on accounting as an information system) with an indication of the type of each transaction. For legal and managerial reasons, it is important to sort these transactions into separate stockholders' equity accounts. Among the most important information that management receives for business planning is a detailed breakdown of revenues and expenses. For income tax reporting, financial reporting, and other reasons, the law requires that capital contributions and dividends be separated from revenues and expenses. Ownership and equity accounts for corporations are covered in much more detail in the chapters on contributed capital and retained earnings. For now, the following accounts, whose relationships are shown in Figure 2-1, are important.

Common Stock When stockholders invest in a corporation, the amount of the investment is recorded in a capital stock account. For instance, in the chapter on accounting as an information system, when James and John Shannon invested their personal resources in a bank account in the name of the corporation in exchange for shares in the corporation, they recorded the amount in the stockholders' equity account titled Common Stock. Any additional investments by the Shannons in their firm would be recorded in this account.

Retained Earnings Retained earnings are the claims of the stockholders against the assets of the company that arise from profitable operations. This account is different from capital stock, which represents the claims against assets brought about by initial and later investments by the stockholders. Both are claims against the general assets of the company, not against any specific assets that may have been set aside. It is important that you do not confuse the assets themselves with the claims against the assets. Retained earnings are increased by profitable operations (revenue and expense activities) and decreased by payments of dividends. They may, of course, be decreased by losses from operations as well. Transactions involving dividends, revenues, and expenses are not recorded directly in the Retained Earnings account but are first recorded in separate accounts and later transferred to Retained Earnings in summary fashion.

Dividends Dividends are distributions of assets that reduce the ownership claims on retained earnings and are shown on the statement of retained earnings. As you learned earlier, they can be declared only by the board of directors. Because the cash that is distributed is made possible by profitable operations, people sometimes say that dividends are "paid out of retained earnings." In fact, the dividends are paid with cash, and the result of this transaction is a reduction in the ownership claim that arose from profitable operations.

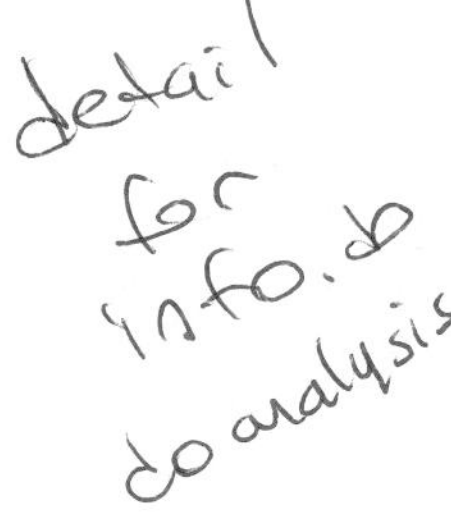

Revenue and Expense Accounts Revenues increase owners' equity, and expenses decrease owners' equity. The greater the revenues, the more the owners' equity is increased. The greater the expenses, the more the owners' equity is decreased. Of course, when revenues are greater than expenses, the company has earned a profit or net income. When expenses are more than revenues, the company has suffered a loss or net loss. Management's major goal is to earn net income, and an important function of accounting is to give management the information that will help it meet this goal. One way of doing this is to have a ledger account for every revenue and expense item. From these accounts, which are included on the income statement, management can identify exactly the source of all reve-

Figure 2-1. Relationships of Stockholders' Equity Accounts

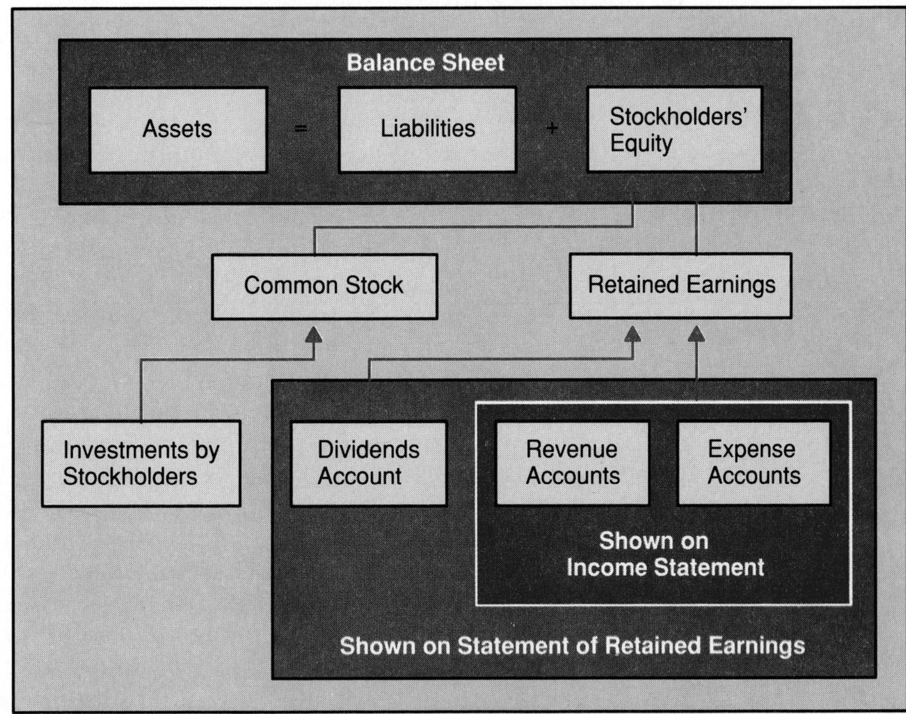

nues and the nature of all expenses. A particular company's revenue and expense accounts will depend on its kind of business and the nature of its operations. A few of the revenue accounts used in this book are Commissions Earned, Advertising Fees Earned, and Sales. Some of the expense accounts are Wages Expense, Supplies Expense, Rent Expense, and Advertising Expense.

Titles of Accounts

The names of accounts are often confusing to beginning accounting students because some of the words are new or have technical meanings. It is also true that the same asset, liability, or owners' equity account may have different names in different companies. This fact is not so strange. People too are often called different names by their friends, families, and associates.

For example, long-term assets may be known in various contexts as Fixed Assets, Plant and Equipment, Capital Assets, Long-Lived Assets, and so forth. Even the most acceptable names change over time in accounting, and out of habit some companies may use names that are out of date. In general, the account title should describe what is recorded in the account. When you encounter an account title that you do not recognize, you should examine the context of the name—whether it is classified as asset, liability, owners' equity, revenue, or expense on the financial statements—and look for the kind of transaction that gave rise to the account.

The Double-Entry System: The Basic Method of Accounting

OBJECTIVE 4 *Define* double-entry system *and state the rules for debit and credit*

The double-entry system, the backbone of accounting, evolved during the Renaissance. The first systematic presentation of double-entry bookkeeping appeared in 1494, two years after Columbus discovered America. It was described in a mathematics book written by Fra Luca Pacioli, a Franciscan monk who was a friend of Leonardo da Vinci. Goethe, the famous German poet and dramatist, referred to double-entry bookkeeping as "one of the finest discoveries of the human intellect." Werner Sombart, an eminent economist-sociologist, expressed the belief that "double-entry bookkeeping is born of the same spirit as the system of Galileo and Newton."

What is the significance of the double-entry system for accounting? The double-entry system is based on the principle of duality, which means that all events of economic importance have two aspects—effort and reward, sacrifice and benefit, sources and uses—that offset or balance each other. In the **double-entry system** each transaction must be recorded with at least one debit and one credit, in such a way that the total dollar amount of debits and the total dollar amount of credits equal each other. Because of the way it is designed, the whole system is always in balance. All accounting systems, no matter how sophisticated, are based on this principle of duality. The T account is a helpful place to begin the study of the double-entry system.

The T Account

In its simplest form, an account has three parts: (1) a title, which describes the asset, liability, or owners' equity account; (2) a left side, which is called the **debit** side; and (3) a right side, which is called the **credit** side. This form of the account, called a **T account** because it resembles the letter *T*, is used to analyze transactions. It appears as follows:

Title of Account	
Left or Debit Side	Right or Credit Side

Thus any entry made on the left side of the account is a debit, or debit entry, and any entry made on the right side of the account is a credit, or credit entry. The terms *debit* (abbreviated Dr., from the Latin *debere*) and *credit* (abbreviated Cr., from the Latin *credere*) are simply the accountant's words for "left" and "right" (not for "increase" or "decrease"). A more formal version of the T account will be presented later in this chapter.

The T Account Illustrated

In the chapter on accounting as an information system, Shannon Realty, Inc. had several transactions that involved the receipt or payment of cash. (See the exhibit "Summary of Effects of Illustrative Transactions on Financial Position" in the chapter on accounting as an information system for a summary of the numbered transactions given below.) These transactions can be summarized in the Cash account by recording receipts on the left or debit side of the account and payments on the right or credit side of the account as follows:

Cash			
(1)	50,000	(2)	35,000
(5)	1,500	(4)	200
(7)	1,000	(8)	1,000
		(9)	400
		(11)	600
	52,500		37,200
Bal.	15,300		

The cash receipts on the left have been totaled as $52,500, and this total is written in small-size figures so that it will not be confused with an actual debit entry. The cash payments are totaled in a similar way on the right side. These figures are simply working totals called **footings**. Footings are calculated at the end of the month as an easy way to determine cash on hand. The difference in dollars between the total debit footing and the total credit footing is called the **balance** or **account balance**. If the balance is a debit, it is written on the left side. If it is a credit, it is written on the right. Notice that Shannon Realty, Inc.'s Cash account has a debit balance of $15,300 ($52,500 – $37,200). This amount represents Shannon's cash on hand at the end of the month.

Analysis of Transactions

The rules of double-entry bookkeeping are that every transaction affects at least two accounts. In other words, there must be one or more accounts debited and one or more accounts credited, and the total dollar amount of the debits must equal the total dollar amount of the credits.

When we look at the accounting equation

Assets = liabilities + owners' equity

we can see that if a debit increases assets, then a credit must be used to increase liabilities or owners' equity. On the other hand, if a credit decreases assets, then a debit must be used to show a decrease in liabilities or owners' equity. These rules are opposite because assets are on the opposite side of the equation from liabilities and owners' equity. These rules can be shown as follows:

Assets		=	**Liabilities**		+	**Owners' Equity**	
Debit for Increases	Credit for Decreases		Debit for Decreases	Credit for Increases		Debit for Decreases	Credit for Increases

1. Increases in assets are debited to asset accounts. Decreases in assets are credited to asset accounts.
2. Increases in liabilities and owners' equity are credited to liability and owners' equity accounts. Decreases in liabilities and owners' equity are debited to liability and owners' equity accounts.

One of the more difficult points to understand is the application of these rules to the owners' equity components of revenues, expenses, and dividends. Since revenues increase owners' equity and expenses and dividends decrease it, the following relationships hold:

Owners' Equity

Decreases (Debits)	Increases (Credits)

Expenses

Increases (Debits)	Decreases (Credits)

Revenues

Decreases (Debits)	Increases (Credits)

Dividends

Increases (Debits)	Decreases (Credits)

Thus, a transaction that increases revenues by a credit also increases owners' equity by a credit. However, expenses and dividends, which are *increased* by debits, *decrease* owners' equity. In other words, the more expenses and dividends are *increased* by debits, the more these debits *decrease* owners' equity; and the more expenses and dividends are *decreased* by credits, the more these credits *increase* owners' equity. The reason for these effects is that expenses and dividends are a component of owners' equity, which is on the right-hand side of the accounting equation.

At this point we can explain how to analyze transactions. Transactions are usually supported by some kind of document, such as an invoice, a receipt, a check, or a contract. These source documents provide the basis for analyzing each transaction. As an example, let us suppose that Jones Corporation borrows $1,000 from its bank on a promissory note. The procedure is as follows:

1. Analyze the effect of the transaction on assets, liabilities, and owners' equity. In this case, both an asset (Cash) and a liability (Notes Payable) were increased.
2. Apply the correct double-entry rule. Increases in assets are recorded by debits. Increases in liabilities are recorded by credits.
3. Make the entry. The increase in assets is recorded by a debit to the Cash account, and the increase in liabilities is recorded by a credit to the Notes Payable account.

Cash			Notes Payable	
1,000				**1,000**

The debit to Cash of $1,000 equals the credit to Notes Payable of $1,000.

Another form of this entry, which will be explained later in this chapter, is as follows:

	Dr.	Cr.
Cash	1,000	
Notes Payable		1,000

Transaction Analysis Illustrated

OBJECTIVE 5
Apply the procedure for transaction analysis to simple transactions

The next few pages consist of the transactions for the Joan Miller Advertising Agency, Inc. during the month of January. We will use these transactions to illustrate the principle of duality and to show how transactions are recorded in the accounts.

January 1: Joan Miller obtained a charter from the state and invested $10,000 in her own advertising agency in exchange for 10,000 shares of $1 par value stock.

Cash	
Jan. 1 10,000	

Common Stock	
	Jan. 1 10,000

Transaction: Investment in business.
Analysis: Assets increased. Owners' equity increased.
Rules: Increases in assets are recorded by debits. Increases in owners' equity are recorded by credits.
Entry: Increase in assets is recorded by a debit to Cash. Increase in owners' equity is recorded by a credit to Common Stock.

	Dr.	Cr.
Cash	10,000	
Common Stock		10,000

If Joan Miller had invested assets other than cash in the business, the appropriate asset accounts would be debited.

January 2: Rented an office, paying two months' rent in advance, $800.

Cash	
Jan. 1 10,000	Jan. 2 800

Prepaid Rent	
Jan. 2 800	

Transaction: Expense paid in advance.
Analysis: Assets increased. Assets decreased.
Rules: Increases in assets are recorded by debits. Decreases in assets are recorded by credits.
Entry: Increase in assets is recorded by a debit to Prepaid Rent. Decrease in assets is recorded by a credit to Cash.

	Dr.	Cr.
Prepaid Rent	800	
Cash		800

January 3: Ordered art supplies, $1,800, and office supplies, $800.

Analysis: No entry is made because no transaction has occurred. According to the recognition issue, there is no liability until the supplies are shipped or received and there is an obligation to pay for them.

January 4: Purchased art equipment for $4,200 cash.

Cash	
Jan. 1 10,000	Jan. 2 800
	4 4,200

Art Equipment	
Jan. 4 4,200	

Transaction: Purchase of equipment.
Analysis: Assets increased. Assets decreased.
Rules: Increases in assets are recorded by debits. Decreases in assets are recorded by credits.
Entry: Increase in assets is recorded by a debit to Art Equipment. Decrease in assets is recorded by a credit to Cash.

	Dr.	Cr.
Art Equipment	4,200	
Cash		4,200

January 5: Purchased office equipment from Morgan Equipment for $3,000, paying $1,500 in cash and agreeing to pay the rest next month.

Cash

Jan. 1	10,000	Jan. 2	800
		4	4,200
		5	1,500

Office Equipment

Jan. 5	3,000		

Accounts Payable

		Jan. 5	1,500

Transaction: Purchase of equipment, partial payment.
Analysis: Assets increased. Assets decreased. Liabilities increased.
Rules: Increases in assets are recorded by debits. Decreases in assets are recorded by credits. Increases in liabilities are recorded by credits.
Entry: Increase in assets is recorded by a debit to Office Equipment. Decrease in assets is recorded by a credit to Cash. Increase in liabilities is recorded by a credit to Accounts Payable.

	Dr.	Cr.
Office Equipment	3,000	
Cash		1,500
Accounts Payable		1,500

January 6: Purchased on credit art supplies for $1,800 and office supplies for $800 from Taylor Supply Company (ordered on January 3).

Art Supplies

Jan. 6	1,800		

Office Supplies

Jan. 6	800		

Accounts Payable

		Jan. 5	1,500
		6	2,600

Transaction: Purchase of supplies on credit.
Analysis: Assets increased. Liabilities increased.
Rules: Increases in assets are recorded by debits. Increases in liabilities are recorded by credits.
Entry: Increase in assets is recorded by debits to Art Supplies and Office Supplies. Increase in liabilities is recorded by a credit to Accounts Payable.

	Dr.	Cr.
Art Supplies	1,800	
Office Supplies	800	
Accounts Payable		2,600

January 8: Paid $480 for a one-year insurance policy with coverage effective January 1.

Cash

Jan. 1	10,000	Jan. 2	800
		4	4,200
		5	1,500
		8	480

Prepaid Insurance

Jan. 8	480		

Transaction: Paid for insurance coverage in advance.
Analysis: Assets increased. Assets decreased.
Rules: Increases in assets are recorded by debits. Decreases in assets are recorded by credits.
Entry: Increase in assets is recorded by a debit to Prepaid Insurance. Decrease in assets is recorded by a credit to Cash.

	Dr.	Cr.
Prepaid Insurance	480	
Cash		480

January 9: Paid Taylor Supply Company $1,000 of the amount owed.

Cash

Jan. 1 10,000	Jan. 2 800
	4 4,200
	5 1,500
	8 480
	9 1,000

Accounts Payable

Jan. 9 1,000	Jan. 5 1,500
	6 2,600

Transaction: Partial payment on a liability.
Analysis: Assets decreased. Liabilities decreased.
Rules: Decreases in assets are recorded by credits. Decreases in liabilities are recorded by debits.
Entry: Decrease in liabilities is recorded by a debit to Accounts Payable. Decrease in assets is recorded by a credit to Cash.

	Dr.	Cr.
Accounts Payable	1,000	
Cash		1,000

January 10: Performed a service by placing advertisements for an automobile dealer in the newspaper and collected a fee of $1,400.

Cash

Jan. 1 10,000	Jan. 2 800
10 1,400	4 4,200
	5 1,500
	8 480
	9 1,000

Advertising Fees Earned

	Jan. 10 1,400

Transaction: Revenue earned and cash collected.
Analysis: Assets increased. Owners' equity increased.
Rules: Increases in assets are recorded by debits. Increases in owners' equity are recorded by credits.
Entry: Increase in assets is recorded by a debit to Cash. Increase in owners' equity is recorded by a credit to Advertising Fees Earned.

	Dr.	Cr.
Cash	1,400	
Advertising Fees Earned		1,400

January 12: Paid the secretary two weeks' wages, $600.

Cash

Jan. 1 10,000	Jan. 2 800
10 1,400	4 4,200
	5 1,500
	8 480
	9 1,000
	12 600

Office Wages Expense

Jan. 12 600	

Transaction: Payment of wages expense.
Analysis: Assets decreased. Owners' equity decreased.
Rules: Decreases in assets are recorded by credits. Decreases in owners' equity are recorded by debits.
Entry: Decrease in owners' equity is recorded by a debit to Office Wages Expense. Decrease in assets is recorded by a credit to Cash.

	Dr.	Cr.
Office Wages Expense	600	
Cash		600

January 15: Accepted $1,000 as an advance fee for art work to be done for another agency.

Cash

Jan. 1	10,000	Jan. 2	800
10	1,400	4	4,200
15	1,000	5	1,500
		8	480
		9	1,000
		12	600

Unearned Art Fees

		Jan. 15	1,000

Transaction: Accepted payment for services to be performed.
Analysis: Assets increased. Liabilities increased.
Rules: Increases in assets are recorded by debits. Increases in liabilities are recorded by credits.
Entry: Increase in assets is recorded by a debit to Cash. Increase in liabilities is recorded by a credit to Unearned Art Fees.

	Dr.	Cr.
Cash	1,000	
Unearned Art Fees		1,000

January 19: Performed a service by placing several major advertisements for Ward Department Stores. The fee of $2,800 is billed now but will be collected next month.

Accounts Receivable

Jan. 19	2,800		

Advertising Fees Earned

		Jan. 10	1,400
		19	2,800

Transaction: Revenue earned, to be received later.
Analysis: Assets increased. Owners' equity increased.
Rules: Increases in assets are recorded by debits. Increases in owners' equity are recorded by credits.
Entry: Increase in assets is recorded by a debit to Accounts Receivable. Increase in owners' equity is recorded by a credit to Advertising Fees Earned.

	Dr.	Cr.
Accounts Receivable	2,800	
Advertising Fees Earned		2,800

January 26: Paid the secretary two more weeks' wages, $600.

Cash

Jan. 1	10,000	Jan. 2	800
10	1,400	4	4,200
15	1,000	5	1,500
		8	480
		9	1,000
		12	600
		26	600

Office Wages Expense

Jan. 12	600		
26	600		

Transaction: Payment of wages expense.
Analysis: Assets decreased. Owners' equity decreased.
Rules: Decreases in assets are recorded by credits. Decreases in owners' equity are recorded by debits.
Entry: Decrease in owners' equity is recorded by a debit to Office Wages Expense. Decrease in assets is recorded by a credit to Cash.

	Dr.	Cr.
Office Wages Expense	600	
Cash		600

January 29: Received and paid the utility bill of $100.

Cash

Jan. 1	10,000	Jan. 2	800
10	1,400	4	4,200
15	1,000	5	1,500
		8	480
		9	1,000
		12	600
		26	600
		29	100

Utility Expense

Jan. 29	100		

Transaction: Payment of expenses.
Analysis: Assets decreased. Owners' equity decreased.
Rules: Decreases in assets are recorded by credits. Decreases in owners' equity are recorded by debits.
Entry: Decrease in owners' equity is recorded by a debit to Utility Expense. Decrease in assets is recorded by a credit to Cash.

	Dr.	Cr.
Utility Expense	100	
Cash		100

January 30: Received (but did not pay) a telephone bill, $70.

Accounts Payable

Jan. 9	1,000	Jan. 5	1,500
		6	2,600
		30	70

Telephone Expense

Jan. 30	70		

Transaction: Expense incurred, payment deferred.
Analysis: Liabilities increased. Owners' equity decreased.
Rules: Increases in liabilities are recorded by credits. Decreases in owners' equity are recorded by debits.
Entry: Decrease in owners' equity is recorded by a debit to Telephone Expense. Increase in liabilities is recorded by a credit to Accounts Payable.

	Dr.	Cr.
Telephone Expense	70	
Accounts Payable		70

January 31: Declared and paid a dividend of $1,400.

Cash

Jan. 1	10,000	Jan. 2	800
10	1,400	4	4,200
15	1,000	5	1,500
		8	480
		9	1,000
		12	600
		26	600
		29	100
		31	1,400

Dividends

Jan. 31	1,400		

Transaction: Declaration and payment of dividends.
Analysis: Assets decreased. Owners' equity decreased.
Rules: Decreases in assets are recorded by credits. Decreases in owners' equity are recorded by debits.
Entry: Decrease in owners' equity is recorded by a debit to Dividends. Decrease in assets is recorded by a credit to Cash.

	Dr.	Cr.
Dividends	1,400	
Cash		1,400

Summary of Transactions

As you may have discovered from the examples, there are only a few ways in which transactions can affect the accounting equation. The following table summarizes them:

Effect	Example Transactions
1. Increase both assets and liabilities	Jan. 6, 15
2. Increase both assets and owners' equity	Jan. 1, 10, 19
3. Decrease both assets and liabilities	Jan. 9
4. Decrease both assets and owners' equity	Jan. 12, 26, 29, 31
5. Increase one asset and decrease another	Jan. 2, 4, 8
6. Increase one liability or owners' equity account and decrease another liability or owners' equity account	Jan. 30
7. No effect	Jan. 3

The January 5 transaction is a slightly more complex transaction; it increases one asset (Office Equipment), decreases another asset (Cash), and increases a liability (Accounts Payable). All the previous transactions are presented in Exhibit 2-2 in their correct accounts. Their relation to the accounting equation is also shown.

DECISION POINT
American Collegiate Sales Corporation

American Collegiate Sales Corporation (ACS) has experienced rapid growth for several years from a simple idea. The company markets grooming aids, casual clothes, and other such products on college campuses through student representatives. These representatives organize parties on campus at which samples of all the products are shown. Students who decide to buy products pay the representative, who in turn orders the products and pays ACS for them. When the products arrive, the student representative delivers them to the buyers. The student representative pays ACS less than he or she charges the students. The difference represents the earnings of representatives who are not employees of ACS. ACS is admired by Wall Street investors because of several years of rapid sales and earnings increases. This year the president of the company has predicted further increases of 30 percent. By December, however, it has become apparent that sales goals will not be met unless something is done. During the last two weeks of December, the company ships $20 million of merchandise to the sales representatives to be held for future sales parties. The student representatives have the right to return all products that they do not sell. The company bills the student representatives and records the shipments as sales. In this way, the company is able to meet its sales goal for the year, with the result that ACS common stock continues to have a high market value on the stock exchange. Were these shipments properly recorded as sales?

Exhibit 2-2. Summary of Illustrative Accounts and Transactions for Joan Miller Advertising Agency, Inc.

Assets = Liabilities + Stockholders' Equity

Assets

Cash

Jan. 1	10,000	Jan. 2	800
10	1,400	4	4,200
15	1,000	5	1,500
		8	480
		9	1,000
		12	600
		26	600
		29	100
		31	1,400
	12,400		**10,680**
Bal.	**1,720**		

Accounts Receivable

Jan. 19	2,800		

Art Supplies

Jan. 6	1,800		

Office Supplies

Jan. 6	800		

Prepaid Rent

Jan. 2	800		

Prepaid Insurance

Jan. 8	480		

Art Equipment

Jan. 4	4,200		

Office Equipment

Jan. 5	3,000		

Liabilities

Accounts Payable

Jan. 9	1,000	Jan. 5	1,500
		6	2,600
		30	70
	1,000		**4,170**
		Bal.	**3,170**

Unearned Art Fees

		Jan. 15	1,000

Stockholders' Equity

Common Stock

		Jan. 1	10,000

Dividends

Jan. 31	1,400		

Advertising Fees Earned

		Jan. 10	1,400
		19	2,800
		Bal.	**4,200**

Office Wages Expense

Jan. 12	600		
26	600		
Bal.	**1,200**		

Utility Expense

Jan. 29	100		

Telephone Expense

Jan. 30	70		

The shipments were improperly recorded as sales. Even though the student representatives are not employees of ACS, the goods have not been ordered by or sold to actual customers and the student representatives have the right to return all the products unconditionally. It is misleading to call them sales. In technical terms, this type of arrangement is called a consignment. To report consignment shipments as legitimate sales is certainly unethical and can be, as in this case, illegal because of the intent to deceive. As it turned out, most of the $20 million of products were returned during January and February, and ACS went into bankruptcy. Officials of the company were later convicted of fraud. ■

Recording Transactions

OBJECTIVE 6 *Record transactions in the general journal*

So far, the analysis of transactions has been illustrated by entering the transactions directly into the T accounts. This method was used because it is a very simple and useful way of analyzing the effects. Advanced accounting students and professional accountants often use T accounts to analyze very complicated transactions. However, there are three steps to be followed in the recording process:

1. Analyze the transactions from the source documents.
2. Enter the transactions into the journal (a procedure usually called journalizing).
3. Post the entries to the ledger (a procedure usually called posting).

The Journal

As illustrated in this chapter, transactions can be recorded directly into the accounts. When this method is used, however, it is very difficult to identify individual transactions, as the debit is recorded in one account and the credit in another. When a large number of transactions is involved, errors in analyzing or recording transactions are very difficult to find. The solution to this problem is to chronologically record all transactions in a **journal**. The journal is sometimes called the book of original entry, because this is where transactions are first recorded. The journal shows the transactions for each day and may contain explanatory information. The debit and credit portions of each transaction can then be transferred to the appropriate accounts.

A separate **journal entry** is used to record each transaction, and the process of recording transactions is called **journalizing**.

The General Journal

It is common for a business to have more than one kind of journal. Several types of journals are discussed in the appendix on special-purpose journals. The simplest and most flexible type is the **general journal**, which is used in the rest of this chapter. The general journal provides for recording the following information about each transaction:

1. The date
2. The names of the accounts debited and the dollar amounts in the debit column on the same lines
3. The names of the accounts credited and the dollar amounts in the credit column on the same lines
4. An explanation of the transaction
5. The account identification numbers, if appropriate

Exhibit 2-3. The General Journal

General Journal — Page 1

Date		Description	Post. Ref.	Debit	Credit
19xx					
Jan.	6	Art Supplies		1,800	
		Office Supplies		800	
		Accounts Payable			2,600
		Purchase of art and office supplies on credit			
	8	Prepaid Insurance		480	
		Cash			480
		Paid one-year insurance premium			

Two transactions for the Joan Miller Advertising Agency, Inc. are recorded in Exhibit 2-3.

The procedure for recording transactions in the general journal is summarized as follows:

1. Record the date by writing the year in small figures on the first line at the top of the first column, the month on the next line of the first column, and the day in the second column opposite the month. For subsequent entries on the same page for the same month and year, the month and year can be omitted.
2. Write the exact names of the accounts debited and credited under the heading "Description." Write the name of the account debited next to the left margin of the second line, and indent the name of the account credited. The explanation is placed on the next line and further indented. It should be brief but sufficient to explain and identify the transaction. A transaction can have more than one debit and/or credit entry; in such a case it is called a **compound entry**. In a compound entry, all debit accounts involved are listed before any credit accounts. (The January 6 transaction of Joan Miller Advertising Agency, Inc. is an example of a compound entry; see Exhibit 2-3.)
3. Write the debit amounts in the appropriate column opposite the accounts to be debited, and write the credit amounts in the appropriate column opposite the accounts to be credited.
4. At the time of recording the transactions, nothing is placed in the Post. Ref. (posting reference) column. (This column is sometimes called LP or Folio.) Later, if the company uses account numbers to identify accounts in the ledger, fill in the account numbers to provide a conven-

Exhibit 2-4. Accounts Payable in the General Ledger

General Ledger

Accounts Payable — Account No. 212

Date		Item	Post. Ref.	Debit	Credit	Balance	
						Debit	Credit
19xx							
Jan.	5		J1		1,500		1,500
	6		J1		2,600		4,100
	9		J1	1,000			3,100
	30		J2		70		3,170

ient cross-reference from general journal to ledger and to indicate that posting to the ledger has been completed. If account numbers are not appropriate, a check (✓) is used.

5. It is customary to skip a line after each journal entry.

The Ledger Account Form

So far, the T form of account has been used as a simple and direct means of recording transactions. In practice, a somewhat more complicated form of the account is needed to record more information. The **ledger account form**, with four columns for dollar amounts, is illustrated in Exhibit 2-4.

The *account title* and *number* appear at the top of the account form. The *date* of the transaction appears in the first two columns, as it does in the journal. The Item column is used only rarely to identify transactions, because an explanation already appears in the journal. The Post. Ref. column is used to note the journal page where the original entry for the transaction can be found. The dollar amount of the entry is entered in the appropriate Debit or Credit column, and a new account balance is computed in the final two columns after each entry. The advantage of this form of account over the T account is that the current balance of the account is readily available.

Relationship Between the Journal and the Ledger

OBJECTIVE 7 *Explain the relationship of the general journal to the general ledger*

After transactions have been entered in the journal, they must be transferred to the general ledger. This process of transferring journal entry information from the journal to the ledger is called **posting**. Posting is usually done, not after each journal entry, but after several entries have been made—for example, at the end of each day or less frequently, depending on the number of transactions.

Through posting, each amount in the Debit column of the journal is transferred into the Debit column of the appropriate account in the ledger, and each amount in the Credit column of the journal is transferred into the Credit column of the appropriate account in the ledger. This procedure is illustrated in Exhibit 2-5. The steps in posting are as follows:

1. Locate in the ledger the debit account named in the journal entry.
2. Enter the date of the transaction and, in the Post. Ref. column of the ledger, the journal page number from which the entry comes.
3. Enter in the Debit column of the ledger account the amount of the debit as it appears in the journal.
4. Enter in the Post. Ref. column of the journal the account number to which the amount was posted.
5. Update the debit or credit balance in the Balance column.
6. Repeat the preceding five steps for the credit side of the journal entry.

Note that Step 4 is the last step in the posting process for each debit and credit. In addition to serving as an easy reference between journal entry and ledger account, this entry in the Post. Ref. column of the journal serves as a check, indicating that all steps for the item are completed. For example, when accountants are called away from their work by telephone calls or other interruptions, they can easily find where they were before the interruption.

In a microcomputer accounting system such as many small businesses have today, the posting is done automatically by the computer after the transactions have been entered. The computer will also do the next step in the accounting cycle, which is to prepare a trial balance.

The Trial Balance

OBJECTIVE 8 *Prepare a trial balance and recognize its value and limitations*

The equality of debit and credit balances in the ledger should be tested periodically by preparing a **trial balance**. Exhibit 2-6 shows a trial balance for the Joan Miller Advertising Agency, Inc. It was prepared from the accounts in Exhibit 2-2, on page 78. The steps in preparing a trial balance follow.

1. Determine the balance of each account in the ledger.
2. List each ledger account that has a balance, with the debit balances in the left column and the credit balances in the right column. Accounts are listed in the order in which they appear in the ledger.
3. Add each column.
4. Compare the totals of each column.

In performing steps **1** and **2**, recall that the account form in the ledger has two balance columns, one for debit balances and one for credit balances. The usual balance for an account is known as the **normal balance**. Consequently, if increases are recorded by debits, the normal balance is a debit balance; if increases are recorded by credits, the normal balance is a credit balance. The table on page 84 summarizes the normal account bal-

Exhibit 2-5. Posting from the General Journal to the Ledger

General Journal ②Page 2

Date		Description	Post. Ref.	Debit	Credit
19xx	②	①	④	③	
Jan.	30	Telephone Expense ⑥	513	70	
		Accounts Payable	212		70
		Received bill for telephone expense			

General Ledger

Accounts Payable — Account No. 212

Date		Item	Post. Ref.	Debit	Credit	Balance Debit	Balance Credit
19xx							
Jan.	5		J1		1,500		1,500
	6		J1		2,600		4,100
	9		J1	1,000			3,100
	30		J2		70		⑤3,170

General Ledger

Telephone Expense — Account No. 513

Date		Item	Post. Ref.	Debit	Credit	Balance Debit	Balance Credit
19xx							
Jan.	30		J2	70		70	

ances of the major account categories. According to the table, the ledger account for Accounts Payable will typically have a credit balance and can be copied into the Trial Balance columns as a credit balance.

Once in a while, a transaction will cause an account to have a balance opposite from its normal balance. Examples are when a customer overpays a bill or when a company overdraws its account at the bank. If this

Exhibit 2-6. Trial Balance

Joan Miller Advertising Agency, Inc.
Trial Balance
January 31, 19xx

Cash	$ 1,720	
Accounts Receivable	2,800	
Art Supplies	1,800	
Office Supplies	800	
Prepaid Rent	800	
Prepaid Insurance	480	
Art Equipment	4,200	
Office Equipment	3,000	
Accounts Payable		$ 3,170
Unearned Art Fees		1,000
Common Stock		10,000
Dividends	1,400	
Advertising Fees Earned		4,200
Office Wages Expense	1,200	
Utility Expense	100	
Telephone Expense	70	
	$18,370	$18,370

happens, the abnormal balance should be copied into the Trial Balance columns as it stands as a debit or credit.

The significance of the trial balance is that it proves whether or not the ledger is in balance. "In balance" means that equal debits and credits have been recorded for all transactions, so that total debits equals total credits. The trial balance proof does not mean, however, that transactions were

	Increases Recorded by		Normal Balance	
Account Category	**Debit**	**Credit**	**Debit**	**Credit**
Asset	x		x	
Liability		x		x
Owners' Equity:				
Common Stock		x		x
Dividends	x		x	
Revenues		x		x
Expenses	x		x	

analyzed correctly or recorded in the proper accounts. For example, there is no way of determining from the trial balance that a debit should have been made in the Art Equipment account rather than the Office Equipment account. Further, if a transaction that should be recorded is omitted, it will not be detected because equal debits and credits will have been omitted. Also, if an error of the same amount is made both as a debit and as a credit, it will not be discovered by the trial balance. The trial balance proves only the equality of the debits and credits in the accounts.

If the debit and credit columns of the trial balance do not equal each other, it may be the result of one or more of the following errors: (1) a debit was entered in an account as a credit, or vice versa, (2) the balance of an account was incorrectly computed, (3) an error was made in carrying the account balance to the trial balance, or (4) the trial balance was incorrectly summed.

Some Notes on Presentation Techniques

Ruled lines appear in financial reports before each subtotal or total to indicate that the amounts above are to be added or subtracted. It is common practice to use a double line under a final total to show that it has been cross checked or verified.

Dollar signs ($) or appropriate currency symbols (for example, £ or ¥) are required in all financial statements, including the balance sheet and income statement, and in schedules such as the trial balance. On these statements, a dollar sign or other currency symbol should be placed before the first amount in each column and before the first amount in a column following a ruled line. Dollar signs and currency symbols are *not* used in journals or ledgers.

On unruled paper, commas and decimal points are used in representing dollar amounts, but when paper with ruled columns is used in journals and ledgers, commas and periods are not needed. In this book, because most problems and illustrations are in whole dollar amounts, the cents column is usually omitted. When professional accountants deal with whole dollars, they will often use a dash in the cents column to indicate whole dollars rather than take the time to write zeros.

Chapter Review

Review of Learning Objectives

1. **Explain in simple terms the generally accepted ways of solving the measurement issues of recognition, valuation, and classification.**
   To measure a business transaction, the accountant must determine when the transaction occurred (the recognition issue), what value should be placed on the transaction (the valuation issue), and how the components of the transaction should be categorized (the classification issue). In gen-

eral, recognition occurs when title passes, and a transaction is valued at the cost or exchange price when the transaction is recognized. Classification refers to the categorizing of transactions according to a system of accounts.

2. **Define and use the terms *account* and *general ledger*.**
   An account is a device for storing data from transactions. There is one account for each asset, liability, and component of owners' equity, including revenues and expenses. The general ledger is a book or file consisting of all of a company's accounts arranged according to a chart of accounts.

3. **Recognize commonly used asset, liability, and stockholders' equity accounts.**
   Commonly used asset accounts are Cash, Notes Receivable, Accounts Receivable, Prepaid Expenses, Land, Buildings, and Equipment. Common liability accounts are Notes Payable, Accounts Payable, and Mortgages Payable. Common stockholders' equity accounts are Common Stock, Retained Earnings, Dividends, Revenues, and Expenses.

4. **Define *double-entry system* and state the rules for debit and credit.**
   In the double-entry system, each transaction must be recorded with at least one debit (left side) and one credit (right side), in such a way that the total dollar amount of the debits equals the total dollar amount of the credits. The rules for debits and credits are (1) increases in assets are debited to asset accounts; decreases in assets are credited to asset accounts; (2) increases in liabilities and owners' equity are credited to those accounts; decreases in liabilities and owners' equity are debited to those accounts.

5. **Apply the procedure for transaction analysis to simple transactions.**
   The procedures for analyzing transactions are to (1) determine the effect of the transaction on assets, liabilities, and owners' equity; (2) apply the appropriate double-entry rule; and (3) make the entry.

6. **Record transactions in the general journal.**
   The general journal is a chronological record of all transactions. The record of a transaction in the general journal contains the date of the transaction, the names of the accounts and dollar amounts debited and credited, an explanation of the journal entries, and the account numbers to which postings have been made.

7. **Explain the relationship of the general journal to the general ledger.**
   After the transactions have been entered in the general journal, they must be posted to the general ledger. Posting is done by transferring each amount in the debit column of the general journal to the debit column of the appropriate account in the general ledger and transferring each amount in the credit column of the general journal to the credit column of the appropriate account in the general ledger.

8. **Prepare a trial balance and recognize its value and limitations.**
   A trial balance is used to test the equality of the debit and credit balances in the ledger. It is prepared by listing each account with its balance in the appropriate debit or credit column. The two columns are added and com-

pared to test their balances. The major limitation of the trial balance is that the equality of debit and credit balances does not necessarily mean that transactions were analyzed correctly or recorded in the proper accounts.

Review of Concepts and Terminology

The following concepts and terms were introduced in this chapter:

(L.O. 2) **Account:** The basic storage unit of accounting. There is a separate account for each asset, liability, and component of owners' equity, including revenues and expenses.

(L.O. 4) **Balance (or account balance):** The difference in total dollars between the total debit footing and the total credit footing of an account.

(L.O. 2) **Chart of accounts:** A numbering scheme that assigns a unique number to each account to facilitate finding the account in the ledger; also the list of account numbers and titles.

(L.O. 1) **Classification:** The process of assigning all transactions to the appropriate accounts.

(L.O. 6) **Compound entry:** A journal entry that has more than one debit and/or credit entry.

(L.O. 1) **Cost:** The exchange price associated with a business transaction at the point of recognition.

(L.O. 1) **Cost principle:** The practice of recording transactions at cost and maintaining this cost in the records until an asset, liability, or owners' equity is sold, expired, consumed, satisfied, or otherwise disposed of.

(L.O. 4) **Credit:** The right side of an account.

(L.O. 4) **Debit:** The left side of an account.

(L.O. 4) **Double-entry system:** An accounting system in which each transaction must be recorded with at least one debit and one credit, in such a way that the total dollar amount of debits and the total dollar amount of credits equal each other.

(L.O. 4) **Footing:** A memorandum total of a column of numbers; to foot, total a column of numbers.

(L.O. 6) **General journal:** The simplest and most flexible type of journal.

(L.O. 2) **General ledger:** The book or file that contains all the company's accounts.

(L.O. 6) **Journal:** A chronological record of all transactions; the place where transactions are first recorded.

(L.O. 6) **Journal entry:** A separate entry in the journal, used to record a single transaction.

(L.O. 6) **Journalizing:** The process of recording transactions in a journal.

(L.O. 2) **Ledger:** A book or file of all a company's accounts, arranged as in the chart of accounts.

(L.O. 6) **Ledger account form:** A form of the account that has four columns, one for debit entries, one for credit entries, and two columns (debit and credit) for showing the balance of the account.

(L.O. 8) **Normal balance:** The balance that one would expect an account to have; the usual balance of an account; also the side (debit or credit) that increases the account.

(L.O. 7) **Posting:** The process of transferring journal entry information from the journal to the ledger.

(L.O. 1) **Recognition:** The determination of when a business transaction is to be recorded.

(L.O. 1) **Recognition point:** The predetermined time at which a transaction is to be recorded. Usually the point at which title passes.

(L.O. 4) **T account:** A form of an account that has a physical resemblance to the letter *T*; used to analyze transactions.

(L.O. 8) **Trial balance:** A listing of accounts in the general ledger with their debit or credit balances in respective columns and a totaling of the columns; used to test the equality of debit and credit balances in the ledger.

(L.O. 1) **Valuation:** The process of assigning a monetary value to all business transactions.

Review Problem
Transaction Analysis, General Journal, Ledger Accounts, and Trial Balance

(L.O. 5, 6, 8) After graduation from veterinary school, Laura Cox entered private practice. The transactions of the business through May 27 are as follows:

19xx
May 1 Laura Cox invested $2,000 in 2,000 shares of $1 par value common stock of her newly chartered company, Pet Clinic, Inc.
3 Paid $300 for two months' rent in advance for an office.
9 Purchased medical supplies for $200 in cash.
12 Purchased $400 of equipment on credit, making a one-fourth down payment.
15 Delivered a calf for a fee of $35.
18 Made a partial payment of $50 on the equipment purchased May 12.
27 Paid a utility bill for $40.

Required

1. Record the above entries in the general journal.
2. Post the entries from the journal to the following accounts in the ledger: Cash (111), Medical Supplies (115), Prepaid Rent (116), Equipment (141), Accounts Payable (211), Common Stock (311), Veterinary Fees Earned (411), Utility Expense (511).
3. Prepare a trial balance.

Answer to Review Problem

1. Recording journal entries:

General Journal					Page 1
Date		Description	Post. Ref.	Debit	Credit
19xx					
May	1	Cash	111	2,000	
		Common Stock	311		2,000
		Laura Cox invested $2,000 in 2,000 shares of $1 par value stock			
	3	Prepaid Rent	116	300	
		Cash	111		300
		Paid two months' rent in advance for an office			
	9	Medical Supplies	115	200	
		Cash	111		200
		Purchased medical supplies for cash			
	12	Equipment	141	400	
		Accounts Payable	211		300
		Cash	111		100
		Purchased equipment on credit, paying 25 percent down			
	15	Cash	111	35	
		Veterinary Fees Earned	411		35
		Collected fee for delivery of a calf			
	18	Accounts Payable	211	50	
		Cash	111		50
		Partial payment for equipment purchased on May 12			
	27	Utility Expense	511	40	
		Cash	111		40
		Paid utility bill			

2. Posting transactions to the ledger accounts:

General Ledger — Page 1

Cash — Account No. 111

Date		Item	Post. Ref.	Debit	Credit	Balance Debit	Balance Credit
19xx							
May	1		J1	2,000		2,000	
	3		J1		300	1,700	
	9		J1		200	1,500	
	12		J1		100	1,400	
	15		J1	35		1,435	
	18		J1		50	1,385	
	27		J1		40	1,345	

Medical Supplies — Account No. 115

Date		Item	Post. Ref.	Debit	Credit	Balance Debit	Balance Credit
19xx							
May	9		J1	200		200	

Prepaid Rent — Account No. 116

Date		Item	Post. Ref.	Debit	Credit	Balance Debit	Balance Credit
19xx							
May	3		J1	300		300	

Equipment — Account No. 141

Date		Item	Post. Ref.	Debit	Credit	Balance Debit	Balance Credit
19xx							
May	12		J1	400		400	

(continued)

Accounts Payable **Account No.** *211*

Date		Item	Post. Ref.	Debit	Credit	Balance Debit	Balance Credit
19xx							
May	12		J1		300		300
	18		J1	50			250

Common Stock **Account No.** *311*

Date		Item	Post. Ref.	Debit	Credit	Balance Debit	Balance Credit
19xx							
May	1		J1		2,000		2,000

Veterinary Fees Earned **Account No.** *411*

Date		Item	Post. Ref.	Debit	Credit	Balance Debit	Balance Credit
19xx							
May	15		J1		35		35

Utility Expense **Account No.** *511*

Date		Item	Post. Ref.	Debit	Credit	Balance Debit	Balance Credit
19xx							
May	27		J1	40		40	

3. Completing trial balance:

Pet Clinic, Inc.
Trial Balance
May 31, 19xx

Cash	$1,345	
Medical Supplies	200	
Prepaid Rent	300	
Equipment	400	
Accounts Payable		$ 250
Common Stock		2,000
Veterinary Fees Earned		35
Utility Expense	40	
	$2,285	$2,285

Chapter Assignments

Discussion Questions

1. What three issues underlie most accounting decisions?
2. Why is recognition an issue to accountants?
3. A customer asks the owner of a store to save an item for him and says that he will pick it up and pay for it next week. The owner agrees to hold it. Should this transaction be recorded as a sale? Explain.
4. Why is it practical for the accountant to rely on original cost for valuation purposes?
5. Comment on the basic limitation of using original cost in accounting measurements.
6. What is an account, and how is it related to the ledger?
7. "Debits are bad; credits are good." Comment on this statement.
8. Why is the system of recording entries called the double-entry system? What is so special about it?
9. Give the rules of debits and credits for (a) assets, (b) liabilities, and (c) owners' equity.
10. Why are the rules the same for liabilities and owners' equity?
11. Explain why debits, which decrease owners' equity, also increase expenses, which are a component of owners' equity.
12. What is the meaning of the statement, "The Cash account has a debit balance of $500"?
13. What are the three steps in transaction analysis?

14. Tell whether each of the following accounts is an asset account, a liability account, or an owners' equity account:
    a. Notes Receivable
    b. Land
    c. Dividends
    d. Bonds Payable
    e. Prepaid Rent
    f. Insurance Expense
    g. Service Revenue
15. List the following six items in a logical sequence to illustrate the flow of events through the accounting system:
    a. Analysis of transaction
    b. Debits and credits posted from the journal to the ledger
    c. Occurrence of business transaction
    d. Preparation of financial statements
    e. Entry made in a journal
    f. Preparation of trial balance
16. What purposes are served by a trial balance?
17. Can errors be present even though the trial balance balances? Comment.
18. In recording entries in a journal, which is written first, the debit or the credit? How is indentation used in the general journal?
19. What is the relationship between the journal and the ledger?
20. Describe each of the following:
    a. Account
    b. Journal
    c. Ledger
    d. Book of original entry
    e. Post. Ref. column
    f. Journalizing
    g. Posting
    h. Footings
    i. Compound entry
21. Does double-entry accounting refer to entering a transaction in both the journal and the ledger? Comment.
22. Is it possible or desirable to forgo the journal and enter transactions directly into the ledger? Comment.
23. What is the normal balance of Accounts Payable? Under what conditions could Accounts Payable have a debit balance?

Communication Skills Exercises

Communication 2-1. Valuation Issue *(L.O. 1)*

The Foxboro Company manufactures and markets a comprehensive family of products for automation of the industrial process. In the company's 1989 annual report under Summary of Significant Accounting Policies, the following statement is made: "Property, plant and equipment was stated at cost."[2] Given the fact that the property, plant, and equipment were undoubtedly purchased over the past several years and that the current value of these assets is likely to be quite different from their original cost, what authoritative basis is there for carrying these assets at cost? Does accounting generally recognize changes in "value" subsequent to the purchase of property, plant, and equipment?

Communication 2-2. Recognition Point *(L.O. 1)*

Paramount Communications Inc. is a major producer of feature films, among them the *Indiana Jones* series and *Another 48 Hours*. The distribution of feature films raises more complex issues than those encountered with products or services that have a single recognition point. Among the significant accounting policies in its 1989 annual report, Paramount states that "Feature films are produced or acquired for distribution, normally, first in the theatrical market followed by, in usual order of priority, videocassettes, pay cable, network televi-

2. Excerpt from the 1989 Annual Report of The Foxboro Company. Used with permission.

sion and syndicated television. On average, the length of the revenue cycle for feature films approximates four years." It states its revenue recognition policy: "Theatrical revenues from domestic and foreign markets are recognized as films are exhibited. Revenues arising from television license agreements are recognized in the year that the films . . . are available for telecast. Revenues from the sale of videocassettes are recognized upon delivery of the merchandise."[3] How do these statements relate to the concept of a recognition point?

Communication 2-3. Recognition Point and Ethical Considerations *(L.O. 1)*

Penn Office Supplies Corporation's sales representative Jerry Hasbrow is compensated on a commission basis and receives a substantial bonus for meeting his annual sales goal. The company's recognition point for sales is the day of shipment. On December 31, Jerry realizes that he needs sales of $2,000 to reach his sales goal and receive the bonus. He calls a purchaser for a local insurance company whom he knows well and asks him to buy $2,000 worth of copier paper today. The purchaser says, "But Jerry, that's more than a year's supply for us." Jerry says, "Buy it today. If you decide it's too much, you can return however much you want for full credit next month." The purchaser says, "Okay, ship it." The paper is shipped on December 31 and recorded as a sale. On January 15, the purchaser returns $1,750 worth of paper for full credit (okayed by Jerry) against the bill. Should the shipment on December 31 be recorded as a sale? Discuss the ethics of Jerry's action.

Communication 2-4. Basic Research Skills *(L.O. 4, 5)*

Obtain a recent issue (or secure a copy in the library) of one of the following business journals: *Barrons, Business Week, Forbes, Fortune,* or the *Wall Street Journal.* Find an article on a company you recognize or on a company in a business that interests you. Read the article carefully noting any references to transactions that the company engages in. These may be normal transactions such as sales and purchases or unusual transactions such as the purchase of another company. Bring a copy of the article to class and be prepared to describe how you would analyze and record the transactions you have noted.

Classroom Exercises

Exercise 2-1. Recognition *(L.O. 1)*

Which of the following events would be recognized and recorded in the accounting records of the Gugini Corporation on the date indicated?

Jan. 15 Gugini Corporation offers to purchase a tract of land for $140,000. There is a high likelihood that the offer will be accepted.

Feb. 2 Gugini Corporation receives notice that its rent will be increased from $500 per month to $600 per month effective March 1.

Mar. 29 Gugini Corporation receives its utility bill for the month of March. The bill is not due until April 9.

Apr. 20 Dan Gugini, a major stockholder in Gugini Corporation, dies. Dan's son, Mike, inherits all of Dan's stock in the company.

May 5 Mike, who inherited Dan's stock in Gugini Corporation, sells 2,000 shares of stock to Sam Lutts for $60,000.

3. Excerpts from the 1989 Annual Report of Paramount Communications Inc. Used with permission.

June 10 Gugini Corporation places a firm order for new office equipment costing $21,000.

July 6 The office equipment ordered on June 10 arrives. Payment is not due until August 1.

Exercise 2-2. Classification of Accounts *(L.O. 3, 4, 8)*

Listed below are the ledger accounts of the Wonder Service Corporation:

a. Cash
b. Wages Expense
c. Accounts Receivable
d. Common Stock
e. Service Revenue
f. Prepaid Rent
g. Accounts Payable
h. Investments in Stocks and Bonds
i. Bonds Payable
j. Income Taxes Expense
k. Land
l. Supplies Expense
m. Prepaid Insurance
n. Utility Expense
o. Fees Earned
p. Dividends
q. Wages Payable
r. Unearned Revenue
s. Office Equipment
t. Rent Payable
u. Notes Receivable
v. Interest Expense
w. Income Taxes Payable
x. Notes Payable
y. Supplies
z. Interest Receivable

Complete the following table, indicating with two Xs for each account its classification and its normal balance (whether a debit or credit increases the account):

			Type of Account					
			Stockholders' Equity				Normal Balance (increases balance)	
				Retained Earnings				
Item	Asset	Liability	Common Stock	Dividends	Revenue	Expense	Debit	Credit
a.	X						X	

Exercise 2-3. Application of Recognition Point *(L.O. 1)*

Skowron's Body Shop, Inc. uses a large amount of supplies in its business. The following table summarizes selected transaction data for orders of supplies purchased.

Order	Date Shipped	Date Received	Amount
a	June 26	July 5	$ 600
b	July 10	15	1,500
c	16	22	800
d	23	30	1,200
e	27	August 2	1,500
f	August 1	5	1,000

Determine the total purchases of supplies for July alone under each of the following assumptions:

1. Skowron's Body Shop recognizes purchases when orders are shipped.
2. Skowron's Body Shop recognizes purchases when orders are received.

Exercise 2-4. Transaction Analysis *(L.O. 5)*

Analyze each of the following transactions, using the form shown in the example below the list.

a. Clarence Davis established Royal Barber Shop, Inc. by incorporating and investing $1,200 in 120 shares of $10 par value common stock.
b. Paid two months' rent in advance, $420.
c. Purchased supplies on credit, $60.
d. Received cash for barbering services, $50.
e. Paid for supplies purchased in **c**.
f. Paid utility bill, $36.
g. Declared and paid a dividend, $50.

Example

a. The asset Cash was increased. Increases in assets are recorded by debits. Debit Cash, $1,200. The owners' equity component Common Stock was increased. Increases in owners' equity are recorded by credits. Credit Common Stock, $1,200.

Exercise 2-5. Recording Transactions in T Accounts *(L.O. 5)*

Open the following T accounts: Cash, Repair Supplies, Repair Equipment, Accounts Payable, Common Stock, Dividends, Repair Fees Earned, Salaries Expense, and Rent Expense. Record the following transactions for the month of June directly in the T accounts; use the letters to identify the transactions in your T accounts. Determine the balance in each account.

a. Michelle Donato opened the Eastmoor Repair Service, Inc. by investing $4,300 in cash and $1,600 in repair equipment in return for 5,900 shares of the company's $1 par value common stock.
b. Paid $400 for current month's rent.
c. Purchased repair supplies on credit, $500.
d. Purchased additional repair equipment for cash, $300.
e. Paid salary to a helper, $450.
f. Paid $200 of amount purchased on credit in **c**.
g. Accepted cash for repairs completed, $860.
h. Declared and paid a dividend, $600.

Exercise 2-6. Trial Balance *(L.O. 8)*

After recording the transactions in Exercise 2-5, prepare a trial balance in proper sequence for Eastmoor Repair Service, Inc., June 30, 19xx.

Exercise 2-7. Analysis of Transactions *(L.O. 5)*

State an explanation for each of the following transactions (identified by letters).

Cash

a.	20,000	b.	5,000
g.	500	e.	1,000
h.	300	f.	1,500

Accounts Receivable

c.	2,000	g.	500

Equipment

b.	5,000	h.	300
d.	3,000		

Accounts Payable

f.	1,500	d.	3,000

Service Revenue

		c.	2,000

Wages Expense

e.	1,000		

Common Stock

		a.	20,000

Exercise 2-8. Analysis of Transactions *(L.O. 5)*

Tap Waste Removal Corporation provided monthly waste removal service for Aaron Corporation, which resulted in the following transactions in Tap's records:

Cash

July 25	500		

Waste Removal Service Revenue

		June 30	750

Accounts Receivable

June 30	750	July 25	500

Using T accounts, prepare the corresponding entries in Aaron Corporation's records.

Exercise 2-9. Analysis of Unfamiliar Transactions *(L.O. 5)*

Managers and accountants often encounter transactions with which they are unfamiliar. Use your analytical skills to analyze and record in general journal form the transactions below, which have not been illustrated thus far in the text.

a. Purchased merchandise inventory on account, $800.
b. Purchased marketable securities for cash, $2,400.
c. Returned part of merchandise inventory purchased earlier for full credit, $250.
d. Sold merchandise inventory on account, $800 (record sale only).
e. Purchased land and a building for $300,000. Payment is $60,000 in cash and a 30-year mortgage for the remainder. The purchase price is allocated $100,000 to land and $200,000 to building.
f. Received an order for $12,000 in services to be provided. With the order was a deposit of $4,000.

Exercise 2-10. Preparation of Ledger Account *(L.O. 7)*

A T account showing the cash transactions for a month follows:

Cash			
Mar. 1	9,400	Mar. 2	900
7	1,200	4	200
14	4,000	8	1,700
21	200	9	5,000
28	6,400	23	600

Prepare the account in ledger form for Cash (Account 111) in a manner similar to the example in Exhibit 2-4.

Exercise 2-11. Recording Transactions in General Journal and Posting to Ledger Accounts *(L.O. 6, 7)*

Open a general journal form like the one in Exhibit 2-3, and label it Page 10. After completing the form, record the following transactions in the journal:

Dec. 14 Purchased an item of equipment for $6,000, paying $2,000 as a cash down payment.
28 Paid $3,000 of the amount owed on the equipment.

Prepare three ledger account forms like those shown in Exhibit 2-4. Use the following account numbers: Cash, 111; Equipment, 143; and Accounts Payable, 212. Then post the two transactions from the general journal to the ledger accounts, at the same time making proper posting references.

Assume that the Cash account has a debit balance of $8,000 a day prior to these transactions.

Exercise 2-12. Preparation of Trial Balance *(L.O. 8)*

The following accounts of the Emory Service Corporation as of March 31, 19xx are listed in alphabetical order. The amount of Accounts Payable is omitted.

Accounts Payable	?	Equipment	$12,000
Accounts Receivable	$ 3,000	Land	5,200
Building	34,000	Notes Payable	20,000
Cash	9,000	Prepaid Insurance	1,100
Common Stock	20,000	Retained Earnings	11,450

Prepare a trial balance with the proper heading and with the accounts listed in the balance sheet sequence (see Exhibit 2-6). Compute the balance of Accounts Payable.

Exercise 2-13. Effect of Errors on Trial Balance *(L.O. 8)*

Which of the following errors would cause a trial balance to have unequal totals? Explain your answers.

a. A payment to a creditor was recorded as a debit to Accounts Payable for $86 and a credit to Cash for $68.
b. A payment of $100 to a creditor for an account payable was debited to Accounts Receivable and credited to Cash.

c. A purchase of office supplies of $280 was recorded as a debit to Office Supplies for $28 and a credit to Cash for $28.
d. A purchase of equipment of $300 was recorded as a debit to Supplies for $300 and a credit to Cash for $300.

Exercise 2-14. Correcting Errors in Trial Balance *(L.O. 8)*

The following trial balance for Engelman Services, Inc. at the end of July does not balance because of a number of errors. The accountant for Engelman has compared the amounts in the trial balance with the ledger, recomputed the account balances, and compared the postings. He found the following errors:

a. The balance of Cash was understated by $200.
b. A cash payment of $210 was credited to Cash for $120.
c. A debit of $60 to Accounts Receivable was not posted.
d. Supplies purchased for $30 were posted as a credit to Supplies.
e. A debit of $90 to Prepaid Insurance was overlooked and not posted.
f. The Accounts Payable account had debits of $2,660 and credits of $4,590.
g. A Notes Payable account with a credit balance of $1,200 was not included in the trial balance.
h. The debit balance of Dividends was listed in the trial balance as a credit.
i. A $100 debit to Dividends was posted as a credit.
j. The Utility Expense of $130 was listed as $13 in the trial balance.

Prepare a correct trial balance.

Engelman Services, Inc.
Trial Balance
July 31, 19xx

Cash	$ 1,920	
Accounts Receivable	2,830	
Supplies	60	
Prepaid Insurance	90	
Equipment	4,200	
Accounts Payable		$ 2,270
Common Stock		2,000
Retained Earnings		3,780
Dividends		350
Revenues		2,960
Salaries Expense	1,300	
Rent Expense	300	
Advertising Expense	170	
Utility Expense	13	
	$10,883	$11,360

Exercise 2-15. Preparation of Trial Balance *(L.O. 8)*

The Viola Construction Corporation builds foundations for buildings and parking lots. The following alphabetical list shows the account balances as of April 30, 19xx:

Accounts Payable	$ 3,900	Office Trailer	$ 2,200
Accounts Receivable	10,120	Prepaid Insurance	4,600
Cash	?	Retained Earnings	10,000
Common Stock	30,000	Revenue Earned	17,400
Construction Supplies	1,900	Supplies Expense	7,200
Dividends	7,800	Utility Expense	420
Equipment	24,500	Wages Expense	8,800
Notes Payable	20,000		

Prepare a trial balance for the company with the proper heading and with the accounts in balance sheet sequence. Determine the correct balance for the Cash account on April 30, 19xx.

Interpretation Cases from Business

ICB 2-1. First Chicago Corporation[4] *(L.O. 3, 5)*

First Chicago Corporation is the largest bank holding company in Illinois. Selected accounts from the company's 1990 annual report are as follows (in millions):

Cash and Due from Banks	$ 3,571
Loans to Customers	27,706
Investment Securities	1,810
Deposits by Customers	32,543

Required

1. Indicate whether each of the above accounts would be an asset, liability, or owners' equity component on First Chicago's balance sheet.
2. Assume that you were in a position to do business with First Chicago. Prepare the general journal entry (in First Chicago's records) to record each of the following transactions:

   a. You sell securities in the amount of $2,000 to the bank.
   b. You deposit the $2,000 received in step **a** in the bank.
   c. You borrow $5,000 from the bank.

ICB 2-2. Stauffer Chemical Company *(L.O. 1)*

Stauffer Chemical Company relies for more than half its profits on agricultural chemicals such as fertilizer and pesticides. Stauffer has been hammered by bad weather, depressed farm prices, and lowered farm output caused by a federal price-support program. In an article in the *Wall Street Journal,* it was reported that Stauffer overstated its 1982 earnings by $31.1 million by improperly accounting for certain sales. In settling a suit brought by the Securities and Exchange Commission (SEC), the company agreed, without admitting or denying the charges, to restate the 1982 financial results, lowering the 1982 profit by 25 percent. The *Wall Street Journal* summarized the situation as follows:

In the summer of 1982, "aware that agricultural chemical sales for its 1982–83 season would probably fall off sharply," Stauffer undertook a plan to accelerate sales of certain products to dealers during fiscal 1982, according to the SEC. . . .

4. Excerpts from the 1990 Annual Report used by permission of First Chicago Corporation. Copyright © 1990.

Stauffer, the SEC charged, offered its dealers incentives to take products during the fourth quarter of 1982. As a result, the company reported $72 million of revenue that ordinarily wouldn't have been booked until early 1983. By March 1983, according to the commission, Stauffer realized that it would have to "offer its distributors relief" from the oversupply of unsaleable products. Stauffer offered dealers refunds for as much as 100% of unsold products taken in 1982, compared with 32% the previous year.

Stauffer ended up refunding nearly 40% of its 1982 agricultural chemical sales, but failed to disclose the "substantial uncertainties" surrounding the sales in the annual report it filed with the SEC in April 1983. The omission was "materially false and misleading," according to the SEC.

"Their business was down and they wanted to accelerate sales," said a government official familiar with the year-long SEC investigation.[5]

Required

1. Prepare the journal entry that Stauffer made in 1982 that the SEC feels should not have been made until 1983.
2. Three issues that must be addressed when recording a transaction are recognition, valuation, and classification. Which of these issues are of most concern to the SEC in the Stauffer case? Explain how each applies to the transaction in part **1**.

ICB 2-3. Yellow Freight System, Inc. of Delaware[6]
(L.O. 5)

Yellow Freight System, Inc. of Delaware operates one of the largest freight transportation and related services companies in the United States. Selected data from the company's 1989 statement of cash flows appears below (in thousands):

Investing Activities:

Acquisition of operating property	$(193,354)
Proceeds from disposal of operating property	11,122
Net cash used in investing activities	$(182,232)

Financing Activities:

Proceeds from issuance of long-term debt	$124,475
Repayment of long-term debt	(104,602)
Exercise of stock options	33
Cash dividends paid to shareholders	(20,967)
Net cash from (used in) financing activities	$ (1,061)

Required

1. Prepare a general journal entry to record each of the above entries (assuming that each is done in a single transaction and that there are no gains or losses on the transactions).

5. Wynter, Leon E., "Stauffer Profit Overstated in '82, SEC Says in Suit," *The Wall Street Journal*, Aug. 14, 1984. Reprinted by permission of *The Wall Street Journal*, © 1984 Dow Jones and Company, Inc. All Rights Reserved Worldwide.
6. Excerpts from the 1989 Annual Report used by permission of Yellow Freight System, Inc. of Delaware. Copyright © 1989.

2. From 1988 to 1989, Yellow Freight's cash balance decreased by only $3,812,000. How is this possible given the figures above?
3. The following statement is made by Yellow Freight's management in its 1989 annual report:

   The projected level of capital expenditures for 1990 is $170 million. It is anticipated that approximately $85 million will be needed for further expansion and improvements to hub and terminal facilities to support Yellow's future growth. The cost of fleet additions and replacements is expected to total $60 million. Additions to other operating property should total $25 million. It is anticipated that 1990 capital expenditures will be financed through internally-generated funds and external financing.

   What do you think is meant by "internally generated funds" versus "external financing"? How will the balance sheet differ at the end of the year if the capital expenditures are paid with internally generated funds as opposed to being paid with external financing?

Problem Set A

Problem 2A-1. Transaction Analysis, T Accounts, and Trial Balance *(L.O. 5, 8)*

Pat McNally opened a secretarial school called VIP Secretarial Training, Inc.

a. As an individual, he contributed the following assets to the business, in exchange for 13,600 shares of $1 par value stock in the corporation:

Cash	$5,700
Word Processors	4,300
Office Equipment	3,600

b. Found a location for his business and paid the first month's rent, $260.
c. Paid $190 for advertisement announcing the opening of the school.
d. Received applications from three students in a four-week secretarial program and two students in a ten-day keyboarding course. The students will be billed later a total of $1,300.
e. Purchased supplies on credit, $330.
f. Billed enrolled students, $1,300.
g. Paid assistant one week's salary, $220.
h. Purchased a word processor, $480, and office equipment, $380, on credit.
i. Paid for supplies purchased on credit in **e** above.
j. Repaired broken word processor, paid cash, $40.
k. Billed new students who enrolled late in the course, $440.
l. Received payment from students previously billed, $1,080.
m. Paid utility bill for current month, $90.
n. Paid assistant one week's salary, $220.
o. Received cash revenue from another new student, $250.
p. Declared and paid a dividend, $300.

Required

1. Set up the following T accounts: Cash, Accounts Receivable, Supplies, Word Processors, Office Equipment, Accounts Payable, Common Stock, Dividends, Revenue from Business, Rent Expense, Advertising Expense, Salaries Expense, Repair Expense, Utility Expense.
2. Record transactions by entering debits and credits directly in the T accounts, using the transaction letter to identify each debit and credit.
3. Prepare a trial balance using the current date.

Problem 2A-2. Transaction Analysis, General Journal, T Accounts, and Trial Balance
(L.O. 1, 5, 6, 8)

John Powers, a house painter, obtained a charter from the state and opened a business called Powers Painting Service, Inc. During the month of April, he completed the following transactions:

Apr. 2 Began his business by contributing equipment valued at $1,230 and depositing $7,100 in a checking account in the name of the corporation in exchange for 833 shares of $10 par value common stock in the corporation.
3 Purchased a used truck costing $1,900. Paid $500 cash and signed a note for the balance.
4 Purchased supplies on account, $320.
5 Completed a painting job and billed the customer, $480.
7 Received cash for painting two rooms, $150.
8 Hired assistant to work with him, to be paid $6 per hour.
10 Purchased supplies for cash, $160.
11 Received check from customer previously billed, $480.
12 Paid $400 on insurance policy for eighteen months' coverage.
13 Billed customer for painting job, $620.
14 Paid assistant for twenty-five hours' work, $150.
15 Purchased a tune-up for truck, $40.
18 Paid for supplies purchased on April 4.
20 Purchased new ladder (equipment) for $60 and supplies for $290, on account.
22 Received telephone bill to be paid next month, $60.
23 Received cash from customer previously billed, $330.
25 Received cash for painting five-room apartment, $360.
27 Paid $200 on note signed for truck.
29 Paid assistant for thirty hours' work, $180.
30 Declared and paid a dividend, $300.

Required

1. Prepare journal entries to record the above transactions in the general journal. Use the accounts listed below.
2. Set up the following T accounts and post all the journal entries: Cash, Accounts Receivable, Supplies, Prepaid Insurance, Equipment, Truck, Notes Payable, Accounts Payable, Common Stock, Dividends, Painting Fees Earned, Wages Expense, Telephone Expense, Truck Expense.
3. Prepare a trial balance for Powers Painting Service, Inc. as of April 30, 19xx.
4. Compare how recognition applies to the transactions of April 5 and 7 and how classification applies to the transactions of April 12 and 14.

Problem 2A-3. Transaction Analysis, General Journal, Ledger Accounts, and Trial Balance
(L.O. 5, 6, 8)

Kwan Lee began a rug cleaning business called Lee Carpet Cleaning Service, Inc. on October 1 and engaged in the following transactions during the month:

Oct. 1 Began business by depositing $6,000 in a business bank account in the name of the corporation in exchange for 600 shares of the $10 par value common stock in the corporation.
2 Ordered cleaning supplies, $500.
3 Purchased cleaning equipment for cash, $1,400.
4 Leased a van by making two months' lease payment in advance, $600.

Oct. 7 Received the cleaning supplies ordered on October 2 and agreed to pay half the amount in ten days and the rest in thirty days.
9 Paid for repairs on the van with cash, $40.
12 Received cash for cleaning carpets, $480.
17 Paid half of the amount owed on supplies purchased on October 7, $250.
21 Billed customers for cleaning carpets, $670.
24 Paid for additional repairs on the van with cash, $40.
27 Received $300 from the customers billed on October 21.
31 Declared and paid a dividend, $350.

Required

1. Prepare journal entries to record the above transactions in the general journal (Pages 1 and 2). Use the accounts listed below.
2. Set up the following ledger accounts and post the journal entries: Cash (111), Accounts Receivable (113), Cleaning Supplies (115), Prepaid Lease (116), Cleaning Equipment (141), Accounts Payable (211), Common Stock (311), Dividends (313), Cleaning Revenues (411), Repair Expense (511).
3. Prepare a trial balance for Lee Carpet Cleaning Service, Inc. as of October 31, 19xx.

Problem 2A-4. Transaction Analysis, General Journal, Ledger Accounts, and Trial Balance
(L.O. 5, 6, 8)

The account balances for Lou's Landscaping Service, Inc. at the end of July are presented in the trial balance shown below.

Lou's Landscaping Service, Inc.
Trial Balance
July 31, 19xx

Cash (111)	$3,100	
Accounts Receivable (113)	220	
Supplies (115)	460	
Prepaid Insurance (116)	400	
Equipment (141)	4,400	
Notes Payable (211)		$3,000
Accounts Payable (212)		700
Common Stock (311)		3,000
Retained Earnings (312)		1,200
Dividends (313)	420	
Service Revenue (411)		1,490
Lease Expense (412)	290	
Pickup Expense (413)	100	
	$9,390	$9,390

During August, Mr. Jacobson completed the following transactions:

Aug. 1 Paid for supplies purchased on credit last month, $140.
2 Billed customers for services, $410.
3 Paid lease on pickup for August, $290.
5 Purchased supplies on credit, $150.

Aug. 7 Received cash from customers not previously billed, $290.
8 Purchased new equipment from Pendleton Manufacturing Company on account, $1,300.
9 Received bill for oil change on pickup, $40.
12 Returned a portion of equipment that was defective, $320. Purchase was made August 8. Reduce equipment and accounts payable.
13 Received payment from customers previously billed, $190.
14 Paid bill received on August 9.
19 Paid for supplies purchased on August 5.
20 Billed customers for services, $270.
23 Purchased equipment on account, $280.
25 Received payment from customers previously billed, $390.
27 Purchased gasoline for pickup with cash, $30.
29 Paid $600 to reduce principal of note payable.
31 Declared and paid a dividend, $110.

Required

1. Prepare journal entries to record the August transactions in the general journal (Pages 11 and 12).
2. Open ledger accounts for the accounts shown in the trial balance. Enter the July 31 trial balance amounts in the ledger accounts.
3. Post the entries to the ledger accounts.
4. Prepare a trial balance as of August 31, 19xx.

Problem 2A-5. Relationship of General Journal, Ledger Accounts, and Trial Balance *(L.O. 6, 7, 8)*

The Other Mother Child Care Corporation provides babysitting and child-care programs. On January 31, 19xx, the corporation had a trial balance as shown below.

Other Mother Child Care Corporation
Trial Balance
January 31, 19xx

Cash (111)	$ 1,870	
Accounts Receivable (113)	1,700	
Equipment (141)	1,040	
Buses (143)	17,400	
Notes Payable (211)		$15,000
Accounts Payable (212)		1,640
Common Stock (311)		4,000
Retained Earnings (312)		1,370
	$22,010	$22,010

During the month of February, the corporation completed the following transactions:

Feb. 2 Paid this month's rent, $270.
3 Received fees for this month's services, $650.
4 Purchased supplies on account, $85.
5 Reimbursed bus driver for gas expenses, $40.

Feb. 6 Ordered playground equipment, $1,000.
7 Paid part-time assistants for two weeks' services, $230.
8 Paid $170 on account.
9 Received $1,200 from customers on account.
10 Billed customers who had not yet paid for this month's services, $700.
11 Paid for supplies purchased on February 4.
13 Purchased playground equipment for cash, $1,000.
17 Equipment invested in business by owner in return for stock, $290.
19 Paid this month's utility bill, $145.
21 Paid part-time assistants for two weeks' services, $230.
22 Received $500 for one month's services from customers previously billed.
27 Purchased gas and oil for bus on account, $35.
28 Paid $290 for a one-year insurance policy.
28 Declared and paid a dividend, $110.

Required

1. Enter the above transactions in the general journal (Pages 17 and 18).
2. Open accounts in the ledger for the accounts in the trial balance plus the following ones: Supplies (115), Prepaid Insurance (116), Dividends (313), Service Revenue (411), Rent Expense (511), Bus Expense (512), Wages Expense (513), Utility Expense (514).
3. Enter the January 31, 19xx account balances from the trial balance.
4. Post the entries to the ledger accounts. Be sure to make the appropriate posting references in the journal and ledger as you post.
5. Prepare a trial balance as of February 28, 19xx.

Problem Set B

Problem 2B-1. Transaction Analysis, T Accounts, and Trial Balance *(L.O. 5, 8)*

Diane Pastore established a small business, Pastore Training Center, Inc., to teach individuals how to use spreadsheet analysis, word processing, and other techniques on microcomputers.

a. Pastore began by transferring the following assets to the business in exchange for 19,600 shares of $1 par value common stock.

Cash	$9,200
Furniture	3,100
Microcomputer	7,300

b. Paid the first month's rent on a small storefront, $280.
c. Purchased computer software on credit, $750.
d. Paid for an advertisement in the school newspaper, $100.
e. Received enrollment applications from five students for a five-day course to start next week. Each student will pay $200 if he or she actually begins the course.
f. Paid wages to a part-time helper, $150.
g. Received cash payment from three of the students enrolled in **e**, $600.
h. Billed the two other students in **e** who attended but did not pay in cash, $400.
i. Paid utility bill for the current month, $110.
j. Made payment toward software purchased in **c**, $250.

k. Received payment from one student billed in **h**, $200.
l. Purchased a second microcomputer for cash, $4,700.
m. Declared and paid a dividend, $300.

Required

1. Set up the following T accounts: Cash, Accounts Receivable, Software, Furniture, Microcomputers, Accounts Payable, Common Stock, Dividends, Tuition Revenue, Rent Expense, Wages Expense, Advertising Expense, Utility Expense.
2. Record transactions by entering debits and credits directly in the T accounts, using the transaction letter to identify each debit and credit.
3. Prepare a trial balance using the proper heading and the current date.

Problem 2B-2. Transaction Analysis, General Journal, T Accounts, and Trial Balance
(L.O. 1, 5, 6, 8)

Hassan Rahim won a concession to rent bicycles in the local park during the summer. During the month of June, Hassan completed the following transactions for his bicycle rental business, Rahim Rentals, Inc.:

June 2 Began business by placing $7,200 in a business checking account in the name of the corporation in exchange for 7,200 shares of $1 par value stock in the corporation.
3 Purchased supplies on account, $150.
4 Purchased 10 bicycles for $2,500, paying $1,200 down and agreeing to pay the rest in thirty days.
5 Purchased for cash a small shed to hold the bicycles and to use for other operations, $2,900.
6 Paid cash for shipping and installation costs (considered as an addition to the cost of the shed) to place the shed at the park entrance, $400.
8 Received cash of $470 for rentals during the first week of operation.
13 Hired a part-time assistant to help out on weekends at $5 per hour.
14 Paid a maintenance person to clean the grounds, $75.
15 Received cash, $500, for rentals during the second week of operation.
16 Paid the assistant for a weekend's work, $80.
20 Paid for the supplies purchased on June 3, $150.
21 Paid repair bill on bicycles, $55.
22 Received cash for rentals during the third week of operation, $550.
23 Paid the assistant for a weekend's work, $80.
26 Billed a company for bicycle rentals for an employee outing, $110.
27 Paid the fee for June to the Park District for the right to the bicycle concession, $100.
29 Received cash for rentals during the week, $410.
30 Paid the assistant for a weekend's work, $80.
30 Declared and paid a dividend, $500.

Required

1. Prepare journal entries to record the above transactions in the general journal.
2. Set up the following T accounts and post all the journal entries: Cash, Accounts Receivable, Supplies, Shed, Bicycles, Accounts Payable, Common Stock, Dividends, Rental Revenue, Wages Expense, Maintenance Expense, Repair Expense, Concession Fee Expense.

3. Prepare a trial balance for Rahim Rentals, Inc. as of June 30, 19xx.
4. Compare how recognition applies to the transactions of June 26 and 29 and how classification applies to the transactions of June 6 and 14.

Problem 2B-3. Transaction Analysis, General Journal, Ledger Accounts, and Trial Balance
(L.O. 5, 6, 8)

Vic Kostro opened a photography and portrait studio on March 1 and completed the following transactions during the month:

Mar.	1	Began business by depositing $17,000 in a bank account in the name of the business in exchange for 1,700 shares of $10 par value stock.
	2	Paid two months' rent in advance for a studio, $900.
	3	Transferred to the business personal photography equipment valued at $4,300 in exchange for stock.
	4	Ordered additional photography equipment, $2,500.
	5	Purchased office equipment for cash, $1,800.
	8	Received and paid for the photography equipment ordered on March 4, $2,500.
	10	Purchased photography supplies on credit, $700.
	15	Received cash for portraits, $380.
	16	Billed customers for portraits, $750.
	21	Paid for one-half the supplies purchased on March 10, $350.
	24	Paid utility bill for March, $120.
	25	Paid telephone bill for March, $70.
	29	Received payment from customers billed on March 16, $250.
	30	Paid wages to assistant, $400.
	31	Declared and paid a dividend, $1,200.

Required

1. Prepare journal entries to record the above transactions in the general journal (Pages 1 and 2).
2. Set up the following ledger accounts and post the journal entries: Cash (111), Accounts Receivable (113), Photography Supplies (115), Prepaid Rent (116), Photography Equipment (141), Office Equipment (143), Accounts Payable (211), Common Stock (311), Dividends (313), Portrait Revenue (411), Wages Expense (511), Utility Expense (512), and Telephone Expense (513).
3. Prepare a trial balance for Kostro Portrait Studio, Inc. as of March 31, 19xx.

Problem 2B-4. Transaction Analysis, General Journal, Ledger Accounts, and Trial Balance
(L.O. 5, 6, 8)

Delta Security Service, Inc. provides ushers and security personnel for athletic events and other functions. Delta's trial balance at the end of April was as shown on page 109. During May, Delta engaged in the following transactions:

May	1	Received cash from customers billed last month, $4,200.
	2	Made payment on accounts payable, $3,100.
	3	Purchased new one-year insurance policy in advance, $3,600.
	5	Purchased supplies on credit, $430.
	6	Billed client for security services, $2,200.
	7	Made rent payment for May, $800.
	9	Received cash from customers for security services, $1,600.
	14	Paid wages for services provided, $1,400.
	16	Ordered equipment, $800.
	17	Paid current month's utility bill, $400.
	18	Received and paid for equipment ordered on May 16, $800.

May 19 Returned for full credit some of the supplies purchased on May 5 because they were defective, $120.
28 Paid for supplies purchased on May 5, less return on May 19, $310.
30 Billed customer for security services performed, $1,800.
31 Paid wages in connection with security services, $1,050.
31 Declared and paid a dividend, $1,000.

Delta Security Service, Inc.
Trial Balance
April 30, 19xx

Cash (111)	$13,300	
Accounts Receivable (113)	9,400	
Supplies (115)	560	
Prepaid Insurance (116)	600	
Equipment (141)	7,800	
Accounts Payable (211)		$ 5,300
Common Stock (311)		10,000
Retained Earnings (312)		11,160
Dividends (313)	2,000	
Security Services Revenue (411)		28,000
Wages Expense (512)	16,000	
Rent Expense (513)	3,200	
Utility Expense (514)	1,600	
	$54,460	$54,460

Required

1. Prepare journal entries to record the above transactions in the general journal (Pages 26 and 27).
2. Open ledger accounts for the accounts shown in the trial balance. Enter the April 30 trial balance amounts in the ledger.
3. Post the journal entries to the ledger.
4. Prepare a trial balance as of May 31, 19xx.

Problem 2B-5. Relationship of General Journal, Ledger Accounts, and Trial Balance
(L.O. 6, 7, 8)

Embassy Communications Corporation is a public relations firm. On July 31, 19xx, the corporation's trial balance was as shown on page 110. During the month of August, the corporation completed the following transactions:

Aug. 2 Paid rent for August, $650.
3 Received cash from customers on account, $2,300.
7 Ordered supplies, $380.
10 Billed customers for services provided, $2,800.
12 Made payment on accounts payable, $1,100.
15 Paid salaries for first half of August, $1,900.
16 Received the supplies ordered on August 7 and agreed to pay for them in thirty days, $380.
17 Discovered some of the supplies were not as ordered and returned them for full credit, $80.
19 Received cash from a customer for services provided, $4,800.

Aug. 24 Paid utility bill for August, $160.
25 Paid telephone bill for August, $120.
26 Received a bill, to be paid in September, for advertisements placed during the month of August in the local newspaper to promote Embassy Communications, $700.
29 Billed customer for services provided, $2,700.
30 Paid salaries for last half of August, $1,900.
31 Declared and paid a dividend, $1,200.

Embassy Communications Corporation
Trial Balance
July 31, 19xx

Cash (111)	$10,200	
Accounts Receivable (113)	5,500	
Supplies (115)	610	
Office Equipment (141)	4,200	
Accounts Payable (211)		$ 2,600
Common Stock (311)		12,000
Retained Earnings (312)		5,910
	$20,510	$20,510

Required

1. Enter the above transactions in the general journal (Pages 22 and 23).
2. Open accounts in the ledger for the accounts in the trial balance plus the following accounts: Dividends (313), Public Relations Fees (411), Salaries Expense (511), Rent Expense (512), Utility Expense (513), Telephone Expense (514), Advertising Expense (515).
3. Enter the July 31 account balances from the trial balance in the appropriate ledger account forms.
4. Post the entries to the ledger accounts. Be sure to make the appropriate posting references in the journal and ledger as you post.
5. Prepare a trial balance as of August 31, 19xx.

Financial Decision Cases

2-1.
Ruiz Repair Service, Inc.
(L.O. 1, 3, 5, 8)

Al and Luis Ruiz engaged an attorney to help them start Ruiz Repair Service, Inc. On March 1, each brother invested $5,750 in return for 575 shares of $10 par value stock. When they paid the attorney's bill of $700, the attorney advised them to hire an accountant to keep their records. However, they were so busy that it was March 31 before they asked you to straighten out their records. Your first task is to develop a trial balance based on the March transactions. You discover the following information.

After the investment and payment to the attorney, the Ruiz brothers borrowed $5,000 from the bank. They later paid $260, including interest of $60, on this loan. They also purchased a pickup truck in the company name, paying $2,500 down and financing $7,400. The first payment on the truck is due April 15. The brothers then rented an office and paid three months' rent of $900 in advance. Credit purchases of office equipment of $700 and repair tools of $500 must be paid by April 10.

In March, Ruiz Repair Service, Inc. completed repairs of $1,300—$400 were cash transactions. Of the credit transactions, $300 was collected during March, and $600 remained to be collected at the end of March. Wages of $400 were paid to employees. On March 31, the company received a $75 bill for March utility expense and a $50 check from a customer for work to be completed in April.

Required

1. Prepare a March 31 trial balance for Ruiz Repair Service, Inc. First you must record the March transactions and determine the balance of each T account.
2. The Ruiz brothers are unsure how to evaluate the trial balance. Their Cash account balance is $12,490, which exceeds their original investment of $11,500 by $990. Did they make a profit of $990? Explain why the Cash account is not an indicator of business earnings. Cite specific examples to show why it is difficult to determine net income by looking solely at figures in the trial balance.

2-2.
Shelley Corporation
(L.O. 3, 4, 6)

The condensed data below are adapted from the annual report of Shelley Corporation, manufacturers of entertainment products. All amounts are in millions of dollars.

	December 31, 1991
Accounts Payable	$ 59.1
Accounts Receivable	166.8
Buildings and Equipment	138.1
Cash	11.7
Common Stock	27.2
Inventories	235.8
Land	13.0
Long-Term Debt	160.0
Marketable Securities	51.6
Other Assets	9.5
Other Liabilities	145.3
Prepaid Expenses	28.9
Retained Earnings	263.8

The following quotations were also taken from the annual report:

Long-Term Obligations:

"Total long-term debt increased to $160 million at December 31, 1991, from $110 million at year-end 1990. In 1991, $50 million of long-term debt due 2008, . . . [was] sold to the public."

Capital Expenditures

"Shelley plans to use the [$50 million in proceeds] from the sale of the long-term debt, described previously, largely for investments in Buildings and Equipment related to product assembly and manufacturing. Pending such use, at year-end 1991, the debt proceeds were invested in marketable securities."

Required

1. Using the data provided, prepare a balance sheet for Shelley at December 31, 1991.
2. What effect did the transaction described under "Long-Term Obligations" have on Shelley's balance sheet? Prepare the entry in general journal form to record the transaction.
3. From reading the information under "Capital Expenditures," you know what Shelley did with the proceeds of the sale of long-term debt in 1991 and what the company plans to do with the proceeds in 1992. Before it can carry out these plans, what transactions must occur? Prepare three entries in general journal form to record the one transaction completed in 1991 and the two transactions planned for 1992. Use the Marketable Securities account to record entries related to the investments.

LEARNING OBJECTIVES

1. *Define* net income *and its two major components,* revenues *and* expenses.
2. *Explain the difficulties of income measurement caused by (a) the accounting period issue, (b) the continuity issue, and (c) the matching issue.*
3. *Define* accrual accounting *and explain two broad ways of accomplishing it.*
4. *State the four principal situations that require adjusting entries.*
5. *Prepare typical adjusting entries.*
6. *Prepare financial statements from an adjusted trial balance.*
7. *State all the steps in the accounting cycle.*

CHAPTER 3

Business Income and Adjusting Entries

In this chapter you will learn how accountants define business income. The chapter should also help you recognize the problems of assigning income to specific time periods. Then, through a realistic example, you can gain an understanding of the adjustment process necessary for measuring periodic business income. Finally, you will prepare financial statements from the adjusted trial balance. After studying this chapter, you should be able to meet the learning objectives listed on the left.

Profitable operation is essential if a business is to succeed or even survive, so earning a profit is an important goal of most businesses. A major function of accounting, of course, is to measure and report a company's success or failure in achieving this goal.

Profit has many meanings. One definition is the increase in owners' equity resulting from business operations. However, even this definition can be interpreted differently by economists, lawyers, business people, and the public. Because the word *profit* has more than one meaning, accountants prefer to use the term *net income,* which has a precise definition from an accounting point of view. To the accountant, net income equals revenues minus expenses, provided revenues exceed expenses.

DECISION POINT
Never Flake, Inc.

Never Flake, Inc., which operated in the northeastern part of the United States, provided a rust prevention coating for the undersides of new automobiles. The company advertised widely and offered its services through new car dealers. When a dealer sold a new car, the dealer attempted to sell the rust prevention coating as an option. The protective coating was supposed to make the cars last longer in the severe northeastern winters. A key selling point was Never Flake's warranty, which stated that it would repair any damage due to rust at no charge as long as the buyer owned the car. During the 1970s and most of the 1980s, Never Flake was very successful in generating enough cash to continue operations, but in 1988 the company suddenly declared bankruptcy. Company officials said that the company had only \$5.5 million in assets against liabilities of \$32.9 million. Most of the liabilities represented potential claims under the company's lifetime warranty. It seemed that owners kept their cars longer in the 1980s than they had in the 1970s. Therefore more damage could be attributed to rust. What accounting decisions could have helped Never Flake to survive under these circumstances?

Under the concepts of accrual accounting and the matching rule, introduced in this chapter, good accounting requires the estimation and recording (accrual) of the expenses associated with a sale even though cash may not be paid out until future years. This procedure enables management to tell whether the company is earning an income and to make informed decisions. In other words, if Never Flake had sold 1,000 rust prevention jobs, there was a warranty expense associated with these jobs that the company could expect to pay in future years. If the warranty expense had been properly estimated and recorded in the years when the sales were made, Never Flake's management would have realized that it was either charging too little for the service or being too generous in the time period covered by the warranty. Failure to follow good accrual accounting practices in the measurement of business income undoubtedly led to poor management decisions, resulting in the bankruptcy of the company. ■

The Measurement of Business Income

Business enterprises engage in continuous activities aimed at earning income. These activities do not naturally coincide with standard periods of time, but the business environment requires a firm to report income or loss regularly. For example, owners must receive income reports every year, and the government requires corporations to pay taxes on annual income. Within the business, management often wants financial statements prepared every month or more often to monitor performance.

Because of these demands, a primary objective of accounting is measuring net income in accordance with generally accepted accounting principles. Readers of financial reports who are familiar with these principles understand how the accountant is defining net income and are aware of its strengths and weaknesses as a measurement of company performance. The following sections present the accounting definition of net income and explain the problems in applying it.

Net Income

OBJECTIVE 1 *Define* net income *and its two major components,* revenues *and* expenses

Net income is the net increase in owners' equity (retained earnings) resulting from the operations of the company. Net income, in its simplest form, is measured by the difference between revenues and expenses:

$$\text{Net income} = \text{revenues} - \text{expenses}$$

If expenses exceed revenues, a **net loss** occurs.

Revenues. **Revenues** "are inflows or other enhancements of assets of an entity or settlement of its liabilities (or a combination of both) from delivering or producing goods, rendering services, or other activities that constitute the entity's ongoing major or central operations."[1] In the simplest case, they equal the price of goods sold and services rendered during a period of time. When a business provides a service or delivers a product to a customer, it usually receives either cash or a promise to pay cash in the near future. The promise to pay is recorded in either Accounts Receivable or Notes Receivable. The revenue for a given period of time equals the total of cash and receivables from goods and services provided to customers during that period.

As shown in the chapter on accounting as an information system, revenues increase owners' equity. Note that liabilities are not generally affected by revenues and that some transactions increase cash and other assets but are not revenues. For example, borrowing money from a bank increases cash and liabilities but does not result in revenue. The collection of accounts receivable, which increases cash and decreases accounts receivable, does not result in revenue either. Remember that when a sale on credit takes place, the asset Accounts Receivable is increased, and at the same time an owners' equity revenue account is increased. So counting the collection of the receivable as revenue later would be counting the same sale twice.

Not all increases in owners' equity arise from revenues. The issuance of common stock results from an investment in the company by an owner. Issuing stock increases owners' equity, but it is not revenue.

Expenses. **Expenses** are "outflows or other using up of assets or incurrences of liabilities (or a combination of both) from delivering or producing goods, rendering services, or carrying out other activities that constitute the entity's ongoing major or central operations."[2] In other words, expenses are the costs of the goods and services used up in the course of gaining revenues. Often called the cost of doing business, expenses include the costs of goods sold, the costs of activities necessary to carry on the business, and the costs of attracting and serving customers. Examples are salaries, rent, advertising, telephone service, and the depreciation (allocation of the cost) of a building or office equipment.

Expenses are the opposite of revenues in that they cause a decrease in owners' equity. They also result in a decrease in assets or an increase in liabilities. Just as not all cash receipts are revenues, not all cash payments are expenses. A cash payment to reduce a liability does not result in an expense. The liability, however, may have come from incurring a previous expense, such as for advertising, that is to be paid later. There may also be two steps before an expenditure of cash becomes an expense. For example, prepaid expenses or plant assets (such as machinery and equipment) are recorded as assets when they are acquired. Later, as their usefulness

1. *Statement of Financial Accounting Concepts No. 6,* "Elements of Financial Statements" (Stamford, Conn.: Financial Accounting Standards Board, December 1985), par. 78.
2. Ibid., par. 80.

expires in the operation of the business, their cost is allocated to expenses. In fact, expenses are sometimes called expired costs. We shall explain these terms and processes further in this chapter.

Not all decreases in owners' equity and retained earnings arise from expenses. Dividends decrease owners' equity and retained earnings, but they are not expenses.

Temporary and Permanent Accounts. As you saw earlier, revenues and expenses can be recorded directly in owners' equity as increases and decreases. In practice, management and others want to know the details of the increases and decreases in owners' equity caused by revenues and expenses. For this reason, separate accounts for each revenue and expense are needed to accumulate the amounts. Because these account balances apply only to the current accounting period, they are sometimes called **temporary** or **nominal accounts**. Temporary accounts show the accumulation of revenues and expenses during the accounting period. At the end of the accounting period, their account balances are transferred to owners' equity. Thus these nominal accounts start each accounting period with zero balances and then accumulate the specific revenues and expenses of that period. On the other hand, the balance sheet accounts, such as assets, liabilities, and stockholders' equity, are called **permanent** or **real accounts** because their balances extend past the end of an accounting period. The process of transferring the totals from the temporary revenue and expense accounts to the permanent owners' equity accounts is found in the chapter on completing the accounting cycle.

The Accounting Period Issue

OBJECTIVE 2a *Explain the difficulties of income measurement caused by the accounting period issue*

The **accounting period issue** addresses the difficulty of assigning revenues and expenses to a short period of time, such as a month or a year. Not all transactions can be easily assigned to specific time periods. Purchases of buildings and equipment, for example, have an effect that extends over many years of a company's life. How many years the buildings or equipment will be in use and how much of the cost should be assigned to each year must of course be an estimate. Accountants solve this problem with an assumption about **periodicity**. The assumption is that the net income for any period of time less than the life of the business must be regarded as tentative but still is a useful estimate of the net income for the period. Generally the time periods are of equal length to make comparisons easier. The time period should be noted in the financial statements.

Any twelve-month accounting period used by a company is called its **fiscal year**. Many companies use the calendar year, January 1 to December 31, for their fiscal year. Many other companies find it convenient to choose a fiscal year that ends during a slack season rather than a peak season. In this case, the fiscal year would correspond to the natural yearly cycle of business activity for the company. The list below shows the diverse fiscal years used by some well-known companies:

Company	Last Month of Fiscal Year
American Greetings Corp.	February
Caesars World, Inc.	July
The Walt Disney Company	September
Eastman Kodak Co.	December
Fleetwood Enterprises, Inc.	April
Lorimar	March
MGM/UA Communications Co.	August
Mattel Inc.	December
Polaroid Corp.	December

Many government and educational units use fiscal years that end September 30 or June 30.

The Continuity Issue

OBJECTIVE 2b
Explain the difficulties of income measurement caused by the continuity issue

Income measurement, as noted above, requires that certain expense and revenue transactions be allocated over several accounting periods. Another problem confronts the accountant, who does not know how long the business entity will last. Many businesses last less than five years, and in any given year, thousands will go bankrupt. This dilemma is called the **continuity issue**. To prepare financial statements for an accounting period, the accountant must make an assumption about the ability of the business to continue. Specifically, the accountant assumes that unless there is evidence to the contrary, the business entity will continue to operate for an indefinite period. This method of dealing with the issue is sometimes called the **going concern** or **continuity** assumption. The justification for all the techniques of income measurement rests on this assumption of continuity.

In measuring net income, the accountant must also make assumptions regarding the life expectancy of assets. The value of assets often is much less if the company is not expected to continue than if it is a going concern. However, we have already pointed out in the chapter on measuring and recording business transactions that the accountant records assets at cost and does not record subsequent changes in their value. Assets become expenses as they are used up. If accountants have evidence that a company will not continue, of course, then their procedures must change. Sometimes accountants are asked, in bankruptcy cases, to drop the continuity assumption and prepare statements based on the assumption that the firm will go out of business and sell all its assets at liquidation values—that is, for what they will bring in cash.

The Matching Issue

OBJECTIVE 2c
Explain the difficulties of income measurement caused by the matching issue

Revenues and expenses may be accounted for on a cash received and cash paid basis. This practice is known as the **cash basis of accounting**. In certain cases, an individual or business may use the cash basis of accounting for income tax purposes. Under this method, revenues are reported as earned in the period in which cash is received; expenses are reported in the period in which cash is paid. Taxable income is therefore calculated as the difference between cash receipts from revenues and cash payments for expenses.

Even though the cash basis of accounting works well for some small businesses and many individuals, it does not meet the needs of most businesses. As explained above, revenues can be earned in a period other than when cash is received, and expenses can be incurred in a period other than when cash is paid. If net income is to be measured adequately, revenues and expenses must be assigned to the appropriate accounting period. The accountant solves this problem by applying the **matching rule**:

Revenues must be assigned to the accounting period in which the goods were sold or the services performed, and expenses must be assigned to the accounting period in which they were used to produce revenue.

Though direct cause-and-effect relationships can seldom be demonstrated for certain, many costs appear to be related to particular revenues. The accountant will recognize such expenses and related revenues in the same accounting period. Examples are the costs of goods sold and sales commissions. When there is no direct means of connecting cause and effect, the accountant tries to allocate costs in a systematic and rational way among the accounting periods that benefit from the cost. For example, a building is converted from an asset to an expense by allocating its cost over the years that benefit from its use.

Accrual Accounting

OBJECTIVE 3 *Define* accrual accounting *and explain two broad ways of accomplishing it*

To apply the matching rule stated above, accountants have developed accrual accounting. **Accrual accounting** "attempts to record the financial effects on an enterprise of transactions and other events and circumstances . . . in the periods in which those transactions, events, and circumstances occur rather than only in the periods in which cash is received or paid by the enterprise."[3] In other words, accrual accounting consists of all the techniques developed by accountants to apply the matching rule. It is done in two general ways: (1) by recognizing revenues when earned and expenses when incurred, and (2) by adjusting the accounts.

Recognizing Revenues When Earned and Expenses When Incurred. The first method of accrual accounting was illustrated several times in the previous chapter. For example, when the Joan Miller Advertising Agency, Inc. made sales on credit by placing advertisements for clients (in the January 19 transaction), revenue was recorded at the time of the sale by debiting Accounts Receivable and crediting Advertising Fees Earned. In this way, the revenue from a credit sale is recognized before the cash is col-

3. *Statement of Financial Accounting Concepts No. 1*, "Objectives of Financial Reporting by Business Enterprises" (Stamford, Conn.: Financial Accounting Standards Board, 1978), par. 44.

lected. Accounts Receivable serves as a holding account until the payment is received. This process of determining when a sale takes place is known as **revenue recognition**.

When the Joan Miller Advertising Agency, Inc. received the telephone bill on January 30, the expense was recognized both as having been incurred and as helping to produce revenue in the current month. The transaction was recorded by debiting Telephone Expense and crediting Accounts Payable. Until the bill is paid, Accounts Payable serves as a holding account. It is important to note that recognition of the expense does *not* depend on payment of cash.

Adjusting the Accounts. An accounting period by definition must end on a particular day. The balance sheet must contain all assets and liabilities as of the end of that day. The income statement must contain all revenues and expenses applicable to the period ending on that day. Although a business is recognized as a continuous process, there must be a cutoff point for the periodic reports. Some transactions invariably span the cutoff point; as a result, some of the accounts need adjustment.

For example, some of the accounts in the end-of-the-period trial balance for the Joan Miller Advertising Agency, Inc. from the chapter on measuring and recording business transactions (also shown in Exhibit 3-1) do not show the proper balances for preparing financial statements. On January 31, the trial balance contains prepaid rent of $800. At $400 per month, this represents rent for the months of January and February. So on January 31, one-half of the $800, or $400, represents rent expense for January, and the remaining $400 represents an asset to be used in February. An adjustment is needed to reflect the $400 balance of the Prepaid Rent account on the balance sheet and the $400 rent expense on the income statement. As you will see in the following section, several other accounts of the Joan Miller Advertising Agency, Inc. do not reflect their proper balances. Like the Prepaid Rent account, they also need adjusting entries.

The Adjustment Process

OBJECTIVE 4
State the four principal situations that require adjusting entries

Accountants use **adjusting entries** to apply accrual accounting to transactions that span more than one accounting period. Adjusting entries have at least one balance sheet (or permanent) account entry and at least one income statement (or temporary) account entry. Adjusting entries will never involve the Cash account. They are needed when deferrals or accruals exist. A **deferral** is the postponement of the recognition of an expense already paid or incurred or of a revenue already received. Deferrals would be needed in the following two cases:

1. There are costs recorded that must be apportioned between two or more accounting periods. Examples are the cost of a building, prepaid insurance, and supplies. The adjusting entry will involve an asset account and an expense account.

Exhibit 3-1. Trial Balance for the Joan Miller Advertising Agency, Inc.

Joan Miller Advertising Agency, Inc.
Trial Balance
January 31, 19xx

Cash	$ 1,720	
Accounts Receivable	2,800	
Art Supplies	1,800	
Office Supplies	800	
Prepaid Rent	800	
Prepaid Insurance	480	
Art Equipment	4,200	
Office Equipment	3,000	
Accounts Payable		$ 3,170
Unearned Art Fees		1,000
Common Stock		10,000
Dividends	1,400	
Advertising Fees Earned		4,200
Office Wages Expense	1,200	
Utility Expense	100	
Telephone Expense	70	
	$18,370	$18,370

2. There are revenues recorded that must be apportioned between two or more accounting periods. An example is commissions collected in advance for services to be rendered in later periods. The adjusting entry will involve a liability account and a revenue account.

An **accrual** is the recognition of an expense or revenue that has arisen but has not yet been recorded. Accruals would be required in the following two cases:

1. There are unrecorded revenues. An example is commissions earned but not yet collected or billed to customers. The adjusting entry will involve an asset account and a revenue account.
2. There are unrecorded expenses. Examples are the wages earned by employees in the current accounting period but after the last pay period. The adjusting entry will involve an expense account and a liability account.

Once again the Joan Miller Advertising Agency, Inc. will be used to illustrate the kinds of adjusting entries that most businesses will have.

Apporioning Recorded Expenses Between Two or More Accounting Periods (Deferrals)

OBJECTIVE 5
Prepare typical adjusting entries

Companies often make expenditures that benefit more than one period. These expenditures are generally debited to an asset account. At the end of the accounting period, the amount that has been used is transferred from the asset account to an expense account. Two of the more important kinds of deferral adjustments are for prepaid expenses and depreciation of plant and equipment.

Prepaid Expenses. Some expenses are customarily paid in advance. These expenditures are called **prepaid expenses**. Among these items are rent, insurance, and supplies. At the end of an accounting period, a portion (or all) of these goods or services most likely will have been used up or will have expired. The part of the expenditure that has benefited current operations is treated as an expense of the period. On the other hand, the part not consumed or expired is treated as an asset applicable to future operations of the company. If adjusting entries for prepaid expenses are not made at the end of the period, both the balance sheet and the income statement will be stated incorrectly. First, the assets of the company will be overstated. Second, the expenses of the company will be understated. For this reason, owners' equity on the balance sheet and net income on the income statement will be overstated.

At the beginning of the month, the Joan Miller Advertising Agency, Inc. paid two months' rent in advance. This expenditure resulted in an asset consisting of the right to occupy the office for two months. As each day in the month passed, part of the asset's costs expired and became an expense. By January 31, one-half had expired and should be treated as an expense. The analysis of this economic event is shown below:

Prepaid Rent (Adjustment a)

Prepaid Rent

Jan. 2	800	**Jan. 31**	400

Rent Expense

Jan. 31	400		

Transaction: Expiration of one month's rent.
Analysis: Assets decreased. Owners' equity decreased.
Rules: Decreases in assets are recorded by credits. Decreases in owners' equity are recorded by debits.
Entries: Decrease in owners' equity is recorded by a debit to Rent Expense. Decrease in assets is recorded by a credit to Prepaid Rent.

	Dr.	Cr.
Rent Expense	400	
Prepaid Rent		400

The Prepaid Rent account now has a balance of $400, which represents one month's rent paid in advance. The Rent Expense account reflects the $400 expense for the month.

Besides rent, the Joan Miller Advertising Agency, Inc. has prepaid expenses for insurance, art supplies, and office supplies, all of which call for adjusting entries.

On January 8, the Joan Miller Advertising Agency, Inc. purchased a one-year insurance policy, paying for it in advance. In a manner similar to the expiration of prepaid rent, prepaid insurance offers protection that expires day by day. By the end of the month, one-twelfth of the protection had expired. The adjustment is analyzed and recorded as shown below:

Prepaid Insurance (Adjustment b)

Prepaid Insurance

Jan. 8 480	Jan. 31 40

Insurance Expense

Jan. 31 40	

Transaction: Expiration of one month's insurance.
Analysis: Assets decreased. Owners' equity decreased.
Rules: Decreases in assets are recorded by credits. Decreases in owners' equity are recorded by debits.
Entries: Decrease in owners' equity is recorded by a debit to Insurance Expense. Decrease in assets is recorded by a credit to Prepaid Insurance.

	Dr.	Cr.
Insurance Expense	40	
Prepaid Insurance		40

The Prepaid Insurance account now has the proper balance of $440, and Insurance Expense reflects the expired cost of $40 for the month.

Early in the month, the Joan Miller Advertising Agency, Inc. purchased art supplies and office supplies. As Joan Miller did art work for various clients during the month, art supplies were consumed. Her secretary also used office supplies. There is no need to account for these supplies every day because the financial statements are not prepared until the end of the month and the recordkeeping would involve too much work.

Instead, Joan Miller makes a careful inventory of the art and office supplies at the end of the month. This inventory records the number and cost of those supplies that are still assets of the company—yet to be consumed. The inventory shows that art supplies costing $1,300 and office supplies costing $600 are still on hand. This means that of the $1,800 of art supplies originally purchased, $500 worth were used up or became an expense. Of the original $800 of office supplies, $200 worth were consumed. These transactions are analyzed and recorded as follows:

Art Supplies and Office Supplies (Adjustments c and d)

Art Supplies

Jan. 6 1,800	Jan. 31 500

Art Supplies Expense

Jan. 31 500	

Office Supplies

Jan. 6 800	Jan. 31 200

Office Supplies Expense

Jan. 31 200	

Transaction: Consumption of supplies.
Analysis: Assets decreased. Owners' equity decreased.
Rules: Decreases in assets are recorded by credits. Decreases in owners' equity are recorded by debits.
Entries: Decreases in owners' equity are recorded by debits to Art Supplies Expense and Office Supplies Expense. Decreases in assets are recorded by credits to Art Supplies and Office Supplies.

	Dr.	Cr.
Art Supplies Expense	500	
Art Supplies		500
Office Supplies Expense	200	
Office Supplies		200

The asset accounts of Art Supplies and Office Supplies now reflect the proper amounts of $1,300 and $600, respectively, yet to be consumed. In addition, the amount of art supplies used up during the accounting period is reflected as $500 and the amount of office supplies used up is reflected as $200.

Depreciation of Plant and Equipment. When a company buys a long-lived asset, such as a building, equipment, trucks, automobiles, a computer, store fixtures, or office furniture, it is basically prepaying for the usefulness of that asset for as long as it benefits the company. In other words, the asset is a deferral of an expense. Proper accounting therefore requires allocating the cost of the asset over its estimated useful life. The amount allocated to any one accounting period is called **depreciation** or **depreciation expense**. Depreciation is an expense like others incurred during an accounting period to obtain revenue.

It is often impossible to tell how long an asset will last or how much of the asset is used in any one period. For this reason, depreciation must be estimated. Accountants have developed a number of methods for estimating depreciation and for dealing with other complex problems concerning it. Only the simplest case is presented in this discussion as an illustration.

Suppose that the Joan Miller Advertising Agency, Inc. estimates that the art equipment and office equipment will last five years (sixty months) and will be worthless at the end of that time. The depreciation of art equipment and office equipment for the month is computed as $70 ($4,200 ÷ 60 months) and $50 ($3,000 ÷ 60 months), respectively. These amounts represent the cost allocated to the month, thus reducing the asset accounts and increasing the expense accounts (reducing owners' equity). These transactions can be analyzed as shown below. The use of the contra-asset account called Accumulated Depreciation is described in the next section.

Art Equipment and Office Equipment (Adjustments e and f)

Art Equipment

Jan. 4 4,200	

Accumulated Depreciation, Art Equipment

	Jan. 31 70

Office Equipment

Jan. 5 3,000	

Accumulated Depreciation, Office Equipment

	Jan. 31 50

Depreciation Expense, Art Equipment

Jan. 31 70	

Depreciation Expense, Office Equipment

Jan. 31 50	

Transaction: Recording depreciation expense.
Analysis: Assets decreased. Owners' equity decreased.
Rules: Decreases in assets are recorded by credits. Decreases in owners' equity are recorded by debits.
Entries: Owners' equity is decreased by debits to Depreciation Expense, Art Equipment, and Depreciation Expense, Office Equipment. Assets are decreased by credits to contra-asset accounts Accumulated Depreciation, Art Equipment, and Accumulated Depreciation, Office Equipment.

	Dr.	Cr.
Depreciation Expense, Art Equipment	70	
Accumulated Depreciation, Art Equipment		70
Depreciation Expense, Office Equipment	50	
Accumulated Depreciation, Office Equipment		50

Accumulated Depreciation—A Contra Account. Note that in the analysis above, the asset accounts were not credited directly. Instead, new accounts—Accumulated Depreciation, Art Equipment, and Accumulated Depreciation, Office Equipment—were credited. These **accumulated depreciation** accounts are contra-asset accounts used to total the past depreciation expense on a specific long-lived asset. A **contra account** is one that is paired with and deducted from another related account in the financial statements. There are several types of contra accounts. In this case, the balance of Accumulated Depreciation, Art Equipment, is a deduction from the associated account Art Equipment. Likewise, Accumulated Depreciation, Office Equipment, is a deduction from Office Equipment. After these adjusting entries have been made, the plant and equipment section of the balance sheet for the Joan Miller Advertising Agency, Inc. appears as in Exhibit 3-2.

The contra account is used for two very good reasons. First, it recognizes that depreciation is an estimate. Second, the use of the contra ac-

Exhibit 3-2. Plant and Equipment Section of Balance Sheet

Joan Miller Advertising Agency, Inc.
Partial Balance Sheet
January 31, 19xx

Plant and Equipment		
Art Equipment	$4,200	
Less Accumulated Depreciation	70	$4,130
Office Equipment	$3,000	
Less Accumulated Depreciation	50	2,950
Total Plant and Equipment		$7,080

count preserves the original cost of the asset and shows how much of the asset has been allocated as an expense as well as the balance left to be depreciated. As the months pass, the amount of the accumulated depreciation will grow, and the net amount shown as an asset will decline. In six months, for instance, Accumulated Depreciation, Art Equipment, will have a total of $420; when this amount is subtracted from Art Equipment, a net amount of $3,780 will remain. This net amount is referred to as the **carrying value** or book value.

Other names are sometimes used for accumulated depreciation, such as "allowance for depreciation." Accumulated depreciation is the newer, better term.

Apportioning Recorded Revenues Between Two or More Accounting Periods (Deferrals)

Just as expenses may be paid before they are used, revenues may be received before they are earned. When such revenues are received in advance, the company has an obligation to deliver goods or perform services. Therefore, **unearned revenues** would be a liability account. For example, publishing companies usually receive payment in advance for magazine subscriptions. These receipts are recorded in a liability account. If the company fails to deliver the magazines, subscribers are entitled to their money back. As the company delivers each issue of the magazine, it earns a part of the advance payments. This earned portion must be transferred from the Unearned Subscription account to the Subscription Revenue account.

During the month, the Joan Miller Advertising Agency, Inc. received $1,000 as an advance payment for art work to be done for another agency. Assume that by the end of the month, $400 of the art work was done and accepted by the other agency. This transaction is analyzed as shown on the next page.

Unearned Art Fees (Adjustment g)

Unearned Art Fees

Jan. 31 400	Jan. 15 1,000

Art Fees Earned

	Jan. 31 400

Transaction: Performance of services paid for in advance.
Analysis: Liabilities decreased. Owners' equity increased.
Rules: Decreases in liabilities are recorded by debits. Increases in owners' equity are recorded by credits.
Entries: Decrease in liabilities is recorded by a debit to Unearned Art Fees. Increase in owners' equity is recorded by a credit to Art Fees Earned.

	Dr.	Cr.
Unearned Art Fees	400	
Art Fees Earned		400

The liability account Unearned Art Fees now reflects the amount of work still to be performed, or $600. The revenue account Art Fees Earned reflects the amount of services performed and earned during the month, or $400.

Unrecorded or Accrued Revenues

Unrecorded or **accrued revenues** are revenues for which the service has been performed or the goods delivered but for which no entry has been recorded. Any revenues that have been earned but not recorded during the accounting period call for an adjusting entry that debits an asset account and credits a revenue account. For example, the interest on a note receivable is earned day by day but may not in fact be received until another accounting period. Interest Income should be credited and Interest Receivable debited for the interest accrued at the end of the current period.

Suppose that the Joan Miller Advertising Agency, Inc. has agreed to place a series of advertisements for Marsh Tire Company and that the first appears on January 31, the last day of the month. The fee of $200 for this advertisement, which has now been earned but not recorded, should be recorded as shown below:

Unrecorded or Accrued Advertising Fees (Adjustment h)

Fees Receivable

Jan. 31 200	

Advertising Fees Earned

	Jan. 10 1,400
	19 2,800
	31 200

Transaction: Accrual of unrecorded revenue.
Analysis: Assets increased. Owners' equity increased.
Rules: Increases in assets are recorded by debits. Increases in owners' equity are recorded by credits.
Entries: Increase in assets is recorded by a debit to Fees Receivable. Increase in owners' equity is recorded by a credit to Advertising Fees Earned.

	Dr.	Cr.
Fees Receivable	200	
Advertising Fees Earned		200

Asset and revenue accounts now both show the proper balance: $200 in Fees Receivable is owed to the company, and $4,400 in Advertising Fees has been earned by the company during the month. Marsh Tire Company will be billed for the series of advertisements when they are completed. At that time, Accounts Receivable will be debited and Fees Receivable will be credited.

Unrecorded or Accrued Expenses

At the end of an accounting period, there are usually expenses that have been incurred but not recorded in the accounts. These expenses require adjusting entries. One such case is interest on borrowed money. Each day interest accumulates on the debt. An adjusting entry at the end of each accounting period records this accumulated interest, which is an expense of the period, and the corresponding liability to pay the interest. Other comparable expenses are taxes, wages, and salaries. As the expense and the corresponding liability accumulate, they are said to accrue—hence the term **accrued expenses.**

Suppose that the calendar for January appears as follows:

January

Su	M	T	W	Th	F	Sa
	1	2	3	4	5	6
7	8	9	10	11	12	13
14	15	16	17	18	19	20
21	22	23	24	25	26	27
28	29	30	31			

By the end of business on January 31, the Joan Miller Advertising Agency, Inc.'s secretary will have worked three days (Monday, Tuesday, and Wednesday) beyond the last biweekly pay period, which ended on January 26. The employee has earned the wages for these days, but they are not due to be paid until the regular payday in February. The wages for these three days are rightfully an expense for January, and the liabilities should reflect the fact that the company does owe the secretary for those days. Because the secretary's wage rate is $600 every two weeks, or $60 per day ($600 ÷ 10 working days), the expense is $180 ($60 × 3 days). This unrecorded or accrued expense can be analyzed as shown on the next page.

Unrecorded or Accrued Wages (Adjustment i)

Wages Payable

	Jan. 31 180

Office Wages Expense

Jan. 12 600	
26 600	
31 180	

Transaction: Accrual of unrecorded expense.
Analysis: Liabilities increased. Owners' equity decreased.
Rules: Increases in liabilities are recorded by credits. Decreases in owners' equity are recorded by debits.
Entries: Decrease in owners' equity is recorded by a debit to Office Wages Expense. Increase in liabilities is recorded by a credit to Wages Payable.

	Dr.	Cr.
Office Wages Expense	180	
Wages Payable		180

The liability of $180 is now correctly reflected in the Wages Payable account. The actual expense incurred for office wages during the month is also correct at $1,380.

Estimated Income Taxes. As a corporation, Joan Miller Advertising Agency, Inc. is subject to federal income taxes. Although the actual income taxes owed cannot be determined until after net income is computed at the end of the fiscal year, each month should bear its part of the total year's expense in accordance with the matching concept. Therefore, the amount of income taxes expense for the current month must be estimated. Assume that after analyzing the first month's operations and talking over the situation with her CPA, Joan Miller estimates January's share of the federal income taxes for the year to be $400. This estimated expense can be analyzed and recorded as follows:

Estimated Income Taxes (Adjustment j)

Income Taxes Payable

	Jan. 31 400

Income Taxes Expense

Jan. 31 400	

Transaction: Accrual of estimated income taxes.
Analysis: Liabilities increased. Owners' equity decreased.
Rules: Increases in liabilities are recorded by credits. Decreases in owners' equity are recorded by debits.
Entries: Decrease in owners' equity is recorded by a debit to Income Taxes Expense. Increase in liabilities is recorded by a credit to Income Taxes Payable.

	Dr.	Cr.
Income Taxes Expense	400	
Income Taxes Payable		400

Expenses for January will now reflect the estimated income taxes attributable to that month, and the liability for these estimated income taxes will appear on the balance sheet.

DECISION POINT
Joan Miller Advertising Agency, Inc.

In the example used in this chapter, an accrual is made on January 31 for wages payable in the amount of $180. Joan Miller might ask, "Why go to the trouble of making this adjustment? Why worry about it? Doesn't everything come out in the end when the secretary is paid in February? Since wages expense in total is the same for the two months, isn't the net income in total unchanged?" Give at least three reasons why the making of adjusting entries will help Joan Miller to assess the performance of her business.

Adusting entries are important because they help accountants compile information that is useful to management and owners. First, adjusting entries are necessary to measure income and financial position in a relevant and useful way. Joan Miller will want to know how much her advertising agency has earned in each month and what its liabilities and assets are on the last day of the month. For instance, if the three days' accrued wages for Joan Miller's secretary are not recorded, the income of the agency will be overstated by $180 or 11.3 percent ($180/$1,590). Second, adjusting entries allow financial statements to be compared from one accounting period to the next. Joan Miller can see whether the company is making progress toward earning a profit or if the company has improved its financial position. To return to our example, if the adjustment for accrued wages is not recorded, not only will the net income for January be overstated by $180, but the net income for February (the month when payment will be made) will be understated by $180. This error will make February earnings, whatever they may be, appear worse than they actually are. Third, even though one adjusting entry may seem insignificant, the cumulative effect of all adjusting entries can be great. Look back over all the adjustments made by the Joan Miller Advertising Agency, Inc. for prepaid rent and insurance, art and office supplies, depreciation of office and art equipment, unearned art fees, accrued wages and expenses, and accrued advertising fees. These are normal and usual adjustments. Their effect on net income in January is to increase expenses by $1,840 and revenues by $600, for a net effect of minus $1,240 or 78 percent ($1,240/$1,590) of net income. If adjusting entries had not been made, Joan Miller would have had a false impression of the performance of her business. ■

Using the Adjusted Trial Balance to Prepare Financial Statements

OBJECTIVE 6
Prepare financial statements from an adjusted trial balance

In the chapter on measuring and recording business transactions, a trial balance was prepared before any adjusting entries were recorded. It is also desirable to prepare an **adjusted trial balance**, which is a list of the accounts and balances after the recording and posting of the adjusting entries. The adjusted trial balance for the Joan Miller Advertising Agency,

Inc. is shown on the left side of Exhibit 3-3. Note that some accounts, such as Cash and Accounts Receivable, have the same balances as they did in the trial balance (see Exhibit 3-1 on page 120) because no adjusting entries affected these accounts. Other accounts, such as Art Supplies, Office Supplies, Prepaid Rent, and Prepaid Insurance, have different balances from those in the trial balance because adjusting entries affected these accounts. If the adjusting entries have been posted correctly to the accounts, the adjusted trial balance will have equal debit and credit totals.

From the adjusted trial balance, the financial statements can be easily prepared. The income statement is prepared from the revenue and expense accounts, as shown in Exhibit 3-3. Then, in Exhibit 3-4, the balance sheet has been prepared from the asset, liability, and stockholders' equity accounts. In the stockholders' equity section, the amount of retained earnings comes from the statement of retained earnings. Notice that the net income from the income statement is combined with dividends on the statement of retained earnings to give the net increase in Joan Miller's Retained Earnings account of $190. In more complex situations, accountants use a device called a work sheet to prepare financial statements. The preparation of a work sheet is covered in the chapter on completing the accounting cycle.

Summary of the Accounting System

OBJECTIVE 7
State all the steps in the accounting cycle

The **accounting system** encompasses the sequence of steps followed in the accounting process. This chapter and the chapter on measuring and recording business transactions have presented the steps in this system, from analyzing transactions to preparing financial statements. This system is sometimes called the **accounting cycle**. The purpose of the system, as illustrated in Figure 3-1 on page 133, is to treat the business transactions as raw material and develop the finished product of accounting—the financial statements—in a systematic way. The steps in this system may be summarized as follows:

1. The transactions are *analyzed* from the *source documents.*
2. The transactions are *recorded* in the *journal.*
3. The entries are *posted* to the *ledger.*
4. The *accounts* are *adjusted* at the end of the period to achieve the *adjusted trial balance.*
5. *Financial statements* are *prepared* from the adjusted trial balance.
6. The *accounts* are *closed* to conclude the current accounting period and prepare for the beginning of the new accounting period.

Step 6 of the accounting system, closing the accounts, is the only step that has not been presented thus far. Since the closing process is covered in detail in the chapter on completing the accounting cycle, it is necessary here to understand only the nature and function of closing entries. *Closing entries* are journal entries prepared by accountants on the last day of the accounting period for the purpose of transferring the balances of the income statement accounts and the Dividends account to the Retained Earn-

Exhibit 3-3. Relationship of Adjusted Trial Balance to Income Statement

Joan Miller Advertising Agency, Inc.
Adjusted Trial Balance
January 31, 19xx

Cash	$ 1,720	
Accounts Receivable	2,800	
Art Supplies	1,300	
Office Supplies	600	
Prepaid Rent	400	
Prepaid Insurance	440	
Art Equipment	4,200	
Accumulated Depreciation, Art Equipment		$ 70
Office Equipment	3,000	
Accumulated Depreciation, Office Equipment		50
Accounts Payable		3,170
Unearned Art Fees		600
Common Stock		10,000
Dividends	1,400	
Advertising Fees Earned		4,400
Office Wages Expense	1,380	
Utility Expense	100	
Telephone Expense	70	
Rent Expense	400	
Insurance Expense	40	
Art Supplies Expense	500	
Office Supplies Expense	200	
Depreciation Expense, Art Equipment	70	
Depreciation Expense, Office Equipment	50	
Art Fees Earned		400
Fees Receivable	200	
Wages Payable		180
Income Taxes Expense	400	
Income Taxes Payable		400
	$19,270	$19,270

Joan Miller Advertising Agency, Inc.
Income Statement
For the Month Ended January 31, 19xx

Revenues		
Advertising Fees Earned		$4,400
Art Fees Earned		400
Total Revenues		$4,800
Expenses		
Office Wages Expense	$1,380	
Utility Expense	100	
Telephone Expense	70	
Rent Expense	400	
Insurance Expense	40	
Art Supplies Expense	500	
Office Supplies Expense	200	
Depreciation Expense, Art Equipment	70	
Depreciation Expense, Office Equipment	50	
Income Taxes Expense	400	
Total Expenses		3,210
Net Income		$1,590

Exhibit 3-4. Relationship of Adjusted Trial Balance to Balance Sheet

Joan Miller Advertising Agency, Inc.
Adjusted Trial Balance
January 31, 19xx

Cash	$ 1,720	
Accounts Receivable	2,800	
Art Supplies	1,300	
Office Supplies	600	
Prepaid Rent	400	
Prepaid Insurance	440	
Art Equipment	4,200	
Accumulated Depreciation, Art Equipment		$ 70
Office Equipment	3,000	
Accumulated Depreciation, Office Equipment		50
Accounts Payable		3,170
Unearned Art Fees		600
Common Stock		10,000
Dividends	1,400	
Advertising Fees Earned		4,400
Office Wages Expense	1,380	
Utility Expense	100	
Telephone Expense	70	
Rent Expense	400	
Insurance Expense	40	
Art Supplies Expense	500	
Office Supplies Expense	200	
Depreciation Expense, Art Equipment	70	
Depreciation Expense, Office Equipment	50	
Art Fees Earned		400
Fees Receivable	200	
Wages Payable		180
Income Taxes Expense	400	
Income Taxes Payable		400
	$19,270	$19,270

Joan Miller Advertising Agency, Inc.
Balance Sheet
January 31, 19xx

Assets		
Cash		$ 1,720
Accounts Receivable		2,800
Fees Receivable		200
Art Supplies		1,300
Office Supplies		600
Prepaid Rent		400
Prepaid Insurance		440
Art Equipment	$4,200	
Less Accumulated Depreciation	70	4,130
Office Equipment	$3,000	
Less Accumulated Depreciation	50	2,950
Total Assets		$14,540
Liabilities		
Accounts Payable	$3,170	
Unearned Art Fees	600	
Wages Payable	180	
Income Taxes Payable	400	
Total Liabilities		$ 4,350
Stockholders' Equity		
Common Stock	$10,000	
Retained Earnings	190	
Total Stockholders' Equity		10,190
Total Liabilities and Stockholders' Equity		$14,540

Joan Miller Advertising Agency, Inc.
Statement of Retained Earnings
For the Month Ended January 31, 19xx

Retained Earnings, January 1, 19xx	—
Net Income	$1,590
Subtotal	$1,590
Less Dividends	1,400
Retained Earnings, January 31, 19xx	$ 190

From Income Statement in Exhibit 3-3.

Figure 3-1. An Overview of the Accounting System

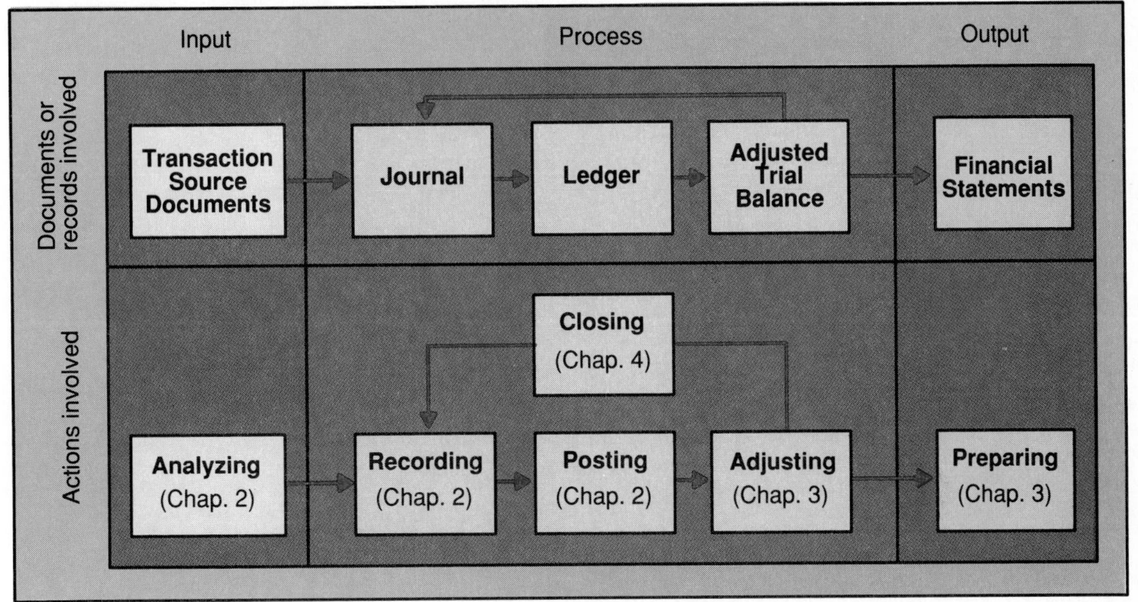

ings account. As a result of this process, the Retained Earnings account will reflect the earnings retained in the business (net income less dividends) as of the last day of the accounting period. In addition, all the revenue and expense accounts as well as the dividends account, are set equal to zero so that they may be used again in the next accounting period.

At this point, a note about journal entries is in order. Throughout the chapter on measuring and recording business transactions and this chapter, all journal entries have been presented with a full analysis of the transaction. This complete analysis was given to show you the thought process behind each entry. By now, you should be fully aware of the effects of transactions on the balance sheet equation and the rules of debit and credit. For this reason, journal entries in the rest of the book will be presented in the standard form that was illustrated in the exhibit "The General Journal" in the chapter on measuring and recording business transactions.

Chapter Review

Review of Learning Objectives

1. **Define *net income* and its two major components, *revenues* and *expenses*.** Net income is the net increase in owners' equity resulting from the profit-seeking operations of a company. Net income equals revenues minus expenses, unless expenses exceed revenues, in which case a net loss results. Revenues are a measure of the asset values received from customers as a result of income-earning activity during a specific period of time. Expenses are the costs of goods and services used up in the process of obtaining revenues.

2. **Explain the difficulties of income measurement caused by (a) the accounting period issue, (b) the continuity issue, and (c) the matching issue.** The accounting period issue recognizes that net income measurements for short periods of time are necessarily tentative. The continuity issue recognizes that even though businesses face an uncertain future, accountants must assume that without evidence to the contrary, a business will continue indefinitely. The matching issue results from the difficulty of assigning revenues and expenses to a period of time and is solved by application of the matching rule. The matching rule states that revenues must be assigned to the accounting period in which the goods are sold or the services performed, and expenses must be assigned to the accounting period in which they were used to produce revenue.

3. **Define *accrual accounting* and explain two broad ways of accomplishing it.** Accrual accounting consists of all the techniques developed by accountants to apply the matching rule. The two general ways of accomplishing it are (1) by recognizing revenue when earned and expenses when incurred and (2) by adjusting the accounts for transactions that span the end of the accounting period.

4. **State the four principal situations that require adjusting entries.** Adjusting entries are required (1) when recorded costs (prepaid assets) are to be apportioned between two or more accounting periods, (2) when recorded liabilities (deferred revenues) are to be apportioned between two or more accounting periods, (3) when unrecorded expenses exist, and (4) when unrecorded revenues exist.

5. **Prepare typical adjusting entries.** The preparation of adjusting entries is summarized in the following table:

Type of Adjusting Entry	Type of Account: Debited	Type of Account: Credited	Examples
Deferrals			
1. Apportioning recorded expenses (recorded, not incurred)	Expense	Asset (or contra asset)	Prepaid Rent Prepaid Insurance Supplies Buildings Equipment
2. Apportioning recorded revenues (recorded, not earned)	Liability	Revenue	Commissions Received in Advance
Accruals			
1. Unrecorded revenues (earned, not received)	Asset	Revenue	Commissions Receivable Interest Receivable
2. Unrecorded expenses (incurred, not paid)	Expense	Liability	Wages Payable Interest Payable

6. **Prepare financial statements from an adjusted trial balance.**
   An adjusted trial balance is prepared after adjusting entries have been posted to the ledger accounts. Its purpose is to test the balance of the ledger after the adjusting entries are made and before financial statements are prepared. The income statement is then prepared from the revenue and expense accounts. The balance sheet is prepared from the balance sheet accounts and from the statement of retained earnings.

7. **State all the steps in the accounting cycle.**
   The steps in the accounting cycle are to (1) analyze the transactions from the source documents, (2) record the transactions in the journal, (3) post the entries to the ledger, (4) adjust the accounts at the end of the period, (5) prepare the financial statements, and (6) close the accounts.

Review of Concepts and Terminology

The following concepts and terms were introduced in this chapter:

(L.O. 2) **Accounting period issue:** The difficulty of assigning revenues and expenses to a short period of time, such as a month or a year; net income must be regarded as tentative but useful.

(L.O. 7) **Accounting system (accounting cycle):** The sequence of steps followed in the accounting process.

(L.O. 4) **Accrual:** The recognition of an expense that has been incurred or a revenue that has been earned but that has not yet been recorded.

(L.O. 3) **Accrual accounting:** The attempt to record the financial effects on an enterprise of transactions and other events in the periods in which those transactions or events occur rather than only in the periods in which cash is received or paid by the enterprise.

(L.O. 5) **Accrued expenses:** Expenses that have been incurred but are not recognized in the accounts, necessitating an adjusting entry; unrecorded expenses.

(L.O. 5) **Accumulated depreciation:** A contra-asset account used to accumulate the total past depreciation of a specific long-lived asset.

(L.O. 6) **Adjusted trial balance:** A trial balance prepared after all adjusting entries have been posted to the accounts.

(L.O. 4) **Adjusting entries:** Entries made to apply accrual accounting to transactions that span more than one accounting period.

(L.O. 5) **Carrying value:** The unexpired portion of the cost of an asset; sometimes called book value.

(L.O. 2) **Cash basis of accounting:** A basis of accounting under which revenues and expenses are accounted for on a cash received and cash paid basis.

(L.O. 2) **Continuity issue:** The difficulty associated with not knowing how long the business entity will last.

(L.O. 5) **Contra account:** An account whose balance is subtracted from an associated account in the financial statements.

(L.O. 4) **Deferral:** The postponement of the recognition of an expense already paid or incurred or of a revenue already received.

(L.O. 5) **Depreciation (depreciation expense):** The periodic allocation of the cost of a tangible long-lived asset over its estimated useful life.

(L.O. 1) **Expenses:** Outflows or other using up of assets or incurrences of liabilities from delivering or producing goods, rendering services, or carrying out other activities that constitute the entity's ongoing major or central operations.

(L.O. 2) **Fiscal year:** Any twelve-month accounting period used by an economic entity.

(L.O. 2) **Going concern (continuity):** Assumption that unless there is evidence to the contrary, the business entity will continue to operate for an indefinite period.

(L.O. 2) **Matching rule:** Revenues must be assigned to the accounting period in which the goods were sold or the services rendered, and expenses must be assigned to the accounting period in which they were used to produce revenue.

(L.O. 1) **Net income:** The net increase in owners' equity resulting from the operations of the company.

(L.O. 1) **Net loss:** Net decrease in owners' equity that develops when expenses exceed revenues.

(L.O. 2) **Periodicity:** The recognition that net income for any period less than the life of the business must be regarded as tentative but is still a useful estimate of the net income for that period.

(L.O. 1) **Permanent (real) accounts:** Balance sheet accounts; accounts whose balances can extend past the end of an accounting period.

(L.O. 5) **Prepaid expenses:** Expenses paid in advance that do not expire during the current accounting period; an asset account.

(L.O. 1) **Profit:** Imprecise term for the earnings of a business enterprise.

(L.O. 3) **Revenue recognition:** The process in accrual accounting of determining when a sale takes place.

(L.O. 1) **Revenues:** Inflows or other enhancements of assets of an entity or settlements of its liabilities from delivering or producing goods, rendering services, or other activities that constitute the entity's ongoing major or central operations.

(L.O. 1) **Temporary (nominal) accounts:** Accounts showing the accumulation of revenues and expenses for only one accounting period; at the end of the accounting period, these account balances are transferred to owners' equity.

(L.O. 5) **Unearned revenues:** A revenue received in advance for which the goods will not be delivered or the services performed during the current accounting period; a liability account.

(L.O. 5) **Unrecorded (accrued) revenues:** Revenues for which the service has been performed or the goods have been delivered but have not been recorded.

Review Problem
Adjusting Entries, T Accounts, and Adjusted Trial Balance

(L.O. 5, 6) The unadjusted trial balance for Certified Answering Service, Inc. appears as follows on December 31, 19x2:

Certified Answering Service, Inc. Trial Balance December 31, 19x2		
Cash	$2,160	
Accounts Receivable	1,250	
Office Supplies	180	
Prepaid Insurance	240	
Office Equipment	3,400	
Accumulated Depreciation, Office Equipment		$ 600
Accounts Payable		700
Unearned Revenue		460
Common Stock		2,000
Retained Earnings		2,870
Dividends	400	
Answering Service Revenue		2,900
Wages Expense	1,500	
Rent Expense	400	
	$9,530	$9,530

The following information is also available:

a. Insurance that expired during December amounted to $40.
b. Office supplies on hand at the end of December totaled $75.
c. Depreciation for the month of December totaled $100.
d. Accrued wages at the end of December totaled $120.
e. Revenues earned for services performed but not yet billed on December 31 totaled $300.
f. Revenues earned for services performed that were paid in advance totaled $160.
g. Income taxes are estimated to be $250.

Required

1. Prepare T accounts for the accounts in the trial balance and enter the balances.
2. Determine the required adjusting entries and record them directly to the T accounts. Open new T accounts as needed.
3. Prepare an adjusted trial balance.
4. Prepare an income statement, a statement of retained earnings, and a balance sheet for the month ended December 31, 19x2.

Answer to Review Problem

1. T accounts set up and amounts from trial balance entered
2. Adjusting entries recorded

Cash

Bal.	2,160		

Accounts Receivable

Bal.	1,250		

Service Revenue Receivable

(e)	300		

Office Supplies

Bal.	180	(b)	105
Bal.	**75**		

Prepaid Insurance

Bal.	240	(a)	40
Bal.	**200**		

Office Equipment

Bal.	3,400		

Accumulated Depreciation, Office Equipment

		Bal.	600
		(c)	100
		Bal.	**700**

Accounts Payable

		Bal.	700

Unearned Revenue

(f)	160	Bal.	460
		Bal.	**300**

Wages Payable

		(d)	120

Income Taxes Payable

		(g)	250

Common Stock

		Bal.	2,000

Retained Earnings

		Bal.	2,870

Dividends

Bal.	400		

Answering Service Revenue

		Bal.	2,900
		(e)	300
		(f)	160
		Bal.	**3,360**

Wages Expense

Bal.	1,500		
(d)	120		
Bal.	**1,620**		

Rent Expense	
Bal. 400	

Insurance Expense	
(a) 40	

Office Supplies Expense	
(b) 105	

Depreciation Expense, Office Equipment	
(c) 100	

Income Taxes Expense	
(g) 250	

3. Adjusted trial balance prepared

Certified Answering Service, Inc.
Adjusted Trial Balance
December 31, 19x2

Cash	$ 2,160	
Accounts Receivable	1,250	
Service Revenue Receivable	300	
Office Supplies	75	
Prepaid Insurance	200	
Office Equipment	3,400	
Accumulated Depreciation, Office Equipment		$ 700
Accounts Payable		700
Unearned Revenue		300
Wages Payable		120
Income Taxes Payable		250
Common Stock		2,000
Retained Earnings		2,870
Dividends	400	
Answering Service Revenue		3,360
Wages Expense	1,620	
Rent Expense	400	
Insurance Expense	40	
Office Supplies Expense	105	
Depreciation Expense, Office Equipment	100	
Income Taxes Expense	250	
	$10,300	$10,300

4. Financial statements prepared

Certified Answering Service, Inc.
Income Statement
For the Month Ended December 31, 19x2

Revenues		
Answering Service Revenue		$3,360
Expenses		
Wages Expense	$1,620	
Rent Expense	400	
Insurance Expense	40	
Office Supplies Expense	105	
Depreciation Expense, Office Equipment	100	
Income Taxes Expense	250	
Total Expenses		2,515
Net Income		$ 845

Certified Answering Service, Inc.
Statement of Retained Earnings
For the Month Ended December 31, 19x2

Retained Earnings, November 30, 19x2	$2,870
Net Income	845
Subtotal	$3,715
Less Dividends	400
Retained Earnings, December 31, 19x2	$3,315

Certified Answering Service, Inc.
Balance Sheet
December 31, 19x2

Assets		
Cash		$2,160
Accounts Receivable		1,250
Service Revenue Receivable		300
Office Supplies		75
Prepaid Insurance		200
Office Equipment	$3,400	
Less Accumulated Depreciation	700	2,700
Total Assets		$6,685
Liabilities		
Accounts Payable		$ 700
Unearned Revenue		300
Wages Payable		120
Income Taxes Payable		250
Total Liabilities		$1,370
Stockholders' Equity		
Common Stock	$2,000	
Retained Earnings	3,315	
Total Stockholders' Equity		5,315
Total Liabilities and Stockholders' Equity		$6,685

Chapter Assignments

Discussion Questions

1. Why does the accountant use the term *net income* instead of *profit*?
2. Define the terms *revenues* and *expenses*.
3. Why are income statement accounts called nominal accounts?
4. Why does the need for an accounting period cause problems?
5. What is the significance of the continuity assumption?
6. "The matching rule is the most significant concept in accounting." Do you agree with this statement? Explain.
7. What is the difference between the cash basis and the accrual basis of accounting?
8. In what two ways is accrual accounting accomplished?
9. Why do adjusting entries need to be made?
10. What are the four situations that require adjusting entries? Give an example of each.
11. Explain the statement, "Some assets are expenses that have not expired."
12. What is a contra account? Give an example.
13. What do plant and equipment, office supplies, and prepaid insurance have in common?
14. What is the difference between accumulated depreciation and depreciation expense?
15. Why are contra accounts used in recording depreciation?
16. How does unearned revenue arise? Give an example.
17. Where does unearned revenue appear on the balance sheet?
18. What accounting problem does a magazine publisher who sells three-year subscriptions have?
19. What is an accrued expense? Give three examples.
20. Under what circumstances might a company have unrecorded revenue? Give an example. What asset arises when the adjustment is made?
21. Why is the income statement usually the first statement prepared from the trial balance?
22. What is the difference between an adjusting entry and a closing entry?
23. Arrange the following activities in proper order by placing the numbers 1 through 6 in the blanks:

    _____ a. The transactions are entered in the journal.
    _____ b. Financial statements are prepared.
    _____ c. The transactions are analyzed from the source documents.
    _____ d. A trial balance and adjusted trial balance are prepared.
    _____ e. Closing entries are prepared.
    _____ f. The transactions are posted to the ledger.

Communication Skills Exercises

Communication 3-1. Account Identification *(L.O. 2, 3, 4)*

Takashimaya Company, Limited, is Japan's largest department store chain. On Takashimaya's balance sheet is an account called Gift Certificates, which contains ¥26,156 million ($176 million).[4] Is this account an asset or a liability? What transaction gives rise to the account? How is this account an example of the application of accrual accounting? Explain what conceptual issues must be resolved in order for this adjustment to be valid.

4. Information from Takashimaya Company, Limited Annual Report.

Communication 3-2. Importance of Adjustments *(L.O. 2, 3, 4)*

Central Appliance Service Co., Inc. has achieved fast growth in the St. Louis area by selling service contracts on large appliances such as washers, driers, and refrigerators. For a fee, Central Appliance will agree to provide all parts and labor on an appliance after the regular warranty runs out. For example, by paying a fee of $200, a person who buys a dishwasher can add two years (years 2 and 3) to the regular one-year (year 1) warranty on the appliance. In 1991, the company sold service contracts in the amount of $1.8 million, all of which applied to future years. Management advocates recording all the sales as revenues in 1991 under the contention that the amount of the contracts can be definitely determined and the cash has been received. Do you agree with this logic? How would you record these cash receipts? What assumptions do you feel must be made?

Communication 3-3. Application of Accrual Accounting *(L.O. 3, 4)*

The Lyric Opera of Chicago is one of the largest and best managed opera companies in the United States. Managing opera productions requires advance planning, including the development of scenery, costumes, and stage properties; sales of tickets; and collection of contributions. To measure how well the company is operating in any given year, accrual accounting must be applied to these and other transactions. At year-end, February 28, 1990, Lyric Opera of Chicago's balance sheet had Deferred Production and Other Costs of $412,858, Deferred Revenue from Sales of Tickets of $3,127,237, and Deferred Revenue from Contributions of $2,314,626.[5] What accounting policies and adjusting entries are applicable to these accounts, and why would they be important to Lyric Opera's management?

Communication 3-4. Nature of Depreciation *(L.O. 2, 3, 4)*

Exxon Corp., a diversified oil, chemical, and energy company, is one of the largest corporations in the world in terms of sales and assets. In 1990, Exxon reported net income of $5.01 billion. In the same year, the company reported depreciation (and related) expense of $5.55 billion.[6] Some people would argue that it is more relevant to think of Exxon as earning $10.56 billion in 1990 because no cash was expended in recording depreciation. According to them, the entry debiting Depreciation Expense and crediting Accumulated Depreciation represents "mere bookkeeping." How do you respond to this view? What assumptions underlie the accounting methods that it favors?

Communication 3-5. Basic Research Skills *(L.O. 4)*

Go to the Yellow Pages of your local telephone directory. Find the names of five different kinds of service businesses. List the types of adjusting entries you think each business will have. Can you think of any types of adjustments that may be unique to each business?

Classroom Exercises

Exercise 3-1. Applications of Accounting Concepts Related to Accrual Accounting *(L.O. 2, 3, 4)*

The accountant for Boulder Company makes the following assumptions or performs the following activities:

a. In estimating the life of a building, assumes that the business will last indefinitely.

5. Reprinted by permission of the Lyric Opera of Chicago.
6. Reprinted by permission of Exxon Corporation.

b. Records a sale at the point in time when the customer is billed.
c. Postpones the recognition as an expense of a one-year insurance policy by initially recording the expenditure as an asset.
d. Recognizes the usefulness of financial statements prepared on a monthly basis even though it is recognized that they are tentative and based on estimates.
e. Recognizes, by making an adjusting entry, wages expense that has been incurred but not yet recorded.
f. Prepares an income statement that shows the revenues earned and the expenses incurred during the accounting period.

Tell which of the following concepts of accrual accounting most directly relates to each of the above actions: (1) periodicity, (2) going concern, (3) matching rule, (4) revenue recognition, (5) deferral, (6) accrual.

Exercise 3-2. Revenue Recognition *(L.O. 5)*

NewsTown, Inc. of Des Moines, Iowa, publishes a monthly magazine featuring local restaurant reviews and upcoming social, cultural, and sporting events. Subscribers pay for subscriptions either one year or two years in advance. Cash received from subscribers is credited to an account called Magazine Subscriptions Received in Advance. At December 31, 19x1, the company's year end, the balance of this account was $1,000,000. Expiration of subscriptions was as follows:

During 19x1	$200,000
During 19x2	500,000
During 19x3	300,000

Prepare the adjusting journal entry, if any is necessary, for December 31, 19x1.

Exercise 3-3. Adjusting Entries for Prepaid Insurance *(L.O. 5)*

An examination of the Prepaid Insurance account shows a balance of $2,056 at the end of an accounting period before adjustments. Prepare journal entries to record the insurance expense for the period under each of the following independent assumptions:

1. An examination of insurance policies shows unexpired insurance that cost $987 at the end of the period.
2. An examination of insurance policies shows that insurance that cost $347 has expired during the period.

Exercise 3-4. Supplies Account: Missing Data *(L.O. 5)*

Determine the amounts indicated by question marks in the columns below. Consider each column a separate problem. Make the adjusting entry for column **a**, assuming that supplies purchased are debited to an asset account.

	a	b	c	d
Supplies on hand July 1	$132	$217	$98	$?
Supplies purchased during month	26	?	87	964
Supplies consumed during month	97	486	?	816
Supplies remaining on July 31	?	218	28	594

Exercise 3-5. Adjusting Entry for Accrued Salaries
(L.O. 5)

Photex, which has a five-day workweek, pays salaries of $35,000 each Friday.

a. Make the adjusting entry required on May 31, assuming that June 1 falls on a Wednesday.
b. Make the entry to pay the salaries on June 3.

Exercise 3-6. Revenue and Expense Recognition
(L.O. 5)

Bellevue Company produces computer software that is sold by Computer Warehouse, Inc. Bellevue receives a royalty of 15 percent of sales. Royalties are paid by Computer Warehouse and received by Bellevue semiannually on April 1 for sales made July through December of the prior year and on October 1 for sales made January through June of the current year. Royalty expense for Computer Warehouse and royalty income for Bellevue in the amount of $12,000 were accrued on December 31, 19x1. Cash in the amounts of $12,000 and $20,000 was paid and received on April 1 and October 1, 19x2, respectively. Software sales during the July to December, 19x2 period totaled $300,000.

1. Calculate the amount of royalty expense for Computer Warehouse and royalty income for Bellevue during 19x2.
2. Prepare the appropriate adjusting entries made by each of the companies on December 31, 19x2.

Exercise 3-7. Adjusting Entries
(L.O. 5)

Prepare year-end adjusting entries for each of the following:

a. Office Supplies had a balance of $84 on January 1. Purchases debited to Office Supplies during the year amount to $415. A year-end inventory reveals supplies of $285 on hand.
b. Depreciation of office equipment is estimated to be $2,130 for the year.
c. Property taxes for six months, estimated to total $875, have accrued but are unrecorded.
d. Unrecorded interest receivable on U.S. government bonds is $850.
e. Unearned Revenue has a balance of $900. The services for $300 received in advance have now been performed.
f. Services totaling $200 have been performed for which the customer has not yet been billed.

Exercise 3-8. Adjusting Entries
(L.O. 5)

Josephina Cordello, computer systems consultant, engaged in the following transactions in 19xx, her initial year of operation:

a. On September 1 Cordello leased an office for one year. The landlord insisted on one year's payment in advance, which was paid in cash, $15,000.
b. On September 1 Cordello purchased office equipment for $3,600 in cash. The office equipment was to be depreciated over a five-year period (60 months) and was estimated to have no value at the end of the five-year period.
c. On October 1 Cordello received an advance payment of $4,800 from TXY Company for a project that will take several months to complete. On December 31, the project was estimated to be 40 percent complete.
d. On December 31 Cordello had completed 90 percent of a $6,000 project for Jacks Corporation that was to be billed to the client in January when the project was completed.

e. On December 31 wages were owed to employees in the amount of $480 that were to be paid in the next accounting period.

1. Prepare general journal entries to record the transactions in **a**, **b**, and **c**.
2. Make the necessary adjusting entries at December 31 for each of the above cases. Assume that no adjusting entries have been made thus far in 19xx.

Exercise 3-9. Relationship of Cash to Expenses Paid *(L.O. 5)*

The 19x1 and 19x2 balance sheets of Target Company showed the following asset and liability amounts at the end of each year after adjusting entries:

	19x1	19x2
Prepaid Insurance	$2,900	$2,400
Wages Payable	2,200	1,200
Unearned Fees	1,900	4,200

From the accounting records, the following amounts of cash disbursements and cash receipts for 19x2 were determined:

Cash disbursed to pay insurance premiums	$ 3,800
Cash disbursed to pay wages	19,500
Cash received for fees	8,900

Calculate the amount of insurance expense, wages expense, and fees earned to be reported on the 19x2 income statement.

Exercise 3-10. Relationship of Expenses to Cash Paid *(L.O. 5)*

The income statement for Gemini Company included the following expenses for 19xx:

Rent Expense	$ 2,600
Interest Expense	3,900
Salaries Expense	41,500

Listed below are the related balance sheet account balances at year end for last year and this year.

	Last Year	This Year
Prepaid Rent	$ 0	$ 450
Interest Payable	600	0
Salaries Payable	2,500	4,800

1. Compute cash paid for rent during the year.
2. Compute cash paid for interest during the year.
3. Compute cash paid for salaries during the year.

Exercise 3-11. Accounting for Revenue Received in Advance *(L.O. 5, 6)*

Michelle Demetri, a lawyer, was paid $24,000 on September 1 to represent a client in certain real estate negotiations during the next twelve months.

Give the entries required in Demetri's records on September 1 and at the end of the year, December 31. How would this transaction be reflected in the balance sheet and income statement on December 31?

Exercise 3-12. Identification of Accruals
(L.O. 5)

Northwest Refrigeration Company has the following liabilities at year end:

Notes Payable	$30,000
Accounts Payable	20,000
Contract Revenue Received in Advance	18,000
Wages Payable	4,900
Interest Payable	1,400
Income Taxes Payable	2,500

1. Which of the above accounts were probably created at year end as a result of an accrual, and which additional account was probably adjusted at year end?
2. Which adjustments probably reduced net income, and which adjustment probably increased net income?

Exercise 3-13. Analysis of Deferrals and Accruals
(L.O. 5)

The following amounts were taken from the balance sheets of Green Bay Corporation:

	December 31	
	19x1	19x2
Prepaid Expenses	$ 45,000	$56,000
Accrued Liabilities	103,000	88,000

During 19x2, $114,000 was expended in cash and charged to Prepaid Expenses, and $212,000 was expended in cash for amounts related to the accrued liabilities. Determine the amount of expense related to Prepaid Expenses and to Accrued Liabilities for 19x2.

Exercise 3-14. Determining Cash Flows
(L.O. 5)

Suburban East News Service, Inc. provides home delivery of day, evening, and Sunday city newspapers to subscribers who live in the suburbs. Customers may pay a yearly subscription fee in advance (at a savings) or pay monthly after delivery of their newspapers. The following data are available for Subscriptions Receivable and Unearned Subscriptions at the beginning and end of May, 19xx:

	May 1	May 31
Subscriptions Receivable	$ 3,800	$4,600
Unearned Subscriptions	11,400	9,800

The income statement shows subscriptions revenue for May of $22,400. Determine the amount of cash received from customers for subscriptions during May.

Exercise 3-15. Preparation of Financial Statements
(L.O. 6)

Prepare the monthly income statement, statement of retained earnings, and balance sheet for Miracle Janitorial Service, Inc. from the data provided in the following adjusted trial balance:

Miracle Janitorial Service, Inc.
Adjusted Trial Balance
June 30, 19xx

Cash	$ 2,295	
Accounts Receivable	1,296	
Prepaid Insurance	190	
Prepaid Rent	100	
Cleaning Supplies	76	
Cleaning Equipment	1,600	
Accumulated Depreciation, Cleaning Equipment		$ 160
Truck	3,600	
Accumulated Depreciation, Truck		360
Accounts Payable		210
Wages Payable		40
Unearned Janitorial Revenue		460
Income Taxes Payable		400
Common Stock		2,000
Retained Earnings		5,517
Dividends	1,000	
Janitorial Revenue		7,310
Wages Expense	2,840	
Rent Expense	600	
Gas, Oil, and Other Truck Expense	290	
Insurance Expense	190	
Supplies Expense	1,460	
Depreciation Expense, Cleaning Equipment	160	
Depreciation Expense, Truck	360	
Income Taxes Expense	400	
	$16,457	$16,457

Interpretation Cases from Business

ICB 3-1. Orion Pictures Corporation[7] *(L.O. 2, 5)*

Orion Pictures Corporation is engaged in the financing, production, and distribution of theatrical motion pictures and television programming. In Orion's 1990 annual report the balance sheet contains an asset called Film Inventories. Film inventories, which consist of the cost associated with producing films less the amount expensed, were $665,966,000 in 1990. The statement of cash flows reveals that the amount of film inventories expensed (amortized) during 1990 was $264,455,000 and the amount spent for new film productions was $370,206,000.

7. Excerpts from the 1990 Annual Report used with the permission of Orion Pictures Corporation.

Required

1. What is the nature of the asset Film Inventories?
2. Prepare an entry to record the amount spent on new film production during 1990 (assume all expenditures are paid for in cash).
3. Prepare the adjusting entry that would be made to record the expense for film productions in 1990.
4. Can you suggest a method by which Orion Pictures Corporation might have determined the expense in **3** in accordance with the matching rule?

ICB 3-2.
The Sperry & Hutchinson Co., Inc.
(L.O. 1, 5)

The Sperry & Hutchinson Co., Inc. is known as "The Green Stamp Company" because its principal business is selling S & H Green Stamps to merchants, who give them to customers, who, in turn, may redeem them for merchandise. When S & H sells green stamps, it incurs a liability to redeem the stamps. It makes a profit to the extent that people do not redeem the stamps. In the past, S & H has assumed that 95 percent of all stamps will be redeemed. Thus, a sale of $1,000 worth of stamps would be recorded as follows:

Cash	1,000	
Liability to Redeem Stamps		950
Stamp Revenue		50

Since it may be years before some stamps are redeemed, the company keeps the liability on its balance sheet indefinitely. An article in *Forbes*, a leading business biweekly magazine, commented on S & H's situation as follows:

> The company [S & H] is sitting on a mountain of money held in reserve to redeem stamps already issued but not yet cashed in. How many of these stamps will ultimately be redeemed? Nobody knows for sure. But Sperry [S & H] has made some assumptions in drawing up its financial statements, and at last count it had stashed away no less than $308 million to match unredeemed stamps. That's more than last year's stamp sales. It's one-third more than the company's total [owners'] equity of $231 million. What's more, to the extent that the company has overestimated the need for that liability—setting aside cash for Green Stamps that have been thrown into the garbage—some of the cash is clearly equity in all but name.[8]

The Liability to Redeem Stamps became so large that in 1979 S & H began setting aside only 90 percent (instead of 95 percent) of stamp sales for redemption. The immediate effect of this change was to boost profits. The reason for this effect is, as stated in *Forbes*, "the extra 5 percent of stamps now assumed to be lost forever goes straight through as pure profit."

Required

1. Assume that S & H has an asset account called Merchandise that represents the goods that can be purchased. What entry would be made if $700 worth of stamps were redeemed for merchandise?
2. What does *Forbes* mean when it says the "some of the cash is clearly equity in all but name"? Is the word "cash" used properly? Show that you know what *Forbes* means by presenting the adjusting entry that would be made if S & H decided to reduce the liability for redemption of stamps.
3. Explain *Forbes*'s comment that the extra 5 percent "goes straight through as pure profit."

8. *Forbes*, October 12, 1981, page 73.

ICB 3-3.
City of Chicago
(L.O. 2, 3)

In 1979, Mayor Jane Byrne won the election in the city of Chicago partly on the basis of her charge that Michael Bilandic, the former mayor, had caused a budget deficit. Taking office in 1980, she hired a major international accounting firm, Peat, Marwick, Mitchell & Co. (now known as KMPG Peat Marwick), to straighten things out. The following excerpt appeared in an article from a leading Chicago business publication:

> [A riddle]
> Q: When is a budget deficit not a deficit?
> A: When it is a surplus, of course.

Chicago Mayor Jane Byrne was once again caught with egg on her face last week as she and her financial advisers tried to defend that riddle. On one hand, Comptroller Daniel J. Grim [Byrne appointee], explaining $75 million in assets the mayor [Byrne] hopes to hold in reserve in the 1981 Chicago city budget, testified in hearings that the city had actually ended 1979 with a $6 million surplus, not the much-reported deficit. He said further that the modest surplus grew to $54 million as a result of tax-enrichment supplements to the 1979 balance sheet.

On the other hand, the mayor stuck by the same guns she used last year on her predecessor. The city had ended 1979, under the Michael Bilandic Administration, not merely without a surplus, but with a deficit. The apparent discrepancy can be explained.[9]

Like most U.S. cities, Chicago operates under the modified accrual accounting basis. This is a combination of the straight cash basis and the accrual basis. The modified accrual basis differs from the accrual method in that an account receivable is recorded only when it is collected in the next accounting period. The collection of Chicago's parking tax, which is assessed on all city parking lots and garages, is an example:

The tax is assessed and collected on a quarterly basis but the city doesn't collect the amount due for the last quarter of 1980 until the first quarter of 1981. Under ideal accrual methods, the parking revenues should be recorded in the 1980 financial statement. Under a cash approach, the revenues would be recorded in the 1981 budget. What the city did before was to record the money whenever it was advantageous politically. That, combined with the infamous revolving funds, allowed the city to hide the fact it was running large deficits under [former] Mayor Bilandic. That also means that no one really knew where the city stood.[10]

The auditors are now reallocating the parking revenues to the 1981 budget but are accruing other revenues by shifting the period of collection from a year in the past. Overall, more revenues were moved into earlier fiscal years than into later years, inflating those budgets. Thus, the 1979 deficit is a surplus. The article concluded:

The upshot is that both Mayor Byrne and Mr. Grim [the comptroller] were correct. There was a deficit in the 1979 corporate or checkbook fund, but because of corrections taking place now, a surplus exists.[11]

9. Reprinted with permission from the December 8, 1980, issue of *Crain's Chicago Business.* Copyright © 1980 by Crain Communications, Inc.
10. Ibid.
11. Ibid.

Required

1. Do you agree with the way the auditors handled parking revenues? Support your answer by explaining which method of accounting you think a city should use.
2. Comment on the statement, "Systematically applied accounting principles will allow all to know exactly where the city stands," made in another part of the article quoted above.

Problem Set A

Problem 3A-1. Preparation of Adjusting Entries *(L.O. 5)*

On June 30, the end of the current fiscal year, the following information was available to aid the Sterling Corporation accountants in making adjusting entries.

a. Among the liabilities of the company is a mortgage payable in the amount of $240,000. On June 30, the accrued interest on this mortgage amounted to $12,000.
b. On Friday, July 2, the company, which is on a five-day workweek and pays employees weekly, will pay its regular salaried employees $19,200.
c. On June 29, the company completed negotiations and signed a contract to provide services to a new client at an annual rate of $3,600.
d. The Supplies account showed a beginning balance of $1,615 and purchases during the year of $3,766. The end-of-year inventory revealed supplies on hand that cost $1,186.
e. The Prepaid Insurance account showed the following entries on June 30:

Beginning Balance	$1,530
January 1	2,900
May 1	3,366

The beginning balance represents the unexpired portion of a one-year policy purchased the previous year. The January 1 entry represents a new one-year policy, and the May 1 entry represents additional coverage in the form of a three-year policy.

f. The table below contains the cost and annual depreciation for buildings and equipment, all of which were purchased before the current year:

Account	Cost	Annual Depreciation
Buildings	$185,000	$ 7,300
Equipment	218,000	21,800

g. On June 1, the company completed negotiations with another client and accepted a payment of $21,000, representing one year's services paid in advance. The $21,000 was credited to Services Collected in Advance.
h. The company calculated that as of June 30 it had earned $3,500 on a $7,500 contract that would be completed and billed in August.
i. Federal income taxes for the year are estimated to be $5,000.

Required

Prepare adjusting entries for each item listed above.

Problem 3A-2. Determining Adjusting Entries, Posting to T Accounts, and Preparing Adjusted Trial Balance *(L.O. 5)*

The schedule below presents the trial balance for the Sigma Consultants Corporation on December 31, 19x2.

Sigma Consultants Corporation
Trial Balance
December 31, 19x2

Cash	$ 12,786	
Accounts Receivable	24,840	
Office Supplies	991	
Prepaid Rent	1,400	
Office Equipment	6,700	
Accumulated Depreciation, Office Equipment		$ 1,600
Accounts Payable		1,820
Notes Payable		10,000
Unearned Fees		2,860
Common Stock		10,000
Retained Earnings		19,387
Dividends	15,000	
Fees Revenue		58,500
Salaries Expense	33,000	
Utility Expense	1,750	
Rent Expense	7,700	
	$104,167	$104,167

The following information is also available:

a. Ending inventory of office supplies, $86.
b. Prepaid rent expired, $700.
c. Depreciation of office equipment for period, $600.
d. Interest accrued on note payable, $600.
e. Salaries accrued at end of period, $200.
f. Fees still unearned at end of period, $1,410.
g. Fees earned but not billed, $600.
h. Estimated federal income taxes for the year, $3,000.

Required

1. Open T accounts for the accounts in the trial balance plus the following: Fees Receivable; Interest Payable; Salaries Payable; Income Taxes Payable; Office Supplies Expense; Depreciation Expense, Office Equipment; Interest Expense; and Income Taxes Expense.
2. Determine adjusting entries and post them directly to the T accounts.
3. Prepare an adjusted trial balance.

Problem 3A-3. Determining Adjusting Entries and Tracing Their Effects to Financial Statements
(L.O. 5, 6)

Having graduated from college with a degree in accounting, Joyce Ozaki opened a small tax preparation service. At the end of its second year of operation, the Ozaki Tax Service, Inc. has the following trial balance:

Ozaki Tax Service, Inc.
Trial Balance
December 31, 19xx

Cash	$ 2,268	
Accounts Receivable	1,031	
Prepaid Insurance	240	
Office Supplies	782	
Office Equipment	4,100	
Accumulated Depreciation, Office Equipment		$ 410
Copier	3,000	
Accumulated Depreciation, Copier		360
Accounts Payable		635
Unearned Tax Fees		219
Common Stock		2,000
Retained Earnings		3,439
Dividends	6,000	
Fees Revenue		21,926
Office Salaries Expense	8,300	
Advertising Expense	650	
Rent Expense	2,400	
Telephone Expense	218	
	$28,989	$28,989

No investments in the business were made during the year. The following information was also available:

a. Supplies on hand, December 31, 19xx, were $227.
b. Insurance still unexpired amounted to $120.
c. Estimated depreciation of office equipment was $410.
d. Estimated depreciation of copier was $360.
e. The telephone expense for December was $19. This bill has been received but not recorded.
f. The services for all unearned tax fees had been performed by the end of the year.
g. Federal income taxes for the year were estimated to be $1,800.

Required

1. Open T accounts for the accounts of the trial balance plus the following: Income Taxes Payable; Insurance Expense; Office Supplies Expense; Depre-

ciation Expense, Office Equipment; Depreciation Expense, Copier; Income Taxes Expense. Record the balances as shown in the trial balance.
2. Determine adjusting entries and post them directly to the T accounts.
3. Prepare an adjusted trial balance, an income statement, a statement of retained earnings, and a balance sheet.

Problem 3A-4. Determining Adjusting Entries and Tracing Their Effects to Financial Statements *(L.O. 5, 6)*

The Elite Livery Service, Inc. was organized to provide limousine service between the airport and various suburban locations. It has just completed its second year of business. Its trial balance appears as follows (account numbers are included):

Elite Livery Service, Inc.
Trial Balance
June 30, 19x2

Cash (111)	$ 9,812	
Accounts Receivable (112)	14,227	
Prepaid Rent (117)	12,000	
Prepaid Insurance (118)	4,900	
Prepaid Maintenance (119)	12,000	
Spare Parts (141)	11,310	
Limousines (142)	200,000	
Accumulated Depreciation, Limousines (143)		$ 25,000
Notes Payable (211)		45,000
Unearned Passenger Service Revenue (212)		30,000
Common Stock (311)		30,000
Retained Earnings (312)		48,211
Dividends (313)	20,000	
Passenger Service Revenue (411)		428,498
Gas and Oil Expense (511)	89,300	
Salaries Expense (512)	206,360	
Advertising Expense (513)	26,800	
	$606,709	$606,709

The following information is also available:

a. To obtain space at the airport, Elite paid two years' rent in advance when it began business.
b. An examination of insurance policies reveals that $2,800 expired during the year.
c. To provide regular maintenance for the vehicles, a deposit of $12,000 was made with a local garage. Examination of maintenance invoices reveals that there are $10,944 in charges against the deposit.
d. An inventory of spare parts shows $1,902 on hand.

e. All of the Elite Livery Service's limousines are to be depreciated at the annual rate of 12.5 percent of cost. There were no limousines purchased during the year.
f. A payment of $10,500 for one full year's interest on notes payable is now due.
g. Unearned Passenger Service Revenue on June 30 includes $17,815 in tickets that were purchased by employers for use by their executives and have not been redeemed.
h. Federal income taxes were expected to be $12,000.

Required

1. Open ledger accounts for the accounts in the trial balance plus the following: Interest Payable (213); Income Taxes Payable (214); Rent Expense (514); Insurance Expense (515); Spare Parts Expense (516); Depreciation Expense, Limousines (517); Maintenance Expense (518); Interest Expense (519); Income Taxes Expense (520). Record the balances as shown in the trial balance.
2. Record the adjusting entries in the general journal (record them on journal Page 14).
3. Post the adjusting entries from the general journal to the ledger accounts, showing proper references.
4. Prepare an adjusted trial balance, an income statement, a statement of retained earnings, and a balance sheet.

Problem 3A-5. Determining Adjusting Entries and Tracing Their Effects to Financial Statements *(L.O. 3, 5, 6)*

At the end of its accounting period, the trial balance for Apollo Cleaners, Inc. appears as shown on page 155. The following information is also available:

a. A study of insurance policies shows that $340 is unexpired at the end of the year.
b. An inventory of cleaning supplies shows $622 on hand.
c. Estimated depreciation for the year was $4,300 on the building and $2,100 on the delivery truck.
d. Accrued interest on the mortgage payable amounted to $500.
e. On August 1, the company signed a contract effective immediately with Stark County Hospital to dry clean, for a fixed monthly charge of $200, the uniforms used by doctors in surgery. The hospital paid for four months of service in advance.
f. Unrecorded plant wages totaled $982.
g. Sales and delivery wages are paid on Saturday. The weekly payroll is $480. September 30 falls on a Thursday, and the company has a six-day pay week.
h. Federal income taxes for the period are estimated to be $500.

Required

1. Open ledger accounts for each account in the trial balance plus the following: Wages Payable (213); Interest Payable (214); Income Taxes Payable (215); Insurance Expense (515); Cleaning Supplies Expense (516); Depreciation Expense, Building (517); Depreciation Expense, Delivery Truck (518); Income Taxes Expense (521). Record the balances as shown in the trial balance.
2. Determine adjusting entries, and enter them in the general journal (Page 42).
3. Post the adjusting entries to the ledger accounts, showing all the proper references.

Apollo Cleaners, Inc.
Trial Balance
September 30, 19x2

Cash (111)	$ 5,894	
Accounts Receivable (112)	13,247	
Prepaid Insurance (115)	1,700	
Cleaning Supplies (116)	3,687	
Land (141)	9,000	
Building (142)	81,000	
Accumulated Depreciation, Building (143)		$ 20,200
Delivery Truck (144)	11,500	
Accumulated Depreciation, Delivery Truck (145)		2,600
Accounts Payable (212)		10,200
Unearned Dry Cleaning Revenue (216)		800
Mortgage Payable (221)		55,000
Common Stock (311)		20,000
Retained Earnings (312)		8,280
Dividends (313)	5,000	
Dry Cleaning Revenue (411)		60,167
Laundry Revenue (412)		18,650
Plant Wages Expense (511)	32,560	
Sales and Delivery Wages Expense (512)	18,105	
Cleaning Equipment Rent Expense (513)	3,000	
Delivery Truck Expense (514)	2,187	
Interest Expense (519)	5,500	
Other Expenses (520)	3,517	
	$195,897	$195,897

4. Prepare an adjusted trial balance.
5. Prepare an income statement, a statement of retained earnings, and a balance sheet for the year ended September 30, 19x2.
6. Give examples of how the techniques of accrual accounting affect the income statement in **5**.

Problem Set B

Problem 3B-1. Preparation of Adjusting Entries *(L.O. 5)*

On November 30, the end of the current fiscal year, the following information was available to assist Pinder Corporation's accountants in making adjusting entries:

a. The Supplies account showed a beginning balance of $2,174. Purchases during the year were $4,526. The end-of-year inventory revealed supplies on hand that cost $1,397.

b. The Prepaid Insurance account showed the following on November 30:

Beginning Balance	$3,580
July 1	4,200
October 1	7,272

The beginning balance represents the unexpired portion of a one-year policy purchased the previous year. The July 1 entry represents a new one-year policy, and the October 1 entry represents additional coverage in the form of a three-year policy.

c. The table below contains the cost and annual depreciation for buildings and equipment, all of which were purchased before the current year.

Account	Cost	Annual Depreciation
Buildings	$286,000	$14,500
Equipment	374,000	35,400

d. On September 1, the company completed negotiations with a client and accepted a payment of $16,800, which represented one year's services paid in advance. The $16,800 was credited to Unearned Services Revenue.
e. The company calculated that as of November 30 it had earned $4,000 on an $11,000 contract that would be completed and billed in January.
f. Among the liabilities of the company is a note payable in the amount of $300,000. On November 30, the interest expense accrued on this note amounted to $15,000.
g. On Saturday, December 2, the company, which is on a six-day workweek, will pay its regular salaried employees $12,300.
h. On November 29, the company completed negotiations and signed a contract to provide services to a new client at an annual rate of $17,500.
i. Management estimates income taxes for the year to be $25,000.

Required

Prepare adjusting entries for each item listed above.

Problem 3B-2. Determining Adjusting Entries, Posting to T Accounts, and Preparing Adjusted Trial Balance *(L.O. 5)*

The schedule on page 157 presents the trial balance for Financial Strategies Service, Inc. on December 31. The following information is also available:

a. Ending inventory of office supplies, $264.
b. Prepaid rent expired, $440.
c. Depreciation of office equipment for period, $660.
d. Accrued interest expense at end of period, $550.
e. Accrued salaries at end of month, $330.
f. Fees still unearned at end of period, $1,166.
g. Fees earned but unrecorded, $2,200.
h. Estimated federal income taxes, $4,000.

Required

1. Open T accounts for the accounts in the trial balance plus the following: Fees Receivable; Interest Payable; Salaries Payable; Income Taxes Payable; Office Supplies Expense; Depreciation Expense, Office Equipment; Interest Expense; and Income Taxes Expense. Enter balances.

Financial Strategies Service, Inc.
Trial Balance
December 31, 19xx

Cash	$ 16,500	
Accounts Receivable	8,250	
Office Supplies	2,662	
Prepaid Rent	1,320	
Office Equipment	9,240	
Accumulated Depreciation, Office Equipment		$ 1,540
Accounts Payable		5,940
Notes Payable		11,000
Unearned Fees		2,970
Common Stock		10,000
Retained Earnings		14,002
Dividends	22,000	
Fees Revenue		72,600
Salaries Expense	49,400	
Rent Expense	4,400	
Utility Expense	4,280	
	$118,052	$118,052

2. Determine adjusting entries and post them directly to the T accounts.
3. Prepare an adjusted trial balance.

Problem 3B-3. Determining Adjusting Entries and Tracing Their Effects to Financial Statements *(L.O. 5, 6)*

The Crescent Custodial Service, Inc. is owned by Mike Podgorney. After six months of operation, the June 30, 19xx trial balance for the company, presented on page 158, was prepared. The following information is also available:

a. Cleaning supplies of $117 are on hand.
b. Prepaid insurance is the cost of a one-year policy purchased on January 1.
c. Prepaid rent represents a $100 payment made on January 1 toward the last month's rent of a three-year lease plus $100 rent per month for each of the six past months.
d. The cleaning equipment and trucks are depreciated at the rate of 20 percent per year (10 percent for each six months).
e. The unearned revenue represents a six-month payment in advance made by a customer on May 1.
f. During the last week of June, Mike completed the first stage of work on a contract that will not be billed until the contract is completed. The price of this stage is $400.
g. On Saturday, July 3, Mike will owe his employees $540 for one week's work (six-day workweek).
h. Federal income taxes for the six months are estimated to be $750.

Crescent Custodial Service, Inc.
Trial Balance
June 30, 19xx

Cash	$ 762	
Accounts Receivable	914	
Prepaid Insurance	380	
Prepaid Rent	700	
Cleaning Supplies	1,396	
Cleaning Equipment	1,740	
Truck	3,600	
Accounts Payable		$ 170
Unearned Janitorial Fees		480
Common Stock		5,095
Dividends	1,000	
Janitorial Fees		7,487
Wages Expense	2,400	
Gas, Oil, and Other Truck Expenses	340	
	$13,232	$13,232

Required

1. Open T accounts for the accounts in the trial balance plus the following: Fees Receivable; Accumulated Depreciation, Cleaning Equipment; Accumulated Depreciation, Truck; Wages Payable; Income Taxes Payable; Rent Expense; Insurance Expense; Cleaning Supplies Expense; Depreciation Expense, Cleaning Equipment; Depreciation Expense, Truck; Income Taxes Expense.
2. Determine adjusting entries and post them directly to the T accounts.
3. Prepare an adjusted trial balance, an income statement, a statement of retained earnings, and a balance sheet.

Problem 3B-4. Determining Adjusting Entries and Tracing Their Effects to Financial Statements
(L.O. 5, 6)

The trial balance for New Wave Dance Studio, Inc. at the end of the current fiscal year appears on page 159. The following information is available to assist in the preparation of adjusting entries:

a. An inventory of supplies reveals $92 still on hand.
b. The prepaid rent reflects the rent for October plus the rent for the last month of the lease.
c. Prepaid insurance consists of a two-year policy purchased on May 1, 19x2.
d. Depreciation on equipment is estimated to be $800.
e. Accrued wages are $65 on October 31.
f. Two-thirds of the unearned dance fees have been earned by October 31.
g. Management estimates federal income taxes for the year to be $3,000.

New Wave Dance Studio, Inc.
Trial Balance
October 31, 19x2

Cash (111)	$ 1,028	
Accounts Receivable (112)	517	
Supplies (115)	170	
Prepaid Rent (116)	400	
Prepaid Insurance (117)	360	
Equipment (141)	9,100	
Accumulated Depreciation, Equipment (142)		$ 400
Accounts Payable (211)		380
Unearned Dance Fees (213)		900
Common Stock (311)		1,500
Retained Earnings (312)		1,000
Dividends (313)	12,000	
Dance Fees (411)		25,995
Wages Expense (511)	3,200	
Rent Expense (512)	2,200	
Utility Expense (515)	1,200	
	$30,175	$30,175

Required

1. Open ledger accounts for the accounts in the trial balance plus the following: Wages Payable (212); Income Taxes Payable (214); Supplies Expense (513); Insurance Expense (514); Depreciation Expense, Equipment (516); Income Taxes Expense (520).
2. Record the adjusting entries in the general journal (use journal Page 53).
3. Post the adjusting entries from the general journal to the ledger accounts, showing proper references.
4. Prepare an adjusted trial balance, an income statement, a statement of retained earnings, and a balance sheet.

Problem 3B-5. Determining Adjusting Entries and Tracing Their Effects to Financial Statements *(L.O. 3, 5, 6)*

At the end of the first three months of operations, the trial balance of the Metropolitan Answering Service, Inc. appeared as shown on page 160. An accountant was engaged to prepare financial statements for the company in order to determine how well the company was doing after three months. Upon examining the accounting records, the accountant found the following items of interest:

a. An inventory of office supplies reveals supplies on hand of $133.
b. The Prepaid Rent account includes the rent for the first three months plus a deposit for the last month's rent.
c. Prepaid Insurance reflects a one-year policy purchased on January 4.
d. Depreciation is computed to be $102 on the office equipment and $106 on the communications equipment for the first three months.

e. The balance of the Unearned Answering Service Revenue account represents a 12-month service contract paid in advance on February 1.
f. On March 31, accrued wages totaled $80.
g. Federal income taxes are estimated to be $1,500.

The balance of the Common Stock account represents investments by the stockholders.

Metropolitan Answering Service, Inc.
Trial Balance
March 31, 19x2

Cash (111)	$ 4,762	
Accounts Receivable (112)	4,236	
Office Supplies (115)	903	
Prepaid Rent (116)	800	
Prepaid Insurance (117)	720	
Office Equipment (141)	2,300	
Communications Equipment (143)	2,400	
Accounts Payable (211)		$ 2,673
Unearned Answering Service Revenue (213)		888
Common Stock (311)		5,933
Dividends (313)	2,130	
Answering Service Revenue (411)		11,002
Wages Expense (511)	1,900	
Office Cleaning Expense (513)	345	
	$20,496	$20,496

Required

1. Open ledger accounts for the accounts in the trial balance plus the following: Accumulated Depreciation, Office Equipment (142); Accumulated Depreciation, Communications Equipment (144); Wages Payable (212); Income Taxes Payable (214); Rent Expense (512); Insurance Expense (514); Office Supplies Expense (515); Depreciation Expense, Office Equipment (516); Depreciation Expense, Communications Equipment (517); Income Taxes Expense (520).
2. Record the adjusting entries in the general journal (use journal Page 12).
3. Post the adjusting entries from the general journal to the ledger accounts, showing proper references.
4. Prepare an adjusted trial balance.
5. Prepare an income statement, a statement of retained earnings, and a balance sheet.
6. Give examples of how the techniques of accrual accounting affect the income statement in **5**.

Financial Decision Cases

3-1. Jamison Hotel/ Restaurant News, Inc.
(L.O. 1, 5)

Karen Jamison, the owner of a newsletter for managers of hotels and restaurants, has prepared the following condensed amounts from the financial statements for 19x3:

Revenues	$346,000
Expenses	282,000
Net Income	$ 64,000
Total Assets	$172,000
Liabilities	$ 48,000
Stockholders' Equity	124,000
Total Liabilities and Stockholders' Equity	$172,000

Given these figures, Karen is planning a cash dividend of $50,000. However, Karen's accountant has found that the following items were overlooked:

a. Although the balance of the printing supplies account is $32,000, only $14,000 in supplies is on hand at the end of the year.
b. Depreciation of $20,000 on equipment has not been recorded.
c. Wages in the amount of $9,400 have been earned by employees but not recognized in the accounts.
d. No provision has been made for estimated income taxes payable of $10,800.
e. A liability account called Unearned Subscriptions has a balance of $16,200, although it is determined that one-third of these subscriptions have been mailed to subscribers.

Required

1. Prepare the necessary adjusting entries.
2. Recast the condensed financial statement figures after making the necessary adjustments.
3. How do you assess the performance of Karen's business after the adjustments have been made? **Hint:** Compare net income to revenues and total assets before and after the adjustments. Do you think that paying the dividend is advisable?

3-2. Lockyer Systems, Inc.
(L.O. 5, 6)

Tim Lockyer filed articles of incorporation with the state on July 1, 19xx, to incorporate his new business. The company, called Lockyer Systems, Inc., is engaged in writing computer programs with special applications for businesses that own small computers. During the first six months of operation, the business has been so successful that Tim has had to hire new employees on several occasions. Yet he has continually had to put off creditors because he lacked the funds to pay them. He wants to apply for a bank loan, but after preparing a statement showing the totals of receipts of cash and payments of cash, he wonders whether a bank will make a loan to him on the basis of such apparently poor results. Deciding that he needs some accounting help, Tim asks you to review the statement and the company's operating results.

Lockyer Systems, Inc.
Statement of Cash Receipts and Payments
For the Six Months Ended December 31, 19xx

Receipts from		
Investment by Tim Lockyer (Common Stock)		$15,000
Customers for Programming Services Provided		25,200
Total Cash Receipts		$40,200
Payments for		
Wages	$9,780	
Insurance	2,400	
Rent	4,200	
Supplies	1,980	
Office Equipment	6,200	
Computer Rental	8,000	
Maintenance	900	
Service Van	5,000	
Oil and Gas Reimbursements	690	
Utility	540	
Telephone	300	
Total Cash Payments		39,990
Bank Balance		$ 210

After verifying the information in Tim's statement, you assemble the following additional facts about Lockyer Systems, Inc.:

a. In addition to the amount received from customers, programming services totaling $9,700 had been performed but were not yet paid for.
b. Employees have been paid all the wages owed to them except for $350 earned since the last payday. The next regular payday is January 3.
c. The insurance account represents a two-year policy purchased on July 1.
d. The rent account represents rent of $600 per month, including the rent for January.
e. In examining the expenditures for supplies, you find invoices for $650 that have not been paid, and an inventory reveals $875 of unused supplies still on hand.
f. The office equipment is fully paid for, and it is estimated it will last five years and be worthless at the end of that time. It was purchased July 1, 19xx.
g. The computer rental agreement provides for a security deposit of $2,000 plus monthly payments of $1,000.

h. The maintenance account represents a one-year maintenance agreement, paid in advance on July 1.
i. The service van account represents the down payment on a van purchased on December 30 for $15,000. Prior to this purchase, the company had reimbursed employees for oil and gas when using their own cars for business. A study of the documents shows that $120 in employee oil and gas receipts must still be reimbursed.

Required

1. From the information given, open T accounts and record the transactions and any adjustments.
2. Prepare an adjusted trial balance, an income statement, and a balance sheet for Lockyer Systems, Inc.
3. What is your assessment of the company's performance? If you were a bank loan officer, would you look favorably on a loan application from Lockyer Systems, Inc.?

LEARNING OBJECTIVES

1. *Prepare a work sheet.*
2. *Identify the three principal uses of a work sheet.*
3. *Prepare financial statements from a work sheet.*
4. *Record the adjusting entries from a work sheet.*
5. *Explain the purposes of closing entries.*
6. *Prepare the required closing entries.*
7. *Prepare the post-closing trial balance.*
8. *Prepare reversing entries as appropriate.*

CHAPTER 4

Completing the Accounting Cycle

You will see the accounting cycle completed in this chapter. First you study the uses and preparation of the work sheet, an important tool for accountants. Then, as the final step in the accounting cycle, you learn how to prepare closing entries.

In previous chapters, the main focus was on the measurement process in accounting. In this chapter, the emphasis is on the accounting system itself and the sequence of steps used by the accountant in completing the accounting cycle. An important part of the accounting system involves the preparation of a work sheet, so we present in detail each step in its preparation. This chapter also explains the uses of the work sheet in accomplishing the end-of-period procedures of recording the adjusting entries, preparing financial statements, and closing the accounts. The optional first step of the next accounting period, preparation of reversing entries, is also discussed. After studying this chapter, you should be able to meet the learning objectives listed on the left.

DECISION POINT
Maintenance Management, Inc.

Shortly after the end of Maintenance Management, Inc.'s December 31, 1990, year-end, the company's accountants provided the financial statements for the past year. The management of this company, which provides janitorial services to major office buildings in the San Francisco area, was surprised to see a fairly substantial loss for the year, and, as a result, determined to pay closer attention to operating results during 1991. The accountants suggested that the company begin preparing interim statements, that is, financial statements that are prepared quarterly or monthly, so that management would see operating results more often than once per year. Management agreed that this sounded like a good idea, but wondered how much effort it would take and how much it would cost to prepare financial statements more frequently.

The preparation of interim financial statements requires more effort than simply preparing one set of financial statements for the year, and it is likely that Maintenance Management, Inc. will have to hire more accounting staff. Each time the financial statements are prepared, adjusting entries will have to be determined, prepared, and recorded. In addition, the ledger accounts will have to be prepared for beginning the next accounting period. The advantages of preparing interim financial statements usually outweigh the costs, however, because management receives timely information that will help it to make the decisions that are necessary to improve the company's operations. This chapter explains these procedures, which are carried out to prepare financial statements at the end of an accounting period, whether that period be a month, a quarter, or a year. ■

The Work Sheet: A Tool of Accountants

OBJECTIVE 1 *Prepare a work sheet*

As seen earlier, the flow of information affecting a business does not arbitrarily stop at the end of an accounting period. In order to prepare the financial reports, accountants must collect relevant data to determine what should be included. For example, accountants must examine insurance policies to see how much prepaid insurance has expired, examine plant and equipment records to determine depreciation, take an inventory of supplies on hand, and calculate the amount of accrued wages. These calculations, together with the other computations, analyses, and preliminary drafts of statements, make up the accountants' **working papers**. Working papers are important for two reasons. First, they aid accountants in organizing their work so that they do not omit important data or steps that affect the accounting statements. Second, they provide evidence of what has been done so that accountants or auditors can retrace their steps and support the basis of the financial statements.

A special kind of working paper is the **work sheet**. The work sheet is used frequently as a preliminary step in the preparation of financial statements. Using a work sheet lessens the possibility of ignoring an adjustment, aids in checking the arithmetical accuracy of the accounts, and facilitates the preparation of financial statements. The work sheet is never published and is rarely seen by management. Nevertheless, it is a useful tool for the accountant. Because preparation of the work sheet is a very mechanical process, accountants often use a microcomputer to assist in its preparation. In some cases, accountants use a spreadsheet to prepare the work sheet. In other cases, general ledger software is used to prepare financial statements from the adjusted trial balance.

Steps in Preparing the Work Sheet

In the chapter on business income and adjusting entries, the adjustments were entered directly in the journal and posted to the ledger, and the financial statements were prepared from the adjusted trial balance. These steps were done rather easily for the Joan Miller Advertising Agency, Inc. because it is a small company. For larger companies, which may require many adjusting entries, a work sheet is essential. To illustrate the preparation of the work sheet, the Joan Miller Advertising Agency, Inc. case will be continued.

A commonly used form of work sheet has one column for account names and/or numbers and ten more columns with headings as shown in Exhibit 4-1. Note that the work sheet is identified by a heading that consists of (1) the name of the company, (2) the title "Work Sheet," and (3) the period of time covered (as on the income statement).

There are five steps in the preparation of a work sheet, as follows:

1. Enter and total the account balances in the Trial Balance columns.
2. Enter and total the adjustments in the Adjustments columns.
3. Enter and total the account balances as adjusted in the Adjusted Trial Balance columns.
4. Extend the account balances from the Adjusted Trial Balance columns to the Income Statement columns or the Balance Sheet columns.
5. Total the Income Statement columns and the Balance Sheet columns. Enter the net income or net loss in both pairs of columns as a balancing figure, and recompute column totals.

1. Enter and total the account balances in the Trial Balance columns. The titles and balances of the accounts as of January 31 are copied directly from the ledger into the Trial Balance columns, as shown in Exhibit 4-1. This trial balance is the same as that illustrated in the chapter on business income and adjusting entries. When a work sheet is prepared, a separate trial balance is not required.

2. Enter and total the adjustments in the Adjustments columns. The required adjustments for the Joan Miller Advertising Agency, Inc. were explained in the last chapter. The same adjustments are entered in the Adjustments columns of the work sheet in Exhibit 4-2. As each adjustment is entered, a letter is used to identify the debit and credit parts of the same entry. The first adjustment, identified by the letter **a**, is for recognition of rent expense, which results in a debit to Rent Expense and a credit to Prepaid Rent. In practice, this letter may be used to refer to supporting computations or documentation underlying the adjusting entry and may simplify the recording of adjusting entries in the general journal.

If an adjustment calls for an account that has not already been used in the trial balance, the new account is added below the accounts listed for the trial balance. The trial balance includes only those accounts that have balances. For example, Rent Expense has been added in Exhibit 4-2. The

Exhibit 4-1. Entering the Account Balances in the Trial Balance Columns

Joan Miller Advertising Agency, Inc.
Work Sheet
For the Month Ended January 31, 19xx

Account Name	Trial Balance		Adjustments		Adjusted Trial Balance		Income Statement		Balance Sheet	
	Debit	Credit	Debit	Credit	Debit	Credit	Debit	Credit	Debit	Credit
Cash	1,720									
Accounts Receivable	2,800									
Art Supplies	1,800									
Office Supplies	800									
Prepaid Rent	800									
Prepaid Insurance	480									
Art Equipment	4,200									
Accumulated Depreciation, Art Equipment										
Office Equipment	3,000									
Accumulated Depreciation, Office Equipment										
Accounts Payable		3,170								
Unearned Art Fees		1,000								
Common Stock		10,000								
Dividends	1,400									
Advertising Fees Earned		4,200								
Office Wages Expense	1,200									
Utility Expense	100									
Telephone Expense	70									
	18,370	18,370								

only exception to this rule is the Accumulated Depreciation accounts, which will have a zero balance only in the initial period of operation. Accumulated Depreciation accounts are listed immediately after their associated asset account.

When all the adjustments have been made, the two Adjustments columns must be totaled. This step proves that the debits and credits of the adjustments are equal and generally reduces errors in the preparation of the work sheet.

3. Enter and total the account balances as adjusted in the Adjusted Trial Balance columns. Exhibit 4-3 (page 169) shows the adjusted trial balance. It is prepared by combining the amount of each account in the original Trial Balance columns with the corresponding amounts in the Adjustments columns and entering the combined amounts on a line-by-line basis in the Adjusted Trial Balance columns.

Exhibit 4-2. Entries in the Adjustments Columns

Joan Miller Advertising Agency, Inc.
Work Sheet
For the Month Ended January 31, 19xx

Account Name	Trial Balance		Adjustments		Adjusted Trial Balance		Income Statement		Balance Sheet	
	Debit	Credit	Debit	Credit	Debit	Credit	Debit	Credit	Debit	Credit
Cash	1,720									
Accounts Receivable	2,800									
Art Supplies	1,800			(c) 500						
Office Supplies	800			(d) 200						
Prepaid Rent	800			(a) 400						
Prepaid Insurance	480			(b) 40						
Art Equipment	4,200									
Accumulated Depreciation, Art Equipment				(e) 70						
Office Equipment	3,000									
Accumulated Depreciation, Office Equipment				(f) 50						
Accounts Payable		3,170								
Unearned Art Fees		1,000	(g) 400							
Common Stock		10,000								
Dividends	1,400									
Advertising Fees Earned		4,200		(h) 200						
Office Wages Expense	1,200		(i) 180							
Utility Expense	100									
Telephone Expense	70									
	18,370	18,370								
Rent Expense			(a) 400							
Insurance Expense			(b) 40							
Art Supplies Expense			(c) 500							
Office Supplies Expense			(d) 200							
Depreciation Expense, Art Equipment			(e) 70							
Depreciation Expense, Office Equipment			(f) 50							
Art Fees Earned				(g) 400						
Fees Receivable			(h) 200							
Wages Payable				(i) 180						
Income Taxes Expense			(j) 400							
Income Taxes Payable				(j) 400						
			2,440	2,440						

Exhibit 4-3. Entries in the Adjusted Trial Balance Columns

Joan Miller Advertising Agency, Inc.
Work Sheet
For the Month Ended January 31, 19xx

	Trial Balance		Adjustments		Adjusted Trial Balance		Income Statement		Balance Sheet	
Account Name	**Debit**	**Credit**	**Debit**	**Credit**	**Debit**	**Credit**	**Debit**	**Credit**	**Debit**	**Credit**
Cash	1,720				1,720					
Accounts Receivable	2,800				2,800					
Art Supplies	1,800			(c) 500	1,300					
Office Supplies	800			(d) 200	600					
Prepaid Rent	800			(a) 400	400					
Prepaid Insurance	480			(b) 40	440					
Art Equipment	4,200				4,200					
Accumulated Depreciation, Art Equipment				(e) 70		70				
Office Equipment	3,000				3,000					
Accumulated Depreciation, Office Equipment				(f) 50		50				
Accounts Payable		3,170				3,170				
Unearned Art Fees		1,000	(g) 400			600				
Common Stock		10,000				10,000				
Dividends	1,400				1,400					
Advertising Fees Earned		4,200		(h) 200		4,400				
Office Wages Expense	1,200		(i) 180		1,380					
Utility Expense	100				100					
Telephone Expense	70				70					
	18,370	18,370								
Rent Expense			(a) 400		400					
Insurance Expense			(b) 40		40					
Art Supplies Expense			(c) 500		500					
Office Supplies Expense			(d) 200		200					
Depreciation Expense, Art Equipment			(e) 70		70					
Depreciation Expense, Office Equipment			(f) 50		50					
Art Fees Earned				(g) 400		400				
Fees Receivable			(h) 200		200					
Wages Payable				(i) 180		180				
Income Taxes Expense			(j) 400		400					
Income Taxes Payable				(j) 400		400				
			2,440	2,440	19,270	19,270				

Some examples from Exhibit 4-3 will illustrate **crossfooting**, or adding and subtracting a group of numbers horizontally. The first line shows Cash with a debit balance of $1,720. Because there are no adjustments to the Cash account, $1,720 is entered in the debit column of the Adjusted Trial Balance. The second line is Accounts Receivable, which shows a debit of $2,800 in the Trial Balance columns. Because there are no adjustments to Accounts Receivable, the $2,800 balance is carried over to the debit column of the Adjusted Trial Balance. The next line is Art Supplies, which shows a debit of $1,800 in the Trial Balance columns and a credit of $500 from adjustment **c** in the Adjustments columns. Subtracting $500 from $1,800 results in a $1,300 debit balance in the Adjusted Trial Balance. This process is followed for all the accounts, including those added below the trial balance. The Adjusted Trial Balance columns are then footed (totaled) to check the accuracy of the crossfooting.

4. Extend the account balances from the Adjusted Trial Balance columns to the Income Statement columns or the Balance Sheet columns. Every account in the adjusted trial balance is either a balance sheet account or an income statement account. Each account is extended to its proper place as a debit or credit in either the Income Statement columns or the Balance Sheet columns. The result of extending the accounts is shown in Exhibit 4-4. Revenue and expense accounts are copied to the Income Statement columns. Assets and liabilities and the Common Stock and Dividends accounts are extended to the Balance Sheet columns. To avoid overlooking an account, extend the accounts line by line, beginning with the first line (which is Cash) and not omitting any subsequent lines. For instance, the Cash debit balance of $1,720 is extended to the debit column of the Balance Sheet; the Accounts Receivable debit balance of $2,800 is extended to the same debit column, and so forth. Each amount is carried across to only one column.

5. Total the Income Statement columns and the Balance Sheet columns. Enter the net income or net loss in both pairs of columns as a balancing figure, and recompute column totals. This last step, as shown in Exhibit 4-5 (page 172), is necessary to compute net income or net loss and to prove the arithmetical accuracy of the work sheet.

Net income (or net loss) is equal to the difference between the debit and credit columns of the Income Statement. It is also equal to the difference between the debit and credit columns of the Balance Sheet.

Revenue (Income Statement credit column total)	$4,800
Expenses (Income Statement debit column total)	(3,210)
Net Income	$1,590

In this case, the revenue (credit column) has exceeded the expenses (debit column). Consequently, the company has a net income of $1,590. The same difference is shown between the debit and credit columns of the Balance Sheet.

Exhibit 4-4. Entries in the Income Statement and Balance Sheet Columns

Joan Miller Advertising Agency, Inc.
Work Sheet
For the Month Ended January 31, 19xx

	Trial Balance		Adjustments		Adjusted Trial Balance		Income Statement		Balance Sheet	
Account Name	Debit	Credit	Debit	Credit	Debit	Credit	Debit	Credit	Debit	Credit
Cash	1,720				1,720				1,720	
Accounts Receivable	2,800				2,800				2,800	
Art Supplies	1,800			(c) 500	1,300				1,300	
Office Supplies	800			(d) 200	600				600	
Prepaid Rent	800			(a) 400	400				400	
Prepaid Insurance	480			(b) 40	440				440	
Art Equipment	4,200				4,200				4,200	
Accumulated Depreciation, Art Equipment				(e) 70		70				70
Office Equipment	3,000				3,000				3,000	
Accumulated Depreciation, Office Equipment				(f) 50		50				50
Accounts Payable		3,170				3,170				3,170
Unearned Art Fees		1,000	(g) 400			600				600
Common Stock		10,000				10,000				10,000
Dividends	1,400				1,400				1,400	
Advertising Fees Earned		4,200		(h) 200		4,400		4,400		
Office Wages Expense	1,200		(i) 180		1,380		1,380			
Utility Expense	100				100		100			
Telephone Expense	70				70		70			
	18,370	18,370								
Rent Expense			(a) 400		400		400			
Insurance Expense			(b) 40		40		40			
Art Supplies Expense			(c) 500		500		500			
Office Supplies Expense			(d) 200		200		200			
Depreciation Expense, Art Equipment			(e) 70		70		70			
Depreciation Expense, Office Equipment			(f) 50		50		50			
Art Fees Earned				(g) 400		400		400		
Fees Receivable			(h) 200		200				200	
Wages Payable				(i) 180		180				180
Income Taxes Expense			(j) 400		400		400			
Income Taxes Payable				(j) 400		400				400
			2,440	2,440	19,270	19,270				

Exhibit 4-5. Entries in the Income Statement and Balance Sheet Columns and Totals

Joan Miller Advertising Agency, Inc.
Work Sheet
For the Month Ended January 31, 19xx

	Trial Balance		Adjustments		Adjusted Trial Balance		Income Statement		Balance Sheet	
Account Name	**Debit**	**Credit**	**Debit**	**Credit**	**Debit**	**Credit**	**Debit**	**Credit**	**Debit**	**Credit**
Cash	1,720				1,720				1,720	
Accounts Receivable	2,800				2,800				2,800	
Art Supplies	1,800			(c) 500	1,300				1,300	
Office Supplies	800			(d) 200	600				600	
Prepaid Rent	800			(a) 400	400				400	
Prepaid Insurance	480			(b) 40	440				440	
Art Equipment	4,200				4,200				4,200	
Accumulated Depreciation, Art Equipment				(e) 70		70				70
Office Equipment	3,000				3,000				3,000	
Accumulated Depreciation, Office Equipment				(f) 50		50				50
Accounts Payable		3,170				3,170				3,170
Unearned Art Fees		1,000	(g) 400			600				600
Common Stock		10,000				10,000				10,000
Dividends	1,400				1,400				1,400	
Advertising Fees Earned		4,200		(h) 200		4,400		4,400		
Office Wages Expense	1,200		(i) 180		1,380		1,380			
Utility Expense	100				100		100			
Telephone Expense	70				70		70			
	18,370	18,370								
Rent Expense			(a) 400		400		400			
Insurance Expense			(b) 40		40		40			
Art Supplies Expense			(c) 500		500		500			
Office Supplies Expense			(d) 200		200		200			
Depreciation Expense, Art Equipment			(e) 70		70		70			
Depreciation Expense, Office Equipment			(f) 50		50		50			
Art Fees Earned				(g) 400		400		400		
Fees Receivable			(h) 200		200				200	
Wages Payable				(i) 180		180				180
Income Taxes Expense			(j) 400		400		400			
Income Taxes Payable				(j) 400		400				400
			2,440	2,440	19,270	19,270	3,210	4,800	16,060	14,470
Net Income							1,590			1,590
							4,800	4,800	16,060	16,060

The $1,590 is entered in the debit side of the Income Statement columns to balance the columns, and it is entered in the credit side of the Balance Sheet columns. This is done because excess revenue (net income) increases owners' equity, and increases in owners' equity are recorded by credits.

If a net loss had occurred, the opposite rule would apply. The excess of expenses (net loss) would be placed in the credit side of the Income Statement columns as a balancing figure. It would then be extended to the debit side of the Balance Sheet columns because a net loss causes a decrease in owners' equity, which would be shown by a debit.

As a final check, the four columns are totaled again. If the Income Statement columns and the Balance Sheet columns do not balance, there may be an account extended or sorted to the wrong column, or an error may have been made in adding the columns. Equal totals in the two pairs of columns, however, are not absolute proof of accuracy. If an asset has been carried to the debit Income Statement column and a similar error involving revenues or liabilities has been made, the work sheet will still balance, but the net income figure will be wrong.

Uses of the Work Sheet

OBJECTIVE 2
Identify the three principal uses of a work sheet

After all the columns of the work sheet are completed, the work sheet assists the accountant in three principal ways: (1) preparing the financial statements, (2) recording the adjusting entries, and (3) recording the closing entries in the general journal in order to prepare the records for the beginning of the next period.

Preparing the Financial Statements

OBJECTIVE 3
Prepare financial statements from a work sheet

After completion of the work sheet, it is simple to prepare the financial statements because the account balances have been sorted into Income Statement and Balance Sheet columns. The income statement shown in Exhibit 4-6 is prepared from the accounts in the Income Statement columns of Exhibit 4-5.

The statement of retained earnings and the balance sheet of the Joan Miller Advertising Agency, Inc. are presented in Exhibits 4-7 and 4-8. The account balances for these statements are drawn from the Balance Sheet columns of the work sheet shown in Exhibit 4-5. Notice that the totals of the assets and of the liabilities and stockholders' equity in the balance sheet do not agree with the totals of the Balance Sheet columns of the work sheet. Accounts such as Accumulated Depreciation and Dividends have normal balances different from their associated accounts on the balance sheet. In addition, the Retained Earnings account on the balance sheet is the amount determined on the statement of retained earnings. At this point, the financial statements have been prepared from the work

Exhibit 4-6. Income Statement for the Joan Miller Advertising Agency, Inc.

Joan Miller Advertising Agency, Inc. Income Statement For the Month Ended January 31, 19xx		
Revenues		
Advertising Fees Earned	$4,400	
Art Fees Earned	400	
Total Revenues		$4,800
Expenses		
Office Wages Expense	$1,380	
Utility Expense	100	
Telephone Expense	70	
Rent Expense	400	
Insurance Expense	40	
Art Supplies Expense	500	
Office Supplies Expense	200	
Depreciation Expense, Art Equipment	70	
Depreciation Expense, Office Equipment	50	
Income Taxes Expense	400	
Total Expenses		3,210
Net Income		**$1,590**

Exhibit 4-7. Statement of Retained Earnings for Joan Miller Advertising Agency, Inc.

Joan Miller Advertising Agency, Inc. Statement of Retained Earnings For the Month Ended January 31, 19xx	
Retained Earnings, January 1, 19xx	$ 0
Net Income	1,590
Subtotal	$1,590
Less Dividends	1,400
Retained Earnings, January 31, 19xx	$ 190

Exhibit 4-8. Balance Sheet for Joan Miller Advertising Agency, Inc.

Joan Miller Advertising Agency, Inc.
Balance Sheet
January 31, 19xx

Assets		
Cash		$ 1,720
Accounts Receivable		2,800
Fees Receivable		200
Art Supplies		1,300
Office Supplies		600
Prepaid Rent		400
Prepaid Insurance		440
Art Equipment	$ 4,200	
Less Accumulated Depreciation	70	4,130
Office Equipment	$ 3,000	
Less Accumulated Depreciation	50	2,950
Total Assets		$14,540
Liabilities		
Accounts Payable	$ 3,170	
Unearned Art Fees	600	
Wages Payable	180	
Income Taxes Payable	400	
Total Liabilities		$ 4,350
Stockholders' Equity		
Common Stock	$10,000	
Retained Earnings	190	
Total Stockholders' Equity		10,190
Total Liabilities and Stockholders' Equity		$14,540

sheet, not from the ledger accounts. For the ledger accounts to show the correct balances, the adjusting entries have to be journalized and posted to the ledger.

Recording the Adjusting Entries

OBJECTIVE 4 *Record the adjusting entries from a work sheet*

For the Joan Miller Advertising Agency, Inc., the adjustments were determined during completion of the work sheet because they are essential to the preparation of the financial statements. The adjusting entries could have been recorded in the general journal at that point. However, it is usually convenient to delay recording them until after the work sheet and the financial statements have been prepared because this task can be done at the same time as the recording of the closing entries, which is described in the next section. Recording the adjusting entries with appropriate explanations in the general journal, as shown in Exhibit 4-9, is an easy step. The information may simply be copied from the work sheet. Adjusting entries are then posted to the general ledger.

Recording the Closing Entries

OBJECTIVE 5
Explain the purposes of closing entries

Closing entries, which are journal entries made at the end of the accounting period, accomplish two purposes. First, closing entries set the stage for the next accounting period by closing or clearing the expense and revenue accounts of their balances. This step must be carried out because an income statement reports the net income for a single accounting period and shows the expenses and revenues only for that period. Therefore, the expense and revenue accounts must be closed or cleared of their balances at the end of the period so that the next period begins with a zero balance in those accounts. The Dividends account is closed in a similar manner.

The second aim of closing entries is to summarize a period's revenues and expenses. This is done by transferring the balances of revenues and expenses to the Income Summary account and recording the net profit or loss in that account. **Income Summary**, a new temporary account, appears in the chart of accounts between the last owners' equity account and the first revenue account. This account provides a place to summarize all revenues and expenses in a single net figure before transferring the result to the Retained Earnings account. It is used only in the closing process and never appears in the financial statements.

The balance of Income Summary equals the net income or loss reported on the income statement. The net income or loss is then transferred to the Retained Earnings account. This step is needed because, even though expenses and revenues are recorded in expense and revenue accounts, they actually represent decreases and increases in stockholders' equity. Thus, closing entries must transfer the net effect of increases (revenues) and decreases (expenses) to stockholders' equity.

As stated in the chapter on business income and adjusting entries, revenue and expense accounts are called temporary or nominal accounts. Nominal accounts begin each period at zero, accumulate a balance during the period, and return to zero by means of closing entries when the balance is transferred to stockholders' equity. The accountant uses these accounts to keep track of the increases and decreases in stockholders' equity in a way that is helpful to management and others interested in the success or progress of the company. Temporary accounts are different from balance sheet accounts. Balance sheet, or permanent, accounts often begin with a balance, increase or decrease during the period, and carry the end-of-period balance into the next accounting period.

Exhibit 4-9. Adjustments on Work Sheet Entered in the General Journal

General Journal — Page 3

Date		Description	Post. Ref.	Debit	Credit
19xx					
Jan.	31	Rent Expense	514	400	
		Prepaid Rent	117		400
		To recognize expiration of one month's rent			
	31	Insurance Expense	515	40	
		Prepaid Insurance	118		40
		To recognize expiration of one month's insurance			
	31	Art Supplies Expense	516	500	
		Art Supplies	115		500
		To recognize art supplies used during the month			
	31	Office Supplies Expense	517	200	
		Office Supplies	116		200
		To recognize office supplies used during the month			
	31	Depreciation Expense, Art Equipment	519	70	
		Accumulated Depreciation, Art Equipment	145		70
		To record depreciation of art equipment for a month			
	31	Depreciation Expense, Office Equipment	520	50	
		Accumulated Depreciation, Office Equipment	147		50
		To record depreciation of office equipment for a month			
	31	Unearned Art Fees	213	400	
		Art Fees Earned	412		400
		To recognize performance of services paid for in advance			
	31	Fees Receivable	114	200	
		Advertising Fees Earned	411		200
		To accrue advertising fees earned but unrecorded			
	31	Office Wages Expense	511	180	
		Wages Payable	214		180
		To accrue unrecorded wages			
	31	Income Taxes Expense	521	400	
		Income Taxes Payable	215		400
		To accrue estimated income taxes			

Required Closing Entries

OBJECTIVE 6
Prepare the required closing entries

Closing entries consist of four important steps:

1. Transferring the credit balances from income statement accounts to Income Summary
2. Transferring the debit balances from income statement accounts to Income Summary
3. Transferring the Income Summary balance to the Retained Earnings account
4. Transferring the Dividends account balance to the Retained Earnings account

With the exception of the Dividends account balance, all the data needed to perform these closing steps are found in the Income Statement columns of the work sheet.

Closing the Credit Balances from Income Statement Accounts to the Income Summary Account

From the credit side of the Income Statement columns of the work sheet in Exhibit 4-5, two revenue accounts have balances. An entry debiting each of these revenue accounts for the amount of its balance is needed to close the account. The Income Summary account is credited for the total (which can be found in the credit side of the Income Statement columns of the work sheet). The compound entry that closes the two revenue accounts for the Joan Miller Advertising Agency, Inc. is as follows:

Jan.	31	Advertising Fees Earned	411	4,400	
		Art Fees Earned	412	400	
		Income Summary	314		4,800
		To close revenue accounts			

The effect of posting the entry is shown in Exhibit 4-10. Note that the dual effect of the entry is to (1) set the balances of the revenue accounts equal to zero, and (2) transfer the total revenues to the credit side of the Income Summary account. If a work sheet is not used, these data may also be found in the appropriate general ledger accounts after the adjusting entries have been posted.

Closing the Debit Balances from Income Statement Accounts to the Income Summary Account

From the debit side of the Income Statement columns of the work sheet in Exhibit 4-5, several expense accounts have balances. A compound entry is needed crediting each of these expense accounts for its balance and debiting the Income Summary for the total (which can be found in the debit side of the Income Statement columns):

Jan.	31	Income Summary	314	3,210	
		Office Wages Expense	511		1,380
		Utility Expense	512		100
		Telephone Expense	513		70
		Rent Expense	514		400
		Insurance Expense	515		40
		Art Supplies Expense	516		500
		Office Supplies Expense	517		200
		Depreciation Expense, Art Equipment	519		70
		Depreciation Expense, Office Equipment	520		50
		Income Taxes Expense	521		400
		To close the expense accounts			

The effect of posting the closing entries to the ledger accounts is shown in Exhibit 4-11. Note again the double effect of (1) reducing expense account balances to zero and (2) transferring the total of the account balances to the debit side of the Income Summary account.

Closing the Income Summary Account to the Retained Earnings Account

After the entries closing the revenue and expense accounts have been posted, the balance of the Income Summary account is equal to the net income or loss for the period. A net income will be indicated by a credit balance and a net loss by a debit balance. At this point, the Income Summary balance, regardless of its nature, must be closed to the Retained

Exhibit 4-10. Posting the Closing Entry of the Credit Balances from the Income Statement Accounts to the Income Summary Account

Advertising Fees Earned — Account No. 411

Date	Item	Post. Ref.	Debit	Credit	Balance Debit	Balance Credit
Jan. 10		J2		1,400		1,400
19		J2		2,800		4,200
31	Adj. (h)	J3		200		4,400
31	Closing	J4	4,400			—

Art Fees Earned — Account No. 412

Date	Item	Post. Ref.	Debit	Credit	Balance Debit	Balance Credit
Jan. 31	Adj. (g)	J3		400		400
31	Closing	J4	400			—

4,400
400
4,800

Income Summary — Account No. 314

Date	Item	Post. Ref.	Debit	Credit	Balance Debit	Balance Credit
Jan. 31	Closing	J4		4,800		4,800

Exhibit 4-11. Posting the Closing Entry of the Expense Accounts to the Income Summary Account

Office Wages Expense — Account No. 511

Date	Item	Post. Ref.	Debit	Credit	Balance Debit	Balance Credit
Jan. 12		J2	600		600	
26		J2	600		1,200	
31	Adj. (i)	J3	180		1,380	
31	Closing	J4		1,380	—	

Utility Expense — Account No. 512

Date	Item	Post. Ref.	Debit	Credit	Balance Debit	Balance Credit
Jan. 29		J2	100		100	
31	Closing	J4		100	—	

Telephone Expense — Account No. 513

Date	Item	Post. Ref.	Debit	Credit	Balance Debit	Balance Credit
Jan. 30		J2	70		70	
31	Closing	J4		70	—	

Rent Expense — Account No. 514

Date	Item	Post. Ref.	Debit	Credit	Balance Debit	Balance Credit
Jan. 31	Adj. (a)	J3	400		400	
31	Closing	J4		400	—	

Insurance Expense — Account No. 515

Date	Item	Post. Ref.	Debit	Credit	Balance Debit	Balance Credit
Jan. 31	Adj. (b)	J3	40		40	
31	Closing	J4		40	—	

Art Supplies Expense — Account No. 516

Date	Item	Post. Ref.	Debit	Credit	Balance Debit	Balance Credit
Jan. 31	Adj. (c)	J3	500		500	
31	Closing	J4		500	—	

Office Supplies Expense — Account No. 517

Date	Item	Post. Ref.	Debit	Credit	Balance Debit	Balance Credit
Jan. 31	Adj. (d)	J3	200		200	
31	Closing	J4		200	—	

Income Summary — Account No. 314

Date	Item	Post. Ref.	Debit	Credit	Balance Debit	Balance Credit
Jan. 31	Closing	J4		4,800		4,800
31	Closing	J4	3,210			1,590

1,380
100
70
400
40
500
400
50
70
200
3,210

Depreciation Expense, Art Equipment — Account No. 519

Date	Item	Post. Ref.	Debit	Credit	Balance Debit	Balance Credit
Jan. 31	Adj. (e)	J3	70		70	
31	Closing	J4		70	—	

Depreciation Expense, Office Equipment — Account No. 520

Date	Item	Post. Ref.	Debit	Credit	Balance Debit	Balance Credit
Jan. 31	Adj. (f)	J3	50		50	
31	Closing	J4		50	—	

Income Taxes Expense — Account No. 521

Date	Item	Post. Ref.	Debit	Credit	Balance Debit	Balance Credit
Jan. 31	Adj. (j)	J3	400		400	
31	Closing	J4		400	—	

Exhibit 4-12. Posting the Closing Entry of the Income Summary Account to the Retained Earnings Account

Income Summary — Account No. 314

Date	Item	Post. Ref.	Debit	Credit	Balance Debit	Balance Credit
Jan. 31	Closing	J4		4,800		4,800
31	Closing	J4	3,210			1,590
31	Closing	J4	1,590			—

Retained Earnings — Account No. 312

Date	Item	Post. Ref.	Debit	Credit	Balance Debit	Balance Credit
Jan. 31	Closing	J4		1,590		1,590

Earnings account. For the Joan Miller Advertising Agency, Inc. the entry is as follows:

Jan. 31	Income Summary	314	1,590	
	Retained Earnings	312		1,590
	To close the Income Summary account			

The effect of posting the closing entry is shown in Exhibit 4-12. Note again the double effect of (1) closing the Income Summary account balance and (2) transferring the balance, net income in this case, to the Retained Earnings account.

Closing the Dividends Account to the Retained Earnings Account

The Dividends account shows the amount by which retained earnings is reduced during the period by cash dividends. The debit balance of the Dividends account is closed to the Retained Earnings account, as follows:

Jan. 31	Retained Earnings	312	1,400	
	Dividends	313		1,400
	To close the Dividends account			

The effect of posting this closing entry is shown in Exhibit 4-13. The double effect of the entry is to (1) close the Dividends account of its balance and (2) transfer the balance to the Retained Earnings account.

Exhibit 4-13. Posting the Closing Entry of the Dividends Account to the Retained Earnings Account

Dividends — Account No. 313

Date	Item	Post. Ref.	Debit	Credit	Balance Debit	Balance Credit
Jan. 25		J2	1,400		1,400	
31	Closing	J4		1,400	—	

Retained Earnings — Account No. 312

Date	Item	Post. Ref.	Debit	Credit	Balance Debit	Balance Credit
Jan. 31	Closing	J4		1,590		1,590
31	Closing	J4	1,400			190

The Accounts After Closing

After all the steps in the closing process have been completed and all the adjusting and closing entries have been posted to the accounts, the stage is set for the next accounting period. The ledger accounts of the Joan Miller Advertising Agency, Inc. as they appear at this point are shown in Exhibit 4-14. The revenue, expense, and Dividends accounts (temporary accounts) have zero balances. Retained Earnings has been increased or decreased depending on net income or loss and dividends paid. The balance sheet accounts (permanent accounts) have the appropriate balances, which are carried forward to the next period.

The Post-Closing Trial Balance

OBJECTIVE 7
Prepare the post-closing trial balance

Because it is possible to make an error in posting the adjustments and closing entries to the ledger accounts, it is necessary to determine that all temporary (nominal) accounts have zero balances and to retest the equality of total debits and credits by preparing a new trial balance. This final trial balance, called a **post-closing trial balance**, is shown in Exhibit 4-15 for the Joan Miller Advertising Agency, Inc. (see page 185). Notice that only balance sheet (permanent) accounts have balances since the income statement accounts and the Dividends account have all been closed.

Reversing Entries: Optional First Step of the Next Accounting Period

OBJECTIVE 8
Prepare reversing entries as appropriate

At the end of each accounting period, adjusting entries are made to bring revenues and expenses into conformity with the matching rule. A **reversing entry** is a general journal entry made on the first day of the new accounting period that is the exact reverse of an adjusting entry made in the previous period. Reversing entries are optional journal entries that are intended to simplify the bookkeeping process for transactions involving certain types of adjustments. Not all adjusting entries may be reversed. For the system of recording used in this book, only adjustments for accruals (accrued revenues and accrued expenses) may be reversed. Deferrals cannot be reversed, as reversing adjustments for deferrals would not simplify the bookkeeping process in future accounting periods.

To show how reversing entries can be helpful, consider the adjusting entry made in the records of the Joan Miller Advertising Agency, Inc. to accrue office wages expense:

Jan.	31	Office Wages Expense	180	
		Wages Payable		180
		To accrue unrecorded wages		

Exhibit 4-14. The Accounts After Closing Entries Are Posted

Cash — Account No. 111

Date	Item	Post. Ref.	Debit	Credit	Balance Debit	Balance Credit
Jan. 1		J1	10,000		10,000	
2		J1		800	9,200	
4		J1		4,200	5,000	
5		J1		1,500	3,500	
8		J1		480	3,020	
9		J1		1,000	2,020	
10		J2	1,400		3,420	
12		J2		600	2,820	
15		J2	1,000		3,820	
26		J2		600	3,220	
29		J2		100	3,120	
31		J2		1,400	1,720	

Accounts Receivable — Account No. 113

Date	Item	Post. Ref.	Debit	Credit	Balance Debit	Balance Credit
Jan. 19		J2	2,800		2,800	

Fees Receivable — Account No. 114

Date	Item	Post. Ref.	Debit	Credit	Balance Debit	Balance Credit
Jan. 31	Adj. (h)	J3	200		200	

Art Supplies — Account No. 115

Date	Item	Post. Ref.	Debit	Credit	Balance Debit	Balance Credit
Jan. 6		J1	1,800		1,800	
31	Adj. (c)	J3		500	1,300	

Office Supplies — Account No. 116

Date	Item	Post. Ref.	Debit	Credit	Balance Debit	Balance Credit
Jan. 6		J1	800		800	
31	Adj. (d)	J3		200	600	

Prepaid Rent — Account No. 117

Date	Item	Post. Ref.	Debit	Credit	Balance Debit	Balance Credit
Jan. 2		J1	800		800	
31	Adj. (a)	J3		400	400	

Prepaid Insurance — Account No. 118

Date	Item	Post. Ref.	Debit	Credit	Balance Debit	Balance Credit
Jan. 8		J1	480		480	
31	Adj. (b)	J3		40	440	

Art Equipment — Account No. 144

Date	Item	Post. Ref.	Debit	Credit	Balance Debit	Balance Credit
Jan. 4		J1	4,200		4,200	

Accumulated Depreciation, Art Equipment — Account No. 145

Date	Item	Post. Ref.	Debit	Credit	Balance Debit	Balance Credit
Jan. 31	Adj. (e)	J3		70		70

Office Equipment — Account No. 146

Date	Item	Post. Ref.	Debit	Credit	Balance Debit	Balance Credit
Jan. 5		J1	3,000		3,000	

Accumulated Depreciation, Office Equipment — Account No. 147

Date	Item	Post. Ref.	Debit	Credit	Balance Debit	Balance Credit
Jan. 31	Adj. (f)	J3		50		50

Accounts Payable — Account No. 212

Date	Item	Post. Ref.	Debit	Credit	Balance Debit	Balance Credit
Jan. 5		J1		1,500		1,500
6		J1		2,600		4,100
9		J1	1,000			3,100
30		J2		70		3,170

Unearned Art Fees — Account No. 213

Date	Item	Post. Ref.	Debit	Credit	Balance Debit	Balance Credit
Jan. 15		J2		1,000		1,000
31	Adj. (g)	J3	400			600

Wages Payable — Account No. 214

Date	Item	Post. Ref.	Debit	Credit	Balance Debit	Balance Credit
Jan. 31	Adj. (i)	J3		180		180

Income Taxes Payable — Account No. 215

Date	Item	Post. Ref.	Debit	Credit	Balance Debit	Balance Credit
Jan. 31	Adj. (j)	J3		400		400

Exhibit 4-14. *(continued)*

Common Stock — Account No. 311

Date	Item	Post. Ref.	Debit	Credit	Balance Debit	Balance Credit
Jan. 1		J1		10,000		10,000

Retained Earnings — Account No. 312

Date	Item	Post. Ref.	Debit	Credit	Balance Debit	Balance Credit
Jan. 31	Closing	J4		1,590		1,590
31	Closing	J4	1,400			190

Dividends — Account No. 313

Date	Item	Post. Ref.	Debit	Credit	Balance Debit	Balance Credit
Jan. 31		J2	1,400		1,400	
31	Closing	J4		1,400	—	

Income Summary — Account No. 314

Date	Item	Post. Ref.	Debit	Credit	Balance Debit	Balance Credit
Jan. 31	Closing	J4		4,800		4,800
31	Closing	J4	3,210			1,590
31	Closing	J4	1,590			—

Advertising Fees Earned — Account No. 411

Date	Item	Post. Ref.	Debit	Credit	Balance Debit	Balance Credit
Jan. 10		J2		1,400		1,400
19		J2		2,800		4,200
31	Adj. (h)	J3		200		4,400
31	Closing	J4	4,400			—

Art Fees Earned — Account No. 412

Date	Item	Post. Ref.	Debit	Credit	Balance Debit	Balance Credit
Jan. 31	Adj. (g)	J3		400		400
31	Closing	J4	400			—

Office Wages Expense — Account No. 511

Date	Item	Post. Ref.	Debit	Credit	Balance Debit	Balance Credit
Jan. 12		J2	600		600	
26		J2	600		1,200	
31	Adj. (i)	J3	180		1,380	
31	Closing	J4		1,380	—	

Utility Expense — Account No. 512

Date	Item	Post. Ref.	Debit	Credit	Balance Debit	Balance Credit
Jan. 29		J2	100		100	
31	Closing	J4		100	—	

Telephone Expense — Account No. 513

Date	Item	Post. Ref.	Debit	Credit	Balance Debit	Balance Credit
Jan. 30		J2	70		70	
31	Closing	J4		70	—	

Rent Expense — Account No. 514

Date	Item	Post. Ref.	Debit	Credit	Balance Debit	Balance Credit
Jan. 31	Adj. (a)	J3	400		400	
31	Closing	J4		400	—	

Insurance Expense — Account No. 515

Date	Item	Post. Ref.	Debit	Credit	Balance Debit	Balance Credit
Jan. 31	Adj. (b)	J3	40		40	
31	Closing	J4		40	—	

Art Supplies Expense — Account No. 516

Date	Item	Post. Ref.	Debit	Credit	Balance Debit	Balance Credit
Jan. 31	Adj. (c)	J3	500		500	
31	Closing	J4		500	—	

Office Supplies Expense — Account No. 517

Date	Item	Post. Ref.	Debit	Credit	Balance Debit	Balance Credit
Jan. 31	Adj. (d)	J3	200		200	
31	Closing	J4		200	—	

Depreciation Expense, Art Equipment — Account No. 519

Date	Item	Post. Ref.	Debit	Credit	Balance Debit	Balance Credit
Jan. 31	Adj. (e)	J3	70		70	
31	Closing	J4		70	—	

Exhibit 4-14. *(continued)*

Depreciation Expense, Office Equipment					Account No. 520	
					Balance	
Date	Item	Post. Ref.	Debit	Credit	Debit	Credit
Jan. 31	Adj. (f)	J3	50		50	
31	Closing	J4		50	—	

Income Taxes Expense					Account No. 521	
					Balance	
Date	Item	Post. Ref.	Debit	Credit	Debit	Credit
Jan. 31	Adj. (j)	J3	400		400	
31	Closing	J4		400	—	

Exhibit 4-15. Post-Closing Trial Balance

Joan Miller Advertising Agency, Inc.
Post-Closing Trial Balance,
January 31, 19xx

Cash	$ 1,720	
Accounts Receivable	2,800	
Fees Receivable	200	
Art Supplies	1,300	
Office Supplies	600	
Prepaid Rent	400	
Prepaid Insurance	440	
Art Equipment	4,200	
Accumulated Depreciation, Art Equipment		$ 70
Office Equipment	3,000	
Accumulated Depreciation, Office Equipment		50
Accounts Payable		3,170
Unearned Art Fees		600
Wages Payable		180
Income Taxes Payable		400
Common Stock		10,000
Retained Earnings		190
	$14,660	$14,660

When the secretary is paid on the next regular payday, the accountant would make the entry below, using the accounting procedure that you know to this point:

Feb. 9	Wages Payable	180	
	Office Wages Expense	420	
	Cash		600
	To record payment of two weeks' wages to secretary, $180 of which accrued in the previous period		

Note that when the payment is made, without a prior reversing entry, the accountant must look in the records to find out how much of the $600 applied to the current accounting period and how much was applicable to the previous period. This step may appear easy in this simple case, but think of how difficult and time-consuming it would be if the company had many employees, especially if some of them are paid on different time schedules, such as weekly or monthly. A reversing entry is an accounting procedure that helps to solve this problem of applying revenues and expenses to the correct accounting period. As noted above, a reversing entry is exactly what its name implies. It is a reversal of the adjusting entry made by debiting the credits and crediting the debits of the adjusting entry. For example, note the following sequence of transactions and their effects on the ledger account for Office Wages Expense.

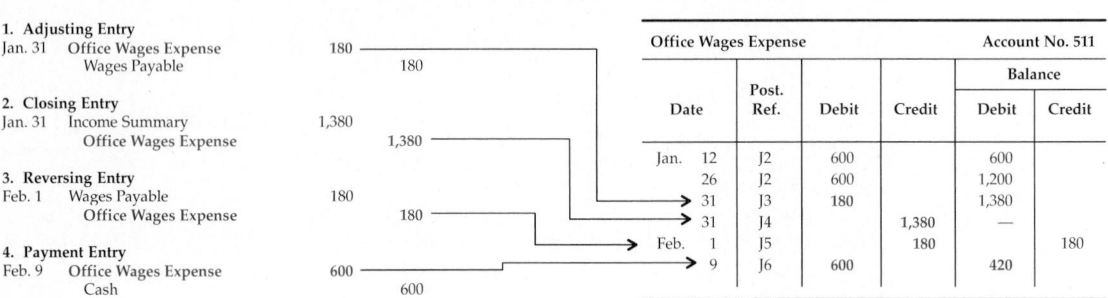

1. Adjusting Entry			
Jan. 31	Office Wages Expense	180	
	Wages Payable		180
2. Closing Entry			
Jan. 31	Income Summary	1,380	
	Office Wages Expense		1,380
3. Reversing Entry			
Feb. 1	Wages Payable	180	
	Office Wages Expense		180
4. Payment Entry			
Feb. 9	Office Wages Expense	600	
	Cash		600

Office Wages Expense — Account No. 511

Date		Post. Ref.	Debit	Credit	Balance Debit	Balance Credit
Jan.	12	J2	600		600	
	26	J2	600		1,200	
	31	J3	180		1,380	
	31	J4		1,380	—	
Feb.	1	J5		180		180
	9	J6	600		420	

These transactions had the following effects on Office Wages Expense:

1. Adjusted Office Wages Expense to accrue $180 in the January accounting period.
2. Closed the $1,380 in total Office Wages Expense for January to Income Summary, leaving a zero balance.
3. Set up a credit balance of $180 on February 1 in Office Wages Expense equal to the expense recognized through the adjusting entry in January (and also reduced the liability account Wages Payable to a zero balance). Note that the reversing entry always sets up a non-normal balance in the income statement account and a zero balance in the balance sheet account.
4. Recorded the $600 payment of two weeks' wages as a debit to Office Wages Expense, automatically leaving a balance of $420, which represents the correct wages expense so far for February.

Making the February 9 payment entry was simplified by the reversing entry. Reversing entries apply to any accrued expenses or revenues. In the case of the Joan Miller Advertising Agency, Inc., Income Taxes Expense is also an accrued expense and thus needs to be reversed. Further, the asset Fees Receivable was created as a result of the adjusting entry made to accrue fees earned but not yet billed. The adjusting entry for this accrued revenue would therefore require a reversing entry. These two additional reversing entries are as follows:

Feb.	1	Income Taxes Payable	400	
		Income Taxes Expense		400
		To reverse adjusting entry for estimated income taxes		
	1	Advertising Fees Earned	200	
		Fees Receivable		200
		To reverse adjusting entry for accrued fees receivable		

When the series of advertisements is finished, the company can credit the entire proceeds to Advertising Fees Earned without regard to the amount accrued in the previous period. The credit will automatically be reduced to the amount earned during February by the $200 debit in the account.

As noted above, under the system of recording used in this book, reversing entries apply only to accruals. Reversing entries do not apply to deferrals, such as those that involve supplies, prepaid rent, prepaid insurance, depreciation, and unearned art fees.

Chapter Review

Review of Learning Objectives

1. **Prepare a work sheet.**
   A work sheet is prepared by first entering the account balances in the Trial Balance columns, the adjustments in the Adjustments columns, and the adjusted account balances in the Adjusted Trial Balance columns. Then the amounts from the Adjusted Trial Balance columns are extended to the Income Statement or Balance Sheet columns as appropriate. Next, the Income Statement and Balance Sheet columns are totaled. Net income or net loss is determined from the Income Statement columns and extended to the Balance Sheet columns. The statement columns are now added to determine that they are in balance.
2. **Identify the three principal uses of a work sheet.**
   A work sheet is useful in (1) preparing the financial statements, (2) recording the adjusting entries, and (3) recording the closing entries.
3. **Prepare financial statements from a work sheet.**
   The balance sheet and income statement can be prepared directly from the Balance Sheet and Income Statement columns of a completed work sheet. The statement of retained earnings is also prepared using dividends, net income, and the beginning balance of Retained Earnings. Note that the ending balance of Retained Earnings does not appear on the work sheet but is a result of it.
4. **Record the adjusting entries from a work sheet.**
   Adjusting entries can be recorded in the general journal directly from the Adjustments columns of the work sheet.

5. **Explain the purposes of closing entries.**
Closing entries have two objectives. First, they transfer the balances of all temporary accounts, including the revenue and expense accounts, and dividends, so that they will have zero balances for the next accounting period. Second, they summarize a period's revenues and expenses in the Income Summary so that the net income or loss for the period may be transferred as a total to Retained Earnings.

6. **Prepare the required closing entries.**
Closing entries are prepared by first transferring the revenue and expense account balances (credit and debit entries in the Income Statement columns of the work sheet) to the Income Summary account. Then the balance of the Income Summary account is transferred to the Retained Earnings account. And finally, the balance of the Dividends account is transferred to the Retained Earnings account.

7. **Prepare the post-closing trial balance.**
As a final check on the balance of the ledger and to ensure that all temporary (nominal) accounts have been closed, a post-closing trial balance is prepared after the closing entries are posted to the ledger accounts.

8. **Prepare reversing entries as appropriate.**
Reversing entries are optional general journal entries made on the first day of a new accounting period. They exactly reverse certain adjusting entries made in the prior period. Under the system used in this text, they apply only to accruals and facilitate routine bookkeeping procedures.

Review of Concepts and Terminology

The following concepts and terms were introduced in this chapter:

(L.O. 5) **Closing entries:** Journal entries made at the end of the accounting period that set the stage for the next accounting period by clearing the temporary accounts of their balances.

(L.O. 1) **Crossfooting:** Horizontal addition and subtraction of adjacent columns on the same row.

(L.O. 5) **Income Summary:** A temporary account used during the closing process in which all revenues and expenses are summarized before the net income or loss is transferred to Retained Earnings.

(L.O. 7) **Post-closing trial balance:** A trial balance prepared at the end of the accounting period after all adjusting and closing entries have been posted. It serves as a final check on the balance of the ledger.

(L.O. 8) **Reversing entry:** Entry made at the beginning of the accounting period after the closing of records for the prior accounting period; used to reverse certain adjusting entries and designed to aid in routine bookkeeping for the next accounting period.

(L.O. 1) **Working papers:** Documents prepared and used by the accountant that aid in organizing the accountant's work and provide evidence to support the financial statements.

(L.O. 1) **Work sheet:** A type of working paper that is used as a preliminary step in and aid to the preparation of financial statements.

Review Problem
Completion of Work Sheet; Preparation of Financial Statements, Adjusting Entries, and Closing Entries

(L.O. 1, 3, 4, 6, 7) This chapter contains an extended example of the preparation of a work sheet and the last two steps of the accounting cycle for the Joan Miller Advertising Agency, Inc. Instead of studying a demonstration problem, carefully review and retrace the steps through the illustrations in the chapter.

Required

1. In Exhibit 4-5, what is the source of the trial balance figures?
2. Trace the entries in the Adjustments columns of Exhibit 4-5 to the journal entries in Exhibit 4-9.
3. Trace the journal entries in Exhibit 4-9 to the ledger accounts in Exhibit 4-14.
4. Trace the amounts in the Income Statement and Balance Sheet columns of Exhibit 4-5 to the income statement in Exhibit 4-6, the statement of retained earnings in Exhibit 4-7, and the balance sheet in Exhibit 4-8.
5. Trace the amounts in the Income Statement columns and the Dividends account balance of Exhibit 4-5 to the closing entries on page 179.
6. Trace the closing entries on page 179 to the ledger accounts in Exhibit 4-14.
7. Trace the balances of the ledger accounts in Exhibit 4-14 to the post-closing trial balance in Exhibit 4-15.

Chapter Assignments

Discussion Questions

1. Why are working papers important to the accountant?
2. Why are work sheets never published and rarely seen by management?
3. Is the work sheet a substitute for the financial statements? Discuss.
4. At the end of the accounting period, does the posting of adjusting entries to the ledger precede or follow the preparation of the work sheet?
5. What is the normal balance of the following accounts in terms of debit and credit? Cash; Accounts Payable; Prepaid Rent; Common Stock; Commission Revenue; Dividends; Rent Expense; Accumulated Depreciation, Office Equipment; Office Equipment.
6. What is the probable cause of a credit balance in the Cash account?
7. Should the Adjusted Trial Balance columns of the work sheet be totaled before or after the adjusted amounts are carried to the Income Statement and Balance Sheet columns? Discuss.
8. What sequence should be followed in extending the Adjusted Trial Balance columns to the Income Statement and Balance Sheet columns? Discuss your answers.
9. Do the totals of the Balance Sheet columns of the work sheet agree with the totals on the balance sheet? Explain.
10. Do the Income Statement columns and Balance Sheet columns of the work sheet balance after the amounts from the Adjusted Trial Balance columns are extended?
11. What is the purpose of the Income Summary account?

12. Should adjusting entries be posted to the ledger accounts before or after the closing entries? Explain.
13. What is the difference between adjusting and closing entries?
14. What are the four basic tasks of closing entries?
15. Which of the following accounts will not have a balance after closing entries are prepared and posted? Insurance Expense, Accounts Receivable, Commission Revenue, Prepaid Insurance, Dividends, Supplies, Supplies Expense.
16. What is the significance of the post-closing trial balance?
17. Which of the following accounts would you expect to find on the post-closing trial balance? Insurance Expense, Accounts Receivable, Commission Revenue, Prepaid Insurance, Dividends, Supplies, Supplies Expense, Retained Earnings.
18. How can reversing entries aid in the bookkeeping process?
19. To what types of adjustments do reversing entries apply? To what types do they not apply?

Communication Skills Exercises

Communication 4-1. Interim Financial Statements *(L.O. 1–8)*

Ocean Oil Services Corporation provides services for offshore drilling operations off the coast of Louisiana. The company has a significant amount of debt to River National Bank in Baton Rouge. The bank requires the company to provide it with financial statements every quarter. What is involved in preparing financial statements every quarter?

Communication 4-2. Accounting Efficiency *(L.O. 4, 5, 8)*

Way Heaters, Inc. is a small, successful manufacturer of industrial heaters located just outside Milwaukee, Wisconsin. The company's heaters are used, for instance, to heat foods such as chocolate for candy manufacturers. The company sells its heaters by making loans to its customers. These loans are usually due six months after purchase. The loans carry a specified interest rate, in this case based on current bank rates. Since the interest on these loans accrues a little bit every day but is not paid until the due date of the note, it is necessary to make an adjusting entry at the end of each accounting period to debit Interest Receivable and credit Interest Income for the amount of the interest accrued but not paid to date. Since the company prepares financial statements every month, keeping track of what has been accrued in the past is a time-consuming problem for the accountant because the notes carry various dates and interest rates. What can the accountant do to make this detailed procedure of making the adjusting entry for accrued interest each month easier?

Communication 4-3. Basic Research Skills *(L.O. 3–8)*

Arrange to interview the owner, manager, or accountant of a local service or retail business for about one hour. Your objective is to learn as much as you can in that time about the accounting system or cycle of the business. Ask the person being interviewed to show you his or her accounting records and to tell you how such transactions as sales, purchases, payments, and payroll are handled. Examine the documents used to support these transactions. Look at any journals, ledgers, or work sheets that he or she may use. Does the business use a computer? Does it use its own accounting system, or does it use an outside or centralized service? Does it use the cash or accrual basis of accounting? When does it prepare adjusting entries? When does it prepare closing entries? How often does it prepare financial statements? Does it prepare reversing entries? How do its procedures differ from those illustrated in the text? When the interview is finished, write up your findings in an organized manner and be prepared to present them to your class.

Classroom Exercises

Exercise 4-1. Preparation of Trial Balance *(L.O. 1)*

The following alphabetical list represents the accounts and balances for Sklar Realty, Inc. on December 31, 19xx. All accounts have normal balances.

Accounts Payable	$ 5,140
Accounts Receivable	2,550
Accumulated Depreciation, Office Equipment	450
Advertising Expense	600
Cash	2,545
Common Stock	10,210
Dividends	9,000
Office Equipment	5,170
Prepaid Insurance	560
Rent Expense	2,400
Revenue from Commissions	19,300
Supplies	275
Wages Expense	12,000

Prepare a trial balance by listing the accounts in proper order, with the balances in the appropriate debit or credit column.

Exercise 4-2. Preparation of Statement of Retained Earnings *(L.O. 3)*

The Retained Earnings, Dividends, and Income Summary accounts for Ruben's Barber Shop, Inc. are presented in T account form below. The closing entries have been recorded for the year ended December 31, 19xx.

Retained Earnings

Debit		Credit	
12/31	9,000	1/1	26,000
		12/31	19,000
		Bal.	**36,000**

Dividends

Debit		Credit	
4/1	3,000	12/31	9,000
7/1	3,000		
10/1	3,000		
Bal.	—		

Income Summary

Debit		Credit	
12/31	43,000	12/31	62,000
12/31	19,000		
Bal.	—		

Prepare a statement of retained earnings for Ruben's Barber Shop, Inc.

Exercise 4-3. Preparation of Adjusting and Reversing Entries from Work Sheet Columns *(L.O. 4, 8)*

The items listed at the top of the next page are from the Adjustments columns of a work sheet as of December 31.

1. Prepare the adjusting entries from the information.
2. If required, prepare appropriate reversing entries.

Account Name	Adjustments	
	Debit	Credit
Prepaid Insurance		(a) 120
Office Supplies		(b) 315
Accumulated Depreciation, Office Equipment		(c) 700
Accumulated Depreciation, Store Equipment		(d) 1,100
Office Salaries Expense	(e) 120	
Store Salaries Expense	(e) 240	
Insurance Expense	(a) 120	
Office Supplies Expense	(b) 315	
Depreciation Expense, Office Equipment	(c) 700	
Depreciation Expense, Store Equipment	(d) 1,100	
Salaries Payable		(e) 360
Income Taxes Expense	(f) 400	
Income Taxes Payable		(f) 400
	2,995	2,995

Exercise 4-4. Preparation of Closing Entries from Work Sheet *(L.O. 6)*

The following items are from the Income Statement columns of the work sheet of the DiPietro Repair Shop, Inc. for the year ended December 31, 19xx.

Account Name	Income Statement	
	Debit	Credit
Repair Revenue		25,620
Wages Expense	8,110	
Rent Expense	1,200	
Supplies Expense	4,260	
Insurance Expense	915	
Depreciation Expense, Repair Equipment	1,345	
Income Taxes Expense	1,000	
	16,830	25,620
Net Income	8,790	
	25,620	25,620

Prepare entries to close the revenue, expense, Income Summary, and Dividends accounts. Dividends of $5,000 were paid during the year.

Exercise 4-5. Completion of Work Sheet *(L.O. 1)*

The following is a list of alphabetically arranged accounts and balances, in highly simplified form. This information is for the month ended October 31, 19xx.

Trial Balance Accounts and Balances

Accounts Payable	$ 4	Office Equipment	$ 8
Accounts Receivable	7	Prepaid Insurance	2
Accumulated Depreciation, Office Equipment	1	Service Revenue	23
Cash	4	Supplies	4
Common Stock	12	Unearned Revenue	3
Dividends	6	Utility Expense	2
		Wages Expense	10

1. Prepare a work sheet, entering the trial balance accounts in the order in which they would normally appear, and arranging the balances in the correct debit or credit column.
2. Complete the work sheet using the following information:
   a. Expired insurance, $1.
   b. Of the unearned revenue balance, $2 has been earned by the end of the month.
   c. Estimated depreciation on office equipment, $1.
   d. Accrued wages, $1.
   e. Unused supplies on hand, $1.
   f. Estimated income taxes, $1.

Exercise 4-6. Derivation of Adjusting Entries from Trial Balance and Income Statement Columns *(L.O. 3, 4)*

Presented below is a partial work sheet in which the Trial Balance and Income Statement columns have been completed. All amounts shown are in dollars.

Account Name	Trial Balance		Income Statement	
	Debit	Credit	Debit	Credit
Cash	8			
Accounts Receivable	12			
Supplies	11			
Prepaid Insurance	8			
Building	25			
Accumulated Depreciation, Building		8		
Accounts Payable		4		
Unearned Revenue		2		
Common Stock		20		
Retained Earnings		12		
Revenue		45		47
Wages Expense	27		30	
	91	91		
Insurance Expense			4	
Supplies Expense			8	
Depreciation Expense, Building			2	
Income Taxes Expense			1	
			45	47
Net Income			2	
			47	47

1. Determine the adjustments that have been made. Assume that no adjustments are made to Accounts Receivable or Accounts Payable.
2. Prepare a balance sheet.

Exercise 4-7.
Reversing Entries
(L.O. 8)

Selected December T accounts for Jefferson Corporation are presented below:

Supplies

12/1 Bal.	430	12/31 Adjust.	640
Dec. purchases	470		
Bal.	**260**		

Supplies Expense

12/31 Adjust.	640	12/31 Closing	640
Bal.	—		

Wages Payable

		12/31 Adjust.	320
		Bal.	**320**

Wages Expense

Dec. wages	1,970	12/31 Closing	2,290
12/31 Adjust.	320		
Bal.	—		

1. In which case is a reversing entry helpful? Why?
2. Prepare the appropriate reversing entry.
3. Prepare the entry to record payments on January 5 for wages totaling $1,570. How much is Wages Expense for January?

Interpretation Cases from Business

ICB 4-1.
H & R Block, Inc.[1]
(L.O. 5, 6)

H & R Block, Inc. is the largest tax preparation services firm. In its 1990 annual report, the statement of earnings (without earnings per share information) for the year ended April 30, 1990, appeared as presented at the top of the next page (in thousands).

It should be noted from H & R Block's statement of retained earnings (not shown here) that cash dividends for 1990 were $69,539,000.

Required

1. Prepare closing entries in general journal form that would have been made by H & R Block on April 30, 1990.
2. On the basis of the way you handled expenses and dividends in **1** and their ultimate effect on Retained Earnings, what theoretical reason can you give for not including expenses and dividends in the same closing entry?

1. Excerpts from the 1990 Annual Report used by permission of H & R Block. Copyright © 1990.

Revenues	
Service Revenues	$ 937,796
Royalties	89,800
Investment Income	15,852
Other Revenues	9,248
Total Revenues	$1,052,696
Expenses	
Employee Compensation and Benefits	$492,840
Occupancy and Equipment Expense	152,370
Marketing and Advertising	69,367
Supplies, Freight, and Postage	43,516
Other Operating Expenses	94,069
Total Expenses	$852,162
Earnings Before Income Taxes	$200,534
Income Taxes	77,005
Net Earnings	$123,529

ICB 4-2. Halliburton Company[2] *(L.O. 4, 5)*

Halliburton Company is one of the world's larger and more diversified oil field services and engineering/construction organizations. The following items appeared on the December 31, 1990, balance sheet of Halliburton Company (in millions). The contracts referred to are contracts to perform services for engineering/construction clients.

Among the assets:	
Unbilled Work on Uncompleted Contracts	$202.1
Among the liabilities:	
Advance Billings on Uncompleted Contracts	$151.3

Contained in Note 1:

Unbilled work on uncompleted contracts generally represents currently billable work, and such work is usually billed during normal billing processes in the next month.

Required

1. Which of the two accounts above arises from an adjusting entry? What would be the debit and credit accounts of the entry?
2. Which of the two accounts above would normally require an adjusting entry at the end of the accounting period? What are the debit and credit accounts of the entry?
3. How does the accounting policy described in Note 1 differ from the general rule covered in this text? Why does it differ?
4. Of the four accounts you mentioned in the adjusting entries in **1** and **2** above, which require closing at the end of the year?

2. Excerpts from the 1990 Annual Report used by permission of Halliburton Company. Copyright © 1990.

Problem Set A

Problem 4A-1. Preparation of Financial Statements and End-of-Period Entries *(L.O. 3, 6, 8)*

Hillcrest Campgrounds, Inc. rents one hundred campsites in a wooded park to campers. The adjusted trial balance for Hillcrest Campgrounds, Inc. on May 31, 19x2, the end of the current fiscal year, is presented below.

Hillcrest Campgrounds, Inc.
Adjusted Trial Balance
May 31, 19x2

Cash	$ 2,040	
Accounts Receivable	3,660	
Supplies	114	
Prepaid Insurance	594	
Land	15,000	
Building	45,900	
Accumulated Depreciation, Building		$ 10,500
Accounts Payable		1,725
Wages Payable		825
Common Stock		20,000
Retained Earnings		26,535
Dividends	18,000	
Campsite Rentals		44,100
Wages Expense	11,925	
Insurance Expense	1,892	
Utility Expense	900	
Supplies Expense	660	
Depreciation Expense, Building	3,000	
Income Taxes Expense	5,000	
Income Taxes Payable		5,000
	$108,685	$108,685

Required

1. From the information given, prepare an income statement, a statement of retained earnings, and a balance sheet. Assume no additional investments by the stockholders.
2. Record the closing entries in the general journal.
3. Assuming Wages Payable and Income Taxes Payable represent wages and taxes accrued at the end of the accounting period, record the reversing entries required on June 1.

Problem 4A-2. Preparation of Work Sheet; Adjusting, Closing, and Reversing Entries
(L.O. 1, 3, 4, 6, 8)

Jose Vargas opened his executive search service on July 1, 19xx. Some customers paid for his services after they were rendered, and others paid in advance for one year of service. After six months of operation, Jose wanted to know how his business stood. The trial balance on December 31 appears below:

Vargas Executive Search Service, Inc.
Trial Balance
December 31, 19xx

Cash	$ 1,713	
Prepaid Rent	1,800	
Office Supplies	413	
Office Equipment	15,750	
Accounts Payable		$ 3,173
Unearned Revenue		1,823
Common Stock		10,000
Dividends	5,200	
Search Revenue		20,140
Telephone and Utility Expense	1,260	
Wages Expense	9,000	
	$35,136	$35,136

Required

1. Enter the trial balance amounts in the Trial Balance columns of the work sheet. Remember that accumulated depreciation is listed with its asset account. Complete the work sheet using the following information:
   a. One year's rent had been paid in advance when Mr. Vargas began business.
   b. Inventory of unused office supplies, $75.
   c. One-half year's depreciation on office equipment, $900.
   d. Service rendered that had been paid for in advance, $863.
   e. Executive search services rendered during the month but not yet billed, $270.
   f. Wages earned by employees but not yet paid, $188.
   g. Estimated income taxes for the half-year, $2,000.
2. From the work sheet, prepare an income statement, a statement of retained earnings, and a balance sheet.
3. From the work sheet, prepare adjusting and closing entries and, if required, reversing entries.
4. What is your evaluation of Mr. Vargas's first six months in business?

Problem 4A-3. Completion of Work Sheet; Preparation of Financial Statements; Adjusting, Closing, and Reversing Entries *(L.O. 1, 3, 4, 6, 8)*

The trial balance below was taken from the ledger of Zolnay Package Delivery Corporation on August 31, 19x2, the end of the company's fiscal year.

Zolnay Package Delivery Corporation
Trial Balance
August 31, 19x2

Cash	$ 5,036	
Accounts Receivable	14,657	
Prepaid Insurance	2,670	
Delivery Supplies	7,350	
Office Supplies	1,230	
Land	7,500	
Building	98,000	
Accumulated Depreciation, Building		$ 26,700
Trucks	51,900	
Accumulated Depreciation, Trucks		15,450
Office Equipment	7,950	
Accumulated Depreciation, Office Equipment		5,400
Accounts Payable		4,698
Unearned Lockbox Fees		4,170
Mortgage Payable		36,000
Common Stock		20,000
Retained Earnings		44,365
Dividends	15,000	
Delivery Services Revenue		141,735
Lockbox Fees Earned		14,400
Truck Drivers' Wages Expense	63,900	
Office Salaries Expense	22,200	
Gas, Oil, and Truck Repairs Expense	15,525	
	$312,918	$312,918

Required

1. Enter the trial balance amounts in the Trial Balance columns of a work sheet and complete the work sheet using the following information:
   a. Expired insurance, $1,530.
   b. Inventory of unused delivery supplies, $715.
   c. Inventory of unused office supplies, $93.
   d. Estimated depreciation, building, $7,200.
   e. Estimated depreciation, trucks, $7,725.
   f. Estimated depreciation, office equipment, $1,350.

General Ledger

Cash

Bal. 13,100	

Prepaid Advertising

Bal. 7,050	

Supplies

Bal. 3,600	

Land

Bal. 372,600	

Equipment

Bal. 78,000	

Accumulated Depreciation, Equipment

	Bal. 19,200

Accounts Payable

	Bal. 151,500

Unearned Revenue, Locker Fees

	Bal. 6,300

Common Stock

	Bal. 100,000

Retained Earnings

	Bal. 135,575

Dividends

Bal. 27,000	

Revenue from Court Fees

	Bal. 339,050

Wages Expense

Bal. 171,000	

Maintenance Expense

Bal. 25,800	

Advertising Expense

Bal. 17,625	

Water and Utility Expense

Bal. 32,400	

Miscellaneous Expense

Bal. 3,450	

East Bend Tennis Club, Inc.
Income Statement
For the Year Ended April 30, 19x2

Revenues		
Revenue from Court Fees	$339,050	
Revenue from Locker Fees	4,800	
Total Revenues		$343,850
Expenses		
Wages Expense	$175,500	
Maintenance Expense	25,800	
Advertising Expense	19,875	
Water and Utility Expense	32,400	
Miscellaneous Expense	3,450	
Property Taxes Expense	11,250	
Supplies Expense	3,000	
Depreciation Expense, Equipment	6,000	
Income Taxes Expense	20,000	
Total Expenses		297,275
Net Income		$ 46,575

2. Reconstruct the adjusting entries and complete the work sheet. Then record the adjusting entries (be certain to provide explanations) in the general journal.
3. Prepare the statement of retained earnings and the balance sheet for April 30, 19x2.

Problem Set B

Problem 4B-1. Preparation of Financial Statements and End-of-Period Entries
(L.O. 3, 6, 8)

Quality Trailer Rental, Inc. owns thirty small trailers that are rented by the day for local moving jobs. The adjusted trial balance for Quality Trailer Rental, Inc. for the year ended June 30, 19x2, which is the end of the current fiscal year, is shown below.

Quality Trailer Rental, Inc.
Adjusted Trial Balance
For the Year Ended June 30, 19x2

Cash	$ 692	
Accounts Receivable	972	
Supplies	119	
Prepaid Insurance	360	
Trailers	12,000	
Accumulated Depreciation, Trailers		$ 7,200
Accounts Payable		271
Wages Payable		200
Common Stock		1,000
Retained Earnings		4,694
Dividends	7,200	
Trailer Rentals		45,546
Wages Expense	23,400	
Insurance Expense	720	
Supplies Expense	266	
Depreciation Expense, Trailers	2,400	
Other Expenses	10,782	
Income Taxes Expense	2,000	
Income Taxes Payable		2,000
	$60,911	$60,911

Required

1. Prepare an income statement, a statement of retained earnings, and a balance sheet. Assume no additional investments by the stockholders.

2. From the information given, record closing entries in the general journal.
3. Assuming Wages Payable and Income Taxes Payable represent wages and interest accrued at the end of the period, record the required reversing entries.

Problem 4B-2. Preparation of Work Sheet, Adjusting Entries, Closing Entries, and Reversing Entries
(L.O. 1, 3, 4, 6, 8)

Roman Patel began his consulting practice immediately after graduating with his M.B.A. To help him get started, several clients paid him retainers (payment in advance) for future services. Other clients paid when service was provided. After one year, the firm had the trial balance that follows.

Roman Patel & Associates, Inc.
Trial Balance
December 31, 19xx

Cash	$ 3,250	
Accounts Receivable	2,709	
Office Supplies	382	
Office Equipment	3,755	
Accounts Payable		$ 1,296
Unearned Retainers		5,000
Common Stock		4,000
Dividends	6,000	
Consulting Fees		18,175
Rent Expense	1,800	
Utility Expense	717	
Wages Expense	9,858	
	$28,471	$28,471

Required

1. Enter the trial balance amounts in the Trial Balance columns of a work sheet, and complete the work sheet using the following information:
   a. Inventory of unused supplies, $58.
   b. Estimated depreciation on equipment, $600.
   c. Services rendered during the month but not yet billed, $725.
   d. Services rendered to clients who paid in advance that should be applied against unearned retainers, $3,150.
   e. Wages earned by employees but not yet paid, $120.
   f. Estimated income taxes for the year, $1,000.
2. Prepare an income statement, statement of retained earnings, and balance sheet.
3. Prepare adjusting, closing, and, if required, reversing entries.
4. How would you evaluate the first year of Mr. Patel's consulting practice?

Problem 4B-3. Completion of Work Sheet; Preparation of Financial Statements; Adjusting, Closing, and Reversing Entries *(L.O. 1, 3, 4, 6, 8)*

At the end of the current fiscal year, the trial balance of the Esquire Theater Corporation appeared as follows:

Esquire Theater Corporation
Trial Balance
December 31, 19x2

Cash	$ 15,900	
Accounts Receivable	9,272	
Prepaid Insurance	9,800	
Office Supplies	390	
Cleaning Supplies	1,795	
Land	10,000	
Building	200,000	
Accumulated Depreciation, Building		$ 19,700
Theater Furnishings	185,000	
Accumulated Depreciation, Theater Furnishings		32,500
Office Equipment	15,800	
Accumulated Depreciation, Office Equipment		7,780
Accounts Payable		22,753
Gift Books Liability		20,950
Mortgage Payable		150,000
Common Stock		100,000
Retained Earnings		56,324
Dividends	30,000	
Ticket Sales Revenue		205,700
Theater Rental Revenue		22,600
Usher Wages Expense	92,000	
Office Wages Expense	12,000	
Utility Expense	56,350	
	$638,307	$638,307

Required

1. Enter the trial balance amounts in the Trial Balance columns of a work sheet and complete the work sheet using the following information:
   a. Expired insurance, $8,700.
   b. Inventory of unused office supplies, $122.
   c. Inventory of unused cleaning supplies, $234.
   d. Estimated depreciation, building, $7,000.
   e. Estimated depreciation on theater furnishings, $18,000.
   f. Estimated depreciation, office equipment, $1,580.
   g. The company credits all gift books sold during the year to a Gift Books Liability account. Gift books are booklets of ticket coupons that are purchased in advance to give to someone. The recipient may then use the

coupons to attend future movies. On December 31 it was estimated that $18,900 worth of the gift books had been redeemed.

h. There are $430 worth of accrued but unpaid usher wages at the end of the accounting period.

i. Management estimates federal income taxes to be $10,000.

2. Prepare an income statement, a statement of retained earnings, and a balance sheet. Assume no additional investments by the stockholders.
3. Prepare adjusting, closing, and, if required, reversing entries.

Problem 4B-4. The Complete Accounting Cycle: Two Months
(L.O. 1, 3, 4, 6, 7)

During its first two months of operation, the Springer Repair Corporation completed the following transactions:

May 1 Began business by depositing $6,000 in a bank account in the name of the company, in exchange for 600 shares of $10 par value common stock.
1 Paid the premium on a one-year insurance policy, $600.
1 Paid current month's rent, $520.
2 Purchased repair equipment from Fisk Company for $2,200. The terms were $300 down payment and $100 per month for nineteen months. The first payment is due June 1.
5 Purchased repair supplies from Cordero Company for $195 on credit.
14 Paid utility expense for the month of May, $77.
15 Cash repair revenue for the first half of May, $681.
20 Paid $100 of the amount owed to Cordero Company.
31 Cash repair revenue for the last half of May, $655.
31 Declared and paid cash dividend, $400.

June 1 Paid the monthly rent, $520.
1 Made the monthly payment to Fisk Company, $100.
9 Purchased repair supplies on credit from Cordero Company, $447.
15 Cash repair revenue for the first half of June, $525.
18 Paid utility expense for June, $83.
19 Paid Cordero Company on account, $200.
30 Cash repair revenue for the last half of June, $687.
30 Declared and paid cash dividend, $200.

Required

1. Prepare journal entries to record the May transactions.
2. Open the following accounts: Cash (111); Prepaid Insurance (117); Repair Supplies (119); Repair Equipment (144); Accumulated Depreciation, Repair Equipment (145); Accounts Payable (212); Income Taxes Payable (213); Common Stock (311); Retained Earnings (312); Dividends (313); Income Summary (314); Repair Revenue (411); Store Rent Expense (511); Utility Expense (512); Insurance Expense (513); Repair Supplies Expense (514); Depreciation Expense, Repair Equipment (515); Income Taxes Expense (516). Post the May journal entries to ledger accounts.
3. Prepare a trial balance in the Trial Balance columns of a work sheet, and complete the work sheet using the following information:

a. One month's insurance has expired.

   b. Remaining inventory of unused repair supplies, $97.
   c. Estimated depreciation on repair equipment, $35.
   d. Estimated income taxes, $20.
4. From the work sheet, prepare an income statement, a statement of retained earnings, and a balance sheet for May.
5. From the work sheet, prepare and post adjusting and closing entries for May.
6. Prepare a post-closing trial balance.
7. Prepare and post journal entries to record June transactions.
8. Prepare a trial balance for June in the Trial Balance columns of a work sheet, and complete the work sheet based on the following information:
   a. One month's insurance has expired.
   b. Inventory of unused repair supplies, $209.
   c. Estimated depreciation on repair equipment, $35.
   d. Estimated income taxes, $20.
9. From the work sheet, prepare an income statement, a statement of retained earnings, and a balance sheet for June.
10. From the work sheet, prepare and post adjusting and closing entries for June.
11. Prepare a post-closing trial balance.

Problem 4B-5. Preparation of Work Sheet from Limited Data *(L.O. 1, 3, 4)*

Presented below are the income statement and trial balance for Whitehead Bowling Lanes, Inc. for the year ended December 31, 19x2.

Whitehead Bowling Lanes, Inc.
Income Statement
For the Year Ended December 31, 19x2

Revenues		$618,263
Expenses		
Wages Expense	$381,076	
Advertising Expense	15,200	
Utility Expense	42,200	
Maintenance Expense	84,100	
Miscellaneous Expense	9,500	
Supplies Expense	1,148	
Insurance Expense	1,500	
Depreciation Expense, Building	4,800	
Depreciation Expense, Equipment	11,000	
Property Taxes Expense	10,000	
Income Taxes Expense	15,000	
Total Expenses		575,524
Net Income		$ 42,739

Whitehead Bowling Lanes, Inc.
Trial Balance
December 31, 19x2

Cash	$ 16,214	
Accounts Receivable	7,388	
Supplies	1,304	
Prepaid Insurance	1,800	
Prepaid Advertising	900	
Land	5,000	
Building	100,000	
Accumulated Depreciation, Building		$ 22,400
Equipment	125,000	
Accumulated Depreciation, Equipment		22,000
Accounts Payable		15,044
Notes Payable		70,000
Unearned Revenues		2,300
Common Stock		20,000
Retained Earnings		40,813
Dividends	24,000	
Revenues		616,263
Wages Expense	377,114	
Advertising Expense	14,300	
Utility Expense	42,200	
Maintenance Expense	84,100	
Miscellaneous Expense	9,500	
	$808,820	$808,820

Required

1. Fill in the Trial Balance and Income Statement columns of a work sheet.
2. Reconstruct the adjustments and complete the work sheet. Assume that there is no adjustment to Accounts Receivable. Then record the adjusting entries with explanations in the general journal.
3. Prepare the statement of retained earnings and the balance sheet as of December 31, 19x2.

Financial Decision Case

Donna's Quik-Type, Inc.
(L.O. 3)

Donna's Quik-Type, Inc. is a very simple business. Donna provides typing services for students at the local university. Her accountant prepared the income statement on the next page for the year ended August 31, 19x2.

In reviewing this statement, Donna is puzzled. She knows that the company paid cash dividends of $7,800 to her, the sole stockholder, and yet the cash balance in the company's bank account increased from $230 to $1,550 from last August 31 to this August 31. She wants to know how her net income could be less than the cash she took out of the business (as dividends) if there is an increase in the cash balance.

Her accountant shows her the balance sheet for August 31, 19x2 and compares it to the one for August 31, 19x1. She explains that besides the change in the cash balance, accounts receivable from customers decreased by $740 and accounts payable increased by $190 (supplies are the only items Donna buys on credit). The only other asset or liability account that changed during the year was accumulated depreciation on office equipment, which increased by $1,100.

Donna's Quik-Type, Inc.
Income Statement
For the Year Ended August 31, 19x2

Revenues		
Typing Services		$10,490
Expenses		
Rent Expense	$1,200	
Depreciation Expense, Office Equipment	1,100	
Supplies Expense	480	
Other Expenses	620	
Total Expenses		3,400
Net Income		$ 7,090

Required

Explain to Donna why the accountant is answering Donna's question by pointing out year-to-year changes in the balance sheet. Verify the cash balance increase by preparing a statement that lists the receipts of cash and the expenditures of cash during the year. How did you treat depreciation expense? Why?

LEARNING OBJECTIVES

1. *Compare the income statements for service and merchandising concerns.*
2. *Record transactions involving revenues for merchandising concerns.*
3. *Calculate cost of goods sold.*
4. *Record transactions involving purchases of merchandise.*
5. *Differentiate the perpetual inventory system from the periodic inventory system.*
6. *Prepare an income statement for a merchandising concern.*
7. *Explain the objectives of handling merchandise inventory at the end of the accounting period and how they are achieved.*
8. *Prepare a work sheet and adjusting and closing entries for a merchandising concern.*
9. *Define* internal control *and identify the three elements of the internal control structure, including seven examples of control procedures.*
10. *Describe the inherent limitations of internal control.*
11. *Apply control procedures to certain merchandising transactions.*

CHAPTER 5

Accounting for Merchandising Operations

Up to this point, you have studied the accounting records and reports for the simplest type of business—the service company. In this chapter, you will study a more complex type of business—the merchandising company. After studying this chapter, you should be able to meet the learning objectives listed on the left.

DECISION POINT
Target Stores

Two key decisions made by management of merchandising companies concern the price at which merchandise will be sold and the level of service that the company will provide. For instance, a department store may set the price of its merchandise at a relatively high level and provide a great deal of service. A discount store, on the other hand, may price its merchandise at a relatively low level and provide limited service.

When Target Stores, a division of Dayton-Hudson Corporation, became a discount merchandiser of brand-name apparel and other products, it had to make decisions about pricing and service. By emphasizing brand-name merchandise at low prices, the company chose to differentiate itself from department and specialty stores that sell at full price and from other discount chains that sell low-priced, but less well known merchandise. Target Stores decided to operate in very large stores that could be controlled efficiently by a minimum number of employees. The company planned to earn a satisfactory net income by selling a large volume of merchandise. By 1990, Target Stores was one of the most successful merchandising companies in the United States. It operated over 400 stores and earned an income (before interest and income taxes) of $466 million on sales of $8.2 billion.[1]

1. Bill Saporito, "Is Wal-Mart Unstoppable?" *Fortune*, May 6, 1991, p. 52.

This chapter focuses on the merchandising income statement, which is structured in a way that makes it easier to evaluate the operations of merchandising companies. The chapter also describes the special buying and selling transactions of merchandising companies and the controls necessary to protect such a company from loss from theft or embezzlement. ■

Income Statement for a Merchandising Concern

OBJECTIVE 1 *Compare the income statements for service and merchandising concerns*

Service companies such as advertising agencies or law firms perform a service for a fee or commission. To determine net income, a simple income statement is often all that is needed. As shown in Figure 5-1, net income is measured as the difference between revenues and expenses.

Figure 5-1. Components of Income Statements for Service and Merchandising Concerns

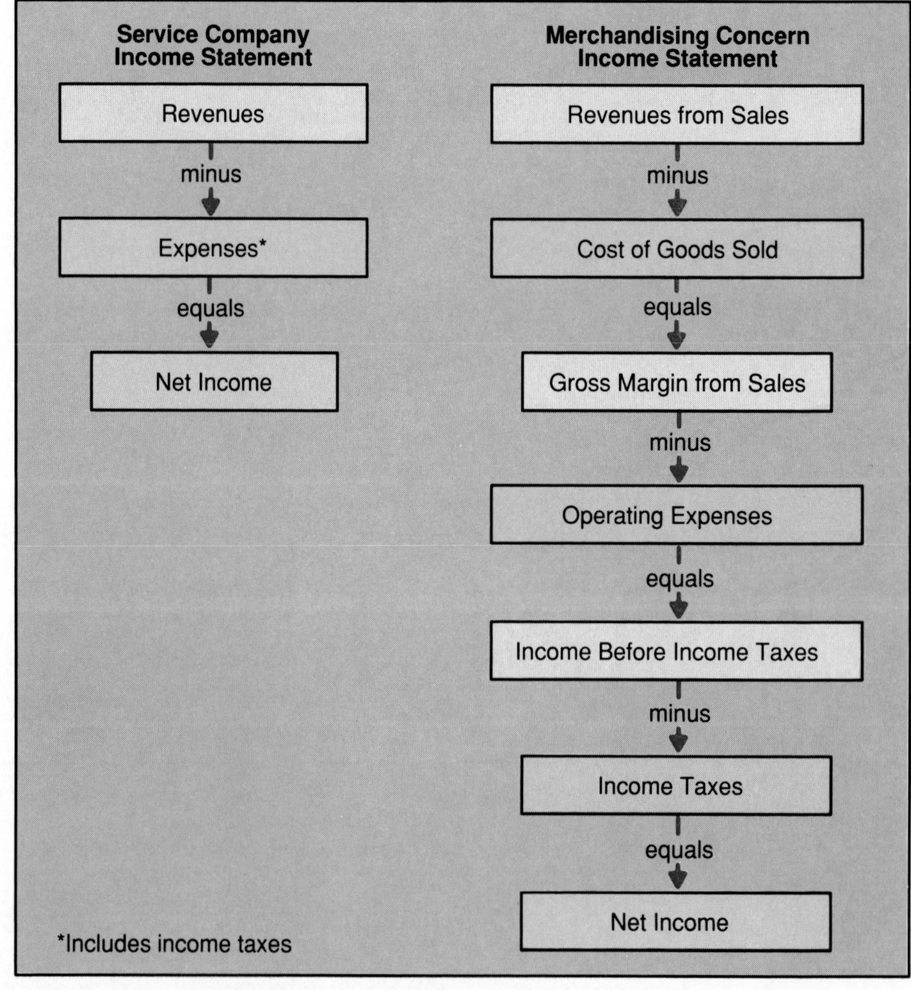

In contrast, many other companies attempt to earn an income by buying and selling products or merchandise. Merchandising companies, whether wholesale or retail, use the same basic accounting methods as service companies, but the process of buying and selling merchandise requires some additional accounts and concepts. This process results in a more complicated income statement than is needed by a service business. As illustrated in Figure 5-1, the income statement for a merchandising concern has three major parts: (1) revenues from sales, (2) cost of goods sold, and (3) operating expenses. Such an income statement differs from the income statement for a service firm in that gross margin from sales must be computed before operating expenses are deducted in order to arrive at net income.

Revenues from sales arise from sales of goods by the merchandising company, and the **cost of goods sold** tells how much the merchant paid for the goods that were sold. The difference between revenues from sales and cost of goods sold is known as **gross margin from sales**, or simply **gross margin** (also referred to as gross profit). To be successful, the merchant must sell the goods for an amount enough greater than cost—that is, gross margin from sales must be large enough—to pay operating expenses and have an adequate income left over. **Operating expenses** are those expenses, other than cost of goods sold, that are incurred in running the business. Operating expenses in a merchandising company are similar to the expenses you have seen in a service company. **Income before income taxes** for a merchandising company is what is left after deducting operating expenses from gross margin. Income taxes are then deducted to arrive at **net income**. Income before income taxes is also referred to as **operating income** or **income from operations** because it represents the income from the company's normal or main business. Note in Exhibit 5-1 that Fenwick Fashions Corporation had a gross margin from sales of \$107,965 (\$239,325 − \$131,360) and net income of \$24,481 (\$107,965 − \$78,484 − \$5,000).

Exhibit 5-1. The Parts of an Income Statement for a Merchandising Concern

Fenwick Fashions Corporation
Income Statement
For the Year Ended December 31, 19xx

Revenues from Sales	$239,325
Cost of Goods Sold	131,360
Gross Margin from Sales	$107,965
Operating Expenses	78,484
Income Before Income Taxes	$ 29,481
Income Taxes	5,000
Net Income	$ 24,481

All parts of the merchandising income statement are important to a company's management. Management is interested both in the percentage of gross margin from sales and in the amount of gross margin. This information is helpful in planning business operations. For instance, management may try to increase total sales dollars by reducing the selling price. This strategy results in a reduction in the percentage of gross margin. It will work if total items sold increase enough to raise gross margin (which raises income from operations). On the other hand, management may increase operating expenses (such as advertising expense) in an effort to increase sales dollars and the amount of gross margin. If the increase in gross margin is greater than the increase in advertising expense, net income will improve. Other strategies, such as reducing cost of goods sold or operating expenses, may also be examined.

In the first portion of this chapter, we discuss the three parts of the merchandising income statement and the transactions that give rise to the amounts in each part. The discussion ends with a comprehensive illustration of the merchandising income statement.

Revenues from Sales

OBJECTIVE 2 *Record transactions involving revenues for merchandising concerns*

The first part of the merchandising income statement is revenues from sales, as presented in Exhibit 5-2. This section requires the computation of **net sales**, which consist of gross proceeds from sales of merchandise less sales returns and allowances and sales discounts. If a business is to succeed or even survive, net sales must be great enough to pay for cost of goods sold and operating expenses and to provide a sufficient net income.

Management, investors, and others often consider the amount and trend of sales to be important indicators of a firm's progress. Increasing sales suggest growth, whereas decreasing sales indicate the possibility of decreased earnings and other financial problems in the future. Thus, to detect trends, comparisons between net sales of different periods are frequently made.

Exhibit 5-2. Partial Income Statement: Revenues from Sales

Fenwick Fashions Corporation
Partial Income Statement
For the Year Ended December 31, 19xx

Revenues from Sales		
Gross Sales		$246,350
Less: Sales Returns and Allowances	$2,750	
Sales Discounts	4,275	7,025
Net Sales		$239,325

Gross Sales

Under accrual accounting, revenues from the sale of merchandise are considered to be earned in the accounting period in which title for the goods passes from seller to buyer. **Gross sales** consist of total sales for cash and total sales on credit during a given accounting period. Even though the cash for the sale may not be collected until the following period, under the revenue recognition rule the revenue is recognized as being earned at the time of the sale. For this reason, there is likely to be a difference between revenues from sales and cash collected from those sales in a given period.

The Sales account is used only for recording sales of merchandise, whether the sale is made for cash or for credit. The journal entry to record a sale of merchandise for cash is as follows:

Sept. 16	Cash	1,286	
	Sales		1,286
	To record the sale of merchandise for cash		

If the sale of merchandise is made on credit, the entry is as follows:

Sept. 16	Accounts Receivable	746	
	Sales		746
	To record the sale of merchandise on credit		

Trade Discounts

In order to avoid reprinting wholesale and retail catalogues and price lists every time there is a price change, some manufacturers and wholesalers quote prices of merchandise at a discount (usually 30 percent or more) off the list or catalogue price. Such discounts are called **trade discounts**. For example, the seller of an article listed at $1,000 with a trade discount of 40 percent, or $400, would record the sale at $600. The buyer would also record the transaction as a purchase of $600. The list price and related trade discounts are used only for convenience in arriving at the agreed-upon price and do not appear in the accounting records.

Sales Returns and Allowances

If a customer receives a defective or otherwise unsatisfactory product, the seller will usually try to accommodate the customer. The business may allow the customer to return the item for a cash refund or credit on account, or it may give the customer an allowance off the sales price. A good accounting system will provide management with information for determining the reasons for sales returns and allowances because such transactions reveal dissatisfied customers. Each return or allowance is recorded as a debit to an account called **Sales Returns and Allowances**. An example of such a transaction follows:

Sept. 17	Sales Returns and Allowances	76	
	Accounts Receivable (or Cash)		76
	To record return or allowance on unsatisfactory merchandise		

If Sales were debited instead of Sales Returns and Allowances, management would not know the extent of customer dissatisfaction. Sales Returns and Allowances is a contra-revenue account with a normal debit balance. Accordingly, it is deducted from gross sales in the income statement (see Exhibit 5-2).

Sales Discounts

When goods are sold on credit, both parties should have an understanding as to the amount and time of payment. These terms are usually printed on the sales invoice and constitute part of the sales agreement. Customary terms differ from industry to industry. In some industries payment is expected in a short period of time, such as ten days or thirty days. In these cases, the invoice may be marked "n/10" or "n/30" (read as "net 10" or "net 30"), meaning that the amount of the invoice is due ten days or thirty days, respectively, after the invoice date. If the payment is due ten days after the end of the month, the invoice may be marked "n/10 eom."

Some industries give discounts for early payment, called **sales discounts**. This practice increases the seller's liquidity by reducing the amount of money tied up in accounts receivable. Examples of these invoice terms are 2/10, n/30 or 2/10, n/60. Terms of **2/10, n/30** mean the debtor may take a 2 percent discount if the invoice is paid within ten days of the invoice date. Otherwise, the debtor may wait thirty days and then pay the full amount of the invoice without the discount.

Because it is usually not possible to know at the time of sale whether the customer will take advantage of the discount by paying within the discount period, sales discounts are recorded only at the time the customer pays. For example, assume that Fenwick Fashions Corporation sells merchandise to a customer on September 20 for $300, on terms of 2/10, n/60. At the time of sale the entry would be:

Sept. 20	Accounts Receivable	300	
	Sales		300
	To record sale of merchandise on credit, terms 2/10, n/60		

The customer may take advantage of the sales discount any time on or before September 30, which is ten days after the date of the invoice. If he or she pays on September 29, the entry in Fenwick's records is:

Sept. 29	Cash	294	
	Sales Discounts	6	
	Accounts Receivable		300
	To record payment for Sept. 20 sale; discount taken		

If the customer does not take advantage of the sales discount but waits until November 19 to pay for the merchandise, the entry would be as follows:

Nov. 19	Cash	300	
	Accounts Receivable		300
	To record payment for Sept. 20 sale; no discount taken		

At the end of the accounting period, the Sales Discounts account has accumulated all the sales discounts taken during the period. Because sales discounts reduce revenues from sales, they are considered a contra-revenue account with a normal debit balance and are deducted from gross sales in the income statement (see Exhibit 5-2).

Cost of Goods Sold

OBJECTIVE 3
Calculate cost of goods sold

Every merchandising business has goods on hand that it holds for sale to customers. The amount of goods on hand at any one time is known as **merchandise inventory**. The cost of **goods available for sale** during the year is the sum of two factors—merchandise inventory at the beginning of the year plus net purchases during the year.

If a company were to sell all the goods available for sale during a given accounting period or year, the cost of goods sold would equal goods that had been available for sale. In most cases, however, the business will have goods still unsold and on hand at the end of the year. To find out how much the merchant paid for the goods that were actually sold (the cost of goods sold), the merchandise inventory at the end of the year must be subtracted from the goods available for sale.

The partial income statement in Exhibit 5-3 shows the cost of goods sold section for Fenwick Fashions Corporation. In this case, goods costing $179,660 were available and could have been sold; Fenwick started with $52,800 in merchandise inventory at the beginning of the year and pur-

Exhibit 5-3. Partial Income Statement: Cost of Goods Sold

Fenwick Fashions Corporation
Partial Income Statement
For the Year Ended December 31, 19xx

Cost of Goods Sold				
Merchandise Inventory, January 1, 19xx			$ 52,800	
Purchases		$126,400		
Less: Purchases Returns and Allowances	$5,640			
Purchases Discounts	2,136	7,776		
		$118,624		
Freight In		8,236		
Net Purchases			126,860	
Goods Available for Sale			$179,660	
Less Merchandise Inventory, December 31, 19xx			48,300	
Cost of Goods Sold				$131,360

chased a net of $126,860 in goods during the year. At the end of the year, $48,300 in goods were left unsold and should appear as merchandise inventory on the balance sheet. When this unsold merchandise inventory is subtracted from the total available goods that could have been sold, the resulting cost of goods sold is $131,360, which should appear on the income statement.

To understand fully the concept of the cost of goods sold, it is necessary to examine net purchases and merchandise inventory.

Net Purchases

OBJECTIVE 4 *Record transactions involving purchases of merchandise*

Net purchases consist of gross purchases less purchases returns and allowances and purchases discounts plus any freight charges on the purchases.

Purchases. Merchandise bought for resale is debited to the Purchases account at the gross purchase price, as shown below.

Nov. 12	Purchases	1,500	
	Accounts Payable		1,500
	To record purchases of merchandise, terms 2/10, n/30		

The **Purchases** account, a temporary or nominal account, is used to accumulate the cost of merchandise purchased for resale. Its sole purpose is to accumulate the total cost of merchandise purchased during an accounting period. Inspection of the Purchases account alone does not indicate whether the merchandise has been sold or is still on hand. Purchases of other assets, such as equipment, should be recorded in the appropriate asset account, not the Purchases account.

Purchases Returns and Allowances. For various reasons, a company may need to return merchandise acquired for resale. The firm may not have been able to sell the merchandise and returns it to the original supplier. Or the merchandise may be defective or damaged in some way and have to be returned. In some cases, the supplier may suggest that an allowance be given as an alternative to returning the goods for full credit. In any event, **purchases returns and allowances** form a separate account and should be recorded in the journal as follows:

Nov. 14	Accounts Payable	200	
	Purchases Returns and Allowances		200
	Return of damaged merchandise purchased on November 12		

Here, the purchaser receives "credit" (in the seller's accounts receivable) for the returned merchandise. The Purchases Returns and Allowances account is used only for returns and allowances of merchandise purchased for resale. Other returns, such as office supplies or equipment, are credited directly to the related asset account, not to a contra account.

Purchases Returns and Allowances is a contra-purchases account with a normal credit balance and is accordingly deducted from purchases in the income statement (see Exhibit 5-3). It is important that a separate account be used to record purchases returns and allowances because management needs the information for making decisions. It can be very costly to return merchandise for credit. There are many costs that cannot be recovered, such as ordering costs, accounting costs, sometimes freight costs, and interest on the money invested in the goods. Sometimes there are lost sales resulting from poor ordering or unusable goods. Excessive returns may indicate a need for new purchasing procedures or new suppliers.

Purchases Discounts. Merchandise purchases are usually made on credit and commonly involve **purchases discounts** for early payment. It is almost always worthwhile for the company to take a discount if one is offered. For example, the terms 2/10, n/30 offer a 2 percent discount for paying only twenty days early (before the period including the eleventh and the thirtieth days). This is an effective interest rate of 36 percent on a yearly basis.[2] Most companies can borrow money for less than this rate. For this reason, management wants to know the amount of discounts taken, which form a separate account and are recorded as follows when the payment is made:

			Debit	Credit
Nov. 22	Accounts Payable		1,300	
	Purchases Discounts			26
	Cash			1,274
	Paid the invoice of Nov. 12			
	Purchase Nov. 12	$1,500		
	Less return	200		
	Net purchase	$1,300		
	Discount: 2%	26		
	Cash	$1,274		

If the purchase is not paid for within the discount period, the entry is as follows:

		Debit	Credit
Dec. 12	Accounts Payable	1,300	
	Cash		1,300
	Paid the invoice of Nov. 12 on due date; no discount taken		

Like Purchases Returns and Allowances, Purchases Discounts is a contra-purchases account with a normal credit balance that is deducted from Purchases on the income statement (see Exhibit 5-3). If a company is able to make only a partial payment on an invoice, most creditors will allow the company to take the discount applicable to the partial payment. The discount usually does not apply to freight, postage, taxes, or other charges that might appear on the invoice.

Good management of cash resources calls for both taking the discount and waiting as long as possible to pay. To accomplish these two objectives, some companies file invoices according to their due dates as they get them. Each day, the invoices due on that day are pulled from the file and paid. In this manner, the company uses cash as long as possible and also

2. (360 days/20 days) × 2% = 36%

takes advantage of the discounts. A method commonly used to control these discounts (the net method) is illustrated on pages 219–220.

Freight In. In some industries, it is customary for the supplier (seller) to pay transportation costs, charging a higher price to include them. In other industries, it is customary for the purchaser to pay transportation charges on merchandise. These charges, called **freight in** or **transportation in**, should logically be included as an addition to purchases, but as in the case of purchases discounts, they should be accumulated in the Freight In account so that management can monitor this cost. The entry for the purchaser is as follows:

Nov. 12	Freight In	134	
	Cash (or Accounts Payable)		134
	Incurred freight charges on merchandise purchased		

Special terms designate whether the supplier or the purchaser is to pay the freight charges. **FOB shipping point** means that the supplier will place the merchandise "free on board" at the point of origin, and the buyer bears the shipping costs from that point. In addition, title to the merchandise passes to the buyer at that point. When purchasing a car, you know that if the sales agreement says "FOB Detroit," you must pay the freight from Detroit to where you are.

On the other hand, **FOB destination** means that the supplier is bearing the transportation costs to the destination. In this case, title remains with the supplier until the merchandise reaches its destination. The supplier normally prepays the amount, in which case the buyer makes no entry for freight. In rare cases, the buyer may pay the charges and then deduct them from the invoice.

The effects of these special shipping terms are summarized below:

Shipping Term	Where Title Passes	Who Bears Cost of Transportation
FOB shipping point	At origin	Buyer
FOB destination	At destination	Seller

In some cases, the supplier pays the freight charges but bills the buyer by including them as a separate item on the sales invoice. When this occurs, the buyer should still record the purchase and the freight in separate accounts. For example, assume that an invoice for purchase of merchandise totaling $1,890 included the cost of merchandise of $1,600, freight charges of $290, and terms of 2/10, n/30. The entry to record this transaction would be:

Nov. 25	Purchases	1,600	
	Freight In	290	
	Accounts Payable		1,890
	Purchased merchandise for $1,600, terms of 2/10, n/30; included in the invoice were freight charges of $290		

If this invoice is paid within ten days, the discount will be $32 ($1,600 × .02), because it would not apply to the freight charges.

It is important not to confuse freight-in costs with freight-out or delivery costs. If you, as seller, agree to pay transportation charges on goods you have sold, this expense is a cost of *selling* merchandise, not a cost of *purchasing* merchandise. Freight Out is shown as an operating expense on the income statement.

Control of Purchases Discounts Using the Net Method

Alternative Method

As noted earlier, it is usually worthwhile to pay invoices promptly in order to qualify for the purchase discount. In fact, it is bad management not to take advantage of such discounts. The system of initially recording purchases at the gross purchase price, called the **gross method** and described earlier, has the disadvantage of telling management only about what discounts were taken. It records no information about the discounts that were not taken, or, in other words, were "lost."

A procedure called the **net method** of recording purchases, which identifies the discounts that are lost, requires that purchases be recorded initially at the net price. Then, if the discount is not taken, a special account is debited for the amount of the lost discount. For example, suppose that a company purchases goods on November 12 for $1,500, with terms of 2/10, n/30, and that it returns $200 worth of merchandise on November 14. Suppose also that payment is not made until December 12, so that the company is not eligible for the 2 percent discount. The entries to record these three transactions are as follows:

Nov. 12	Purchases	1,470	
	Accounts Payable		1,470
	To record purchases of merchandise at net price, terms 2/10, n/30; $1,500 – (.02 × $1,500) = $1,470		
Nov. 14	Accounts Payable	196	
	Purchases Returns and Allowances		196
	Return of damaged merchandise purchased on November 12; recorded at net price: $200 – (.02 × $200) = $196		
Dec. 12	Accounts Payable	1,274	
	Purchases Discounts Lost	26	
	Cash		1,300
	Paid invoice of Nov. 12		
	Purchase Nov. 12 $1,500		
	Less return Nov. 14 200		
	Net purchase $1,300		
	Discount lost: .02 × $1,300 = $26		

If the company pays the invoice by November 22 and uses the net method of recording purchases, it will make a payment of $1,274. Since purchases were recorded at net prices, no Purchases Discounts Lost account would be required, and the entry would be recorded as follows:

Nov. 22	Accounts Payable	1,274	
	Cash		1,274
	Payment of Nov. 12 invoice within discount period		

However, if the company makes the payment after the discount period, management learns of the failure to take the discount by examining the Purchases Discounts Lost account. The amount of Purchases Discounts Lost is shown as an operating expense on the income statement.

Merchandise Inventory

OBJECTIVE 5 *Differentiate the perpetual inventory system from the periodic inventory system*

The inventory of a merchandising concern consists of the goods on hand and available for sale to customers. For a grocery store, inventory would be the meats, vegetables, canned goods, and other items for sale. For a service station, it would be gasoline, oil, and automobile parts. Merchandising concerns purchase their inventories from wholesalers, manufacturers, and other suppliers.

The merchandise inventory on hand at the beginning of the accounting period is called the **beginning inventory**. Conversely, the merchandise inventory on hand at the end of the accounting period is called the **ending inventory**. As we have seen, beginning and ending inventories are used in calculating the cost of goods sold on the income statement. Ending inventory also appears on the balance sheet as an asset. It will become a part of cost of goods sold in a later period when it is sold. This year's beginning inventory was last year's ending inventory.

Measuring Merchandise Inventory. Merchandise inventory is a key factor in determining cost of goods sold. Because merchandise inventory represents goods available for sale that are still unsold, there must be a method for determining both the quantity and the cost of these goods on hand. The two basic systems of accounting for the number of items in the merchandise inventory are the periodic inventory system and the perpetual inventory system.

Under the **periodic inventory system**, a count of the physical inventory takes place periodically, usually at the end of the accounting period, and no detailed records of the physical inventory on hand are maintained during the period. Under the **perpetual inventory system**, records are kept of the quantity and, usually, the cost of individual items of inventory as they are bought and sold.

Cost of goods sold under the periodic inventory system is determined at the end of the accounting period in a manner similar to the method of accounting for supplies expense, with which you are already familiar. In the simplest case, the cost of inventory purchased is accumulated in a Purchases account. Then, at the end of the accounting period, the actual count of the physical inventory is deducted from the total of purchases plus beginning merchandise inventory to determine cost of goods sold.

Under the perpetual inventory system, on the other hand, the cost of each item is debited to the Merchandise Inventory account as it is purchased. As items are sold, the Merchandise Inventory account is credited and the Cost of Goods Sold account is debited for the cost of the items sold. In this way the balance of the Merchandise Inventory account always equals the cost of goods on hand at a point in time, and the Cost of Goods Sold account equals total cost associated with items sold to that point in time.

Traditionally, the periodic inventory system has been used by companies that sell items of low value and high volume because of the difficulty and expense of accounting for the purchase and sale of each item. Examples of such companies are drugstores, automobile parts stores, department stores, discount companies, and grain companies. In contrast, companies that sell items of high unit value, such as appliances or automobiles, have tended to use the perpetual inventory system. This distinction between high and low unit value for inventory systems has blurred considerably in recent years because of the widespread use of the computer. Although the periodic inventory system is still widely used, use of the perpetual inventory system has increased greatly. For example, many grocery stores, which traditionally used the periodic inventory system, can now, through the use of electronic markings on each product, update the physical inventory as items are sold by linking their cash registers to a computer. It has become common for some retail businesses to use the perpetual system for keeping track of the physical flow of inventory and the periodic system for preparing the financial statements.

The periodic inventory system for determining cost of goods sold is described in this chapter. The perpetual inventory system is discussed further in the chapter on inventories.

The Periodic Inventory System. Most companies rely on an actual count of goods on hand at the end of an accounting period to determine ending inventory and, indirectly, the cost of goods sold. The procedure for determining the merchandise inventory under the periodic inventory system can be summarized as follows:

1. Make a physical count of merchandise on hand at the end of the accounting period.
2. Multiply the quantity of each type of merchandise by its unit cost.
3. Add the resulting costs for each type of merchandise to obtain a total. This amount is the ending merchandise inventory.

The cost of the ending merchandise inventory is deducted from goods available for sale to determine cost of goods sold. The ending inventory of one period is the beginning inventory of the next period. Entries are made in the adjusting or closing process at the end of the accounting period to remove the beginning inventory (the last period's ending inventory) and to enter the ending inventory of the current period. These entries are the only ones made to the Merchandise Inventory account during the period.

Consequently, only on the balance sheet date and after the closing entries does the Inventory account represent the actual inventory on hand. As soon as purchases or sales are made, the figure becomes a historical amount and remains so until the new inventory is entered at the end of the accounting period.

Taking the Physical Inventory. Making a physical count of all merchandise on hand is referred to as **taking a physical inventory**. It can be a difficult task, since it is easy to omit or miscount items.

Merchandise inventory includes all salable goods owned by the concern, regardless of where they are located. It includes all goods on shelves, in storerooms, in warehouses, and in trucks en route between warehouses and stores. It includes goods in transit from suppliers if title to the goods has passed to the merchant. Ending inventory does not include merchandise sold to customers but not delivered or goods that cannot be sold because they are damaged or obsolete. If the damaged or obsolete goods can be sold at a reduced price, however, they should be included in ending inventory at the reduced value.

The actual count is usually taken after the close of business on the last day of the fiscal year. Many companies end their fiscal year in a slow season to facilitate taking the physical inventory. Retail department stores often end their fiscal year in January or February, for example. After hours, at night or on the weekend, employees count and record all items on numbered inventory tickets or sheets. Sometimes a store will close for all or part of a day for inventory taking. They follow established procedures to make sure that no items are missed.

DECISION POINT
High Country, Inc. (Part 1)

High Country, Inc. operates a chain of specialty stores that feature outdoor clothing. All of its stores are located in shopping malls. The company gears its merchandising strategy to the four seasons of the year. Four times a year each store receives a shipment of clothing for the upcoming quarter. Using the periodic inventory system, the company takes a quarterly physical inventory before preparing financial statements at the end of each quarter. The company lost money for the last two quarters of 1990 and the first quarter of 1991, in part, management believed, because some stores ran out of merchandise, while other stores had more than they could sell. If financial statements were prepared each month, so as to give more timely information, the company would be better able to adapt to varying sales patterns during the quarters. What type of inventory system would help management achieve these goals?

The company changed to the perpetual inventory system in the second quarter of 1991 and began preparing financial statements at the end of every month. To this end, each piece of clothing was tagged with an identification label. Under the new system, when sales are made, the identification labels are removed and returned to the central accounting office, where the merchandise inventory records are maintained. Trends in sales of clothing are monitored for the purpose of adapting purchases, shipments, and promotions among stores and products on a monthly basis. Taking a monthly physical inventory has not been necessary because the amount of the ending merchandise inventory is available from the perpetual inventory records. An immediate increase in sales and income has resulted. ■

Inventory Losses

Many companies have substantial losses in merchandise inventory from spoilage, shoplifting, and employee pilferage. Management will, of course, want to take steps to prevent such losses from occurring. But if they do occur, the periodic inventory system provides no means of determining such losses because these costs are automatically included in the cost of goods sold. For example, assume that a company lost $1,250 during an accounting period because merchandise had been stolen or spoiled. When the physical inventory is taken, the missing items will not be in stock and cannot be counted. Because the ending inventory will not contain these items, the amount subtracted from goods available for sale is less than it would be if the goods were in stock. Cost of goods sold, therefore, is greater by $1,250. In a sense, cost of goods sold is inflated by the amount of merchandise that has been lost. If the perpetual inventory system is used, it is easier to identify these types of losses. Since the Merchandise Inventory account is continuously updated for sales, purchases, and returns, the loss will show up as the difference between the inventory records and the physical inventory at the end of the accounting period.

Operating Expenses

Operating expenses make up the third major part of the income statement for a merchandising concern. As noted earlier, they are the expenses, other than the cost of goods sold, that are necessary to run the business. It is customary to group operating expenses into useful categories. Selling expenses and general and administrative expenses are common categories. Selling expenses include all expenses of storing and preparing goods for sale; displaying, advertising, and otherwise promoting sales; making the sales; and delivering the goods to the buyer if the seller bears the cost of delivery. Among the general and administrative expenses are general office expenses; those for accounting, personnel, and credit and collections; and any other expenses that apply to the overall operation of the company. Although general occupancy expenses, such as rent expense and utility expense, are often classified as general and administrative, they are sometimes allocated or divided between the selling and the general and administrative categories on a basis determined by management.

Income Statement Illustrated

OBJECTIVE 6
Prepare an income statement for a merchandising concern

The major parts of the income statement for a merchandising concern have now been presented and the transactions pertaining to each part discussed. Exhibit 5-4 (page 225) pulls the parts together and shows the complete income statement for Fenwick Fashions Corporation. The statement may be prepared by referring to the accounts in the ledger that pertain to the income statement; or when a work sheet is prepared, the accounts and their balances may be taken from the Income Statement columns of the work sheet. In practice, the statement of retained earnings and the balance sheet would also be prepared. They are not presented here because they are like those of service companies, except that merchandise inventory is listed among the assets on the balance sheet.

Handling Merchandise Inventory at the End of the Accounting Period

OBJECTIVE 7
Explain the objectives of handling merchandise inventory at the end of the accounting period and how they are achieved

Recall that under the periodic inventory system, purchases of merchandise are accumulated in the Purchases account. During the accounting period, no entries are made to the Merchandise Inventory account. Its balance at the end of the period, before adjusting and closing entries, is the same as it was at the beginning of the period. Thus, its balance at this point represents beginning merchandise inventory. Recall also that the cost of goods sold is determined by adding beginning merchandise inventory to net purchases and then subtracting ending merchandise inventory. The objectives of handling merchandise inventory at the end of the period are to (1) remove the beginning balance from the Merchandise Inventory account, (2) enter the ending balance into the Merchandise Inventory account, and (3) enter the beginning inventory as a debit and the ending inventory as a credit to the Income Summary account to properly calculate net income. Using the figures for Fenwick Fashions Corporation, these objectives can be accomplished if the following effects on the Merchandise Inventory and Income Summary accounts are achieved:

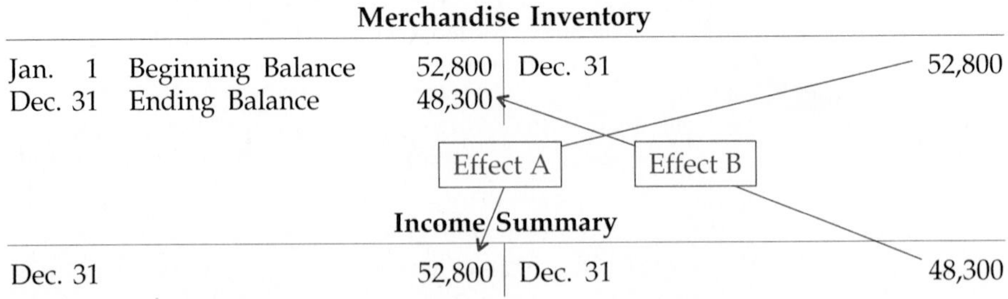

In this example, merchandise inventory was $52,800 at the beginning of the year and $48,300 at the end of the year. Effect A removes the $52,800 from Merchandise Inventory, leaving a zero balance, and transfers it to Income Summary. In Income Summary, the $52,800 is in effect added to

Exhibit 5-4. Income Statement for Fenwick Fashions Corporation

Fenwick Fashions Corporation
Income Statement
For the Year Ended December 31, 19xx

Revenues from Sales				
Gross Sales				$246,350
Less: Sales Returns and Allowances			$ 2,750	
Sales Discounts			4,275	7,025
Net Sales				$239,325
Cost of Goods Sold				
Merchandise Inventory, January 1, 19xx			$ 52,800	
Purchases		$126,400		
Less: Purchases Returns and Allowances	$5,640			
Purchases Discounts	2,136	7,776		
		$118,624		
Freight In		8,236		
Net Purchases			126,860	
Goods Available for Sale			$179,660	
Less Merchandise Inventory, December 31, 19xx			48,300	
Cost of Goods Sold				131,360
Gross Margin from Sales				$107,965
Operating Expenses				
Selling Expenses				
Sales Salaries Expense		$ 22,500		
Freight Out Expense		5,740		
Advertising Expense		10,000		
Insurance Expense, Selling		1,600		
Store Supplies Expense		1,540		
Total Selling Expenses			$ 41,380	
General and Administrative Expenses				
Office Salaries Expense		$ 26,900		
Insurance Expense, General		4,200		
Office Supplies Expense		1,204		
Depreciation Expense, Building		2,600		
Depreciation Expense, Office Equipment		2,200		
Total General and Administrative Expenses			37,104	
Total Operating Expenses				78,484
Income Before Income Taxes				$ 29,481
Income Taxes				5,000
Net Income				$ 24,481

net purchases because, like expenses, the balance of the Purchases account is debited to Income Summary by a closing entry. Effect B establishes the ending balance of Merchandise Inventory of $48,300 and enters it as a credit in the Income Summary account. The credit entry in Income Summary has the effect of deducting the ending inventory from goods available for sale because both purchases and beginning inventory were entered on the debit side. In other words, beginning merchandise inventory and purchases are debits to Income Summary, and ending merchandise inventory is a credit to Income Summary.

Thus, the three objectives stated above are accomplished if effects A and B both occur. The question then arises as to how to achieve the effects. Two acceptable methods are available: the adjusting entry method and the closing entry method. Each method produces exactly the same result, so a company would use only one of them. However, since practice varies in different regions of the country as to which method is most used, both are described here. Each method is simply a bookkeeping technique designed to deal with the Merchandise Inventory account under the periodic inventory system.

The Adjusting Entry Method

Using the adjusting entry method, the two entries indicated by effects A and B are prepared at the same time the other adjusting entries are made, as follows:

Adjusting Entries

Dec. 31	Income Summary	52,800	
	Merchandise Inventory		**52,800**
	To remove beginning balance of Merchandise Inventory and transfer it to Income Summary		
31	**Merchandise Inventory**	**48,300**	
	Income Summary		48,300
	To establish ending balance of Merchandise Inventory and deduct it from goods available for sale in Income Summary		

The Closing Entry Method

The closing entry method makes the debit and the credit to Merchandise Inventory by including them among the closing entries, as follows:

Closing Entries

Dec. 31	Income Summary	Total of credits	
	Merchandise Inventory		**52,800**
	Expenses and Other Income Statement Accounts with Debit Balances		Various amounts
	To close temporary expense and revenue accounts that have debit balances and to remove beginning inventory		

Dec. 31	**Merchandise Inventory**	48,300	
	Revenues and Other Income Statement Accounts with Credit Balances	Various amounts	
	Income Summary		Total of debits
	To close temporary expense and revenue accounts that have credit balances and to establish the ending merchandise inventory		

Notice that under both methods, Merchandise Inventory is credited for the beginning balance and debited for the ending balance, and the opposite entries are made to Income Summary.

Work Sheet for a Merchandising Concern: Closing Entry Method

OBJECTIVE 8
Prepare a work sheet and adjusting and closing entries for a merchandising concern

In the chapter on completing the accounting cycle, the work sheet was presented as a useful tool in preparing adjusting entries, closing entries, and financial statements. The work sheet of a merchandising business is basically the same as that of a service business, except that it has to deal with the new accounts that are needed to handle merchandising transactions. These accounts include Sales, Sales Returns and Allowances, Sales Discounts, Purchases, Purchases Returns and Allowances, Purchases Discounts, Freight In, and Merchandise Inventory. Except for Merchandise Inventory, these accounts are treated much as revenue and expense accounts are for a service company. They are transferred to the Income Summary account in the closing process. On the work sheet, they are extended to the Income Statement columns.

The work sheet for Fenwick Fashions Corporation using the closing entry method is presented in Exhibit 5-5. Each pair of columns in the work sheet and the adjusting and closing entries are discussed on the following pages.

Trial Balance Columns. The first step in the preparation of the work sheet is to enter the balances from the ledger accounts into the Trial Balance columns. You are already familiar with this procedure.

Adjustments Columns. Under the closing entry method of handling merchandise inventory, the adjusting entries for Fenwick Fashions Corporation are entered in the Adjustments columns in the same way that they were for service companies. They involve insurance expired during the period (adjustment **a**), store and office supplies used during the period (adjustments **b** and **c**), depreciation of building and office equipment (adjustments **d** and **e**), and accrued income taxes (adjustment **f**). No adjusting entry is made for merchandise inventory. After the adjusting entries are entered on the work sheet, the columns are totaled to prove the equality of the debits and credits.

Omission of Adjusted Trial Balance Columns. These two columns, which appeared in the work sheet for a service company, may be omitted.

Exhibit 5-5. Work Sheet for Fenwick Fashions Corporation: Closing Entry Method

Fenwick Fashions Corporation
Work Sheet
For the Year Ended December 31, 19xx

Account Name	Trial Balance		Adjustments		Income Statement		Balance Sheet	
	Debit	Credit	Debit	Credit	Debit	Credit	Debit	Credit
Cash	29,410						29,410	
Accounts Receivable	42,400						42,400	
Merchandise Inventory	52,800				52,800	48,300	48,300	
Prepaid Insurance	17,400			(a) 5,800			11,600	
Store Supplies	2,600			(b) 1,540			1,060	
Office Supplies	1,840			(c) 1,204			636	
Land	4,500						4,500	
Building	20,260						20,260	
Accumulated Depreciation, Building		5,650		(d) 2,600				8,250
Office Equipment	8,600						8,600	
Accumulated Depreciation, Office Equipment		2,800		(e) 2,200				5,000
Accounts Payable		25,683						25,683
Common Stock		50,000						50,000
Retained Earnings		68,352						68,352
Dividends	20,000						20,000	
Sales		246,350				246,350		
Sales Returns and Allowances	2,750				2,750			
Sales Discounts	4,275				4,275			
Purchases	126,400				126,400			
Purchases Returns and Allowances		5,640				5,640		
Purchases Discounts		2,136				2,136		
Freight In	8,236				8,236			
Sales Salaries Expense	22,500				22,500			
Freight Out Expense	5,740				5,740			
Advertising Expense	10,000				10,000			
Office Salaries Expense	26,900				26,900			
	406,611	406,611						
Insurance Expense, Selling			(a) 1,600		1,600			
Insurance Expense, General			(a) 4,200		4,200			
Store Supplies Expense			(b) 1,540		1,540			
Office Supplies Expense			(c) 1,204		1,204			
Depreciation Expense, Building			(d) 2,600		2,600			
Depreciation Expense, Office Equipment			(e) 2,200		2,200			
Income Taxes Expense			(f) 5,000		5,000			
Income Taxes Payable				(f) 5,000				5,000
			18,344	18,344	277,945	302,426	186,766	162,285
Net Income					24,481			24,481
					302,426	302,426	186,766	186,766

These columns are optional and are used when there are many adjusting entries to record. When only a few adjusting entries are required, as is the case for Fenwick Fashions Corporation, these columns are not necessary and may be omitted to save time.

Income Statement and Balance Sheet Columns. After the Trial Balance columns have been totaled, the adjustments entered, and the equality of the columns proved, the balances are extended to the statement columns. This process is accomplished most efficiently by beginning with the Cash account at the top of the work sheet and moving sequentially down the work sheet one account at a time. Each account balance is entered in the proper Income Statement or Balance Sheet column.

The extension that may not be obvious is in the Merchandise Inventory row. The beginning inventory balance of $52,800 (which is already in the trial balance) is first extended to the debit column of the Income Statement, as illustrated in Exhibit 5-5. This procedure has the effect of adding beginning inventory to net purchases because the Purchases account is also in the debit column of the Income Statement. The ending inventory balance of $48,300 (which is determined by the physical inventory and is not in the trial balance) is then inserted in the credit column of the Income Statement. This procedure has the effect of subtracting the ending inventory from goods available for sale in order to calculate the cost of goods sold. Finally, the ending merchandise inventory ($48,300) is inserted in the debit column of the Balance Sheet because it will appear on the balance sheet.

After all the items have been extended into the proper statement columns, the four columns are totaled. The net income or net loss is determined as the difference in the debit and credit Income Statement columns. In this case, Fenwick Fashions Corporation has earned a net income of $24,481, which is extended to the credit column of the Balance Sheet. The four columns are then added to prove the equality of the debits and credits.

Adjusting Entries. The adjusting entries are now entered into the general journal from the work sheet and posted to the ledger as they would be in a service company. Under the closing entry method, there is no difference in this procedure between a service company and a merchandising company.

Closing Entries. The closing entries for Fenwick Fashions Corporation under the closing entry method appear in Exhibit 5-6. Note that Merchandise Inventory is credited in the first entry for the amount of beginning inventory ($52,800) and debited in the second entry for the amount of the ending inventory ($48,300), as shown on pages 226–227. Otherwise, these closing entries are very similar to those for a service company except that the new merchandising accounts introduced in this chapter must also be closed to Income Summary. All income statement accounts with debit balances—for instance, Sales Returns and Allowances, Sales Discounts, Purchases, and Freight In—are credited in the first entry. The total of these accounts equals the total of the debit column in the Income Statement col-

Exhibit 5-6. Closing Entries for a Merchandising Concern: Closing Entry Method

General Journal — Page 1

Date		Description	Post. Ref.	Debit	Credit
19xx		*Closing entries:*			
Dec.	31	Income Summary		277,945	
		Merchandise Inventory			52,800
		Sales Returns and Allowances			2,750
		Sales Discounts			4,275
		Purchases			126,400
		Freight In			8,236
		Sales Salaries Expense			22,500
		Freight Out Expense			5,740
		Advertising Expense			10,000
		Office Salaries Expense			26,900
		Insurance Expense, Selling			1,600
		Insurance Expense, General			4,200
		Store Supplies Expense			1,540
		Office Supplies Expense			1,204
		Depreciation Expense, Building			2,600
		Depreciation Expense, Office Equipment			2,200
		Income Taxes Expense			5,000
		To close temporary expense and revenue accounts having debit balances			
	31	Merchandise Inventory		48,300	
		Sales		246,350	
		Purchases Returns and Allowances		5,640	
		Purchases Discounts		2,136	
		Income Summary			302,426
		To close temporary expense and revenue accounts having credit balances			
	31	Income Summary		24,481	
		Retained Earnings			24,481
		To close the Income Summary account			
	31	Retained Earnings		20,000	
		Dividends			20,000
		To close the Dividends account			

umns of the work sheet. All income statement accounts with credit balances—namely, Sales, Purchases Returns and Allowances, and Purchases Discounts—are debited in the second entry. The total of these accounts equals the total of the Income Statement credit column in the work sheet. The third and fourth entries are used to close the Income Summary account and transfer net income to the Retained Earnings account and to close the Dividends account to Retained Earnings.

Internal Control Structure: Basic Elements and Procedures

Accounting for merchandising companies, as you have seen, focuses on buying and selling. These transactions involve asset accounts—Cash, Accounts Receivable, and Merchandise Inventory—that are vulnerable to theft or embezzlement. There are two reasons for this vulnerability. One is that cash and inventory are fairly easy to steal. The other is that these assets involve a large number of transactions—cash sales, receipts on account, payments for purchases, receipts and shipments of inventory, and so on. A merchandising company can have high losses of cash and inventory if it does not take steps to protect the assets. The best way to do so is to set up and maintain a good internal control structure.

DECISION POINT
High Country, Inc. (Part 2)

High Country, Inc., a specialty retailer of outdoor clothing, installed the perpetual inventory system in the second quarter of 1991 to adjust merchandise inventories to sales patterns more effectively and to prepare monthly financial statements to give management more timely information. Although this system led to an improvement in sales and income, the gross margin on the monthly income statements was falling below both management expectations and the industry average. At the end of 1991 a physical inventory revealed that actual merchandise inventory was considerably lower than the perpetual inventory records indicated. The merchandise inventories of some stores were off more than others, but all had deficiencies. Management wondered what caused these losses and what steps might be taken to prevent them in the future.

The merchandise inventory losses are probably due to shoplifting and embezzlement. Management must carefully review its controls at the individual stores and install a system that will protect its merchandise inventory from these forms of theft. As will be seen in the next section, this goal can be accomplished through an internal control structure that provides an environment that encourages compliance with company policies, a good accounting system, and specific procedures designed to safeguard the merchandise inventory. ■

Internal Control Defined

OBJECTIVE 9
Define internal control *and identify the three elements of the internal control structure, including seven examples of control procedures*

Internal control has traditionally been defined as all the policies and procedures by which management protects the assets and assures the accuracy and reliability of the accounting records. It includes controls that deal with operating efficiency and adherence to management policies. In other words, management wants not only to safeguard assets and have reliable records, but also to maintain an efficient operation that follows its policies. To achieve this, management should establish an **internal control structure** consisting of three elements: the control environment, the accounting system, and the control procedures.[3]

The **control environment** reflects the overall attitude, awareness, and actions of the owners and management of the business. It includes such things as management's philosophy and operating style, the company's organizational structure, methods of assigning authority and responsibility, and personnel policies and practices. Personnel should be qualified to handle responsibilities, which means that employees must be trained and informed. For example, the manager of a retail store should train employees to follow prescribed procedures for handling cash sales, credit card sales, and returns and refunds. It is clear that an accounting system, no matter how well designed, is only as good as the people who run it. The control environment also includes regular reviews for compliance with procedures. For example, large companies often have a staff of internal auditors who review the company's system of internal control to see that it is working properly and that procedures are being followed. In smaller businesses, the owners and managers should conduct such reviews.

The **accounting system** consists of methods and records established by management to identify, assemble, analyze, classify, record, and report a company's transactions, and to provide assurance that the objectives of internal control are achieved. There are many **control procedures** in management's toolbox to ensure the safeguarding of the company's assets and the reliability of the accounting records. Examples of these control procedures are presented below:

1. **Authorization** All transactions and activities should be properly authorized by management. In a retail store, for example, some transactions, such as normal cash sales, are routinely authorized, but others, such as issuing a refund, may require the manager's approval.
2. **Recording of transactions** All transactions should be recorded to facilitate preparation of financial statements and to establish accountability for assets. In a retail store, for example, the cash register records sales, refunds, and other transactions internally on a paper tape or computer disk so that the cashier may be held responsible for the cash that has been received, and merchandise that has been removed, during his or her shift.
3. **Documents and records** Design and use of adequate documents help ensure the proper recording of transactions. For example, to ensure

3. *Professional Standards* (New York: American Institute of Certified Public Accountants, June 1, 1989), Vol. 1, Sec. AU 319.06–.11.

that all transactions are recorded, invoices should be prenumbered and all numbers accounted for.

4. **Limited access** Access to assets should be permitted only in accordance with management's authorization. For example, retail stores should use cash registers, and only the cashier responsible for the cash in a particular register should have access to it. Other employees should not be able to open the cash drawer if the cashier is not present. Likewise, warehouses and storerooms should be accessible only to authorized personnel. Access to accounting records, including company computers, should also be controlled.
5. **Periodic independent verification** The records should be checked against the assets by someone other than the person responsible for the records and the assets. For example, at the end of each shift or day, the owner or store manager should count the cash in the cash drawer and compare the amount with the amount recorded in the cash register on the tape or computer disk. Other examples of independent verification are the monthly bank reconciliation (described later in this chapter) and periodic counts of physical inventory.
6. **Separation of duties** Separation of duties means that the plan of organization should describe the proper separation of functional responsibilities. Authorizing transactions, operating a department, handling assets, and keeping the records of assets for the department should not all be the responsibility of one person. For example, in an appliance or stereo store, each employee should oversee only a single part of a transaction. A sales employee takes the order and writes out an invoice. Another employee receives the customer's money or credit card. Once the customer has a paid receipt, and only then, a third employee obtains the item from the warehouse and gives it to the customer. A person in the accounting department subsequently records the sales from the tape in the cash register, comparing them with the sales invoices and updating the inventory in the records. In other words, separation of duties should mean that a mistake, honest or not, cannot be made without having been seen by at least one other person.
7. **Sound personnel procedures** Sound practices should be followed in managing the people who carry out the duties and functions of each department. Among these practices are good supervision, rotation of key people among different jobs, insistence that employees take vacations, and bonding of personnel who handle cash or inventories. **Bonding** means carefully checking on an employee's background and insuring the company against any theft by that person. Bonding will not prevent theft, but it will prevent or reduce economic loss if theft occurs.

Limitations of Internal Control

OBJECTIVE 10
Describe the inherent limitations of internal control

No system of internal control is without certain weaknesses. As long as people must carry out control procedures, the internal control system is open to human error. Errors may arise because of a misunderstanding of instructions, mistakes in judgment, carelessness, distraction, or fatigue. The separation of duties can be defeated through collusion—that is, when employees secretly agree to deceive the company. Also, procedures designed by management may be ineffective against employee errors or dishonesty. Or, controls that may have been effective at first may become ineffective because of changing conditions.[4] In some cases, the costs of establishing and maintaining elaborate systems may exceed the benefits. In a small business, for example, active involvement by the owner may be a practical substitute for certain separation of duties.

Internal Control Over Merchandising Transactions

OBJECTIVE 11
Apply control procedures to certain merchandising transactions

Sound internal control procedures are needed in all aspects of a business, but particularly when assets are involved. Assets are especially vulnerable when they enter or leave the business. When sales are made, for example, cash or other assets enter the business, and goods or services leave the business. Procedures must be set up to prevent theft during these transactions. Likewise, purchases of assets and payments of liabilities must be controlled. The majority of these transactions can be safeguarded by adequate purchasing and payroll systems. In addition, assets on hand, such as cash, investments, inventory, plant, and equipment, must be protected.

In this and the following sections, internal control procedures will be applied to such merchandising transactions as sales, cash receipts, purchases, and cash payments. Internal control for other kinds of transactions will be covered later in the book. As mentioned previously, similar procedures are applicable to service and manufacturing businesses.

When a system of internal control is applied effectively to merchandising transactions, it can achieve important goals for accounting as well as for general management. Examples of two goals for accounting follow:

1. To prevent losses of cash or inventory from theft or fraud
2. To provide accurate records of merchandising transactions and account balances

Examples of broader management goals are as follows:

1. To keep just enough inventory on hand to sell to customers without overstocking
2. To keep enough cash on hand to pay for purchases in time to receive purchases discounts
3. To keep credit losses as low as possible by restricting credit sales to those customers who are likely to pay on time

One control to meet broad management goals is the cash budget, which projects future cash receipts and disbursements. By maintaining adequate cash balances, the company is able to take advantage of discounts on purchases, prepare for borrowing money when necessary, and avoid the damaging effects of not being able to pay bills when they are due. On the other hand, if the company has excess cash at a particular time, it can be invested, earning interest until it is needed.

4. Ibid., Sec. AU 320.35.

A more specific accounting control is the separation of duties involving the control of cash. This separation means that theft without detection is impossible except through the collusion of two or more employees. The subdivision of duties is easier in large businesses than in small ones, where one person may have to carry out several duties. The effectiveness of internal control over cash will vary depending on the size and nature of the company. Most firms, however, should use the following procedures:

1. The functions of authorization, recordkeeping, and the custodianship of cash should be kept separate.
2. The number of persons who have access to cash should be limited.
3. Persons who are to have responsibility for handling cash should be specifically designated.
4. Banking facilities should be used as much as possible, and the amount of cash on hand should be kept to a minimum.
5. All employees having access to cash should be bonded.
6. Cash on hand should be protected physically by the use of such devices as cash registers, cashiers' cages, and safes.
7. Surprise audits of cash on hand should be made by a person who does not handle or record cash.
8. All cash receipts should be recorded promptly.
9. All cash receipts should be deposited promptly.
10. All cash payments should be made by check.
11. The cash account should be reconciled monthly by a person who does not authorize, handle, or record cash.

Note that each of the above procedures helps to safeguard cash by making it more difficult for any one person to have access to cash and to steal or misuse it undetected. These procedures may be specifically related to the control of cash receipts and cash disbursements.

Control of Cash Sales Receipts

Cash receipts for sales of goods and services may be received by mail or over the counter in the form of checks or currency. Whatever the source, cash should be recorded immediately upon receipt. This is generally done by making an entry in a special-purpose journal for recording cash receipts. This step establishes a written record of the receipt of cash and should prevent errors and make theft more difficult.

Control of Cash Received Through the Mail. Cash receipts received through the mail are vulnerable to being stolen by the employees who receive them. This way of doing business is increasing, however, because of the expansion of mail order sales. To control these receipts, customers should always be urged to pay in the form of checks instead of currency. Also, cash that comes in through the mail should be handled by two or more employees. The employee who opens the mail should make a list in triplicate of the money received. This list should contain each payer's name, the purpose for which the money was sent, and the amount. One copy goes with the cash to the cashier, who deposits the money. The second copy goes to the accounting department to be recorded in the cash receipts journal. The person who opens the mail keeps the third copy of the list. Errors can be caught easily because the amount deposited by the cashier must agree with the amount received and the amount recorded in the cash receipts journal.

Control of Cash Sales Received Over the Counter. Two common means of controlling cash sales are through the use of cash registers and prenumbered sales tickets. Amounts from cash sales should be rung up on a cash register at the time of each sale. The cash register should be placed so that the customer can see the amount recorded. Each cash register should have a locked-in tape on which it prints the day's transactions. At the end of the day, the cashier counts the cash in the cash register and turns it in to the cashier's office. Another employee takes the tape out of the cash register and records the cash receipts for the day in the cash receipts journal. The amount of cash turned in and the amount recorded on the tape should be in agreement; if not, any differences must be accounted for. Large retail chains commonly perform this function by having each cash register tied directly into a computer. In this way each transaction is recorded as it occurs. The separation of duties involving cash receipts, cash deposits, and recordkeeping is thus achieved, ensuring good internal control.

In some stores, internal control is strengthened further by the use of prenumbered sales tickets and a central cash register or cashier's office, where all sales are rung up and collected by a person who does not participate in the sale. Under this procedure, the salesperson completes a prenumbered sales ticket at the time of sale, giving one copy to the customer and keeping a copy. At the end of the day, all sales tickets must be accounted for, and the sales total computed from the sales tickets should equal the total sales recorded on the cash register.

Control of Purchases and Cash Disbursements

Cash disbursements are very vulnerable to fraud and embezzlement. In a recent and notable case, the treasurer of one of the nation's largest jewelry retailers was charged with having stolen over one-half million dollars by systematically overpaying federal income taxes and pocketing the refund checks as they came back to the company.

To avoid this kind of theft, cash should be paid only on the basis of specific authorization that is supported by documents establishing the validity and amount of the claim. In addition, maximum possible use should be made of the principle of separation of duties in the purchase of goods and services and the payments for them. The amount of separation of duties will vary depending on the size of the business. Figure 5-2 shows how this kind of control can be achieved in companies large enough for maximum separation of duties. In this example, five internal units (the requesting department, the purchasing department, the accounting department, the receiving department, and the treasurer) and two external contacts (the supplier and the banking system) all play a role in the internal control plan. Note that business documents also play an important role in the plan. The plan is summarized in Table 5-1. Under this plan, every action is documented and subject to verification by at least one other person. For

Figure 5-2. Internal Control for Purchasing and Paying for Goods and Services

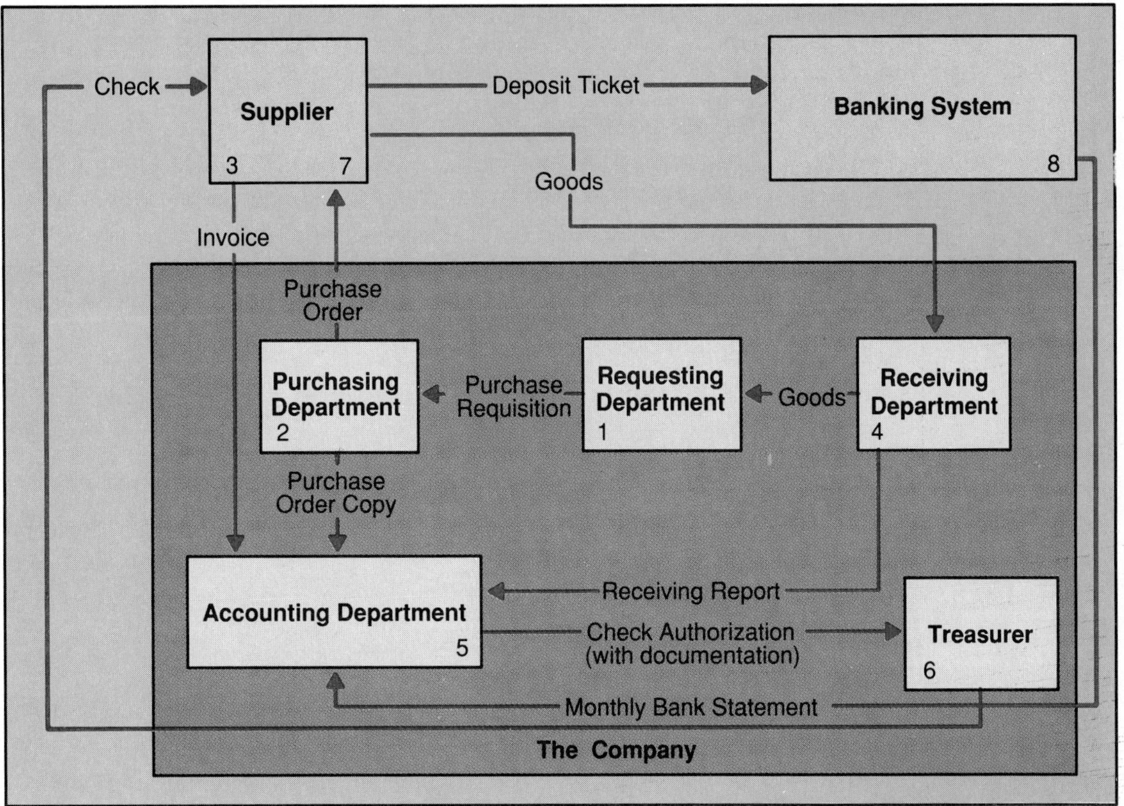

instance, the requesting department cannot work out a kickback scheme with the supplier because the receiving department independently records receipts and the accounting department verifies prices. The receiving department cannot steal goods because the receiving report must equal the invoices. For the same reason, the supplier cannot bill for more goods than were shipped. The accounting department's work is verified by the treasurer, and the treasurer is ultimately checked by the accounting department.

Figures 5-3 through 5-7, which show typical documents used in this plan, use as an example the purchase of twenty boxes of fax paper rolls. In Figure 5-3 the credit office of Martin Maintenance Company fills out a **purchase requisition** for twenty boxes of fax paper rolls. The department head approves it and forwards it to the purchasing department. The people in the purchasing department prepare a **purchase order**, as illustrated in Figure 5-4. The purchase order is addressed to the vendor (seller) and contains a description of the items ordered; their expected price, terms, and shipping date; and other shipping instructions. Martin Maintenance Company will not pay any bill that is not accompanied by a purchase order number.

After receiving the purchase order, the vendor, Henderson Supply Company, ships the goods (in this case delivers them) and sends an **invoice**, or bill (Figure 5-5, page 240), to Martin Maintenance Company. The invoice gives the quantity and a description of the goods delivered, the terms of payment, and the corresponding purchase order number. If the goods cannot all be shipped immediately, the estimated date for shipment of the remainder is indicated.

When the goods reach the receiving department of Martin Maintenance Company, an employee of this department writes the description, quantity, and condition of the goods on the **receiving report**. The receiving department does not receive a copy of the purchase order or invoice, so the people in that department do not know what is to be received. Thus they are not tempted to steal any excess that may be delivered.

Table 5-1. Internal Control Plan for Cash Disbursements

Business Document	Prepared by	Sent to	Verifications and Related Procedures
1. Purchase requisition	Requesting department	Purchasing department	Purchasing verifies authorization.
2. Purchase order	Purchasing department	Supplier	Supplier sends goods or services in accordance with purchase order.
3. Invoice	Supplier	Accounting department	Accounting receives invoice from supplier.
4. Receiving report	Receiving department	Accounting department	Accounting compares invoice, purchase order, and receiving report. Accounting verifies prices.
5. Check authorization (or voucher)	Accounting department	Treasurer	Accounting attaches check authorization to invoice, purchase order, and receiving report.
6. Check	Treasurer	Supplier	Treasurer verifies all documents before preparing check.
7. Deposit ticket	Supplier	Supplier's bank	Supplier compares check with invoice. Bank deducts check from buyer's account.
8. Bank statement	Buyer's bank	Accounting department	Accounting compares amount and payee's name on returned check with check authorization.

Figure 5-3. Purchase Requisition

PURCHASE REQUISITION No. 7077

Martin Maintenance Company

From: Credit Office Date September 6, 19xx

To: Purchasing Department Suggested Vendor: Henderson Supply Company

Please purchase the following items:

Quantity	Number	Description
20 boxes	X 144	Fax paper rolls

Reason for Request

Six months' supply for office

Approved BM

To be filled in by Purchasing Department

Date ordered 9/8/xx P.O. No. J 102

Figure 5-4. Purchase Order

PURCHASE ORDER No. J 102

Martin Maintenance Company
8428 Rocky Island Avenue
Chicago, Illinois 60643

To: Henderson Supply Company
2525 25th Street
Mesa, Illinois 61611

Date September 8, 19xx

FOB Destination

Ship by September 12, 19xx

Ship to: Martin Maintenance Company
Above Address

Terms 2/10, n/30

Please ship the following:

Quantity	✓	Number	Description	Price	Per	Amount
20 boxes		X 144	Fax paper rolls	12.00	box	$240.00

Purchase order number must appear on all shipments and invoices.

Ordered by Marsha Owen

Figure 5-5. Invoice

INVOICE No. 0468

Henderson Supply Company
2525 25th Street
Mesa, Illinois 61611

Date September 12, 19xx

Your Order No. J 102

Sold to:

Martin Maintenance Company
8428 Rocky Island Avenue
Chicago, Illinois 60643

Ship to:

Same

Sales Representative: Joe Jacobs

Quantity		Description	Price	Per	Amount
Ordered	Shipped				
20	20	X144 Fax Paper Rolls	12.00	box	$240.00

FOB Delivered | Terms: 2/10,n/30 | Date Shipped: 9/12/xx Via: Self

Figure 5-6. Check Authorization

CHECK AUTHORIZATION

	NO.	CHECK
Requisition	7077	✓
Purchase Order	J 102	✓
Receiving Report	JR 065	✓
INVOICE	0468	
Price		✓
Calculations		✓
Terms		✓
Approved for Payment	J. Joseph	

The receiving report is sent to the accounting department, where it is compared with the purchase order and the invoice. If all is correct, the accounting department completes a **check authorization** and attaches it to the three supporting documents. The check authorization form shown in Figure 5-6 has a space for each item to be checked off as it is examined. Note that the accounting department has all the documentary

Figure 5-7. Check with Attached Remittance Advice

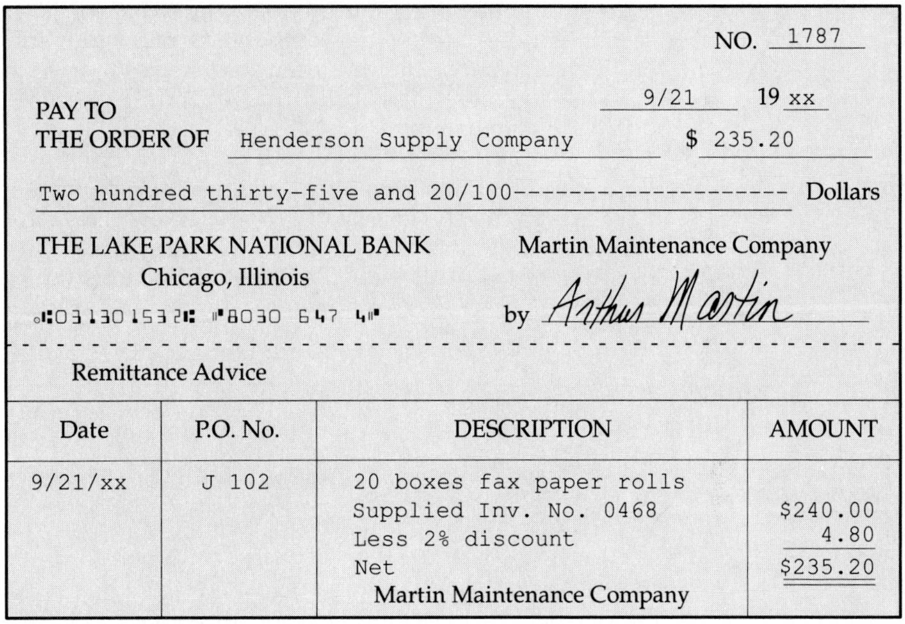

NO. 1787

9/21 19 xx

PAY TO
THE ORDER OF Henderson Supply Company $ 235.20

Two hundred thirty-five and 20/100------------------- Dollars

THE LAKE PARK NATIONAL BANK
Chicago, Illinois

Martin Maintenance Company

⑆031301532⑆ ⑈8030 647 4⑈

by Arthur Martin

Remittance Advice

Date	P.O. No.	DESCRIPTION	AMOUNT
9/21/xx	J 102	20 boxes fax paper rolls	
		Supplied Inv. No. 0468	$240.00
		Less 2% discount	4.80
		Net	$235.20
		Martin Maintenance Company	

evidence for the transaction but does not have access to the assets purchased. Nor does it write the checks for payment. For this reason, the people performing the accounting function cannot gain by falsifying documents in an effort to conceal fraud.

Finally, the treasurer again examines all the evidence and issues a **check** (Figure 5-7 above) for the amount of the invoice less any appropriate discount. In some systems, the accounting department fills out the check, so that all the treasurer has to do is inspect and sign it. The check is then sent to the supplier, with remittance advice, which shows what the check is paying. A supplier who is not paid the proper amount will complain, of course, thus providing a form of outside control over the payment. The supplier will deposit the check in the bank, which will return the canceled check with Martin Maintenance Company's next bank statement. If the treasurer has made the check for an incorrect amount (or altered a prefilled-in check), it will show up at this point.

There are many variations of the system just described. This example is offered as a simple system that provides adequate internal control.

Chapter Review

Review of Learning Objectives

1. **Compare the income statements for service and merchandising concerns.** The merchandising company differs from the service company in that it attempts to earn income by buying and selling merchandise rather than by offering services. In the simplest case, the income statement for a service

company consists only of revenues and expenses. The income statement for a merchandising company has three major parts: (1) revenues from sales, (2) cost of goods sold, and (3) operating expenses. The cost of goods sold section is necessary for the computation of gross margin from sales made on the merchandise that has been sold. Merchandisers must sell their merchandise for more than cost to pay operating expenses and have an adequate profit remaining.

2. **Record transactions involving revenues for merchandising concerns.** Revenues from sales consist of gross sales less sales returns and allowances and sales discounts. The amount of a sales discount can be determined from the terms of the sale. Revenue transactions for merchandising firms may be summarized as follows:

	Related Accounting Entries	
Transaction	**Debit**	**Credit**
Sell merchandise to customer.	Cash (or Accounts Receivable)	Sales
Collect for merchandise sold on credit.	Cash (and Sales Discounts, if applicable)	Accounts Receivable
Permit customers to return merchandise or grant a reduction on original price.	Sales Returns and Allowances	Cash (or Accounts Receivable)

3. **Calculate cost of goods sold.** To compute cost of goods sold under the periodic inventory system, add beginning merchandise inventory to the net purchases to determine goods available for sale. Then subtract ending merchandise inventory from the total, as follows:

$$\text{Beginning Merchandise Inventory} + \text{Net Purchases} = \text{Goods Available for Sale}$$

$$\text{Goods Available for Sale} - \text{Ending Merchandise Inventory} = \text{Cost of Goods Sold}$$

Net purchases are calculated by subtracting the purchases discounts and purchases returns and allowances from gross purchases and then adding any freight-in charges on the purchases, as follows:

$$\text{Gross Purchases} - \text{Purchases Discounts} - \text{Purchases Returns and Allowances} + \text{Freight In} = \text{Net Purchases}$$

The Purchases account is debited only for merchandise purchased for resale. Its sole purpose is to accumulate the total cost of merchandise purchased during an accounting period.

4. **Record transactions involving purchases of merchandise.**
The transactions involving purchases of merchandise may be summarized as follows:

	Related Accounting Entries	
Transaction	**Debit**	**Credit**
Purchase merchandise for resale.	Purchases	Cash (or Accounts Payable)
Incur transportation charges on merchandise purchased for resale.	Freight In	Cash (or Accounts Payable)
Return unsatisfactory merchandise to supplier, or obtain a reduction from original price.	Cash (or Accounts Payable)	Purchases Returns and Allowances
Pay for merchandise purchased on credit.	Accounts Payable	Cash (and Purchases Discounts, if applicable)

5. **Differentiate the perpetual inventory system from the periodic inventory system.**
Merchandise inventory may be determined by one of two systems. (1) Under the perpetual inventory system, records are kept of the quantity and usually the cost of individual items of inventory throughout the year as items are bought and sold. Cost of goods sold is recorded as goods are transferred to customers, and the inventory balance is kept current throughout the year as items are bought and sold. (2) Under the periodic inventory system, the company usually waits until the end of the accounting period to take a physical inventory and does not maintain detailed records of physical inventory on hand during the period. Cost of goods sold is computed after a physical inventory is taken. Merchandise inventory includes all salable goods owned, regardless of where they are located.

6. **Prepare an income statement for a merchandising concern.**
The income statement of a merchandising company comprises three major sections. The revenues from sales section will show gross sales, with contra-revenue accounts deducted from it to arrive at net sales. The cost of goods sold section will show the accounts that make up goods available for sale and ending inventory. Net sales less cost of goods sold equals gross margin from sales. The operating expenses section will divide the expenses into useful categories, such as selling expenses and general and administrative expenses. Net income is revenues from sales less cost of goods sold (gross margin from sales) less operating expenses.

7. **Explain the objectives of handling merchandise inventory at the end of the accounting period and how they are achieved.**
At the end of the accounting period under a periodic inventory system, it is necessary to (1) remove the beginning balance from the Merchandise Inventory account, (2) enter the ending balance in the Merchandise Inventory

account, and (3) enter these two amounts in the Income Summary account so that the proper calculation of net income results. These objectives are accomplished by crediting Merchandise Inventory and debiting Income Summary for the beginning balance and debiting Merchandise Inventory and crediting Income Summary for the ending balance, as shown:

Inventory Procedures at End of Period	Related Accounting Entries	
	Debit	**Credit**
Transfer the balance of the beginning inventory to the Income Summary account.	Income Summary	Merchandise Inventory
Take a physical inventory of goods on hand at the end of the period, and establish the balance of ending inventory.	Merchandise Inventory	Income Summary

8. **Prepare a work sheet and adjusting and closing entries for a merchandising concern.**
The major difference between preparing a work sheet for a merchandising concern and preparing one for a service company is the accounts relating to merchandising transactions. The accounts necessary to compute cost of goods sold appear in the Income Statement columns. Under the closing entry method, the beginning inventory from the trial balance is extended to the debit column of the Income Statement, and the ending balance of Merchandise Inventory is inserted in the credit column of the Income Statement and the debit column of the Balance Sheet.
Under the closing entry method, the adjusting entries for a merchandising concern are similar to those for a service business. The greatest difference in the closing entries is in the handling of merchandise inventory. Merchandise Inventory is credited for the amount of the beginning inventory to remove the beginning inventory from the records. The corresponding debit is to Income Summary. Then, Merchandise Inventory is debited for the amount of the ending inventory with a corresponding credit to Income Summary.

9. **Define *internal control* and identify the three elements of the internal control structure, including seven examples of control procedures.**
Internal controls are the methods and procedures employed primarily to protect assets and ensure the accuracy and reliability of the accounting records, but also to achieve efficient operation and compliance with management policies. The internal control structure consists of three elements: the control environment, the accounting system, and the control procedures. Examples of control procedures are proper authorization of transactions; recording of transactions to facilitate preparation of financial statements and to establish accountability for assets; use of well-designed documents and records; access to assets limited to authorized personnel; periodic in-

dependent comparison of records and assets; appropriate separation of duties into the functions of authorization, operations and custody of assets, and recordkeeping; and use of sound personnel policies.

10. **Describe the inherent limitations of internal control.**
To be effective, a system of internal control must rely on the people who perform the duties assigned. Thus, the effectiveness of internal control is limited by the people involved. Human errors, collusion, management interference, and failure to recognize changed conditions can all contribute to a system failure.

11. **Apply control procedures to certain merchandising transactions.**
Internal control over sales, cash receipts, purchases, and cash disbursements is strengthened if the attributes of effective internal control are applied. First, the functions of authorization, recordkeeping, and custody should be kept separate. Second, the accounting system should provide for physical protection of assets (especially cash and merchandise inventory), prompt recording and depositing of cash receipts, and payment by check only on the basis of documentary support. Third, persons who have access to cash and merchandise inventory should be specifically designated and their number limited. Fourth, personnel should be trained and bonded. Fifth, the Cash account should be reconciled monthly, and surprise audits of cash on hand should be made by an individual who does not handle or record cash.

Review of Concepts and Terminology

The following concepts and terms were introduced in this chapter:

(L.O. 9) **Accounting system:** The methods and records established to identify, assemble, analyze, classify, and report a company's transactions and to provide assurance that the objectives of internal control are achieved.

(L.O. 5) **Beginning inventory:** Merchandise (for sale to customers) on hand at the beginning of the accounting period.

(L.O. 9) **Bonding:** The careful checking of an employee's background and insuring the company against theft by that person.

(L.O. 11) **Check:** A written order to a bank to pay the amount specified from funds on deposit.

(L.O. 11) **Check authorization:** A form prepared by the accounting department after it has compared the receiving report for goods received with the purchase order and the invoice.

(L.O. 9) **Control environment:** The overall attitude, awareness, and actions of the owners and management of a business, as reflected in philosophy and operating style, organizational structure, methods of assigning authority and responsibility, and personnel policies and practices.

(L.O. 9) **Control procedures:** Additional procedures and policies established by management to provide assurance that the objectives of internal control are achieved.

(L.O. 1) **Cost of goods sold:** The amount paid for goods that were sold during an accounting period.

(L.O. 5) **Ending inventory:** Merchandise (for sale to customers) on hand at the end of the accounting period.

(L.O. 4) **FOB destination:** Term relating to transportation charges meaning that the seller bears the transportation costs to the destination.

(L.O. 4) **FOB shipping point:** Term relating to transportation charges meaning that the buyer bears the transportation costs from the point of origin.

(L.O. 4) **Freight in (transportation in):** Transportation charges on merchandise purchased for resale.

(L.O. 3) **Goods available for sale:** The total goods during the accounting period that could have been sold to customers; the beginning merchandise inventory plus net purchases.

(L.O. 1) **Gross margin from sales (or gross profit):** The amount of revenues from sales, after deducting cost of goods sold, that is available for operating expenses, income taxes, and net income.

(L.O. 4) **Gross method:** The system of initially recording purchases at the gross purchase price.

(L.O. 2) **Gross sales:** Total sales for cash and on credit for a given accounting period.

(L.O. 1) **Income before income taxes:** For a merchandising concern, gross margin less operating expenses.

(L.O. 9) **Internal control:** Plan of organization and all policies and procedures adopted within a company to safeguard its assets, check the accuracy and reliability of its accounting data, promote operational efficiency, and encourage adherence to prescribed managerial policies.

(L.O. 9) **Internal control structure:** A structure established to safeguard the assets of a business and provide reliable accounting records; consists of the control environment, the accounting system, and the control procedures.

(L.O. 11) **Invoice:** A form sent or delivered to the purchaser by the vendor (seller) giving the quantity and price as well as a description of goods delivered and the terms of payment.

(L.O. 3) **Merchandise inventory:** Goods on hand available for sale to customers.

(L.O. 1) **Net income:** The net increase in owners' equity resulting from the profit-seeking operations of a company; net income = revenue − expenses. For merchandising companies, what is left after deducting operating expenses and income taxes from gross margin.

(L.O. 4) **Net method:** A method of recording purchases that, in order to identify the discounts that are lost, requires that purchases be recorded initially at the net price.

(L.O. 4) **Net purchases:** Under the periodic inventory system, gross purchases less purchases discounts and purchases returns and allowances plus any freight charges on the purchases.

(L.O. 2) **Net sales:** Gross proceeds from sales of merchandise less sales returns and allowances and sales discounts.

(L.O. 1) **Operating expenses:** Those expenses, other than cost of goods sold, that are incurred in running the business.

(L.O. 1) **Operating income (income from operations):** Same as income before income taxes; gross margin less operating expenses.

(L.O. 5) **Periodic inventory system:** Determination of cost of goods sold by deducting the ending inventory, which has been determined by a physical count of

the physical inventory, from the total of purchases plus beginning merchandise inventory.

(L.O. 5) **Perpetual inventory system:** Determination of cost of goods sold by keeping continuous records of the physical inventory as goods are bought and sold.

(L.O. 11) **Purchase order:** A form addressed by the purchasing department of a company to a vendor (seller) containing a description of the items ordered; their expected price, terms, and shipping date; and other shipping instructions.

(L.O. 11) **Purchase requisition:** A formal written request for a purchase.

(L.O. 4) **Purchases:** An account used under the periodic inventory system in which the cost of all merchandise bought for resale is recorded.

(L.O. 4) **Purchases discounts:** Allowances made for prompt payment for merchandise purchased for resale; a contra-purchases account.

(L.O. 4) **Purchases Returns and Allowances:** Account used to accumulate cash refunds and other allowances made by suppliers on merchandise originally purchased for resale; a contra-purchases account.

(L.O. 11) **Receiving report:** A form prepared by the receiving department of a company giving the description, quantity, and condition of goods received.

(L.O. 1) **Revenues from sales:** Sales of goods by a merchandising company.

(L.O. 2) **Sales discounts:** Discounts given to customers for early payment for sales made on credit; a contra-revenue account.

(L.O. 2) **Sales Returns and Allowances:** Account used to accumulate the amount of cash refunds granted to customers or other allowances related to prior sales; a contra-revenue account.

(L.O. 5) **Taking a physical inventory:** The act of making a physical count of all merchandise on hand at the end of an accounting period.

(L.O. 2) **Trade discounts:** Prices for merchandise quoted at a discount (usually 30 percent or more) when manufacturers and wholesalers wish to avoid reprinting catalogues and price lists every time there is a price change.

(L.O. 2) **2/10, n/30:** Credit terms enabling the debtor to take a 2 percent discount if the invoice is paid within ten days of the invoice date; otherwise, the debtor must pay the full amount of the invoice within thirty days.

Review Problem
Methods of Recording Purchases and Sales Contrasted

(L.O. 2, 4) Newcomb Discount Warehouse Corporation purchased $80,000 of merchandise, terms 2/10, n/30, from Videotex Corporation on September 14.

Required

1. Give the entries in Newcomb's records to record the purchase and payment under each of the following situations.
   a. Purchases are recorded at gross amount, and payment is made on September 24.
   b. Purchases are recorded at gross amount, and payment is made on October 14.
   c. Purchases are recorded at net amount, and payment is made on September 24.

d. Purchases are recorded at net amount, and payment is made on October 14.

2. Give the entries on Videotex's records to record the sale and its collection under each of the four situations above. Assume all sales are recorded at their gross amounts.

Answer to Review Problem

Situation	Date	1. Newcomb's Records			2. Videotex's Records		
a.	Sept. 14	Purchases	80,000		Accounts Receivable	80,000	
		Accounts Payable		80,000	Sales		80,000
		To record purchase—gross method			To record sales		
	Sept. 24	Accounts Payable	80,000		Cash	78,400	
		Purchases Discounts		1,600	Sales Discounts	1,600	
		Cash		78,400	Accounts Receivable		80,000
		To record payment—gross method			To record collection		
b.	Sept. 14	Purchases	80,000		Accounts Receivable	80,000	
		Accounts Payable		80,000	Sales		80,000
		To record purchase—gross method			To record sales		
	Oct. 14	Accounts Payable	80,000		Cash	80,000	
		Cash		80,000	Accounts Receivable		80,000
		To record payment—gross method			To record collection		
c.	Sept. 14	Purchases	78,400		Accounts Receivable	80,000	
		Accounts Payable		78,400	Sales		80,000
		To record purchase—net method			To record sales		
	Sept. 24	Accounts Payable	78,400		Cash	78,400	
		Cash		78,400	Sales Discounts	1,600	
		To record payment—net method			Accounts Receivable		80,000
					To record collection		
d.	Sept. 14	Purchases	78,400		Accounts Receivable	80,000	
		Accounts Payable		78,400	Sales		80,000
		To record purchase—net method			To record sales		
	Oct. 14	Accounts Payable	78,400		Cash	80,000	
		Purchases Discounts Lost	1,600		Accounts Receivable		80,000
		Cash		80,000	To record collection		
		To record payment—net method					

Chapter Assignments

Discussion Questions

1. What is the primary difference between the operations of a merchandising concern and those of a service concern, and how is it reflected on the income statement?

2. What is the source of revenues for a merchandising concern?
3. Define gross margin from sales. Why is it important?
4. Kumler Nursery had a cost of goods sold during its first year of $64,000 and a gross margin from sales equal to 40 percent of sales. What was the dollar amount of the company's sales?
5. Could Kumler Nursery (in question **4**) have a net loss for the year? Explain your answer.
6. Why is it advisable to maintain an account for Sales Returns and Allowances when the same result could be obtained by debiting each return or allowance to the Sales account?
7. What is a sales discount? If the terms are 2/10, n/30, what is the length of the credit period? What is the length of the discount period?
8. What two related transactions are reflected in the T accounts below?

Cash

(b)	980		

Accounts Receivable

(a)	1,000	(b)	1,000

Sales

		(a)	1,000

Sales Discounts

(b)	20		

9. What is the normal balance of the Sales Discounts account? Is it an asset, liability, expense, or contra-revenue account?
10. In counting the ending inventory, a clerk counts a $200 item of inventory twice. What effect does this error have on the balance sheet and income statement?
11. Hornberger Hardware purchased the following items: (a) a delivery truck, (b) two dozen hammers, (c) supplies for its office workers, (d) a broom for the janitor. Which item(s) should be debited to the Purchases account?
12. What three related transactions are reflected in the T accounts that are shown below?

Cash

		(c)	441

Accounts Payable

(b)	50	(a)	500
(c)	450		

Purchases

(a)	500		

Purchases Returns and Allowances

		(b)	50

Purchases Discounts

		(c)	9

13. How would the transactions in question **12** differ if the net method of recording purchases were used?
14. Is Freight In an operating expense? Explain.
15. Prices and terms quoted by two companies on fifty units of product are as follows: Supplier A—50 at $20 per unit, FOB shipping point; Supplier

B—50 at $21 per unit, FOB destination. Which supplier has quoted the better deal? Explain.

16. Does the beginning or ending inventory appear in the year-end unadjusted trial balance prepared by a company that uses the periodic inventory system?
17. Under the periodic inventory system, how is the amount of inventory at the end of the year determined?
18. What is your assessment of the following statement: "The perpetual inventory system is the best system because management always needs to know how much inventory it has"?
19. Why is the handling of merchandise inventory at the end of the accounting period of special importance in the determination of net income? What must be achieved in the account?
20. What are the principal differences between the work sheet for a merchandising company and that for a service company? Discuss in terms of the closing entry method.
21. Most people think of internal control as making fraud harder to commit and easier to detect. Can you think of some other important purposes of internal control?
22. What are the three elements of the internal control structure?
23. What are some examples of control procedures?
24. Why is a separation of duties policy necessary to ensure sound internal control?
25. At Thrifty Variety Store, each sales clerk counts the cash in his or her cash drawer at the end of the day and then removes the cash register tape and prepares the daily cash form, noting any discrepancies. This information is checked by an employee in the cashier's office, who counts the cash, compares the total with the form, and takes the cash to the cashier's office. What is the weakness in this system of internal control?
26. How does a movie theater control cash receipts?
27. One of the basic principles of internal control is separation of duties. What does this principle assume about the relationships of employees in a company and the possibility of two or more of them stealing from the company?

Communication Skills Exercises

Communication 5-1. Merchandising Income Statement
(L.O. 1, 6)

Village TV and ***TV Warehouse*** sell television sets and other video equipment in the Phoenix area. Village TV gives each customer individual attention, with employees explaining the features, advantages, and disadvantages of each video component. When a customer buys a television set or video system, Village provides free delivery to the customer's house, installs and adjusts the equipment, and teaches the family how to use it. TV Warehouse sells the same video components through showroom display. If a customer wants to buy a video component or a system, he or she fills out a form and takes it to the cashier for payment. After paying, the customer drives around to the back of the warehouse to pick up the component, which he or she then takes home and installs. Village TV charges higher prices than TV Warehouse for the same components. How would you expect the income statements of Village TV and TV Warehouse to differ? Is it possible to tell which approach is more profitable?

Communication 5-2. Periodic vs. Perpetual Inventory Systems
(L.O. 5)

The Book Nook is a well-established chain of twenty book stores in eastern Michigan. In recent years the company has grown rapidly, adding five new stores in regional malls. Management has relied on the manager of each store to place orders keyed to the market in his or her neighborhood, selected from a master list of available titles provided by the central office. Every six months, a physical inventory is taken and financial statements are prepared using the periodic inventory system. At that time, books that have not sold well are placed on sale or, whenever possible, returned to the publisher. As a result of the company's fast growth, management has found that the newer store managers do not have the same ability to judge the market as managers of the older, established stores. Thus, management is considering a recommendation to implement a perpetual inventory system and carefully monitor sales from the central office. Do you think The Book Nook should switch to the perpetual inventory system or stay with the current periodic inventory system? What are the advantages and disadvantages of each?

Communication 5-3. Basic Control Procedures
(L.O. 9)

The Book Nook, which is described in the previous communication skills exercise, sets up its stores so that each has one cash register and accepts cash, checks, or approved credit cards in payment. In addition to the store manager, the employees include a cashier and several stock clerks. Suggest control procedures for authorization, recording of transactions, documents and records, limited access, periodic independent verification, separation of duties, and sound personnel policies for control of sales for The Book Nook.

Communication 5-4. Basic Research Skills
(L.O. 9)

Visit a local outlet of a national retail chain, such as a fast-food restaurant, music store, or jeans or other clothing store. Observe for one hour and record as much as you can about the company's internal control structure. It is usually best to conduct the observation at a busy time of day. How do you go about assessing the control environment? Are any aspects of the company's accounting system apparent? What control procedures, including authorization, recording of transactions, documents and records, limited access, periodic independent verification, separation of duties, and sound personnel policies, can you observe? Be prepared to discuss your observations in class.

Classroom Exercises

Exercise 5-1. Computation of Net Sales
(L.O. 2)

During 19xx, the Nexus Corporation had total credit sales of $220,000. Of this amount, $180,000 was collected during the year. In addition, the corporation had cash sales of $120,000. Furthermore, customers returned merchandise for credit of $8,000, and cash discounts of $4,000 were allowed. How much would 19xx net sales be for the Nexus Corporation?

Exercise 5-2. Sales Transactions
(L.O. 2)

On June 15, the Jackson Company sold merchandise for $2,600 on terms of 2/10, n/30 to Clement Company. Give the entries to record (1) the sale, (2) a return of merchandise of $600, June 20, (3) receipt of the balance from Clement Company, assuming payment on June 25, (4) balance from Clement Company, assuming receipt of a check on July 15.

Exercise 5-3. Parts of the Income Statement: Missing Data *(L.O. 2, 3, 4)*

Compute the dollar amount of each item indicated by a letter in the table below. Treat each horizontal row of numbers as a separate problem.

Sales	Beginning Inventory	Net Purchases	Ending Inventory	Cost of Goods Sold	Gross Margin	Operating Expenses	Income (or Loss)
$125,000	$ a	$ 35,000	$10,000	$ b	$40,000	$ c	$12,000
d	12,000	e	18,000	108,000	60,000	40,000	20,000
230,000	22,000	167,000	f	g	50,000	h	(1,000)
390,000	40,000	i	60,000	j	k	120,000	40,000

Exercise 5-4. Gross Margin from Sales Computation: Missing Data *(L.O. 3)*

Determine the amount of gross purchases by preparing a partial income statement showing the calculation of gross margin from sales from the following data: Purchases Discounts, $3,500; Freight In, $13,000; Cost of Goods Sold, $185,000; Sales, $275,000; Beginning Inventory, $25,000; Purchases Returns and Allowances, $4,000; Ending Inventory, $12,000.

Exercise 5-5. Purchases and Sales Involving Discounts *(L.O. 2, 4)*

The Orosco Company purchased $4,600 of merchandise, terms 2/10, n/30, from the Garber Company and paid for the merchandise within the discount period. Give the entries (1) by the Orosco Company to record the purchase and payment, assuming purchases are recorded at gross purchase price, and (2) by the Garber Company to record the sale and receipt.

Exercise 5-6. Gross and Net Methods of Recording Purchases Contrasted *(L.O. 4)*

Westland Corporation purchased $9,400 of merchandise, terms 2/10, n/30, on June 10. Give the entries to record purchase and payment under each of the four assumptions below.

1. Purchases are recorded at gross amount, and payment is made June 20.
2. Purchases are recorded at gross amount, and payment is made July 10.
3. Purchases are recorded at net amount, and payment is made June 20.
4. Purchases are recorded at net amount, and payment is made July 20.

Exercise 5-7. Recording Purchases: Gross and Net Methods *(L.O. 4)*

Give the entries to record each of the following transactions, first using the gross method and then using the net method:

1. Purchased merchandise on credit, terms 2/10, n/30, FOB shipping point, $2,500.
2. Paid freight on shipment in transaction **1**, $135.
3. Purchased merchandise on credit, terms 2/10, n/30, FOB destination, $1,400.
4. Purchased merchandise on credit, terms 2/10, n/30, FOB shipping point, $2,600, which includes freight paid by supplier of $200.
5. Returned merchandise pertaining to transaction **3**, $500.
6. Paid the amount owed on the purchases in transactions **1** and **4**, respectively, within the discount periods. Record as two transactions.
7. Paid the amount owed on the purchase in transaction **3** less return, but not within the discount period.

Exercise 5-8. Preparation of Income Statement from Work Sheet *(L.O. 6)*

Selected items from the Income Statement columns of the December 31, 19xx work sheet of the Mill Pond General Store for the year ended December 31, 19xx appear below:

Account Name	Income Statement	
	Debit	Credit
Sales		297,000
Sales Returns and Allowances	11,000	
Sales Discounts	4,200	
Purchases	114,800	
Purchases Returns and Allowances		1,800
Purchases Discounts		2,200
Freight In	5,600	
Selling Expenses	48,500	
General and Administrative Expenses	37,200	
Income Taxes Expense	15,000	

Beginning merchandise inventory was $26,000, and ending merchandise inventory is $22,000. From the information given, prepare a 19xx income statement for the company.

Exercise 5-9. Merchandising Income Statement: Missing Data, Multiple Years *(L.O. 6)*

Determine the missing data for each letter in the following three income statements for Belden Wholesale Paper Company (in thousands):

	19x3	19x2	19x1
Gross Sales	$ p	$ h	$286
Sales Returns and Allowances	19	12	14
Sales Discounts	5	7	a
Net Sales	q	317	b
Merchandise Inventory, Jan. 1	r	i	38
Purchases	192	169	c
Purchases Returns and Allowances	23	j	13
Purchases Discounts	8	5	4
Freight In	s	29	22
Net Purchases	189	k	d
Goods Available for Sale	222	212	182
Merchandise Inventory, Dec. 31	39	l	42
Cost of Goods Sold	t	179	e
Gross Margin from Sales	142	m	126
Selling Expenses	u	78	f
General and Administrative Expenses	39	n	33
Total Operating Expenses	130	128	g
Income Before Income Taxes	v	o	27
Income Taxes Expense	2	2	5
Net Income	w	8	22

Exercise 5-10. Preparation of Closing Entries *(L.O. 8)*

Using the closing entry method, prepare closing entries from the information given in Exercise 5-8, assuming that Mill Pond General Store declared and paid dividends of $34,000 during the year.

Exercise 5-11. Preparation of Work Sheet *(L.O. 8)*

Simplified trial balance accounts and their balances for Lane Office Supplies, Inc. for the period ended December 31, 19xx follow in alphabetical order: Accounts Payable, $3; Accounts Receivable, $25; Accumulated Depreciation, Store Equipment, $6; Cash, $12; Common Stock, $40; Dividends, $12; Freight In, $2; General Expenses, $15; Merchandise Inventory (Beginning), $8; Prepaid Insurance, $2; Purchases, $35; Purchases Returns and Allowances, $2; Retained Earnings, $27; Sales, $97; Sales Discounts, $3; Selling Expenses, $22; Store Equipment, $30; Store Supplies, $9.

Copy the trial balance accounts and amounts onto a work sheet in the same order as they appear above. Complete the work sheet, using the closing entry method and the following information: (a) estimated depreciation on store equipment, $3; (b) ending inventory of store supplies, $2; (c) expired insurance, $1; (d) estimated income taxes, $2; (e) ending merchandise inventory, $7.

Exercise 5-12. Use of Accounting Records in Internal Control *(L.O. 9)*

Careful scrutiny of the accounting records and financial statements may lead to the discovery of fraud or embezzlement. Each of the following situations may indicate a breakdown in internal control. Indicate what the possible fraud or embezzlement may be in each situation.

a. Wages Expense for a branch office was 30 percent higher in 19x2 than in 19x1, even though the office was authorized to employ only the same four employees and raises were only 5 percent in 19x2.
b. Sales Returns and Allowances increased from 5 percent to 20 percent of sales in the first two months of 19x2, after record sales in 19x1 resulted in large bonuses being paid to the sales staff.
c. Gross Margin decreased from 40 percent of net sales to 30 percent even though there was no change in pricing. Ending inventory was 50 percent less than that at the beginning of the year. There is no immediate explanation for the decrease in inventory.
d. A review of daily cash register receipts records shows that one cashier consistently accepts more discount coupons for purchases than other cashiers.

Exercise 5-13. Control Procedures *(L.O. 9)*

Sean O'Mara, who operates a small grocery store, has established the following policies with regard to the check-out cashiers:

_____ 1. Each cashier has his or her own cash drawer, to which no one else has access.

_____ 2. Each cashier may accept checks for purchases under $50 with proper identification. Checks over $50 must be approved by O'Mara before they are accepted.

_____ 3. Every sale must be rung up on the cash register and a receipt given to the customer. Each sale is recorded on a tape inside the cash register.

_____ 4. At the end of each day O'Mara counts the cash in the drawer and compares it with the amount on the tape inside the cash register.

Identify by letter which of the following conditions for internal control apply to each of the above policies:

a. Transactions are executed in accordance with management's general or specific authorization.
b. Transactions are recorded as necessary to (1) permit preparation of financial statements and (2) maintain accountability for assets.
c. Access to assets is permitted only as allowed by management.
d. The recorded accountability for assets is compared with the existing assets at reasonable intervals.

Exercise 5-14. Internal Control Procedures *(L.O. 9)*

Ruth's Video Store maintains the following policies with regard to purchases of new video tapes at each of its branch stores:

_____ 1. Employees are required to take vacations, and duties of employees are rotated periodically.
_____ 2. Once each month a person from the home office visits each branch to examine the receiving records and to compare the inventory of tapes with the accounting records.
_____ 3. Purchases of new tapes must be authorized by purchase order in the home office and paid for by the treasurer in the home office. Receiving reports are prepared in each branch and sent to the home office.
_____ 4. All new personnel receive a one-hour training orientation on receiving and cataloguing new tapes.
_____ 5. The company maintains a perpetual inventory system that keeps track of all tapes purchased, sold, and on hand.

Indicate by letter which of the following control procedures apply to each of the above policies:

a. Authorization
b. Recording
c. Documents and records
d. Limited access
e. Periodic independent verification
f. Separation of duties
g. Sound personnel policies

Exercise 5-15. Internal Control Evaluation *(L.O. 9)*

Developing a convenient means of providing sales representatives with cash for their incidental expenses, such as entertaining a client at lunch, is a problem many companies face. One company has a plan whereby the sales representatives receive advances in cash from the petty cash fund. Each advance is supported by an authorization from the sales manager. The representative returns the receipt for the expenditure and any unused cash, which is replaced in the petty cash fund. The cashier of the petty cash fund is responsible for seeing that the receipt and the cash returned equal the advance. At the time that the petty cash fund is reimbursed, the amount of the representatives' expenditures is debited to Direct Sales Expense.

What is the weak point of the procedure, and what fundamental principle of internal control has been ignored? What improvement in the procedure can you suggest?

Exercise 5-16. Internal Control Evaluation
(L.O. 11)

An accountant and his assistants are responsible for the following procedures: (a) receipt of all cash; (b) maintenance of the general ledger; (c) maintenance of the accounts receivable ledger; (d) maintenance of the journals for recording sales, cash receipts, and purchases; and (e) preparation of monthly statements to be sent to customers. As a service to customers and employees, the company allows the accountant to cash checks of up to $50 with money from the cash receipts. The accountant may approve the cashing of such checks for current employees and customers. When the deposits are made, the checks are included in place of the cash receipts.

What weakness in internal control exists in this system?

Interpretation Cases from Business

ICB 5-1. Wal-Mart[5] vs. Kmart[6]
(L.O. 1)

Wal-Mart Stores, Inc. and Kmart Corp., two of the largest and most successful retailers in the United States, have different approaches to retailing. The difference may be revealed by analyzing their respective income statements and merchandise inventories. Selected information from their annual reports for the year ended January 31, 1990 is presented below. (All amounts are in millions.)

Wal-Mart: Net Sales, $25,810; Cost of Goods Sold, $20,070; Operating Expenses, $4,069; Ending Inventory, $4,428.

Kmart: Net Sales, $29,793; Cost of Goods Sold, $21,745; Operating Expenses, $7,282; Ending Inventory, $6,933.

Required

1. Prepare a schedule computing gross margin from sales and net income (ignore income taxes) for both companies as dollar amounts and as percentages of net sales. Also, compute inventory as a percentage of cost of goods sold.
2. From what you know about the different retailing approaches of these two companies, do the gross margin and net income computations from **1** seem compatible with these approaches? What is it about the nature of Kmart's operations that results in less gross margin from sales and operating expenses in percentages than Wal-Mart? Which company's approach is more successful for this year? Explain.
3. Both companies choose a fiscal year that ends on January 31. Why do you suppose they made this choice? How realistic do you think the inventory figures are as indicators of inventory levels during the rest of the year?

ICB 5-2. Best Products, Inc.[7]
(L.O. 1, 6)

Best Products, Inc. is one of the nation's largest discount retailers, operating 194 stores in 27 states. In a letter to the stockholders in the 1986 annual report (fiscal year ended January 31, 1987), the chairman and chief executive officer of the company states, "Our operating plan for fiscal 1987 (year ended Janu-

5. Information from the Wal-Mart Annual Report is reprinted by permission of Wal-Mart Stores, Inc.
6. Excerpts from the Annual Report used by permission of Kmart Corporation. All rights reserved.
7. Excerpts from the 1987 Annual Report used by permission of Best Products, Inc. Copyright © 1987.

ary 30, 1988) calls for moderate sales increases, continued improvement in gross margins, and a continuation of aggressive expense reduction programs." The following data are taken from the income statements presented in the 1987 annual report (in millions):

	Year Ended		
	January 30, 1988	January 31, 1987	February 1, 1986
Net Sales	$2,067	$2,142	$2,235
Cost of Goods Sold	1,500	1,593	1,685
Operating Expenses	466	486	502

Required

Has Best Products, Inc. achieved the objective stated by its chairman? **Hint:** Prepare an income statement for each year and compute gross margin and operating expenses as percentages of net sales.

ICB 5-3. J. Walter Thompson Co.[8] *(L.O. 9)*

J. Walter Thompson Co. (JWT) is one of the world's largest advertising agencies, with more than $1 billion in billings per year. One of its smaller units is a television syndication unit that acquires rights to distribute television programming and sells those rights to local television stations, receiving in exchange advertising time that is sold to the agency's clients. Cash rarely changes hands between the unit and the television station, but the unit is supposed to recognize revenue when the television programs are exchanged for advertising time that will be used by clients at a later date.

The *Wall Street Journal* reported on February 17, 1982, that the company "had discovered 'fictitious' accounting entries that inflated revenue at the television program syndication unit." The article went on to say that "the syndication unit booked revenue of $29.3 million over a five-year period, but that $24.5 million of that amount was fictitious" and that "the accounting irregularities didn't involve an outlay of cash . . . and its [JWT's] advertising clients weren't improperly billed. . . . The fictitious sales were recorded in such a manner as to prevent the issuance of billings to advertising clients. The sole effect of these transactions was to overstate the degree to which the unit was achieving its revenue and profit objectives."

The chief financial officer of JWT indicated that "the discrepancies began to surface . . . when the company reorganized so that all accounting functions reported to the chief financial officer's central office. Previously, he said, 'we had been decentralized in accounting,' with the unit keeping its own books."

Required

1. Show an example entry to recognize revenue from the exchange of the right to televise a show for advertising time and an example entry to bill a client for using the advertising time. Explain how the fraud was accomplished.
2. What would motivate the head of the syndication unit to perpetrate this fraud if no cash or other assets were stolen?

8. Based on information from the *Wall Street Journal*, February 17, 1982.

3. What principles of internal control were violated that would allow this fraud to exist for five years, and how did correction of the weaknesses in internal control allow the fraud to be discovered?

Problem Set A

Problem 5A-1. Merchandising Transactions *(L.O. 2, 4)*

Dawkins Company, which uses the periodic inventory system, engaged in the following transactions:

Oct. 1 Sold merchandise to Ernie Devlin on credit, terms 2/10, n/30, $1,050.
2 Purchased merchandise on credit from Ruland Company, terms 2/10, n/30, FOB shipping point, $1,900.
2 Paid Custom Freight $145 for freight charges on merchandise received.
6 Purchased store supplies on credit from Arizin Supply House, terms n/20, $318.
8 Purchased merchandise on credit from PG Company, terms 2/10, n/30, FOB shipping point, $1,200.
8 Paid Custom Freight $97 for freight charges on merchandise received.
9 Purchased merchandise on credit from LNP Company, terms 2/10, n/30, FOB shipping point, $1,800, including $100 freight costs paid by LNP Company.
11 Received full payment from Ernie Devlin for his October 1 purchase.
12 Paid Ruland Company for purchase of October 2.
13 Sold merchandise on credit to Otis King, terms 2/10, n/30, $600.
14 Returned for credit $300 of merchandise received on October 8.
15 Returned for credit $100 of store supplies purchased on October 6.
16 Sold merchandise for cash, $500.
19 Paid LNP Company for purchase of October 9.
22 Paid PG Company for purchase of October 8 less return of October 14.
23 Received full payment from Otis King for his October 13 purchase.
26 Paid Arizin Supply House for purchase of October 6, less return on October 15.
31 Sold merchandise for cash, $675.

Required

1. Prepare general journal entries to record the transactions, assuming purchases are recorded initially at the gross purchase price.
2. Which entries would differ if the purchases were recorded initially at the net purchase price and purchases discounts lost were recognized? What advantages does this method have over the gross method?

Problem 5A-2. Journalizing Transactions of a Merchandising Company *(L.O. 2, 4)*

Following is a list of transactions for the month of January 19xx.

Jan. 2 Purchased merchandise on credit from DEF Company, terms 2/10, n/30, FOB destination, $7,400.
3 Sold merchandise on credit to A. Molina, terms 1/10, n/30, FOB shipping point, $1,000.

Jan. 5 Sold merchandise for cash, $700.
6 Purchased and received merchandise on credit from Stockton Company, terms 2/10, n/30, FOB shipping point, $4,200.
7 Received freight bill from Eastline Express for shipment received on January 6, $570.
9 Sold merchandise on credit to C. Parish, terms 1/10, n/30, FOB destination, $3,800.
10 Purchased merchandise from DEF Company, terms 2/10, n/30, FOB shipping point, $2,650, including freight costs of $150.
11 Received freight bill from Eastline Express for sale to C. Parish on January 9, $291.
12 Paid DEF Company for purchase of January 2.
13 Received payment in full for A. Molina's purchase of January 3.
14 Returned faulty merchandise worth $300 to DEF Company for credit against purchase of January 10.
15 Purchased office supplies from Quaker Co. for $478, terms n/10.
16 Paid Stockton Company one-half of the amount owed from purchase of January 6.
17 Sold merchandise to D. Healy on credit, terms 2/10, n/30, FOB shipping point, $780.
18 Returned for credit several items of office supplies received on Jan. 15, $128.
19 Received payment from C. Parish for one-half of the purchase of January 9.
20 Paid DEF Company in full for amount owed on purchase of January 10, less return on January 14.
22 Gave credit to D. Healy for returned merchandise, $180.
25 Paid for purchase of January 15, less return on January 18.
26 Paid freight company for freight charges, January 7 and 11.
27 Received payment of amount owed by D. Healy from purchase of January 17, less credit of January 22.
28 Paid Stockton Company for balance of January 6 purchase.
31 Sold merchandise for cash, $973.

Required

1. Prepare general journal entries to record the transactions, assuming that the periodic inventory system is used and that purchases are recorded initially at gross purchase price.
2. Tell how the entries would differ if the net method of recording purchases were used.

Problem 5A-3. Income Statement for a Merchandising Concern
(L.O. 6)

Data from Rafi's Camera Store, Inc.'s adjusted trial balance as of the year ended June 30, 19x3 appears on page 260.

The company's beginning inventory was $81,222, and the ending merchandise inventory is $76,664.

Rafi's Camera Store, Inc.
Partial Adjusted Trial Balance
June 30, 19x3

Sales		433,912
Sales Returns and Allowances	11,250	
Purchases	221,185	
Purchases Returns and Allowances		26,450
Purchases Discounts		3,788
Freight In	10,078	
Store Salaries Expense	107,550	
Office Salaries Expense	26,500	
Advertising Expense	18,200	
Rent Expense	14,400	
Insurance Expense	2,800	
Utility Expense	18,760	
Store Supplies Expense	464	
Office Supplies Expense	814	
Depreciation Expense, Store Equipment	1,800	
Depreciation Expense, Office Equipment	1,850	
Income Taxes Expense	5,000	

Required

1. Prepare an income statement for Rafi's Camera Store, Inc. Store Salaries Expense; Advertising Expense; Store Supplies Expense; and Depreciation Expense, Store Equipment, are considered to be selling expenses. The other expenses are considered to be general and administrative expenses.
2. Based on your knowledge at this point in the course, how might you use Rafi's income statement to evaluate the company's profitability?

Problem 5A-4. Internal Control *(L.O. 9)*

Greenwood Company, a small concern, is attempting to organize its accounting department to achieve maximum internal control, subject to the constraint of limited resources. There are three employees (1, 2, and 3) in the accounting department, each of whom has some accounting experience. The accounting department must accomplish the following functions: (a) maintain the general ledger, (b) maintain the accounts payable ledger, (c) maintain the accounts receivable ledger, (d) prepare checks for signature, (e) maintain the cash payments journal, (f) issue credits on returns and allowances, (g) reconcile the bank account, and (h) handle and deposit cash receipts.

Required

1. Assuming that each employee will do only the jobs assigned, assign the functions to the three employees in a way that will ensure the highest degree of internal control possible.
2. Identify four possible unsatisfactory combinations of functions.

Problem 5A-5. Work Sheet, Financial Statements, and Closing Entries for a Merchandising Company *(L.O. 6, 8)*

The following trial balance was taken from the ledger of Conner Book Store, Inc. at the end of its annual accounting period:

Conner Book Store, Inc.
Trial Balance
June 30, 19x2

Cash	$ 6,025	
Accounts Receivable	9,280	
Merchandise Inventory	29,450	
Store Supplies	1,911	
Prepaid Insurance	1,600	
Store Equipment	37,200	
Accumulated Depreciation, Store Equipment		$ 15,600
Accounts Payable		12,300
Common Stock		10,000
Retained Earnings		31,994
Dividends	12,000	
Sales		102,250
Sales Returns and Allowances	987	
Purchases	63,200	
Purchases Returns and Allowances		19,655
Purchases Discounts		1,356
Freight In	2,261	
Sales Salaries Expense	21,350	
Rent Expense	3,600	
Other Selling Expenses	2,614	
Utility Expense	1,677	
	$193,155	$193,155

Required

1. Enter the trial balance on a work sheet, and complete the work sheet using the following information: (a) ending store supplies inventory, $304; (b) ending prepaid insurance, $200; (c) estimated depreciation on store equipment, $4,300; (d) sales salaries payable, $80; (e) accrued utility expense, $150; (f) estimated income taxes expense, $5,000. Also, ending merchandise inventory is $33,227. Use the closing entry method to account for the merchandise inventory of Conner Book Store, Inc.
2. Prepare an income statement, a statement of retained earnings, and a balance sheet. Sales Salaries Expense; Other Selling Expenses; Store Supplies Expense; and Depreciation Expense, Store Equipment, are to be considered selling expenses.
3. From the work sheet, prepare closing entries.

Problem 5A-6. Work Sheet, Income Statement, and Closing Entries for a Merchandising Concern
(L.O. 6, 8)

The year-end trial balance for Lima's Shoe Store, Inc. appears below:

Lima's Shoe Store, Inc.
Trial Balance
June 30, 19x2

Cash	$ 5,215	
Accounts Receivable	19,307	
Merchandise Inventory	26,500	
Store Supplies	951	
Prepaid Insurance	2,600	
Store Equipment	72,000	
Accumulated Depreciation, Store Equipment		$ 18,400
Accounts Payable		22,366
Common Stock		20,000
Retained Earnings		43,601
Dividends	15,000	
Sales		145,540
Sales Returns and Allowances	2,150	
Purchases	60,015	
Purchases Returns and Allowances		17,310
Purchases Discounts		1,300
Freight In	2,144	
Rent Expense	4,800	
Store Salaries Expense	41,600	
Advertising Expense	14,056	
Utility Expense	2,179	
	$268,517	$268,517

Required

1. Copy the trial balance amounts into the Trial Balance columns of a work sheet, and complete the work sheet using the following information: (a) ending store supplies inventory, $288; (b) expired insurance, $2,400; (c) estimated depreciation, store equipment, $8,800; (d) advertising expenses include $1,470 for July clearance sale advertisements, which will begin appearing on July 2; (e) accrued store salaries, $320; (f) estimated income taxes expense, $7,000. Also, ending merchandise inventory is $30,640. Use the closing entry method to account for the merchandise inventory of Lima's Shoe Store, Inc.
2. Prepare an income statement for the shoe store. Store Salaries Expense; Advertising Expense; Store Supplies Expense; and Depreciation Expense, Store Equipment, are to be considered selling expenses. The other expenses are to be considered general and administrative expenses.
3. From the work sheet you prepared for Lima's Shoe Store, Inc. in **1** above, derive closing entries.

Problem Set B

Problem 5B-1. Merchandising Transactions
(L.O. 2, 4)

Lazzer Company, which uses the periodic inventory system, engaged in the following transactions:

Mar. 1 Purchased merchandise on credit from Rivers Company, terms 2/10, n/30, FOB shipping point, $1,950.
1 Paid Oakley Company $109 for shipping charges on merchandise received.
3 Sold merchandise on credit to Wes Short, terms 2/10, n/60, $1,500.
6 Purchased merchandise on credit from North Company, terms 2/10, n/30, FOB shipping point, $4,800, including $300 freight costs paid by North.
7 Purchased merchandise on credit from Sun Company, terms 1/10, n/30, FOB shipping point, $3,000.
7 Paid Oakley Company $127 for shipping charges on merchandise received.
8 Purchased office supplies on credit from La Russo Company, terms n/10, $1,200.
10 Sold merchandise on credit to Steven Wong, terms 2/10, n/30, $1,200.
11 Paid Rivers Company for purchase of March 1.
12 Returned for credit $300 of damaged merchandise received from Sun Company on March 7.
13 Received check from Wes Short for his purchase of merchandise on March 3.
14 Returned a portion of the office supplies received on March 8 for credit because the wrong items were received, $200.
15 Sold merchandise for cash, $900.
16 Paid North Company for purchase of March 6.
19 Paid Sun Company the balance from transactions of March 7 and March 12.
20 Received payment in full from Steven Wong for sale of merchandise on March 10.
23 Paid La Russo Company for purchase of March 8, less the return on March 14. The terms were n/10.
31 Sold merchandise for cash, $750.

Required

1. Prepare general journal entries to record the transactions, assuming purchases are recorded initially at the gross purchase price.
2. Which entries would differ if the purchases were recorded initially at net purchase price and discounts lost were recognized? What advantages does this method have over the gross method?

Problem 5B-2. Journalizing Transactions of a Merchandising Company
(L.O. 2, 4)

Following is a list of transactions for the month of June 19xx.

June 1 Sold merchandise on credit to B. Holder, terms 2/10, n/60, FOB shipping point, $1,100.
2 Purchased merchandise on credit from Eagle Company, terms 2/10, n/30, FOB shipping point, $6,400.
3 Received freight bill for shipment received on June 2, $450.

June 4 Sold merchandise for cash, $550.
5 Sold merchandise on credit to T. Kuo, terms 2/10, n/60, $1,200.
6 Purchased merchandise from Reliable Company, terms 1/10, n/30, FOB shipping point, $3,090, including freight costs of $200.
7 Sold merchandise on credit to A. Rodriguez, terms 2/10, n/20, $2,200.
8 Purchased merchandise from Eagle Company, terms 2/10, n/30, FOB shipping point, $8,200.
9 Received freight bill for shipment of June 8, $730.
10 Received check from B. Holder for payment in full for sale of June 1.
11 Returned for credit merchandise of the June 6 shipment that was the wrong size and color, $290.
12 Paid Eagle Company for purchase of June 2.
13 A. Rodriguez returned some of merchandise sold to him on June 7 for credit, $200.
15 Received payment from T. Kuo for one-half of his purchase on June 5. A discount is allowed on partial payment.
16 Paid Reliable Company balance due on account from transactions on June 6 and 11.
17 In checking the purchase of June 8 from Eagle Company, the accounting department found an overcharge of $400. Eagle agreed to give credit.
20 Paid freight company for freight charges of June 3 and 9.
22 Purchased on credit cleaning supplies from Goldman Company, terms n/5, $250.
23 Discovered that $50 of the cleaning supplies purchased on June 22 were items not ordered. Returned to Goldman Company for credit.
25 Sold merchandise for cash, $800.
26 Paid Goldman Company for the June 22 purchase less the June 23 return.
27 Received payment in full from A. Rodriguez for transactions on June 7 and 13.
28 Paid Eagle Company for purchase of June 8, less allowance of June 17.
30 Received payment for balance of amount owed from T. Kuo from transactions of June 5 and 15.

Required

1. Prepare general journal entries to record the transactions, assuming that the periodic inventory system is used and that purchases are recorded initially at gross purchase price.
2. Tell how the entries would differ if the net method of recording purchases were used.

Problem 5B-3. Income Statement for a Merchandising Concern
(L.O. 6)

At the end of the fiscal year, August 31, 19x2, selected accounts from the adjusted trial balance for Irma's Fashion Shop, Inc. appeared as shown on page 265.

In addition to the figures shown in the partial adjusted trial balance, the merchandise inventory for Irma's Fashion Shop, Inc. was $38,200 at the beginning of the year and $29,400 at the end of the year.

Irma's Fashion Shop, Inc.
Partial Adjusted Trial Balance
August 31, 19x2

Sales		165,000
Sales Returns and Allowances	2,000	
Purchases	70,200	
Purchases Returns and Allowances		1,400
Purchases Discounts		1,200
Freight In	2,300	
Store Salaries Expense	32,625	
Office Salaries Expense	12,875	
Advertising Expense	24,300	
Rent Expense	2,400	
Insurance Expense	1,200	
Utility Expense	1,560	
Store Supplies Expense	2,880	
Office Supplies Expense	1,175	
Depreciation Expense, Store Equipment	1,050	
Depreciation Expense, Office Equipment	800	
Income Taxes Expense	1,000	

Required

1. Using the information given, prepare an income statement for Irma's Fashion Shop, Inc. Store Salaries Expense; Advertising Expense; Store Supplies Expense; and Depreciation Expense, Store Equipment, are considered to be selling expenses. The other expenses are considered to be general and administrative expenses.
2. Based on your knowledge at this point in the course, how might you use the income statement for Irma's Fashion Shop, Inc. to evaluate the company's profitability?

Problem 5B-4. Internal Control *(L.O. 9)*

Ostrowski Company, a large merchandising concern that stocks over 85,000 different items in inventory, has just installed a new computer system for inventory control. The computer's data storage system has random access processing and carries all pertinent data relating to individual items of inventory. The system is equipped with fifteen remote computer terminals, distributed at various locations throughout the warehouse and sales areas. Using these terminals, employees can obtain information from the computer system about the status of any inventory item. To make an inquiry, they use a keyboard similar to a typewriter's. The answer is relayed back instantaneously on the screen. As inventory is received, shipped, or transferred, employees update the inventory records in the computer system by means of the remote terminals.

Required

1. What potential weakness in internal control exists in the system?
2. What suggestions do you have for improving the internal control?

Problem 5B-5. Work Sheet, Financial Statements, and Closing Entries for a Merchandising Company
(L.O. 6, 8)

The year-end trial balance shown below was taken from the ledger of Kirby Party Costumes Corporation at the end of its annual accounting period on June 30, 19x2.

Kirby Party Costumes Corporation
Trial Balance
June 30, 19x2

Cash	$ 7,050	
Accounts Receivable	24,830	
Merchandise Inventory	71,400	
Store Supplies	3,800	
Prepaid Insurance	4,800	
Store Equipment	151,300	
Accumulated Depreciation, Store Equipment		$ 25,500
Accounts Payable		38,950
Common Stock		50,000
Retained Earnings		111,350
Dividends	24,000	
Sales		475,250
Sales Returns and Allowances	4,690	
Sales Discounts	3,790	
Purchases	251,600	
Purchases Returns and Allowances		3,150
Purchases Discounts		2,900
Freight In	10,400	
Sales Salaries Expense	64,600	
Rent Expense	48,000	
Other Selling Expenses	32,910	
Utility Expense	3,930	
	$707,100	$707,100

Required

1. Enter the trial balance on a work sheet, and complete the work sheet using the following information: (a) ending store supplies inventory, $550; (b) expired insurance, $2,400; (c) estimated depreciation on store equipment, $5,000; (d) sales salaries payable, $650; (e) accrued utility expense, $100; (f) estimated income taxes expense, $20,000. Also, ending merchandise inventory is $88,900. Use the closing entry method to account for the merchandise inventory of Kirby Party Costumes Corporation.
2. Prepare an income statement, a statement of retained earnings, and a balance sheet. Sales Salaries Expense; Other Selling Expenses; Store Supplies Expense; and Depreciation Expense, Store Equipment, are to be considered selling expenses.
3. From the work sheet, prepare closing entries.

Problem 5B-6. Work Sheet, Income Statement, and Closing Entries for a Merchandising Concern *(L.O. 6, 8)*

A year-end trial balance for Dumars Sporting Goods Store, Inc. appears below.

Dumars Sporting Goods Store, Inc.
Trial Balance
May 31, 19x2

Cash	$ 8,250	
Accounts Receivable	6,322	
Merchandise Inventory	93,750	
Store Supplies	7,170	
Prepaid Insurance	5,400	
Store Equipment	151,800	
Accumulated Depreciation, Store Equipment		$ 42,200
Accounts Payable		53,670
Common Stock		80,000
Retained Earnings		46,337
Dividends	27,000	
Sales		985,710
Sales Returns and Allowances	8,100	
Purchases	703,475	
Purchases Returns and Allowances		12,375
Purchases Discounts		11,850
Freight In	4,800	
Rent Expense	37,200	
Store Salaries Expense	113,250	
Advertising Expense	56,655	
Utility Expense	8,970	
	$1,232,142	$1,232,142

Required

1. Copy the trial balance amounts into the Trial Balance columns of a work sheet, and complete the work sheet using the following information: (a) ending store supplies inventory, $870; (b) insurance unexpired at end of period, $2,700; (c) estimated depreciation, store equipment, $15,900; (d) accrued store salaries, $375; (e) estimated income taxes expense, $10,000. Also, ending merchandise inventory is $86,240. Use the closing entry method to account for the merchandise inventory of Dumars Sporting Goods Store, Inc.
2. Prepare an income statement for the store. Store Salaries Expense; Advertising Expense; Store Supplies Expense; and Depreciation Expense, Store Equipment, are selling expenses. The other expenses are general and administrative expenses.
3. From the work sheet, prepare closing entries.

Financial Decision Cases

5-1. Jefferson Jeans Company
(L.O. 3, 9, 11)

In 19x1, Joseph "JJ" Jefferson opened a small retail store in a suburban mall. Called Jefferson Jeans Company, the shop sold designer jeans to rather well-to-do customers. JJ worked fourteen hours a day and was in control of all aspects of the operation. All sales were made for cash or bank credit card. The business was such a success that in 19x2 JJ decided to expand by opening a second outlet in another mall. Since the new shop needed his attention, he hired a manager for the original store to work with the two sales clerks who had been helping JJ in the store.

During 19x2, the new store was successful, but the operations of the original store did not match the first year's performance. Concerned about this turn of events, JJ compared the two years' results for the original store. The figures are as follows:

	19x2	19x1
Net Sales	$325,000	$350,000
Cost of Goods Sold	225,000	225,000
Gross Margin from Sales	$100,000	$125,000
Operating Expenses	75,000	50,000
Net Income	$ 25,000	$ 75,000

In addition, JJ's analysis revealed that the cost and selling price of jeans were about the same in both years and that the level of operating expenses was roughly the same in both years except for the $25,000 salary of the new manager. Sales returns and allowances were insignificant amounts in both years.

Studying the situation further, JJ discovered the following facts about cost of goods sold:

	19x2	19x1
Gross purchases	$200,000	$271,000
Total purchases returns, allowances, and discounts	15,000	20,000
Freight in	19,000	27,000
Physical inventory	32,000	53,000

Still not satisfied, JJ went through all the individual sales and purchase records for the year. Both sales and purchases were verified. However, the 19x2 ending inventory should have been $57,000, given the unit purchases and sales during the year. After puzzling over all this information, JJ comes to you for accounting help.

Required

1. Using JJ's new information, recompute cost of goods sold for 19x1 and 19x2, and account for the difference in net income between 19x1 and 19x2.
2. Suggest at least two reasons that might have caused the difference. (Assume that the new manager's salary is proper.) How might JJ improve his management of the original store?

5-2.
Gabhart's
(L.O. 10, 11)

Gabhart's is a retail department store with several departments. Its internal control procedures for cash sales and purchases are described below.

Cash Sales. Every cash sale is rung up by the sales clerk assigned to a particular department on the cash register for that department. The cash register produces a sales slip to be given to the customer with the merchandise. A carbon copy of the sales ticket is made on a continuous tape locked inside the machine. At the end of each day, a "total" key is pressed, and the machine prints the total sales for the day on the continuous tape. Then the sales clerk unlocks the machine, takes off the total sales figure, makes the entry in the accounting records for the day's cash sales, counts the cash in the drawer, retains $50 so as to have funds to make change on sales the next day, and gives the cash received to the cashier. The sales clerk then files the cash register tape and is ready for the next business day.

Purchases. All goods are ordered by the purchasing agent upon the request of the various department heads. When the goods are received, the receiving clerk prepares a receiving report in triplicate. One copy is sent to the purchasing agent, one copy is forwarded to the department head, and one copy is kept by the receiving clerk. Invoices are forwarded immediately to the accounting department to ensure payment before the discount period elapses. After payment, the invoice is forwarded to the purchasing agent for comparison with the purchase order and the receiving report and is then returned to the accounting office for filing.

Required

For each of the above situations, identify at least one major internal control weakness, and tell what you would suggest to improve the situation.

Part Two

Measuring and Reporting Assets, Liabilities, and Stockholders' Equity

Accounting, as you have seen, is an information system that measures, processes, and communicates information for decision making. Part I presented the principles and practices of the basic accounting system. Part II begins with an overview of classified financial statements and then considers each of the major kinds of assets, liabilities, and stockholders' equity, with special attention to the effect of their measurement on net income and to their presentation in the financial statements.

Chapter 6 introduces the objectives and qualitative aspects of financial information, and it shows how much more useful classified and general-purpose financial statements are than simple financial statements in presenting information to statement users.

Chapter 7 focuses on four kinds of short-term assets: cash, short-term investments, accounts receivable, and notes receivable.

Chapter 8 presents a detailed discussion of inventories.

Chapter 9 discusses property, plant, equipment, natural resources, and intangible assets, as well as the concepts and techniques of depreciation, depletion, and amortization.

Chapter 10 presents the concepts and techniques associated with current liabilities and the time value of money.

Chapter 11 introduces the long-term liabilities of corporations, paying special attention to accounting for bond liabilities. It also deals with other long-term liabilities, such as mortgages, installment notes, and postretirement benefits.

Chapter 12 presents accounting for the contributed capital section of stockholders' equity.

Chapter 13 focuses on accounting for retained earnings, a number of other transactions that affect stockholders' equity, and the components of the corporate income statement.

LEARNING OBJECTIVES

1. *State the objectives of financial reporting.*
2. *State the qualitative characteristics of accounting information, and describe their interrelationships.*
3. *Define and describe the use of the conventions of comparability and consistency, materiality, conservatism, full disclosure, and cost-benefit.*
4. *Summarize the concepts underlying financial accounting and their relationship to ethical financial reporting.*
5. *Identify and describe the basic components of a classified balance sheet.*
6. *Prepare the multistep and single-step types of classified income statements.*
7. *Use classified financial statements for the simple evaluation of liquidity and profitability.*
8. *Identify the major components of a corporate annual report.*

CHAPTER 6

Accounting Concepts and Classified Financial Statements

Financial statements are the most important means of communicating accounting information to decision makers. For decision makers external to the business, the financial statements, which are usually audited by independent accountants, are often the only information available directly from the company. As a result, it is essential that all business students have a thorough knowledge of the objectives and concepts underlying financial reporting, as well as the forms and evaluation of financial statements. This knowledge provides the foundation for the further study of accounting.

DECISION POINT

The Gap, Inc.[1]

Corporations issue annual reports in order to distribute their financial statements and communicate other relevant information to stockholders and others outside the business. Since these users have no direct access to the accounting records, they must depend on the information contained in this report. Beyond the financial statements and accompanying notes and text, management must devise its own methods to make the data in the statements more understandable to the reader.

The management of The Gap, Inc., one of the most successful U.S. specialty retailers of casual and active wear for men, women, and children, assists readers of its 1989 annual report by presenting on the first page a series of statistics called "Financial Highlights." Most of the statistics in this series are based on figures from the financial statements for the past three years. Along with such important information as net sales, net earnings, and total assets, a number of ratios appear, including working capital, current ratio,

1. Information is based on The Gap, Inc. 1989 Annual Report.

debt to equity, net earnings as a percentage of net sales, and return on average stockholders' equity. Unfortunately, these ratios are meaningless unless someone knows their components and understands their implications. Because learning how to read and interpret financial statements is so important, this chapter describes the categories or classifications used in balance sheets and income statements and explains some of the most important financial analysis ratios.

The chapter begins by describing the objectives, qualities, and conventions that underlie the preparation of financial statements. It ends with a concrete example: The annotated financial statements of Toys "R" Us, Inc., a major U.S. corporation. ■

Objectives of Financial Information[2]

OBJECTIVE 1
State the objectives of financial reporting

The United States has a highly developed exchange economy. In such an economy, most goods and services are exchanged for money or claims to money instead of being used or bartered by their producers. Most business is carried on through corporations, including many extremely large firms that buy, sell, and obtain financing in U.S. and world markets.

By issuing stocks and bonds that are traded in the market, businesses can raise capital for production and marketing activities through financial institutions, small groups, and the public at large. Investors are interested mainly in returns from dividends and in the market prices of their investments, rather than in managing the company's business. Creditors want to know whether the business can repay a loan according to its terms. Thus, investors and creditors both need to know whether a company can generate favorable cash flows. Financial statements are important to both groups in making this judgment. They offer valuable information that helps investors and creditors judge a company's ability to pay dividends and repay debts with interest. In this way, the market puts scarce resources to work in those companies that can use them most efficiently.

The needs of users and the general business environment described above are the basis for the Financial Accounting Standards Board's three objectives of financial reporting:[3]

1. *To furnish information useful in making investment and credit decisions* Financial reporting should offer information that is useful to present and potential investors and creditors as well as to others in making rational investment and credit decisions. The reports should be in a form that makes sense to those who have some understanding of business and are willing to study the information carefully.
2. *To provide information useful in assessing cash flow prospects* Financial reporting should supply information to help present and potential inves-

2. This discussion is based on *Statement of Financial Accounting Concepts No. 1,* "Objectives of Financial Reporting by Business Enterprises" (Stamford, Conn.: Financial Accounting Standards Board, 1978), pars. 6–16 and 28–40.
3. Ibid., pars. 32–54.

tors (owners), creditors, and others judge the amounts, timing, and risk of expected cash receipts from dividends or interest and the proceeds from the sale, redemption, or maturity of stocks or loans.

3. *To provide information about business resources, claims to those resources, and changes in them* Financial reporting should give information about a company's assets, its liabilities and owners' equity, and the effects of transactions that change its assets, liabilities, and owners' equity.

General-purpose external financial statements are the most important way of periodically presenting to parties outside the business the information that has been gathered and processed in the accounting system. For this reason, these statements—the balance sheet, the income statement, the statement of retained earnings, and the statement of cash flows—are the most important output of the accounting system. These financial statements are called "general purpose" because of their wide audience. They are "external" because the users are outside the business. Because of a potential conflict of interest between managers, who must prepare the statements, and the investors or creditors, who invest in or lend money to the businesses, these statements are often audited by outside accountants to increase confidence in their reliability.

Qualitative Characteristics of Accounting Information[4]

OBJECTIVE 2
State the qualitative characteristics of accounting information, and describe their interrelationships

It is easy for a student in the first accounting course to get the idea that accounting is 100 percent accurate. This idea is reinforced by the fact that all the problems in this and other introductory books can be solved. The numbers all add up, what is supposed to equal something else does, and so forth. Accounting seems very much like mathematics in its perfection. In this course, the basics of accounting are presented in a simple form at first to promote better understanding. In practice, however, accounting information is neither simple nor perfect and rarely satisfies all criteria. The FASB emphasizes this fact in the following statement:

> The information provided by financial reporting often results from approximate, rather than exact, measures. The measures commonly involve numerous estimates, classifications, summarizations, judgments and allocations. The outcome of economic activity in a dynamic economy is uncertain and results from combinations of many factors. Thus, despite the aura of precision that may seem to surround financial reporting in general and financial statements in particular, with few exceptions the measures are approximations, which may be based on rules and conventions, rather than exact amounts.[5]

4. The discussion in this section is based on *Statement of Financial Accounting Concepts No. 2*, "Qualitative Characteristics of Accounting Information" (Stamford, Conn.: Financial Accounting Standards Board, 1980). Copyright by Financial Accounting Standards Board, High Ridge Park, Stamford, CT 06905, USA. Reprinted with permission. Copies of the complete document are available from the FASB.
5. *Statement of Financial Accounting Concepts No. 1*, par. 20.

The goal of accounting information—to provide the basic data that different users need to make informed decisions—is an ideal. The gap, however, between the ideal and the actual provides much of the interest and controversy in accounting. The information needs to be both useful and understandable. Therefore, the burden of interpreting and using the information falls partly on the decision maker. The decision maker not only must judge what information to use and how to use it but also must understand it. How useful and understandable accounting information is depends on both the decision maker and the accountant. The accountant prepares the financial statements in accordance with accepted practices and presents information that is believed to be generally useful. But the decision maker must interpret the information and use it in making the decision. To aid in understanding this process of interpretation, the FASB has described the qualitative characteristics of accounting information. **Qualitative characteristics** are the standards for judging the information. In addition, there are generally accepted conventions for recording and reporting that facilitate interpretation. The relationships among these concepts are shown in Figure 6-1.

If accounting information is to be useful, it must have two major qualitative characteristics: relevance and reliability. **Relevance** means that the information makes a difference to the outcome of a decision. In other words, another decision would be made if the relevant information were not available. To be relevant, information must provide feedback, give help in predicting future conditions, and be timely. For example, the in-

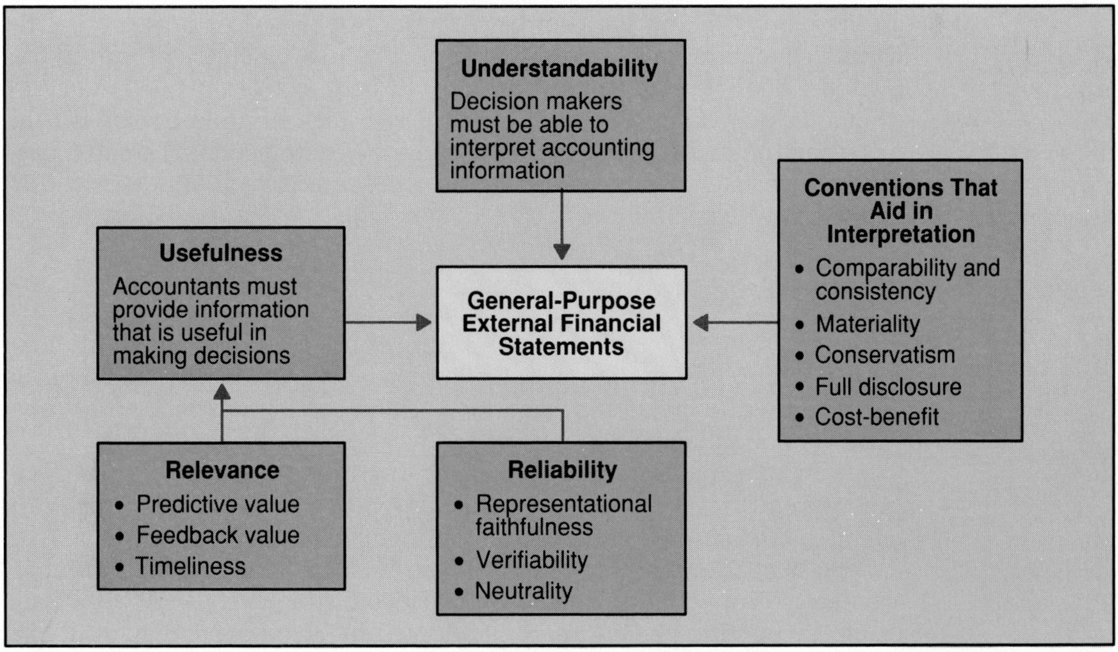

Figure 6-1. Qualitative Characteristics and Conventions of Accounting Information

come statement provides information about how a company did in the past year (feedback), and it helps in making plans for the next year (prediction). To be useful, however, it must also be communicated soon enough after the first year to affect the operations of the second year (timeliness).

In addition to being relevant, accounting information must have **reliability**. In other words, the user must be able to depend on the information. It must represent what it is meant to represent. It must be regarded as credible or verifiable by independent parties using the same methods of measuring. It must also be neutral or objective. Accounting should convey business activity as faithfully as possible without coloring the picture being presented in order to influence anyone in a certain direction. For example, the balance sheet should represent the economic resources, obligations, and stockholders' equity of a business as faithfully as possible in accordance with generally accepted accounting principles, and this balance sheet should be verifiable by an auditor.

Conventions to Aid Interpretation of Financial Information

OBJECTIVE 3
Define and describe the use of the conventions of comparability and consistency, materiality, conservatism, full disclosure, and cost-benefit

To a large extent, financial statements are based on estimates and rather arbitrary rules of recognition and allocation. In this book we point out a number of difficulties that financial statements may have. One is failing to recognize the changing value of the dollar due to inflation. Another is treating intangibles, like research and development costs, as assets if they are purchased outside the company, but treating them as expenses if they are developed within the company. These problems do not mean that financial statements are useless; they are, of course, essential. However, users must know how to interpret them. To help in this interpretation, accountants depend on five conventions or rules of thumb that aid in recording transactions and preparing financial statements: (1) comparability and consistency, (2) materiality, (3) conservatism, (4) full disclosure, and (5) cost-benefit.

Comparability and Consistency

A characteristic that adds to the usefulness of accounting information is comparability. Information about a company is more useful if it can be compared with similar facts about the same company over several time periods or about another company for the same time period. **Comparability** means that the information is presented in such a way that the decision maker can recognize similarities, differences, and trends between different companies or between different time periods.

Consistent use of accounting measures and procedures is important in achieving comparability. The **consistency** convention requires that a particular accounting procedure, once adopted by a company, remain in use from one period to the next unless users are informed of the change.

Thus, without a statement to the contrary, users of financial statements may assume that there has been no arbitrary change in the treatment of a particular account or item that may affect the interpretation of the statements.

If management decides that a certain procedure is not appropriate and should be changed, generally accepted accounting principles require that the change and its dollar effect be described in the notes to the financial statements:

> The nature of and justification for a change in accounting principle and its effect on income should be disclosed in the financial statements of the period in which the change is made. The justification for the change should explain clearly why the newly adopted accounting principle is preferable.[6]

For example, during the current year, a company might report that it had changed its method of accounting for inventories because management felt the new method reflected actual cost flows more realistically.

Materiality

The term **materiality** refers to the relative importance of an item or event. If an item or event is material, it is likely to be relevant to the user of the financial statements. In other words, an item is material if the user would have done something differently if he or she had not known about the item. The accountant is often faced with many small items or events that make little difference to users no matter how they are handled. For example, in the chapter on long-term assets it is suggested that it is more practical to charge small tools as expenses than to depreciate them. Also, small capital expenditures of less than $100 or $500 may be charged as expenses rather than recorded as equipment and depreciated.

In general, an item is material if there is a reasonable expectation that knowing about it would influence the decisions of users of financial statements. The materiality of an item is normally determined by relating its dollar value to parts of the financial statements, such as net income or total assets. However, materiality also depends on the nature of the item as well as the amount. For example, in a multimillion-dollar company, a mistake in recording an item of $5,000 may not be important, but discovering a $5,000 bribe or theft may be very significant. Also, a great many small errors combined may result in a material amount. Accountants judge the materiality of many things, and the users of financial statements depend on their judgment being fair and accurate.

Conservatism

Accountants try to base their decisions on logic and evidence that will lead to the fairest report of what happened. In judging and estimating, however, accountants are often faced with uncertainties or doubts. In these cases, they look to the convention of **conservatism**. This convention means that when accountants face major uncertainties as to which ac-

6. Accounting Principles Board, *Opinion No. 20*, "Accounting Changes" (New York: American Institute of Certified Public Accountants, 1971), par. 17.

counting procedure to use, they generally choose the one that will be least likely to overstate assets and income.

One of the most common applications of the conservatism convention is the use of the lower-of-cost-or-market method in accounting for short-term investments, described in a later chapter, and for inventories, presented in the chapter on inventories. Under this method, if the market value is greater than cost, the more conservative cost figure is used. If the market value is less than cost, then the more conservative market value is used.

Conservatism can be a useful tool in doubtful cases, but the abuse of this convention will certainly lead to incorrect and misleading financial statements. Suppose that someone incorrectly applied the conservatism convention by expensing a long-term asset in the period of purchase. In this case, there is no uncertainty. Income and assets for the current period would be understated, and income of future periods would be overstated. For this reason, accountants depend on the conservatism convention only as a last resort.

Full Disclosure

The convention of **full disclosure** requires that financial statements and their footnotes present all information relevant to the users' understanding of the case. In other words, accounting information should offer any explanation that is needed to keep it from being misleading. Such explanations in the notes are considered an integral part of the financial statements. For instance, as noted in the previous section on consistency, a change from one accounting procedure to another should be reported. In general, the form of the financial statements, as described later in this chapter, may affect their usefulness in making certain decisions. Also, certain items, such as the amount of depreciation expense on the income statement and the accumulated depreciation on the balance sheet, are considered essential to readers of financial statements.

Other examples of disclosures required by the Financial Accounting Standards Board and other official bodies are the accounting procedures used in preparing the statements, important terms of the company's debt, commitments and contingencies, and important events taking place after the date of the statements. However, there is a point where the statements become so cluttered that they impede rather than aid understanding. Beyond required disclosures, the application of the full-disclosure convention is based not on definite standards, but on the judgment of management and of the accountants who prepare the financial statements.

The principle of full disclosure has also been influenced by users of accounting information in recent years. To protect the investor, independent auditors, the stock exchanges, and the SEC have made more demands for disclosure by publicly owned companies. The SEC has been pushing especially hard for the enforcement of full disclosure. So today more and better information about corporations is available to the public than ever before.

Cost-Benefit

The **cost-benefit** convention underlies all the qualitative characteristics and conventions. It holds that the benefits to be gained from providing new accounting information should be greater than the costs of providing it. Of course, certain minimum levels of relevance and reliability must be reached for accounting information to be useful. Beyond these minimum levels, however, it is up to the FASB and the SEC, which require the information, and the accountant, who provides the information, to judge the costs and benefits in each case. Most of the costs of providing information fall at first on the preparers, though the benefits are reaped by both preparers and users. Finally, both the costs and the benefits are passed on to society in the form of prices and social benefits from more efficient allocation of resources. The costs and benefits of a particular required accounting disclosure are both direct and indirect, immediate and deferred. For example, it is hard to judge the final costs and benefits of a far-reaching and costly regulation. The FASB, for instance, allows certain large companies to make a supplemental disclosure in their financial statements of the effects of price changes on current costs. Most companies have chosen not to present this information because they view the costs of producing and providing it as exceeding the benefits to the readers of their financial statements. Cost-benefit is a question faced by all regulators, including the FASB and the SEC. Even though there are no definitive ways of measuring costs and benefits, much of an accountant's work deals with these concepts.

Financial Accounting Concepts and Ethical Reporting

OBJECTIVE 4
Summarize the concepts underlying financial accounting and their relationship to ethical financial reporting

In the presentation of accounting thus far, the relationships of financial accounting concepts to accounting techniques and procedures as well as the judgment underlying their application have been emphasized. The next sections summarize the financial accounting concepts presented to this point and make clear that the use of judgment in their application places an ethical responsibility on the preparer.

Summary of Financial Accounting Concepts

The first figure in this textbook introduced accounting as an information system for business decision making. That information system is expanded in Figure 6-2 to include the financial accounting concepts introduced thus far. In overview, Figure 6-2 shows the information system as a circular, continuous process. People make decisions and take actions; these decisions and actions affect economic activities that in turn are measured, processed, and communicated back to the decision makers in the form of financial statements in accordance with their information needs or objectives.

Figure 6-2. Summary of Financial Accounting Concepts

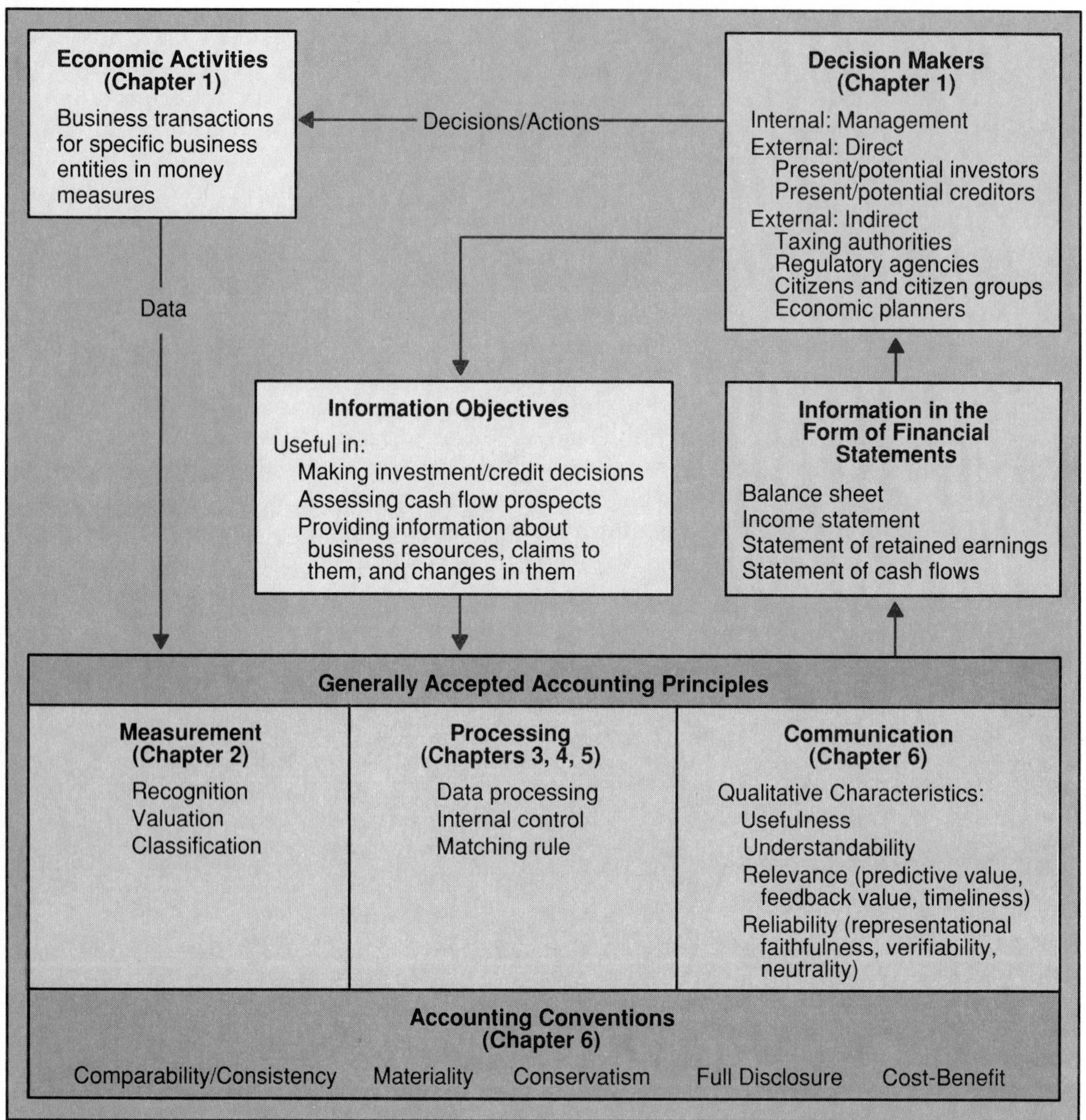

The decision makers consist of internal users (management) and direct and indirect external users of accounting information. Present and potential investors and creditors are direct users; and taxing authorities, regulatory agencies, citizens and citizen groups, and economic planners are indirect users. Accountants measure some but not all economic activities for various economic entities (businesses, government units, not-for-profit organizations, and individuals). In the case of specific business entities, accountants measure business transactions in terms of money.

The measurement, processing, and communication of accounting information is governed by generally accepted accounting principles (GAAP) that encompass all the rules, procedures, and conventions necessary to define accounting practices at a given point in time. The most important source of GAAP is the Financial Accounting Standards Board (FASB), but other sources include authoritative bodies such as the American Institute of CPAs (AICPA), as well as traditional practices.

In measuring a business transaction, three characteristics must be identified. First, recognition focuses on when a transaction took place. Second, valuation focuses on what value to place on the transaction. The usual value assigned to a transaction is cost (the value exchanged at the time the transaction is recognized). Third, classification requires the identification of the specific accounts in which the transaction is to be recorded. When these three determinations are made in accordance with GAAP, the transaction may be properly recorded in the accounting records.

The processing of accounting data is facilitated if the data are stored in a manner that permits quick and easy retrieval for preparing reports and financial statements. Furthermore, it is important to establish internal accounting controls over the processing so that assets are safeguarded and accurate records are maintained. Lastly, the matching rule is applied through accrual accounting so that the income earned by the business is properly reported.

In this chapter, you have learned the qualitative characteristics of accounting information and the accounting conventions that direct the application of GAAP. A knowledge of these characteristics and conventions is essential to interpreting the financial statements that are communicated to decision makers. Finally, it is important to understand that the accounting process is driven by information objectives communicated by the decision makers to accountants. This link reinforces the primary function of accounting, which is to provide useful information to decision makers.

Ethics and Financial Reporting

The users of financial statements depend on the good judgment of preparers in applying accounting concepts to the preparation of financial statements. This dependence places a responsibility on a company's management and its accountants to act ethically in the reporting process. The intentional preparation of misleading financial statements is referred to as **fraudulent financial reporting**[7] and can result from distortion of company records, such as the manipulation of inventory records; falsified transactions, such as fictitious sales or orders; or misapplication of accounting principles, such as treating as an asset an item that should be expensed.

The motivation for fraudulent reporting may spring from various sources, for instance the desire to obtain a higher price in the sale of the company, meet the expectations of the owners, or obtain a loan. Other

7. National Commission on Fraudulent Financial Reporting, *Report of the National Commission on Fraudulent Financial Reporting* (Washington, D.C., 1987), p. 2.

times the incentive is personal gain, such as additional compensation, promotion, or avoidance of penalties for poor performance by the managers or accountants. The personal costs of such actions can be high—criminal penalties and financial loss can fall to the individuals who authorize or prepare the financial statements. Others, including investors and lenders to the company, other employees, and customers, suffer from fraudulent financial reporting as well.

The motivations for fraudulent financial reporting exist to some extent in every company. It is the responsibility of management to insist upon honest financial reporting, but it is also the responsibility of the accountants within the organization to maintain high ethical standards in the performance of their duties to avoid being linked to fraudulent financial statements. To be ethical in financial reporting, the accountant should seek to apply financial accounting concepts in a way that will present a fair view of the operations and financial position of the company and not mislead the readers of the financial statements.

Classified Balance Sheet

OBJECTIVE 5
Identify and describe the basic components of a classified balance sheet

So far in this book, balance sheets have listed the accounts in categories of assets, liabilities, and owners' equity. Because even a fairly small company may have hundreds of accounts, simply listing accounts by these broad categories is not particularly helpful to a statement user. Setting up subcategories within the major categories will often make the financial statements much more useful. Investors and creditors study and evaluate the relationships among the subcategories. When general-purpose external financial statements are divided into useful subcategories, they are called **classified financial statements.**

The balance sheet presents the financial position of a company at a particular time. The subdivisions of the classified balance sheet shown in Exhibit 6-1 are typical of most companies in the United States. The subdivisions under owners' or stockholders' equity, of course, depend on the form of business.

Assets

The assets of a company are often divided into four categories: (1) current assets; (2) investments; (3) property, plant, and equipment; and (4) intangible assets. Some companies use a fifth category called other assets if there are miscellaneous assets that do not fall into any of the other groups. These categories are listed in the order of their presumed liquidity (the ease with which an asset can be converted into cash). For example, current assets are considered more liquid than property, plant, and equipment.

Current Assets. **Current assets** are cash or other assets that are reasonably expected to be realized in cash, sold, or consumed during the next year or during a normal operating cycle of a business, if the cycle is longer than a year. The normal operating cycle of a company is the average time

Exhibit 6-1. Classified Balance Sheet for Shafer Auto Parts Corporation

Shafer Auto Parts Corporation
Balance Sheet
December 31, 19xx

Assets			
Current Assets			
Cash		$10,360	
Short-Term Investments		2,000	
Notes Receivable		8,000	
Accounts Receivable		35,300	
Merchandise Inventory		60,400	
Prepaid Insurance		6,600	
Store Supplies		1,060	
Office Supplies		636	
Total Current Assets			$124,356
Investments			
Land Held for Future Use			5,000
Property, Plant, and Equipment			
Land		$ 4,500	
Building	$20,650		
Less Accumulated Depreciation	8,640	12,010	
Delivery Equipment	$18,400		
Less Accumulated Depreciation	9,450	8,950	
Office Equipment	$ 8,600		
Less Accumulated Depreciation	5,000	3,600	
Total Property, Plant, and Equipment			29,060
Intangible Assets			
Trademark			500
Total Assets			$158,916
Liabilities			
Current Liabilities			
Accounts Payable		$25,683	
Notes Payable		15,000	
Salaries Payable		2,000	
Total Current Liabilities			$ 42,683
Long-Term Liabilities			
Mortgage Payable			17,800
Total Liabilities			$ 60,483
Stockholders' Equity			
Contributed Capital			
Common Stock, $10 par value 5,000 shares issued and outstanding		$50,000	
Paid-in Capital in Excess of Par Value		10,000	
Total Contributed Capital		$60,000	
Retained Earnings		38,433	
Total Stockholders' Equity			98,433
Total Liabilities and Stockholders' Equity			$158,916

that is needed to go from cash to cash. As illustrated in Figure 6-3, cash is used to buy merchandise inventory, which is sold for cash or for a promise of cash (a receivable) if the sale is made on account (for credit). If the sales are on account, the resulting receivables must be collected before the cycle is completed.

The normal operating cycle for most companies is less than one year, but there are exceptions. Tobacco companies, for example, must cure the tobacco for two or three years before their inventory can be sold. The tobacco inventory is still considered a current asset because it will be sold within the normal operating cycle. Another example is a company that sells on an installment basis. The collection payments for a television set or stove may be extended over twenty-four or thirty-six months, but these receivables are still considered current assets.

Cash is obviously a current asset. Temporary investments, accounts and notes receivable, and inventory are also current assets because they are expected to be converted to cash within the next year or during the normal operating cycle of the firm, if the cycle is longer than one year. They are listed in the order of the ease of their conversion into cash. Accounting for these short-term assets is presented in a later chapter.

Prepaid expenses, such as rent and insurance paid for in advance, and inventories of various supplies bought for use rather than for sale should also be classified as current assets. These kinds of assets are current in the sense that, if they had not been bought earlier, a current outlay of cash

Figure 6-3. The Operating Cycle

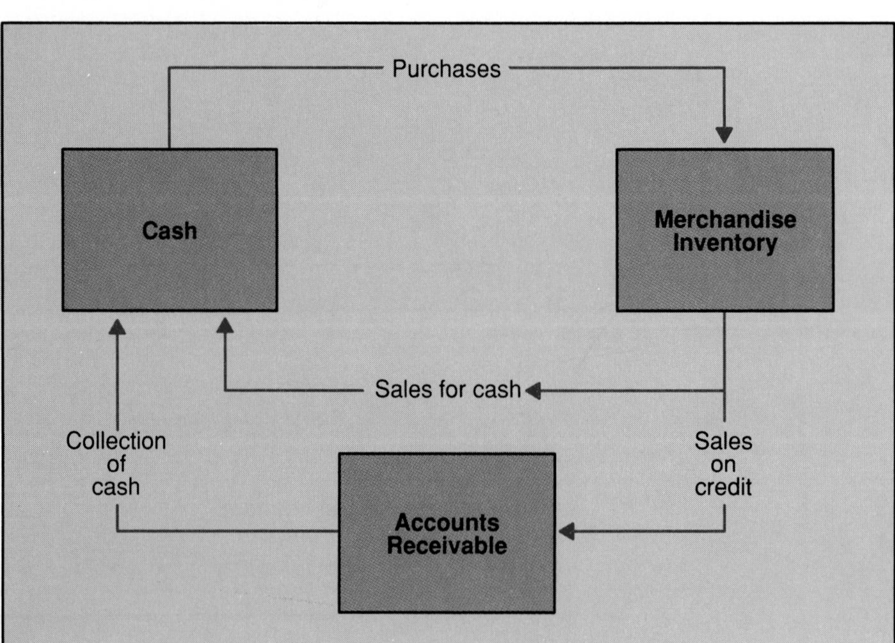

would be needed to obtain them. They are an exception to the current asset definition presented earlier.[8]

In deciding whether an asset is current or noncurrent, the idea of "reasonable expectation" is important. For example, Short-Term Investments is an account used for temporary investments of idle cash or cash not immediately required for operating purposes. Management can reasonably expect to sell these securities as cash needs arise over the next year or operating cycle. Investments in securities that management does not expect to sell within the next year and that do not involve the temporary use of idle cash should be shown in the investments category of a classified balance sheet.

Investments. The **investments** category includes assets, generally of a long-term nature, that are not used in the normal operation of a business and that management does not plan to convert to cash within the next year. Items in this category are securities held for long-term investment, long-term notes receivable, land held for future use, plant or equipment not used in the business, and special funds such as to pay off a debt or buy a building. Also in this category are large permanent investments in another company for the purpose of controlling that company. These topics are covered in the chapter on international accounting and intercompany investments.

Property, Plant, and Equipment. The **property, plant, and equipment** category includes long-term assets that are used in the continuing operation of the business. They represent a place for the business to operate (land and buildings) and equipment to produce, sell, deliver, and service its goods. For this reason, these assets are often called operating assets or sometimes fixed assets, tangible assets, or long-lived assets. We have seen earlier in the book that, through depreciation, the cost of these assets (except land) is spread over the periods they benefit. Past depreciation is recorded in the Accumulated Depreciation accounts. The exact order in which property, plant, and equipment are listed is not the same everywhere in practice, and often various accounts are combined to make the financial statement less cluttered, perhaps in the following manner:

Property, Plant, and Equipment

Land		$ 4,500
Buildings and Equipment	$47,650	
Less Accumulated Depreciation	23,090	24,560
Total Property, Plant, and Equipment		$29,060

Property, plant, and equipment also includes natural resources owned, such as forest lands, oil and gas properties, or coal mines. Assets of this

8. *Accounting Research and Terminology Bulletin,* Final Edition (New York: American Institute of Certified Public Accountants, 1961), p. 20.

type not used in the regular course of business should be listed in the investments category, as noted above. The chapter on long-term assets is devoted largely to property, plant, and equipment.

Intangible Assets. **Intangible assets** are long-term assets that have no physical substance but have a value based on rights or privileges that belong to the owner. Examples are patents, copyrights, goodwill, franchises, and trademarks. These assets are recorded at cost, which is spread over the expected life of the right or privilege. These assets are explained further in the chapter on long-term assets.

Other Assets. Some companies use the category **other assets** to group all the assets owned by a company other than current assets and property, plant, and equipment. Other assets might include investments and intangible assets.

Liabilities

Liabilities are divided into two categories: current liabilities and long-term liabilities.

Current Liabilities. The category **current liabilities** consists of obligations due within the normal operating cycle of the business or within a year, whichever is longer. These liabilities are generally paid from current assets or by incurring new short-term liabilities. Under this heading are notes payable, accounts payable, the current portion of long-term debt, wages payable, taxes payable, and customer advances (unearned revenues). Current liabilities are presented in more detail in the chapter on current liabilities and the time value of money.

Long-Term Liabilities. Debts of a business that fall due more than one year ahead or beyond the normal operating cycle, or that are to be paid out of noncurrent assets, are **long-term liabilities**. Mortgages payable, long-term notes, bonds payable, employee pension obligations, and long-term lease liabilities generally fall in this category. Long-term liabilities are presented in a later chapter.

Owners' Equity

The owners' equity section for a corporation would appear as shown in the balance sheet for Shafer Auto Parts Corporation. As you learned earlier, corporations are separate, legal entities. The owners are the stockholders. The stockholders' equity section of a balance sheet has two parts: contributed or paid-in capital and retained earnings, which are covered in the chapters on contributed capital and on retained earnings and corporate income statements.

Other Forms of Business Organization

The accounting treatment of assets and liabilities is not usually affected by the form of business organization. However, the owners' equity section of the balance sheet is very different for a business that is organized as a sole proprietorship or partnership than it is for a corporation.

Sole Proprietorship. The owner's equity section for a sole proprietorship simply shows the capital in the owner's name at an amount equal to the net assets of the company. The owner's equity section for a sole proprietorship might appear as follows:

Owner's Equity

Fred Shafer, Capital	$98,433

Since there is no legal separation between an owner and his or her sole proprietorship, there is no need for contributed capital to be separated from earnings retained for use in the business. This capital account is increased by both the owner's investments and net income. It is decreased by net losses and withdrawals of assets from the business for personal use by the owner. In this kind of business, the formality of declaring and paying dividends is not required.

In fact, the terms *owner's equity, proprietorship, capital,* and *net worth* are used interchangeably. They all stand for the owner's interest in the company. The first three terms are felt to be better usage than *net worth* because most assets are recorded at original cost rather than at current value. For this reason, the ownership section will not represent "worth." It is really a claim against the assets of the company.

Partnership. The owners' equity section of the balance sheet for a partnership is called partners' equity and is much like that of the sole proprietorship. It might appear as follows:

Partners' Equity

A. J. Martin, Capital	$21,666	
R. C. Moore, Capital	35,724	
Total Partners' Equity		$57,390

Forms of the Income Statement

OBJECTIVE 6 *Prepare the multistep and single-step types of classified income statements*

For internal management, a detailed income statement such as the one you learned about in the chapter on merchandising operations and internal control and the one for Shafer Auto Parts Corporation in Exhibit 6-2 is helpful in analyzing the company's performance. In the Shafer statement, gross margin from sales less operating expenses is called **income from operations**, and a new section, **other revenues and expenses**, is added to the

Exhibit 6-2. Income Statement for Shafer Auto Parts Corporation

Shafer Auto Parts Corporation
Income Statement
For the Year Ended December 31, 19xx

Revenues from Sales			
Sales			$299,156
Less: Sales Returns and Allowances		$ 6,300	
Sales Discounts		3,200	9,500
Net Sales			$289,656
Cost of Goods Sold			
Merchandise Inventory, January 1, 19xx		$ 64,800	
Purchases	$168,624		
Freight In	8,236	176,860	
Goods Available for Sale		$241,660	
Merchandise Inventory, December 31, 19xx		60,400	
Cost of Goods Sold			181,260
Gross Margin from Sales			$108,396
Operating Expenses			
Selling Expenses			
Sales Salaries Expense	$ 22,500		
Rent Expense, Store Fixtures	5,600		
Freight Out Expense	5,740		
Advertising Expense	10,000		
Insurance Expense, Selling	1,600		
Store Supplies Expense	1,540		
Depreciation Expense, Building	2,600		
Depreciation Expense, Delivery Equipment	5,200		
Total Selling Expenses		$ 54,780	
General and Administrative Expenses			
Office Salaries Expense	$ 26,900		
Insurance Expense, General	4,200		
Office Supplies Expense	1,204		
Depreciation Expense, Office Equipment	2,200		
Total General and Administrative Expenses		34,504	
Total Operating Expenses			89,284
Income from Operations			$ 19,112
Other Revenues and Expenses			
Interest Income		$ 1,400	
Less Interest Expense		2,631	
Excess of Other Expenses over Other Revenues			1,231
Income Before Income Taxes			$ 17,881
Income Taxes			3,381
Net Income			$ 14,500
Earnings per share			$ 2.90

statement to include nonoperating revenues and expenses. This latter section includes revenues from investments (such as dividends and interest from stocks and bonds and savings accounts) and interest earned on credit or notes extended to customers. It also includes interest expense and other expenses that result from borrowing money or from credit being extended to the company. If the company has other revenues and expenses unrelated to normal business operations, they too are classified in this part of the income statement. Thus, an analyst wanting to compare two companies independent of their financing methods, that is, before considering other revenues and expenses, would focus on income from operations.

Income taxes, also called **income taxes expense** or **provision for income taxes**, represents the expense for federal and state income taxes on corporate income. This account would not appear in the income statements of sole proprietorships and partnerships because they are not taxpaying units. The individuals who own these businesses are the taxpaying units, and they pay income taxes on their share of the business income. Corporations, however, must report and pay income taxes on earnings. For this reason, income taxes expense is always shown as a separate item on the income statement of a corporation. The amount of the federal income tax is based on taxable net income as defined by the Internal Revenue Code, which may or may not agree with the income as determined by generally accepted accounting principles. Because federal, state, and local income taxes for corporations are substantial, they have a significant effect on business decisions. Most other taxes, such as property taxes, employment taxes, licenses, and fees, are shown among the operating expenses. Corporate income taxes are discussed in more detail in the chapter on retained earnings and corporate income statements.

Earnings per share, often called **net income per share** of common stock, is also unique to corporate reporting. Ownership in corporations is represented by shares of stock, and the net income per share is reported immediately below net income on the income statement. In the simplest case, it is computed by dividing the net income by the number of shares of common stock outstanding. For example, Shafer's earnings per share of $2.90 was computed by dividing the net income of $14,500 by the 5,000 shares of common stock outstanding as reported in the stockholders' equity section of the balance sheet (Exhibit 6-1). Investors find the figure useful as a shorthand way of assessing a company's profit-earning success and also in evaluating the earnings in relation to the market price of the stock.

For external reporting purposes, the income statement is usually presented in condensed form. **Condensed financial statements** present only the major categories of the financial statement. There are two common forms of the condensed income statement, the multistep form and the single-step form. The **multistep form**, illustrated in Exhibit 6-3, derives net income in the same step-by-step fashion as the detailed income statement for Shafer Auto Parts Corporation in Exhibit 6-2 except that only the totals of significant categories are given. Usually, some breakdown is shown for operating expenses, such as the totals for selling expenses and for general and administrative expenses. Other revenues and expenses are also usually broken down. The **single-step form**, illustrated in Exhibit 6-4, derives net income in a single step by putting the major categories of revenues in the first part of the statement and the major categories of costs and expenses in the second part. Each of these forms has its advantages. The multistep form shows the components used in deriving net income, while the single-step form has the advantage of simplicity. About an equal number of large U.S. companies use each form in their public reports.

Other Financial Statements

Two other statements that are necessary to an understanding of a company's financial operations are the statement of retained earnings and the statement of cash flows.

Exhibit 6-3. Condensed Multistep Income Statement for Shafer Auto Parts Corporation

Shafer Auto Parts Corporation
Income Statement
For the Year Ended December 31, 19xx

Revenues from Sales		$289,656
Cost of Goods Sold		181,260
Gross Margin from Sales		$108,396
Operating Expenses		
Selling Expenses	$54,780	
General and Administrative Expenses	34,504	
Total Operating Expenses		89,284
Income from Operations		$ 19,112
Other Revenues and Expenses		
Interest Income	$ 1,400	
Less Interest Expense	2,631	
Excess of Other Expenses over Other Revenues		1,231
Income Before Income Taxes		$ 17,881
Income Taxes		3,381
Net Income		$ 14,500
Earnings per share		$ 2.90

Exhibit 6-4. Condensed Single-Step Income Statement for Shafer Auto Parts Corporation

Shafer Auto Parts Corporation
Income Statement
For the Year Ended December 31, 19xx

Revenues		
Net Sales	$289,656	
Interest Income	1,400	
Total Revenues		$291,056
Costs and Expenses		
Cost of Goods Sold	$181,260	
Selling Expenses	54,780	
General and Administrative Expenses	34,504	
Interest Expense	2,631	
Income Taxes Expense	3,381	
Total Costs and Expenses		276,556
Net Income		$ 14,500
Earnings per share		$ 2.90

The statement of retained earnings for Shafer Auto Parts Corporation is shown in Exhibit 6-5.

A simple form of the statement of cash flows was shown in the first chapter. A more complicated one appears in Figure 6-7 near the end of this chapter. This important statement is explained in detail in the chapter on the statement of cash flows.

Exhibit 6-5. Statement of Retained Earnings for Shafer Auto Parts Corporation

Shafer Auto Parts Corporation
Statement of Retained Earnings
For the Year Ended December 31, 19xx

Retained Earnings, January 1, 19xx	$43,933
Net Income	14,500
Subtotal	$58,433
Less Dividends	20,000
Retained Earnings, December 31, 19xx	$38,433

Using Classified Financial Statements

OBJECTIVE 7
Use classified financial statements for the simple evaluation of liquidity and profitability

A major reason for classifying financial statements is to aid in evaluating a business. Though the analysis and interpretation of financial statements is the subject of a later chapter, it is helpful at this point to explain briefly how classified financial statements can be used to show meaningful relationships. Earlier in this chapter you learned that the objectives of financial reporting, according to the Financial Accounting Standards Board, are to provide information that is useful in making investment and credit decisions, in judging cash flow prospects, and in understanding business resources, claims to those resources, and changes in them. These objectives are related to two of the more important goals of management—those of (1) maintaining adequate liquidity and (2) achieving satisfactory profitability—because the decisions made by investors and creditors are based largely on their assessment of the company's potential liquidity and profitability. The following analysis focuses on these two important goals.

Beginning in this section and continuing at appropriate points in future chapters, a series of charts shows average ratios for six industries based on data obtained from *Industry Norms and Ratios* published by Dun and Bradstreet. There are two examples from service industries, accounting and bookkeeping services and interstate trucking; two from merchandising industries, auto and home supply and grocery stores; and two from manufacturing, pharmaceuticals and household appliances. Shafer Auto Parts Corporation, the example used in this chapter, falls into the category of auto and home supply.

Evaluation of Liquidity

Liquidity means having enough money on hand to (1) pay a company's bills when they are due and (2) take care of unexpected needs for cash. Two measures of liquidity are working capital and the current ratio.

Working Capital. The first measure, **working capital**, is the amount by which total current assets exceed total current liabilities. This is an important measure of liquidity, because current liabilities are debts to be paid within one year and current assets are assets to be realized in cash or used up within one year or one operating cycle, whichever is longer. By definition, current liabilities will be paid out of current assets. So the excess of current assets over current liabilities is, in fact, the net current assets on hand to continue business operations. It is the funds or working capital that can be used to buy inventory, obtain credit, and finance expanded sales. Lack of working capital can lead to the failure of a company. For Shafer Auto Parts Corporation, the working capital is computed as follows:

Current Assets	\$124,356
Less Current Liabilities	42,683
Working Capital	\$ 81,673

Current Ratio. The second measure of liquidity, called the current ratio, is closely related to working capital and is believed by many bankers and other creditors to be a good indicator of a company's ability to pay its bills and to repay outstanding loans. The **current ratio** is the ratio of current assets to current liabilities. For Shafer Auto Parts Corporation, it would be computed as follows:

$$\text{Current ratio} = \frac{\text{current assets}}{\text{current liabilities}} = \frac{\$124{,}356}{\$42{,}683} = 2.9$$

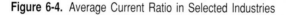

Based on this result, Shafer has \$2.90 of current assets for each \$1.00 of current liabilities. Judging whether this rate is good or bad involves comparing this year's ratio with those of earlier years and with similar measures for successful companies in the same industry. The average current ratio can vary widely from industry to industry, as can be seen in Figure 6-4. For interstate trucking companies, which have no merchandise inventory, the current ratio is 1.4 times. In contrast, accounting and bookkeeping and pharmaceuticals have current ratios of 2.6 times. Shafer Auto Parts Corporation exceeds the auto and home supply industry average of 2.4, having an average of 2.9. A very low current ratio can, of course, be unfavorable, but so can a very high one. The latter may indicate that the company is not using its assets effectively.

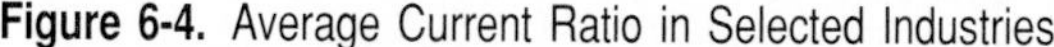

Figure 6-4. Average Current Ratio in Selected Industries

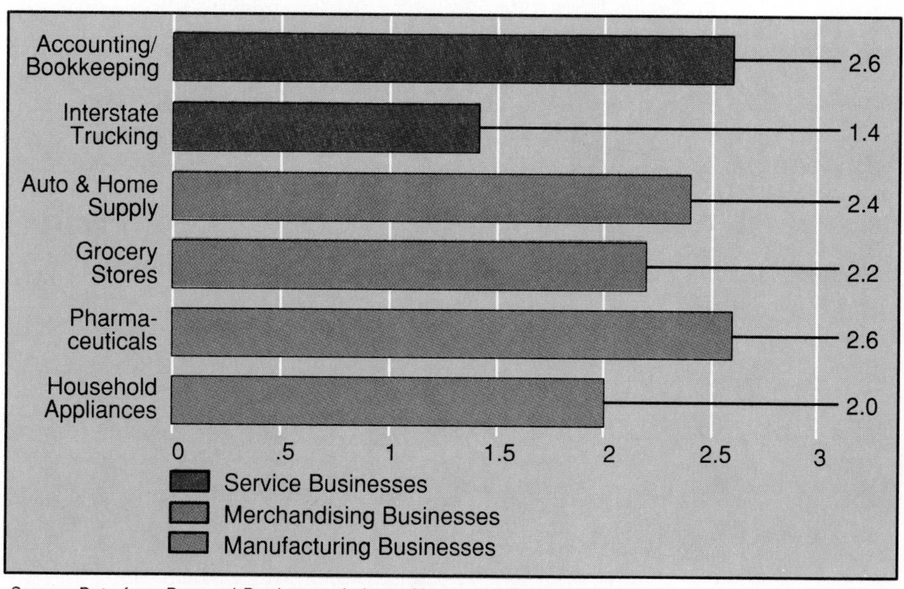

Source: Data from Dun and Bradstreet, *Industry Norms and Ratios*, 1990–91.

Evaluation of Profitability

Equally as important as paying one's bills on time is the goal of **profitability**—the ability to earn a satisfactory level of earnings. As a goal, profitability competes with liquidity for managerial attention because liquid assets, while important, are not the best profit-producing resources. Cash, for example, means purchasing power, but a satisfactory profit will result only if purchasing power is used to buy profit-producing (and less liquid) assets such as inventory and long-term assets.

Among the common measures that have to do with a company's ability to earn an income are (1) profit margin, (2) asset turnover, (3) return on assets, (4) debt to equity, and (5) return on equity. To evaluate a company meaningfully, one must relate a company's profit performance to its past and prospects for the future as well as to the norms (averages) of other companies competing in the same industry.

Profit Margin. The **profit margin** shows the percentage of each sales dollar that results in net income. It is figured by dividing net income by net sales. It should not be confused with gross margin, which is not a ratio, but rather the amount by which revenues exceed cost of goods sold. For Shafer Auto Parts Corporation, the profit margin is as follows:

$$\text{Profit margin} = \frac{\text{net income}}{\text{net sales}} = \frac{\$14{,}500}{\$289{,}656} = .05\ (5\%)$$

On each dollar of sales, Shafer Auto Parts Corporation made 5¢. A difference of 1 or 2 percent in a company's profit margin may mean the difference between a fair year and a very profitable one.

Asset Turnover. **Asset turnover** measures how efficiently assets are used to produce sales. It is computed by dividing net sales by average total assets and shows how many dollars of sales were generated by each dollar of assets. A company with a higher asset turnover uses its assets more productively than one with a lower asset turnover. Average total assets is computed by adding total assets at the beginning of the year to total assets at the end of the year and dividing by 2. Assuming that total assets for Shafer Auto Parts Corporation were $148,620 at the beginning of the year, the asset turnover is computed as follows:

$$\text{Asset turnover} = \frac{\text{net sales}}{\text{average total assets}}$$

$$= \frac{\$289{,}656}{(\$148{,}620 + \$158{,}916)/2}$$

$$= \frac{\$289{,}656}{\$153{,}768} = 1.88 \text{ times}$$

Shafer Auto Parts Corporation produced $1.88 in sales for each dollar in average total assets. This ratio shows the relationship between an income statement figure and a balance sheet figure.

Return on Assets. Both the profit margin and asset turnover ratios have deficiencies. The profit margin ratio does not take into consideration the assets necessary to produce income, and the asset turnover ratio does not take into account the amount of income produced. The **return on assets** ratio overcomes these deficiencies by relating net income to average total assets. It is computed as follows:

$$\text{Return on assets} = \frac{\text{net income}}{\text{average total assets}}$$

$$= \frac{\$14{,}500}{(\$148{,}620 + \$158{,}916)/2}$$

$$= \frac{\$14{,}500}{\$153{,}768} = .094 \text{ (or } 9.4\%)$$

For each dollar invested, Shafer Auto Parts Corporation's assets generated 9.4¢ of net income. This ratio indicates the income-generating strength (profit margin) of the company's resources and how efficiently the company is using all its assets (asset turnover). This conclusion may be demonstrated as follows:

$$\text{Profit margin} \times \text{asset turnover} = \text{return on assets}$$

$$5\% \times 1.88 \text{ times} = 9.4\%$$

Thus, a company's management may improve overall profitability by increasing the profit margin, the asset turnover, or both. Similarly, in evaluating a company's overall profitability, the financial statement user must consider the interaction of both ratios to produce return on assets.

Careful study of Figure 6-5 shows the different ways in which the selected industries combine profit margin and asset turnover to produce return on assets. For instance, grocery stores and pharmaceutical companies have a similar return on assets, but they achieve it in very different ways. Grocery stores have a very small profit margin, 1.4 percent, which when combined with a high asset turnover, 5.6, gives a return on assets of 7.8 percent. Pharmaceutical manufacturers, on the other hand, have a high profit margin, 7.8 percent, combined with a low asset turnover, 1.1, producing a return on assets of 8.6 percent. Accounting and bookkeeping services have the best return on assets, 28.8 percent, because they have a good profit margin, 13.1 percent, combined with a fairly good asset turnover, 2.2.

Shafer Auto Parts Corporation's profit margin of 5 percent is not quite double the auto and home supply industry average of 2.7 percent, but its turnover of 1.88 times lags behind the industry average of 2.6 times. Shafer is sacrificing asset turnover to achieve a high profit margin. It is clear that this strategy is working, because Shafer's return on assets of 9.4 percent exceeded the industry average of 6.9 percent.

Debt to Equity. Another useful measure is the **debt to equity ratio**, which shows the proportion of the company financed by creditors in com-

Figure 6-5. Average Profit Margin, Asset Turnover, and Return on Assets for Selected Industries

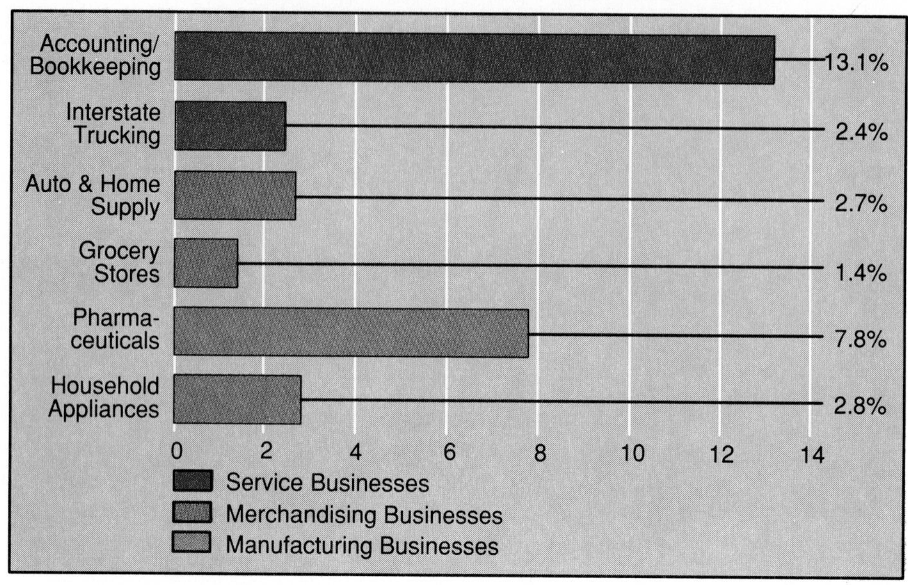

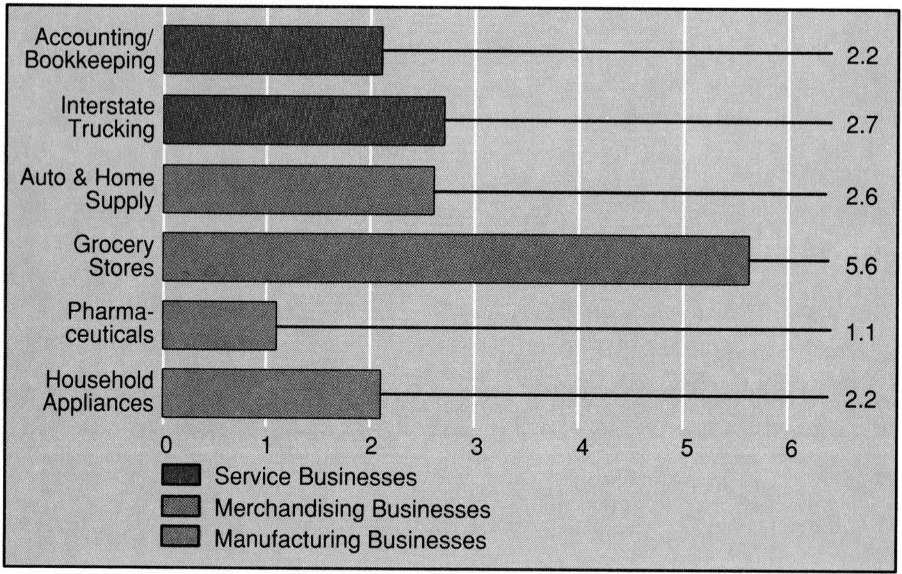

Figure 6-5. *Continued*

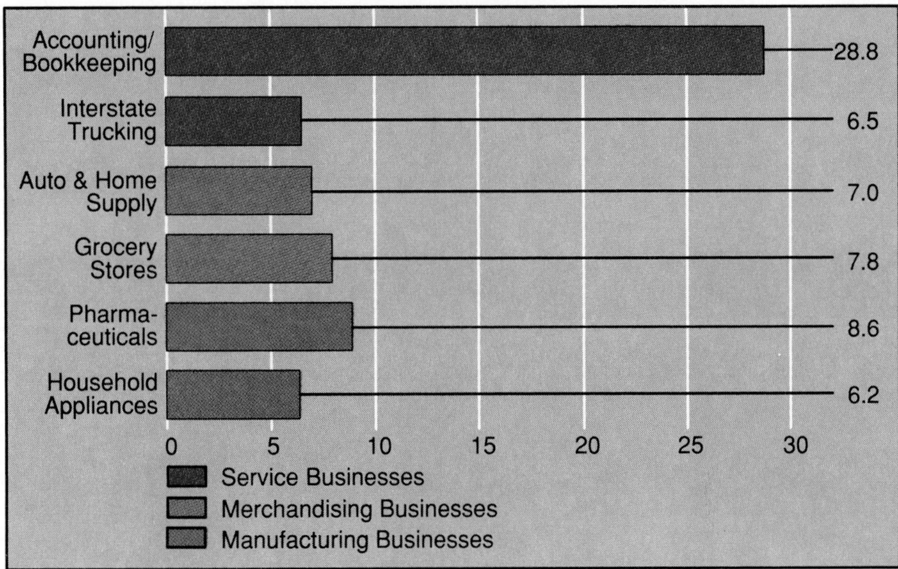

Source: Data from Dun and Bradstreet, *Industry Norms and Ratios*, 1990–91.

parison to that financed by the owners. This ratio is computed by dividing total liabilities by stockholders' equity. A debt to equity ratio of 1.0 means that total liabilities equal stockholders' equity and that one-half of the company's assets are financed by creditors. A ratio of .5 would mean that one-third of the assets was financed by creditors. A company with a high debt to equity ratio is more vulnerable in poor economic times because it must continue to repay creditors. Stockholders' investments, on the other hand, do not have to be repaid and dividends can be deferred if the company is suffering because of a poor economy. The debt to equity ratio for Shafer Auto Parts Corporation is computed as follows:

$$\text{Debt to equity} = \frac{\text{total liabilities}}{\text{stockholders' equity}} = \frac{\$60{,}483}{\$98{,}433} = .614 \text{ (or 61.4\%)}$$

Because its ratio of debt to equity is 61.4 percent, about 40 percent of Shafer Auto Parts Corporation is financed by creditors and roughly 60 percent is financed by investors' capital.

The debt to equity ratio does not fit neatly into either the liquidity or profitability category. It is clearly very important to liquidity analysis because it relates to debt and its repayment. However, it is also relevant to profitability for two reasons. First, creditors are interested in the proportion of the business that is debt financed because the more debt a company has, the more profit it must earn to ensure the payment of interest to the creditors. Second, stockholders are interested in the proportion of the business that is debt financed. The amount of interest that must be paid on the debt affects the amount of profit that is left to provide a return on stockholders' investments. The debt to equity ratio also shows how much expansion might be possible by borrowing additional long-term funds. In Figure 6-6, it may be seen that the debt to equity ratio in our selected industries varies from a low of 52.8 percent in the pharmaceutical industry to 109.2 percent in the interstate trucking industry.

Return on Equity. Of course, stockholders are interested in how much they earned on their investment in the business. Their **return on equity** is measured by the ratio of net income to average stockholders' equity. Taking ending stockholders' equity from the balance sheet and assuming beginning stockholders' equity is \$100,552, the return on equity for the company is computed as follows:

$$\text{Return on equity} = \frac{\text{net income}}{\text{average stockholders' equity}}$$

$$= \frac{\$14{,}500}{(\$100{,}552 + \$98{,}433)/2}$$

$$= \frac{\$14{,}500}{\$99{,}492.50} = .146 \text{ (or 14.6\%)}$$

So in 19xx Shafer Auto Parts Corporation has earned 14.6¢ for every dollar of stockholders' equity. Judging whether or not this is an acceptable return will depend on several factors, such as how much the company

Figure 6-6. Average Debt to Equity for Selected Industries

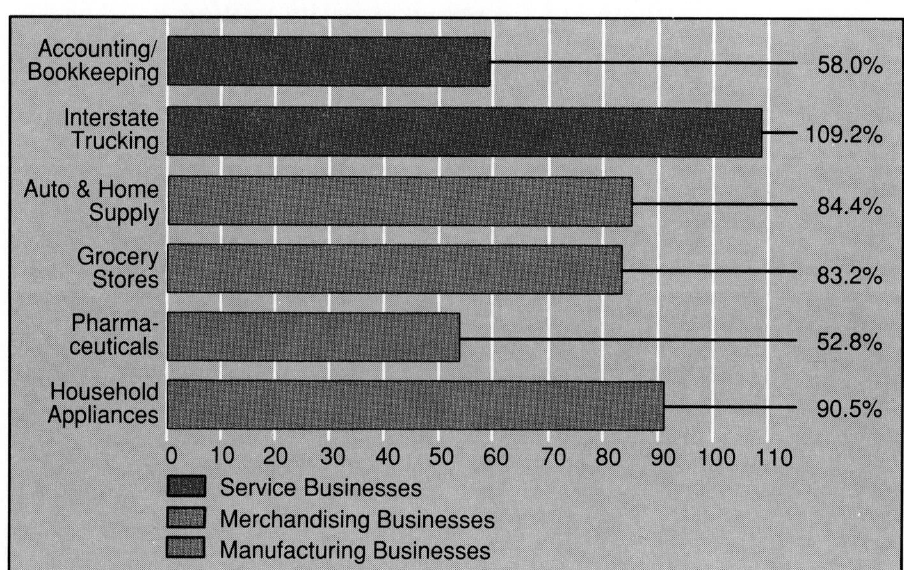

Source: Data from Dun and Bradstreet, *Industry Norms and Ratios*, 1990–91.

earned in prior years and how much other companies in the same industry earned. As measured by return on equity, as shown in Figure 6-7, accounting and bookkeeping services is the most profitable of our sample industries, with a return on equity of 30.8 percent. Household appliances are the least profitable, with a return on equity of 8.2 percent. Shafer Auto Parts Corporation's average return on equity of 14.5 percent exceeds the auto and home supply industry average of 11.5 percent.

The Annual Report of a Major Corporation

OBJECTIVE 8
Identify the major components of a corporate annual report

So far, simple financial statements have been presented. Statements for major corporations, however, can be quite complicated and have many other features. The management of a corporation has a responsibility each year to report to the stockholders on the company's performance. This report, called the **annual report**, contains the annual financial statements, the notes related to these financial statements, and other information about the company. In addition to the financial statements and related notes, the annual report usually contains a letter to the stockholders, a multiyear summary of financial highlights, a description of the business, management's discussion of operating results and financial condition, a report of management's responsibility, the auditors' report, and a list of directors and officers of the company. This report and other data must also be filed annually with the Securities and Exchange Commission.

To illustrate the annual report of a major corporation, excerpts from the 1990 annual report of Toys "R" Us, Inc. will be used in the following sec-

Figure 6-7. Average Return on Owners' Equity

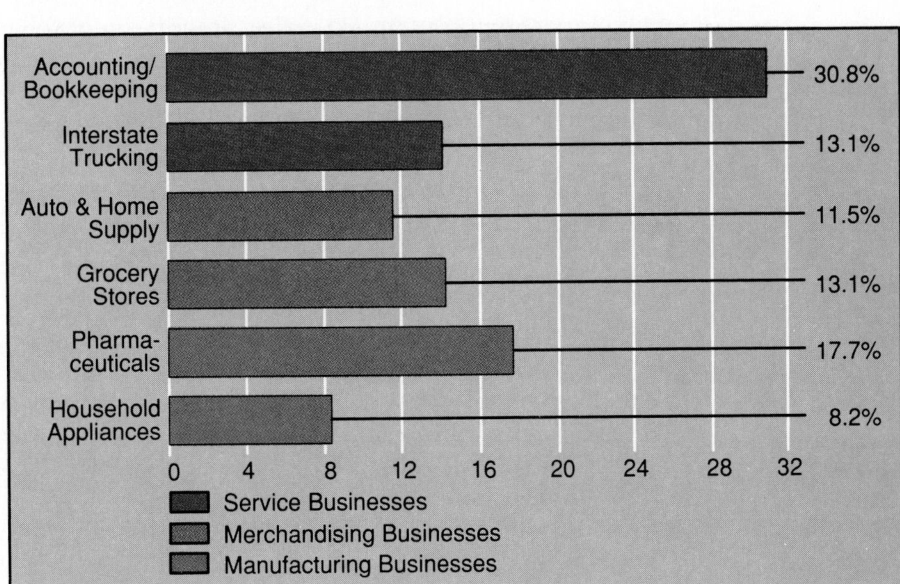

Source: Data from Dun and Bradstreet, *Industry Norms and Ratios*, 1990–91.

tions of this chapter.[9] Toys "R" Us, Inc. is one of the most successful retailers of this generation and is famous for its stores filled with huge inventories of toys and other items for children. In recent years, the company has opened a chain of stores that sell children's clothes, called Kids "R" Us.

Letter to the Stockholders

Traditionally, the top officers of corporations address the stockholders about the performance and prospects for the company in a letter at the beginning of the annual report. The president and the chairman of the board of Toys "R" Us wrote to the stockholders about the highlights of the past year, the outlook for the new year, human resources, and expansion plans. For example, they reported on the prospects for the 1991 season as follows:

> We look forward to a much stronger year in 1991, with declining profits in the first half of the year more than offset by a vibrant second half. Our assessment of the February Toy Fair indicates another strong year in categories such as dolls, action figures, juvenile and pre-school.

Financial Highlights (Figure 6-8)

The financial highlights section of the annual report presents key financial statistics for a ten-year period and is often accompanied by graphical presentations. Note, for example, that Figure 6-8 shows key figures for operations, financial position, and number of stores at year end for Toys "R" Us. Net sales is presented graphically. Other key figures are also shown graphically at appropriate points in the report. Note that the financial highlights section often includes nonfinancial data, such as number of stores or number of employees. In addition to the financial highlights, the annual report will contain a detailed description of the products and divisions of the company. Some analysts scoff at this section of the annual report because of the glossy photographs, but many companies provide useful information about past results and future plans.

Consolidated Statements of Earnings (Figure 6-9)

1. Toys "R" Us calls its income statements the consolidated statements of earnings. The word **consolidated** used in the title means that Toys "R" Us consists of several companies that are combined for financial reporting purposes.
2. The consolidated statements of earnings contain data for the years ended in 1991, 1990, and 1989, shown in the columns at the right, to aid in the evaluation of the company over the years. Financial statements presented in this fashion are called **comparative financial statements**. This form of reporting is in accordance with generally accepted accounting principles. For Toys "R" Us, the fiscal year for 1990 and 1989 ends on the Sunday nearest the end of January. Beginning in 1991, it is the Saturday nearest the end of January.

9. Excerpts reprinted courtesy of Toys "R" Us, Inc.

Figure 6-8. Financial Highlights for Toys "R" Us, Inc.

TOYS"R"US, INC. AND SUBSIDIARIES

FINANCIAL HIGHLIGHTS

(In millions except per share information) *Fiscal Year Ended*

	Feb. 2 1991	Jan. 28 1990	Jan. 29 1989	Jan. 31 1988	Feb. 1 1987	Feb. 2 1986	Feb. 3 1985	Jan. 29 1984	Jan. 30 1983	Jan. 31 1982
OPERATIONS:										
Net Sales	$5,510	$4,788	$4,000	$3,137	$2,445	$1,976	$1,702	$1,320	$1,042	$783
Net Earnings	326	321	268	204	152	120	111	92	64	49
Net Earnings Per Share*	1.11	1.09	.91	.69	.52	.41	.39	.32	.23	.19
FINANCIAL POSITION AT YEAR-END:										
Working Capital	177	238	255	225	155	181	222	220	157	137
Real Estate-Net	1,433	1,142	952	762	601	423	279	185	121	79
Total Assets	3,582	3,075	2,555	2,027	1,523	1,226	1,099	820	559	442
Long-Term Obligations	195	173	174	177	85	88	88	55	42	88
Stockholders' Equity	2,046	1,705	1,424	1,135	901	717	579	460	323	206
NUMBER OF STORES AT YEAR-END:										
Toys"R"Us - United States	451	404	358	313	271	233	198	169	144	120
Toys"R"Us - International	97	74	52	37	24	13	5	—	—	—
Kids"R"Us	164	137	112	74	43	23	10	2	—	—

*Restated to reflect the three-for-two stock split effected on June 29, 1990.

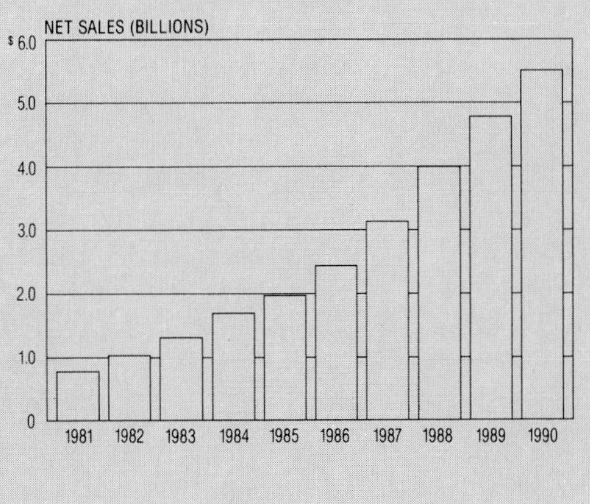

Reprinted courtesy of Toys "R" Us, Inc. The footnotes to the financial statement, which are an integral part of the report, are not included.

Figure 6-9. Consolidated Statements of Earnings for Toys "R" Us, Inc.

TOYS"R"US, INC. AND SUBSIDIARIES

(1) CONSOLIDATED STATEMENTS OF EARNINGS

(2)

(In thousands except per share information)	February 2 1991	January 28 1990	Year Ended January 29 1989
(3) Net sales	$ 5,510,001	$ 4,787,830	$ 4,000,192
Costs and expenses:			
Cost of sales	3,820,840	3,309,653	2,766,543
Selling, advertising, general and administrative	1,024,809	866,399	736,329
Depreciation and amortization	79,093	65,839	54,564
Interest expense	73,304	44,309	25,812
Interest and other income	(11,233)	(12,050)	(11,880)
	4,986,813	4,274,150	3,571,368
(4) Earnings before taxes on income	523,188	513,680	428,824
Taxes on income	197,200	192,600	160,800
Net earnings	$ 325,988	$ 321,080	$ 268,024
(5) Net earnings per share	$ 1.11	$ 1.09	$ .91

(6) See notes to consolidated financial statements.

Reprinted courtesy of Toys "R" Us, Inc. The footnotes to the financial statement, which are an integral part of the report, are not included.

3. Toys "R" Us uses the single-step form of the income statement and so includes all costs and expenses as a deduction from sales to arrive at Earnings Before Taxes on Income.
4. Income taxes are the expense for federal and state taxes on Toys "R" Us's corporate income. Income taxes for corporations are substantial, often exceeding 35 percent of the income before income taxes, and thus have a significant effect on company decisions. Most other taxes, such as property taxes and employment taxes, are shown among the operating expenses.
5. Earnings per share is reported by Toys "R" Us as **net earnings per share**, a term used by some companies to emphasize that the figure is based on net earnings. Its calculation is based on the average number of common shares outstanding during the year.
6. At the bottom of each page of financial statements, the company reminds the reader in a footnote that the notes accompanying the financial statements are an integral part of the statements and must be consulted in interpreting the financial statements.

Consolidated Balance Sheets (Figure 6-10)

1. Toys "R" Us also presents consolidated balance sheets in comparative form. In contrast to the statements of consolidated earnings, only two years of comparative data are used for the balance sheet.
2. Toys "R" Us has a typical set of current assets for a merchandising company.
3. Toys "R" Us has a large investment in property and equipment. More details on property and equipment including the amounts for accumulated depreciation and amortization are provided in the notes and shown in the discussion of explanatory notes on page 307.
4. Toys "R" Us has some leased property that is recorded on the balance sheet as an asset. Also, in place of an investment category and an intangible asset category, Toys "R" Us has a catchall group named Other Assets.
5. The current liabilities section contains typical current liabilities.
6. Another liability in the Toys "R" Us balance sheet is Long-Term Debt and Obligations Under Capital Leases (excluding the current portions). Also included is Deferred Income Taxes, an account that is sometimes hard to understand. In general, deferred income taxes are income tax expenses that will not have to be paid until sometime in the future. The subject of deferred income taxes is covered in a later chapter.
7. There are several items in the stockholders' equity section. You are familiar with Common Stock and Retained Earnings. Additional paid-in capital represents amounts invested by stockholders in excess of the par value of the common stock. The foreign currency translation adjustment occurs because Toys "R" Us has foreign operations (see the chapter on international accounting). Treasury shares is a contra shareholders' equity account that represents the cost of previously issued shares that have been bought back by the company. Finally, the receivable from exercise of stock options represents stock purchased by management and employees but not yet paid for.

The Consolidated Statements of Stockholders' Equity

Instead of a simple statement of retained earnings, Toys "R" Us presents a statement of stockholders' equity. This statement, which is too complex to present at this point in the text, explains the changes in each of the six components of stockholders' equity. The statement is covered in the chapter on retained earnings.

The Consolidated Statements of Cash Flows (Figure 6-11)

1. The preparation of the consolidated statement of cash flows is presented in a later chapter. However, its importance makes it worthwhile for you to look at its major sections at this point. Whereas the income statement reflects the profitability of the company, the statement of cash

Figure 6-10. Consolidated Balance Sheets for Toys "R" Us, Inc.

TOYS"R"US, INC. AND SUBSIDIARIES

CONSOLIDATED BALANCE SHEETS

(In thousands)

	(1) *February 2 1991*	*January 28 1990*
ASSETS		
(2) Current Assets:		
Cash and short-term investments	$ 35,005	$ 40,895
Accounts and other receivables	73,170	53,098
Merchandise inventories	1,275,169	1,230,394
Prepaid expenses	20,981	13,965
Total Current Assets	1,404,325	1,338,352
(3) Property and Equipment:		
Real estate, net	1,433,489	1,141,690
Other, net	700,481	553,104
Leased property under capital leases, net	7,371	8,180
(4) Total Property and Equipment	2,141,341	1,702,974
Other Assets	36,777	33,362
	$ 3,582,443	$ 3,074,688
LIABILITIES AND STOCKHOLDERS' EQUITY		
(5) Current Liabilities:		
Short-term notes payable to banks	$ 386,470	$ 205,513
Accounts payable	483,948	517,903
Accrued expenses, taxes and other liabilities	275,579	280,517
Income taxes	81,591	96,033
Total Current Liabilities	1,227,588	1,099,966
(6) Deferred Income Taxes	113,405	96,391
Long-Term Debt	182,695	159,518
Obligations Under Capital Leases	12,462	13,467
(7) Stockholders' Equity:		
Common stock	29,794	19,797
Additional paid-in capital	353,924	324,616
Retained earnings	1,752,800	1,436,855
Foreign currency translation adjustments	40,428	23,010
Treasury shares, at cost	(129,340)	(96,973)
Receivable from exercise of stock options	(1,313)	(1,959)
	2,046,293	1,705,346
	$ 3,582,443	$ 3,074,688

See notes to consolidated financial statements.

Reprinted courtesy of Toys "R" Us, Inc. The footnotes to the financial statement, which are an integral part of the report, are not included.

Figure 6-11. Consolidated Statements of Cash Flows for Toys "R" Us, Inc.

TOYS"R"US, INC. AND SUBSIDIARIES

CONSOLIDATED STATEMENTS OF CASH FLOWS

(In thousands)		(1)	*Year Ended*
	February 2 1991	*January 28 1990*	*January 29 1989*
CASH FLOWS FROM OPERATING ACTIVITIES			
(2) Net income	$ 325,988	$ 321,080	$ 268,024
Adjustments to reconcile net income to net cash provided by operating activities:			
Depreciation and amortization	79,093	65,839	54,564
Deferred taxes	17,014	17,572	25,463
Change in operating assets and liabilities:			
Accounts and other receivables	(20,072)	14,932	(5,886)
Merchandise inventories	(44,775)	(299,274)	(158,287)
Prepaid expenses and other assets	(10,431)	(11,391)	(14,366)
Accounts payable, accrued expenses and taxes	(53,529)	92,316	158,802
Total adjustments	(32,700)	(120,006)	60,290
Net cash provided by operating activities	293,288	201,074	328,314
CASH FLOWS FROM INVESTING ACTIVITIES			
(3) Capital expenditures – net	(517,460)	(371,851)	(327,010)
Other – net	17,385	(5,114)	4,463
Net cash used in investing activities	(500,075)	(376,965)	(322,547)
CASH FLOWS FROM FINANCING ACTIVITIES			
(4) Short-term borrowings – net	180,957	129,380	58,476
Long-term borrowings	33,152	—	693
Long-term debt repayments	(10,864)	(1,199)	(3,899)
Exercise of stock options	30,344	19,861	52,429
Share repurchase program	(32,692)	(54,168)	(36,550)
Net cash provided by financing activities	200,897	93,874	71,149
CASH AND SHORT-TERM INVESTMENTS			
(5) Increase (decrease) during year	(5,890)	(82,017)	76,916
Beginning of year	40,895	122,912	45,996
End of year	$ 35,005	$ 40,895	$ 122,912

SUPPLEMENTAL DISCLOSURES OF CASH FLOW INFORMATION

(6) The Company considers all highly liquid investments purchased as part of its daily cash management activities to be short-term investments.

During the years ended February 2, 1991, January 28, 1990 and January 29, 1989, the Company made income tax payments of $180,943, $116,770 and $110,079 and interest payments (net of amounts capitalized) of $77,570, $44,265 and $25,738, respectively.

See notes to consolidated financial statements.

Reprinted courtesy of Toys "R" Us, Inc. The footnotes to the financial statement, which are an integral part of the report, are not included.

flows reflects the liquidity of the company. The statement provides information about a company's cash receipts and cash payments and about its investing and financing activities during an accounting period. Three years of comparative statements are presented in Figure 6-11.

2. The first section of the consolidated statements of cash flows shows cash flows from operating activities. It begins with the net income (earnings) from the consolidated statements of earnings (Figure 6-9) and adjusts that figure, which is based on accrual accounting, to a figure that represents the net cash flows provided by operating activities. Among the adjustments are increases for depreciation and amortization, which are expenses that do not require the use of cash, and increases and decreases for the changes in the various working capital accounts. In the year ended February 2, 1991, Toys "R" Us had net income of $325,988,000, and its net cash inflow from these operations was $293,288,000. Added to net income are expenses that do not require a current outlay of cash such as depreciation and amortization ($79,093,000) and deferred taxes ($17,014,000). Cash was also used to increase accounts and other receivables ($20,072,000), inventories ($44,775,000), and prepaid expenses and other assets ($10,431,000). It was also used to decrease Accounts Payable ($53,529,000). Because of these increases in current assets and decreases in accounts payable, net cash provided by operating activities was less than net income.
3. The second major section of the consolidated statements of cash flows is cash flows from investing activities. The main item in this category is capital expenditures, net, of $517,460,000. This shows that Toys "R" Us is a growing company.
4. The third major section of the consolidated statements of cash flows is cash flows from financing activities. You can see here that the primary sources of cash from financing activities are short-term borrowings of $180,957,000, long-term borrowings of $33,152,000, and exercise of stock options of $30,344,000, which was helpful in paying for part of the capital expenditures in the investing activities section. In total, the company raised $200,897,000 from financing activities during the year.
5. At the bottom of the consolidated statements of cash flows, the net effect of the operating, investing, and financing activities on the cash balance may be seen. Toys "R" Us had a decrease in cash (and short-term investments) during the year of $5,890,000 and ended the year with $35,005,000 of cash (and short-term investments) on hand.
6. The supplemental disclosures of cash flow information explain that Toys "R" Us intends the word cash to include not only cash but also highly liquid short-term investments, which earn a return on cash that is not needed at the moment. This section also explains other significant investing and financing transactions.

Notes to Consolidated Financial Statements

To meet the requirements of full disclosure, the company must add **notes to the financial statements** to help the user interpret some of the more complex items in the published financial statements. The notes are considered an integral part of the financial statements. In recent years, the need for explanation and further details has become so great that the notes often take more space than the statements themselves. The notes to the financial statements can be put into three broad groups: summary of significant accounting policies, explanatory notes, and supplementary information notes.

Summary of Significant Accounting Policies. In its *Opinion No. 22,* the Accounting Principles Board requires that the financial statements include a **summary of significant accounting policies**. In most cases, this summary is presented in the first note to the financial statements or as a separate part just before the notes. In this part, the company tells which generally accepted accounting principles it has followed in preparing the statements. For example, in the Toys "R" Us report the company states the principles followed for property and equipment:

Property and equipment are recorded at cost. Depreciation and amortization are provided using the straight-line method over the estimated useful lives of the assets, or where applicable, the terms of the respective leases, whichever is shorter.

Other important accounting policies listed by Toys "R" Us deal with fiscal year, principles of consolidation, merchandise inventories, preopening costs, and capitalized interest.

Explanatory Notes. Other notes explain some of the items in the financial statements. For example, Toys "R" Us showed the details of its Property and Equipment account in the second note, as follows:

(In thousands)	Useful Life (In years)	February 2, 1991	January 28, 1990
Land		$ 479,802	$ 403,997
Buildings	20–50	961,892	742,120
Furniture and equipment	5–15	581,971	463,341
Leaseholds and leasehold improvements	12½–50	364,065	281,471
Construction in progress		66,334	52,189
Leased property under capital leases		21,172	21,172
		$2,475,236	$1,964,290
Less accumulated depreciation and amortization		333,895	261,316
		$2,141,341	$1,702,974

Other notes had to do with long-term debt, leases, stock options, stock option plan, taxes on income, profit sharing plan, net earnings per share, and foreign operations.

Supplementary Information Notes. In recent years, the FASB and SEC have ruled that certain supplemental information must be presented with financial statements. An example is the quarterly report that most companies make to their stockholders and to the Securities and Exchange Commission. These quarterly reports, which are called **interim financial statements**, are in most cases reviewed but not audited by the company's independent CPA firm. In its annual report, Toys "R" Us presented unaudited quarterly financial data from its 1991 quarterly statements, which are shown in the following table (dollars in thousands, except per share amounts).

Year ended February 2, 1991:

	First Quarter	Second Quarter	Third Quarter	Fourth Quarter
Net Sales	$944,802	$964,034	$1,052,607	$2,548,558
Cost of Sales	653,384	668,267	722,327	1,776,862
Net Earnings	33,228	26,494	28,725	237,541
Net Earnings per Share	$.11	$.09	$.10	$.81

Interim data were presented for 1990 as well. Toys "R" Us also provides supplemental information on the market price of its common stock during the years. Other companies that are engaged in more than one line or type of business may present information for each business segment.

Report of Management's Responsibilities

A statement of management's responsibility for the financial statements and the system of internal control may accompany the financial statements. A part of the statement by Toys "R" Us management is as follows:

Responsibility for the integrity and objectivity of the financial information presented in this Annual Report rests with Toys "R" Us management. The accompanying financial statements have been prepared from accounting records which management believes fairly and accurately reflect the operations and financial position of the Company. Management has established a system of internal controls to provide reasonable assurance that assets are maintained and accounted for in accordance with its policies and that transactions are recorded accurately on the Company's books and records.

Management's Discussion and Analysis

A discussion and analysis by management of financial conditions and results of operations is also presented. In this section, management explains the difference from one year to the next. For example, the management of

Toys "R" Us describes the company's sales performance in the following way:

The Company has experienced sales growth in each of its last three years; sales were up 15.1% in 1990, 19.7% in 1989 and 27.5% in 1988. Part of the growth is attributable to the opening of 138 new U.S. toy stores, 60 international toy stores and 90 children's clothing stores during the three-year period, and a portion of the increase is due to comparable U.S. toy store sales increases of .3%, 6.7% and 11.3% in 1990, 1989 and 1988, respectively.

Its management of cash flows is described as follows:

Because of the seasonal nature of the business (approximately 46% of sales take place in the fourth quarter), cash typically declines from the beginning of the year through October as inventory is built up for the Christmas season and funds are used for land purchases and construction of new stores which usually open in the first ten months of the year. In this connection, the Company has commitments and backup lines from numerous financial institutions to adequately support its short-term financing needs. Management expects that seasonal cash requirements will continue to be met primarily through operations, issuance of short-term commercial paper and bank borrowings for its foreign subsidiaries.

Report of Certified Public Accountants (Figure 6-12)

1. The **accountants' report** (or **auditors' report**) deals with the credibility of the financial statements. This report by independent public accountants gives the accountants' opinion about how fairly these statements have been presented. Using financial statements prepared by managers without an independent audit would be like having a judge hear a case in which he or she was personally involved or having a member of a team taking part in a football game act as a referee. Management, through its internal accounting system, is logically responsible for recordkeeping because it needs similar information for its own use in operating the business. The certified public accountant, acting independently, adds the necessary credibility to management's figures for interested third parties. Note that the certified public accountant reports to the board of directors and the stockholders rather than to management.

   In form and language, most auditors' reports are like the one shown in Figure 6-12. Usually such a report is short, but its language is very important. The report is divided into three parts.
2. The first paragraph identifies the financial statements subject to the auditors' report. This paragraph also identifies responsibilities. Company management is responsible for financial statements, and the auditor is responsible for expressing an opinion on the financial statements based on the audit.
3. The second paragraph or **scope section** states that the examination was made in accordance with generally accepted auditing standards. These standards call for an acceptable level of quality in ten areas established by the American Institute of Certified Public Accountants. This paragraph also contains a brief description of the objectives and nature of the audit.

Figure 6-12. Auditors' Report for Toys "R" Us, Inc.

INDEPENDENT AUDITORS' REPORT

(1) To the Board of Directors and Stockholders
Toys "R" Us, Inc.
Paramus, New Jersey

(2) We have audited the accompanying consolidated balance sheets of Toys "R" Us, Inc. and subsidiaries as of February 2, 1991 and January 28, 1990, and the related consolidated statements of earnings, stockholders' equity and cash flows for each of the three years in the period ended February 2, 1991. These financial statements are the responsibility of the Company's management. Our responsibility is to express an opinion on these financial statements based on our audits.

(3) We conducted our audits in accordance with generally accepted auditing standards. Those standards require that we plan and perform the audit to obtain reasonable assurance about whether the financial statements are free of material misstatement. An audit includes examining, on a test basis, evidence supporting the amounts and disclosures in the financial statements. An audit also includes assessing the accounting principles used and significant estimates made by management, as well as evaluating the overall financial statement presentation. We believe that our audits provide a reasonable basis for our opinion.

(4) In our opinion, such consolidated financial statements present fairly, in all material respects, the financial position of Toys"R"Us, Inc. and subsidiaries as of February 2, 1991 and January 28, 1990, and the results of their operations and their cash flows for each of the three years in the period ended February 2, 1991 in conformity with generally accepted accounting principles.

Deloitte & Touche

March 13, 1991
New York, New York

Reprinted courtesy of Toys "R" Us, Inc. The footnotes to the financial statement, which are an integral part of the report, are not included.

4. The third paragraph or **opinion section** states the results of the auditors' examination. The use of the word *opinion* is very important, because the auditor does not certify or guarantee that the statements are absolutely correct. To do so would go beyond the truth, because many items such as depreciation are based on estimates. Instead, the auditors simply give an opinion as to whether, overall, the financial statements "present fairly," in all material respects, the financial position and results of operations. This means that the statements are prepared in accordance with generally accepted accounting principles. If in the auditors' opinion they are not, the auditors must explain why and to what extent they do not meet the standards.

This report reflects a change made by the American Institute of Certified Public Accountants in the language of the auditors' report to emphasize management's responsibility for the financial statements and to clarify the nature and purpose of the audit.

Chapter Review

Review of Learning Objectives

1. **State the objectives of financial reporting.**
The objectives of financial reporting are that financial statements should provide (1) information useful in making investment and credit decisions, (2) information useful in assessing cash flow prospects, and (3) information about business resources, claims to those resources, and changes in them.

2. **State the qualitative characteristics of accounting information, and describe their interrelationships.**
Understandability depends on the user's knowledge and the accountant's ability to provide useful information. Usefulness is a function of two primary characteristics, relevance and reliability. Relevance depends on the information's predictive value, feedback value, and timeliness. Reliability depends on the information's representational faithfulness, verifiability, and neutrality.

3. **Define and describe the use of the conventions of comparability and consistency, materiality, conservatism, full disclosure, and cost-benefit.**
Because accountants' measurements are not exact, certain conventions have come to be applied in current practice to aid in interpreting the financial statements. One of these conventions is consistency, which requires the use of the same accounting procedures from period to period and enhances the comparability of financial statements. The second is materiality, which involves the relative importance of an item. The third is conservatism, which entails using the procedure that will be least likely to overstate assets and income. The fourth is full disclosure, which means including all relevant information in the financial statements. The fifth is cost-benefit, which suggests that after providing a minimum level of information, additional information should be provided only if the benefits derived from the information exceed the costs of providing it.

4. **Summarize the concepts underlying financial accounting and their relationship to ethical financial reporting.**
   Accounting is an information system that facilitates the making of business decisions by measuring, processing, and communicating to decision makers information in the form of financial statements about the transactions of a business entity. To interpret and use the financial statements, it is important to understand the generally accepted accounting principles (GAAP), qualitative characteristics, and accounting conventions that underlie the accounting information system. Ethical financial reporting means that these concepts are applied with the intent to enlighten, not to mislead.

5. **Identify and describe the basic components of a classified balance sheet.**
   The classified balance sheet is subdivided as follows:

Assets	Liabilities
Current Assets	Current Liabilities
Investments	Long-Term Liabilities
Property, Plant, and Equipment	
Intangible Assets	**Owners' Equity**
(Other Assets)	(Categories depend on form of business)

   A current asset is an asset that can reasonably be expected to be realized in cash during the next year or normal operating cycle. In general, assets are listed in the order of the ease of their conversion into cash. A current liability is a liability that can reasonably be expected to be paid during the next year or normal operating cycle, whichever is longer. The owners' (stockholders') equity section for a corporation differs from that of a proprietorship in that it has subdivisions of contributed capital and retained earnings.

6. **Prepare the multistep and single-step types of classified income statements.**
   Condensed income statements for external reporting may be in multistep or single-step form. The multistep form arrives at net income through a series of steps, whereas the single-step form arrives at net income in a single step. The single-step form often separates out income taxes. There is usually a separate section in the multistep form for other revenues and expenses below income from operations.

7. **Use classified financial statements for the simple evaluation of liquidity and profitability.**
   One major use of classified financial statements is to evaluate the company's liquidity and profitability. Two simple measures of liquidity are working capital and the current ratio. Five simple measures of profitability are profit margin, asset turnover, return on assets, debt to equity, and return on equity.

8. **Identify the major components of a corporate annual report.**
   A corporation's annual report is the mechanism by which management reports to the stockholders the company's financial results for the year. The annual report has the following principal components: letter to the stockholders, financial highlights, the four basic financial statements, notes to the financial statements, report of management's responsibilities, manage-

ment's discussion and analysis of earnings, and the report of the certified public accountant.

Review of Concepts and Terminology

The following concepts and terms were introduced in this chapter:

(L.O. 8) **Accountants' (auditors') report:** The medium by which the independent public accountants communicate to the users of the financial statements the nature of the audit (scope section) and the conclusion as to the fair presentation of the financial statements (opinion section).

(L.O. 8) **Annual report:** The medium by which the general-purpose external financial statements of a business are communicated once a year to stockholders and other interested parties.

(L.O. 7) **Asset turnover:** A ratio that measures how efficiently assets are used to produce sales; net sales divided by average total assets.

(L.O. 5) **Classified financial statements:** General-purpose external financial statements that are divided into useful subcategories.

(L.O. 3) **Comparability:** The convention of presenting information in such a way that decision makers can recognize similarities, differences, and trends.

(L.O. 8) **Comparative financial statements:** Financial statements in which data for two or more years are presented in adjacent columnar form.

(L.O. 6) **Condensed financial statements:** Financial statements for external reporting purposes that present only the major categories of information.

(L.O. 3) **Conservatism:** The convention that mandates that, in the face of two equally acceptable alternatives, the accountant will choose the one less likely to overstate assets and income.

(L.O. 3) **Consistency:** The convention that an accounting procedure, once adopted, will not be changed from one period to another unless users are informed of the change.

(L.O. 8) **Consolidated (financial statements):** The combined financial statements of a parent company and its subsidiaries.

(L.O. 3) **Cost-benefit:** The convention that the benefits gained from providing accounting information should be greater than the costs of providing that information.

(L.O. 5) **Current assets:** Cash or other assets that are reasonably expected to be realized in cash, sold, or consumed during a normal operating cycle of a business, or within one year, whichever is longer.

(L.O. 5) **Current liabilities:** Obligations due within the normal operating cycle of the business or within one year, whichever is longer.

(L.O. 7) **Current ratio:** A measure of liquidity; current assets divided by current liabilities.

(L.O. 7) **Debt to equity ratio:** A ratio that measures the relationship of assets provided by creditors to those provided by owners; total liabilities divided by stockholders' equity.

(L.O. 6, 8) **Earnings per share (net income per share or net earnings per share):** Item on corporate income statements that shows the net income earned on each share of common stock; net income divided by the weighted average of common shares outstanding.

(L.O. 4) **Fraudulent financial reporting:** The intentional preparation of misleading financial statements.

(L.O. 3) **Full disclosure:** The convention that requires financial statements and the notes to them to present all information relevant to the users' understanding of the company's financial condition.

(L.O. 1) **General-purpose external financial statements:** The medium through which information that has been gathered and processed in the accounting system is periodically communicated to investors, creditors, and other interested parties outside the business.

(L.O. 6) **Income from operations:** The excess of gross margin from sales over operating expenses.

(L.O. 6, 8) **Income taxes (income taxes expense or provision for income taxes):** An account that represents the expense for federal and state income taxes on corporate income; this account appears only on income statements of corporations.

(L.O. 5) **Intangible assets:** Long-term assets that have no physical substance but have a value based on rights or privileges accruing to the owner.

(L.O. 8) **Interim financial statements:** Financial statements prepared on a condensed basis for an accounting period of less than one year.

(L.O. 5) **Investments:** Assets, generally of a long-term nature, that are not used in the normal operation of a business and that management does not intend to convert to cash within the next year.

(L.O. 7) **Liquidity:** Having enough money on hand to (1) pay a company's bills when they are due and (2) take care of unexpected needs for cash.

(L.O. 5) **Long-term liabilities:** Debts of a business that fall due more than one year ahead or beyond the normal operating cycle, or that are to be paid out of noncurrent assets.

(L.O. 3) **Materiality:** The convention that requires an item or event in a financial statement to be important to the decisions made by users of the financial statements.

(L.O. 6) **Multistep form:** Form of the income statement that arrives at net income in steps.

(L.O. 8) **Notes to the financial statements:** A section of a corporate annual report containing notes that aid the user in interpreting the financial statements.

(L.O. 8) **Opinion section:** Section of the auditors' report that states the results of the examination.

(L.O. 5) **Other assets:** All the assets owned by a company other than current assets and property, plant, and equipment.

(L.O. 6) **Other revenues and expenses:** The section of a classified income statement that includes nonoperating revenues and expenses.

(L.O. 7) **Profitability:** The ability of a business to earn a satisfactory level of earnings.

(L.O. 7) **Profit margin:** A measure of profitability; the percentage of each sales dollar that results in net income; net income divided by net sales.

(L.O. 5) **Property, plant, and equipment:** Tangible assets of a long-term nature used in the continuing operation of the business.

(L.O. 2) **Qualitative characteristics:** Standards for judging the information that accountants give to decision makers.

(L.O. 2) **Relevance:** A qualitative characteristic of accounting information that makes a difference to or bears directly on the economic outcome of a decision for which it is used.

(L.O. 2) **Reliability:** The qualitative characteristic of accounting information that has the traits of representational faithfulness, verifiability, and neutrality.

(L.O. 7) **Return on assets:** A measure of profitability that shows how efficiently a company is using its assets; net income divided by average total assets.

(L.O. 7) **Return on equity:** A measure of profitability related to the amount earned by a business in relation to the stockholders' investments in the business; net income divided by average stockholders' equity.

(L.O. 8) **Scope section:** Part of the auditors' report that tells that the examination was made in accordance with generally accepted auditing standards.

(L.O. 6) **Single-step form:** Form of the income statement that arrives at net income in a single step.

(L.O. 8) **Summary of significant accounting policies:** Section of a corporate annual report that discloses which generally accepted accounting principles the company has followed in preparing the financial statements.

(L.O. 7) **Working capital:** The amount by which total current assets exceed total current liabilities.

Review Problem
Analyzing Liquidity and Profitability Using Ratios

(L.O. 7) Flavin Shirt Company has faced increased competition from imported shirts in recent years.

Presented below is summary information for the past two years:

	19x2	19x1
Current Assets	$ 200,000	$ 170,000
Total Assets	880,000	710,000
Current Liabilities	90,000	50,000
Long-Term Liabilities	150,000	50,000
Stockholders' Equity	640,000	610,000
Sales	1,200,000	1,050,000
Net Income	60,000	80,000

Total assets and stockholders' equity at the beginning of 19x1 were $690,000 and $590,000, respectively.

Required Use liquidity and profitability analyses to document the declining financial position of Flavin Shirt Company.

Answer to Review Problem

Liquidity analysis:

	Current Assets	Current Liabilities	Working Capital	Current Ratio
19x1	$170,000	$50,000	$120,000	3.40
19x2	200,000	90,000	110,000	2.22
Increase (decrease) in working capital			$ (10,000)	
Decrease in current ratio				1.18

Both working capital and the current ratio declined because, although current assets increased by $30,000 ($200,000 – $170,000), current liabilities increased by the greater amount of $40,000 ($90,000 – $50,000) from 19x1 to 19x2.

		Sales		Average Total Assets			Average Stockholders' Equity	
	Net Income	Sales	Profit Margin	Amount	Asset Turnover	Return on Assets	Amount	Return on Equity
19x1	$ 80,000	$1,050,000	7.6%	$700,000[1]	1.50	11.4%	$600,000[3]	13.3%
19x2	60,000	1,200,000	5.0%	795,000[2]	1.51	7.5%	625,000[4]	9.6%
Increase (Decrease)	$(20,000)	$ 150,000	(2.6)%	$ 95,000	0.01	(3.9)%	$ 25,000	(3.7)%

[1] ($690,000 + $710,000) ÷ 2
[2] ($710,000 + $880,000) ÷ 2
[3] ($590,000 + $610,000) ÷ 2
[4] ($610,000 + $640,000) ÷ 2

Net income decreased by $20,000 in spite of an increase in sales of $150,000 and an increase in average total assets of $95,000. The results were decreases in profit margin from 7.6 percent to 5.0 percent and in return on assets from 11.4 percent to 7.5 percent. Asset turnover had almost no change and thus did not contribute to the decline in profitability. The decrease in return on equity from 13.3 percent to 9.6 percent was not as great as the decrease in return on assets because the growth in total assets was financed by debt instead of stockholders' equity, as shown by the following capital structure analysis:

	Total Liabilities	Stockholders' Equity	Debt to Equity Ratio
19x1	$100,000	$610,000	16.4%
19x2	240,000	640,000	37.5%
Increase	$140,000	$ 30,000	21.1%

Total liabilities increased by $140,000, while stockholders' equity increased by $30,000. As a result, the amount of the business financed by debt in relation to stockholders' equity increased from 16.4 percent to 37.5 percent.

Chapter Assignments

Discussion Questions

1. What are the three objectives of financial reporting?
2. What are the qualitative characteristics of accounting information, and what is their significance?
3. What are the accounting conventions, and how does each aid in the interpretation of financial information?
4. What is the relationship among the objectives of financial information, financial statements, decision makers, economic activities, and ethical financial reporting?
5. What is the purpose of classified financial statements?
6. What are four common categories of assets?
7. What criterion must an asset meet to be classified as current? Under what condition will an asset be considered current even though it will not be realized as cash within a year? What are two examples of assets that fall into this category?
8. In what order should current assets be listed?
9. What is the difference between a short-term investment in the current assets section and a security in the investments section of the balance sheet?
10. What is an intangible asset? Give at least three examples.
11. Name the two major categories of liabilities.
12. What are the primary differences between the owners' equity section for a sole proprietorship or partnership and the corresponding section for a corporation?
13. Explain the difference between contributed capital and retained earnings.
14. Explain how the multistep form of the income statement differs from the single-step form. What are the relative merits of each?
15. Why are other revenues and expenses separated from operating revenues and expenses on the multistep income statement?
16. Define liquidity and name two measures.
17. How is the current ratio computed, and why is it important?

18. Which is the more important goal—liquidity or profitability? Explain.
19. Name five measures of profitability.
20. Evaluate this statement: "Return on assets is a better measure of profitability than profit margin."
21. What are some of the differences between the income statement for a sole proprietorship and that for a corporation?
22. Explain earnings per share and how this figure appears on the income statement.
23. What is the purpose of the accountants' report?
24. Why are notes to financial statements necessary?

Communication Skills Exercises

Communication 6-1. Materiality
(L.O. 3)

Mackey Electronics operates a chain of consumer electronics stores in the Atlanta area. This year the company achieved annual sales of $50 million, on which it earned a net income of $2 million. Until this year, the company used the periodic inventory system for financial reporting. At the beginning of the year, management implemented a new inventory system that enabled it to track all purchases and sales. At the end of the year, a physical inventory revealed that the actual inventory was $80,000 below what the new system indicated it should be. The inventory loss, which probably resulted from shoplifting, is reflected in a higher cost of goods sold. This problem concerns management but seems to be less important to the company's auditors. What is materiality? Why might the inventory loss concern management more than it does the auditors? Do you think the amount is material?

Communication 6-2. Accounting Conventions
(L.O. 3)

Mason Parking, which operates a seven-story parking building in downtown Chicago, has a calendar year end. It serves daily and hourly parkers, as well as monthly parkers who pay a fixed monthly rate in advance. The company has traditionally recorded all cash receipts as revenues when received. Most monthly parkers pay in full during the month prior to that in which they have the right to park. The company's auditors have said that, beginning in 1991, the company should consider recording the cash receipts from monthly parking on an accrual basis, debiting Prepaid Parking. Total cash receipts for 1991 were $2,500,000, and the cash receipts received in 1991 and applicable to January 1992 were $125,000. Discuss the relevance of the accounting conventions of consistency, materiality, and full disclosure to the decision on recording the monthly parking revenues on an accrual basis.

Communication 6-3. Ethics and Financial Reporting
(L.O. 4)

Salem Software, located outside Boston, develops computer software and licenses it to financial institutions. Salem Software uses an aggressive accounting method that books revenues from the systems it has sold on a percentage of completion basis. This means that revenue for partially completed projects is recognized based on the proportion of the project that is completed. If a project is 50 percent completed, then 50 percent of the contracted revenue is recognized. In 1991, preliminary estimates for a major $5 million project are that the project is 75 percent complete. Since the estimate of completion is a matter of judgment, management asks for a new report showing the project to be 90 percent complete. This change will enable management to meet its financial goals for the year and thus receive substantial year-end bonuses. Do you think management's action is ethical? If you were the company controller and were asked to prepare the new report, would you do it? What action would you take?

Communication 6-4. Ethics and Financial Reporting *(L.O. 4)*

Treon Microsystems, Inc., a Silicon Valley manufacturer of microchips for personal computers, has just completed its year-end physical inventory in advance of preparing financial statements. To celebrate, the entire accounting department goes out for a New Year's Eve party at a local establishment. As senior accountant, you join the fun. At the party, you fall into conversation with an employee of one of your main competitors. After a while, the employee reveals that the competitor plans to introduce a new product in sixty days that will make Treon's principal product obsolete.

On Monday morning, you go to the financial vice president with this information, stating that the inventory may have to be written down and net income reduced. To your surprise, the financial vice president says that you were right to come to him, but urges you to say nothing about the problem. He says, "It is probably a rumor, and even if it is true, there will be plenty of time to write down the inventory in sixty days." You wonder if this is the appropriate thing to do. You feel confident that your source knew what he was talking about. You know that the salaries of all top managers, including the financial vice president, are tied to net income. What is fraudulent financial reporting? Is this an example of fraudulent financial reporting? What action would you take?

Communication 6-5. Basic Research Skills *(L.O. 7, 8)*

Most college and public libraries file annual reports of major public corporations. In some libraries these annual reports are on microfiche. Go to the library and obtain the annual report for a company that you recognize. In the annual report, identify the four basic financial statements, the notes to the financial statements, the letter to stockholders, the multiyear summary of financial highlights, the description of the business, management's discussion of operating results and financial condition, the report of management's responsibility, the auditors' report, and the list of directors and officers of the company. Perform a liquidity analysis, including the calculation of working capital and the current ratio. Perform a profitability analysis, calculating profit margin, asset turnover, return on assets, debt to equity, and return on equity.

Classroom Exercises

Exercise 6-1. Accounting Concepts and Conventions *(L.O. 3)*

Each of the statements below violates a convention in accounting. State which of the following concepts or conventions is violated: comparability and consistency, materiality, conservatism, full disclosure, or cost-benefit.

1. A series of reports that are time-consuming and expensive to prepare are presented to the board of directors each month even though the reports are never used.
2. A company changes its method of accounting for depreciation.
3. The company in **2** does not indicate in the financial statements that the method of depreciation was changed, nor does it specify the effect of the change on net income.

4. A new office building next to the factory is debited to the Factory account because it represents a fairly small dollar amount in relation to the factory.
5. The asset account for a pickup truck still used in the business is written down to salvage value even though the carrying value under conventional depreciation methods is higher.

Exercise 6-2. Financial Accounting Concepts *(L.O. 1, 2, 3, 4)*

The lettered items below represent a classification scheme for the concepts of financial accounting. Match each term with the letter indicating the category in which it belongs.

a. Decision makers (users of accounting information)
b. Business activities or entities relevant to accounting measurement
c. Objectives of accounting information
d. Accounting measurement considerations
e. Accounting processing considerations
f. Qualitative characteristics
g. Accounting conventions
h. Financial statements

____ 1. Conservatism
____ 2. Verifiability
____ 3. Statement of cash flows
____ 4. Materiality
____ 5. Reliable
____ 6. Recognition
____ 7. Cost-benefit
____ 8. Understandable
____ 9. Business transactions
____ 10. Consistency
____ 11. Full disclosure
____ 12. To furnish information useful to investors and creditors
____ 13. Specific business entities
____ 14. Classification
____ 15. Management
____ 16. Neutral (objective)
____ 17. Internal accounting control
____ 18. Valuation
____ 19. Investors
____ 20. Timely
____ 21. Relevance
____ 22. To furnish information useful in assessing cash flow prospects

Exercise 6-3. Classification of Accounts: Balance Sheet *(L.O. 5)*

The lettered items below represent a classification scheme for a balance sheet, and the numbered items are account titles. Match each account with the letter indicating the category in which it belongs.

a. Current assets
b. Investments
c. Property, plant, and equipment
d. Intangible assets
e. Current liabilities
f. Long-term liabilities
g. Stockholders' equity
h. Not on balance sheet

____ 1. Patent
____ 2. Building Held for Sale
____ 3. Prepaid Rent
____ 4. Wages Payable
____ 5. Note Payable in Five Years
____ 6. Building Used in Operations
____ 7. Fund Held to Pay Off Long-Term Debt
____ 8. Inventory
____ 9. Prepaid Insurance
____ 10. Depreciation Expense
____ 11. Accounts Receivable
____ 12. Interest Expense
____ 13. Revenue Received in Advance
____ 14. Short-Term Investments
____ 15. Accumulated Depreciation
____ 16. Retained Earnings

Exercise 6-4. Classification of Accounts: Income Statement *(L.O. 6)*

Using the classification scheme below for a multistep income statement, match each account with the category in which it belongs.

a. Revenues
b. Cost of goods sold
c. Selling expenses
d. General and administrative expenses
e. Other revenue or expense
f. Not on income statement

_____ 1. Purchases
_____ 2. Sales Discounts
_____ 3. Beginning Merchandise Inventory
_____ 4. Dividend Income
_____ 5. Advertising Expense
_____ 6. Office Salaries Expense
_____ 7. Freight Out Expense
_____ 8. Prepaid Insurance
_____ 9. Utility Expense
_____ 10. Sales Salaries Expense
_____ 11. Rent Expense
_____ 12. Purchases Returns and Allowances
_____ 13. Freight In
_____ 14. Depreciation Expense, Delivery Equipment
_____ 15. Taxes Payable
_____ 16. Interest Expense

Exercise 6-5. Classified Balance Sheet Preparation *(L.O. 5)*

The following data pertain to a corporation: Cash, $31,200; Investment in Six-Month Government Securities, $16,400; Accounts Receivable, $38,000; Inventory, $40,000; Prepaid Rent, $1,200; Investment in Corporate Securities (long-term), $20,000; Land, $8,000; Building, $70,000; Accumulated Depreciation, Building, $14,000; Equipment, $152,000; Accumulated Depreciation, Equipment, $17,000; Copyright, $6,200; Accounts Payable, $51,000; Revenue Received in Advance, $2,800; Bonds Payable, $60,000; Common Stock—$10 par, 10,000 shares authorized, issued, and outstanding, $100,000; Paid-in Capital in Excess of Par Value, $50,000; and Retained Earnings, $88,200.

Prepare a classified balance sheet; omit the statement heading.

Exercise 6-6. Preparation of Income Statements *(L.O. 6)*

The following data pertain to a corporation: Sales, $810,000; Cost of Goods Sold, $440,000; Selling Expenses, $180,000; General and Administrative Expenses, $120,000; Income Taxes Expense, $15,000; Interest Expense, $8,000; Interest Income, $6,000; and Common Stock Outstanding, 100,000 shares.

1. Prepare a condensed single-step income statement.
2. Prepare a condensed multistep income statement.

Exercise 6-7. Condensed Multistep Income Statement *(L.O. 6)*

A condensed single-step income statement appears on the following page. Present this information in a condensed multistep income statement, and tell what insights may be obtained from the multistep form as opposed to the single-step form.

Dawson Furniture Corporation
Income Statement
For the Year Ended December 31, 19xx

Revenues		
Net Sales	$598,566	
Interest Income	2,860	
Total Revenues		$601,426
Costs and Expenses		
Cost of Goods Sold	$388,540	
Selling Expenses	101,870	
General and Administrative Expenses	50,344	
Interest Expense	6,780	
Income Taxes Expense	12,000	
Total Costs and Expenses		559,534
Net Income		$ 41,892
Earnings per share		$4.19

Exercise 6-8.
Liquidity Ratios
(L.O. 7)

The following accounts and balances are taken from the general ledger of West Hills Corporation:

Accounts Payable	$16,600
Accounts Receivable	10,200
Cash	1,500
Current Portion of Long-Term Debt	10,000
Long-Term Investments	10,400
Short-Term Securities	12,600
Merchandise Inventory	25,400
Notes Payable, 90 days	15,000
Notes Payable, 2 years	20,000
Notes Receivable, 90 days	26,000
Notes Receivable, 2 years	10,000
Prepaid Insurance	400
Property, Plant, and Equipment	60,000
Retained Earnings	28,300
Salaries Payable	850
Supplies	350
Taxes Payable	1,250
Unearned Revenue	750

Compute (1) working capital and (2) the current ratio.

Exercise 6-9.
Profitability Ratios
(L.O. 7)

The following end-of-year amounts are taken from the financial statements of Lewiston Corporation: Total Assets, $426,000; Total Liabilities, $172,000; Stockholders' Equity, $254,000; Net Sales, $782,000; Cost of Goods Sold, $486,000; Operating Expenses, $182,000; Income Taxes, $20,000; and Dividends, $40,000.

During the past year, total assets increased by $75,000. Total stockholders' equity was affected only by net income and dividends.

Compute (1) profit margin, (2) asset turnover, (3) return on assets, (4) debt to equity, and (5) return on equity.

Exercise 6-10. Analysis Using Ratios
(L.O. 7)

The following ratios were computed from the 19x1 classified financial statements of Revkin Company: Profit margin, 6.0 percent; asset turnover, 1.25; return on assets, 7.5 percent; return on equity, 9.375 percent; debt to equity, 25 percent. Assume that the ratios are computed on 19x1 year-end balances. Using the ratios given and assuming net sales of $400,000, calculate net income, total assets, total liabilities, and stockholders' equity.

Exercise 6-11. Computation of Ratios
(L.O. 7)

The simplified balance sheet and income statement for a corporation appear as follows:

Balance Sheet
December 31, 19xx

Assets		Liabilities	
Current Assets	$100,000	Current Liabilities	$ 40,000
Investments	20,000	Long-Term Liabilities	60,000
Property, Plant, and Equipment	293,000	Total Liabilities	$100,000
Intangible Assets	27,000		
		Stockholders' Equity	
		Common Stock	$200,000
		Retained Earnings	140,000
		Total Stockholders' Equity	$340,000
Total Assets	$440,000	Total Liabilities and Stockholders' Equity	$440,000

Income Statement
For the Year Ended December 31, 19xx

Revenue from Sales (net)	$820,000
Cost of Goods Sold	500,000
Gross Margin from Sales	$320,000
Operating Expenses	260,000
Net Income Before Taxes	$ 60,000
Income Taxes	10,000
Net Income	$ 50,000

Total assets and stockholders' equity at the beginning of 19xx were $360,000 and $280,000, respectively.

1. Compute the following liquidity measures: (a) working capital and (b) current ratio.
2. Compute the following profitability measures: (a) profit margin, (b) asset turnover, (c) return on assets, (d) debt to equity, and (e) return on equity.

Exercise 6-12. Comprehensive Ratio Analysis *(L.O. 7)*

Florida Fashions, Inc. has experienced rapid growth in the past two years. Selected summary information for the past three years is presented below:

	19x2	19x1	19x0
Current Assets	$ 400,000	$ 170,000	
Total Assets	1,400,000	800,000	$760,000
Current Liabilities	220,000	60,000	
Long-Term Liabilities	420,000	100,000	
Stockholders' Equity	760,000	640,000	540,000
Sales	2,400,000	1,200,000	
Net Income	120,000	100,000	

Determine whether Florida's financial situation has improved from 19x1 to 19x2 as a result of its growth by conducting a liquidity analysis (working capital and current ratio) and profitability analysis (profit margin, asset turnover, return on assets, return on equity, and debt to equity).

Interpretation Cases from Business

ICB 6-1. Toys "R" Us, Inc.[10] *(L.O. 5, 6, 7, 8)*

The questions in this exercise pertain to the financial statements of Toys "R" Us, Inc. in Figures 6-8 to 6-12. (Note that 1991 refers to the year ended February 2, 1991, and 1990 refers to the year ended January 28, 1990.)

Required

1. Consolidated balance sheets: (a) Did the amount of working capital increase or decrease from 1990 to 1991? By how much? (b) Did the current ratio improve from 1990 to 1991? (c) Does the company have long-term investments or intangible assets? (d) Did the capital structure of Toys "R" Us change from 1990 to 1991? (e) What is the contributed capital for 1991? How does it compare with retained earnings?
2. Consolidated statements of earnings: (a) Did Toys "R" Us use a multistep or single-step form of income statement? (b) Is it a comparative statement? (c) What is the trend of net earnings? (d) How significant are income taxes for Toys "R" Us? (e) What is the trend of net earnings per share? (f) Did the profit margin increase from 1990 to 1991? (g) Did asset turnover improve from 1990 to 1991? (h) Did the return on assets increase from 1990 to 1991? (i) Did the return on equity increase from 1990 to 1991? Total assets and total stockholders' equity for 1991 may be obtained from Figure 6-10.
3. Consolidated statements of cash flows: (a) Compare net income with cash provided by operating activities. Why is there a difference? (b) What are the most important investment activities in 1991? (c) What are the most important financing activities in 1991? (d) How did these investing and financing activities compare with those in prior years? (e) Where did Toys "R" Us get cash to pay for the capital expenditures? (f) How did the change in Cash and Short-Term Investments in 1991 compare to that in other years?

10. Excerpts from the 1991 Annual Report used by permission of Toys "R" Us, Inc. Copyright © 1991.

4. Auditors' report: (a) What was the name of Toys "R" Us's independent auditor? (b) Who is responsible for the financial statements? (c) What is the auditor's responsibility? (d) Does the auditor examine all the company's records? (e) Did the accountants think that the financial statements presented fairly the financial situation of the company? (f) Did the company comply with generally accepted accounting principles?

ICB 6-2. Albertson's, Inc., A&P, and American Stores Co.[11]
(L.O. 7)

Three of the largest chains of grocery/drug stores in the United States are Albertson's, Inc., The Great Atlantic & Pacific Tea Company, Inc. (A&P), and American Stores Co. (Jewel, Alpha Beta, Osco, Skaggs, and others). In fiscal years ending in 1990, Albertson's, A&P, and American had net income of $196.6 million, $146.7 million, and $118.1 million, respectively. It is difficult to judge which company is the most profitable from these figures alone, because they do not take into account the relative sales, sizes, and investments of the companies. The three companies, respectively, have 1990 net sales of $7,422.7 million, $11,148.0 million, and $22,004.1 million; 1990 total assets of $1,591.0 million, $2,831.6 million, and $7,398.0 million; 1989 total assets of $1,862.7 million, $2,640.4 million, and $7,010.4 million; 1990 total liabilities of $933.2 million, $1,739.4 million, and $6,196.2 million; 1989 total liabilities of $790.5 million, $1,669.5 million, and $5,892.0 million; 1990 stockholders' equity of $929.5 million, $1,092.2 million, and $1,201.8 million; and 1989 stockholders' equity of $800.5 million, $970.8 million, and $1,118.4 million.

Required

1. Determine which company is most profitable by computing profit margin, asset turnover, return on assets, debt to equity, and return on equity for the three companies. Comment on the relative profitability of the three companies.
2. What do the calculations in **1** tell you about the factors that go into achieving an adequate return on assets in the grocery industry?
3. How would you characterize the use of debt financing in the grocery industry and the use of debt by the three companies?

ICB 6-3. Toys "R" Us, Inc. II[12]
(L.O. 6, 7)

Toys "R" Us, Inc. has consistently been one of the best and fastest growing retailers in the country. Management is proud of its record of cost control, as witnessed by the following quotation from the company's 1987 annual report:

> Toys "R" Us expense levels are among the best controlled in retailing.... For example, in 1986 (year ended February 1, 1987) our expenses as a percentage of sales declined by almost 3% from 21.7% to 18.8%. As a result, we were able to operate with lower merchandise margins and still increase our earnings and return on sales.

The company's condensed single-step income statements appear in Figure 6-9 on page 302.

Required

1. Prepare multistep income statements for Toys "R" Us for 1990 and 1991, and compute the ratios of gross margin from sales, operating expenses, income from operations, and net earnings to net sales.

11. Excerpts from the 1990 Annual Reports are reprinted by permission of Albertson's, Copyright © 1990; Great Atlantic & Pacific Tea Company, Inc.; and American Stores.
12. Excerpts from the 1991 Annual Report used by permission of Toys "R" Us, Inc. Copyright © 1991.

2. Comment on whether the trend indicated by management in 1987 continued to be true in 1991. In 1987, gross margin was 31.2 percent, total operating expenses were 20.0 percent of net sales, and net earnings were 9.9 percent of sales.

ICB 6-4.
Wellcome plc[13]
(L.O. 5, 7)

Presented below is the classified balance sheet for the British company Wellcome plc, a major pharmaceutical firm with marketing and manufacturing operations in eighteen countries.

Wellcome plc
Group Company Balance Sheets
as at 1 September 1990

	1990 £m	1989 £m
Fixed Assets		
Tangible assets	677.1	575.0
Investments	4.5	17.2
	681.6	592.2
Current Assets		
Stocks	223.8	205.5
Debtors	355.5	353.3
Investments	229.4	253.3
Cash at bank	18.5	14.3
	827.2	826.4
Creditors—Amounts Falling Due Within One Year:		
Loans and overdrafts	(109.4)	(68.7)
Other	(302.1)	(276.4)
Net Current Assets	415.7	481.3
Total Assets Less Current Liabilities	1,097.3	1,073.5
Creditors—amounts falling due after one year:		
Loans	(121.1)	(168.5)
Other	(2.9)	(4.5)
Provisions for liabilities and charges	(85.4)	(75.5)
Minority interests	(20.1)	(3.8)
Total Net Assets	867.8	821.2
Capital and Reserves		
Called up share capital	212.2	211.9
Share premium account	41.4	39.1
Profit and loss account	614.2	570.2
Shareholders' Funds	867.8	821.2

13. Excerpts from the 1990 Annual Report are reprinted with permission of Wellcome plc.

In the United Kingdom, the format used for classified financial statements is usually different from that used in the United States. In order to compare the financial statements of companies in different countries, it is important to be able to interpret a variety of formats.

Required

1. For each line on Wellcome plc's balance sheet, indicate the corresponding term that would be found on a U.S. balance sheet. (For this exercise, consider Provisions for Liabilities and Charges and Minority Interests to be long-term liabilities.) What is the focus or rationale behind the format of the U.K. balance sheet?
2. Assuming that Wellcome plc earned a net income of £181.6 million and £178.9 million in 1989 and 1990, respectively, compute the current ratio, debt to equity, return on assets, and return on equity for 1989 and 1990. (Use year-end amounts to compute ratios.)

Problem Set A

Problem 6A-1. Accounting Conventions *(L.O. 3)*

In each case below, accounting conventions may have been violated.

1. Figuero Manufacturing Company uses the cost method for computing the balance sheet amount of inventory unless the market value of the inventory is less than the cost, in which case the market value is used. At the end of the current year, the market value is $77,000 and the cost is $80,000. Figuero uses the $77,000 figure to compute net income because management feels it is the more cautious approach.
2. Margolis Company has annual sales of $5,000,000. It follows the practice of charging any items costing less than $100 to expenses in the year purchased. During the current year, it purchased several chairs for the executive conference rooms at $97 each, including freight. Although the chairs were expected to last for at least ten years, they were charged as an expense in accordance with company policy.
3. Choi Company closed its books on December 31, 19x8, before preparing its annual report. On December 30, 19x8, a fire destroyed one of the company's two factories. Although the company had fire insurance and would not suffer a loss on the building, a significant decrease in sales in 19x9 was expected because of the fire. The fire damage was not reported in the 19x8 financial statements because the operations for that year were not affected by the fire.
4. Shumate Drug Company spends a substantial portion of its profits on research and development. The company has been reporting its $2,500,000 expenditure for research and development as a lump sum, but management recently decided to begin classifying the expenditures by project even though the recordkeeping costs will increase.
5. During the current year, McMillan Company changed from one generally accepted method of accounting for inventories to another method.

Required

In each case, state the convention that is applicable, and explain briefly whether or not the treatment is in accord with the convention and generally accepted accounting principles.

Problem 6A-2. Forms of the Income Statement
(L.O. 6)

Income statement accounts from the June 30, 19x2 year-end adjusted trial balance of Tasheki Hardware Corporation appear as follows. Beginning merchandise inventory was $175,200, and ending merchandise inventory is $157,650. The company had 20,000 shares of common stock outstanding throughout the year.

Account Name	Debit	Credit
Sales		541,230
Sales Returns and Allowances	10,228	
Sales Discounts	5,070	
Purchases	212,336	
Purchases Returns and Allowances		4,282
Purchases Discounts		1,877
Freight In	11,221	
Sales Salaries Expense	102,030	
Sales Supplies Expense	1,642	
Rent Expense, Selling Space	18,000	
Utility Expense, Selling Space	11,256	
Advertising Expense	21,986	
Depreciation Expense, Selling Fixtures	6,778	
Office Salaries Expense	47,912	
Office Supplies Expense	782	
Rent Expense, Office Space	4,000	
Depreciation Expense, Office Equipment	3,251	
Utility Expense, Office Space	3,114	
Postage Expense	626	
Insurance Expense	2,700	
Miscellaneous Expense	481	
Interest Expense	3,600	
Interest Income		800
Income Taxes Expense	15,000	

Required

From the information provided, prepare the following:

1. A detailed income statement.
2. A condensed income statement in multistep form.
3. A condensed income statement in single-step form.

Problem 6A-3. Classified Balance Sheet
(L.O. 5)

Accounts from the June 30, 19x2 post-closing trial balance of Tasheki Hardware Corporation appear on page 329.

Required

From the information provided, prepare a classified balance sheet.

Account Name	Debit	Credit
Cash	24,000	
Short-Term Investments	13,150	
Notes Receivable	45,000	
Accounts Receivable	76,570	
Merchandise Inventory	156,750	
Prepaid Rent	2,000	
Prepaid Insurance	1,200	
Sales Supplies	426	
Office Supplies	97	
Land Held for Future Expansion	11,500	
Selling Fixtures	72,400	
Accumulated Depreciation, Selling Fixtures		22,000
Office Equipment	24,100	
Accumulated Depreciation, Office Equipment		12,050
Trademark	4,000	
Accounts Payable		109,745
Salaries Payable		787
Interest Payable		600
Notes Payable (due in three years)		36,000
Common Stock, $1 par value		20,000
Paid-in Capital in Excess of Par Value		130,000
Retained Earnings		100,011

Problem 6A-4. Ratio Analysis: Liquidity and Profitability *(L.O. 7)*

A summary of data taken from the income statements and balance sheets for Heard Construction Supply, Inc. for the past two years appears as follows.

	19x2	19x1
Current Assets	$ 183,000	$ 155,000
Total Assets	1,160,000	870,000
Current Liabilities	90,000	60,000
Long-Term Liabilities	400,000	290,000
Stockholders' Equity	670,000	520,000
Net Sales	2,300,000	1,740,000
Net Income	150,000	102,000

Total assets and stockholders' equity at the beginning of 19x1 were $680,000 and $420,000, respectively.

Required

1. Compute the following liquidity measures for 19x1 and 19x2: (a) working capital and (b) current ratio. Comment on the differences between the years.
2. Compute the following measures of profitability for 19x1 and 19x2: (a) profit margin, (b) asset turnover, (c) return on assets, (d) debt to equity, and (e) return on equity. Comment on the change in performance from 19x1 to 19x2.

Problem 6A-5. Classified Financial Statement Preparation and Evaluation *(L.O. 5, 6, 7)*

The following accounts (in alphabetical order) and amounts were taken or calculated from the December 31, 19x2 year-end adjusted trial balance of Blossom Lawn Equipment Center, Inc.: Accounts Payable, $36,300; Accounts Receivable, $84,700; Accumulated Depreciation, Building, $26,200; Accumulated Depreciation, Equipment, $17,400; Building, $110,000; Cash, $10,640; Common Stock ($10 par value), $40,000; Cost of Goods Sold, $246,000; Depreciation Expense, Building, $4,500; Depreciation Expense, Equipment, $6,100; Dividend Income, $1,280; Dividends, $23,900; Equipment, $75,600; Income Taxes Expense, $6,000; Interest Expense, $6,200; Inventory, $56,150; Investment in General Motors, 100 shares (short-term), $6,500; Land Held for Future Use, $20,000; Land Used in Operations, $29,000; Mortgage Payable, $90,000; Notes Payable (short-term), $25,000; Notes Receivable, $12,000; Operating Expenses Excluding Depreciation, $151,350; Paid-in Capital in Excess of Par Value, $60,000; Retained Earnings, $111,210; Sales (net), $448,000; and Trademark, $6,750. Total assets and total stockholders' equity at the beginning of the year were $343,950 and $211,210, respectively.

Required

1. From the information above, prepare (a) an income statement in condensed multistep form, (b) a statement of retained earnings, and (c) a classified balance sheet.
2. Calculate the following measures of liquidity: (a) working capital and (b) current ratio.
3. Calculate the following measures of profitability: (a) profit margin, (b) asset turnover, (c) return on assets, (d) debt to equity, and (e) return on equity.

Problem Set B

Problem 6B-1. Accounting Conventions *(L.O. 3)*

In each case below, accounting conventions may have been violated.

1. After careful study, Hawthorne Company, which has offices in forty states, has determined that, in the future, the depreciation of its office furniture should be changed. The new method is adopted for the current year, and the change is noted in the financial statements.
2. Regalado Corporation has in the past recorded operating expenses in general accounts for each classification, such as Salaries Expense, Depreciation Expense, and Utility Expense. Management has determined that in spite of the additional recordkeeping costs, the company's income statement should break down each operating expense into its selling expense and administrative expense components.
3. Watts, the auditor of Burleson Corporation, discovered that an official of the company may have authorized the payment of a $1,000 bribe to a local official. Management argued that, because the item was so small in relation to the size of the company ($1,000,000 in sales), the illegal payment should not be disclosed.
4. Kuberski's Book Store built a small addition to the main building to house a new computer games division. Because of uncertainty about whether the computer games division would succeed, a conservative approach was taken by recording the addition as expense.
5. Since its origin ten years ago, Hsu Company has used the same generally accepted inventory method. Because there has been no change in the inventory method, the company does not declare in its financial statements what inventory method it uses.

Required

In each case, state the convention that is applicable, explain briefly whether or not the treatment is in accord with the convention and generally accepted accounting principles, and explain why.

Problem 6B-2. Forms of the Income Statement *(L.O. 6)*

The March 31, 19x2 year-end income statement accounts that follow are for O'Dell Hardware Corporation. Beginning merchandise inventory was $86,400, and ending merchandise inventory is $72,500. The corporation had 100,000 shares of common stock outstanding throughout the year.

Account Name	Debit	Credit
Sales		491,100
Sales Returns and Allowances	21,200	
Sales Discounts	5,700	
Purchases	224,500	
Purchases Returns and Allowances		8,120
Purchases Discounts		3,800
Freight In	17,400	
Sales Salaries Expense	62,160	
Sales Supplies Expense	1,640	
Rent Expense, Selling Space	7,200	
Utility Expense, Selling Space	2,960	
Advertising Expense	16,800	
Depreciation Expense, Delivery Equipment	4,400	
Office Salaries Expense	29,240	
Office Supplies Expense	9,760	
Rent Expense, Office Space	2,400	
Utility Expense, Office Space	1,000	
Postage Expense	2,320	
Insurance Expense	2,680	
Miscellaneous Expense	1,440	
General Management Salaries Expense	42,000	
Interest Expense	5,600	
Interest Income		420
Income Taxes Expense	7,000	

Required

From the information provided, prepare the following:

1. A detailed income statement.
2. A condensed income statement in multistep form.
3. A condensed income statement in single-step form.

Problem 6B-3. Classified Balance Sheet *(L.O. 5)*

Accounts from the March 31, 19x2 post-closing trial balance of O'Dell Hardware Corporation appear on page 332.

Account Name	Debit	Credit
Cash	15,500	
Short-Term Investments	16,500	
Notes Receivable	5,000	
Accounts Receivable	138,000	
Merchandise Inventory	72,500	
Prepaid Rent	800	
Prepaid Insurance	2,400	
Sales Supplies	640	
Office Supplies	220	
Prepaid Advertising	1,840	
Building, Not in Use	24,800	
Land	11,200	
Delivery Equipment	20,600	
Accumulated Depreciation, Delivery Equipment		14,200
Franchise Fee	2,000	
Accounts Payable		57,300
Salaries Payable		2,600
Interest Payable		420
Long-Term Notes Payable		40,000
Common Stock, $1 par value		10,000
Paid-in Capital in Excess of Par Value		80,000
Retained Earnings		107,480

Required

From the information provided, prepare a classified balance sheet.

Problem 6B-4. Ratio Analysis: Liquidity and Profitability *(L.O. 7)*

Sambito Products Corporation has been disappointed with its operating results for the past two years. As accountant for the company, you have the following information available:

	19x2	19x1
Current Assets	$ 90,000	$ 70,000
Total Assets	290,000	220,000
Current Liabilities	40,000	20,000
Long-Term Liabilities	40,000	—
Stockholders' Equity	210,000	200,000
Net Sales	524,000	400,000
Net Income	32,000	22,000

Total assets and stockholders' equity at the beginning of 19x1 were $180,000 and $160,000, respectively.

Required

1. Compute the following measures of liquidity for 19x1 and 19x2: (a) working capital and (b) current ratio. Comment on the differences between the years.
2. Compute the following measures of profitability for 19x1 and 19x2: (a) profit margin, (b) asset turnover, (c) return on assets, (d) debt to equity, and (e) return on equity. Comment on the change in performance from 19x1 to 19x2.

Problem 6B-5. Classified Financial Statement Preparation and Evaluation
(L.O. 5, 6, 7)

Wedman Corporation sells outdoor sports equipment. At the end of the year 19x2, the following financial information was available from the income statement: Administrative Expenses, $80,800; Cost of Goods Sold, $350,420; Income Taxes Expense, $7,000; Interest Expense, $22,640; Interest Income, $2,800; Net Sales, $714,390; and Selling Expenses, $220,200.

The following information was available from the balance sheet (after closing entries): Accounts Payable, $32,600; Accounts Receivable, $104,800; Accumulated Depreciation, Delivery Equipment, $17,100; Accumulated Depreciation, Store Fixtures, $42,220; Cash, $28,400; Common Stock—$1 par value, 10,000 shares issued and outstanding, $10,000; Delivery Equipment, $88,500; Dividends, $60,000; Inventory, $136,540; Investment in Gray Corporation (long-term), $56,000; Investment in U.S. Government Securities (short-term), $39,600; Notes Payable (long-term), $100,000; Notes Payable (short-term), $50,000; Paid-in Capital in Excess of Par Value, $90,000; Retained Earnings, $259,300 (ending balance); Short-Term Prepaid Expenses, $5,760; and Store Fixtures, $141,620.

Total assets and total stockholders' equity at the beginning of 19x2 were $524,400 and $283,170, respectively.

Required

1. From the information above, prepare the following: (a) an income statement in single-step form, (b) a statement of retained earnings, and (c) a classified balance sheet.
2. From the statements you have prepared, compute the following measures: (a) for liquidity—working capital and current ratio, and (b) for profitability—profit margin, asset turnover, return on assets, debt to equity, and return on equity.

Financial Decision Cases

6-1. Josephina Tapestries, Inc.
(L.O. 7)

Josephina Mancilla is the principal stockholder and president of Josephina Tapestries, Inc., which wholesales fine tapestries to retail stores. Because Josephina was not satisfied with the earnings of the company in 19x2, she raised prices in 19x3 so that gross margin from sales was 35 percent in 19x3, compared with 30 percent in 19x2. Josephina is pleased that net income did in fact go up from 19x2 to 19x3, as shown in the following comparative income statements:

	19x3	19x2
Revenues		
Net Sales	$1,222,600	$1,386,400
Costs and Expenses		
Cost of Goods Sold	$ 794,690	$ 970,480
Selling and Administrative Expenses	278,520	277,280
Income Taxes Expense	29,878	27,728
Total Costs and Expenses	$1,103,088	$1,275,488
Net Income	$ 119,512	$ 110,912

Total assets for Josephina Tapestries, Inc. for 19x1, 19x2, and 19x3 were $1,246,780, $1,386,810, and $1,536,910, respectively.

Required

1. Has Josephina Tapestries, Inc.'s profitability really improved? **Hint:** Compute profit margin and return on assets, and comment.
2. What factors has Josephina overlooked in evaluating the profitability of the company? **Hint:** Compute asset turnover, and comment on the role it plays in profitability.

6-2.
First National Bank
(L.O. 7)

Steve Sullivan was recently promoted to loan officer at the First National Bank. He has authority to issue loans up to $50,000 without approval from a higher bank official. This week two small companies, Handy Harvey, Inc. and Sheila's Fashions, Inc., have each submitted a proposal for a six-month $50,000 loan. In order to prepare a financial analysis of the two companies, Steve has obtained the information summarized below.

Handy Harvey, Inc. is a local lumber and home improvement company. Because sales have increased so much during the past two years, Handy Harvey has had to raise additional working capital, especially as represented by receivables and inventory. The $50,000 loan is needed to assure the company of enough working capital for the next year. Handy Harvey began the year with total assets of $740,000 and stockholders' equity of $260,000, and during the past year the company had a net income of $40,000 on sales of $760,000. The company's current unclassified balance sheet appears as follows:

Assets		Liabilities and Stockholders' Equity	
Cash	$ 30,000	Accounts Payable	$200,000
Accounts Receivable (net)	150,000	Note Payable (short-term)	100,000
Inventory	250,000	Mortgage Payable	200,000
Land	50,000	Common Stock	250,000
Buildings (net)	250,000	Retained Earnings	50,000
Equipment (net)	70,000		
Total Assets	$800,000	Total Liabilities and Stockholders' Equity	$800,000

Sheila's Fashions, Inc. has for three years been a successful clothing store for young professional women. The leased store is located in the downtown financial district. Sheila's loan proposal asks for $50,000 to pay for stocking a new line of professional suits for working women during the coming season. At the beginning of the year, the company had total assets of $200,000 and total stockholders' equity of $114,000. Over the past year, the company earned a net income of $36,000 on sales of $480,000. The firm's unclassified balance sheet at the current date appears as follows:

Assets		Liabilities and Stockholders' Equity	
Cash	$ 10,000	Accounts Payable	$ 80,000
Accounts Receivable (net)	50,000	Accrued Liabilities	10,000
Inventory	135,000	Common Stock	50,000
Prepaid Expenses	5,000	Retained Earnings	100,000
Equipment (net)	40,000		
Total Assets	$240,000	Total Liabilities and Stockholders' Equity	$240,000

Required

1. Prepare a financial analysis of both companies' liquidity before and after receiving the proposed loan. Also, compute profitability ratios before and after as appropriate. Write a brief summary of the effect of the proposed loan on each company's financial position.
2. To which company do you suppose Steve would be more willing to make a $50,000 loan? What are the positive and negative factors related to each company's ability to pay back the loan in the next year? What other information of a financial or nonfinancial nature would be helpful for making a final decision?

LEARNING OBJECTIVES

1. *Account for cash and short-term investments.*
2. *Define* accounts receivable, *and explain the relationships among credit policies, sales, and uncollectible accounts.*
3. *Apply the allowance method of accounting for uncollectible accounts, including using the percentage of net sales method and the accounts receivable aging method to estimate uncollectible accounts.*
4. *Identify methods of financing accounts receivable and other issues related to accounts receivable.*
5. *Define and describe a promissory note, and make calculations involving promissory notes.*
6. *Journalize entries involving notes receivable.*
7. *Demonstrate control of cash by preparing a bank reconciliation.*
8. *Demonstrate the use of a simple imprest system.*

CHAPTER 7

Short-Term Liquid Assets

In the chapters on accounting as an information system and on accounting concepts and classified financial statements, profitability and liquidity were identified as two major concerns of management. In this chapter you will study the assets that are most closely associated with the liquidity of a business. **Short-term liquid assets** are financial assets that arise from cash transactions, the investment of cash, and the extension of credit. They include cash, short-term investments, accounts receivable, and notes receivable. They are useful because they are usually quickly available for paying current obligations. Other assets—such as inventories; property, plant, and equipment; natural resources; and intangibles—are less liquid. After studying this chapter, you should be able to meet the learning objectives listed on the left.

DECISION POINT

Bell Atlantic Corporation[1]

Management must use a company's assets to maximize income earned while maintaining the liquidity of the business. This responsibility applies to the company's short-term liquid assets as well as to productive assets such as property, plant, and equipment. Bell Atlantic Corporation, a leading provider of voice and data communications, mobile telephone services, computer maintenance, and equipment leasing and financing products, is faced with the challenge of managing almost $3 billion in short-term liquid assets. At the end of 1989, as reported on the balance sheet in the company's 1989 annual report, these assets were as follows (in millions):

Cash and Cash Equivalents	$ 164.2
Short-Term Investments	278.9
Accounts Receivable, net of allowances of $104	1,907.8
Notes Receivable, Net	493.5
Total Short-Term Liquid Assets	$2,844.4

Although these assets make up only a little more than 10 percent of Bell Atlantic's total assets, they are very important to achieving the company's goals. The asset management

1. Excerpts from the 1989 Annual Report used with permission of Bell Atlantic Corporation. All rights reserved.

techniques employed at Bell Atlantic ensure that these assets provide liquidity for the company's operations. These techniques also maximize the interest earned on the assets and minimize losses from any decrease in the market value of investments or from the failure of customers to pay their bills. Moreover, the company seeks to keep cash at a minimum by investing the cash that is not currently needed. This chapter emphasizes the accounting for, and management of, these short-term liquid assets. ■

Accounting for Cash and Short-Term Investments

OBJECTIVE 1
Account for cash and short-term investments

The annual report of Bell Atlantic Corporation refers to *cash and cash equivalents*. Of these two terms, *cash* is the easier to understand. It is the most liquid of all assets and the most readily available to pay debts. We discussed the control of cash receipts and payments in the chapter on accounting for merchandising operations, but we did not deal with the content of the Cash account on the balance sheet. **Cash** normally consists of coin and currency on hand, checks and money orders received from customers, and deposits in bank checking accounts. Cash may also include an amount that is not entirely free to be spent called a **compensating balance**. A compensating balance is a minimum amount that a bank requires a company to keep in its bank account as part of a credit-granting arrangement. Such an arrangement restricts cash and may reduce a company's liquidity. Therefore, the SEC requires companies to disclose in a note to the financial statements the amount of any compensating balance.

The term *cash equivalents* is a little harder to understand. Consider that at various times a company may find it has more cash on hand than it needs to pay current obligations. This excess cash should not be permitted to remain idle, especially in periods of high interest rates. Thus, management may periodically invest the idle funds in time deposits or certificates of deposit in banks and other financial institutions, in government securities such as U.S. Treasury notes, or in other securities. These actions are rightfully called investments. However, if they carry a term of less than ninety days, such investments are often called **cash equivalents**, because the funds revert to cash so quickly that they are regarded as cash on the balance sheet. Bell Atlantic follows this practice. Its policy is stated as follows: "The Company considers all highly liquid investments with a maturity of 90 days or less when purchased to be cash equivalents. Cash equivalents are stated at cost, which approximates market value." A recent survey of the practices of 600 large U.S. corporations found that 134 of them, or 22 percent, used the term *cash* as the balance sheet caption and 358, or 60 percent, used the phrase *cash and cash equivalents* or *cash and equivalents*. Ninety-three companies, or 16 percent, combined cash with marketable securities.[2] The average amount of cash held can also vary by industry, as can be seen in the data on our sample industries in Figure 7-1.

2. *Accounting Trends & Techniques* (New York: American Institute of CPAs, 1990), p. 88.

Figure 7-1. Cash as a Percentage of Total Assets in Selected Industries

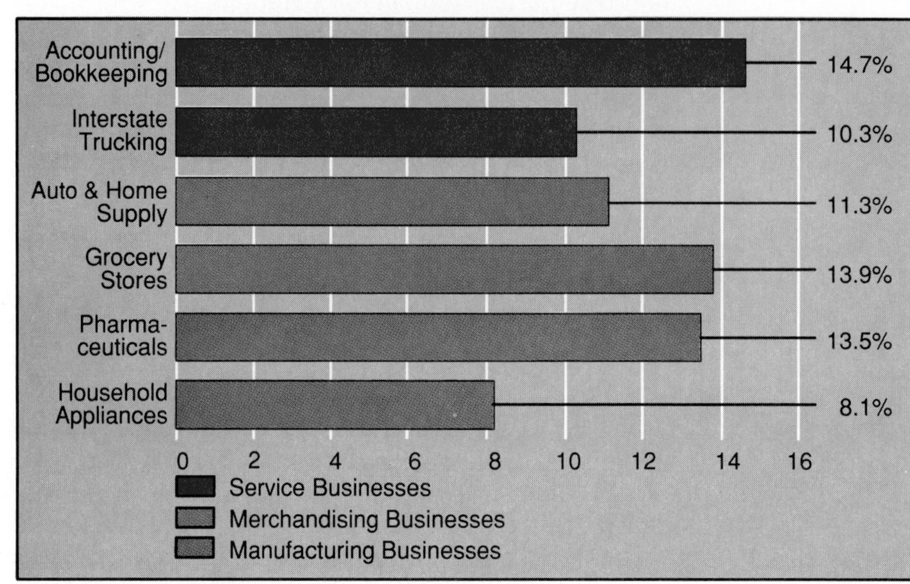

Source: Data from Dun and Bradstreet, *Industry Norms and Ratios*, 1990–91.

When investments carry a maturity of longer than ninety days but are intended to be held only until cash is needed for current operations, they are called **short-term investments** or **marketable securities**. Bell Atlantic states its policy on short-term investments as follows: "Short-term investments consist of investments that mature in 91 days to 12 months from the date of purchase." Investments that are intended to be held for more than one year are called long-term investments. As discussed in the chapter on accounting concepts and classified financial statements, these holdings are classified in an investments section of the balance sheet, not in the current assets section. Although these investments may be just as *marketable* as short-term assets, management intends to hold them for an indefinite period of time.

Short-term investments are first recorded at cost. Suppose that on March 1, ST Company purchased U.S. Treasury bills, which are short-term debt of the U.S. government, for $97,000. The bills will mature in 120 days at $100,000. The following entry would be made by ST Company:

Mar. 1	Short-Term Investments	97,000	
	Cash		97,000
	Purchase of U.S. Treasury bills that mature in 120 days at $100,000		

Income on short-term investments is recorded as received. For example, dividends and interest on stocks and bonds held as short-term investments would be recorded as Dividend Income or Interest Income when received. In the case of the investment by ST Company, the interest is received when the bills are paid at maturity, as shown in the entry below:

June 29	Cash	100,000	
	Interest Income		3,000
	Short-Term Investments		97,000
	Receipt of cash on U.S. Treasury bills and recognition of related income		

When short-term investments are sold, a gain or loss usually results. Suppose that ST Company sells 5,000 shares of an investment in Mobil Corporation on December 5. It bought the shares for $70 per share, including broker's commission. When it sells them at $60 per share net of (after) broker's commissions, the entry below results:

Dec. 5	Cash	300,000	
	Loss on Sale of Investments	50,000	
	Short-Term Investments		350,000
	Sale of 5,000 shares of Mobil Corporation at $60, net of commissions		

In *Statement of Financial Accounting Standards No. 12,* the Financial Accounting Standards Board requires that investments in debt securities, such as U.S. Treasury bills or corporate debt, be listed at cost unless there is reason to believe that the value of the security is permanently impaired. However, the board requires that investments in equity securities, such as capital stock, be reported at the lower of historical cost or the market value determined at the balance sheet date.[3] For example, assume that at its year end of December 31, ST Company still owns 10,000 shares of Mobil Corporation that it purchased for $70 per share and that are now worth $60 per share. An adjusting entry is made to recognize the loss in value and to reduce the asset amount by means of a contra account, as follows:

Dec. 31	Loss on Decline in Short-Term Investments	100,000	
	Allowance to Reduce Short-Term Investments to Market		100,000
	To recognize decline in market value of short-term investments		

The loss is reported on the income statement, and although it is not usually shown as a separate item, the allowance account is reflected in the value assigned to short-term investments on the balance sheet, as follows:

Current Assets

Short-Term Investments (at lower of cost or market; cost equals $700,000)	$600,000

Subsequent increases in the market value of the investment in Mobil may be recorded, but only to the extent that they bring the short-term invest-

3. *Statement of Financial Accounting Standards No. 12,* "Accounting for Certain Marketable Securities" (Stamford, Conn.: Financial Accounting Standards Board, 1975).

ment back up to cost. Increases in market value per share above cost are not recorded. When investments that previously have been written down are sold, as was done in this case, the gain or loss is measured by the difference between the sale price and the original purchase cost, regardless of any balance in Allowance to Reduce Short-Term Investments to Market. For instance, if ST Company sells 2,000 of the Mobil shares it owned at year end on January 15 for $62 per share, the entry would be:

Jan. 15	Cash	124,000	
	Loss on Sale of Investments	16,000	
	Short-Term Investments		140,000
	Sale of 2,000 shares of Mobil at a loss: 2,000 shares × ($70 – $62) = $16,000		

At the end of the next accounting period the balance in the allowance account is adjusted up or down to reflect any difference between the cost and the lower market value of any short-term investments held at the end of the accounting period. The credit balance in the allowance account may be reduced to zero (resulting in a gain) if the market value exceeds the cost of the short-term investments. In no case, however, are short-term investments increased to a value above cost. If the company has more than one investment, then these rules are applied to the total value of the investments at the end of each accounting period.

Note that accounting for investments is inconsistent with the concept of historical cost. Under historical cost, the cost value would be maintained on the balance sheet until the asset is sold. Accountants justify this inconsistency on the basis of the conservatism convention. That is, they recognize the potential loss immediately but put off recognition of any potential gain until it is actually realized.

Accounting for Accounts Receivable

OBJECTIVE 2
Define accounts receivable, *and explain the relationships among credit policies, sales, and uncollectible accounts*

The other major types of short-term liquid assets are accounts receivable and notes receivable. Both result from credit sales to customers. Retail companies such as Sears, Roebuck and Co. have made credit available to nearly every responsible person in the United States. Every field of retail trade has expanded by allowing customers the right to make payments a month or more after the date of sale. What is not so apparent is that credit has expanded even more in the wholesale and manufacturing industries than at the retail level. This is apparent from Figure 7-2, which shows accounts receivable as a percentage of total assets for selected industries. The low ratio of 4.8 percent for grocery stores is expected, but even auto and home supply stores have a lower ratio than the service and household appliance manufacturing industries. This result is no doubt partly due to the widespread use of credit cards by retail stores, including auto and home supply outlets (see the discussion on financing of accounts receivable later in this chapter). The rest of this chapter shows the accounting for accounts receivable and notes receivable, which play a key role in this credit expansion.

Figure 7-2. Accounts Receivable as a Percentage of Total Assets in Selected Industries

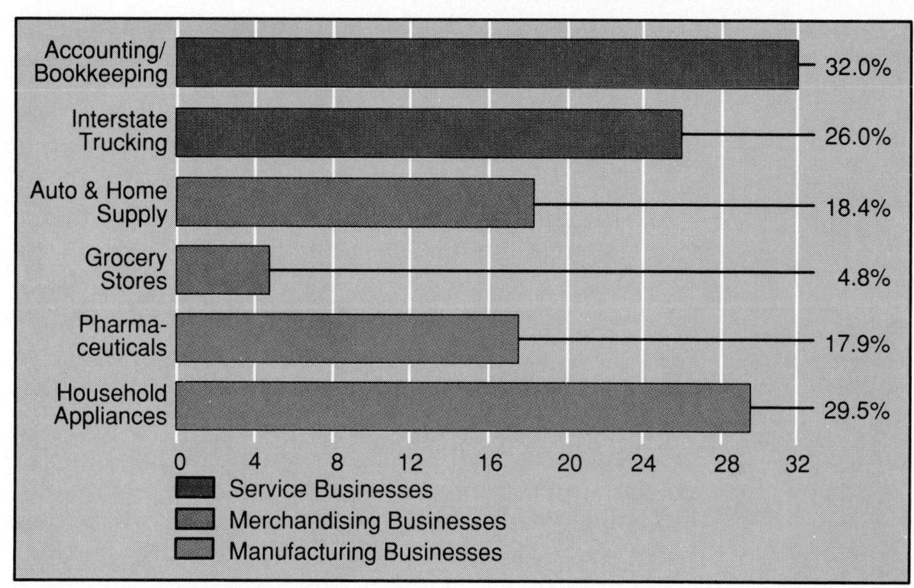

Source: Data from Dun and Bradstreet, *Industry Norms and Ratios*, 1990–91.

Accounts receivable are short-term liquid assets that arise from sales on credit to customers by wholesalers or retailers. This type of credit is often called **trade credit**.

Accounts Receivable and Its Subsidiary Ledger

In previous chapters, all such transactions have been posted to Accounts Receivable. However, this single accounts receivable entry does not readily tell how much each customer bought and paid for or how much each customer owes. In practice, almost all companies that sell to customers on credit keep an individual accounts receivable record for each customer. If the company has 6,000 credit customers, there are 6,000 accounts receivable. To include all these accounts in the ledger with the other assets, liabilities, and stockholders' equity accounts would make it very bulky. Consequently, most companies take the individual customers' accounts out of the general ledger, which contains the financial statement accounts, and place them in a separate ledger called a **subsidiary ledger**. The customers' accounts are filed alphabetically in this accounts receivable ledger.

When a company puts its individual customers' accounts in an accounts receivable ledger, there is still a need for an Accounts Receivable account in the general ledger to maintain its balance. This Accounts Receivable account in the general ledger is said to control the subsidiary ledger and is called a **controlling** or **control account**. It is a controlling account in the sense that its balance should equal the total of the individual account balances in the subsidiary ledger. This is true because in transactions involving accounts receivable, such as credit sales, there must be postings to the individual subsidiary customer accounts every day and to the controlling account in the general ledger in total each month. If an error has been made in posting, the sum of all customer account balances in the subsidiary accounts receivable ledger will not equal the balance of the Accounts Receivable controlling account in the general ledger. When these amounts do not match, the accountant knows that there is an error and can find and correct it.

Most companies, as you will see, use an accounts payable subsidiary ledger as well. It is also possible to use a subsidiary ledger for almost any account in the general ledger where management wants a specific account for individual items, such as Notes Receivable, Short-term Investments, and Equipment.

Credit Policies and Uncollectible Accounts

Companies that sell on credit naturally want customers who will pay. Therefore, most companies develop control procedures to increase the likelihood of selling only to customers who will pay when they are supposed to. As a result of these procedures, a company generally has a credit department. This department's responsibilities include the examination of each person or company that applies for credit and the approval or rejection of a credit sale to that customer. Typically, the credit department will ask for information on the customer's financial resources and debts. In addition, it may check personal references and established credit bureaus, which may have information about the customer. On the basis of this information, the credit department will decide whether to sell on credit to that customer. It may recommend the amount of payment, limit the amount of credit, or ask the customer to put up certain assets as security.

Regardless of how thorough and efficient its credit control system is, a company will always have some customers who will not pay. The accounts owed by such customers are called **uncollectible accounts**, or bad debts, and are a loss or an expense of selling on credit. Why does a company sell on credit if it expects that some of its accounts will not be paid? The answer is that the company expects to sell much more than it would if it did not sell on credit and, as a result, to increase its earnings.

Matching Losses on Uncollectible Accounts with Sales

Accounting for uncollectible accounts depends on the matching rule. Expenses should be matched against the sales they help to produce. If bad debt losses are incurred in the process of increasing sales revenues, they should be charged against those sales revenues. A company does not know at the time of a credit sale that the debt will not be collected. In fact, it may take a year or more to exhaust every possible means of collection. However, even though the loss may not be specifically identified until a later accounting period, it is still an expense of the period of the sale. Therefore, losses from the uncollectible accounts must be estimated, and this estimate becomes an expense in the fiscal year of the sale.

For example, let us assume that Cottage Sales Company made most of its sales on credit during its first year of operation. At the end of the year, accounts receivable amounted to $100,000. On this date, management reviewed the collectible status of the accounts receivable. Approximately $6,000 of the $100,000 of accounts reviewed were estimated to be uncollectible. Thus the uncollectible accounts expense for the first year of operation was estimated to be $6,000. The following adjusting entry would be made on December 31 of that year:

Dec. 31	Uncollectible Accounts Expense	6,000	
	Allowance for Uncollectible Accounts		6,000
	To record the estimated uncollectible accounts expense for the year 19xx		

Uncollectible Accounts Expense appears on the income statement as an operating expense. The **Allowance for Uncollectible Accounts** appears in the balance sheet as a contra account that is deducted from the face value of accounts receivable.[4] It reduces the accounts receivable to the amount that is expected to be realized, or collected in cash, as follows:

Current Assets		
Cash		$ 10,000
Short-Term Investments		15,000
Accounts Receivable	**$100,000**	
Less Allowance for Uncollectible Accounts	**6,000**	**94,000**
Inventory		56,000
Total Current Assets		$175,000

The allowance method of accounting for uncollectible accounts argues that in accordance with the matching rule, a business should assume that losses from an uncollectible account occur at the moment the sale is made to the customer. The Allowance for Uncollectible Accounts is used because the company does not know until after the sale that a particular customer will not pay. Since the amount of the loss must be estimated if it is to be matched against the sales or revenue for the period, it is not possible to credit the account of any particular customer. Also, it is not possible to credit the Accounts Receivable controlling account in the general ledger because doing so would cause the controlling account to be out of balance with the total of customers' accounts in the subsidiary ledger.

The Allowance for Uncollectible Accounts will often have other titles, such as Allowance for Doubtful Accounts or Allowance for Bad Debts. Once in a while, the older phrase Reserve for Bad Debts will be seen, but in modern practice it should not be used. Bad Debts Expense is often used as another title for Uncollectible Accounts Expense.

4. Note that although the purpose of the Allowance for Uncollectible Accounts is to reduce the gross accounts receivable to the amount collectible (estimated value), the purpose of the Accumulated Depreciation account, another contra account, is *not* to reduce the gross plant and equipment accounts to realizable value. The purpose of the Accumulated Depreciation account is to show how much of the cost of the plant and equipment has been allocated as an expense to previous accounting periods.

Estimating Uncollectible Accounts Expense

Because it is impossible to know which accounts will be uncollectible at the time financial statements are prepared, it is necessary to estimate the expense to cover the expected losses for the year. Of course, estimates can vary widely. If one takes an optimistic view and projects a small loss from uncollectible accounts, the resulting net accounts receivable will be larger than if one takes a pessimistic view. Also, the net income will be larger under the optimistic view because the estimated expense will be smaller. The company's accountant makes an estimate based on past experience, modified by current economic conditions. For example, losses from uncollectible accounts are normally expected to be greater in a recession than during a period of economic growth. The final decision on what the estimated expense will be, made by management, will depend on objective information, such as the accountant's analyses, and on certain qualitative factors, such as how investors, bankers, creditors, and others may view the performance of the company. Regardless of the qualitative considerations, the estimated losses from uncollectible accounts should be realistic.

The accountant has two common methods available for estimating uncollectible accounts expense for an accounting period. The first is the percentage of net sales method, and the second is the accounts receivable aging method.

OBJECTIVE 3
Apply the allowance method of accounting for uncollectible accounts, including using the percentage of net sales method and the accounts receivable aging method to estimate uncollectible accounts

Percentage of Net Sales Method. The **percentage of net sales method** asks the question, How much of this year's net sales will not be collected? The answer determines the amount of uncollectible accounts expense for the year.

For example, assume that the following balances represent the ending figures for Hassel Company for the year 19x9:

Sales	
	645,000

Sales Returns and Allowances	
40,000	

Sales Discounts	
5,000	

Allowance for Uncollectible Accounts	
	3,600

Assume that actual losses from uncollectible accounts for the past three years have been as follows:

Year	Net Sales	Losses from Uncollectible Accounts	Percentage
19x6	$ 520,000	$10,200	1.96
19x7	595,000	13,900	2.34
19x8	585,000	9,900	1.69
Total	$1,700,000	$34,000	2.00

Management believes that uncollectible accounts will continue to average about 2 percent of net sales. The uncollectible accounts expense for the year 19x9 is therefore estimated to be:

$$.02 \times (\$645{,}000 - \$40{,}000 - \$5{,}000) = .02 \times \$600{,}000 = \$12{,}000$$

The entry to record this estimate is:

Dec. 31	Uncollectible Accounts Expense	12,000	
	Allowance for Uncollectible Accounts		12,000
	To record uncollectible accounts expense at 2 percent of $600,000 net sales		

The Allowance for Uncollectible Accounts will have a balance of $15,600 after the above entry is posted, as follows:

Allowance for Uncollectible Accounts

				Balance	
Date	**Item**	**Debit**	**Credit**	**Debit**	**Credit**
Dec. 31	Balance				3,600
31	Adjustment		12,000		15,600

The balance consists of the $12,000 estimated uncollectible accounts receivable from 19x9 sales and the $3,600 estimated uncollectible accounts receivable from previous years. The latter have not yet been matched with specific uncollectible accounts receivable resulting from sales in those years.

Accounts Receivable Aging Method. The **accounts receivable aging method** asks the question, How much of the year-end balance of accounts receivable will not be collected? The answer determines the year-end balance of Allowance for Uncollectible Accounts. The difference between this amount and the actual balance of the Allowance for Uncollectible Accounts is the expense for the year. In theory, this method should produce the same result as the percentage of net sales method, but in practice it rarely does in any one year.

The **aging of accounts receivable** is the process of listing each accounts receivable customer according to the due date of the account. If a customer is past due on the account, there is a greater possibility that the account will not be paid. The further past due an account is, the greater the likelihood that the customer will not pay. The aging of accounts receivable is useful to management in evaluating its credit and collection policies and alerting it to possible problems. The aging of accounts receivable for Myer Company is shown in Exhibit 7-1. Each account receivable is classified as being not yet due, or 1–30 days, 31–60 days, 61–90 days, or over 90 days past due. The percentage uncollectible in each category is also shown.

The aging of accounts receivable method is useful to the accountant in determining the proper balance of the Allowance for Uncollectible Accounts. In Exhibit 7-2, estimates based on past experience show that only

Exhibit 7-1. Analysis of Accounts Receivable by Age

Myer Company
Analysis of Accounts Receivable by Age
December 31, 19xx

Customer	Total	Not Yet Due	1–30 Days Past Due	31–60 Days Past Due	61–90 Days Past Due	Over 90 Days Past Due
A. Arnold	$ 150		$ 150			
M. Benoit	400			$ 400		
J. Connolly	1,000	$ 900	100			
R. Deering	250				$ 250	
Others	42,600	21,000	14,000	3,800	2,200	$1,600
Totals	$44,400	$21,900	$14,250	$4,200	$2,450	$1,600
Percentage Uncollectible		1.0	2.0	10.0	30.0	50.0

1 percent of the accounts not yet due and 2 percent of the 1–30 days past due accounts will not be collected. Past experience also indicates that of the 31–60 days, 61–90 days, and over 90 days past due accounts, 10 percent, 30 percent, and 50 percent, respectively, will not be collected. In total, it is estimated that $2,459 of the $44,400 in accounts receivable will not be collected.

Exhibit 7-2. Calculation of Estimated Uncollectible Accounts

Myer Company
Estimated Uncollectible Accounts
December 31, 19xx

	Amount	Percentage Considered Uncollectible	Allowance for Uncollectible Accounts
Not yet due	$21,900	1	$ 219
1–30 days	14,250	2	285
31–60 days	4,200	10	420
61–90 days	2,450	30	735
Over 90 days	1,600	50	800
Totals	$44,400		$2,459

Let us assume that the December 31 credit balance of the Allowance for Uncollectible Accounts for Myer Company is $800. Thus, the estimated uncollectible accounts expense for the year is $1,659, which is calculated as follows:

Estimated Uncollectible Accounts	$2,459
Less Credit Balance—Allowance for Uncollectible Accounts	800
Uncollectible Accounts Expense	$1,659

The uncollectible accounts expense is recorded as follows:

Dec. 31	Uncollectible Accounts Expense	1,659	
	Allowance for Uncollectible Accounts		1,659
	To increase the allowance for uncollectible accounts to the level of estimated losses		

The resulting balance of the Allowance for Uncollectible Accounts is $2,459, as follows:

Allowance for Uncollectible Accounts

				Balance	
Date	Item	Debit	Credit	Debit	Credit
Dec. 31	Balance				800
31	Adjustment		1,659		2,459

Since an $800 credit balance in this account was carried over because fewer accounts than anticipated had been written off thus far, an adjustment of only $1,659 is needed to bring the Allowance for Uncollectible Accounts to its estimated level. However, if we assume the same facts except that the balance of the Allowance for Uncollectible Accounts for Meyer Company is a debit balance of $800, the estimated uncollectible accounts expense for the year will be $3,259, calculated as follows:

Estimated Uncollectible Accounts	$2,459
Plus Debit Balance—Allowance for Uncollectible Accounts	800
Uncollectible Accounts Expense	$3,259

This uncollectible accounts expense is recorded as follows:

Dec. 31	Uncollectible Accounts Expense	3,259	
	Allowance for Uncollectible Accounts		3,259
	To increase the allowance for uncollectible accounts to the level of estimated losses		

After this entry, the balance of the Allowance for Uncollectible Accounts is a credit of $2,459, as follows:

Allowance for Uncollectible Accounts

Date	Item	Debit	Credit	Balance Debit	Balance Credit
Dec. 31	Balance			800	
31	Adjustment		3,259		2,459

In this case, $800 more in accounts were written off because of uncollectibility than had been provided by the adjustment for estimated uncollectible accounts in the prior period. In order to bring the Allowance for Uncollectible Accounts to the new estimate of $2,459, the uncollectible accounts expense for the period had to be $3,259.

Comparison of the Two Methods. Both methods of estimation try to determine the uncollectible accounts expense for the current period in accordance with the matching rule, but they do so in different ways. The percentage of net sales method represents an income statement viewpoint. It is based on the proposition that of each dollar of sales, a certain proportion will not be collected, and this proportion is the expense for the year. Because this method matches expenses against revenues, it is in accordance with the matching rule. However, this way of determining expense is independent of the current balance of the Allowance for Uncollectible Accounts. The estimated proportion of net sales not expected to be collected is added to the current balance of the allowance account.

The aging of accounts receivable represents a balance sheet viewpoint and is a more direct valuation method. It is based on the proposition that of each dollar of accounts receivable outstanding, a certain proportion will not be collected, and this proportion should be the balance of the allowance account at the end of the year. This method also agrees with the matching rule because the expense is the difference between what the account is and what it should be. The difference is assumed to be applicable to the current year.

Writing Off an Uncollectible Account

When it becomes clear that a specific account will not be collected, the amount should be written off to the Allowance for Uncollectible Accounts. Remember that it was already accounted for as an expense when the allowance was established. For example, assume that R. Deering, who owes the Myer Company $250, is declared bankrupt by a federal court. The entry to *write off* this account is as follows:

Jan. 15	Allowance for Uncollectible Accounts	250	
	Accounts Receivable, R. Deering		250
	To write off receivable from R. Deering as uncollectible; Deering declared bankruptcy on January 15		

Note that the write-off does not affect the estimated net amount of accounts receivable because there is no expense involved and because the related allowance for uncollectible accounts has already been deducted from the receivables. The write-off simply reduces R. Deering's account to zero and reduces the Allowance for Uncollectible Accounts by a similar amount, as the following table shows:

	Balances Before Write-off	Balances After Write-off
Accounts Receivable	$44,400	$44,150
Less Allowance for Uncollectible Accounts	2,459	2,209
Estimated Net Value of Accounts Receivable	$41,941	$41,941

Why Accounts Written Off Will Differ from Estimates. The total of accounts receivable written off in any given year will rarely equal the estimated amount credited to the Allowance for Uncollectible Accounts. The allowance account will show a credit balance when the accounts written off are less than the estimated uncollectible accounts. The allowance account will show a debit balance when the accounts written off are greater than the estimated uncollectible accounts. The adjusting entry that is made to record the estimated uncollectible accounts expense for the current year will eliminate any debit balance at the end of the accounting period.

If the percentage of net sales method is used, the new balance of the allowance account after the adjusting entry will equal the percentage of sales estimated to be uncollectible minus the old debit balance. If the accounts receivable aging method is used, the amount of the adjustment must equal the estimated uncollectible accounts plus the debit balance in the Allowance for Uncollectible Accounts. Of course, if the estimates are consistently wrong, the balance of the allowance account will become unusually large, indicating that management should reexamine the company's estimation rates.

Recovery of Accounts Receivable Written Off. Sometimes a customer whose account has been written off as uncollectible will later be able to pay the amount in full or in part. When this happens, it is necessary to make two journal entries: one to reverse the earlier write-off, which is now incorrect, and another to show the collection of the account.

For example, assume that on September 1, R. Deering, after his bankruptcy on January 15, notified the company that he would be able to pay $100 of his account and sent a check for $50. The entries to record this transaction are as follows:

Sept. 1	Accounts Receivable, R. Deering	100	
	Allowance for Uncollectible Accounts		100
	To reinstate the portion of the account of R. Deering now considered collectible, which had been written off January 15		
1	Cash	50	
	Accounts Receivable, R. Deering		50
	To record collection from R. Deering		

The collectible portion of R. Deering's account must be restored to his account and credited to the Allowance for Uncollectible Accounts for two reasons. First, it was an error in judgment to write off the full $250 on January 15 because only $150 was actually uncollectible. Second, the accounts receivable subsidiary account for R. Deering should reflect his ability to pay a portion of the money he owed in spite of his bankruptcy. Documentation of this action will give a clear picture of his credit record for future credit action.

DECISION POINT
Fleetwood Enterprises, Inc.[5]

In 1987, Fleetwood Enterprises, Inc., the nation's leading producer of recreational vehicles and manufactured homes, established Fleetwood Credit Corporation to finance sales of its RV products. This business has grown rapidly, and in 1989 it financed 25 percent of all Fleetwood sales. Since buyers of recreational vehicles and manufactured homes can take several years to pay, management decided to sell significant amounts of the receivables held by Fleetwood Credit Corporation to provide the company with financial flexibility and to provide funds for future growth. In 1988, $75 million of its receivables were sold to public investors and $55 million were sold to a private investor. In the first case, the investors have recourse up to a maximum of 13 percent, and in the second, up to 7 percent. ■

Financing Accounts Receivable

OBJECTIVE 4
Identify methods of financing accounts receivable and other issues related to accounts receivable

Financial flexibility is important to most companies. Companies that have significant amounts of assets tied up in accounts receivable may be unwilling or unable to wait until the receivables are collected to receive the cash they represent. Many companies have set up finance companies to help their customers finance the purchase of their products. For example, Ford Motor Co. has Ford Motor Credit Company (FMCC), General Motors Corp. has General Motors Acceptance Corporation (GMAC), and Sears has Sears Roebuck Acceptance Corporation (SRAC). Some companies borrow funds by pledging their accounts receivable as collateral for the loans. If the company does not pay back the loan, the creditor can take the collateral, in this case the accounts receivable, and convert it to cash to satisfy the loan.

Another way to raise funds is to sell or transfer accounts receivable to another entity, called a **factor**. This sale or transfer of accounts receivable is called **factoring**; it can be done with or without recourse. *Without recourse* means that the factor who buys the accounts receivable bears any losses from uncollectible accounts. The acceptance by companies of credit cards like VISA, MasterCard, or American Express is an example of factoring without recourse because the credit card companies accept the risk of nonpayment. *With recourse* means that the seller of the receivables is

5. Excerpts from the 1989 Annual Report used with permission of Fleetwood Enterprises, Inc.

liable to the purchaser if the receivable is not collected. The factor, of course, charges a fee for its service. In the case of sales with recourse, the fee is usually about 1 percent of the accounts receivable. The fee is higher for sales without recourse because the factor's risk is greater.

Other Issues Related to Receivables

Installment Accounts Receivable. Installment sales make up a significant portion of the accounts receivable of many retail companies. Department stores, appliance stores, and retail chains all sell goods that are paid for in a series of time payments. Companies such as J. C. Penney and Sears have millions of dollars in these **installment accounts receivable**. Although the payment period may be twenty-four months or more, installment accounts receivable are classified as current assets if such credit policies are customary in the industry. There are special accounting rules that apply to installment sales. Because these rules can be very complicated, their study is usually deferred until a more advanced accounting course.

Credit Card Sales. Many retailers allow customers to charge their purchases to a third-party company that the customer will pay later. These transactions are normally handled with credit cards. The five most widely used credit cards are American Express, Carte Blanche, Diners Club, MasterCard, and VISA. The customer establishes credit with the lender and receives a plastic card to use in making charge purchases. If the seller accepts the card, the seller uses the charge card to imprint an invoice that is signed by the customer at the time of the sale. The seller then sends the invoice to the lender and receives cash. Because the seller does not have to establish the customer's credit, collect from the customer, or tie money up in accounts receivable, the seller receives an economic benefit from the lender (the credit card company). For this reason, the credit card company does not pay 100 percent of the total amount of the credit card sales invoices, but takes a discount of 2 to 6 percent.

One of two procedures is used in accounting for credit card sales, depending on whether the merchant must wait for collection from the credit card company or may deposit the sales invoices in a checking account immediately. The following example illustrates the procedure used in the first case. Assume that, at the end of the day, a restaurant has American Express invoices totaling $1,000 and that the discount charged by American Express is 4 percent. These sales are recorded as follows:

Accounts Receivable, American Express	960	
Credit Card Discount Expense	40	
Sales		1,000
Sales made on American Express cards; discount fee is 4 percent		

The seller sends the American Express invoices to American Express and later receives payment for them at 96 percent of their face value. When cash is received, the entry shown on page 352 is made.

Cash	960	
Accounts Receivable, American Express		960
Receipt of payment from American Express for invoices at 96 percent of face value		

The second case is typical of sales made through bank credit cards such as VISA and MasterCard. For example, assume that the restaurant made sales of $1,000 on VISA credit cards and that VISA takes a 4 percent discount on the sales. Assume also that the sales invoices can be deposited in a special VISA bank account in the name of the company in much the same way that checks from cash sales are deposited. These sales are recorded as follows:

Cash	960	
Credit Card Discount Expense	40	
Sales		1,000
Sales on VISA cards		

Direct Charge-off Method. Some companies record uncollectible accounts by debiting expenses directly when bad debts are discovered instead of using the Allowance for Uncollectible Accounts. The **direct charge-off method** is not in accordance with good accounting theory because it makes no attempt to match revenues and expenses. Uncollectible accounts are charged to expenses in the accounting period in which they are discovered rather than in the period of the sale. On the balance sheet the accounts receivable are shown at gross value, not realizable value, because there is no Allowance for Uncollectible Accounts. Only the direct charge-off method, however, is allowable in computing taxable income under federal income tax regulations. The allowance method is still used for financial reporting because it is better from the standpoint of accounting theory.

Credit Balances in Accounts Receivable. Sometimes customers overpay their accounts because of mistakes or in anticipation of future purchases, or they may return merchandise for credit after payment has been made. When customer accounts show credit balances in the accounts receivable ledger, the balance of the Accounts Receivable controlling account should not appear on the balance sheet as the amount of the accounts receivable. The total of the customers' accounts with credit balances should be shown as a current liability because the company is liable to these customers for their overpayments.

Other Accounts Receivable. The title Accounts Receivable on the balance sheet should be reserved for sales made to regular customers in the ordinary course of business. If loans or sales that do not fall in this category are made to employees, officers of the corporation, or owners, they should be shown separately on the balance sheet with an asset title such as Receivables from Employees and Officers.

Accounting for Notes Receivable

OBJECTIVE 5
Define and describe a promissory note, and make calculations involving promissory notes

A **promissory note** is an unconditional promise to pay a definite sum of money on demand or at a future date. The person who signs the note and thereby promises to pay is called the *maker* of the note. The person to whom payment is to be made is called the *payee*. The promissory note in Figure 7-3 is dated May 20, 19x1, and is an unconditional promise by the maker, Samuel Mason, to pay a definite sum or principal ($1,000) to the payee, Cook County Bank & Trust Company, at the future date of August 18, 19x1. The promissory note bears an interest rate of 8 percent. The payee regards all promissory notes it holds that are due in less than a year as **notes receivable** in the current asset section of the balance sheet. The makers regard them as **notes payable** in the current liability section of the balance sheet.

In this chapter, we are concerned primarily with notes received from customers. The nature of a business generally determines how frequently promissory notes are received from customers. Firms selling durable goods of high value, such as farm machinery and automobiles, will often accept promissory notes. Among the advantages of promissory notes are that they produce interest income and represent a stronger legal claim against the creditor than accounts receivable. In addition, promissory notes can be resold to banks as a financing method. Almost all companies will occasionally receive a note, and many companies obtain notes receivable in settlement of past-due accounts.

Figure 7-3. A Promissory Note

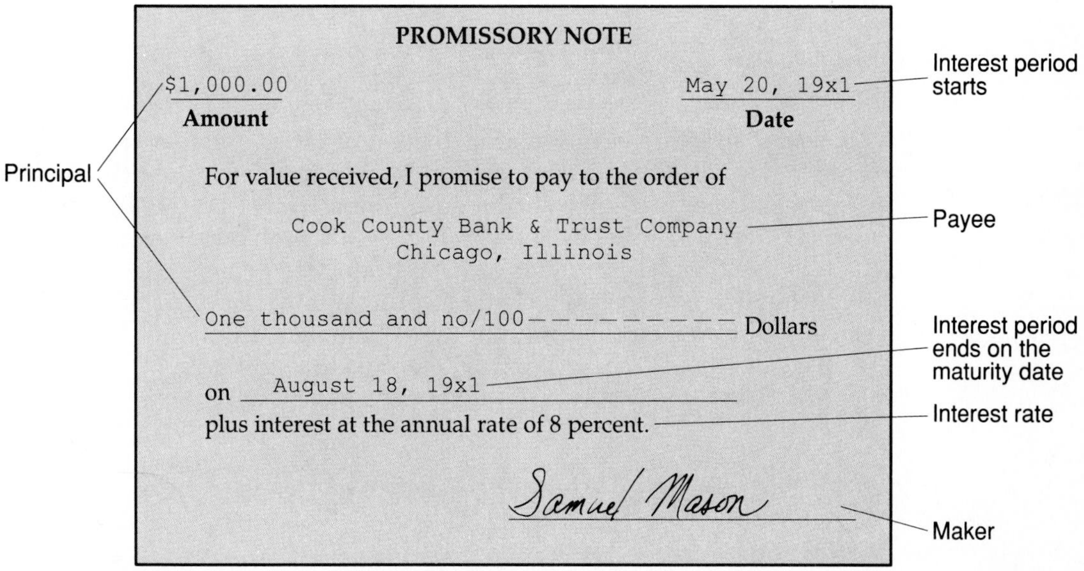

PROMISSORY NOTE

$1,000.00 — **Amount** May 20, 19x1 — **Date**

For value received, I promise to pay to the order of

Cook County Bank & Trust Company
Chicago, Illinois

One thousand and no/100 ---------- Dollars

on August 18, 19x1

plus interest at the annual rate of 8 percent.

Samuel Mason

Principal
Interest period starts
Payee
Interest period ends on the maturity date
Interest rate
Maker

Computations for Promissory Notes

In accounting for promissory notes, several terms are important to remember. These terms are (1) maturity date, (2) duration of note, (3) interest and interest rate, (4) maturity value, (5) discount, and (6) proceeds from discounting.

Maturity Date. The **maturity date** is the date on which the note must be paid. It must either be stated on the promissory note or be determinable from the facts stated on the note. Among the most common statements of maturity date are the following:

1. A specific date, such as "November 14, 19xx"
2. A specific number of months after the date of the note, for example, "3 months after date"
3. A specific number of days after the date of the note, for example, "60 days after date"

There is no problem in determining the maturity date when it is stated. When the maturity date is a number of months from date of note, one simply uses the same day in the appropriate future month. For example, a note dated January 20 that is due in two months would be due on March 20.

When the maturity date is stated as a specific number of days, it must be based on the exact number of days. In computing the maturity, it is important to exclude the date of the note and to include the maturity day. For example, a note dated May 20 and due in 90 days would be due on August 18, computed as follows:

Days remaining in May (31 − 20)	11
Days in June	30
Days in July	31
Days in August	18
Total days	90

Duration of Note. Determining the **duration of note**, or its length of time in days, is the opposite problem from determining the maturity date. This calculation is important because interest must be calculated on the basis of the exact number of days. There is no problem when the maturity date is based on the number of days from date of note. However, if the maturity date is a specified date, the exact number of days must be determined. Assume that the length of time of a note is from May 10 to August 10. The length of time is 92 days, determined as follows:

Days remaining in May (31 − 10)	21
Days in June	30
Days in July	31
Days in August	10
Total days	92

Interest and Interest Rate. The **interest** is the cost of borrowing money or the return for lending money, depending on whether one is the borrower or the lender. The amount of interest is based on three factors: the principal (the amount of money borrowed or lent), the rate of interest, and the loan's length of time. The formula used in computing interest is as follows:

Principal × rate of interest × time = interest

Interest rates are usually stated on an annual basis. For example, the interest on a $1,000, one-year, 8 percent note is computed as follows: $1,000 × 8/100 × 1 = $80.

If the term of the note were three months instead of a year, the interest charge would be $20, computed as follows: $1,000 × 8/100 × 3/12 = $20.

When the terms of a note are expressed in days, the exact number of days must be used in computing the interest. To keep the computation simple, let us compute interest on the basis of 360[6] days per year. Therefore, if the term of the above note were 45 days, the interest would be $10, computed as follows: $1,000 × 8/100 × 45/360 = $10.

Maturity Value. It is necessary to determine the **maturity value** of a note, or the total proceeds of the note at the maturity date. The maturity value is the face value of the note plus interest. The maturity value of a 90-day, 8 percent, $1,000 note is computed as follows:

Maturity value = principal + interest
= $1,000 + ($1,000 × 8/100 × 90/360)
= $1,000 + $20
= $1,020

Occasionally, one will encounter a so-called noninterest-bearing note. The maturity value is the face value or principal amount. In this case, the principal amount includes an implied interest cost.

Discount. To **discount** a note means to take out the interest in advance. The **discount** is the amount of interest deducted. It is very common for banks to use this method when lending money on promissory notes. The amount of the discount is computed as follows:

Discount = maturity value × interest rate × time

For example, assume that a note has a maturity value of $1,000, is due in 90 days, and is discounted at a 10 percent rate of interest:

Discount = $1,000 × 10/100 × 90/360 = $25

6. Practice varies in the computation of interest. Many banks use a 360-day year for commercial loans and a 365-day year for consumer loans. Other banks use a 365-day year for all loans. In Europe, use of a 360-day year is common. In this book, we use 360 days in a year to keep the computations simple.

Proceeds from Discounting. Normally when someone borrows money on a note, the amount he or she receives or borrows is the face value or principal. But when a note receivable is discounted, the amount the borrower receives is called the **proceeds from discounting** and must be computed as follows:

Proceeds = maturity value – discount

Thus, in the preceding example, the proceeds would be computed as follows:

$$
\begin{aligned}
\text{Proceeds} &= \$1{,}000 - (\$1{,}000 \times 10/100 \times 90/360) \\
&= \$1{,}000 - \$25 \\
&= \$975
\end{aligned}
$$

This calculation is very simple when the maturity value is given, as illustrated here. However, the calculation is more complicated when the maturity value must be calculated, as when an interest-bearing note from a customer is discounted to the bank. In this situation, the maturity value must first be computed using the formula for computing maturity value. Then the discount must be computed on the basis of the maturity value. Finally, the proceeds are determined by deducting the discount from the maturity value. For example, the proceeds of a \$2,000, 8 percent, 90-day note, discounted on the date it is drawn at the bank at 10 percent, would be \$1,989:

$$
\begin{aligned}
\textbf{Maturity value} &= \textbf{principal + interest} \\
&= \$2{,}000 + (\$2{,}000 \times 8/100 \times 90/360) \\
&= \$2{,}000 + \$40 \\
&= \$2{,}040
\end{aligned}
$$

$$
\begin{aligned}
\textbf{Discount} &= \textbf{maturity value} \times \textbf{discount rate} \times \textbf{time} \\
&= \$2{,}040 \times 10/100 \times 90/360 \\
&= \$51
\end{aligned}
$$

$$
\begin{aligned}
\textbf{Proceeds} &= \textbf{maturity value – discount} \\
&= \$2{,}040 - \$51 \\
&= \$1{,}989
\end{aligned}
$$

In this example, the note was discounted to the bank on the same day it was written. Usually time will pass between the date the note is written and the date it is discounted. In such a case, the number of days used in computing the discount should be the number of days remaining until the maturity date of the note, because that is the length of time for which the bank is lending the money to the company holding the note. For example, assume the same facts as above except that the company holding the note waits 30 days to discount the note to the bank. In other words, at the date of discounting, there are 60 (90 – 30) days remaining until the maturity date. The proceeds are determined as follows:

$$\begin{aligned}
\text{Maturity value} &= \text{principal} + \text{interest} \\
&= \$2{,}040 \text{ (from page 356)} \\
\text{Discount} &= \text{maturity value} \times \text{discount rate} \times \text{time} \\
&= \$2{,}040 \times 10/100 \times 60/360 \\
&= \$34 \\
\text{Proceeds} &= \text{maturity value} - \text{discount} \\
&= \$2{,}040 - \$34 \\
&= \$2{,}006
\end{aligned}$$

The difference in discount of $17 ($51 – $34) between the two cases is equal to the discount on the 30 days that have elapsed between writing and discounting the note ($2,040 × 10/100 × 30/360 = $17).

Illustrative Accounting Entries

OBJECTIVE 6 *Journalize entries involving notes receivable*

The accounting entries for promissory notes receivable fall into five groups: (1) receipt of a note, (2) collection on a note, (3) recording a dishonored note, (4) selling or discounting a note, and (5) recording adjusting entries.

Receipt of a Note. Assume that a 12 percent, 30-day note is received from a customer, J. Halsted, in settlement of an existing account receivable of $4,000, on June 1. The entry for this transaction is as follows:

June	1	Notes Receivable	4,000	
		Accounts Receivable, J. Halsted		4,000
		Received 12 percent, 30-day note in payment of account		

Collection on a Note. When the note plus interest is collected 30 days later, the entry is as follows:

July	1	Cash	4,040	
		Notes Receivable		4,000
		Interest Income		40
		Collected 12 percent, 30-day note from J. Halsted		

Recording a Dishonored Note. When the maker of a note does not pay the note at maturity, the note is said to be dishonored. In the case of a **dishonored note**, an entry should be made by the holder or payee to transfer the total amount due from the Notes Receivable account to an account receivable from the debtor. If J. Halsted did not pay his note on July 1 but dishonored it, the following entry would be made:

July	1	Accounts Receivable, J. Halsted	4,040	
		Notes Receivable		4,000
		Interest Income		40
		To record 12 percent, 30-day note dishonored by J. Halsted		

The interest earned is recorded because although J. Halsted did not pay the note, he is still obligated to pay both the principal amount and the interest.

Two things are accomplished by transferring dishonored notes receivable into an Accounts Receivable account. First, it leaves the Notes Receivable account with only notes that have not matured and are presumably negotiable and collectible. Second, it establishes a record in the borrower's account receivable that he or she has dishonored a note receivable. This information may be helpful in deciding whether to extend future credit to this customer.

Selling or Discounting a Note. Many companies raise cash for operations by selling unmatured notes receivable to banks or finance companies. This type of financing is common in the sales of equipment and other products where the customer does not have a strong credit rating, as in sales of videogame machines to convenience stores. It is usually called discounting because the bank or other purchaser deducts the interest from the maturity value of the note to determine the proceeds. The holder of the note (usually the payee) signs his or her name on the back of the note (as in endorsing a check) and delivers the note to the bank. The bank or other purchaser expects to collect the maturity value of the note (principal plus interest) on the maturity date but also has recourse against the endorser or seller of the note. Therefore, if the maker fails to pay, the endorser is liable to the bank or other purchaser for payment. In accounting terminology, the endorser is said to be contingently liable. A **contingent liability** is a potential liability that can develop into a real liability if a possible subsequent event occurs. In this case, the subsequent event would be the nonpayment of the note by the maker.

Although sales of notes receivable are made to many different purchasers, we will assume for this example that a $1,000, 12 percent, 90-day note is taken to the bank 60 days before maturity and that the bank discounts it at 15 percent for cash. The cash to be received (proceeds from discounting) is calculated as the maturity value less the discount, recorded as follows:

Cash	1,004.25	
Notes Receivable		1,000.00
Interest Income		4.25
To record discounting of a 12 percent, 90-day note with 60 days left at 15 percent		
Maturity value:		
$1,000 + ($1,000 × 12/100 × 90/360)	= $1,030.00	
Less discount:		
$1,030 × 15/100 × 60/360	= 25.75	
Proceeds from discounted note receivable	$1,004.25	

Since the interest of $30 to be received exceeds the interest cost or discount, the difference of $4.25 is credited to Interest Income. If the proceeds had been less than the note receivable, the difference would have been recorded as a debit to Interest Expense. For example, if the proceeds had been $995.75 instead of $1,004.25, Interest Expense would have been debited for $4.25, and there would have been no entry to Interest Income.

Note that neither the length of the discounting period nor the discount rate is the same as the term or the rate of interest of the note. This situation is typical. Also, notice that the account Notes Receivable is credited. Although this entry removes the note from the records, remember that if the maker cannot or will not pay the bank, the endorser is liable to the bank for the note.

Before the maturity date of the discounted note, the bank will notify the maker that it is holding the note and that payment should be made directly to the bank. If the maker pays the bank as agreed, then no entry is required in the records of the endorser. If the maker does not pay the note and interest on the due date, the note is dishonored. To hold the endorser liable for the note, the bank must notify the endorser that the note is dishonored. The bank will normally notify the endorser by protesting the note. The bank does this by preparing and mailing a notice of protest to the endorser. The **notice of protest** is a sworn statement that the note was presented to the maker for payment and the maker refused to pay. The bank typically charges a **protest fee** for protesting the note, which must be paid when the endorser pays the bank the amount due on the dishonored note.

If the note discounted in this example is dishonored by the maker on the maturity date, the following entry should be made by the endorser when paying the obligation:

Accounts Receivable, Name of Maker	1,040	
Cash		1,040
To record payment of principal and interest on discounted note (maturity value of $1,030), plus a protest fee of $10 to bank; the note was dishonored by the maker		

Additional interest usually accrues on the maturity value plus the protest fee until the note is paid or written off as uncollectible.

Recording Adjusting Entries. A promissory note received in one period may not be due until a following accounting period. Because a small amount of the interest on the note accrues each day of the note's duration, it is necessary, according to the matching rule, to apportion the interest earned to the period to which it belongs. For example, assume that on August 31 a 60-day, 8 percent, $2,000 note was received and that the company prepares financial statements monthly. The following adjusting entry on September 30 is necessary to show how the interest earned for September has accrued:

Sept. 30	Interest Receivable	13.33	
	Interest Income		13.33
	To accrue 30 days' interest earned on note receivable $2,000 × 8/100 × 30/360 = $13.33		

The account Interest Receivable is a current asset on the balance sheet. Upon receiving payment of the note plus interest on October 30, the following entry is made:[7]

Oct. 30	Cash	2,026.67	
	Note Receivable		2,000.00
	Interest Receivable		13.33
	Interest Income		13.34
	To record receipt of note receivable plus interest		

As seen from these transactions, September and October each receives the benefit of one-half the interest earned.

DECISION POINT
Marriott Corporation[8]

Marriott Corporation is the world's largest operator of hotels and a leader in food and services management. The company has investments in various affiliated companies that own hotel properties, and it assists in the financing of some of their operations. To provide cash for various purposes, management has sold portions of the notes receivable from affiliates. In the company's 1989 annual report, the notes to the financial statements show that the company sold $61 million of the notes receivable in 1989 and $128 million in 1988. At December 29, 1989, the aggregate unpaid balance of notes receivable sold with recourse was $55 million. This $55 million represents a contingent liability. ■

Control of Cash Transactions

OBJECTIVE 7
Demonstrate control of cash by preparing a bank reconciliation

Banking facilities are also an important aid to businesses in controlling both cash receipts and cash disbursements. Banks are safe depositories of cash, negotiable instruments, and other valuable business documents such as stocks and bonds. The use of bank checks for disbursements improves a company's control by minimizing the amount of currency on hand and by providing a permanent record of all cash payments. Furthermore, banks can serve as agents for a company in a variety of important transactions, such as the collection and payment of certain kinds of debts and the exchange of foreign currencies.

Once a month the bank sends a statement to each depositor and returns the canceled checks that it has paid and charged to the depositor's account. The returned checks are said to be "canceled" because the bank stamps, or cancels, them to show that they have been paid. The **bank statement** shows the balance at the beginning of the month, the deposits,

7. Some firms may follow the practice of reversing the September 30 adjusting entry. Here we assume that a reversing entry is not made.
8. Excerpts from the 1989 Annual Report used with permission of Marriott Corporation.

the checks paid, other debits and credits during the month, and the balance at the end of the month. A bank statement is illustrated in Figure 7-4.

Preparing a Bank Reconciliation

Rarely will the balance of a company's Cash account exactly equal the cash balance as shown on the bank statement. Certain transactions shown in the company's records may not be recorded by the bank, and certain bank transactions may not appear in the company's records. Therefore, a necessary step in internal control is to prove both the balance of the bank

Figure 7-4. Bank Statement

Statement of Account with
THE LAKE PARK NATIONAL BANK
Chicago, Illinois

Martin Maintenance Company
8428 Rocky Island Avenue
Chicago, Illinois 60643

Checking Acct No
8030-647-4
Period covered
Sept.30-Oct.31,19xx

Previous Balance	Checks/Debits—No.	Deposits/Credits—No.	S.C.	Current Balance
$2,645.78	$4,319.33 --15	$5,157.12 --7	$12.50	$3,471.07

CHECKS/DEBITS			DEPOSITS/CREDITS		DAILY BALANCES	
Posting Date	Check No.	Amount	Posting Date	Amount	Date	Amount
					09/30	2,645.78
10/01	564	100.00	10/01	586.00	10/01	2,881.78
10/01	565	250.00	10/05	1,500.00	10/04	2,825.60
10/04	567	56.18	10/06	300.00	10/05	3,900.46
10/05	566	425.14	10/16	1,845.50	10/06	4,183.34
10/06	568	17.12	10/21	600.00	10/12	2,242.34
10/12	569	1,705.80	10/24	300.00CM	10/16	3,687.84
10/12	570	235.20	10/31	25.62IN	10/17	3,589.09
10/16	571	400.00			10/21	4,189.09
10/17	572	29.75			10/24	3,745.59
10/17	573	69.00			10/25	3,586.09
10/24	574	738.50			10/28	3,457.95
10/24		5.00DM			10/31	3,471.07
10/25	575	7.50				
10/25	577	152.00				
10/28		128.14NSF				
10/31		12.50SC				

Explanation of Symbols:

CM – Credit Memo
DM – Debit Memo
NSF – Non-Sufficient Funds

SC – Service Charge
EC – Error Correction
OD – Overdraft
IN – Interest on Average Balance

The last amount in this column is your balance.

Please examine; if no errors are reported within ten (10) days, the account will be considered to be correct.

and the balance of Cash in the accounting records. A **bank reconciliation** is the process of accounting for the differences between the balance appearing on the bank statement and the balance of Cash according to the company's records. This process involves making additions to and subtractions from both balances to arrive at the adjusted cash balance.

The most common examples of transactions shown in the company's records but not entered in the bank's records are the following:

1. **Outstanding checks** These are checks that have been issued and recorded by the company, but do not yet appear on the bank statement.
2. **Deposits in transit** These are deposits that were mailed or taken to the bank but were not received in time to be recorded on the statement.

Transactions that may appear on the bank statement but have not been recorded by the company include the following:

1. **Service Charges (SC)** Banks cannot profitably handle small accounts without making a service charge. Many banks base the service charge on a number of factors, such as the average balance of the account during the month or the number of checks drawn.
2. **NSF (Non-Sufficient Funds) checks** An NSF check is a check deposited by the company that is not paid when the company's bank presents it to the maker's bank. The bank charges the company's account and returns the check so that the company can try to collect the amount due. If the bank has deducted the NSF check from the bank statement but the company has not deducted it from its book balance, an adjustment must be made in the bank reconciliation. The depositor usually reclassifies the NSF check from Cash to Accounts Receivable because the company must now collect from the person or company that wrote the check.
3. **Interest income** It is very common for banks to pay interest on a company's average balance. These accounts are sometimes called N.O.W. or money market accounts but can take other forms. Such interest is reported on the bank statement.
4. **Miscellaneous charges and credits** Banks also charge for other services, such as collection and payment of promissory notes, stopping payment on checks, and printing checks. The bank notifies the depositor of each deduction by including a debit memorandum with the monthly statement. A bank will sometimes serve as an agent in collecting on promissory notes for the depositor. In such a case, a credit memorandum will be included.

An error by either the bank or the depositor will, of course, require immediate correction.

Steps in Reconciling the Bank Balance. The steps to be followed in achieving a bank reconciliation are as follows:

1. Compare the deposits listed on the bank statement with deposits shown in the accounting records. Any deposits in transit should be

added to the bank balance. (Immediately investigate any deposits in transit from last month still not listed on the bank statement.)
2. Trace returned checks to the bank statement, making sure that all checks have been issued by the company, properly charged to the company's account, and properly signed.
3. Arrange the canceled checks returned with the bank statement in numerical order, and compare them with the record of checks issued. List checks issued but not on the bank statement. (Be sure to include any checks still outstanding from prior months; investigate any checks outstanding for more than a few months.) Deduct outstanding checks from the bank balance.
4. Deduct from the balance per books any debit memoranda issued by the bank, such as NSF checks and service charges, that are not yet recorded on the company's records.
5. Add to the balance per books any interest earned or credit memoranda issued by the bank, such as collection of a promissory note that is not yet recorded on the company's books.
6. Make journal entries for any items on the bank statement that have not been recorded in the company's books.

Illustration of a Bank Reconciliation. The October bank statement for Martin Maintenance Company, as shown in Figure 7-4, indicates a balance on October 31 of $3,471.07. We shall assume that Martin Maintenance Company has a cash balance in its records on October 31 of $2,405.91. The purpose of a bank reconciliation is to identify the items that make up the difference between these amounts and to determine the correct cash balance. The bank reconciliation for Martin Maintenance Company is given in Exhibit 7-3. The numbered items in the exhibit refer to the following:

1. A deposit in the amount of $276.00 was mailed to the bank on October 31 and had not been recorded by the bank.
2. Five checks issued in October or prior months have not yet been paid by the bank, as follows:

Check No.	Date	Amount
551	Sept. 14	$150.00
576	Oct. 30	40.68
578	Oct. 31	500.00
579	Oct. 31	370.00
580	Oct. 31	130.50

3. The deposit for cash sales of October 6 was incorrectly recorded in Martin Maintenance Company's records as $330.00. The bank correctly recorded the deposit as $300.00.
4. Among the returned checks was a credit memorandum showing that the bank had collected a promissory note from A. Jacobs in the amount of $280.00, plus $20.00 in interest on the note. A debit memorandum

was also enclosed for the $5.00 collection fee. No entry had been made on Martin Maintenance Company's records.

5. Also returned with the bank statement was an NSF check for $128.14. This check had been received from a customer named Arthur Clubb. The NSF check from Clubb was not reflected in the company's accounting records.
6. A debit memorandum was enclosed for the regular monthly service charge of $12.50. This charge was not yet recorded by Martin Maintenance Company.
7. Interest earned by the company on the average balance was reported as $25.62.

Note in Exhibit 7-3 that, starting from their separate balances, both the bank and book amounts are adjusted to the amount of $2,555.89. This ad-

Exhibit 7-3. Bank Reconciliation

Martin Maintenance Company
Bank Reconciliation
October 31, 19xx

Balance per bank, October 31		$3,471.07
① Add deposit of October 31 in transit		276.00
		$3,747.07
② Less outstanding checks:		
No. 551	$150.00	
No. 576	40.68	
No. 578	500.00	
No. 579	370.00	
No. 580	130.50	1,191.18
Adjusted bank balance, October 31		**$2,555.89**
Balance per books, October 31		$2,405.91
Add:		
④ Notes receivable collected by bank, including $20.00 of interest income	$300.00	
⑦ Interest income	25.62	325.62
		$2,731.53
Less:		
③ Overstatement of deposit of October 6	$ 30.00	
④ Collection fee	5.00	
⑤ NSF check of Arthur Clubb	128.14	
⑥ Service charge	12.50	175.64
Adjusted book balance, October 31		**$2,555.89**

Note: The circled numbers refer to the items listed in the text on pages 363 and 364 (above).

justed balance is the amount of cash owned by the company on October 31 and thus is the amount that should appear on its October 31 balance sheet.

Recording Transactions After Reconciliation. The adjusted balance of cash differs from both the bank statement and Martin Maintenance Company's records. The bank balance will automatically become correct when outstanding checks are presented for payment and the deposit in transit is received and recorded by the bank. Entries are necessary, however, to reflect in the company's records the transactions necessary to correct the book balance. All the items reported by the bank but not yet recorded by the company must be recorded in the general journal by means of the following entries:

Date	Account	Debit	Credit
Oct. 31	Cash	300.00	
	Notes Receivable		280.00
	Interest Income		20.00
	Note receivable of $280.00 and interest of $20.00 collected by bank from A. Jacobs		
31	Cash	25.62	
	Interest Income		25.62
	Interest on average bank account balance		
31	Sales	30.00	
	Cash		30.00
	Correction of error in recording a $300.00 deposit as $330.00		
31	Accounts Receivable, Arthur Clubb	128.14	
	Cash		128.14
	NSF check of Arthur Clubb returned by bank		
31	Bank Service Charges Expense	17.50	
	Cash		17.50
	Bank service charge ($12.50) and collection fee ($5.00) for October		

It is acceptable to record these entries in one or two compound entries to save time and space, as follows:

Date	Account	Debit	Credit
Oct. 31	Cash	149.98	
	Sales	30.00	
	Accounts Receivable, Arthur Clubb	128.14	
	Bank Service Charges Expense	17.50	
	Notes Receivable		280.00
	Interest Income		45.62
	To record items from bank reconciliation		

Controlling Cash with an Imprest System

OBJECTIVE 8 *Demonstrate the use of a simple imprest system*

Under some circumstances, it is not practical to make all cash disbursements by check. A company may facilitate certain operations by providing cash to individuals to spend on operations. For example, cash might be advanced to traveling sales representatives for expenses, to other employees for travel expenses, to divisions to pay the payroll or to conduct other operations. One way to control these cash expenditures is through the use of an **imprest system**. Under this system a cash fund or advance is established at a fixed amount and is periodically reimbursed based on documented expenditures for the exact amount necessary to bring it back to the fixed amount.

One of the simplest examples of an imprest system is the use of a **petty cash fund** to make small payments of cash for such things as postage stamps, incoming postage, shipping charges due, or minor purchases of supplies. The use of a petty cash fund will be used here to illustrate the imprest system, but the basic idea can be used to control cash in any situation where cash is advanced in anticipation of expenditures.

Establishing the Petty Cash Fund. Some companies have a regular cashier, secretary, or receptionist to administer the petty cash fund. To establish the petty cash fund, the company issues a check for an amount that is intended to cover two to four weeks of small expenditures. The check is cashed, and the money is placed in the petty cash box, drawer, or envelope.

The only entry required when the fund is established is to record the issuance of the check, as follows:

Oct. 14	Petty Cash	100.00	
	Cash		100.00
	To establish petty cash fund		

Making Disbursements from the Petty Cash Fund. The custodian of the petty cash fund should prepare a **petty cash voucher**, or written authorization, for each expenditure. On each petty cash voucher the custodian enters the date, amount, and purpose of the expenditure. The voucher is signed by the person receiving the payment.

The custodian should be informed that surprise audits of the fund will be made occasionally. The cash in the fund plus the sum of the petty cash vouchers should equal the amount shown in the Petty Cash account at all times.

Reimbursing the Petty Cash Fund. At specified intervals, when the fund becomes low, and at the end of an accounting period, the petty cash fund is replenished by a check issued to the custodian for the exact amount of the expenditures. From time to time there may be minor discrepancies in the amount of cash left in the fund at the time of reimbursement. In these cases, the amount of the discrepancy should be recorded in Cash Short or Over as a debit if short or as a credit if over.

Assume that after two weeks the petty cash fund established earlier had a cash balance of $14.27 and petty cash vouchers as follows: postage, $25.00; supplies, $30.55; freight in, $30.00. The entry to replenish, or replace, the fund is as follows:

Oct. 28	Postage Expense	25.00	
	Supplies	30.55	
	Freight In	30.00	
	Cash Short or Over	.18	
	Cash		85.73
	To replenish petty cash fund		

Note that the Petty Cash account is debited only when the fund is first established. Expense or asset accounts will be debited each time the fund is replenished. In most cases, no further entries to the Petty Cash account are needed unless there is a desire to change the original fixed amount of the fund.

The petty cash fund should be replenished at the end of an accounting period to bring it up to its fixed amount and to ensure that the other accounts involved will be properly reflected in the current period's financial statements. If through an oversight the petty cash fund is not replenished at the end of the period, expenditures for the period must still appear on the income statement. They are shown through an adjusting entry debiting the expense accounts and crediting Petty Cash. The result is a reduction in the petty cash fund and the Petty Cash account by the amount of the adjusting entry. For financial statement presentation, the balance of the Petty Cash account is usually combined with other cash accounts.

Chapter Review

Review of Learning Objectives

1. **Account for cash and short-term investments.**
Cash consists of coin and currency on hand, checks and money orders received from customers, and deposits in bank accounts. Short-term investments, sometimes called marketable securities, including time deposits, certificates of deposit, government securities, stocks, and other securities intended to be held for short periods of time (usually less than a year), are first recorded at cost. Afterwards, investments in debt securities are carried at cost unless there is a permanent drop in the market value. Investments in equity securities are reported at the lower of cost or market. If the cost of equity securities exceeds market value, an allowance to reduce short-term investments to market value is established.

2. **Define *accounts receivable*, and explain the relationships among credit policies, sales, and uncollectible accounts.**
Accounts receivable are amounts still to be collected from credit sales to customers. The amounts still owed by individual customers are found in the subsidiary ledger.
Because credit is offered to increase sales, bad debts associated with the sales should be charged as expenses in the period in which the sales are

made. However, because of the time lag between the sales and the time the accounts are judged to be uncollectible, the accountant must estimate the amount of bad debts in any given period.

3. **Apply the allowance method of accounting for uncollectible accounts, including using the percentage of net sales method and the accounts receivable aging method to estimate uncollectible accounts.**
Uncollectible accounts expense is estimated by either the percentage of net sales method or the accounts receivable aging method. When the first method is used, bad debts are judged to be a certain percentage of sales during the period. When the second method is used, certain percentages are applied to groups of the accounts receivable that have been arranged by due dates. A third method, the direct charge-off method, is required when filing federal income tax returns but is not used in the accounting records because it does not follow the matching rule.
   Allowance for Uncollectible Accounts is a contra account to Accounts Receivable. When the estimate of uncollectible accounts is made, debit Uncollectible Accounts Expense and credit the allowance account. When an individual account is determined to be uncollectible, it is removed from Accounts Receivable by debiting the allowance account and crediting Accounts Receivable. If this account should later be collected, the earlier entry should be reversed and the collection recorded in the normal way.

4. **Identify methods of financing accounts receivable and other issues related to accounts receivable.**
Methods of financing accounts receivable include pledging accounts receivable as collateral for a loan and selling or factoring accounts receivable with or without recourse.
   Accounts of customers with credit balances should not be classified as negative accounts receivable but as current liabilities on the balance sheet. Installment accounts receivable are classified as current assets if such credit policies are followed in the industry. Receivables from credit card companies should be classified as current assets. Receivables from employees, officers, stockholders, and others made outside the normal course of business should not be listed among accounts receivable. They may be either short- or long-term assets depending on when collection is expected to take place.

5. **Define and describe a promissory note, and make calculations involving promissory notes.**
A promissory note is an unconditional promise to pay a definite sum of money on demand or at a future date. Companies selling durable goods of high value, such as farm machinery and automobiles, will often take promissory notes, which can be sold to banks as a financing method.
   In accounting for promissory notes, it is important to know how to calculate the following: maturity date, duration of note, interest and interest rate, maturity value, discount, and proceeds from discounting. Discounting is the act by which the lender takes out the interest in advance when making a loan on a note.

6. **Journalize entries involving notes receivable.**
The accounting entries for promissory notes receivable fall into five groups: receipt of a note, collection on a note, recording a dishonored note, selling or discounting a note, and recording adjusting entries.

7. **Demonstrate control of cash by preparing a bank reconciliation.**
   The term *bank reconciliation* means accounting for the difference between the balance appearing on the bank statement and the balance of the Cash account according to the company's records. It involves adjusting both balances to arrive at the adjusted cash balance. The bank balance is adjusted for outstanding checks and deposits in transit. The depositor's book balance is adjusted for service charges, NSF checks, interest earned, and miscellaneous charges and credits.

8. **Demonstrate the use of a simple imprest system.**
   An imprest system is a method of controlling cash expenditures by setting up a fund at a fixed amount. A petty cash system, one example of an imprest system, is established by a debit to Petty Cash and a credit to Cash. It is replenished by debits to various expense or asset accounts and a credit to Cash. Each expenditure should be supported by a petty cash voucher.

Review of Concepts and Terminology

The following concepts and terms were introduced in this chapter:

(L.O. 2) **Accounts receivable:** Short-term liquid assets that arise from sales on credit at the wholesale or the retail level.

(L.O. 3) **Accounts receivable aging method:** A method of estimating uncollectible accounts based on the assumption that a predictable portion of accounts receivable will not be collected.

(L.O. 3) **Aging of accounts receivable:** The process of listing each customer in accounts receivable according to the due date of the account.

(L.O. 2) **Allowance for Uncollectible Accounts:** A contra account that serves to reduce accounts receivable to the amount that is expected to be collected in cash.

(L.O. 7) **Bank reconciliation:** A procedure to account for the difference between the cash balance appearing on the bank statement and the balance of the Cash account in the depositor's record.

(L.O. 7) **Bank statement:** A statement showing the balance in a bank account at the beginning of the month, the deposits, the checks paid, other debits and credits during the month, and the balance at the end of the month.

(L.O. 1) **Cash:** Coins and currency on hand, checks and money orders from customers, and deposits in bank checking accounts.

(L.O. 1) **Cash equivalents:** Short-term investments that will revert to cash in less than ninety days.

(L.O. 1) **Compensating balance:** A minimum amount required by a bank to be kept in an account as part of a credit-granting arrangement.

(L.O. 6) **Contingent liability:** A potential liability that can develop into a real liability if a possible subsequent event occurs.

(L.O. 2) **Controlling (or control) account:** An account in the general ledger that summarizes the total balance of a group of related accounts in a subsidiary ledger.

(L.O. 4) **Direct charge-off method:** A method of accounting for uncollectible accounts by debiting expenses directly when bad debts are discovered instead

of using the allowance method; the method violates the matching rule but is required for federal income tax computations.

(L.O. 5) **Discount:** (Verb) to take out interest in advance; (noun) the interest amount deducted in advance.

(L.O. 6) **Dishonored note:** A promissory note that the maker cannot or will not pay at the maturity date.

(L.O. 5) **Duration of note:** Length of time in days between the making of a promissory note and its maturity date.

(L.O. 4) **Factor:** An entity that buys accounts receivable.

(L.O. 4) **Factoring:** The selling or transferring of accounts receivable.

(L.O. 8) **Imprest system:** A system for controlling cash by establishing a fund at a fixed amount and periodically reimbursing the fund by the amount necessary to bring the fund back to the fixed amount.

(L.O. 4) **Installment accounts receivable:** Accounts receivable that are payable in a series of time payments.

(L.O. 5) **Interest:** The cost of borrowing money or the return for lending money, depending on whether one is the borrower or the lender.

(L.O. 5) **Maturity date:** The due date of a promissory note.

(L.O. 5) **Maturity value:** The total proceeds of a promissory note, including principal and interest at the maturity date.

(L.O. 5) **Notes payable:** Collective term for promissory notes owed by the maker to other entities.

(L.O. 5) **Notes receivable:** Collective term for promissory notes held by the entity (payee) to whom payment is promised.

(L.O. 6) **Notice of protest:** A sworn statement that a promissory note was presented to the maker for payment and the maker refused to pay.

(L.O. 3) **Percentage of net sales method:** A method of estimating uncollectible accounts based on the assumption that a predictable portion of sales will not be collected.

(L.O. 8) **Petty cash fund:** A fund established by a business for making small payments of cash for minor purchases when it is inconvenient to pay with a check.

(L.O. 8) **Petty cash voucher:** A form signed by each person receiving a cash payment from a business, listing the date, amount, and purpose of the expenditure.

(L.O. 5) **Proceeds from discounting:** The amount received by the borrower when a promissory note is discounted; proceeds = maturity value – discount.

(L.O. 5) **Promissory note:** An unconditional promise to pay a definite sum of money on demand or at a future date.

(L.O. 6) **Protest fee:** The charge made by a bank for preparing and mailing a notice of protest.

(L.O. 1) **Short-term investments (marketable securities):** Temporary investments of excess cash, invested until needed to pay current obligations.

(L.O. 1) **Short-term liquid assets:** Financial assets that arise from cash transactions, the investment of cash, and the extension of credit.

(L.O. 2) **Subsidiary ledger:** A ledger separate from the general ledger; contains a group of related accounts the total of whose balances equals the balance of a controlling account in the general ledger.

(L.O. 2) **Trade credit:** Credit granted to customers by wholesalers or retailers.

(L.O. 2) **Uncollectible accounts:** Accounts receivable from customers who cannot or will not pay.

Review Problem
Entries for Uncollectible Accounts Expense and Notes Receivable Transactions

(L.O. 3, 5, 6) The Farm Implement Company sells merchandise on credit and also accepts notes for payment, which are discounted to the bank. During the year ended June 30, the company had net credit sales of $1,200,000 and at the end of the year had Accounts Receivable of $400,000 and a debit balance in the Allowance for Uncollectible Accounts of $2,100. In the past, approximately 1.5 percent of net sales have proved uncollectible. Also, an aging analysis of accounts receivable reveals that $17,000 in accounts receivable appears to be uncollectible.

The Farm Implement Company sold a tractor to R. C. Sims. Payment was received in the form of a $15,000, 9 percent, 90-day note dated March 16. On March 31, the note was discounted to the bank at 10 percent. On June 14, the bank notified the company that Sims had dishonored the note. The company paid the bank the maturity value of the note plus a fee of $15. On June 29, the company received payment in full from Sims plus additional interest from the date of the dishonored note.

Required

1. Prepare journal entries to record uncollectible accounts expense using (a) the percentage of net sales method and (b) the accounts receivable aging method.
2. Prepare journal entries relating to the note received from R. C. Sims.

Answer to Review Problem

1. Journal entries for uncollectible accounts prepared:

a. Percentage of net sales method:

June 30	Uncollectible Accounts Expense	18,000	
	Allowance for Uncollectible Accounts		18,000
	To record estimated uncollectible accounts expense at 1.5 percent of $1,200,000		

b. Accounts receivable aging method:

June 30	Uncollectible Accounts Expense	19,100	
	Allowance for Uncollectible Accounts		19,100
	To record estimated uncollectible accounts expense. The debit balance in the allowance account must be added to the estimated uncollectible accounts: $2,100 + $17,000 = $19,100		

2. Journal entries related to note prepared:

March	16	Notes Receivable	15,000.00	
		Sales		15,000.00
		Tractor sold to R. C. Sims; terms of note: 9 percent, 90 days		
	31	Cash	15,017.97	
		Notes Receivable		15,000.00
		Interest Income		17.97
		To record note discounted at bank at 10 percent		
		Maturity value: $15,000 + ($15,000 × 9/100 × 90/360)	= $15,337.50	
		Less discount: $15,337.50 × 10/100 × 75/360	= 319.53	
		Proceeds from discounted note receivable	$15,017.97	
June	14	Accounts Receivable, R. C. Sims	15,352.50	
		Cash		15,352.50
		To record payment of principal and interest on discounted note (maturity value $15,337.50), plus a $15 fee to bank; the note was dishonored by Sims		
	29	Cash	15,410.07	
		Accounts Receivable, R. C. Sims		15,352.50
		Interest Income		57.57
		Received payment in full from R. C. Sims $15,352.50 + ($15,352.50 × 9/100 × 15/360) $15,352.50 + $57.57 = $15,410.07		

Chapter Assignments

Discussion Questions

1. What items are included in the Cash account? What is a compensating balance?
2. Why does a business need short-term liquid assets? Why is it acceptable to account for certain short-term investments by the lower-of-cost-or-market method?
3. Why does a company sell on credit if it expects that some of the accounts will not be paid? What role does a credit department play in selling on credit?
4. According to generally accepted accounting principles, at what point in the cycle of selling and collecting does the bad debt loss occur?
5. If management estimates that $5,000 of the year's sales will not be collected, what entry should be made at year end?
6. After adjusting and closing entries at the end of the year, suppose that Accounts Receivable is $176,000 and the Allowance for Uncollectible Accounts is $14,500. (a) What is the collectible value of Accounts Receivable? (b) If the $450 account of a bankrupt customer is written off in the first month of the new year, what will be the resulting collectible value of Accounts Receivable?

7. What is the effect on net income of an optimistic versus a pessimistic view by management of estimated uncollectible accounts?
8. In what ways is the Allowance for Uncollectible Accounts similar to Accumulated Depreciation? In what ways is it different?
9. What procedure for estimating uncollectible accounts also gives management a view of the status of collections and the overall quality of accounts receivable?
10. What is the underlying reasoning behind the percentage of net sales method and the accounts receivable aging method of estimating uncollectible accounts?
11. Are the following terms different in any way: allowance for bad debts, allowance for doubtful accounts, allowance for uncollectible accounts?
12. Why should the entry for an account that has been written off as uncollectible be reinstated if the amount owed is subsequently collected?
13. What is a factor, and what does factoring with and without recourse mean?
14. What accounting rule is violated by the direct charge-off method of recognizing uncollectible accounts? Why?
15. Which of the lettered items below should be in Accounts Receivable? For those that do not belong in Accounts Receivable, tell where on the balance sheet they do belong: (a) installment accounts receivable from regular customers, due monthly for three years; (b) debit balances in customers' accounts; (c) receivables from employees; (d) credit balances in customers' accounts; (e) receivables from officers of the company; (f) accounts payable to a company that are less than accounts receivable from the same company.
16. What is a promissory note? Who is the maker? Who is the payee?
17. What are the due dates of the following notes: (a) a 3-month note dated August 16, (b) a 90-day note dated August 16, (c) a 60-day note dated March 25?
18. What is the difference between a cash discount and a discount on a note?
19. What is the difference between the interest on a note and the discount on a note?
20. Why is a bank reconciliation prepared?
21. Assume that each of the numbered items below appeared on a bank reconciliation. Which item(s) would be (a) an addition to the balance on the bank statement? (b) a deduction from the balance on the bank statement? (c) an addition to the balance on the books? (d) a deduction from the balance on the books? Write the correct letter after each numbered item.
    (1) Outstanding checks
    (2) Deposits in transit
    (3) Bank service charge
    (4) NSF check returned with statement
    (5) Note collected by bank

    Which of the above items require a journal entry?
22. What is the purpose of a petty cash fund, and, from the standpoint of internal control, what is the significance of the total of the fund (the level at which the fund is established)?
23. What account or accounts are debited when a petty cash fund is established? What account or accounts are debited when a petty cash fund is replenished?
24. Should a petty cash fund be replenished as of the last day of the accounting period? Explain.

Communication Skills Exercises

Communication 7-1. Management of Cash
(L.O. 1)

Academia Publishing Company publishes college textbooks in the sciences and humanities. More than 50 percent of the company's sales occur in July, August, and December. Its cash balances are largest in August, September, and January. During the rest of the year, its cash receipts are low. The corporate treasurer keeps the cash in a bank checking account that pays little or no interest. Bills are paid from this account as they come due. In order to survive, the company has needed to borrow money during some slow sales months. The loans were repaid in the months when cash receipts were largest. A management group has suggested that the company institute a new cash management plan under which cash would be invested in marketable securities as it is received and securities would be sold when the funds are needed. In this way, the cash will earn an income and perhaps the company will realize a gain through an increase in the value of the securities, reducing the need for borrowing. What are the accounting implications of this cash management plan? Are there any disadvantages to the plan?

Communication 7-2. Role of Credit Sales
(L.O. 2)

Mitsubishi Corporation[9], a broadly diversified Japanese corporation, instituted a credit plan, called Three Diamond, for customers who buy its major electronic products, such as large-screen televisions and videotape recorders, from specified retail dealers. Under this plan, which was introduced in 1990, approved customers who make purchases in November do not have to make any payments until April and no interest is charged for the intervening months. Mitsubishi pays the dealer the full amount less a small fee, sends the customer a Mitsubishi credit card, and collects from the customer at the specified time. What is Mitsubishi's motivation for establishing these generous credit terms? What costs are involved? What are the accounting implications?

Communication 7-3. Asset Financing
(L.O. 4, 6)

Siegel Appliances, Inc. is a small manufacturer of washing machines and dryers located in central Michigan. Siegel sells most of its appliances to large, established discount retail companies that market the appliances under their own names. Siegel sells the appliances on trade credit terms of n/60. If a customer wants a longer term, however, Siegel will accept notes for a period of up to nine months in payment. At present, the company is having cash flow troubles. The company needs $5 million immediately. Its cash balance is $200,000, its accounts receivable balance is $2.3 million, and its notes receivable balance is $3.7 million. How might Siegel's management use its accounts receivable and notes receivable to raise the cash it needs? What are the company's prospects for raising the needed cash?

Communication 7-4. Basic Research Skills
(L.O. 1)

Find a recent issue of the *Wall Street Journal* in your school library. Turn to the third or C section, entitled "Money & Investing," and take notes on the stock and treasury investments, as instructed. Find in the index at the top of the page the location of New York Stock Exchange (NYSE) stocks and turn to that page. From the listing of stock, find five companies you have heard of. They may be companies like IBM, Deere, Ford, or McDonald's. Copy down the range of the stock price for the last year and the current closing price. Also, copy down the dividend, if any, per share. How much did the market values of these common stocks you picked vary in the last year? Do these data dem-

9. Information based on promotional brochures received from Mitsubishi Corporation.

onstrate the need to value short-term investments of this type at the lower of cost or market? How does accounting for short-term investments in these common stocks differ from accounting for short-term investments in U.S. government Treasury bills? How are dividends received on investments in these common stocks accounted for? Be prepared to hand in your notes and to discuss the results of your investigation in class.

Classroom Exercises

Exercise 7-1. Accounting for Short-Term Investments in Equities *(L.O. 1)*

On October 16, 19x1, Jetline Corporation acquired the following short-term securities:

150 shares of IBM	$15,000
280 shares of General Motors	14,000
Total acquisition cost	$29,000

Jetline received dividends from IBM of $4.80 per share and from General Motors of $1.60 per share on December 15. IBM stock is selling for $110 per share and General Motors is selling for $40 at the end of the year. On January 9, 19x2 Jetline sells the General Motors shares for $13,000. Assume the October transaction was the first investment by Jetline.

1. Prepare the journal entry to record the acquisition.
2. Prepare the journal entry to record receipt of the dividends.
3. Calculate the market value of the portfolio on December 31, 19x1 and prepare the journal entry to record the loss.
4. Prepare the balance sheet presentation for short-term investments on the December 31, 19x1 balance sheet.
5. Prepare the journal entry for January 9, 19x2 to record the sale.

Exercise 7-2. Accounting for Short-Term Investments *(L.O. 1)*

During certain periods of its fiscal year, Nicks Company invests its excess cash until it is needed. On January 16, the company invested $146,000 in 90-day U.S. Treasury bills that had a maturity value of $150,000. On April 15, Nicks purchased 10,000 shares of Goodrich Paper common stock at $40 per share and 5,000 shares of Keuron Power common stock at $30 per share. The Treasury bills matured on April 16, and the company received $150,000 in cash. On May 15, it received quarterly dividends of 92.25 cents per share from Keuron Power and 60 cents per share from Goodrich Paper. On June 15, the company sold all the shares of Goodrich Paper for $48 per share. On June 30, the value of the Keuron Power stock was $28 per share.

Prepare journal entries to record the transactions on January 16, April 15, April 16, May 15, June 15, and June 30. Also, show the balance sheet presentations of short-term investments on June 30. Round to the nearest whole dollar. Assume there is no balance in the Allowance to Reduce Short-Term Investments to Market at the beginning of January.

Exercise 7-3. Adjusting Entries: Accounts Receivable Aging Method *(L.O. 3)*

Accounts Receivable of Herrera Company shows a debit balance of $104,000 at the end of the year. An aging method analysis of the individual accounts indicates estimated uncollectible accounts to be $6,700.

Give the general journal entry to record the uncollectible accounts expense under each of the following independent assumptions: (a) The Allowance for

Uncollectible Accounts has a credit balance of $800 before adjustment. (b) The Allowance for Uncollectible Accounts has a debit balance of $800 before adjustment.

Exercise 7-4. Adjusting Entry: Percentage of Net Sales Method *(L.O. 3)*

At the end of the year, Marin Enterprises estimates the uncollectible accounts expense to be .7 percent of net sales of $10,100,000. The current credit balance of the Allowance for Uncollectible Accounts is $17,200. Give the general journal entry to record the uncollectible accounts expense.

Exercise 7-5. Aging Method and Net Sales Method Contrasted *(L.O. 3)*

At the beginning of 19xx, the balances of Accounts Receivable and the Allowance for Uncollectible Accounts were $860,000 and $62,800, respectively. During the current year, credit sales were $6,400,000 and collections on account were $5,900,000. In addition, $70,000 in uncollectible accounts were written off. Using T accounts, determine the year-end balances of Accounts Receivable and Allowance for Uncollectible Accounts. Then make the year-end adjusting entry to record the uncollectible accounts expense, and show the year-end balance sheet presentation of Accounts Receivable and the Allowance for Uncollectible Accounts under each of the following conditions:

a. Management estimates the percentage of uncollectible credit sales to be 1.2 percent of total credit sales.
b. Based on an aging of accounts receivable, management estimates the end-of-year uncollectible accounts receivable to be $77,400.

Post the results of each entry to the Allowance for Uncollectible Accounts.

Exercise 7-6. Entries for Uncollectible Accounts Expense *(L.O. 3)*

The Schumacker Office Supply Company sells merchandise on credit. During the year ended December 31, the company had net sales of $2,300,000. At the end of the year it had Accounts Receivable of $600,000 and a debit balance in the Allowance for Uncollectible Accounts of $3,400. In the past, approximately 1.4 percent of net sales have proved uncollectible. Also, an aging analysis of accounts receivable reveals that $30,000 of the receivables appear to be uncollectible. Prepare journal entries to record uncollectible accounts expense using (a) the percentage of net sales method and (b) the accounts receivable aging method.

What is the resulting balance of the Allowance for Uncollectible Accounts under each method? How would your answers change if the Allowance for Uncollectible Accounts had begun with a credit balance of $3,400 instead of a debit balance?

Exercise 7-7. Accounts Receivable Transactions *(L.O. 3)*

Assuming that the allowance method is being used, prepare journal entries to record the following transactions:

May 17, 19x8	Sold merchandise to Holly Fox for $900, terms n/10.
Sept. 20, 19x8	Received $300 from Holly Fox on account.
June 25, 19x9	Wrote off as uncollectible the balance of the Holly Fox account when she was declared bankrupt.
July 27, 19x9	Unexpectedly received a check for $100 from Holly Fox.

Exercise 7-8. Credit Card Sales Transactions *(L.O. 4)*

Prepare journal entries to record the following transactions for Maggie's Specialty Shop:

Dec. 4 A tabulation of invoices at the end of the day showed $1,100 in American Express invoices and $600 in Diners Club invoices. American Express takes a discount of 4 percent, and Diners Club takes a 5 percent discount.

8 Received payment from American Express at 96 percent of face value and from Diners Club at 95 percent of face value.

9 A tabulation of invoices at the end of the day showed $400 in VISA invoices, which are deposited in a special bank account at full value less 5 percent discount.

Exercise 7-9. Interest Computations *(L.O. 5)*

Determine the interest on the following notes:

a. $11,400 at 10 percent for 90 days
b. $8,000 at 12 percent for 60 days
c. $9,000 at 9 percent for 30 days
d. $15,000 at 15 percent for 120 days
e. $5,400 at 6 percent for 60 days

Exercise 7-10. Discounting Notes *(L.O. 5)*

In an effort to raise cash, Chao Company discounted two notes at the bank on September 15. The bank charged a discount rate of 15 percent applied to the maturity value. Compute the proceeds from discounting of each of the following notes:

Date of Note	Amount	Interest Rate	Life of Note
a. Aug. 1	$ 9,500	10	120 days
b. July 20	$18,000	12	90 days

Exercise 7-11. Notes Receivable Transactions *(L.O. 6)*

Prepare general journal entries to record the following transactions:

Jan. 16 Sold merchandise to Brighton Corporation on account for $36,000, terms n/30.

Feb. 15 Accepted a $36,000, 10 percent, 90-day note from Brighton Corporation in lieu of payment on account.

Mar. 17 Discounted Brighton Corporation note at bank at 12 percent.

May 16 Received notice that Brighton dishonored the note. Paid the bank the maturity value of the note plus a protest fee of $15.

June 15 Received payment in full from Brighton Corporation, including interest at 10 percent from the date the note was dishonored.

Exercise 7-12. Adjusting Entries: Interest Expense *(L.O. 6)*

Prepare journal entries (assuming reversing entries were not made) to record the following:

Dec. 1 Received a 90-day, 12 percent note for $5,000 from a customer for a sale of merchandise.

31 Made end-of-year adjustment for interest income.

Mar. 1 Received payment in full for note and interest.

Exercise 7-13. Comprehensive Notes Receivable Transactions *(L.O. 6)*

Prepare general journal entries to record these transactions:

Jan.	5	Accepted a $2,400, 60-day, 10 percent note dated this day in granting a time extension on the past-due account of A. Jones.
Mar.	6	A. Jones paid the maturity value of his $2,400 note.
	9	Accepted a $1,500, 60-day, 12 percent note dated this day in granting a time extension on the past-due account of S. Smith.
May	8	S. Smith dishonored his note when presented for payment.
	12	Accepted a $1,800, 90-day, 12 percent note in granting a time extension on the past-due account of R. Johnson.
	16	Discounted the R. Johnson note at the bank at 15 percent.
Aug.	14	Since notice protesting the R. Johnson note had not been received, assumed that it had been paid.
	14	Accepted a $1,200, 60-day, 10 percent note dated August 14 in granting a time extension on the past-due account of E. Cummings.
Sept.	6	Discounted the E. Cummings note at the bank at 15 percent.
Oct.	13	Received notice protesting the E. Cummings note. Paid the bank the maturity value of the note plus a $20 protest fee.
	14	Accepted a $3,000, 60-day, 12 percent note dated this day from J. Carlos in granting a time extension on his past-due account.
Nov.	13	Discounted the J. Carlos note at the bank at 15 percent.
Dec.	14	Received notice protesting the J. Carlos note. Paid the bank the maturity value of the note plus a $20 protest fee.
	25	Received payment from J. Carlos of the maturity value of his dishonored note, the protest fee, and the interest on both for 12 days beyond maturity at 15 percent.
	31	Wrote off the account of S. Smith against the allowance for uncollectible accounts.

Exercise 7-14. Bank Reconciliation *(L.O. 7)*

Prepare a bank reconciliation from the following information:

a. Balance per bank statement as of May 31, $4,227.27
b. Balance per books as of May 31, $3,069.02
c. Deposits in transit, $567.21
d. Outstanding checks, $1,727.96
e. Bank service charge, $2.50

Exercise 7-15. Bank Reconciliation: Missing Data *(L.O. 7)*

Compute the correct amount to replace each letter in the following table:

Balance per bank statement	$ a	$8,900	$315	$1,990
Deposits in transit	600	b	50	125
Outstanding checks	1,500	1,000	c	75
Balance per books	3,450	9,400	225	d

Exercise 7-16. Collection of Note by Bank *(L.O. 7)*

Nicks Corporation received a notice with its bank statement that the bank had collected a note for $2,000.00 plus $10.00 interest from R. Maggio and credited Nicks Corporation's account for the total less a collection charge of $15.00.

Explain the effect that these items have on the bank reconciliation. Prepare a general journal entry to record the information on the books.

Exercise 7-17.
Petty Cash Entries
(L.O. 8)

The petty cash fund of Martinez Company appeared as follows on December 31, 19xx (the end of the accounting period):

Cash on Hand		$ 61.23
Petty Cash vouchers		
Freight In	$22.86	
Postage	21.19	
Flowers for a sick employee	18.50	
Office Supplies	26.22	88.77
Total		$150.00

Because there is cash on hand, is there a need to replenish the petty cash fund on December 31? Explain. Prepare in general journal form an entry to replenish the fund.

Exercise 7-18.
Petty Cash Transactions
(L.O. 8)

A small company maintains a petty cash fund for minor expenditures. The following transactions occurred:

a. The fund was established in the amount of $100.00 on September 1 from the proceeds of check no. 2707.
b. On September 30, the petty cash fund had cash of $15.46 and the following receipts on hand: postage, $40.00; supplies, $24.94; delivery service, $12.40; and rubber stamp, $7.20. Check no. 2778 was drawn to replenish the fund.
c. On October 31, the petty cash fund had cash of $22.06 and the following receipts on hand: postage, $34.20; supplies, $32.84; and delivery service, $6.40. The petty cash custodian could not account for the shortage. Check no. 2847 was written to replenish the fund.

Prepare the general journal entries necessary to record each transaction.

Interpretation Cases from Business

ICB 7-1.
Winton Sharrer Co.
(L.O. 3)

Winton Sharrer Co. is a major consumer goods company that sells over 3,000 products in 135 countries. From the company's annual report to the Securities and Exchange Commission, data pertaining to net sales and accounts related to accounts receivable for 1989, 1990, and 1991 were as follows (in thousands):

	1991	1990	1989
Net Sales	$4,910,000	$4,865,000	$4,888,000
Accounts Receivable	523,000	524,000	504,000
Allowance for Doubtful Accounts	18,600	21,200	24,500
Uncollectible Accounts Expense	15,000	16,700	15,800
Uncollectible Accounts Written Off	19,300	20,100	17,700
Recoveries of Accounts Previously Written Off	1,700	100	1,000

Required

1. Compute the ratios of Uncollectible Accounts Expense to Net Sales and to Accounts Receivable and of the Allowance for Doubtful Accounts to Accounts Receivable for 1989, 1990, and 1991. What appears to be management's attitude with respect to the collectibility of accounts receivable over the three-year period?

2. Make the general journal entries for 1991 related to the Allowance for Doubtful Accounts and to recoveries of accounts previously written off.

ICB 7-2.
AmeriBank
(L.O. 2, 3, 5)

AmeriBank is a large banking and financial institution with branches throughout the world. The following data about AmeriBank's loans and lease financing come from its 1990 and 1991 annual reports.

(in millions of dollars)	December 31, 1991	December 31, 1990
Loans and Lease Financing, Net (Notes 2, 3, and 4)		
Consumer (Net of unearned discount of $3,674 in 1991 and $4,154 in 1990)	$ 78,959	$ 68,243
Commercial (Net of unearned discount of $598 in 1991 and $467 in 1990)	55,754	59,439
Lease Financing	3,372	3,222
Loan and Lease Financing, Net of Unearned Discount	$138,085	$130,904
Allowance for Possible Credit Losses	(4,618)	(1,698)
Total Loans and Lease Financing, Net	$133,467	$129,206

The following additional data come from Note 4 of the same report:

4. Changes in the Allowance for Possible Credit Losses

(in millions of dollars)	1991	1990
Balance at Beginning of Year	$1,698	**$1,235**
Deductions		
Consumer loan and lease losses	$1,271	**$1,172**
Consumer loan and lease recoveries	(247)	**(214)**
Net consumer loan and lease losses	$1,024	**$ 958**
Commercial loan and lease losses	$ 617	**$ 489**
Commercial loan and lease recoveries	(144)	**(76)**
Net commercial loan and lease losses	$ 473	**$ 413**
Additions		
Provision for possible credit losses	$4,410	**$1,825**
Other (Principally from allowance balances of acquired companies and translation of overseas allowance balances)	7	**9**
Balance at End of Year	$4,618	**$1,698**

Required

1. Does AmeriBank experience a higher loss rate for commercial loans or for consumer loans? Has AmeriBank's loss experience improved from 1990 to 1991? **Hint:** Compute the ratio of net consumer loan and lease losses to consumer loans and the ratio of net commercial loans and lease losses to commercial loans for both years. Ignore the effects of lease financing as immaterial.
2. Has AmeriBank's expectation about overall future losses become more optimistic or more pessimistic from 1990 to 1991? **Hint:** Calculate the ratio of the Allowance for Possible Credit Losses to Loans and Lease Financing, net of unearned discount, for both years.
3. Prepare the general journal entries for 1991 to record the losses and recoveries for commercial loans and leases and consumer loans and leases and the provision for possible credit losses.
4. Both the consumer and commercial loans are listed as net of unearned discount. What is an unearned discount? Assuming that AmeriBank made a ninety-day commercial loan with a maturity value of $1,200 at an annual discount rate of 12 percent, how would the entry be recorded? What entry would be made when the loan is collected in full?

ICB 7-3. Chrysler Corporation[10]
(L.O. 1, 2)

The automobile industry, especially Chrysler Corporation, had difficult financial problems in the early 1980s. Chrysler incurred operating losses of over $1 billion in both 1979 and 1980. At that time it received U.S. government loan guarantees of $1 billion and more. Chrysler's short-term liquid assets for 1979 and 1980 were presented in its annual report as follows (in millions of dollars):

	1980	1979
Cash	$101.1	$ 188.2
Time Deposits	2.6	120.8
Marketable Securities—at lower of cost or market	193.6	165.3
Accounts Receivable (less allowance for doubtful accounts: 1980—$40.3 million; 1979—$34.9 million)	476.2	610.3
Total Short-Term Liquid Assets	$773.5	$1,084.6

The company also reported current liabilities of $3,231.6 million in 1979 and $3,029.3 million in 1980. Sales totaled $12,001.9 million in 1979 and $9,225.3 million in 1980. In management's discussion and analysis of financial conditions and results of operations, it was noted that "Chrysler had to defer paying its major suppliers until it received the proceeds from the additional $400 million of federally guaranteed debt. Chrysler's liquidity and its long-term viability are predicated on a return to sustained profitable operations."

Epilogue: At the end of 1983, Lee A. Iacocca, chief executive officer of Chrysler, could state in the annual report, "We repaid the $1.2 billion in loans guaranteed by the Federal Government. This action was taken seven years early." At the end of 1983, Chrysler had total short-term liquid assets of $1,360.6 mil-

10. Excerpts from the 1980, 1983 and 1990 Annual Reports used by permission of Chrysler Corporation. Copyright © 1980, 1983, and 1990.

lion, consisting of Cash and Time Deposits of $111.6 million; Marketable Securities of $957.8 million; and Accounts Receivable (less allowance for uncollectible accounts of $25.5 million) of $291.2. Current liabilities were $3,453.9 million, and sales for 1983 were $13,240.4 million. By 1990, short-term liquid assets were $3,597 million, consisting of Cash and Time Deposits of $1,491 million, Marketable Securities of $1,473 million, and Accounts Receivable of $633 million. Current liabilities were $7,096 million, and sales for 1990 were $26,965 million. For comparison purposes, 1990 figures are shown for Chrysler operations without the finance and rental subsidiaries included. A separate allowance for uncollectible accounts was not disclosed for Chrysler operations.

Required

1. Compute Chrysler's ratio of short-term liquid assets to current liabilities for 1979 and 1980. Did Chrysler's short-term liquidity position improve or deteriorate from 1979 to 1980? What apparent effect did the 1980 federally guaranteed loan of $400 million have on the balance sheet and on the liquidity position?
2. It is important to Chrysler's survival that its customers pay their debts, and pay them on time. Compute for 1979 and 1980 the ratio of the allowance for doubtful accounts to *gross* accounts receivable and the ratio of *net* accounts receivable to sales. What can you conclude from these computations about Chrysler's ability to collect from its customers?
3. Compute for 1983 the three ratios you computed in questions **1** and **2** for 1979 and 1980; for 1990, compute the first and third ratios. Comment on Chrysler's situation in 1983 and 1990 compared to 1979–1980.

Problem Set A

Problem 7A-1. Percentage of Net Sales Method *(L.O. 3)*

Chappell Company had an Accounts Receivable balance of $320,000 and a credit balance in the Allowance for Uncollectible Accounts of $16,700 at January 1, 19xx. During the year, the company recorded the following transactions:

a. Sales on account, $1,052,000.
b. Sales returns and allowances by credit customers, $53,400.
c. Collections from customers, $993,000.
d. Worthless accounts written off, $19,800.
e. Written-off accounts collected, $4,200.

The company's past history indicates that, in addition, 2.5 percent of net credit sales will not be collected.

Required

1. Open ledger accounts for the Accounts Receivable controlling account (112) and the Allowance for Uncollectible Accounts (113). Then enter the beginning balances in these accounts.
2. Record a single general journal entry for each of the five items listed above, summarizing the year's activity.
3. Record the general journal entry on December 31 for the estimated uncollectible accounts expense for the year.
4. Post the appropriate parts of the transactions in **2** and **3** to Accounts Receivable and the Allowance for Uncollectible Accounts.

Problem 7A-2. Accounts Receivable Aging Method
(L.O. 3)

The DiPalma Jewelry Store uses the accounts receivable aging method to estimate uncollectible accounts. The balances of Accounts Receivable and Allowance for Uncollectible Accounts were $446,341 and $43,000, respectively, at February 1, 19x1. During the year, the store had sales on account of $3,724,000, sales returns and allowances of $63,000, worthless accounts written off of $44,300, and collections from customers of $3,214,000. As part of end-of-year (January 31, 19x2) procedures, an aging analysis of accounts receivable is prepared. The analysis is partially complete. The totals of the analysis appear below.

Customer Account	Total	Not Yet Due	1–30 Days Past Due	31–60 Days Past Due	61–90 Days Past Due	Over 90 Days Past Due
Balance Forward	$793,791	$438,933	$149,614	$106,400	$57,442	$41,402

The following accounts remain to be classified in order to finish the analysis:

Account	Amount	Due Date
H. Caldwell	$10,977	January 15
D. Carlson	9,314	February 15 (next fiscal year)
M. Guokas	8,664	December 20
F. Javier	780	October 1
B. Loo	14,810	January 4
S. Qadri	6,316	November 15
A. Rosenthal	4,389	March 1 (next fiscal year)
	$55,250	

From past experience, the company has found that the following rates for estimating uncollectible accounts produce an adequate balance for the Allowance for Uncollectible Accounts:

Time Past Due	Percentage Considered Uncollectible
Not yet due	2
1–30 days	5
31–60 days	15
61–90 days	25
Over 90 days	50

Required

1. Complete the aging analysis of accounts receivable.
2. Determine the end-of-year balances (before adjustments) of the Accounts Receivable controlling account and the Allowance for Uncollectible Accounts.
3. Prepare an analysis, computing the estimated uncollectible accounts.
4. Prepare a general journal entry to record the estimated uncollectible accounts expense for the year (round the adjustment to the nearest whole dollar).

Problem 7A-3. Notes Receivable Transactions
(L.O. 5, 6)

Sharman Manufacturing Company sells truck beds to various companies. To improve its liquidity, Sharman discounts any promissory notes it receives. The company engaged in the following transactions involving promissory notes:

Jan. 10 Sold beds to Hudson Company for $30,000, terms n/10.
20 Accepted a 90-day, 12 percent promissory note in settlement of the account from Hudson.
31 Discounted the note from Hudson Company at the bank at 14 percent.
Apr. 20 Having received no notice that the note had been dishonored, assumed Hudson Company paid the bank.
May 5 Sold beds to Monroe Company for $20,000, terms n/10.
15 Received $4,000 cash and a 60-day, 13 percent note for $16,000 in settlement of the Monroe account.
25 Discounted the note from Monroe to the bank at 14 percent.
July 14 Received notice that Monroe dishonored the note. Paid the bank the maturity value of the note plus a protest fee of $20.
Aug. 2 Wrote off the Monroe account as uncollectible after news that the company declared bankruptcy.
5 Received a 90-day, 11 percent note for $15,000 from Circle Company in settlement of an account receivable.
15 Discounted the note from Circle at the bank at 14 percent.
Nov. 3 Received notice that Circle dishonored the note. Paid the bank the maturity value of the note plus a protest fee of $20.
9 Received payment in full from Circle, including 15 percent interest for the 6 days since the note was dishonored.

Required

Prepare general journal entries to record the above transactions.

Problem 7A-4. Notes Receivable Transactions
(L.O. 5, 6)

The Alvarado Company accepts notes as payment for sales to key customers. The transactions involving notes for August and October are presented below.

Aug. 6 Accepted a $9,000, 60-day, 10 percent note from Cronin Company in payment for merchandise.
8 Accepted a $7,000, 60-day, 11 percent note from La Russo's Electronics in payment for merchandise.
13 Discounted the Cronin Company note at the bank at 15 percent.
23 Discounted the La Russo's Electronics note at the bank at 15 percent.
28 Accepted a $21,000, 60-day, 9 percent note from Ramsey Company in payment for merchandise.
30 Accepted a $14,000, 60-day, 12 percent note from Lee Company in payment for merchandise.
Oct. 5 Receiving no notice of dishonor by Cronin Company, assumed Cronin paid its obligation to the bank.
7 Received notice from the bank that La Russo's Electronics dishonored its note. Paid the bank the maturity value plus a protest fee of $18.
27 Ramsey Company paid its note and interest.
29 Lee Company dishonored its note.

Required

Prepare general journal entries to record the above transactions.

Problem 7A-5. Short-Term Financing by Discounting Customers' Notes
(L.O. 5, 6)

The management of Gerrin Lawn Products sells its goods to distributors 120 days before the summer season. Mr. Gerrin has worked out a plan with his bank to finance receivables from sales. The plan calls for the company to receive a 120-day, 10 percent note for each sale to a distributor. Each note will be discounted at the bank at the rate of 12 percent. This plan will provide Gerrin with adequate cash flow to operate his company.

During January and February, Gerrin made the following sales under the plan:

Company	Amount of Note	Date of Note	Discount Date*
Gold Hardware	$460,000	Jan. 7	Jan. 9
Kedzie Stores	820,000	12	15
Howell's Markets	290,000	19	Feb. 18

*Assume 28 days in February

During May, all the distributors paid on their respective due dates except Kedzie Stores, which defaulted on its note. The account was paid in full 30 days late, including additional interest at 9 percent and a bank protest fee of $50.

Required

1. Prepare general journal entries to record Gerrin Lawn Products' transactions (round calculations to nearest dollar) for January 7, 9, 12, 15, 19 and February 18.
2. What was the total amount of cash generated in January by discounting the notes receivable?
3. Prepare general journal entries to record the transactions on Gerrin Lawn Products' records for May 12 and June 11.
4. What is your evaluation of the plan? What risk is management taking?

Problem 7A-6. Bank Reconciliation
(L.O. 7)

The following information is available for Jorge Mendoza Company as of October 31, 19xx.

a. Cash on the books as of October 31 amounted to $21,327.08. Cash on the bank statement for the same date was $26,175.73.
b. A deposit of $2,610.47, representing cash receipts of October 31, did not appear on the bank statement.
c. Outstanding checks totaled $1,968.40.
d. A check for $960.00 returned with the statement was recorded incorrectly in the check register as $690.00. The check was made for a cash purchase of merchandise.
e. Bank service charges for October amounted to $12.50.
f. The bank collected for Jorge Mendoza Company $6,120.00 on a note. The face value of the note was $6,000.00.
g. An NSF check for $91.78 from a customer, Beth Franco, was returned with the statement.
h. The bank mistakenly charged to the company account a check for $425.00 drawn by another company.
i. The bank reported that it had credited the account for $170.00 in interest on the average balance for October.

Required

1. Prepare a bank reconciliation for Jorge Mendoza Company as of October 31, 19xx.
2. Prepare the journal entries necessary to adjust the accounts.
3. State the amount that should appear on the balance sheet as of October 31.

Problem 7A-7. Bank Reconciliation *(L.O. 7)*

The information presented below comes from the records of the Janesville Company:

From the Cash Receipts Journal Page 22

Date	Debit Cash
Feb. 1	1,416
8	14,486
15	13,214
22	10,487
28	7,802
	47,405

From the Cash Payments Journal Page 106

Date	Check Number	Credit Cash
Feb. 1	2076	1,218
3	2077	22
6	2078	6
7	2079	19,400
8	2080	2,620
12	2081	9,135
16	2082	14
17	2083	186
18	2084	5,662
		38,263

From the General Ledger

Cash **Account No. 111**

Date		Item	Post. Ref.	Debit	Credit	Balance Debit	Balance Credit
Jan.	31	Balance				10,570	
Feb.	28		CR22	47,405		57,975	
	28		CP106		38,263	19,712	

The bank statement for Janesville Company is shown on page 387. The NSF check was received from customer T. Lambeth for merchandise. The credit memorandum represents a $1,600 note, plus interest collected by the bank. The February 2 deposit, recorded by Janesville as $1,416 in cash sales, was recorded correctly by the bank as $1,614. On February 1, there were the following outstanding checks: no. 2056 at $510, no. 2072 at $4, no. 2073 at $35, no. 2074 at $1,265, and no. 2075 at $32.

Required

1. Prepare a bank reconciliation as of February 28, 19xx.
2. Prepare journal entries to update the accounts.

3. What amount should appear on the balance sheet for cash as of February 28?

FIRST NATIONAL BANK					Statement of Janesville Company Janesville, OH	
Checks/Debits			Deposits/Credits		Daily Balances	
Posting Date	Check No.	Amount	Posting Date	Amount	Date	Amount
02/02	2056	510.00	02/02	1,614.00	02/01	12,416.00
02/02	2075	32.00	02/09	14,486.00	02/02	13,488.00
02/03	2076	1,218.00	02/12	1,654.00CM	02/03	12,266.00
02/03	2072	4.00	02/16	13,214.00	02/05	12,244.00
02/05	2077	22.00	02/23	10,487.00	02/09	26,730.00
02/10	2079	19,400.00	02/28	101.00IN	02/10	6,065.00
02/10	2074	1,265.00			02/11	3,445.00
02/11	2080	2,620.00			02/12	5,099.00
02/17	2081	9,135.00			02/16	18,313.00
02/17	2082	14.00			02/17	9,164.00
02/18		40.00NSF			02/18	9,124.00
02/24	2084	5,662.00			02/23	19,611.00
02/28		17.00SC			02/24	13,949.00
					02/28	14,033.00

Code: CM–Credit Memo, DM–Debit Memo; IN–Interest, SC–Service Charge; NSF–Non-Sufficient Funds

Problem Set B

Problem 7B-1. Percentage of Net Sales Method *(L.O. 3)*

On December 31 of last year, the balance sheet of Marzano Company had Accounts Receivable of $298,000 and a credit balance in the Allowance for Uncollectible Accounts of $20,300. During the current year, the company's records included the following selected activities: sales on account, $1,195,000; sales returns and allowances, $73,000; collections from customers, $1,150,000; accounts written off as worthless, $16,000; written-off accounts unexpectedly collected, $2,000. In the past, the company had found that 1.6 percent of net sales would not be collected.

Required

1. Open ledger accounts for the Accounts Receivable controlling account (112) and the Allowance for Uncollectible Accounts (113). Then enter the beginning balances in these accounts.
2. Give a single general journal entry to record in summary form each of the five items listed above.
3. Give the general journal entry on December 31 of the current year to record the estimated uncollectible accounts expense for the year.
4. Post the appropriate parts of the transactions in **2** and **3** to these accounts.

Problem 7B-2. Accounts Receivable Aging Method
(L.O. 3)

Pokorny Company uses the accounts receivable aging method to estimate uncollectible accounts. The Accounts Receivable controlling account and the Allowance for Uncollectible Accounts had balances of $88,430 and $7,200, respectively, at the beginning of the year. During the year, the company had sales on account of $473,000, sales returns and allowances of $4,200, worthless accounts written off of $7,900, and collections from customers of $450,730. At the end of the year (December 31), a junior accountant for the company was preparing an aging analysis of accounts receivable. At the top of page 6 of his report, his totals appeared as follows:

Customer Account	Total	Not Yet Due	1–30 Days Past Due	31–60 Days Past Due	61–90 Days Past Due	Over 90 Days Past Due
Balance Forward	$89,640	$49,030	$24,110	$9,210	$3,990	$3,300

He had the following accounts remaining to finish the analysis:

Account	Amount	Due Date
K. Foust	$ 930	Jan. 14 (next year)
K. Groth	620	Dec. 24
R. Mejias	1,955	Sept. 28
C. Polk	2,100	Aug. 16
M. Spears	375	Dec. 14
J. Yong	2,685	Jan. 23 (next year)
A. Zorr	295	Nov. 5
	$8,960	

The company has found from past experience that the following rates of estimated uncollectible accounts produce an adequate balance for the Allowance for Uncollectible Accounts:

Time Past Due	Percentage Considered Uncollectible
Not yet due	2
1–30 days	4
31–60 days	20
61–90 days	30
Over 90 days	50

Required

1. Complete the aging analysis of accounts receivable.
2. Determine the end-of-year balances (before adjustments) of the Accounts Receivable controlling account and the Allowance for Uncollectible Accounts.
3. Prepare an analysis computing the estimated uncollectible accounts.
4. Prepare a general journal entry to record the estimated uncollectible accounts expense for the year. (Round adjustment to the nearest dollar.)

Problem 7B-3. Notes Receivable Transactions *(L.O. 5, 6)*

Hopson Manufacturing Company engaged in the following transactions involving promissory notes:

Jan. 14 Sold merchandise to Barbara Reid Company for $18,500, terms n/30.
Feb. 13 Received $4,200 in cash from Barbara Reid Company and received a 90-day, 8 percent promissory note for the balance of the account.
23 Discounted the note at the bank at 15 percent.
May 14 Because no notice that the note had been dishonored was received, assumed that Barbara Reid Company had paid the bank.
15 Received a 60-day, 12 percent note from Ralph Sarkis Company in payment of a past-due account, $6,000.
30 Discounted the note at the bank at 15 percent.
July 14 Received notice that Ralph Sarkis Company dishonored the note. Paid the bank the maturity value of the note plus a protest fee of $20.
20 Received a check from Ralph Sarkis Company for payment of the maturity value of the note, the $20 protest fee, and interest at 12 percent for the six days beyond maturity.
25 Sold merchandise to James Flowers Company for $18,000, with payment of $3,000 cash down and the remainder on account.
31 Received a $15,000, 45-day, 10 percent promissory note from James Flowers Company for the outstanding account.
Aug. 5 Discounted the note at the bank at 15 percent.
Sept. 14 Received notice that James Flowers Company dishonored the note. Paid the bank the maturity value of the note plus a protest fee of $20.
25 Wrote off the James Flowers Company account as uncollectible following news that the company had been declared bankrupt.

Required

Prepare general journal entries to record the above transactions.

Problem 7B-4. Notes Receivable Transactions *(L.O. 5, 6)*

Roman's Auto Store engaged in the following transactions:

Jan. 2 Accepted a $9,400, 90-day, 14 percent note from Willis Daniels as an extension on his past-due account.
5 Accepted a $2,900, 90-day, 12 percent note from Sharon Kelly in payment of a past-due account receivable.
10 Accepted a $4,500, 90-day, 10 percent note from Charles Suggs as an extension of a past-due account.
12 Discounted Willis Daniels' note at the bank at 14 percent.
25 Discounted Charles Suggs' note at the bank at 14 percent.
30 Accepted a $5,200, 90-day, 12 percent note from Linda Pate in lieu of payment of a past-due account.
Apr. 2 Received notice that Willis Daniels had dishonored his note. Paid the bank the maturity value plus a protest fee of $25.
5 Sharon Kelly dishonored her note.
10 Received no notice of dishonor by Charles Suggs and assumed he paid his obligation to the bank.
22 Received payment from Willis Daniels for the total amount owed including maturity value, protest fee, and interest at 15 percent for the twenty days past maturity.

Apr. 25 Wrote off the Sharon Kelly account as uncollectible because she could not be located.
30 Linda Pate paid her note plus interest in full.

Required

Prepare general journal entries to record the above transactions.

Problem 7B-5. Short-Term Financing by Discounting Customers' Notes
(L.O. 5, 6)

The Ling Company is faced with a severe cash shortage because of slowing sales and past-due accounts. The financial vice president has studied the situation and has found a number of large past-due accounts. He makes the following recommendations: (a) that the company seek promissory notes from past-due accounts to encourage the customers to pay on time and to earn interest on these accounts, and (b) that the company generate cash by discounting the notes at the bank at the going rate of interest. During the first month of this program, the company was successful, as indicated by the following table:

Company	Amount of Note	Length of Note	Date of Note	Interest Rate	Discount Date	Discount Rate
Blue Manufacturing Company	$210,000	60 days	Apr. 5	15%	Apr. 7	15%
Norris Company	170,000	60 days	Apr. 10	12%	Apr. 13	15%
Lazaro Corporation	110,000	60 days	Apr. 15	14%	Apr. 20	15%

Blue Manufacturing Company and Norris Company paid their notes on the due dates. Lazaro Corporation dishonored its note on the due date. The latter note was paid by Ling Company, including a bank protest fee of $50.

Required

1. Prepare appropriate general journal entries for April 5, 7, 10, 13, 15, and 20.
2. What was the total cash generated during April by the vice president's plan?
3. Prepare appropriate general journal entries for June 4, 9, and 14.
4. What is your evaluation of the plan? What offsetting factors occur in later months such as June?

Problem 7B-6. Bank Reconciliation
(L.O. 7)

The following information is available for Pagan Company as of June 30, 19xx:

a. Cash on the books as of June 30 amounted to $56,837.64. Cash on the bank statement for the same date was $70,858.54.
b. A deposit of $7,124.92, representing cash receipts of June 30, did not appear on the bank statement.
c. Outstanding checks totaled $3,646.82.
d. A check for $1,210.00 returned with the statement was recorded in the cash payments journal as $1,012.00. The check was for advertising.
e. Bank service charges for June amounted to $13.00.
f. The bank collected for Pagan Company $18,200.00 on a note left for collection. The face value of the note was $18,000.00.

g. An NSF check for $570.00 from a customer, Louise Bryant, was returned with the statement.
h. The bank mistakenly deducted a check for $400.00 drawn by Sherod Corporation.
i. The bank reported a credit of $480.00 for interest on the average balance.

Required

1. Prepare a bank reconciliation for Pagan Company as of June 30, 19xx.
2. Prepare the journal entries necessary from the reconciliation.
3. State the amount of cash that should appear on the balance sheet as of June 30.

Problem 7B-7. Bank Reconciliation *(L.O. 7)*

The information presented below comes from the records of the Lightman Company:

From the Cash Receipts Journal — Page 9

Date	Debit Cash
Nov. 1	1,828
7	2,024
14	6,480
21	5,292
30	3,884
	19,508

From the Cash Payments Journal — Page 12

Date	Check Number	Credit Cash
Nov. 1	721	28
2	722	566
3	723	832
4	724	54
	725	(voided)
5	726	10
10	727	11,492
11	728	1,418
20	729	2,492
21	730	152
		17,044

From the General Ledger

Cash — Account No. 111

Date		Item	Post. Ref.	Debit	Credit	Balance Debit	Balance Credit
Oct.	31	Balance				4,930	
Nov.	30		CR9	19,508		24,438	
	30		CP12		17,044	7,394	

SHORELINE NATIONAL BANK					Statement of Lightman Company Davis and Wells Streets	
Checks/Debits			Deposits/Credits		Daily Balances	
Posting Date	Check No.	Amount	Posting Date	Amount	Date	Amount
11/02	700	200.00	11/02	1,828.00	11/01	7,570.00
11/02	707	1,000.00	11/08	2,024.00	11/02	8,198.00
11/04	720	920.00	11/15	6,480.00	11/04	7,250.00
11/04	721	28.00	11/22	5,292.00	11/06	6,418.00
11/06	723	832.00	11/26	816.00CM	11/08	8,388.00
11/08	724	54.00	11/30	84.00IN	11/12	8,348.00
11/12	726	10.00			11/14	6,534.00
11/12		30.00NSF			11/15	13,014.00
11/14	728	1,814.00			11/22	18,306.00
11/24	727	11,492.00			11/24	6,814.00
11/26	730	152.00			11/26	7,478.00
11/30		8.00SC			11/30	7,554.00

Code: CM–Credit Memo   IN–Interest   NSF–Non-Sufficient Funds
DM–Debit Memo   SC–Service Charge

The NSF check was received from customer G. Soto for merchandise. The credit memorandum represents an $800 note, plus interest, collected by the bank. Check number 725 was prepared improperly and has been voided. Check number 728 for a purchase of merchandise was incorrectly recorded in the cash payments journal as $1,418 instead of $1,814. On November 1, there were the following outstanding checks: no. 700 at $200, no. 707 at $1,000, no. 719 at $520, and no. 720 at $920.

Required

1. Prepare a bank reconciliation as of November 30, 19xx.
2. Prepare the general journal entries.
3. What amount should appear on the balance sheet for cash as of November 30?

Financial Decision Cases

7-1. Golina Christmas Tree Company *(L.O. 1)*

Golina Christmas Tree Company engages in a seasonal business, the growing and selling of Christmas trees. By January 1, after a successful season, the company has cash on hand that will not be needed for several months. The company has minimal expenses from January to October and heavy expenses during the harvest and shipping months of November and December. The company's management follows the practice of investing the idle cash in marketable securities, which can be sold as the funds are needed for operations. The company's fiscal year ends on June 30. On January 10 of the current year the company has cash of $372,800 on hand. It keeps $20,000 on hand for operating expenses and invests the rest as follows:

$100,000 3-month Treasury bill	$ 97,800
1,000 shares of Ford Motor Co. ($40 per share)	40,000
2,500 shares of McDonald's ($40 per share)	100,000
1,000 shares of IBM ($115 per share)	115,000
Total of short-term investments	$352,800

During the next few months the company receives quarterly cash dividends of $.75 per share from Ford, $.085 from McDonald's, and $1.20 from IBM twice from each company (assume February 10 and May 10). The Treasury bill is redeemed at face value on April 10. On June 1 management sells 500 shares of McDonald's at $45 per share. On June 30 the market values of the investments are as follows:

Ford Motor Co.	$ 51 per share
McDonald's	$ 36 per share
IBM	$105 per share

Another quarterly dividend is received from each company (assume August 10). All the remaining shares are sold on November 1 at the following prices:

Ford Motor Co.	$ 45 per share
McDonald's	$ 34 per share
IBM	$126 per share

Required

1. Record the investment transactions that occurred on January 10, February 10, April 10, May 10, and June 1. Prepare the required adjusting entry on June 30, and record the investment transactions on August 10 and November 1.
2. How would the short-term investments be shown on the balance sheet on June 30?
3. After November 1, what is the balance of the account called Allowance to Reduce Short-Term Investments to Market, and what will happen to this account next June?
4. What is your assessment of Golina Christmas Tree Company's strategy with regard to idle cash?

7-2. Elliot Electronics, Inc. *(L.O. 1, 2)*

Two years ago Mark and Prudence Elliot began Elliot Electronics, Inc. on a shoestring budget. Hard work and personal attention have brought success to their business, which sells television sets, VCRs, and other electronic entertainment devices. However, because of insufficient funds to finance credit sales, they have accepted only cash and bank credit cards. They are now considering a new policy of offering installment sales on terms of 25 percent down and 25 percent per month for three months, as well as continuing to accept cash and bank credit cards. They feel that this policy will boost sales greatly during the coming fall season. But to follow through on the new policy, they will need a bank loan. To apply for the loan, they must make financial projections showing the effects of the new policy.

The Elliots project sales for the last third of 19xx as follows:

September	October	November	December
$30,000	$50,000	$80,000	$100,000

They also expect 20 percent of sales to be for cash; 30 percent to be by credit card, on which a 5 percent fee is paid; and 50 percent to be on installment sales.

The Elliots have a financial agreement with their suppliers that requires them to buy and pay for their inventory in the month that they sell the items. This arrangement is called buying on consignment. Part of the Elliots' success has stemmed from their policy of selling at a discount price. They set the price at one-third above cost. (In other words, cost equals 75 percent of selling price.) This price is lower than that charged by most retail stores, and they intend to continue this policy. The Elliots feel that other costs associated with the new policy will increase cash outlays for operating expenses to $7,000 per month.

Required

1. Prepare a schedule that shows the impact of the new credit policy on cash receipts and payments for each of the four months. How much money in total will the Elliots need to borrow by December 31 to finance the new credit policy?
2. What will the level of accounts receivable be on December 31 if the Elliots' projections are met? What factors have they ignored? How would you change their projections to make them more realistic? What technique would you apply to accounts receivable at the end of each month to determine whether the assumptions about collectibility are being met?

LEARNING OBJECTIVES

1. *Define* merchandise inventory, *and show how inventory measurement affects income determination.*
2. *Define* inventory cost, *and relate it to goods flow and cost flow.*
3. *Calculate the pricing of inventory, using the cost basis according to the (a) specific identification method; (b) average-cost method; (c) first-in, first-out (FIFO) method; (d) last-in, first-out (LIFO) method.*
4. *State the effects of each method on income determination and income taxes in periods of changing prices.*
5. *Apply the perpetual inventory system to accounting for inventories and cost of goods sold.*
6. *Apply the lower-of-cost-or-market rule to inventory valuation.*
7. *Estimate the cost of ending inventory using (a) the retail inventory method and (b) the gross profit method.*

CHAPTER 8

Inventories

The major source of revenues for retail and wholesale businesses is the sale of merchandise. In terms of dollars, the inventory of goods held for sale is one of the largest assets of a merchandising business. The cost of goods sold is the largest deduction from sales because merchandise is continually bought and sold by these companies. In fact, this cost is often larger than the total of other expenses. Inventories are also important to manufacturing companies. These companies have three kinds of inventory: raw materials to be used in making products, partly complete products (often called work in process), and finished goods ready for sale. Figure 8-1 illustrates the importance of inventory as an asset to the merchandising and manufacturing industries (service business examples are omitted because these businesses do not have inventories for sale). The ratio varies from a low of 21.2 percent for pharmaceutical companies to a high of 42.5 percent for auto and home supply stores. This chapter deals with inventory measurement, emphasizing its importance to income determination and explaining several different ways of determining, valuing, and estimating inventories. Although the examples used in this chapter mostly relate to merchandising businesses, the concepts and techniques are also applicable to manufacturing companies. After studying this chapter, you should be able to meet the learning objectives listed on the left.

Assets may be divided into two categories. There are financial assets, such as those studied in the chapter on short-term liquid assets, including cash, short-term investments, accounts receivable, and notes receivable. These assets represent a right to cash or can be easily converted into cash. The second type of asset represents an unexpired cost that has not yet been matched against revenues. Among these assets are prepaid expenses; inventories; property, plant, and equipment; natural resources; and intangibles.

DECISION POINT
Amoco Corporation[1] *(Part 1)*

The most important accounting issue faced by management in connection with the second type of assets is how to apply

1. Excerpts from the 1989 Annual Report are reprinted with permission of Amoco Corporation.

the matching rule for the purpose of measuring income. In applying the matching rule, two important questions must be answered: (1) How much of the asset is used up or has expired during the current accounting period and should be shown as an expense on the income statement? (2) How much of the asset is still unused or unexpired and should remain on the balance sheet as an asset? These accounting issues are particularly important to companies like Amoco Corporation, one of the largest companies in the world. This leading petroleum and chemical company has huge investments in inventories, prepaid expenses, and long-term assets. In 1989, Amoco had more than $24 billion invested in these assets. Variations in the application of the matching rule to these assets can have an effect of $1 billion or more in any one year on Amoco's net income, which totaled $1.6 billion in 1989. In this chapter you learn to apply the matching rule to inventories. Later you will learn to apply the matching rule to long-term assets, including property, plant, and equipment; natural resources; and intangibles. ■

Inventories and Income Determination

OBJECTIVE 1 *Define* merchandise inventory, *and show how inventory measurement affects income determination*

Merchandise inventory consists of all goods that are owned and held for sale in the regular course of business, including goods in transit. Because it will normally be converted into cash within a year's time, merchandise inventory is considered a current asset. It is shown on the balance sheet just below Accounts Receivable because it is less liquid.

The American Institute of Certified Public Accountants states, "A major objective of accounting for inventories is the proper determination of income through the process of matching appropriate costs against reve-

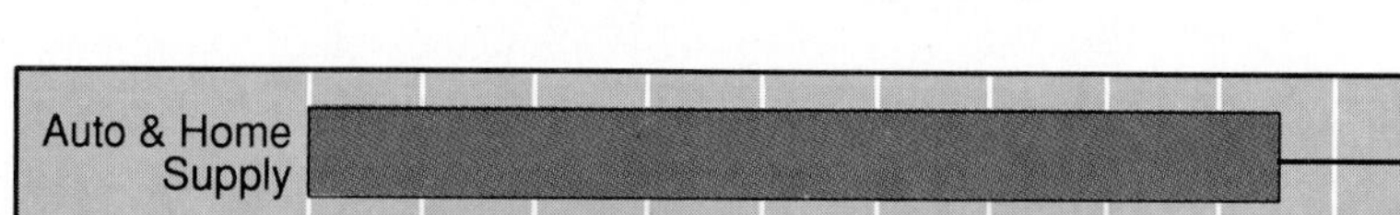

Figure 8-1. Inventory as a Percentage of Total Assets in Selected Industries

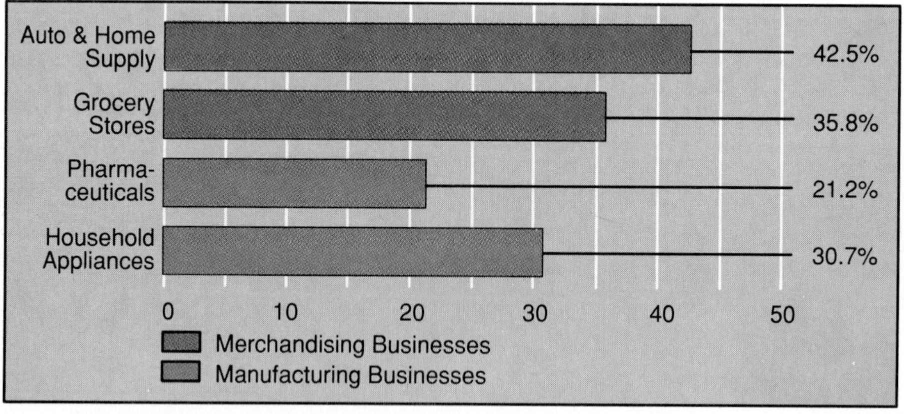

Source: Data from Dun and Bradstreet, *Industry Norms and Ratios*, 1990–91.

nues."[2] Note that the objective is to determine the best measure of income, not the most realistic inventory value. As you will see, the two objectives are sometimes incompatible, in which case the objective of income determination takes precedence over a realistic inventory figure for the balance sheet.

Review of Gross Margin and Cost of Goods Sold Computations

A review should show how the cost assigned to inventory is related to the computations of gross margin and cost of goods sold. The gross margin on sales is computed by deducting cost of goods sold from the net sales for the period. Cost of goods sold is measured by deducting ending inventory from cost of goods available for sale. Because of these relationships, the higher the cost of ending inventory, the lower the cost of goods sold will be and the higher the resulting gross margin. Conversely, the lower the value assigned to ending inventory, the higher the cost of goods sold will be and the lower the gross margin. *In effect, the value assigned to the ending inventory determines what portion of the cost of goods originally available for sale will be deducted from net sales as cost of goods sold and what portion will be carried to the next period as beginning inventory.* Remember that the amount of goods available for sale includes the beginning inventory (unexpired costs passed from the last period to this period) plus net purchases during this period. The effects on income of errors in the cost of ending inventory are demonstrated in the next section.

Effects of Errors in Inventory Measurement

As seen above, the basic problem of separating goods available for sale into the two components, goods sold and goods not sold, is that of assigning a cost to the goods not sold, the ending inventory. This, in turn, determines the cost of goods sold because whatever portion of the cost of goods available for sale is assigned to the ending inventory, the remainder is cost of goods sold.

For this reason, an error in determining the inventory figure at the end of the period will cause an equal error in gross margin and net income in the income statement. The amounts of assets and owners' equity in the balance sheet will also be misstated by the same amount. The consequences of overstatement and understatement of inventory are illustrated in the following three simplified examples. In each case, beginning inventory, purchases, and cost of goods available for sale are correctly stated. In the first example, ending inventory has been stated correctly. In the second example, ending inventory is overstated by $6,000, and in the third example, ending inventory is understated by $6,000.

2. American Institute of Certified Public Accountants, *Accounting Research Bulletin No. 43* (New York: AICPA, 1953), Ch. 4.

Example 1. Ending Inventory Correctly Stated at $10,000

Cost of Goods Sold for the Year		Income Statement for the Year	
Beginning Inventory	$12,000	Net Sales	$100,000
Net Purchases	58,000	Cost of Goods Sold	60,000
Cost of Goods Available for Sale	$70,000	Gross Margin from Sales	$ 40,000
Ending Inventory	10,000	Operating Expenses	32,000
Cost of Goods Sold	$60,000	Net Income	$ 8,000

Example 2. Ending Inventory Overstated by $6,000

Cost of Goods Sold for the Year		Income Statement for the Year	
Beginning Inventory	$12,000	Net Sales	$100,000
Net Purchases	58,000	Cost of Goods Sold	54,000
Cost of Goods Available for Sale	$70,000	Gross Margin from Sales	$ 46,000
Ending Inventory	16,000	Operating Expenses	32,000
Cost of Goods Sold	$54,000	Net Income	$ 14,000

Example 3. Ending Inventory Understated by $6,000

Cost of Goods Sold for the Year		Income Statement for the Year	
Beginning Inventory	$12,000	Net Sales	$100,000
Net Purchases	58,000	Cost of Goods Sold	66,000
Cost of Goods Available for Sale	$70,000	Gross Margin from Sales	$ 34,000
Ending Inventory	4,000	Operating Expenses	32,000
Cost of Goods Sold	$66,000	Net Income	$ 2,000

In these examples, the total cost of goods available for sale amounted to $70,000 in each case. The difference in net income resulted from how this $70,000 was divided between ending inventory and cost of goods sold.

Because the ending inventory in one period becomes the beginning inventory in the following period, it is important to recognize that an error in inventory valuation affects not only the current period but also the following period. Using the same figures as Examples **1** and **2** above, the income statements for two successive years in Exhibit 8-1 illustrate this carryover effect.

Exhibit 8-1. Effect of Error in Ending Inventory on Current and Succeeding Year

Effect of Error in Inventory
Income Statement
For the Year Ended December 31, 19x1

	Correct Statement of Ending Inventory		Overstatement of Ending Inventory	
Net Sales		$100,000		$100,000
Cost of Goods Sold				
Beginning Inventory, Jan. 1, 19x1	$12,000		$12,000	
Net Purchases	58,000		58,000	
Cost of Goods Available for Sale	$70,000		$70,000	
Less Ending Inventory, Dec. 31, 19x1	10,000		16,000	
Cost of Goods Sold		60,000		54,000
Gross Margin from Sales		$ 40,000		$ 46,000
Operating Expenses		32,000		32,000
Net Income		$ 8,000		$ 14,000

Effect on Succeeding Year
Income Statement
For the Year Ended December 31, 19x2

	Correct Statement of Beginning Inventory		Overstatement of Beginning Inventory	
Net Sales		$130,000		$130,000
Cost of Goods Sold				
Beginning Inventory, Jan. 1, 19x2	$10,000		$16,000	
Net Purchases	68,000		68,000	
Cost of Goods Available for Sale	$78,000		$84,000	
Less Ending Inventory, Dec. 31, 19x2	13,000		13,000	
Cost of Goods Sold		65,000		71,000
Gross Margin from Sales		$ 65,000		$ 59,000
Operating Expenses		50,000		50,000
Net Income		$ 15,000		$ 9,000

Note that over a period of two years the errors in net income will offset or counterbalance each other. In Exhibit 8-1, for example, the overstatement of ending inventory in 19x1 caused a $6,000 overstatement of beginning inventory in the following year, resulting in an understatement of income by $6,000 in the second year. This offsetting effect is shown as follows:

	With Inventory Correctly Stated	With Inventory at Dec. 31, 19x1 Overstated	
		Reported Net Income Will Be	Reported Net Income Will Be Overstated (Understated)
Net Income for 19x1	$ 8,000	$14,000	$ 6,000
Net Income for 19x2	15,000	9,000	(6,000)
Total Net Income for Two Years	$23,000	$23,000	—

Because the total income for the two years is the same, there may be a tendency to think that one does not need to worry about inventory errors. This idea is not correct because it violates the matching rule and because many management decisions as well as creditor and investor decisions are made on an annual basis and depend on the accountant's determination of net income. The accountant has an obligation to make the net income figure for each year as useful as possible.

The effects of errors in inventory on net income are as follows:

Year 1	Year 2
Ending Inventory overstated	**Beginning Inventory overstated**
Cost of Goods Sold understated	Cost of Goods Sold overstated
Net Income overstated	Net Income understated
Ending Inventory understated	**Beginning Inventory understated**
Cost of Goods Sold overstated	Cost of Goods Sold understated
Net Income understated	Net Income overstated

If we assume no income tax effects, a change or error in inventory results in a change or error in net income of the same amount. Thus, the measurement of inventory is an important problem and is the subject of the remainder of this chapter.

Inventory Measurement

The cost assigned to ending inventory depends on two measurements: quantity and price. At least once each year, a business must take an actual physical count of all items of merchandise held for sale. This process is called taking a physical inventory, or simply taking inventory, as described in the chapter on accounting for merchandising operations. Although companies may take inventory at other times during the year, most companies take inventory only at the end of each year. Taking the inventory consists of (1) counting, weighing, or measuring the items on hand, (2) pricing each item, and (3) extending (multiplying) to determine the total cost.

Merchandise in Transit

Because merchandise inventory includes items owned by the company and held for sale, purchased merchandise in transit should be included in the inventory count if title to the goods has passed. As explained in the chapter on accounting for merchandising operations, the terms of the shipping agreement must be examined to determine whether title has passed. For example, outgoing goods shipped FOB destination would be included in merchandise inventory, whereas those shipped FOB shipping point would not. Conversely, incoming goods shipped FOB shipping point would be included in merchandise inventory, but those shipped FOB destination would not.

Merchandise on Hand Not Included in Inventory

At the time a physical inventory is taken, there may be merchandise on hand to which the company does not hold title. One category of such goods is an order for a customer on which the sale is completed and the goods in question now belong to the buyer and await delivery. This sale should be recorded and the goods segregated for delivery. A second category is goods held on consignment. A **consignment** is the placing of goods by the owner of the goods (known as the *consignor*) on the premises of another company (the *consignee*). Title to consigned goods remains with the consignor until the consignee sells the goods. Thus, if consigned goods are on hand, they should not be included in the physical inventory because they still belong to the consignor.

Pricing the Inventory at Cost

OBJECTIVE 2
Define inventory cost, *and relate it to goods flow and cost flow*

The pricing of inventory is one of the most interesting and most widely debated problems in accounting. As demonstrated, the value placed on ending inventory may have a dramatic effect on net income for each of two consecutive years. Federal income taxes are based on income, so the valuation of inventory can also have a considerable effect on the income taxes to be paid. Federal income tax authorities have, therefore, been interested in the effects of various inventory valuation procedures and have specific regulations about the acceptability of different methods. So the accountant is sometimes faced with the problem of balancing the goals of proper income determination with those of minimizing income taxes.

There are a number of acceptable methods of valuing inventories on the financial statements. Most are based either on cost or on the lower of cost or market. Both methods are acceptable for income tax purposes. We will first explain variations of the cost basis of inventory valuation and then turn to the lower-of-cost-or-market method.

Cost Defined

According to the AICPA, "The primary basis of accounting for inventories is cost, which has been defined generally as the price paid or consideration given to acquire an asset."[3] This definition of **inventory cost** has

3. Ibid.

generally been interpreted to include the following costs: (1) invoice price less purchases discounts; (2) freight or transportation in, including insurance in transit; and (3) applicable taxes and tariffs. Other costs, such as those for purchasing, receiving, and storing, should in principle also be included in inventory cost. In practice, however, it is so hard to allocate these costs to specific inventory items that they are usually considered an expense of the accounting period instead of an inventory cost.

Methods of Pricing Inventory at Cost

The prices of most kinds of merchandise vary during the year. Identical lots of merchandise may have been purchased at different prices. Also, when identical items are bought and sold, it is often impossible to tell which have been sold and which are still in inventory. For this reason, it is necessary to make an assumption about the order in which items have been sold. Because the assumed order of sale may or may not be the same as the actual order of sale, the assumption is really an assumption about the *flow of costs* rather than the *flow of physical inventory.*

Thus, the term **goods flow** refers to the actual physical movement of goods in the operations of the company, and the term **cost flow** refers to the association of costs with their *assumed* flow in the operations of the company. The assumed cost flow may or may not be the same as the actual goods flow. Though this statement may seem strange at first, there is nothing wrong with it. Several assumed cost flows are available under generally accepted accounting principles. In fact, it is sometimes preferable to use an assumed cost flow that bears no relationship to goods flow because it gives a better estimate of income, which, as stated earlier, is the major goal of inventory valuation.

Accountants usually price inventory by using one of the following generally accepted methods, each based on a different assumption of cost flow: (1) specific identification method; (2) average-cost method; (3) first-in, first-out method (FIFO); and (4) last-in, first-out method (LIFO).

To illustrate the four methods, the following data for the month of June will be used:

Inventory Data, June 30

June 1	Inventory	50 units @ $1.00	$ 50
6	Purchased	50 units @ $1.10	55
13	Purchased	150 units @ $1.20	180
20	Purchased	100 units @ $1.30	130
25	Purchased	150 units @ $1.40	210
Goods Available for Sale		500 units	$625
Sales		280 units	
On hand June 30		220 units	

Note that the total available for sale is 500 units, at a total cost of $625. Stated simply, the problem of inventory pricing is to divide the $625 between the 280 units sold and the 220 units on hand.

OBJECTIVE 3a
Calculate the pricing of inventory, using the cost basis according to the specific identification method

Specific Identification Method. If the units in the ending inventory can be identified as coming from specific purchases, the **specific identification method** may be used to price the inventories. For instance, assume that the June 30 inventory consisted of 50 units from the inventory on hand June 1, 100 units of the purchase of June 13, and 70 units of the purchase of June 25. The cost to be assigned to the inventory under the specific identification method would be $268, and it can be determined as follows:

Inventory, June 30—Specific Identification Method

50 units @ $1.00	$ 50	Cost of Goods Available for Sale	$625
100 units @ $1.20	120		
70 units @ $1.40	98	→ **Less June 30 Inventory**	268
220 units at cost of	**$268** ←	Cost of Goods Sold	$357

The specific identification method might be used in the purchase and sale of high-priced articles, such as automobiles, heavy equipment, and works of art. Although this method may appear logical, it is not used by many companies because it has two definite disadvantages. First, in most cases it is difficult and impractical to keep track of the purchase and sale of individual items. Second, when a company deals in items of an identical nature, deciding which items are to be sold becomes arbitrary; thus, the company can raise or lower income by choosing to sell the high- or low-cost items.

OBJECTIVE 3b
Calculate the pricing of inventory, using the cost basis according to the average-cost method

Average-Cost Method. Under the **average-cost method**, it is assumed that the cost of inventory is the average cost of goods on hand at the beginning of the period plus all goods purchased during the period. Average cost is computed by dividing the total cost of goods available for sale by the total units available for sale. This gives a weighted-average unit cost that is applied to the units in the ending inventory. The ending inventory in our illustration would be $1.25 per unit, or a total of $275, determined as follows:

Inventory, June 30—Average-Cost Method

June 1	Inventory	50 @ $1.00	$ 50
6	Purchased	50 @ $1.10	55
13	Purchased	150 @ $1.20	180
20	Purchased	100 @ $1.30	130
25	Purchased	150 @ $1.40	210
Totals		500 units	$625

Average unit cost: $625 ÷ 500 = $1.25
→ **Ending inventory: 220 units @ $1.25 = $275**

Cost of Goods Available for Sale	$625
→ **Less June 30 Inventory**	275
Cost of Goods Sold	$350

The cost figure obtained for the ending inventory under the average-cost method is influenced by all the prices paid during the year and the beginning inventory price, which tends to level out the effects of cost increases and decreases. Some, however, criticize the average-cost method because they feel that recent costs should receive more attention and are more relevant for income measurement and decision making.

OBJECTIVE 3c *Calculate the pricing of inventory, using the cost basis according to the first-in, first-out (FIFO) method*

First-In, First-Out (FIFO) Method. The **first-in, first-out (FIFO) method** is based on the assumption that the costs of the first items acquired should be assigned to the first items sold. The costs of the goods on hand at the end of a period are assumed to be from the most recent purchases, and the costs assigned to goods that have been sold are assumed to be from the earliest purchases. The FIFO method of determining inventory cost may be adopted by any business, regardless of the actual physical flow of goods, because the assumption is made regarding the flow of costs and not the flow of goods.

In our illustration, the June 30 inventory would be $301 when the FIFO method is used. It is computed as follows:

Inventory, June 30—First-In, First-Out Method

150 units at $1.40 from the purchase of June 25	$210
70 units at $1.30 from the purchase of June 20	91
220 units at a cost of	**$301**
Cost of Goods Available for Sale	$625
Less June 30 Inventory	**301**
Cost of Goods Sold	$324

The effect of the FIFO method is to value the ending inventory at the most recent costs and include earlier costs in cost of goods sold. During periods of consistently rising prices, the FIFO method yields the highest possible amount of net income, since cost of goods sold will show costs closer to the price level at the time the goods were purchased. Another reason for this result is that businesses tend to increase selling prices as costs rise, regardless of the fact that inventories may have been purchased before the price rise. The reverse effect occurs in periods of price decreases. For these reasons a major criticism of FIFO is that it magnifies the effects of the business cycle on income.

Last-In, First-Out (LIFO) Method. The **last-in, first-out (LIFO) method** of costing inventories is based on the assumption that the costs of the last items purchased should be assigned to the first items used or sold and that the cost of the ending inventory is the cost of merchandise purchased earliest.

OBJECTIVE 3d
Calculate the pricing of inventory, using the cost basis according to the last-in, first-out (LIFO) method

Under this method, the June 30 inventory would be $249, computed as follows:

Inventory, June 30—Last-In, First-Out Method

50 units at $1.00 from June 1 inventory	$ 50
50 units at $1.10 from purchase of June 6	55
120 units at $1.20 from purchase of June 13	144
220 units at a cost of	**$249**
Cost of Goods Available for Sale	$625
Less June 30 Inventory	249
Cost of Goods Sold	$376

The effect of LIFO is to value inventory at the earliest prices and to include in cost of goods sold the cost of the most recently purchased goods. This assumption, of course, does not agree with the actual physical movement of goods in most businesses.

However, there is a strong logical argument to support this method, based on the fact that an inventory of a certain size is necessary in a going concern. When inventory is sold, it must be replaced with more goods. The supporters of LIFO reason that the fairest determination of income occurs if the current costs of merchandise are matched against current sales prices, regardless of which physical units of merchandise are sold. When prices are moving either upward or downward, under LIFO the cost of goods sold will show costs closer to the price level at the time the goods were sold. As a result, the LIFO method tends to produce a smaller net income during inflationary times and a larger net income during deflationary times than other methods of inventory valuation. Thus, the peaks and valleys of the business cycle tend to be smoothed out. The important factor here is that in inventory valuation the flow of costs and hence income determination is more important than the physical movement of goods and balance sheet valuation.

An argument may also be made against the LIFO method. Because the inventory valuation on the balance sheet reflects earlier prices, this value is often unrealistic with respect to the current value of the inventory. Thus, such balance sheet measures as working capital and current ratio may be distorted and must be interpreted carefully.

Comparison and Effects of the Alternative Methods of Pricing Inventory

The specific identification, average-cost, FIFO, and LIFO methods of pricing inventory have now been illustrated. The specific identification method is based on actual costs, whereas the other three methods are based on assumptions regarding the flow of costs. Let us now compare the effects of the four methods on net income using the same data as before and assuming sales during June of $500.

	Specific Identification Method	Average-Cost Method	First-In, First-Out Method	Last-In, First-Out Method
Sales	$500	$500	$500	$500
Cost of Goods Sold				
Beginning Inventory	$ 50	$ 50	$ 50	$ 50
Purchases	575	575	575	575
Cost of Goods Available for Sale	$625	$625	$625	$625
Less Ending Inventory	**268**	**275**	**301**	**249**
Costs of Goods Sold	**$357**	**$350**	**$324**	**$376**
Gross Margin from Sales	**$143**	**$150**	**$176**	**$124**

OBJECTIVE 4
State the effects of each method on income determination and income taxes in periods of changing prices

Keeping in mind that in the illustration June was a period of rising prices, we can see that LIFO, which charges the most recent and in this case the highest prices to cost of goods sold, resulted in the lowest gross margin. Conversely, FIFO, which charges the earliest and in this case the lowest prices to cost of goods sold, produced the highest gross margin. The gross margin under the average-cost method is somewhere between those computed under LIFO and FIFO. Thus, it is clear that this method has a less pronounced effect.

During a period of declining prices, the reverse would occur. The LIFO method would produce a higher gross margin than the FIFO method. It is apparent that the method of inventory valuation has the greatest importance during prolonged periods of price changes in one direction, either up or down.

Effect on the Financial Statements. Each of the four methods of inventory pricing presented above is acceptable for use in published financial statements. The FIFO, LIFO, and average-cost methods are widely used, as can be seen in Figure 8-2, which shows the inventory cost methods used by six hundred large companies. Each has its advantages and disadvantages, and none can be considered best or perfect. The factors that should be considered in choosing an inventory method are the effects of each method on the balance sheet, the income statement, income taxes, and management decisions.

A basic problem in determining the best inventory measure for a particular company is that inventory appears on both the balance sheet and the income statement. As we have seen, the LIFO method is best suited for the income statement because it matches revenues and cost of goods sold. But it is not the best measure of the current balance sheet value of inventory, particularly during a prolonged period of price increases or decreases. The FIFO method, on the other hand, is best suited to the balance

Figure 8-2. Inventory Cost Methods Used by 600 Large Companies

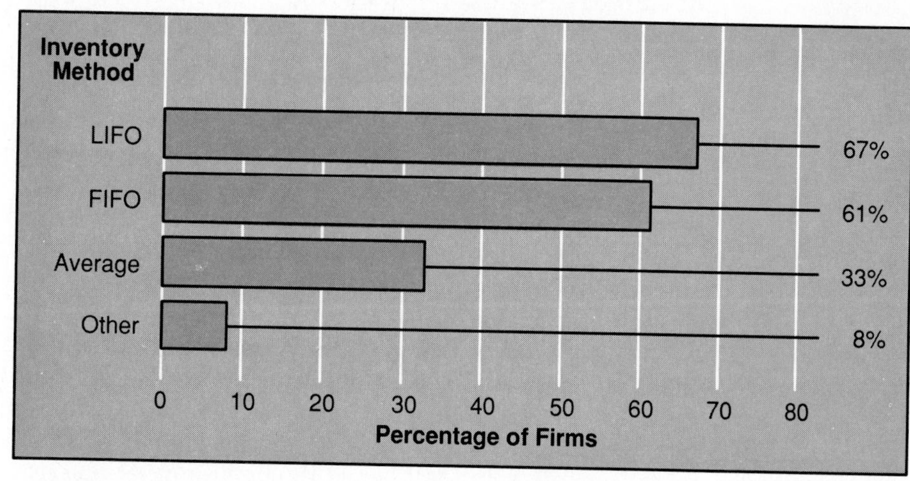

Total percentage exceeds 100 because some companies used different methods for different types of inventory.

Source: American Institute of Certified Public Accountants, *Accounting Trends and Techniques* (New York: AICPA, 1990).

sheet because the ending inventory is closest to current values and thus gives a more realistic view of the current financial assets of a business. Readers of financial statements must be alert to inventory methods and be able to assess their effects.

Effect on Income Taxes. The Internal Revenue Service has developed several rules for valuing inventories for federal income tax purposes. A company has a wide choice of methods, including specific identification, average cost, FIFO, and LIFO as well as lower of cost or market. But once a method is chosen, it must be used consistently from one year to the next. The IRS must approve any changes in inventory valuation method for income tax purposes.[4] This requirement is in agreement with the rule of consistency in accounting in that changes in inventory method would cause income to fluctuate too much and would make income statements hard to interpret from year to year. A company may change its inventory method if there is a good reason for doing so. The nature and effect of the change must be shown on its financial statements.

Many accountants believe that the use of the FIFO or the average-cost method in periods of rising prices causes businesses to report more than their true profit, resulting in the payment of excess income taxes. The profit is overstated because cost of goods sold is understated, relative to current prices. The company must buy replacement inventory at higher prices, but additional funds are also needed to pay income taxes. During the rapid inflation of 1979 to 1982, billions of dollars reported as profits

4. A single exception to this rule is that taxpayers must notify the IRS of a change to LIFO from another method, but do not have to have advance IRS approval.

and paid in income taxes were believed to be the result of poor matching of current costs and revenues under the FIFO and average-cost methods. Consequently, many companies have since switched to the LIFO inventory method, encouraged by the belief that prices will continue to rise.

If a company uses the LIFO method in reporting income for tax purposes, the IRS requires that the LIFO method also be used in the accounting records. Also, the IRS will not allow the use of the lower-of-cost-or-market rule if the method of determining cost is the LIFO method. In this case, only the LIFO cost can be used. This rule, however, does not preclude a company from using lower of LIFO cost or market for financial reporting purposes. (The use of lower of cost or market is discussed later in this chapter.)

Over a period of rising prices, a business that uses the LIFO basis may find that its inventory is valued for balance sheet purposes at a cost figure far below what it currently pays for the same items. Management must monitor this situation carefully, because, if it should let the inventory quantity at year end fall below the beginning-of-the-year level, it will find itself paying income taxes on the difference between the current cost and the old LIFO cost in the records. When this occurs, it is called a **LIFO liquidation** because sales have reduced inventories below the levels established in prior years. A LIFO liquidation may be prevented by making enough purchases prior to year end to restore the desired inventory level. Sometimes a LIFO liquidation cannot be avoided because the products are discontinued or supplies are interrupted, as in the case of a strike.

DECISION POINT

Amoco Corporation[5] *(Part 2)*

As pointed out above, the inventory methods used by a company affect not only the company's reported profitability but also its reported liquidity. In the case of a large company like Amoco Corporation, the effects can be complex and material. Like many companies, Amoco uses three of the methods in this chapter to cost its various types of inventory, which in 1989 totaled $1.1 billion. In its statement of accounting policies, management explains its inventory methods in this way: "Cost is determined under the last-in, first-out (LIFO) method for the majority of inventories of crude oil, petroleum products, and chemical products. The costs of remaining inventories are determined on the first-in, first-out (FIFO) or average cost methods." In a subsequent note on inventories, more detail is given:

> Inventories carried under the LIFO method represented approximately 52 percent of total year-end inventory carrying values in 1989 and 1988. It is estimated that inventories would have been approximately $1.3 billion higher than reported on December 31, 1989, and approximately $1.1 billion

5. Excerpts from the 1989 Annual Report are reprinted with permission of Amoco Corporation.

> higher on December 31, 1988, if the quantities valued on the LIFO basis were instead valued on the FIFO basis.

The information in the note allows the reader to determine what Amoco's net income for 1989 would have been if FIFO had been used excluding tax and currency effects and other variables. In this case, Amoco's net income of $1.6 billion would have been increased by $.2 billion ($1.3 billion – $1.1 billion) to $1.8 billion, an increase of 12.5 percent, if FIFO had been used. Finally, in management's discussion and analysis, the following clarifying remark is made:

> Amoco's short-term liquidity position is better than the reported figures indicate since the inventory component of working capital is largely valued under the LIFO method, whereas other elements of working capital are reported at amounts more indicative of their current values. If inventories were valued at current replacement costs, the level of working capital would rise and an increase in the current ratio would result. ■

Application of the Perpetual Inventory System

OBJECTIVE 5
Apply the perpetual inventory system to accounting for inventories and cost of goods sold

The system of inventories used so far in this book has been the **periodic inventory system**. Under this system, no detailed record of inventory is kept during the year, and a physical inventory must be taken at the end of the year to establish ending inventory. The cost of goods sold cannot be determined until the physical inventory has been completed. Cost of goods sold is computed by adding the net cost of purchases to beginning inventory and then subtracting the ending inventory.

Periodic inventory systems are used in many retail and wholesale businesses because they do not require a large amount of clerical work. The primary disadvantage of periodic inventory systems is the lack of detailed records of what items of inventory are on hand at a point in time. Such detailed data would enable management to respond to customers' inquiries concerning product availability, order inventory more effectively to avoid being out of stock, and control the financial costs associated with the money invested in the inventory. The system that provides this type of data is the **perpetual inventory system**. Under this system, a continuous record of the inventory is maintained by keeping detailed records of the purchases and sales of inventory. As a result, the amount of inventory on hand and the cost of goods sold are known throughout the accounting period. In the past, the high clerical cost of maintaining this type of system meant that it was used primarily for goods of high value and low volume. However, with the advent of the computer and of electronic tags and markings, the perpetual inventory system has become easier and less expensive to operate and, consequently, much more prevalent. For example, electronic marking of grocery items enables grocery stores to maintain perpetual inventory records; and the tags attached to products sold by clothing, department, and discount stores such as Sears and Kmart enable them to have tight controls over inventory and ordering.

Handling the Perpetual Inventory System in the Accounting Records

The primary difference in accounting between the perpetual and the periodic inventory systems is that under the perpetual inventory system, the Merchandise Inventory account is continually adjusted by entering purchases, sales, and other inventory transactions as they occur. Under the periodic inventory system, on the other hand, the Merchandise Inventory account stays at the beginning level until the physical inventory is recorded at the end of the period. As a result, accounts you are familiar with under the periodic inventory system, such as Purchases, Purchases Returns and Allowances, Purchases Discounts, and Freight In, are not used under the perpetual system. Also, under the perpetual system, as sales occur, the Cost of Goods Sold account is used to accumulate the cost of goods sold to customers. To illustrate these differences, the transactions of an office supply wholesaler are recorded under both the periodic and the perpetual inventory systems as follows:

1. Received 100 cases of floppy disks for word processors at a cost of $12,000; terms 2/10, n/30, FOB destination. The net method of recording purchases is used.

Perpetual Inventory System			Periodic Inventory System		
Merchandise Inventory	**11,760**		**Purchases**	**11,760**	
Accounts Payable		11,760	Accounts Payable		11,760
Purchase of merchandise at net purchase price (terms 2/10, n/30, FOB destination)			Purchase of merchandise at net purchase price (terms 2/10, n/30, FOB destination)		

2. Sold 20 cases of floppy disks to a retailer at a total price of $3,000, terms n/10, FOB shipping point.

Perpetual Inventory System			Periodic Inventory System		
Accounts Receivable	3,000		Accounts Receivable	3,000	
Sales		3,000	Sales		3,000
Sale of 20 cases; terms n/10, FOB shipping point			Sale of 20 cases; terms n/10, FOB shipping point		
Cost of Goods Sold	**2,352**				
Merchandise Inventory		**2,352**			
To record cost of goods sold 20 cases × $117.60 = $2,352					

3. Arranged to return 10 cases of the floppy disks to supplier for full credit.

Perpetual Inventory System			Periodic Inventory System		
Accounts Payable	1,176		Accounts Payable	1,176	
Merchandise Inventory		1,176	Purchases Returns and Allowances		1,176
To record purchase return 10 cases × $117.60 = $1,176			To record purchase return 10 cases × $117.60 = $1,176		

4. Paid supplier in full within the discount period.

Perpetual Inventory System			Periodic Inventory System		
Accounts Payable	10,584		Accounts Payable	10,584	
Cash		10,584	Cash		10,584
Payment to supplier $11,760 − $1,176 = $10,584			Payment to supplier $11,760 − $1,176 = $10,584		

Note the differences in the first three transactions. In each case, under the perpetual inventory system, the Merchandise Inventory account is updated for the effect on the physical inventory; the Purchases and Purchases Returns and Allowances accounts are not used. Also, in transaction **2**, the Cost of Goods Sold account is updated at the time of a sale.

At the end of the year, neither adjustments to Merchandise Inventory nor corresponding debits or credits to Income Summary are needed under the perpetual inventory system. Because the Merchandise Inventory account has been continually updated during the year, there is no need to establish the ending inventory in the records. The required entry closes Cost of Goods Sold to Income Summary.

Maintaining the Detailed Perpetual Inventory Records

To keep track of the quantities and costs of the individual items stocked in merchandise inventory under the perpetual inventory system, it is necessary to maintain an individual record for each type of inventory. The Merchandise Inventory account is a controlling account for a subsidiary file of individual inventory records. This mechanism is similar to the Accounts Receivable controlling account and its subsidiary ledger. In the Inventory subsidiary file, each item has a card (or file in a computer system) on which purchases and sales are entered as they take place. A sample perpetual inventory card is shown in Exhibit 8-2 for another item held for sale by our office supply wholesaler. At any time, the card will show the number of pencil sharpeners on hand, and the total of all the cards is equal to the merchandise inventory.

As shown in Exhibit 8-2, on June 1 there is a balance of 60 pencil sharpeners that cost $5 each. A sale on June 4 reduces the balance by 10 pencil sharpeners. On June 10, 100 pencil sharpeners are purchased at $6 each. Now the inventory consists of 50 pencil sharpeners purchased at $5 each and 100 pencil sharpeners purchased at $6 each. The method of inventory

Exhibit 8-2. Perpetual Inventory Record Card, FIFO

Item: Pencil Sharpener, Model D-222

	Purchased			Sold			Balance		
Date	Units	Cost	Total	Units	Cost	Total	Units	Cost	Balance
June 1							60	5.00	300.00
4				10	5.00	50.00	50	5.00	250.00
10	100	6.00	600.00				50 100	5.00 6.00	850.00
20				30	5.00	150.00	20 100	5.00 6.00	700.00

valuation in Exhibit 8-2 is first-in, first-out, as can be determined by looking at the June 20 sale. The entire sale of 30 pencil sharpeners is taken from the 50 sharpeners still left from the beginning inventory. If the LIFO method were used, the sale would be deducted from the latest purchase of 100 pencil sharpeners at $6 each. Under LIFO the resulting balance would be $670 [(50 × $5) + (70 × $6)]. An example showing both the FIFO and the LIFO methods appears in the review problem at the end of this chapter.

Need for Physical Inventories Under the Perpetual Inventory System

The use of the perpetual inventory system does not eliminate the need for a physical inventory at the end of the accounting period. The perpetual inventory records show what should be on hand, not necessarily what is on hand. There may be losses due to spoilage, employee pilferage, theft, or other causes. If a loss has occurred, it is reflected in the accounts by a debit to Inventory Shortage Expense and a credit to Merchandise Inventory. The individual inventory cards, which may also be the subsidiary ledger, must also be adjusted.

Valuing the Inventory at the Lower of Cost or Market (LCM)

OBJECTIVE 6 *Apply the lower-of-cost-or-market rule to inventory valuation*

Although cost is usually the most appropriate basis for valuation of inventory, there are times when inventory may properly be shown in the financial statements at less than its cost. If by reason of physical deterioration, obsolescence, or decline in price level the market value of the inventory falls below the cost, a loss has occurred. This loss may be recognized by writing the inventory down to market. The term **market** is used here to mean current replacement cost. For a merchandising company, market is the amount that the company would pay at the present time for the same goods, purchased from the usual suppliers and in the usual quantities. It may help in applying the **lower-of-cost-or-market (LCM) rule** to think of it as the "lower-of-cost-or-replacement-cost" rule.[6]

Methods of Applying LCM

There are three basic methods of valuing inventories at the lower of cost or market, as follows: (1) the item-by-item method, (2) the major category method, and (3) the total inventory method.

For example, a stereo shop could determine lower of cost or market for each kind of speaker, receiver, and turntable (item by item); for all speakers, all receivers, and all turntables (major categories); or for all speakers, receivers, and turntables together (total inventory).

Item-by-Item Method. When the **item-by-item method** is used, cost and market are compared for each item in the inventory. The individual items are then valued at their lower price.

Lower of Cost or Market with Item-by-Item Method

	Quantity	Per Unit Cost	Per Unit Market	Lower of Cost or Market
Category I				
Item a	200	**$1.50**	$1.70	$ 300
Item b	100	2.00	**1.80**	180
Item c	100	**2.50**	2.60	250
Category II				
Item d	300	5.00	**4.50**	1,350
Item e	200	**4.00**	4.10	800
Inventory at the lower of cost or market				**$2,880**

Major Category Method. Under the **major category method**, the total cost and total market for each category of items are compared. Each category is then valued at its lower amount.

6. In some cases, *market value* is determined by the *realizable value* of the inventory—the amount for which the goods can be sold rather than the amount for which the goods can be replaced. The circumstances in which realizable value determines market value are encountered in practice only occasionally, and the valuation procedures are technical enough to be addressed in a more advanced accounting course.

Lower of Cost or Market with Major Category Method

	Quantity	Per Unit Cost	Per Unit Market	Total Cost	Total Market	Lower of Cost or Market
Category I						
Item a	200	$1.50	$1.70	$ 300	$ 340	
Item b	100	2.00	1.80	200	180	
Item c	100	2.50	2.60	250	260	
Totals				**$ 750**	$ 780	**$ 750**
Category II						
Item d	300	5.00	4.50	$1,500	$1,350	
Item e	200	4.00	4.10	800	820	
Totals				$2,300	**$2,170**	**$2,170**
Inventory at the lower of cost or market						**$2,920**

Total Inventory Method. Under the **total inventory method**, the entire inventory is valued at both cost and market, and the lower price is used to value inventory. Since this method is not acceptable for federal income tax purposes, it is not illustrated here.

Valuing Inventory by Estimation

It is sometimes necessary or desirable to estimate the value of ending inventory. The methods most commonly used for this purpose are the retail method and the gross profit method.

Retail Method of Inventory Estimation

OBJECTIVE 7a *Estimate the cost of ending inventory using the retail inventory method*

The **retail method**, as its name implies, is used in retail merchandising businesses. There are two principal reasons for the use of the retail method. First, management usually requires that financial statements be prepared at least once a month, and, as it is time-consuming and expensive to take a physical inventory each month, the retail method is used to estimate the value of inventory on hand. Second, because items in a retail store normally have a price tag, it is a common practice to take the physical inventory at retail from these price tags and reduce the total value to cost through use of the retail method. The term *at retail* means the amount of the inventory at the marked selling prices of the inventory items.

When the retail method is used to estimate an ending inventory, the records must show the beginning inventory at cost and at retail. The records must also show the amount of goods purchased during the period both at cost and at retail. The net sales at retail is, of course, the balance of the Sales account less returns and allowances. A simple example of the retail method is shown below.

The Retail Method of Inventory Valuation

	Cost	Retail
Beginning Inventory	$ 40,000	$ 55,000
Net Purchases for the Period (excluding Freight In)	107,000	145,000
Freight In	3,000	
Merchandise Available for Sale	**$150,000**	**$200,000**
Ratio of Cost to Retail Price: $\frac{\$150{,}000}{\$200{,}000} = 75\%$		
Net Sales During the Period		160,000
Estimated Ending Inventory at Retail		$ 40,000
Ratio of Cost to Retail	75%	
Estimated Cost of Ending Inventory	$ 30,000	

Merchandise available for sale is determined both at cost and at retail by listing beginning inventory and net purchases (excluding freight in) for the period both at cost and at the expected selling price of the goods, adding freight to the cost column, and totaling. The ratio of these two amounts (cost to retail price) provides an estimate of the cost of each dollar of retail sales value. The estimated ending inventory at retail is then determined by deducting sales for the period from the retail price of the goods that were available for sale during the period. The inventory at retail is now converted to cost on the basis of the ratio of cost to retail.

The cost of ending inventory may also be estimated by applying the ratio of cost to retail to the total retail value of the physical count of the inventory. Applying the retail method is often more difficult in practice than in this simple example because of certain complications such as changes in the retail price during the year, different markups on different types of merchandise, and varying volumes of sales for different types of merchandise.

Gross Profit Method of Inventory Estimation

The **gross profit method** assumes that the ratio of gross margin for a business remains relatively stable from year to year. It is used in place of the retail method when records of the retail prices of beginning inventory

OBJECTIVE 7b
Estimate the cost of ending inventory using the gross profit method

and purchases are not kept. It is considered acceptable for estimating the cost of inventory for interim reports, but is not an acceptable method for valuing inventory in the annual financial statements. It is also useful in estimating the amount of inventory lost or destroyed by theft, fire, or other hazards. Insurance companies often use this method to verify loss claims.

The gross profit method is very simple to use. First, figure the cost of goods available for sale in the usual way (add purchases to beginning inventory). Second, estimate the cost of goods sold by deducting the estimated gross margin from sales. Third, deduct the estimated cost of goods sold from the goods available for sale in order to estimate the cost of ending inventory. This method is shown below.

The Gross Profit Method of Inventory Valuation

1. Beginning Inventory at Cost		$ 50,000
Net Purchases at Cost		290,000
Goods Available for Sale		$340,000
2. Less Estimated Cost of Goods Sold		
Sales at Selling Price	$400,000	
Less Estimated Gross Margin of 30%	120,000	
Estimated Cost of Goods Sold		280,000
3. Estimated Cost of Ending Inventory		$ 60,000

Chapter Review

Review of Learning Objectives

1. **Define *merchandise inventory,* and show how inventory measurement affects income determination.**
   Merchandise inventory consists of all goods owned and held for sale in the regular course of business. The objective of accounting for inventories is the proper determination of income. If the value of ending inventory is understated or overstated, a corresponding error—dollar for dollar—will be made in net income. Furthermore, because the ending inventory of one period is the beginning inventory of the next, the misstatement affects two accounting periods, although the effects are opposite.

2. **Define *inventory cost,* and relate it to goods flow and cost flow.**
   The cost of inventory includes (1) invoice price less purchases discounts, (2) freight or transportation in, including insurance in transit, and (3) applicable taxes and tariffs. Goods flow relates to the actual physical flow of merchandise, whereas cost flow refers to the assumed flow of costs in the operation of the business.

3. **Calculate the pricing of inventory, using the cost basis according to the (a) specific identification method; (b) average-cost method; (c) first-in, first-out (FIFO) method; (d) last-in, first-out (LIFO) method.**
The value assigned to the ending inventory is the result of two measurements: quantity and price. Quantity is determined by taking a physical inventory. The pricing of inventory is usually based on the assumed cost flow of the goods as they are bought and sold. One of four assumptions is usually made regarding cost flow. These assumptions are represented by four inventory methods. Inventory pricing could be determined by the specific identification method, which associates the actual cost with each item of inventory but is rarely used. The average-cost method assumes that the cost of inventory is the average cost of goods available for sale during the period. The first-in, first-out (FIFO) method assumes that the costs of the first items acquired should be assigned to the first items sold. The last-in, first-out (LIFO) method assumes that the costs of the last items acquired should be assigned to the first items sold. The inventory method chosen may or may not be equivalent to the actual physical flow of goods.

4. **State the effects of each method on income determination and income taxes in periods of changing prices.**
During periods of rising prices, the LIFO method will show the lowest net income; FIFO, the highest; and average cost, in between. The opposite effects occur in periods of falling prices. No generalization can be made regarding the specific identification method. The Internal Revenue Service requires that if LIFO is used for tax purposes, it must also be used for book purposes, and that the lower-of-cost-or-market rule cannot be applied to the LIFO method.

5. **Apply the perpetual inventory system to accounting for inventories and cost of goods sold.**
Under the periodic inventory system, the one used earlier in this book, inventory is determined by a physical count at the end of the accounting period. Under the perpetual inventory system, the Inventory control account is constantly updated as sales and purchases are made during the accounting period. Also, as sales are made, the Cost of Goods Sold account is used to accumulate the costs of those sales.

6. **Apply the lower-of-cost-or-market rule to inventory valuation.**
The lower-of-cost-or-market rule can be applied to the above methods of determining inventory at cost. This rule states that if the replacement cost (market) of the inventory is lower than what the inventory cost, the lower figure should be used.

7. **Estimate the cost of ending inventory using (a) the retail inventory method and (b) the gross profit method.**
Two methods of estimating the value of inventory are the retail inventory method and the gross profit method. Under the retail inventory method, inventory is determined at retail prices and is then reduced to estimated cost by applying a ratio of cost to retail price. Under the gross profit method, cost of goods sold is estimated by reducing sales by estimated gross margin. The estimated cost of goods sold is then deducted from cost of goods available for sale to estimate the inventory.

Review of Concepts and Terminology

The following concepts and terms were introduced in this chapter:

(L.O. 3) **Average-cost method:** An inventory cost method that assumes that the cost of inventory is the average cost of all goods available for sale.

(L.O. 1) **Consignment:** The placing of goods by the owner of the goods (known as the consignor) on the premises of another company (the consignee).

(L.O. 2) **Cost flow:** Association of costs with their assumed flow within the operations of the company.

(L.O. 3) **First-in, first-out (FIFO) method:** An inventory cost method based on the assumption that the costs of the first items acquired should be assigned to the first items sold.

(L.O. 2) **Goods flow:** The actual physical movement of goods in the operations of the company.

(L.O. 7) **Gross profit method:** A method of inventory estimation that assumes that the ratio of gross margin for a business remains relatively stable from year to year.

(L.O. 2) **Inventory cost:** The price paid or consideration given to acquire an asset; it includes invoice price less purchases discounts, plus freight or transportation in and applicable taxes or tariffs.

(L.O. 6) **Item-by-item method:** A lower-of-cost-or-market method of valuing inventory in which cost and market are compared for each item in the inventory, with each item then valued at its lower price.

(L.O. 3) **Last-in, first-out (LIFO) method:** An inventory cost method that assumes that the costs of the last items purchased should be assigned to the first items sold.

(L.O. 4) **LIFO liquidation:** The reduction of inventory below previous levels so that income is increased by the amount by which current prices exceed the historical cost of the inventory under LIFO.

(L.O. 6) **Lower-of-cost-or-market (LCM) rule:** A method of valuing inventory at an amount below cost if the replacement (market) value is less than cost.

(L.O. 6) **Major category method:** A lower-of-cost-or-market method of valuing inventory in which the total cost and total market for each category of items are compared, with each category then valued at its lower amount.

(L.O. 6) **Market:** Current replacement cost of inventory.

(L.O. 1) **Merchandise inventory:** All goods that are owned and held for sale in the regular course of business.

(L.O. 5) **Periodic inventory system:** The method of accounting for the physical quantity of inventory by taking a count at the end of the period and then adjusting the inventory account for the new balance.

(L.O. 5) **Perpetual inventory system:** The method of accounting for the physical quantity and costs of inventory by keeping continuous detailed records of purchases and sales.

(L.O. 7) **Retail method:** A method of inventory estimation used in retail businesses; inventory at retail value is reduced by the ratio of cost to retail price.

(L.O. 3) **Specific identification method:** Determining the cost of inventory by identifying the cost of each item.

(L.O. 6) **Total inventory method:** A lower-of-cost-or-market method of valuing inventory in which the entire inventory is valued at both cost and market, and the lower price is used; not an acceptable method for federal income tax purposes.

Review Problem
Periodic and Perpetual Inventory Systems

(L.O. 3, 5) The following table summarizes the beginning inventory, purchases, and sales of Psi Company's single product during January.

	Beginning Inventory			Purchases			
Date	**Units**	**Cost**	**Total**	**Units**	**Cost**	**Total**	**Sales Units**
Jan. 1	1,400	$19	$26,600				
4							300
8				600	$20	$12,000	
10							1,300
12				900	21	18,900	
15							150
18				500	22	11,000	
24				800	23	18,400	
31							1,350
Totals	1,400		$26,600	2,800		$60,300	3,100

Required

1. Assuming that the company uses the periodic inventory system, compute the cost that should be assigned to ending inventory using (a) a FIFO basis and (b) a LIFO basis.
2. Assuming that the company uses the perpetual inventory system, compute the cost that should be assigned to ending inventory using (a) a FIFO basis and (b) a LIFO basis. (**Hint:** It is helpful to use a form similar to the perpetual inventory card in Exhibit 8-2.)

Answer to Review Problem

	Units	Dollars
Beginning Inventory	1,400	$26,600
Purchases	2,800	60,300
Available for Sale	4,200	$86,900
Sales	3,100	
Ending Inventory	1,100	

1. Periodic inventory system
   a. FIFO basis
      Ending inventory consists of

January 24 purchases (800 × $23)	$18,400	
January 18 purchases (300 × $22)	6,600	$25,000

   b. LIFO basis
      Ending inventory consists of

Beginning inventory (1,100 × $19)	$20,900

2. Perpetual inventory system
   a. FIFO basis

	Purchased			Sold			Balance		
Date	Units	Cost	Total	Units	Cost	Total	Units	Cost	Total
Jan. 1							1,400	$19	$26,600
4				300	$19	$ 5,700	1,100	19	20,900
8	600	$20	$12,000				1,100	19	
							600	20	32,900
10				1,100	19				
				200	20	24,900	400	20	8,000
12	900	21	18,900				400	20	
							900	21	26,900
15				150	20	3,000	250	20	
							900	21	23,900
18	500	22	11,000				250	20	
							900	21	
							500	22	34,900
24	800	23	18,400				250	20	
							900	21	
							500	22	
							800	23	53,300
31				250	20				
				900	21				
				200	22	28,300	**300**	**22**	
							800	**23**	**25,000**

b. LIFO basis

	Purchased			Sold			Balance		
Date	Units	Cost	Total	Units	Cost	Total	Units	Cost	Total
Jan. 1							1,400	$19	$26,600
4				300	$19	$ 5,700	1,100	19	20,900
8	600	$20	$12,000				1,100 600	19 20	32,900
10				600 700	20 19	25,300	400	19	7,600
12	900	21	18,900				400 900	19 21	26,500
15				150	21	3,150	400 750	19 21	23,350
18	500	22	11,000				400 750 500	19 21 22	34,350
24	800	23	18,400				400 750 500 800	19 21 22 23	52,750
31				800 500 50	23 22 21	30,450	**400** **700**	**19** **21**	**22,300**

Chapter Assignments

Discussion Questions

1. How does inventory differ from short-term liquid assets, and what measurements of inventory must be taken to make a proper income determination? What is the relationship of inventory to the matching rule?
2. What is merchandise inventory, and what is the primary objective of inventory measurement?
3. If the merchandise inventory is mistakenly overstated at the end of 19x8, what is the effect on (a) 19x8 net income, (b) 19x8 year-end balance sheet value, (c) 19x9 net income, and (d) 19x9 year-end balance sheet value?
4. Fargo Sales Company is very busy at the end of its fiscal year on June 30. There is an order for 130 units of product in the warehouse. Although the shipping department tries, it cannot ship the product by June 30, and title has not yet passed. Should the 130 units be included in the year-end count of inventory? Why or why not?
5. What does the term *taking a physical inventory* mean?
6. What items are included in the cost of inventory?

7. In periods of steadily rising prices, which of the three inventory methods—average-cost, FIFO, or LIFO—will give the (a) highest inventory cost, (b) lowest inventory cost, (c) highest net income, and (d) lowest net income?
8. May a company change its inventory costing method from year to year? Explain.
9. Do the FIFO and LIFO inventory methods result in different quantities of ending inventory?
10. Under which method of cost flow are (a) the earliest costs assigned to inventory, (b) the latest costs assigned to inventory, (c) the average costs assigned to inventory?
11. What are the relative advantages and disadvantages of FIFO and LIFO from management's point of view?
12. Which is more expensive to maintain, a perpetual inventory system or a periodic inventory system? Why?
13. What differences occur in recording sales, purchases, and closing entries under the perpetual and periodic inventory systems?
14. In the phrase "lower of cost or market," what is meant by the word "market"?
15. What methods can be used to determine lower of cost or market?
16. What effects do income taxes have on inventory valuation?
17. What are some reasons management may use the gross profit method of determining inventory?
18. Does using the retail inventory method mean that inventories are measured at retail value on the balance sheet? Explain.
19. Which of the following inventory systems do not require taking a physical inventory: (a) perpetual, (b) periodic, (c) retail, (d) gross profit?

Communication Skills Exercises

Communication 8-1. Inventories, Income Determination, and Ethics *(L.O. 1)*

Flare, Inc., which has a December 31 year end, designs and sells fashions for young professional women. Sandra Mason, president of the company, feared that the forecasted 1991 profitability goals would not be reached. She was pleased when Flare received a large order on December 30 from The Executive Woman, a retail chain of upscale stores for businesswomen. Mason immediately directed the controller to record the sale, which represented 13 percent of Flare's annual sales, but directed the inventory control department not to separate the goods for shipment until after January 1. Separated goods are not included in inventory because they have been sold. On December 31, the company's auditors arrived to observe the year-end taking of the physical inventory under the periodic inventory system. What will be the effect of Mason's action on Flare's 1991 profitability? What will be the effect on 1992 profitability? Is Mason's action ethical?

Communication 8-2. LIFO Inventory Method *(L.O. 4)*

In 1989, 96 percent of paper companies used the LIFO inventory method for the costing of inventories, whereas only 24 percent of electronic equipment companies used LIFO.[7] Describe the LIFO inventory method. What effects does it have on reported income and income taxes during periods of price changes? Can you think of a reason why the paper industry would use LIFO and most of the electronics industry would not?

7. American Institute of Certified Public Accountants, *Accounting Trends and Techniques* (New York: AICPA, 1990), p. 106.

Communication 8-3. Periodic Versus Perpetual Inventory Systems *(L.O. 5)*

The Foot Joint, Inc. operates four sports shoe stores in Omaha-area malls. The company uses the periodic inventory system and takes a quarterly physical inventory in order to prepare financial statements at the end of each quarter. The company lost money during the last two quarters of 1991 and the first quarter of 1992. Part of the problem, management believes, is that some stores have run out of merchandise while other stores have too much on hand. Top management is certain that if more timely monthly financial statements were prepared, the company could adapt to varying sales patterns during a quarter. Managers have proposed that the company switch to the perpetual inventory system in the second quarter of 1992 and prepare financial statements at the end of each month. Every shoe will be tagged with a machine-readable identification label, which will be scanned as each sale is made. Trends in shoe sales will be monitored so that purchases, shipments, and promotions for each store can be modified on a monthly basis. Monthly physical inventories will be unnecessary under this plan because the amount of the ending merchandise inventory will be available from perpetual inventory records. What changes in the method of recording transactions will be needed in order to adopt the perpetual inventory system? What advantages do you see in the new system? What disadvantages? Will quarterly physical inventories still be necessary?

Communication 8-4. Basic Research Skills *(L.O. 2, 5)*

Visit a local retail business—a grocery, clothing, book, music, or appliance store, for example—and make an appointment to interview the manager for thirty minutes about the company's inventory accounting system. The store may be a branch of a larger company. Find out answers to the following questions, summarize the answers in a paper to be handed in, and be prepared to discuss your results in class.

What is the physical flow of merchandise into the store and what documents are used in connection with this flow?

What documents are prepared when merchandise is sold?

Does the store keep perpetual inventory records? If so, are the records in units only or do they keep track of cost as well? If not, what system do they use?

How often does the company take a physical inventory?

How are financial statements generated for the store?

What method does the company use to price its inventory for financial statements?

Classroom Exercises

Exercise 8-1. Effects of Inventory Errors *(L.O. 1)*

Condensed income statements for Rodriguez Company for two years are shown on page 424. After the end of 19x2, it was discovered that an error had been made that resulted in a $3,000 understatement of the 19x1 ending inventory.

Compute the corrected net income for 19x1 and 19x2. What effect will the error have on net income and owners' equity for 19x3?

	19x2	19x1
Sales	$42,000	$35,000
Cost of Goods Sold	25,000	18,000
Gross Margin on Sales	$17,000	$17,000
Operating Expenses	10,000	10,000
Net Income	$ 7,000	$ 7,000

Exercise 8-2. Inventory Cost Methods *(L.O. 3)*

Helen's Farm Store had the purchases and sales of fertilizer during the year that are presented below:

Jan. 1	Beginning Inventory	250 cases @ $23	$ 5,750
Feb. 25	Purchased	100 cases @ $26	2,600
June 15	Purchased	400 cases @ $28	11,200
Aug. 15	Purchased	100 cases @ $26	2,600
Oct. 15	Purchased	300 cases @ $28	8,400
Dec. 15	Purchased	200 cases @ $30	6,000
Total Goods Available for Sale		1,350	$36,550
Total Sales		1,000 cases	
Dec. 31	Ending Inventory	350 cases	

Assume that all of the June 15 purchase and 200 cases each from the January 1 beginning inventory, the October 15 purchase, and the December 15 purchase were sold.

Determine the costs that should be assigned to ending inventory and cost of goods sold under each of the following assumptions: (1) costs are assigned by the specific identification method; (2) costs are assigned on an average-cost basis; (3) costs are assigned on a FIFO basis; (4) costs are assigned on a LIFO basis. What conclusions can be drawn as to the effect of each method on the income statement and the balance sheet of Helen's Farm Store?

Exercise 8-3. Inventory Cost Methods *(L.O. 3)*

During its first year of operation, Jefferson Company purchased 5,600 units of a product at $21 per unit. During the second year, it purchased 6,000 units of the same product at $24 per unit. During the third year, it purchased 5,000 units at $30 per unit. Jefferson Company managed to have an ending inventory each year of 1,000 units. The company sells goods at a 100 percent markup over cost.

Prepare cost of goods sold statements that compare the value of ending inventory and the cost of goods sold for each of the three years using (1) the FIFO method and (2) the LIFO method. What conclusions can you draw from the resulting data about the relationships between changes in unit price and changes in the value of ending inventory?

Exercise 8-4. Effects of Inventory Methods on Cash Flows *(L.O. 4)*

Ross Products, Inc. sold 120,000 cases of glue at $40 per case during 19x1. Its beginning inventory consisted of 20,000 cases at a cost of $24 per case. During 19x1 it purchased 60,000 cases at $28 per case and later 50,000 cases at $30 per case. Operating expenses were $1,100,000, and the applicable income tax rate is 30 percent.

Using the periodic inventory system, compute net income using the FIFO basis and the LIFO basis for costing inventory. Which alternative produces the larger cash flow? The company is considering a purchase of 10,000 cases at $30 per case just before the year end. What effect on net income and on cash flow will this proposed purchase have under each basis? **Hint:** What are the income tax consequences?

Exercise 8-5. Inventory Costing Method Characteristics
(L.O. 3, 4)

The lettered items below represent inventory costing methods. In the blank next to each numbered statement, write the letter of the method to which the statement is *most* applicable.

a. Specific identification
b. Average-cost
c. First-in, first-out (FIFO)
d. Last-in, first-out (LIFO)

_____ 1. Matches recent costs with recent revenues
_____ 2. Assumes that each item of inventory is identifiable
_____ 3. Results in most realistic balance sheet valuation
_____ 4. Results in lowest net income in periods of deflation
_____ 5. Results in lowest net income in periods of inflation
_____ 6. Matches oldest costs with recent revenues
_____ 7. Results in highest net income in periods of inflation
_____ 8. Results in highest net income in periods of deflation
_____ 9. Tends to level out the effects of inflation
_____ 10. Is unpredictable as to the effects of inflation

Exercise 8-6. Inventory Costing Methods: Periodic and Perpetual Systems
(L.O. 3, 5)

During July 19x2, Servex, Inc. sold 250 units of its product Dervex for $2,000 from the following units available:

	Units	Cost
Beginning Inventory	100	$1
Purchase 1	40	2
Purchase 2	60	3
Purchase 3	70	4
Purchase 4	80	5
Purchase 5	90	6

A sale of 100 units was made after purchase 1, and a sale of 150 units was made after purchase 4. Of the units sold, 100 came from beginning inventory and 150 from purchases 3 and 4.

Determine cost of goods available for sale and ending inventory in units. Then determine the costs that should be assigned to cost of goods sold and ending inventory under each of the following assumptions: (1) Costs are assigned under the periodic inventory system using (a) the specific identification method, (b) the average-cost method, (c) the FIFO method, and (d) the LIFO method. (2) Costs are assigned under the perpetual inventory system using (a) the FIFO method, (b) the LIFO method. For each alternative, show the gross margin from sales.

Exercise 8-7.
Perpetual and Periodic Inventory Methods
(L.O. 5)

Record general journal entries using the net purchase method to record the following transactions under (1) the perpetual inventory system and (2) the periodic inventory system.

March 11 Received 4,000 cases of chloride tablets at a cost of $200 per case, terms 2/10, n/30, FOB destination.
15 Sold 200 cases of tablets for $300 per case, terms n/10, FOB shipping point.
17 Returned 50 cases of tablets that were damaged to suppliers for full credit.
20 Paid the supplier in full for the amount owed on the purchase of March 11.

Exercise 8-8.
Periodic Inventory System and Inventory Cost Methods
(L.O. 3, 4)

In chronological order, the inventory, purchases, and sales of a single product for a recent month appear as follows:

			Units	Amount per Unit
June	1	Beginning Inventory	300	$10
	4	Purchase	800	11
	8	Sale	400	20
	12	Purchase	1,000	12
	16	Sale	700	20
	20	Sale	500	22
	24	Purchase	1,200	13
	28	Sale	600	22
	30	Sale	400	22

Using the periodic inventory system, compute the cost of ending inventory, cost of goods sold, and gross margin from sales. Use the FIFO and LIFO inventory costing methods. Explain the difference in gross margin from sales produced by the two methods.

Exercise 8-9.
Perpetual Inventory System and Inventory Cost Methods
(L.O. 3, 5)

Using the data provided in Exercise 8-8 and assuming the perpetual inventory system, compute the cost of ending inventory, cost of goods sold, and gross margin from sales. Use the FIFO and LIFO inventory costing methods. Explain the difference in gross margin from sales produced by the two methods.

Exercise 8-10.
Lower-of-Cost-or-Market Method
(L.O. 6)

Tillman Company values its inventory, shown on page 427, at the lower of cost or market. Compute Tillman's inventory value using (1) the item-by-item method and (2) the major category method.

	Quantity	Per Unit Cost	Per Unit Market
Category I			
Item aa	200	$1.00	$0.90
Item bb	240	2.00	2.20
Item cc	400	4.00	3.75
Category II			
Item dd	300	6.00	6.50
Item ee	400	9.00	9.10

Exercise 8-11. Retail Method *(L.O. 7)*

Jamie's Dress Shop had net retail sales of $250,000 during the current year. Additional information obtained from the accounting records follows:

	At Cost	At Retail
Beginning Inventory	$ 40,000	$ 60,000
Net Purchases (excluding Freight In)	140,000	220,000
Freight In	10,400	

1. Estimate the company's ending inventory at cost using the retail method.
2. Assume that a physical inventory taken at year end revealed an inventory on hand of $18,000 at retail value. What is the estimated amount of inventory shrinkage (loss due to theft, damage, and so forth) at cost?
3. Prepare the journal entry to record the inventory shrinkage.

Exercise 8-12. Gross Profit Method *(L.O. 7)*

Dale Nolan was at home watching television when he received a call from the fire department. His business was a total loss from fire. The insurance company asked him to prove his inventory loss. For the year, until the date of the fire, Dale's company had sales of $450,000 and purchases of $280,000. Freight in amounted to $13,700, and the beginning inventory was $45,000. It was Dale's custom to price goods in such a way as to have a gross margin of 40 percent on sales.

Compute Dale's estimated inventory loss.

Interpretation Cases from Business

ICB 8-1. Crazy Eddie Inc.[8] *(L.O. 1)*

The *Wall Street Journal* reported on November 20, 1987, that Crazy Eddie, Inc., a discount consumer electronics chain, seemed to be missing $45 million in merchandise inventory. "It was a shock," Elias Zinn, the new president and chief executive officer, was quoted as saying.

The article went on to say that Mr. Zinn headed a management team that took control of Crazy Eddie after a new board of directors was elected at a shareholders' meeting on November 6. A count on November 9 turned up

8. Based on Ann Hagedorn, "Crazy Eddie Says About $45 Million of Goods Missing," *Wall Street Journal*, November 20, 1987, p. 47.

only $75 million compared with $126.7 million reported by the old management on August 30. Net sales could account for only $6.7 million of the difference. Mr. Zinn said he didn't know whether bookkeeping errors or an actual physical loss created the shortfall, although at least one store manager felt it was a bookkeeping error, because security is strong. "It would be hard for someone to steal anything," he says.

Required

1. What has been the effect of the misstatement of inventory on Crazy Eddie's reported earnings in prior accounting periods?
2. Is this a situation you would expect in a company that is experiencing financial difficulty? Explain.

ICB 8-2. Hershey Foods Corporation[9] *(L.O. 2, 4)*

A portion of the income statements for 1990 and 1989 for Hershey Foods Corporation, famous for its chocolate and confectionery products, appears as shown below (in thousands).

In a note on supplemental balance sheet information, Hershey indicated that most of its inventories are maintained on a last-in, first-out (LIFO) basis. The company also reported that inventories on a LIFO cost basis were $309,837 in 1989 and $379,108 in 1990. In addition, it reported that if valued on a first-in, first-out (FIFO) basis, inventories would have been $371,697 in 1989 and $434,774 in 1990.

	1990	1989
Net Sales	$2,715,609	$2,420,988
Cost of Goods Sold	1,588,360	1,455,612
Gross Margin	$1,127,249	$ 965,376
Selling, General, and Administrative Expense	776,668	655,040
Gain from Business Restructuring—Net	35,540	
Income from Operations	$ 386,121	$ 310,336
Interest Expense	24,603	20,414
Income Before Income Taxes	$ 361,518	$ 289,922
Provision for Income Taxes	145,636	118,868
Net Income (from operations)	$ 215,882	$ 171,054

Required

1. Prepare a schedule comparing net income for 1990 on a LIFO basis with what it would have been on a FIFO basis. Use a corporate income tax rate of 40.3 percent (Hershey's average tax rate in 1990).
2. Why do you suppose the management of Hershey chooses to use the LIFO inventory method? On what economic conditions, if any, do these reasons depend? Given your calculations in **1** above, do you believe the economic conditions relevant to Hershey were advantageous for using LIFO in 1990? Explain your answer.

ICB 8-3. General Motors[10] *(L.O. 4)*

In 1985 and 1986 General Motors Corp. experienced what is called a LIFO liquidation, as explained in its 1986 annual report: "Certain LIFO inventories carried at lower costs prevailing in prior years, as compared with the costs of

9. The income statements are reprinted by permission of the copyright owner, Hershey Foods Corporation, Hershey, Pennsylvania, U.S.A.

10. Excerpts from the 1986 Annual Report used by permission of General Motors. Copyright 1986.

current purchases, were liquidated in 1986 and 1985. These inventory adjustments favorably affected income before income taxes by approximately $38.2 million in 1986 and $20.9 million in 1985." General Motors' average income tax rate for 1985 and 1986 was 22 percent.

Required

1. Explain why a reduction in the quantity of inventory resulted in favorable effects on income before income taxes. Would the same result have occurred if General Motors had used the FIFO method to value inventory? Explain your answer.
2. What is the income tax effect of the LIFO liquidation? Is it really a "favorable" outcome?

Problem Set A

Problem 8A-1. Inventory Costing Methods
(L.O. 3)

Palaggi Company merchandises a single product called Compak. The following data represent beginning inventory and purchases of Compak during the past year: January 1 inventory, 68,000 units at $11.00; February purchases, 80,000 units at $12.00; March purchases, 160,000 units at $12.40; May purchases, 120,000 units at $12.60; July purchases, 200,000 units at $12.80; September purchases, 160,000 units at $12.60; and November purchases, 60,000 units at $13.00. Sales of Compak totaled 786,000 units at $20 per unit. Selling and administrative expenses totaled $5,102,000 for the year, and Palaggi Company uses a periodic inventory system.

Required

1. Prepare a schedule to compute the cost of goods available for sale.
2. Prepare an income statement under each of the following assumptions: (a) costs are assigned to inventory on an average-cost basis; (b) costs are assigned to inventory on a FIFO basis; (c) costs are assigned to inventory on a LIFO basis.

Problem 8A-2. Lower-of-Cost-or-Market Method
(L.O. 6)

After taking the physical inventory, the accountant for McFarlane Company prepared the inventory schedule shown below:

	Quantity	Per Unit	
		Cost	Market
Product line 1			
Item 11	190	$ 9	$10
Item 12	270	4	5
Item 13	210	8	7
Product line 2			
Item 21	160	15	17
Item 22	400	21	20
Item 23	70	18	20
Product line 3			
Item 31	290	26	20
Item 32	310	30	28
Item 33	120	34	39

Required

Determine the value of the inventory at lower of cost or market using (1) the item-by-item method and (2) the major category method.

Problem 8A-3.
Periodic Inventory System
(L.O. 3)

The beginning inventory of Product M and data on purchases and sales for a two-month period are presented below. The company closes its books at the end of each month. It uses a periodic inventory system.

Apr. 1	Inventory	50 units @ $102
5	Sale	30 units
10	Purchase	100 units @ $110
17	Sale	60 units
May 2	Purchase	100 units @ $108
8	Sale	110 units
14	Purchase	50 units @ $112
18	Sale	40 units
22	Purchase	60 units @ $117
26	Sale	30 units
31	Sale	20 units

Required

1. Compute the value of the ending inventory of Product M on April 30 and May 31 on a FIFO basis. In addition, determine cost of goods sold for April and May.
2. Compute the value of the ending inventory of Product M on April 30 and May 31 on a LIFO basis. In addition, determine cost of goods sold for April and May.
3. Prepare a general journal entry to record the sale on May 31 to Alou Corporation on credit for $4,000.

Problem 8A-4.
Perpetual Inventory System
(L.O. 3, 5)

Assume the data presented in Problem 8A-3, except that the company uses a perpetual inventory system.

Required

1. Assume that the company maintains inventory on a FIFO basis and uses perpetual inventory cards similar to the one illustrated in Exhibit 8-2. Record the transactions on a card, using two or more lines as needed. Also, determine cost of goods sold for April and May.
2. Assuming that the company keeps its records on a LIFO basis, record the transactions on a second record card and determine cost of goods sold for both months.
3. Assuming that the May 31 sale was made to Alou Corporation on credit for $4,000, prepare a general journal entry to record the sale and cost of goods sold on a LIFO basis.
4. Assuming that the company takes a periodic physical inventory on May 31, that the value of the Product M inventory was $6,900, and that the FIFO basis of evaluating inventory is used, record an inventory shrinkage if necessary.

Problem 8A-5.
Retail Inventory Method
(L.O. 7)

Ramirez Company operates a large discount store and uses the retail inventory method to estimate the cost of ending inventory. Management suspects that in recent weeks there have been unusually heavy losses from shoplifting or employee pilferage. To estimate the amount of the loss, the company has taken a physical inventory and will compare the results with the estimated cost of inventory. Data from the accounting records of Ramirez Company are as follows:

	At Cost	At Retail
October 1 Beginning Inventory	$51,488	$ 74,300
Purchases	71,733	108,500
Purchases Returns and Allowances	(2,043)	(3,200)
Freight In	950	
Sales		109,183
Sales Returns and Allowances		(933)
October 31 Physical Inventory		62,450

Required

1. Prepare a schedule to estimate the dollar amount of the store's year-end inventory using the retail method.
2. Use the store's cost ratio to reduce the retail value of the physical inventory to cost.
3. Calculate the estimated amount of inventory shortage at cost and at retail.

Problem 8A-6. Gross Profit Method
(L.O. 7)

Holmes Brothers is a large retail furniture company that operates in two adjacent warehouses. One warehouse is a showroom, and the other is used for storage of merchandise. On the night of April 22, a fire broke out in the storage warehouse and destroyed the merchandise. Fortunately, the fire did not reach the showroom, so all the merchandise on display was saved.

Although the company maintained a perpetual inventory system, its records were rather haphazard, and the last reliable physical inventory was taken on December 31. In addition, there was no control of the flow of the goods between the showroom and the warehouse. Thus it was impossible to tell what goods should be in either place. As a result, the insurance company required an independent estimate of the amount of loss. The insurance company examiners were satisfied when they were provided with the following information:

1. Merchandise Inventory on December 31	$ 727,400
2. Purchases, January 1 to April 22	1,206,100
3. Purchases Returns, January 1 to April 22	(5,353)
4. Freight In, January 1 to April 22	26,550
5. Sales, January 1 to April 22	1,979,525
6. Sales Returns, January 1 to April 22	(14,900)
7. Merchandise inventory in showroom on April 22	201,480
8. Average gross profit margin	44 percent

Required

Prepare a schedule that estimates the amount of the inventory lost in the fire.

Problem Set B

Problem 8B-1. Inventory Costing Methods
(L.O. 3)

The Highland Door Company sold 2,200 doors during 19x8 at $160 per door. Its beginning inventory on January 1 was 130 doors at $56. Purchases during the year were as follows on the next page:

February	225 doors @ $62
April	350 doors @ $65
June	700 doors @ $70
August	300 doors @ $66
October	400 doors @ $68
November	250 doors @ $72

The company's selling and administrative expenses for the year were $101,000, and the company uses the periodic inventory system.

Required

1. Prepare a schedule to compute the cost of goods available for sale.
2. Prepare an income statement under each of the following assumptions: (a) costs are assigned to inventory on an average-cost basis; (b) costs are assigned to inventory on a FIFO basis; (c) costs are assigned to inventory on a LIFO basis.

Problem 8B-2. Lower-of-Cost-or-Market Method
(L.O. 6)

The employees of Garland's Shoes completed their physical inventory as shown below.

	Pairs of Shoes	Per Unit Cost	Per Unit Market
Men			
Black	400	$22	$24
Brown	325	21	21
Blue	100	25	23
Tan	200	19	10
Women			
White	300	26	32
Red	150	23	20
Yellow	100	30	25
Blue	250	25	33
Brown	100	20	30
Black	150	20	25

Required

Determine the value of inventory at lower of cost or market using (1) the item-by-item method and (2) the major category method.

Problem 8B-3. Periodic Inventory System
(L.O. 3)

The beginning inventory, purchases, and sales of Product SLT for August and September are presented below. The company closes its books at the end of each month. It uses the periodic inventory system.

Aug.	1	Beginning Inventory	60 units @ $49
	7	Sales	20 units
	10	Purchases	100 units @ $52
	19	Sales	70 units

Sept.	4	Purchases	120 units @ $53
	11	Sales	110 units
	15	Purchases	50 units @ $54
	23	Sales	80 units
	25	Purchases	100 units @ $55
	27	Sales	100 units

Required

1. Compute the cost of the ending inventory on August 31 and September 30 on a FIFO basis. In addition, determine cost of goods sold for August and September.
2. Compute the cost of the ending inventory on August 31 and September 30 on a LIFO basis. In addition, determine cost of goods sold for August and September.
3. Prepare a general journal entry to record the sale on September 27 to Karimi Company on credit for $9,100.

Problem 8B-4. Perpetual Inventory System
(L.O. 3, 5)

Assume the data presented in Problem 8B-3, except that the company uses the perpetual inventory system.

Required

1. Assume that the company maintains inventory on a FIFO basis and uses perpetual inventory cards similar to the one illustrated in Exhibit 8-2. Record the transactions on a card, using two or more lines as needed. Also, determine cost of goods sold for August and September.
2. Assuming that the company keeps its records on a LIFO basis, record the transactions on a second record card and determine cost of goods sold for both months.
3. Prepare general journal entries to record the credit purchase on September 15 and the credit sale on September 27 for $9,100, assuming the LIFO basis of costing inventory. What are the amount and LIFO cost of the inventory at the end of September?
4. On September 30, the company counted a physical inventory of 22 units. Record any inventory shrinkage necessary, assuming a LIFO basis.

Problem 8B-5. Retail Inventory Method
(L.O. 7)

Steelcraft switched recently to the retail inventory method to estimate the cost of ending inventory. To test this method, the company took a physical inventory one month after its implementation. Cost, retail, and the physical inventory data are presented below:

	At Cost	At Retail
March 1 Beginning Inventory	$236,066	$311,400
Purchases	375,000	504,200
Purchases Returns and Allowances	(12,600)	(17,400)
Freight In	4,175	
Sales		530,000
Sales Returns and Allowances		(14,000)
March 31 Physical Inventory		254,100

Required

1. Prepare a schedule to estimate the dollar amount of Steelcraft's March 31 inventory using the retail method.
2. Use Steelcraft's cost ratio to reduce the retail value of the physical inventory to cost.
3. Calculate the estimated amount of inventory shortage at cost and at retail.

Problem 8B-6. Gross Profit Method *(L.O. 7)*

Raleigh Oil Products warehouses its oil field products in a West Texas warehouse. The warehouse and most of its inventory were completely destroyed by a tornado on May 11. The company found some of its records, but it does not keep perpetual inventory records. The warehouse manager must estimate the amount of the loss. He found the information presented below in the records:

January 1 Beginning Inventory	$660,000
Purchases, January 2 to May 11	390,000
Purchases Returns, January 2 to May 11	(15,000)
Freight In since January 2	8,000
Sales, January 2 to May 11	920,000
Sales Returns, January 2 to May 11	(20,000)

Inventory costing $210,000 was recovered and could be sold. The manager remembers that the average gross margin on oil field products is 48 percent.

Required

Prepare a schedule to estimate the inventory destroyed by the tornado.

Financial Decision Cases

8-1. RTS Company *(L.O. 3, 4)*

Refrigerated Truck Sales Company (RTS Company) buys large refrigerated trucks from the manufacturer and sells them to companies and independent truckers who haul perishable goods for long distances. RTS has been successful in this specialized niche of the industry because it provides a unique product and service. Because of the high cost of these trucks and of financing inventory, RTS tries to maintain as small an inventory as possible. In fact, at the beginning of March, the company had no inventory or liabilities, as shown by the following balance sheet:

RTS Company
Balance Sheet
March 1, 19xx

Assets		Stockholders' Equity	
Cash	$400,000	Common Stock	$400,000
Total Assets	$400,000	Total Stockholders' Equity	$400,000

On March 5, RTS takes delivery of a truck at a price of $150,000. On March 15, after a rise in price, an identical truck is delivered to the company at a price of

$160,000. On March 25, the company sells one of the trucks for $195,000. During March, expenses totaled $15,000. All transactions were paid in cash.

Required

1. Prepare income statements and balance sheets for RTS on March 31 using (a) the FIFO method of inventory valuation and (b) the LIFO method of inventory valuation. Assume an income tax rate of 40 percent. Explain the effects that each method has on the financial statements.
2. Assume that Robert Trinker, owner of RTS Company, follows the policy of declaring a cash dividend each period that is exactly equal to net income. What effect does this action have on each balance sheet prepared in **1**, and how do they compare with the balance sheet at the beginning of the month? Which inventory method, if either, do you feel is more realistic in representing RTS's income?
3. Assume that RTS receives notice of another price increase of $10,000 on refrigerated trucks, to take effect on April 1. How does this information relate to the dividend policy of the owner, and how will it affect next month's operations?

8-2.
Kyoto Trading Company
(L.O. 4)

The Kyoto Trading Company began business in 19x1 for the purpose of importing and marketing an electronics component used widely in digital appliances. During the course of the year, the Kyoto Trading Company imported the following components:

	Units	Price per Unit
Jan. 14	200,000	$2
Aug. 18	400,000	3

During 19x1 the company sold 500,000 units at $6 per unit and had operating expenses of $1,200,000.

It is now December 20, 19x1, and management is considering its options. Among its considerations is which inventory method to choose. It has decided to choose either the FIFO or the LIFO cost basis. Also, management has an option to purchase an additional 100,000 units of inventory before year end at a price of $4 per unit, the price that is expected to prevail during 19x2. The income tax rate applicable to the company in 19x1 is 30 percent.

Business conditions are expected to be favorable in 19x2, as they were in 19x1. Management has asked you to advise it as to which inventory method to choose and whether to order the additional inventory.

Required

1. Using the periodic inventory system, compute net income for 19x1 using the FIFO basis and the LIFO basis, assuming that the additional inventory is not purchased in 19x1.
2. Using the periodic inventory system, compute net income for 19x1 using the FIFO basis and the LIFO basis, assuming that the additional inventory is purchased.
3. What is the difference in cash flows under the four alternatives presented in **1** and **2**?
4. Should management choose a FIFO or a LIFO basis for costing inventory, and should a purchase be made prior to December 31?

LEARNING OBJECTIVES

1. *Describe the nature, types, and issues of accounting for long-term assets.*
2. *Account for the cost of property, plant, and equipment.*
3. *Define* depreciation, *state the factors that affect its computation, and show how to record it.*
4. *Compute periodic depreciation under (a) the straight-line method, (b) the production method, and (c) accelerated methods, including (1) the sum-of-the-years'-digits method and (2) the declining-balance method.*
5. *Apply depreciation methods to problems of partial years, revised rates, items of low unit cost, groups of similar items, and accelerated cost recovery.*
6. *Apply the matching rule to the allocation of expired costs for capital expenditures and revenue expenditures.*
7. *Account for disposal of depreciable assets not involving exchanges.*
8. *Account for disposal of depreciable assets involving exchanges.*
9. *Identify natural resource accounting issues and compute depletion.*
10. *Apply the matching rule to intangible asset accounting issues.*

CHAPTER 9

Long-Term Assets: Acquisition and Depreciation

Long-term assets present management and accountants with many challenges. This chapter focuses on the acquisition, depreciation or amortization, and disposal of long-term assets and other special accounting issues related to these assets. After studying this chapter, you should be able to meet the learning objectives listed on the left.

DECISION POINT
H. J. Heinz Company[1]

The effects of management's decisions regarding long-term assets are most apparent in the areas of reported total assets and net income. An idea of the extent and importance of these assets can be gained from the following figures taken from the 1989 annual report of the H. J. Heinz Company, one of the world's largest food companies. Of the company's more than $4 billion in assets, about one-third consists of property, plant, and equipment, and another 15 percent is intangible assets. The depreciation and amortization associated with these assets are equal to more than one-third of the company's $408 million in net income. Further, the company spent $323 million on new long-term assets. Differences in methods of accounting for these assets and expenditures can make a difference of millions of dollars in reported net income and income taxes paid. Among the issues management and the company's accountants must consider are how to account for acquisition costs, how to estimate how long the assets will last, what methods should be used in allocating the cost, how special capital and revenue expenditures are to be handled, how gains and losses are to

1. Excerpts from the 1989 Annual Report used by permission of H. J. Heinz Company. Copyright © 1989.

be accounted for when these assets are sold or otherwise disposed of, and how intangible assets, such as trademarks, are to be accounted for. The purpose of this chapter is to provide answers to these questions. ■

Long-Term Assets

Let us take a closer look at long-term assets, which were defined briefly in the chapter on inventories. **Long-term assets** are assets that (1) have a useful life of more than one year, (2) are acquired for use in the operation of the business, and (3) are not intended for resale to customers. For many years, it was common to refer to long-term assets as **fixed assets**, but use of this term is declining because the word *fixed* implies that they last forever. The relative importance of long-term assets to various industries is shown in Figure 9-1. Long-term assets range from 16.3 percent of total assets in auto and home supply to 34.2 percent in interstate trucking.

Although there is no strict minimum length of time for an asset to be classified as long term, the most common criterion is that the asset must be capable of repeated use for a period of at least a year. Included in this category is equipment that is used only in peak or emergency periods, such as a generator.

Assets not used in the normal course of business should not be included in this category. Thus, land held for speculative reasons or buildings that are no longer used in ordinary business operations should not be included

Figure 9-1. Long-Term Assets as a Percentage of Total Assets in Selected Industries

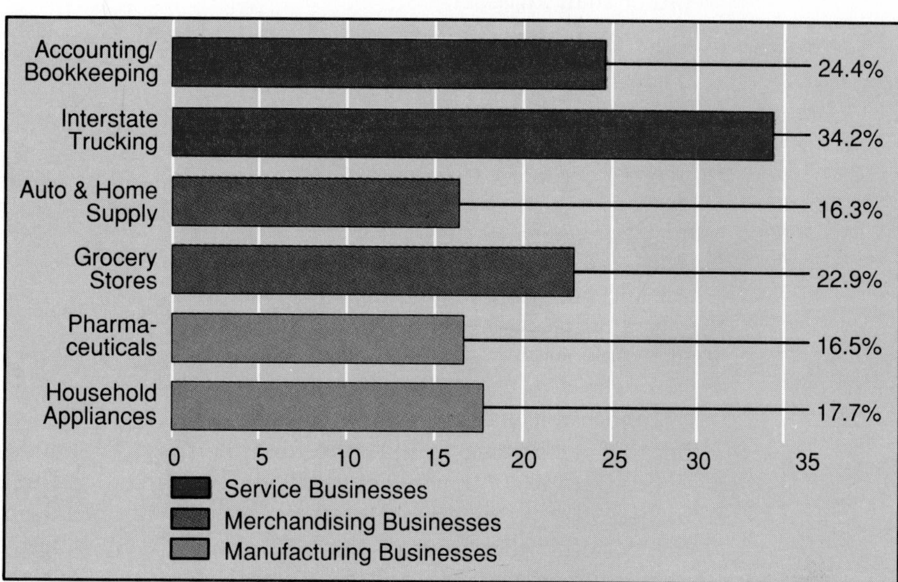

Source: Data from Dun and Bradstreet, *Industry Norms and Ratios*, 1990–91.

in the property, plant, and equipment category. Instead, they should be classified as long-term investments.

Finally, if an item is held for resale to customers, it should be classified as inventory, not plant and equipment—no matter how durable it is. For example, a printing press held for sale by a printing press manufacturer would be considered inventory, whereas the same printing press would be plant and equipment for a printing company that buys the press to use in its operations.

Life of Long-Term Assets

OBJECTIVE 1 *Describe the nature, types, and issues of accounting for long-term assets*

The primary accounting issue in dealing with short-term assets such as inventory and prepaid assets was to determine how much of the asset benefited the current period and how much should be carried forward as an asset to benefit future periods. Costs must be allocated to the periods that benefit from the use of the asset to satisfy the matching rule. Note that exactly the same matching issue applies to long-term assets, since they are long-term unexpired costs.

It is helpful to think of a long-term asset as a bundle of services that are to be used in the operation of the business over a period of years. A delivery truck may provide 100,000 miles of service over its life. A piece of equipment may have the potential to produce 500,000 parts. A building may provide shelter for fifty years. As each of these assets is purchased, the company is paying in advance (prepaying) for 100,000 miles, capacity to produce 500,000 parts, or fifty years of service. In essence, each of these assets is a type of long-term prepaid expense. The accounting problem is to spread the cost of these services over the useful life of the asset. As the services benefit the company over the years, the cost becomes an expense rather than an asset.

Types of Long-Term Assets

Long-term assets are customarily divided into the following categories:

Asset	Expense
Tangible Assets	
Land	None
Plant, buildings, and equipment (plant assets)	Depreciation
Natural resources	Depletion
Intangible Assets	Amortization

Tangible assets have physical substance. Land is a tangible asset, and because it has an unlimited life it is the only tangible asset not subject to depreciation or other expense. Plant, buildings, and equipment (referred to hereafter as plant assets) are subject to depreciation. **Depreciation** is the periodic allocation of the cost of a tangible long-lived asset over its useful life. The term applies to manmade assets only. Note that accounting for depreciation is an allocation process, not a valuation process. This point is discussed in more detail later.

Natural resources differ from land in that they are purchased for the substances that can be taken from the land and used up rather than for the value of their location. Among natural resources are ore from mines, oil and gas from oil and gas fields, and lumber from forests. Natural resources are subject to depletion rather than to depreciation. The term **depletion** refers to the exhaustion of a natural resource through mining, cutting, pumping, or otherwise using up the resource, and to the way in which the cost is allocated.

Intangible assets are long-term assets that do not have physical substance and in most cases have to do with legal rights or advantages held. Among them are patents, copyrights, trademarks, franchises, organization costs, leaseholds, leasehold improvements, and goodwill. The allocation of the cost of intangible assets to the periods that they benefit is called **amortization**. Even though the current assets accounts receivable and prepaid expenses do not have physical substance, they are not intangible assets because they are not long term.

The unexpired part of the cost of an asset is generally called its book value or *carrying value*. The latter term is used in this book when referring to long-term assets. The carrying value of plant assets, for instance, is cost less accumulated depreciation.

Issues of Accounting for Long-Term Assets

As with inventories and prepaid expenses, there are two important accounting problems connected with long-term assets. The first is determining how much of the total cost should be allocated to expense in the current accounting period. The second is figuring how much should remain on the balance sheet as an asset to benefit future periods. To solve these problems, four important questions (shown in Figure 9-2) must be answered:

1. How is the cost of the long-term assets determined?
2. How should the expired portion of the cost of the long-term assets be allocated against revenues over time?
3. How should later expenditures such as repairs, maintenance, and additions be treated?
4. How should disposal of long-term assets be recorded?

The first part of this chapter deals with the answers to questions **1** and **2**. The discussion of questions **3** and **4** and specific discussion of natural resources and intangibles are included at the end of the chapter.

Acquisition Cost of Property, Plant, and Equipment

The acquisition cost of property, plant, and equipment includes all expenditures reasonable and necessary to get them in place and ready for use. For example, the cost of installing and testing a machine is a legitimate cost of the machine. However, if the machine is damaged during instal-

Figure 9-2. Issues of Accounting for Long-Term Assets

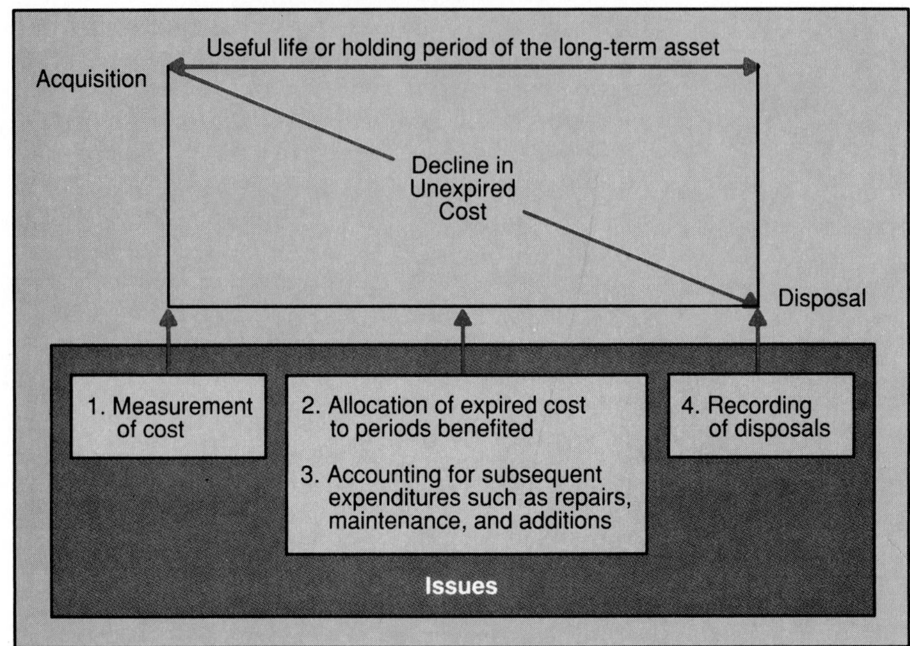

OBJECTIVE 2 *Account for the cost of property, plant, and equipment*

lation, the cost of repairing the machine is an operating expense and not a cost of the machine.

Cost is easiest to determine when a transaction is made for cash. In this case, the cost of the asset is equal to the cash paid for the asset plus expenditures for freight, insurance while in transit, installation, and other necessary related costs. If a debt is incurred in the purchase of the asset, the interest charges are not a cost of the asset but a cost of borrowing the money to buy the asset. They are therefore an expense for the period. An exception to this principle is that interest costs during the construction of an asset are properly included as a cost of the asset.[2]

Expenditures such as freight, insurance while in transit, and installation are included in the cost of the asset because these expenditures are necessary for the asset to function. In accordance with the matching rule, they are allocated to the useful life of the asset rather than charged as an expense in the current period.

Some of the problems of determining the cost of a long-lived asset are demonstrated in the illustrations for land, buildings, equipment, land improvements, and group purchases presented in the next few sections.

Land

There are often expenditures in addition to the purchase price of the land that should be debited to the Land account. Some examples are commissions to real estate agents; lawyers' fees; accrued taxes paid by the pur-

2. "Capitalization of Interest Cost," *Statement of Financial Accounting Standards No. 34* (Stamford, Conn.: Financial Accounting Standards Board, 1979), par. 9–11.

chaser; cost of draining, clearing, and grading; and assessments for local improvements such as streets and sewage systems. The cost of landscaping is usually debited to the Land account also because these improvements are relatively permanent.

Let us assume that a company buys land for a new retail operation. It pays a net purchase price of $170,000, pays brokerage fees of $6,000 and legal fees of $2,000, pays $10,000 to have an old building on the site torn down, receives $4,000 salvage from the old building, and pays $1,000 to have the site graded. The cost of the land will be $185,000, determined as follows:

Net purchase price		$170,000
Brokerage fees		6,000
Legal fees		2,000
Tearing down old building	$10,000	
Less salvage	4,000	6,000
Grading		1,000
		$185,000

Land Improvements

Improvements to real estate such as driveways, parking lots, and fences have a limited life and so are subject to depreciation. They should be recorded in an account called Land Improvements rather than in the Land account.

Buildings

When an existing building is purchased, its cost includes the purchase price plus all repairs and other expenses required to put it in usable condition. When a business constructs its own building, the cost includes all reasonable and necessary expenditures, such as those for materials, labor, part of the overhead and other indirect costs, the architects' fees, insurance during construction, interest on construction loans during the period of construction, the lawyers' fees, and building permits. If outside contractors are used in the construction, the net contract price plus other expenditures necessary to put the building in usable condition are included.

Equipment

The cost of equipment includes all expenditures connected with purchasing the equipment and preparing it for use. These expenditures include the invoice price less cash discounts; freight or transportation, including insurance; excise taxes and tariffs; buying expenses; installation costs; and test runs to ready the equipment for operation.

Group Purchases

Sometimes land and other assets will be purchased for a lump sum. Because land is a nondepreciable asset and has an unlimited life, separate ledger accounts must be kept for land and the other assets. For this reason, the lump-sum purchase price must be apportioned between the land and the other assets. For example, assume that a building and the land on which it is situated are purchased for a lump-sum payment of $85,000. The apportionment can be made by determining the price of each if purchased separately and applying the appropriate percentages to the lump-sum price. Assume that appraisals yield estimates of $10,000 for the land and $90,000 for the building, if purchased separately. In that case, 10 percent, or $8,500, of the lump-sum price would be allocated to the land and 90 percent, or $76,500, would be allocated to the building, as follows:

	Appraisal	Percentage	Apportionment
Land	$ 10,000	10	$ 8,500
Building	90,000	90	76,500
Totals	$100,000	100	$85,000

Accounting for Depreciation

OBJECTIVE 3 *Define depreciation, state the factors that affect its computation, and show how to record it*

Depreciation accounting is described by the AICPA as follows:

> The cost of a productive facility is one of the costs of the services it renders during its useful economic life. Generally accepted accounting principles require that this cost be spread over the expected useful life of the facility in such a way as to allocate it as equitably as possible to the periods during which services are obtained from the use of the facility. This procedure is known as depreciation accounting, a system of accounting which aims to distribute the cost or other basic value of tangible capital assets, less salvage (if any), over the estimated useful life of the unit . . . in a systematic and rational manner. It is a process of allocation, not of valuation.[3]

This description contains several important points. First, all tangible assets except land have a limited useful life. Because of this limited useful life, the cost of these assets must be distributed as expenses over the years they benefit. Physical deterioration and obsolescence are the major causes of the limited useful life of a depreciable asset. The **physical deterioration** of tangible assets results from use and from exposure to the elements, such as wind and sun. Periodic repairs and a sound maintenance policy may keep buildings and equipment in good operating order and extract the maximum useful life from them, but every machine or building at some point must be discarded. The need for depreciation is not eliminated by repairs. **Obsolescence** is the process of becoming out of date. With fast-changing technology as well as fast-changing demands, machinery and even buildings often become obsolete before they wear out. Accountants do not distinguish between physical deterioration and obsolescence because they are interested in the length of the useful life of the asset regardless of what limits that useful life.

3. *Financial Accounting Standards: Original Pronouncements as of July 1, 1977* (Stamford, Conn.: Financial Accounting Standards Board, 1977), ARB No. 43, Chapt. 9, Sec. C, par. 5.

Second, the term *depreciation,* as used in accounting, does not refer to the physical deterioration of an asset or the decrease in market value of an asset over time. Depreciation means the allocation of the cost of a plant asset to the periods that benefit from the services of the asset. The term is used to describe the gradual conversion of the cost of the asset into an expense.

Third, depreciation is not a process of valuation. Accounting records are kept in accordance with the cost principle and thus are not meant to be indicators of changing price levels. It is possible that, through an advantageous buy and specific market conditions, the market value of a building may rise. Nevertheless, depreciation must continue to be recorded because it is the result of an allocation, not a valuation, process. Eventually the building will wear out or become obsolete regardless of interim fluctuations in market value.

Factors That Affect the Computation of Depreciation

Four factors affect the computation of depreciation. They are: (1) cost, (2) residual value, (3) depreciable cost, and (4) estimated useful life.

Cost. As explained above, cost is the net purchase price plus all reasonable and necessary expenditures to get the asset in place and ready for use.

Residual Value. The **residual value** of an asset is its estimated net scrap, salvage, or trade-in value as of the estimated date of disposal. Other terms often used to describe residual value are **salvage value** and **disposal value**.

Depreciable Cost. The **depreciable cost** of an asset is its cost less its residual value. For example, a truck that costs $12,000 and has a residual value of $3,000 would have a depreciable cost of $9,000. Depreciable cost must be allocated over the useful life of the asset.

Estimated Useful Life. The **estimated useful life** of an asset is the total number of service units expected from the asset. Service units may be measured in terms of years the asset is expected to be used, units expected to be produced, miles expected to be driven, or similar measures. In computing the estimated useful life of an asset, the accountant should consider all relevant information, including (1) past experience with similar assets, (2) the asset's present condition, (3) the company's repair and maintenance policy, (4) current technological and industry trends, and (5) local conditions such as weather.

As introduced in the chapter on business income and adjusting entries, depreciation is recorded at the end of the accounting period by an adjusting entry that takes the following form:

Depreciation Expense, Asset Name	xxx	
Accumulated Depreciation, Asset Name		xxx
To record depreciation for the period		

Methods of Computing Depreciation

OBJECTIVE 4
Compute periodic depreciation under each of four methods

Many methods are used to allocate the cost of plant and equipment to accounting periods through depreciation. Each of them is proper for certain circumstances. The most common methods are (1) the straight-line method, (2) the production method, and (3) two accelerated methods known as the sum-of-the-years'-digits method and the declining-balance method.

Straight-Line Method

OBJECTIVE 4a
Compute periodic depreciation under the straight-line method

When the **straight-line method** is used to allocate depreciation, the depreciable cost of the asset is spread evenly over the life of the asset. The straight-line method is based on the assumption that depreciation depends only on the passage of time. The depreciation expense for each period is computed by dividing the depreciable cost (cost of the depreciating asset less its estimated residual value) by the number of accounting periods in the estimated useful life. The rate of depreciation is the same in each year. Suppose, for example, that a delivery truck costs \$10,000 and has an estimated residual value of \$1,000 at the end of its estimated useful life of five years. In this case, the annual depreciation would be \$1,800 under the straight-line method. This calculation is as follows:

$$\frac{\text{Cost} - \text{residual value}}{\text{Estimated useful life}} = \frac{\$10{,}000 - \$1{,}000}{5\text{ years}} = \$1{,}800 \text{ per year}$$

The depreciation for the five years would be as follows:

Depreciation Schedule, Straight-Line Method

	Cost	Yearly Depreciation	Accumulated Depreciation	Carrying Value
Date of purchase	\$10,000	—	—	\$10,000
End of first year	10,000	\$1,800	\$1,800	8,200
End of second year	10,000	1,800	3,600	6,400
End of third year	10,000	1,800	5,400	4,600
End of fourth year	10,000	1,800	7,200	2,800
End of fifth year	10,000	1,800	9,000	1,000

There are three important points to note from the schedule for the straight-line depreciation method. First, the depreciation is the same each year. Second, the accumulated depreciation increases uniformly. Third, the carrying value decreases uniformly until it reaches the estimated residual value.

Production Method

The **production method** of depreciation is based on the assumption that depreciation is solely the result of use and that the passage of time plays no role in the depreciation process. If we assume that the delivery truck

OBJECTIVE 4b
Compute periodic depreciation under the production method

from the previous example has an estimated useful life of 90,000 miles, the depreciation cost per mile would be determined as follows:

$$\frac{\text{Cost} - \text{residual value}}{\text{Estimated units of useful life}} = \frac{\$10{,}000 - \$1{,}000}{90{,}000 \text{ miles}} = \$.10 \text{ per mile}$$

If we assume that the mileage use of the truck was 20,000 miles for the first year, 30,000 miles for the second, 10,000 miles for the third, 20,000 miles for the fourth, and 10,000 miles for the fifth, the depreciation schedule for the delivery truck would appear as follows:

Depreciation Schedule, Production Method

	Cost	Miles	Yearly Deprecia-tion	Accumulated Deprecia-tion	Carrying Value
Date of purchase	$10,000	—	—	—	$10,000
End of first year	10,000	20,000	$2,000	$2,000	8,000
End of second year	10,000	30,000	3,000	5,000	5,000
End of third year	10,000	10,000	1,000	6,000	4,000
End of fourth year	10,000	20,000	2,000	8,000	2,000
End of fifth year	10,000	10,000	1,000	9,000	1,000

Note the direct relation between the amount of depreciation each year and the units of output or use. Also, the accumulated depreciation increases each year in direct relation to units of output or use. Finally, the carrying value decreases each year in direct relation to units of output or use until it reaches the estimated residual value.

Under the production method, the unit of output or use that is used to measure estimated useful life for each asset should be appropriate for that asset. For example, the number of items produced may be appropriate for one machine, whereas the number of hours of use may be a better indicator of depreciation for another. The production method should be used only when the output of an asset over its useful life can be estimated with reasonable accuracy.

Accelerated Methods

Accelerated methods of depreciation result in relatively large amounts of depreciation in the early years and smaller amounts in later years. These methods, which are based on the passage of time, assume that many kinds of plant assets are most efficient when new, so they provide more and better service in the early years of useful life. It is consistent with the matching rule to allocate more depreciation to the early years than to later years if the benefits or services received in the early years are greater.

The accelerated methods also recognize that changing technologies make some equipment lose service value rapidly. Thus, it is realistic to allocate more to depreciation in current years than in future years. New inventions and products result in obsolescence of equipment bought earlier, making it necessary to replace equipment sooner than if our technology changed more slowly.

Another argument in favor of accelerated methods is that repair expense is likely to be greater in future years than in current years. Thus, the total of repair and depreciation expense remains fairly constant over a period of years. This result naturally assumes that the services received from the asset are roughly equal from year to year.

OBJECTIVE 4c(1) *Compute periodic depreciation under the sum-of-the-years'-digits method*

Sum-of-the-Years'-Digits Method. Under the **sum-of-the-years'-digits method**, the years in the service life of an asset are added. Their sum becomes the denominator of a series of fractions that are applied against the depreciable cost of the asset in allocating the total depreciation over the estimated useful life. The numerators of the fractions are the individual years in the estimated useful life of the asset in their reverse order.

For the delivery truck used in the illustrations above, the estimated useful life is five years. The sum of the years' digits is as follows:[4]

$$1 + 2 + 3 + 4 + 5 = 15$$

The annual depreciation is then determined by multiplying the depreciable cost of $9,000 ($10,000 – $1,000) by each of the following fractions: 5/15, 4/15, 3/15, 2/15, 1/15. The depreciation schedule for the sum-of-the-years'-digits method is as follows:

Depreciation Schedule, Sum-of-the-Years'-Digits Method

	Cost	Yearly Depreciation		Accumulated Depreciation	Carrying Value
Date of purchase	$10,000		—	—	$10,000
End of first year	10,000	(5/15 × $9,000)	$3,000	$3,000	7,000
End of second year	10,000	(4/15 × $9,000)	2,400	5,400	4,600
End of third year	10,000	(3/15 × $9,000)	1,800	7,200	2,800
End of fourth year	10,000	(2/15 × $9,000)	1,200	8,400	1,600
End of fifth year	10,000	(1/15 × $9,000)	600	9,000	1,000

From the schedule, note that the yearly depreciation is greatest in the first year and declines each year after that. Also, the accumulated depreciation increases by a smaller amount each year. Finally, the carrying value decreases each year by the amount of depreciation until it reaches the residual value.

4. The denominator used in the sum-of-the-years'-digits method can be computed quickly from the following formula:

$$S = \frac{N(N + 1)}{2}$$

where S equals the sum of the digits and N equals the number of years in the estimated useful life. For example, for an asset with an estimated useful life of ten years, the sum of the digits equals 55, calculated as follows:

$$S = \frac{10(10 + 1)}{2} = \frac{110}{2} = 55$$

OBJECTIVE 4c(2)
Compute periodic depreciation under the declining-balance method

Declining-Balance Method. The **declining-balance method** is an accelerated method of depreciation in which depreciation is computed by applying a fixed rate to the carrying value (the declining balance) of a long-lived asset. It is based on the same assumption as the sum-of-the-years'-digits method. Both methods result in higher depreciation charges during the early years of an asset's life. Though any fixed rate might be used under the method, the most common rate is a percentage equal to twice the straight-line percentage. When twice the straight-line rate is used, the method is usually called the **double-declining-balance method**.

In our earlier example, the delivery truck had an estimated useful life of five years. Consequently, under the straight-line method, the percentage depreciation for each year was 20 percent (100 percent ÷ 5 years).

Under the double-declining-balance method, the fixed percentage rate is therefore 40 percent (2 × 20 percent). This fixed rate of 40 percent is applied to the *remaining carrying value* at the end of each year. Estimated residual value is not taken into account in figuring depreciation except in the last year of an asset's useful life, when depreciation is limited to the amount necessary to bring the carrying value down to the estimated residual value. The depreciation schedule for this method is as follows:

Depreciation Schedule, Double-Declining-Balance Method

	Cost	Yearly Depreciation		Accumulated Depreciation	Carrying Value
Date of purchase	$10,000		—	—	$10,000
End of first year	10,000	(40% × $10,000)	$4,000	$4,000	6,000
End of second year	10,000	(40% × $6,000)	2,400	6,400	3,600
End of third year	10,000	(40% × $3,600)	1,440	7,840	2,160
End of fourth year	10,000	(40% × $2,160)	864	8,704	1,296
End of fifth year	10,000		296*	9,000	1,000

* Depreciation limited to amount necessary to reduce carrying value to residual value.
$296 = $1,296 (previous carrying value) – $1,000 (residual value)

Note that the fixed rate is always applied to the carrying value of the previous year. Next, the depreciation is greatest in the first year and declines each year after that. Finally, the depreciation in the last year is limited to the amount necessary to reduce carrying value to residual value.

Comparing the Four Methods

A visual comparison may provide a better understanding of the four depreciation methods described above. Figure 9-3 compares periodic depreciation and carrying value under the four methods. In the graph that shows yearly depreciation, straight-line depreciation is uniform over the five-year period at $1,800. However, both accelerated depreciation meth-

Figure 9-3. Graphical Comparison of Four Methods of Determining Depreciation

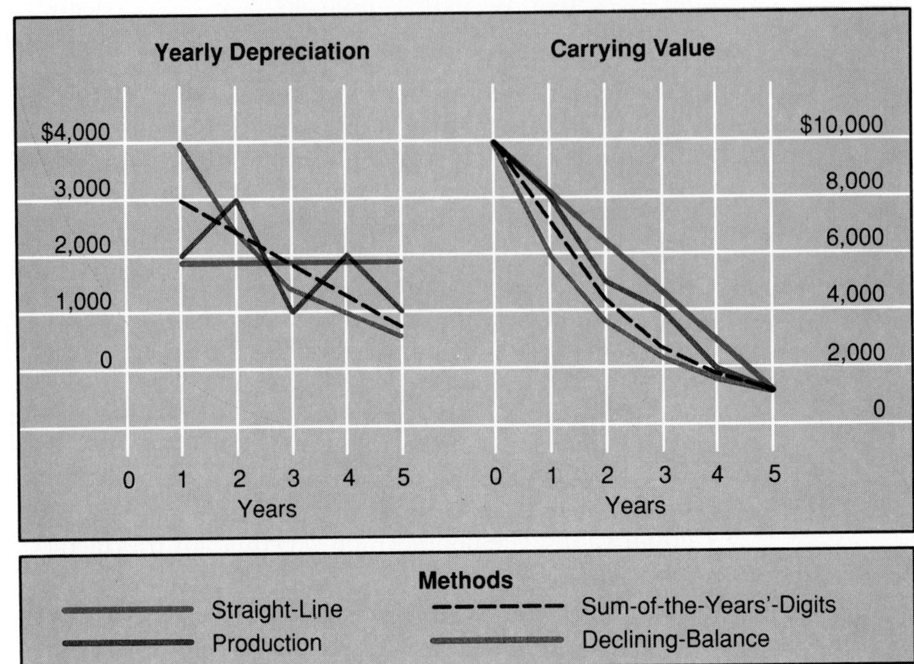

ods (sum-of-the-years'-digits and declining-balance) begin at amounts greater than straight-line ($3,000 and $4,000, respectively), and decrease each year to amounts less than straight-line ($600 and $296, respectively). The production method does not produce a regular pattern of depreciation because of the random fluctuation of the depreciation from year to year. These yearly depreciation patterns are reflected in the carrying value graph. For instance, the carrying value for the straight-line method is always greater than that for the accelerated methods. However, in the latter graph, each method starts in the same place (cost of $10,000) and ends at the same place (residual value of $1,000). It is the patterns during the useful life of the asset that differ for each method.

Special Problems of Depreciating Plant Assets

The illustrations used so far in this chapter have been simplified to explain the concepts and methods of depreciation. In real business practice, there is often a need to (1) calculate depreciation for partial years, (2) revise depreciation rates on the basis of new estimates of the useful life or residual value, (3) develop more practical ways of depreciating items of low unit cost, (4) group together items that are alike in order to calculate depreciation, and (5) use the accelerated cost recovery method for tax purposes. The next sections discuss these five cases.

Depreciation for Partial Years

OBJECTIVE 5
Apply depreciation methods to problems of partial years, revised rates, items of low unit cost, groups of similar items, and accelerated cost recovery

So far, the illustrations of the depreciation methods have assumed that the plant assets were purchased at the beginning or end of an accounting period. However, business people do not often buy assets exactly at the beginning or end of an accounting period. In most cases, they buy the assets when they are needed and sell or discard them when they are no longer useful or needed. The time of the year is normally not a factor in the decision. Consequently, it is often necessary to calculate depreciation for partial years.

For example, assume that a piece of equipment is purchased for $3,500 and that it has an estimated useful life of six years, with an estimated residual value of $500. Assume also that it is purchased on September 5 and that the yearly accounting period ends on December 31. Depreciation must be recorded for four months, or four-twelfths of the year. This factor is applied to the calculated depreciation for the entire year. The four months' depreciation under the straight-line method is calculated as follows:

$$\frac{\$3{,}500 - \$500}{6 \text{ years}} \times 4/12 = \$167$$

For the other depreciation methods, most companies will compute the first year's depreciation and then multiply by the partial year factor. For example, if the company used the double-declining-balance method on the above equipment, the depreciation on the asset would be computed as follows:

$$\$3{,}500 \times .33 \times 4/12 = \$385$$

Typically, the depreciation calculation is rounded off to the nearest whole month because a partial month's depreciation is not usually material and it makes the calculation easier. In this case, depreciation was recorded from the beginning of September even though the purchase was made on September 5. If the equipment had been purchased on September 16 or thereafter, depreciation would be charged beginning October 1, as if the equipment were purchased on that date. Some companies round off all partial years to the nearest one-half year for ease of calculation (half-year convention).

When an asset is disposed of, the depreciation on it must be brought up to date. For example, if the asset is not disposed of at the beginning or end of the year, depreciation must be recorded for a partial year, reflecting the time to the date of disposal. The accounting treatment of disposals is covered later in this chapter.

Revision of Depreciation Rates

Because depreciation rates are based on an estimate of the useful life of an asset, the periodic depreciation charge is seldom precisely accurate. Sometimes it is very inadequate or excessive. This situation may result from an underestimate or overestimate of the asset's useful life or perhaps from a wrong estimate of the residual value. What action should be taken when it is found, after using a piece of equipment for several years, that the equipment will not last as long as—or will last longer than—originally thought? Sometimes it is necessary to revise the estimate of the useful life, so that the periodic depreciation expense increases or decreases. In such a case, the method for correcting depreciation is to spread the undepreciated cost of the asset over the years of remaining useful life.

Under this method, the annual depreciation expense is increased or decreased so that the remaining depreciation of the asset will reduce its carrying value to residual value at the end of the remaining useful life. To illustrate, assume that a delivery truck was purchased for a price of $7,000, with a residual value of $1,000. At the time of the purchase, it was thought that the truck would last six years, and it was depreciated on the straight-line basis. However, after two years of intensive use, it is determined that the delivery truck will last only two more years and will continue to carry an estimated residual value of $1,000 at the end of the two years. In other words, at the end of the second year, the estimated useful life has been reduced from six years to four years. At that time, the asset account and its related accumulated depreciation account would appear as follows:

Delivery Truck	
Cost 7,000	

Accumulated Depreciation, Delivery Truck	
	Depreciation, year 1 1,000
	Depreciation, year 2 1,000

The remaining depreciable cost is computed as follows:

cost	minus	depreciation already taken	minus	residual value		
$7,000	−	$2,000	−	$1,000	=	$4,000

The new annual periodic depreciation charge is computed by dividing the remaining depreciable cost of $4,000 by the remaining useful life of two years. Therefore, the new periodic depreciation charge is $2,000. The annual adjusting entry for depreciation for the next two years would be as follows:

Dec. 31	Depreciation Expense, Delivery Truck	2,000	
	Accumulated Depreciation, Delivery Truck		2,000
	To record depreciation expense for the year		

This method of revising depreciation is used widely in industry. It is also supported by the Accounting Principles Board of the AICPA in Accounting Principles Board *Opinion No. 9* and *Opinion No. 20*.

Accounting for Assets of Low Unit Cost

Some classes of plant assets are made up of many individual items of low unit cost. In this category are included small tools such as hammers, wrenches, and drills, as well as dies, molds, patterns, and spare parts. Because of their large numbers, hard usage, breakage, and pilferage, assets such as these are relatively short-lived and require constant replacement. It is impractical to use the ordinary depreciation methods for such assets, and it is often costly to keep records of individual items.

There are two basic methods for accounting for plant assets of low unit cost. The first method is simply to charge the items as expenses when they are purchased. This method assumes that the annual loss on these items from use, depreciation, breakage, and other causes will approximately equal the amount of these items purchased during the year.

The second method used for plant assets of low unit cost is to account for them on an inventory basis. This method is best used when the amounts of items purchased vary greatly from year to year. The inventory basis of accounting for items of low unit cost is very similar to the method of accounting for supplies, which you already know. Let us assume that a company's asset account for Spare Parts on hand at the beginning of the accounting period is represented by a debit balance. As spare parts are purchased during the accounting period, their cost is debited to this account. At the end of the period, a physical inventory of usable spare parts on hand in the factory is taken. This inventory amount is subtracted from the end-of-period balance in the Spare Parts account to determine the cost of spare parts lost, broken, and used during this period. This cost, assumed in this case to be $700, is then charged to an expense account as a work sheet adjustment with the adjusting entry as follows:

Dec. 31	Spare Parts Expense	700	
	Spare Parts		700
	To record cost of spare parts used or lost during the period		

Group Depreciation

To say that the estimated useful life of an asset, such as a piece of equipment, is six years means that the average piece of equipment of that type is expected to last six years. In reality, some pieces of equipment may last only two or three years, and other pieces of equipment may last eight or nine years, or longer. For this reason, and also for reasons of convenience, large companies will group together items of similar assets, such as trucks, power lines, office equipment, or transformers, for purposes of calculating depreciation. This method is called **group depreciation**. Group depreciation is used widely in all fields of industry and business. A recent survey of large businesses indicated that 65 percent used group depreciation for all or part of their plant assets.[5]

5. Edward P. McTague, "Accounting for Trade-Ins of Operational Assets," *The National Public Accountant* (January 1986), p. 39.

Cost Recovery for Federal Tax Purposes

In 1981, Congress dramatically changed the rules for tax depreciation by substituting for depreciation methods similar to those used for financial reporting a new method called the **Accelerated Cost Recovery System (ACRS)**. ACRS was a completely new and mandatory cost recovery system that for tax purposes discarded the concepts of estimated useful life and residual value and instead required that a cost recovery allowance be computed (1) on the unadjusted cost of property being recovered, and (2) over a period of years prescribed by the law for all property of similar types. Recovery allowances could be calculated by the straight-line method or by prescribed percentages that approximated 150 percent of the declining-balance method with a half-year convention. ACRS recovery property is generally defined as tangible property subject to depreciation and placed in service after December 31, 1980, and before January 1, 1987. Property purchased before January 1, 1981 is subject to the accounting depreciation methods presented earlier in this chapter.

In 1986, Congress passed the **Tax Reform Act of 1986**, arguably the most sweeping revision of federal tax laws since the original enactment of the Internal Revenue Code in 1913. The new **Modified Accelerated Cost Recovery System (MACRS)** retains the ACRS concepts of prescribed recovery periods for different classes of property, calculation of recovery allowances on the basis of the unadjusted cost of property, and elective use of the straight-line method or an accelerated method of cost recovery. The accelerated method prescribed under MACRS for most property other than real estate is 200 percent declining balance with a half-year convention (only one half-year's depreciation is allowed in the year of purchase and one half-year is taken in the last year). In addition, the period over which the cost may be recovered has been increased. Recovery of the cost of property placed in service after December 31, 1986 will be calculated as prescribed in the new law. Recovery of the cost of property placed in service before January 1, 1987 will continue to be calculated under ACRS. There is one exception. For property placed in service after July 31, 1986, the new law can be elected based on a property-by-property evaluation. In summary,

Date Property Purchased	Applicable Methods
Before January 1, 1981	Accounting depreciation methods
After December 31, 1980 but before January 1, 1987	ACRS
January 1, 1987 or after	MACRS

The intent of Congress, in both ACRS and MACRS, was to encourage businesses to invest in new plant and equipment by allowing them to write the assets off rapidly. Both ACRS and MACRS accelerate the write-off of these investments in two ways. First, the recovery periods they prescribe are often shorter than the estimated useful lives used for calculat-

Table 9-1. Old and New Depreciation Rates for Federal Income Tax Purposes

	ACRS		MACRS*	
Year	3-Year Property	5-Year Property	3-Year Property	5-Year Property
1	25%	15%	33.33%	20%
2	38	22	44.45	32
3	37	21	14.81	19.2
4		21	7.41	11.52
5		21		11.52
6				5.76

* Because of the half-year convention, an additional year is added on to each property year category (e.g., there are four depreciation percentages in the three-year category).

ing book depreciation. Second, the accelerated methods allowed under ACRS and the new law provide for recovery of most of the cost of the investments early in the recovery period. Recovery will generally be more rapid under MACRS than under ACRS because of the faster accelerated method allowed. In some cases, however, MACRS provides longer recovery periods. For example, automobiles, light trucks, and light tools were classified as three-year property under ACRS. Under the new law, light tools continue to be three-year property, but automobiles and light trucks are five-year property. Table 9-1 shows the percentages of asset costs that can be written off under ACRS and MACRS.

The use of ACRS may be demonstrated using a delivery truck with a cost of $7,000, an estimated useful life of six years, and an estimated residual value of $1,000. Under ACRS, the delivery truck is a three-year property. The depreciation expense for federal income tax purposes is determined for each year as follows:

Year	Computation	Depreciation Expense	Accumulated Depreciation	Carrying Value
				$7,000
1	(25% × $7,000)	$1,750	$1,750	5,250
2	(38% × $7,000)	2,660	4,410	2,590
3	(37% × $7,000)	2,590	7,000	0

Note that three years, rather than the estimated useful life of six years, is used to calculate depreciation under ACRS. In addition, the estimated residual value is ignored, and the truck is depreciated to a carrying value of zero. No fractional-year computations are made, regardless of when during the year the truck was put into service.

Under MACRS, the truck is five-year property and is depreciated for tax purposes using the 200 percent declining-balance method with a half-year convention. Depreciation expense for federal income tax purposes is calculated as follows:

Year	Computation	Depreciation Expense*	Accumulated Depreciation	Carrying Value
				7,000
1	($7,000 × 20%)	$1,400	$1,400	5,600
2	($7,000 × 32%)	2,240	3,640	3,360
3	($7,000 × 19.2%)	1,344	4,984	2,016
4	($7,000 × 11.52%)	806	5,790	1,210
5	($7,000 × 11.52%)	806	6,596	404
6	($7,000 × 5.76%)	404	7,000	0

* Rounded to nearest dollar

Note that cost recovery under the new law is less rapid, despite the use of the 200 percent declining-balance method, because the truck is now classified as five-year property. Also note that six years are required to write off the five-year property because of the half-year convention that allowed only a half-year's recovery in the first year.

Tax methods of depreciation are not usually acceptable for financial reporting under generally accepted accounting principles because the recovery periods used are shorter than the depreciable assets' estimated useful lives. Accounting for the effects of differences between tax and book depreciation is discussed in the chapter on retained earnings and corporate income statements.

DECISION POINT

Choice of Depreciation Methods and Income Taxes: 600 Large Companies

Most companies choose the straight-line method of depreciation for financial reporting purposes, as shown in Figure 9-4. This chart, however, tends to be misleading about the importance of accelerated depreciation methods. As discussed in the previous section, federal income tax laws allow either the straight-line method or an accelerated method at 150 or 200 percent of the straight-line rate. According to *Accounting Trends and Techniques*, 454, or about 75 percent, of the 600 large companies studied chose the accelerated method for tax purposes. Although the straight-line method used for financial reporting usually produces the highest net income, the accelerated method results in lower income taxes. ■

Capital Expenditures and Revenue Expenditures

The term **expenditure** refers to a payment or incurrence of an obligation to make future payment for an asset, such as a truck, or a service received, such as a repair. When the payment or debt is for an asset or a service, it is correctly called an expenditure. A **capital expenditure** is an

Figure 9-4. Depreciation Methods Used by 600 Large Companies

Depreciation Method	Percentage of Companies Using Method
Straight-Line	94%
Accelerated Method Type Not Specified	12%
Units of Production	8%
Declining-Balance	7%
Sum-of-the-Years'-Digits	3%

Total percentage exceeds 100 because some companies used different methods for different types of depreciable assets.

Source: American Institute of Certified Public Accountants, *Accounting Trends and Techniques* (New York: AICPA, 1990), p. 261

expenditure for the purchase or expansion of long-term assets and is recorded in the asset accounts. Expenditures for repairs, maintenance, fuel, or other things needed to maintain and operate plant and equipment are called **revenue expenditures** because they are immediately charged as expenses against revenues. They are recorded by debits to expense accounts. Revenue expenditures are charged to expense because the benefits from the expenditures will be used up in the current period. For this reason, they will be deducted from the revenues of the current period in determining net income. In summary, any expenditure that will benefit several accounting periods is considered a capital expenditure. Any expenditure that will benefit only the current accounting period is called a revenue expenditure.

It is important to note this careful distinction between capital and revenue expenditures. In accordance with the matching rule, expenditures of any type should be charged to the period that they benefit. For example, if the purchase of an automobile is mistakenly charged as a revenue expenditure, the expense for the current period is overstated on the income statement. As a result, current net income is understated, and in future periods net income will be overstated. If, on the other hand, a revenue expenditure such as the painting of a building were charged to an asset account, the expense of the current period would be understated. Current net income would be overstated by the same amount, and net income of future periods would be understated.

OBJECTIVE 6
Apply the matching rule to the allocation of expired costs for capital expenditures and revenue expenditures

For practical purposes many companies establish policies stating what constitutes a revenue or capital expenditure. For example, small expenditures for items that normally would be treated as capital expenditures may be treated as revenue expenditures because the amounts involved are not material in relation to net income. Thus, a wastebasket, which might last for years, would be recorded as a supplies expense rather than as a depreciable asset.

In addition to acquisition of plant assets, natural resources, and intangible assets, capital expenditures also include additions and betterments. **Additions** are enlargements to the physical layout of a plant asset. If a new wing is added to a building, the benefits from the expenditure will be received over several years, and the amount paid for it should be debited to the asset account. **Betterments** are improvements to plant assets that do not add to the physical layout of the asset. Installation of an air-conditioning system is an example of an expenditure for a betterment or improvement that will offer benefits over a period of years and so should be charged to an asset account.

Among the more usual kinds of revenue expenditures relating to plant equipment are the ordinary repairs, maintenance, lubrication, cleaning, and inspection necessary to keep an asset in good working condition.

Repairs fall into two categories: ordinary repairs and extraordinary repairs. **Ordinary repairs** are expenditures that are necessary to maintain an asset in good operating condition. Trucks must have tune-ups, tires and batteries must be replaced regularly, and other ordinary repairs must be made. Offices and halls must be painted regularly and have broken tiles or woodwork replaced. Ordinary repairs consist of any expenditures needed to maintain a plant asset in its normal state of operation. Such repairs are a current expense.

Extraordinary repairs are repairs of a more significant nature—they affect the estimated residual value or estimated useful life of an asset. For example, a boiler for heating a building may receive a complete overhaul, at a cost of several thousand dollars, that will extend the useful life of the boiler five years.

Typically, extraordinary repairs are recorded by debiting the Accumulated Depreciation account, under the assumption that some of the depreciation previously recorded has now been eliminated. The effect of this reduction in the Accumulated Depreciation account is to increase the book or carrying value of the asset by the cost of the extraordinary repair. Consequently, the new carrying value of the asset should be depreciated over the new estimated useful life. Let us assume that a machine costing $10,000 had no estimated residual value and an original estimated useful life of ten years. After eight years, the accumulated depreciation (straight-line method assumed) would be $8,000, and the carrying value would be $2,000 ($10,000 – $8,000). Assume that, at this point in time, the machine was given a major overhaul costing $1,500. This expenditure extends the useful life three years beyond the original ten years. The entry for extraordinary repair would be as follows:

Mar. 14	Accumulated Depreciation, Machinery	1,500	
	Cash		1,500
	To record extraordinary repair to machinery		

The annual periodic depreciation for each of the five years remaining in the machine's useful life would be calculated as follows:

Carrying value before extraordinary repairs	$2,000
Extraordinary repairs	1,500
Total	$3,500

$$\text{Annual periodic depreciation} = \frac{\$3{,}500}{5 \text{ years}} = \$700$$

If the machine remains in use for the five years expected after the major overhaul, the annual periodic depreciation charges of $700 will exactly write off the new carrying value, including the cost of extraordinary repairs.

Disposal of Depreciable Assets

OBJECTIVE 7 Account for disposal of depreciable assets not involving exchanges

When items of plant assets are no longer useful in a business because they are worn out or obsolete, they may be discarded, sold, or traded in on the purchase of new plant and equipment. A comprehensive illustration is used in the following sections to show how these disposals are recorded in the accounting records.

Assumptions for the Comprehensive Illustration

For accounting purposes, a plant asset may be disposed of in three ways: (1) discarded, (2) sold for cash, or (3) exchanged for another asset. To illustrate how each of these cases is recorded, assume the following facts. MGC Corporation purchased a machine on January 1, 19x0, for $6,500 and depreciated it on a straight-line basis over an estimated useful life of ten years. The residual value at the end of ten years was estimated to be $500. On January 1, 19x7, the balances of the relevant accounts in the plant ledger appear as follows:

Machinery		Accumulated Depreciation, Machinery	
6,500			4,200

On September 30, management disposes of the asset. The next few sections illustrate the accounting treatment to record depreciation for the partial year and the disposal under several assumptions.

Depreciation for Partial Year Prior to Disposal

When items of plant assets are discarded or disposed of in some other way, it is necessary to record depreciation expense for the partial year up to the date of disposal. This step is required because the asset was used until that date, and under the matching rule the accounting period should receive the proper allocation of depreciation expense.

The depreciation expense for the partial year before disposal is calculated in exactly the same way as it is calculated for the partial year after purchase.

In this comprehensive illustration, MGC Corporation disposes of the machinery on September 30. The entry to record the depreciation for the first nine months of 19x7 is as follows:

Sept. 30	Depreciation Expense, Machinery	450	
	Accumulated Depreciation, Machinery		450
	To record depreciation up to date of disposal:		
	$\frac{\$6{,}500 - \$500}{10} \times \frac{9}{12} = \$450$		

The relevant accounts in the plant ledger accounts appear as follows after the entry is posted:

Machinery	
6,500	

Accumulated Depreciation, Machinery	
	4,650

Recording Discarded Plant Assets

Even though it is depreciated over its estimated life, a plant asset rarely lasts exactly as long as its estimated life. If it lasts longer than its estimated life, it is not depreciated past the point at which its carrying value equals its residual value. The purpose of depreciation is to spread the depreciable cost of the asset over the future life of the asset. Thus the total accumulated depreciation should never exceed the total depreciable cost. If the asset is still used in the business, this fact should be supported by its cost and accumulated depreciation remaining in the ledger accounts. Proper records will thus be available for maintaining control over plant assets. If the residual value is zero, the carrying value of a fully depreciated asset is zero until the asset is disposed of. If such an asset is discarded, no gain or loss results.

In the comprehensive illustration, however, the discarded equipment has a carrying value of $1,850 at the time of disposal. A loss equal to the carrying value should be recorded when the machine is discarded:

Sept. 30	Accumulated Depreciation, Machinery	4,650	
	Loss on Disposal of Machinery	1,850	
	Machinery		6,500
	Discarded machine no longer used in the business		

Gains and losses on disposals of long-term assets are classified as other income and expenses on the income statement.

Recording Plant Assets Sold for Cash

The entry to record the sale of an asset for cash is similar to the one illustrated above except that the receipt of cash must also be recorded. The following entries show how to record the sale of a machine under three assumptions about the selling price. In the first case, the $1,850 of cash received is exactly equal to the carrying value of the machine ($1,850), so no gain or loss results:

Sept. 30	Cash	1,850	
	Accumulated Depreciation, Machinery	4,650	
	Machinery		6,500
	Sale of machine at carrying value; no gain or loss		

In the second case, the $1,000 cash received is less than the carrying value of $1,850, so a loss of $850 is recorded:

Sept. 30	Cash	1,000	
	Accumulated Depreciation, Machinery	4,650	
	Loss on Sale of Machinery	850	
	Machinery		6,500
	Sale of machine at less than carrying value; loss of $850 ($1,850 – $1,000) recorded		

In the third case, the $2,000 cash received exceeds the carrying value of $1,850, so a gain of $150 is recorded:

Sept. 30	Cash	2,000	
	Accumulated Depreciation, Machinery	4,650	
	Gain on Sale of Machinery		150
	Machinery		6,500
	Sale of machine at more than the carrying value, gain of $150 ($2,000 – $1,850) recorded		

Recording Exchanges of Plant Assets

OBJECTIVE 8
Account for disposal of depreciable assets involving exchanges

Businesses also dispose of plant assets by trading them in on the purchase of other plant assets. Exchanges may involve similar assets, such as an old machine traded in on a newer model, or dissimilar assets, such as a machine being traded in on a truck. In either case, the purchase price is reduced by the amount of the trade-in allowance given for the asset traded in.

The basic accounting for exchanges of plant assets is similar to accounting for sales of plant assets for cash. If the trade-in allowance received is greater than the carrying value of the asset surrendered, there has been a gain. If the allowance is less, there has been a loss. There are special rules for recognizing these gains and losses depending on the nature of the assets exchanged.

Exchange	Losses Recognized	Gains Recognized
For financial accounting purposes		
Of dissimilar assets	Yes	Yes
Of similar assets	Yes	No
For income tax purposes		
Of dissimilar assets	Yes	Yes
Of similar assets	No	No

Both gains and losses are recognized when a company exchanges dissimilar assets. Assets are dissimilar when they perform different functions and are similar when they perform the same function. For financial accounting purposes, gains on exchanges of similar assets are not recognized because the earning lives of the assets surrendered are not considered to be completed. When a company trades in an older machine on a newer machine of the same type, the economic substance of the transaction is the same as a major renovation and upgrading of the older machine. One can think of the trade-in as an extension of the life and usefulness of the original machine. Instead of recognizing a gain at the time of the exchange, the company records the new machine at the sum of the book value of the older machine plus any cash paid.[6]

Accounting for exchanges of similar assets is complicated by the fact that neither gains nor losses are recognized for income tax purposes. This is important because many companies choose to follow this practice in their accounting records. The reason usually given is for convenience. Thus, in practice, accountants face cases where both gains and losses are recognized (exchanges of dissimilar assets), where losses are recognized and gains are not (exchanges of similar assets), and where neither gains nor losses are recognized (income tax exchanges of similar assets). Since all these options are used in practice, they are all illustrated in the following paragraphs.

Loss Recognized on the Exchange. A loss is recognized for accounting purposes on all exchanges in which a material loss occurs. To illustrate the recognition of a loss, let us assume that the firm in our comprehensive example exchanges the machine for a newer, more modern machine on the following terms:

Price of new machine	**$12,000**
Trade-in allowance for old machine	(1,000)
Cash payment required	$11,000

6. Accounting Principles Board, *Opinion No. 29,* "Accounting for Nonmonetary Transactions" (New York: American Institute of Certified Public Accountants, 1973); also see James B. Hobbs and D. R. Bainbridge, "Nonmonetary Exchange Transactions: Clarification of APB Opinion No. 29," *The Accounting Review* (January 1982).

In this case, the trade-in allowance ($1,000) is less than the carrying value ($1,850) of the old machine. Thus, there is a loss on the exchange of $850 ($1,850 – $1,000). The following journal entry records this transaction under the assumption that the loss is to be recognized:

Sept. 30	**Machinery (new)**	**12,000**	
	Accumulated Depreciation, Machinery	4,650	
	Loss on Exchange of Machinery	850	
	Machinery (old)		6,500
	Cash		11,000
	Exchange of machines—cost of old machine and its accumulated depreciation removed from the records; new machine recorded at purchase price; loss recognized		

Loss Not Recognized on the Exchange. In the previous example in which a loss was recognized, the new asset was recorded at the purchase price of $12,000 and a loss of $850 was recorded. If the transaction is for similar assets and is to be recorded for income tax purposes, the loss should not be recognized. In this case, the cost basis of the new asset will reflect the effect of the unrecorded loss. The cost basis is computed by adding the cash payment to the carrying value of the old asset:

Carrying value of old machine	$ 1,850
Cash paid	11,000
Cost basis of new machine	**$12,850**

Note that no loss is recognized in the entry to record this transaction:

Sept. 30	**Machinery (new)**	**12,850**	
	Accumulated Depreciation, Machinery	4,650	
	Machinery (old)		6,500
	Cash		11,000
	Exchange of machines—cost of old machine and its accumulated depreciation removed from the records; new machine recorded at amount equal to carrying value of old machine plus cash paid; no loss recognized		

Note that the new machinery is reported at the purchase price of $12,000 plus the unrecognized loss of $850. The nonrecognition of the loss on the exchange is, in effect, a postponement of the loss. Since depreciation of the new machine will be computed based on a cost of $12,850 instead of $12,000, the "unrecognized" loss is reflected by more depreciation each year than if the loss had been recognized.

Gain Recognized on the Exchange. Gains are recognized for accounting purposes on exchanges when dissimilar assets are exchanged. To illustrate the recognition of a gain, we will continue with the same example, assuming the following terms for the exchange in which the machines serve different functions:

Price of new machine	$12,000
Trade-in allowance for old machine	(3,000)
Cash payment required	$ 9,000

Here the trade-in allowance ($3,000) exceeds the carrying value ($1,850) of the old machine by $1,150. Thus, there is a gain on the exchange if we assume that the price of the new machine has not been inflated for the purpose of allowing an excessive trade-in value. In other words, a gain exists if the trade-in allowance represents the fair market value of the old machine. Assuming that this condition is true, the entry to record the transaction is as follows:

Sept. 30	Machinery (new)	12,000	
	Accumulated Depreciation, Machinery	4,650	
	Gain on Exchange of Machinery		1,150
	Machinery (old)		6,500
	Cash		9,000
	Exchange of machines—cost of old machine and its accumulated depreciation removed from the records; new machine recorded at sales price; gain recognized		

Gain Not Recognized on the Exchange. A gain on an exchange should not be recognized in the accounting records if the machines perform similar functions. The cost basis of the new machine must indicate the effect of the unrecorded gain. This cost basis is computed by adding the cash payment to the carrying value of the old asset:

Carrying value of old machine	$ 1,850
Cash paid	9,000
Cost basis of new machine	$10,850

The entry to record the transaction is as follows:

Sept. 30	Machinery (new)	10,850	
	Accumulated Depreciation, Machinery	4,650	
	Machinery (old)		6,500
	Cash		9,000
	Exchange of machine—cost of old machine and its accumulated depreciation removed from the records; new machine recorded at amount equal to carrying value of old machine plus cash paid; no gain recognized		

Similar to the nonrecognition of losses, the nonrecognition of the gain on exchange is, in effect, a postponement of the gain. In the illustration above, when the new machine is eventually discarded or sold, its cost basis will be $10,850 instead of its original price of $12,000. Since depreciation will be computed on the cost basis of $10,850, the "unrecognized" gain is reflected in less depreciation each year than if the gain had been recognized.

Accounting for Natural Resources

OBJECTIVE 9
Identify natural resource accounting issues and compute depletion

Natural resources are also known as **wasting assets**. Examples of natural resources are standing timber, oil and gas fields, and mineral deposits. The distinguishing characteristic of these wasting assets is that they are converted into inventory by cutting, pumping, or mining. For example, an oil field is a reservoir of unpumped oil, and a coal mine is a deposit of unmined coal.

Natural resources are shown on the balance sheet as long-term assets with descriptive titles such as Timber Lands, Oil and Gas Reserves, and Mineral Deposits. When the timber is cut, the oil is pumped, or the coal is mined, it becomes an inventory of the product to be sold. Natural resources are recorded at acquisition cost, which may also include some costs of development. As the resource is converted through the process of cutting, pumping, or mining, the asset account must be proportionally reduced. The carrying value of oil reserves on the balance sheet, for example, is reduced by a small amount for each barrel of oil pumped. As a result, the original cost of the oil reserves is gradually reduced, and depletion is recognized by the amount of the decrease.

Depletion

The term **depletion** is used to describe not only the exhaustion of a natural resource but also the proportional allocation of the cost of a natural resource to the units extracted. The costs are allocated in a way that is much like the production method used for depreciation. When a natural resource is purchased or developed, there must be an estimate of the total units that will be available, such as barrels of oil, tons of coal, or board-feet of lumber. The depletion cost per unit is determined by dividing the cost (less residual value, if any) of the natural resource by the estimated number of units available. The amount of the depletion cost for each accounting period is then computed by multiplying the depletion cost per unit by the number of units pumped, mined, or cut. For example, for a mine having an estimated 1,500,000 tons of coal, a cost of $1,800,000, and an estimated residual value of $300,000, the depletion charge per ton of coal is $1. Thus, if 115,000 tons of coal are mined and sold during the first year, the depletion charge for the year is $115,000. It is recorded as follows:

Dec. 31	Depletion Expense, Coal Mine	115,000	
	Accumulated Depletion, Coal Mine		115,000
	To record depletion of coal mine: 115,000 tons mined and sold and depleted at the rate of $1 per ton		

On the balance sheet, the mine would be presented as follows:

Coal Mine	$1,800,000	
Less Accumulated Depletion	115,000	$1,685,000

A natural resource that is extracted in one year may sometimes not be sold until a later year. It is important to note that it would then be recorded as a depletion *expense* in the year it is *sold*. The part not sold is considered inventory.

Depreciation of Closely Related Plant Assets

Natural resources often require special on-site buildings and equipment, such as conveyors, roads, tracks, and drilling and pumping devices that are necessary to extract the resource. If the useful life of these assets is longer than the estimated time it will take to deplete the resource, a special problem arises. Because these long-term assets are often abandoned and have no useful purpose beyond the time when the resources are extracted, they should be depreciated on the same basis as the depletion is computed. For example, if machinery with a useful life of ten years is installed on an oil field that is expected to be depleted in eight years, the machinery should be depreciated over the eight-year period using the production method. In other words, each year's depreciation charge should be proportional to the depletion charge. If one-sixth of the oil field's total reserves is pumped in one year, then the depreciation should be one-sixth of the machinery's depreciable cost. If the useful life of a long-term asset is less than the expected life of the depleting asset, the shorter life should be used to compute depreciation. In this case or when an asset is not to be abandoned when the reserves are fully depleted, other depreciation methods such as straight-line or accelerated methods are appropriate.

Development and Exploration Costs in the Oil and Gas Industry

The costs of exploration and development of oil and gas resources can be accounted for under either of the following methods. Under **successful efforts accounting**, successful exploration—for example, the cost of a producing oil well—is a cost of the resource. This cost should be recorded as an asset and depleted over the estimated life of the resource. On the other hand, an unsuccessful exploration—such as the cost of a dry well—is written off immediately as a loss. Because of these immediate write-offs, successful efforts accounting is considered the more conservative method and is used by most large oil companies.

Exploration-minded independent oil companies, on the other hand, argue that the cost of the dry wells is part of the overall cost of the systematic development of the oil field and thus a part of the cost of producing wells. Under this **full-costing** method, all costs including the cost of dry wells are recorded as assets and depleted over the estimated life of the producing resources. This method tends to improve earnings performance in the early years of companies using it. Either method is permitted by the Financial Accounting Standards Board.[7]

what 40 years amort,

Accounting for Intangible Assets

OBJECTIVE 10
Apply the matching rule to intangible asset accounting issues

The purchase of an intangible asset is a special kind of capital expenditure. An intangible asset is long term, but it has no physical substance. Its value comes from the long-term rights or advantages that it offers to the owner. Among the most common examples are patents, copyrights, leaseholds, leasehold improvements, trademarks and brand names, franchises, licenses, formulas, processes, and goodwill. Some current assets, such as accounts receivable and certain prepaid expenses, have no physical nature, but they are not called intangible assets because they are short term. Intangible assets are both long term and nonphysical.

Intangible assets are accounted for at acquisition cost, that is, the amount paid for them. Some intangible assets such as goodwill or trademarks may have been acquired at little or no cost. Even though they may have great value and are needed for profitable operations, they should not appear on the balance sheet unless they have been purchased from another party at a price established in the marketplace.

The accounting issues connected with intangible assets are the same as those connected with other long-lived assets. The Accounting Principles Board, in its *Opinion No. 17*, lists them as follows:

1. Determining an initial carrying amount
2. Accounting for that amount after acquisition under normal business conditions—that is, through periodic write-off or amortization—in a manner similar to depreciation
3. Accounting for that amount if the value declines substantially and permanently[8]

Besides these three problems, an intangible asset has no physical qualities and so in some cases may be impossible to identify. For these reasons, its value and its useful life may be quite hard to estimate.

The Accounting Principles Board has decided that a company should record as assets the costs of intangible assets acquired from others. However, the company should record as expenses the costs of developing intangible assets. Also, intangible assets that have a determinable life, such as patents, copyrights, and leaseholds, should be written off through periodic amortization over that useful life in much the same way that plant assets are depreciated. Even though some intangible assets, such as goodwill and trademarks, have no measurable limit on their lives, they should also be amortized over a reasonable length of time (not to exceed forty years).

7. *Statement of Financial Accounting Standards No. 25*, "Suspension of Certain Accounting Requirements for Oil and Gas Producing Companies" (Stamford, Conn.: Financial Accounting Standards Board, 1979).
8. Adapted from Accounting Principles Board, *Opinion No. 17*, "Intangible Assets" (New York: American Institute of Certified Public Accountants, 1970), par. 2.

To illustrate these procedures, assume that Soda Bottling Company purchases a patent on a unique bottle cap for $18,000. The entry to record the patent would be

Patent	18,000	
Cash		18,000
Purchase of bottle cap patent		

Note that if this company had developed the bottle cap internally instead of purchasing it from an outside party, the costs of developing the cap, such as salaries of researchers, supplies used in testing, and costs of equipment, would have been expensed as incurred.

Assume now that Soda's management determines that, although the patent for the bottle cap will last for seventeen years, the product using the cap will be sold only for the next six years. The entry to record the annual amortization would be

Amortization of Patent	3,000	
Patent		3,000
Annual amortization of patent: $18,000 ÷ 6 years = $3,000		

Note that the Patent account is reduced directly by the amount of the amortization expense. This is in contrast to other long-term asset accounts, for which depreciation or depletion is accumulated in a separate contra account.

If the patent becomes worthless before it is fully amortized, the remaining carrying value is written off as a loss. For instance, assume that after the first year Soda's chief competitor offers a bottle with a new type of cap that makes Soda's cap obsolete. The entry to record the loss would be

Loss on Patent	15,000	
Patent		15,000
To record loss resulting from patent's becoming worthless		

Accounting for the different types of intangible assets is outlined in Table 9-2.

Research and Development Costs

Most successful companies carry out activities, possibly within a separate department, involving research and development. Among these activities are development of new products, testing of existing and proposed products, and pure research. In the past, some companies would record as an asset those costs of research and development that could be directly traced to the development of certain patents, formulas, or other rights. Other costs, such as those for testing and pure research, were treated as expenses of the accounting period and deducted from income.

The Financial Accounting Standards Board has stated that all research and development costs should be treated as revenue expenditures and

Table 9-2. Accounting for Intangible Assets

Type	Description	Special Accounting Problems
Patent	An exclusive right granted by the federal government for a period of 17 years to make a particular product or use a specific process.	The cost of successfully defending a patent in a patent infringement suit is added to the acquisition cost of the patent. Amortize over the useful life, which may be less than the legal life of 17 years.
Copyright	An exclusive right granted by the federal government to the possessor to publish and sell literary, musical, and other artistic materials for a period of the author's life plus 50 years. Includes computer programs.	Record at acquisition cost and amortize over the useful life, but not to exceed 40 years, which is often much shorter than the legal life. For example, the cost of paperback rights to a popular novel would typically be amortized over a useful life of two to four years.
Leasehold	A right to occupy land or buildings under a long-term rental contract. For example, Company A, which owns but does not want to use a prime retail location, sells Company B the right to use it for ten years in return for one or more rental payments. Company B has purchased a leasehold.	Debit Leasehold for the amount of the payment, and amortize it over the remaining life of the lease. Payments to the lessor during the life of the lease should be debited to Lease Expense.
Leasehold Improvements	Improvements to leased property that become the property of the lessor (the person who owns the property) at the end of the lease.	Debit Leasehold Improvements for the cost of improvements, and amortize the cost of the improvements over the remaining life of the lease.
Trademark, Brand Name	A registered symbol or name giving the holder the right to use it to identify a product or service.	Debit the trademark or brand name for the acquisition cost, and amortize it over a reasonable life, not to exceed 40 years.
Franchise, License, Formula, Process	A right to an exclusive territory or to exclusive use of a formula, technique, or design.	Debit the franchise, license, formula, or process for the acquisition cost, and amortize it over a reasonable life, not to exceed 40 years.
Goodwill	The excess of the cost of a group of assets (usually a business) over the market value of the assets individually.	Debit Goodwill for the acquisition cost, and amortize it over a reasonable life, not to exceed 40 years.

charged to expense in the period when incurred.[9] The board argues that it is too hard to trace specific costs to specific profitable developments. Also, the costs of research and development are continuous and necessary for the success of a business and so should be treated as current expenses. To support this conclusion, the board cites studies showing that 30 to 90 percent of all new products fail and that three-fourths of new product expenses go to unsuccessful products. Thus, their costs do not represent future benefits.

Computer Software Costs

Many companies develop computer programs or software to be sold or leased to individuals and companies. The costs incurred in creating a computer software product are considered research and development costs until the product has been proved to be technologically feasible. As a result, costs incurred to this point in the process should be charged to expense as incurred. A product is deemed to be technologically feasible when a detailed working program has been designed. After the working program has been developed, all software production costs are recorded as assets and amortized as expense over the estimated economic life of the product using the straight-line method. If at any time the company cannot expect to realize from the software product the amount of its unamortized costs on the balance sheet, the asset should be written down to the amount expected to be realized.[10]

Goodwill

The term **goodwill** is widely used by business people, lawyers, and the public to mean different things. In most cases one thinks of goodwill as meaning the good reputation of a company. From an accounting standpoint, goodwill exists when a purchaser pays more for a business than the fair market value of the assets if purchased separately. Because the purchaser has paid more than the fair market value of the physical assets, there must be intangible assets. If the company being purchased does not have patents, copyrights, trademarks, or other identifiable intangible assets of value, one must conclude that the excess payment is for goodwill. One would pay for goodwill because most businesses are worth more as going concerns than as collections of assets. Goodwill reflects all the factors, including customer satisfaction, good management, manufacturing efficiency, the advantages of holding a monopoly, good locations, and good employee relations, that allow a company to earn a higher than market rate of return on its assets. The payment above and beyond the fair

9. *Statement of Financial Accounting Standards No. 2*, "Accounting for Research and Development Costs" (Stamford, Conn.: Financial Accounting Standards Board, 1974), par. 12.
10. *Statement of Financial Accounting Standards No. 86*, "Accounting for the Costs of Computer Software to Be Sold, Leased, or Otherwise Marketed" (Stamford, Conn.: Financial Accounting Standards Board, 1985).

market value of the tangible assets and other specific intangible assets is properly recorded in the Goodwill account.

In *Opinion No. 17,* the Accounting Principles Board states that the benefits arising from purchased goodwill will in time disappear. It is hard for a company to keep having above-average earnings unless new factors of goodwill replace the old ones. For this reason, goodwill should be amortized or written off by systematic charges to income over a reasonable number of future time periods. The time period should in no case be more than forty years.[11]

Chapter Review

Review of Learning Objectives

1. **Describe the nature, types, and issues of accounting for long-term assets.**
   Long-term assets are unexpired costs that are used in the operation of the business, are not intended for resale, and have a useful life of more than one year. Long-term assets are either tangible or intangible. In the former category are land, plant assets, and natural resources. In the latter are trademarks, patents, franchises, goodwill, and other rights. The issues associated with accounting for long-term assets are the determination of cost, the allocation of expired cost, and the handling of repairs, maintenance, additions, and disposals.
2. **Account for the cost of property, plant, and equipment.**
   The acquisition cost of property, plant, and equipment includes all expenditures reasonable and necessary to get the asset in place and ready for use. These expenditures include such payments as purchase price, installation cost, freight charges, and insurance.
3. **Define *depreciation,* state the factors that affect its computation, and show how to record it.**
   Depreciation is the periodic allocation of the cost of a plant asset over its estimated useful life. It is recorded by debiting Depreciation Expense and crediting a related contra-asset account called Accumulated Depreciation. Factors that affect its computation are the asset's cost, residual value, depreciable cost, and estimated useful life.
4. **Compute periodic depreciation under (a) the straight-line method, (b) the production method, and (c) accelerated methods, including (1) the sum-of-the-years'-digits method and (2) the declining-balance method.**
   Depreciation is commonly computed by the straight-line method, the production method, or one of the accelerated methods. The two most widely used accelerated methods are the sum-of-the-years'-digits method and the declining-balance method. The straight-line method is related directly to the passage of time, whereas the production method is related directly to use. Accelerated methods, which result in relatively large amounts of depreciation in the early years and reduced amounts in later years, are based on the assumption that plant assets provide greater economic benefit in their early years than in later years.

11. Accounting Principles Board, *Opinion No. 17,* par. 29.

5. **Apply depreciation methods to problems of partial years, revised rates, items of low unit cost, groups of similar items, and accelerated cost recovery.**
   In the application of depreciation methods, it may be necessary to calculate depreciation for partial years and to revise depreciation rates. In addition, it may be practical to apply these methods to groups of similar assets and to apply an inventory method to items of low unit cost. For income tax purposes, rapid write-offs of depreciable assets are allowed through the accelerated cost recovery system and the modified accelerated cost recovery system.

6. **Apply the matching rule to the allocation of expired costs for capital expenditures and revenue expenditures.**
   It is important to distinguish between capital expenditures, which are recorded as assets, and revenue expenditures, which are recorded as expenses. The error of classifying one as the other will have an important effect on net income. Expenditures for plant assets, additions, betterments, and intangible assets are capital expenditures. Extraordinary repairs, which increase the residual value or extend the life of an asset, are also treated as capital expenditures, whereas ordinary repairs are revenue expenditures.

7. **Account for disposal of depreciable assets not involving exchanges.**
   Long-term assets may be disposed of by being discarded, sold, or exchanged. In the disposal of long-term assets, it is necessary to bring the depreciation up to the date of disposal and to remove the carrying value from the accounts by removing the cost from the asset account and the depreciation to date from the accumulated depreciation account. If a long-term asset is sold at a price different from its carrying value, there is a gain or loss that must be recorded and reported on the income statement.

8. **Account for disposal of depreciable assets involving exchanges.**
   In recording exchanges of similar plant assets, a gain or loss may also arise. According to the Accounting Principles Board, losses, but not gains, should be recognized at the time of the exchange. When a gain is not recognized, the new asset is recorded at the carrying value of the old asset plus any cash paid. For income tax purposes, neither gains nor losses are recognized in the exchange of similar assets. When dissimilar assets are exchanged, gains and losses are recognized under both accounting and income tax rules.

9. **Identify natural resource accounting issues and compute depletion.**
   Natural resources are wasting assets, which are converted to inventory by cutting, pumping, mining, or other forms of extraction. Natural resources are recorded at cost as long-term assets. They are allocated as expenses through depletion charges as the resources are sold. The depletion charge is based on the ratio of the resource extracted to the total estimated resource. A major issue related to this subject is accounting for oil and gas reserves.

10. **Apply the matching rule to intangible asset accounting issues.**
   Purchases of intangible assets should be treated as capital expenditures and recorded at acquisition cost, which in turn should be amortized over the useful life of the assets (but not more than forty years). The FASB requires that research and development costs be treated as revenue expenditures and charged as expense in the period of the expenditure. Software costs are treated as research and development costs and expensed until a

feasible working program is developed, after which time the costs may be capitalized and amortized over a reasonable estimated life. Goodwill is the excess of the amount over the fair market value of the net assets paid to purchase a business and is usually related to the superior earning potential of the business. It should be recorded only in connection with the purchase of a business and should be amortized over a period not to exceed forty years.

Review of Concepts and Terminology

The following concepts and terms were introduced in this chapter:

(L.O. 5) **Accelerated Cost Recovery System (ACRS):** A mandatory system enacted by Congress in 1981 that requires that a cost recovery allowance be computed (1) on the unadjusted cost of property being recovered, and (2) over a period of years prescribed by the law for all property of similar types.

(L.O. 4) **Accelerated methods:** Methods of depreciation that allocate relatively large amounts of the depreciable cost of the asset to earlier years and reduced amounts to later years.

(L.O. 6) **Additions:** Enlargements to the physical layout of a plant asset.

(L.O. 1) **Amortization:** The periodic allocation of the cost of an intangible asset over its useful life.

(L.O. 6) **Betterments:** Improvements to plant assets that do not add to the physical layout of the asset.

(L.O. 6) **Capital expenditure:** An expenditure for the purchase or expansion of long-term assets, recorded in the asset accounts.

(L.O. 10) **Copyright:** An exclusive right granted by the federal government to the possessor to publish and sell literary, musical, and other artistic materials for a period of the author's life plus fifty years.

(L.O. 4) **Declining-balance method:** An accelerated method of depreciation in which depreciation is computed by applying a fixed rate to the carrying value (the declining balance) of a tangible long-lived asset.

(L.O. 1, 9) **Depletion:** The proportional allocation of the cost of a natural resource to the units removed; the exhaustion of a natural resource through mining, cutting, pumping, or otherwise using up the resource.

(L.O. 3) **Depreciable cost:** The cost of an asset less its residual value.

(L.O. 1) **Depreciation:** The periodic allocation of the cost of a tangible long-lived asset over its estimated useful life.

(L.O. 4) **Double-declining-balance method:** An accelerated method of depreciation that applies a fixed rate percentage equal to twice the straight-line percentage to the carrying value of a tangible long-term asset.

(L.O. 3) **Estimated useful life:** The total number of service units expected from a long-term asset.

(L.O. 6) **Expenditure:** A payment or incurrence of an obligation to make future payment for an asset or a service received.

(L.O. 6) **Extraordinary repairs:** Repairs that affect the estimated residual value or estimated useful life of an asset.

(L.O. 1) **Fixed assets:** Another name, no longer in wide use, for long-term assets.

(L.O. 10) **Franchise:** The right to an exclusive territory or market.

(L.O. 9) **Full-costing:** Method of accounting for the costs of exploration and development of oil and gas resources in which all costs are recorded as assets and depleted over the estimated life of the producing resources.

(L.O. 10) **Goodwill:** The excess of the cost of a group of assets (usually a business) over the market value of the assets individually.

(L.O. 5) **Group depreciation:** The grouping of items of similar plant assets together for purposes of calculating depreciation.

(L.O. 1) **Intangible assets:** Long-term assets that have no physical substance but have a value based on rights or privileges accruing to the owner.

(L.O. 10) **Leasehold:** A right to occupy land or buildings under a long-term rental contract.

(L.O. 10) **Leasehold improvement:** An improvement to leased property that becomes the property of the lessor at the end of the lease.

(L.O. 10) **License:** Official or legal permission to do or own a specific thing.

(L.O. 1) **Long-term assets:** Assets that (1) have a useful life of more than one year, (2) are acquired for use in the operation of the business, and (3) are not intended for resale to customers.

(L.O. 5) **Modified Accelerated Cost Recovery System (MACRS):** A modification of the accelerated cost recovery system (ACRS) made by the Tax Reform Act of 1986.

(L.O. 1) **Natural resources:** Long-term assets purchased for the physical substances that can be taken from the land and used up rather than for the value of their location.

(L.O. 3) **Obsolescence:** The process of becoming out of date; a contributor, together with physical deterioration, to the limited useful life of tangible assets.

(L.O. 6) **Ordinary repairs:** Expenditures, usually of a recurring nature, that are necessary to maintain an asset in good operating condition.

(L.O. 10) **Patent:** An exclusive right granted by the federal government to make a particular product or use a specific process.

(L.O. 3) **Physical deterioration:** Limitations on the useful life of a depreciable asset resulting from use and from exposure to the elements.

(L.O. 4) **Production method:** A method of depreciation that bases the depreciation charge for a period of time solely on the amount of use of the asset during the period of time.

(L.O. 3) **Residual value (salvage value or disposal value):** The estimated net scrap, salvage, or trade-in value of a tangible asset at the estimated date of disposal.

(L.O. 6) **Revenue expenditure:** An expenditure for repairs, maintenance, or other services needed to maintain or operate plant assets.

(L.O. 4) **Straight-line method:** A method of depreciation that assumes that depreciation is dependent on the passage of time and that allocates an equal amount of depreciation to each period of time.

(L.O. 9) **Successful efforts accounting:** Method of accounting in which successful exploration for oil and gas resources is recorded as an asset and depleted over

the estimated life of the resource and all unsuccessful efforts are immediately written off as a loss.

(L.O. 4) **Sum-of-the-years'-digits method:** An accelerated method of depreciation in which the years in the service life of an asset are added; their sum becomes the denominator of a series of fractions that are applied against the depreciable cost of the asset in allocating the total depreciation over the estimated useful life.

(L.O. 1) **Tangible assets:** Long-term assets that have physical substance.

(L.O. 5) **Tax Reform Act of 1986:** Arguably the most sweeping revision of federal tax laws since the original enactment of the Internal Revenue Code in 1913.

(L.O. 10) **Trademark:** A registered symbol that gives the holder the right to use it to identify a product or service.

(L.O. 9) **Wasting assets:** Another term for natural resources; long-term assets purchased for the physical substances that can be taken from the land and used up rather than for the value of their location.

Review Problem
Depreciation Methods and Partial Years

(L.O. 3, 4, 5) Norton Construction Company purchased a cement mixer for $14,500. The mixer is expected to have a useful life of five years and a residual value of $1,000. The company engineers estimate that the mixer will have a useful life of 7,500 hours, of which 2,625 hours were used in 19x2. The company's year end is December 31.

Required

1. Compute the depreciation expense for 19x2 assuming that the cement mixer was purchased on January 1, 19x1, using the following four methods: (a) straight-line, (b) production, (c) sum-of-the-years'-digits, (d) double-declining-balance.
2. Compute the depreciation expense for 19x2 assuming that the cement mixer was purchased on July 1, 19x1, using the following methods: (a) straight-line, (b) production, (c) sum-of-the-years'-digits, (d) double-declining-balance.
3. Prepare the adjusting entry to record the depreciation calculated in **1 (a)**.
4. Show the balance sheet presentation for the cement mixer after the entry in **3** on December 31, 19x2.

Answer to Review Problem

1. Depreciation expense for 19x2 assuming purchase on January 1, 19x1:
   a. Straight-line method
      ($14,500 – $1,000) ÷ 5 = $2,700
   b. Production method
      $(\$14{,}500 - \$1{,}000) \times \frac{2{,}625}{7{,}500} = \$4{,}725$
   c. Sum-of-the-years'-digits method
      $(\$14{,}500 - \$1{,}000) \times \frac{4}{15} = \$3{,}600$
   d. Double-declining-balance method
      First year: $14,500 × .4 = $5,800
      Second year: ($14,500 – $5,800) × .4 = $3,480

2. Depreciation expense for 19x2 assuming purchase on July 1, 19x1:
   a. Straight-line method
      First half: [($14,500 − $1,000) ÷ 5] × 1/2 = $1,350
      Second half: [($14,500 − $1,000) ÷ 5] × 1/2 = 1,350
      19x2 Total $2,700

      (Note that depreciation is the same for each half-year under the straight-line method.)
   b. Production method

      $$(\$14,500 - \$1,000) \times \frac{2,625}{7,500} = \$4,725$$

   c. Sum-of-the-years'-digits method
      First half: ($14,500 − $1,000) × 5/15 × 1/2 = $2,250
      Second half: ($14,500 − $1,000) × 4/15 × 1/2 = 1,800
      19x2 Total $4,050

   d. Double-declining-balance method
      First half: ($14,500 × .4) × 1/2 = $2,900
      Second half: [($14,500 − $5,800*) × .4] × 1/2 = 1,740
      19x2 Total $4,640

      *First full year's depreciation: $14,500 × .4 = $5,800

3. Adjusting entry for depreciation prepared:

19x2			
Dec. 31	Depreciation Expense, Cement Mixer	2,700	
	Accumulated Depreciation, Cement Mixer		2,700
	To record depreciation for 19x2 under the straight-line method		

4. Balance sheet presentation shown for December 31, 19x2:

Cement Mixer	$14,500
Less Accumulated Depreciation	5,400
	$ 9,100

Chapter Assignments

Discussion Questions

1. What are the characteristics of long-term assets?
2. Which of the following items would be classified as plant assets on the balance sheet: (a) a truck held for sale by a truck dealer, (b) an office building that was once the company headquarters but is now to be sold, (c) a typewriter used by a secretary of the company, (d) a machine that is used in the manufacturing operations but is now fully depreciated, (e) pollution-control equipment that does not reduce the cost or improve the efficiency of the factory, (f) a parking lot for company employees?
3. Why is it useful to think of plant assets as a bundle of services?
4. Why is land different from other long-term assets?

5. What in general is included in the cost of a long-term asset?
6. Which of the following expenditures incurred in connection with the purchase of a computer system would be charged to the asset account? (a) Purchase price of the equipment, (b) interest on debt incurred to purchase the equipment, (c) freight charges, (d) installation charges, (e) cost of special communications outlets at the computer site, (f) cost of repairing a door that was damaged during installation, (g) cost of adjustments to the system during the first month of operation.
7. Hale's Grocery obtained bids on the construction of a dock for receiving goods at the back of its store. The lowest bid was $22,000. The company, however, decided to build the dock itself and was able to do it for $20,000, which it borrowed. The activity was recorded as a debit to Buildings for $22,000 and credits to Notes Payable for $20,000 and Gain on Construction for $2,000. Do you agree with the entry?
8. What do accountants mean by the term *depreciation*, and what is its relationship to depletion and amortization?
9. A firm buys a piece of technical equipment that is expected to last twelve years. Why might the equipment have to be depreciated over a shorter period of time?
10. A company purchased a building five years ago. The market value of the building is greater now than it was when the building was purchased. Explain why the company should continue depreciating the building.
11. Evaluate the following statement: "A parking lot should not be depreciated because adequate repairs will make it last forever."
12. Is the purpose of depreciation to determine the value of equipment? Explain your answer.
13. Contrast the assumptions underlying the straight-line depreciation method with the assumptions underlying the production depreciation method.
14. What is the principal argument supporting accelerated depreciation methods?
15. What does the balance of the Accumulated Depreciation account represent? Does it represent funds available to purchase new plant assets?
16. If a plant asset is sold during the year, why should depreciation be computed for the partial year prior to the date of the sale?
17. What basic procedure should be followed in revising a depreciation rate?
18. Explain why and how plant assets of low unit cost can be accounted for on a basis similar to the handling of supplies inventory.
19. On what basis can depreciation be taken on a group of assets rather than on individual items?
20. What is the difference between depreciation for accounting purposes and accelerated cost recovery for income tax purposes?
21. What is the distinction between revenue expenditures and capital expenditures, and why is this distinction important?
22. What will be the effect on future years' income of charging an addition to a building as repair expense?
23. In what ways do an addition, a betterment, and an extraordinary repair differ?
24. How does an extraordinary repair differ from an ordinary repair? What is the accounting treatment for each?
25. If a plant asset is discarded before the end of its useful life, how is the amount of loss measured?

26. When similar assets are exchanged, at what amount is the new asset recorded for federal income tax purposes?
27. When an exchange of similar assets in which there is an unrecorded loss occurs, is the taxpayer ever able to deduct or receive federal income tax credit for the loss?
28. Old Stake Mining Company computes the depletion rate to be $2 per ton. During 19xx, the company mined 400,000 tons of ore and sold 370,000 tons. What is the total depletion for the year?
29. Under what circumstances can a mining company depreciate its plant assets over a period of time that is less than their useful lives?
30. Because accounts receivable have no physical substance, can they be classified as intangible assets?
31. Under what circumstances can a company have intangible assets that do not appear on the balance sheet?
32. When the Accounting Principles Board indicates that accounting for intangible assets involves the same problems as accounting for tangible assets, what problems is it referring to?
33. How does the Financial Accounting Standards Board recommend that research and development costs be treated?
34. How is accounting for software development cost similar to and different from accounting for research and development costs?
35. Under what conditions should goodwill be recorded? Should it remain in the records permanently once it is recorded?

Communication Skills Exercises

Communication 9-1. Nature of Depreciation and Amortization and Estimated Useful Lives *(L.O. 3)*

General Motors Corp., in its 1987 annual report, states, "In the third quarter of 1987, the Corporation revised the estimated service lives of its plants and equipment and special tools retroactive to January 1, 1987. These revisions, which were based on 1987 studies of actual useful lives and periods of use, recognized current estimates of service lives of the assets and had the effect of reducing 1987 depreciation and amortization charges by $1,236.6 million or $2.55 per share of $1-2/3 par value common stock."[12] In 1987, General Motors' income before income taxes was $2,005.4 million. What is the purpose of depreciation and amortization? What is the estimated service life, and on what basis did General Motors change the estimates of the service lives of plants and equipment and special tools? What was the effect of this change on the corporation's income before income taxes? Is it likely that the company is in better condition economically as a result of the change? Does the company have more cash at the end of the year as a result? (Ignore income tax effects.)

Communication 9-2. Choice of Depreciation Methods *(L.O. 4)*

Ford Motor Co., one of the nation's largest manufacturers of automobiles, does not use the straight-line depreciation method for financial reporting purposes even though, as shown in Figure 9-4, most companies do choose this depreciation method. As noted in Ford's 1990 annual report:

12. Excerpts from the 1987 Annual Report used by permission of General Motors. Copyright © 1987.

Depreciation is computed using an accelerated method that results in accumulated depreciation of approximately two-thirds of asset cost during the first half of the asset's estimated useful life.[13]

What reasons can you give for Ford's choosing this method over the straight-line method? What is the role of the matching rule? Which method is the more conservative?

Communication 9-3. Depreciation Method and Income Taxes *(L.O. 5)*

The Goodyear Tire & Rubber Company describes its accounting policies for properties and plants in its 1989 annual report: "Properties and plants are stated at cost. Depreciation is computed on the straight line method. Accelerated depreciation is used for income tax purposes, where permitted."[14] Why do you think management chooses this combination of depreciation methods? What condition must hold for the advantages of this policy to become apparent?

Communication 9-4. Trademarks *(L.O. 10)*

The Quaker Oats Company's advertising campaign, "Gatorade is thirst aid for that deep down body thirst," infringed on a trademark held by Sands Taylor & Wood of Norwich, Vermont, according to a 1990 ruling by a federal judge. Sands Taylor & Wood had acquired the trademark "thirst aid" in a 1973 acquisition but did not use the trademark at the time the ruling was handed down. The judge determined that Gatorade had produced $247.3 million in income over the previous six years and reasoned that the advertising campaign was responsible for 10 percent of the product's sales. As a result, he awarded Sands Taylor & Wood $24.7 million plus legal fees and interest from 1984. He also prohibited Quaker from further use of the phrase "thirst aid" in any advertising campaign for Gatorade, its largest-selling product.[15]

What is a trademark, and why is it considered an intangible asset? Why does a trademark have value? To whom does a trademark have value? How do your answers apply to the case of Quaker Oats' use of "thirst aid"?

Communication 9-5. Basic Research Skills *(L.O. 7)*

Public corporations are required not only to communicate with their stockholders by means of an annual report, but also to submit an annual report to the Securities & Exchange Commission (SEC). The annual report to the SEC is called a 10-K and contains information in addition to that provided to stockholders. Most college and university libraries provide access to at least a selected number of 10-Ks. These 10-Ks may be on microfiche or on file with the companies' annual reports to stockholders. In your school's library, find the 10-K for a single company. In that 10-K, Schedule 5 will contain information about the dispositions and acquisitions of property, plant, and equipment at book value. Schedule 6 will show the increases and decreases in the accumulated depreciation accounts. In the statement of cash flows under investing

13. Excerpts from 1990 Annual Report used by permission of Ford Motor Co. Copyright © 1990.
14. Excerpt from the 1989 Annual Report used by permission of Goodyear Tire & Rubber Company.
15. James P. Miller, "Quaker Oats Loses Trademark Battle Over Gatorade Ad," *Wall Street Journal*, Dec. 19, 1990.

activities, the cash proceeds from dispositions of property, plant, and equipment will be shown. Using the information from these three related schedules and the statement, determine whether or not the company had a gain or loss from dispositions of property, plant, and equipment during the year. Be prepared to discuss your results in class.

Classroom Exercises

Exercise 9-1. Determining Cost of Long-Term Assets *(L.O. 2)*

Rosemond Manufacturing purchased land next to its factory to be used as a parking lot. Expenditures incurred by the company were as follows: purchase price, $75,000; broker's fees, $6,000; title search and other fees, $550; demolition of a shack on the property, $2,000; general grading of property, $1,050; paving parking lots, $10,000; lighting for parking lots, $8,000; and signs for parking lots, $1,600. Determine the amount that should be debited to the Land account and to the Land Improvements account.

Exercise 9-2. Cost of Long-Term Asset and Depreciation *(L.O. 2, 3, 4)*

Jason Farm purchased a used tractor for $17,500. Before the tractor could be used, it required new tires, which cost $1,100, and an overhaul, which cost $1,400. Its first tank of fuel cost $75. The tractor is expected to last six years and have a residual value of $2,000. Determine the cost and depreciable cost of the tractor, and calculate the first year's depreciation under the straight-line method.

Exercise 9-3. Group Purchase *(L.O. 2)*

Ellen Briggs went into business by purchasing a car wash business for $240,000. The car wash assets included land, building, and equipment. If purchased separately, the land would have cost $60,000, the building $135,000, and the equipment $105,000. Determine the amount that should be recorded by Briggs in the new business's records for land, building, and equipment.

Exercise 9-4. Depreciation Methods *(L.O. 3, 4)*

Logan Oil Corporation purchased a drilling truck for $45,000. The company expected the truck to last five years or 200,000 miles, with an estimated residual value of $7,500 at the end of that time. During 19x2, the truck was driven 48,000 miles. The company's year end is December 31.

Compute the depreciation for 19x2 under each of the following methods, assuming that the truck was purchased on January 13, 19x1: (1) straight-line, (2) production, (3) sum-of-the-years'-digits, and (4) double-declining-balance. Using the amount computed in **4**, prepare the general journal entry to record depreciation expense for the second year and show how drilling trucks would appear on the balance sheet.

Exercise 9-5. Depreciation Methods: Partial Years *(L.O. 4, 5)*

Using the same data given for Logan Oil Corporation in Exercise 9-4, compute the depreciation for 19x2 under each of the following methods, assuming that the truck was purchased on July 1, 19x1: (1) straight-line, (2) production, (3) sum-of-the-years'-digits, (4) double-declining-balance.

Exercise 9-6. Declining-Balance Method *(L.O. 4)*

Quadri Burglar Alarm Systems Company purchased a word processor for $4,480. It has an estimated useful life of four years and an estimated residual value of $480. Compute the depreciation charge for each of the four years using the double-declining-balance method.

Exercise 9-7. Straight-Line Method: Partial Years *(L.O. 4, 5)*

Strauss Manufacturing Corporation purchased three machines during the year, as follows:

February 10	Machine 1	$ 1,800
July 26	Machine 2	12,000
October 11	Machine 3	21,600

The machines are assumed to last six years and to have no estimated residual value. The company's fiscal year corresponds to the calendar year. Using the straight-line method, compute the depreciation charge to the nearest month for each machine for the year.

Exercise 9-8. Revision of Depreciation Rates *(L.O. 4, 5)*

Eastmoor Hospital purchased a special x-ray machine for its operating room. The machine, which cost $155,780, was expected to last ten years, with an estimated residual value of $15,780. After two years of operation (and depreciation charges using the straight-line rate), it became evident that the x-ray machine would last a total of only seven years. The estimated residual value, however, would remain the same. Given this information, determine the depreciation charge for the third year on the basis of the new estimated useful life.

Exercise 9-9. Accounting for Items of Low Unit Cost *(L.O. 5)*

Newgard Air Conditioner Service Company maintains a large supply of small tools for servicing air conditioners. The company uses the inventory basis for accounting for the tools and assumes that annual expense is approximately equal to the cost of tools lost and discarded during the year. At the beginning of the year, the company had an inventory of small tools on hand in the amount of $8,765. During the year, small tools were purchased in the amount of $4,780. At the end of the year (December 31), a physical inventory revealed small tools in the amount of $6,585 on hand. Prepare a general journal entry to record small tools expense for the year for Newgard Air Conditioner Service Company.

Exercise 9-10. Capital and Revenue Expenditures *(L.O. 6)*

For each of the following transactions related to an office building, tell whether the transaction is a revenue expenditure (RE) or a capital expenditure (CE). In addition, indicate whether each transaction is an ordinary repair (OR), an extraordinary repair (ER), an addition (A), a betterment (B), or none of these (N).

_____ a. The hallways and ceilings in the building are repainted at a cost of $8,300.
_____ b. The hallways, which have tile floors, are carpeted at a cost of $28,000.
_____ c. A new wing is added to the building at a cost of $175,000.

_____ d. Furniture is purchased for the entrance to the building at a cost of $16,500.

_____ e. The air conditioning system is overhauled at a cost of $28,500. The overhaul extends the useful life of the air conditioning system by ten years.

_____ f. A cleaning firm is paid $200 per week to clean the newly installed carpets.

Exercise 9-11. Extraordinary Repairs *(L.O. 6)*

Sharif Manufacturing has an incinerator that originally cost $93,600 and now has accumulated depreciation of $66,400. The incinerator just completed its fifteenth year of service in an estimated useful life of twenty years. At the beginning of the sixteenth year, the company spent $21,400 repairing and modernizing the incinerator to comply with pollution control standards. Therefore, instead of five years, the incinerator is now expected to last ten more years. It will not, however, have more capacity than it did in the past or a residual value at the end of its useful life.

1. Prepare the entry to record the cost of the repairs.
2. Compute the book value of the incinerator after the entry.
3. Prepare the entry to record the depreciation (assuming the straight-line method) for the current year.

Exercise 9-12. Disposal of Plant Assets *(L.O. 7, 8)*

A piece of equipment that cost $32,400 and on which $18,000 of accumulated depreciation had been recorded was disposed of on January 2, the first day of business of the current year. Give general journal entries to record the disposal under each of the following independent assumptions:

1. It was discarded as having no value.
2. It was sold for $6,000 cash.
3. It was sold for $18,000 cash.
4. The equipment was traded in on dissimilar equipment having a list price of $48,000. A $15,600 trade-in was allowed, and the balance was paid in cash. Gains and losses are to be recognized.
5. The equipment was traded in on dissimilar equipment having a list price of $48,000. A $7,200 trade-in was allowed, and the balance was paid in cash. Gains and losses are to be recognized.
6. Same as **5** except that the items are similar and gains and losses are not to be recognized.

Exercise 9-13. Disposal of Plant Assets *(L.O. 7, 8)*

A commercial vacuum cleaner costing $4,900, with accumulated depreciation of $3,600, was traded in on a new model that had a list price of $6,100. A trade-in allowance of $1,000 was given.

1. Compute the carrying value of the old vacuum cleaner.
2. Determine the amount of cash required to purchase the new vacuum cleaner.
3. Compute the amount of loss on the exchange.
4. Determine the cost basis of the new vacuum cleaner assuming that (a) the loss is recognized and (b) the loss is not recognized.

5. Compute the yearly depreciation on the new vacuum cleaner for both assumptions in **4**, assuming a useful life of five years, a residual value of $1,600, and straight-line depreciation.

Exercise 9-14. Disposal of Plant Assets *(L.O. 7, 8)*

A microcomputer was purchased by Juniper Company on January 1, 19x1 at a cost of $5,000. It is expected to have a useful life of five years and a residual value of $500. Assuming that the computer is disposed of on July 1, 19x4 and the straight-line method is used, record the partial year's depreciation for 19x4, and record the disposal under each of the following assumptions:

1. The microcomputer is discarded.
2. The microcomputer is sold for $800.
3. The microcomputer is sold for $2,200.
4. The microcomputer is exchanged for a new microcomputer with a list price of $9,000. A $1,200 trade-in is allowed on the cash purchase. The accounting approach to gains and losses is followed.
5. Same as **4** except that a $2,400 trade-in is allowed.
6. Same as **4** except that the income tax approach is followed.
7. Same as **5** except that the income tax approach is followed.
8. Same as **4** except that the microcomputer is exchanged for dissimilar office equipment.
9. Same as **5** except that the microcomputer is exchanged for dissimilar office equipment.

Exercise 9-15. Natural Resource Depletion and Depreciation of Related Plant Assets *(L.O. 9)*

Church Mining Corporation purchased land containing an estimated 10 million tons of ore for a cost of $8,800,000. The land is estimated to be worth $1,600,000 without the ore. The company expects that all the usable ore can be mined in ten years. Buildings costing $800,000 with an estimated useful life of thirty years were erected on the site. Equipment costing $960,000 with an estimated useful life of ten years was installed. Because of the remote location, neither the buildings nor the equipment has an estimated residual value. During its first year of operation, the company mined and sold 800,000 tons of ore.

1. Compute the depletion charge per ton.
2. Compute the depletion expense that Church Mining Corporation should record for the year.
3. Determine the annual depreciation expense for the buildings, making it proportional to the depletion.
4. Determine the annual depreciation expense for the equipment under two alternatives: (a) using the straight-line method and (b) making the expense proportional to the depletion.

Exercise 9-16. Comprehensive Natural Resources Entries *(L.O. 9)*

On January 3, 19x2, Ben Green purchased a piece of property with sand deposits for $6,510,000. He estimated that the sand deposits contained 4,700,000 cubic yards of sand. The sand is used for making concrete and as foundations for sidewalks, driveways, and other prepared surfaces. After the sand is gone, the land will be worth only about $400,000. The equipment required to extract the sand cost $1,452,000. In addition, Green decided to build a small frame building to house the site office and a small dining hall for the workers. The building cost $152,000 and would have no residual value after its estimated useful life of ten years. It cannot be moved from the site. The equipment has an estimated useful life of six years (with no residual value) and also cannot be removed from the site. Trucks for the project cost $308,000 (estimated life, six years; residual value, $20,000). The trucks, of course, can be used at a different site. Green estimated that in five years all the sand would be extracted and the site would be shut down. During 19x2, 1,175,000 cubic yards of sand were extracted and sold.

1. Prepare general journal entries to record the purchase of the property and all the buildings and equipment associated with the site. Assume purchases are made with cash.
2. Prepare adjusting entries to record depletion and depreciation for the first year of operation (19x2). Assume that the depreciation rate is equal to the percentage of the total sand sold during the year unless the asset is movable. For movable assets, use the straight-line method.

Exercise 9-17. Amortization of Copyrights and Trademarks *(L.O. 10)*

1. Fortunato Publishing Company purchased the copyright to a basic computer textbook for $20,000. The usual life of a textbook is about four years. However, the copyright will remain in effect for another fifty years. Calculate the annual amortization of the copyright.
2. Guzman Company purchased a trademark from a well-known supermarket for $160,000. The management of the company argued that the trademark value would last forever and might even increase, and so no amortization should be charged. Calculate the minimum amount of annual amortization that should be charged, according to guidelines of the appropriate Accounting Principles Board opinion.

Interpretation Cases from Business

ICB 9-1. Century Steelworks Company *(L.O. 5)*

Depreciation expense is a significant expense for companies in industries that have a high proportion of plant assets to other assets. Also, the amount of depreciation expense in a given year is affected by estimates of useful life and by choice of depreciation method. In 1990, Century Steelworks Company, a major integrated steel producer, changed both the estimates of depreciable lives for major production assets and the method of depreciation from straight-line to the production method for other steel-making assets.

The company's 1990 annual report states, "A recent study conducted by management shows that actual years-in-service figures for our major production equipment and machinery are, in most cases, higher than the estimated useful lives assigned to these assets. We have recast the depreciable lives of such assets so that equipment previously assigned a useful life of 8 to 26 years now has an extended depreciable life of 10 to 32 years." The report goes on to explain that the new production method of depreciation "recognizes that depreciation of production equipment and machinery correlates directly to both physical wear and tear and the passage of time. The production method of depreciation, which we have now initiated, more closely allocates the cost of these assets to the periods in which products are manufactured."

The report also summarized the effects of both actions on the year 1990 as follows:

Incremental Increase in Net Income	In Millions	Per Share
Lengthened lives	$11.0	$ .80
Production method		
Current year	7.3	.53
Prior years	2.8	.20
Total increase	$21.1	$1.53

During 1990, Century Steelworks reported a net loss of $83,156,500 ($6.03 per share). Depreciation expense for 1990 was $87,707,200.

In explaining the changes, the controller of Century Steelworks was quoted in an article in *Business Journal* as follows: "There is no reason why Century Steelworks should continue to depreciate our assets more conservatively than our competitors do." But the article quotes an industry analyst who argues that, by slowing its method of depreciation, Century Steelworks could be viewed as reporting lower quality earnings.

Required

1. Explain the accounting treatment when there is a change in the estimated lives of depreciable assets. What circumstances must exist for the production method to produce the effect it did in relation to the straight-line method? What would have been Century Steelworks' net income or loss if the changes had not been made? What may have motivated management to make the changes?
2. What does the controller of Century Steelworks mean when he says that Century had been depreciating "more conservatively than our competitors"? Why might the changes at Century Steelworks indicate, as the analyst asserts, "lower quality earnings"? What risks might Century face as a result of its decision to use the production method of depreciation?

ICB 9-2. Pan American World Airways, Inc.[16] ***(L.O. 7)***

The *Wall Street Journal* reported on October 14, 1983, that "Pan American World Airways and American Airlines are in the final stages of negotiating the biggest swap in the industry's history. . . . According to industry sources, Pan Am would trade fifteen of its DC 10's to American Airlines. In return, Pan Am would get eight of American's much bigger Boeing 747 jumbo jets."

The article also stated that "New Boeing 747's currently sell for about $85 million, indicating that the eight involved in the swap could be valued at nearly $700 million. But the market for used wide-body jets is weak. One industry source estimated that a used 747 might fetch only about $20 million, indicating the eight could be valued as low as $160 million."

A note to Pan Am's 1983 annual report indicated that by the end of 1983 the title to fifteen DC 10's had been transferred to American Airlines, but that only one of the eight Boeing 747's had been received from American. It reported, "An Aircraft Exchange Receivable of approximately $111,652,000 has been recorded on the balance sheet at December 31, 1983, in connection with the exchange. No gain or loss has been recorded on the exchange."

Required

1. Since no gain or loss was recognized on the exchange, how did Pan Am arrive at a value to be placed on the Boeing 747's? Assuming that each Boe-

16. William M. Carley, "American Air, Pan Am Prepare to Swap Planes," *Wall Street Journal*, October 14, 1983, pp. 3, 18.

ing 747 was valued at the same amount, what was the total value of the exchange? How does this amount compare with the market value of the planes? Why was market value not used to value the transaction?

2. Prepare as completely as possible the journal entry Pan Am made to record the exchange. How would the account Aircraft Exchange Receivable be classified in the financial statements? Assume that Pan Am received delivery of two Boeing 747's on February 1, 1984. What entry would be made?

ICB 9-3. Ocean Drilling and Exploration Company (ODECO)[17] *(L.O. 1, 6)*

Selected accounting policies involving long-term assets of ODECO, one of the largest oil and gas contract drilling companies, appear below:

1. Provisions are made for major repairs on the company's drilling barges by monthly charges to expense. The cost of major repairs incurred is charged against the related allowance created by the monthly provisions.
2. All other maintenance and repair costs are charged to expense.
3. Renewals (extraordinary repairs) are capitalized by reducing accumulated depreciation, and betterments are capitalized by increasing the asset account.

The following data apply to the year 1986:

Major Barge Repairs

Provisions	$ 4,451,000
Charges	2,588,000
Repairs and maintenance	27,165,000
Renewals to drilling barges (estimated)	10,000,000
Betterments to drilling barges (estimated)	20,000,000

Required

1. Explain the reasoning behind each of the accounting policies listed above.
2. Prepare journal entries to record each of the amounts listed (assume that expenditures are made in cash).

Problem Set A

Problem 9A-1. Determining Cost of Assets *(L.O. 2, 3, 4, 5)*

Flair Corporation began operation on January 1, 19xx. At the end of the year, the company's auditor discovered that all expenditures involving long-term assets had been debited to an account called Fixed Assets. An analysis of the account, which has a balance at the end of the year of $2,644,972, disclosed that it contained the items presented on page 485.

The timber that was cleared from the land was sold to a firewood dealer for $5,000. This amount was credited to Miscellaneous Income. During the construction period, two supervisors devoted their full time to the construction project. These people earn annual salaries of $48,000 and $42,000, respectively. They spent two months on the purchase and preparation of the land, six months on the construction of the building (approximately one-sixth of which was devoted to improvements on the grounds), and one month on installation of machinery. The plant began operation on October 1, and the supervisors returned to their regular duties. Their salaries were debited to Factory Salary Expense.

17. Excerpts from the 1986 Annual Report used by permission of Ocean Drilling and Exploration Company. Copyright © 1986.

Cost of land	$ 316,600
Surveying costs	4,100
Transfer of title and other fees required by the county	920
Broker's fees	21,144
Attorney's fees associated with land acquisition	7,048
Cost of removing unusable timber from land	50,400
Cost of grading land	4,200
Cost of digging building foundation	34,600
Architect's fee for building and land improvements (80 percent building)	64,800
Cost of building	710,000
Cost of sidewalks	11,400
Cost of parking lots	54,400
Cost of lighting for grounds	80,300
Cost of landscaping	11,800
Cost of machinery	989,000
Shipping cost on machinery	55,300
Cost of installing machinery	176,200
Cost of testing machinery	22,100
Cost of changes in building due to safety regulations required because of machinery	12,540
Cost of repairing building that was damaged in the installation of machinery	8,900
Cost of medical bill for injury received by employee while installing machinery	2,400
Cost of water damage to building during heavy rains prior to opening the plant for operation	6,820
Account Balance	$2,644,972

Required

1. Prepare a schedule with the following column headings: Land, Land Improvements, Buildings, Machinery, and Losses. List the items appropriate to each of these accounts in the proper columns. Negative amounts should be shown in parentheses. Total the columns.
2. Prepare an entry to adjust the accounts based on all the information given, assuming that the company's accounts have not been closed at the end of the year.
3. Assume that the plant was in operation for three months during the year. Prepare an adjusting entry to record depreciation expense, assuming that the land improvements are depreciated over twenty years with no residual value, that the buildings are depreciated over thirty years with no estimated residual value, and that the machinery is depreciated over twelve years with the estimated residual value equal to 10 percent of cost. The company uses the straight-line method. Round your answers to the nearest dollar.

Problem 9A-2. Comparison of Depreciation Methods *(L.O. 3, 4)*

Riggio Construction Company purchased a new crane for $360,500. The crane has an estimated residual value of $35,000 and an estimated useful life of six years. The crane is expected to last 10,000 hours. It was used 1,800 hours in year 1; 2,000 in year 2; 2,500 in year 3; 1,500 in year 4; 1,200 in year 5; and 1,000 in year 6.

Required

1. Compute the annual depreciation and carrying value for the new crane for each of the six years (round to nearest dollar where necessary) under each of the following methods: (a) straight-line, (b) production, (c) sum-of-the-years'-digits, (d) double-declining-balance.
2. Prepare the adjusting entry that would be made each year to record the depreciation calculated under the straight-line method.
3. Show the balance sheet presentation for the crane after the adjusting entry in year 2 using the straight-line method.
4. What conclusions can you draw from the patterns of yearly depreciation and carrying value in **1**?

Problem 9A-3. Depreciation Methods and Partial Years *(L.O. 4, 5)*

Wu Corporation operates four types of equipment. Because of their varied functions, company accounting policy requires the application of four different depreciation methods to the equipment. Data on this equipment are summarized below.

Equipment	Date Purchased	Cost	Installation Cost	Estimated Residual Value	Estimated Life	Depreciation Method
1	1/12/x1	$57,000	$3,000	$ 6,000	10 years	Double-declining-balance
2	1/7/x1	76,675	2,750	7,500	6 years	Sum-of-the-years'-digits
3	7/9/x1	63,700	5,300	7,000	10 years	Straight-line
4	10/2/x1	96,900	2,700	11,200	20,000 hours	Production

Required

Assuming that the fiscal year ends December 31, compute the depreciation charges for 19x1, 19x2, and 19x3 to the nearest month by filling in a table with the headings shown below.

		Depreciation		
Equipment No.	**Computations**	**19x1**	**19x2**	**19x3**

Assume that production for Equipment 4 was 2,000 hours in 19x1; 4,200 hours in 19x2; and 3,200 hours in 19x3. Show your computations.

Problem 9A-4. Plant Asset Transactions, Revised Depreciation, and Spare Parts *(L.O. 2, 3, 4, 5)*

Rita Carrasquel entered the jewelry refinishing business in January 19x1. She was able to purchase refinishing equipment for $59,275 on January 2. It cost her $6,400 to have the equipment moved to her building and $2,340 to have it installed. It cost another $1,585 to adjust the equipment. She estimated that the equipment would have a useful life of ten years and a residual value of $6,000. Small tools were purchased on May 14 at a cost of $580, and regular maintenance of the equipment on September 16 came to $1,485. At the end of the year, an inventory revealed that $240 in small tools were still on hand. During 19x2, small tools costing $725 were purchased on April 18, and the physical inventory disclosed $230 on hand at the end of the year. Regular maintenance costs expended on October 4 were $2,070. At the end of 19x2 it became apparent that the equipment would last a total of only six years instead of the ten years originally estimated and that the estimated residual value at the end of six years would be only $2,500.

Required

1. Prepare general journal entries for 19x1 to record the purchase of the equipment, the costs associated with the purchase, the transaction involving small tools, the upkeep costs, the year-end depreciation charge, and the small tools expense. Carrasquel's company uses the inventory method of recording small tools expense and the straight-line method for computing depreciation expense. Assume that all purchases are made with cash.
2. Prepare general journal entries for 19x2 for small tools, maintenance, and depreciation expense. The depreciation expense should be based on the new estimates regarding the equipment.

Problem 9A-5. Comprehensive Capital and Revenue Expenditure Entries *(L.O. 6, 7)*

Nieman's, Inc. operates a chain of self-service gasoline stations in several southern states. The transactions below describe the capital and revenue expenditures for one station.

Construction of the station was completed on July 1, 1970, at a cost of $355,000. It was estimated that the station would have a useful life of thirty-five years and a residual value of $40,000. On September 15, 1974, scheduled painting and minor repairs affecting the appearance of the station were completed at a cost of $4,650. On July 9, 1975, a new gasoline tank was added at a cost of $80,000. The tank did not add to the useful life of the station, but it did add $11,000 to its estimated residual value. On October 22, 1979, the driveway of the station was resurfaced at a cost of $1,900. The cost of major repairs and renovation, as part of the company's planned maintenance completed on July 3, 1980, was $55,000. It was estimated that this work would extend the life of the station by five years and would not increase the residual value. A change in the routing of a major highway led to the sale of the station on January 2, 1983, for $230,000. The company received $30,000 in cash and a note for the balance of the $230,000.

Required

1. Prepare general journal entries for the following dates: (a) July 1, 1970; (b) September 15, 1974; (c) July 9, 1975; (d) October 22, 1979; and (e) July 3, 1980.
2. Open ledger accounts for Station (143) and for Accumulated Depreciation, Station (144), and post the relevant portions of the entries in **1**.
3. Compute depreciation expense for each year and partial year until the date of sale, assuming that the straight-line method is used and that the company's fiscal year ends on June 30. Enter the amounts in the account for Accumulated Depreciation, Station.
4. Prepare a general journal entry to record the sale of the station on January 2, 1983. Post the relevant portions of the entries to the two accounts opened in **2**.

Problem 9A-6. Recording Disposals *(L.O. 7, 8)*

Robles Construction Company purchased a road grader for $29,000. The road grader is expected to have a useful life of five years and a residual value of $2,000 at the end of that time.

Required

Prepare journal entries to record the disposal of the road grader at the end of the second year, assuming that the straight-line method is used and making the following additional independent assumptions:

a. The road grader is sold for $20,000 cash.
b. It is sold for $16,000 cash.
c. It is traded in on a dissimilar item (machinery) having a price of $33,000, a trade-in allowance of $20,000 is given, the balance is paid in cash, and gains or losses are recognized.
d. It is traded in on a dissimilar item (machinery) having a price of $33,000, a trade-in allowance of $16,000 is given, the balance is paid in cash, and gains or losses are recognized.
e. Same as **c** except that it is traded for a similar road grader and Robles Construction Company follows APB accounting rules with regard to the recognition of gains or losses.
f. Same as **d** except that it is traded for a similar road grader and Robles Construction Company follows APB accounting rules with regard to the recognition of gains or losses.
g. Same as **c** except that it is traded for a similar road grader and gains or losses are not recognized (income tax purposes).
h. Same as **d** except that it is traded for a similar road grader and gains or losses are not recognized (income tax purposes).

Problem 9A-7. Amortization of Exclusive License, Leasehold, and Leasehold Improvements *(L.O. 10)*

Part 1

On January 1, Future Play, Inc. purchased the exclusive license to make dolls based on the characters in a new hit series on television called "Sky Pirates." The exclusive license cost $2,100,000, and there was no termination date on the rights. Immediately after signing the contract, the company sued a rival firm that claimed it had already received the exclusive license to the series characters. Future Play successfully defended its rights at a cost of $360,000. During the first year and the next, Future Play marketed toys based on the series. Because a successful television series lasts about five years, the company felt it could market the toys for three more years. However, before the third year of the series could get under way, a controversy arose between the two stars of the series and the producer. As a result, the stars refused to do the third year and the show was canceled, rendering the exclusive rights worthless.

Required

Prepare journal entries to record the following: (a) purchase of the exclusive license; (b) successful defense of the license; (c) amortization expense, if any, for the first year; and (d) news of the series cancellation.

Part 2

Pamela Newell purchased a six-year sublease on a building from the estate of the former tenant, who had died suddenly. It was a good location for her business, and the annual rent of $3,600, which had been established ten years before, was low for such a good location. The cost of the sublease was $9,450. To use the building, Newell had to make certain alterations. First she moved some panels at a cost of $1,700 and installed others for $6,100. Then she added carpet, lighting fixtures, and a sign at costs of $2,900, $3,100, and $1,200, respectively. All items except the carpet would last for at least twelve years. The expected life of the carpet was six years. None of the improvements would have a residual value at the end of those times.

Required

Prepare general journal entries to record the following: (a) the payment for the sublease; (b) the payments for the alterations, panels, carpet, lighting fixtures, and sign; (c) the lease payment for the first year; (d) the expense, if any, associated with the sublease; and (e) the expense, if any, associated with the alterations, panels, carpet, lighting fixtures, and sign.

Problem Set B

Problem 9B-1. Determining Cost of Assets *(L.O. 2, 3, 4, 5)*

Moline Computers, Incorporated constructed a new training center in 19x7. You have been hired to manage the training center. A review of the accounting records lists the following expenditures debited to the Training Center account:

Attorney's fee, land acquisition	$ 17,450
Cost of land	299,000
Architect's fee, building design	51,000
Contractor's cost, building	510,000
Contractor's cost, parking lot and sidewalk	67,800
Contractor's cost, electrical	82,000
Landscaping	27,500
Costs of surveying land	4,600
Training equipment, tables, and chairs	68,200
Contractor's cost, installing training equipment	34,000
Cost of grading the land	7,000
Cost of changes in building to soundproof rooms	29,600
Total Account Balance	$1,198,150

During the center's construction, someone from Moline Computers, Incorporated worked full time on the project. He spent two months on the purchase and preparation of the site, six months on the construction, one month on land improvements, and one month on equipment installation and training room furniture purchase and set-up. His salary of $32,000 during this ten-month period was charged to Administrative Expense. The training center was placed in operation on November 1.

Required

1. Prepare a schedule with the following four column (Account) headings: Land, Land Improvements, Building, and Equipment. Place each item in the appropriate column. Total the columns.
2. Prepare an entry on December 31 to correct the accounts associated with the training center, assuming that the company's accounts have not been closed at the end of the year.
3. Assume that the center was in operation for two months during the year. Prepare an adjusting entry to record depreciation expense, assuming that the land improvements are depreciated over twenty years with no residual value, that the buildings are depreciated over thirty years with no residual value, and that the equipment is depreciated over twelve years with an estimated residual value equal to 10 percent of cost. The company uses the straight-line method. Round your answers to the nearest dollar.

Problem 9B-2. Comparison of Depreciation Methods
(L.O. 3, 4)

Hoekstra Manufacturing Company purchased a robot for its manufacturing operations at a cost of $720,000 at the beginning of year 1. The robot has an estimated useful life of four years and an estimated residual value of $60,000. The robot is expected to last 20,000 hours. The robot was operated 6,000 hours in year 1; 8,000 hours in year 2; 4,000 hours in year 3; and 2,000 hours in year 4.

Required

1. Compute the annual depreciation and carrying value for the robot for each year assuming the following depreciation methods: (a) straight-line, (b) production, (c) sum-of-the-years'-digits, and (d) double-declining-balance.
2. Prepare the adjusting entry that would be made each year to record the depreciation calculated under the straight-line method.
3. Show the balance sheet presentation for the robot after the adjusting entry in year 2 using the straight-line method.
4. What conclusions can you draw from the patterns of yearly depreciation and carrying value in **1**?

Problem 9B-3. Depreciation Methods and Partial Years
(L.O. 4, 5)

Ada Pinkston purchased a laundry company that caters to young college students. In addition to the washing machines, Ada installed a tanning machine, a video game machine, and a bar. Because each type of asset performs a different function, she has decided to use different depreciation methods. Data on each type of asset are summarized below:

Asset	Date Purchased	Cost	Installation Cost	Residual Value	Estimated Life	Depreciation Method
Washing machines	3/5/x7	$15,000	$2,000	$2,600	4 years	Straight-line
Tanning machine	4/1/x7	34,000	3,000	1,000	7,500 hours	Production
Video game	6/30/x7	10,000	1,000	800	4 years	Sum-of-the-years'-digits
Bar	10/1/x7	3,400	600	600	10 years	Double-declining-balance

The tanning machine was operated 2,100 hours in 19x7, 3,000 hours in 19x8, and 2,400 hours in 19x9.

Required

Assuming that the fiscal year ends December 31, compute the depreciation charges for 19x7, 19x8, and 19x9. Round your answers to the nearest dollar and present them by filling in a table with the headings shown below:

		Depreciation		
Asset	**Computations**	**19x7**	**19x8**	**19x9**

Problem 9B-4. Plant Asset Transactions, Revised Depreciation, and Spare Parts *(L.O. 2, 3, 4, 5)*

Fernandez Auto Repair Company installed auto repair equipment on January 2, 19x7, which was purchased for $94,000. Delivery cost was $3,500, and installation cost was $2,500. Mr. Fernandez estimated that the equipment would have a useful life of six years and a residual value of $10,000. On April 2, small tools for auto repairs were purchased for $1,475. Regular maintenance in 19x7 was $480, expended on November 1. At the end of the year, an inventory revealed $760 of small tools still on hand. Regular maintenance for the equipment was $750 in 19x8. This expenditure was made on May 10. At that time Mr. Fernandez determined that the equipment would last only four years instead of the originally estimated six years. The new estimated residual value would be only $5,000. On June 10, 19x8, $420 of small tools were purchased, and the inventory of small tools showed $1,020 on hand at the end of the year.

Required

1. Prepare general journal entries for 19x7 to record the purchase of the equipment, costs associated with the purchase, maintenance costs, the transactions involving small tools, and year-end depreciation assuming the straight-line method of depreciation. Use the inventory method of recording small tools expense, and assume that all purchases are made with cash.
2. Prepare general journal entries for 19x8 for maintenance, small tools, and depreciation expense using Mr. Fernandez's revised estimates.

Problem 9B-5. Capital and Revenue Expenditure Entries *(L.O. 6, 7)*

Gary Kubiak operates several low-budget motels in the Midwest. The transactions below describe the capital and revenue expenditures for the first motel he purchased:

Dec. 21, 19x1	Purchased the motel at a cost of $940,000. The estimated life of the motel is twenty years, and the residual value is $140,000.
Dec. 31, 19x1	The motel was repainted and some minor roof problems were corrected at a cost of $40,000. These costs were necessary before the motel was opened to the public.
Jan. 12, 19x5	Made a small addition to the motel at a cost of $38,250. This cost did not affect the life or residual value of the motel.
May 20, 19x5	Minor repairs were made to the doors of each room for $5,300.
Sept. 17, 19x5	Minor resurfacing was performed on the parking lot at a cost of $6,100.
Jan. 9, 19x8	Major repairs and renovation of $74,500 were completed. It was estimated that this work would extend the life of the motel by five years and increase the residual value by $10,000.

Required

1. Prepare general journal entries for each transaction. Assume that all transactions are made with cash.
2. Open ledger accounts for Motel (150) and Accumulated Depreciation, Motel (151), and post the relevant entries in **1** and other necessary entries above through 19x8.
3. Compute depreciation expense for each year and partial year assuming that the straight-line method is used and the company's fiscal year ends on December 31. Enter the amounts in the accounts for Accumulated Depreciation, Motel.

4. Prepare general journal entries to record the partial year's depreciation and the sale of the motel on June 30, 19x9, for $880,000, including $80,000 in cash and the remaining amount as a mortgage note. Post the relevant portions of the entry to the two accounts opened in **2**.

Problem 9B-6. Recording Disposals *(L.O. 7, 8)*

Ingram Designs, Inc. purchased a computer to assist it in designing factory layouts. The cost of the computer was $47,000. The expected useful life is six years. The company can probably sell the computer for $5,000 at the end of six years.

Required

Prepare journal entries to record the disposal of the computer at the end of the third year, assuming that it was depreciated using the straight-line method and making the following independent assumptions.

a. The computer is sold for $38,000.
b. It is sold for $20,000.
c. It is traded in on a dissimilar item (equipment) costing $72,000, a trade-in allowance of $35,000 is given, the balance is paid in cash, and gains and losses are recognized.
d. Same as **c**, except that the trade-in allowance is $22,000.
e. Same as **c**, except that it is traded for a similar computer and APB accounting rules are followed with regard to the recognition of gains or losses.
f. Same as **d**, except that it is traded for a similar computer and APB accounting rules are followed with regard to the recognition of gains or losses.
g. Same as **c**, except that it is traded for a similar computer and gains and losses are not recognized (income tax method).
h. Same as **d**, except that it is traded for a similar computer and gains and losses are not recognized (income tax method).

Problem 9B-7. Leasehold, Leasehold Improvements, and Amortization of Patent *(L.O. 10)*

Part 1

At the beginning of the fiscal year, Dempsey Company purchased an eight-year sublease on a warehouse in Nashville for $24,000. Dempsey will also pay rent of $500 a month. The warehouse needs the following improvements to meet Dempsey's needs:

Lighting fixtures	$ 9,000	Heating system	$15,000
Replacement of a wall	12,500	Break room	6,100
Office carpet	7,200	Loading dock	4,200

The expected life of the loading dock and carpet is eight years. The other items are expected to last ten years. None of the improvements will have a residual value.

Required

Prepare general journal entries to record the following: (a) payment for the sublease; (b) first-year lease payment; (c) payments for the improvements; (d) amortization of leasehold for the year; (e) leasehold improvement amortization for the year.

Part 2

At the beginning of the fiscal year, Fellner Company purchased a patent for $515,000 that applies to the manufacture of a unique tamper-proof lid for medicine bottles. Fellner incurred legal costs of $225,000 in successfully defending the patent against use of the lid by a competitor. Fellner estimated that the patent would be valuable for at least ten years. During the first two years of operation, Fellner successfully marketed the lid. At the beginning of the third year, a study appeared in a consumers' magazine showing that the lid could, in fact, be removed by children. As a result, all orders for the lids were canceled, and the patent was rendered worthless.

Required

Prepare journal entries to record the following: (a) purchase of the patent; (b) successful defense of the patent; (c) amortization expense for the first year; and (d) write-off of the patent as worthless.

Financial Decision Cases

9-1. Hyde Computer Company *(L.O. 4)*

The Hyde Computer Company manufactures computers for sale or rent. On January 2, 19x1, the company completed the manufacture of a computer for a total cost of $190,000. A customer leased the computer on the same day for a five-year period at a monthly rental of $5,000. Although the computer will last longer than five years, it is likely but not certain that it will be technologically obsolete by the end of the five-year period. Hyde's management estimates that if the computer is obsolete, it can be sold for $20,000 at the end of the lease, and if it is not obsolete, it can be sold for $40,000 because it would probably last for another two years. On the basis of its experience in leasing many computers, management estimates that the expenses associated with the lease of this computer will be as follows:

	Insurance and Property Taxes	Repairs and Maintenance
19x1	$7,000	$3,000
19x2	6,400	4,500
19x3	5,800	6,000
19x4	5,200	7,500
19x5	4,600	9,000

Required

1. What estimated useful life and estimated residual value do you recommend that Hyde use for the computer? Explain.
2. Prepare two schedules that show for each year the lease revenue, expenses, and income before income taxes. Also, show on each schedule for each year the carrying value of the computer at the end of the year, and compute the ratio of income before income taxes to carrying value (return on assets). Round components to one decimal place. The first schedule should compute depreciation using the straight-line method, and the second schedule should use the sum-of-the-years'-digits method.
3. Compare the two schedules in **2**, and discuss the results. Which of the methods do you feel produces the most realistic pattern of income before taxes, and why?
4. If you were asked to determine the amount of cash generated each year from this lease (cash received minus cash disbursed), what effect, if any, would the method of depreciation have on your computations? Ignore income tax effects.

9-2.
Daniels Gravel Company
(L.O. 4, 9)

Billy Bob Daniels is in the gravel business in Oklahoma and has engaged you to assist in evaluating his company. Your first step is to collect the facts about the company's operations. On January 3, 19x2, Billy Bob purchased a piece of property with gravel deposits for $6,310,000. He estimated that the gravel deposits contained 4,700,000 cubic yards of gravel. The gravel is used for making roads. After the gravel is gone, the land, which is in the desert, will be worth only about $200,000.

The equipment required to extract the gravel cost $1,452,000. In addition, Billy Bob had to build a small frame building to house the mine office and a small dining hall for the workers. The building cost $152,000 and will have no residual value after its estimated useful life of ten years. It cannot be moved from the mine site. The equipment has an estimated useful life of six years (with no residual value) and also cannot be moved from the mine site.

Trucks for the project cost $308,000 (estimated life, six years; residual value, $20,000). The trucks, of course, can be used at a different site.

Billy Bob estimated that in five years all the gravel would be mined and the mine would be shut down. During 19x2, 1,175,000 cubic yards of gravel were mined. The average selling price during the year was $2.66 per cubic yard, and at the end of the year 125,000 cubic yards remained unsold. Operating expenses were $852,000 for labor and $232,000 for other expenses.

Required

1. Prepare general journal entries to record the purchase of the property and all the buildings and equipment associated with the mine. Assume purchases are made with cash on January 3.
2. Prepare adjusting entries to record depletion and depreciation for the first year of operation (19x2). Assume that the depreciation rate is equal to the percentage of the total gravel mined during the year unless the asset is movable. For movable assets, use the straight-line method.
3. Prepare an income statement for 19x2 for the Daniels Gravel Company.
4. What is your evaluation of the company's operations? What are the reasons for your evaluation? Ignore income tax effects.

9-3.
Conway Enterprises
(L.O. 10)

Stan Johnson, president of Johnson Company, had been looking for a good business to purchase. He found one in Conway Enterprises, which had earned an average of $46,000 a year for the last five years. Johnson proposed that he purchase all the assets, except for cash, of Conway Enterprises and assume the liabilities of Conway. He would pay $150,000 cash and give a one-year note for the balance. He was willing to pay for goodwill equal to four times those earnings that exceeded the industry average earnings of 10 percent of net tangible assets, excluding cash.

Information from the current balance sheet for Conway Enterprises is on page 495.

Stan Johnson and Bob Conway agree to adjust the Conway Enterprises books in two ways. First of all, the land, which had been purchased many years before by the Conway family, was not realistically valued and should have a value of $25,000. Second, the trademark and franchise had been on the books for many years without being amortized and should not be considered to have any value.

Conway Enterprises
Balance Sheet

Cash		$ 22,000
Other Current Assets		164,000
Plant Assets		
Land		5,000
Buildings	$124,000	
Less Accumulated Depreciation	42,000	82,000
Equipment	$289,000	
Less Accumulated Depreciation	106,000	183,000
Trademark		22,000
Franchise		17,000
Total Assets		$495,000
Current Liabilities		$ 46,000
Long-Term Note Payable		100,000
Common Stock		100,000
Retained Earnings		249,000
Total Liabilities and Stockholders' Equity		$495,000

Required

1. Prepare a general journal entry to adjust the Conway Enterprises books in accordance with the agreement. The net effect increases or decreases Retained Earnings.
2. Compute the net tangible assets exclusive of cash.
3. Compute the amount of goodwill to be purchased.
4. Prepare a general journal entry in Johnson Company's records to show the purchase of Conway Enterprises.

LEARNING OBJECTIVES

1. Explain how the issues of recognition, valuation, and classification apply to liabilities.
2. Identify, compute, and record definitely determinable and estimated current liabilities.
3. Define a contingent liability.
4. Distinguish simple from compound interest.
5. Use compound interest tables to compute the future value of a single invested sum at compound interest and of an ordinary annuity.
6. Use compound interest tables to compute the present value of a single sum due in the future and of an ordinary annuity.
7. Apply the concept of present value to accounting situations.

CHAPTER 10

Current Liabilities and the Time Value of Money

Liabilities are one of the three major parts of the balance sheet. The two major kinds of liabilities are current and long-term liabilities. This chapter deals with the nature and measurement of current liabilities. The subject of long-term liabilities is covered later. After studying this chapter, you should be able to meet the learning objectives listed on the left.

DECISION POINT

USAir Group Inc.[1]

Liabilities are the result of a company's past transactions; they are legal obligations for the future payment of assets or the future performance of services. For example, at the end of 1990, USAir Group Inc., one of ten major U.S. airlines, with total assets of $6,574 million, had Accounts Payable of $474 million and Accrued Expenses of $815 million, most of which would require an outlay of cash in 1991. In addition, Traffic Balances Payable and Unused Tickets were listed at $481 million. The unused tickets represent future services that must be performed. Air travel must be provided to people who have bought tickets, or the value of the tickets must be refunded if they are not used. These are regarded as **current liabilities** because they are debts and obligations that are expected to be satisfied in one year or within the normal operating cycle, whichever is longer. USAir's management incurred these debts to provide for the smooth operation of the business. Thus, it must plan to pay or to satisfy these obligations out of current assets or with cash generated by the company's operations.

USAir also has **long-term liabilities** of $2,263 million. These liabilities are not due during the next year or normal operating cycle. Management's purpose in incurring these liabilities is very different from its purpose in incurring current liabilities. Long-term liabilities are used to finance long-term assets, such as aircraft. Management has many options

1. Excerpts from the 1990 Annual Report are reprinted by permission of USAir.

for financing the business through current liabilities and long-term liabilities. This chapter and the next explore these options from the accounting point of view. ■

Nature and Measurement of Liabilities

The problems of recognition, valuation, and classification apply to liabilities as they do to assets.

Recognition of Liabilities

OBJECTIVE 1
Explain how the issues of recognition, valuation, and classification apply to liabilities

Timing is important in the recognition of liabilities. Very often failure to record a liability in an accounting period goes along with failure to record an expense. Thus it leads to an understatement of expense and an overstatement of income. Liabilities are recorded when an obligation occurs. This rule is harder to apply than it might appear. When a transaction obligates the company to make future payments, a liability arises and is recognized, as when goods are bought on credit. However, current liabilities often are not represented by a direct transaction. One of the major reasons for adjusting entries at the end of an accounting period is to recognize unrecorded liabilities. Among these accrued liabilities are salaries payable and interest payable. Other liabilities that can only be estimated, such as taxes payable, must also be recognized by adjusting entries.

On the other hand, a company may sometimes enter into an agreement for future transactions. For instance, a company may agree to pay an executive $50,000 a year for a period of three years, or a public utility may agree to buy an unspecified quantity of coal at a certain price over the next five years. These contracts, though they are definite commitments, are not considered liabilities because they are for future—not past—transactions. As there is no current obligation, no liability is recognized.

Valuation of Liabilities

Liabilities are generally valued on the balance sheet at the amount of money needed to pay the debt or at the fair market value of goods or services to be delivered. For most liabilities the amount is definitely known, but for some it must be estimated. For example, an automobile dealer who sells a car with a one-year warranty must provide parts and services during the year. The obligation is definite because the sale of the car has occurred, but the amount must be estimated. Additional disclosures of the market value of liabilities may be required in the notes to the financial statement as explained below.

Classification of Liabilities

The classification of current liabilities directly matches the classification of current assets. Two important measures of liquidity are working capital (current assets less current liabilities) and the current ratio (current assets divided by current liabilities). Long-term liabilities are usually designated in such a way that the reader of the financial statement can compute the debt to equity ratio.

Disclosure of Liabilities

Because it found past disclosure practices inadequate, the FASB required increased disclosure by corporations about all their financial instruments.[2] **Financial instruments** include cash, evidences of ownership such as common stock, and any contract that results in an asset to one entity and a liability to another entity. As such, they include financial assets. However, the FASB is more concerned with the disclosure of financial liabilities, such as loans, mortgages, bonds, leases, and other forms of debt financing, especially **off-balance-sheet liabilities**, which do not appear on the balance sheet as liabilities but that expose the company to possible loss through a credit risk. A credit risk is the possibility, however remote, that a loss might be incurred through failure of another party to perform according to the terms of a financial instrument. For example, if Maas Company guarantees the loan of Chona Corporation, no liability is recorded in the records of Maas Company, even though if Chona fails to pay the loan, Maas will have to pay it and will suffer a loss. The FASB requires that this kind of agreement be disclosed in the notes to Maas Company's financial statements.

The FASB has proposed that all companies be required to disclose information about the market value of their financial instruments, both assets and liabilities.[3] Quoted market prices generally provide the most reliable measure of market value. Market price is defined as the amount at which a single trading unit of the instrument could be sold or bought between a willing buyer and a willing seller, other than a forced or liquidation sale. For instance, if the market value of a company's outstanding debt changes because of changing interest rates (see the chapter on long-term liabilities), the amount of the company's liability would not change on the balance sheet but the disclosure in the notes to the financial statements would show the current market value. If market prices are not available, estimates based on the present value of future cash flows (discussed later in this chapter) or the market value of similar instruments could be used. The FASB is expected to reach its final decision in late 1991.

Common Categories of Current Liabilities

Current liabilities usually equal about one-fourth to one-third of total assets across all industries, as may be seen in Figure 10-1. They fall into two major groups: (1) definitely determinable liabilities and (2) estimated liabilities. Discussions of each follow.

2. *Statement of Financial Accounting Standards No. 105,* "Disclosure of Information About Financial Instruments with Concentrations of Credit Risk" (Stamford, Conn.: Financial Accounting Standards Board, 1990).
3. *Exposure Draft,* "Disclosures About Market Value of Financial Instruments" (Stamford, Conn.: Financial Accounting Standards Board, 1990).

Figure 10-1. Current Liabilities as a Percentage of Total Assets

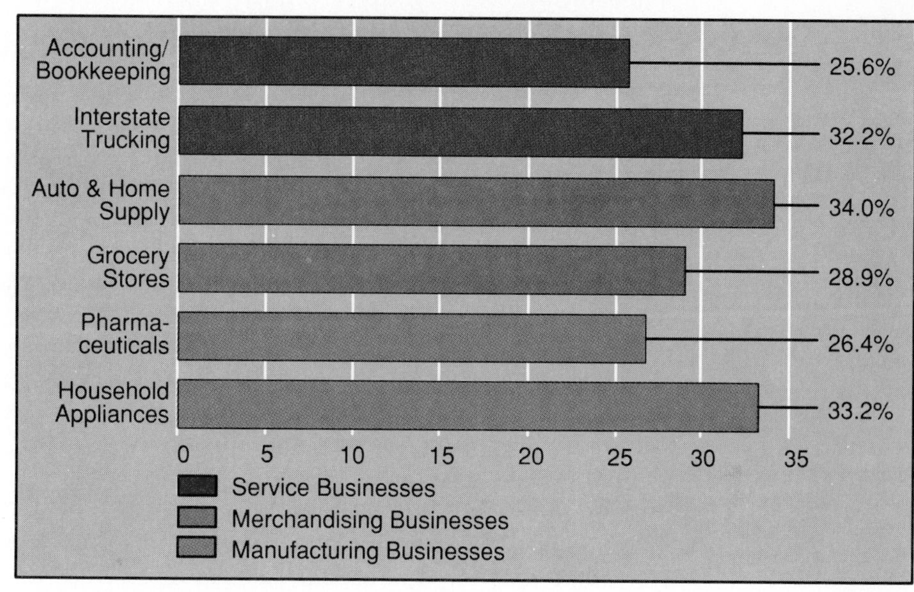

Source: Data from Dun and Bradstreet, *Industry Norms and Ratios*, 1990–91.

Definitely Determinable Liabilities

OBJECTIVE 2 *Identify, compute, and record definitely determinable and estimated current liabilities*

Current liabilities that are set by contract or by statute and can be measured exactly are called **definitely determinable liabilities**. The accounting problems connected with these liabilities are to determine the existence and amount of the liability and to see that the liability is recorded properly. Definitely determinable liabilities include trade accounts payable, bank loans and commercial paper, notes payable, accrued liabilities, dividends payable, sales and excise taxes payable, current portions of long-term debt, payroll liabilities, and deferred revenues.

Trade Accounts Payable. Trade accounts payable are short-term obligations to suppliers for goods and services. The amount in the Trade Accounts Payable account is generally supported by an accounts payable subsidiary ledger, which contains an individual account for each person or company to whom money is owed. Accounting for trade accounts payable has been treated at length earlier in the book.

Bank Loans and Commercial Paper. Management will often establish a **line of credit** from a bank; this arrangement allows the company to borrow funds when they are needed to finance current operations. For example, Nordstrom, a chain of quality department stores, reported in its 1990 annual report that the finance division had "a $150 [million] unsecured line of credit with a group of commercial banks which is available as liquidity support for short-term debt."[4] A promissory note for the full amount of the line of credit is signed when the line of credit is granted, but the company has great flexibility in using the line of credit. The company can increase its borrowing up to the limit when it needs cash and reduce the amount borrowed when it obtains cash. Both the amount of the borrowing and the interest rate charged by the bank may change on a daily basis. The bank may require the company to meet certain financial goals (such as maintaining certain profit margins, current ratios, or debt to equity ratios) to retain the line of credit. Companies with excellent credit ratings may also borrow short-term funds by issuing **commercial paper**. Commercial paper constitutes unsecured loans that are sold to the public, usually through professionally managed investment firms. The portion of a line of credit that has currently been borrowed and the amount of commercial paper issued are usually combined with notes payable in the current liabilities section of the balance sheet. Details are disclosed in a note to the financial statements.

Notes Payable. Short-term notes payable, which also arise out of the ordinary course of business, are obligations represented by promissory notes. These notes may be used to secure bank loans, to pay suppliers for goods and services, and to secure credit from other sources.

As with notes receivable, presented in the chapter on short-term liquid assets, the interest on notes may be stated separately on the face of the note (Case 1 in Figure 10-2), or it may be deducted in advance by discounting it from the face value of the note (Case 2). The entries to record the note in each case are as follows:

Case 1—Interest stated separately

Aug. 31	Cash	5,000	
	Notes Payable		5,000
	To record 60-day, 12% promissory note with interest stated separately		

Case 2—Interest in face amount

Aug. 31	Cash	4,900	
	Discount on Notes Payable	100	
	Notes Payable		5,000
	To record 60-day, 12% promissory note with prepaid interest included in face amount		

$$\$5{,}000 \times \frac{60}{360} \times .12 = \$100$$

Note that in Case 1 the money borrowed equaled the face value of the note, whereas in Case 2 the money borrowed ($4,900) was less than the face value ($5,000) of the note. The amount of the discount equals the amount of the interest for sixty days. Discount on Notes Payable is a contra account to Notes Payable and is deducted from Notes Payable on the balance sheet.

4. Nordstrom 1990 Annual Report.

Figure 10-2. Two Promissory Notes: One with Interest Stated Separately; One with Interest in Face Amount

Case 1 ***Interest Stated Separately***

Chicago, Illinois August 31, 19xx

Sixty days after date I promise to pay First Federal Bank the sum of $5,000 with interest at the rate of 12% per annum.

Sandra Caron

Caron Corporation

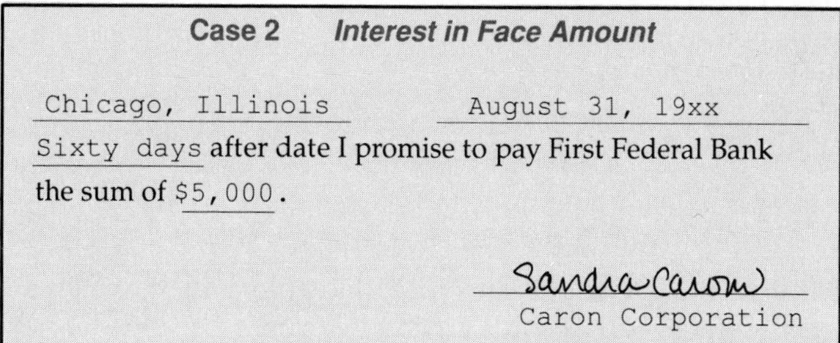

Case 2 ***Interest in Face Amount***

Chicago, Illinois August 31, 19xx

Sixty days after date I promise to pay First Federal Bank the sum of $5,000.

Sandra Caron

Caron Corporation

On October 30, when the note is paid, each alternative is recorded as follows:

Case 1—Interest stated separately

Oct.	30	Notes Payable	5,000	
		Interest Expense	100	
		Cash		5,100
		Payment of note with interest stated separately		

Case 2—Interest in face amount

Oct.	30	Notes Payable	5,000	
		Cash		5,000
		Payment of note with interest included in face amount		
	30	Interest Expense	100	
		Discount on Notes Payable		100
		To record interest expense on matured note		

Accrued Liabilities. A principal reason for adjusting entries at the end of an accounting period is to recognize and record liabilities that are not already recorded in the accounting records. This practice applies to any type of liability. For example, in previous chapters, adjustments relating to salaries payable were made. As you will see, accrued liabilities can also include estimated liabilities.

Here the focus is on interest payable, a definitely determinable liability. Interest accrues daily on interest-bearing notes. At the end of the accounting period, an adjusting entry should be made in accordance with the matching rule to record the interest obligation up to that point in time. Let us again use the example of the two notes presented earlier in this chapter. If we assume that the accounting period ends on September 30, or thirty days after the issuance of the sixty-day notes, the adjusting entries for each case would be as follows:

Case 1—Interest stated separately

Sept. 30	Interest Expense	50	
	Interest Payable		50
	To record interest expense for 30 days on note with interest stated separately		
	$\$5{,}000 \times \frac{30}{360} \times .12 = \$50$		

Case 2—Interest in face amount

Sept. 30	Interest Expense	50	
	Discount on Notes Payable		50
	To record interest expense for 30 days on note with interest included in face amount		
	$\$5{,}000 \times \frac{30}{360} \times .12 = \$50$		

In Case 2, Discount on Notes Payable will now have a debit balance of $50, which will become interest expense during the next thirty days.

Dividends Payable. Cash dividends are a distribution of earnings by a corporation. The payment of dividends is solely the decision of the corporation's board of directors. A liability does not exist until the board declares the dividends. There is usually a short time between the date of declaration and the date of payment of dividends. During that short time, the dividends declared are current liabilities of the corporation. Accounting for dividends is treated extensively in the chapter on retained earnings and corporate income statements.

Sales and Excise Taxes Payable. Most states and many cities levy a sales tax on retail transactions. There are federal excise taxes on some products, such as automobile tires. The merchant who sells goods subject to these taxes must collect the taxes and remit, or pay, them periodically to the appropriate government agency. The amount of tax collected represents a current liability until it is remitted to the government. For example, assume that a merchant makes a $100 sale that is subject to a 5 percent sales tax and a 10 percent excise tax. Assuming that the sale took place on June 1, the correct entry to record the sale is as follows:

June 1	Cash	115	
	Sales		100
	Sales Tax Payable		5
	Excise Tax Payable		10
	To record sale of merchandise and collection of sales and excise taxes		

The sale is properly recorded at $100, and the tax collections are recorded as liabilities to be remitted at the proper time to the appropriate government agency.

Current Portions of Long-Term Debt. If a portion of long-term debt is due within the next year and is to be paid from current assets, then this current portion of long-term debt is properly classified as a current liability. For example, suppose that a $500,000 debt is to be paid in installments of $100,000 per year for the next five years. The $100,000 installment due in the current year should be classified as a current liability. The remaining $400,000 should be classified as a long-term liability. Note that no journal entry is necessary. The total debt of $500,000 is simply reclassified when the financial statements are prepared, as follows:

Current Liabilities	
Current Portion of Long-Term Debt	$100,000
Long-Term Liabilities	
Long-Term Debt	400,000

Payroll Liabilities. A number of current liabilities are associated with payroll accounting. These liabilities are discussed in the appendix on payroll accounting.

Unearned or Deferred Revenues. **Unearned** or **deferred revenues** represent obligations for goods or services that the company must provide or deliver in a future accounting period in return for an advance payment from a customer. For example, a publisher of a monthly magazine who receives annual subscriptions totaling $240 would make the following entry:

Cash	240	
Unearned Subscriptions		240
Receipt of annual subscriptions in advance		

The publisher now has a liability of $240 that will be gradually reduced as monthly issues of the magazine are delivered, as follows:

Unearned Subscriptions	20	
Subscription Revenues		20
Delivery of monthly magazine issues		

Many businesses, such as repair companies, construction companies, and special-order firms, ask for a deposit or advance from a customer before they will begin work. These advances are also current liabilities until the goods or services are delivered.

Estimated Liabilities

Estimated liabilities are definite debts or obligations of a company for which the exact amount cannot be known until a later date. Since there is no doubt as to the existence of the legal obligation, the primary accounting problem is to estimate and record the amount of the liability. Examples of estimated liabilities are income taxes, property taxes, product warranties, and vacation pay.

Income Tax. The income of a corporation is taxed by the federal government, most state governments, and some cities and towns. The amount of income tax liability depends on the results of operations. Often it is not certain until after the end of the year. However, because income taxes are an expense in the year in which income is earned, an adjusting entry is necessary to record the estimated tax liability. An example of this entry follows:

Dec. 31	Federal Income Tax Expense	53,000	
	Federal Income Tax Payable		53,000
	To record estimated federal income tax		

Remember that the income of sole proprietorships and partnerships is *not* subject to income taxes. Their owners must report their share of the firm's income on their individual tax returns.

Property Taxes Payable. Property taxes are taxes levied on real property, such as land and buildings, and on personal property, such as inventory and equipment. Property taxes are a main source of revenue for local governments. Usually they are assessed annually against the property involved. Because the fiscal years of local governments and their assessment dates rarely correspond to those of the firm, it is necessary to estimate the amount of property taxes that applies to each month of the year. Assume, for instance, that a local government has a fiscal year of July 1 to June 30, that its assessment date is November 1 for the current fiscal year that began on July 1, and that its payment date is December 15. Assume also that on July 1, Janis Corporation estimates that its property tax assessment for the coming year will be $24,000. The adjusting entry to be made on July 31, which would be repeated on August 31, September 30, and October 31, would be as follows:

July 31	Property Taxes Expense	2,000	
	Estimated Property Taxes Payable		2,000
	To record estimated property taxes expense for the month $24,000 ÷ 12 months = $2,000		

On November 1, the firm receives a property tax bill for $24,720. The estimate made in July was too low. The monthly charge should have been $2,060 per month. Because the difference between the actual and the estimate is small, the company decides to absorb in November the amount undercharged in the previous four months. Therefore, the property tax expense for November is $2,300 [$2,060 + 4($60)] and is recorded as follows:

Nov. 30	Property Taxes Expense	2,300	
	Estimated Property Taxes Payable		2,300
	To record estimated property taxes		

The Estimated Property Taxes Payable account now has a balance of $10,300. The entry to record payment on December 15 would be made as follows:

Dec. 15	Estimated Property Taxes Payable	10,300	
	Prepaid Property Taxes	14,420	
	Cash		24,720
	To record payment of property taxes		

Beginning December 31 and each month afterward until June 30, property tax expense is recorded by a debit to Property Taxes Expense and a credit to Prepaid Property Taxes in the amount of $2,060. The total of these seven entries will reduce the Prepaid Property Taxes account to zero on June 30.

Product Warranty Liability. When a firm places a warranty or guarantee on its product at the time of sale, a liability exists for the length of the warranty. The cost of the warranty is properly debited to an expense account in the period of sale because it is a feature of the product or service sold and thus is included in the price paid by the customer for the product. On the basis of experience, it should be possible to estimate the amount the warranty will cost in the future. Some products or services will require little warranty service; others may require much. Thus there will be an average cost per product or service.

For example, assume that a muffler company guarantees that it will replace any muffler free of charge if it fails any time as long as you own your car. The company charges a small service fee for replacing the muffler. This guarantee is an important selling feature for the firm's mufflers. In the past, 6 percent of the mufflers sold have been returned for replacement under the guarantee. The average cost of a muffler is $25. Assume that during July, 350 mufflers were sold. This accrued liability would be recorded as an adjustment at the end of July as follows:

July 31	Product Warranty Expense	525	
	Estimated Product Warranty Liability		525
	To record estimated product warranty expense:		
	Number of units sold	350	
	Rate of replacements under warranty	× .06	
	Estimated units to be replaced	21	
	Estimated cost per unit	×$ 25	
	Estimated liability for product warranty	$525	

When a muffler is returned for replacement under the product warranty, the cost of the muffler is charged against the estimated product warranty liability account. For example, assume that a customer returns on December 5 with a defective muffler and pays a $10 service fee to have the muffler replaced. Assume that this particular muffler cost $20. The entry is as follows:

Dec. 5	Cash	10	
	Estimated Product Warranty Liability	20	
	Service Revenue		10
	Merchandise Inventory		20
	To record replacement of muffler under warranty		

Vacation Pay Liability. In most companies, employees earn the right to paid vacation days or weeks as they work during the year. For example, an employee may earn two weeks of paid vacation for each fifty weeks of work. Therefore, she or he is paid fifty-two weeks' salary for fifty weeks' work. Theoretically, the cost of the two weeks' vacation should be allocated as expense over the whole year so that month-to-month costs will not be distorted. So vacation pay represents 4 percent (two weeks' vacation divided by fifty weeks) of a worker's pay. Every week worked earns the employee a small fraction (4 percent) of his or her vacation pay. Vacation pay liability can be a substantial amount of money. For example, Delta Airlines reported at its 1989 year end a vacation pay liability of $83,083,000.

Suppose that a company with this vacation policy has a payroll of $21,000, of which $1,000 was paid to employees on vacation for the week ended April 20. Since not all employees in every company will collect vacation pay because of turnover and rules regarding term of employment, it is assumed that 75 percent of employees will ultimately collect vacation pay. The computation of vacation pay expense based on the payroll of employees not on vacation ($20,000 – $1,000) is as follows: $20,000 × 4 percent × 75 percent = $600.

The entry to record vacation pay expense for the week ended April 20 is as follows:

Apr. 20	Vacation Pay Expense	600	
	Estimated Liability for Vacation Pay		600
	To record estimated vacation pay expense		

At the time employees receive their vacation pay, an entry is made debiting Estimated Liability for Vacation Pay and crediting Cash or Wages Payable. For example, the entry to record the $1,000 paid to employees on vacation is as follows:

Aug. 31	Estimated Liability for Vacation Pay	1,000	
	Cash (or Wages Payable)		1,000
	To record wages of employees on vacation		

The treatment presented here for vacation pay may also be applied to other payroll costs, such as bonus plans and contributions to pension plans.

Contingent Liabilities

OBJECTIVE 3
Define a contingent liability

A **contingent liability** is not an existing liability. Rather, it is a potential liability because it depends on a future event arising out of a past transaction. For instance, a construction company that built a bridge may have been sued by the state for using poor materials. The past transaction is the building of the bridge under contract. The future event whose outcome is not known is the suit against the company. Two conditions have been established by the FASB for determining when a contingency should be entered in the accounting records. They are that the liability must be probable and that it must be reasonably estimated.[5] Estimated liabilities such as the estimated income taxes liability, warranty liability, and vacation pay liability that were described earlier in this chapter meet these conditions. Therefore, they are accrued in the accounting records. Potential liabilities that do not meet both conditions are reported in the notes to the financial statements. Losses from such potential liabilities are recorded when the conditions set by the FASB are met. The following example comes from the notes in a recent annual report of Humana Inc., one of the largest health services organizations:

> The company continuously evaluates contingencies based upon the best available evidence. In addition, allowances for loss are provided currently for disputed items that have continuing significance, such as certain third-party reimbursements and tax deductions and credits that continue to be claimed in current cost reports and tax returns. Management believes that allowances for loss have been provided to the extent necessary and that its assessment of contingencies is reasonable. To the extent that resolution of contingencies results in amounts that vary from management's estimates, future earnings will be charged or credited. The principal contingencies are described below:
>
> *Third-Party Revenues.* Cost reimbursements and certain other third-party payments are subject to examination by agencies administering the programs. The Company is contesting certain issues raised in audits of prior-year cost reports.
>
> *Income Taxes.* The Internal Revenue Service has proposed additional taxes for prior years. The more significant issues include current deductibility of liability insurance premiums paid to an insurance subsidiary, cash-basis tax accounting, depreciable lives and investment tax credits. Settlement of these issues is not expected to have a material adverse effect on earnings. However, deferred tax credits could be reduced as a result of any such resolution.
>
> *Insurance Activities.* Certain levels of professional liability risks have been underwritten by a subsidiary. Company hospitals have paid premiums, and the subsidiary has provided loss allowances, based upon actuarially-determined estimates. In addition, the Company's Group Health Division has entered into group accident and health contracts that involve actuarial estimation of medical claims reserves. Actual claim settlements and expenses incident thereto may differ from the provisions for loss.

5. *Statement of Financial Accounting Standards No. 5,* "Accounting for Contingencies" (Stamford, Conn.: Financial Accounting Standards Board, 1975).

Litigation. Various suits and claims arising in the ordinary course of business are pending against the Company.[6]

Contingent liabilities may also arise from failure to follow government regulations, from discounted notes receivable, and from guarantees of the debt of other companies.

The Time Value of Money

Interest is an important cost to the debtor and an important revenue to the creditor. Because interest is a cost associated with time, and "time is money," it is also an important consideration in any business decision. For example, an individual who holds $100 for one year without putting that $100 in a savings account has forgone the interest that could have been earned. Thus, there is a cost associated with holding this money equal to the interest that could have been earned. Similarly, a business person who accepts a noninterest-bearing note instead of cash for the sale of merchandise is not forgoing the interest that could have been earned on that money but is including the interest implicitly in the price of the merchandise. These examples illustrate the point that the timing of the receipt and payment of cash must be considered in making business decisions.

Simple Interest and Compound Interest

OBJECTIVE 4
Distinguish simple from compound interest

Interest is the cost associated with the use of money for a specific period of time. **Simple interest** is the interest cost for one or more periods if we assume that the amount on which the interest is computed stays the same from period to period. **Compound interest** is the interest cost for two or more periods if we assume that after each period the interest of that period is added to the amount on which interest is computed in future periods. In other words, compound interest is interest earned on a principal sum that is increased at the end of each period by the interest of that period.

Example: Simple Interest. Joe Sanchez accepts an 8 percent, $30,000 note due in ninety days. How much will he receive in total at that time? Remember the formula for calculating simple interest, which was presented in the chapter on short-term liquid assets as part of the discussion of notes receivable:

$$\text{Interest} = \text{principal} \times \text{rate} \times \text{time}$$
$$\text{Interest} = \$30{,}000 \times 8/100 \times 90/360$$
$$\text{Interest} = \$600$$

6. Excerpts from the 1988 Annual Report used by permission of Humana Inc.

The total that Sanchez will receive is computed as follows:

Total = principal + interest
Total = $30,000 + $600
Total = $30,600

Example: Compound Interest. Ann Clary deposits $5,000 in a savings account that pays 6 percent interest. She expects to leave the principal and accumulated interest in the account for three years. How much will her account total at the end of three years? Assume that the interest is paid at the end of the year and is added to the principal at that time and that this total in turn earns interest. The amount at the end of three years may be computed as follows:

(1) Year	(2) Principal Amount at Beginning of Year	(3) Annual Amount of Interest (col. 2 x .06)	(4) Accumulated Amount at End of Year (col. 2 + col. 3)
1	$5,000.00	$300.00	$5,300.00
2	5,300.00	318.00	5,618.00
3	5,618.00	337.08	5,955.08

At the end of three years, Clary will have $5,955.08 in her savings account. Note that the annual amount of interest increases each year by the interest rate times the interest of the previous year. For example, between year 1 and year 2, the interest increased by $18 ($318 – $300), which exactly equals .06 times $300.

Future Value of a Single Invested Sum at Compound Interest

OBJECTIVE 5
Use compound interest tables to compute the future value of a single invested sum at compound interest and of an ordinary annuity

Another way to ask the question in the example of compound interest above is, What is the future value of a single sum ($5,000) at compound interest (6 percent) for three years? **Future value** is the amount that an investment will be worth at a future date if invested at compound interest. A business person often wants to know future value, but the method of computing the future value illustrated above is too time-consuming in practice. Imagine how tedious the calculation would be if the example were ten years instead of three. Fortunately, there are tables that make problems involving compound interest much simpler and quicker to solve. Table 10-1, showing the future value of $1 after a given number of time periods, is an example. It is actually part of the first table in the appendix on future value and present value tables. Suppose that we want to

Table 10-1. Future Value of $1 after a Given Number of Time Periods

Periods	1%	2%	3%	4%	5%	6%	7%	8%	9%	10%	12%	14%	15%
1	1.010	1.020	1.030	1.040	1.050	1.060	1.070	1.080	1.090	1.100	1.120	1.140	1.150
2	1.020	1.040	1.061	1.082	1.103	1.124	1.145	1.166	1.188	1.210	1.254	1.300	1.323
3	1.030	1.061	1.093	1.125	1.158	1.191	1.225	1.260	1.295	1.331	1.405	1.482	1.521
4	1.041	1.082	1.126	1.170	1.216	1.262	1.311	1.360	1.412	1.464	1.574	1.689	1.749
5	1.051	1.104	1.159	1.217	1.276	1.338	1.403	1.469	1.539	1.611	1.762	1.925	2.011
6	1.062	1.126	1.194	1.265	1.340	1.419	1.501	1.587	1.677	1.772	1.974	2.195	2.313
7	1.072	1.149	1.230	1.316	1.407	1.504	1.606	1.714	1.828	1.949	2.211	2.502	2.660
8	1.083	1.172	1.267	1.369	1.477	1.594	1.718	1.851	1.993	2.144	2.476	2.853	3.059
9	1.094	1.195	1.305	1.423	1.551	1.689	1.838	1.999	2.172	2.358	2.773	3.252	3.518
10	1.105	1.219	1.344	1.480	1.629	1.791	1.967	2.159	2.367	2.594	3.106	3.707	4.046

Source: Excerpt from the first table in the appendix on future value and present value tables.

solve the problem of Clary's savings account above. We simply look down the 6 percent column in Table 10-1 until we reach period 3 and find the factor 1.191. This factor, when multiplied by $1, gives the future value of that $1 at compound interest of 6 percent for three periods (years in this case). Thus we solve the problem:

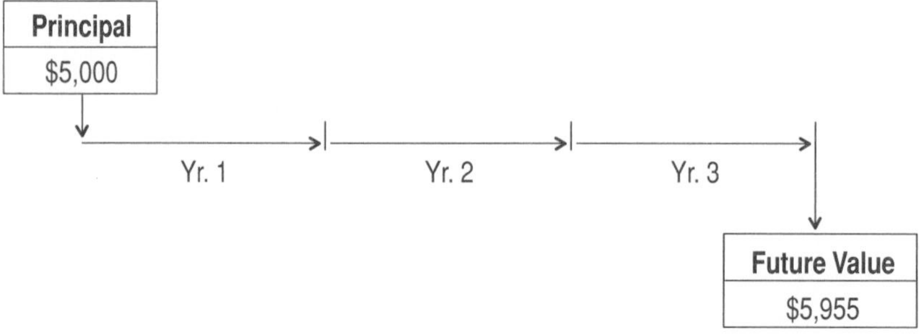

Principal × factor = future value
$5,000 × 1.191 = $5,955

Except for a rounding error of $.08, the answer is exactly the same as that calculated previously.

Future Value of an Ordinary Annuity

Another common problem involves an **ordinary annuity**, which is a series of equal payments made at the end of equal intervals of time, with compound interest on these payments.

The following example shows how to find the future value of an ordinary annuity. Assume that Ben Katz deposits $200 at the end of each of the next three years in a savings account that pays 5 percent interest. How much money will he have in his account at the end of the three years? One way of computing the amount is shown in the following table:

(1) Year	(2) Beginning Balance	(3) Interest Earned (5% x col. 2)	(4) Periodic Payment	(5) Accumulated at End of Period (col. 2 + col. 3 + col. 4)
1	$ —	$ —	$200	$200.00
2	200.00	10.00	200	410.00
3	410.00	20.50	200	630.50

Katz would have $630.50 in his account at the end of three years, consisting of $600 in periodic payments and $30.50 in interest.

This calculation can also be simplified by using Table 10-2. We look down the 5 percent column until we reach period 3 and find the factor 3.153. This factor, when multiplied by $1, gives the future value of a series of three $1 payments (years in this case) at compound interest of 5 percent. Thus, we solve the problem:

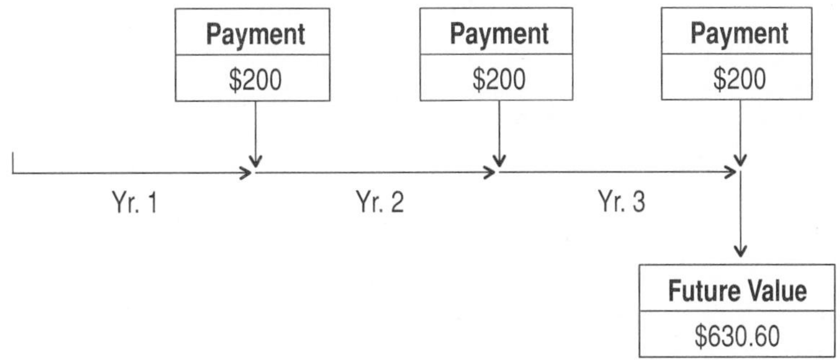

$$\begin{array}{ccc} \text{Periodic payment} \times \text{factor} & = & \text{future value} \\ \$200 \times 3.153 & = & \$630.60 \end{array}$$

Except for a rounding error of $.10, this result is the same as the one above.

Present Value

Suppose that you had the choice of receiving $100 today or one year from today. Intuitively, you would choose to receive the $100 today. Why? You know that if you have the $100 today, you can put it in a savings account to earn interest, and you will have more than $100 a year from today. Therefore, we can say that an amount to be received in the future (future value) is not worth as much today as an amount to be received today (present value) because of the cost associated with the passage of time. In fact, present value and future value are closely related. **Present value** is

Table 10-2. Future Value of an Ordinary Annuity of $1 Paid in Each Period for a Given Number of Time Periods

Periods	1%	2%	3%	4%	5%	6%	7%	8%	9%	10%	12%	14%	15%
1	1.000	1.000	1.000	1.000	1.000	1.000	1.000	1.000	1.000	1.000	1.000	1.000	1.000
2	2.010	2.020	2.030	2.040	2.050	2.060	2.070	2.080	2.090	2.100	2.120	2.140	2.150
3	3.030	3.060	3.091	3.122	3.153	3.184	3.215	3.246	3.278	3.310	3.374	3.440	3.473
4	4.060	4.122	4.184	4.246	4.310	4.375	4.440	4.506	4.573	4.641	4.779	4.921	4.993
5	5.101	5.204	5.309	5.416	5.526	5.637	5.751	5.867	5.985	6.105	6.353	6.610	6.742
6	6.152	6.308	6.468	6.633	6.802	6.975	7.153	7.336	7.523	7.716	8.115	8.536	8.754
7	7.214	7.434	7.662	7.898	8.142	8.394	8.654	8.923	9.200	9.487	10.09	10.73	11.07
8	8.286	8.583	8.892	9.214	9.549	9.897	10.26	10.64	11.03	11.44	12.30	13.23	13.73
9	9.369	9.755	10.16	10.58	11.03	11.49	11.98	12.49	13.02	13.58	14.78	16.09	16.79
10	10.46	10.95	11.46	12.01	12.58	13.18	13.82	14.49	15.19	15.94	17.55	19.34	20.30

Source: Excerpt from the second table in the appendix on future value and present value tables.

the amount that must be invested now at a given rate of interest to produce a given future value.

For example, assume that Sue Dapper needs $1,000 one year from now. How much should she invest now to achieve that goal if the interest rate is 5 percent? From earlier examples, this equation may be established:

$$\begin{aligned}
\text{Present value} \times (1.0 + \text{interest rate}) &= \text{future value} \\
\text{Present value} \times \quad 1.05 &= \$1{,}000 \\
\text{Present value} &= \$1{,}000 \div 1.05 \\
\text{Present value} &= \$952.38
\end{aligned}$$

Thus, to achieve a future value of $1,000, a present value of $952.38 must be invested. Interest of 5 percent of $952.38 for one year equals $47.62, and these two amounts added together equal $1,000.

Present Value of a Single Sum Due in the Future

OBJECTIVE 6
Use compound interest tables to compute the present value of a single sum due in the future and of an ordinary annuity

When more than one time period is involved, the calculation of present value is more complicated. Consider the following example. Don Riley wants to be sure of having $4,000 at the end of three years. How much must he invest today in a 5 percent savings account to achieve this goal? Adapting the above equation, we compute the present value of $4,000 at compound interest of 5 percent for three years in the future.

Year	Amount at End of Year		Divide by		Present Value at Beginning of Year
3	$4,000.00	÷	1.05	=	$3,809.52
2	3,809.52	÷	1.05	=	3,628.11
1	3,628.11	÷	1.05	=	3,455.34

Table 10-3. Present Value of $1 to Be Received at the End of a Given Number of Time Periods

Periods	1%	2%	3%	4%	5%	6%	7%	8%	9%	10%
1	0.990	0.980	0.971	0.962	0.952	0.943	0.935	0.926	0.917	0.909
2	0.980	0.961	0.943	0.925	0.907	0.890	0.873	0.857	0.842	0.826
3	0.971	0.942	0.915	0.889	0.864	0.840	0.816	0.794	0.772	0.751
4	0.961	0.924	0.888	0.855	0.823	0.792	0.763	0.735	0.708	0.683
5	0.951	0.906	0.883	0.822	0.784	0.747	0.713	0.681	0.650	0.621
6	0.942	0.888	0.837	0.790	0.746	0.705	0.666	0.630	0.596	0.564
7	0.933	0.871	0.813	0.760	0.711	0.665	0.623	0.583	0.547	0.513
8	0.923	0.853	0.789	0.731	0.677	0.627	0.582	0.540	0.502	0.467
9	0.914	0.837	0.766	0.703	0.645	0.592	0.544	0.500	0.460	0.424
10	0.905	0.820	0.744	0.676	0.614	0.558	0.508	0.463	0.422	0.386

Source: Excerpt from the third table in the appendix on future value and present value tables.

Riley must invest a present value of $3,455.34 to achieve a future value of $4,000 in three years.

This calculation is again made much easier by using the appropriate table. In Table 10-3, we look down the 5 percent column until we reach period 3 and find the factor 0.864. This factor, when multiplied by $1, gives the present value of the $1 to be received three years from now at 5 percent interest. Thus we solve the problem:

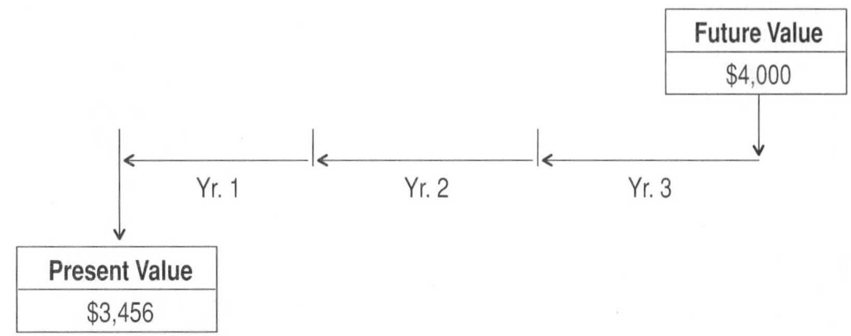

Future value × factor	=	present value
$4,000 × 0.864	=	$3,456

Except for a rounding error of $.66, this result is the same as the one above.

Present Value of an Ordinary Annuity

It is often necessary to compute the present value of a series of receipts or payments. When we calculate the present value of equal amounts equally spaced over a period of time, we are computing the present value of an ordinary annuity.

For example, assume that Kathy Foster has sold a piece of property and is to receive $15,000 in three equal annual payments of $5,000, beginning one year from today. What is the present value of this sale, assuming a current interest rate of 5 percent? This present value may be computed by calculating a separate present value for each of the three payments (using Table 10-3) and summing the results, as shown below.

Future Receipts (Annuity) Year 1	Year 2	Year 3		Present Value Factor at 5 Percent (from Table 10-3)		Present Value
$5,000			×	0.952	=	$ 4,760
	$5,000		×	0.907	=	4,535
		$5,000	×	0.864	=	4,320
Total Present Value						$13,615

The present value of this sale is $13,615. Thus there is an implied interest cost (given the 5 percent rate) of $1,385 associated with the payment plan that allows the purchaser to pay in three installments.

We can make this calculation more easily by using Table 10-4. We look down the 5 percent column until we reach period 3 and find the factor 2.723. This factor, when multiplied by $1, gives the present value of a series of three $1 payments (spaced one year apart) at compound interest of 5 percent. Thus we solve the problem:

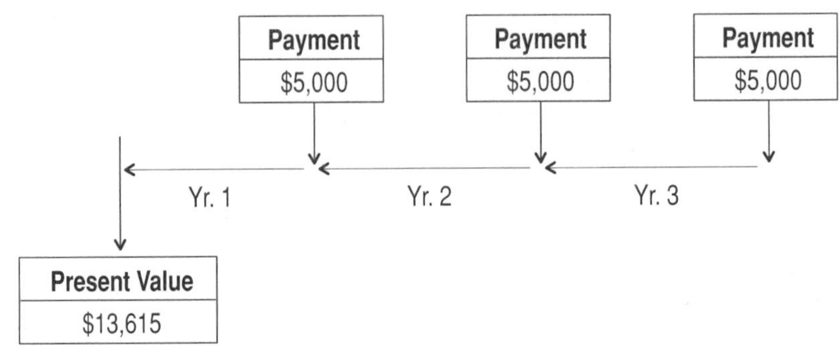

$$\begin{array}{ccc} \text{Periodic payment} \times \text{factor} & = & \text{present value} \\ \$5{,}000 \times 2.723 & = & \$13{,}615 \end{array}$$

This result is the same as the one computed previously.

Time Periods

In all the examples above and in most other cases, the compounding period is one year, and the interest rate is stated on an annual basis. However, in each of the four tables, the left-hand column refers not to years, but to periods. This wording is intended to accommodate compounding periods of less than one year. Savings accounts that record interest quar-

Table 10-4. Present Value of an Ordinary Annuity of $1 Received Each Period for a Given Number of Time Periods

Periods	1%	2%	3%	4%	5%	6%	7%	8%	9%	10%
1	0.990	0.980	0.971	0.962	0.952	0.943	0.935	0.926	0.917	0.909
2	1.970	1.942	1.913	1.886	1.859	1.833	1.808	1.783	1.759	1.736
3	2.941	2.884	2.829	2.775	2.723	2.673	2.624	2.577	2.531	2.487
4	3.902	3.808	3.717	3.630	3.546	3.465	3.387	3.312	3.240	3.170
5	4.853	4.713	4.580	4.452	4.329	4.212	4.100	3.993	3.890	3.791
6	5.795	5.601	5.417	5.242	5.076	4.917	4.767	4.623	4.486	4.355
7	6.728	6.472	6.230	6.002	5.786	5.582	5.389	5.206	5.033	4.868
8	7.652	7.325	7.020	6.733	6.463	6.210	5.971	5.747	5.535	5.335
9	8.566	8.162	7.786	7.435	7.108	6.802	6.515	6.247	5.995	5.759
10	9.471	8.983	8.530	8.111	7.722	7.360	7.024	6.710	6.418	6.145

Source: Excerpt from the fourth table in the appendix on future value and present value tables.

terly and bonds that pay interest semiannually are cases in which the compounding period is less than one year. In order to use the tables in such cases, it is necessary to (1) divide the annual interest rate by the number of periods in the year, and (2) multiply the number of periods in one year by the number of years.

For example, assume that a $6,000 note is to be paid in two years and carries an annual interest rate of 8 percent. Compute the maturity (future) value of the note, assuming that the compounding period is semiannual. Before using the table, it is necessary to compute the interest rate that applies to each compounding period and the total number of compounding periods. First, the interest rate to use is 4 percent (8% annual rate ÷ 2 periods per year). Second, the total number of compounding periods is 4 (2 periods per year × 2 years). From Table 10-1, therefore, the maturity value of the note may be computed as follows:

Principal × factor = future value
$6,000 × 1.170 = $7,020

The note will be worth $7,020 in two years.

This procedure for determining the interest rate and the number of periods when the compounding period is less than one year may be used with all the tables.

DECISION POINT
Safety-Net Corporation

The fair market value of individual assets is sometimes difficult to determine. Valuing a business is even more difficult. The seller and buyer may have different views of a business's value. Present value methods may be useful in resolving the differences between buyer and seller because they illuminate the effects of each party's assumptions. Robert Taft, president of Safety-Net Corporation, a manufacturer of a car safety restraint for children, wants to sell the business. He wants to receive $12,000,000 for the company, which has a stockholders' equity (net assets) of $10,000,000. He argues that this price is a bargain because the company will generate annual cash flows of $2,000,000 for twenty years. Given an annual return of 15 percent, he says, the present value of the business should be $12,518,000, calculated from Table 4 in the appendix "Future Value and Present Value Tables" (20 years, 15 percent) as follows:

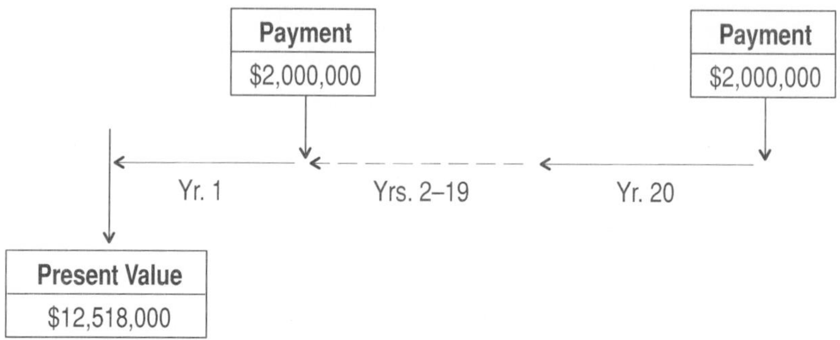

$$\begin{array}{ccc} \text{Periodic cash flow} \times \text{factor} & = & \text{present value} \\ \$2{,}000{,}000 \times 6.259 & = & \$12{,}518{,}000 \end{array}$$

Susan Arnett, who represents a group of investors, is willing to pay no more than $10,000,000, the amount of stockholders' equity, because she believes Taft's assumptions are overly optimistic. First, she would reduce the twenty-year time period to twelve years because she is convinced that after that time, prospects for the business become uncertain. Using the same table as Taft did, she recalculates the present value of the business based on twelve years (12 years, 15 percent) as follows:

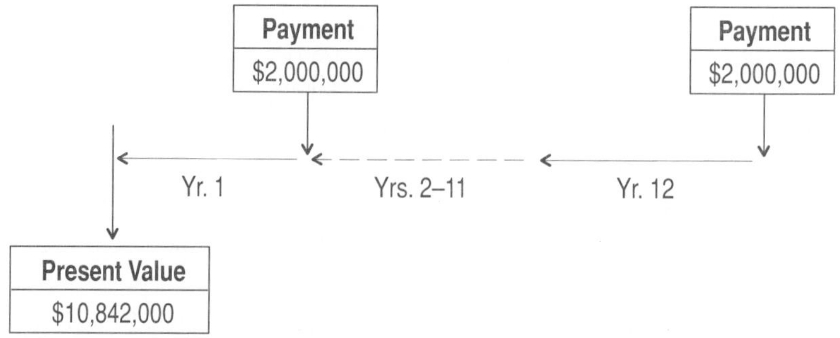

$$\begin{array}{ccc} \text{Periodic cash flow} \times \text{factor} & = & \text{present value} \\ \$2{,}000{,}000 \times 5.421 & = & \$10{,}842{,}000 \end{array}$$

Under Arnett's assumptions, the present value of the business decreases by $1,676,000 ($12,518,000 – $10,842,000). Note that under the present value method, the effect of decreasing the time frame from twenty to twelve years is much less than the $16,000,000 ($2,000,000 × 8 years) realized through cash flows because the cash flows from distant years have low present values.

Second, Arnett questions whether the company can produce an annual cash flow of $2,000,000. She believes that an annual cash flow of $1,800,000 is more realistic. The present value of the business, using the same factor from the same table (12 years, 15 percent), would be calculated as follows:

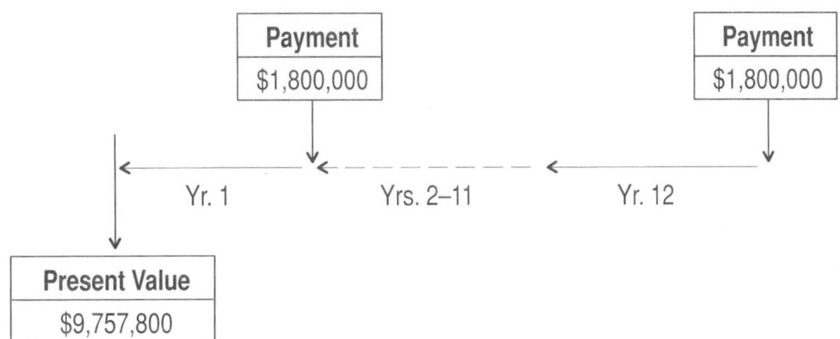

Periodic cash flow × factor = present value
$1,800,000 × 5.421 = $9,757,800

Under this assumption of reduced annual cash flow, the present value of the business drops by another $1,084,200 ($10,842,000 – $9,757,800) to $9,757,800, an amount that is very much in line with Arnett's offer. Taft and Arnett now have a bargaining range within which they may be able to resolve their differences. Whether or not the two parties will be able to reach an agreement is open to question, but at least they know the source of their differences: the number of years over which the annual cash flows should be projected, and the amount of the annual cash flows. ■

Applications of Present Value to Accounting

OBJECTIVE 7
Apply the concept of present value to accounting situations

The concept of present value is widely applicable in the discipline of accounting. Here, the purpose is to demonstrate its usefulness in some simple applications. In-depth study of present value is deferred to more advanced courses.

Imputing Interest on Noninterest-Bearing Notes

Clearly there is no such thing as interest-free debt, whether or not the interest rate is explicitly stated. The Accounting Principles Board has declared that when a long-term note does not explicitly state an interest rate (or if the interest rate is unreasonably low), a rate based on the normal interest cost of the company in question should be assigned, or imputed.[7]

The following example applies the principle stated above. On January 1, 19x8, Gato purchases merchandise from Haines by issuing an $8,000 noninterest-bearing note due in two years. Gato can borrow money from the bank at 9 percent interest. Gato pays the note in full after two years.

Note that the $8,000 note represents partly a payment for merchandise and partly a payment of interest for two years. In recording the purchase and sale, it is necessary to use Table 10-3 to determine the present value of the note. The calculation follows.

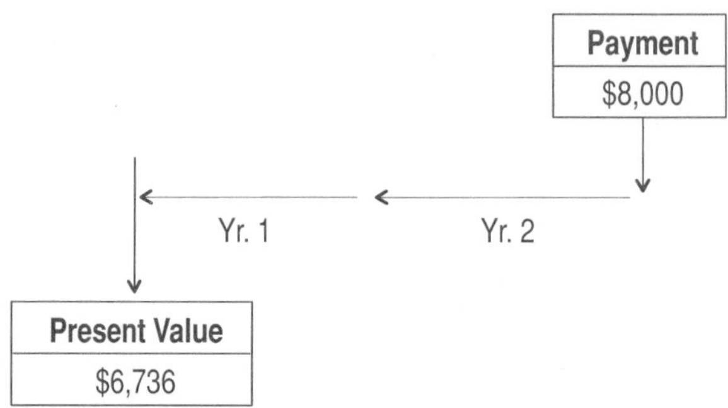

Future payment	×	present value factor (9%, 2 years)	=	present value
$8,000	×	0.842	=	$6,736

The imputed interest cost is $1,264 ($8,000 – $6,736), and this is recorded as a discount on notes payable in Gato's records and a discount on notes receivable in Haines's records. The entries necessary to record the purchase in the Gato records and the sale in the Haines records are shown below.

Gato Journal			Haines Journal		
Purchases	6,736		Notes Receivable	8,000	
Discount on Notes Payable	1,264		Discount on Notes Receivable		1,264
Notes Payable		8,000	Sales		6,736

On December 31, 19x8, the adjustments to recognize the interest expense and interest income will be:

Gato Journal			Haines Journal		
Interest Expense	606.24		Discount on Notes Receivable	606.24	
Discount on Notes Payable		606.24	Interest Income		606.24

The interest is calculated by multiplying the original purchase by the interest for one year ($6,736 × .09 = $606.24). When payment is made on

7. Accounting Principles Board, *Opinion No. 21,* "Interest on Receivables and Payables" (New York: American Institute of Certified Public Accountants, 1971), par. 13.

December 31, 19x9, the following entries will be made in the respective journals:

Gato Journal

Interest Expense	657.76	
Notes Payable	8,000.00	
Discount on Notes Payable		657.76
Cash		8,000.00

Haines Journal

Discount on Notes Receivable	657.76	
Cash	8,000.00	
Interest Income		657.76
Notes Receivable		8,000.00

The interest entries represent the remaining interest to be expensed or realized ($1,264 – $606.24 = $657.76). This amount approximates (because of rounding errors in the table) the interest for one year on the purchases plus last year's interest [($6,736 + $606.24) × .09 = $660.80].

Valuing an Asset

An asset is recorded because it will provide future benefits to the company that owns it. These future benefits are the basis for the definition of an asset. Usually, the purchase price of the asset represents the present value of these future benefits. It is possible to evaluate a proposed purchase price of an asset by comparing that price with the present value of the asset to the company.

For example, Sam Hurst is thinking of buying a new labor-saving machine that will reduce his annual labor cost by $700 per year. The machine will last eight years. The interest rate that Hurst assumes for making managerial decisions is 10 percent. What is the maximum amount (present value) that Hurst should pay for the machine?

The present value of the machine to Hurst is equal to the present value of an ordinary annuity of $700 per year for eight years at compound interest of 10 percent. From Table 10-4, we compute the value as follows:

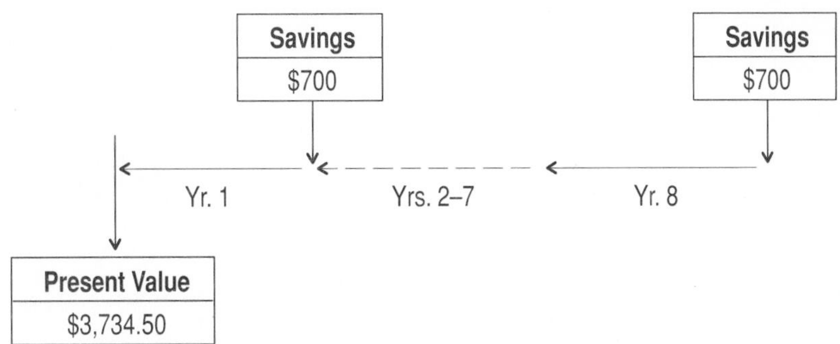

Periodic savings × factor = present value
$700 × 5.335 = $3,734.50

Hurst should not pay more than $3,734.50 for the new machine because this amount equals the present value of the benefits that will be received from owning the machine.

Deferred Payment

A seller will sometimes agree to defer payment for a sale in order to encourage the buyer to make the purchase. This practice is common, for example, in the farm implement industry, where the farmer needs the equipment in the spring but cannot pay for it until the fall crop is in. Assume that Plains Implement Corporation sells a tractor to Samuel Washington for $50,000 on February 1, agreeing to take payment ten months later on December 1. When this type of agreement is made, the future payment includes not only the sales price of the tractor but also an implied (imputed) interest cost. If the prevailing annual interest rate for such transactions is 12 percent compounded monthly, the actual sale (purchase) price of the tractor would be the present value of the future payment, computed according to Table 10-3 (10 periods, 1 percent), as follows:

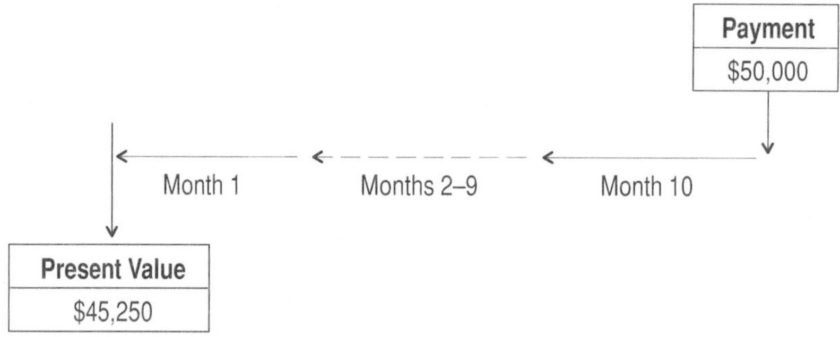

Future payment	× factor	= present value
$50,000	× 0.905 =	$45,250

The purchase in Washington's records and the sale in Plains' records are recorded at the present value, $45,250. The balance consists of interest expense or interest income. The entries necessary to record the purchase in Washington's records and the sale in Plains' records are as follows:

		Washington's Journal			Plains' Journal		
Feb.	1	Tractor	45,250		Accounts Receivable	45,250	
		Accounts Payable		45,250	Sales		45,250
		Purchase of tractor			To record sale of tractor		

When Washington pays for the tractor, the entries are as follows:

		Washington's Journal			Plains' Journal		
Dec.	1	Accounts Payable	45,250		Cash	50,000	
		Interest Expense	4,750		Accounts Receivable		45,250
		Cash		50,000	Interest Income		4,750
		Payment on account including imputed interest			Receipt on account from Washington including imputed interest earned		

Investment of Idle Cash

Childware Corporation, a toy manufacturer, has just completed a successful fall selling season and has $10,000,000 in cash to invest for six months. The company places the cash in a money market account that is expected to pay 12 percent annual interest. Interest is compounded monthly and credited to the company's account each month. How much cash will the company have at the end of six months, and what entries will be made to record the investment and the monthly interest? From Table 10-1, the future value factor is based on six monthly periods of 1 percent (12 percent divided by 12 months), and the future value is computed as follows:

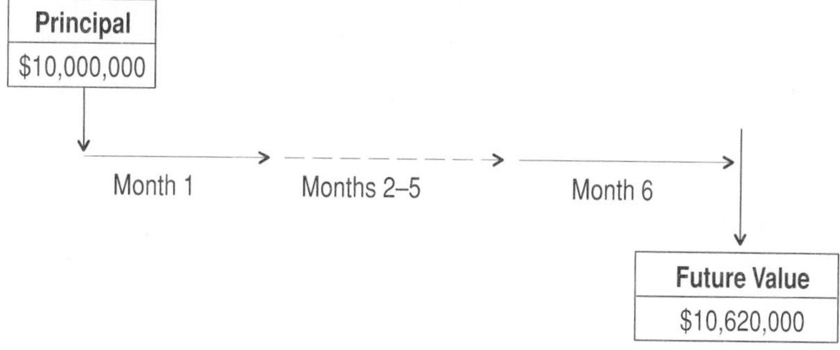

Investment × factor	=	future value
$10,000,000 × 1.062	=	$10,620,000

When the investment is made, the journal entry is as follows:

Short-Term Investment	10,000,000	
Cash		10,000,000
To record investment of cash		

After the first month, the interest is recorded by increasing the Short-Term Investments account, as follows:

Short-Term Investments	100,000	
Interest Income		100,000
To record one month's interest income $10,000,000 × .01 = $100,000		

After the second month, the interest is earned on the new balance of the Short-Term Investments account, as follows:

Short-Term Investments	101,000	
Interest Income		101,000
To record one month's interest income $10,100,000 × .01 = $101,000		

Entries would continue in a similar manner for four more months, at which time the balance of Short-Term Investments would be about $10,620,000. The actual amount accumulated may vary from this total because the interest rate paid on money market accounts can vary over time as a result of changes in market conditions.

Accumulation of a Fund

When a company owes a large fixed amount in several years, management would be wise to accumulate a fund with which to pay off the debt at maturity. Sometimes creditors, when they agree to provide a loan, require that such a fund be established. In establishing the fund, management must determine how much cash to set aside each period in order to pay the debt. The amount will depend on the estimated rate of interest the investments will earn. Assume that Vason Corporation agrees with a creditor to set aside cash at the end of each year to accumulate enough to pay off a $100,000 note due in six years. Since the first contribution to the fund will be made in one year, five annual contributions will be made by the time the note is due. Assume also that the fund is projected to earn 8 percent, compounded annually. The amount of each annual payment is calculated from Table 10-2 (5 periods, 8 percent), as follows:

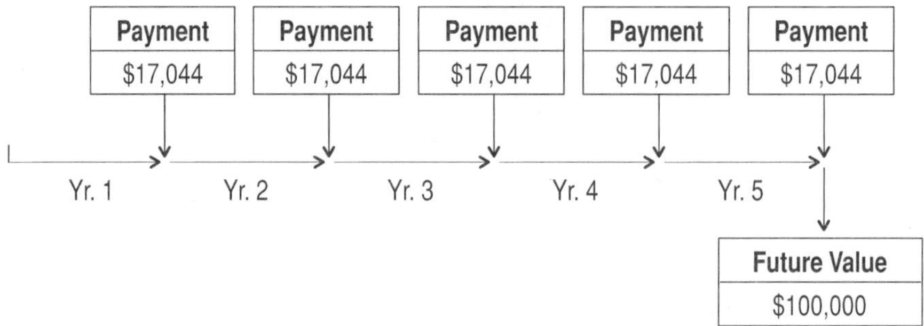

Future value of fund ÷ factor = annual investment
$100,000 ÷ 5.867 = $17,044 (rounded)

Each year's contribution to the fund is $17,044. This contribution is recorded as follows:

Loan Repayment Fund	17,044	
Cash		17,044
To record an annual contribution to loan repayment fund		

Other Accounting Applications

There are many other applications of present value in accounting. The uses of present value in accounting for installment notes, valuing a bond, and recording lease obligations are shown in the chapter on long-term liabilities. Present value is also applied in such areas as pension obligations; premium and discount on debt; depreciation of property, plant, and equipment; capital expenditure decisions; and generally any problem where time is a factor.

Chapter Review

Review of Learning Objectives

1. **Explain how the issues of recognition, valuation, and classification apply to liabilities.**
   Liabilities represent present legal obligations of the firm for future payment of assets or the future performance of services. They result from past transactions, and should be recognized when there is a transaction that obligates the company to make future payments. Liabilities are valued at the amount of money necessary to satisfy the obligation or the fair market value of goods or services that must be delivered. Liabilities are classified as current or long term.

2. **Identify, compute, and record definitely determinable and estimated current liabilities.**
   Two principal categories of current liabilities are definitely determinable liabilities and estimated liabilities. Although definitely determinable liabilities such as accounts payable, notes payable, dividends payable, accrued liabilities, and the current portion of long-term debt can be measured exactly, the accountant must still be careful not to overlook existing liabilities in these categories. Estimated liabilities such as liabilities for income taxes, property taxes, product warranties, and others definitely exist, but the amounts must be estimated and recorded properly.

3. **Define a contingent liability.**
   A contingent liability is a potential liability arising from a past transaction and dependent on a future event. Examples are lawsuits, income tax disputes, discounted notes receivable, guarantees of debt, and the potential cost of changes in government regulations.

4. **Distinguish simple from compound interest.**
   In computing simple interest, the amount on which the interest is computed stays the same from period to period. However, in computing compound interest, the interest for a period is added to the principal amount before the interest for the next period is computed.

5. **Use compound interest tables to compute the future value of a single invested sum at compound interest and of an ordinary annuity.**
   Future value is the amount that an investment will be worth at a future date if invested at compound interest. An ordinary annuity is a series of equal payments made at the end of equal intervals of time, with compound interest on these payments. Use Table 1 in the appendix on future value and present value tables to compute future values and Table 2 in the same appendix to compute ordinary annuities.

6. **Use compound interest tables to compute the present value of a single sum due in the future and of an ordinary annuity.**
   Present value is the amount that must be invested now at a given rate of interest to produce a given future value. The present value of an ordinary annuity is the present value of a series of payments. Use Table 3 in the appendix on future value and present value tables to compute present values and Table 4 in the same appendix to compute the present value of an ordinary annuity.

7. **Apply the concept of present value to accounting situations.**
Present value may be used to compute interest on noninterest-bearing notes, to value a bond or other asset, to compute the present value of deferred payments, to determine a bargaining range in negotiating the sale of a business, to determine the future value of an investment of idle cash or the accumulation of a fund, to record lease obligations, and in other accounting situations.

Review of Concepts and Terminology

The following concepts and terms were introduced in this chapter:

(L.O. 2) **Commercial paper:** A means of borrowing funds directly from the public.

(L.O. 4) **Compound interest:** Interest cost for two or more periods if we assume that after each period the interest of that period is added to the amount on which interest is computed in future periods.

(L.O. 3) **Contingent liability:** A potential liability that depends on a future event arising out of a past transaction.

(L.O. 1) **Current liabilities:** Debts and obligations that are expected to be satisfied in one year or within the normal operating cycle, whichever is longer.

(L.O. 2) **Definitely determinable liabilities:** Current liabilities that are set by contract or by statute and can be measured exactly.

(L.O. 2) **Estimated liabilities:** Definite debts or obligations for which the exact amounts cannot be known until a later date.

(L.O. 1) **Financial instruments:** Cash, evidences of ownership, and any contract that results in an asset in one entity's records and a liability in another entity's records.

(L.O. 5) **Future value:** The amount an investment will be worth at a future date if invested at compound interest.

(L.O. 4) **Interest:** The cost associated with the use of money for a specific period of time.

(L.O. 1) **Liabilities:** Legal obligations for the future payment of assets or the future performance of services that result from past transactions.

(L.O. 2) **Line of credit:** A preapproved arrangement with a commercial bank that allows a company to borrow as it needs cash.

(L.O. 1) **Long-term liabilities:** Debts or obligations that will not be due during the next year or the normal operating cycle.

(L.O. 1) **Off-balance-sheet liabilities:** Agreements that do not show up on the balance sheet as liabilities but that expose the company to possible loss through a credit risk.

(L.O. 5) **Ordinary annuity:** A series of equal payments made at the end of equal intervals of time, with compound interest on these payments.

(L.O. 5) **Present value:** The amount that must be invested now at a given rate of interest to produce a given future value.

(L.O. 4) **Simple interest:** Interest cost for one or more periods if we assume that the amount on which the interest is computed stays the same from period to period.

(L.O. 2) **Unearned or deferred revenues:** Revenues received in advance for which the goods will not be delivered nor the services performed during the current accounting period.

Review Problem
Notes Payable Transactions and End-of-Period Entries

(L.O. 2) McLaughlin, Inc., whose fiscal year ends June 30, completed the following transactions involving notes payable:

May 11 Purchased a small crane by issuing a sixty-day, 12 percent note for $54,000. The face of the note does not include interest.
16 Obtained a $40,000 loan from the bank to finance a temporary increase in receivables by signing a ninety-day, 10 percent note. The face value includes prepaid interest.
June 30 Made end-of-year adjusting entry to accrue interest expense.
30 Made end-of-year adjusting entry to record accrued interest expense on note with interest included in face amount.
30 Made end-of-year closing entry pertaining to interest expense.
July 1 Made appropriate reversing entry.
10 Paid the note plus interest on the crane purchase.
Aug. 14 Paid off the note to the bank.

Required

1. Prepare general journal entries for the above transactions (journal Page 36).
2. Open general ledger accounts for Notes Payable (212), Discount on Notes Payable (213), Interest Payable (214), and Interest Expense (721). Post the relevant portions of the entries to these general ledger accounts.

Answer to Review Problem

1. Journal entries prepared

General Journal **Page 36**

Date		Description	Post. Ref.	Debit	Credit
19xx					
May	11	Equipment		54,000	
		Notes Payable	212		54,000
		Purchase of crane with 60-day, 12% note			
	16	Cash		39,000	
		Discount on Notes Payable	213	1,000	
		Notes Payable	212		40,000
		Loan from bank obtained by signing 90-day, 10% note; discount $40,000 × .1 × 90/360 = $1,000			

(continued)

General Journal					Page 36
Date		Description	Post. Ref.	Debit	Credit
June	30	Interest Expense	721	900	
		Interest Payable	214		900
		To accrue interest expense			
		$54,000 × .12 × 50/360 = $900			
	30	Interest Expense	721	500	
		Discount on Notes Payable	213		500
		To recognize prepaid interest expired			
		$1,000 × 45/90 = $500			
	30	Income Summary		1,400	
		Interest Expense	721		1,400
		To close interest expense			
July	1	Interest Payable	214	900	
		Interest Expense	721		900
		To reverse interest expense accrual			
	10	Notes Payable	212	54,000	
		Interest Expense	721	1,080	
		Cash			55,080
		Payment of note on equipment			
		$54,000 × .12 × 60/360 = $1,080			
Aug.	14	Notes Payable	212	40,000	
		Cash			40,000
		Payment of bank loan			
	14	Interest Expense	721	500	
		Discount on Notes Payable	213		500
		To record interest expense on matured note			
		$1,000 − $500 = $500			

2. Accounts opened and amounts posted

Notes Payable						Account No. 212	
						Balance	
Date		Item	Post. Ref.	Debit	Credit	Debit	Credit
May	11		J36		54,000		54,000
	16		J36		40,000		94,000
July	10		J36	54,000			40,000
Aug.	14		J36	40,000			—

(continued)

Discount on Notes Payable — Account No. 213

Date		Item	Post. Ref.	Debit	Credit	Balance Debit	Balance Credit
May	16		J36	1,000		1,000	
June	30		J36		500	500	
Aug.	14		J36		500	—	

Interest Payable — Account No. 214

Date		Item	Post. Ref.	Debit	Credit	Balance Debit	Balance Credit
June	30		J36		900		900
July	1		J36	900			—

Interest Expense — Account No. 721

Date		Item	Post. Ref.	Debit	Credit	Balance Debit	Balance Credit
June	30		J36	900		900	
	30		J36	500		1,400	
	30		J36		1,400	—	
July	1		J36		900		900
	10		J36	1,080		180	
Aug.	14		J36	500		680	

Chapter Assignments

Discussion Questions

1. What are liabilities?
2. Why is the timing of liability recognition important in accounting?
3. At the end of the accounting period, Janson Company had a legal obligation to accept delivery and pay for a truckload of hospital supplies the following week. Is this legal obligation a liability?
4. Ned Johnson, a star college basketball player, received a contract from the Midwest Blazers to play professional basketball. The contract calls for a salary of $300,000 a year for four years, dependent on his making the team

in each of those years. Should this contract be considered a liability and recorded on the books of the basketball team?
5. What is a financial instrument? Give three examples.
6. What are off-balance-sheet liabilities? Give an example.
7. What is the rule for determining a current liability?
8. What are a line of credit and commercial paper? Where do they appear on the balance sheet?
9. Where should the Discount on Notes Payable account appear on the balance sheet?
10. When can a portion of long-term debt be classified as a current liability?
11. Why are deferred revenues classified as liabilities?
12. What is definite about an estimated liability?
13. Why are income taxes payable considered to be estimated liabilities?
14. When does a company incur a liability for a product warranty?
15. What is a contingent liability, and how does it differ from an estimated liability?
16. What are some examples of contingent liabilities, and why is each a contingent liability?
17. What is interest, and how does simple interest differ from compound interest?
18. What is the key variable that distinguishes present value from future value?
19. What is an ordinary annuity?
20. How does the use of a compounding period of less than one year affect the computation of present value?
21. Why is present value important to accounting? (Illustrate your answer by giving concrete examples of applications in accounting.)

Communication Skills Exercises

Communication 10-1. Identification of Current Liabilities *(L.O. 2)*

Several businesses and organizations and a current liability from the balance sheet of each are listed below. Explain the nature of each current liability (whether it is a definitely determinable or an estimated liability), how each arose, and how the obligation is likely to be fulfilled.

Institute of Management Accountants: Deferred Revenues—Membership Dues

The Foxboro Company: Advances on Sales Contracts

UNC Incorporated: Current Portion of Long-Term Debt

Hurco Companies, Inc.: Accrued Warranty Expense

Affiliated Publications, Inc.: Deferred Subscription Revenues

Geo. A Hormel & Company: Accrued Advertising

Communication 10-2. Identification of Current Liabilities *(L.O. 2)*

Stanhome Inc.'s current liabilities section of its 1989 balance sheet[8] appears as follows:

8. *Accounting Trends and Techniques* (New York: American Institute of Certified Public Accountants, 1990), p. 155. Excerpts from Stanhome's 1989 Annual Report used by permission of Stanhome Inc.

Current Liabilities:	
Notes and loans payable	$ 20,369,757
Accounts payable	48,718,671
Customer deposits	4,241,481
Federal, state, and foreign taxes on income	22,489,295
Unredeemed coupons and certificates	932,823
Accrued expenses—	
Payroll and commissions	11,736,468
Pensions and profit sharing	7,809,380
Vacation, sick leave, and retirement insurance	7,668,911
Payroll taxes	2,343,858
Other	19,978,163
Dividends payable	3,872,911
Total current liabilities	$150,161,718

Explain the nature of each current liability (whether it is a definitely determinable or an estimated liability), how each arose, and how the obligation will be fulfilled.

Communication 10-3. Frequent Flyer Plan *(L.O. 2)*

America South Airways instituted a frequent flyer program, under which passengers accumulate points based on the number of miles they fly on America South Airways. One point is awarded for each mile flown, with a minimum of 750 miles given for any flight. Because of competition and a drop in passenger air travel in 1991, the company began a triple mileage bonus plan, under which passengers received triple the normal mileage points. In the past, about 1.5 percent of passenger miles were flown by passengers who had converted points to free flights. Under the triple mileage program, it is expected that a 2.5 percent rate will be more appropriate for future years. During 1991 the company had passenger revenues of $966.3 million and passenger transportation operating expenses of $802.8 million before depreciation and amortization. Operating income was $86.1 million. The AICPA is considering requiring airline companies to recognize frequent flyer plans in their accounting records. What is the appropriate rate to use to estimate free miles? What would be the effect of the estimated liability for free travel by passengers under the frequent flyer program on 1991 net income? Describe several ways to estimate the amount of this liability. What are the arguments for and against recognizing this liability?

Communication 10-4. Baseball Contract *(L.O. 7)*

The St. Louis Browns' fifth-year center fielder Carlos Hayes made the All-Star team and won the most valuable player award in 1991. St. Louis, a major league ball club, went to the World Series and lost to Oakland in six games. Hayes has three years left on a contract that is to pay him $800,000 per year. He wants to renegotiate his contract because other players who have equally outstanding records (although they do have more experience) are receiving as much as $3.5 million per year for five years. Management has a policy of never renegotiating a current contract but is willing to consider extending the contract to additional years. In fact, the Browns have offered Hayes an additional three years at $2.0 million, $3.0 million, and $4.0 million, respectively. In addition, they have added an option year at $5.0 million. Management points out that this package is worth $14.0 million, or $3.5 million per year on average. Hayes is considering this offer and is also considering asking for a bonus to be paid upon the signing of the contract. Comment on management's position. What is your evaluation of the offer, assuming a current prime (best bank rate) interest rate of 10 percent? (**Hint:** Use present values.) Hayes is considering asking for a signing bonus. Propose a range for the signing bonus. What other considerations may affect the value of the offer?

Communication 10-5. Basic Research Skills *(L.O. 4)*

Banks pay interest to depositors on the basis of how long the depositors are willing to commit their money to the bank. Checking accounts and money market accounts allow the depositor to take money out whenever he or she desires it. Longer commitments in the form of certificates of deposit have a definite term, such as six months, one year, two years, or longer. Certificates of deposit usually carry a substantial penalty for taking money out of the bank before the end of the term. Obtain a list or schedule of the current interest rates paid on money market accounts and certificates of deposit from your local bank. Also, find out if the money market accounts or certificates of deposit pay simple or compound interest. Prepare a graph that shows the relationship of the length of time of the commitment to the rate of interest. What conclusions can you draw? Be prepared to discuss your results in class.

Classroom Exercises

Exercise 10-1. Interest Expense: Interest Not Included in Face Value of Note *(L.O. 2)*

On the last day of October, Gross Company borrows $60,000 on a bank note for sixty days at 12 percent interest. Assume that interest is not included in the face amount. Prepare the following general journal entries: (1) October 31, recording of note; (2) November 30, accrual of interest expense; (3) November 30, closing entry; (4) December 1, reversing entry; (5) December 30, payment of note plus interest.

Exercise 10-2. Interest Expense: Interest Included in Face Value of Note *(L.O. 2)*

Assume the same facts as in Exercise 10-1, except that interest is included in the face amount of the note and the note is discounted at the bank on October 31. Prepare the following general journal entries: (1) October 31, recording of note; (2) November 30, recognize interest accrued on note with interest included in face amount; (3) November 30, closing entry; (4) December 30, payment of note and recording of interest expense.

Exercise 10-3. Sales and Excise Taxes *(L.O. 2)*

Quik Dial Service billed its customers for a total of $490,200 for the month of May, including 9 percent federal excise tax and 5 percent sales tax.

1. Determine the proper amount of revenue to report for the month.
2. Prepare a general journal entry to record the revenue and related liabilities for the month.

Exercise 10-4. Product Warranty Liability *(L.O. 2)*

Rainbow manufactures and sells electronic games. Each game costs $50 to produce and sells for $90. In addition, each game carries a warranty that provides for free replacement if it fails for any reason during the two years following the sale. In the past, 7 percent of the games sold have had to be replaced under the warranty. During October, Rainbow sold 52,000 games, and 2,800 games were replaced under the warranty.

1. Prepare a general journal entry to record the estimated liability for product warranties during the month.
2. Prepare a general journal entry to record the games replaced under warranty during the month.

Exercise 10-5.
Vacation Pay Liability
(L.O. 2)

Outland Corporation currently allows each employee three weeks' paid vacation after working at the company for one year. On the basis of studies of employee turnover and previous experience, management estimates that 65 percent of the employees will qualify for vacation pay this year.

1. Assume that the August payroll for Outland is $320,000, of which $20,000 is paid to employees on vacation. Figure the estimated employee benefit for the month.
2. Prepare a general journal entry to record the employee benefit for August.
3. Prepare a general journal entry to record the pay to employees on vacation.

Exercise 10-6.
Estimated Liability
(L.O. 2)

Southeast Airways has initiated a frequent flyer program in which enrolled passengers accumulate miles of travel that may be redeemed for rewards such as free trips or upgrades from coach to first class. Southeast estimates that approximately 2 percent of its passengers are traveling free as a result of this program. During 19x3, Southeast Airways had total revenues of $8,000,000,000.

In January 19x4, passengers representing tickets of $150,000 flew free. Prepare the December year-end adjusting entry to record the estimated liability for this program and the January entry for the free tickets. Can you suggest how these transactions would be recorded if the estimate of the free tickets were to be considered a deferred revenue (revenue received in advance) rather than an estimated liability? How is each treatment an application of the matching rule?

Exercise 10-7.
Future Value Calculations
(L.O. 5)

Naber receives a one-year note that carries a 12 percent annual interest rate on $1,500 for the sale of a used car.

Compute the maturity value under each of the following assumptions: (1) The interest is simple interest. (2) The interest is compounded semiannually. (3) The interest is compounded quarterly. (4) The interest is compounded monthly.

Exercise 10-8.
Future Value Calculations
(L.O. 5)

Find the future value of (1) a single payment of $10,000 at 7 percent for ten years, (2) ten annual payments of $1,000 at 7 percent, (3) a single payment of $3,000 at 9 percent for seven years, and (4) seven annual payments of $3,000 at 9 percent.

Exercise 10-9.
Present Value Calculations
(L.O. 6)

Find the present value of (1) a single payment of $12,000 at 6 percent for twelve years, (2) twelve annual payments of $1,000 at 6 percent, (3) a single payment of $2,500 at 9 percent for five years, and (4) five annual payments of $2,500 at 9 percent.

Exercise 10-10. Future Value Calculations *(L.O. 5)*

Assume that $20,000 is invested today. Compute the amount that would accumulate at the end of seven years when the interest is (1) 8 percent annual interest compounded annually, (2) 8 percent annual interest compounded semiannually, and (3) 8 percent annual interest compounded quarterly.

Exercise 10-11. Future Value Calculations *(L.O. 5)*

Calculate the accumulation of periodic payments of $500 made at the end of each of four years, assuming (1) 10 percent annual interest compounded annually, (2) 10 percent annual interest compounded semiannually, (3) 4 percent annual interest compounded annually, and (4) 16 percent annual interest compounded quarterly.

Exercise 10-12. Future Value Applications *(L.O. 5)*

a. Two parents have $10,000 to invest for their child's college tuition, which they estimate will cost $20,000 when the child enters college twelve years from now.
   Calculate the approximate rate of annual interest that the investment must earn to reach the $20,000 goal in twelve years. (**Hint**: Make a calculation, then use Table 1 in the appendix on future value and present value tables.)
b. Bill Roister is saving to purchase a summer home that will cost about $32,000. He has $20,000 now, on which he can earn 7 percent annual interest.
   Calculate the approximate length of time he will have to wait to purchase the summer home. (**Hint**: Make a calculation, then use Table 1 in the appendix on future value and present value tables.)

Exercise 10-13. Working Backward from a Future Value *(L.O. 5)*

May Marquez has a debt of $45,000 due in four years. She wants to save money to pay it off by making annual deposits in an investment account that earns 8 percent annual interest.

Calculate the amount she must deposit each year to reach her goal. (**Hint**: Use Table 2 in the appendix on future value and present value tables, then make a calculation.)

Exercise 10-14. Present Value of a Lump-Sum Contract *(L.O. 6)*

A contract calls for a lump-sum payment of $30,000. Find the present value of the contract, assuming that (1) the payment is due in five years, and the current interest rate is 9 percent; (2) the payment is due in ten years, and the current interest rate is 9 percent; (3) the payment is due in five years, and the current interest rate is 5 percent; and (4) the payment is due in ten years, and the current interest rate is 5 percent.

Exercise 10-15. Present Value of an Annuity Contract *(L.O. 6)*

A contract calls for annual payments of $600. Find the present value of the contract, assuming that (1) the number of payments is seven, and the current interest rate is 6 percent; (2) the number of payments is fourteen, and the current interest rate is 6 percent; (3) the number of payments is seven, and the current interest rate is 8 percent; and (4) the number of payments is fourteen, and the current interest rate is 8 percent.

Exercise 10-16. Determining an Advance Payment *(L.O. 6)*

Ellen Saber is contemplating paying five years' rent in advance. Her annual rent is $4,800. Calculate the single sum that would have to be paid now for the advance rent, if we assume compound interest of 8 percent.

Exercise 10-17. Noninterest-Bearing Note *(L.O. 7)*

On January 1, 19x8, Olson purchases a machine from Carter by signing a two-year, noninterest-bearing $16,000 note. Olson currently pays 12 percent interest to borrow money at the bank.

Prepare journal entries in Olson's and Carter's records to (1) record the purchase and the note, (2) adjust the accounts after one year, and (3) record payment of the note after two years (on December 31, 19x9).

Exercise 10-18. Valuing an Asset for the Purpose of Making a Purchasing Decision *(L.O. 7)*

Kubo owns a service station and has the opportunity to purchase a car wash machine for $15,000. After carefully studying projected costs and revenues, Kubo estimates that the car wash will produce a net cash flow of $2,600 annually and will last for eight years. Kubo feels that an interest rate of 14 percent is adequate for his business.

Calculate the present value of the machine to Kubo. Does the purchase appear to be a correct business decision?

Exercise 10-19. Deferred Payment *(L.O. 7)*

Johnson Equipment Corporation sells a precision tool machine with computer controls to Borst Corporation for $800,000 on January 1, agreeing to take payment nine months later, on September 1. Assuming that the prevailing annual interest rate for such a transaction is 16 percent compounded quarterly, what will the actual sales (purchase) price of the machine tool be, and what journal entries will be made at the time of the purchase (sale) and at the time of the payment (receipt) on the records of both Borst and Johnson?

Exercise 10-20. Investment of Idle Cash *(L.O. 7)*

Scientific Publishing Company, a publisher of college books, has just completed a successful fall selling season and has $5,000,000 in cash to invest for nine months, beginning on January 1. The company places the cash in a money market account that is expected to pay 12 percent annual interest compounded monthly. Interest is credited to the company's account each month. How much cash will the company have at the end of nine months, and what entries are made to record the investment and the first two monthly (February 1 and March 1) interest amounts?

Exercise 10-21. Accumulation of a Fund *(L.O. 7)*

Laferia Corporation borrows $3,000,000 from an insurance company on a five-year note. Management agrees to set aside enough cash at the end of each year to accumulate the amount needed to pay off the note at maturity. Since the first contribution to the fund will be made in one year, four annual contributions are needed. Assuming that the fund will earn 10 percent compounded annually, how much will the annual contribution to the fund be (round to nearest dollar), and what will be the journal entry for the first contribution?

Exercise 10-22. Negotiating the Sale of a Business *(L.O. 7)*

Horace Johnson is attempting to sell his business to Ernando Ruiz. The company has assets of $900,000, liabilities of $400,000, and stockholders' equity of $500,000. Both parties agree that the proper rate of return to expect is 12 percent; however, they differ on other assumptions. Johnson believes that the business will generate at least $100,000 per year of cash flows for twenty years. Ruiz thinks that $80,000 in cash flows per year is more reasonable and that only ten years in the future should be considered. Using Table 4 in the appendix on future value and present value tables, determine the range for negotiation by computing the present value of Johnson's offer to sell and of Ruiz's offer to buy.

Interpretion Cases from Business

ICB 10-1. Trans World Airlines, Inc. (TWA)[9] *(L.O. 1, 2)*

Trans World Airlines, Inc. is a major airline that experienced financial difficulties in 1988 and 1989. In TWA's 1989 annual report, management refers to the company's deteriorating liquidity situation as follows:

> TWA's net working capital deficit was $55.5 million at December 31, 1989, representing a reduction of $82.6 million from net working capital of $27.1 million at December 31, 1988. Working capital deficits are not unusual in the airline industry because of the large advance ticket sales current liability account.

The company's current liabilities and current assets at December 31 for the two years are as follows (in thousands):

	1989	1988
Current liabilities:		
Current maturities of long-term debt	$ 127,301	$ 242,914
Current obligations under capital leases	93,194	60,574
Advance ticket sales	276,549	280,206
Accounts payable, principally trade	387,256	337,460
Accounts payable to affiliated companies	8,828	69,697
Securities sold, not yet purchased	82,302	240,044
Accrued expenses:		
Employee compensation and vacations earned	148,175	128,902
Contributions to retirement and pension trusts	14,711	36,766
Interest on debt and capital leases	86,761	78,795
Taxes	33,388	29,401
Other accrued expenses	122,295	140,320
Total	$1,380,760	$1,645,079

9. Excerpts from the 1989 Annual Report used by permission of Trans World Airlines, Inc. Copyright © 1989.

Current assets:		
Cash and cash equivalents	$ 454,415	$ 632,311
Marketable securities	10,355	77,556
Receivables, less allowance for doubtful accounts, $13,432 in 1989 and $14,132 in 1988	435,061	427,092
Receivables from affiliated companies	15,506	—
Due from brokers	70,636	233,050
Spare parts, materials, and supplies, less allowance for obsolescence, $38,423 in 1989 and $32,380 in 1988	227,098	193,550
Prepaid expenses and other	112,232	108,667
Total	$1,325,303	$1,672,226

Required

1. Identify any current liabilities that do not require a current outlay of cash and identify any current estimated liabilities for 1989 and 1988. Why is management not worried about the cash flow consequences of advance ticket sales?
2. For 1989 and 1988, which current assets will not generate cash inflow, and which will most likely be available to pay for the remaining current liabilities? Compare the amount of these current assets to the amount of current liabilities other than those identified in **1** as not requiring a cash outlay.
3. In light of the calculations in **2**, comment on TWA's liquidity position for 1989 and 1988, and identify several alternative sources of additional cash.

ICB 10-2.
Texaco, Inc.[10]
(L.O. 3)

Texaco, one of the largest integrated oil companies in the world, reported its loss of the largest damage judgment in history in its 1986 annual report as follows:

Note 17. Contingent Liabilities
Pennzoil Litigation
State Court Action. On December 10, 1985, the 151st District Court of Harris County, Texas, entered judgment for Pennzoil Company of $7.5 billion actual damages, $3 billion punitive damages, and approximately $600 million prejudgment interest in *Pennzoil Company v. Texaco, Inc.*, an action in which Pennzoil claims that Texaco, Inc., tortiously interfered with Pennzoil's alleged contract to acquire a 3/7ths interest in Getty. Interest began accruing on the judgment at the simple rate of 10% per annum from the date of judgment. Texaco, Inc., believes that there is no legal basis for the judgment, which it believes is contrary to the evidence and applicable law. Texaco, Inc., is pursuing all available remedies to set aside or to reverse the judgment.

* * *

The outcome of the appeal on the preliminary injunction and the ultimate outcome of the Pennzoil litigation are not presently determinable, but could have a material adverse effect on the consolidated financial position and the results of the consolidated operations of Texaco, Inc.

10. Excerpts from the 1986 Annual Report used by permission of Texaco, Inc. Copyright © 1986.

At December 31, 1986, Texaco's retained earnings were $12.882 billion, and its cash and marketable securities totaled $3.0 billion. The company's net income for 1986 was $.725 billion.

After a series of court reversals and filing for bankruptcy in 1987, Texaco announced in December 1987 an out-of-court settlement with Pennzoil for $3.0 billion. Although less than the original amount, it is still the largest damage payment in history.

Required

1. The FASB has established two conditions that a contingent liability must meet before it is recorded in the accounting records. What are the two conditions? Does the situation described in "Note 17: Contingent Liabilities" meet those conditions? Explain your answer.
2. Do the events of 1987 change your answer to **1**? Explain your answer.
3. What will be the effect of the settlement on Texaco's retained earnings, cash and marketable securities, and net income?

ICB 10-3.
Internal Revenue Service
(L.O. 6)

When an asset is sold on credit, the purchaser usually pays interest on the amount owed, and the seller must include the interest received in income. The seller must pay income taxes on this interest income. Some taxpayers have tried to understate interest in reported income by using an unrealistically low stated interest rate. For example, an asset was sold on January 1, 1991, for $28,000 under a contract that provides for four equal payments of principal and a stated interest rate of 9 percent as follows:

Date of Payment	Payment	Stated Interest (9%)	Total Paid	Balance Due
Jan. 1, 1991				$28,000
Jan. 1, 1992	$ 7,000	$2,520	$ 9,520	21,000
Jan. 1, 1993	7,000	1,890	8,890	14,000
Jan. 1, 1994	7,000	1,260	8,260	7,000
Jan. 1, 1995	7,000	630	7,630	—
	$28,000	$6,300	$34,300	

Every six months the Internal Revenue Service (IRS) determines a "federal" rate of interest based on the average yield of certain marketable securities of the U.S. government. Any sale such as the one above must have an effective interest rate at least equal to 110 percent of the "federal" rate. If it does not, the IRS will use a rate equal to 120 percent of the "federal" rate to compute the amount of unstated interest that must be reported as interest income in addition to the stated interest.

If the 110 percent test is not met, the amount of unstated interest that must be reported as income may be determined by substituting the present value of the total payments using present value factors based on 120 percent of the "federal" rate from the original sale price.

Required

Assuming that the "federal" rate is 10 percent, does the agreement in this question meet the IRS test for stated interest? If not, use the third present value table in the appendix on future value and present value tables to determine the present value of the four payments. Then determine the total unstated interest that must be reported as taxable interest income in addition to the stated interest.

Problem Set A

Problem 10A-1. Notes Payable Transactions and End-of-Month Period Entries *(L.O. 2)*

Prentiss Paper Company, whose fiscal year ends December 31, completed the following transactions involving notes payable:

Nov. 25 Purchased a new loading cart by issuing a sixty-day, 10 percent note for $21,600.
Dec. 16 Borrowed $25,000 from the bank to finance inventory by signing a ninety-day, 12 percent note. The face value of the note includes interest. Proceeds received were $24,250.
31 Made end-of-year adjusting entry to accrue interest expense.
31 Made end-of-year adjusting entry to recognize discount on note payable expired.
31 Made end-of-year closing entry pertaining to interest expense.
Jan. 2 Made appropriate reversing entry.
24 Paid off the loading cart note.
Mar. 16 Paid off the inventory note to the bank.

Required

1. Prepare general journal entries for these transactions (journal Page 41).
2. Open general ledger accounts for Notes Payable (212), Discount on Notes Payable (213), Interest Payable (214), and Interest Expense (721). Post the relevant portions of the entries to these general ledger accounts.

Problem 10A-2. Property Tax and Vacation Pay Liabilities *(L.O. 2)*

Chin Corporation accrues estimated liabilities for property taxes and vacation pay. The company's fiscal year ends June 30. The property taxes for the previous year were $36,000, and they are expected to increase 6 percent this year. Two weeks' vacation pay is given to each employee after one year of service. Chin management estimates that 75 percent of its employees will qualify for this benefit in the current year. In addition, the following information is available:

The property tax bill of $39,552 was received in September and paid on November 1.

Total payroll for July was $98,200. This amount includes $9,200 paid to employees on paid vacations.

Required

1. Prepare the monthly journal entries to record accrued property taxes for July through November and actual property taxes paid. (Round to nearest dollar.)
2. a. Prepare a general journal entry to record the vacation accrual expense for July.
   b. Prepare a general journal entry to record the wages of employees on vacation in July (ignore payroll deductions and taxes).

Problem 10A-3. Product Warranty Liability *(L.O. 2)*

The Citation Company manufactures and sells food processors. The company guarantees the processors for five years. If a processor fails, the customer is charged a percentage of the retail price for replacement. That percentage is based on the age of the processor. In the past, management has found that only 3 percent of the processors sold require replacement under the warranty. Of those replaced, an average of 20 percent of the cost is collected under the replacement pricing policy. The average food processor costs the company $120. At the beginning of September, the account for estimated liability for product warranties had a credit balance of $104,000. During September, 250 processors were returned under the warranty. The cost of replacement was $27,000, of which $4,930 was recovered under the replacement pricing policy. During the month, the company sold 2,800 food processors.

Required

1. Prepare general journal entries to record the cost of food processors replaced under warranty and the estimated liability for product warranties for processors sold during the month.
2. Compute the balance of the estimated product warranty liabilities at the end of the month.

Problem 10A-4. Product Warranty Liability *(L.O. 2)*

Western Tire Company guarantees the tires it sells until they wear out. If a tire fails, the customer is charged a percentage of the retail price based on the percentage of the tire that is worn, plus a service charge for putting the tire on the car. In the past, management has found that only 2 percent of the tires sold require replacement under warranty, and of those replaced, an average of 20 percent of the cost is collected under the percentage pricing system. The average tire costs the company $70. At the beginning of July, the account for estimated liability for product warranties had a credit balance of $45,492. During July, 250 tires were returned under the warranty. The cost of the replacement tires was $9,250, of which $2,250 was recovered under the percentage-worn formula. Service revenue amounted to $1,062. During the month, the company sold 7,050 tires.

Required

1. Prepare general journal entries to record each of the following: (a) the warranty work completed during the month, including related revenue; (b) the estimated liability for product warranties for tires sold during the month.
2. Compute the balance of the estimated product warranty liabilities at the end of the month.

Problem 10A-5. Noninterest-bearing Note and Valuing an Asset for the Purpose of Making a Purchasing Decision *(L.O. 2, 6)*

Part A: Fender, a candy manufacturer, needs a machine to heat chocolate. On January 1, 19x1, Fender purchases a machine to accomplish this task from Royce by signing a two-year, noninterest-bearing $32,000 note. Fender currently pays 12 percent interest to borrow money at the bank.

Required

Prepare journal entries in Fender's and Royce's records to (1) record the purchase and the note; (2) adjust the accounts after one year; and (3) record payment of the note after two years (on December 31, 19x2). (Assume that reversing entries are not made by either party.)

Part B: Sanchez owns a printing service and has the opportunity to purchase a high-speed copy machine for $20,000. After carefully studying projected costs and revenues, Sanchez estimates that the copy machine will produce a net cash flow of $3,000 annually and will last for eight years. Sanchez feels that an interest rate of 14 percent is adequate for his business.

Required

Calculate the present value of the machine to Sanchez. Does the purchase appear to be a correct business decision?

Problem 10A-6. Time Value of Money Applications *(L.O. 5, 6, 7)*

Neiman Corporation's management took several actions, each of which was to be effective on January 1, 19x1, and each of which involved an application of the time value of money:

a. Established a new retirement plan to take effect in three years and authorized three annual payments of $500,000 starting January 1, 19x2, to establish the retirement fund.
b. Approved plans for a new distribution center to be built for $1,000,000 and authorized five annual payments, starting January 1, 19x2, to accumulate the funds for the new center.
c. Bought out the contract of a member of top management for a payment of $50,000 per year for four years beginning January 1, 19x2.
d. Accepted a two-year noninterest-bearing note for $100,000 as payment for equipment that the company sold.
e. Set aside $300,000 for possible losses from lawsuits over a defective product. The lawsuits are not expected to be settled for three years.

Required

Assuming an annual interest rate of 10 percent and using Tables 10-1, 10-2, 10-3, and 10-4, answer the following questions:

1. In action **a**, how much will the retirement fund accumulate in three years?
2. In action **b**, how much must the annual payment be to reach the goal?
3. In action **c**, what is the cost (present value) of the buy-out?
4. In action **d**, assuming that interest is compounded semiannually, what is the selling price (present value) of the equipment?
5. In action **e**, how much will the fund accumulate to in three years?

Problem Set B

Problem 10B-1. Notes Payable Transactions and End-of-Period Entries *(L.O. 2)*

Fairbrooks Corporation, whose fiscal year ends June 30, completed the following transactions involving notes payable:

May 11 Signed a ninety-day, 12 percent, $132,000 note payable to Village Bank for a working capital loan. The face value included interest. Proceeds received were $128,040.

21 Obtained a sixty-day extension on a $36,000 trade account payable owed to a supplier by signing a sixty-day, $36,000 note. Interest is in addition to the face value, at the rate of 14 percent.

June	30	Made end-of-year adjusting entry to accrue interest expense.
	30	Made end-of-year adjusting entry to recognize prepaid interest expense.
	30	Made end-of-year closing entry pertaining to interest expense.
July	1	Made appropriate reversing entry.
	20	Paid off the note plus interest due the supplier.
Aug.	9	Paid amount due bank on ninety-day note.

Required

1. Prepare general journal entries for the above transactions (journal Page 28).
2. Open general ledger accounts for Notes Payable (212), Discount on Notes Payable (213), Interest Payable (214), and Interest Expense (721). Post the relevant portions of the entries to these general ledger accounts.

Problem 10B-2. Property Tax and Vacation Pay Liabilities *(L.O. 2)*

Brett Corporation prepares monthly financial statements and ends its fiscal year on June 30. In July, your first month as accountant for the company, you find that the company has not previously accrued estimated liabilities. In the past, the company, which has a large property tax bill, has charged property taxes to the month in which the bill is paid. The tax bill for last year was $36,000, and it is estimated that the tax will increase by 8 percent in the coming year. The tax bill is usually received on September 1, to be paid November 1.

You also discover that the company allows employees who have worked for the company for one year to take two weeks' paid vacation each year. The cost of these vacations has been charged to expense in the month of payment. Approximately 80 percent of the employees qualify for this benefit. You suggest to management that proper accounting treatment of these expenses is to spread their cost over the entire year. Management agrees and asks you to make the necessary adjustments.

Required

1. Figure the proper monthly charge to Property Taxes Expense, and prepare general journal entries for the following:

July 31	Accrual of property tax expense
Aug. 31	Accrual of property tax expense
Sept. 30	Accrual of property tax expense (assume actual bill is $40,860)
Oct. 31	Accrual of property tax expense
Nov. 1	Payment of property tax
Nov. 30	Accrual of property tax expense

2. Assume that the total payroll for July is $568,000. This amount includes $21,000 paid to employees on paid vacations. (a) Compute the vacation pay expense for July. (b) Prepare a general journal entry to record the accrual of vacation pay expense for July. (c) Prepare a general journal entry to record the wages of employees on vacation in July (ignore payroll deductions and taxes).

Problem 10B-3. Product Warranty Liability *(L.O. 2)*

Lighthouse Company is engaged in the retail sale of washing machines. Each machine has a twenty-four-month warranty on parts. If a repair under warranty is required, a charge for the labor is made. Management has found that 20 percent of the machines sold require some work before the warranty expires. Furthermore, the average cost of replacement parts has been $80 per repair. At the beginning of February, the account for the estimated liability for product warranties had a credit balance of $14,300. During February, 112 machines were returned under the warranty. The cost of the parts used in repairing the machines was $8,765, and $9,442 was collected as service revenue for the labor involved. During the month, Lighthouse Company sold 450 new machines.

Required

1. Prepare general journal entries to record each of the following: (a) the warranty work completed during the month, including related revenue; (b) the estimated liability for product warranties for machines sold during the month.
2. Compute the balance of the estimated product warranty liabilities at the end of the month.

Problem 10B-4. Product Warranty Liability *(L.O. 2)*

Among other things, Broadway Car Outlet, Inc. sells tires and guarantees them as long as the customer owns them. If a tire fails, the customer is charged a percentage of the retail price based on the percentage of the tire that is worn, plus a service charge for putting the tire on the car. In the past, management has found that only 2 percent of the tires sold require replacement under warranty, and of those replaced, an average of 20 percent of the cost is collected under the percentage pricing system. The average tire costs the company $55. At the beginning of July, the account for estimated liability for product warranties had a credit balance of $22,746. During July, 125 tires were returned under the warranty. The cost of the replacement tires was $4,625, of which $1,125 was recovered under the percentage-worn formula. Service revenue amounted to $531. During the month, the company sold 3,525 tires.

Required

1. Prepare general journal entries to record each of the following: (a) the warranty work completed during the month including related revenues; (b) the estimated liability for product warranties for tires sold during the month.
2. Compute the balance of the estimated product warranty liabilities at the end of the month.

Problem 10B-5. Noninterest-bearing Note and Valuing an Asset for the Purpose of Making a Purchasing Decision *(L.O. 2, 6)*

Part A: Munro, Inc. provides heavy-duty industrial cleaning services to manufacturing companies. On July 1, 19x1, Munro, Inc. purchases a new truck for servicing its accounts from Lake Corporation by signing a two-year, noninterest-bearing $24,000 note. Lake currently pays 15 percent interest to borrow money at the bank.

Required

Prepare journal entries in Munro's and Lake's records to (1) record the purchase and the note; (2) adjust the accounts after one year (assuming June 30 year end); and (3) record payment of the note after two years (on June 30, 19x3). (Reversing entries are not made by either company.)

Part B: Becker Corporation is in the lawn care business. Management is considering the purchase of a special type of spraying machine for $38,000. After carefully studying projected costs and revenues, management estimates that the machine will produce a net cash flow of $10,500 for the next seven years. Management also believes that an interest rate of 18 percent is appropriate for this analysis.

Required

Calculate the present value of the machine to Becker Corporation. Does the purchase appear to be a correct business decision?

Problem 10B-6. Time Value of Money Applications *(L.O. 5, 6, 7)*

Effective January 1, 19x1, the board of directors of Riordan, Inc. approved the following actions, each of which is an application of the time value of money:

a. Established in a single payment of $100,000 a contingency fund for the possible settlement of a lawsuit. The suit is expected to be settled in two years.
b. Asked for another fund to be established by a single payment to accumulate to $300,000 in four years.
c. Approved purchase of a parcel of land for future plant expansion. Payments are to start January 1, 19x2, at $50,000 per year for 5 years.
d. Determined that a new building to be built on the property in **c** would cost $800,000 and authorized annual payments to be paid starting January 1, 19x2, into a fund for its construction.
e. Purchased Riordan common stock from a stockholder who wanted to be bought out by issuing a four-year noninterest-bearing note for $200,000.

Required

Assuming an annual interest rate of 8 percent and using Tables 10-1, 10-2, 10-3, and 10-4, answer the following questions:

1. In action **a**, how much will the fund accumulate to in two years?
2. In action **b**, how much will need to be deposited initially to accumulate the desired amount?
3. In action **c**, what is the purchase price (present value) of the land?
4. In action **d**, how much would the equal annual payments need to be to accumulate enough money to build the building?
5. In action **e**, assuming semiannual compounding of interest, what is the actual purchase price of the stock (present value of the note)?

Financial Decision Cases

10-1. Highland Television Repair *(L.O. 1, 2)*

Jerry Highland opened a small television repair shop on January 2, 19xx. He also sold a small line of television sets. Jerry's wife, Jane, was the sole salesperson for the television sets, and Jerry was the only person doing repairs. (Jerry had worked for another television repair store for twenty years, where he was the supervisor for six repairpersons.) The new business was such a success that he hired two assistants on March 1, 19xx. In October, Jerry received a letter from the Internal Revenue Service informing him that he had failed to file any tax reports for his business since its inception, and probably owed a considerable amount of taxes. Since Jerry has limited experience in maintaining business records, he has brought the letter and all his business records to you for help. The records include a checkbook, canceled checks, deposit slips, invoices from his suppliers, notice of annual property taxes of $4,620 due to the city November 1, 19xx, and a promissory note to his father-in-law for $5,000. He wants you to determine what his business owes to the government and other parties.

You analyze all his records and determine the following:

Unpaid supplies invoices	$ 3,160
Sales (excluding sales tax)	88,540
Workers' salaries	20,400
Repair revenues	120,600

You learn that the company has deducted $952.00 from employees' salaries for federal income tax withholding, which is owed to the government. In addition, a total of $3,064.80 is owed to the federal government for social security taxes (FICA). Further, the company must pay a state unemployment tax and a federal unemployment tax ("FUTA") of 5.4 percent of salaries to the state and 0.8 percent to the federal government. The latter two taxes apply only to the first $7,000 earned by each of the two employees. Jerry has not filed a sales tax report to the state (5 percent of sales).

Required

1. Given these limited facts, determine Highland Television Repair's liabilities as of October 31, 19xx.
2. What additional information would you want from Jerry to satisfy yourself that all liabilities have been identified?

10-2.
O'Hara Machine Works, Inc.
(L.O. 6, 7)

O'Hara Machine Works, Inc. has just been notified that it was successful in signing a subcontract to manufacture parts for a new military aircraft. The parts are to be delivered over the next five years, and O'Hara will be paid as the parts are delivered. In order to make the parts, new equipment will have to be purchased. Two types of equipment arrangements are available. One type (A) uses conventional equipment that can be put into service immediately, and the other type (B) requires one year to be put into service but is more efficient. Type A requires an immediate cash investment of $500,000 and will produce enough parts to provide net cash receipts of $170,000 each year for the five years. Type B may be purchased by signing a two-year noninterest-bearing note for $673,000. It is projected that Type B will produce net cash receipts of zero in year 1, $250,000 in year 2, $300,000 in year 3, $300,000 in year 4, and the remaining $100,000 in year 5. Neither type of equipment can be used on other contracts or will have any useful life remaining at the end of the contract. O'Hara currently pays an interest rate of 16 percent to borrow money.

Required

1. What is the present value of the investment required for each type of equipment? (Use Table 3 in the appendix on future value and present value tables.)
2. Compute the present value of the net cash receipts projected to be received from each type of equipment. (Use Tables 3 and 4 in the same appendix.)
3. Which option appears to be best for O'Hara, based on your analysis, and why?

CHAPTER 11

Long-Term Liabilities

LEARNING OBJECTIVES

1. *Identify and contrast the major characteristics of bonds.*
2. *Record the issuance of bonds at face value and at a discount or premium.*
3. *Determine the value of bonds using present values.*
4. *Amortize (a) bond discounts and (b) bond premiums by using the straight-line and effective interest methods.*
5. *Account for bonds issued between interest dates and make year-end adjustments.*
6. *Account for the retirement of bonds and the conversion of bonds into stock.*
7. *Explain the basic features of mortgages payable, installment notes payable, long-term leases, pensions, and postretirement benefits as long-term liabilities.*

This chapter introduces long-term liabilities. It describes the nature of bonds and the accounting treatment for bonds payable and other long-term liabilities, such as mortgages, long-term leases, pension liabilities, and postretirement benefits. After studying this chapter, you should be able to meet the learning objectives listed on the left.

A corporation has many sources of funds from which to finance operations and expansion. As you learned earlier, corporations can acquire cash and other assets by conducting profitable operations, obtaining short-term credit, and issuing stock. Another source of funds for a business is long-term debt in the form of bonds or notes. When a company issues bonds or notes, it promises to pay the creditor periodic interest plus the principal of the debt on a certain date in the future. Notes and bonds are long-term if they are due more than one year from the balance sheet date. In practice, long-term notes can range from two to ten years to maturity, and long-term bonds and mortgages from ten to fifty years to maturity. Although some companies carry an amount of long-term debt that exceeds 50 percent of total assets, the average company carries much less. As will be seen in Figure 11-1, the average ratio of long-term debt to total assets ranged from 13.0 percent for pharmaceutical companies to more than 22 percent for interstate trucking firms and for grocery stores.

DECISION POINT
RJR Nabisco

During the 1980s, there was an explosion in the amount of long-term debt issued by companies either to refinance their own operations or to finance takeovers of other companies. Much of this financing was accomplished through so-called **junk bonds**, unsecured, high-risk, long-term bonds with high rates of interest. Carrying a large amount of debt is risky for a company, because the interest charges on the debt will be very high in relation to earnings and cash flows. If a company is unable to pay the interest on the bonds, it may be forced to declare bankruptcy. Even if the company can pay the interest, its ability to improve and expand operations may be severely limited. RJR Nabisco

Figure 11-1. Average Long-Term Debt as a Percentage of Total Assets

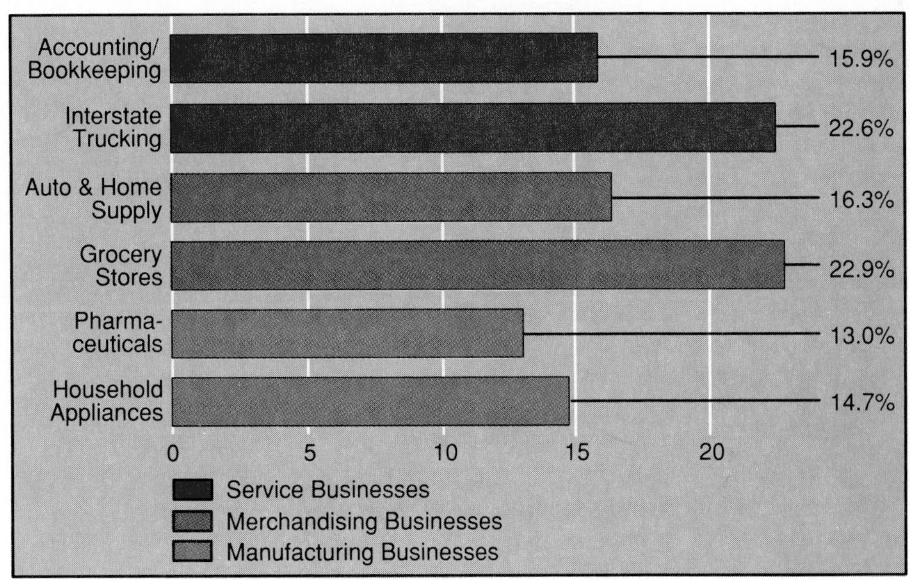

Source: Data from Dun and Bradstreet, *Industry Norms and Ratios*, 1990–91.

set a record when it issued $26 billion in junk bonds in its takeover by the securities firm of Kohlberg Kravis Roberts & Co. in February 1989. The heavy debt load proved to be a burden to RJR Nabisco. The biggest problem the company faced involved bonds whose interest rate had to be increased if the prices of the bonds on the open market declined, as they did in 1990. Some interest rates would have had to be reset at 20 percent or higher, more than double the interest rates on less risky bonds. Management now had to decide how to alleviate this situation or face the potential bankruptcy or breakup of the company.

As reported in the *Asian Wall Street Journal*, after six months of intense negotiation RJR Nabisco's management resolved its immediate problems through a $6.9 billion refinancing plan.[1] This large refinancing package was designed to strengthen the balance sheet and ward off a potential financial crisis. Louis Gerstner, RJR Nabisco's chief financial officer, called the refinancing package "a comprehensive, creative program." Under the plan, RJR Nabisco would have billions of dollars at its disposal. Among the components of the plan were new long-term bonds, adjustments of interest rates on existing bonds, new issues of capital stock, new bank loans, and expansion of existing bank lines of credit. While this financing is among the most complex in history, the plan may be understood using concepts developed in this chapter. ■

1. George Anders, "RJR Nabisco Moves to Retire Most Troublesome Junk Bonds," *Asian Wall Street Journal*, July 17, 1990.

Nature of Bonds

OBJECTIVE 1 Identify and contrast the major characteristics of bonds

A **bond** is a security, usually long-term, representing money borrowed by a corporation from the investing public. (Other kinds of bonds are issued by the United States government, state and local governments, and foreign companies and countries to raise money.) Bonds must be repaid at a certain time and require periodic payments of interest. Interest is usually paid semiannually, or twice a year. Bonds must not be confused with stocks. Because stocks are shares of ownership, stockholders are owners. Bondholders, however, are creditors. Bonds are promises to repay the amount borrowed, called the principal, and a certain rate of interest at specified future dates.

The holder of a bond receives a **bond certificate** as evidence of the company's debt to the bondholder. In most cases, the face value (denomination) of the bond is $1,000 or some multiple of $1,000. A **bond issue** is the total number of bonds that are issued at one time. For example, a $1,000,000 bond issue may consist of a thousand $1,000 bonds. The issue may be bought and held by many investors. So the corporation usually enters into a supplementary agreement, called a **bond indenture**. The bond indenture defines the rights, privileges, and limitations of bondholders. The bond indenture will generally describe such things as the maturity date of the bonds, interest payment dates, the interest rate, and characteristics of the bonds such as call features. Repayment plans and restrictions may also be covered.

The prices of bonds are stated in terms of a percentage of face value. If a bond issue is quoted at 103½, this means that a $1,000 bond would cost $1,035 ($1,000 × 103½%). When a bond sells at exactly 100, it is said to sell at face or par value. When it sells above 100, it is said to sell at a premium; below 100, at a discount. A $1,000 bond quoted at 87.62 would be selling at a discount and would cost the buyer $876.20.

A bond indenture can be written to fit the financing needs of an individual company. As a result, the bonds being issued by corporations in today's financial markets have many different features. Several of the more important ones are described here.

Secured or Unsecured Bonds

Bonds may be either secured or unsecured. If they are issued on the general credit of the company, they are **unsecured bonds** (also called **debentures**). **Secured bonds** give the bondholders a pledge of certain assets of the company as a guarantee of repayment. The security identified by a secured bond may be any specific asset of the company or a general category of assets, such as property, plant, and equipment.

Term or Serial Bonds

When all the bonds of an issue mature at the same time, they are called **term bonds**. For example, a company may issue $1,000,000 worth of bonds, all due twenty years from the date of issue. If the maturity dates of a bond issue are spread over several different dates, the bonds are **serial bonds**. A company may issue serial bonds to ease the task of retiring its debt. An example of serial bonds would be a $1,000,000 issue that calls for retiring $200,000 of the principal every five years. This arrangement means that after the first $200,000 payment is made, $800,000 of the bonds would remain outstanding for the next five years. In other words, $1,000,000 is outstanding for the first five years, $800,000 for the second five years, and so on.

Registered or Coupon Bonds

Most bonds that are issued today are **registered bonds**. The names and addresses of the owners of these bonds must be recorded with the issuing company. The company keeps a register of the owners and pays interest by check to the bondholders of record on the interest payment date. **Coupon bonds** generally are not registered with the corporation, but instead bear interest coupons stating the amount of interest due and the payment date. The coupons are removed from the bond on the interest payment dates and presented at a bank for collection. In this way the interest is paid to the holder of the coupon.

Accounting for Bonds Payable[2]

OBJECTIVE 2
Record the issuance of bonds at face value and at a discount or premium

When the board of directors decides to issue bonds, it generally presents the proposal to the stockholders. If the stockholders agree to the issue, the company prints the certificates and draws up a deed of trust. The bonds are then authorized for issuance. It is not necessary to make on a journal entry for the authorization, but most companies prepare a memorandum in the Bonds Payable account describing the issue. This note gives the amount of bonds authorized, the interest rate, the interest payment dates, and the life of the bonds.

Once the bonds are issued, the corporation must pay interest to the bondholders during the life of the bonds (in most cases semiannually) and must repay the principal of the bonds at maturity.

Balance Sheet Disclosure of Bonds

Bonds payable and either unamortized discount or unamortized premium (which will be explained later) are generally shown on a company's balance sheet as long-term liabilities. However, as explained in the chapter on current liabilities, if the maturity date of the bond issue is one year or less and the bonds will be retired by the use of current assets, bonds payable should be listed as current liabilities. If the issue is to be paid with segregated assets or replaced by another bond issue, then bonds should still be shown as long-term liabilities.

2. At the time this chapter was being written, the market interest rates on corporate bonds were volatile. Therefore, the examples and problems in this chapter use a variety of interest rates that are convenient for demonstrating the concepts.

Important provisions of the bond indenture are reported in the notes to the financial statements. Often reported with them is a list of all bond issues, the kind of bond, the interest rate, any security connected with the bonds, interest payment dates, maturity date, and effective interest rate.

Bonds Issued at Face Value

As an example, suppose that the Vason Corporation has authorized the issuance of $100,000 of 9 percent, five-year bonds on January 1, 19x0. Interest is to be paid on January 1 and July 1 of each year. Assume that the bonds are sold on January 1, 19x0 for their face value. The entry to record the issuance is as follows:

Jan. 1	Cash	100,000	
	Bonds Payable		100,000
	Sold $100,000 of 9%, 5-year bonds at face value		

As stated above, interest is paid on July 1 and January 1 of each year. Thus the corporation would owe the bondholders $4,500 interest on July 1, 19x0. The interest computation would be:

$$\begin{aligned} \text{interest} &= \text{principal} \times \text{rate} \times \text{time} \\ &= \$100{,}000 \times .09 \times 1/2 \text{ year} \\ &= \$4{,}500 \end{aligned}$$

The interest paid to the bondholders on each semiannual interest payment date (January 1 or July 1) would be recorded as follows:

Bond Interest Expense	4,500	
Cash (or Interest Payable)		4,500
Paid (or accrued) semiannual interest to bondholders of 9%, 5-year bonds		

Face Interest Rate and Market Interest Rate

When issuing bonds, most companies try to set the face interest rate as close as possible to the market interest rate. The **face interest rate** is the rate of interest paid to the bondholders based on the face value or principal of the bonds. The rate and amount are fixed over the life of the bond. The **market interest rate** is the rate of interest paid in the market on bonds of similar risk. The market interest rate fluctuates on a day-by-day basis. However, a company must decide in advance what the face interest rate will be to allow time to file with regulatory bodies, publicize the issue, and print the certificates. Since the company has no control over the market rate of interest, there is often a difference between the market or effective rate of interest and the face rate of interest on the issue date. The result is that the issue price of the bond does not always equal the principal or face value of the bond. If the market rate of interest is greater than the face interest rate, the issue price will be less than the face value, and the bonds are said to be issued at a **discount.** The discount equals the excess of the face value over the issue price. On the other hand, if the market rate of interest is less than the face interest rate, the issue price will be more than the face value, and the bonds are said to be issued at a **premium**. The premium is equal to the excess of the issue price over the face value.

Bonds Issued at a Discount

Suppose that the Vason Corporation issues its $100,000 of five-year, 9 percent bonds at 96.149 on January 1, 19x0, when the market rate of interest is 10 percent. In this case a discount exists, because the market rate of interest exceeds the face interest rate. The entry to record the issuance of the bonds at a discount is:

Jan.	1	Cash		96,149	
		Unamortized Bond Discount		3,851	
		Bonds Payable			100,000
		Sold $100,000 of 9%, 5-year bonds			
		Face Amount of Bonds	$100,000		
		Less Purchase Price of Bonds ($100,000 × .96149)	96,149		
		Unamortized Bond Discount	$ 3,851		

As shown, Cash is debited for the amount received ($96,149), Bonds Payable is credited for the face amount ($100,000) of the bond liability, and the difference ($3,851) is debited to Unamortized Bond Discount. If a balance sheet is prepared right after this issuance of bonds at a discount, the liability for bonds payable is as follows:

Long-Term Liabilities		
9% Bonds Payable, due 1/1/x5	$100,000	
Less Unamortized Bond Discount	3,851	$96,149

Unamortized Bond Discount is a contra-liability account that is deducted from the face amount of the bonds to arrive at the carrying value or present value of the bonds. The bond discount is described as unamortized because it will be amortized (written off) over the life of the bonds.

Bonds Issued at a Premium

When bonds have a face interest rate that is above the market rate for similar investments, they will be issued at a price above the face value, or at a premium. For example, assume that the Vason Corporation issues $100,000 of 9 percent, five-year bonds for $104,100 on January 1, 19x0, when the market rate of interest is 8 percent. This means that they will be purchased by investors at 104.1 percent of their face value. The entry to record their issuance would be as follows:

Jan.	1	Cash	104,100	
		Unamortized Bond Premium		4,100
		Bonds Payable		100,000
		Sold $100,000 of 9%, 5-year bonds at 104.1 ($100,000 × 1.04)		

Right after this entry is made, bonds payable would be presented on the balance sheet as follows:

Long-Term Liabilities		
9% Bonds Payable, due 1/1/x5	$100,000	
Unamortized Bond Premium	4,100	$104,100

The carrying value of the bonds payable is $104,100, which is equal to the face value of the bonds plus the unamortized bond premium. The cash received from the issuance of the bonds is also $104,100. This means that the purchasers were willing to pay a premium of $4,100 to get these bonds because the face interest on them was greater than the market rate.

Bond Issue Costs

Most bonds are sold through underwriters, who receive a fee for taking care of the details of marketing the issue and for guaranteeing that the company will receive a certain minimum price. These costs are connected with the issuance of bonds. Since bond issue costs benefit the whole life of the bond issue, it makes sense to spread these costs over that period. It is generally accepted practice to establish a separate account for bond issue costs and amortize them over the life of the bonds. However, issue costs decrease the amount of money received by the company for the bond issue. Thus they have the effect of raising the discount or lowering the premium on the issue. As a result, bond issue costs may be spread over the life of the bonds through the amortization of the discount or premium. Because this method simplifies the recordkeeping, it is assumed in the text and problems of this book that all bond issue costs increase discounts or decrease premiums of the bond issues.

Using Present Value to Value a Bond

OBJECTIVE 3 *Determine the value of bonds using present values*

Present value is relevant here because the value of a bond is based on the present value of two components of cash flow: (1) a series of fixed interest payments and (2) a single payment at maturity. The amount of interest that a bond pays is fixed over its life. During its life, however, the market rate of interest varies from day to day. Thus the amount that investors are willing to pay for the bond changes as well.

Assume, for example, that a particular bond has a face value of $10,000 and pays a fixed amount of interest of $450 (9 percent annual rate) every six months. The bond is due in five years. If the market rate of interest today is 14 percent, what is the present value of the bond?

To determine the present value of the bond, we use Tables 3 and 4 in the appendix on future value and present value tables. Because the compounding period is shorter than a year, it is necessary to convert the annual rate to a semiannual rate of 7 percent (14 percent divided by two six-month periods per year) and to use ten periods (five years multiplied by two six-month periods per year). Using this information, we compute the present value of the bond:

Present value of 10 periodic payments at 7% (from Table 4 in the appendix on future value and present value tables): $450 × 7.024	=	$3,160.80
Present value of a single payment at end of 10 periods at 7% (from Table 3 in the appendix on future value and present value tables): $10,000 × 0.508	=	5,080.00
Present value of $10,000 bond	=	$8,240.80

The market rate of interest has increased so much since the bond was issued (from 9 percent to 14 percent) that the value of the bond is only $8,240.80 today. This amount is all that investors would be willing to pay at this time for an income from this bond of $450 every six months and return of the $10,000 principal in five years.

If the market rate of interest falls below the face interest rate, say to 8 percent, the present value of the bond will be greater than the face value of $10,000, as shown in the calculation below:

Present value of 10 periodic payments at 4% (from Table 4 in the appendix on future value and present value tables): $450 × 8.111	=	$ 3,649.95
Present value of a single payment at end of 10 periods at 4% (from Table 3 in the appendix on future value and present value tables): $10,000 × .676	=	6,760.00
Present value of $10,000 bond	=	$10,409.95

Amortizing Bond Discounts

OBJECTIVE 4a *Amortize bond discounts by using the straight-line and effective interest methods*

Recall that in the illustration on page 549 Vason Corporation issued $100,000 of five-year bonds at a discount because the market interest rate of 10 percent exceeded the face interest rate of 9 percent. The bonds were sold for $96,149, resulting in an unamortized bond discount of $3,851. Since this discount, as we will see, affects interest expense in each year of the bond issue, it should be amortized or reduced gradually over the life of the bond issue. As a result, the unamortized bond discount will gradually decrease over time, and the carrying value of the bond issue (face value less unamortized discount) will gradually increase. By the maturity date of the bond, the carrying value of the issue will equal its face value, and the unamortized bond discount will be zero.

In the next two sections the calculation of total interest cost is explained and the straight-line and effective interest methods of amortizing a bond discount are presented.

Calculation of Total Interest Cost

When bonds are issued at a discount, the effective interest rate paid by the company is greater than the face interest rate on the bonds. The reason is that the interest cost to the company is the stated interest payments *plus* the amount of the bond discount. That is, though the company does not receive the full face value of the bonds upon issue, it must still pay back the full face amount at maturity. The difference between the issue price and the face value must be added to the total interest payments to arrive at the actual interest expense. The full cost to the Vason Corporation of issuing the bonds at a discount is as follows:

Cash to be paid to bondholders	
Face value at maturity	$100,000
Interest payments ($100,000 × .09 × 5 years)	45,000
Total cash paid to bondholders	$145,000
Less cash received from bondholders	96,149
Total interest cost	**$ 48,851**

Or alternatively:

Interest payments ($100,000 × .09 × 5 years)	$ 45,000
Bond discount	3,851
Total interest cost	**$ 48,851**

The total interest cost of $48,851 is made up of $45,000 in interest payments and the $3,851 bond discount. So the bond discount increases the interest paid on the bonds from the stated to the effective interest rate. The effective interest rate is the real interest cost of the bond over its life.

In order for each year's interest expense to reflect the effective interest rate, the discount must be spread or allocated over the remaining life of the bonds as an increase in the interest expense each period. This process of allocation is called amortization of the bond discount. Thus interest expense for each period will exceed the actual payment of interest by the amount of bond discount amortized during the period.

It is interesting to note that some companies and governmental units have begun to issue bonds that do not have periodic interest payments. These bonds, called **zero coupon bonds**, are simply a promise to pay a fixed amount at the maturity date. They are issued at a large discount, because the only interest earned by the buyer or paid by the issuer is the discount. For example, a five-year, $100,000 bond issued at a time when the market rate is 14 percent, compounded semiannually, would sell for only $50,800. This amount is the present value of a single payment of $100,000 at the end of five years (from Table 3 in the appendix on future value and present value tables: 7 percent for ten periods equals 0.508). The discount of $49,200 ($100,000 – $50,800) is the total interest cost and is amortized over the life of the bond. Methods of amortizing a discount are shown in the following sections.

Methods of Amortizing Bond Discounts

There are two ways of amortizing bond discounts or premiums: the straight-line method and the effective interest method. These methods are first applied to the amortization of bond discounts.

Straight-Line Method. The **straight-line method** is the easier of the two, with equal amortization of the discount for each interest period. In this case, suppose that the interest payment dates for the Vason bond issue are January 1 and July 1. The amount of the bond discount amortized and the interest cost for each semiannual period are figured in four steps, as follows:

1. Total interest payments = interest payments per year × life of bonds
   = 2 × 5 = 10

2. Amortization of bond discount per interest payment

$$= \frac{\text{bond discount}}{\text{total interest payments}} = \frac{\$3{,}851}{10} = \$385^*$$

   * Rounded

3. Regular cash interest payment
   = face value × face interest rate × time
   = $100,000 × .09 × ½ = $4,500

4. Total interest cost per interest date
   = interest payment + amortization of bond discount
   = $4,500 + $385 = $4,885

On July 1, 19x0, the semiannual interest date, the entry would be as follows:

July	1	Bond Interest Expense	4,885	
		Unamortized Bond Discount		385
		Cash (or Interest Payable)		4,500
		Paid (or accrued) semiannual interest to bondholders and amortized discount on 9%, 5-year bonds		

Note that the bond interest expense is $4,885, but the amount paid to the bondholders is the $4,500 face interest payment. The difference of $385 is the credit to Unamortized Bond Discount. This will lower the debit balance of the Unamortized Bond Discount account and raise the carrying value of the bonds payable by $385 each interest period. Assuming that no changes occur in the bond issue, this entry will be made every six months for the life of the bond. When the bond issue matures, there will be no balance in the Unamortized Bond Discount account, and the carrying value of the bonds will be $100,000. This is exactly equal to the amount due the bondholders.

Though the straight-line method has long been used, it has a certain weakness. Because the carrying value goes up each period and the bond interest expense stays the same, the straight-line method leads to a decreasing rate of interest over time. Conversely, using the straight-line method to amortize a premium leads to a rising rate of interest over time. For this reason, the APB has ruled that the straight-line method can be used only when it does not lead to a material difference from the effective interest method.[3] As will be seen, the effective interest rate method presupposes a constant rate of interest over the life of the bond. This rate will be constant if the total interest expense changes a little each interest period in response to the changing carrying value of the bond.

Alternative Method

Effective Interest Method. To compute the interest and amortization of bond discount for each interest period under the **effective interest method**, one must apply a constant interest rate to the carrying value of the bonds at the beginning of the interest period. This constant rate is equal to the market rate at the time the bonds are issued and is called the **effective rate**. The amount to be amortized becomes the difference between the interest computed using the effective rate and the actual interest paid to the bondholders.

As an example of this method, let us use the same facts presented earlier (a $100,000 bond issued at 9 percent, with a five-year maturity, interest to be paid twice a year). The market or effective rate of interest at the time was 10 percent. The bonds were sold for $96,149, at a discount of $3,851. The resulting amounts of interest and amortization of the bond discount are shown in Table 11-1.

Note the following explanations of how the amounts in the table are computed:

Column A: The carrying value of the bonds is the face value of the bonds less unamortized bond discount ($100,000 – $3,851 = **$96,149**).

Column B: The interest expense to be recorded is the effective interest. It is found by multiplying the carrying value of the bonds by the effective interest rate for one-half year ($96,149 × .10 × ½ = **$4,807**).

Column C: The interest paid in the period is the face value of the bonds multiplied by the face interest rate for the bonds multiplied by the interest time period ($100,000 × .09 × ½ = **$4,500**).

Column D: The discount amortized is the difference between the effective interest expense to be recorded and the interest to be paid on the interest payment date ($4,807 – $4,500 = **$307**).

Column E: The unamortized bond discount is the balance of the bond discount at the beginning of the period less the current period amortization of the discount ($3,851 – $307 = **$3,544**). The unamortized discount decreases each interest payment period because it is amortized as a portion of interest expense.

Column F: The carrying value of the bonds at the end of the period is the carrying value at the beginning of the period plus the amortization during the period ($96,149 + $307 = **$96,456**). Notice that the sum of the carrying value and unamortized discount (column F + column E) always equals the face value of the bonds ($96,456 + $3,544 = $100,000).

The entry to record the interest expense is exactly like the one used when the straight-line method is applied. However, the amounts debited

3. Accounting Principles Board, *Opinion No. 21*, "Interest on Receivables and Payables" (New York: American Institute of Certified Public Accountants, 1971), par. 15.

Table 11-1. Interest and Amortization of Bond Discount: Effective Interest Method

	A	B	C	D	E	F
Semi-annual Interest Period	Carrying Value at Beginning of Period	Semiannual Interest Expense at 10% to Be Recorded* (5% × A)	Semiannual Interest to Be Paid to Bondholders (4½% × $100,000)	Amortization of Discount (B – C)	Unamortized Bond Discount at End of Period	Carrying Value at End of Period (A + D)
0					$3,851	$ 96,149
1	$96,149	$4,807	$4,500	$307	3,544	96,456
2	96,456	4,823	4,500	323	3,221	96,779
3	96,779	4,839	4,500	339	2,882	97,118
4	97,118	4,856	4,500	356	2,526	97,474
5	97,474	4,874	4,500	374	2,152	97,848
6	97,848	4,892	4,500	392	1,760	98,240
7	98,240	4,912	4,500	412	1,348	98,652
8	98,652	4,933	4,500	433	915	99,085
9	99,085	4,954	4,500	454	461	99,539
10	99,539	4,961 **	4,500	461	—	100,000

* Rounded to nearest dollar
** Error due to rounding

and credited to the various accounts are different. The entry for July 1, 19x0, using the effective interest method, would be:

July 1	Bond Interest Expense	4,807	
	Unamortized Bond Discount		307
	Cash (or Interest Payable)		4,500
	Paid (or accrued) semiannual interest to bondholders and amortized discount on 9%, 5-year bonds		

Note that an interest and amortization table does not have to be prepared to determine the amortization of discount for any one interest payment period. It is necessary only to multiply the carrying value by the effective interest rate and subtract the interest payment from the result. For example, the amount of discount to be amortized in the seventh interest payment period equals $412 [($98,240 × .05) – $4,500].

Visual Summary of Effective Interest Method. The effect of the amortization of bond discount using the effective interest method on carrying value and interest expense may be seen visually in Figure 11-2 (based on the data from Table 11-1). Note that initially the carrying value (issue price) is less than the face value, but that it gradually increases toward the face value over the life of the bond issue. Note also that interest expense

Figure 11-2. Carrying Value and Interest Expense—Bonds Issued at a Discount

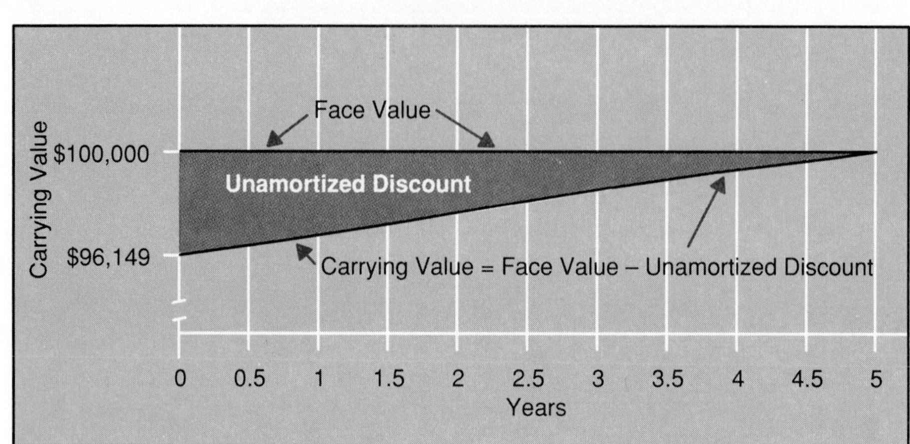

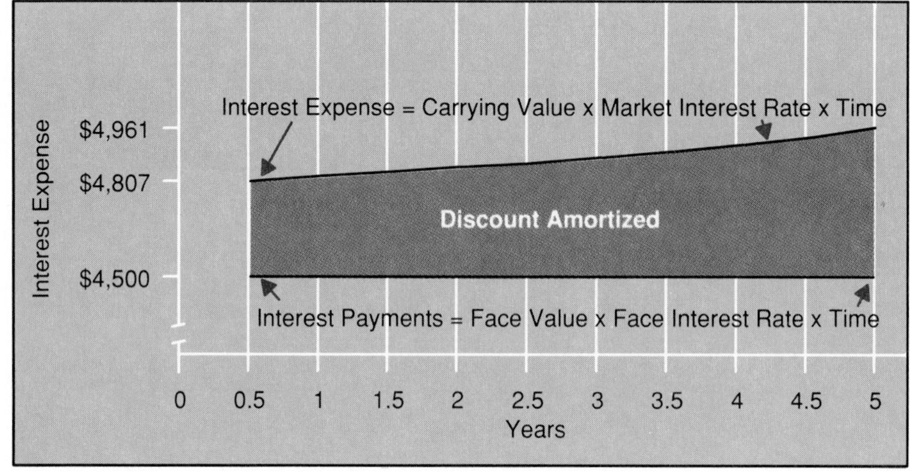

exceeds interest payments by the amount of the discount amortized. Interest expense increases gradually over the life of the bond because it is based on the gradually increasing carrying value (multiplied by the market interest rate).

Amortizing Bond Premiums

OBJECTIVE 4b *Amortize bond premiums by using the straight-line and effective interest methods*

Recall that under another assumption (page 549) Vason Corporation issued $100,000 of five-year bonds at a premium because the market rate of interest of 8 percent was less than the face interest rate of 9 percent. The bonds were sold for $104,100, resulting in an unamortized bond premium of $4,100. In a manner similar to the methods shown for amortizing bond discounts, the bond premium must be amortized over the life of the bond in order that it may be matched to its effects on interest expense during that period. In the following sections, the total interest cost is calculated and the bond premium is amortized using the straight-line and effective interest methods.

Calculation of Total Interest Cost

Since the bondholders paid in excess of face value for the bonds, the premium of $4,100 ($104,100 – $100,000) represents an amount that the bondholders will not receive at maturity. The premium is in effect a reduction, in advance, of the total interest paid on the bonds over the life of the bond issue. The total interest cost over the issue's life may be computed as follows:

Cash to be paid to bondholders	
Face value at maturity	$100,000
Interest payments ($100,000 × .09 × 5 years)	45,000
Total cash paid to bondholders	$145,000
Less cash received from bondholders	104,100
Total interest cost	$ 40,900

Or alternatively:

Interest payments ($100,000 × .09 × 5 years)	$ 45,000
Less bond premium	4,100
Total interest cost	$ 40,900

Note that total interest payments of $45,000 exceed total interest costs of $40,900 by $4,100, or the amount of the bond premium.

Methods of Amortizing Bond Premiums

As with bond discounts, the two methods of amortizing the bond premium are the straight-line method and the effective interest method. Both are discussed below.

Straight-Line Method. Under the straight-line method, the bond premiums are spread evenly over the life of the bond issue. As with bond discounts, the amount of the bond premium amortized and the interest cost for each semiannual period are computed in the following four steps:

1. Total interest payments = interest payments per year × life of bonds
$$= 2 \times 5$$
$$= 10$$

2. Amortization of bond premium per interest payment
$$= \frac{\text{bond premium}}{\text{total interest payments}}$$
$$= \frac{\$4{,}100}{10}$$
$$= \$410$$

3. Regular cash interest payment
   = face value × face interest rate × time
   = $100,000 × .09 × ½
   = $4,500

4. Total interest cost per interest date
   = interest payment – amortization of bond premium
   = $4,500 – $410
   = $4,090

On July 1, 19x0, the semiannual interest date, the entry would be as follows:

July	1	Bond Interest Expense	4,090	
		Unamortized Bond Premium	410	
		Cash (or Interest Payable)		4,500
		Paid (or accrued) semiannual interest to bondholders and amortized premium on 9%, 5-year bonds		

Note that the bond interest expense is $4,090, but the amount received by the bondholders is the $4,500 face interest payment. The difference of $410 is the debit to Unamortized Bond Premium. This will lower the credit balance of the Unamortized Bond Premium account and the carrying value of the bonds payable by $410 each interest period. Assuming that the bond issue remains unchanged, the same entry will be made every six months over the life of the bond issue. When the bond issue matures, there will be no balance in the Unamortized Bond Premium account, and the carrying value of the bonds payable will be $100,000. This is exactly equal to the amount due the bondholders. As noted before, the straight-line method should be used only when it does not lead to a material difference from the effective interest method.

Alternative Method

Effective Interest Method. Under the straight-line method, the real or effective interest rate is constantly changing even though the interest expense is fixed, because the effective interest rate is determined by comparing the fixed interest expense with a carrying value that is changing as a result of amortizing the discount or premium. To apply a fixed interest rate over the life of the bonds based on the actual market rate at the time of the bond issue requires the use of the effective interest method, as was shown previously in regard to the amortization of bond discounts. Under this method the interest expense decreases slightly each period (see Table 11-2, column B) because the amount of the bond premium amortized increases slightly (column D). This occurs because a fixed rate is applied each period to the gradually decreasing carrying value (see column A).

Table 11-2. Interest and Amortization of Bond Premium: Effective Interest Method

	A	B	C	D	E	F
Semiannual Interest Period	Carrying Value at Beginning of Period	Semiannual Interest Expense at 8% to Be Recorded* (4% × A)	Semiannual Interest to Be Paid to Bondholders (4½% × $100,000)	Amortization of Premium (C – B)	Unamortized Bond Premium at End of Period	Carrying Value at End of Period (A – D)
0					$4,100	$104,100
1	$104,100	$4,164	$4,500	$336	3,764	103,764
2	103,764	4,151	4,500	349	3,415	103,415
3	103,415	4,137	4,500	363	3,052	103,052
4	103,052	4,122	4,500	378	2,674	102,674
5	102,674	4,107	4,500	393	2,281	102,281
6	102,281	4,091	4,500	409	1,872	101,872
7	101,872	4,075	4,500	425	1,447	101,447
8	101,447	4,058	4,500	442	1,005	101,005
9	101,005	4,040	4,500	460	545	100,545
10	100,545	3,955 **	4,500	545	—	100,000

* Rounded to nearest dollar
** Error due to rounding

The first interest payment is recorded as follows:

July 1	Bond Interest Expense	4,164	
	Unamortized Bond Premium	336	
	Cash (or Interest Payable)		4,500
	Paid (or accrued) semiannual interest to bondholders and amortized premium on 9%, 5-year bonds		

Note that the unamortized bond premium (column E) decreases gradually to zero as the carrying value decreases to the face value (column F). To find the amount of premium amortization in any one interest payment period, we subtract the effective interest expense (the carrying value times the effective interest rate, column B) from the interest payment (column C). In semiannual interest period 5, for example, the amortization of premium equals $393 [$4,500 – ($102,674 × .04)].

Visual Summary of Effective Interest Method. The effect of the amortization of bond premium using the effective interest method on carrying value and interest expense may be seen visually in Figure 11-3 (based on data from Table 11-2). Note that initially the carrying value (issue price) is greater than the face value, but that it gradually decreases toward the face

Figure 11-3. Carrying Value and Interest Expense—Bonds Issued at a Premium

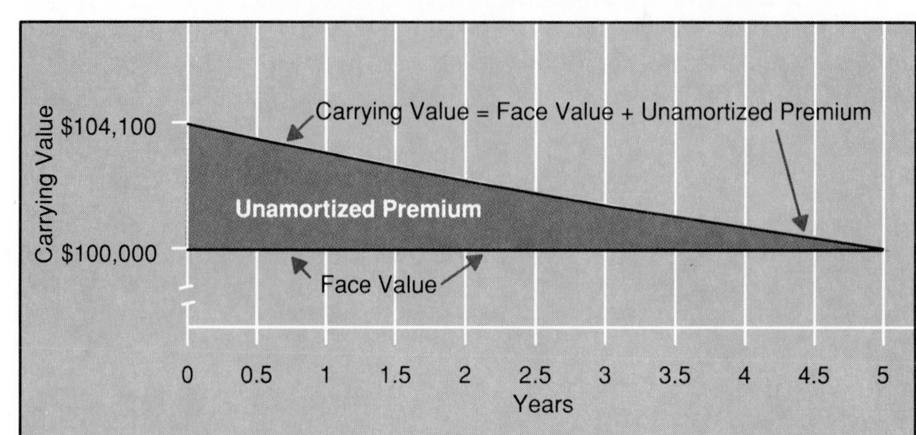

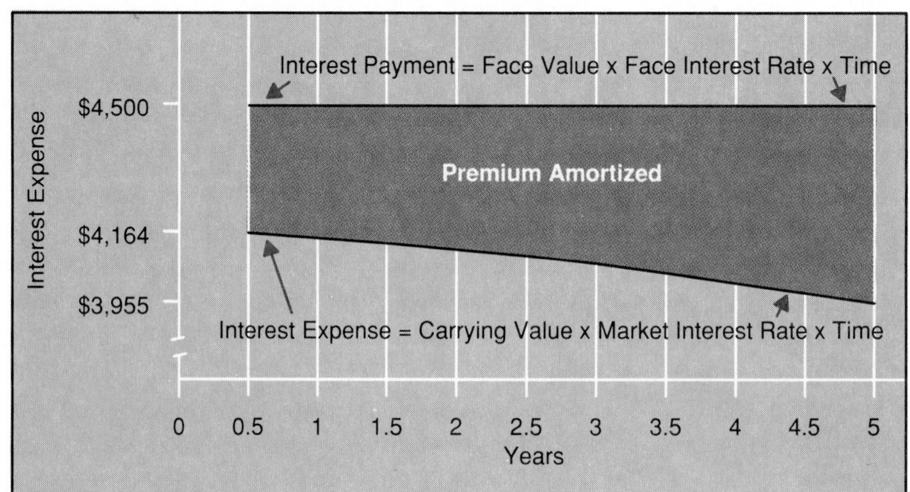

value over the life of the bond issue. Note also that interest payments exceed interest expense by the amount of the premium amortized, and that interest expense decreases gradually over the life of the bond because it is based on the gradually decreasing carrying value (multiplied by the market interest rate).

Other Bonds Payable Issues

Several other issues arise in accounting for bonds payable. Among these are sales of bonds between interest payment dates, year-end accrual of bond interest expense, retirement of bonds, and conversion of bonds into common stock.

Sales of Bonds Between Interest Dates

OBJECTIVE 5 *Account for bonds issued between interest dates and make year-end adjustments*

Bonds may be issued on their interest date, as in the example above, but many times they are issued between interest payment dates. The generally accepted method of handling bonds issued in this manner is to collect from the investor the interest that has accrued since the last interest payment date. Then when the next interest period arrives, the corporation pays the investor the interest for the entire period. Thus the interest collected when bonds are sold is returned to the investor on the next interest payment date.

There are two reasons for following this procedure. The first is a practical one. If a company were to issue bonds on several different days and did not collect the accrued interest, records would have to be maintained for each bondholder and date of purchase. In such a case, the interest due each bondholder would have to be computed on the basis of different time periods. Clearly, large bookkeeping costs would be incurred under such a system. On the other hand, if accrued interest is collected when the bonds are sold, then on the interest payment date the corporation can pay the interest due for the entire period, eliminating the extra computations and costs.

The second reason for collecting accrued interest in advance is that when this amount is netted against the full interest paid on the interest payment date, the resulting interest expense is the amount for the time the money has been borrowed.

For example, assume that the Vason Corporation sold $100,000 of 9 percent, five-year bonds for face value on May 1, 19x0, rather than on January 1, 19x0, the issue date. The entries to record the sale of the bonds and payment of interest on July 1, 19x0 follow:

May 1	Cash	103,000	
	Bond Interest Expense		3,000
	Bonds Payable		100,000
	Sold 9%, 5-year bonds at face value plus four months' accrued interest $100,000 × .09 × 4/12 = $3,000		

As shown, Cash is debited for the amount received, $103,000 (face value of $100,000 plus four months' accrued interest of $3,000). Bond Interest Expense is credited for the $3,000 of accrued interest, and Bonds Payable is credited for the face value of $100,000. When the first semiannual interest payment date arrives, the following entry is made:

July 1	Bond Interest Expense	4,500	
	Cash (or Interest Payable)		4,500
	Paid (or accrued) semiannual interest $100,000 × .09 × 1/2 = $4,500		

Note that here the entire half-year interest is both debited to Bond Interest Expense and credited to Cash, because the corporation only pays bond

Figure 11-4. Effect on Bond Interest Expense When Bonds Are Issued Between Interest Dates

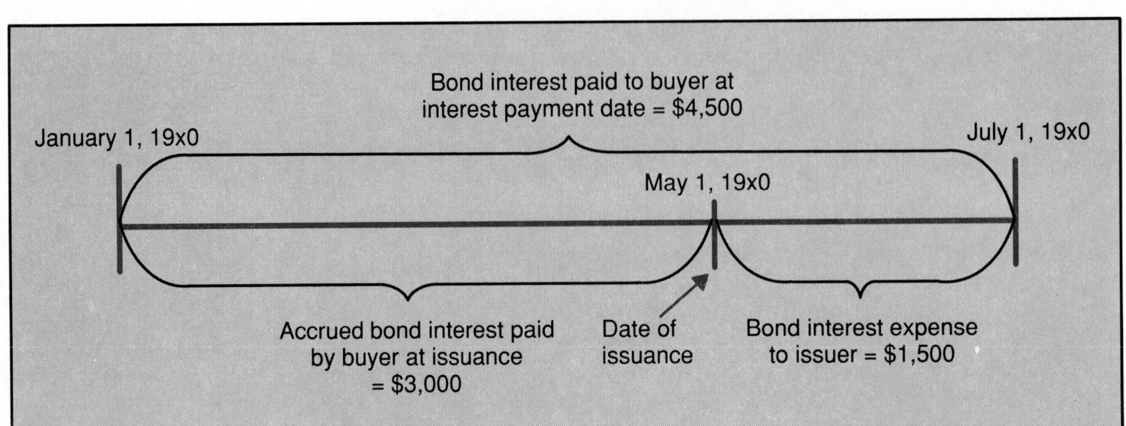

interest once every six months, in full six-month amounts. This process is illustrated by Figure 11-4. The actual interest expense for the two months that the bonds were outstanding is $1,500. This amount is the net balance of the $4,500 debit to Bond Interest Expense on July 1 less the $3,000 credit to Bond Interest Expense on May 1. We can also see these steps clearly in the posted entries in the ledger account for Bond Interest Expense.

Bond Interest Expense — **Account No. 723**

Date		Item	Post. Ref.	Debit	Credit	Balance Debit	Balance Credit
19x0							
May	1				3,000		3,000
July	1			4,500		**1,500**	

Year-End Accrual for Bond Interest Expense

It is not often that bond interest payment dates will correspond to a company's fiscal year. An adjustment therefore must be made at the end of the accounting period to accrue the interest expense on the bonds from the last payment date to the end of the fiscal year. Further, if there is any discount or premium on the bonds, it must also be amortized for the fractional period.

Remember that in an earlier example, Vason Corporation issued $100,000 in bonds on January 1, 19x0 at 104.1 (see page 549). The company's fiscal year ends September 30, 19x0. In the period since the interest payment and amortization of premium on July 1, three months' interest has accrued, and the following adjusting entry under the effective interest method must be made:

Sept. 30	Bond Interest Expense	2,075.50	
	Unamortized Bond Premium	174.50	
	Interest Payable		2,250.00
	Accrued interest on 9% bonds payable for 3 months and amortized one-half of the premium for second interest payment period		

This entry covers one-half of the second interest period. Unamortized Bond Premium is debited for $174.50, which is one-half of $349, the amortization of premium for the second period from Table 11-2. Interest Payable is credited for $2,250, three months' interest on the face value of the bonds ($100,000 × .09 × 1/4). The net debit figure of $2,075.50 ($2,250 – $174.50) is the bond interest expense for the three-month period.

When the January 1, 19x1 payment date arrives, the entry to pay the bondholders and amortize the premium is as follows:

Jan. 1	Bond Interest Expense	2,075.50	
	Interest Payable	2,250.00	
	Unamortized Bond Premium	174.50	
	Cash		4,500.00
	Paid semiannual interest including interest previously accrued and amortized the premium for the period since the end of the fiscal year		

As shown here, one-half ($2,250) of the amount paid ($4,500) was accrued on September 30. Unamortized Bond Premium is debited for the remaining amount to be amortized for the period ($349.00 – $174.50 = $174.50). The resulting bond interest expense is the amount that applies to the three-month period from October 1 to January 1.

Bond discounts are recorded at year end in the same way as bond premiums. The difference is that the amortization of bond discounts will increase interest expense instead of decreasing it as a premium does.

Retirement of Bonds

OBJECTIVE 6
Account for the retirement of bonds and the conversion of bonds into stock

Most bond issues provide a call feature. This feature gives the corporation a chance to buy back and retire the bonds at a given price, usually above face value, before maturity. Such bonds are known as **callable bonds**. They give the corporation flexibility in financing its operations. For example, if bond interest rates drop, the company can call its bonds and reissue debt at a lower interest rate. The bond indenture will state the time period and the prices at which the bonds can be redeemed. When a bond issue is retired before its maturity date, it is called **early extinguishment of debt**.

As an illustration of this feature, assume that Vason Corporation may call or retire the $100,000 bond issued at a premium (page 549) at 105, and that it decides to do so on July 1, 19x3. To avoid complexity, this illustration assumes retirement on an interest payment date. Because the bonds were issued on January 1, 19x0, the retirement takes place on the seventh interest payment date. Assume that the entry for the interest payment (which must be made) and the amortization of premium have been made. The entry to retire the bonds is as follows:

19x3				
July	1	Bonds Payable	100,000	
		Unamortized Bond Premium	1,447	
		Loss on Retirement of Bonds	3,553	
		Cash		105,000
		Retired 9% bonds at 105		

In this entry, the cash paid is the face value times the call price ($100,000 × 1.05 = $105,000). The unamortized bond premium can be found in column E of Table 11-2. The loss on retirement of bonds occurs because the call price of the bonds is greater than the carrying value ($105,000 – $101,447 = $3,553). The loss, if material, is presented as an extraordinary item on the income statement, as explained in the chapter on retained earnings and corporate income statements.

Sometimes a rise in the market interest rate will cause the market value of the bonds to fall considerably below their face amount. If it has the cash to do so, the company may find it advantageous to purchase the bonds on the open market and retire them, rather than waiting and paying them off at face value. A gain is recognized for the difference between the purchase price of the bonds and the face value of the retired bonds. For example, assume that because of a rise in interest rates, Vason Corporation was able to purchase the $100,000 bond issue on the open market at 85, making it unnecessary to call the bonds at the higher price of 105. Then the entry would be as follows:

19x3				
July	1	Bonds Payable	100,000	
		Unamortized Bond Premium	1,447	
		Cash		85,000
		Gain on Retirement of Bonds		16,447
		Purchased and retired 9% bonds at 85		

Conversion of Bonds into Common Stock

Bonds that may be exchanged for other securities of the corporation (in most cases common stock) are called **convertible bonds**. The conversion feature gives the investor a chance to make more money, because if the market price of the common stock rises, the value of the bond rises. However, if the price of the common stock does not rise, the investor still holds the bond and receives the periodic interest payment as well as the principal at the maturity date.

When a bondholder wishes to convert bonds into common stock, the rule is that the common stock is recorded at the carrying value of the bonds. The bond liability and associated unamortized discount or premium are written off the books. For this reason, no gain or loss is recorded on the transaction. For example, suppose that Vason Corporation's bonds are not called on July 1, 19x3. Instead, the corporation's bondholders decide to convert all the bonds to $8 par value common stock under a convertible provision of 40 shares of common stock for each $1,000 bond. The entry would be:

19x3				
July	1	Bonds Payable	100,000	
		Unamortized Bond Premium	1,447	
		Common Stock		32,000
		Paid-in Capital in Excess of Par Value, Common		69,447
		Converted 9% bonds payable into common stock at a rate of 40 shares for each $1,000 bond		

The unamortized bond premium is found in column E of Table 11-2. At a rate of 40 shares for each $1,000 bond, 4,000 shares will be issued at a total par value of $32,000 (4,000 × $8). The Common Stock account is credited for the amount of the par value of the stock issued. Another account, called Paid-in Capital in Excess of Par Value, Common, is credited for the difference between the carrying value of the bonds and the par value of the stocks issued ($101,447 − $32,000 = $69,447). No gain or loss is recorded.

DECISION POINT

Inco Limited

The *Wall Street Journal* reported that Inco Limited was issuing that day $172.5 million in 7¾ percent convertible debentures (unsecured bonds) due in 2016. The debentures, which are callable, could be converted into common shares of the company at a conversion price of $38.25. In other words, a holder of a $1,000 bond could convert it into 26.14 ($1,000 ÷ $38.25) shares of common stock.[4] On the previous day, March 19, the company's common stock sold on the New York Stock Exchange for $31.50. What advantages and disadvantages did Inco's management have to weigh in deciding to issue convertible bonds rather than another security, such as nonconvertible bonds or common stock?

Several factors are favorable to the issuance of convertible bonds. First, the interest rate of 7¾ percent is less than the company would have to offer if the bonds were not convertible, because an investor is willing to give up some current interest for the prospect that the value of the underlying stock will increase, and therefore the value of the bonds will also increase. For example, if the common stock rises from a price of $31.50 to above $38.25 per share, the value of the bond will begin to rise, based on changes in the price of the common stock, not on changes in interest rates. If the

4. "$172,500,000 Inco Limited 7¾% Convertible Debentures Due 2016," *Wall Street Journal*, March 20, 1991.

common stock were to rise to $50, the market value of a $1,000 bond would rise to $1,307 (26.14 shares × $50). A second advantage of issuing convertible bonds is that Inco does not have to give up any current control of the company. Bondholders do not have voting rights. Only stockholders do. A third benefit is tax savings. Interest paid on bonds is fully deductible for income tax purposes, whereas cash dividends on common stock are not deductible. Fourth, the company's income will be favorably affected if the company earns a return that exceeds the interest cost of the debentures. For example, if the company uses the funds for a purpose that earns 16 percent, this return will be more than twice the interest cost of 7 3/4 percent. Successful use of debt in this way is called *leverage*. Finally, the convertible feature offers financial flexibility. If the price of the stock rises above $38.25, management can avoid repaying the bonds by calling them for redemption, thereby forcing the bondholders to convert their bonds into common stock. The bondholders will agree to convert because the common stock they will receive will be worth more than the amount they would receive if the bonds were redeemed.

One major disadvantage of convertible debentures is that interest must be paid semiannually. Inability to make an interest payment could force the company into bankruptcy. Common stock dividends are declared and paid only when the board of directors decides to do so. Another disadvantage is that when the bonds are converted, they become new outstanding common stock and no longer carry the features of bonds. Inco's management obviously feels that the advantages of its choice outweigh the disadvantages. ■

Other Long-Term Liabilities

A company may have long-term liabilities other than bonds. The most common are mortgages payable, installment notes payable, long-term leases, pensions, and postretirement benefits.

Mortgages Payable

OBJECTIVE 7
Explain the basic features of mortgages payable, installment notes payable, long-term leases, pensions, and postretirement benefits as long-term liabilities

A **mortgage** is a long-term debt secured by real property. It is usually paid in equal monthly installments. Each monthly payment includes interest on the debt and a reduction in the debt. To illustrate this point, Table 11-3 shows the first three monthly payments on a $50,000, 12 percent mortgage. The mortgage was obtained on June 1, and the monthly payments are $800. According to the table, the entry to record the July 1 payment would be as follows:

July	1	Mortgage Payable	300	
		Mortgage Interest Expense	500	
		Cash		800
		Made monthly mortgage payment		

Table 11-3. Monthly Payment Schedule on $50,000, 12 Percent Mortgage

	A	B	C	D	E
Payment Date	Unpaid Balance at Beginning of Period	Monthly Payment	Interest for 1 Month at 1% on Unpaid Balance* (1% × A)	Reduction in Debt (B – C)	Unpaid Balance at End of Period (A – D)
June 1					$50,000
July 1	$50,000	$800	$500	$300	49,700
Aug. 1	49,700	800	497	303	49,397
Sept. 1	49,397	800	494	306	49,091

* Rounded to nearest dollar

Note from the entry and from Table 11-3 that the July 1 payment represents interest expense of $500 ($50,000 × .12 × 1/12) and a reduction in the debt of $300 ($800 – $500). Therefore, the unpaid balance is reduced by the July payment to $49,700. The interest expense for August is slightly less than July's because of this decrease in the debt.

Installment Notes Payable

Long-term notes may be paid at the maturity date by making a lump sum payment that includes the amount borrowed plus interest. Often, however, the terms of the note call for a series of periodic payments. When this occurs, the notes payable are called **installment notes payable** because each payment includes the interest from the previous payment to date plus a repayment of part of the amount borrowed. For example, assume that on December 31, 19x1, $100,000 is borrowed on a 15 percent installment note to be paid annually over five years. The entry to record the note is as follows:

19x1			
Dec. 31	Cash	100,000	
	Notes Payable		100,000
	Borrowed $100,000 at 15% on 5-year installment note		

Payments of Accrued Interest Plus Equal Amounts of Principal. Installment notes most often call for payments consisting of accrued interest plus equal amounts of principal repayment. The amount of each installment will decrease because the amount of principal on which the accrued interest is owed decreases by the amount of the principal repaid. Banks use installment notes to finance equipment purchases by businesses; these notes are also common for other kinds of purchases when payment is spread over several years. They can be set up on a revolving basis, whereby the borrower may borrow additional funds as the installments are paid. Moreover, the interest rate charged on the note may be adjusted periodically by the bank as market rates of interest change.

Under this method of payment, the principal declines by an equal amount each year for five years, or by $20,000 per year ($100,000 ÷ 5 years). The interest is calculated on the balance of the note that remains each year. Since the balance of the note declines each year, the amount of interest will also decline. For example, the entries for the first two payments of the installment note are as follows:

19x2			
Dec. 31	Notes Payable	20,000	
	Interest Expense	15,000	
	Cash		35,000
	First installment payment on note $100,000 × .15 = $15,000		
19x3			
Dec. 31	Notes Payable	20,000	
	Interest Expense	12,000	
	Cash		32,000
	Second installment payment on note $80,000 × .15 = $12,000		

Note that the amount of the payment has decreased from $35,000 to $32,000 because the amount owed on the note has decreased from $100,000 to $80,000. The difference of $3,000 is the interest on the $20,000 that was repaid in 19x2. Each subsequent payment will decrease by $3,000, as the note itself decreases by $20,000 each year until it is fully paid. This example assumes that the repayment of principal and the interest rate remain the same from year to year.

Accrued Interest Plus Increasing Amounts of Principal. Less commonly, the terms of an installment note, like those used for leasing of equipment, may call for equal periodic payments, such as monthly or yearly, of accrued interest plus increasing amounts of principal. Under this method, the interest is deducted from the equal payments to determine the amount by which the principal will be reduced each year. This procedure, presented in Table 11-4, is very similar to that shown above for mortgages. Each equal payment of $29,833 is allocated between interest and reduction in debt (principal). Each year the interest is calculated on the remaining principal. As the principal decreases, the annual interest also decreases, and since the payment remains the same, the amount by which the principal decreases becomes larger each year. The entries for the first two years, with data taken from Table 11-4, are as follows:

19x2			
Dec. 31	Notes Payable	14,833	
	Interest Expense	15,000	
	Cash		29,833
	First installment payment on note		

19x3			
Dec. 31	Notes Payable	17,058	
	Interest Expense	12,775	
	Cash		29,833
	Second installment payment on note		

Similar entries will be made for the next three years.

A natural question to ask is: How is the equal annual payment calculated? Since the $100,000 borrowed is the present value of the five equal annual payments at 15 percent interest, present value tables may be used to calculate the annual payments. Using Table 4 from the appendix on future value and present value tables, the calculation is made as follows:

Periodic payment × factor (Table 4 in the present value appendix: 15%, 5 years) = present value
Periodic payment × 3.352 = $100,000
Periodic payment = $100,000 ÷ 3.352 = $29,833

Table 11-4 shows that five equal annual payments of $29,833 at 15 percent will reduce the principal balance to zero (except for the error due to rounding).

Long-Term Leases

There are several ways in which a company may obtain new operating assets. One way is to borrow the money and buy the asset. Another is to rent the equipment on a short-term lease. A third way is to obtain the

Table 11-4. Payment Schedule on $100,000, 15 Percent Installment Note

	A	B	C	D	E
Payment Date	Unpaid Principal at Beginning	Equal Annual Payment	Interest for 1 Year at 15% on Unpaid Principal* (15% × A)	Reduction in Principal (B – C)	Unpaid Principal at End of Period (A – D)
					$100,000
19x2	$100,000	$29,833	$15,000	$14,833	85,167
19x3	85,167	29,833	12,775	17,058	68,109
19x4	68,109	29,833	10,216	19,617	48,492
19x5	48,492	29,833	7,274	22,559	25,933
19x6	25,933	29,833	3,900**	25,933	—

* Rounded to the nearest dollar

** The last year's interest equals the installment payment minus the remaining unpaid principal ($29,833 – $25,933 = $3,900) and does not exactly equal $3,890 ($25,933 × .15) because of cumulative rounding errors.

equipment on a long-term lease. The first two methods cause no unusual accounting problems. In the first case, the asset and liability are recorded at the amount paid, and the asset is subject to periodic depreciation. In the second case, the lease is short-term or cancelable, and the risks of ownership lie with the lessor. This type of lease is called an **operating lease**. It is proper accounting to treat operating lease payments as an expense and to debit the amount of each monthly payment to Rent Expense.

The third case, a long-term lease, is one of the fastest-growing ways of financing operating equipment in the United States today. It has several advantages. For instance, it requires no immediate cash payment. The rental payment is deducted in full for tax purposes. And it costs less than a short-term lease. Acquiring the use of a plant asset under a long-term lease does cause several accounting problems, however. Often, such leases may not be canceled. Also, their length may be about the same as the useful life of the asset. Finally, they may provide for the lessee to buy the asset at a nominal price at the end of the lease. The lease is much like an installment purchase because the risks of ownership lie with the lessee. Not only the lessee company's available assets but its legal obligations (liabilities) increase, because it must make a number of payments over the life of the asset.

Noting this problem, the Financial Accounting Standards Board has described such a long-term lease as a **capital lease**. This term reflects the provisions of the lease, which make the transaction more like a purchase or sale on installment. The FASB has ruled that in the case of a capital lease, the lessee must record an asset and a long-term liability equal to the present value of the total lease payments during the lease term. In doing so, the lessee must use the present value at the beginning of the lease.[5] In much the same way as mortgage payments, each lease payment becomes partly interest expense and partly a repayment of debt. Further, depreciation expense is figured on the asset and entered on the records of the lessee.

Suppose, for example, that Isaacs Company enters into a long-term lease for a machine used in its manufacturing operations. The lease terms call for an annual payment of $4,000 for six years, which approximates the useful life of the machine. (See Table 11-5.) At the end of the lease period, the title to the machine passes to Isaacs. This lease is clearly a capital lease and should be recorded according to FASB *Statement No. 13*.

A lease is a periodic payment for the right to use an asset or assets. Present value techniques, explained in the chapter on current liabilities and the time value of money, can be used to value the asset and the corresponding liability associated with a capital lease. If Isaacs' usual interest cost is 16 percent, the present value of the lease payments may be computed as follows:

Periodic payment	×	factor (Table 4 in the present value appendix: 16%, 6 years)	=	present value
$4,000	×	3.685	=	$14,740

5. *Statement of Financial Accounting Standards No. 13*, "Accounting for Leases" (Stamford, Conn.: Financial Accounting Standards Board, 1976), par. 10.

Table 11-5. Payment Schedule on 16 Percent Capital Lease

	A	B	C	D
Year	Lease Payment	Interest (16%) on Unpaid Obligation (16% of D)	Reduction of Lease Obligation (A – B)	Balance of Lease Obligation
Beginning				$14,740.00
1	$ 4,000	$2,358.40	$ 1,641.60	13,098.40
2	4,000	2,095.74	1,904.26	11,194.14
3	4,000	1,791.06	2,208.94	8,985.20
4	4,000	1,437.63	2,562.37	6,422.83
5	4,000	1,027.65	2,972.35	3,450.48
6	4,000	549.52*	3,450.48	—
	$24,000	$9,260.00	$14,740.00	

* The last year's interest equals the lease payment minus the remaining balance of the lease obligation ($549.52 = $4,000 – $3,450.48) and does not exactly equal $552.08 ($3,450.48 × 0.16) because of cumulative rounding errors.

The entry to record the lease contract is

Equipment Under Capital Lease	14,740	
Obligations Under Capital Lease		14,740

Equipment Under Capital Lease is classified as a long-term asset; Obligations Under Capital Lease is classified as a long-term liability. Each year, Isaacs must record depreciation on the leased asset. If we assume straight-line depreciation, a six-year life, and no salvage value, the entry will be

Depreciation Expense	2,456.67	
Accumulated Depreciation, Leased Equipment Under Capital Lease		2,456.67

The amount of interest expense for each year would be computed by multiplying the interest rate (16 percent) by the amount of the remaining lease obligation. Table 11-5 shows these calculations. Using the data presented in Table 11-5, the first lease payment would be recorded as follows:

Interest Expense (col. B)	2,358.40	
Obligations Under Capital Lease (col. C)	1,641.60	
Cash		4,000.00

Pensions

Most employees who work for medium-sized and large companies are covered by some sort of pension plan. A **pension plan** is a contract between the company and its employees wherein the company agrees to pay benefits to employees after retirement. Most companies contribute the full cost of the pension, but sometimes the employees also pay part of their salary or wages toward their pension. The contributions from both parties are generally paid into a **pension fund**, from which benefits are paid out to retirees. In most cases, pension benefits consist of monthly payments to employees after retirement and other payments on death or disability.

There are two kinds of pension plans. Under *defined contribution plans*, the employer is required to contribute an annual amount determined in the current year on the basis of agreements between the company and its employees or resolution of the board of directors. Retirement payments will depend on the amount of pension payments the accumulated contributions can support. Under *defined benefit plans*, the employer's required annual contribution is the amount required to fund pension liabilities that arise as a result of employment in the current year but whose amount will not be finally determined until the retirement and death of the persons currently employed. Here the amount of the contribution required in the current year depends on a fixed amount of future benefits but uncertain current contributions, whereas under a defined contribution plan, the uncertain future amount of pension liabilities depends on the cumulative amounts of fixed current contributions.

Accounting for annual pension expense under defined contribution plans is simple. After determining what contribution is required, Pension Expense is debited and a liability (or Cash) is credited.

Accounting for annual expense under defined benefit plans is one of the most complex topics in accounting; thus the intricacies are reserved for advanced courses. In concept, however, the procedure is simple.

First, the amount of pension expense is determined. Then, if the amount of cash contributed to the fund is less than the pension expense, a liability results, which is reported on the balance sheet. If the amount of cash paid to the pension plan exceeds the pension expense, a prepaid expense arises and appears on the asset side of the balance sheet. For example, the December 31, 1986 annual report for The Goodyear Tire & Rubber Company included among other assets on the balance sheet deferred pension plan costs of $320.2 million.

In accordance with *Statement No. 87*, all companies should use the same actuarial method to compute pension expense.[6] However, because many factors, such as average remaining service life of active employees, expected long-run return on pension plan assets, and expected future salary increases, must be estimated, the computation of pension expense is not simple. In addition, actuarial terminology further complicates pension accounting. In nontechnical terms, the pension expense for the year includes not only the cost of the benefits earned by people working during the year but interest costs on the total pension obligation (which is calculated as the present value of future benefits to be paid) and other adjustments. These costs are reduced by the expected return on the pension fund assets.

6. *Statement of Financial Accounting Standards No. 87*, "Employers' Accounting for Pensions" (Stamford, Conn.: Financial Accounting Standards Board, 1985).

Beginning in 1989, all employers whose pension plans do not have sufficient assets to cover the present value of their pension benefit obligations (on a termination basis) must record the amount of the shortfall as a liability on their balance sheets. The investor will no longer have to read the notes to the financial statements to learn whether the pension plan is fully funded. However, if a pension plan does have sufficient assets to cover its obligations, then no balance sheet reporting is required or permitted.

Other Postretirement Benefits

In addition to pension benefits, many companies provide health care and other benefits for employees after retirement. In the past, these **other postretirement benefits** were accounted for on a cash basis; that is, they were expensed when the benefits were paid, after the employee had retired. The FASB has concluded, however, that these benefits are earned by the employee, and that, in accordance with the matching rule, they should be estimated and accrued while the employee is still working.[7] These estimates must take into account assumptions about retirement age, mortality, and, most significantly, future trends in health care benefits. As in accounting for pension benefits, these future benefits should also be discounted to the current period. In a field test conducted by the Financial Executives Research Foundation, it was determined that this move to accrual accounting increases postretirement benefits by two to seven times the amount recognized on a cash basis. Although the new requirement will not be effective for businesses until 1993, some companies are electing to implement it early. For example, IBM Corporation reported its first quarterly loss ever in the first quarter of 1991 when it recorded a one-time $2.26 billion charge associated with the adoption of Statement No. 106.[8] This charge covers costs of postretirement benefits earned by employees in the past up to the current date. Future quarters will bear only costs associated with earnings in those quarters.

Chapter Review

Review of Learning Objectives

1. **Identify and contrast the major characteristics of bonds.**
   When bonds are issued, the corporation enters into a contract with the bondholders, called a bond indenture. The bond indenture identifies the major conditions of the bonds. A corporation may issue several types of

7. *Statement of Financial Accounting Standards No. 106*, "Employers' Accounting for Postretirement Benefits Other Than Pensions" (Stamford, Conn.: Financial Accounting Standards Board, 1990).
8. "Earnings Drop and One-Time Charge Produce $1.7 Billion Loss at IBM," *International Herald Tribune*, April 13–14, 1991.

bonds, each having different characteristics. For example, a bond issue may or may not require security (secured versus unsecured). It may be payable at a single time (term) or at several times (serial). The holder may receive interest automatically (registered) or may have to return coupons to receive interest (coupon bond). The bond may be callable or convertible into other securities.

2. **Record the issuance of bonds at face value and at a discount or premium.**
When bonds are issued, the bondholders will pay an amount equal to, greater than, or less than the face value of the bonds. A bondholder will pay face value for the bonds when the interest rate on the bonds approximates the market rate for similar investments. The issuing corporation records the issuance of bonds as a long-term liability, called Bonds Payable, equal to the face value of the bonds.
Bonds are issued at less than face value when the bond interest rate is below the market rate for similar investments. The difference between face value and issue price is called a discount and is debited to Unamortized Bond Discount.
If the interest rate on bonds is greater than the return on similar investments, investors will be willing to pay more than face value for the bonds. The difference between issue price and face value is called a premium and is credited to Unamortized Bond Premium.

3. **Determine the value of bonds using present values.**
The value of a bond may be determined by summing the present values of (a) the series of fixed interest payments of a bond issue and (b) the single payment of the face value at maturity. The third and fourth tables in the appendix on future value and present value tables should be used in making those computations.

4. **Amortize (a) bond discounts and (b) bond premiums by using the straight-line and effective interest methods.**
When bonds are sold at a premium or discount, the result is an adjustment of the interest rate on the bonds from the face rate to an effective rate that is close to the market rate when the bonds were issued. Therefore, bond discounts or premiums have the effect of increasing or decreasing the interest paid on the bonds over their life. Under these conditions, it is necessary to amortize the premium or discount over the life of the bonds by either the straight-line or the effective interest method.
The straight-line method allocates a fixed portion of the bond discount or premium each interest period to adjust the interest payment to interest expense. The effective interest method, which is used when the effects of amortization are material, results in a constant rate of interest on the carrying value of the bonds. To find the interest and the amortization of premiums or discounts, we apply the effective interest rate to the carrying value (face value plus premium or minus discount) of the bonds at the beginning of the interest period. The amount of premium or discount to be amortized is the difference between the interest figured by using the effective rate and that obtained by using the stated or face rate. The effects of the effective interest method on bonds issued at par value, at a discount, and at a premium may be summarized as follows:

	Bonds Issued at		
	Face Value	Discount	Premium
Trend in Carrying Value over Bond Term	Constant	Increasing	Decreasing
Trend in Interest Expense over Bond Term	Constant	Increasing	Decreasing
Interest Expense vs. Interest Payments	Interest expense = interest payments	Interest expense > interest payments	Interest expense < interest payments
Classification of Bond Discount or Premium		Contra-liability (deducted from Bonds Payable)	Liability (added to Bonds Payable)

5. **Account for bonds issued between interest dates and make year-end adjustments.**
   If bonds are sold on a date between the interest payment dates, the issuing corporation collects from the investors the interest that has accrued since the last interest payment date. When the next interest payment date arrives, the corporation pays the bondholders interest for the entire interest period.
   When the end of a corporation's fiscal year does not correspond to interest payment dates, the corporation must accrue bond interest expense from the last interest payment date to the end of the company's fiscal year. This accrual results in the inclusion of the interest expense in the year incurred.

6. **Account for the retirement of bonds and the conversion of bonds into stock.**
   Callable bonds may be retired before maturity at the option of the issuing corporation. The call price is usually greater than the face value of the bonds, so the corporation usually recognizes a loss on the retirement of the bonds. An extraordinary gain may also be recognized on early extinguishment of debt, which occurs when a company purchases its bonds on the open market. This retirement method can be used when a rise in the market interest rate causes the market value of the bonds to fall.
   Convertible bonds allow the bondholder to convert bonds to stock in the issuing corporation. In this case, the common stocks issued are recorded at the carrying value of the bonds being converted. No gain or loss is recognized.

7. **Explain the basic features of mortgages payable, installment notes payable, long-term leases, pensions, and postretirement benefits as long-term liabilities.**
A mortgage is a type of long-term debt secured by real property. It is usually paid in equal monthly installments. Each payment is partly interest expense and partly debt repayment. Installment notes payable are long-term notes that are paid in a series of payments. Part of each payment is interest and part is repayment of principal. If a long-term lease is a capital lease, the risks of ownership lie with the lessee. Like a mortgage payment, each lease payment is partly interest and partly reduction of debt. For a capital lease, then, both an asset and a long-term liability should be recorded. The liability should be equal to the present value at the beginning of the lease of the total lease payments during the lease term. The recorded asset is subject to depreciation. Pension expense must be recorded in the current period. Other postretirement benefits should be estimated and accrued in the period when the employee is working.

Review of Concepts and Terminology

The following concepts and terms were introduced in this chapter:

(L.O. 1) **Bond:** A security, usually long-term, representing money borrowed by a corporation from the investing public.

(L.O. 1) **Bond certificate:** Evidence of a company's debt to the bondholder.

(L.O. 1) **Bond indenture:** A supplementary agreement to a bond issue that defines the rights, privileges, and limitations of bondholders.

(L.O. 1) **Bond issue:** The total number of bonds that are issued at one time.

(L.O. 6) **Callable bonds:** Bonds that a corporation may buy back and retire at a given price, usually above face value, before maturity.

(L.O. 7) **Capital lease:** A long-term lease in which the risk of ownership lies with the lessee, and whose terms resemble a purchase or sale.

(L.O. 6) **Convertible bonds:** Bonds that may be exchanged for other securities of the corporation, usually common stock.

(L.O. 1) **Coupon bonds:** Bonds that generally are not registered with the issuing corporation but instead bear interest coupons stating the amount of interest due and the payment date.

(L.O. 2) **Discount:** The amount by which the face value of a bond exceeds the issue price, for bonds issued when the market rate of interest is greater than the face interest rate.

(L.O. 6) **Early extinguishment of debt:** The purchase by a company of its own bonds on the open market in order to retire the debt at less than face value.

(L.O. 4) **Effective interest method:** A method of amortizing bond discounts or premiums in which a constant interest rate, the effective rate (market rate) at the time the bonds were issued, is applied to the carrying value of the bonds at the beginning of each interest period.

(L.O. 4) **Effective rate:** The interest rate used to amortize bond interest discounts and premiums under the effective interest method; equal to the market rate of interest at the time the bonds are issued.

(L.O. 2) **Face interest rate:** The rate of interest paid to the bondholders based on the face value or principal of the bonds.

(L.O. 7) **Installment notes payable:** Long-term notes payable in a series of payments, of which part of each is interest and part is repayment of principal.

(L.O. 1) **Junk bonds:** Unsecured, high-risk, long-terms bonds that carry high rates of interest.

(L.O. 2) **Market interest rate:** The rate of interest paid in the market on bonds of similar risk.

(L.O. 7) **Mortgage:** A type of long-term debt secured by real property that is usually paid in equal monthly installments.

(L.O. 7) **Operating lease:** A short-term, cancelable lease for which the risks of ownership lie with the lessor, and whose payments are recorded as a rent expense.

(L.O. 7) **Other postretirement benefits:** Health care and other nonpension benefits that are paid for a worker after retirement but that are earned while the employee is working.

(L.O. 7) **Pension fund:** A fund established through contributions from an employer and sometimes employees that pays pension benefits to employees after retirement or on their death or disability.

(L.O. 7) **Pension plan:** A contract between a company and its employees under which the company agrees to pay benefits to employees after their retirement.

(L.O. 2) **Premium:** The amount by which the issue price of a bond exceeds the face value; for bonds issued when the market rate of interest is less than the face interest rate.

(L.O. 1) **Registered bonds:** Bonds for which the names and addresses of the bond owners are recorded with the issuing company.

(L.O. 1) **Secured bonds:** Bonds that give the bondholders a pledge of certain assets of the company as a guarantee of repayment.

(L.O. 1) **Serial bonds:** A bond issue with several different maturity dates.

(L.O. 4) **Straight-line method:** A method of amortizing bond discounts or premiums in which amortization of the discount or premium is equal for each interest period over the life of the bond.

(L.O. 1) **Term bonds:** Bonds of a bond issue that all mature at the same time.

(L.O. 1) **Unsecured bonds (debentures):** Bonds issued on the general credit of a company.

(L.O. 4) **Zero coupon bonds:** Bonds that do not pay periodic interest, but are simply a promise to pay a fixed amount at the maturity date. The only interest earned by the buyer or paid by the issuer is the discount on the issue date.

Review Problem
Interest and Amortization of Bond Discount, Bond Retirement, and Bond Conversion

(L.O. 2, 4, 6) When the Merrill Manufacturing Company was expanding its metal window division in Utah, the company did not have enough capital to finance the expansion. Thus, management sought and received approval from the board of directors to issue bonds for the activity. The company planned to issue

$5,000,000 of 8 percent, five-year bonds in 19x1. Interest would be paid on December 31 and June 30 of each year. The bonds would be callable at 104, and each $1,000 bond would be convertible into 30 shares of $10 par value common stock.

The bonds were sold at 96 on January 1, 19x1 because the market rate for similar investments was 9 percent. The company decided to amortize the bond discount by using the effective interest method. On July 1, 19x3, management called and retired half the bonds, and investors converted the other half into common stock.

Required

1. Prepare an interest and amortization schedule for the first five interest payment dates.
2. Prepare the journal entries to record the sale of the bonds, the first two interest payments, the bond retirement, and the bond conversion.

Answer to Review Problem

1. Schedule for first five periods prepared

Interest and Amortization of Bond Discount

Semiannual Interest Payment	Carrying Value of Beginning of Period	Semiannual Interest Expense* (9% × ½)	Semiannual Interest Paid per Period (8% × ½)	Amortization of Discount	Unamortized Bond Discount at End of Period	Carrying Value at End of Period
Jan. 1, 19x1					$200,000	$4,800,000
June 30, 19x1	$4,800,000	$216,000	$200,000	$16,000	184,000	4,816,000
Dec. 31, 19x1	4,816,000	216,720	200,000	16,720	167,280	4,832,720
June 30, 19x2	4,832,720	217,472	200,000	17,472	149,808	4,850,192
Dec. 31, 19x2	4,850,192	218,259	200,000	18,259	131,549	4,868,451
June 30, 19x3	4,868,451	219,080	200,000	19,080	112,469	4,887,531

* Rounded to nearest dollar

2. Journal entries prepared

19x1			
Jan. 1	Cash	4,800,000	
	Unamortized Bond Discount	200,000	
	Bonds Payable		5,000,000
	Sold $5,000,000 of 8% bonds at 96		
June 30	Bond Interest Expense	216,000	
	Unamortized Bond Discount		16,000
	Cash		200,000
	Paid semiannual interest and amortized discount on 8%, five-year bonds		

Date		Account	Debit	Credit
Dec.	31	Bond Interest Expense	216,720	
		Unamortized Bond Discount		16,720
		Cash		200,000
		Paid semiannual interest and amortized discount on 8%, five-year bonds		
19x3				
July	1	Bonds Payable	2,500,000	
		Loss on Retirement of Bonds Payable	156,235	
		Unamortized Bond Discount		56,235
		Cash		2,600,000
		Called \$2,500,000 of 8% bonds and retired them at 104 \$112,469 × ½ = \$56,235*		
	1	Bonds Payable	2,500,000	
		Unamortized Bond Discount		56,234
		Common Stock		750,000
		Paid-in Capital in Excess of Par Value		1,693,766
		Converted \$2,500,000 of 8% bonds into common stock: 2,500 × 30 shares = 75,000 shares 75,000 shares × \$10 = \$750,000 \$112,469 − \$56,235 = \$56,234* \$2,500,000 − (\$56,234 + \$750,000) = \$1,693,766		

* Rounded

Chapter Assignments

Discussion Questions

1. What is the difference between a bond certificate, a bond issue, and a bond indenture? What are some examples of items found in a bond indenture?
2. What are the essential differences between (a) secured versus debenture bonds, (b) term versus serial bonds, and (c) registered versus coupon bonds?
3. Napier Corporation sold \$500,000 of 5 percent bonds on the interest payment date. What would the proceeds from the sale be if the bonds were issued at 95, at 100, and at 102?
4. If you were buying a bond on which the face interest rate was less than the market interest rate, would you expect to pay more or less than par value for the bonds? Why?
5. Why does the amortization of a bond discount increase interest expense to an amount greater than interest paid? Why does a premium have the opposite effect?
6. When the effective interest rate method of amortizing a bond discount or premium is used, why does the amount of interest expense change from period to period?
7. When bonds are issued between interest dates, why is it necessary for the issuer to collect an amount equal to accrued interest from the buyer?
8. Why would a company want to exercise the callable provision of a bond when it can wait longer to pay off the debt?

9. What are the advantages of convertible bonds to the company issuing them and to the investor?
10. What are the two components of a uniform monthly mortgage payment?
11. Under what conditions is a long-term lease called a capital lease? Why should the accountant record both an asset and a liability in connection with this type of lease? What items should appear on the income statement as the result of such a lease?
12. What is a pension plan? What assumptions must be made to account for the expenses of such a plan?
13. What is the difference between a defined contribution plan and a defined benefit plan? In general, how is expense determined under each?
14. What are other postretirement benefits, and how does the matching rule apply to them?

Communication Skills Exercises

Communication 11-1. Bond Interest Rates and Market Prices *(L.O. 1)*

RJR Nabisco's debt restructuring was the subject of the decision point that appeared at the beginning of this chapter. The following statement relates to this plan:

> The refinancing plan's chief objective is to purge away most of the reset bonds of 2007 and 2009. These bonds have proved to be an immense headache for RJR. . . . That's because the bonds' interest rate must be reset so that they trade at full face value. The bonds had sunk to a deep discount earlier this year, raising the prospect that RJR might have to accept a painfully high reset rate of 20% or more to meet its reset obligations.[9]

What is a "deep discount," and what causes bonds to sell at a deep discount? Who loses when they do? What does "the bonds' interest rate must be reset so that they trade at full value" mean? Why would this provision in the covenant be "an immense headache" to RJR Nabisco?

Communication 11-2. Pros and Cons of Convertible Bonds *(L.O. 6)*

Sumitomo Corporation, a Japanese company that is one of the world's leading merchandisers of commodities, industrial goods, and consumer goods, has a number of issues of long-term debt. Among these issues are almost ¥20,000 million ($142 million) of $1\frac{3}{5}$% convertible bonds payable in Japanese yen in the year 2002.[10] (The interest rate illustrates the historically low rates in Japan.) The bonds are unsecured and are convertible into common stock at ¥1,074.60 per share. What reasons can you suggest for the company's issuing bonds that are convertible into common stock rather than simply issuing nonconvertible bonds or issuing common stock directly? Are there any disadvantages to this approach?

Communication 11-3. Lease Financing *(L.O. 7)*

Federal Express Corporation, known for overnight delivery and distribution of high-priority goods and documents throughout the world, has an extensive fleet of aircraft and vehicles. Under lease commitments in its 1989 annual report, the company states that it "utilizes certain aircraft, land, facilities, and equipment under capital and operating leases which expire at various dates through 2026. In addition, supplemental aircraft are leased under agreements

9. Based on George Anders, "RJR Nabisco Moves to Retire Most Troublesome Junk Bonds," *The Asian Wall Street Journal*, July 17, 1990. Reprinted by permission of *The Asian Wall Street Journal*, © 1990 Dow Jones & Company, Inc. All Rights Reserved Worldwide.
10. Excerpts from the 1989 Annual Report of Sumitomo Corporation. Used with permission.

which generally provide for cancellation upon 60 days' notice." The annual report further states that the minimum commitments for capital leases and noncancelable operating leases for 1992 are $67,135,000 and $265,712,000, respectively.[11] What is the difference between a capital lease and an operating lease? How does the accounting treatment for the two types of leases differ? How do you interpret management's reasoning in placing some aircraft under capital leases and others under operating leases? Why do you think the management of Federal Express leases most of its aircraft instead of buying them?

Communication 11-4. Effects of Taxes on Business Decisions *(L.O. 7)*

MidStates Financial Corporation is seeing substantial effects from recent tax law changes. *Crain's Chicago Business* reports:

> The new tax laws, which increase the length of time over which a business must depreciate capital equiment, have decreased the tax benefits of outright purchases. Lease payments are deductible as company expenses and do not appear as liabilities on a company's balance sheet. . . .
>
> Says Gerald Tax, president of the 12-year-old Mid-States Financial Corp. of Schaumburg: "Our industry used to specialize in business startups. Now we are dealing more with established companies with a track record of creditworthiness."
>
> Businesses most likely to lease equipment are in the printing, machine tool, computer or telecommunications industries, Mr. Tax says. . . .
>
> "In some cases the monthly leasing rate is less than a company would pay to a bank on a loan basis for the same equipment," Mr. Tax says.
>
> "When we write up a lease, we figure in the future residual value of the equipment. When the lease expires, we can resell or release the equipment."[12]

Why does a longer required useful life decrease the tax advantage of owning equipment? What advantage arises when lease payments are deductible as expenses and do not appear as liabilities on the balance sheet? Why are lease payments sometimes smaller than what would have to be paid on a bank loan? Can you think of an advantage to the longer useful lives of the new tax laws?

Communication 11-5. Basic Research Skills *(L.O. 2)*

In your school or local library, obtain a copy of a recent issue of the *Wall Street Journal*. In the newspaper, find Section C, "Money & Investing," and turn to the page where the New York Exchange Bonds are listed. Note, first, the Dow Jones Bond Averages of 20 bonds, 10 utilities, and 10 industrials. Are the averages above or below 100? Is this a premium or a discount? Is the market rate of interest above or below the face rate of the average bond? Now identify three bonds from those listed. Choose one that sells at a discount, one that sells at a premium, and one that sells for approximately 100. For each bond, write the name of the company, the face interest rate, the year the bond is due, the current yield, and the current closing market price. (Some bonds have the letters *cv* in the yield column. This means the bonds are convertible.) For each bond, explain the relationship among the face interest rate, the current yield, and the closing price. What other factors affect the current yield of a bond? Be prepared to discuss your results in class.

11. Excerpts from the 1989 Annual Report used by permission of Federal Express Corporation.
12. Excerpts reprinted with permission from the May 23, 1988 issue of *Crain's Chicago Business*. Copyright © 1991 by Crain Communications Inc.

Classroom Exercises[13]

Exercise 11-1. Journal Entries for Interest Using the Straight-Line Method
(L.O. 2, 4)

Plantation Corporation issued $2,000,000 in 10½ percent, ten-year bonds on February 1, 19x1, at 104. The semiannual interest payment dates are February 1 and August 1.

Prepare journal entries for the issue of the bonds by Plantation on February 1, 19x1 and the first two interest payments on August 1, 19x1 and February 1, 19x2, using the straight-line method (ignore year-end accruals).

Exercise 11-2. Journal Entries for Interest Using the Straight-Line Method
(L.O. 2, 4)

Brennan Corporation issued $4,000,000 in 8½ percent, five-year bonds on March 1, 19x1, at 96. The semiannual interest payment dates are March 1 and September 1.

Prepare journal entries for the issue of the bonds by Brennan on March 1, 19x1 and the first two interest payments on September 1, 19x1 and March 1, 19x2, using the straight-line method (ignore year-end accruals).

Exercise 11-3. Journal Entries for Interest Using the Effective Interest Method
(L.O. 2, 4)

The Mayfair Drapery Company sold $500,000 of its 9½ percent, twenty-year bonds on April 1, 19xx, at 106. The semiannual interest payment dates are April 1 and October 1. The effective interest rate is approximately 8.9 percent. The company's fiscal year ends September 30.

Prepare journal entries to record the sale of the bonds on April 1, the accrual of interest and amortization of premium on September 30, and the first interest payment on October 1. Use the effective interest method to amortize the premium.

Exercise 11-4. Journal Entries for Interest Using the Effective Interest Method
(L.O. 2, 4)

On March 1, 19x1, the Clayton Corporation issued $600,000 of five-year, 10 percent bonds. The semiannual interest payment dates are March 1 and September 1. Because the market rate for similar investments was 11 percent, the bonds had to be issued at a discount. The discount on the issuance of the bonds was $24,335. The company's fiscal year ends February 28.

Prepare journal entries to record the bond issue on March 1, 19x1; the payment of interest and amortization of the discount on September 1, 19x1; the accrual of interest and amortization of the discount on February 28, 19x2; and the payment of interest on March 1, 19x2. Use the effective interest method.

Exercise 11-5. Journal Entries for Interest Payments Using the Effective Interest Method
(L.O. 4)

The long-term debt section of the Discovery Corporation's balance sheet at the end of its fiscal year, December 31, 1991, is as follows:

Long-Term Liabilities		
Bonds Payable—8%, interest payable 1/1 and 7/1, due 12/31/06	$500,000	
Less Unamortized Bond Discount	40,000	$460,000

Prepare the journal entries relevant to the interest payments on July 1, 1992, December 31, 1993, and January 1, 1994. Assume an effective interest rate of 10 percent.

13. Bond interest rates are most often quoted in eighths of a percent. Some exercises and problems in this chapter quote the rates in tenths of a percent to ease the burden of computation.

Exercise 11-6. Valuing Bonds Using Present Value *(L.O. 3)*

Lakeshore, Inc. is considering two bond issues. (a) One is a $400,000 bond issue that pays semiannual interest of $32,000 and is due in twenty years. (b) The other is a $400,000 bond issue that pays semiannual interest of $30,000 and is due in fifteen years. Assume that the market rate of interest for each bond is 12 percent.

Calculate the amount that Lakeshore, Inc. will receive if both bond issues occur. (Calculate the present value of each bond issue and sum.)

Exercise 11-7. Valuing Bonds Using Present Value *(L.O. 3)*

Using the present value tables in the appendix on future value and present value tables, calculate the issue price of a $600,000 bond issue in each of the following independent cases, assuming that interest is paid semiannually:

a. a ten-year, 8% bond issue; market rate of interest is 10%.
b. a ten-year, 8% bond issue; market rate of interest is 6%.
c. a ten-year, 10% bond issue; market rate of interest is 8%.
d. a twenty-year, 10% bond issue; market rate of interest is 12%.
e. a twenty-year, 10% bond issue; market rate of interest is 6%.

Exercise 11-8. Zero Coupon Bonds *(L.O. 3)*

The Commonwealth of Kentucky needs to raise $50,000,000 for highway repairs. Officials are considering issuing zero coupon bonds, which have no periodic interest payments. The current market rate of interest for the bonds is 10 percent. What face value of bonds must be issued to raise the needed funds, assuming that the bonds will be due in thirty years and compounded annually? How would your answer change if the bonds were due in fifty years?

How would both answers change if the market rate of interest were 8 percent instead of 10 percent?

Exercise 11-9. Time Value of Money and Early Extinguishment of Debt *(L.O. 3, 6)*

Nelson, Inc. has a $700,000, 8 percent bond issue that was issued a number of years ago at face value. There are now ten years left on the bond issue, and the market rate of interest is 16 percent. Interest is paid semiannually.

1. Figure the current market value of the bond issue, using present value tables.
2. Record the retirement of the bonds, assuming that the company purchases the bonds on the open market at the calculated value.

Exercise 11-10. Bond Issue Entries *(L.O. 2, 5)*

Microfilm is authorized to issue $900,000 in bonds on June 1. The bonds carry a face interest rate of 9 percent, which is to be paid on June 1 and December 1.

Prepare journal entries for the issue of the bonds by Microfilm under the independent assumptions that (a) the bonds are issued on September 1 at 100 and (b) the bonds are issued on June 1 at 105.

Exercise 11-11. Sales of Bonds Between Interest Dates *(L.O. 5)*

Tripp Corporation sold $200,000 of 12 percent, ten-year bonds for face value on September 1, 19xx. The issue date of the bonds was May 1, 19xx.

1. Record the sale of the bonds on September 1 and the first semiannual interest payment on November 1, 19xx.

2. The company's fiscal year ends on December 31 and the above is its only bond issue. What is the bond interest expense for the year ending December 31, 19xx?

Exercise 11-12. Year-End Accrual of Bond Interest *(L.O. 2, 4, 5)*

Rex Corporation issued $500,000 of 9 percent bonds on October 1, 19x1, at 96. The bonds are dated October 1 and pay interest semiannually. The market rate of interest is 10 percent, and the company's year end is December 31.

Prepare the entries to record the issuance of the bonds, the accrual of the interest on December 31, 19x1, and the payment of the first semiannual interest on April 1, 19x2. Assume that the company does not use reversing entries and uses the effective interest method to amortize bond discount.

Exercise 11-13. Bond Retirement Journal Entry *(L.O. 6)*

The Figaro Corporation has outstanding $800,000 of 8 percent bonds callable at 104. On September 1, immediately after recording the payment of the semiannual interest and amortization of discount, the unamortized bond discount equaled $21,000. On that date, $480,000 of the bonds were called and retired.

Prepare the entry to record the retirement of the bonds on September 1.

Exercise 11-14. Bond Conversion Journal Entry *(L.O. 6)*

The Gallery Corporation has $400,000 of 6 percent bonds outstanding. There is $20,000 of unamortized discount remaining on these bonds after the July 1, 19x8 semiannual interest payment. The bonds are convertible at the rate of 40 shares of $5 par value common stock for each $1,000 bond. On July 1, 19x8, bondholders presented $300,000 of the bonds for conversion.

Prepare the journal entry to record the conversion of the bonds.

Exercise 11-15. Mortgage Payable *(L.O. 7)*

Inland Corporation purchased a building by signing a $150,000 long-term mortgage with monthly payments of $2,000. The mortgage carries an interest rate of 12 percent.

1. For the first three months, prepare a monthly payment schedule showing the monthly payment, the interest for the month, the reduction in debt, and the unpaid balance. (Round to the nearest dollar.)
2. Prepare a journal entry to record the purchase and the first two monthly payments.

Exercise 11-16. Recording Lease Obligations *(L.O. 7)*

Profile Corporation has leased a piece of equipment that has a useful life of twelve years. The terms of the lease are $21,500 per year for twelve years. Profile is currently able to borrow money at a long-term interest rate of 15 percent.

1. Calculate the present value of the lease.
2. Prepare the journal entry to record the lease agreement.
3. Prepare the entry to record depreciation of the equipment for the first year using the straight-line method.
4. Prepare the entries to record the lease payments for the first two years.

Exercise 11-17. Installment Notes Payable: Unequal Payments *(L.O. 7)*

Assume that on December 31, 19x1, $40,000 is borrowed on a 12 percent installment note, to be paid annually over four years. Prepare the entry to record the note and the first two annual payments, assuming that the principal is paid in equal annual installments and the interest on the unpaid balance accrues annually. How would your answer change if the interest rate changed to 13 percent in the second year?

Exercise 11-18. Installment Notes Payable: Equal Payments *(L.O. 7)*

Assume that on December 31, 19x1, $40,000 is borrowed on a 12 percent installment note, to be paid in equal annual payments over four years. Calculate to the nearest dollar the amount of each equal payment, using the appropriate present value table (Table 4 from the appendix on future value and present value tables). Prepare a payment schedule table similar to Table 11-4, and record the first two annual payments.

Interpretation Cases from Business

ICB 11-1. The Times Mirror Company[14] *(L.O. 2, 4)*

The Times Mirror Company, publisher of the *Los Angeles Times*, *Newsday*, and other publications, engaged in the following long-term debt transactions in 1986, according to the long-term debt note in its annual report:

a. On April 1, 1986, the company issued $100,000,000 of ten-year, $8\frac{1}{4}$ percent notes with semiannual interest payments on April 1 and October 1 at face value.
b. On October 15, 1986, the company redeemed, prior to maturity dates, all its outstanding 10 percent notes that had been issued in connection with the acquisition of Call-Chronicle Newspapers, Inc. The redemption price was $65,000,000 plus accrued interest. The carrying value of the notes on October 15 was $65,000,000 less unamortized discount of $7,223,000. The semiannual interest dates are June 15 and December 15.
c. On December 8, 1986, the company issued $100,000,000 of 8 percent notes due December 15, 1996, with semiannual interest payments on June 15 and December 15. The notes were issued at face value plus accrued interest.

Required

1. Prepare journal entries to record the above three transactions.
2. Prepare the entries on the interest payment dates of October 1 and December 15, 1986, and the year-end adjustment on December 31, 1986.
3. What was the total interest expense during 1986 for the three long-term notes issued, assuming that Unamortized Discount was $7,493,000 at the beginning of the year?

ICB 11-2. Franklin Savings Association *(L.O. 2, 3, 4)*

A notice appeared in the November 16, 1984, *Wall Street Journal* stating that Franklin Savings Association of Kansas was issuing $2.9 billion in zero coupon bonds. "The Bonds do not pay interest periodically. The only scheduled payment to the holder of a Bond will be the amount at maturity," the ad read. The details of two components of the issue were as follows:

$500,000,000 Bonds due December 12, 2014, at 3.254%
$500,000,000 Bonds due December 12, 2024, at 1.380%

14. Excerpts from the 1986 Annual Report used by permission of the Times Mirror Company. Copyright © 1986.

plus accrued amortization, if any, of the original issue discount from December 12, 1984, to date of delivery.

Required

1. Assuming all the bonds were issued on December 12, 1984, make the general journal entry to record each component shown above.
2. Determine the approximate effective interest rate on each of the two components of the bond issue. Assume that interest is compounded annually. **Hint:** Use Table 3 in the appendix on future value and present value tables.
3. Prepare general journal entries to record bond interest expense for each of the first two years (December 12, 1985 and 1986) on the component of the bond due in 2014 (ignore effects of fiscal year ends). What advantages or disadvantages are there to Franklin in issuing zero coupon bonds?

ICB 11-3.
UAL Corporation[15]
(L.O. 7)

UAL Corporation, owner of United Airlines, states in its 1990 annual report that it leased 203 of its aircraft, 24 of which were capital leases. United has leased many of these planes for terms of ten to twenty-two years. Some leases carry the right of first refusal to purchase the aircraft at fair market value at the end of the lease term and others at fair market value or a percentage of cost.

On United's December 31, 1990, balance sheet the following accounts appear (in thousands):

Owned—Flight Equipment	$5,677,428
Capital Leases—Flight Equipment	420,452
Current Obligations Under Capital Leases	27,174
Long-Term Obligations Under Capital Leases	361,246

Expected payments in 1991 for operating leases are $652,691 and for capital leases are $64,889.

Required

1. How would you characterize the differences in aircraft leases described in the first paragraph as operating leases or those as capital leases? Explain your answer.
2. Explain in general the difference in accounting (a) for operating and capital leases and (b) for Owned—Flight Equipment and Capital Leases—Flight Equipment.

Problem Set A

Problem 11A-1.
Bond Transactions—Straight-Line Method
(L.O. 2, 4, 5)

Marconi Corporation has $10,000,000 of 10½ percent, twenty-year bonds dated June 1, with interest payment dates of May 30 and November 30. The company's fiscal year ends December 31. It uses the straight-line method to amortize premium or discount.

Required

1. Assume that the bonds were issued at 103 on June 1. Prepare general journal entries for June 1, November 30, and December 31.
2. Assume that the bonds were issued at 97 on June 1. Prepare general journal entries for June 1, November 30, and December 31.

15. Excerpts from the 1990 Annual Report used by permission of UAL Corporation. Copyright © 1990 by UAL, Inc.

3. Assume that the bonds were issued at face value plus accrued interest on August 1. Prepare general journal entries for August 1, November 30, and December 31.

Problem 11A-2. Bond Transactions—Effective Interest Method
(L.O. 2, 4, 5)

Aparicio Corporation has $8,000,000 of 9½ percent, twenty-five-year bonds dated March 1, with interest payable on March 1 and September 1. The company's fiscal year ends on November 30. It uses the effective interest method to amortize premium or discount. Round amounts to nearest dollar.

Required

1. Assume that the bonds were issued at 102.5 on March 1, to yield an effective interest rate of 9.2 percent. Prepare general journal entries for March 1, September 1, and November 30.
2. Assume that the bonds were issued at 97.5 on March 1, to yield an effective interest rate of 9.8 percent. Prepare general journal entries for March 1, September 1, and November 30.
3. Assume that the bonds were issued on June 1 at face value plus accrued interest. Prepare general journal entries for June 1, September 1, and November 30.

Problem 11A-3. Bonds Issued at Discount and at Premium
(L.O. 2, 4, 5)

Chambliss Corporation sold bonds twice during 19x2. A summary of the transactions involving these bonds follows.

19x2

Jan. 1 Issued $3,000,000 of 9⁹⁄₁₀ percent, ten-year bonds dated January 1, 19x2, with interest payable on December 31 and June 30. The bonds were sold at 102.6, resulting in an effective interest rate of 9.4 percent.

Mar. 1 Issued $2,000,000 of 9⅕ percent, ten-year bonds dated March 1, 19x2, with interest payable March 1 and September 1. The bonds were sold at 98.2, resulting in an effective interest rate of 9.5 percent.

June 30 Paid semiannual interest on the January 1 issue and amortized the premium, using the effective interest method.

Sept. 1 Paid semiannual interest on the March 1 issue and amortized the discount, using the effective interest method.

Dec. 31 Paid the semiannual interest on the January 1 issue and amortized the premium, using the effective interest method.

31 Made an end-of-year adjusting entry to accrue the interest on the March 1 issue and amortize two-thirds of the discount applicable to the second interest period.

19x3

Mar. 1 Paid the semiannual interest on the March 1 issue and amortized the remainder of the discount applicable to the second interest period.

Required

Prepare general journal entries to record the bond transactions. Round amounts to nearest dollar.

Problem 11A-4. Bond and Mortgage Transactions Contrasted *(L.O. 2, 4, 5, 7)*

Munson Grocery Stores, Inc. is expanding its operations by buying a chain of four outlets in another city. To finance this purchase of land and buildings, Munson is getting a $2,000,000 mortgage that carries an interest rate of 12 percent and requires monthly payments of $27,000. To finance the rest of the purchase, Munson is issuing $2,000,000 of 12½ percent unsecured bonds due in twenty years, with interest payable December 31 and June 30.

The company's fiscal year ends March 31. Selected transactions related to these two financing activities are as follows:

Jan. 1 Issued the bonds for cash at 104 to yield an effective rate of 12 percent.
Feb. 1 Issued the mortgage in exchange for land and buildings. The land represents 15 percent of the purchase price.
Mar. 1 Made first mortgage payment.
31 Made the year-end adjusting entry to accrue interest on the bonds and amortize the premium, using the effective interest method.
Apr. 1 Made second mortgage payment.
May 1 Made third mortgage payment.
June 1 Made fourth mortgage payment.
30 Made the first semiannual interest payment on the bonds and amortized the premium for the time period since the end of the fiscal year.
July 1 Made fifth mortgage payment.
Dec. 1 Made tenth mortgage payment.
31 Made the second semiannual interest payment on the bonds and amortized the premium for the time period since the last payment.

Required

1. Prepare a payment schedule for the mortgage for ten months using these headings (round amounts to the nearest dollar): Payment Date, Unpaid Balance at Beginning of Period, Monthly Payment, Interest for One Month at 1% on Unpaid Balance, Reduction in Debt, and Unpaid Balance at End of Period.
2. Prepare the journal entries for the selected transactions. (Ignore the mortgage payments for August 1 through November 1.)

Problem 11A-5. Bond Interest and Amortization Table and Bond Retirements *(L.O. 2, 4, 6)*

In 19x1 Sharief Corporation was authorized to issue $3,000,000 of unsecured bonds, due March 31, 19x6. The bonds carried a face interest rate of 11⅗ percent, payable semiannually on March 31 and September 30, and were callable at 104 any time after March 31, 19x4. All the bonds were issued on April 1, 19x1 at 102.261, a price that yielded an effective interest of 11 percent.

On April 1, 19x4, Sharief Corporation called one-half of the outstanding bonds and retired them.

Required

1. Prepare a table similar to Table 11-2 to show the interest and amortization of the bond premium for ten interest payment periods, using the effective interest method (round results to nearest dollar).
2. Prepare general journal entries for the bond issue, interest payments and amortization of bond premium, and bond retirement on the following dates: April 1, 19x1; September 30, 19x1; March 31, 19x4; April 1, 19x4; and September 30, 19x4.

Problem 11A-6. Comprehensive Bond Transactions
(L.O. 2, 4, 5, 6)

Over a period of three years, Henley Corporation, a company with a December 31 year end, engaged in the following transactions involving two bond issues:

19x1

July 1 Issued $10,000,000 of 12 percent convertible bonds at 96. The bonds are convertible into $20 par value common stock at the rate of 20 shares of stock for each $1,000 bond. Interest is payable on June 30 and December 31, and the market rate of interest is 13 percent.

Dec. 31 Made semiannual interest payment and amortized bond discount.

19x2

June 1 Issued $20,000,000 of 9 percent bonds at face value plus accrued interest. Interest is payable on February 28 and August 31. The bonds are callable at 105, and the market rate of interest is 9 percent.

30 Made semiannual interest payment on 12 percent bonds and amortized the bond discount.

Aug. 31 Made semiannual interest payment on 9 percent bonds.

Dec. 31 Made semiannual interest payment on 12 percent bonds, amortized discount, and accrued interest on 9 percent bonds.

19x3

Feb. 28 Made semiannual interest payment on 9 percent bonds.

June 30 Made semiannual interest payment on 12 percent bonds and amortized the bond discount.

July 1 Accepted for conversion into common stock all 12 percent bonds.

31 Called and retired all 9 percent bonds, including accrued interest.

Required

Prepare general journal entries to record the bond transactions, making all necessary accruals and using the effective interest method. (Round calculations to the nearest dollar.)

Problem Set B

Problem 11B-1. Bond Transactions— Straight-Line Method
(L.O. 2, 4, 5)

Dunston Corporation has $4,000,000 of $9\frac{1}{2}$ percent, twenty-five-year bonds dated March 1, with interest payable on March 1 and September 1. The company's fiscal year ends on November 30. It uses the straight-line method to amortize premium or discount.

Required

1. Assume that the bonds were issued at 103.5 on March 1. Prepare general journal entries for March 1, September 1, and November 30.
2. Assume that the bonds were issued at 96.5 on March 1. Prepare general journal entries for March 1, September 1, and November 30.
3. Assume that the bonds were issued on June 1 at face value plus accrued interest. Prepare general journal entries for June 1, September 1, and November 30.

Problem 11B-2. Bond Transactions—Effective Interest Method
(L.O. 2, 4, 5)

Marino Corporation has $10,000,000 of 10½ percent, twenty-year bonds dated June 1, with interest payment dates of May 30 and November 30. The company's fiscal year ends December 31. It uses the effective interest method to amortize premium or discount. Round amounts to nearest dollar.

Required

1. Assume that the bonds were issued at 103 on June 1, to yield an effective interest rate of 10.1 percent. Prepare general journal entries for June 1, November 30, and December 31.
2. Assume that the bonds were issued at 97 on June 1, to yield an effective interest rate of 10.9 percent. Prepare general journal entries for June 1, November 30, and December 31.
3. Assume that the bonds were issued at face value plus accrued interest on August 1. Prepare general journal entries for August 1, November 30, and December 31.

Problem 11B-3. Bonds Issued at Discount and at Premium
(L.O. 2, 4, 5)

Perennial Corporation issued bonds twice during 19x1. The transactions were as follows:

19x1

Jan. 1 Issued $1,000,000 of 9⅕ percent, ten-year bonds dated January 1, 19x1, with interest payable on June 30 and December 31. The bonds were sold at 98.1, resulting in an effective interest rate of 9.5 percent.

Apr. 1 Issued $2,000,000 of 9⅘ percent, ten-year bonds dated April 1, 19x1, with interest payable on March 31 and September 30. The bonds were sold at 102, resulting in an effective interest rate of 9.5 percent.

June 30 Paid semiannual interest on the January 1 issue and amortized the discount, using the effective interest method.

Sept. 30 Paid semiannual interest on the April 1 issue and amortized the premium, using the effective interest method.

Dec. 31 Paid semiannual interest on the January 1 issue and amortized the discount, using the effective interest method.

31 Made an end-of-year adjusting entry to accrue interest on the April 1 issue and amortize one-half the premium applicable to the second interest period.

19x2

Mar. 31 Paid semiannual interest on the April 1 issue and amortized the premium applicable to the second half of the second interest period.

Required

Prepare general journal entries to record the bond transactions. Round amounts to nearest dollar.

Problem 11B-4. Bond and Mortgage Transactions Contrasted
(L.O. 2, 4, 5, 7)

Shah Manufacturing Company, a company with a June 30 fiscal year, is expanding its operations by building and equipping a new plant. It is financing the building and land with a $10,000,000, thirty-year mortgage, which carries an interest rate of 12 percent and requires monthly payments of $118,000. The company is financing the equipment and working capital for the new plant with a $10,000,000, twenty-year bond, which carries a face interest rate of 11 percent, payable semiannually on March 31 and September 30. To date, selected transactions related to these two issues have been as follows:

19x1

Jan.	1	Signed mortgage in exchange for land and building. Land represents 10 percent of total price.
Feb.	1	Made first mortgage payment.
Mar.	1	Made second mortgage payment.
	31	Issued bonds for cash at 96, resulting in an effective interest rate of 11.5 percent.
Apr.	1	Made third mortgage payment.
May	1	Made fourth mortgage payment.
June	1	Made fifth mortgage payment.
	30	Made end-of-year adjusting entry to accrue interest on bonds and amortize the discount, using the effective interest method.
July	1	Made sixth mortgage payment.
Aug.	1	Made seventh mortgage payment.
Sept.	1	Made eighth mortgage payment.
	30	Made first interest payment on bonds and amortized the discount for the time period since the end of the fiscal year.

19x2

Mar.	31	Made second interest payment on bonds and amortized the discount for the time period since the last interest payment.

Required

1. Prepare a monthly payment schedule for the mortgage for ten months using these headings (round amounts to the nearest dollar): Payment Date, Unpaid Balance at Beginning of Period, Monthly Payment, Interest for One Month at 1% on Unpaid Balance, Reduction in Debt, and Unpaid Balance at End of Period.
2. Prepare the journal entries for the selected transactions. (Ignore mortgage payments made after September 1, 19x1.)

Problem 11B-5. Bond Interest and Amortization Table and Bond Retirements
(L.O. 2, 4, 6)

In 19x1 the Vallejo Corporation was authorized to issue $30,000,000 of six-year unsecured bonds. The bonds carried a face interest rate of 9 percent, payable semiannually on June 30 and December 31. Each $2,000 bond was convertible into 40 shares of $20 par value common stock. The bonds were callable at 105 any time after June 30, 19x4. All bonds were issued on July 1, 19x1, at 95.568, a price yielding an effective interest rate of 10 percent. On July 1, 19x4 the company called and retired one-half the outstanding bonds.

Required

1. Prepare a table similar to Table 11-1, showing the interest and amortization of bond discount for twelve interest payment periods. Use the effective interest method (round results to the nearest dollar).
2. Prepare general journal entries for the bond issue, interest payments and amortization of bond discount, and bond retirement on the following dates: July 1, 19x1; December 31, 19x1; June 30, 19x4; July 1, 19x4; and December 31, 19x4.

Problem 11B-6. Comprehensive Bond Transactions *(L.O. 2, 4, 5, 6)*

The Ozaki Corporation, a company with a June 30 fiscal year end, engaged in the following long-term bond transactions over a three-year period:

19x5

Nov. 1 Issued $20,000,000 of 12 percent debenture bonds at face value plus accrued interest. Interest is payable on January 31 and July 31, and the bonds are callable at 104.

19x6

Jan. 31 Made the semiannual interest payment on the 12 percent bonds.

June 30 Made the year-end accrual of interest on the 12 percent bonds.

July 31 Issued $10,000,000 of 10 percent, fifteen-year convertible bonds at 105 plus accrued interest. Interest is payable on June 30 and December 31, and each $1,000 bond is convertible into 30 shares of $10 par value common stock. The market rate of interest is 9 percent.

31 Made the semiannual interest payment on the 12 percent bonds.

Dec. 31 Made the semiannual interest payment on the 10 percent bonds and amortized the bond premium.

19x7

Jan. 31 Made the semiannual interest payment on the 12 percent bonds.

Feb. 28 Called and retired all the 12 percent bonds, including accrued interest.

June 30 Made the semiannual interest payment on the 10 percent bonds and amortized the bond premium.

July 1 Accepted for conversion into common stock all the 10 percent bonds.

Required

Prepare general journal entries to record the bond transactions, making all necessary accruals and using the effective interest method. (Round all calculations to the nearest dollar.)

Financial Decision Cases

11-1. J.C. Penney Company, Inc. *(L.O. 2, 3)*

A bond or note with no periodic interest payments sounds like a car with no motor. But some large companies are issuing this kind of bond. For example, in 1981, J.C. Penney Company, Inc. advertised in the business press and sold $200,000,000 of zero coupon (no periodic interest) bonds due in 1989. The price, however, was not $200,000,000 but only 33.247 percent of $200,000,000. In other words, the investor pays about $332,470 now and in eight years collects $1,000,000. The advantage to J.C. Penney is that it does not have to pay a cent of interest for eight years. It does, of course, have to come up with the full face value of the notes at the maturity date. For the investor, a return is guaranteed no matter what the market rate of interest may be over the next eight years, as long as J.C. Penney is able to pay off the notes at the maturity date. The J.C. Penney zero coupon bonds can be contrasted with the financing transactions taking place at about the same time at two other companies of similar quality: Transamerica Corporation and Greyhound Corporation. Transamerica sold $200,000,000 (face value) of thirty-year bonds with a 6½ percent coupon at a price of $480.67 per $1,000 bond. Greyhound issued $75,000,000 of ten-year notes carrying an interest rate of 14¼ percent at 100.

Required

1. Using Tables 3 and 4 in the appendix on future value and present value tables, compute the effective interest rates for the three debt issues. Which issue appears to be the most attractive to the investor?
2. Federal tax laws require the payment of income taxes on interest income that is amortized on low-coupon bonds and notes as well as on interest that is actually paid. In light of this, would your answer to **1** change? What factors other than the effective interest rate and income taxes would you consider important in deciding which of these bonds to invest in?

11-2.
Gianni Chemical Corporation
(L.O. 2, 4, 7)

The Gianni Chemical Corporation plans to build a new plant that will produce liquid fertilizer for the agricultural market. The plant is expected to cost \$200,000,000 and will be located in the southwestern part of the United States. The company's chief financial officer, Julio Bassi, has spent the last several weeks studying different means of financing the plant's construction. From his talks with bankers and other financiers, he has decided that there are two basic choices. The plant can be financed through the issuance of a long-term bond or through a long-term lease. The two options follow:

a. Issuance of a \$200,000,000, twenty-five-year, 16 percent bond secured by the new plant. Interest on the bonds would be payable semiannually.
b. Signing of a twenty-five-year lease calling for semiannual lease payments of \$16,350,000.

Bassi wants to know what the effect of each choice will be on the company's financial statements. He estimates that the useful life of the plant is twenty-five years, at which time it is expected to have an estimated residual value of \$20,000,000.

Required

1. Prepare the entries to record issuance of the bonds at face value in exchange for the fertilizer plant. Assume that the transaction occurs on the first day of the fiscal year, which is July 1. Also prepare entries to pay the interest expense and interest payable and to record depreciation on the plant during the first year. Assume that the straight-line method is used. Describe the effects that these transactions will have on the balance sheet and income statement.
2. Prepare the entries required to treat the long-term lease as a capital lease. Assume that the plant is occupied on the first day of the fiscal year, July 1, and that an interest rate of 16 percent applies. Also prepare entries to record the lease payments and to record depreciation during the first year. Describe the effects that these transactions will have on the balance sheet and income statement. (A knowledge of present value, which is dealt with in the chapter on current liabilities and the time value of money and in Table 4 in the appendix on future value and present value tables, is necessary to do this part of the question.)
3. What factors would you consider important in deciding which alternative to choose? Contrast the annual cash requirements of the two alternatives.

CHAPTER 12

Contributed Capital

LEARNING OBJECTIVES

1. Define a corporation, and state the advantages and disadvantages of the corporate form of business.
2. Account for organization costs.
3. Identify the components of stockholders' equity.
4. Account for cash dividends.
5. Calculate the division of dividends between common and preferred stockholders.
6. Account for the issuance of common and preferred stock for cash and other assets.
7. Account for stock subscriptions.
8. Account for the exercise of stock options.

There are fewer corporations than sole proprietorships and partnerships in the United States. However, the corporate form of business dominates the economy in total dollars of assets and output of goods and services. The corporate form of business is also well suited to today's trends toward large organizations, international trade, and professional management. After studying this chapter, you should be able to meet the learning objectives listed on the left.

DECISION POINT
Time Warner, Inc.

A major reason for the dominance of corporations in the U.S. economy is their ability to amass a large amount of capital. This characteristic is illustrated by Figure 12-1, which shows the amounts and sources of new funds raised by corporations over the most recent five years for which data are available. In 1989, the amount of new corporate capital reached $304.9 billion, of which $274.3 billion, or 90 percent, came from new bond issues; $22.9 billion, or 7.5 percent, came from common stock issues; and $7.7 billion, or 2.5 percent, came from preferred stock issues. As pointed out in the chapter on long-term liabilities, bonds are a popular way for corporations to raise new capital, for reasons such as income tax advantages, flexibility, and leverage. Although much less popular than bonds, capital stock issues are still favored by many corporations. The *Wall Street Journal* recently reported that Time Warner, Inc., a major publishing and entertainment company, had been successful in raising about $2.7 billion from its common stock.[1] In light of the advantages of bond financing, what are some possible reasons for Time Warner's decision to issue common stock?

As a means of financing, common stock has disadvantages. Dividends paid on stock are not tax deductible, unlike interest expense on bonds. Moreover, current shareholders yield some control to the new stockholders. On the

1. Randall Smith, "Time Warner's Offer Expires; Demand Is High," *Wall Street Journal*, August 6, 1991.

Figure 12-1. Sources of Capital Raised by Corporations in the United States

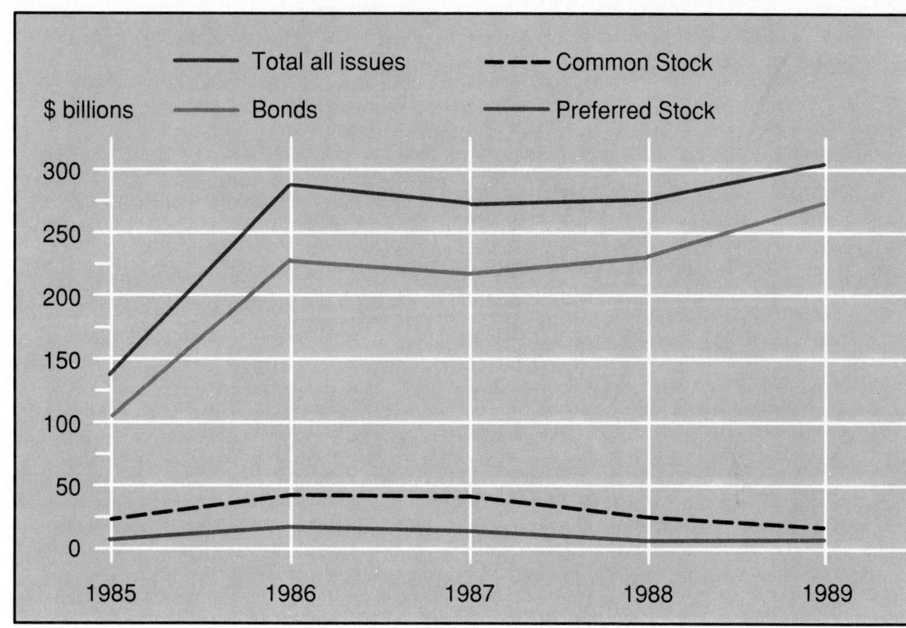

Source: Data from *Securities Industry Handbook* (New York: Securities Industry Association, 1990), p. 753.

other hand, definite advantages to financing with common stock exist. First, financing with common stock issues is less risky than financing with bonds, because dividends on common stock are not paid unless management and the board of directors decide to pay them. In contrast, if the interest on bonds is not paid, a company can be forced into bankruptcy. Second, when a company does not pay a cash dividend, the cash generated by profitable operations may be invested in company operations rather than paid out to the investors. Third, and most important for Time Warner, Inc., the company needed the proceeds to reduce its debt and achieve a better balance between liabilities and stockholders' equity. For these and other reasons, it is important to understand the nature and characteristics of corporations as well as the process of accounting for the issuance of stock and other stock transactions. ■

The Corporation

A **corporation** is defined as "a body of persons granted a charter legally recognizing them as a separate entity having its own rights, privileges, and liabilities distinct from those of its members."[2] In other words, the corporation is a legal entity separate and distinct from its owners.

2. Copyright © 1985 Houghton Mifflin Company. Adapted and reprinted by permission from *The American Heritage Dictionary*, Second College Edition.

Advantages of a Corporation

OBJECTIVE 1 *Define a corporation, and state the advantages and disadvantages of the corporate form of business*

The corporate form of business organization has several advantages over the sole proprietorship and the partnership. Among these advantages are separate legal entity, limited liability, ease of capital generation, ease of transfer of ownership, lack of mutual agency, continuous existence, centralized authority and responsibility, and professional management.

Separate Legal Entity. A corporation is a separate legal entity that has most of the rights of a person except those of voting and marrying. As such, it may buy, sell, or own property; sue and be sued; enter into contracts with all parties; hire and fire employees; and be taxed.

Limited Liability. Because a corporation is a separate legal entity, it is responsible for its own actions and liabilities. For this reason, a corporation's creditors generally cannot look beyond the assets of the company to satisfy their claims. In other words, the creditors can satisfy their claims only against the assets of the corporation, not against the personal property of the owners of the company. Because owners of a corporation are not responsible for the debts of the company, their liability is limited to the amount of their investment. The personal property of sole proprietors and partners, however, may be available to creditors.

Ease of Capital Generation. It is fairly easy for a corporation to raise money because many people can take part in the ownership of the business by investing small amounts of money. As a result, a single corporation may be owned by many people.

Ease of Transfer of Ownership. The ownership of a corporation is represented by a transferable unit called a share of stock. An owner of shares of stock, or a stockholder, can normally buy and sell these shares without affecting the activities of the corporation or needing the approval of other owners.

Lack of Mutual Agency. There is no mutual agency with the corporate form of business as there is in a partnership, in which any partner can bind the partnership. If a stockholder, acting as an owner, tries to enter into a contract for the corporation, the corporation will not be bound by the contract. But a partnership, where there is mutual agency, can be bound by a partner's actions.

Continuous Existence. Another advantage of the corporation's being a legal entity separate from its owners is that an owner's death, incapacity, or withdrawal does not affect the life of the corporation. The life of a corporation is set by its charter and regulated by state laws.

Centralized Authority and Responsibility. The board of directors represents the stockholders and delegates the responsibility and authority for the day-to-day operation of the corporation to a single person, usually the president of the organization. This power is not divided among the many owners of the business. The president may delegate authority for certain segments of the business to others, but he or she is held accountable to the board of directors for the business. If the board is dissatisfied with the performance of the president, he or she can be replaced.

Professional Management. Large corporations are owned by many people who probably do not have the time or training to make timely operating decisions for the business. So, in most cases, management and ownership are separated in the manner described in the previous paragraph. This arrangement allows the corporation to hire the best talent available for managing the business.

Disadvantages of a Corporation

The corporate form of business also has its disadvantages. Among the more important ones are government regulation, taxation, limited liability, and separate ownership and control.

Government Regulation. When corporations are created, they must meet the requirements of state laws. For this reason, they are said to be "creatures of the state" and are subject to greater control and regulation by the state than other forms of business. Corporations must file many reports with the states in which they are chartered. Also, corporations that are publicly held must file reports with the Securities and Exchange Commission and with the stock exchanges. Meeting these requirements becomes very costly.

Taxation. A major disadvantage of a corporation is **double taxation**. Because the corporation is a separate legal entity, its earnings are subject to federal and state income taxes. These taxes may approach 35 percent of the corporate earnings. If the corporation's after-tax earnings are then paid out to its stockholders as dividends, these earnings are again taxed as income to the stockholders who receive them. Taxation is different for the sole proprietorship and the partnership, whose earnings are taxed only as personal income to the owners.

Limited Liability. Earlier, limited liability was listed as an advantage of a corporation. This same feature, however, may limit the ability of a small corporation to borrow money. The credit of a small corporation is reduced because the stockholders have limited liability and the creditors will have claims only on the assets of the corporation. In such cases, the creditors will limit their loans to the level secured by the assets of the corporation or ask the stockholders to personally guarantee the loans.

Separation of Ownership and Control. Just as limited liability may be a drawback, so may the separation of ownership and control. Sometimes management makes decisions that are not good for the corporation as a whole. Poor communication can also make it hard for stockholders to exercise control over the corporation or even to recognize that management's decisions are harmful.

Organization Costs

OBJECTIVE 2
Account for organization costs

The costs of forming a corporation are called **organization costs**. These costs, which are incurred prior to the start of the corporation, include such items as state incorporation fees and attorneys' fees for drawing up the articles of incorporation to establish the corporation. They also include the cost of printing stock certificates, accountants' fees for services rendered in registering the firm's initial stock, and other expenditures necessary for forming the corporation.

Theoretically, these costs benefit the entire life of the organization. For this reason, a case can be made for recording organization costs as intangible assets and amortizing them over the years of the life of the corporation. However, the life of a corporation is normally unknown, so accountants amortize these costs over the early years of a corporation's life. Because federal income tax regulations allow organization costs to be amortized over five years or more, most companies amortize these costs over a five-year (sixty-month) period, although the FASB will allow a period of up to forty years. Organization costs normally appear as Other Assets or as Intangible Assets on the balance sheet.

To illustrate accounting practice for organization costs, we will assume that a corporation pays a lawyer $5,000 for services rendered in July in preparing the application for a charter from the state. The entry to record this cost would be as follows:

19x0				
July	1	Organization Costs	5,000	
		Cash		5,000
		To record $5,000 lawyer's fee for services rendered in corporate organization		

If the corporation amortizes the organization costs over a five-year period, the entry to record the amortization at the end of the fiscal year on June 30, 19x1 would be:

19x1				
June	30	Amortization Expense, Organization Costs	1,000	
		Organization Costs		1,000
		To record one year's costs: $5,000 ÷ 5 years = $1,000		

The Components of Stockholders' Equity

OBJECTIVE 3
Identify the components of stockholders' equity

In a corporation's balance sheet, the owners' claims to the business are called stockholders' equity, as follows:

Stockholders' Equity		
Contributed Capital		
Preferred Stock—$50 par value, 1,000 shares authorized and issued		$ 50,000
Common Stock—$5 par value, 30,000 shares authorized, 20,000 shares issued	$100,000	
Paid-in Capital in Excess of Par Value, Common	50,000	150,000
Total Contributed Capital		$200,000
Retained Earnings		60,000
Total Stockholders' Equity		$260,000

The stockholders' equity section is divided into two parts: (1) contributed capital and (2) retained earnings. Contributed capital represents the investments made by the stockholders in the corporation. The retained earnings are the earnings of the business that have not been distributed to the stockholders. Instead, the retained earnings have been reinvested in the business.

The contributed capital part of stockholders' equity on the balance sheet, in keeping with the convention of full disclosure, gives a great deal of information about the stock of a corporation. For example, the kinds of stock, their par value, and the number of shares authorized and issued are reported in this part of stockholders' equity. This information in the contributed capital part of stockholders' equity is the subject of the rest of this chapter. Retained earnings will be explained fully in the chapter on retained earnings and corporate income statements.

Capital Stock

A unit of ownership in a corporation is called a share of stock. A **stock certificate** will be issued to the owner. It shows the number of shares of the corporation's stock owned by the stockholder. Stockholders can transfer their ownership at will, but they must sign their stock certificates and send them to the corporation's secretary. In large corporations listed on the organized stock exchanges, it is hard to maintain stockholders' records. Such companies may have millions of shares of stock, several thousand of which may change ownership every day. Therefore, these corporations often appoint independent registrars and transfer agents to aid in performing the secretary's duties. The registrars and the transfer agents are usually banks and trust companies. They are responsible for transferring the corporation's stock, maintaining stockholders' records, preparing a list of stockholders for stockholders' meetings, and paying the dividends. To help with the initial issue of capital stock, corporations often engage an underwriter. The underwriter is an intermediary, or contact, between the corporation and the investing public. For a fee—usually less than 1 percent of the selling price—the underwriter guarantees the sale of the stock. The corporation records the amount of the net proceeds of the offering—what the public paid less the underwriter's fee, legal and printing expenses, and any other direct costs of the offering—in its Capital Stock and Additional Paid-in Capital Accounts.

Authorization of Stock. When a corporation applies for a charter, the articles of incorporation indicate the maximum number of shares of stock a corporation will be allowed to issue. This number represents **authorized stock.** Most corporations get an authorization to issue more shares of stock than are necessary at the time of organization. This action enables the corporation to issue stock in the future to raise additional capital. For example, if a corporation is planning to expand later, a possible source of capital would be the unissued shares of stock that were authorized in its charter. If all authorized stock is issued immediately, the corporation must change its charter by applying to the state to increase the number of shares of authorized stock if it wants to issue more. The charter also shows the par value of the stock that has been authorized. The **par value** is an arbitrary amount to be printed on each share of stock. It must be recorded in the capital stock accounts and constitutes the **legal capital** of a corporation. Legal capital equals the number of shares issued times the par value and is the minimum amount that can be reported as contributed capital. It usually bears little if any relationship to the market value or book value of the shares. When the corporation is formed, a memorandum entry may be made in the general journal giving the number and description of authorized shares.

Issued and Outstanding Stock. The **issued stock** of a corporation is the shares sold or otherwise transferred to the stockholders. For example, a corporation may have been authorized to issue 500,000 shares of stock but chose to issue only 300,000 shares when the company was organized. The holders of those 300,000 issued shares own 100 percent of the corporation. The remaining 200,000 shares of stock are unissued shares. No rights or privileges are associated with them until they are issued. Shares of stock are said to be **outstanding stock** if they have been issued and are still in circulation. A share of stock would not be outstanding if it had been repurchased by the issuing corporation or given back to the company that issued it by a stockholder. In such cases, a company can have more shares issued than are currently outstanding or held by the stockholders. Issued shares that have been bought back and are still held by the corporation are called *treasury stock*, which is explained in the chapter on retained earnings and corporate income statements.

Common Stock

A corporation may issue two basic types of stock: common stock and preferred stock. If only one kind of stock is issued by the corporation, it is called **common stock**. The common stock is the **residual equity** of a company. This term means that all other creditors' and preferred stockholders' claims to the company's assets rank ahead of those of the common stockholders in case of liquidation. Because common stock is generally the only stock carrying voting rights, it represents the means of controlling the corporation.

Dividends

OBJECTIVE 4
Account for cash dividends

A **dividend** is a distribution of assets of a corporation to its stockholders. Each stockholder receives assets, usually cash, in proportion to the number of shares of stock held. The board of directors has sole authority to declare dividends.

Dividends may be paid quarterly, semiannually, annually, or at other times decided on by the board. Most states do not allow the board to declare a dividend that exceeds retained earnings. Where such a dividend is declared, the corporation is essentially returning to the stockholders a part of their contributed capital. This is called a **liquidating dividend** and is normally paid when a company is going out of business or is reducing its operations. However, having sufficient retained earnings does not in itself justify the distribution of a dividend. Cash or other readily distributable assets may not be available for distribution. In such a case the company might have to borrow money in order to pay a dividend. This is an action the board of directors may want to avoid.

There are three important dates associated with dividends. In order of occurrence, these are (1) the date of declaration, (2) the date of record, and (3) the date of payment. The date of declaration is the date on which the board of directors takes formal action declaring that a dividend will be paid. The date of record is the date on which ownership of the stock of a company, and therefore of the right to receive a dividend, is determined. Those individuals who own the stock on the date of record will be the ones to receive the dividend. After that date, the stock is said to be **ex-dividend** because if one person sells the shares of stock to another, the right to the cash dividend remains with the first person and does not transfer with the shares to the second person. The date of payment is the date on which the dividend will be paid to the stockholders of record.

Cash Dividends. To illustrate the accounting for cash dividends, we will assume that the board of directors has decided that sufficient cash is available to pay a $56,000 cash dividend to the common stockholders. To do this, a two-step process is followed. First, the dividend is declared by the board of directors for stockholders as of a certain date. Second, the dividend is paid. Assume that the dividend is declared on February 21, 19xx, for stockholders of record on March 10, 19xx, to be paid on March 31,

19xx. The entries to record the declaration and payment of the cash dividend follow:

Date of Declaration

Feb. 21	Dividends Declared	56,000	
	Dividends Payable		56,000
	To record the declaration of a cash dividend to common stockholders		

Date of Record

Mar. 10	No entry is required because this date is used simply to determine the owners of the stock who will receive the dividends. After this date (starting March 11), the shares are ex-dividend.

Date of Payment

Mar. 31	Dividends Payable	56,000	
	Cash		56,000
	To record the payment of cash dividends		

Note that the liability for the dividend was recorded on the date of declaration because the legal obligation to pay the dividend was established on that date. No entry was required on the date of record, and the liability was liquidated, or settled, on the date of payment. The Dividends Declared account is a stockholders' equity account that is closed at the end of the accounting period by debiting Retained Earnings and crediting Dividends Declared. Retained earnings are thereby reduced by the total dividends declared during the period.

Some companies do not pay dividends very often. For one reason, the company may not have any earnings. For another, the company may be growing, and thus the assets generated by the earnings are kept in the company for business purposes such as expansion of the plant. Investors in such growth companies expect a return on their investment in the form of an increased market value of their stock. Stock dividends, another kind of return, will be discussed in the chapter on retained earnings and corporate income statements.

Preferred Stock

The second kind of stock, called **preferred stock**, may be issued so that the company can obtain money from investors who have different investment goals. Preferred stock has preference over common stock in one or more areas. There may be several different classes of preferred stock, each with distinctive characteristics to attract different investors. Most preferred stock has one or more of the following characteristics: preference as to dividends, preference as to assets of the business in liquidation, convertibility or nonconvertibility, and a callable option.

OBJECTIVE 5
Calculate the division of dividends between common and preferred stockholders

Preference as to Dividends. Preferred stocks ordinarily have a *preference* over common stock in the receipt of dividends; that is, the holders of preferred shares must receive a certain amount of dividends before the holders of common shares may receive dividends. The amount that preferred stockholders must be paid before common stockholders may be paid is usually stated in dollars per share or as a percentage of the face value of the preferred shares. For example, a corporation may issue a preferred stock and pay a dividend of $4 per share, or it might issue a preferred stock of $50 par value and pay a yearly dividend of 8 percent of par value, which amounts to a $4 annual dividend.

Preferred stockholders have no guarantee of ever receiving dividends; the company must have earnings and the board of directors must declare dividends on preferred shares before any liability to pay them arises. The consequences of not declaring a dividend to preferred stockholders in the current year vary, however, according to the exact terms under which the shares were issued. To have **noncumulative** preferred shares means that if the board of directors fails to declare a dividend to preferred stockholders in a given year, it is under no obligation to make up the missed dividend in future years. If the shares are **cumulative**, however, the fixed preference amount per preferred share accumulates from year to year, and the whole amount must be paid before any common dividends may be paid. The dividends that are not paid in the year they are due are called **dividends in arrears.**

Assume that the preferred stock of a corporation is as follows: preferred stock, 5 percent cumulative, 10,000 shares authorized, issued, and outstanding, $100 par value, $1,000,000. If in 19x1 no dividends were paid, at the end of that year there would be preferred dividends of $50,000 in arrears (10,000 shares × $100 × 5% = $50,000). Thus if dividends are paid next year, the preferred stockholders' dividends in arrears plus the 19x2 preferred dividends must be paid before any dividends on common stock can be paid in 19x2.

Dividends in arrears are not recognized as liabilities of a corporation because there is no liability until the board declares a dividend. A corporation cannot be sure of making a profit. So, of course, it cannot promise dividends to stockholders. However, if a company has dividends in arrears, they should be reported either in the body of the financial statements or in a footnote. It is important to give this information to the users of these statements. The following footnote appeared in a steel company's annual report a few years ago:

> On January 1, 19xx, the company was in arrears by $37,851,000 ($1.25 per share) on dividends to its preferred stockholders. The company must pay all dividends in arrears to preferred stockholders before paying any dividends to common stockholders.

As an illustration, let us assume the following facts. On January 1, 19x1, a corporation issued 10,000 shares of $10 par, 6 percent cumulative preferred stock and 50,000 shares of common stock. The first year's operations resulted in income of only $4,000. The board of directors declared a

$3,000 cash dividend to the preferred stockholders. The dividend picture at the end of 19x1 appears as follows:

19x1 dividends due preferred stockholders ($100,000 × 6%)	$6,000
19x1 dividends declared to preferred stockholders	(3,000)
Preferred stock dividends in arrears	$3,000

Let us suppose that in 19x2 the company earned income of $30,000 and wished to pay dividends to both the preferred and the common stockholders. But the preferred stock is cumulative. So the corporation must pay the $3,000 in arrears on the preferred stock, plus the current year's dividends, before the common stockholders can receive a dividend. For example, assume that the corporation's board of directors declared a $12,000 dividend to be distributed to the preferred and common stockholders. Under these circumstances, the distribution of the dividend would be as follows:

19x2 declaration of dividends	$12,000	
Less 19x1 preferred stock dividends in arrears	3,000	
Available for 19x2 dividends		$9,000
Less 19x2 preferred stock dividend ($100,000 × 6%)		6,000
Remainder available to common stockholders		$3,000

The entry below is made when the dividend is declared:

Dec. 31	Dividends Declared	12,000	
	Dividends Payable		12,000
	To record declaration of a $9,000 cash dividend to preferred stockholders and a $3,000 cash dividend to common stockholders		

Preference as to Assets. Many preferred stocks have preference as to the assets of the corporation in the case of liquidation of the business. So when the business is ended, the preferred stockholders have a right to receive the par value of their stock or a larger stated liquidation value per share before the common stockholders receive any share of the company's assets. This preference may also include any dividends in arrears owed to the preferred stockholders.

Convertible Preferred Stock. A corporation may make its preferred stock more attractive to investors by adding a convertibility feature. Those who hold **convertible preferred stock** can exchange their shares of preferred stock, if they wish, for shares of the company's common stock at a ratio stated in the preferred stock contract. Convertibility is attractive to investors for two reasons. (1) Like all preferred stockholders, owners of convertible stock can be surer of regular dividends than can common stockholders. (2) If the market value of a company's common stock rises, the conversion feature will allow the preferred stockholders to share in this increase. The rise in value would come either through equal increases in the value of the preferred stock or through conversion to common stock.

For example, suppose that a company issues 1,000 shares of 8 percent, $100 par value convertible preferred stock for $100 per share. Each share of stock can be converted into five shares of the company's common stock at any time. The market value of the common stock is now $15 a share. In the past, dividends on the common stock had been about $1 per share per year. The stockholder owning one share of preferred stock, on the other hand, now holds an investment that is worth about $100 on the market, and the probability of dividends is higher than with common stock.

Assume that in the next several years the corporation's earnings increase, and the dividends paid to common stockholders also increase, to $3 per share. In addition, the market value of a share of common stock increases from $15 to $30. The preferred stockholders can convert each of their preferred shares into five common shares and increase their dividends from $8 on each preferred share to the equivalent of $15 ($3 on each of five common shares). Furthermore, the market value of each share of preferred stock will be close to the $150 value of the five shares of common stock because the share may be converted into the five shares of common stock.

Callable Preferred Stock. Most preferred stocks are **callable preferred stocks**. That is, they may be redeemed or retired at the option of the issuing corporation at a certain price stated in the preferred stock contract. The stockholder must surrender a nonconvertible preferred stock to the corporation when requested to do so. If the preferred stock is convertible, the stockholder may either surrender the stock to the corporation or convert it into common stock when the corporation calls the stock. The call price, or redemption price, is usually higher than the par value of the stock. For example, a $100 par value preferred stock might be callable at $103 per share. When preferred stock is called and surrendered, the stockholder is entitled to (1) the par value of the stock, (2) the call premium, (3) the dividends in arrears, and (4) a prorated (by the proportion of the year to the call date) portion of the current period's dividend.

There are several reasons why a corporation may call its preferred stock. First, it may wish to force conversion of the preferred stock to common because the cash dividend to be paid on the equivalent common stock is less than the dividend being paid on the preferred shares. Second, it may be possible to replace the outstanding preferred stock on the current market with a preferred stock at a lower dividend rate or with long-term debt that may have a lower after-tax cost. Third, the company may simply be profitable enough to retire the preferred stock.

DECISION POINT

J.C. Penney Company, Inc.

Preferred stock issues can be used strategically to accomplish management's objectives. For instance, an article in the *Wall Street Journal* reported that J.C. Penney Company, the large retailer, planned to sell an issue of preferred stock to its newly created Employee Stock Ownership Plan (ESOP) and use the $700 million in proceeds to buy back up to 11 percent of its outstanding common stock. The plan would result in the employees' owning about 24 percent of the company. The new preferred stock would pay a dividend of 7.9 percent and would be convertible into common shares at $60 per share. The stock market reacted positively to the plan; the company's common stock rose almost $2 per share to $48 on the date of the announcement. What benefits to the company does management see from this elaborate plan?

As reported by the *Wall Street Journal*, "Analysts said the move should make the company less attractive as a takeover candidate by increasing its share price and per share earnings as well as by putting more shares in employees' hands."[3] Further, the company feels that its common stock is undervalued and that because there will be less common stock outstanding after the plan is put into effect, the market value of the company's stock will be enhanced. ■

Retained Earnings

Retained earnings, the other component of stockholders' equity, represents the claim of stockholders to the assets of the company resulting from profitable operations. The chapter on retained earnings and corporate income statements explains in detail the retained earnings section of the balance sheet.

Accounting for Stock Issuance

OBJECTIVE 6
Account for the issuance of common and preferred stock for cash and other assets

A share of capital stock is either a par or a no-par stock. If the capital stock is par stock, the corporation charter states the par value, and this value must be printed on each share of stock. Par value may be 10¢, $1, $5, $100, or any other amount worked out by the organizers of the corporation. The par values of common stocks tend to be lower than those of preferred stocks.

Par value is the amount per share that is entered into the corporation's Capital Stock account and makes up the legal capital of the corporation. A corporation may not declare a dividend that would cause stockholders' equity to fall below the legal capital of the firm. Therefore, the par value is a minimum cushion of capital that protects creditors. Any amount in

3. Karen Blumenthal, "J.C. Penney Plans to Buy Back Stock with ESOP Gains," *Wall Street Journal*, Aug. 31, 1988.

excess of par value received from the issuance of stock is recorded as Paid-in Capital in Excess of Par Value and represents a portion of the company's contributed capital.

No-par stock is capital stock that does not have a par value. There are several reasons for issuing stock without a par value. One is that some investors have confused par value with the market value of stock instead of recognizing it as an arbitrary figure. Another reason is that most states will not allow an original issuance of stock below par value and thereby limit a corporation's flexibility in obtaining capital.

No-par stock may be issued with or without a stated value. The board of directors of the corporation issuing the no-par stock may be required by state law to place a **stated value** on each share of stock or may wish to do so as a matter of convenience. The stated value can usually be any value set by the board, but some states do indicate a minimum stated value per share. The stated value may be set before or after the shares are issued if the state law does not specify this point.

If a company issues a no-par stock without a stated value, then all proceeds of the stock's issuance are recorded in the Capital Stock account. This amount becomes the corporation's legal capital unless the amount is specified by state law. Because additional shares of the stock may be issued at different prices, the credit to the Capital Stock account per share will not be uniform. In this way it differs from par value stock or no-par stock with a stated value.

When no-par stock with a stated value is issued, the shares are recorded in the Capital Stock account at the stated value. Any amount received in excess of the stated value is recorded as Paid-in Capital in Excess of Stated Value. The excess of the stated value is a part of the corporation's contributed capital. However, the stated value is normally considered to be the legal capital of the corporation.

Issuance of Par Value Stock

When par value stock is issued, the appropriate capital stock account (usually Common Stock or Preferred Stock) is credited for the par value (legal capital) regardless of whether the proceeds are more or less than the par value. For example, assume that Bradley Corporation is authorized to issue 20,000 shares of $10 par value common stock and actually issues 10,000 shares at $10 per share on January 1. The entry to record the issuance of the stock at par value would be as follows:

Jan.	1	Cash	100,000	
		Common Stock		100,000
		Issued 10,000 shares of $10 par value common stock for $10 per share		

Cash is debited for $100,000 (10,000 shares × $10), and Common Stock is credited for an equal amount because the stock was sold for par value (legal capital). If the stock had been issued for a price greater than par, the proceeds in excess of par would be credited to a capital account entitled

Paid-in Capital in Excess of Par Value, Common. For example, assume that the 10,000 shares of Bradley common stock were sold for $12 per share on January 1. The entry to record the issuance of the stock at the price in excess of par value would be as follows:

Jan.	1	Cash	120,000	
		Common Stock		100,000
		Paid-in Capital in Excess of Par Value, Common		20,000
		Issued 10,000 shares of $10 par value common stock for $12 per share		

Cash is debited for the proceeds of $120,000 (10,000 shares × $12), and Common Stock is credited at total par value of $100,000 (10,000 shares × $10). Paid-in Capital in Excess of Par Value, Common, is credited for the difference of $20,000 (10,000 shares × $2). The latter amount is a part of the corporation's contributed capital and will be added to Common Stock in the stockholders' equity section of the balance sheet. The stockholders' equity section for Bradley Corporation immediately following the stock issue would appear as follows:

Contributed Capital	
Common Stock—$10 par value, 20,000 shares authorized, 10,000 shares issued and outstanding	$100,000
Paid-in Capital in Excess of Par Value, Common	20,000
Total Contributed Capital	$120,000
Retained Earnings	—
Total Stockholders' Equity	$120,000

If a corporation issues stock for less than par, an account entitled Discount on Capital Stock should be debited for the discount. The issuance of stock at a discount rarely occurs because it is illegal in many states; it is thus not illustrated in this text.

Issuance of No-Par Stock

As mentioned earlier, stock may be issued without a par value. However, most states require that all or part of the proceeds from the issuance of no-par stock be designated as legal capital not subject to withdrawal, except in liquidation. The purpose is to protect the corporation's assets for the creditors. Assume that the Bradley Corporation's capital stock is no-par common and that 10,000 shares are issued on January 1, 19xx, at $15 per share. The $150,000 (10,000 shares at $15) in proceeds would be recorded as shown in the following entry:

Jan.	1	Cash	150,000	
		Common Stock		150,000
		Issued 10,000 shares of no-par common stock for $15 per share		

Since the stock does not have a stated or par value, all proceeds of the issue are credited to Common Stock and are part of the company's legal capital.

Most states allow the board of directors to put a stated value on no-par stock, and this value represents the legal capital. Assume that Bradley's board puts a $10 stated value on its no-par stock. The entry to record the issue of 10,000 shares of no-par common stock with a $10 stated value for $15 per share would change from that in the last paragraph to the following:

Jan.	1	Cash	150,000	
		Common Stock		100,000
		Paid-in Capital in Excess of Stated Value, Common		50,000
		Issued 10,000 shares of no-par common stock of $10 stated value for $15 per share		

Note that the legal capital credited to Common Stock is the stated value as decided by the board of directors. Note also that the account Paid-in Capital in Excess of Stated Value, Common, is credited for $50,000. The $50,000 is the difference between the proceeds ($150,000) and the total stated value ($100,000). Paid-in Capital in Excess of Stated Value, Common, is presented on the balance sheet in the same way that Paid-in Capital in Excess of Par Value, Common, is presented on the balance sheet for par value stock.

Issuance of Stock for Noncash Assets

In many stock transactions, stock is issued for assets or services other than cash. As a result, a problem arises as to what dollar amount should be recorded for the exchange. The generally preferred rule for such a transaction is to record the transaction at the fair market value of what is given up—in this case, the stock. If the fair market value of the stock cannot be determined, the fair market value of the assets or services may be used to record the transaction. Transactions of this kind usually include the use of stock to pay for land or buildings or for services of attorneys and others who helped organize the company.

Where there is an exchange of stock for noncash assets, the board of directors has the right to determine the fair market value of the property. Thus, when the Bradley Corporation was formed on January 1, its attorney agreed to accept 100 shares of its $10 par value common stock for services rendered. At the time of the issuance, the market value of the stock could not be determined. However, for similar services the attorney would have billed the company for $1,500. The entry to record the noncash transaction follows:

Jan.	1	Organization Costs	1,500	
		Common Stock		1,000
		Paid-in Capital in Excess of Par Value, Common		500
		Issued 100 shares of $10 par value common stock for attorney's services		

Assume further that the Bradley Corporation exchanged 1,000 shares of its $10 par value common stock for a piece of land two years later. At the time of the exchange, the stock was selling on the market for $16 per share and the value of the land could not be determined. The entry to record this exchange would be:

Jan.	1	Land	16,000	
		Common Stock		10,000
		Paid-in Capital in Excess of Par Value, Common		6,000
		Issued 1,000 shares of $10 par value common stock for a piece of land; market value of the stock $16 per share		

Stock Subscriptions

OBJECTIVE 7
Account for stock subscriptions

In some states, corporations may sell stock on a subscription basis. In a **stock subscription**, the investor agrees to pay for the stock on some future date or in installments at an agreed price. When a subscription is received, a contract exists and the corporation acquires an asset, Subscriptions Receivable, which represents the amount owed on the stock, and a capital item, Capital Stock Subscribed. The latter account is used because it represents the par or stated value of the stock not yet fully paid for and issued. The Common Stock account is reserved for the par value of stock that has been issued. The Subscriptions Receivable account should be identified as either common or preferred stock. The Capital Stock Subscribed account should also be identified as either common or preferred stock. Whether or not the subscriber is entitled to dividends on the subscribed stock depends on the laws of the state in which the company is incorporated. In certain states, the stock is considered to be legally issued when a subscription contract is accepted, thereby making the subscriber a legal stockholder. However, in accounting for stock subscriptions, capital stock is not issued and recorded until the subscriptions receivable pertaining to the shares are collected in full and the stock certificate is delivered to the stockholder. Likewise, it may be assumed that dividends are not paid on common stock subscribed until it is fully paid for and the certificates issued.

To illustrate stock subscriptions, we will assume that on January 1, 19xx the Bradley Corporation received subscriptions for 15,000 shares of $10 par value common stock at $15 per share. The entry to record the subscriptions would be as follows:

Jan.	1	Subscriptions Receivable, Common	225,000	
		Common Stock Subscribed		150,000
		Paid-in Capital in Excess of Par Value, Common		75,000
		Received subscriptions for 15,000 shares of $10 par value common stock for $15 per share		

If the full subscription price for 10,000 shares was collected on January 21, 19xx, the entry for the collection of the subscription would be as shown below:

Jan. 21	Cash	150,000	
	Subscriptions Receivable, Common		150,000
	Collected subscriptions in full for 10,000 shares of $10 par value common stock at $15 per share		

Because the 10,000 shares are fully paid for, it is appropriate to issue the common stock, as follows:

Jan. 21	Common Stock Subscribed	100,000	
	Common Stock		100,000
	Issued 10,000 shares of $10 par value common stock		

Note that since the paid-in capital in excess of par value was recorded in the January 1 entry, there is no need to record it again.

Assume that the financial statements are prepared on January 31, 19xx, before the remaining subscriptions are collected. The Subscriptions Receivable account of $75,000 ($225,000 – $150,000) would be classified as a current asset unless there was some reason why it would not be collected in the next year. The balance of $50,000 ($150,000 – $100,000) in the Common Stock Subscribed account represents the par value of the stock yet to be issued and is a temporary capital account. As such, it is properly shown as a part of stockholders' equity under Contributed Capital, as in the following illustration:

Contributed Capital		
Common Stock—$10 par value, 80,000 shares authorized		
Issued and outstanding, 10,000 shares	$100,000	
Subscribed but not issued, 5,000 shares	**50,000**	$150,000
Paid-in Capital in Excess of Par Value, Common		75,000
Total Contributed Capital		$225,000

Assume that one-half payment of $37,500 is received on February 5 for the remaining subscriptions receivable. The entry for the collection would be as follows:

Feb. 5	Cash	37,500	
	Subscriptions Receivable, Common		37,500
	Collected one-half payment for subscriptions to 5,000 common shares		

In this case, there is no entry to issue common stock because the subscription for the stock is not paid in full. If the subscriptions receivable are paid in full on February 20, the entries are as follows:

Feb. 20	Cash	37,500	
	Subscriptions Receivable, Common		37,500
	Collected remaining subscriptions in full for 5,000 shares of $10 par value common stock for $15 per share		

Because the subscriptions are now paid in full, the common stock can be issued as follows:

Feb. 20	Common Stock Subscribed	50,000	
	Common Stock		50,000
	Issued 5,000 shares of $10 par value common stock		

Exercise of Stock Options

OBJECTIVE 8 *Account for the exercise of stock options*

Many companies encourage ownership of the company's common stock through a **stock option plan**. A stock option plan is an agreement to issue stock to employees according to the terms of the plan. Under some plans, the option to purchase stock may apply to all employees equally, and the purchase of stock is made at a price that is approximately market value at the time of purchase. When this situation exists, the issuance of stock is recorded in the same way any stock issue to an outsider is recorded. If, for example, we assume that on March 30 the employees of a company purchased 2,000 shares of $10 par value common stock at the current market value of $25 per share, the entry would be as follows:

Mar. 30	Cash	50,000	
	Common Stock		20,000
	Paid-in Capital in Excess of Par Value, Common		30,000
	Issued 2,000 shares of $10 par value common stock under employee stock option plan		

In other cases, the stock option plan may give the employee the right to purchase stock in the future at a fixed price. This type of plan, which usually applies to management personnel, serves to compensate and motivate the employee, because if the company's performance is such that the market value of the stock goes up, the employee can purchase the stock at the option price and sell it at the higher market price. The amount of compensation to the employee is measured by the difference between the option price and the market price on the date of granting the option, not on the date of issuing the stock. If there is no difference between the option price and the market price on the date of grant, no compensation exists. When the option is eventually exercised on the stock and it is issued, the entry is similar to the previous entry. For example, assume that a company grants to key management personnel on July 1, 19x1 the option to purchase 50,000 shares of $10 par value common stock at the market value of $15 per share on that date. Assume that a company vice president exercises the option to purchase 2,000 shares on March 30, 19x2, when the market price is $25 per share. The entry to record the issue would be

Mar. 30	Cash	30,000	
	Common Stock		20,000
	Paid-in Capital in Excess of Par Value, Common		10,000
	Issue 2,000 shares of $10 par value common stock under employee stock option plan		

Although the vice president has a gain of $20,000 ($50,000 market value minus $30,000 option price), no compensation expense is recorded. Compensation expense would have been recorded only if the option price were less than the $15 market price on July 1, 19x1, the date of grant. The handling of compensation when this situation exists is covered in more advanced courses.[4] Information pertaining to the employee stock option plans should be discussed in the notes to the financial statements.

Chapter Review

Review of Learning Objectives

1. **Define a corporation, and state the advantages and disadvantages of the corporate form of business.**
   Corporations, whose ownership is represented by shares of stock, are separate entities for both legal and accounting purposes. The corporation is a separate legal entity having its own rights, privileges, and liabilities distinct from those of its owners. Like other forms of business entities, it has several advantages and disadvantages. The more common advantages are that (a) a corporation is a separate legal entity, (b) stockholders have limited liability, (c) it is easy to generate capital for a corporation, (d) stockholders can buy and sell shares of stock with ease, (e) there is a lack of mutual agency, (f) the corporation has a continuous existence, (g) authority and responsibility are centralized, and (h) it is run by a professional management team. Disadvantages of corporations include (a) a large amount of government regulation, (b) double taxation, (c) limited liability, and (d) the separation of ownership and control.
2. **Account for organization costs.**
   The costs of organizing a corporation are recorded on a historical cost basis. As an intangible asset, organization costs are amortized over a reasonable period of time, usually five years but not more than forty years.
3. **Identify the components of stockholders' equity.**
   Stockholders' equity consists of contributed capital and retained earnings. Contributed capital may include more than one type of stock. Two of the most common types of stock are common stock and preferred stock. When only one type of security is issued, it is common stock. The holders of com-

4. Stock options are discussed here in the context of employee compensation. They can also be important features of complex corporate capitalization arrangements.

mon stock have the right to elect the board of directors and vote on key issues of the corporation. In addition, common stockholders share in the earnings of the corporation and share in the assets of the corporation in case of liquidation.

Preferred stock is issued to investors whose investment objectives differ from those of common stockholders. To attract these investors, corporations give them a preference as to certain items. Preferred stockholders' rights normally include the privilege of receiving dividends ahead of common stockholders and the right to assets in liquidation ahead of common stockholders. Sometimes they have the right of convertibility to common stock.

Retained earnings, the other component of stockholders' equity, represents the claim of stockholders to the assets of the company resulting from profitable operations.

4. **Account for cash dividends.**
A liability for payment of cash dividends arises on the date of declaration by the board of directors. The date of record, on which no entry is required, establishes the stockholders who will receive the cash dividend on the date of payment.

5. **Calculate the division of dividends between common and preferred stockholders.**
Most preferred stock is preferred as to dividends. This preference means that in allocating total dividends between common and preferred stockholders, the amount for the preferred stock is figured first. Then the remainder goes to common stock. If the preferred stock is cumulative and in arrears, the amount in arrears also has to be allocated to preferred before any allocation is made to common.

6. **Account for the issuance of common and preferred stock for cash and other assets.**
A corporation's stock will normally be issued for cash and other assets or by subscription. The majority of states require that stock be issued at a minimum value called legal capital. Legal capital is represented by the par or stated value of the stock.

   When stock is issued for cash or other assets, the par or stated value of the stock is recorded as Common or Preferred Stock. When the stock is sold at an amount greater than the par or stated value, the excess is recorded as Paid-in Capital in Excess of Par or Stated Value.

   Sometimes stock is issued for noncash assets. In these transactions, it is necessary to decide what value to use in recording the issuance of the stock. The general rule is to record the stock at the market value of the stock issued. If this value cannot be determined, then the fair market value of the asset received will be used to record the transaction.

7. **Account for stock subscriptions.**
When stock is not fully paid for at the time of sale, it is not issued. However, the transaction is recorded by debiting Subscriptions Receivable (a current asset) and crediting Capital Stock Subscribed (a stockholders' equity account) for the par or stated value and crediting Paid-in Capital in

Excess of Par or Stated Value for any difference. When the stock has been fully paid for and is issued, Capital Stock Subscribed is debited and Capital Stock is credited.

8. **Account for the exercise of stock options.**
Stock option plans are established to allow a company's employees to own a part of the company. Usually the issue of stock to employees under stock option plans is recorded in a manner similar to the issue of stock to any outsider.

Review of Concepts and Terminology

The following concepts and terms were introduced in this chapter:

(L.O. 3) **Authorized stock:** The maximum number of shares a corporation may issue without changing its charter with the state.

(L.O. 5) **Callable preferred stock:** Preferred stock that may be redeemed and retired by the corporation at its option.

(L.O. 3) **Common stock:** The stock representing the most basic rights to ownership of a corporation.

(L.O. 5) **Convertible preferred stock:** Preferred stock that may be exchanged for common stock at the option of the holder.

(L.O. 1) **Corporation:** A body of persons granted a charter legally recognizing the corporation as a separate entity having its own rights, privileges, and liabilities distinct from those of its members.

(L.O. 5) **Cumulative stock:** Preferred stock on which unpaid dividends accumulate over time and must be satisfied in any given year before a dividend may be paid to common stockholders.

(L.O. 4) **Dividend:** A distribution of assets (usually cash) of a corporation to its stockholders.

(L.O. 5) **Dividends in arrears:** The accumulated unpaid dividends on cumulative preferred stock from prior years.

(L.O. 1) **Double taxation:** A term referring to the fact that earnings of a corporation are taxed twice, both as the net income of the corporation and as the dividends distributed to the stockholders.

(L.O. 4) **Ex-dividend:** A description of capital stock when the right to a dividend already declared on the stock remains with the person who sells the stock and does not transfer to the person who buys it.

(L.O. 3) **Issued stock:** The shares of stock sold or otherwise transferred to stockholders.

(L.O. 3) **Legal capital:** The minimum amount that can be reported as contributed capital; usually equal to par value or stated value.

(L.O. 4) **Liquidating dividend:** A dividend that exceeds retained earnings.

(L.O. 5) **Noncumulative:** Preferred stock on which the dividend may lapse and does not have to be paid if not paid within a given year.

(L.O. 6) **No-par stock:** Capital stock that does not have a par value.

(L.O. 2) **Organization costs:** The costs of forming a corporation.

(L.O. 3) **Outstanding stock:** The shares of a corporation's stock held by stockholders.

(L.O. 3) **Par value:** The amount printed on each share of stock that must be recorded in the capital stock accounts; used in determining the legal capital of a corporation.

(L.O. 4) **Preferred stock:** A type of stock that has some preference over common stock, usually including dividends.

(L.O. 3) **Residual equity:** The common stock of a corporation.

(L.O. 6) **Stated value:** A value assigned by the board of directors of a corporation to no-par stock.

(L.O. 3) **Stock certificate:** A document issued to a stockholder in a corporation indicating the number of shares of stock owned by the stockholder.

(L.O. 8) **Stock option plan:** An agreement to issue stock to employees according to the terms of the plan.

(L.O. 7) **Stock subscription:** An issuance of stock where the investor agrees to pay for the stock on some future date or in installments at an agreed price.

Review Problem
Stock Journal Entries and Stockholders' Equity

(L.O. 4, 5, 6, 7) The Beta Corporation was organized in 19xx in the state of Arizona. The charter of the corporation authorized the issuance of 1,000,000 shares of $1 par value common stock and an additional 25,000 shares of 4 percent, $20 par value cumulative convertible preferred stock. Transactions that relate to the stock of the company for 19xx are as follows:

Feb. 12 Issued 100,000 shares of common stock for $125,000.
20 Issued 3,000 shares of common stock for accounting and legal services. The services were billed to the company at $3,600.
Mar. 15 Issued 120,000 shares of common stock to Edward Jackson in exchange for a building and land that had an appraised value of $100,000 and $25,000, respectively.
Apr. 2 Accepted subscriptions for 200,000 shares of common stock at $1.30 per share.
July 1 Issued 25,000 shares of preferred stock for $500,000.
Sept. 30 Collected in full subscriptions related to 60 percent of the common stock subscribed, and issued the appropriate stock to common stock subscribers. Make two separate entries.
Dec. 31 The company reported net income of $40,000 for 19xx, and the board declared dividends of $25,000, payable on January 15 to stockholders of record on January 8. Dividends include preferred stock cash dividends for one-half year.

Required

1. Prepare the journal entries necessary to record these stock-related transactions, including closing net income and Dividends Declared to Retained Earnings. Following the December 31 entry to record dividends, show dividends payable for each class of stock.

2. Prepare the stockholders' equity section of the Beta Corporation balance sheet as of December 31, 19xx.

Answer to Review Problem

1. Journal entries prepared:

Date	Account	Debit	Credit
Feb. 12	Cash	125,000	
	Common Stock		100,000
	Paid-in Capital in Excess of Par Value, Common		25,000
	To record the sale of 100,000 shares of $1 par value common stock for $1.25 per share		
20	Organization Costs	3,600	
	Common Stock		3,000
	Paid-in Capital in Excess of Par Value, Common		600
	To record issuance of 3,000 shares of $1 par value common stock for billed accounting and legal services of $3,600		
Mar. 15	Building	100,000	
	Land	25,000	
	Common Stock		120,000
	Paid-in Capital in Excess of Par Value, Common		5,000
	To record issuance of 120,000 shares of $1 par value common stock for a building and tract of land appraised at $100,000 and $25,000		
Apr. 2	Subscriptions Receivable, Common Stock	260,000	
	Common Stock Subscribed		200,000
	Paid-in Capital in Excess of Par Value, Common		60,000
	To record subscription for 200,000 shares of $1 par value stock at $1.30 a share		
July 1	Cash	500,000	
	Preferred Stock		500,000
	To record sale of 25,000 shares of $20 par value preferred stock for $20 per share		
Sept. 30	Cash	156,000	
	Subscriptions Receivable, Common Stock		156,000
	To record collection in full of 60 percent of subscriptions receivable: $260,000 × .60 = $156,000		

Sept. 30	Common Stock Subscribed		120,000	
	Common Stock			120,000
	To record issuance of common stock $200,000 × .60 = $120,000			
Dec. 31	Income Summary		40,000	
	Retained Earnings			40,000
	To close net income to Retained Earnings			
31	Dividends Declared		25,000	
	Dividends Payable			25,000
	To record the declaration of a $25,000 cash dividend to preferred and common stockholders:			
	Total dividend	$25,000		
	Less preferred stock cash dividend: $500,000 × .04 × .5 =	10,000		
	Common stock cash dividend	$15,000		
31	Retained Earnings		25,000	
	Dividends Declared			25,000
	To close the Dividends Declared account for the year ended Dec. 31, 19xx			

2. Stockholders' equity section of balance sheet prepared:

Beta Corporation
Stockholders' Equity
December 31, 19xx

Contributed Capital		
4% Cumulative Convertible Preferred Stock—$20 par value, 25,000 shares authorized, issued, and outstanding		$ 500,000
Common Stock—$1 par value, 1,000,000 shares authorized, 343,000 shares issued and outstanding	$343,000	
Common Stock Subscribed	80,000	
Paid-in Capital in Excess of Par Value, Common	90,600	513,600
Total Contributed Capital		$1,013,600
Retained Earnings		15,000
Total Stockholders' Equity		$1,028,600

Chapter Assignments

Discussion Questions

1. What is a corporation, and how is it formed?
2. What is the role of the board of directors in a corporation, and how does it differ from the role of management?
3. What are the typical officers in the management of a corporation, and what are their duties?
4. What are several advantages of the corporate form of business? Explain.
5. What are several disadvantages of the corporate form of business? Explain your answer.
6. What are organization costs of a corporation?
7. What is the proper accounting treatment of organization costs?
8. What is the legal capital of a corporation, and what is its significance?
9. How is the value determined for recording stock issued for noncash assets?
10. Describe the significance of the following dates as they relate to dividends: (a) date of declaration, (b) date of record, and (c) date of payment.
11. Explain the accounting treatment of cash dividends.
12. What are stock subscriptions, and how are Subscriptions Receivable and Common Stock Subscribed classified on the balance sheet?
13. What does it mean for preferred stock to be cumulative, convertible, and/or callable?
14. What are dividends in arrears, and how should they be disclosed in the financial statements?
15. What is the proper classification of the following accounts on the balance sheet? (a) Organization Costs; (b) Common Stock; (c) Subscriptions Receivable, Preferred; (d) Preferred Stock Subscribed; (e) Paid-in Capital in Excess of Par Value, Common; (f) Paid-in Capital in Excess of Stated Value, Common; (g) Discount on Common Stock; (h) Retained Earnings.
16. What reasons can you think of for a corporation to have a stock option plan? Why would an employee want to participate in one?

Communication Skills Exercises

Communication 12-1. The Corporate Form of Business and Ethical Considerations for the Accounting Profession *(L.O. 1)*

Traditionally, accounting firms have organized as partnerships or as professional corporations, a form of corporation that in many ways resembles a partnership. In recent years, some accounting firms have suffered large judgments as a result of lawsuits by investors who lost money when they invested in companies that went bankrupt. In one case, a large international accounting firm went bankrupt largely because of liabilities that were anticipated to arise from problems in the savings and loan industry. The partners dissolved the firm rather than put up the additional capital needed to keep it going. Because of the increased risk of large losses from malpractice suits, there is a movement to allow accounting firms to incorporate as long as they maintain a minimum level of partners' capital and carry malpractice insurance. Some accounting practitioners feel that incorporating would be a violation of their responsibility to the public. What features of the corporate form of business would be most advantageous to the partners of an accounting firm? Do you think it would be a violation of the public trust for an accounting firm to incorporate? (**Hint:** If you want to refresh your memory of the characteristics of partnerships, refer to the introductory chapter or to the appendix on unincorporated businesses.)

Communication 12-2. Reasons for Stock Issue
(L.O. 1, 6)

UAL Corporation, the *Wall Street Journal* reported, planned to issue 1.5 million shares of common stock to raise more than $225 million. The company could take advantage of the fact that the price of its stock had risen to above $150 recently, up more than 35 percent from the previous year. At the time, the company did not pay a dividend on its common stock and had a relatively large debt. The article reported: "Proceeds from the offering . . . would be used to acquire international routes, aircraft, facilities, and also pay for UAL's proposed purchase of Pan Am Corp.'s London Heathrow Airport operations and Eastern Airlines' operations at Chicago's O'Hare International Airport. . . . The offering comes as the carrier, stung by heavy financial losses, enters an ambitious five-year plan."[5] What reasons can you think of for UAL's decision to raise new capital through the issuance of common stock rather than long-term or other forms of debt?

Communication 12-3. Effect of Omission of Preferred Dividend
(L.O. 6)

Tucson Electric Company, the *Wall Street Journal* disclosed, omitted all its preferred stock dividends indefinitely in an effort to improve liquidity. All the company's cumulative preferred stock was affected. According to the article, "Some interpreted the drastic action as a requisite for the cash-strapped utility to secure a new credit agreement. . . . If the credit agreement falls through, the omission of preferred-stock dividends would suggest Tucson Electric is perilously close to filing for bankruptcy."[6] What are cumulative preferred shares? Why is the omission of the dividend on these shares a "drastic action"? If new bank financing is not obtained, why would the company have to consider declaring bankruptcy?

Communication 12-4. Basic Research Skills
(L.O. 5, 6, 8)

In your library, select the annual reports of three corporations. You may choose them from the same industry or at random, at the direction of your instructor. (**Note:** These companies will be used again for the basic research skills exercises in later chapters.) Prepare a table with a column for each corporation. Then answer the following questions: Does the corporation have preferred stock? If so, what are the par value and the indicated dividend, and is the preferred stock cumulative or convertible? Is the common stock par value or no-par? What is the par value or stated value? What cash dividends, if any, were paid in the past year? From the notes to the financial statements, determine whether the company has an employee stock option plan. What are some of the provisions? Be prepared to discuss the characteristics of the stocks and dividends for your selected companies in class.

Classroom Exercises

Exercise 12-1. Journal Entries for Organization Costs
(L.O. 2)

The Korman Corporation was organized during 19x7. At the beginning of the fiscal year, the company incurred the following costs in organizing the company: (1) Attorney's fees, market value of services $3,000; paid with 2,000

5. Asra Q. Nomani, "UAL Stock Sale Seeks Proceeds of $225 Million," *Wall Street Journal,* March 6, 1991.
6. Rick Wartzman, "Tucson Electric Omits Dividends on Preferred Stock," *Wall Street Journal,* Dec. 10, 1990.

shares of $1 par common stock. (2) Incorporation fees paid to the state, $2,500. (3) Accountant's services that would normally be billed at $1,500 paid with 1,100 shares of $1 par value common stock.

Prepare the separate journal entries necessary to record these transactions and to amortize organization costs for the first year, assuming that the company elects to write off organization costs over five years.

Exercise 12-2. Characteristics of Common and Preferred Stock *(L.O. 3, 5)*

For each of the characteristics listed below, indicate whether it is more closely associated with common stock (C) or with preferred stock (P):

_____ a. Often receives dividends at an unchanging rate
_____ b. Is known as the residual equity of a company
_____ c. May be callable
_____ d. May be convertible
_____ e. Amount of dividend more likely to vary from year to year
_____ f. May be entitled to receive dividends not paid in past years
_____ g. Likely to have full voting rights
_____ h. May receive assets first in a liquidation
_____ i. May be entitled to receive dividends before other classes of stock

Exercise 12-3. Journal Entries and Stockholders' Equity *(L.O. 3, 6)*

The Winkler Hospital Supply Corporation was organized in 19xx. The company was authorized to issue 100,000 shares of no-par common stock with a stated value of $5 per share, and 20,000 shares of $100 par value, 6 percent noncumulative preferred stock. On March 1 the company sold 60,000 shares of its common stock for $15 per share and 8,000 shares of its preferred stock for $100 per share.

1. Prepare the journal entries to record the sale of the stock.
2. Prepare the company's stockholders' equity section of the balance sheet immediately after the common and preferred stock were issued.

Exercise 12-4. Stockholders' Equity *(L.O. 3)*

The accounts and balances that follow were taken from the records of Aguilar Corporation on December 31, 19xx.

	Balance	
Account Name	**Debit**	**Credit**
Preferred Stock—$100 par value, 9% cumulative, 10,000 shares authorized, 6,000 shares issued and outstanding		$600,000
Common Stock—$12 par value, 60,000 shares authorized, 30,000 shares issued and outstanding		360,000
Common Stock Subscribed, 2,000 shares		24,000
Paid-in Capital in Excess of Par Value, Common		170,000
Retained Earnings		23,000
Subscriptions Receivable, Common	$30,000	

Prepare a stockholders' equity section for Aguilar Corporation's balance sheet.

Exercise 12-5. Cash Dividends *(L.O. 4)*

Downey Corporation has authorized 200,000 shares of $10 par value common stock. There are 160,000 shares issued and 140,000 shares outstanding. On June 5, the board of directors declares a $.50 per share cash dividend to be paid on June 25 to stockholders of record on June 15. Prepare the journal entries necessary to record these events.

Exercise 12-6. Cash Dividends *(L.O. 4)*

Gayle Corporation has authorized 500,000 shares of $1 par value common stock, of which 400,000 are issued and 360,000 are outstanding. On October 15, the board of directors declares a cash dividend of $.25 per share payable on November 15 to stockholders of record on November 1. Prepare the entries, as necessary, for each of the three dates.

Exercise 12-7. Preferred Stock Dividends with Dividends in Arrears *(L.O. 5)*

The Matsuta Corporation has 10,000 shares of its $100, 7 percent cumulative preferred stock outstanding, and 50,000 shares of its $1 par value common stock outstanding. In its first four years of operation, the board of directors of Matsuta Corporation paid cash dividends as follows: 19x1, none; 19x2, $120,000; 19x3, $140,000; 19x4, $140,000.

Determine the total cash dividends and dividends per share paid to the preferred and common stockholders during each of the four years.

Exercise 12-8. Preferred and Common Stock Dividends *(L.O. 5)*

The Goss-Carterly Corporation pays dividends at the end of each year. The dividends paid for 19x1, 19x2, and 19x3 were $40,000, $30,000, and $90,000, respectively.

Calculate the total amount of dividends paid each year to the common and preferred stockholders if each of the following capital structures is assumed: (1) 10,000 shares of $100 par, 6 percent noncumulative preferred stock and 30,000 shares of $10 par common stock; (2) 5,000 shares of $100 par, 7 percent cumulative preferred stock and 30,000 shares of $10 par common stock. There were no dividends in arrears at the beginning of 19x1.

Exercise 12-9. Issuance of Stock *(L.O. 6)*

Foth Company is authorized to issue 200,000 shares of common stock. On August 1, the company sold 10,000 shares at $25 per share. Prepare journal entries to record the sale of stock for cash under each of the following independent alternatives:

1. The stock has a par value of $25.
2. The stock has a par value of $10.
3. The stock has no par value.
4. The stock has no par value but a stated value of $1 per share.

Exercise 12-10. Journal Entries: Stated Value Stock *(L.O. 6)*

The Sayre Corporation is authorized to issue 100,000 shares of no-par stock. The company recently sold 40,000 shares for $13 per share in cash.

1. Prepare the journal entry to record the sale of the stock if there is no stated value.
2. Prepare the entry if a $10 stated value is authorized by the company's board of directors.

Exercise 12-11. Issuance of Stock for Noncash Assets *(L.O. 6)*

On July 1, 19xx, Wayside, a new corporation, issued 20,000 shares of its common stock for a corporate headquarters building. The building has a fair market value of $300,000 and a book value of $200,000. Because the corporation is new, it is not possible to establish a market value for the common stock.

Record the issuance of stock for the building, assuming the following independent conditions: (1) the par value of the stock is $5 per share; (2) the stock is no-par stock; and (3) the stock is no-par stock but has a stated value of $2 per share.

Exercise 12-12. Issuance of Stock for Noncash Assets *(L.O. 6)*

The Probst Corporation issued 2,000 shares of its $10 par value common stock for some land. The land had a fair market value of $30,000.

Prepare the journal entries necessary to record the issuance of the stock for the land under each of the following independent conditions: (1) the stock was selling for $14 per share on the day of the transaction; and (2) management attempted to place a value on the common stock but could not do so.

Exercise 12-13. Stock Subscriptions *(L.O. 7)*

The Spangler Corporation sold 15,000 shares of its $2 par value common stock by subscription for $8 per share on February 15, 19xx. Cash was received in installments from the purchasers: 50 percent on April 1 and 50 percent on June 1.

Prepare the entries necessary to record these transactions.

Exercise 12-14. Stock Subscriptions *(L.O. 7)*

The Pinto Corporation sold 50,000 shares of its no-par, $10 stated value common stock by subscription for $18 per share on March 12, 19xx. The purchasers paid for the stock in installments of 60 percent on April 1 and 40 percent on May 1.

Prepare journal entries to record these transactions.

Exercise 12-15. Exercise of Stock Options *(L.O. 8)*

Record the following equity transaction of the Evans Company in 19xx:

May 5 Walter Evans exercised his option to purchase 10,000 shares of $1 par value common stock at an option price of $12. The market price per share was $12 on the grant date and $24 on the exercise date.

Interpretation Cases from Business

ICB 12-1. United Airlines[7] *(L.O. 3, 6)*

UAL Corporation is the holding company whose primary subsidiary is United Airlines, which provides passenger and cargo air transportation to 141 airports worldwide. On March 20, 1991, UAL announced an issuance of common stock in the *Wall Street Journal*, as shown below:

1,500,000 Shares
UAL Corporation
Common Stock
($5 par value)
Price $146 per share

7. Excerpts from the 1990 Annual Report used by permission of UAL Corporation. Copyright © 1990.

In fact, UAL sold 1,733,100 shares of stock at $146 for net proceeds of $247.2 million.

A portion of the stockholders' equity section of the balance sheet from UAL's 1990 annual report appeared as follows:

	1990	1989
	(in thousands)	
Common stock, $5 par value; authorized 125,000,000 shares; issued 23,467,880 shares in 1990 and 23,419,953 shares in 1989	117,339	117,100
Additional Paid-in Capital	52,391	47,320
Retained earnings	1,620,885	1,526,534

Required

1. Based on the actual shares sold and actual net proceeds, prepare the entry in UAL's accounting records to record the stock issue.
2. Prepare the portion of the stockholders' equity section of the balance sheet shown above after the issue of the common stock, based on the information given. Did UAL have to increase the authorized shares to undertake this stock issue?
3. What amount per share did UAL receive and how much would an investor pay if UAL's underwriter kept a fee of $2.50 per share to assist it in issuing the stock?

ICB 12-2. Navistar International Corporation I[8]
(L.O. 4, 5)

Navistar International Corporation, a manufacturer of medium and heavy-duty diesel trucks, had several different types of preferred stock on October 31, 1986. Two different series of preferred stock outstanding with different terms and amounts are as follows:

Series C: No-par, cumulative preferred, $5.76 dividend per share rate, 3,000,000 shares outstanding

Series E: No-par, noncumulative, convertible preferred, $120 dividend rate, commencing at the start of the first semiannual period in which a dividend is payable on common stock, in addition, a dividend not payable until all arrears are paid on Series C, conversion rate 100 shares of common stock per share of preferred stock, 160,960 shares outstanding.

There are 108,524,400 shares of no-par value common stock outstanding. As of October 31, 1986, there were $86.4 million ($28.80 per share) in cumulative dividends in arrears on Series C preferred stock.

Navistar, which suffered greatly from the farm recession in the 1980s, lost $12,240,000 in 1986 and has a deficit in Retained Earnings of $1,889,168,000.

Required

1. How likely is it that investors in Navistar common stock will receive cash dividends? Explain your answer.
2. Assume that in 1987 Navistar returned to profitable operations and eliminated the deficit in retained earnings. What amount of dividends in total must be declared before the common stockholders would be eligible to receive a dividend? Assuming that total dividends of $154,575,000 were declared by the board of directors in 1987, what would be the dividends per share paid to the common stockholders?

8. Excerpts from the 1986 Annual Report used by permission of Navistar International Corporation. Copyright © 1986.

ICB 12-3.
Navistar International Corporation II[9]
(L.O. 5, 6, 8)

At the beginning of fiscal 1986, Navistar International, described in the preceding case, had 685,000 shares of Series A no-par, callable, convertible, cumulative preferred stock outstanding. During fiscal 1986, 16,000 shares were called at $25.67 per share and retired. In addition, 669,000 shares were converted to 2,500,000 shares of no-par common stock. The total carrying value of the preferred stock after the redemption and before the conversion was $17,600,000.

In addition, employees exercised employee stock options on 56,000 shares of no-par common stock at $3.60 per share.

Required

1. There are four adjectives that describe Navistar's Series A preferred stock. Explain what each means.
2. Prepare journal entries to record the call and the conversion of preferred shares.
3. Prepare the entry to record the exercise of stock options.
4. In 1986 Navistar had a net loss of $12,240,000 and a deficit in Retained Earnings of $1,889,168,000. The company has not paid a cash dividend since 1981. Why would the preferred stockholders and the employees want to own Navistar common stock?

ICB 12-4.
The Limited, Inc.[10]
(L.O. 8)

The Limited, Inc., one of the most successful specialty retailers, offers officers and key employees options to buy its $.50 par value common stock, as described in the following excerpt from its 1990 annual report:

Stock options are granted to officers and key employees based upon fair market value at the date of grant. The Company had approximately 9.0 million shares available for grant at February 2, 1991 as compared to 10.7 million shares available at February 3, 1990. Approximately 5.8 million shares of the Company's common stock were reserved for outstanding options, of which 2.3 million were exercisable as of February 2, 1991. Option activity for 1990, as adjusted for the June 8, 1990 stock split, follows:

	Number of Shares	Weighted Average Option Price Per Share
Outstanding Options, February 3, 1990	4,968,000	$10.52
Activity during 1989:		
Granted	2,083,000	$20.03
Exercised	(927,000)	$ 6.81
Canceled	(328,000)	$15.26
Outstanding Options, February 2, 1991	5,796,000	$14.26

Required

1. Prepare the general journal entry to record the exercise of employee stock options in 1990.
2. Why was it advantageous for employees to exercise these options in 1990? At what price were new options granted? Why is no journal entry made for the granting of stock options in 1990? Why do The Limited and other successful companies grant stock options to their employees?

9. Excerpts from the 1986 Annual Report used by permission of Navistar International Corporation. Copyright © 1986.
10. Excerpts from the 1990 Annual Report used by permission of The Limited, Inc. Copyright © 1990.

Problem Set A

Problem 12A-1. Organization Costs, Stock and Dividend Journal Entries, and Stockholders' Equity
(L.O. 2, 3, 4, 6)

On March 1, 19xx, Benson Corporation began operations with a charter from the state that authorized 100,000 shares of $2 par value common stock and engaged in the following transactions:

Mar. 1 Issued 30,000 shares of common stock, $100,000.
2 Paid fees associated with obtaining the charter and organizing the corporation, $12,000.
Apr. 10 Issued 13,000 shares of common stock, $65,000.
May 31 Closed the Income Summary account. Net income earned during the first quarter was $12,000.
31 The board of directors declared a $.10 per share cash dividend to be paid on June 15 to shareholders of record on June 10. Closed Dividends Declared to Retained Earnings.

Required

1. Prepare general journal entries to record the above transactions and closing entries as indicated.
2. Prepare the stockholders' equity section of Benson Corporation's balance sheet on May 31, 19xx.
3. Assuming that the payment for organization costs on March 2 was to be amortized over five years, what adjustment was made on May 31 to record three months' amortization? Describe the resulting balance sheet presentation of organization costs.

Problem 12A-2. Stock Journal Entries and Stockholders' Equity
(L.O. 3, 6, 7)

Lau Company, Inc. has been authorized by the state of Indiana to issue 1,000,000 shares of $1 par value common stock. The company began issuing its common stock in May of 19xx.

During May the company had the following stock transactions:

May 10 Issued 30,000 shares of stock for a building and land with fair market values of $32,000 and $7,000, respectively.
15 Accepted subscriptions for 500,000 shares of its stock for $650,000.
20 Collected full payment on 200,000 shares of the common stock subscribed on May 15. Issued the appropriate shares.
23 Sold 15,000 shares of stock for $20,000 cash.
27 Collected full payment on 100,000 shares of the common stock subscribed on May 15 and issued the shares.

Required

1. Prepare the general journal entries to record the stock transactions of Lau Company, Inc. for the month of May.
2. Prepare the stockholders' equity section of Lau's balance sheet as of May 31. Assume that the company had net income of $18,000 for May and paid no dividends.

Problem 12A-3. Preferred and Common Stock Dividends
(L.O. 5)

The Sabatino Corporation had the following stock outstanding for 19x1 through 19x4:

Preferred stock—$50 par value, 8 percent cumulative, 10,000 shares authorized, issued, and outstanding

Common stock—$5 par value, 200,000 shares authorized, issued, and outstanding

The company paid $30,000, $30,000, $94,000, and $130,000 in dividends during 19x1, 19x2, 19x3, and 19x4, respectively.

Required

1. Determine the dividend per share paid to common stockholders and preferred stockholders in 19x1, 19x2, 19x3, and 19x4.
2. Perform the same computations assuming that the preferred stock is noncumulative.

Problem 12A-4. Comprehensive Stockholders' Equity Transactions *(L.O. 2, 3, 4, 6, 7)*

Cabrini, Inc. was organized and authorized to issue 10,000 shares of $100 par value 9 percent preferred stock and 100,000 shares of no-par, $5 stated value common stock on July 1, 19xx. Stock-related transactions for Cabrini are as follows:

July 1 Issued 20,000 shares of common stock at $11 per share.
1 Issued 1,000 shares of common stock at $11 per share for services rendered in connection with the organization of the company.
2 Issued 2,000 shares of preferred stock at par value for cash.
10 Received subscriptions for 10,000 shares of common stock at $12 per share.
10 Issued 5,000 shares of common stock for land on which the asking price was $60,000. Market value of the stock was $12. Management wishes to record the land at full market value of the stock.
31 Closed the Income Summary account. Net income earned during July was $13,000.

Aug. 2 Received payment in full for 6,000 shares of the stock subscriptions of July 10. Issued the appropriate stock.
10 Declared a cash dividend for one month on the outstanding preferred stock and $.02 per share on common stock outstanding, payable on August 22 to stockholders of record on August 12.
12 Date of record for cash dividends.
22 Paid cash dividends.
31 Closed the Income Summary and Dividends Declared accounts. Net income during August was $12,000.

Required

1. Prepare general journal entries to record the above transactions.
2. Prepare the stockholders' equity section of the balance sheet as it would appear on August 31, 19xx.

Problem 12A-5. Comprehensive Stockholders' Equity Transactions *(L.O. 2, 3, 4, 6, 7, 8)*

In January 19xx, Abelman Corporation was organized and authorized to issue 2,000,000 shares of no-par common stock and 50,000 shares of 5 percent, $50 par value, noncumulative preferred stock. The stock-related transactions of the first year's operations follow.

Jan. 19 Sold 15,000 shares of the common stock for $31,500. State law requires a minimum of $1 stated value per share.
21 Issued 5,000 shares of common stock to attorneys and accountants for services valued at $11,000 provided during the organization of the corporation.
26 Accepted subscriptions for 20,000 shares of the common stock for $2.50 per share.

Feb. 7	Issued 30,000 shares of common stock for a building that had an appraised value of $78,000.
Mar. 22	Collected full payment for 12,000 shares of the common stock subscribed on January 26, 19xx, and issued the stock.
June 30	Closed the Income Summary account. Reported $80,000 income for the first six months of operations, ended June 30.
July 15	Issued 5,000 shares of common stock to employees under a stock option plan that allows any employee to buy shares at the current market price, which today is $3 per share.
Aug. 1	Collected the full amount on the remaining 8,000 shares of common stock subscribed and issued the stock.
Sept. 1	Declared a cash dividend of $.15 per common share to be paid on September 25 to stockholders of record on September 15.
15	Cash dividend date of record.
25	Paid cash dividend to stockholders of record on September 15.
Oct. 30	Issued 4,000 shares of common stock for a piece of land. The stock is selling for $3 per share, and the land has a fair market value of $12,500.
Nov. 10	Accepted subscriptions for 10,000 shares of the common stock for $3.50 per share.
Dec. 15	Issued 2,200 shares of preferred stock for $50 per share.
31	Closed the Income Summary account and Dividends Declared account. Reported $20,000 income for the past six months of operations.

Required

1. Prepare the journal entries to record all the above transactions of Abelman Corporation during 19xx.
2. Prepare the stockholders' equity section of Abelman Corporation's balance sheet as of December 31, 19xx.

Problem Set B

Problem 12B-1. Organization Costs, Stock and Dividend Journal Entries, and Stockholders' Equity
(L.O. 2, 3, 4, 6)

Forsyth Corporation began operations on September 1, 19xx. The corporation's charter authorized 300,000 shares of $4 par value common stock. Forsyth Corporation engaged in the following transactions during the first quarter:

Sept. 1	Issued 50,000 shares of common stock, $250,000.
1	Paid an attorney $16,000 to assist in organizing the corporation and obtaining the corporate charter from the state.
Oct. 2	Issued 80,000 shares of common stock, $480,000.
Nov. 30	The board of directors declared a cash dividend of $.20 per share to be paid on December 15 to stockholders of record on December 10.
30	Closed the Income Summary and Dividends Declared accounts for the first quarter. Revenues were $210,000 and expenses $170,000. (Assume that revenues and expenses have already been closed to Income Summary.)

Required

1. Prepare general journal entries to record the first-quarter transactions and closing entries as indicated.
2. Prepare the stockholders' equity section of Forsyth Corporation's November 30, 19xx balance sheet.

3. Assuming that the payment to the attorney on September 1 was to be amortized over five years, what adjusting entry was made on November 30? Also, describe the resulting balance sheet presentation for organization costs.

Problem 12B-2. Stock Journal Entries and Stockholders' Equity
(L.O. 3, 6, 7)

The corporate charter for Waldman Corporation states that the company is authorized to issue 500,000 shares of $3 par value common stock. The company was involved in several stock transactions during June 19x8, as shown in the following list. Assume no prior transactions.

June 3 Accepted subscriptions for 200,000 shares of its common stock at $5.50 per share.
12 Issued 24,000 shares of stock for land and warehouse. The land and warehouse had a fair market value of $25,000 and $100,000, respectively.
22 Sold 50,000 shares of stock for $325,000.
25 Collected full payment on 60,000 shares of the common stock subscribed on June 3 and issued the shares.

Required

1. Prepare the general journal entries to record the June transactions of Waldman Corporation.
2. Prepare the stockholders' equity section of Waldman Corporation's balance sheet as of June 30, 19x8. Assume that the company had net income of $8,000 during June and paid no dividends (and all necessary entries have been made).

Problem 12B-3. Preferred and Common Stock Dividends
(L.O. 5)

The Jefferson Corporation had both common stock and preferred stock outstanding from 19x4 through 19x6. Information about each stock for the three years is as follows:

Type	Par Value	Shares Outstanding	Other
Preferred	$100	20,000	7 percent cumulative
Common	10	600,000	

The company paid $70,000, $400,000, and $550,000 in dividends for 19x4 through 19x6, respectively.

Required

1. Determine the dividend per share paid to the common and preferred stockholders each year.
2. Repeat the computation performed in **1**, assuming that the preferred stock was noncumulative.

Problem 12B-4. Comprehensive Stockholders' Equity Transactions
(L.O. 2, 3, 4, 6, 7)

The Specialty Plastics Corporation was chartered in the state of Michigan. The company was authorized to issue 10,000 shares of $100 par value 6 percent preferred stock and 100,000 shares of no-par common stock. The common stock has a $1 stated value. The stock-related transactions for March and April, 19xx were as follows:

Mar. 3 Issued 10,000 shares of common stock for $60,000 worth of services rendered in organizing and chartering the corporation.
10 Received subscriptions for 40,000 shares of common stock at $6 a share.
15 Issued 16,000 shares of common stock for land, which has an asking price of $100,000. The common stock has a market value of $6 per share.
22 Issued 5,000 shares of preferred stock for $500,000.
31 Closed the Income Summary account. Net income for March was $9,000.
Apr. 4 Issued 10,000 shares of common stock for $60,000.
10 Received payment in full for 30,000 shares of the stock subscriptions of March 10 and issued the appropriate stock.
15 Declared a cash dividend for one month on the outstanding preferred stock and $.05 per share on the common stock outstanding, payable on April 30 to stockholders of record on April 25.
25 Date of record for cash dividends.
30 Paid cash dividends.
30 Closed the Income Summary and Dividends Declared accounts. Net income for April was $14,000.

Required

1. Prepare general journal entries for March and April.
2. Prepare the stockholders' equity section of the company's balance sheet as of April 30, 19xx.

Problem 12B-5. Comprehensive Stockholders' Equity Transactions *(L.O. 2, 3, 4, 6, 7, 8)*

Sun Lighting Corporation was organized and authorized to issue 100,000 shares of 6 percent, $100 par value, noncumulative preferred stock and 3,000,000 shares of $5 par value common stock. The stock-related transactions for the first six months of 19xx are as follows:

Apr. 3 Issued 12,000 shares of common stock for legal and other organizational fees valued at $60,000.
29 Sold 300,000 shares of common stock for $6 a share.
May 5 Issued 40,000 shares of common stock for a building and land appraised at $150,000 and $80,000, respectively.
17 Received subscriptions for 300,000 shares of common stock at $8 a share.
June 17 Received full payment for 200,000 shares of common stock subscribed on May 17 and issued the stock.
30 Closed the Income Summary account for the first quarter of operations. Net income for the first quarter was $200,000. (Assume that the revenues and expenses have already been closed into Income Summary.)
July 10 Issued 2,000 shares of common stock to employees under a stock option plan. The plan provides for employees to purchase the stock at the current market price, which was $6.
17 Collected the full amount for the remaining 100,000 shares of common stock subscribed on May 17 and issued the stock.
Aug. 8 Issued 10,000 shares of common stock for $8 a share.
Sept. 11 Declared a cash dividend of $.10 per common share to be paid on September 25 to stockholders of record on September 18.
18 Cash dividend date of record.

Sept. 25 Paid the cash dividend to stockholders of record on September 18.
26 Issued 5,000 shares of preferred stock at par value.
29 Accepted subscriptions for 20,000 shares of common stock at $9 per share.
30 Closed the Income Summary and Dividends Declared accounts for the second quarter of operations. Net income for the second quarter was $125,000.

Required

1. Prepare general journal entries to record the stock-related transactions of Sun Lighting Corporation.
2. Prepare the stockholders' equity section of Sun Lighting Corporation's balance sheet as of September 30, 19xx.

Financial Decision Case

Northeast Servotech Corporation *(L.O. 3)*

Companies offering services to the computer technology industry are growing quickly. Participating in this growth, Northeast Servotech Corporation has expanded rapidly in recent years. Because of its profitability, the company has been able to grow without obtaining external financing. This fact is reflected in its current balance sheet, which contains no long-term debt. The liabilities and stockholders' equity sections of the balance sheet are as follows.

Northeast Servotech Corporation
Partial Balance Sheet

Liabilities		
Current Liabilities		$ 500,000
Stockholders' Equity		
Common Stock—$10 par value, 500,000 shares authorized, 100,000 shares issued and outstanding	$1,000,000	
Paid-in Capital in Excess of Par Value, Common	1,800,000	
Retained Earnings	1,700,000	
Total Stockholders' Equity		4,500,000
Total Liabilities and Stockholders' Equity		$5,000,000

The company is now faced with the possibility of doubling its size by purchasing the operations of a rival company for $4,000,000. If the purchase goes through, Northeast will become the top company in its specialized industry in the northeastern part of the country. The problem for management is how to finance the purchase. After much study and discussion with bankers and underwriters, management prepares three financing alternatives to present to the board of directors, which must authorize the purchase and the financing.

Alternative A: The company could issue $4,000,000 of long-term debt. Given the company's financial rating and the current market rates, it is believed that the company will have to pay an interest rate of 17 percent on the debt.

Alternative B: The company could issue 40,000 shares of 12 percent, $100 par value preferred stock.

Alternative C: The company could issue 100,000 additional shares of $10 par value common stock at $40.

Management explains to the board that the interest on the long-term debt is tax deductible and that the applicable income tax rate is 40 percent. The board members know that a dividend of $.80 per share of common stock was paid last year, up from $.60 and $.40 per share in the two years before that. The board has had a policy of regular increases in dividends of $.20 per share. The board feels that each of the three financing alternatives is feasible and now wishes to study the financial effects of each alternative.

Required

1. Prepare a schedule to show how the liabilities and stockholders' equity side of Northeast Servotech's balance sheet will look under each alternative, and figure the debt to equity ratio (total liabilities ÷ total stockholders' equity) for each.
2. Compute and compare the cash needed to pay the interest or dividend for each kind of financing net of income taxes in the first year. How may this requirement change in future years?
3. Evaluate the alternatives, giving the arguments for and against each one.

LEARNING OBJECTIVES

1. *Define* retained earnings, *and prepare a statement of retained earnings.*
2. *Account for stock dividends and stock splits.*
3. *Account for treasury stock transactions.*
4. *Describe the disclosure of restrictions on retained earnings.*
5. *Prepare a statement of stockholders' equity.*
6. *Calculate book value per share, and distinguish it from market value.*
7. *Prepare a corporate income statement.*
8. *Show the relationships among income taxes expense, deferred income taxes, and net of taxes.*
9. *Describe the disclosure on the income statement of discontinued operations, extraordinary items, and accounting changes.*
10. *Compute earnings per share.*

CHAPTER 13

Retained Earnings and Corporate Income Statements

This chapter continues the study of the stockholders' equity section of the balance sheet. It first covers the retained earnings of a corporation, the transactions that affect them, and the statement of stockholders' equity. The rest of the chapter examines the components of the corporate income statement. After studying this chapter, you should be able to meet the learning objectives listed on the left.

DECISION POINT

International Business Machines Corporation (IBM)

A note to IBM's 1989 annual report outlines the company's stock repurchase plan, which has already resulted in the repurchase of a substantial number of IBM's common shares and projects the repurchase of many more shares, as follows:

> Under programs for purchasing IBM stock 16,085,900 shares were purchased during 1989 at a cost of $1,759 million, 8,611,396 shares were repurchased during 1988 at a cost of $992 million and 11,252,000 shares during 1987 at a cost of $1,425 million. The repurchased shares were retired and restored to the status of authorized but unissued shares. In late 1989, the Board of Directors authorized the company to purchase from time to time shares of its capital stock not to exceed $5,000 million. At December 31, 1989, $4,887 million of that authorization remained.[1]

Why would management want to repurchase its company's common shares, and what would be the effects of these repurchases on the company's financial statements?

1. Excerpt used by permission from the 1989 Annual Report of IBM Corporation.

There are several good reasons for a company to repurchase its common stock, as will be seen later in this chapter. The goal of IBM management is to increase the value of the company's stock, as revealed in the following excerpt from the letter to stockholders in the annual report:

> To further enhance shareholder value, IBM has, since 1986, repurchased shares of its common stock—a total of 47 million shares through the end of 1989. Repurchase reduces shareholders' equity, distributing earnings over a smaller base and increasing returns. The benefit to IBM shareholders has been to increase return on equity by approximately 6 percent in 1988 and 1989. . . . We regard IBM stock as an attractive investment.[2]

Examination of the statement of stockholders' equity reveals that large amounts of common stock were indeed retired in 1987, 1988, and 1989, resulting in decreases in common stock and retained earnings. The decrease in retained earnings in 1989, for example, was $1,582 million. The retirement of common stock is just one of several important transactions that affect retained earnings. The following sections explore these transactions. ■

Retained Earnings Transactions

OBJECTIVE 1
Define retained earnings, *and prepare a statement of retained earnings*

Stockholders' equity, as presented earlier, has two parts: contributed capital and retained earnings. The **retained earnings** of a company are the part of the stockholders' equity that represents claims to assets arising from the earnings of the business. Retained earnings equal the profits of a company since the date of its beginning less any losses, dividends to stockholders, or transfers to contributed capital. Exhibit 13-1 shows a statement of retained earnings of Caprock Corporation for 19x2. The beginning balance of retained earnings of $854,000 is increased by net income of $76,000 and decreased by cash dividends of $30,000, so that the ending balance is $900,000. This statement may also disclose other transactions that are explained in the chapter.

It is important to note that retained earnings are not the assets themselves, but the existence of retained earnings means that assets generated by profitable operations have been kept in the company to help it grow or to meet other business needs. However, a credit balance in Retained Earnings does *not* mean that cash or any designated set of assets is directly associated with retained earnings. The fact that earnings have been retained means that assets as a whole have been increased.

Retained Earnings may carry a debit balance. Generally, this happens when a company's losses and distributions to stockholders are greater than its profits from operations. In such a case, the firm is said to have a

2. Excerpt used by permission from the 1989 Annual Report of IBM Corporation.

Exhibit 13-1. A Statement of Retained Earnings

Caprock Corporation
Statement of Retained Earnings
For the Year Ended December 31, 19x2

Retained Earnings, December 31, 19x1	$854,000
Net Income, 19x2	76,000
Subtotal	$930,000
Less Cash Dividends, Common	30,000
Retained Earnings, December 31, 19x2	$900,000

deficit (debit balance) in retained earnings. This is shown in the stockholders' equity section of the balance sheet as a deduction from contributed capital.

Accountants have used various terms for the retained earnings of a business. One term is *surplus,* which implies that there are excess assets available for dividends. This is poor terminology, as the existence of retained earnings carries no connotation of "excess" or "surplus." Because of possible misinterpretation, the American Institute of Certified Public Accountants recommends more fitting terms, such as *retained income, retained earnings, accumulated earnings,* or *earnings retained for use in the business.*[3]

Prior period adjustments are events or transactions that relate to earlier accounting periods but were not determinable in the earlier period. When they occur, they are shown on the statement of retained earnings as an adjustment in the account's beginning balance. The Financial Accounting Standards Board identifies only two kinds of prior period adjustments. The first is to correct an error in the financial statements of a prior year. The second is needed if a company realizes an income tax gain from carrying forward a preacquisition operating loss of a purchased subsidiary.[4] Prior period adjustments are rare in accounting.

Stock Dividends

OBJECTIVE 2
Account for stock dividends and stock splits

A **stock dividend** is a proportional distribution of shares of the company's stock to the corporation's stockholders. The distribution of stock does not change the assets and liabilities of the firm because there is not a

3. Committee on Accounting Terminology, *Accounting Terminology Bulletin No. 1,* "Review and Resume" (New York: American Institute of Certified Public Accountants, 1953), par. 69.
4. *Statement of Financial Accounting Standards No. 16,* "Prior Period Adjustments" (Stamford, Conn.: Financial Accounting Standards Board, 1977), par. 11.

distribution of assets as in a cash dividend. The board of directors may declare a stock dividend for several reasons:

1. It may wish to give stockholders some evidence of the success of the company without paying a cash dividend, which would affect the firm's working capital position.
2. The board's aim may be to reduce the market price of the stock by increasing the number of shares outstanding, though this goal is more often met by stock splits.
3. It may want to make a nontaxable distribution to stockholders. Stock dividends that meet certain conditions are not considered income, so a tax is not levied on this type of transaction.
4. It communicates that the permanent capital of the company has increased by transferring an amount from Retained Earnings to Contributed Capital.

The total stockholders' equity is not affected by a stock dividend. The effect of a stock dividend is to transfer a dollar amount from Retained Earnings to the Contributed Capital section on the date of declaration. The amount to be transferred is the fair market value (usually market price) of the additional shares to be issued. The laws of most states specify the minimum value of each share to be transferred under a stock dividend, which is normally the minimum legal capital (par or stated value). However, generally accepted accounting principles state that market value reflects the economic effect of small stock distributions (less than 20 or 25 percent of a company's outstanding common stock) better than the par or stated value does. For this reason, the market price should be used for proper accounting for small stock dividends.[5]

To illustrate the accounting for a stock dividend, we will assume that Caprock Corporation has the following stockholders' equity structure:

Contributed Capital	
Common Stock—$5 par value, 100,000 shares authorized, 30,000 shares issued and outstanding	$ 150,000
Paid-in Capital in Excess of Par Value, Common	30,000
Total Contributed Capital	$ 180,000
Retained Earnings	900,000
Total Stockholders' Equity	$1,080,000

Assume further that the board of directors declares a 10 percent stock dividend on February 24, distributable on March 31 to stockholders of record on March 15. The market price of the stock on February 24 was $20 per share. The entries to record the stock dividend declaration and distribution are as follows:

5. *Accounting Research Bulletin No. 43* (New York: American Institute of Certified Public Accountants, 1953), Chapter 7, Section B, par. 10.

Date of Declaration

Feb. 24	Retained Earnings	60,000	
	Common Stock Distributable		15,000
	Paid-in Capital in Excess of Par Value, Common		45,000
	To record the declaration of a 10% stock dividend on common stock, distributable on March 31 to stockholders of record on March 15: 30,000 shares × 10% = 3,000 shares 3,000 shares × $20/share = $60,000 3,000 shares × $5/share = $15,000		

Note that Retained Earnings is reduced directly rather than through a Dividends Declared account as was done for cash dividends in the chapter on contributed capital. The reason for this treatment is that cash dividends are usually declared on several occasions during the year. The Dividends Declared account is useful in accumulating the total cash dividends declared during the year. Stock dividends are usually declared only once per year, if at all.

Date of Record

Mar. 15 No entry required

Date of Distribution

Mar. 31	Common Stock Distributable	15,000	
	Common Stock		15,000
	To record the distribution of stock dividend of 3,000 shares		

The effect of the above stock dividend is to transfer permanently the market value of the stock, $60,000, from Retained Earnings to Contributed Capital and to increase the number of shares outstanding by 3,000. Common Stock Distributable is credited for the par value of the stock to be distributed (3,000 × $5 = $15,000). In addition, when the market value of the stock is greater than the par value, Paid-in Capital in Excess of Par Value, Common, must be credited for the amount by which market value exceeds par value. In this case, the total market value of the stock dividend ($60,000) exceeds the total par value ($15,000) by $45,000. No entry is required on the date of record. On the distribution date, the common stock is issued by debiting Common Stock Distributable and crediting Common Stock for the par value of the stock ($15,000).

Common Stock Distributable is not a liability because there is no obligation to distribute cash or other assets. The obligation is to distribute additional shares of capital stock. If financial statements are prepared between the date of declaration and the distribution of stock, Common Stock Distributable should be reported as part of Contributed Capital, as follows:

Contributed Capital	
Common Stock—$5 par value, 100,000 shares authorized, 30,000 shares issued and outstanding	$ 150,000
Common Stock Distributable, 3,000 shares	15,000
Paid-in Capital in Excess of Par Value, Common	75,000
Total Contributed Capital	$ 240,000
Retained Earnings	840,000
Total Stockholders' Equity	$1,080,000

Three points can be made from this example. First, total stockholders' equity is unchanged before and after the stock dividend. Second, the assets of the corporation are not reduced as in the case of a cash dividend. Third, the proportionate ownership in the corporation of any individual stockholder is unchanged before and after the stock dividend. To illustrate these points, we will assume that a stockholder owns 1,000 shares before the stock dividend. After the 10 percent stock dividend is distributed, this stockholder would own 1,100 shares.

Stockholders' Equity	Before Dividend	After Dividend
Common Stock	$ 150,000	$ 165,000
Paid-in Capital in Excess of Par Value	30,000	75,000
Total Contributed Capital	$ 180,000	$ 240,000
Retained Earnings	900,000	840,000
Total Stockholders' Equity	$1,080,000	$1,080,000
Shares Outstanding	30,000	33,000
Book Value per Share	$36.00	$32.73
Stockholders' Investment		
Shares owned	1,000	1,100
Shares outstanding	30,000	33,000
Percentage of ownership	3⅓%	3⅓%
Book value of investment (3⅓% × $1,080,000)	$ 36,000	$ 36,000

Both before and after the stock dividend, the stockholders' equity totals $1,080,000 and the stockholder owns 3⅓ percent of the company. Book value of the investment stays at $36,000.

All stock dividends have an effect on the market price of a company's stock. But some stock dividends are so large that they have a material effect on the price per share of the stock. For example, a 50 percent stock dividend would cause the market price of the stock to drop about 33 percent. The AICPA has arbitrarily decided that large stock dividends, those greater than 20 to 25 percent, should be accounted for by transferring the par or stated value of the stock on the date of declaration from Retained Earnings to Contributed Capital.[6]

Stock Splits

A **stock split** occurs when a corporation increases the number of issued shares of stock and reduces the par or stated value proportionally. A company may plan a stock split when it wishes to lower the market value per share of its stock and increase the liquidity of the stock. This action may be necessary if the market value per share has become so high that it hinders the trading of the company's stock on the market. For example, suppose that the Caprock Corporation has 30,000 shares of $5.00 par value stock outstanding. The market value is $70.00 per share. The corporation plans a 2 for 1 split. This split will lower the par value to $2.50 and increase the number of shares outstanding to 60,000. If a stockholder previously owned 400 shares of the $5.00 par stock, he or she would own 800 shares of the $2.50 par stock after the split. When a stock split occurs, the market value tends to fall in proportion to the increase in outstanding shares of stock. For example, a 2 for 1 stock split would cause the price of the stock to drop by approximately 50 percent, to about $35.00. The lower price plus the increase in shares tends to promote the buying and selling of shares.

A stock split does not, in itself, increase the number of shares authorized. Nor does it change the balances in the stockholders' equity section. It simply changes the par value and number of shares outstanding. Therefore, an entry is not necessary. However, it is appropriate to document the change by making a memorandum entry in the general journal, as follows:

July 15 The 30,000 shares of $5 par value common stock that are issued and outstanding were split 2 for 1, resulting in 60,000 shares of $2.50 par value common stock issued and outstanding.

The change for the Caprock Corporation is as follows:

Before Stock Split (from page 636)

Contributed Capital	
Common Stock—$5 par value, **100,000 shares authorized, 30,000 shares issued and outstanding**	$ 150,000
Paid-in Capital in Excess of Par Value, Common	30,000
Total Contributed Capital	$ 180,000
Retained Earnings	900,000
Total Stockholders' Equity	$1,080,000

6. Ibid., par. 13.

After Stock Split

Contributed Capital	
Common Stock—$2.50 par value, 100,000 shares authorized, 60,000 shares issued and outstanding	$ 150,000
Paid-in Capital in Excess of Par Value, Common	30,000
Total Contributed Capital	$ 180,000
Retained Earnings	900,000
Total Stockholders' Equity	$1,080,000

In cases where the number of split shares will exceed the number of authorized shares, the board of directors will have to authorize, with appropriate state approval, additional shares at the time of the split.

Treasury Stock Transactions

OBJECTIVE 3
Account for treasury stock transactions

Treasury stock is capital stock, either common or preferred, that has been issued and reacquired by the issuing company but has not been sold or retired. The company normally gets the stock back by purchasing the shares on the market or through donations by stockholders. It is common for companies to buy and hold their own stock. In 1989, 393, or 66 percent, of 600 large companies held treasury stock.[7] There are several reasons why a company may purchase its own stock. (1) It may want to have stock available to distribute to employees through stock option plans. (2) It may be trying to maintain a favorable market for the company's stock. (3) It may want to increase the company's earnings per share. (4) It may want to have additional shares of the company's stock available for such activities as purchasing other companies. (5) It may be used as a strategy to prevent a hostile takeover.

The effect of a treasury stock purchase is to reduce the assets and the stockholders' equity of the company. It is not considered a purchase of assets, as purchase of the shares of another company would be. Treasury stock is capital stock that has been issued but is no longer outstanding. Treasury shares may be held for an indefinite period of time, reissued, or retired. Thus treasury stock is somewhat similar to unissued stock. That is, it has no rights until the stock is reissued. Treasury stock does not have voting rights, preemptive rights, rights to cash dividends, or rights to share in assets during liquidation of the company, and it is not considered to be outstanding in the calculation of book value. However, there is one major difference between unissued shares and treasury shares. If a share of stock was originally issued at par value or greater and fully paid for, and then reacquired as treasury stock, it may be reissued at less than par value without a discount liability attaching to it.

Purchase of Treasury Stock. When treasury stock is purchased, it is normally recorded at cost. The transaction reduces both the assets and the stockholders' equity of the firm. For example, assume that on September 15 the Caprock Corporation purchases 1,000 shares of its common stock

7. *Accounting Trends and Techniques* (New York: American Institute of Certified Public Accountants, 1990), p. 201.

on the market at a price of $50 per share. The purchase would be recorded as follows:

Sept. 15	Treasury Stock, Common	50,000	
	Cash		50,000
	Acquired 1,000 shares of company's common stock for $50 per share		

Note that the treasury shares are recorded at cost. Any par value, stated value, or original issue price of the stock is ignored.

The stockholders' equity section of Caprock's balance sheet shows the cost of the treasury stock as a deduction from the total of Contributed Capital and Retained Earnings, as follows:

Contributed Capital	
Common Stock—$5 par value, 100,000 shares authorized, 30,000 shares issued, 29,000 shares outstanding	$ 150,000
Paid-in Capital in Excess of Par Value, Common	30,000
Total Contributed Capital	$ 180,000
Retained Earnings	900,000
Total Contributed Capital and Retained Earnings	$1,080,000
Less Treasury Stock, Common (1,000 shares at cost)	50,000
Total Stockholders' Equity	$1,030,000

Note that the number of shares issued, and thus the legal capital, has not changed, although the number of outstanding shares has decreased as a result of the transaction.

Sale of Treasury Stock. The treasury shares may be sold at cost, above cost, or below cost. For example, assume that on November 15 the 1,000 treasury shares of the Caprock Corporation are sold for $50 per share. The entry to record this transaction is

Nov. 15	Cash	50,000	
	Treasury Stock, Common		50,000
	Reissued 1,000 shares of treasury stock for $50 per share		

When treasury shares are sold for an amount greater than their cost, the excess of the sales price over cost should be credited to Paid-in Capital, Treasury Stock. No gain should be recorded. For example, suppose that on November 15 the 1,000 treasury shares of the Caprock Corporation are sold for $60 per share. The entry for the reissue would be

Nov. 15	Cash	60,000	
	Treasury Stock, Common		50,000
	Paid-in Capital, Treasury Stock		10,000
	To record the sale of 1,000 shares of treasury stock for $60 per share; cost was $50 per share		

If the treasury shares are sold below their cost, the difference should be deducted from Paid-in Capital, Treasury Stock. When this account does not exist or is insufficient to cover the excess of cost over reissuance price, Retained Earnings should absorb the excess. No loss should be recorded. For example, suppose that on September 15 the Caprock Corporation bought 1,000 shares of its common stock on the market at a price of $50 per share. The company sold 400 shares of its stock on October 15 for $60 per share and the remaining 600 shares on December 15 for $42 per share. The entries to record these transactions are presented as follows:

Date	Account	Debit	Credit
Sept. 15	Treasury Stock, Common	50,000	
	Cash		50,000
	To record the purchase of 1,000 shares of treasury stock at $50 per share		
Oct. 15	Cash	24,000	
	Treasury Stock, Common		20,000
	Paid-in Capital, Treasury Stock		4,000
	To record the sale of 400 shares of treasury stock for $60 per share; cost was $50 per share		
Dec. 15	Cash	25,200	
	Paid-in Capital, Treasury Stock	4,000	
	Retained Earnings	800	
	Treasury Stock, Common		30,000
	To record the sale of 600 shares of treasury stock for $42 per share; cost was $50 per share		

In the December 15 entry, Retained Earnings is debited for $800 because the 600 shares were sold for $4,800 less than cost. That amount is $800 greater than the $4,000 of paid-in capital generated by the sale of the 400 shares on October 15.

Retirement of Treasury Stock. If a company determines that it will not reissue stock it has purchased, it may, with the approval of its stockholders, decide to retire the stock. When shares of stock are retired, all items related to those shares should be removed from the related capital accounts. When stock that cost less than the original contributed capital is retired, the difference is recognized as Paid-in Capital, Retirement of Stock. However, if stock that cost more than was received when the shares were first issued is retired, the difference is a reduction in stockholders' equity and is debited to Retained Earnings. For instance, suppose that instead of selling the 1,000 shares of treasury stock purchased for $50,000, Caprock decides to retire the shares on November 15. Assuming that the $5 par value common stock was originally issued at $6 per share, the entry to record the retirement is

Date	Account	Debit	Credit
Nov. 15	Common Stock	5,000	
	Paid-in Capital in Excess of Par Value	1,000	
	Retained Earnings	44,000	
	Treasury Stock		50,000
	To record the retirement of 1,000 shares that cost $50 per share and were originally issued at $6 per share		

Restrictions on Retained Earnings

OBJECTIVE 4 *Describe the disclosure of restrictions on retained earnings*

A corporation may wish or be required to restrict all or a portion of retained earnings. A **restriction on retained earnings** means that dividends may be declared only to the extent of the *unrestricted* retained earnings. The following are several reasons why a corporation might do this:

1. *A contractual agreement.* For example, bond indentures may place a limitation on the dividends to be paid by the company.
2. *State law.* Many states will not allow dividends or the purchase of treasury stock if doing so impairs the legal capital of a company.
3. *Voluntary action by the board of directors.* Many times a board will decide to retain assets in the business for future needs. For example, the company may be planning to build a new plant and may wish to show that dividends will be limited to save enough money for the building. The company may also restrict retained earnings to show the possible future loss of assets resulting from a lawsuit.

There are two ways of reporting retained earnings restrictions to readers of financial statements. First, the restriction of retained earnings may be shown in the stockholders' equity section of the balance sheet. Second, the restricted retained earnings may be disclosed by means of a note to the financial statements.

A restriction on retained earnings does not change the total retained earnings or stockholders' equity of the company. It simply divides retained earnings into two parts, restricted and unrestricted. The restricted part indicates that assets in that amount may not be used for payment of dividends. The unrestricted amount represents earnings kept in the business that could be used for dividends and other purposes. Assuming that Caprock's board of directors has decided to restrict retained earnings of $300,000 because of plans for plant expansion, the disclosure in Caprock's stockholders' equity section would be as follows:

Contributed Capital		
Common Stock—$5 par value, 100,000 shares authorized, 30,000 shares issued and outstanding		$ 150,000
Paid-in Capital in Excess of Par Value, Common		30,000
Total Contributed Capital		$ 180,000
Retained Earnings		
Restricted for Plant Expansion	$300,000	
Unrestricted	600,000	
Total Retained Earnings		900,000
Total Stockholders' Equity		$1,080,000

The same facts about restricted retained earnings could also be presented by reference to a note to the financial statements. For example:

Retained Earnings (Note 15)	$900,000

Note 15:
Because of plans for expanding the capacity of the clothing division, the board of directors has restricted retained earnings available for dividends by $300,000.

Note that the restriction of retained earnings does not restrict cash in any way. It simply explains to the readers of the financial statements that a certain amount of assets generated by earnings will remain in the business for the purpose stated. It is still management's job to make sure that there is enough cash or assets on hand to satisfy the restriction, and the subsequent removal of the restriction does not necessarily mean that the board of directors will now declare a dividend.

Statement of Stockholders' Equity

OBJECTIVE 5
Prepare a statement of stockholders' equity

The statement of stockholders' equity, also called the statement of changes in stockholders' equity, summarizes the changes in the components of the stockholders' equity section of the balance sheet. Companies are increasingly using this statement in place of the statement of retained earnings because it reveals much more about the year's stockholders' equity transactions. In Exhibit 13-2, for example, note that in the Tri-State Corporation's statement of stockholders' equity, the first line contains the beginning balances (last period's ending balances) of each account in the

Exhibit 13-2. A Statement of Stockholders' Equity

Tri-State Corporation
Statement of Stockholders' Equity
For the Year Ended December 31, 19x2

	Preferred Stock $100 Par Value 8% Convertible	Common Stock $10 Par Value	Paid-in Capital in Excess of Par Value	Retained Earnings	Treasury Stock	Total
Balance, December 31, 19x1	$400,000	$300,000	$300,000	$600,000	—	$1,600,000
Issuance of 5,000 Shares of Common Stock		50,000	200,000			250,000
Conversion of 1,000 Shares of Preferred Stock into 3,000 Shares of Common Stock	(100,000)	30,000	70,000			—
10 Percent Stock Dividend on Common Stock, 3,800 Shares		38,000	152,000	(190,000)		—
Purchase of 500 Shares of Treasury Stock					$(24,000)	(24,000)
Net Income				270,000		270,000
Cash Dividends						
Preferred Stock				(33,000)		(33,000)
Common Stock				(38,600)		(38,600)
Balance, December 31, 19x2	$300,000	$418,000	$722,000	$608,400	$(24,000)	$2,024,400

stockholders' equity section. Each additional line in the statement discloses the effects of transactions that affect the accounts. It is possible to determine from this statement that during 19x2 Tri-State Corporation issued 5,000 shares of common stock for $250,000, had a conversion of $100,000 of preferred stock into common stock, declared and issued a 10 percent stock dividend on common stock, had a net purchase of treasury shares of $24,000, earned net income of $270,000, and paid cash dividends on both preferred and common stock. The ending balances of the accounts are presented at the bottom of the statement. These accounts and balances will make up the stockholders' equity section of Tri-State's balance sheet at December 31, 19x2, as shown below. Also, note that the Retained Earnings column has the same components as would the statement of retained earnings, if it were prepared separately.

Tri-State Corporation
Stockholders' Equity
December 31, 19x2

Contributed Capital		
Preferred Stock—$100 par value, 8% convertible, 10,000 shares authorized, 3,000 shares outstanding		$ 300,000
Common Stock—$10 par value, 100,000 shares authorized, 41,800 shares issued, 41,300 shares outstanding	$418,000	
Paid-in Capital in Excess of Par Value, Common	722,000	1,140,000
Total Contributed Capital		$1,440,000
Retained Earnings		608,400
Total Contributed Capital and Retained Earnings		$2,048,400
Less Treasury Stock, Common (500 shares)		24,000
Total Stockholders' Equity		$2,024,400

Stock Values

The word *value* is associated with shares of stock in several ways. The terms *par value* and *stated value* have already been explained. They are each values per share that establish the legal capital of a company. Par value or stated value is arbitrarily set when the stock is authorized. Neither has any relationship to the book value or the market value.

Book Value

OBJECTIVE 6 *Calculate book value per share, and distinguish it from market value*

The **book value** of a company's stock represents the total assets of the company less liabilities. Thus, it is simply the owners' equity of the company or, to look at it another way, the company's net assets. The book value per share, therefore, represents the equity of the owner of one share of stock in the net assets of the corporation. This value, of course, does not necessarily equal the amount the shareholders would receive if the company were sold or liquidated. It is probably different, because most assets are recorded at historical cost, not at the current value at which they could be sold. To learn the book value per share when the company has only common stock outstanding, divide the total stockholders' equity by the total common shares outstanding. In computing shares outstanding, shares subscribed but not issued are included, but treasury stock (shares previously issued now held by the company) is not included. For example, on page 641, Caprock Corporation has total stockholders' equity of $1,030,000 and 29,000 shares outstanding after recording the purchase of treasury shares. The book value per share of Caprock's common stock is $35.52 ($1,030,000 ÷ 29,000 shares).

If a company has both preferred and common stock, the determination of book value per share is not so simple. The general rule is that the call value (or par value, if a call value is not specified) of the preferred stock plus any dividends in arrears is subtracted from total stockholders' equity to figure the equity pertaining to common stock. As an illustration, refer to the stockholders' equity section for Tri-State Corporation on page 645. Assuming that there are no dividends in arrears and that the preferred stock is callable at $105, the equity pertaining to common stock is figured as follows:

Total stockholders' equity	$2,024,400
Less equity allocated to preferred shareholders ($105 × 3,000 shares)	315,000
Equity pertaining to common shareholders	**$1,709,400**

There are 41,300 shares of common stock outstanding (41,800 shares issued less 500 shares of treasury stock). The book values per share would be as follows:

Preferred Stock: $315,000 ÷ 3,000 shares = $105 per share
Common Stock: $1,709,400 ÷ 41,300 shares = $41.39 per share

If we assume the same facts except that the preferred stock is cumulative and that one year of dividends is in arrears, the stockholders' equity would be allocated as follows:

Total Stockholders' Equity		$2,024,400
Less: Call value of outstanding preferred shares	$315,000	
Dividends in arrears (8% × $300,000)	24,000	
Equity allocated to preferred shareholders		**339,000**
Equity pertaining to common shareholders		**$1,685,400**

The book values per share under this assumption are:

Preferred Stock: $339,000 ÷ 3,000 shares = $113 per share
Common Stock: $1,685,400 ÷ 41,300 shares = $40.81 per share

Undeclared preferred dividends fall into arrears on the last day of the fiscal year (the date when the financial statements are prepared). Also, dividends in arrears do not apply to unissued preferred stock.

Market Value

The **market value** is the price that investors are willing to pay for a share of stock on the open market. Whereas the book value is based on historical cost, the market value is usually determined by investors' expectations for the particular company and general economic conditions. That is, what people expect about the company's future profitability and dividends per share, how risky they view the company and its current financial condition to be, and the state of the money market will all play a part in determining the market value of a corporation's stock. Although the book value per share often has little relationship to the market value per share, some investors use the relationship of the two measures as a rough indicator of the relative values of shares. For example, in early 1991 a major oil company, Texaco, had a market value per share of $65 compared with a book value per share of $34. At the same time, a large automobile company, Chrysler, had a market value per share of $14 and a book value per share of $31.

DECISION POINT
Eastman Kodak Company

Someone who does not understand the structure and use of corporate income statements may be confused by corporate earnings reports in the financial press. For example, the *Wall Street Journal* recently reported, "Eastman Kodak Co. recorded a third-quarter net loss of $206 million, or 64 cents a share, but posted a 22 percent rise in operating earnings as the company continued to benefit from restructuring moves that began in 1989."[8] How could Eastman Kodak, a well-known photographic film, chemical, and health company, have both a large net loss and an increase in operating earnings?

As will be explained in the following section, the corporate income statement has several components. Eastman Kodak's net loss reflects a $909.5 million charge for costs associated with a ruling against the company for its infringement on Polaroid Corporation's instant photography patents. This loss, however, is reported on the income statement below the earnings from current or continuing operations, which in one year rose by 22 percent, from $682 million to $835 million. The *Wall Street Journal* report indicates that Eastman Kodak's continuing operations are doing well, but the adverse ruling brought on a serious one-time loss. This fact would be apparent to a reader who knows how to evaluate corporate income statements. ■

8. James S. Hirsch, "Eastman Kodak Posts Net Loss for 3rd Quarter," *Wall Street Journal*, Nov. 1, 1990.

Corporate Income Statement

OBJECTIVE 7
Prepare a corporate income statement

This chapter and the chapter on contributed capital show how certain transactions are reflected in the stockholders' equity section of the corporate balance sheet and in the retained earnings statement. A separate chapter deals with the statement of cash flows. The following sections will briefly describe some of the features of the corporate income statement.

The format of the income statement has not been specified by the accounting profession because flexibility has been considered more important than a standard format. Either the single-step or multistep form may be used (see the chapter on accounting concepts and classified financial statements). However, the accounting profession has taken the position that income for a period shall be an all-inclusive or **comprehensive income.**[9] This rule means that income or loss for a period should include all revenues, expenses, gains, and losses of the period, except for prior period adjustments. This approach to the measurement of income has resulted in several items being added to the income statement. These items include discontinued operations, extraordinary items, and accounting changes. In addition, earnings per share figures should be disclosed. Exhibit 13-3 illustrates the corporate income statement and the disclosures required. The following sections discuss these components of the corporate income statement, beginning with income taxes expense.

Income Taxes Expense

OBJECTIVE 8
Show the relationships among income taxes expense, deferred income taxes, and net of taxes

Corporations determine their taxable income (the amount on which taxes will be paid) by subtracting allowable business deductions from includable gross income. The federal tax laws determine what business deductions are allowed and what must be included in gross income.[10]

The tax rates that apply to a corporation's taxable income are shown in Table 13-1. A corporation with a taxable income of $70,000 would have a federal income tax liability of $12,500. This amount is computed by adding $7,500 (the tax on the first $50,000 of taxable income) to $5,000 (25 percent times the $20,000 earned in excess of $50,000).

Income Taxes Expense is the expense recognized in the accounting records on an accrual basis as applicable to income from continuing operations. This expense may or may not be equal to the amount of taxes actually paid by the corporation. The amount payable is determined from taxable income, which is measured according to the rules and regulations of the income tax code. For most small businesses, it is convenient to keep accounting records on the same basis as tax records so that the income taxes expense on the income statement equals the income taxes liability to

9. *Statement of Financial Accounting Concepts No. 6,* "Elements of Financial Statements" (Stamford, Conn.: Financial Accounting Standards Board, 1985), pars. 70–77.

10. Rules for calculating and reporting taxable income in specialized industries such as banking, insurance, mutual funds, and cooperatives are highly technical and may vary significantly from those shown in this chapter.

Exhibit 13-3. A Corporate Income Statement

Junction Corporation
Income Statement
For the Year Ended December 31, 19xx

Revenues		$925,000
Less Costs and Expenses		500,000
Income from Continuing Operations Before Taxes		$425,000
Income Taxes Expense		119,000
Income from Continuing Operations		$306,000
Discontinued Operations		
Income from Operations of Discontinued Segment (net of taxes, $35,000)	$90,000	
Loss on Disposal of Segment (net of taxes, $42,000)	(73,000)	17,000
Income Before Extraordinary Items and Cumulative Effect of Accounting Change		$323,000
Extraordinary Gain (net of taxes, $17,000)		43,000
Subtotal		$366,000
Cumulative Effect of a Change in Accounting Principle (net of taxes, $5,000)		(6,000)
Net Income		$360,000
Earnings per Common Share:		
Income from Continuing Operations		$3.06
Discontinued Operations (net of taxes)		.17
Income Before Extraordinary Items		$3.23
Extraordinary Gain (net of taxes)		.43
Cumulative Effect of Accounting Change (net of taxes)		(.06)
Net Income		$3.60

be paid to the Internal Revenue Service (IRS). This practice is usually acceptable when there is no material difference between income on an accounting basis and income on an income tax basis. However, the purpose of accounting is to determine net income in accordance with generally accepted accounting principles, whereas the purpose of the tax code is to determine taxable income and tax liability.

Management has an incentive to use methods that will minimize the tax liability, but accountants, who are bound by accrual accounting and the materiality concept, cannot let the tax procedures dictate the method of preparing financial statements if the result would be misleading. As a consequence, a material difference can occur between accounting and taxable incomes, especially in larger businesses. This difference in accounting and taxable incomes may result from a difference in the timing of the rec-

Table 13-1. Tax Rate Schedule for Corporations*

Taxable Income		Tax Liability	
Over	But Not Over		Of the Amount Over
$ 0	$ 50,000	0 + 15%	$ 0
50,000	75,000	$ 7,500 + 25%	50,000
75,000	100,000	13,750 + 34%	75,000
100,000	335,000	22,250 + 39%	100,000
335,000	—	113,900 + 34%	335,000

*Tax rates are subject to change because they vary on an annual basis and among industries.

ognition of revenues and expenses because of different methods used in determining the respective incomes. Some possible alternatives are as follows:

	Accounting Method	Tax Method
Expense recognition	Accrual or deferral	At time of expenditure
Accounts receivable	Allowance	Direct charge-off
Inventories	Average cost	FIFO
Depreciation	Straight-line	Accelerated cost recovery system (see the chapter on inventories)

Accounting for the difference between income taxes expense based on accounting income and the actual income taxes payable based on taxable income is accomplished by an accounting technique called **income tax allocation**. The amount by which income taxes expense differs from income taxes payable is reconciled in an account called **Deferred Income Taxes**. For example, if the Junction Corporation had income taxes expense of $119,000 shown on the income statement and actual income taxes payable to the IRS of $92,000, the entry to record the Income Taxes Expense applicable to income from continuing operations using the income tax allocation procedure would be as follows:

Dec. 31	Income Taxes Expense	119,000	
	Income Taxes Payable		92,000
	Deferred Income Taxes		27,000
	To record current and deferred income taxes		

In other years, it is possible for Income Taxes Payable to exceed Income Taxes Expense, in which case the same entry is made except that the Deferred Income Taxes account is debited.

The Financial Accounting Standards Board has issued new rules for recording, measuring, and classifying deferred income taxes.[11] When the Deferred Income Taxes account has a credit balance, which is the normal situation, it is classified as a liability on the balance sheet. Whether it is classified as a current or a long-term (noncurrent) liability depends on when the timing difference is expected to reverse or have the opposite effect. For instance, if an income tax deferral is caused by an expenditure that is deducted for income tax purposes in one year but will not be an expense for accounting purposes until the next year, an income tax deferral is present in the first year that will reverse in the second year. The income tax deferral in the first year is classified as a current liability. On the other hand, if the deferral is not expected to reverse for more than one year, the deferred income taxes are classified as a long-term (noncurrent) liability. This latter situation may occur, for example, when the income tax deferral is caused by a difference in depreciation methods for items of plant and equipment that have useful lives of more than one year. In other words, the income tax liability is classified as short-term or long-term based on the nature of the transactions that gave rise to the deferrals and their corresponding expected dates of reversal.

The Deferred Income Taxes account may at times have a debit balance, in which case it should be classified as an asset. In this situation, the company has prepaid its income taxes because total income taxes paid have exceeded income taxes expensed. Classification of the debit balance as a current asset or as a long-term asset follows the same rules as for liabilities, but the amount of the asset is subject to certain limitations that are reserved for more advanced courses.

Each year the balance of the deferred taxes account is evaluated to determine whether it represents the expected asset or liability in light of the legislated changes in income tax laws and regulations in the current year. If changes have occurred in the income tax laws, an adjusting entry is required to bring the account balance into line with the current laws. For example, a decrease in corporate income tax rates, as occurred in 1987, means that companies with deferred income tax liabilities will pay less taxes in future years than indicated by the credit balances of their Deferred Income Taxes accounts. As a result, they would debit Deferred Income Taxes to reduce the liability and credit Gain from Reduction in Income Taxes Rates. The latter amount increases the reported income on the income statement. If there are tax increases in future years, a loss would be recorded and the deferred income tax liability increased.

In any given year, the amount of a company's income taxes paid is determined by subtracting (or adding, as the case may be) the Deferred Income Taxes for that year (as reported in the notes to the financial statements) from (or to) the Income Taxes Expense, which is also reported in the notes to the financial statements. In subsequent years, the amount of deferred income taxes can vary based on changes in the income tax laws and rates.

11. *Statement of Financial Accounting Standards No. 96*, "Accounting for Income Taxes" (Stamford, Conn.: Financial Accounting Standards Board, 1987).

Some understanding of the importance of deferred income taxes to financial reporting may be gained from studying the financial statements of six hundred large companies surveyed in a recent year. About 82 percent reported Deferred Income Taxes with a credit balance in the noncurrent or long-term liability section.[12] About 7 percent reported deferred income taxes as a current liability.[13]

Net of Taxes

The phrase **net of taxes**, as used in Exhibit 13-3 and in the discussion below, means that the effect of applicable taxes (usually income taxes) has been considered when determining the overall effect of the item on the financial statements. The phrase is used on the corporate income statement when a company has items (such as those explained below) that must be disclosed in a separate section of the income statement. Each of these items should be reported at net of the income taxes applicable to that item to avoid distorting the net operating income figure. For example, assume that a corporation with $120,000 operating income before taxes has a total tax liability of $66,000 based on taxable income, which is higher because it includes a capital gain of $100,000 on which a tax of $30,000 is due. Assume also that the gain is an extraordinary item (see Extraordinary Items, page 653) and must be disclosed as such. Thus,

Operating Income Before Taxes	$120,000
Income Taxes Expense **(actual taxes are $66,000, of which $30,000 is applicable to extraordinary gain)**	36,000
Income Before Extraordinary Item	$ 84,000
Extraordinary Gain (net of taxes) **($100,000 − $30,000)**	70,000
Net Income	$154,000

If all the taxes payable were deducted from operating income before taxes, both the income before extraordinary items and the extraordinary gain would be distorted. A company follows the same procedure in the case of an extraordinary loss. For example, assume the same facts as before except that total tax liability is only $6,000 because of a $100,000 extraordinary loss, which results in a $30,000 tax saving, as shown below.

Operating Income Before Taxes	$120,000
Income Taxes Expense **(actual taxes of $6,000 as a result of an extraordinary loss)**	36,000
Income Before Extraordinary Item	$ 84,000
Extraordinary Loss (net of taxes) **($100,000 − $30,000)**	(70,000)
Net Income	$ 14,000

If we apply these ideas to Junction Corporation in Exhibit 13-3, the total of the income tax items is $124,000. This amount is allocated among five statement components, as follows:

12. *Accounting Trends and Techniques* (New York: American Institute of Certified Public Accountants, 1990), p. 178.
13. Ibid., p. 153.

Income Taxes Expense on Income from Continuing Operations	$119,000
Income Tax on Income of Discontinued Segment	35,000
Income Tax Saving on Loss on Disposal of Segment	(42,000)
Income Tax on Extraordinary Gain	17,000
Income Tax Saving on Cumulative Effect of Change in Accounting Principle	(5,000)
Total Income Taxes Expense	$124,000

Discontinued Operations

OBJECTIVE 9
Describe the disclosure on the income statement of discontinued operations, extraordinary items, and accounting changes

Large companies in the United States usually have many segments. A segment of a business may be a separate major line of business or a separate class of customer. For example, a company that makes heavy drilling equipment may also have another line of business, such as the manufacturing of mobile homes. These large companies may discontinue or otherwise dispose of certain segments of their business that are not profitable. **Discontinued operations** are segments of a business that are no longer part of the ongoing operations of the company. Generally accepted accounting principles require that gains and losses from discontinued operations be reported separately in the income statement. The reasoning behind the separate disclosure requirement is that the income statement will be more useful in evaluating the ongoing activities of the business if results from continuing operations are reported separately from discontinued operations.

In Exhibit 13-3, the disclosure of discontinued operations has two parts. One part shows that the income during the year from operations of the segment of business that has been disposed of (or will be disposed of) after the decision date to discontinue was $90,000 (net of $35,000 taxes). The other part shows that the loss from disposal of the segment of business was $73,000 (net of $42,000 tax savings). The computation of the gains or losses will be covered in more advanced accounting courses. The disclosure has been described, however, to give a complete view of the content of the corporate income statement.

Extraordinary Items

The Accounting Principles Board, in its *Opinion No. 30,* defines **extraordinary items** as those "events or transactions that are distinguished by their unusual nature *and* by the infrequency of their occurrence."[14] As stated in the definition, the major criteria for these extraordinary items are that they must be unusual and they must not happen very often. Unusual and infrequent occurrences are explained in the opinion as follows:

> Unusual Nature—the underlying event or transaction should possess a high degree of abnormality and be of a type clearly unrelated to, or only incidentally related to, the ordinary and typical activities of the entity, taking into account the environment in which the entity operates.

14. Accounting Principles Board, *Opinion No. 30,* "Reporting the Results of Operations" (New York: American Institute of Certified Public Accountants, 1973), par. 20.

Infrequency of Occurrence—the underlying event or transaction should be of a type that would not reasonably be expected to recur in the foreseeable future, taking into account the environment in which the entity operates.[15]

If these items are both unusual and infrequent (and material in amount), they should be reported separately from continuing operations on the income statement. This disclosure will allow the reader of the statement to identify those gains or losses shown in the computation of income that would not be expected to happen again soon. Examples of items that usually are treated as extraordinary are (1) uninsured losses from floods, earthquakes, fires, and theft; (2) gains and losses resulting from the passing of a new law; (3) expropriation (taking) of property by a foreign government; and (4) gains or losses from early retirement of debt. These items should be reported in the income statement after discontinued operations. Also, the gain or loss should be shown net of applicable taxes. In a recent year, 49 (8 percent) of six hundred large companies reported extraordinary items on the income statement.[16] In Exhibit 13-3, the extraordinary gain was $43,000 after applicable taxes of $17,000.

Accounting Changes

Consistency, one of the basic conventions of accounting, means that, for accounting purposes, companies should apply the same accounting principles from year to year. However, a company is allowed to make accounting changes if current procedures are incorrect or inappropriate. For example, a change from the FIFO to the LIFO inventory method may be made if there is adequate justification for the change. Adequate justification usually means that, if the change occurs, the financial statements will better show the financial activities of the company. A company's desire to lower the amount of income taxes to be paid is not seen as an adequate justification for an accounting change. If justification does exist and an accounting change is made during an accounting period, generally accepted accounting principles require the disclosure of the change in the financial statements.

The **cumulative effect of an accounting change** is the effect that the new accounting principle would have had on net income of prior periods if it, instead of the old principle, had been applied in past years; this effect is shown on the income statement immediately after extraordinary items.[17] For example, assume in Exhibit 13-3 that for the prior five years the Junction Corporation has used the straight-line method in depreciating its machinery. The company changes to the sum-of-the-years'-digits method of depreciation this year. The following depreciation charges (net of taxes) were arrived at by the controller:

15. Ibid.
16. *Accounting Trends and Techniques* (New York: American Institute of Certified Public Accountants, 1990), p. 291.
17. Accounting Principles Board, *Opinion No. 20*, "Accounting Changes" (New York: American Institute of Certified Public Accountants, 1971), par. 20.

Cumulative, 5-year sum-of-the-years'-digits depreciation	$16,000
Less cumulative, 5-year straight-line depreciation	10,000
Cumulative effect of accounting change	$ 6,000

Relevant information about the accounting change is shown in the notes to the financial statements. The $6,000 difference (net of $5,000 income taxes) is the cumulative effect of the change in depreciation methods. The change results in an additional $6,000 (net of taxes) depreciation expense for prior years being deducted in the current year in addition to the current year's depreciation costs included in the $500,000 costs and expenses section of the income statement. This expense must be shown in the current year's income statement as a reduction in income (see Exhibit 13-3). In a recent year, 174 (29 percent) of six hundred large companies reported changes in accounting procedures.[18] Further study of accounting changes is left for more advanced accounting courses.

Earnings per Share

OBJECTIVE 10
Compute earnings per share

Readers of financial statements use earnings per share information to judge the performance of the company and to compare its performance with that of other companies. The Accounting Principles Board recognized the importance of this information in its *Opinion No. 15.* There it concluded that earnings per share of common stock should be presented on the face of the income statement.[19] As shown in Exhibit 13-3, the information is generally disclosed just below the net income figure. An earnings per share amount is always shown for (1) income from continuing operations, (2) income before extraordinary items and cumulative effect of accounting changes, (3) cumulative effect of accounting changes, and (4) net income. If the statement has a gain or loss from discontinued operations or a gain or loss on extraordinary items, earnings per share amounts may also be presented for these items.

A basic earnings per share amount is found when a company has only common stock and the same number of shares are outstanding throughout the year. For example, it is assumed in Exhibit 13-3 that Junction Corporation, with a net income of $360,000, had 100,000 shares of common stock outstanding for the entire year. The earnings per share of common stock were computed as follows:

$$\text{Earnings per share} = \frac{\text{net income}}{\text{shares outstanding}} = \frac{\$360{,}000}{100{,}000 \text{ shares}} = \$3.60 \text{ per share}$$

18. *Accounting Trends and Techniques* (New York: American Institute of Certified Public Accountants, 1990), p. 419.
19. Accounting Principles Board, *Opinion No. 15,* "Earnings per Share" (New York: American Institute of Certified Public Accountants, 1969), par. 12.

If, however, the number of shares outstanding changes during the year, it is necessary to figure a weighted-average number of shares outstanding for the year. Let us now suppose some different facts about Junction Corporation's outstanding shares. Let us assume that the common shares outstanding during various periods of the year were as follows: January–March, 100,000 shares; April–September, 120,000 shares; and October–December, 130,000 shares. The weighted-average number of common shares outstanding and earnings per share would be found as shown:

100,000 shares × 1/4 year	25,000
120,000 shares × 1/2 year	60,000
130,000 shares × 1/4 year	32,500
Weighted-average shares outstanding	117,500

$$\text{Earnings per share} = \frac{\$360{,}000}{117{,}500 \text{ shares}}$$
$$= \$3.06 \text{ per share}$$

If a company has nonconvertible preferred stock outstanding, the dividend for this stock must be subtracted from net income before computing earnings per share for common stock. If we suppose that Junction Corporation has preferred stock on which the annual dividend is $23,500, earnings per share on common stock would be $2.86 [($360,000 – $23,500) ÷ 117,500 shares].

Companies with a capital structure in which there are no bonds, stocks, or stock options that could be converted into common stock are said to have a **simple capital structure**. The earnings per share for these companies are computed as shown above. Many companies, however, have a **complex capital structure**, which includes convertible stock and bonds. These convertible securities have the potential of diluting the earnings per share of common stock. Potential dilution means that a person's proportionate share of ownership in the company may be reduced by an increase in total shares outstanding through a conversion of stocks or bonds, or exercise of stock options. For example, suppose that a person owns 10,000 shares of a company, which equals 2 percent of the 500,000 outstanding shares. Now suppose that holders of convertible bonds convert the bonds into 100,000 shares of stock. The person's 10,000 shares would then be only 1.67 percent (10,000 ÷ 600,000) of the outstanding shares. In addition, the added shares outstanding would result in lower earnings per share and most likely a lower market price per share.

Since stock options and convertible preferred stocks or bonds have the potential to dilute earnings per share, they are referred to as **potentially dilutive securities**. A special subset of these convertible securities is called **common stock equivalents** because these securities are considered to be similar to common stock. A convertible stock or bond is considered a common stock equivalent if the conversion feature is an important part of determining its original issue price. Special rules are applied by the accountant to determine whether a convertible stock or bond is a common stock equivalent. A stock option, on the other hand, is by definition a common stock equivalent. The significance of common stock equivalents is that, when they exist, they are used in the earnings per share calculations explained in the next paragraph.

When a company has a complex capital structure, it must present two earnings per share figures. The company must report **primary earnings per share** and **fully diluted earnings per share**. Primary earnings per share are calculated by including in the denominator the total of weighted-average common shares outstanding and common stock equivalents. On the other hand, fully diluted earnings per share are calculated by including in the denominator the additional potentially dilutive securities that are not common stock equivalents. The latter figure thus shows stockholders the maximum potential effect of dilution of their ownership in the company. An example of this type of disclosure is as follows:

	19x2	19x1
Net Income	$280,000	$200,000
Earnings per Share of Common Stock		
Primary	$2.25	$1.58
Fully Diluted	$2.00	$1.43

The computation of these figures is a complex process reserved for more advanced courses.

Chapter Review

Review of Learning Objectives

1. **Define *retained earnings*, and prepare a statement of retained earnings.**
   Retained earnings are the part of stockholders' equity that comes from retaining assets earned in business operations. They are the claims of the stockholders against the assets of the company that arise from profitable operations. This account is different from contributed capital, which represents the claims against assets brought about by the initial and later investments by the stockholders. Both are claims against the general assets of the company, not against any specific assets that may have been set aside. It is important not to confuse the assets themselves with the claims against the assets. The statement of retained earnings will always show the beginning and ending balance of retained earnings, net income or loss, and cash dividends. It may also show prior period adjustments, stock dividends, and other transactions affecting retained earnings.

2. **Account for stock dividends and stock splits.**
   A stock dividend is a proportional distribution of shares of the company's stock by a corporation to its stockholders. A summary of the key dates and accounting treatment for stock dividends follows:

Key Date	Stock Dividend
Declaration date	Debit Retained Earnings for the market value of the stock to be distributed, if it is a small stock dividend, and credit Common Stock Distributable (par value) and Paid-in Capital in Excess of Par Value for the excess of market value over the stock's par value.
Record date	No entry.
Payment date	Debit Common Stock Distributable and credit Common Stock for the par value of the stock that was distributed.

A stock split is usually undertaken to reduce the market value and improve the liquidity of a company's stock. Since there is normally a decrease in the par value of the stock proportionate to the number of additional shares issued, there is no effect on the dollar amounts in the stockholders' equity accounts. The split should be recorded in the general journal by a memorandum entry only.

3. **Account for treasury stock transactions.**
Treasury stock of a company is stock that has been issued and reacquired but not resold or retired. A company acquires its own stock for reasons such as creating stock option plans, maintaining a favorable market for the stock, increasing earnings per share, and purchasing other companies. Treasury stock is similar to unissued stock in that it does not have rights until it is reissued. However, treasury stock can be resold at less than par value without incurring a discount liability. The accounting treatment for treasury stock is summarized as follows:

Treasury Stock Transaction	Accounting Treatment
Purchase of treasury stock	Debit Treasury Stock and credit Cash for the cost of the shares.
Sale of treasury stock at cost	Debit Cash and credit Treasury Stock for the cost of the shares.
Sale of treasury stock at an amount greater than the cost of the shares	Debit Cash for the reissue price of the shares, and credit Treasury Stock for the cost of the shares and Paid-in Capital, Treasury Stock, for the excess.
Sale of treasury stock at an amount less than the cost of the shares	Debit Cash for the reissue price; debit Paid-in Capital, Treasury Stock, for the difference between reissue price and the cost of the shares; and credit Treasury Stock, for the cost of the shares. If Paid-in Capital, Treasury Stock, does not exist or is not large enough to cover the difference, Retained Earnings should absorb the difference.

4. **Describe the disclosure of restrictions on retained earnings.**
For reasons such as plant expansion, a company may need to retain a portion of its assets in the business rather than distribute them to the stockholders as dividends. Management may communicate such plans to stockholders and other users of the company's financial statements by restricting

retained earnings. This restriction may be disclosed in two ways: in the stockholders' equity section of the balance sheet, or more commonly as a note to the financial statements. When the reason for the restriction no longer exists, its disclosure may be removed from the financial statements.

5. **Prepare a statement of stockholders' equity.**
The statement of stockholders' equity shows the changes during the year in each component of the stockholders' equity section of the balance sheet.

6. **Calculate book value per share, and distinguish it from market value.**
Book value per share is the owners' equity per share, calculated by dividing stockholders' equity by the number of common shares outstanding plus shares subscribed and shares distributable. When preferred stock exists, the call or par value plus any dividends in arrears are deducted from total stockholders' equity before dividing by common shares outstanding plus shares subscribed. Market value per share is the price investors are willing to pay based on their expectations about general economic conditions and the future earning ability of the company.

7. **Prepare a corporate income statement.**
The corporate income statement is prepared under the all-inclusive or comprehensive income philosophy and thus includes all revenues, expenses, gains, and losses for the accounting period, except for prior period adjustments. The top part of the corporate income statement includes all revenues, costs and expenses, and income taxes that pertain to continuing operations. The bottom part of the statement may contain any or all of the following: discontinued operations, extraordinary items, and cumulative effect of a change in accounting principle. Earnings per share data should be shown below the statement.

8. **Show the relationships among income taxes expense, deferred income taxes, and net of taxes.**
Income taxes expense are the taxes applicable to income from operations on an accrual basis. Income tax allocation is necessary when differences between accrual-based accounting income and taxable income cause a material difference in income taxes expense as shown on the income statement and the actual income tax liability. The difference between the income taxes payable and income taxes expense is debited or credited to an account called Deferred Income Taxes. Net of taxes is a phrase used to indicate that the effect of taxes has been considered when showing an item on the income statement.

9. **Describe the disclosure on the income statement of discontinued operations, extraordinary items, and accounting changes.**
There are several accounting items that must be disclosed separately from continuing operations and net of income taxes on the income statement because of their unusual nature. These items include a gain or loss on discontinued operations, extraordinary items, and the cumulative effect of accounting changes.

10. **Compute earnings per share.**
Stockholders and other users of financial statements use earnings per share data to evaluate the performance of a company, estimate future earnings, and evaluate their investment opportunities. Therefore, earnings per share data are presented on the face of the income statement. The amounts are computed by dividing the income applicable to common stock by the common shares outstanding for the year. If the number of

shares outstanding has varied during the year, then the weighted-average shares outstanding should be used in the computation. When the company has a complex capital structure, a dual presentation of primary and fully diluted earnings per share data must be disclosed on the face of the income statement.

Review of Concepts and Terminology

The following concepts and terms were introduced in this chapter:

(L.O. 6) **Book value:** Total assets of a company less total liabilities; owners' equity.

(L.O. 10) **Common stock equivalents:** Convertible stocks or bonds whose conversion feature is an important part of determining the original issue price.

(L.O. 10) **Complex capital structure:** A capital structure with additional securities (convertible stocks and bonds) that can be converted into common stock.

(L.O. 7) **Comprehensive income:** The change in equity (net assets) of an entity during a period from transactions and other events and circumstances from nonowner sources. It includes all changes in equity during a period except those resulting from investments by the owners and distributions to or withdrawals by owners.

(L.O. 9) **Cumulative effect of an accounting change:** The effect that a new accounting principle would have had on net income of prior periods if it had been used instead of the old principle.

(L.O. 8) **Deferred Income Taxes:** An account used to record the difference between Income Taxes Expense and current Income Taxes Payable accounts.

(L.O. 1) **Deficit:** A debit balance in the Retained Earnings account.

(L.O. 9) **Discontinued operations:** Segments of a business that are no longer part of the ongoing operations of the company.

(L.O. 9) **Extraordinary items:** Events or transactions that are distinguished by their unusual nature and by the infrequency of their occurrence.

(L.O. 10) **Fully diluted earnings per share:** Net income applicable to common stock divided by the sum of the weighted-average common stock and common stock equivalents and other potentially dilutive securities.

(L.O. 8) **Income tax allocation:** An accounting method designed to accrue income tax expense on the basis of accounting income whenever there are differences in accounting and taxable income.

(L.O. 6) **Market value:** The price investors are willing to pay for a share of stock on the open market.

(L.O. 8) **Net of taxes:** Taking into account the effect of applicable taxes (usually income taxes) on an item to determine the overall effect of the item on the financial statements.

(L.O. 10) **Potentially dilutive securities:** Term referring to stock options and convertible preferred stocks or bonds because of their potential to dilute earnings per share.

(L.O. 10) **Primary earnings per share:** Net income applicable to common stock divided by the sum of the weighted-average common shares and common stock equivalents.

(L.O. 1) **Prior period adjustments:** Events or transactions that relate to earlier accounting periods but were not determinable in the earlier periods.

(L.O. 4) **Restriction on retained earnings:** An indication that a portion of a company's assets is to be used for purposes other than paying dividends.

(L.O. 1) **Retained earnings:** The stockholders' equity that has arisen from retaining assets from earnings in the business; the accumulated earnings of a corporation from its inception minus any losses, dividends, or transfers to contributed capital.

(L.O. 10) **Simple capital structure:** A capital structure with no other securities (either stocks or bonds) that can be converted into common stock.

(L.O. 5) **Statement of stockholders' equity:** A financial statement that summarizes changes in the components of the stockholders' equity section of the balance sheet; also called a statement of changes in stockholders' equity.

(L.O. 2) **Stock dividend:** A proportional distribution of shares of a corporation's stock to the corporation's stockholders.

(L.O. 2) **Stock split:** An increase in the number of outstanding shares of stock accompanied by a proportionate reduction in the par or stated value.

(L.O. 3) **Treasury stock:** Capital stock, either common or preferred, that has been issued and reacquired by the issuing company but has not been sold or retired.

Review Problem
Comprehensive Stockholders' Equity Transactions

(L.O. 1, 2, 3, 4, 5, 6) The stockholders' equity of the Szatkowski Company on June 30, 19x5 is as follows:

Contributed Capital	
Common Stock—no par value, $6 stated value, 1,000,000 shares authorized, 250,000 shares issued and outstanding	$1,500,000
Paid-in Capital in Excess of Stated Value, Common	820,000
Total Contributed Capital	$2,320,000
Retained Earnings	970,000
Total Stockholders' Equity	$3,290,000

Stockholders' equity transactions for the next fiscal year were as follows:

a. The board of directors declared a 2 for 1 split.
b. The board of directors obtained authorization to issue 50,000 shares of $100 par value 6 percent noncumulative preferred stock that is callable at $104.
c. Issued 12,000 shares of common stock for a building appraised at $96,000.
d. Purchased 8,000 shares of the company's common stock for $64,000.
e. Issued 20,000 shares of the preferred stock for $100 per share.
f. Sold 5,000 shares of the treasury stock for $35,000.
g. Declared cash dividends of $6 per share on the preferred stock and $.20 per share on the common stock.
h. Date of record.
i. Paid the preferred and common stock cash dividends.

j. Declared a 10 percent stock dividend on the common stock. The market value was $10 per share. The stock dividend is distributable after the end of the fiscal year.
k. Net income for the year was $340,000.
l. Closed Dividends Declared to Retained Earnings.

Due to a loan agreement, the company is not allowed to reduce retained earnings below $100,000. The board of directors determined that this restriction should be disclosed in the notes to the financial statements.

Required

1. Make the general journal entries as appropriate to record the transactions above.
2. Prepare the company's statement of retained earnings at June 30, 19x6.
3. Prepare the stockholders' equity section of the company's balance sheet at June 30, 19x6, including appropriate disclosure of the restriction on retained earnings.
4. Compute the book values per share of common stock on June 30, 19x5 and 19x6 and preferred stock on June 30, 19x6.

Answer to Review Problem

1. Journal entries prepared:

a. Memorandum entry: 2 for 1 stock split, common, resulting in 500,000 shares issued and outstanding of no par value common stock with a stated value of $3

b. No entry required

	Debit	Credit
c. Building	96,000	
Common Stock		36,000
Paid-in Capital in Excess of Stated Value, Common		60,000
To record issuance of 12,000 shares of common stock for a building appraised at $96,000		
d. Treasury Stock, Common	64,000	
Cash		64,000
To record the purchase of 8,000 shares of common stock for the treasury for $8.00 per share		
e. Cash	2,000,000	
Preferred Stock		2,000,000
To record the sale of 20,000 shares of $100 par value preferred stock at $100		
f. Cash	35,000	
Retained Earnings	5,000	
Treasury Stock, Common		40,000
To record the sale of 5,000 shares of treasury stock for $35,000, originally purchased for $8.00 per share		

	Debit	Credit
g. Dividends Declared	221,800	
Dividends Payable		221,800
To record the declaration of cash dividends of $6 per share on 20,000 shares of preferred stock and $.20 per share on 509,000 shares of common stock:		
$6 × 20,000 = $120,000		
$.20 × 509,000 = 101,800		
$221,800		
h. No entry required		
i. Dividends Payable	221,800	
Cash		221,800
Paid cash dividend to preferred and common stockholders		
j. Retained Earnings	509,000	
Common Stock Distributable		152,700
Paid-in Capital in Excess of Stated Value, Common		356,300
To record the declaration of a 50,900 share stock dividend (10% × 509,000) on $3 stated value common stock at market value of $509,000 (50,900 × $10)		
k. Income Summary	340,000	
Retained Earnings		340,000
To close Income Summary		
l. Retained Earnings	221,800	
Dividends Declared		221,800
To close Dividends Declared to Retained Earnings		

2. Statement of Retained Earnings prepared:

Szatkowski Company
Statement of Retained Earnings
For the Year Ended June 30, 19x6

Retained Earnings, June 30, 19x5		$ 970,000
Net Income, 19x6		340,000
Subtotal		$1,310,000
Less: Cash Dividends		
Preferred	$120,000	
Common	101,800	
Stock Dividends	509,000	
Treasury Stock Transaction	5,000	735,800
Retained Earnings, June 30, 19x6		$ 574,200

3. Stockholders' equity section of balance sheet prepared:

Szatkowski Company
Stockholders' Equity
June 30, 19x6

Contributed Capital		
Preferred Stock—$100 par value, 6% noncumulative, 50,000 shares authorized, 20,000 shares outstanding		$2,000,000
Common Stock—no par value, $3 stated value, 1,000,000 shares authorized, 512,000 shares issued, 509,000 shares outstanding	$1,536,000	
Common Stock Distributable, 50,900 shares	152,700	
Paid-in Capital in Excess of Stated Value, Common	1,236,300	2,925,000
Total Contributed Capital		$4,925,000
Retained Earnings (Note x)		574,200
Total Contributed Capital and Retained Earnings		$5,499,200
Less Treasury Stock, Common (3,000 shares at cost)		24,000
Total Stockholders' Equity		$5,475,200

Note x: The board of directors has restricted retained earnings available for dividends by the amount of $100,000 as required under a loan agreement.

4. Book values computed:

June 30, 19x5
Common Stock: $3,290,000 ÷ 250,000 shares = $13.16 per share
June 30, 19x6
Preferred Stock:
Call price of $104 per share equals book value per share
Common Stock:
($5,475,200 − $2,080,000) ÷ (509,000 shares + 50,900 shares) =
$3,395,200 ÷ 559,900 shares = $6.06 per share

Chapter Assignments

Discussion Questions

1. What are retained earnings, and how do they relate to the assets of a corporation?
2. When does a company have a deficit in retained earnings?
3. What items are identified by generally accepted accounting principles as prior period adjustments?
4. How does the accounting treatment of stock dividends differ from that of cash dividends?
5. What is the difference between a stock dividend and a stock split? What is the effect of each on the capital structure of a corporation?
6. What is the purpose of restricting retained earnings?

7. Define treasury stock, and explain why a company would purchase its own stock.
8. What is the difference between the statement of stockholders' equity and the stockholders' equity section of the balance sheet?
9. Would you expect a corporation's book value per share to equal its market value per share? Why or why not?
10. "Accounting income should be geared to the concept of taxable income because the public understands the concept of taxable income." Comment on this statement, and tell why income tax allocation is necessary.
11. Santa Fe Southern Pacific Railroad had about $1.8 billion of deferred income taxes in 1982, equal to about 31 percent of total liabilities. By 1984, deferred income taxes had reached almost $2.3 billion, or about 38 percent of total liabilities. Given management's desire to put off the payment of taxes as long as possible, the long-term growth of the economy and inflation, and the definition of a liability (probable future sacrifices of economic benefits arising from present obligations), can you give an argument for not accounting for deferred income taxes?
12. Explain the two major criteria for extraordinary items. How should extraordinary items be disclosed in financial statements?
13. How are earnings per share disclosed in financial statements?
14. When an accounting change occurs, what financial statement disclosures are necessary?
15. When does a company have a simple capital structure? a complex capital structure?
16. What is the difference between primary and fully diluted earnings per share?
17. Why should a gain or loss on discontinued operations be disclosed separately on the income statement?

Communication Skills Exercises

Communication 13-1. Motivation for Stock Dividends *(L.O. 2)*

Athey Products Corporation, a small, successful, and rapidly growing public corporation, has followed the practice in recent years of issuing an annual 10 percent stock dividend. Although the company's net income has been almost $4 million in each of the last three years, retained earnings have declined from about $10 million to about $6 million.[20] What is the probable motivation for Athey's management to issue an annual 10 percent stock dividend? What is the most likely explanation for the decrease in retained earnings? Given your explanation, would stockholders' equity also decrease by a like amount?

Communication 13-2. Purpose of Treasury Stock *(L.O. 3)*

Atlantic Richfield Company, in its 1989 annual report, indicated that the number of common shares held in the treasury decreased from 45,546,171 in 1988 to 3,397,381 in 1989. The following was also reported:

> By Board authorization, effective December 31, 1989 the Company cancelled 50 million shares of common stock held in treasury. As a result of the cancellation, common stock decreased by $125 million, capital in excess of par value of stock decreased by $228 million, and retained earnings decreased by $3,119 million.[21]

20. *Accounting Trends and Techniques* (New York: American Institute of Certified Public Accountants, 1990), p. 307.
21. Excerpt used by permission from Atlantic Richfield Company's 1989 Annual Report.

The shares canceled or retired represent almost 25 percent of the shares of common stock issued by Atlantic Richfield. Explain the accounting for the treasury shares by Atlantic Richfield. Did the company buy any treasury shares during the year? What journal entry was made to record the cancellation or retirement of the treasury shares? At what average price were the treasury shares purchased, and at what average price were they originally issued? What do you think was management's reason for purchasing the treasury shares?

Communication 13-3. Interpretation of Earnings Reports
(L.O. 7, 9)

McDonnell Douglas Corporation, the large aerospace and defense company based in St. Louis, was the subject of an article in the *Wall Street Journal* reporting on its third-quarter 1990 results of operations. The following are excerpts from that article:

McDonnell Douglas Corp. posted a sharp rise in third-quarter net income after an accounting adjustment, but financial problems related to its C-17 military transport program raised questions about the strength of operating results.

Net soared to $248 million, or $6.46 a share, from $38 million, or $.98 a share, in the year-earlier period on a 13% rise in revenue to $4.18 billion from $3.71 billion.

The accounting adjustment, which stems from the settlement of certain pension fund obligations announced in September, contributed $234 million, or $6.11 a share, leaving operating profit of only $14 million, or $.35 a share.

While McDonnell Douglas hailed its "improved performance," some Wall Street analysts weren't quite so upbeat. They took particular issue with the company's effort to paint a $58 million reversal of earnings on the C-17 program as a one-time, nonoperating adjustment, when in fact far more serious write-downs remain possible.

"I would consider the C-17 adjustment an operational issue because it stemmed from cost problems," said Lawrence Harris, an analyst.

. . . In making the C-17 adjustment, the company wiped out profit recorded on the program between 1985 and the first quarter of this year, indicating that it expects to bump against the $6.6 billion cost ceiling when the project is completed in the 1990s. Should it pierce that ceiling, things would get much worse. At that point, the company could begin absorbing all expenses with the federal government no longer obliged to reimburse it.[22]

Is the increase shown by McDonnell Douglas's net income misleading? Why or why not? Defend your position by explaining the structure of McDonnell Douglas's income statement as suggested by the excerpt.

Communication 13-4. Basic Research Skills
(L.O. 2, 3, 5, 6, 7, 8, 9)

In your library, select the annual reports of three corporations. You may choose them from the same industry or at random, at the direction of your instructor. (If you completed the related basic research skills exercise in the chapter on contributed capital, use the same three companies.) Prepare a table with a column for each corporation. Then, for any year covered by the balance sheet, the statement of stockholders' equity, and the income statement, answer the following questions: Does the company own treasury stock? Was any

22. Rick Wartzman, "McDonnell's Net Rose in 3rd Period; Special Items Cited," *The Wall Street Journal*, October 24, 1990. Reprinted by permission of *The Wall Street Journal*, © 1990 Dow Jones & Company, Inc. All Rights Reserved Worldwide.

treasury stock bought or retired? Did the company declare a stock dividend or a stock split? What other transactions appear in the statement of stockholders' equity? Has the company deferred any income taxes? Were there any discontinued operations, extraordinary items, or accounting changes? Compute the book value per common share for the company. In the financial section of a daily newspaper or the *Wall Street Journal*, find the current market price of each company's common stock and compare it to the book value you computed. Should there be any relationship between these values? Be prepared to discuss your answers to the above questions in class.

Classroom Exercises

Exercise 13-1. Statement of Retained Earnings *(L.O. 1)*

The Snadhu Corporation had a Retained Earnings balance on January 1, 19x2 of $260,000. During 19x2, the company reported a profit of $112,000 after taxes. In addition, the company located a $44,000 (net of taxes) error that resulted in an overstatement of prior years' income and meets the criteria for a prior period adjustment. During 19x2, the company declared cash dividends totaling $16,000.

Prepare the company's statement of retained earnings for the year ended December 31, 19x2.

Exercise 13-2. Journal Entries: Stock Dividends *(L.O. 2)*

The Geyer Company has 30,000 shares of its $1 par value common stock outstanding. Record the following transactions as they relate to the company's common stock:

July 17	Declared a 10 percent stock dividend on common stock to be distributed on August 10 to stockholders of record on July 31. Market value of the stock was $5 per share on this date.
31	Record date.
Aug. 10	Distributed the stock dividend declared on July 17.
Sept. 1	Declared a $.50 per share cash dividend on common stock to be paid on September 16 to stockholders of record on September 10.

Exercise 13-3. Journal Entries: Stock Dividends *(L.O. 2)*

On August 26, Shipley Corporation's board of directors declared a 2 percent stock dividend applicable to the outstanding shares of its $5 par value common stock, of which 150,000 shares are authorized, 130,000 are issued, and 10,000 are held in the treasury. The stock dividend was distributable on September 25 to stockholders of record on September 10. On August 26, the market value of the common stock was $12. On November 26, the board of directors declared a $.20 per share cash dividend. No other stock transactions have occurred. Record the transactions on August 26, September 10, September 25, and November 26.

Exercise 13-4. Stock Split *(L.O. 2)*

The Colson Company currently has 200,000 shares of $1 par value common stock outstanding. The board of directors declared a 2 for 1 split on May 15, when the market value of the common stock was $2.50 per share. The Retained Earnings balance on May 15 was $700,000. Paid-in Capital in Excess of Par Value, Common Stock, on this date was $20,000.

Prepare the stockholders' equity section of the company's balance sheet before and after the stock split. What journal entry, if any, is necessary to record the stock split?

Exercise 13-5.
Stock Split
(L.O. 2)

On January 15, the board of directors of Fuquat International declared a 3 for 1 stock split of its $12 par value common stock, of which 800,000 shares were authorized and 200,000 were issued and outstanding. The market value on this date was $45 per share. On the same date, the balance of Paid-in Capital in Excess of Par Value was $4,000,000, and the balance of Retained Earnings was $8,000,000.

Prepare the stockholders' equity section of the company's balance sheet before and after the stock split. What journal entry, if any, is needed to record the stock split?

Exercise 13-6.
Treasury Stock Transactions
(L.O. 3)

Prepare the journal entries necessary to record the following stock transactions of the Henderson Company during 19xx:

May 5 Purchased 400 shares of its own $1 par value common stock for $10, the current market price.
17 Sold 150 shares of treasury stock purchased on May 5 for $11 per share.
21 Sold 100 shares of treasury stock purchased on May 5 for $10 per share.
28 Sold the remaining 150 shares of treasury stock purchased on May 5 for $9.50 per share.

Exercise 13-7.
Treasury Stock Transactions Including Retirement
(L.O. 3)

Prepare the journal entries necessary to record the following stock transactions of Nakate Corporation, which represent all treasury stock transactions entered into by the company.

June 1 Purchased 2,000 shares of its own $15 par value common stock for $35, the current market price.
10 Sold 500 shares of treasury stock purchased on June 1 for $40 per share.
20 Sold 700 shares of treasury stock purchased on June 1 for $29 per share.
30 Retired the remaining shares purchased on June 1. The original issue price was $21 per share.

Exercise 13-8.
Restriction of Retained Earnings
(L.O. 4)

The board of directors of the Hollander Company has approved plans to acquire another company during the coming year. The acquisition should cost approximately $550,000. The board has taken action to restrict retained earnings of the company in the amount of $550,000 on July 17, 19x1. On July 31, the company has retained earnings of $975,000.

1. Show two ways the restriction of retained earnings may be disclosed.
2. Assuming the purchase takes place as planned, what effect will it have on retained earnings and future disclosures?

Exercise 13-9. Statement of Stockholders' Equity
(L.O. 5)

The stockholders' equity section of Network Corporation's balance sheet on December 31, 19x2 appears as follows:

Contributed Capital	
Common Stock—$1 par value, 500,000 shares authorized, 400,000 shares issued and outstanding	$ 400,000
Paid-in Capital in Excess of Par Value, Common	600,000
Total Contributed Capital	$1,000,000
Retained Earnings	2,100,000
Total Stockholders' Equity	$3,100,000

Prepare a statement of stockholders' equity at December 31, 19x3, assuming the following transactions occurred in sequence during 19x3:

a. Issued 5,000 shares of $100 par value, 9 percent cumulative preferred stock at par after obtaining authorization from the state.
b. Issued 40,000 shares of common stock in connection with the conversion of bonds having a carrying value of $300,000.
c. Declared and issued a 2 percent common stock dividend. The market value on the date of declaration is $7 per share.
d. Purchased 10,000 shares of common stock for the treasury at a cost of $8 per share.
e. Earned net income of $230,000.
f. Paid the full year's dividend on preferred stock and a dividend of $.20 per share on common stock outstanding at the end of the year.

Exercise 13-10. Book Value for Preferred and Common Stock
(L.O. 6)

The stockholders' equity section of the Colombus Corporation's balance sheet is shown below.

Contributed Capital		
Preferred Stock—$100 per share, 6 percent cumulative, 10,000 shares authorized, 200 shares issued and outstanding		$ 20,000
Common Stock—$5 par value, 100,000 shares authorized, 10,000 shares issued, 9,000 shares outstanding	$50,000	
Paid-in Capital in Excess of Par Value, Common	28,000	78,000
Total Contributed Capital		$ 98,000
Retained Earnings		95,000
Total Contributed Capital and Retained Earnings		$193,000
Less Treasury Stock, Common (1,000 shares at cost)		15,000
Total Stockholders' Equity		$178,000

Determine the book value per share for both the preferred stock and the common stock under each of the following conditions:

1. The preferred stock does not have a call price, and there are no preferred stock dividends in arrears.
2. The preferred stock has a call price of $105, and there are no preferred stock dividends in arrears.

3. The preferred stock does not have a call price, and one year's preferred stock dividends are in arrears.
4. The preferred stock has a call price of $105, and one year's preferred stock dividends are in arrears.

Exercise 13-11. Corporate Income Statement *(L.O. 7)*

Assume that the Jaeger Furniture Company's chief financial officer gave you the following information: Net Sales, $1,900,000; Cost of Goods Sold, $1,050,000; Extraordinary Gain (applicable income tax on gain of $3,500), $16,000; Loss from Discontinued Operations (applicable income tax benefit of $30,000), $82,000; Loss on Disposal of Discontinued Operations (applicable income tax benefit of $13,000), $48,000; Selling Expenses, $50,000; Administrative Expenses, $40,000; Income Taxes Expense on Continuing Operations, $300,000.

From this information, prepare the company's income statement for the year ended June 30, 19xx. (Ignore earnings per share information.)

Exercise 13-12. Use of Corporate Income Tax Rate Schedule *(L.O. 8)*

Using the corporate tax rate schedule on page 650, compute the income tax liability for the following situations:

Situation	Taxable Income
A	$ 70,000
B	85,000
C	320,000

Exercise 13-13. Income Tax Allocation *(L.O. 8)*

The Theus Corporation reported the following accounting income before income taxes, income taxes expense, and net income for 19x2 and 19x3:

	19x2	19x3
Accounting income before taxes	$140,000	$140,000
Income taxes expense	44,150	44,150
Net income	$ 95,850	$ 95,850

Also on the balance sheet, deferred income taxes liability increased by $19,200 in 19x2 and decreased by $9,400 in 19x3.

1. How much did Theus Corporation actually pay in income taxes in 19x2 and 19x3?
2. Prepare journal entries to record income taxes expense in 19x2 and 19x3.

Exercise 13-14. Earnings per Share *(L.O. 10)*

During 19x1, the Heath Corporation reported a net income of $1,529,500. On January 1, Heath had 700,000 shares of common stock outstanding. The company issued an additional 420,000 shares of common stock on October 1. In 19x1, the company had a simple capital structure. During 19x2, there were no transactions involving common stock, and the company reported net income of $2,016,000.

1. Determine the weighted-average number of common shares outstanding each year.
2. Compute earnings per share for each year.

Exercise 13-15. Corporate Income Statement
(L.O. 7, 8, 9, 10)

The following items are components in the income statement of Cohen Corporation for the year ended December 31, 19x1:

Sales	$500,000
Cost of Goods Sold	(275,000)
Operating Expenses	(112,500)
Income Taxes Expense	(82,350)
Income from Operations of a Discontinued Segment	80,000
Gain on Disposal of Segment	70,000
Extraordinary Gain on Retirement of Bonds	36,000
Cumulative Effect of a Change in Accounting Principle	(24,000)
Net Income	$192,150
Earnings per Share	$.96

Recast the 19x1 income statement in proper multistep form, including allocating income taxes to appropriate items (assume a 30 percent income tax rate) and showing earnings per share figures (200,000 shares outstanding).

Interpretation Cases from Business

ICB 13-1. Lockheed Corporation
(L.O. 7, 9)

Presented below are several excerpts from an article that appeared in the February 2, 1982, *Wall Street Journal* entitled "Lockheed Had Loss in 4th Quarter, Year; $396 Million TriStar Write-Off is Cited."

As expected, Lockheed Corp. took a $396 million write-off to cover expenses of its production phase-out of L-1011 TriStar commercial jets, resulting in a net loss of . . . $289 million for the year.

Roy A. Anderson, Lockheed Chairman, said he believed the company had "recognized all costs, including those yet to be incurred, that are associated with the phase-out of the TriStar program." He said he thinks the company now is in a sound position to embark on a program of future growth and earnings improvement.

Included in the $396 million total write-off are remaining deferred production start-up costs, adjustments for redundant inventories, and provisions for losses and other costs expected to be incurred while TriStar production is completed. In addition to the write-off, discontinued operations include a $70 million after-tax loss associated with 1981 L-1011 operations. The comparable 1980 L-1011 loss was $108 million.

The $289 million 1981 net loss consists of the TriStar losses, reduced by the previously reported [extraordinary after-tax] gain of $23 million from the exchange of debentures.

For the year, Lockheed had earnings from continuing operations of $154 million, a 14% gain from $135 million in 1980. In 1981 the company had a $466 million loss from discontinued operations, resulting in a net loss of $289 million. A year earlier, the concern had a $108 million loss from discontinued operations, resulting in a net profit of $28 million.[23]

Required

1. Interpret the financial information from the *Wall Street Journal* by preparing a partial income statement for Lockheed for 1981, beginning with "income from continuing operations." Be prepared to explain the nature of each item on the income statement.
2. How do you explain the fact that on the New York Stock Exchange, Lockheed common stock closed at $50 per share, up 75¢ on the day after the quoted announcement of a net loss of $289 million and up from $41 per share two months earlier?

ICB 13-2. Jackson Electronics, Inc. *(L.O. 4)*

The consolidated statements of stockholders' equity for Jackson Electronics, Inc., a manufacturer of a broad line of electrical components, appear as presented below.

Jackson Electronics, Inc.
Consolidated Statements of Stockholders' Equity
(in thousands)

	Preferred Stock	Common Stock	Paid-in Capital in Excess of Par Value	Retained Earnings	Common Stock in Treasury	Total
Balance at September 30, 1990	$2,756	$3,902	$14,149	$119,312	$ (942)	$139,177
Year Ended September 30, 1991:						
Net income	—	—	—	18,753	—	18,753
Redemption and retirement of Preferred Stock (27,560 shares)	(2,756)	—	—	—	—	(2,756)
Stock options exercised (89,000 shares)	—	89	847	—	—	936
Purchases of Common Stock for treasury (501,412 shares)	—	—	—	—	(12,552)	(12,552)
Issuance of Common Stock (148,000 shares) in exchange for convertible subordinated debentures	—	148	3,635	—	—	3,783
Issuance of Common Stock (715,000 shares) for cash	—	715	24,535	—	—	25,250
Issuance of 500,000 shares of Common Stock in exchange for investment interest in Electrix Company	—	500	17,263	—	—	17,763
Cash dividends—Common Stock ($.80 per share)	—	—	—	(3,086)	—	(3,086)
Balance at September 30, 1991	$ —	$5,354	$60,429	$134,979	$(13,494)	$187,268

23. "Lockheed Had Loss in 4th Quarter, Year; $396 Million TriStar Write-Off Is Cited," *Wall Street Journal*, Feb. 2, 1982. Reprinted by permission of *The Wall Street Journal*, © Dow Jones & Company, Inc. 1982. All Rights Reserved Worldwide.

Required

Jackson Electronics, Inc.'s statement of stockholders' equity has eight summary transactions. Show that you understand this statement by preparing a general journal entry with an explanation for each. In each case, if applicable, determine the average price per common share. Sometimes you will also have to make assumptions about an offsetting part of the entry. For example, assume that there are no premiums or discounts on debentures (long-term bonds) and that employees pay cash for stock purchased under Jackson Electronics, Inc.'s employee incentive plans.

ICB 13-3. Sara Lee Corporation[24] *(L.O. 8)*

In its 1989 annual report, Sara Lee Corporation, an international food and packaged products company based in Chicago, provided the following data about its current and deferred income tax provisions (in thousands):

	1989	
	Current	**Deferred**
Federal	$ 89,336	$31,964
Foreign	78,510	9,817
State	13,124	6,238
	$180,970	$48,019

Required

1. How much in income taxes was paid in 1989? What was the income tax expense? Prepare a journal entry to record the overall income tax liability for 1989, using income tax allocation procedures.
2. In the long-term liability section of the balance sheet, Sara Lee shows deferred income taxes of $346,470,000 in 1989 versus $298,952,000 in 1988, and $280,527,000 in 1987. This shows the amount of deferred income taxes to have grown every year for several years. How do such deferred income taxes arise? Give an example of this process. Given the definition of a liability, do you see a potential problem with the company's classifying deferred income taxes as a liability while it is continuing to grow?

ICB 13-4. Ford Motor Company[25] *(L.O. 2, 3)*

In November 1987, Ford Motor Company announced a plan to buy up to $2 billion of its common stock in the open market, constituting the company's second large-scale stock repurchase since 1984. At the current market price of $71.75, Ford estimated that it could purchase more than 27 million shares, which would effectively reduce the number of outstanding shares by more than 11 percent.

24. Excerpts from the 1989 Annual Report are used by permission of Sara Lee Corporation.
25. Excerpts from the 1986 Annual Report used by permission of Ford Motor Company. Copyright © 1986.

The plan represented management's belief that Ford stock was undervalued and would be an exceptional investment for both the company and its shareholders. It was an action that demonstrated management's confidence in Ford's future in the highly competitive market for automobiles.

Another interpretation of the action might be that Ford had generated a tremendous amount of cash for which the company had limited investment opportunities other than its own stock. By the close of 1987, it was estimated that the company would have $8 billion in cash reserves.

On October 8, eleven days before the stock market crash of October 19, Ford proposed to shareholders a 2-for-1 stock split; the new shares were expected to be issued January 12. The calculations for the buyback move were based on pre-split figures. October 8 was also the day of Ford's ninth dividend increase in the past seventeen quarters; the company's quarterly dividend rose from 75¢ to $1.00 a share on a pre-split basis.

The condensed balance sheet for Ford at December 31, 1986, was as follows:

Ford Motor Company
Condensed Balance Sheet
December 31, 1986
(in billions)

Current Assets	$18.5	Current Liabilities	$15.6
Long-Term Assets	19.4	Long-Term Liabilities	7.5
		Stockholders' Equity	
		Common Stock ($2 par value)	.5
		Paid-in Capital in Excess of Par Value	.6
		Retained Earnings	13.7
Total Assets	$37.9	Total Liabilities and Stockholders' Equity	$37.9

Required

1. Assuming that the buyback was completed as planned (prior to December 31, 1987), prepare the journal entry to record the purchase of treasury stock (use the total dollar amount and date given in the article).
2. Prepare the condensed balance sheet after the buyback in **1** is recorded, assuming that the balance sheet at December 31, 1986 is the same as the balance sheet immediately prior to the buyback.
3. Tell whether the buyback would increase or decrease the following ratios: current ratio, debt to equity, return on assets, return on equity, and earnings per share. Also indicate whether the increase or decrease is favorable or unfavorable.
4. Assuming that Ford decides to retire the repurchased stock, prepare the appropriate journal entry.
5. Assume that Ford does not retire the repurchased stock but goes through with the proposed stock split. How will the balance sheet differ from the one you prepared in **2**, and how much would be the total quarterly dividends paid?

Problem Set A

Problem 13A-1. Treasury Stock Transactions *(L.O. 3)*

The following treasury stock transactions occurred during 19xx for the Arroyo Company: (a) Purchased 26,000 shares of its $1 par value common stock on the market for $20 per share. (b) Sold 8,000 shares of the treasury stock for $21 per share. (c) Sold 6,000 shares of the treasury stock for $19 per share. (d) Sold 10,000 shares of the treasury stock remaining for $17 per share. (e) Purchased an additional 4,000 shares for $18 per share. (f) Retired all the remaining shares of treasury stock. All shares were originally issued at $4 per share.

Required

Record these transactions in general journal form.

Problem 13A-2. Stock Dividend and Treasury Stock Transactions *(L.O. 2, 3, 5)*

The stockholders' equity section of Linden Cotton Mills, Inc. as of December 31, 19x2 is as follows:

Contributed Capital	
Common Stock—$6 par value, 500,000 shares authorized, 80,000 shares issued and outstanding	$ 480,000
Paid-in Capital in Excess of Par Value, Common	150,000
Total Contributed Capital	$ 630,000
Retained Earnings	480,000
Total Stockholders' Equity	$1,110,000

A review of the stockholders' equity records of Linden Cotton Mills, Inc. disclosed the following transactions during 19x3:

Jan. 30	Purchased 20,000 shares of the company's $6 par value common stock for $10.50. The stock was originally issued at $9.
Feb. 16	Sold 6,000 shares of the company's stock purchased on January 30 for $12 per share.
Mar. 25	The board of directors declared a 5 percent stock dividend to stockholders of record on April 20 to be distributed on May 1. The market value of common stock is $11 per share.
Apr. 20	Date of record for stock dividend.
May 1	Issued stock dividend.
Aug. 17	Sold 1,000 shares of the company's stock purchased on January 30 for $9 per share.
Sept. 10	Declared a 3 for 1 stock split. Assume that the stock split applies to shares held in the treasury.
Oct. 5	Sold 6,000 shares of the company's stock purchased on January 30 for $2 per share. (**Hint:** Note effect of stock split on cost of shares.)
Nov. 20	Decided to retire, effective immediately, 20,000 of the remaining shares held in the treasury.
Dec. 15	Declared a 10 percent stock dividend to stockholders of record on January 15 to be distributed on February 15. The market price on this date is $3.50 per share.

Required

1. Record the transactions for Linden Cotton Mills, Inc. in general journal form.

2. Prepare the stockholders' equity section of the company's balance sheet as of December 31, 19x3. Assume that net income for 19x3 is $47,000.

Problem 13A-3. Dividend Transactions, Retained Earnings, and Stockholders' Equity
(L.O. 1, 2, 4, 5)

The balance sheet of the Shimer Clothing Company disclosed the following stockholders' equity as of September 30, 19x1:

Contributed Capital	
Common Stock—$2 par value, 1,000,000 shares authorized, 300,000 shares issued and outstanding	$ 600,000
Paid-in Capital in Excess of Par Value, Common	370,000
Total Contributed Capital	$ 970,000
Retained Earnings	350,000
Total Stockholders' Equity	$1,320,000

The following stockholders' equity transactions were completed during the next fiscal year in the order presented:

19x1		
Dec.	17	Declared a 10 percent stock dividend to be distributed January 20 to stockholders of record on January 1. The market value per share on the date of declaration was $4.
19x2		
Jan.	1	Date of record.
	20	Distributed the stock dividend.
Apr.	14	Declared a 25¢ per share cash dividend. Cash dividend payable May 15 to stockholders of record on May 1.
May	1	Date of record.
	15	Paid the cash dividend.
June	17	Split its stock 2 for 1.
Sept.	15	Declared a cash dividend of 10¢ per share payable October 10 to stockholders of record October 1.
	30	Closed Income Summary with a credit balance of $150,000 to Retained Earnings.
	30	Closed Dividends Declared to Retained Earnings.

On September 14, the board of directors restricted retained earnings for plant expansion in the amount of $150,000. The restriction is shown within the balance sheet.

Required

1. Record the above transactions in general journal form.
2. Prepare a statement of retained earnings.
3. Prepare the stockholders' equity section of the company's balance sheet as of September 30, 19x2, with appropriate disclosure of the restriction of retained earnings.

Problem 13A-4. Corporate Income Statement *(L.O. 7, 8, 9, 10)*

Information concerning operations of the Daniels Shoe Corporation during 19xx is as follows: (a) administrative expenses, $90,000; (b) cost of goods sold, $420,000; (c) cumulative effect of an accounting change in depreciation methods that increased income (net of taxes, $20,000), $42,000; (d) extraordinary loss from earthquake (net of taxes, $36,000), $60,000; (e) sales (net), $900,000; (f) selling expenses, $80,000; and (g) income taxes expense applicable to continuing operations, $105,000.

Required

Prepare the corporation's income statement for the year ended December 31, 19xx, including earnings per share information. Assume a weighted average of 100,000 common stock shares outstanding during the year.

Problem 13A-5. Stockholders' Equity and Comprehensive Stockholders' Equity Transactions *(L.O. 1, 2, 3, 4, 5, 6)*

On December 31, 19x1, the stockholders' equity section of the Skolnick Company's balance sheet appeared as follows:

Contributed Capital	
Common Stock—$4 par value, 200,000 shares authorized, 60,000 shares issued and outstanding	$ 240,000
Paid-in Capital in Excess of Par Value, Common	640,000
Total Contributed Capital	$ 880,000
Retained Earnings	412,000
Total Stockholders' Equity	$1,292,000

Selected transactions involving stockholders' equity in 19x2 are as follows: On January 4, the board of directors obtained authorization for 20,000 shares of $20 par value noncumulative preferred stock that carried an indicated dividend rate of $2 per share and was callable at $21 per share. On January 14, the company sold 12,000 shares of the preferred stock at $20 per share and issued another 2,000 in exchange for a building valued at $40,000. On March 8, the board of directors also declared a 2 for 1 stock split on the common stock. On April 20, after the stock split, the company purchased 3,000 shares of common stock for the treasury at an average price of $6 per share; 1,000 of these shares were subsequently sold on May 4 at an average price of $8 per share. On July 15, the board of directors declared a cash dividend of $2 per share on preferred stock and $.20 per share on common stock. The date of record was July 25. The dividends were paid on August 15. The board of directors declared a 15 percent stock dividend on November 28 when the common stock was selling for $10. The record date for the stock dividend was December 15, and the dividend was to be distributed on January 5. Net loss for 19x2 was $109,000. On December 31, Income Summary and Dividends Declared were closed. The board of directors noted that footnote disclosure must be made of a bank loan agreement that requires minimum retained earnings. No cash dividends may be declared or paid if retained earnings falls below $50,000.

Required

1. Prepare journal entries to record the above transactions.
2. Prepare the company's statement of retained earnings for the year ended December 31, 19x2.

3. Prepare the stockholders' equity section of the company's balance sheet as of December 31, 19x2, including appropriate disclosure of the restriction on retained earnings.
4. Compute book value per share for preferred and common stock on December 31, 19x1 and 19x2.

Problem Set B

Problem 13B-1. Treasury Stock Transactions *(L.O. 3)*

The Oliva Corporation was involved in the following treasury stock transactions during 19x7: (a) purchased 40,000 shares of its $1 par value common stock at $2.50 per share; (b) purchased 8,000 shares of its common stock at $2.80 per share; (c) sold 22,000 shares purchased in **a** for $65,500; (d) sold the other 18,000 shares purchased in **a** for $36,000; (e) sold 3,000 of the remaining shares of treasury stock for $1.60 per share; and (f) retired all the remaining shares of treasury stock. All shares were originally issued at $1.50 per share.

Required

Record the treasury stock transactions in general journal form.

Problem 13B-2. Stock Dividend and Treasury Stock Transactions *(L.O. 2, 3, 5)*

The stockholders' equity section of the balance sheet of Packer Corporation as of December 31, 19x6, is as follows:

Contributed Capital	
Common Stock—$2 par value, 500,000 shares authorized, 200,000 shares issued and outstanding	$ 400,000
Paid-in Capital in Excess of Par Value, Common	500,000
Total Contributed Capital	$ 900,000
Retained Earnings	600,000
Total Stockholders' Equity	$1,500,000

The following transactions occurred in 19x7 for Packer Corporation:

Jan. 21	Purchased 10,000 shares of the company's $2 par value common stock at $6 per share.
Feb. 28	The board of directors declared a 10 percent stock dividend to stockholders of record on March 25 to be distributed on April 5. The market value on this date is $8.
Mar. 25	Date of record for stock dividend.
Apr. 5	Issued stock dividend.
May 16	Sold 4,000 shares of the treasury stock purchased on January 21 for $7 per share.
June 15	Sold 5,000 shares of the treasury stock purchased on January 21 for $3.50 per share.
July 15	Decided to retire, effective immediately, the remaining shares held in the treasury. The shares were originally issued at $3 per share.
Aug. 3	Declared a 2 for 1 stock split.
Nov. 20	Purchased 20,000 shares of the company's common stock at $4 per share for the treasury.

Dec. 31 Declared a 5 percent stock dividend to stockholders of record on January 25 to be distributed on February 5. The market value per share is $4.50.

Required

1. Record the transactions for Packer Corporation in general journal form.
2. Prepare the stockholders' equity section of the company's balance sheet as of December 31, 19x7. Assume net income for 19x7 is $54,000.

Problem 13B-3. Dividend Transactions, Retained Earnings, and Stockholders' Equity
(L.O. 1, 2, 4, 5)

The stockholders' equity section of the Hughes Blind and Awning Company's balance sheet as of December 31, 19x6 is as follows:

Contributed Capital	
Common Stock—$1 par value, 3,000,000 shares authorized, 500,000 shares issued and outstanding	$ 500,000
Paid-in Capital in Excess of Par Value, Common	200,000
Total Contributed Capital	$ 700,000
Retained Earnings	540,000
Total Stockholders' Equity	$1,240,000

The company was involved in the following stockholders' equity transactions during 19x7:

Mar. 5	Declared a $.20 per share cash dividend to be paid on April 6 to stockholders of record on March 20.
20	Date of record.
Apr. 6	Paid the cash dividend.
June 17	Declared a 10 percent stock dividend to be distributed August 17 to stockholders of record on August 5. The market value of the stock was $7 per share.
Aug. 5	Date of record.
17	Distributed the stock dividend.
Oct. 2	Split its stock 3 for 1.
Dec. 27	Declared a cash dividend of $.05 payable January 27, 19x8 to stockholders of record on January 14, 19x8.
31	Closed Income Summary with a credit balance of $200,000 to Retained Earnings.
31	Closed Dividends Declared to Retained Earnings.

On December 9, the board of directors restricted retained earnings for a pending lawsuit in the amount of $100,000. The restriction is to be shown within the balance sheet.

Required

1. Record the 19x7 transactions in general journal form.
2. Prepare a statement of retained earnings.
3. Prepare the stockholders' equity section of the company's balance sheet as of December 31, 19x7, with appropriate disclosure of the restriction of retained earnings.

Problem 13B-4. Corporate Income Statement
(L.O. 7, 8, 9, 10)

Income statement information for Walker Corporation during 19x1 is as follows:

a. administrative expenses, $110,000
b. cost of goods sold, $440,000
c. cumulative effect of accounting change in inventory methods that decreased income (net of taxes, $28,000), $60,000
d. extraordinary loss from storm (net of taxes, $10,000), $20,000
e. income taxes expense, continuing operations, $42,000
f. net sales, $890,000
g. selling expenses, $190,000.

Required

Prepare Walker Corporation's income statement for 19x1, including earnings per share information assuming a weighted average of 200,000 shares of common stock outstanding for 19x1.

Problem 13B-5. Comprehensive Stockholders' Equity Transactions
(L.O. 1, 2, 3, 4, 5)

The stockholders' equity of the Roper Company on June 30, 19x5 is as shown below:

Contributed Capital	
Common Stock—no par value, $2 stated value, 500,000 shares authorized, 200,000 shares issued and outstanding	$ 400,000
Paid-in Capital in Excess of Stated Value, Common	640,000
Total Contributed Capital	$1,040,000
Retained Earnings	420,000
Total Stockholders' Equity	$1,460,000

Stockholders' equity transactions for the next fiscal year are as follows:

a. The board of directors declared a 2 for 1 split.
b. The board of directors obtained authorization to issue 100,000 shares of $100 par value $4 noncumulative preferred stock that is callable at $105.
c. Issued 10,000 shares of common stock for a building appraised at $22,000.
d. Purchased 6,000 shares of the company's common stock for $15,000.
e. Issued 15,000 shares, $100 par value, of the preferred stock for $100 per share.
f. Sold 4,000 shares of the treasury stock for $9,000.
g. Declared cash dividends of $4 per share on the preferred stock and $.10 per share on the common stock.
h. Date of record.
i. Paid the preferred and common stock cash dividends.
j. Declared a 5 percent stock dividend on the common stock. The market value was $9 per share. The stock dividend was distributable after the end of the fiscal year.
k. Net income for the year was $210,000.
l. Closed dividends declared to Retained Earnings. Because of a loan agreement, the company is not allowed to reduce retained earnings below

$100,000. The board of directors determined that this restriction should be disclosed in the notes to the financial statements.

Required

1. Make the appropriate general journal entries to record the transactions.
2. Prepare the company's statement of retained earnings at June 30, 19x6.
3. Prepare the stockholders' equity section of the company's balance sheet at June 30, 19x6, including appropriate disclosure of the restriction on retained earnings.
4. Compute the book values per share of preferred and common stock (including common stock distributable) on June 30, 19x5 and 19x6.

Financial Decision Cases

13-1.
Dasbol Corporation
(L.O. 7, 8, 9)

During 19x3 Dasbol Corporation engaged in a number of complex transactions to restructure the business—selling off a division, retiring bonds, and changing accounting methods. The company has always issued a simple single-step income statement, and the accountant has accordingly prepared the following December 31 year-end income statements for 19x2 and 19x3:

Dasbol Corporation
Income Statements
For the Years Ended December 31, 19x2 and 19x3

	19x3	19x2
Sales	$1,000,000	$1,200,000
Cost of Goods Sold	(550,000)	(600,000)
Operating Expenses	(225,000)	(150,000)
Income Taxes Expense	(164,700)	(135,000)
Income from Operations of a Discontinued Segment	160,000	
Gain on Disposal of Segment	140,000	
Extraordinary Gain on Retirement of Bonds	72,000	
Cumulative Effect of a Change in Accounting Principle	(48,000)	
Net Income	$ 384,300	$ 315,000
Earnings per share	$1.92	$1.58

The president of the company, Joseph Dasbol, is pleased to see that both net income and earnings per share increased by 22 percent from 19x2 to 19x3 and intends to announce to the stockholders that the restructuring is a success.

Required

1. Recast the 19x3 income statement in proper multistep form, including allocating income taxes to appropriate items (assume a 30 percent income tax rate) and showing earnings per share figures (200,000 shares outstanding).
2. What is your assessment of the restructuring plan?

13-2. Metzger Steel Corporation *(L.O. 2, 3, 6)*

Metzger Steel Corporation (MSC) is a small specialty steel manufacturer located in northern Alabama that has been owned by the Metzger family for several generations. Arnold Metzger III is a major shareholder in MSC by virtue of having inherited 200,000 shares of common stock in the company. Previously, Arnold has not shown much interest in the business because of his enthusiasm for archaeology, which takes him to far parts of the world. However, when he received minutes of the last board of directors meeting, he questioned a number of transactions involving the stockholders' equity of MSC. He asks you, as a person with a knowledge of accounting, to help him interpret the effect of these transactions on his interest in MSC.

First, you note that at the beginning of 19xx the stockholders' equity of MSC appeared as follows (in thousands):

Metzger Steel Corporation
Stockholders' Equity
January 1, 19xx

Contributed Capital	
Common Stock—$10 par value, 5,000,000 shares authorized, 1,000,000 shares issued and outstanding	$10,000
Paid-in Capital in Excess of Par Value, Common	25,000
Total Contributed Capital	$35,000
Retained Earnings	20,000
Total Stockholders' Equity	$55,000

Then you read the relevant parts of the minutes of the December 15, 19xx meeting of the board of directors of MSC:

Item A: The president reported the following transactions involving the company's stock during the last quarter:

October 15. Sold 500,000 shares of authorized common stock through the investment banking firm of A. B. Abbott at a net price of $50 per share.

November 1. Purchased 100,000 shares for the corporate treasury from Sharon Metzger at a price of $55 per share.

Item B: The board declared a 2 for 1 stock split (accomplished by halving the par value, doubling each stockholder's shares, and increasing authorized shares to 10,000,000), followed by a 10 percent stock dividend. The board then declared a cash dividend of $2.00 per share on the resulting shares. All these transactions are applicable to stockholders of record on December 20 and are payable on January 10. The market value of Metzger stock on the board meeting date after the stock split was estimated to be $30.

Item C: The chief financial officer stated that he expected the company to report a net income for the year of $4,000,000.

Required

1. Prepare a stockholders' equity section of MSC's balance sheet as of December 31, 19xx that reflects the above transactions. (**Hint:** Use T accounts to analyze the transactions. Also, use a T account to keep track of the shares of common stock outstanding.)
2. Compute the book value per share and Arnold's percentage of ownership of the company at the beginning and at the end of the year. Explain the differences. Would you say that Arnold's position has improved during the year or not?

COMPREHENSIVE PROBLEM

Sundial Corporation

Sundial Corporation filed articles of incorporation and obtained authorization for 500,000 shares of no-par common stock with a stated value of \$1 per share and 10,000 shares of 9 percent cumulative preferred stock with a par value of \$100 and a call price of \$104. The company began business on January 1, 19xx as a high-tech startup in the business of making sophisticated time measuring devices. The company's first year of operation was an exciting and profitable one in which the company engaged in a number of transactions involving its stockholders' equity, which are listed below.

19xx		
Jan.	1	Issued for cash 100,000 shares of common stock at a price of \$5 per share.
	2	Issued 12,000 shares of common stock to attorneys and others who assisted with the organization of the corporation. The value of these services was put at \$60,000.
	3	Issued for cash 10,000 shares of preferred stock at par value.
Feb.	6	Accepted subscriptions for 60,000 shares of common stock at a price of \$6 per share.
Mar.	7	Issued 8,000 shares of common stock in exchange for a patent that had a value set at \$50,000.
Apr.	2	Received full payment for half the stock subscription of February 6 and issued the stock.
May	5	Purchased 30,000 common shares from a stockholder for \$8 per share.
	19	Sold 13,000 of the common shares purchased on May 5 for \$9 per share.
June	30	Transferred by a closing entry the net income for the first half of the year to retained earnings, \$250,000.
July	8	Sold 7,000 more of the common shares purchased on May 5 for \$7.
Aug.	4	Declared a 10 percent common stock dividend distributable on Aug. 24 to stockholders of record Aug. 14. At this time the company's common stock is selling for \$8 per share.
	14	Date of record for stock dividend.
	24	Date of distribution for stock dividend.

Sept. 9	Issued common stock for cash in connection with the exercise by management of employee stock options on 40,000 shares of common stock at $5 per share.
Oct. 10	Purchased 10,000 shares of common stock from a stockholder for $9 per share.
20	Retired the shares purchased on October 10. The shares were originally issued at $6 per share.
Nov. 1	Declared cash dividends representing the annual dividend on preferred stock and $0.25 per share on common stock to stockholders of record November 11, payable on November 21.
11	Date of record for cash dividends.
21	Date of payment for cash dividends.
Dec. 16	Declared a 2 for 1 stock split. Assume the stock split applies to treasury stock and common stock subscribed.
31	Transferred by closing entry the net income for the second half of the year of $230,000 to retained earnings and closed dividends to retained earnings.
31	Because of litigation and potential loss from a lawsuit over patent infringement, the board of directors voted to restrict retained earnings to the extent of $100,000 and to disclose this information in a note to the financial statements.

Required

1. Record the above entries for Sundial Corporation in the general journal.
2. Prepare the statement of retained earnings for 19xx for Sundial Corporation.
3. Prepare the stockholders' equity section of Sundial's balance sheet on December 31, 19xx, including proper disclosure of the restriction of retained earnings.
4. Compute book value for preferred stock and common stock at year end.

This Comprehensive Problem covers all of the Learning Objectives in Chapter 12 and Learning Objectives 1 through 6 in Chapter 13.

Part Three
Special Reports and Analyses of Accounting Information

Because business organizations are so complex today, special reports are needed to present important information about their activities. In order to understand and evaluate financial statements, it is necessary to learn how to analyze them.

Part Three deals with these important special reports and with the analysis of financial statements.

Chapter 14 presents the statement of cash flows, which explains the major operating, financing, and investing activities of a business. The chapter presents this statement using both the direct approach and the indirect approach.

Chapter 15 explains the objectives and techniques of financial statement analysis from the standpoint of the financial analyst. As an extended illustration, the financial statements of Eastman Kodak are analyzed.

Chapter 16 addresses two areas of relevance to most corporations in today's complex and global environment. The first is international accounting, including the effects of changing rates of exchange for foreign currencies and of diversity of international accounting standards on the interpretation of financial statements. The second is accounting for investments by one company in the capital stock of another, including consolidated financial statements.

LEARNING OBJECTIVES

1. *Describe the statement of cash flows, and define* cash *and* cash equivalents.
2. *State the principal purposes and uses of the statement of cash flows.*
3. *Identify the principal components of the classifications of cash flows, and state the significance of noncash investing and financing transactions.*
4. *Determine cash flows from operating activities using the (a) direct and (b) indirect methods.*
5. *Determine cash flows from (a) investing activities and (b) financing activities.*
6. *Prepare a statement of cash flows using the (a) direct and (b) indirect methods.*
7. *Interpret the statement of cash flows.*
8. *Prepare a work sheet for the statement of cash flows.*

CHAPTER 14

The Statement of Cash Flows

Earlier in this book you studied the balance sheet, the income statement, and the statement of stockholders' equity. In this chapter you will learn to prepare a fourth major financial statement, the statement of cash flows. After studying this chapter, you should be able to meet the learning objectives listed on the left.

DECISION POINT

Marriott Corporation[1]

Marriott Corporation is a world leader in lodging and contract services. The company's annual report provides an excellent picture of management's philosophy and performance. The company's balance sheet—like that of any company—shows, at a point in time, how management has invested the company's assets, and how those assets are financed by liabilities and stockholders' equity. The income statement shows how much the company earned on its assets during the year. The statement of stockholders' equity shows changes in the ownership of the business, including the cumulative income retained in the business.

While these three financial statements are essential to the evaluation of a company, several questions that they do not cover are answered by a fourth financial statement, the statement of cash flows. For example, how much cash was generated by the company's operations during the year? Marriott answers this question with the following narrative and chart (see Figure 14-1) based on the company's statement of cash flows:

> Cash provided by continuing operations increased to $423 million in 1989, reflecting higher income after adjustment for depreciation and other noncash charges.
>
> Operating cash flows, appropriately leveraged with debt, provide the company with substantial investment capacity. *Because maintaining excess investment capacity is inconsistent with the goal of maximizing shareholder value, management is continually challenged to identify investment opportunities that offer attractive returns.*

1. Excerpts reprinted by permission from the 1989 Annual Report of Marriott Corporation.

Figure 14-1. Cash Provided by Continuing Operations *(in millions)*

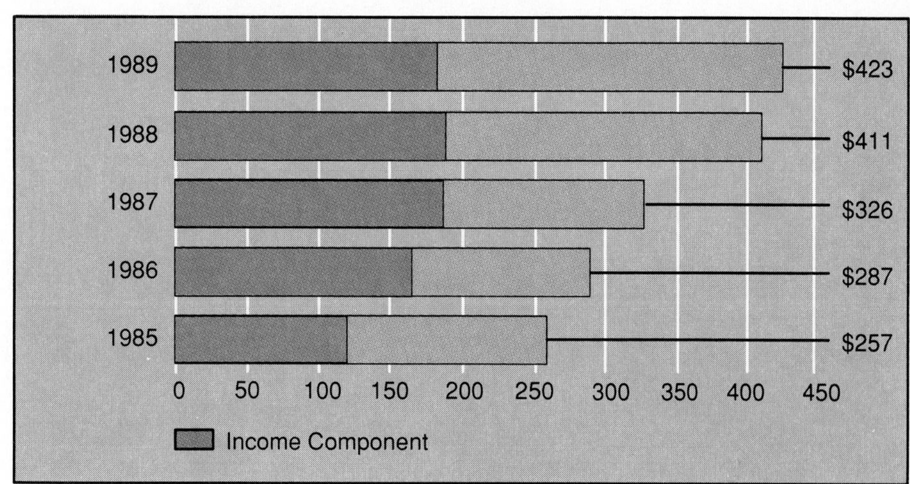

This information is provided in the first part of the discussion of cash flows and indicates that Marriott is very successful in generating cash for further investment. The chart shows that cash flows from continuing operations greatly exceed net income. Other parts of the statement and discussion report where management invested the funds and the other sources of financing used by the company. In the investing and financing areas, the statement of cash flows demonstrates management's commitments for the company in ways that are not readily apparent in the other financial statements. In effect, the statement of cash flows is the most future-directed of the basic financial statements. It is required by the FASB[2] and satisfies the FASB's long-held position that a primary objective of financial statements is to provide investors and creditors with information on a company's cash flows.[3] ■

Purposes, Uses, and Components of the Statement of Cash Flows

OBJECTIVE 1
Describe the statement of cash flows, and define cash *and* cash equivalents

The **statement of cash flows** shows the effect on cash of the operating, investing, and financing activities of a company for an accounting period. It explains the net increase (or decrease) in cash during the accounting period. For purposes of preparing this statement, **cash** is defined to include both cash and cash equivalents. **Cash equivalents** are defined by the FASB as short-term, highly liquid investments, including money market

2. *Statement of Financial Accounting Standards No. 95,* "Statement of Cash Flows" (Stamford, Conn.: Financial Accounting Standards Board, 1987).
3. *Statement of Financial Accounting Concepts No. 1,* "Objectives of Financial Reporting for Business Enterprises" (Stamford, Conn.: Financial Accounting Standards Board, 1978), par. 37–39.

accounts, commercial paper, and U.S. Treasury bills. A company maintains cash equivalents in order to earn interest while cash temporarily lies idle. Suppose, for example, that a company has $1,000,000 that it will not need for thirty days. To earn a return on this sum, the company may place the cash in an account that earns interest (for example, a money market account); it may loan the cash to another corporation by purchasing that corporation's short-term note (commercial paper); or it may purchase a short-term obligation of the U.S. government (a Treasury bill). In this context, short-term is defined as original maturities of ninety days or less. Since cash and cash equivalents are considered the same, transfers between the Cash account and cash equivalents are not treated as cash receipts or cash payments.

Cash equivalents should not be confused with short-term investments or marketable securities, which are not combined with the Cash account on the statement of cash flows. Purchases of marketable securities are treated as cash outflows and sales of marketable securities as cash inflows on the statement of cash flows. In this chapter, cash will be assumed to include both cash and cash equivalents.

Purposes of the Statement of Cash Flows

OBJECTIVE 2
State the principal purposes and uses of the statement of cash flows

The primary purpose of the statement of cash flows is to provide information about a company's cash receipts and cash payments during an accounting period. A secondary purpose of the statement is to provide information about a company's operating, investing, and financing activities during the accounting period. Some of the information on these activities may be inferred by examining other financial statements, but it is on the statement of cash flows that all the transactions affecting cash are summarized.

Internal and External Uses of the Statement of Cash Flows

The statement of cash flows is useful internally to management and externally to investors and creditors. Management may use the statement of cash flows to assess the liquidity of the business, to determine dividend policy, and to evaluate the effects of major policy decisions involving investments and financing. In other words, management will use the statement of cash flows to determine whether or not short-term financing is needed to pay current liabilities, to decide whether to raise or lower dividends, and to plan for investing and financing needs.

Investors and creditors will find the statement useful in assessing the company's ability to manage cash flows, to generate positive future cash flows, to pay its liabilities, and to pay dividends, as well as its need for additional financing. In addition, they may use the statement to explain the differences between net income on the income statement and the net cash flows generated from operations. The statement shows both the cash and noncash effects of investing and financing activities during the accounting period.

Classification of Cash Flows

OBJECTIVE 3
Identify the principal components of the classifications of cash flows, and state the significance of noncash investing and financing transactions

The statement of cash flows classifies cash receipts and cash payments into the categories of operating, investing, and financing activities. The components of these activities are illustrated in Figure 14-2 and are summarized as follows:

1. **Operating activities** include the cash effects of transactions and other events that enter into the determination of net income. Included in this category as cash inflows are cash receipts from customers for goods and services and interest and dividends received on loans and investments. Included as cash outflows are cash payments for wages, goods and services, interest, and taxes applied to employees, suppliers, government bodies, and others. In effect, the income statement is changed from an accrual to a cash basis.

Figure 14-2. Classification of Cash Inflows and Cash Outflows

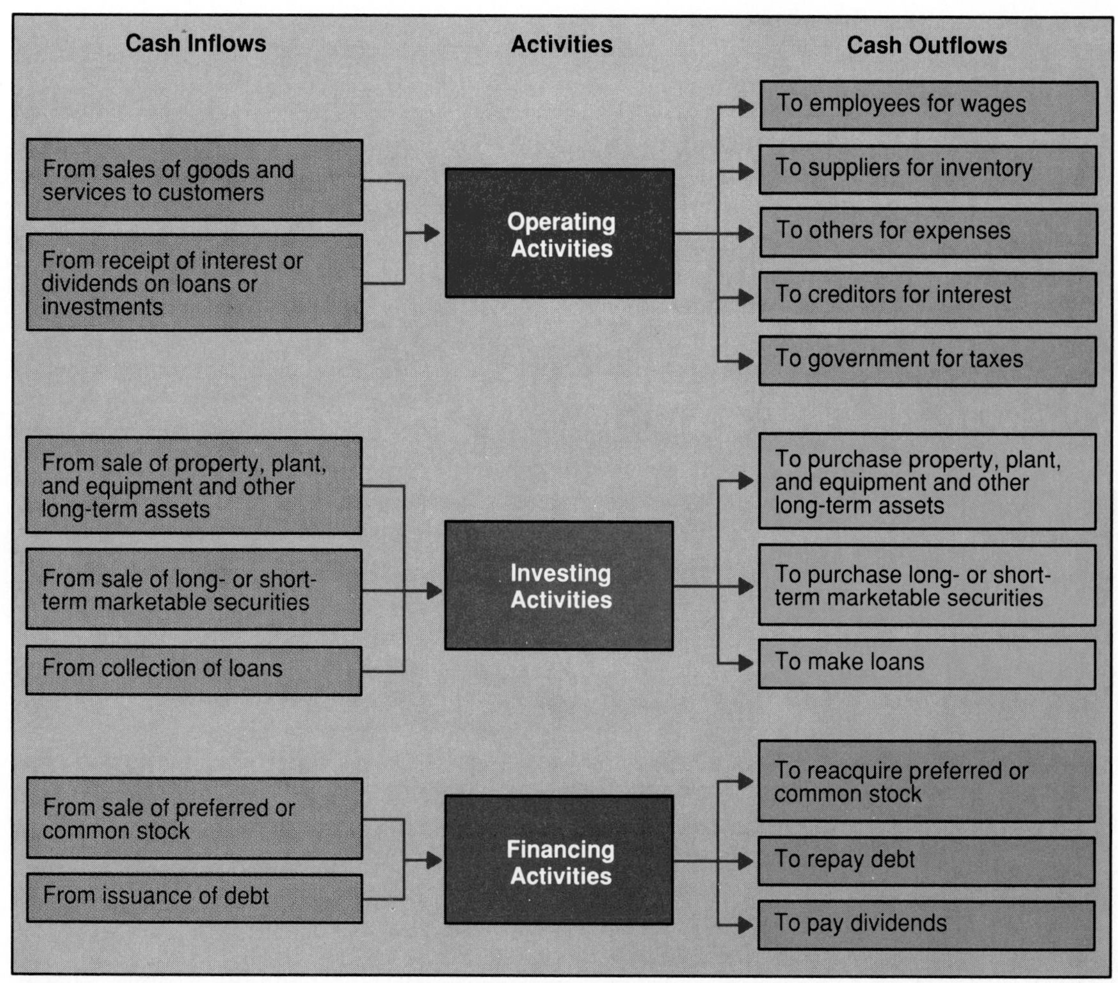

2. **Investing activities** include the acquiring and selling of long-term assets, the acquiring and selling of marketable securities other than cash equivalents, and the making and collecting of loans. Cash inflows include the cash received from selling long-term assets and marketable securities and from collecting loans. Cash outflows include the cash expended for purchases of long-term assets and marketable securities and the cash loaned to borrowers.
3. **Financing activities** include (1) obtaining or returning resources from or to owners and providing the owners with a return on their investment and (2) obtaining resources from creditors and repaying the amounts borrowed, or otherwise settling the obligation. Cash inflows include the proceeds from issues of stocks and from short-term and long-term borrowing. Cash outflows include repayments of loans and payments to owners, including cash dividends. Treasury stock transactions are also considered financing activities. Repayments of accounts payable or accrued liabilities are not considered repayments of loans under financing activities, but are classified as cash outflows under operating activities.

A company will occasionally engage in significant **noncash investing and financing transactions** involving only long-term assets, long-term liabilities, or stockholders' equity, such as the exchange of a long-term asset for a long-term liability or the settlement of a debt by issuing capital stock. For instance, a company might issue a long-term mortgage for the purchase of land and a building. Or it might convert long-term bonds into common stock. These transactions represent significant investing and financing activities, but they would not be reflected on the statement of cash flows because they do not involve either cash inflows or cash outflows. However, since one purpose of the statement of cash flows is to show investing and financing activities, and since transactions like these will have future effects on cash flows, the FASB has determined that they should be disclosed in a separate schedule as part of the statement of cash flows. In this way, the reader of the statement will see clearly the company's investing and financing activities.

Format of the Statement of Cash Flows

The general format of the statement of cash flows, shown in Exhibit 14-1, is divided into three categories corresponding to the three activities discussed above. The cash flows from operating activities are followed by cash flows from investing activities and cash flows from financing activities. The individual inflows and outflows from investing and financing activities are shown separately in their respective categories. For instance, cash inflows from the sale of property, plant, and equipment are shown separately from cash outflows for the purchase of property, plant, and equipment. Similarly, cash inflows from borrowing are shown separately from cash outflows to retire loans. A reconciliation of the beginning and ending balances of cash is shown at the end of the statement. A list of noncash transactions appears in the schedule at the bottom of the statement.

Exhibit 14-1. Format for the Statement of Cash Flows

Company Name
Statement of Cash Flows
Period Covered

Cash Flows from Operating Activities		
(List of individual inflows and outflows)	xxx	
Net Cash Flows from Operating Activities		xxx
Cash Flows from Investing Activities		
(List of individual inflows and outflows)	xxx	
Net Cash Flows from Investing Activities		xxx
Cash Flows from Financing Activities		
(List of individual inflows and outflows)	xxx	
Net Cash Flows from Financing Activities		xxx
Net Increase (Decrease) in Cash		xx
Cash at Beginning of Year		xx
Cash at End of Year		xx

Schedule of Noncash Investing and Financing Transactions

(List of individual transactions)	xxx

Preparing the Statement of Cash Flows

To demonstrate the preparation of the statement of cash flows, we will work an example step by step. The data for this example are presented in Exhibits 14-2 (on page 694) and 14-3 (on page 695). They are the Ryan Corporation's balance sheets for December 31, 19x1 and 19x2, and its 19x2 income statement. Since the changes in the balance sheet accounts will be used in analyzing the various accounts, those changes are shown in Exhibit 14-2. For each individual account, an indication is made as to whether the change is an increase or a decrease. In addition, Exhibit 14-3 contains data about transactions that occurred during the year that affected noncurrent accounts. These transactions would be identified by the company's accountants from the records.

There are four steps in preparing the statement of cash flows:

1. Determine cash flows from operating activities.
2. Determine cash flows from investing activities.
3. Determine cash flows from financing activities.
4. Present the information obtained in the first three steps in the form of the statement of cash flows.

Exhibit 14-2. Balance Sheet with Changes in Accounts Indicated for Ryan Corporation

Ryan Corporation
Balance Sheets
December 31, 19x2 and 19x1

	19x2	19x1	Change	Increase or Decrease
Assets				
Current Assets				
Cash	$ 46,000	$ 15,000	$ 31,000	Increase
Accounts Receivable (net)	47,000	55,000	(8,000)	Decrease
Inventory	144,000	110,000	34,000	Increase
Prepaid Expenses	1,000	5,000	(4,000)	Decrease
Total Current Assets	$238,000	$185,000	$ 53,000	
Investments	$115,000	$127,000	$(12,000)	Decrease
Plant Assets				
Plant Assets	$715,000	$505,000	$210,000	Increase
Accumulated Depreciation	(103,000)	(68,000)	(35,000)	Increase
Total Plant Assets	$612,000	$437,000	$175,000	
Total Assets	$965,000	$749,000	$216,000	
Liabilities				
Current Liabilities				
Accounts Payable	$ 50,000	$ 43,000	$ 7,000	Increase
Accrued Liabilities	12,000	9,000	3,000	Increase
Income Taxes Payable	3,000	5,000	(2,000)	Decrease
Total Current Liabilities	$ 65,000	$ 57,000	$ 8,000	
Long-Term Liabilities				
Bonds Payable	$295,000	$245,000	$ 50,000	Increase
Total Liabilities	$360,000	$302,000	$ 58,000	
Stockholders' Equity				
Common Stock, $5 par value	$276,000	$200,000	$ 76,000	Increase
Paid-in Capital in Excess of Par Value	189,000	115,000	74,000	Increase
Retained Earnings	140,000	132,000	8,000	Increase
Total Stockholders' Equity	$605,000	$447,000	$158,000	
Total Liabilities and Stockholders' Equity	$965,000	$749,000	$216,000	

Exhibit 14-3. Income Statement and Other Information on Noncurrent Accounts for Ryan Corporation

Ryan Corporation
Income Statement
For the Year Ended December 31, 19x2

Sales		$698,000
Cost of Goods Sold		520,000
Gross Margin		$178,000
Operating Expenses (including Depreciation Expense of $37,000)		147,000
Operating Income		$ 31,000
Other Income (Expenses)		
Interest Expense	$(23,000)	
Interest Income	6,000	
Gain on Sale of Investments	12,000	
Loss on Sale of Plant Assets	(3,000)	(8,000)
Income Before Income Taxes		$ 23,000
Income Taxes		7,000
Net Income		$ 16,000

Other transactions affecting noncurrent accounts during 19x2:

1. Purchased investments in the amount of $78,000.
2. Sold investments for $102,000. These investments cost $90,000.
3. Purchased plant assets in the amount of $120,000.
4. Sold plant assets that cost $10,000 with accumulated depreciation of $2,000 for $5,000.
5. Issued $100,000 of bonds at face value in a noncash exchange for plant assets.
6. Repaid $50,000 of bonds at face value at maturity.
7. Issued 15,200 shares of $5 par value common stock for $150,000.
8. Paid cash dividends in the amount of $8,000.

Determining Cash Flows from Operating Activities

The income statement indicates the success or failure of a business in earning an income from its operating activities, but it does not reflect the inflow and outflow of cash from those activities. The reason for this is that the income statement is prepared on an accrual basis. Revenues are recorded even though the cash for them may not have been received, and expenses are incurred and recorded even though cash may not yet have been expended for them. As a result, to arrive at cash flows from operations, one must convert the figures on the income statement from an accrual basis to a cash basis by adjusting earned revenues to cash received from sales and incurred costs and expenses to cash expended, as shown in Figure 14-3 (see page 696).

Figure 14-3. Relationship of Accrual and Cash Bases of Accounting

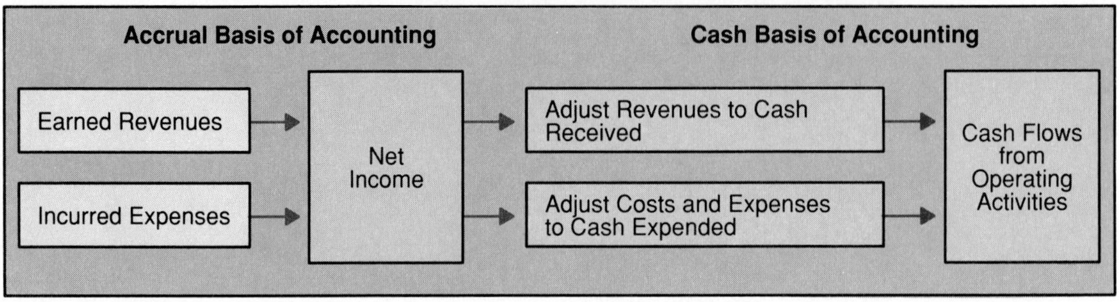

Accrual Basis of Accounting | **Cash Basis of Accounting**

Earned Revenues → Net Income → Adjust Revenues to Cash Received → Cash Flows from Operating Activities

Incurred Expenses → Net Income → Adjust Costs and Expenses to Cash Expended → Cash Flows from Operating Activities

OBJECTIVE 4a *Determine cash flows from operating activities using the direct method*

There are two methods of converting the income statement from an accrual basis to a cash basis: the direct method and the indirect method. The **direct method** is accomplished by adjusting each item in the income statement in turn from the accrual basis to the cash basis. The result is a statement that begins with cash receipts from sales and then deducts cash payments for purchases, operating expenses, interest payments, and income taxes, to arrive at net cash flows from operating activities:

Cash Flows from Operating Activities		
Cash Receipts from		
Sales	XXX	
Interest and Dividends Received	XXX	XXX
Cash Payments for		
Purchases	XXX	
Operating Expenses	XXX	
Interest Payments	XXX	
Income Taxes	XXX	XXX
Net Cash Flows from Operating Activities		XXX

OBJECTIVE 4b *Determine cash flows from operating activities using the indirect method*

The **indirect method**, on the other hand, does not involve adjustment of each item in the income statement individually; only those adjustments necessary to convert net income to cash flows from operations are listed, as follows:

Cash Flows from Operating Activities		
Net Income		XXX
Adjustments to Reconcile Net Income to Net Cash Flows from Operating Activities		
(List of individual items)	XXX	XXX
Net Cash Flows from Operating Activities		XXX

Both adjustments are derived from an analysis of certain income statement items and changes in certain current assets and current liabilities.

DECISION POINT
Survey of Large Companies

The direct method and the indirect method of determining cash flows from operating activities produce the same results. Although it will accept either method, the FASB recommends that the direct method be used, with a supplemental reconciliation to the indirect method. Given these facts, it is interesting to learn which method the majority of companies choose to follow.

A survey of large companies in 1989 showed that an overwhelming majority of 97 percent chose to use the indirect method. Of 600 companies, only seventeen chose the direct approach.[4] Why did so many choose the indirect approach? The reasons for this choice may vary, but chief financial officers tend to prefer the indirect method because it is easier and less expensive to prepare. Moreover, because the FASB requires reconciliation of the direct to the indirect method, the indirect method has to be implemented anyway.

A knowledge of the direct method helps the manager and the reader of financial statements to perceive the underlying causes for the difference between reported net income and cash flows from operations. The indirect method is a practical way of presenting the differences. Since both methods have merit, the direct method will be used in the sections that follow to illustrate the conversion of the income statement to a cash basis, and the indirect method will be used to summarize the process. Finally, to show the preparation of the statement of cash flows, a work sheet approach using the indirect method is presented. ■

Cash Receipts from Sales. Sales result in a positive cash flow for a company. Cash sales are direct increases in the cash flows of the company. Credit sales are not, because they are recorded originally as accounts receivable. When they are collected, they become inflows of cash. One cannot, however, assume that credit sales are automatically inflows of cash, because the collections of accounts receivable in any one accounting period are not likely to equal credit sales. Receivables may prove to be uncollectible, sales from a prior period may be collected in the current period, or sales from the current period may be collected in the next period. For example, if accounts receivable increases from one accounting period to the next, cash receipts from sales will not be as great as sales. On the other hand, if accounts receivable decreases from one accounting period to the next, cash receipts from sales will exceed sales.

4. *Accounting Trends and Techniques* (New York: American Institute of Certified Public Accountants, 1990), p. 350.

The relationships among sales, changes in accounts receivable, and cash receipts from sales are reflected in the following formula.

$$\text{Cash Receipts from Sales} = \text{Sales} \begin{cases} + \text{Decrease in accounts receivable} \\ \text{or} \\ - \text{Increase in accounts receivable} \end{cases}$$

Refer to the balance sheets and income statement for Ryan Corporation in Exhibits 14-2 and 14-3. Note that sales were $698,000 in 19x2, and accounts receivable decreased by $8,000. Thus, cash received from sales is $706,000, calculated as follows:

$$\$706{,}000 = \$698{,}000 + \$8{,}000$$

Ryan Corporation collected $8,000 more from sales than it sold during the year. This relationship may be illustrated as follows:

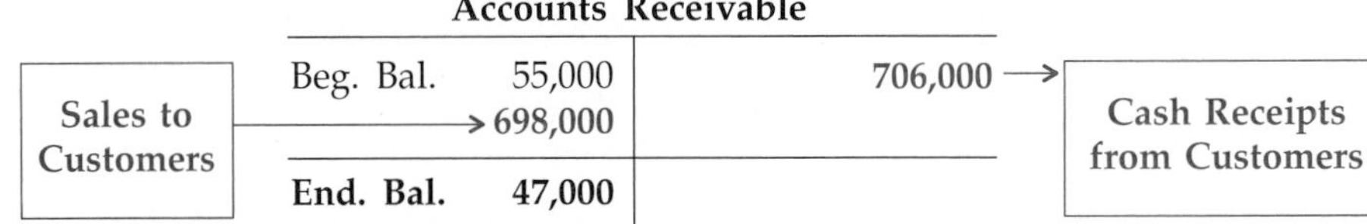

If Ryan Corporation had unearned revenues or advances from customers, an adjustment would be made for changes in those items as well.

Cash Receipts from Interest and Dividends Received. Although interest and dividends received are most closely associated with investment activity and are often called investment income, the FASB has decided to classify the cash received from these items as operating activities. To simplify the examples in this text, it is assumed that interest income equals interest received and that dividend income equals dividends received. Thus, from Exhibit 14-3, interest received by Ryan Corporation is assumed to equal $6,000, which is the amount of interest income.

Cash Payments for Purchases. Cost of goods sold (from the income statement) must be adjusted for changes in two balance sheet accounts to arrive at cash payments for purchases. First, cost of goods sold must be adjusted for changes in inventory to arrive at net purchases. Then, net purchases must be adjusted for the change in accounts payable to arrive at cash payments for purchases. If inventory has increased from one accounting period to another, net purchases will be greater than cost of goods sold; if inventory has decreased, net purchases will be less than cost of goods sold. Conversely, if accounts payable has increased, cash payments for purchases will be less than net purchases; if accounts payable has decreased, cash payments for purchases will be greater than net purchases.

These relationships may be stated in equation form as follows:

$$\text{Cash Payments for Purchases} = \text{Cost of Goods Sold} \begin{cases} + \text{ Increase in Inventory} \\ \text{or} \\ - \text{ Decrease in Inventory} \end{cases} \begin{cases} + \text{ Decrease in Accounts Payable} \\ \text{or} \\ - \text{ Increase in Accounts Payable} \end{cases}$$

From Exhibits 14-2 and 14-3, cost of goods sold is $520,000; inventory increased by $34,000; and accounts payable increased by $7,000. Thus, cash payments for purchases is $547,000, as the following calculation shows:

$$\$547{,}000 = \$520{,}000 + \$34{,}000 - \$7{,}000$$

In this example, Ryan Corporation purchased $34,000 more inventory than it sold and paid out $7,000 less in cash than it purchased. The net result is that cash payments for purchases exceeded cost of goods sold by $27,000 ($547,000 − $520,000). These relationships may be visualized as follows:

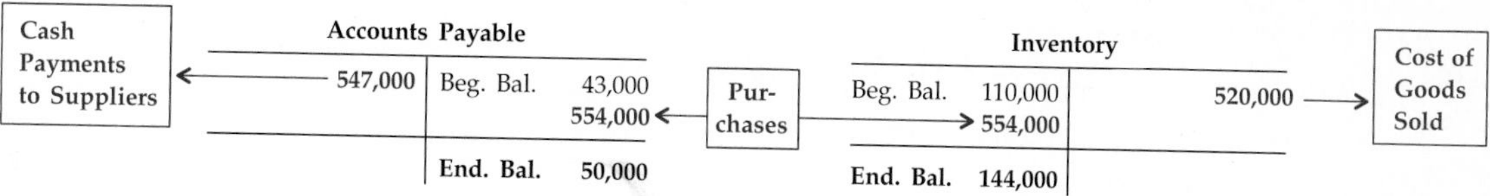

Cash Payments for Operating Expenses. Just as cost of goods sold does not represent the amount of cash paid for purchases during an accounting period, operating expenses will not match the amount of cash paid to employees, suppliers, and others for goods and services. Three adjustments must be made to operating expenses to arrive at the cash flows. The first adjustment is for changes in prepaid expenses, such as prepaid insurance or prepaid rent. If prepaid assets increase during the accounting period, more cash will have been paid out than appears on the income statement in the form of expenses. If prepaid assets decrease, more expenses will appear on the income statement than cash was spent.

The second adjustment is for changes in liabilities resulting from accrued expenses, such as wages payable and payroll taxes payable. If accrued liabilities increase during the accounting period, operating expenses on the income statement will exceed the cash spent. And if accrued liabilities decrease, operating expenses will fall short of cash spent.

The third adjustment is made because certain expenses do not require a current outlay of cash; these expenses must be subtracted from operating expenses to arrive at cash payments for operating expenses. The most common expenses in this category are depreciation expense, amortization expense, and depletion expense. Expenditures for plant assets, intangibles, and natural resources occur when they are purchased and are classified as an investing activity at that time. Depreciation expense, amortization expense, and depletion expense are simply allocations of the costs of those original purchases to the current accounting period, and do not affect cash flows in the current period. For example, Ryan Corporation recorded 19x2 depreciation expense as follows:

Depreciation Expense	37,000	
Accumulated Depreciation		37,000
To record depreciation on plant assets		

No cash payment is made in this transaction. Thus, to the extent that operating expenses include depreciation and similar items, an adjustment is needed to reduce operating expenses to the amount of cash expended.

The three adjustments to operating expenses are summarized in the following equation.

$$\begin{array}{l}\text{Cash Payments}\\ \text{for Operating}\\ \text{Expenses}\end{array} = \begin{array}{l}\text{Operating}\\ \text{Expenses}\end{array} \left\{\begin{array}{l}+\text{ Increase in}\\ \quad\text{Prepaid}\\ \quad\text{Expenses}\\ \quad\text{or}\\ -\text{ Decrease in}\\ \quad\text{Prepaid}\\ \quad\text{Expenses}\end{array}\right. \left\{\begin{array}{l}+\text{ Decrease in}\\ \quad\text{Accrued}\\ \quad\text{Liabilities}\\ \quad\text{or}\\ -\text{ Increase in}\\ \quad\text{Accrued}\\ \quad\text{Liabilities}\end{array}\right. \left\{\begin{array}{l}-\text{Depreciation}\\ \text{and Other Non-}\\ \text{cash Expenses}\end{array}\right.$$

From Exhibits 14-2 and 14-3, Ryan's operating expenses (including depreciation of \$37,000) were \$147,000; prepaid expenses decreased by \$4,000; and accrued liabilities increased by \$3,000. As a result, Ryan Corporation's cash payments for operating expenses are \$103,000, computed as follows:

\$103,000 = \$147,000 – \$4,000 – \$3,000 – \$37,000

If prepaid expenses and accrued liabilities that are *not* related to specific operating expenses exist, they are not to be used in these computations. An example of such a case is income taxes payable, which is the accrued liability related to income taxes expense. The cash payment for income taxes is discussed in a later section.

Cash Payments for Interest. The FASB classifies cash payments for interest as operating activities in spite of the fact that some authorities argue that they should be considered financing activities because of their association with loans incurred to finance the business. The FASB feels that interest expense is a cost of operating the business. We follow the FASB position in this text. Also, for the sake of simplicity, all examples in this text assume that interest payments are equal to interest expense on the income statement. Thus, from Exhibit 14-3, Ryan Corporation's interest payments are assumed to be \$23,000 in 19x2.

Cash Payments for Income Taxes. The amount of income taxes expense that appears on the income statement rarely equals the amount of income taxes actually paid during the year. One reason for this difference is that the final payments for the income taxes of one year are not due until some time in the following year. A second reason is that there may be differences between what is deducted from, or included in, income for accounting purposes and what is included or deducted for purposes of calculating income tax liability. The latter reason often results in a deferred income tax liability. Its effects on cash flows are discussed in the chapter on retained earnings and corporate income statements. Here, we deal only with the changes that result from increases or decreases in income taxes payable.

To determine cash payments for income taxes, income taxes expense (from the income statement) is adjusted by the change in income taxes payable. If income taxes payable increased during the accounting period, cash payments for taxes will be less than the expense shown on the income statement. If income taxes payable decreased, cash payments for taxes will exceed income taxes on the income statement. In other words, the following equation is applicable.

$$\text{Cash Payments for Income Taxes} = \text{Income Taxes} \begin{cases} + \text{ Decrease in Income Taxes Payable} \\ \text{or} \\ - \text{ Increase in Income Taxes Payable} \end{cases}$$

In 19x2, Ryan Corporation showed income taxes of $7,000 on its income statement and a decrease of $2,000 in income taxes payable on its balance sheets (see Exhibits 14-2 and 14-3). As a result, cash payments for income taxes during 19x2 were $9,000, calculated as follows:

$$\$9{,}000 = \$7{,}000 + \$2{,}000$$

Other Income and Expenses. In computing cash flows from operations, some items classified on the income statement as other income and expenses are not considered operating items because they are more closely related to financing and investing activities than to operating activities. Items must be analyzed individually to determine their proper classification on the statement of cash flows. For instance, we have already dealt with interest income and interest expense as operating activities. Unlike the effects of interest, however, the effects on cash flows of gains and losses are considered with the item that gave rise to the gain or loss. The effects of gains or losses on the sale of assets are considered with investing activities, and the effects of gains and losses related to liabilities are considered with financing activities. Consequently, the effects of the gain on sale of investments and of the loss on sale of plant assets reported on Ryan Corporation's income statement (Exhibit 14-3) are considered under cash flows from investing activities.

Schedule of Cash Flows from Operating Activities—Direct Method. It is now possible to prepare a schedule of cash flows from operations using the direct method and the calculations made in the preceding paragraphs. In Exhibit 14-4, Ryan Corporation had Cash Receipts from Sales and Interest Received of $712,000 and Cash Payments for Purchases, Operating Expenses, Interest Payments, and Income Taxes of $682,000, resulting in Net Cash Flows from Operating Activities of $30,000 in 19x2.

Exhibit 14-4. Schedule of Cash Flows from Operating Activities—Direct Method

Ryan Corporation
Schedule of Cash Flows from Operating Activities
For the Year Ended December 31, 19x2

Cash Flows from Operating Activities		
Cash Receipts from		
Sales	$706,000	
Interest Received	6,000	$712,000
Cash Payments for		
Purchases	$547,000	
Operating Expenses	103,000	
Interest Payments	23,000	
Income Taxes	9,000	682,000
Net Cash Flows from Operating Activities		**$ 30,000**

Exhibit 14-5. Schedule of Cash Flows from Operating Activities—Indirect Method

Ryan Corporation
Schedule of Cash Flows from Operating Activities
For the Year Ended December 31, 19x2

Cash Flows from Operating Activities		
Net Income		$16,000
Adjustments to Reconcile Net Income to Net Cash Flows from Operating Activities		
Depreciation	$ 37,000	
Gain on Sale of Investments	(12,000)	
Loss on Sale of Plant Assets	3,000	
Decrease in Accounts Receivable	8,000	
Increase in Inventory	(34,000)	
Decrease in Prepaid Expenses	4,000	
Increase in Accounts Payable	7,000	
Increase in Accrued Liabilities	3,000	
Decrease in Income Taxes Payable	(2,000)	14,000
Net Cash Flows from Operating Activities		**$30,000**

Schedule of Cash Flows from Operating Activities—Indirect Method. It is also possible to calculate net cash flows from operations using the indirect method, as shown in Exhibit 14-5. Note that the amount for Net Cash Flows from Operating Activities is the same as it was under the direct method (Exhibit 14-4). Under the indirect method, the same adjustments for the changes in current assets and current liabilities are made as under the direct method, except that they are made as additions to or subtractions from net income instead of as adjustments to the individual income statement items. For instance, under the direct method, the decrease in accounts receivable was added to Sales to adjust sales from an accrual basis to a cash basis. Since sales are included in the computation of net income, the same effect is achieved by adding the decrease in Accounts Receivable to Net Income. The same logic applies to adjustments to Cost of Goods Sold, Operating Expenses, and Income Taxes, except that the signs will be opposite for these adjustments. The following table summarizes these adjustments.

	Adjustments to Convert Net Income to Net Cash Flows from Operating Activities	
	Add to Net Income	**Deduct from Net Income**
Current Assets		
Accounts Receivable (net)	Decrease	Increase
Inventory	Decrease	Increase
Prepaid Expenses	Decrease	Increase
Current Liabilities		
Accounts Payable	Increase	Decrease
Accrued Liabilities	Increase	Decrease
Income Taxes Payable	Increase	Decrease

Net income must also be adjusted for expenses such as depreciation expense, amortization expense, depletion expense, and other income and expenses such as gains and losses in accordance with the same logic. These items are added or deducted as follows:

	Adjustments to Convert Net Income to Net Cash Flows from Operating Activities
	Add to (Deduct from) Net Income
Depreciation Expense	Add
Amortization Expense	Add
Depletion Expense	Add
Losses	Add
Gains	Deduct

Note that these adjustments to net income are made for several reasons. Depreciation expense is added because it is a noncash expense that was deducted in the income statement to arrive at net income. Adjustments are made for gains and losses because of reasons that will become clear when investing and financing activities are discussed in the next section. Finally, the additions or deductions for increases and decreases in current assets and current liabilities are included because each is necessary to adjust an income statement item from an accrual basis to a cash basis.

Determining Cash Flows from Investing Activities

OBJECTIVE 5a *Determine cash flows from investing activities*

The second step in preparation of the statement of cash flows is to determine cash flows from investing activities. The procedure followed in this step is to examine individually the accounts that involve cash receipts and cash payments from investing activities. The objective in each case is to explain the change in the account balance from one year to the next.

Investing activities center on the long-term assets shown on the balance sheet, but they also include transactions affecting short-term investments from the current asset section of the balance sheet and investment income from the income statement. From the balance sheet in Exhibit 14-2, we can see that Ryan Corporation has long-term assets including investments and plant, but no short-term investments. From the income statement in Exhibit 14-3, we see that it has investment income in the form of interest income, a gain on sale of investments, and a loss on sale of plant assets. Also, from the schedule at the bottom of Exhibit 14-3, we find the following five items pertaining to investing activities in 19x2:

1. Purchased investments in the amount of $78,000.
2. Sold investments that cost $90,000 for $102,000, resulting in a gain of $12,000.
3. Purchased plant assets in the amount of $120,000.
4. Sold plant assets that cost $10,000 with accumulated depreciation of $2,000 for $5,000, resulting in a loss of $3,000.
5. Issued $100,000 of bonds at face value in a noncash exchange for plant assets.

The following paragraphs analyze the accounts related to investing activities for the purpose of determining their effects on Ryan Corporation's cash flows.

Investments. The objective here is to explain the $12,000 decrease in investments (from Exhibit 14-2) by analyzing the increases and decreases in investments to determine the effects on the Cash account. Purchases increase investments and sales decrease investments. Item **1** in the list of Ryan's investing activities shows purchases of $78,000 during 19x2. This transaction was recorded as follows:

Investments	78,000	
Cash		**78,000**
To record purchase of investments		

As we can see from the entry, the effect of this transaction is a $78,000 decrease in cash flows.

Item **2** in the list shows a sale of investments at a gain. It was recorded as follows:

Cash	**102,000**	
Investments		90,000
Gain on Sale of Investments		12,000
To record sale of investments for a gain		

The effect of this transaction is a $102,000 increase in cash flows. Note that the gain on sale of investments is included in the $102,000. This is the reason it was excluded earlier in computing cash flows from operations. If it had been included in that section, it would have been counted twice.

The $12,000 decrease in the Investments account during 19x2 has now been explained, as may be seen in the following T account:

Investments

Beg. Bal.	127,000	Sales	90,000
Purchases	78,000		
End. Bal.	**115,000**		

The cash flow effects from these transactions will be shown in the Cash Flows from Investing Activities section on the statement of cash flows, as follows:

Purchase of Investments	$ (78,000)
Sale of Investments	102,000

Note that purchases and sales are disclosed separately as cash outflows and cash inflows. They are not netted against each other into a single figure. This disclosure gives the reader of the statement a more complete view of investing activity.

If Ryan Corporation had short-term investments or marketable securities, the analysis of cash flows would be the same.

Plant Assets. In the case of plant assets, it is necessary to explain the changes in both the asset account and the related accumulated depreciation account. From Exhibit 14-2, Plant Assets increased by $210,000 and Accumulated Depreciation increased by $35,000. Purchases increase plant assets and sales decrease plant assets. Accumulated Depreciation is increased by the amount of depreciation expense and decreased by the removal of the accumulated depreciation associated with plant assets that are sold. Three items listed in Exhibit 14-3 affect plant assets. Item **3** in the list on page 704 indicates that Ryan Corporation purchased plant assets in the amount of $120,000 during 19x2, as shown by this entry:

Plant Assets	120,000	
Cash		120,000
To record purchase of plant assets		

This transaction results in a cash outflow of $120,000.

Item **4** states that Ryan Corporation sold plant assets for $5,000 that had cost $10,000 and had accumulated depreciation of $2,000. The entry to record this transaction was

Cash	5,000	
Accumulated Depreciation	2,000	
Loss on Sale of Plant Assets	3,000	
Plant Assets		10,000
To record sale of plant assets at a loss		

Note that in this transaction the positive cash flow is equal to the amount of cash received, or $5,000. The loss on sale of plant assets is considered here rather than in the operating activities section, where it was deleted from the income statement when computing cash flows from operating activities. The amount of loss or gain on the sale of an asset is determined by the amount of cash received.

The disclosure of these two transactions in the investing activities section of the statement of cash flows is as follows:

Purchase of Plant Assets	**$(120,000)**
Sale of Plant Assets	**5,000**

As with investments, cash outflows and cash inflows are not netted, but are presented separately to give full information to the statement reader.

Item **5** on the list of Ryan's investing activities is a noncash exchange that affects two long-term accounts, Plant Assets and Bonds Payable. It was recorded as follows:

Plant Assets	100,000	
Bonds Payable		100,000
Issued bonds at face value for plant assets		

Although this transaction is not an inflow or outflow of cash, it is a significant transaction involving both an investing activity (the purchase of plant assets) and a financing activity (the issue of bonds payable). Because one purpose of the statement of cash flows is to show important investing and financing activities, it is listed in a separate schedule at the bottom of the statement of cash flows (see Exhibit 14-6 on page 710) or accompanying the statement, as follows:

Schedule of Noncash Investing and Financing Transactions

Issue of Bonds Payable for Plant Assets	**$100,000**

Through our analysis of these transactions and the depreciation expense for plant assets of $37,000, all the changes in the plant assets accounts have now been accounted for, as shown in these T accounts:

Plant Assets

Beg. Bal.	505,000	Sale	10,000
Purchase	120,000		
Noncash Purchase	100,000		
End. Bal.	**715,000**		

Accumulated Depreciation

Sale	2,000	Beg. Bal.	68,000
		Dep. Exp.	37,000
		End. Bal.	**103,000**

If the balance sheet had included specific plant asset accounts such as Buildings and Equipment and their related accumulated depreciation accounts, or other long-term asset accounts such as intangibles or natural resources, the analysis would be the same.

Determining Cash Flows from Financing Activities

OBJECTIVE 5b *Determine cash flows from financing activities*

The third step in preparation of the statement of cash flows is to determine cash flows from financing activities. The procedure followed in this step is the same as that applied to the analysis of investing activities, including related gains and/or losses. The only difference between the two is that the accounts to be analyzed are the long-term liability and stockholders' equity accounts. Also to be taken into account are short-term borrowings and cash dividends. The following items from Exhibit 14-3 pertain to Ryan Corporation's financing activities in 19x2:

5. Issued $100,000 of bonds at face value in a noncash exchange for plant assets.
6. Repaid $50,000 of bonds at face value at maturity.
7. Issued 15,200 shares of $5 par value common stock for $150,000.
8. Paid cash dividends in the amount of $8,000.

Bonds Payable. Exhibit 14-2 shows that Bonds Payable increased by $50,000 in 19x2. This account is affected by items **5** and **6**. Item **5** was analyzed in connection with plant assets. It is reported on the schedule of noncash investing and financing transactions (see Exhibit 14-6), but it must be remembered here in preparing the T account for Bonds Payable. Item **6** results in a cash outflow, a point that can be seen in the following transaction:

Bonds Payable	50,000	
Cash		**50,000**
To record repayment of bonds at face value at maturity		

This cash outflow is shown in the financing activities section of the statement of cash flows as follows:

Repayment of Bonds	**$(50,000)**

From these transactions, the change in the Bonds Payable account can be explained as follows:

Bonds Payable

Repayment	50,000	Beg. Bal.	245,000
		Noncash Issue	**100,000**
		End. Bal.	**295,000**

If Ryan Corporation had notes payable, either short-term or long-term, the analysis would be the same.

Common Stock. As with plant assets, related stockholders' equity accounts should be analyzed together. For example, Paid-in Capital in Excess of Par Value should be examined together with Common Stock. In 19x2 Ryan Corporation's Common Stock account increased by $76,000 and Paid-in Capital in Excess of Par Value increased by $74,000. These increases are explained by item **7**, which states that Ryan Corporation issued 15,200 shares of stock for $150,000. The entry to record this cash inflow was as follows:

Cash	150,000	
Common Stock		76,000
Paid-in Capital in Excess of Par Value		74,000
Issue of 15,200 shares of $5 par value common stock		

This cash inflow is shown in the financing activities section of the statement of cash flows as follows:

Issue of Common Stock	$150,000

The analysis of this transaction is all that is needed to explain the changes in the two accounts during 19x2, as follows:

Common Stock

	Beg. Bal.	200,000
	Issue	76,000
	End. Bal.	**276,000**

Paid-in Capital in Excess of Par Value

	Beg. Bal.	115,000
	Issue	74,000
	End. Bal.	**189,000**

Retained Earnings. At this point in the analysis, several items that affected Retained Earnings have already been dealt with. For instance, in the case of Ryan Corporation, net income was used as part of the analysis of cash flows from operating activities. The only other item affecting the retained earnings of Ryan Corporation was the payment of $8,000 in cash dividends (item **8** on the list on page 707), as reflected by the following transaction:

Retained Earnings	8,000	
Cash		8,000
To record cash dividends for 19x2		

Ryan Corporation may have declared the dividend before paying it and debited the Dividends Declared account instead of Retained Earnings, but after paying the dividend and closing the Dividends Declared account to Retained Earnings, the effect is as shown. Cash dividends are displayed in the financing activities section of the statement of cash flows as follows:

Dividends Paid	$(8,000)

The change in the Retained Earnings account is explained in the T account below:

Retained Earnings

Dividends	8,000	Beg. Bal.	132,000
		Net Income	16,000
		End. Bal.	**140,000**

Presenting the Information in the Form of the Statement of Cash Flows

OBJECTIVE 6
Prepare a statement of cash flows using the (a) direct and (b) indirect methods

At this point in the analysis, all income statement items have been analyzed, all balance sheet changes have been explained, and all additional information has been taken into account. The resulting information may now be assembled into a statement of cash flows for Ryan Corporation, as shown in Exhibit 14-6. The direct approach is used because the operating activities section contains the data from Exhibit 14-4, which shows the net cash flows from operating activities as determined by the direct approach. The statement is just as easily prepared using the indirect approach and the data in Exhibit 14-5, as presented in Exhibit 14-7 (located on page 711). The only difference in the main part of the two statements is the approach used in the operating activities section. The Schedule of Noncash Investing and Financing Transactions is presented at the bottom of each statement. When the direct method is used, a schedule reconciling or explaining the difference between reported net income and net cash flows from operating activities must be provided as shown in Exhibit 14-6. This reconciliation is the same as the cash flows from operating activities section of the indirect method form of the statement, as shown in Exhibits 14-5 and 14-7.

Interpretation of the Statement of Cash Flows

OBJECTIVE 7
Interpret the statement of cash flows

Now that the statement has been prepared, it is important to know how to interpret and use it. What can one learn about Ryan Corporation and its management by reading its statement of cash flows?

Starting with the first section of the statement in Exhibits 14-6 and 14-7, note that Ryan Corporation generated net cash flows from operating activities of $30,000, which compares very favorably with its net income of $16,000. We can see from Exhibit 14-7 that the largest positive factor is the depreciation expense of $37,000. This expense did not require a current

Exhibit 14-6. The Statement of Cash Flows—Direct Method

Ryan Corporation
Statement of Cash Flows
For the Year Ended December 31, 19x2

Cash Flows from Operating Activities		
Cash Receipts from		
Sales	$706,000	
Interest Received	6,000	$712,000
Cash Payments for		
Purchases	$547,000	
Operating Expenses	103,000	
Interest Payments	23,000	
Income Taxes	9,000	682,000
Net Cash Flows from Operating Activities		$ 30,000
Cash Flows from Investing Activities		
Purchase of Investments	$ (78,000)	
Sale of Investments	102,000	
Purchase of Plant Assets	(120,000)	
Sale of Plant Assets	5,000	
Net Cash Flows from Investing Activities		(91,000)
Cash Flows from Financing Activities		
Repayment of Bonds	$ (50,000)	
Issue of Common Stock	150,000	
Dividends Paid	(8,000)	
Net Cash Flows from Financing Activities		92,000
Net Increase (Decrease) in Cash		$ 31,000
Cash at Beginning of Year		15,000
Cash at End of Year		$ 46,000

Schedule of Noncash Investing and Financing Transactions

Issue of Bonds Payable for Plant Assets	$100,000

Reconciliation of Net Income to Net Cash Flows from Operating Activities

Net Income		$16,000
Adjustments to Reconcile Net Income to Net Cash Flows from Operating Activities		
Depreciation	$ 37,000	
Gain on Sale of Investments	(12,000)	
Loss on Sale of Plant Assets	3,000	
Decrease in Accounts Receivable	8,000	
Increase in Inventory	(34,000)	
Decrease in Prepaid Expenses	4,000	
Increase in Accounts Payable	7,000	
Increase in Accrued Liabilities	3,000	
Decrease in Income Taxes Payable	(2,000)	14,000
Net Cash Flows from Operating Activities		$30,000

Exhibit 14-7. Statement of Cash Flows—Indirect Method

Ryan Corporation
Statement of Cash Flows
For the Year Ended December 31, 19x2

Cash Flows from Operating Activities		
Net Income		$ 16,000
Adjustments to Reconcile Net Income to Net Cash Flows from Operating Activities		
Depreciation	$ 37,000	
Gain on Sale of Investments	(12,000)	
Loss on Sale of Plant Assets	3,000	
Decrease in Accounts Receivable	8,000	
Increase in Inventory	(34,000)	
Decrease in Prepaid Expenses	4,000	
Increase in Accounts Payable	7,000	
Increase in Accrued Liabilities	3,000	
Decrease in Income Taxes Payable	(2,000)	14,000
Net Cash Flows from Operating Activities		$ 30,000
Cash Flows from Investing Activities		
Purchase of Investments	$ (78,000)	
Sale of Investments	102,000	
Purchase of Plant Assets	(120,000)	
Sale of Plant Assets	5,000	
Net Cash Flows from Investing Activities		(91,000)
Cash Flows from Financing Activities		
Repayment of Bonds	$ (50,000)	
Issue of Common Stock	150,000	
Dividends Paid	(8,000)	
Net Cash Flows from Financing Activities		92,000
Net Increase (Decrease) in Cash		$ 31,000
Cash at Beginning of Year		15,000
Cash at End of Year		$ 46,000

Schedule of Noncash Investing and Financing Transactions

Issue of Bonds Payable for Plant Assets	$100,000

cash outlay, and is thus an important cause of the difference between net income and cash flows from operating activities.

The largest drain on cash in the operating activities section is the $34,000 increase in inventory. Management may want to explore ways of reducing inventory during the next year, unless this increase was for increased sales activities next year. Other changes in current assets and current liabilities, except for the small decrease in income taxes payable, have positive effects on cash flows in this section.

Investors and creditors may want to compare net cash flows from operating activities to dividends paid in the financing activities section to determine whether the company has adequate cash flows from operations to cover its payments to investors. Ryan Corporation is in good condition in this regard. Dividends paid are $8,000, compared to $30,000 in net cash flows from operating activities. The remaining $22,000 is available for other purposes and provides a cushion for payment of dividends.

Moving to the investing activities, it is apparent that the company is expanding because there is a net cash outflow of $91,000 in this section. The company has expanded by purchasing plant assets of $120,000. Various other investing activities have reduced the cash need to $91,000. This is not the whole story on the expansion of the business, however, because the schedule of noncash investing and financing transactions reveals that the company bought another $100,000 in plant assets by issuing bonds. In other words, total purchases of plant assets were $220,000. Part of this expansion was financed by issuing bonds in exchange for plant assets, and most of the rest was financed through other activities.

Net cash inflows of $92,000 were provided by financing activities to offset the $91,000 net cash outflows needed for investing activities. The company looked to its owners for financing by issuing common stock for $150,000 while repaying $50,000 in bonds payable. Taking into account the noncash transaction, bonds payable increased by $50,000.

In summary, Ryan Corporation has paid for its expansion with a combination of cash flows from operating activities, net sales of investment assets, issuance of common stock, and a net increase in bonds payable.

Preparing the Work Sheet

OBJECTIVE 8 *Prepare a work sheet for the statement of cash flows*

Previous sections illustrated the preparation of the statement of cash flows for Ryan Corporation, a relatively simple company. To assist in preparing the statement of cash flows in more complex companies, accountants have developed a work sheet approach. The work sheet approach employs a special format that allows for the systematic analysis of all the changes in the balance sheet accounts to arrive at the statement of cash flows. In this section, the work sheet approach is demonstrated using the statement of cash flows for Ryan Corporation. The work sheet approach uses the indirect method of determining cash flows from operating activities because of its basis in changes in the balance sheet accounts.

Procedures in Preparing the Work Sheet

Alternative Method

The work sheet for Ryan Corporation is presented in Exhibit 14-8. The work sheet has four columns, labeled as follows:

Column A: Description

Column B: Account balances for the end of the prior year (19x1)

Column C: Analysis of transactions for the current year

Column D: Account balances for the end of the current year (19x2)

Exhibit 14-8. Work Sheet for the Statement of Cash Flows

Ryan Corporation
Work Sheet for Statement of Cash Flows
For the Year Ended December 31, 19x2

(A) Description	(B) Account Balances 12/31/x1	(C) Analysis of Transactions: Debit	Analysis of Transactions: Credit	(D) Account Balances 12/31/x2
Debits				
Cash	15,000	(x) **31,000**		46,000
Accounts Receivable (net)	55,000		(b) 8,000	47,000
Inventory	110,000	(c) 34,000		144,000
Prepaid Expenses	5,000		(d) 4,000	1,000
Investments	127,000	(h) 78,000	(i) 90,000	115,000
Plant Assets	505,000	(j) 120,000	(k) 10,000	715,000
		(l) 100,000		
Total Debits	817,000			1,068,000
Credits				
Accumulated Depreciation	68,000	(k) 2,000	(m) 37,000	103,000
Accounts Payable	43,000		(e) 7,000	50,000
Accrued Liabilities	9,000		(f) 3,000	12,000
Income Taxes Payable	5,000	(g) 2,000		3,000
Bonds Payable	245,000	(n) 50,000	(l) 100,000	295,000
Common Stock	200,000		(o) 76,000	276,000
Paid-in Capital	115,000		(o) 74,000	189,000
Retained Earnings	132,000	(p) 8,000	(a) 16,000	140,000
Total Credits	817,000	425,000	425,000	1,068,000
Cash Flows from Operating Activities				
Net Income		(a) 16,000		
Decrease in Accounts Receivable		(b) 8,000		
Increase in Inventory			(c) 34,000	
Decrease in Prepaid Expenses		(d) 4,000		
Increase in Accounts Payable		(e) 7,000		
Increase in Accrued Liabilities		(f) 3,000		
Decrease in Income Taxes Payable			(g) 2,000	
Gain on Sale of Investments			(i) 12,000	
Loss on Sale of Plant Assets		(k) 3,000		
Depreciation Expense		(m) 37,000		
Cash Flows from Investing Activities				
Purchase of Investments			(h) 78,000	
Sale of Investments		(i) 102,000		
Purchase of Plant Assets			(j) 120,000	
Sale of Plant Assets		(k) 5,000		
Cash Flows from Financing Activities				
Repayment of Bonds			(n) 50,000	
Issue of Common Stock		(o) 150,000		
Dividends Paid			(p) 8,000	
		335,000	304,000	
Net Increase in Cash			(x) 31,000	
		335,000	335,000	

Five steps are followed in the preparation of the work sheet. As you read each one, refer to Exhibit 14-8.

1. Enter the account names from the balance sheet (Exhibit 14-2 on page 694) in column A. Note that all accounts with debit balances are listed first, followed by all accounts with credit balances.
2. Enter the account balances for 19x1 in column B and the account balances for 19x2 in column D. In each column, total the debits and the credits. The total debits should equal the total credits in each column. (This is a check of whether all accounts were transferred from the balance sheet correctly.)
3. Below the data entered in Step 2, insert the captions Cash Flows from Operating Activities, Cash Flows from Investing Activities, and Cash Flows from Financing Activities, leaving several lines of space between each one. As you do the analysis in Step 4, write the results in the appropriate categories.
4. Analyze the changes in each balance sheet account, using information both from the income statement (see Exhibit 14-3) and from other appropriate transactions. (The procedures for this analysis are presented in the next section.) Enter the results in the debit and credit columns in column C. Identify each item with a letter. On the first line, identify the change in cash with an (x). In a complex situation, these letters will refer to a list of explanations on another working paper.
5. When all the changes in the balance sheet accounts have been explained, add the debit and credit columns in both the top and bottom portions of column C. The debit and credit columns in the top portion should equal each other. They should *not* be equal in the bottom portion. If no errors have been made, the difference between the columns in the bottom portion should equal the increase or decrease in the Cash account, identified with an (x) on the first line of the work sheet. Add this difference to the lesser of the two columns, and identify it as either an increase or a decrease in cash. Label the change with an (x) and compare it with the change in cash on the first line of the work sheet, also labeled (x). The amounts should be equal, as they are in Exhibit 14-8, where the net increase in cash is $31,000.

When the work sheet is complete, the statement of cash flows may be prepared using the information in the lower half of the work sheet, as shown previously in Exhibit 14-7.

Analyzing the Changes in Balance Sheet Accounts

The most important step in the preparation of the work sheet is the analysis of the changes in the balances of the balance sheet accounts (Step 4). Although there are a number of transactions and reclassifications to analyze and record, the overall procedure is systematic and not overly complicated. It is as follows:

1. Record net income.
2. Account for changes in current assets and current liabilities.

3. Account for changes in noncurrent accounts using the information about other transactions.
4. Reclassify any other income and expense items not already dealt with. In the following explanations, the identification letters refer to the corresponding transactions and reclassifications in the work sheet.

a. ***Net Income.*** Net income results in an increase in Retained Earnings. It is also the starting point under the indirect method for determining cash flows from operating activities. Under this method, additions and deductions are made to net income to arrive at cash flows from operating activities. Work sheet entry **a** is as follows:

		Debit	Credit
(a)	Cash Flows from Operations: Net Income	16,000	
	Retained Earnings		16,000

b–g. ***Changes in Current Assets and Current Liabilities.*** Entries **b** to **g** record the effects on cash flows of the changes in current assets and current liabilities. In each case, there is a debit or credit to the current asset or current liability to account for the change during the year and a corresponding debit or credit in the operating activities section of the work sheet. Recall that in the prior analysis, each item on the accrual-based income statement was adjusted for the change in the related current asset or current liability to arrive at the cash-based figure. The same reasoning applies in recording these changes in accounts as debits or credits in the operating activities section. For example, work sheet entry **b** records the decrease in Accounts Receivable as a credit (decrease) to Accounts Receivable and as a debit in the operating activities section because the decrease has a positive effect on cash flows, as follows:

		Debit	Credit
(b)	Cash Flows from Operating Activities:		
	Decrease in Accounts Receivable	8,000	
	Accounts Receivable		8,000

Work sheet entries **c–g** reflect the effects of the changes in the other current assets and current liabilities on cash flows from operating activities. As you study these entries, note how the effects of each entry on cash flows are automatically determined by debits or credits reflecting changes in the balance sheet accounts.

		Debit	Credit
(c)	Inventory	34,000	
	Cash Flows from Operating Activities:		
	Increase in Inventory		34,000
(d)	Cash Flows from Operating Activities:		
	Decrease in Prepaid Expenses	4,000	
	Prepaid Expenses		4,000
(e)	Cash Flows from Operating Activities:		
	Increase in Accounts Payable	7,000	
	Accounts Payable		7,000
(f)	Cash Flows from Operating Activities:		
	Increase in Accrued Liabilities	3,000	
	Accrued Liabilities		3,000

(g) Income Taxes Payable	2,000	
Cash Flows from Operating Activities:		
Decrease in Income Taxes Payable		2,000

h–i. ***Investments.*** Among the other transactions affecting noncurrent accounts during 19x2 (see Exhibit 14-3), two items pertain to investments. One is the purchase for $78,000, and the other is the sale at $102,000. The purchase is recorded on the work sheet as a cash flow in the investing activities section, as follows:

(h) Investments	78,000	
Cash Flows from Investing Activities:		
Purchase of Investments		78,000

Note that instead of crediting Cash, a credit entry with the appropriate designation is made in the appropriate section in the lower half of the work sheet. The sale transaction is more complicated because it involves a gain that appears on the income statement and is included in net income. The work sheet entry accounts for this gain as follows:

(i) Cash Flows from Investing Activities:		
Sale of Investments	102,000	
Investments		90,000
Cash Flows from Operating Activities:		
Gain on Sale of Investments		12,000

This entry records the cash inflow in the investing activities section, accounts for the remaining difference in the Investments account, and removes the gain on sale of investments from net income.

j–m. ***Plant Assets and Accumulated Depreciation.*** Four transactions affect plant assets and the related accumulated depreciation. These are the purchase of plant assets, the sale of plant assets at a loss, the noncash exchange of plant assets for bonds, and the depreciation expense for the year. Because these transactions may appear complicated, it is important to work through them systematically when preparing the work sheet. First, the purchase of plant assets for $120,000 is entered (entry **j**) in the same way the purchase of investments was entered in entry **h**. Second, the sale of plant assets is similar to the sale of investments, except that instead of a gain, a loss is involved, as follows:

(k) Cash Flows from Investing Activities:		
Sale of Plant Assets	5,000	
Cash Flows from Operating Activities:		
Loss on Sale of Plant Assets	3,000	
Accumulated Depreciation	2,000	
Plant Assets		10,000

The cash inflow from this transaction is $5,000. The rest of the entry is necessary to add the loss back into net income in the operating activities section of the statement (since it was deducted to arrive at net income) and to record the effects on plant assets and accumulated depreciation.

The third transaction (entry l) is the noncash issue of bonds for the purchase of plant assets, as follows:

(l) Plant Assets	100,000	
Bonds Payable		100,000

Note that this transaction does not affect cash. Still, it needs to be recorded because the objective is to account for all the changes in the balance sheet accounts. It is listed at the end of the statement of cash flows (Exhibit 14-7) in the schedule of noncash investing and financing transactions.

At this point the increase of $210,000 ($715,000 – $505,000) in plant assets has been explained by the two purchases less the sale ($120,000 + $100,000 – $10,000 = $210,000), but the change in Accumulated Depreciation has not been completely explained. The depreciation expense for the year needs to be entered, as follows:

(m) Cash Flows from Operating Activities:		
Depreciation Expense	37,000	
Accumulated Depreciation		37,000

The debit is to the operating activities section of the work sheet because, as explained earlier in the chapter, no current cash outflow is required for depreciation expense. The effect of this debit is to add the amount for depreciation expense back into net income. The $35,000 increase in Accumulated Depreciation has now been explained by the sale transaction and the depreciation expense (– $2,000 + $37,000 = $35,000).

n. ***Bonds Payable.*** Part of the change in Bonds Payable was explained in entry **l** when a noncash transaction, a $100,000 issue of bonds in exchange for plant assets, was entered. All that remains is to enter the repayment, as follows:

(n) Bonds Payable	50,000	
Cash Flows from Financing Activities:		
Repayment of Bonds		50,000

o. ***Common Stock and Paid-in Capital in Excess of Par Value.*** One transaction affects both these accounts. It is an issue of 15,200 shares of $5 par value common stock for a total of $150,000. The work sheet entry is:

(o) Cash Flows from Financing Activities:		
Issue of Common Stock	150,000	
Common Stock		76,000
Paid-in Capital in Excess of Par Value		74,000

p. ***Retained Earnings.*** Part of the change in Retained Earnings was recognized when net income was entered (entry **a**). The only remaining effect to be recognized is that of the $8,000 in cash dividends paid during the year, as follows:

(p) Retained Earnings	8,000	
Cash Flows from Financing Activities:		
Dividends Paid		8,000

x. The final step is to total the debit and credit columns in the top and bottom portions of the work sheet and then to enter the net change in cash at the bottom of the work sheet. The columns in the upper half equal $425,000. In the lower half, the debit column totals $335,000 and the credit column totals $304,000. The credit difference of $31,000 (entry **x**) equals the debit change in cash on the first line of the work sheet.

Chapter Review

Review of Learning Objectives

1. **Describe the statement of cash flows, and define *cash* and *cash equivalents*.**
   The statement of cash flows explains the changes in cash and cash equivalents from one accounting period to the next by showing cash outflows and cash inflows from the operating, investing, and financing activities of a company for an accounting period. For purposes of preparing the statement of cash flows, *cash* is defined to include cash and cash equivalents. *Cash equivalents* are short-term (ninety days or less), highly liquid investments, including money market accounts, commercial paper, and U.S. Treasury bills.

2. **State the principal purposes and uses of the statement of cash flows.**
   The primary purpose of the statement of cash flows is to provide information about a company's cash receipts and cash payments during an accounting period. Its secondary purpose is to provide information about a company's operating, investing, and financing activities. It is useful to management as well as to investors and creditors in assessing the liquidity of a business, including the ability of the business to generate future cash flows and to pay its debts and dividends.

3. **Identify the principal components of the classifications of cash flows, and state the significance of noncash investing and financing transactions.**
   Cash flows may be classified as operating activities, which include the cash effects of transactions and other events that enter into the determination of net income; as investing activities, which include the acquiring and selling of long- and short-term marketable securities, property, plant, and equipment, and the making and collecting of loans, excluding interest; or as financing activities, which include the obtaining and returning or repaying of resources, excluding interest, to owners and creditors. Noncash investing and financing transactions are particularly important because they are exchanges of assets and/or liabilities that are of interest to investors and creditors when evaluating the financing and investing activities of the business.

4. **Determine cash flows from operating activities using the (a) direct and (b) indirect methods.**
In the direct method of determining cash flows from operating activities, each item in the income statement is adjusted from an accrual basis to a cash basis, in the following form:

Cash Flows from Operating Activities		
Cash Receipts from		
Sales	xxx	
Interest and Dividends Received	xxx	xxx
Cash Payments for		
Purchases	xxx	
Operating Expenses	xxx	
Interest Payments	xxx	
Income Taxes	xxx	xxx
Net Cash Flows from Operating Activities		xxx

In the indirect method, net income is adjusted for all noncash effects to arrive at a cash flow basis, as follows:

Cash Flows from Operating Activities		
Net Income		xxx
Adjustments to Reconcile Net Income to Net Cash Flows from Operating Activities		
(List of individual items)	xxx	xxx
Net Cash Flows from Operating Activities		xxx

5. **Determine cash flows from (a) investing activities and (b) financing activities.**
Cash flows from investing activities are determined by identifying the cash flow effects of the transactions that affect each account relevant to investing activities. These accounts include all long-term assets and short-term marketable securities. The same procedure is followed for financing activities, except that the accounts involved are short-term notes payable, long-term liabilities, and owners' equity accounts. The effects on related accounts of gains and losses reported on the income statement must also be considered. When the change in a balance sheet account from one accounting period to the next has been explained, all the cash flow effects should have been identified.

6. **Prepare a statement of cash flows using the (a) direct and (b) indirect methods.**
The statement of cash flows lists cash flows from operating activities, investing activities, and financing activities, in that order. The section on operating activities may be prepared using either the direct or the indirect method of determining cash flows from operating activities. The sections on investing and financing activities are prepared by examining individual accounts involving cash receipts and cash payments in order to explain year-to-year changes in the account balances. Significant noncash transactions are included in a schedule of noncash investing and financing transactions that accompanies the statement of cash flows.

7. **Interpret the statement of cash flows.**
Interpretation of the statement of cash flows begins with an examination of the cash flows from operations, to determine whether they are positive and to assess the differences between net income and net cash flows from operating activities. It is usually informative to relate cash flows from operations to dividend payments in the financing section to see whether the company is comfortably covering these important cash outflows. It is also useful to examine investing activities to determine whether the company is expanding, and if so, in what areas of business it is investing; or if not, in what areas it is contracting. Based on the analysis of investing, one should then look at the financing section to evaluate how the company is financing its expansion, or if it is not expanding, how it is reducing its financing obligations. Finally, it is important to evaluate the impact of the noncash investing and financing transactions listed in the lower portion of the statement of cash flows.

8. **Prepare a work sheet for the statement of cash flows.**
A work sheet is useful in preparing the statement of cash flows for complex companies. The basic procedures in the work sheet approach are to analyze the changes in the balance sheet accounts for their effects on cash flows (in the top portion of the work sheet) and to classify those effects according to the format of the statement of cash flows (in the lower portion of the work sheet). When all the changes in the balance sheet accounts have been explained and entered on the work sheet, the change in the Cash account will also be explained, and the information will be available to prepare the statement of cash flows. The work sheet approach lends itself to the indirect method of preparing the statement of cash flows.

Review of Concepts and Terminology

The following concepts and terms were introduced in this chapter:

(L.O. 1) **Cash:** Cash and cash equivalents.

(L.O. 1) **Cash equivalents:** Short-term (ninety days or less), highly liquid investments, including money market accounts, commercial paper, and U.S. Treasury bills.

(L.O. 4a) **Direct method:** The procedure for converting the income statement from an accrual basis to a cash basis by adjusting each item in the income statement separately.

(L.O. 3) **Financing activities:** Business activities that involve obtaining or returning resources from or to owners and providing them with a return on their investment.

(L.O. 4b) **Indirect method:** The procedure for converting the income statement from an accrual basis to a cash basis by adjusting net income for items that do not affect cash flows, including depreciation, amortization, depletion, gains, losses, and changes in current assets and current liabilities.

(L.O. 3) **Investing activities:** Business activities that include the acquiring and selling of long-term assets, the acquiring and selling of marketable securities other than cash equivalents, and the making and collecting of loans.

(L.O. 3) **Noncash investing and financing transactions:** Significant investing and financing transactions that do not involve an actual cash inflow or outflow but involve only long-term assets, long-term liabilities, or stockholders' eq-

uity, such as the exchange of a long-term asset for a long-term liability or the settlement of a debt by the issue of capital stock.

(L.O. 3) **Operating activities:** Business activities that include the cash effects of transactions and other events that enter into the determination of net income.

(L.O. 1) **Statement of cash flows:** A primary financial statement that shows the effect on cash of the operating, investing, and financing activities of a company for an accounting period.

Review Problem
The Statement of Cash Flows

(L.O. 4, 5, 6) The comparative balance sheets for Northwest Corporation for the years 19x7 and 19x6 are presented below; the 19x7 income statement is shown on page 722.

Northwest Corporation
Comparative Balance Sheets
December 31, 19x7 and 19x6

	19x7	19x6	Change	Increase or Decrease
Assets				
Cash	$ 115,850	$ 121,850	$ (6,000)	Decrease
Accounts Receivable (net)	296,000	314,500	(18,500)	Decrease
Inventory	322,000	301,000	21,000	Increase
Prepaid Expenses	7,800	5,800	2,000	Increase
Long-Term Investments	36,000	86,000	(50,000)	Decrease
Land	150,000	125,000	25,000	Increase
Building	462,000	462,000	—	—
Accumulated Depreciation, Building	(91,000)	(79,000)	(12,000)	Increase
Equipment	159,730	167,230	(7,500)	Decrease
Accumulated Depreciation, Equipment	(43,400)	(45,600)	2,200	Decrease
Intangible Assets	19,200	24,000	(4,800)	Decrease
Total Assets	$1,434,180	$1,482,780	$ (48,600)	
Liabilities and Stockholders' Equity				
Accounts Payable	$ 133,750	$ 233,750	$(100,000)	Decrease
Notes Payable (current)	75,700	145,700	(70,000)	Decrease
Accrued Liabilities	5,000	—	5,000	Increase
Income Taxes Payable	20,000	—	20,000	Increase
Bonds Payable	210,000	310,000	(100,000)	Decrease
Mortgage Payable	330,000	350,000	(20,000)	Decrease
Common Stock—$10 par value	360,000	300,000	60,000	Increase
Paid-in Capital in Excess of Par Value, Common	90,000	50,000	40,000	Increase
Retained Earnings	209,730	93,330	116,400	Increase
Total Liabilities and Stockholders' Equity	$1,434,180	$1,482,780	$ (48,600)	

Northwest Corporation Income Statement For the Year Ended December 31, 19x7		
Sales		$1,650,000
Cost of Goods Sold		920,000
Gross Margin		$ 730,000
Operating Expenses (including Depreciation Expense of $12,000 on Buildings and $23,100 on Equipment and Amortization Expense of $4,800)		470,000
Operating Income		$ 260,000
Other Income (Expense)		
Interest Expense	$(55,000)	
Dividend Income	3,400	
Gain on Sale of Investments	12,500	
Loss on Disposal of Equipment	(2,300)	(41,400)
Income Before Income Taxes		$ 218,600
Income Taxes		52,200
Net Income		$ 166,400

The following additional information was taken from the company's records:

a. Long-term investments that cost $70,000 were sold at a gain of $12,500; additional long-term investments were made in the amount of $20,000.
b. Five acres of land were purchased for $25,000 for a parking lot.
c. Equipment that cost $37,500 with accumulated depreciation of $25,300 was sold at a loss of $2,300; new equipment in the amount of $30,000 was purchased.
d. Notes payable in the amount of $100,000 were repaid; an additional $30,000 was borrowed by signing notes payable.
e. Bonds payable in the amount of $100,000 were converted into 6,000 shares of common stock.
f. The Mortgage Payable account was reduced by $20,000 during the year.
g. Cash dividends declared and paid were $50,000.

Required

1. Prepare a schedule of cash flows from operating activities using (a) the direct method and (b) the indirect method.
2. Prepare a statement of cash flows using the indirect method.

Answer to Review Problem

1. (a) Schedule of cash flows from operating activities—direct method prepared

Northwest Corporation
Schedule of Cash Flows from Operating Activities
For the Year Ended December 31, 19x7

Cash Flows from Operating Activities		
Cash Receipts from		
Sales	$1,668,500 [1]	
Dividends Received	3,400	$1,671,900
Cash Payments for		
Purchases	$1,041,000 [2]	
Operating Expenses	427,100 [3]	
Interest Payments	55,000	
Income Taxes	32,200 [4]	1,555,300
Net Cash Flows from Operating Activities		$ 116,600

[1] $1,650,000 + $18,500 = $1,668,500
[2] $920,000 + $100,000 + $21,000 = $1,041,000
[3] $470,000 + $2,000 − $5,000 − ($12,000 + $23,100 + $4,800) = $427,100
[4] $52,200 − $20,000 = $32,200

1. (b) Schedule of cash flows from operating activities—indirect method prepared

Northwest Corporation
Schedule of Cash Flows from Operating Activities
For the Year Ended December 31, 19x7

Net Income		$166,400
Adjustments to Reconcile Net Income to Net Cash Flows from Operating Activities		
Depreciation Expense, Buildings	$ 12,000	
Depreciation Expense, Equipment	23,100	
Amortization Expense, Intangible Assets	4,800	
Gain on Sale of Investments	(12,500)	
Loss on Disposal of Equipment	2,300	
Decrease in Accounts Receivable	18,500	
Increase in Inventory	(21,000)	
Increase in Prepaid Expenses	(2,000)	
Decrease in Accounts Payable	(100,000)	
Increase in Accrued Liabilities	5,000	
Increase in Income Taxes Payable	20,000	(49,800)
Net Cash Flows from Operating Activities		$116,600

2. Statement of cash flows—indirect method prepared

Northwest Corporation
Statement of Cash Flows
For the Year Ended December 31, 19x7

Cash Flows from Operating Activities		
Net Income		$166,400
Adjustments to Reconcile Net Income to Net Cash Flows from Operating Activities		
Depreciation Expense, Buildings	$ 12,000	
Depreciation Expense, Equipment	23,100	
Amortization Expense, Intangible Assets	4,800	
Gain on Sale of Investments	(12,500)	
Loss on Disposal of Equipment	2,300	
Decrease in Accounts Receivable	18,500	
Increase in Inventory	(21,000)	
Increase in Prepaid Expenses	(2,000)	
Decrease in Accounts Payable	(100,000)	
Increase in Accrued Liabilities	5,000	
Increase in Income Taxes Payable	20,000	(49,800)
Net Cash Flows from Operating Activities		$ 116,600
Cash Flows from Investing Activities		
Sale of Long-Term Investments	$ 82,500*	
Purchase of Long-Term Investments	(20,000)	
Purchase of Land	(25,000)	
Sale of Equipment	9,900**	
Purchase of Equipment	(30,000)	
Net Cash Flows from Investing Activities		17,400
Cash Flows from Financing Activities		
Repayment of Notes Payable	$ (100,000)	
Issuance of Notes Payable	30,000	
Reduction in Mortgage	(20,000)	
Dividends Paid	(50,000)	
Net Cash Flows from Financing Activities		(140,000)
Net Increase (Decrease) in Cash		$ (6,000)
Cash at Beginning of Year		121,850
Cash at End of Year		$ 115,850

Schedule of Noncash Investing and Financing Transactions

Conversion of Bonds Payable into Common Stock	$ 100,000

* $70,000 + $12,500 (gain) = $82,500
**$37,500 – $25,300 = $12,200 (book value)
$12,200 – $2,300 (loss) = $9,900

Chapter Assignments

Discussion Questions

1. What is the term *cash* in the statement of cash flows understood to mean and include?
2. In order to earn a return on cash on hand during 19x3, Sallas Corporation transferred $45,000 from its checking account to a money market account, purchased a $25,000 Treasury bill, and bought $35,000 in common stocks. How will each of these transactions affect the statement of cash flows?
3. What are the purposes of the statement of cash flows?
4. Why is the statement of cash flows needed when most of the information in it is available from a company's comparative balance sheets and the income statement?
5. What are the three classifications of cash flows? Give some examples of each.
6. Why is it important to disclose certain noncash transactions? How should they be disclosed?
7. Cell-Borne Corporation had a net loss of $12,000 in 19x1 but had positive cash flows from operations of $9,000. What conditions may have caused this situation?
8. What are the essential differences between the direct method and the indirect method of determining cash flows from operations?
9. Glen Corporation has the following other income and expense items: interest expense, $12,000; interest income, $3,000; dividend income, $5,000; and loss on retirement of bonds, $6,000. How does each of these items appear on or affect the statement of cash flows?
10. What are the effects of the following items on cash flows from operations: (a) an increase in accounts receivable, (b) a decrease in inventory, (c) an increase in accounts payable, (d) a decrease in wages payable, (e) depreciation expense, and (f) amortization of patents?
11. What is the proper treatment on the statement of cash flows of a transaction in which a building that cost $50,000 with accumulated depreciation of $32,000 is sold for a loss of $5,000?
12. What is the proper treatment on the statement of cash flows of (a) a transaction in which buildings and land are purchased by the issuance of a mortgage for $234,000 and (b) a conversion of $50,000 in bonds payable into 2,500 shares of $6 par value common stock?
13. In interpreting the statement of cash flows, what are some comparisons that can be made with cash flows from operations? Prepare a list of reasons why a company would have a decrease in cash flows from investing activities.
14. Why is the work sheet approach considered to be more compatible with the indirect method of determining cash flows from operations than with the direct method?
15. Assuming in each of the following independent cases that only one transaction occurred, what transactions would likely cause (1) a decrease in investments and (2) an increase in common stock? How would each case be treated on the work sheet for the statement of cash flows?

Communication Skills Exercises

Communication 14-1. Direct Versus Indirect Method
(L.O. 4)

United States Surgical Corporation, a leading manufacturer of devices used in surgery, uses the direct method of presenting the cash flows from operating activities in its statement of cash flows.[5] As noted in the text, 97 percent of large companies use the indirect method. State clearly the difference between the direct and indirect methods of presenting cash flows from operating activities. Then take either the direct or the indirect method and develop an argument for it as the best way of presenting cash flows from operations.

Communication 14-2. Definitions and Interpretations of Cash Flows
(L.O. 7)

Tandy Corporation may not look the same to every analyst. Analysts tend to define and interpret cash flows in different ways. One interpretation of cash flows, presented in a *Business Week* article, is as follows:

Cash Flow = Net Income + Depreciation + Depletion + Amortization
Operating Cash Flow = Cash Flow + Interest + Income Tax Expense
Free Cash Flow = Cash Flow − Capital Expenditures − Dividends

According to the article, "Takeover artists and LBO operators hunt for 'operating cash flow [OCF].' That's the money generated by the company before the cost of financing and taxes comes into play. . . . While OCF is the broadest measure of a company's funds, some prefer to zero in on the narrower 'free cash flow.' That measures truly discretionary funds—company money that an owner could pocket without harming the business."[6]

The 1990 Statement of Cash Flows for Tandy Corporation, the owner of Radio Shack and other store chains, is on page 727. From the statement, compute cash flow, operating cash flow, and free cash flow as defined above. (Interest and Income Tax Expense from the income statement are $5,939,000 and $183,592,000, respectively.) How does the definition of cash flow in the formula differ from the concept followed in the statement of cash flows? (Assume that "cash and short-term investments" is equivalent to "cash and cash equivalents.") Is the definition of cash flow in the formula a substitute for net cash flows from operations? Is the concept of free cash flow, as defined, useful?

Communication 14-3. Basic Research Skills
(L.O. 7)

In your library, select the annual reports of three corporations. You may choose them from the same industry or at random, at the direction of your instructor. (If you did a related exercise in a previous chapter, use the same three companies.) Prepare a table with a column for each corporation. Then, for any year covered by the statement of cash flows, answer the following questions: Does the company use the direct or the indirect approach? Is net income more or less than net cash flows from operating activities? What are the major causes of differences between net income and net cash flows from operating activities? Compare net cash flows from operating activities to dividends paid. Does the dividend appear secure? Did the company make signifi-

5. *Accounting Trends and Techniques* (New York: American Institute of Certified Public Accountants, 1990), p. 352.
6. Jeffrey Laderman, "Earnings, Schmernings—Look at the Cash," *Business Week,* July 24, 1989, p. 56.

Tandy Corporation and Subsidiaries
Consolidated Statements of Cash Flows[7]
Year Ended June 30, 1990
(in thousands)

Cash flows from operating activities:	
Net income	$290,347
Adjustments to reconcile net income to net cash provided by operating activities:	
Depreciation and amortization	92,115
Deferred income taxes and other items	(3,206)
Provision for credit losses	33,073
Changes in operating assets and liabilities, excluding the effect of businesses acquired:	
Receivables	(273,921)
Inventories	(110,336)
Other current assets	(15,110)
Accounts payable, accrued expenses and income taxes	45,445
Net cash provided by operating activities	58,407
Investing activities:	
Additions to property, plant and equipment, net of retirements	(112,515)
Acquisition of Victor Technologies	(112,856)
Payment received on InterTAN note	35,906
Other investing activities	7,853
Net cash used by investing activities	(181,612)
Financing activities:	
Purchases of treasury stock	(369,982)
Sales of treasury stock to employee stock purchase program	52,019
Dividends paid	(49,760)
Changes in short-term borrowings—net	479,325
Additions to long-term borrowings	133,751
Repayments of long-term borrowings	(45,349)
Net cash provided (used) by financing activities	200,004
Increase (decrease) in cash and short-term investments	76,799
Cash and short-term investments at the beginning of the year	58,398
Cash and short-term investments at the end of the year	$135,197

7. Excerpt used with written permission from the 1990 Annual Report of Tandy Corporation. Copyright © 1990 by Tandy Corporation.

cant capital expenditures during the year? How were the expenditures financed? Do you notice anything unusual about the investing and financing activities of your companies? Do the investing and financing activities provide any insights into management's plan for each company? If so, what are they? Be prepared to discuss the answers to these questions in class.

Classroom Exercises

Exercise 14-1. Classification of Cash Flow Transactions *(L.O. 3)*

Horizon Corporation engaged in the following transactions. Identify each as (1) an operating activity, (2) an investing activity, (3) a financing activity, (4) a noncash transaction, or (5) none of the above.

a. Declared and paid a cash dividend.
b. Purchased an investment.
c. Received cash from customers.
d. Paid interest.
e. Sold equipment at a loss.
f. Issued long-term bonds for plant assets.
g. Received dividends on securities held.
h. Issued common stock.
i. Declared and issued a stock dividend.
j. Repaid notes payable.
k. Paid employees for wages.
l. Purchased a sixty-day Treasury bill.
m. Purchased land.

Exercise 14-2. Cash Receipts from Sales *(L.O. 4a)*

During 19x2, Union Chemical Company, a distributor of farm fertilizers and herbicides, had sales of $6,500,000. The ending balances of Accounts Receivable were $850,000 in 19x1 and $1,200,000 in 19x2. Calculate cash receipts from sales in 19x2.

Exercise 14-3. Cash Payments for Purchases *(L.O. 4a)*

During 19x2, Union Chemical Company had cost of goods sold of $3,800,000. The ending balances of Inventory were $510,000 in 19x1 and $420,000 in 19x2. The ending balances of Accounts Payable were $360,000 in 19x1 and $480,000 in 19x2. Calculate cash payments for purchases in 19x2.

Exercise 14-4. Cash Payments for Operating Expenses and Income Taxes *(L.O. 4a)*

During 19x2, Union Chemical Company had operating expenses of $1,900,000 and income taxes expense of $200,000. Depreciation expense of $410,000 for 19x2 was included in operating expenses. The ending balances of Prepaid Expenses were $90,000 in 19x1 and $130,000 in 19x2. The ending balances of Accrued Liabilities (excluding Income Taxes Payable) were $50,000 in 19x1 and $30,000 in 19x2. The ending balances of Income Taxes Payable were $60,000 in 19x1 and $70,000 in 19x2. Calculate cash payments for operating expenses and income taxes in 19x2.

Exercise 14-5. Cash Flows from Operating Activities—Direct Method *(L.O. 4a)*

Using the computations you made in Exercises 14-2, 14-3, and 14-4, prepare in good form a schedule of cash flows from operating activities for 19x2, using the direct method. The company has a December 31 year end.

Exercise 14-6. Cash Flows from Operating Activities —Indirect Method *(L.O. 4b)*

The condensed single-step income statement of Union Chemical Company, a distributor of farm fertilizers and herbicides, appears as follows:

Sales		$6,500,000
Less: Cost of Goods Sold	$3,800,000	
Operating Expenses (including depreciation of $410,000)	1,900,000	
Income Taxes	200,000	5,900,000
Net Income		$ 600,000

Selected accounts from the company's balance sheets for 19x1 and 19x2 appear as follows:

	19x2	19x1
Accounts Receivable	$1,200,000	$850,000
Inventory	420,000	510,000
Prepaid Expenses	130,000	90,000
Accounts Payable	480,000	360,000
Accrued Liabilities	30,000	50,000
Income Taxes Payable	70,000	60,000

Present in good form a schedule of cash flows from operating activities, using the indirect method.

Exercise 14-7. Computing Cash Flows from Operating Activities— Direct Method *(L.O. 4a)*

Europa Corporation engaged in the following transactions in 19x2. Using the direct method, compute the various cash flows from operating activities as required.

a. During 19x2, Europa Corporation had cash sales of $41,300 and sales on credit of $123,000. During the same year, Accounts Receivable decreased by $18,000. Determine the cash received from customers during 19x2.
b. During 19x2, Europa Corporation's cost of goods sold was $119,000. During the same year, Merchandise Inventory increased by $12,500 and Accounts Payable decreased by $4,300. Determine the cash payments for purchases during 19x2.
c. During 19x2, Europa Corporation had operating expenses of $45,000, including depreciation of $15,600. Also during 19x2, related prepaid expenses decreased by $3,100 and relevant accrued liabilities increased by $1,200. Determine the cash payments for operating expenses to suppliers of goods and services during 19x2.
d. Europa Corporation's Income Taxes Expense for 19x2 was $4,300. Income Taxes Payable decreased by $230 that year. Determine the cash payment for income taxes during 19x2.

Exercise 14-8. Computing Cash Flows from Operating Activities— Indirect Method *(L.O. 4b)*

During 19x1, Mayfair Corporation had a net income of $41,000. Included on the income statement was Depreciation Expense of $2,300 and Amortization Expense of $300. During the year, accounts receivable increased by $3,400, inventories decreased by $1,900, prepaid expenses decreased by $200, accounts payable increased by $5,000, and accrued liabilities decreased by $450. Determine cash flows from operating activities using the indirect method.

Exercise 14-9. Preparing a Schedule of Cash Flows from Operating Activities—Direct Method *(L.O. 4a)*

The income statement for the Ridge Corporation follows.

Ridge Corporation
Income Statement
For the Year Ended June 30, 19xx

Sales		$61,000
Cost of Goods Sold		30,000
Gross Margin from Sales		$31,000
Other Expenses		
Salaries Expense	$16,000	
Rent Expense	8,400	
Depreciation Expense	1,000	25,400
Income Before Income Taxes		$ 5,600
Income Taxes		1,200
Net Income		$ 4,400

Additional information: (a) All sales were on credit, and accounts receivable increased by $2,200 during the year. (b) All merchandise purchased was on credit. Inventories increased by $3,500, and accounts payable increased by $7,000 during the year. (c) Prepaid rent decreased by $700, and salaries payable increased by $500. (d) Income taxes payable decreased by $300 during the year. Prepare a schedule of cash flows from operating activities using the direct method.

Exercise 14-10. Preparing a Schedule of Cash Flows from Operating Activities—Indirect Method *(L.O. 4b)*

Using the data provided in Exercise 14-9, prepare a schedule of cash flows from operating activities using the indirect method.

Exercise 14-11. Computing Cash Flows from Investing Activities—Investments *(L.O. 5)*

The T account for the Investments account for Krieger Company at the end of 19x3 follows:

Investments

Beg. Bal.	38,500	Sales	39,000
Purchases	58,000		
End. Bal.	**57,500**		

In addition, Krieger's income statement shows a loss on the sale of investments of $6,500. Compute the amounts to be shown as cash flows from investing activities, and show how they are to appear on the statement of cash flows.

Exercise 14-12. Computing Cash Flows from Investing Activities— Plant Assets *(L.O. 5)*

The T accounts for the Plant Assets and Accumulated Depreciation accounts for Krieger Company at the end of 19x3 are as follows:

Plant Assets

Beg. Bal.	65,000	Disposals	23,000
Purchases	33,600		
End. Bal.	**75,600**		

Accumulated Depreciation

Disposals	14,700	Beg. Bal.	34,500
		19x3 Depreciation	10,200
		End. Bal.	**30,000**

In addition, Krieger Company's income statement shows a gain on sale of plant assets of $4,400. Compute the amounts to be shown as cash flows from investing activities, and show how they are to appear on the statement of cash flows.

Exercise 14-13. Determining Cash Flows from Investing and Financing Activities *(L.O. 5)*

All transactions involving Notes Payable and related accounts engaged in by Krieger Company during 19x3 are as follows:

Cash	18,000	
Notes Payable		18,000
Bank loan		
Patent	30,000	
Notes Payable		30,000
Purchase of patent by issuing note payable		
Notes Payable	5,000	
Interest Expense	500	
Cash		5,500
Repayment of note payable at maturity		

Determine the amounts and how these transactions are to be shown in the statement of cash flows for 19x3.

Exercise 14-14. Preparing the Statement of Cash Flows *(L.O. 6a)*

Javier Corporation's comparative balance sheets for June 30, 19x2 and 19x1, and its 19x2 income statement follow on page 732.

Additional information: (a) issued $22,000 note payable for purchase of furniture; (b) sold furniture that cost $27,000 with accumulated depreciation of $15,300 at carrying value; (c) recorded depreciation on the furniture during the year, $19,300; (d) repaid a note in the amount of $20,000; (e) issued $25,000 of common stock at par value; and (f) declared and paid dividends of $4,300. Without using a work sheet, prepare a statement of cash flows for 19x2 using the direct method. Omit the reconciliation of net income to net cash flows from operating activities.

Javier Corporation
Comparative Balance Sheets
June 30, 19x2 and 19x1

	19x2	19x1
Assets		
Cash	$ 69,900	$ 12,500
Accounts Receivable (net)	21,000	26,000
Inventory	43,400	48,400
Prepaid Expenses	3,200	2,600
Furniture	55,000	60,000
Accumulated Depreciation, Furniture	(9,000)	(5,000)
Total Assets	$183,500	$144,500
Liabilities and Stockholders' Equity		
Accounts Payable	$ 13,000	$ 14,000
Income Taxes Payable	1,200	1,800
Notes Payable (long-term)	37,000	35,000
Common Stock—$5 par value	115,000	90,000
Retained Earnings	17,300	3,700
Total Liabilities and Stockholders' Equity	$183,500	$144,500

Javier Corporation
Income Statement
For the Year Ended June 30, 19x2

Sales	$234,000
Cost of Goods Sold	156,000
Gross Margin	$ 78,000
Operating Expenses	45,000
Operating Income	$ 33,000
Interest Expense	2,800
Income Before Income Taxes	$ 30,200
Income Taxes	12,300
Net Income	$ 17,900

Exercise 14-15. Preparing a Work Sheet for the Statement of Cash Flows *(L.O. 6b, 8)*

Using the information in Exercise 14-14, prepare a work sheet for the statement of cash flows for Javier Corporation for 19x2. From the work sheet, prepare a statement of cash flows using the indirect method.

Interpretation Cases from Business

ICB 14-1. National Communications, Inc.
(L.O. 6, 7)

The following statements of cash flows from the annual report of National Communications, Inc., a major television network broadcaster and publisher, do not follow the format recommended by the FASB.

National Communications, Inc.
Statements of Cash Flows
For the Years Ended January 31, 1991 and 1990
(in thousands)

	1991	1990
Cash provided		
Operations		
Net income	$ 267,693	$242,222
Depreciation	95,202	37,992
Amortization of intangible assets	63,403	19,712
Other noncash items, net	28,930	23,370
Total cash from operations	$ 455,228	$323,296
Capital expenditures for operations	(153,087)	(75,383)
Program licenses and rights, net	(2,732)	(1,734)
Available cash flow from operations	$ 299,409	$246,179
Issuance of common stock	517,500	—
Issuance of common stock warrants	97,197	—
Issuance of long-term debt	1,350,503	493,322
Long-term debt assumed on acquisitions	123,678	—
Disposition of operating properties, net of current taxes	625,677	7,229
Disposition of real estate	162,166	—
Other dispositions, net	29,495	3,114
	$3,205,625	$749,844
Cash applied		
Acquisition of television stations	$3,270,972	$ —
Common stock warrants purchased and redeemed	16,688	—
Acquisition of other operating properties	12,599	103,109
Reduction of long-term debt	367,521	7,874
Changes in other working capital items	86,645	2,322
Purchase of common stock for treasury	1,079	485
Dividends	3,210	2,594
	$3,758,714	$116,384
(Decrease) increase in cash and cash investments	(553,089)	$633,460
Cash and cash equivalents		
Beginning of period	687,413	53,953
End of period	$ 134,324	$687,413

Required

1. Recast the statements of cash flows using the indirect method as shown in this chapter (ignore noncash investing and financing transactions).

2. National Communications, Inc. places an emphasis on "available cash flow from operations." Evaluate this approach as compared to "net cash flows from operating activities" in the statement of cash flows.

3. Although net cash flow from operating activities increased from 1990 to 1991, cash and cash equivalents decreased significantly (from $687,413,000 to $134,324,000). What are the primary causes of this decline in cash and cash equivalents?

ICB 14-2. Airborne Freight Corporation[8] *(L.O. 7)*

Airborne Freight Corporation, which is known as Airborne Express, is an air express transportation company, providing next-day, morning delivery of small packages and documents throughout the United States. Airborne Express is one of three major participants, along with Federal Express and United Parcel Service, in the air express industry. The following statement appears in "Management's discussion and analysis of results of operations and financial condition" from the company's 1990 annual report: "Capital expenditures and financing associated with those expenditures continued to be the primary factor affecting the financial condition of the company." The company's statements of cash flows for 1990, 1989, and 1988 are presented on page 735.

Required

1. Have operations provided significant cash flows over the past three years? What is the role of net earnings in this provision? Other than net earnings, what is the most significant factor in providing the cash flows? Have changes in working capital accounts been a significant factor?

2. Does Airborne Express generate enough net cash flows from operating activities to both pay dividends and provide additional funds for expansion?

3. Is management's statement about capital expenditures and associated financing substantiated by the figures? If your answer is yes, what were Airborne's primary means of financing the expansion in 1990?

8. Excerpts from the 1990 Annual Report used by permission of Airborne Freight Corporation, P.O. Box 662, Seattle, Washington 98111. Copyright © 1990.

Airborne Freight Corporation and Subsidiaries
Consolidated Statements of Cash Flows
Year Ended December 31

	1990	1989	1988
		(in thousands)	
Operating Activities:			
Net Earnings	$ 33,577	$ 19,083	$ 7,036
Adjustments to reconcile net earnings to net cash provided by operating activities:			
Depreciation and amortization	69,055	55,082	46,462
Provision for aircraft engine overhauls	6,224	5,703	5,823
Deferred income taxes	536	(136)	1,795
Provision for lease expense	—	4,088	—
Gain on disposition of aircraft	—	—	(1,717)
Cash Provided by Operations	109,392	83,820	59,399
Change in:			
Receivables	(19,722)	(20,152)	(16,874)
Inventories and prepaid expenses	(6,496)	(1,316)	(8,229)
Accounts payable	14,514	13,720	20,243
Accrued expenses, salaries and taxes payable	12,447	13,043	6,077
Net Cash Provided by Operating Activities	110,135	89,115	60,616
Investing Activities:			
Additions to property and equipment	(217,926)	(145,008)	(85,831)
Disposition of property and equipment	2,286	1,315	2,142
Expenditures for engine overhauls	(7,483)	(8,155)	(6,525)
Other	(1,679)	444	(1,730)
Net Cash Used in Investing Activities	(224,802)	(151,404)	(91,944)
Financing Activities:			
Proceeds from sale-leaseback of aircraft	28,464	83,904	—
Increase (decrease) in bank notes payable	(6,800)	(12,700)	37,800
Principal payments of long-term debt and capital lease obligations	(8,642)	(4,010)	(3,165)
Issuance of redeemable preferred stock	40,000	—	—
Issuance of common stock	69,461	1,410	78
Dividends paid	(7,609)	(4,168)	(4,141)
Net Cash Provided by Financing Activities	114,874	64,436	30,572
Net Increase (Decrease) in Cash	207	2,147	(756)
Cash at Beginning of Year	8,588	6,441	7,197
Cash at End of Year	$ 8,795	$ 8,588	$ 6,441

Problem Set A

Problem 14A-1. Classification of Transactions *(L.O. 3)*

Analyze the transactions presented in the schedule that follows and place an X in the appropriate column to indicate the classification of each transaction and its effect on cash flows using the direct method.

Transaction	Cash Flow Classification: Operating Activity	Investing Activity	Financing Activity	Noncash Transactions	Effect on Cash: Increase	Decrease	No Effect
a. Incurred a net loss.							
b. Declared and issued a stock dividend.							
c. Paid a cash dividend.							
d. Collected accounts receivable.							
e. Purchased inventory with cash.							
f. Retired long-term debt with cash.							
g. Sold investment for a loss.							
h. Issued stock for equipment.							
i. Purchased a one-year insurance policy for cash.							
j. Purchased treasury stock with cash.							
k. Retired a fully depreciated truck (no gain or loss).							
l. Paid interest on note.							
m. Received dividend on investment.							
n. Sold treasury stock.							
o. Paid income taxes.							
p. Transferred cash to money market account.							
q. Purchased land and building with a mortgage.							

Problem 14A-2.
Cash Flows from Operating Activities
(L.O. 4)

The income statement for Milos Food Corporation is shown as follows:

Milos Food Corporation
Income Statement
For the Year Ended December 31, 19xx

Sales		$490,000
Cost of Goods Sold		
Beginning Inventory	$220,000	
Purchases (net)	400,000	
Goods Available for Sale	$620,000	
Ending Inventory	250,000	
Cost of Goods Sold		370,000
Gross Margin from Sales		$120,000
Selling and Administrative Expenses		
Selling and Administrative Salaries Expense	$ 50,000	
Other Selling and Administrative Expenses	11,500	
Depreciation Expense	18,000	
Amortization Expense (Intangible Assets)	1,500	81,000
Income Before Income Taxes		$ 39,000
Income Taxes		12,500
Net Income		$ 26,500

Additional information: (a) accounts receivable (net) increased by $18,000 and accounts payable decreased by $26,000 during the year; (b) salaries payable at the end of the year were $7,000 more than last year; (c) the expired amount of prepaid insurance for the year is $500 and equals the decrease in the Prepaid Insurance account; and (d) income taxes payable decreased by $5,400 from last year.

Required

1. Prepare a schedule of cash flows from operating activities using the direct method.
2. Prepare a schedule of cash flows from operating activities using the indirect method.

Problem 14A-3.
Cash Flows from Operating Activities
(L.O. 4)

The income statement of Gardner Electronics, Inc. appears on page 738. Relevant accounts from the comparative balance sheets for February 28, 19x3 and 19x2 are as follows:

	19x3	19x2
Accounts Receivable (net)	$65,490	$ 48,920
Inventory	98,760	102,560
Prepaid Expenses	10,450	5,490
Accounts Payable	42,380	55,690
Accrued Liabilities	3,560	8,790
Income Taxes Payable	24,630	13,800

Gardner Electronics, Inc.
Income Statement
For the Year Ended February 28, 19x3

Sales		$919,000
Cost of Goods Sold		643,500
Gross Margin from Sales		$275,500
Operating Expenses (including Depreciation Expense of $21,430)		176,900
Operating Income		$ 98,600
Other Income (Expenses)		
Interest Expense	$(27,800)	
Dividend Income	14,200	
Loss on Sale of Investments	(12,100)	(25,700)
Income Before Income Taxes		$ 72,900
Income Taxes		21,500
Net Income		$ 51,400

Required

1. Prepare a schedule of cash flows from operating activities using the direct method.
2. Prepare a schedule of cash flows from operating activities using the indirect method.

Problem 14A-4. The Statement of Cash Flows—Direct Method *(L.O. 6a, 7)*

Meridian Corporation's 19x2 income statement and its comparative balance sheets as of December 31, 19x2 and 19x1 appear as follows:

Meridian Corporation
Income Statement
For the Year Ended December 31, 19x2

Sales		$804,500
Cost of Goods Sold		563,900
Gross Margin from Sales		$240,600
Operating Expenses (including Depreciation Expense of $23,400)		224,700
Income from Operations		$ 15,900
Other Income (Expenses)		
Gain on Disposal of Furniture and Fixtures	$ 3,500	
Interest Expense	(11,600)	(8,100)
Income Before Income Taxes		$ 7,800
Income Taxes		2,300
Net Income		$ 5,500

Meridian Corporation
Comparative Balance Sheets
December 31, 19x2 and 19x1

	19x2	19x1
Assets		
Cash	$ 82,400	$ 25,000
Accounts Receivable (net)	82,600	100,000
Merchandise Inventory	175,000	225,000
Prepaid Rent	1,000	1,500
Furniture and Fixtures	74,000	72,000
Accumulated Depreciation, Furniture and Fixtures	(21,000)	(12,000)
Total Assets	$394,000	$411,500
Liabilities and Stockholders' Equity		
Accounts Payable	$ 71,700	$100,200
Notes Payable (long-term)	20,000	10,000
Bonds Payable	50,000	100,000
Income Taxes Payable	700	2,200
Common Stock—$10 par value	120,000	100,000
Paid-in Capital in Excess of Par Value	90,720	60,720
Retained Earnings	40,880	38,380
Total Liabilities and Stockholders' Equity	$394,000	$411,500

Additional information about 19x2: (a) furniture and fixtures that cost $17,800 with accumulated depreciation of $14,400 were sold at a gain of $3,500; (b) furniture and fixtures were purchased in the amount of $19,800; (c) a $10,000 note payable was paid and $20,000 was borrowed on a new note; (d) bonds payable in the amount of $50,000 were converted into 2,000 shares of common stock; and (e) $3,000 in cash dividends were declared and paid.

Required

1. Prepare a statement of cash flows using the direct method. Include a supporting schedule of noncash investing and financing transactions, but omit the reconciliation of net income to net cash flow from operating activities. (Do not use a work sheet.)
2. What are the primary reasons for Meridian Corporation's large increase in cash from 19x1 to 19x2, despite its low net income?

Problem 14A-5. The Work Sheet and the Statement of Cash Flows—Indirect Method *(L.O. 6b, 8)*

Use the information for Meridian Corporation given in Problem 14A-4 to answer the requirements on page 740.

Required

1. Prepare a work sheet for gathering information for the preparation of the statement of cash flows.
2. From the information on the work sheet, prepare a statement of cash flows using the indirect approach. Include a supporting schedule of noncash investing and financing transactions.

Problem 14A-6. The Work Sheet and the Statement of Cash Flows—Indirect Method
(L.O. 6b, 7, 8)

The comparative balance sheets for Gregory Fabrics, Inc. for December 31, 19x3 and 19x2 appear as follows.

Gregory Fabrics, Inc.
Comparative Balance Sheets
December 31, 19x3 and 19x2

	19x3	19x2
Assets		
Cash	$ 38,560	$ 27,360
Accounts Receivable (net)	102,430	75,430
Inventory	112,890	137,890
Prepaid Expenses	—	20,000
Land	25,000	—
Building	137,000	—
Accumulated Depreciation, Building	(15,000)	—
Equipment	33,000	34,000
Accumulated Depreciation, Equipment	(14,500)	(24,000)
Patents	4,000	6,000
Total Assets	$423,380	$276,680
Liabilities and Stockholders' Equity		
Accounts Payable	$ 10,750	$ 36,750
Notes Payable	10,000	—
Accrued Liabilities (current)	—	12,300
Mortgage Payable	162,000	—
Common Stock	180,000	150,000
Paid-in Capital in Excess of Par Value	57,200	37,200
Retained Earnings	3,430	40,430
Total Liabilities and Stockholders' Equity	$423,380	$276,680

Additional information about Gregory Fabrics' operations during 19x3: (a) net loss, $28,000; (b) building and equipment depreciation expense amounts, $15,000 and $3,000, respectively; (c) equipment that cost $13,500 with accumulated depreciation of $12,500, sold for a gain of $5,300; (d) equipment purchases, $12,500; (e) patent amortization, $3,000; purchase of patent, $1,000; (f) borrowed funds by issuing notes payable, $25,000; notes payable repaid, $15,000; (g) land and building purchased for $162,000 by signing a mortgage for the total cost; (h) 3,000 shares of $10 par value common stock issued for a total of $50,000; and (i) cash dividend, $9,000.

Required

1. Prepare a work sheet for the statement of cash flows for Gregory Fabrics.
2. Prepare a statement of cash flows from the information in the work sheet using the indirect method. Include a supporting schedule on noncash investing and financing transactions.
3. Why did Gregory Fabrics have an increase in Cash in a year in which it recorded a net loss of $28,000? Discuss and interpret.

Problem Set B

Problem 14B-1. Classification of Transactions *(L.O. 3)*

Analyze the transactions in the schedule below, and place an X in the appropriate column to indicate the classification of each transaction and its effect on cash flows using the direct method.

	Cash Flow Classification				Effect on Cash		
Transaction	Operating Activity	Investing Activity	Financing Activity	Noncash Transactions	Increase	Decrease	No Effect
a. Recorded net income.							
b. Declared and paid cash dividend.							
c. Issued stock for cash.							
d. Retired long-term debt by issuing stock.							
e. Paid accounts payable.							
f. Purchased inventory.							
g. Purchased a one-year insurance policy.							
h. Purchased a long-term investment with cash.							
i. Sold marketable securities at a gain.							
j. Sold a machine at a loss.							
k. Retired fully depreciated equipment.							

(continued)

Transaction	Cash Flow Classification				Effect on Cash		
	Operating Activity	Investing Activity	Financing Activity	Noncash Transactions	Increase	Decrease	No Effect
l. Paid interest on debt.							
m. Purchased marketable securities.							
n. Received dividend income.							
o. Received cash on account.							
p. Converted bonds to common stock.							
q. Purchased short-term (ninety-day) Treasury bill.							

Problem 14B-2. Cash Flows from Operating Activities *(L.O. 4)*

The income statement for Falcone Clothing Store is as follows.

Falcone Clothing Store
Income Statement
For the Year Ended June 30, 19xx

Sales		$2,450,000
Cost of Goods Sold		
Beginning Inventory	$ 620,000	
Purchases (net)	1,520,000	
Goods Available for Sale	$2,140,000	
Ending Inventory	700,000	
Cost of Goods Sold		1,440,000
Gross Margin from Sales		$1,010,000
Operating Expenses		
Sales and Administrative Salaries Expense	$ 556,000	
Other Sales and Administrative Expenses	312,000	
Total Operating Expenses		868,000
Income Before Income Taxes		$ 142,000
Income Taxes		39,000
Net Income		$ 103,000

Additional information: (a) other sales and administrative expenses include depreciation expense of $52,000 and amortization expense of $18,000; (b) at the end of the year, accrued liabilities for salaries were $12,000 less than the previous year and prepaid expenses were $20,000 more than the previous year; and (c) during the year accounts receivable (net) increased by $144,000, accounts payable increased by $114,000, and income taxes payable decreased by $7,200.

Required

1. Prepare a schedule of cash flows from operating activities using the direct method.
2. Prepare a schedule of cash flows from operating activities using the indirect method.

Problem 14B-3. Cash Flows from Operating Activities *(L.O. 4)*

The income statement for Malamud Greeting Card Company follows:

Malamud Greeting Card Company
Income Statement
For the Year Ended December 31, 19x2

Sales		$472,000
Cost of Goods Sold		286,700
Gross Margin from Sales		$185,300
Operating Expenses (including Depreciation Expense of $21,430)		87,400
Operating Income		$ 97,900
Other Income (Expenses)		
Interest Expense	$(8,400)	
Interest Income	4,300	
Loss on Sale of Investments	(5,800)	(9,900)
Income Before Income Taxes		$ 88,000
Income Taxes		18,500
Net Income		$ 69,500

Relevant accounts from the balance sheets for December 31, 19x2 and 19x1 are as follows:

	19x2	19x1
Accounts Receivable (net)	$18,530	$23,670
Inventory	39,640	34,990
Prepaid Expenses	2,400	8,900
Accounts Payable	34,940	22,700
Accrued Liabilities	4,690	8,830
Income Taxes Payable	4,750	17,600

Required

1. Prepare a schedule of cash flows from operating activities using the direct method.
2. Prepare a schedule of cash flows from operating activities using the indirect method.

Problem 14B-4. The Statement of Cash Flows—Direct Method
(L.O. 6a, 7)

Plath Corporation's comparative balance sheets as of June 30, 19x7 and 19x6 appear below and its 19x7 income statement appears on page 745:

Plath Corporation
Comparative Balance Sheets
June 30, 19x7 and 19x6

	19x7	19x6
Assets		
Cash	$167,000	$ 20,000
Accounts Receivable (net)	100,000	120,000
Finished Goods Inventory	180,000	220,000
Prepaid Expenses	600	1,000
Property, Plant, and Equipment	628,000	552,000
Accumulated Depreciation, Property, Plant, and Equipment	(183,000)	(140,000)
Total Assets	$892,600	$773,000
Liabilities and Stockholders' Equity		
Accounts Payable	$ 64,000	$ 42,000
Notes Payable (due in 90 days)	30,000	80,000
Income Taxes Payable	26,000	18,000
Mortgage Payable	360,000	280,000
Common Stock—$5 par value	200,000	200,000
Retained Earnings	212,600	153,000
Total Liabilities and Stockholders' Equity	$892,600	$773,000

Additional information about 19x7: (a) equipment that cost $24,000 with accumulated depreciation of $17,000 was sold at a loss of $4,000; (b) land and building costing $100,000 were purchased through an increase of $100,000 in the mortgage payable; (c) a $20,000 payment was made on the mortgage; (d) the notes were repaid, but the company borrowed an additional $30,000 through the issuance of a new note payable; and (e) a $60,000 cash dividend was declared and paid.

Required

1. Prepare a statement of cash flows using the direct method. Include a supporting schedule of noncash investing and financing transactions, but omit the reconciliation of net income to net cash flows from operating activities.
2. What are the primary reasons for Plath Corporation's large increase in cash from 19x6 to 19x7?

Plath Corporation
Income Statement
For the Year Ended June 30, 19x7

Sales		$1,040,900
Cost of Goods Sold		656,300
Gross Margin from Sales		$ 384,600
Operating Expenses (including Depreciation Expense of $60,000)		189,200
Income from Operations		$ 195,400
Other Income (Expenses)		
Loss on Disposal of Equipment	$ (4,000)	
Interest Expense	(37,600)	(41,600)
Income Before Income Taxes		$ 153,800
Income Taxes		34,200
Net Income		$ 119,600

Problem 14B-5. The Work Sheet and the Statement of Cash Flows—Indirect Method *(L.O. 6b, 8)*

Use the information for Plath Corporation given in Problem 14B-4 to answer the requirements below.

Required

1. Prepare a work sheet for gathering information for the preparation of the statement of cash flows.
2. From the information on the work sheet, prepare a statement of cash flows using the indirect method. Include a supporting schedule of noncash investing and financing transactions.

Problem 14B-6. The Work Sheet and the Statement of Cash Flows—Indirect Method *(L.O. 6b, 7, 8)*

The comparative balance sheets for Willis Ceramics, Inc. for December 31, 19x3 and 19x2 appear on page 746. Additional information about Willis Ceramics' operations during 19x3: (a) net income was $48,000; (b) building and equipment depreciation expense amounts were $40,000 and $30,000, respectively; (c) intangible assets were amortized in the amount of $10,000; (d) investments in the amount of $58,000 were purchased; (e) investments were sold for $75,000, on which a gain of $17,000 was made; (f) the company issued $120,000 in long-term bonds at face value; (g) a small warehouse building with the accompanying land was purchased through the issue of a $160,000 mortgage; (h) the company paid $20,000 to reduce the mortgage payable during 19x7; (i) the company borrowed funds in the amount of $30,000 by issuing notes payable and repaid notes payable in the amount of $90,000; and (j) cash dividends in the amount of $18,000 were declared and paid.

Required

1. Prepare a work sheet for the statement of cash flows for Willis Ceramics.
2. Prepare a statement of cash flows from the information in the work sheet using the indirect method. Include a supporting schedule of noncash investing and financing transactions.
3. Why did Willis Ceramics experience a decrease in cash in a year in which it had a net income of $48,000? Discuss and interpret.

Willis Ceramics, Inc.
Comparative Balance Sheets
December 31, 19x3 and 19x2

	19x3	19x2
Assets		
Cash	$ 138,800	$ 152,800
Accounts Receivable (net)	369,400	379,400
Inventory	480,000	400,000
Prepaid Expenses	7,400	13,400
Long-Term Investments	220,000	220,000
Land	180,600	160,600
Building	600,000	460,000
Accumulated Depreciation, Building	(120,000)	(80,000)
Equipment	240,000	240,000
Accumulated Depreciation, Equipment	(58,000)	(28,000)
Intangible Assets	10,000	20,000
Total Assets	$2,068,200	$1,938,200
Liabilities and Stockholders' Equity		
Accounts Payable	$ 235,400	$ 330,400
Notes Payable (current)	20,000	80,000
Accrued Liabilities	5,400	10,400
Mortgage Payable	540,000	400,000
Bonds Payable	500,000	380,000
Common Stock	600,000	600,000
Paid-in Capital in Excess of Par Value	40,000	40,000
Retained Earnings	127,400	97,400
Total Liabilities and Stockholders' Equity	$2,068,200	$1,938,200

Financial Decision Cases

14-1. Dru's Exercise Shop *(L.O. 6a, 7)*

Dru Travalley opened a retail store that sells exercise equipment on January 1, 19x2. At the end of the year Dru prepared the following statement of cash flows for the company.

Dru's Exercise Shop
Statement of Cash Flows
For the Year Ended December 31, 19x2

Sources of Cash		
From sale of capital stock	$600,000	
From sales of merchandise	550,000	
From sale of investments	50,000	
From depreciation	80,000	
From issuance of note for delivery truck	25,000	
From dividends on investments	5,000	
Total sources of cash		$1,310,000
Uses of Cash		
For purchase of fixtures and equipment	$450,000	
For merchandise purchased for resale	400,000	
For operating expenses (including depreciation)	235,000	
For purchase of investments	60,000	
For purchase of delivery truck by issuance of note	25,000	
For purchase of treasury stock	27,000	
For interest on note	3,000	
Total uses of cash		1,200,000
Net increase in cash		$ 110,000

Dru is excited about the successful year she has had as shown by her statement of cash flows. She is happy that cash has increased by $110,000. However, based on your recent study of the new statement of cash flows, you see that this statement is incorrectly prepared and that what seems to be cash flow is not. You offer to help Dru in assessing her company's operations.

Required

1. Prepare a statement of cash flows in good form (use the direct method without a schedule reconciling net income to net cash flows from operating activities).
2. Write an assessment of the Exercise Shop's first year of operations.

14-2.
Adams Print Gallery
(L.O. 6a, 7)

Bernadette Adams, President of Adams Print Gallery, Inc., is examining the income statement presented on page 748, which has just been handed to her by her accountant, Jason Rosenberg, CPA. After looking at the statement, Ms. Adams said to Mr. Rosenberg, "Jason, the statement seems to be well done, but what I need to know is why I don't have enough cash to pay my bills this month. You show that I earned $60,000 in 19x2, but I have only $12,000 in the bank. I know I bought a building on a mortgage and paid a cash dividend of $24,000, but what else is going on?" Mr. Rosenberg replied, "To answer your question, Bernadette, we have to look at comparative balance sheets and prepare another type of statement. Here, take a look at these balance sheets." The statements handed to Ms. Adams are shown on page 748.

Adams Print Gallery, Inc.
Income Statement
For the Year Ended December 31, 19x2

Sales	$442,000
Cost of Goods Sold	254,000
Gross Margin	$188,000
Operating Expenses (including Depreciation Expense of $10,000)	102,000
Operating Income	$ 86,000
Interest Expense	12,000
Income Before Income Taxes	$ 74,000
Income Taxes	14,000
Net Income	$ 60,000

Adams Print Gallery, Inc.
Comparative Balance Sheets
December 31, 19x2 and 19x1

	19x2	19x1
Assets		
Cash	$ 12,000	$ 20,000
Accounts Receivable (net)	89,000	73,000
Inventory	120,000	90,000
Prepaid Expenses	5,000	7,000
Building	200,000	—
Accumulated Depreciation	(10,000)	—
Total Assets	$416,000	$190,000
Liabilities and Stockholders' Equity		
Accounts Payable	$ 37,000	$ 48,000
Income Taxes Payable	3,000	2,000
Mortgage Payable	200,000	—
Common Stock	100,000	100,000
Retained Earnings	76,000	40,000
Total Liabilities and Stockholders' Equity	$416,000	$190,000

Required

1. To what statement is Mr. Rosenberg referring? From the information given, prepare the additional statement using the direct method.
2. Explain why Adams has a cash problem despite profitable operations.

LEARNING OBJECTIVES

1. *Describe and discuss the objectives of financial statement analysis.*
2. *Describe and discuss the standards for financial statement analysis.*
3. *State the sources of information for financial statement analysis.*
4. *Identify the issues related to the evaluation of the quality of a company's earnings.*
5. *Apply horizontal analysis, trend analysis, and vertical analysis to financial statements.*
6. *Apply ratio analysis to financial statements in the study of an enterprise's liquidity, profitability, long-term solvency, and market tests.*

CHAPTER 15

Financial Statement Analysis

This chapter presents a number of techniques intended to aid in decision making by highlighting important relationships in the financial statements. This process is called financial statement analysis. After studying this chapter, you should be able to meet the learning objectives listed on the left.

Effective decision making calls for the ability to sort out relevant information from a great many facts and to make adjustments for changing conditions. Very often, financial statements in a company's annual report run twenty or more pages, including footnotes and other necessary disclosures. If these statements are to be useful in making decisions, decision makers must be able to see important relationships among figures and to make comparisons from year to year and from company to company. The many techniques that together are called **financial statement analysis** accomplish this goal.

DECISION POINT
Moody's Investors Service

Moody's Investors Service rates the bonds and other debt of companies on the basis of safety, that is, the likelihood of repayment. Investors rely on this service in making investments in bonds and other long-term company debt. The *Wall Street Journal* reported on September 19, 1990 that Moody's was reviewing $40 million of Ford Motor Company's debt for possible downgrade.[1] Moody's cited the softness in the U.S. auto market. Ford replied that the action was not warranted and questioned the rating agency's decision to review this debt because of what might be a short-term situation. One month later, on October 25, 1990, Moody's did in fact lower the rating on Ford's long-term

1. "Ford Motor's Debt Reviewed by Moody's; Downgrade Is Possible," *Wall Street Journal*, September 19, 1990.

debt. The rating was still in the high-grade area, but the downgrade meant that Ford would pay higher interest rates because, according to Moody's, its debt was not quite as secure as it had been. On what basis would Moody's decide to upgrade or lower the bond rating of a company?

According to the *Wall Street Journal,* "Moody's said it took the actions because Ford's returns and cash flow are vulnerable to a weaker U.S. economy, softer European sales, and volatile fuel prices. At the same time, Moody's said, Ford has committed to huge capital spending plans."[2] Ford Motor Company officials, according to the same article, said they were disappointed with the decision, as the reasons given were cyclical and transitional in nature. This case demonstrates several features of the evaluation of a company's financial prospects. First, the analysis is rooted in the financial statements (for example, returns and cash flow). Second, it is directed toward the future (for example, capital spending plans). Third, the operating environment must be taken into consideration (for example, a weaker U.S. economy, softer European sales, and volatile fuel prices). Fourth, judgment is involved (for example, the disagreement between Moody's and Ford as to the seriousness of the situation). ■

Objectives of Financial Statement Analysis

Users of financial statements fall into two broad categories: internal and external. Management is the main internal user. The tools of financial analysis are, of course, useful in management's operation of the business. However, because those who run the company have inside information on operations, other techniques are available to them. Since these techniques are covered in managerial accounting courses, the main focus here is on the external use of financial analysis.

Creditors make loans in the form of trade accounts, notes, or bonds, on which they receive interest. They expect a loan to be repaid according to its terms. Investors buy capital stock, from which they hope to receive dividends and an increase in value. Both groups face risks. The creditor faces the risk that the debtor will fail to pay back the loan. The investor faces the risk that dividends will be reduced or not paid or that the market price of the stock will drop. In each case, the goal is to achieve a return that makes up for the risk taken. In general, the greater the risk taken, the greater the return required as compensation.

Any one loan or any one investment can turn out badly. As a result, most creditors and investors put their funds into a **portfolio**, or group of loans or investments. The portfolio allows them to average both the return and the risk. Nevertheless, the portfolio is made up of a number of

2. Bradley A. Stertz, "Ratings on Ford and Units' Debt Cut by Moody's," *Wall Street Journal*, October 25, 1990.

loans or stocks on which individual decisions must be made. It is in making these individual decisions that financial statement analysis is most useful. Creditors and investors use financial statement analysis in two general ways: (1) They use it to judge past performance and current position, and (2) they use it to judge future potential and the risk connected with the potential.

Assessment of Past Performance and Current Position

OBJECTIVE 1
Describe and discuss the objectives of financial statement analysis

Past performance is often a good indicator of future performance. Therefore, an investor or creditor is interested in the trend of past sales, expenses, net income, cash flow, and return on investment. These trends offer a means for judging management's past performance and are a possible indicator of future performance. In addition, an analysis of current position will tell where the business stands today. For example, it will tell what assets the business owns and what liabilities must be paid. It will tell what the cash position is, how much debt the company has in relation to equity, and how reasonable the inventories and receivables are. Knowing a company's past performance and current position is often important in achieving the second general objective of financial analysis.

Assessment of Future Potential and Related Risk

Information about the past and present is useful only to the extent that it has bearing on decisions concerning the future. An investor judges the potential earning ability of a company because that ability will affect the value of the investment (the market price of the company's stock) and the amount of dividends the company will pay. A creditor judges the potential debt-paying ability of the company.

The potentials of some companies are easier to predict than those of others, and so there is less risk associated with these companies. The riskiness of an investment or loan depends on how easy it is to predict future profitability or liquidity. If an investor can predict with confidence that a company's earnings per share will be between $2.50 and $2.60 next year, the investment is less risky than if the earnings per share are expected to fall between $2.00 and $3.00. For example, the potential associated with an investment in an established and stable electric utility, or a loan to it, is relatively easy to predict on the basis of the company's past performance and current position. The potential associated with a small microcomputer manufacturer, on the other hand, may be much harder to predict. For this reason, the investment or loan to the electric utility is less risky than the investment or loan to the small computer company.

Often, in return for taking the greater risk, the investor in the microcomputer company will demand a higher expected return (increase in market price plus dividends) than will the investor in the utility company. Also, a creditor of the microcomputer company will need a higher interest rate and possibly more assurance of repayment (a secured loan, for instance) than a creditor to the utility company. The higher interest rate is payment to the creditor for assuming a higher risk.

Standards for Financial Statement Analysis

OBJECTIVE 2
Describe and discuss the standards for financial statement analysis

In using financial statement analysis, decision makers must judge whether the relationships they have found are favorable or unfavorable. Three standards of comparison often used are (1) rule-of-thumb measurements, (2) past performance of the company, and (3) industry norms.

Rule-of-Thumb Measurements

Many financial analysts and lenders use ideal or rule-of-thumb measurements for key financial ratios. For example, it has long been thought that a current ratio (current assets divided by current liabilities) of 2:1 is acceptable. The credit-rating firm of Dun & Bradstreet, in its *Key Business Ratios,* offers these guidelines:

Current debt to tangible net worth. Ordinarily, a business begins to pile up trouble when this relationship exceeds 80%.

Inventory to net working capital. Ordinarily, this relationship should not exceed 80%.

Although such measures may suggest areas that need further investigation, there is no proof that they are the best for any individual company. A company with a current ratio higher than 2:1 may have a poor credit policy (resulting in accounts receivable being too large), too much or out-of-date inventory, or poor cash management. Another company may have a lower than 2:1 ratio as a result of excellent management in these three areas. Thus, rule-of-thumb measurements must be used with great care.

Past Performance of the Company

An improvement over the rule-of-thumb method is the comparison of financial measures or ratios of the same company over a period of time. This standard will at least give the analyst some basis for judging whether the measure or ratio is getting better or worse. It may also be helpful in showing possible future trends. However, since trends do reverse at times, such projections must be made with care. Another disadvantage is that the past may not be a good measure of adequacy. In other words, past performance may not be enough to meet present needs. For example, even if return on total investment improved from 3 percent last year to 4 percent this year, the 4 percent return may not be adequate.

Industry Norms

One way of making up for the limitations of using past performance as a standard is to use industry norms. This standard will tell how the company being analyzed compares with other companies in the same industry. For example, suppose that other companies in an industry have an average rate of return on total investment of 8 percent. In such a case, 3 and 4 percent returns are probably not adequate. Industry norms can also be used to judge trends. Suppose that because of a downward turn in the economy, a company's profit margin dropped from 12 to 10 percent. A finding that other companies in the same industry had an average drop in profit margin from 12 to 4 percent would indicate that the company being analyzed did relatively well.

There are three limitations to using industry norms as standards. First, two companies that seem to be in the same industry may not be strictly comparable. Consider two companies said to be in the oil industry. The main business of one may be marketing oil products it buys from other producers through service stations. The other, an international company, may discover, produce, refine, and market its own oil products. The operations of these two companies cannot be compared because they are different.

Second, most large companies today operate in more than one industry. Some of these **diversified companies**, or **conglomerates**, operate in many unrelated industries. The individual segments of a diversified company generally have different rates of profitability and degrees of risk. In using the consolidated financial statements of these companies for financial analysis, it is often impossible to use industry norms as standards. There are simply no other companies that are similar enough. One partial solution to this problem is a requirement by the Financial Accounting Standards Board in *Statement No. 14*. This requirement states that diversified companies must report revenues, income from operations, and identifiable assets for each of their operating segments. Depending on specific criteria, segment information may be reported for operations in different industries, in foreign markets, or to major customers.[3]

The third limitation of industry norms is that companies in the same industry with similar operations may use different acceptable accounting procedures. That is, inventories may be valued using different methods, or different depreciation methods may be used for similar assets. Even so, if little information about a company's prior performance is available, industry norms probably offer the best available standards for judging a company's current performance. They should be used with care.

DECISION POINT
Eastman Kodak Company

Most people think of Eastman Kodak Company as a maker of photographic film when in fact the company has diversified from its traditional business, which it calls imaging, into the information, chemical, and health businesses. Since these businesses are very different, the overall success of Eastman Kodak as reflected in its financial statements will be affected by the relative amount of investment and earnings in each of them. How is a financial analyst to assess the impact of these four businesses on the company's overall financial performance?

In accordance with FASB *Statement No. 14*, Eastman Kodak Company reports the information about these four segments, shown in

3. *Statement of Financial Accounting Standards No. 14*, "Financial Reporting for Segments of a Business Enterprise" (Stamford, Conn.: Financial Accounting Standards Board, 1976).

Exhibit 15-1, in a note to the financial statements in its annual report. The analyst can learn much about the company from this information. For example, although the traditional imaging segment makes up only about 38 percent of sales ($7,128 of $18,908) in 1990, it still produces the lion's share, about 57 percent ($1,611 of $2,844), of earnings. Information produces sales about equal to the chemicals segment and the health segment but is much less profitable. In terms of assets, more assets are devoted to the health segment than any other segment. Profitability ratios, such as profit margin, asset turnover, and return on assets can be computed for each segment. The section on capital expenditures shows the analyst where the company is investing for the future. Although management is investing heavily in all segments, the largest increases in the last three years have been in the information and health segments. ■

Sources of Information

OBJECTIVE 3
State the sources of information for financial statement analysis

The external analyst is often limited to publicly available information about a company. The major sources of information about publicly held corporations are published reports, SEC reports, business periodicals, and credit and investment advisory services.

Published Reports

The annual report of a publicly held corporation is an important source of financial information. As previously discussed in the chapter on classified financial statements, the major parts of this annual report are (1) management's analysis of the past year's operations, (2) the financial statements, (3) the notes to the statements, including the principal accounting procedures used by the company, (4) the auditors' report, and (5) a summary of operations for a five- or ten-year period. Also, most publicly held companies publish **interim financial statements** each quarter. These reports present limited information in the form of condensed financial statements, which may be subject to a limited review or a full audit by the independent auditor. The interim statements are watched closely by the financial community for early signs of important changes in a company's earnings trend.[4]

SEC Reports

Publicly held corporations must file annual reports, quarterly reports, and current reports with the Securities and Exchange Commission (SEC). All such reports are available to the public at a small charge. The SEC calls for a standard form for the annual report (Form 10-K). This report is fuller than the published annual report. Form 10-K is, for this reason, a valuable

4. Accounting Principles Board, *Opinion No. 28*, "Interim Financial Reporting" (New York: American Institute of Certified Public Accountants, 1973); and *Statement of Financial Accounting Standards No. 3*, "Reporting Accounting Change in Interim Financial Statements" (Stamford, Conn.: Financial Accounting Standards Board, 1974).

Exhibit 15-1. Segment Information (in millions)

	1990	1989	1988
Sales, including intersegment sales			
Imaging	$ 7,128	$ 6,998	$ 6,642
Information	4,140	4,200	3,937
Chemicals	3,588	3,522	3,123
Health	4,349	4,009	3,597
Intersegment sales			
Imaging	(6)	(13)	(4)
Chemicals	(291)	(318)	(261)
Sales to unaffiliated customers	$18,908	$18,398	$17,034
Earnings (Losses) from operations[1]			
Imaging	$ 1,611	$ 821	$ 1,280
Information	5	(360)	311
Chemicals	602	643	630
Health	626	487	591
Earnings from operations	2,844	1,591	2,812
Interest and other income (charges)			
Imaging	10	108	78
Information	(8)	(35)	2
Chemicals	(6)	5	(4)
Health	(2)	3	(27)
Corporate	119	148	72
Interest expense	(812)	(895)	(697)
Litigation judgment	(888)	—	—
Earnings before income taxes	$ 1,257	$ 925	$ 2,236
Assets			
Imaging[2]	$ 6,623	$ 7,039	$ 7,186
Information	3,943	4,331	4,319
Chemicals	3,952	3,238	2,967
Health	8,464	7,793	7,278
Corporate[2] [3]	1,561	1,744	1,493
Intersegment receivables	(418)	(493)	(279)
Total assets at year end	$24,125	$23,652	$22,964
Depreciation expense			
Imaging	$ 371	$ 401	$ 345
Information	347	379	371
Chemicals	289	264	226
Health	161	137	115
Total depreciation expense	$ 1,168	$ 1,181	$ 1,057
Amortization expense			
Imaging	$ 18	$ 19	$ 20
Information	5	12	12
Chemicals	1	1	1
Health	117	113	93
Total amortization expense	$ 141	$ 145	$ 126
Capital expenditures			
Imaging	$ 679	$ 902	$ 854
Information	468	453	393
Chemicals	610	514	515
Health	280	249	152
Total capital expenditures	$ 2,037	$ 2,118	$ 1,914

(1) Earnings (Losses) from operations for 1989 are shown after deducting restructuring costs of $388 million for Imaging, $417 million for Information, $17 million for Chemicals and $53 million for Health.
(2) Data for 1989 and 1988 have been restated to conform to the 1990 presentation.
(3) Includes Cash, Marketable Securities and Eastman Kodak Credit Corporation assets.
Source: All information from Eastman Kodak Company reports reprinted by permission of Eastman Kodak Company. Copyright © 1988, 1989, 1990.

source of information. It is available, free of charge, to stockholders of the company. The quarterly report (Form 10-Q) presents important facts about interim financial performance. The current report (Form 8-K) must be filed within a few days of the date of certain major events. It is often the first indicator of important changes that may affect the company's financial performance in the future.

Business Periodicals and Credit and Investment Advisory Services

Financial analysts must keep up with current events in the financial world. Probably the best source of financial news is the *Wall Street Journal*, which is published daily and is the most complete financial newspaper in the United States. Some helpful magazines, published every week or every two weeks, are *Forbes*, *Barron's*, *Fortune*, and the *Commercial and Financial Chronicle*.

For further details about the financial history of companies, the publications of such services as Moody's Investors Service and Standard & Poor's Industrial Surveys are useful. Data on industry norms, average ratios and relationships, and credit ratings are available from such agencies as the Dun & Bradstreet Corporation. Dun & Bradstreet offers, among other useful services, an annual analysis using 14 ratios of 125 industry groups classified as retailing, wholesaling, manufacturing, and construction in its *Key Business Ratios*. Another important source of industry data is the *Annual Statement Studies*, published by Robert Morris Associates, which presents many facts and ratios for 223 different industries. Also, a number of private services are available to the analyst for a yearly fee.

Evaluating a Company's Quality of Earnings

OBJECTIVE 4
Identify the issues related to the evaluation of the quality of a company's earnings

It is clear from the preceding sections that the current and expected earnings of a company play an important role in the analysis of the company's prospects. In fact, a recent survey of two thousand members of the Association for Investment Management and Research indicated that the two most important economic indicators in evaluating common stocks were expected changes in earnings per share and expected return on equity.[5] Net income is an important component of both measures. Because of the importance of net income, or the "bottom line," in measures of a company's prospects, interest in evaluating the quality of the net income figure, or the *quality of earnings*, has become an important topic. The quality of a company's earnings may be affected by (1) the accounting methods and estimates the company's management chooses and/or (2) the nature of nonoperating items in the income statement.

Choice of Accounting Methods and Estimates

There are two aspects to the choice of accounting methods that affect the quality of earnings. First, some accounting methods are by nature more

5. Cited in *The Week in Review* (Deloitte Haskins & Sells), February 28, 1985.

conservative than others because they tend to produce a lower net income in the current period. Second, there is considerable latitude in the choice of the estimated useful life over which assets are written off and in the amount of estimated residual value. In general, an accounting method or estimated useful life and/or residual value that results in lower current earnings is considered to produce better quality earnings.

In earlier chapters, various acceptable alternative methods were used in the application of the matching rule. These methods are based on allocation procedures, which in turn are based on certain assumptions. Here are some of these procedures:

1. For estimating uncollectible accounts expense: percentage of net sales method and accounts receivable aging method
2. For pricing the ending inventory: average-cost method; first-in, first-out method (FIFO); and last-in, first-out method (LIFO)
3. For estimating depreciation expense: straight-line method, production method, sum-of-the-years'-digits method, and declining-balance method
4. For estimating depletion expense: production (extraction) method
5. For estimating amortization of intangibles: straight-line method

All these procedures are designed to allocate the costs of assets to the periods in which those costs contribute to the production of revenue. They are based on a determination of the benefits to the current period (expenses) versus the benefits to future periods (assets). They are estimates, and the period or periods benefited cannot be demonstrated conclusively. They are also subjective, because in practice it is hard to justify one method of estimation over another.

For this reason, it is important for both the accountant and the financial statement user to understand the possible effects of different accounting procedures on net income and financial position. For example, suppose that two companies have similar operations, but that one uses FIFO for inventory pricing and the straight-line (SL) method for computing depreciation and the other uses LIFO for inventory pricing and the sum-of-the-years'-digits (SYD) method for computing depreciation. The income statements of the two companies might appear as follows:

	FIFO and SL	LIFO and SYD
Sales	$500,000	$500,000
Goods Available for Sale	$300,000	$300,000
Less Ending Inventory	60,000	50,000
Cost of Goods Sold	$240,000	$250,000
Gross Margin	$260,000	$250,000
Less: Depreciation Expense	$ 40,000	$ 70,000
Other Expenses	170,000	170,000
Total Operating Expenses	$210,000	$240,000
Net Income	$ 50,000	$ 10,000

This fivefold difference in income stems only from the differences in accounting methods. Differences in the estimated lives and residual values of the plant assets could cause an even greater variation. In practice, of course, differences in net income occur for many reasons, but the user must be aware of the discrepancies that can occur as a result of the methods chosen by management.

The existence of these alternatives could cause problems in the interpretation of financial statements were it not for the conventions of full disclosure and consistency described in the chapter on accounting concepts and classified financial statements. Full disclosure requires that management explain the significant accounting policies used in preparing the financial statements in a note to the statements. Consistency requires that the same accounting procedures be followed from year to year. If a change in procedure is made, the nature of the change and its monetary effect must be explained in a note.

Nature of Nonoperating Items

As seen in the chapter on retained earnings and corporate income statements, the corporate income statement has several components. The top of the statement presents earnings from current ongoing operations, called income from operations. The lower part of the statement can contain such nonoperating items as discontinued operations, extraordinary gains and losses, and effects of accounting changes. These items may drastically affect the bottom line, or net income, of the company. For example, Eastman Kodak Company had an unusual charge of $888 million in 1990 that related primarily to the loss of a patent suit with Polaroid. The loss had a detrimental effect on reported net earnings in 1990.

Such nonoperating items should be taken into consideration when interpreting a company's earnings. For example, in 1983, U.S. Steel (now USX) made an apparent turnaround by reporting first quarter earnings of $1.35 a share versus a deficit of $1.31 a year earlier. However, the "improved" earnings included a gain from sales of assets of $.45 per share and sale of tax benefits on newly acquired assets of $.40 per share, as well as other items totaling $.61 per share. These items total $1.46, an amount greater than the reported earnings for the year.[6] The opposite effect can also occur. For the first six months of 1984, Texas Instruments reported a loss of $112 million compared with a profit of $64.5 million the previous year. The loss was caused by write-offs of $58 million for nonoperating losses, $83 million for inventory, and $37 million for increased reserves for rebates, price protection for retailers, and returned inventory.[7] In reality, this large write-off was a positive step on Texas Instruments' part because getting out of the low-profit home computer business meant that TI's future cash flows would not be drained by those operations.

6. Dan Dorfman, "Three Well-Known Stocks with Earnings of Dubious Quality," *Chicago Tribune*, June 28, 1984, p. 11.
7. "Loss at Texas Instruments Hits $119.2 Million," *Wall Street Journal*, November 14, 1984.

For practical reasons, the trends and ratios in the sections that follow are based on the assumption that net income and other components are comparable from year to year and company to company. However, the astute analyst will always look beyond the ratios to the quality of the components in making interpretations.

Tools and Techniques of Financial Analysis

Few numbers by themselves mean very much. It is their relationship to other numbers or their change from one period to another that is important. The tools of financial analysis are intended to show relationships and changes. Among the more widely used of these financial analysis techniques are horizontal analysis, trend analysis, vertical analysis, and ratio analysis.

Horizontal Analysis

OBJECTIVE 5 *Apply horizontal analysis, trend analysis, and vertical analysis to financial statements*

Generally accepted accounting principles call for presenting comparative financial statements that give the current year's and past year's financial information. A common starting point for studying such statements is **horizontal analysis**, which involves the computation of dollar amount changes and percentage changes from the previous to the current year. The percentage change must be figured to show how the size of the change relates to the size of the amounts involved. A change of $1 million in sales is not so drastic as a change of $1 million in net income, because sales is a larger amount than net income.

Exhibits 15-2 and 15-3 present the comparative balance sheets and income statements, respectively, for Eastman Kodak Company, with the dollar and percentage changes shown. The percentage change is computed as follows:

$$\text{Percentage change} = 100\left(\frac{\text{amount of change}}{\text{previous year amount}}\right)$$

The **base year** in any set of data is always the first year being studied. For example, from 1989 to 1990, Kodak's total assets increased by $473 million, from $23,652 million to $24,125 million, or by 2.0 percent, computed as follows:

$$\text{Percentage increase} = 100\left(\frac{\$473 \text{ million}}{\$23{,}652 \text{ million}}\right) = 2.0\%$$

An examination of the comparative balance sheet in Exhibit 15-2 shows little change in the asset categories from 1989 to 1990. As shown above, there was an overall growth in total assets of 2.0 percent. Although overall total liabilities and deferred credits shows about the same increase, there was a change in the composition of liabilities. Current liabilities increased by 9.0 percent, whereas long-term borrowings decreased by 5.2 percent.

Several interesting observations can be made about the income statement. Sales outside the United States were strong, showing an 8.6 percent

Exhibit 15-2. Comparative Balance Sheets with Horizontal Analysis

Eastman Kodak Company
Consolidated Balance Sheets (Statements of Financial Position)
December 31, 1990, and 1989

	(In millions)		Increase (Decrease)	
	1990	**1989**	**Amount**	**Percentage**
Assets				
Current Assets				
Cash and cash equivalents	$ 735	$ 1,095	$(360)	(32.9)
Marketable securities	181	184	(3)	(1.6)
Receivables	4,333	4,245	88	2.1
Inventories	2,425	2,507	(82)	(3.3)
Deferred income tax charges	653	306	347	113.4
Prepaid charges applicable to future operations	281	254	27	10.6
Total Current Assets	$ 8,608	$ 8,591	$ 17	.2
Properties				
Land, buildings, machinery, and equipment at cost	$17,648	$16,774	$ 874	5.2
Less Accumulated depreciation	8,670	8,146	524	6.4
Net Properties	$ 8,978	$ 8,628	$ 350	4.1
Other Assets				
Unamortized goodwill	4,448	4,579	(131)	(2.9)
Long-term receivables and other noncurrent assets	2,091	1,854	237	12.8
Total Assets	$24,125	$23,652	$ 473	2.0
Liabilities and Shareowners' Equity				
Current Liabilities				
Payables	$ 6,413	$ 6,073	$ 340	5.6
Taxes—income and other	588	338	250	74.0
Dividends payable	162	162	0	0.0
Total Current Liabilities	$ 7,163	$ 6,573	$ 590	9.0
Other Liabilities and Deferred Credits				
Long-term borrowings	6,989	7,376	(387)	(5.2)
Other long-term liabilities	1,406	1,371	35	2.6
Deferred income tax credits	1,830	1,690	140	8.3
Total Liabilities and Deferred Credits	$17,388	$17,010	$ 378	2.2
Shareowners' Equity				
Common stock, par value $2.50 per share	$ 941	$ 940	$ 1	0.1
Retained earnings	7,855	7,761	94	1.2
	$ 8,796	$ 8,701	$ 95	1.1
Less Treasury stock at cost	2,059	2,059	0	0.0
Total Shareowners' Equity	$ 6,737	$ 6,642	$ 95	1.4
Total Liabilities and Shareowners' Equity	$24,125	$23,652	$ 473	2.0

* Certain amounts have been restated as a result of the consolidation of the Eastman Kodak Credit Corporation.

Exhibit 15-3. Comparative Income Statements with Horizontal Analysis

Eastman Kodak Company
Consolidated Statements of Earnings
For the Years Ended December 31, 1990, and 1989

	(In millions*)		Increase (Decrease)	
	1990	**1989**	**Amount**	**Percentage**
Sales to: Customers in the United States	$10,118	$10,302	**$ (184)**	**(1.8)**
Customers outside the United States	8,790	8,096	**694**	**8.6**
Total Sales	$18,908	$18,398	**$ 510**	**2.8**
Cost of goods sold	$10,966	$11,075	**$ (109)**	**(1.0)**
Sales, advertising, distribution and administrative expenses	5,098	4,857	**241**	**5.0**
Restructuring costs	—	875	**(875)**	**(100.0)**
Total costs and expenses	$16,064	$16,807	**$ (743)**	**(4.4)**
Earnings from Operations	$ 2,844	$ 1,591	**$1,253**	**78.8**
Investment income	167	148	**19**	**12.8**
Interest expense	(812)	(895)	**83**	**(9.3)**
Litigation judgment	(888)	—	**(888)**	**—**
Other income (charges)	(54)	81	**(135)**	**(166.7)**
Earnings before income taxes	$ 1,257	$ 925	**$ 332**	**35.9**
Provision for United States, foreign, and other income taxes	554	396	**158**	**39.9**
Net Earnings	$ 703	$ 529	**$ 174**	**32.9**
Average number of common shares outstanding	324.5	324.3	**.2**	**0.1**
Net earnings per share	$2.17	$1.63	**$0.54**	**33.1**

* Except per share data

increase, but sales in the United States declined by 1.8 percent. Earnings from operations showed a strong increase of 78.8 percent. This was mostly caused by the restructuring costs of $875 million, which lowered earnings in 1989. The notes to the financial statements reveal that the restructuring costs consisted primarily of write-offs of inventory and other assets as well as a provision for separation costs for employees leaving the company. Despite the increase in earnings from operations, earnings before income taxes and net earnings were up only 35.9 percent and 32.9 percent, respectively, because of a litigation judgment in 1990. The restructuring costs in 1989 and the litigation costs in 1990 are important considerations in analyzing the comparative income statements.

Care also has to be taken in the analysis of percentage changes. For example in Exhibit 15-3, one might view the 12.8 percent increase in investment income as greater than the 9.3 percent decrease in interest expense.

In dollar amount, though, the decrease in interest expense was more than four times the increase in investment income ($83 million versus $19 million). Dollar amounts and percentages must be considered together.

Trend Analysis

A variation of horizontal analysis is **trend analysis**, in which percentage changes are calculated for several successive years instead of two years. Trend analysis is important because, with its long-run view, it may point to basic changes in the nature of the business. Besides comparative financial statements, most companies give out a summary of operations and data on other key indicators for five or more years. Selected items from Kodak's summary of operations together with trend analysis are presented in Exhibit 15-4.

Trend analysis uses an **index number** to show changes in related items over a period of time. For index numbers, one year, the base year, is equal to 100 percent. Other years are measured in relation to that amount. For example, the 1990 index of 163.7 for sales was figured as follows:

$$\text{Index} = 100\left(\frac{\text{index year amount}}{\text{base year amount}}\right) = 100\left(\frac{\$18{,}908}{\$11{,}550}\right) = 163.7$$

An index number of 163.7 means that 1990 sales are 163.7 percent or 1.637 times 1986 sales.

Exhibit 15-4. Trend Analysis

Eastman Kodak Company
Summary of Operations
Selected Data
(Sales and Net Earnings in Millions)

	1990	1989	1988	1987	1986
Sales	$18,908	$18,398	$17,034	$13,305	$11,550
Earnings from Operations	2,844	1,591	2,812	2,078	724
Per Common Share*					
Net Earnings*	2.17	1.63	4.31	3.52	1.10
Dividends*	2.00	2.00	1.90	1.71	1.63
Trend Analysis (in percentages)					
Sales	163.7	159.3	147.5	115.2	100.0
Earnings from Operations	392.8	219.8	388.4	287.0	100.0
Per Common Share					
Net Earnings	197.3	148.2	391.8	320.0	100.0
Dividends	122.7	122.7	116.6	104.9	100.0

* Per share data restated to reflect 3-for-2 stock splits in 1985 and 1987

A study of the trend analysis in Exhibit 15-4 shows that earnings from operations has been more volatile than sales and that net earnings per common share has been more volatile than dividends per share. Sales rose steadily over the five-year period, while dividends per share rose over the first four years and remained the same in years four and five. After a decrease in 1989, earnings from operations and net earnings per share rebounded in 1990. Over the five-year period, earnings from operations increased more rapidly than sales (392.8 versus 163.7). The contrasting volatility and steadiness are dramatically shown when graphed in Figure 15-1.

Vertical Analysis

In **vertical analysis** percentages are used to show the relationship of the different parts to the total in a single statement. The accountant sets a total figure in the statement equal to 100 percent and computes the percentage of the total of each component of that figure. (The figure would be total assets or total liabilities and stockholders' equity in the case of the balance sheet, and revenues or sales in the case of the income statement.) The resulting statement of percentages is called a **common-size statement**. Common-size balance sheets and income statements for Kodak are shown graphically in pie chart form in Figures 15-2 and 15-3, and in financial statement form in Exhibits 15-5 and 15-6 (pages 765 and 766).

Vertical analysis is useful for comparing the importance of certain components in the operation of the business. It is also useful for pointing out

Figure 15-1. Trend Analysis for Eastman Kodak Company

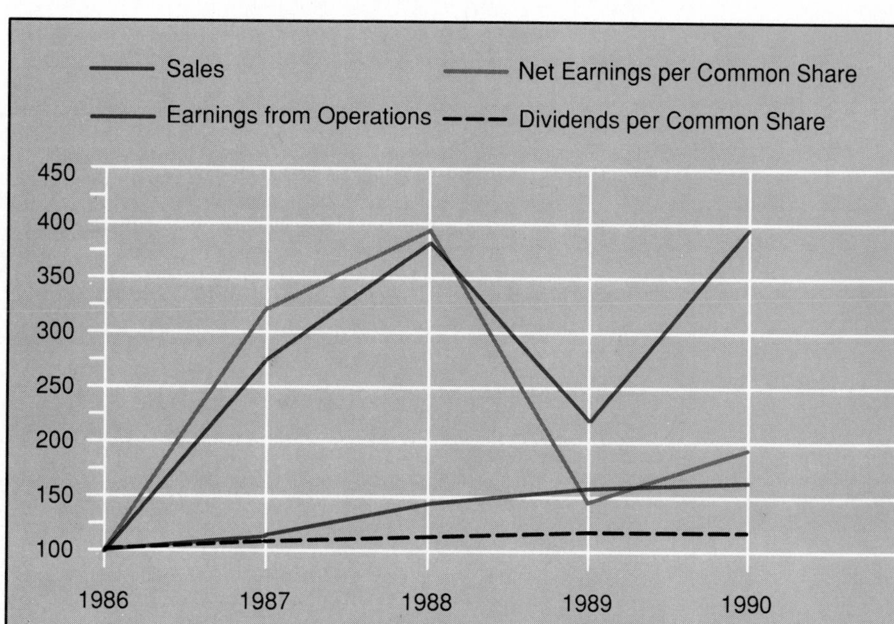

Figure 15-2. Common-Size Balance Sheets Presented Graphically

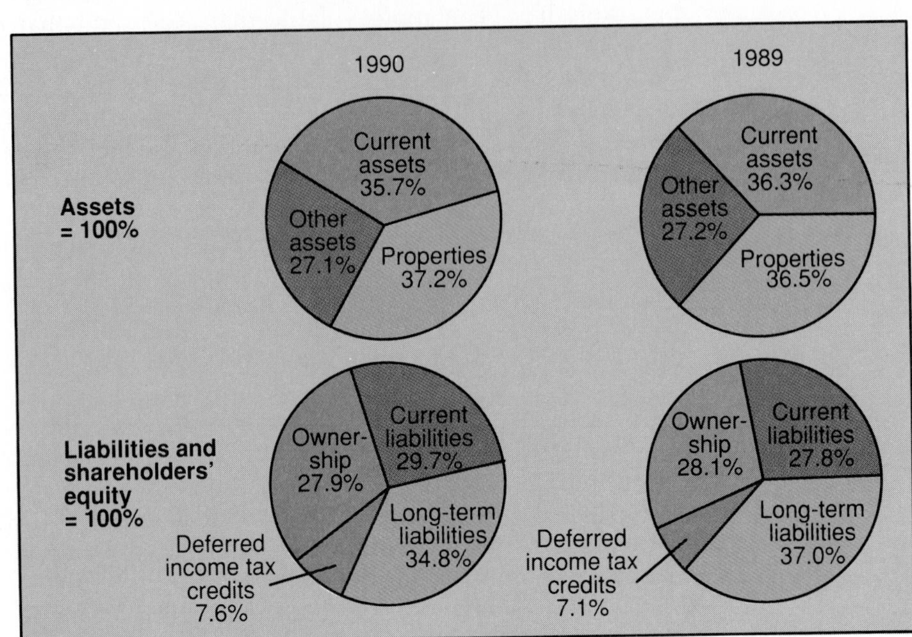

important changes in the components from one year to the next in comparative common-size statements. For Kodak, the composition of assets in Exhibit 15-5 did not change significantly from 1989 to 1990. About the same proportion of assets were in properties (37.2 percent versus 36.5 percent) and in current assets (35.7 percent versus 36.3 percent) in 1990 as in 1989. The composition of liabilities shows more change. The part of total liabilities made up of current liabilities increased from 27.8 percent to 29.7

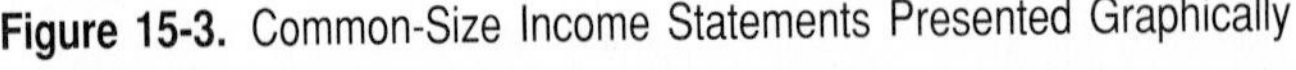

Figure 15-3. Common-Size Income Statements Presented Graphically

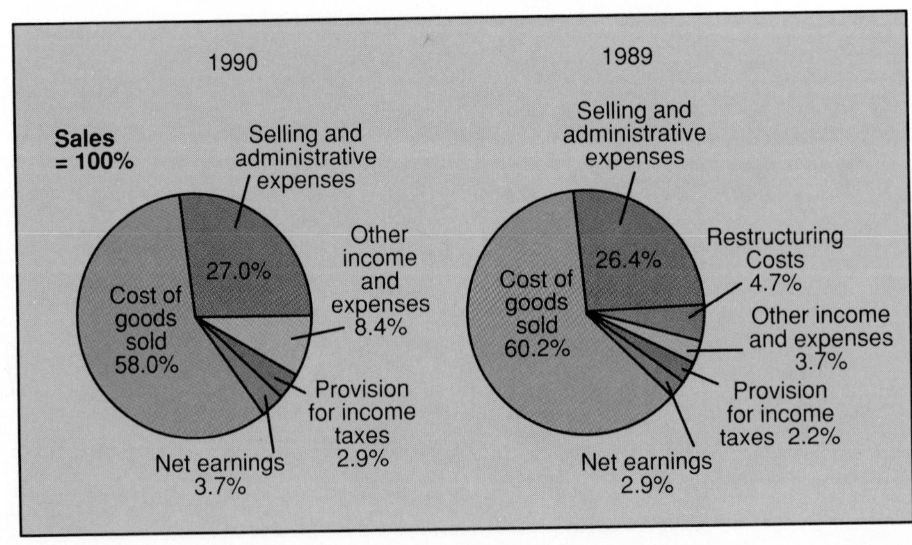

percent. Correspondingly, long-term liabilities decreased from 37.0 percent to 34.8 percent.

The common-size statements of earnings (Exhibit 15-6) show the importance of the decrease in costs and expenses from 91.3 to 85.0 percent of sales. Two factors cause this decrease. One was the one-time decrease in restructuring costs, but the other was a very favorable decrease in cost of goods sold from 60.2 percent of sales to 58.0 percent. This decrease was a major cause of the increase in earnings from operations from 8.6 to 15.0 percent of sales. Note, however, the negative impact of the increase in other income and expenses from 3.7 percent of sales to 8.4 percent and the increase in income taxes from 2.2 percent of sales to 2.9 percent. Consequently, earnings as a percent of sales actually increased from 2.9 percent of sales in 1989 to only 3.7 percent of sales in 1990.

Common-size statements are often used to make comparisons between companies. They allow an analyst to compare the operating and financing

Exhibit 15-5. Common-Size Balance Sheets

Eastman Kodak Company
Common-Size Balance Sheets
December 31, 1990, and 1989

	1990*	1989*
Assets		
Current Assets	35.7%	36.3%
Properties (less Accumulated Depreciation)	37.2	36.5
Other Assets	27.1	27.2
Total Assets	100.0%	100.0%
Liabilities		
Current Liabilities	29.7%	27.8%
Long-Term Liabilities	34.8	37.0
Deferred Income Tax Credits	7.6	7.1
Total Liabilities	72.1%	71.9%
Ownership		
Common Stock	3.9%	4.0%
Retained Earnings	32.6	32.8
Treasury Stock at Cost	(8.5)	(8.7)
Total Ownership	27.9%	28.1%
Total Liabilities and Ownership	100.0%	100.0%

* Results are rounded in some cases to equal 100%.

Exhibit 15-6. Common-Size Income Statements

Eastman Kodak Company
Common-Size Income Statements (Statements of Earnings)
For Years Ended December 31, 1990, and 1989

	1990*	1989*
Sales	100.0%	100.0%
Costs and Expenses		
Cost of Goods Sold	58.0%	60.2%
Selling and Administrative Expenses	27.0	26.4
Restructuring Costs	—	4.7
Total Costs and Expenses	85.0%	91.3%
Earnings from Operations	15.0%	8.6%
Other Income and (Expenses)	(8.4)	(3.7)
Earnings before Income Taxes	6.6%	5.0%
Provision for Income Taxes	2.9	2.2
Net Earnings	3.7%	2.9%

* Rounding causes some additions and subtractions not to total.

characteristics of two companies of different size in the same industry. For example, the analyst may want to compare Kodak to other companies in terms of the percentage of total assets financed by debt or the percentage of general administrative and selling expenses to sales and revenues. Common-size statements would show these and other relationships.

Ratio Analysis

Ratio analysis is an important way to state meaningful relationships between two components of a financial statement. To be most useful, a ratio must also include a study of the underlying data. Ratios are guides or short cuts that are useful in evaluating the financial position and operations of a company and in comparing them to results in previous years or to other companies. The primary purpose of ratios is to point out areas needing further investigation. They should be used in connection with a general understanding of the company and its environment. Ratios for financial analysis were introduced in the chapter on classified financial statements. The following section briefly reviews the ratios covered in that chapter and expands the analysis to cover new ratios.

Ratios may be stated in several ways. For example, a ratio of net income of $100,000 to sales of $1,000,000 may be stated as (1) net income is 1/10 or 10 percent of sales, (2) the ratio of sales to net income is 10 to 1 (10:1) or 10 times net income, or (3) for every dollar of sales, the company has an average net income of 10 cents.

Survey of Commonly Used Ratios

In the following sections, ratio analysis is applied to four objectives: the evaluation of (1) liquidity, (2) profitability, (3) long-term solvency, and (4) market strength. The chapter on accounting concepts and classified financial statements addressed the first two objectives in an introductory way. Here we expand the evaluation to include other ratios related to those objectives and to introduce two new objectives. Data for the analyses come from the financial statements of Kodak presented in Exhibits 15-2 and 15-3. Other data are presented as needed.

Evaluating Liquidity

OBJECTIVE 6
Apply ratio analysis to financial statements in the study of an enterprise's liquidity, profitability, long-term solvency, and market tests

Liquidity is the ability to pay bills when they are due and to meet unexpected needs for cash. The ratios that relate to this goal all have to do with working capital or some part of it, because it is out of working capital that debts are paid as they mature. Some common ratios connected with evaluating liquidity are the current ratio, the quick ratio, receivable turnover, and inventory turnover.

Current Ratio. The **current ratio** expresses the relationship of current assets to current liabilities. It is widely used as a broad indicator of a company's liquidity and short-term debt-paying ability. The ratio for Kodak for 1990 and 1989 is figured as follows:

Current Ratio	1990	1989
$\frac{\text{Current assets}}{\text{Current liabilities}}$	$\frac{\$8{,}608}{\$7{,}163} = 1.20$	$\frac{\$8{,}591}{\$6{,}573} = 1.31$

The current ratio for Kodak suggests a decrease in the company's liquidity from 1989 to 1990.

Quick Ratio. One of the current ratio's faults is that it does not take into account the make-up of current assets. They may appear to be large enough, but they may not have the proper balance. Clearly, a dollar of cash or even accounts receivable is more readily available to meet obligations than is a dollar of most kinds of inventory. The **quick ratio** is designed to overcome this problem by measuring short-term liquidity. That is, it measures the relationship of the more liquid current assets (cash, marketable securities or short-term investments, and receivables) to current liabilities. This ratio for Kodak for 1990 and 1989 is figured as follows:

Quick Ratio	1990	1989
$\frac{\text{Cash + marketable securities + receivables}}{\text{Current liabilities}}$	$\frac{\$735 + \$181 + \$4{,}333}{\$7{,}163}$	$\frac{\$1{,}095 + \$184 + \$4{,}245}{\$6{,}573}$
	$= \frac{\$5{,}249}{\$7{,}163} = 0.73$	$= \frac{\$5{,}524}{\$6{,}573} = 0.84$

This ratio too suggests a decrease in liquidity from 1989 to 1990.

Receivable Turnover. The ability of a company to collect for credit sales in a timely way affects the company's liquidity. The **receivable turnover** ratio measures the relative size of a company's accounts receivable and the success of its credit and collection policies. It shows how many times, on average, the receivables were turned into cash during the period. However, it can also be affected by external factors, such as economic conditions and interest rates.

Turnover ratios usually consist of one balance sheet account and one income statement account. The receivable turnover is computed by dividing net sales by average accounts receivable. Theoretically, the numerator should be net credit sales, but the amount of net credit sales is rarely made available in public reports. So we will use total net sales. Further, in this ratio and others in which an average is required, we will take the beginning and ending balances and divide by 2. If we had internal financial data, it would be better to use monthly balances to find the average, because the balances of receivables, inventories, and other accounts can vary widely during the year. In fact, many companies choose a fiscal year that begins and ends at a low period of the business cycle, when inventories and receivables may be at the lowest levels of the year. When the previous year's balance is not available for computing the average, it is common practice to use the ending balance for the current year.

Using a 1988 accounts receivable ending balance of $4,071 million, Kodak's receivable turnover is computed as follows:

Receivable Turnover	1990	1989
$\frac{\text{Net sales}}{\text{Average accounts receivable}}$	$\frac{\$18,908}{(\$4,333 + \$4,245)/2}$	$\frac{\$18,398}{(\$4,245 + \$4,071)/2}$
	$= \frac{\$18,908}{\$4,289} = \frac{4.41}{\text{times}}$	$= \frac{\$18,398}{\$4,158} = \frac{4.42}{\text{times}}$

Within reasonable ranges, the higher the turnover ratio the better. With a higher turnover, the company is turning receivables into cash at a faster pace. The speed at which receivables are turned over depends on the company's credit terms. Since a company's credit terms are usually stated in days, such as 2/10, n/30, it is helpful to convert the receivable turnover to **average days' sales uncollected**. This conversion is made by dividing the length of the accounting period (usually 365 days) by the receivable turnover (as computed above), as follows:

Average Days' Sales Uncollected	1990	1989
$\frac{\text{Days in year}}{\text{Receivable turnover}}$	$\frac{365 \text{ days}}{4.41} = 82.8 \text{ days}$	$\frac{365 \text{ days}}{4.42} = 82.6 \text{ days}$

In the case of Kodak, both the receivable turnover and the average days' sales uncollected were about the same in 1989 and 1990. The average accounts receivable was turned over about 4.4 times both years. This means Kodak had to wait on average about 82 or 83 days to receive payment for credit sales.

Inventory Turnover. Inventory is two steps removed from cash (sale and collection). The **inventory turnover** ratio measures the relative size of inventory. The proportion of assets tied up in inventory, of course, affects the amount of cash available to pay maturing debts. Inventory should be maintained at the best level to support production and sales. In general, however, a smaller, faster-moving inventory means that the company has less cash tied up in inventory. It also means that there is less chance for the inventory to become spoiled or out of date. A build-up in inventory may mean that a recession or some other factor is preventing sales from keeping pace with purchasing and production.

Using a 1988 ending inventory balance of $3,025 million, inventory turnover for 1990 and 1989 at Kodak is computed as follows:

Inventory Turnover	1990	1989
Cost of goods sold / Average inventory	$10,966 / ($2,425 + $2,507)/2	$11,075 / ($2,507 + $3,025)/2
	= $10,966 / $2,466 = 4.45 times	= $11,075 / $2,766 = 4.00 times

There was an increase in inventory turnover from 1989 to 1990.

Evaluating Profitability

A company's long-run survival depends on its being able to earn a satisfactory income. Investors become and remain stockholders for only one reason: They believe that the dividends and capital gains they will receive will be greater than the returns on other investments of about the same risk. An evaluation of a company's past earning power may give the investor a better basis for decision making. Also, as pointed out in the chapter on accounting concepts and classified financial statements, a company's ability to earn an income usually affects its liquidity position. For this reason, evaluating profitability is important to both investors and creditors. In judging the profitability of Kodak, five ratios will be presented: profit margin, asset turnover, return on assets, return on equity, and earnings per share. Except for earnings per share, all these ratios were introduced in the discussion of classified financial statements.

Profit Margin. The **profit margin** ratio measures the percentage of each revenue dollar that contributes to net income. It is computed for Kodak as follows:

Profit Margin[8]	1990	1989
Net income / Net sales	$703 / $18,908 = 3.7%	$529 / $18,398 = 2.9%

8. In comparing companies in an industry, some analysts use net income before income taxes as the numerator to eliminate the effect of differing tax rates among firms.

The ratio confirms what was clear from the common-size income statements (Exhibit 15-6): that the profit margin increased from 1989 (2.9 percent) to 1990 (3.7 percent).

Asset Turnover. **Asset turnover** is a measure of how efficiently assets are used to produce sales. It shows how many dollars in sales are produced by each dollar invested in assets. In other words, it tells how many times in the period assets were "turned over" in sales. The higher the asset turnover, the more concentrated is the use of assets. Using the data for Kodak from Exhibits 15-2 and 15-3 and 1988 total assets of $22,964 million, the asset turnover for 1990 and 1989 is computed as follows:

Asset Turnover	1990	1989
$\frac{\text{Net sales}}{\text{Average total assets}}$	$\frac{\$18,908}{(\$24,125 + \$23,652)/2}$	$\frac{\$18,398}{(\$23,652 + \$22,964)/2}$
	$= \frac{\$18,908}{\$23,888.50}$	$= \frac{\$18,398}{\$23,308}$
	= .79 times	= .79 times

Compared to companies in other industries, Kodak needs a large investment in assets for each dollar of sales. A retailer may have an asset turnover of between 4.0 and 6.0. In Kodak's case, however, asset turnover was only .79 in 1989 and in 1990. This means that Kodak makes sales of a little less than one dollar for each dollar of assets.

Return on Assets. The best overall measure of the earning power or profitability of a company is **return on assets**, which measures the amount earned on each dollar of assets invested. The return on assets for 1990 and 1989 for Kodak is computed as follows:

Return on Assets[9]	1990	1989
$\frac{\text{Net income}}{\text{Average total assets}}$	$\frac{\$703}{\$23,888.50} = 2.9\%$	$\frac{\$529}{\$23,308} = 2.3\%$

Kodak's return on assets increased from 2.3 percent in 1989 to 2.9 percent in 1990. Although it is a favorable change, the level of return would be considered low by most analysts.

One reason why return on assets is a good measure of profitability is that it combines the effects of profit margin and asset turnover. The 1990 and 1989 results for Kodak can be analyzed as follows:

9. Some authorities would add interest expense to the numerator because they view interest expense as a cost of acquiring capital rather than a cost of operations.

	Profit Margin		Asset Turnover		Return on Assets
Ratios:	net income / net sales	×	net sales / average total assets	=	net income / average total assets
1990	3.7%	×	.79	=	2.9%
1989	2.9%	×	.79	=	2.3%

From this analysis, it is clear that the increase in return on assets in 1990 can be attributed to the increase in profit margin.

Return on Equity. An important measure of profitability from the stockholders' standpoint is **return on equity**. This ratio measures how much was earned for each dollar invested by owners. For Kodak, this ratio for 1990 and 1989 is figured as follows (1988 owners' equity equals $6,780 million):

Return on Equity	1990	1989
Net income / Average owners' equity	$703 / (\$6,737 + \$6,642)/2	$529 / (\$6,642 + \$6,780)/2
	= $703 / $6,689.50	= $529 / $6,711
	= 10.5%	= 7.9%

This ratio also improved from 1989 to 1990. The increase was greater than the increase in return on assets because, although average owners' equity declined slightly from 1989 to 1990, average total assets increased.

A natural question is, Why is there a difference between return on assets and return on equity? The answer lies in the company's use of **leverage**, or debt financing. A company that has interest-bearing debt is said to be leveraged. If the company earns more with its borrowed funds than it must pay in interest for those funds, then the difference is available to increase the return on equity. Leverage may work against the company as well. Thus an unfavorable situation occurs when the return on assets is less than the rate of interest paid on borrowed funds. Because of Kodak's leverage, the return on assets in 1990 of 2.9 percent created a larger return on equity of 10.5 percent for the same year. (The debt to equity ratio is presented later in this chapter.)

Earnings per Share. One of the most widely quoted measures of profitability is **earnings per share** of common stock. Exhibit 15-3 shows that the net earnings per share for Kodak improved from $1.63 to $2.17, reflecting the increase in net earnings from 1989 to 1990. These disclosures must be made in financial statements; calculations of this kind were presented in the chapter on retained earnings and corporate income statements.

Evaluating Long-Term Solvency

Long-term solvency has to do with a company's ability to survive over many years. The aim of long-term solvency analysis is to point out early if a company is on the road to bankruptcy. Studies have shown that accounting ratios can show as much as five years in advance that a company may fail.[10] Declining profitability and liquidity ratios are key signs of possible business failure. Two other ratios that analysts often consider as indicators of long-term solvency are the debt to equity ratio and the interest coverage ratio.

Debt to Equity Ratio. The existence of increasing amounts of debt in a company's capital structure is thought to be risky. The company has a legal obligation to make interest payments on time and to pay the principal at the maturity date. And this obligation holds no matter what the level of the company's earnings is. If the payments are not made, the company may be forced into bankruptcy. In contrast, dividends and other distributions to equity holders are made only when the board of directors declares them. The **debt to equity ratio** shows the amount of the company's assets provided by creditors in relation to the amount provided by stockholders. Thus it measures the extent to which the company is leveraged. The larger the debt to equity ratio, the more fixed obligations the company has, and so the riskier the situation.

The ratio is computed as follows:

Debt to Equity Ratio	1990	1989
$\frac{\text{Total liabilities}}{\text{Owners' equity}}$	$\frac{\$17,388}{\$6,737} = 2.58$	$\frac{\$17,010}{\$6,642} = 2.56$

From 1989 to 1990, the debt to equity ratio for Kodak remained almost the same. This finding agrees with the analysis of the common-size balance sheets (Exhibit 15-5).

Interest Coverage Ratio. One question that usually arises at this point is, If debt is bad, why have any? The answer is that, as with many ratios, the level of debt is a matter of balance. In spite of its riskiness, debt is a flexible means of financing certain business operations. Also, because it usually carries a fixed interest charge, it limits the cost of financing and creates a situation in which leverage can be used to advantage. Thus, if the company is able to earn a return on assets greater than the cost of the interest, it makes an overall profit.[11] However, the company runs the risk

10. William H. Beaver, "Alternative Accounting Measures as Indicators of Failure," *Accounting Review* (January 1968); and Edward Altman, "Financial Ratios, Discriminant Analysis and the Prediction of Corporate Bankruptcy," *Journal of Finance* (September 1968).
11. In addition, there are advantages to being a debtor in periods of inflation because the debt, which is fixed in dollar amount, may be repaid with cheaper dollars.

of not earning a return on assets equal to the cost of financing those assets, and thereby incurring a loss.

One measure of the degree of protection creditors have from a default on interest payments is the **interest coverage ratio**, which is computed as follows:

Interest Coverage Ratio	1990	1989
$\dfrac{\text{Net income before taxes + interest expense}}{\text{Interest expense}}$	$\dfrac{\$1{,}257 + \$812}{\$812}$	$\dfrac{\$925 + \$895}{\$895}$
	= 2.55 times	= 2.03 times

Although interest coverage improved in 1990, interest payments were protected by a ratio of only 2.55 times in 1990 because of the large amount of interest expense in relation to net income before taxes and interest expense.

Market Test Ratios

The market price of a company's stock is of interest to the analyst because it represents what investors as a whole think of a company at a point in time. Market price is the price at which people are willing to buy and sell the stock. It provides information about how investors view the potential return and risk connected with owning the company's stock. This information cannot be obtained simply by considering the market price of the stock by itself, however. Companies differ in number of outstanding shares and amount of underlying earnings and dividends. Thus the market price must be related to the earnings per share, dividends per share, and price of other companies' shares. This is accomplished through the price/earnings ratio, the dividends yield, and an analysis of market risk.

Price/Earnings Ratio. The **price/earnings (P/E) ratio** measures the relationship of the current market price of a stock to the company's earnings per share. Assuming a current market price of $40 and using the 1990 earnings per share for Eastman Kodak Company of $2.17 from Exhibit 15-3, we can compute the price/earnings ratio as follows:

$$\frac{\text{Market price per share}}{\text{Earnings per share}} = \frac{\$40}{\$2.17} = 18.4 \text{ times}$$

At this time, Kodak's P/E ratio is 18.4 times its underlying earnings. The price/earnings ratio changes from day to day and from quarter to quarter as market price and earnings change. It tells how much, at any particular time, the investing public as a whole is willing to pay for $1 of a company's earnings per share.

This price/earnings ratio is very useful and widely applied because it allows companies to be compared. When a company's P/E ratio is higher than the P/E ratios for other companies, it *usually* means that investors feel that the company's earnings are going to grow at a faster rate than those of the other companies. On the other hand, a lower P/E ratio *usually* means a more negative assessment by investors. To compare two well-known companies, the market was less favorable toward IBM (11 times earnings per share) than it was toward AT&T (14 times earnings per share) in 1991.

Dividends Yield. The **dividends yield** is a measure of the current return to an investor in a stock. It is found by dividing the current annual dividend by the current market price of the stock. Assuming the same $40 per share and using the 1990 dividends of $2.00 per share for Kodak from Exhibit 15-4, we can compute the dividends yield thus:

$$\frac{\text{Dividends per share}}{\text{Market price per share}} = \frac{\$2.00}{\$40} = 5.0\%$$

Thus an investor who owns Kodak stock at $40 had a return from dividends in 1990 of 5.0 percent.

The dividends yield is only one part of the investor's total return from investing in Eastman Kodak Company. The investor must add to or subtract from the dividends yield the percentage change (either up or down) in the market value of the stock.

Market Risk. It was pointed out earlier that besides assessing the potential return from an investment, the investor must also judge the risk associated with the investment. Many factors may be brought into assessing risk—the nature of the business, the quality of the business, the track record of the company, and so forth. One measure of risk that has gained increased attention among analysts in recent years is market risk. **Market risk** is the volatility of (or changes up and down in) the price of a stock in relation to the volatility of the prices of other stocks.

The computation of market risk is complex, involving computers and sophisticated statistical techniques such as regression analysis. The idea, however, is simple. Consider the following data on the changes in the prices of the stocks of Company A and Company B compared to the average change in price of all stocks in the market:

Average Percentage Change in Price of All Stocks	Percentage Change in Price of Company A's Stock	Percentage Change in Price of Company B's Stock
+10	+15	+5
–10	–15	–5

In this example, when the average price of all stocks went up by 10 percent, Company A's price increased 15 percent whereas Company B's increased only 5 percent. When the average price of all stocks went down by 10 percent, Company A's price decreased 15 percent but Company B's decreased only 5 percent. Thus, relative to all stocks, Company A's stock is more volatile than Company B's. If the prices of stocks go down, the risk of loss is greater in the case of Company A than in the case of Company B. If the market goes up, however, the potential for gain is greater in the case of Company A than in the case of Company B.

Market risk can be approximated by dividing the percentage change in price of a particular stock by the average percentage change in the price of all stocks, as follows:

$$\text{Company A} \quad \frac{\text{specific change}}{\text{average change}} = \frac{15}{10} = 1.5$$

$$\text{Company B} \quad \frac{\text{specific change}}{\text{average change}} = \frac{5}{10} = .5$$

This means that an investor can generally expect the value of an investment in Company A to increase or decrease 1.5 times as much as the average change in the price of all stocks. An investment in Company B can be expected to increase or decrease only .5 times as much as the price of all stocks.

Analysts call this measure of market risk **beta** (β), after the mathematical symbol used in the formula for calculating the relationships of stock prices. The actual betas used by analysts are based on several years of data and are continually updated. Because the calculations require the use of computers, betas are usually provided by investment services.

The market risk or beta for USX in a recent year was 1.01. This means that, other things being equal, a person who invests in the stock of USX can expect its volatility or risk to be about the same as that of the stock market as a whole (which has a beta of 1.0). When one considers that USX is a mature company and the largest steel producer, with output closely related to the ups and downs in the economy as a whole, its near-neutral beta makes sense.

If the investor's objective is to assume less risk than that of the market as a whole, other companies in the steel industry might be considered. The second largest steel company in the United States, Bethlehem Steel, can be eliminated because its beta of 1.25 makes it riskier than USX. National Steel, the third largest steel processor, has been more stable over the years than its competitors, with a beta of only .75. It is a less risky stock in that there is less potential for a loss in a "down" market; but there is also less potential for gain in an "up" market. National Steel's beta is very low and compares favorably with that of major utilities such as American Telephone and Telegraph, which has a beta of .65.

Typically, growth stocks and speculative stocks are riskier than the stock market as a whole. Tandy Corporation (Radio Shack), a good example of a growth company, has had a beta of 1.45 in recent years. Tandy Corporation has rewarded investors' patience over the long term, but has been much more volatile and thus riskier than the average stock with a beta of 1.00.

Investment decisions are not made on the basis of market risk alone, of course. First, other risk factors such as those indicated by the ratios discussed in this chapter, as well as industry, national, and world economic outlooks, must be considered. Second, the expected return must be considered. Further, most investors try to assemble a portfolio of stocks whose average beta corresponds to the degree of risk they are willing to assume in relation to their average expected return.

Chapter Review

Review of Learning Objectives

1. **Describe and discuss the objectives of financial statement analysis.** Creditors and investors, as well as managers, use financial statement analysis to judge the past performance and current position of a company. In this way they also judge its future potential and the risk associated with it. Creditors use the information gained from their analysis to make reliable loans that will be repaid with interest. Investors use the information to make investments that provide a return that is worth the risk.
2. **Describe and discuss the standards for financial statement analysis.** Three commonly used standards for financial statement analysis are rule-of-thumb measurements, past performance of the company, and industry norms. Rule-of-thumb measurements are weak because of the lack of evidence that they can be applied widely. The past performance of a company can offer a guideline for measuring improvement but is not helpful in judging performance relative to other companies. Although the use of industry norms overcomes this last problem, its disadvantage is that firms are not always comparable, even in the same industry.
3. **State the sources of information for financial statement analysis.** The major sources of information about publicly held corporations are published reports such as annual reports and interim financial statements, SEC reports, business periodicals, and credit and investment advisory services.
4. **Identify the issues related to the evaluation of the quality of a company's earnings.** Current and prospective net income is an important component in many ratios used to evaluate a company. The user should recognize that the quality of reported net income can be influenced by certain choices made by a company's management. First, management exercises judgment in choosing the accounting methods and estimates used in computing net income. Second, discontinued operations, extraordinary gains or losses, and accounting changes may affect net income positively or negatively.
5. **Apply horizontal analysis, trend analysis, and vertical analysis to financial statements.** Horizontal analysis involves the computation of dollar amount changes and percentage changes from year to year. Trend analysis is an extension of horizontal analysis in that percentage changes are calculated for several years. The changes are usually computed by setting a base year equal to 100 and calculating the results for subsequent years as a percentage of that base year. Vertical analysis uses percentages to show the relationship of the component parts to the total in a single statement. The resulting statements, expressed entirely in percentages, are called common-size statements.
6. **Apply ratio analysis to financial statements in the study of an enterprise's liquidity, profitability, long-term solvency, and market tests.** The following table summarizes the basic information on ratio analysis.

Ratio	Components	Use or Meaning
Liquidity Ratios		
Current ratio	$\frac{\text{Current assets}}{\text{Current liabilities}}$	Measure of short-term debt-paying ability
Quick ratio	$\frac{\text{Cash + marketable securities + receivables}}{\text{Current liabilities}}$	Measure of short-term liquidity
Receivable turnover	$\frac{\text{Net sales}}{\text{Average accounts receivable}}$	Measure of relative size of accounts receivable balance and effectiveness of credit policies
Average days' sales uncollected	$\frac{\text{Days in year}}{\text{Receivable turnover}}$	Measure of average time taken to collect receivables
Inventory turnover	$\frac{\text{Cost of goods sold}}{\text{Average inventory}}$	Measure of relative size of inventory
Profitability Ratios		
Profit margin	$\frac{\text{Net income}}{\text{Net sales}}$	Net income produced by each dollar of sales
Asset turnover	$\frac{\text{Net sales}}{\text{Average total assets}}$	Measure of how efficiently assets are used to produce sales
Return on assets	$\frac{\text{Net income}}{\text{Average total assets}}$	Overall measure of earning power or profitability of all assets employed in the business
Return on equity	$\frac{\text{Net income}}{\text{Average owners' equity}}$	Profitability of owners' investment
Earnings per share	$\frac{\text{Net income}}{\text{Weighted average outstanding shares}}$	Means of placing earnings on a common basis for comparison
Long-Term Solvency Ratios		
Debt to equity ratio	$\frac{\text{Total liabilities}}{\text{Owners' equity}}$	Measure of relationship of debt financing to equity financing
Interest coverage ratio	$\frac{\text{Net income before taxes + interest expense}}{\text{Interest expense}}$	Measure of protection of creditors from default on interest payments

(continued)

Ratio	Components	Use or Meaning
Market Test Ratios		
Price/earnings (P/E) ratio	$\frac{\text{Market price per share}}{\text{Earnings per share}}$	Measure of amount the market will pay for a dollar of earnings
Dividends yield	$\frac{\text{Dividends per share}}{\text{Market price per share}}$	Measure of current return to investor
Market risk	$\frac{\text{Specific change in market price}}{\text{Average change in market price}}$	Measure of volatility of the market price of a stock in relation to that of other stocks

Review of Concepts and Terminology

The following concepts and terms were introduced in this chapter:

(L.O. 6) **Asset turnover:** Net sales divided by average total assets. Used to measure how efficiently assets are used to produce sales.

(L.O. 6) **Average days' sales uncollected:** The length of the accounting period, usually 365 days, divided by the receivable turnover. Shows the speed at which receivables are turned over—literally, the number of days, on the average, a company must wait to receive payment for credit sales.

(L.O. 5) **Base year:** In financial analysis, the first year to be considered in any set of data.

(L.O. 6) **Beta (β):** A measure of the market risk of an individual stock in relation to the average market risk of all stocks.

(L.O. 5) **Common-size statement:** A financial statement in which the components of a total figure are stated in terms of percentages of the total.

(L.O. 6) **Current ratio:** The relationship of current assets to current liabilities. Used as an indicator of a company's liquidity and short-term debt-paying ability.

(L.O. 6) **Debt to equity ratio:** Total liabilities divided by owners' equity. Used to measure the relationship of debt financing to equity financing, or the extent to which a company is leveraged.

(L.O. 2) **Diversified companies (conglomerates):** Companies that operate in more than one industry.

(L.O. 6) **Dividends yield:** The current annual dividend divided by the current market price of a stock. Used as a measure of the current return to an investor in a stock.

(L.O. 6) **Earnings per share:** Net income divided by the weighted-average number of outstanding shares of common stock. Used as a measure of profitability and a means of comparison among stocks.

(L.O. 1) **Financial statement analysis:** A collective term for the techniques used to show important relationships among figures in financial statements.

(L.O. 5) **Horizontal analysis:** A technique for analyzing financial statements that involves the computation of dollar amount changes and percentage changes from the previous to the current year.

(L.O. 5) **Index number:** In trend analysis, a number against which changes in related items over a period of time are measured. Calculated by setting the base year equal to 100 percent.

(L.O. 6) **Interest coverage ratio:** Net income before taxes plus interest expense, divided by interest expense. Used as a measure of the degree of protection creditors have from a default on interest payments.

(L.O. 3) **Interim financial statements:** Financial statements issued for a period of less than one year, usually monthly or quarterly.

(L.O. 6) **Inventory turnover:** The cost of goods sold divided by average inventory. Used to measure the relative size of inventory.

(L.O. 6) **Leverage:** Debt financing. The amount of debt financing in relation to equity financing is measured by the debt to equity ratio.

(L.O. 6) **Market risk:** The volatility of the price of a stock in relation to the volatility of the prices of other stocks.

(L.O. 1) **Portfolio:** A group of loans or investments designed to average the return and risks of a creditor or investor.

(L.O. 6) **Price/earnings (P/E) ratio:** Current market price per share divided by earnings per share. Used as a measure of investor confidence in a company, and as a means of comparison among stocks.

(L.O. 6) **Profit margin:** Net income divided by net sales. Used to measure the percentage of each net sales dollar that is contributed to net income.

(L.O. 6) **Quick ratio:** The relationship of the more liquid current assets—cash, marketable securities or short-term investments, and receivables—to current liabilities. Used as a measure of short-term liquidity.

(L.O. 6) **Ratio analysis:** A technique for analyzing financial statements in which meaningful relationships are shown between components of financial statements. (For a summary of ratios see the Review of Learning Objectives, pages 777–778.)

(L.O. 6) **Receivable turnover:** The relationship of net sales to average accounts receivable. Used as a measure of the relative size of a company's accounts receivable and the success of its credit and collection policies; shows how many times, on the average, receivables were turned into cash during the period.

(L.O. 6) **Return on assets:** Net income divided by average total assets. Used to measure the amount earned on each dollar of assets invested. An overall measure of earning power or profitability.

(L.O. 6) **Return on equity:** Net income divided by average owners' equity. Used to measure how much income was earned for each dollar invested by owners.

(L.O. 5) **Trend analysis:** A type of horizontal analysis in which percentage changes are calculated for several successive years instead of two years.

(L.O. 5) **Vertical analysis:** A technique for analyzing financial statements that uses percentages to show the relationship of the different parts to the total in a single statement.

Review Problem
Comparative Analysis of Two Companies

(L.O. 6) Maggie Washington is considering an investment in one of two fast-food restaurant chains because she believes the trend toward eating out more often will continue. Her choices have been narrowed to Quik Burger and Big Steak, whose income statements and balance sheets are shown below and on page 781.

In addition to the information on the financial statements, dividends paid were $500,000 for Quik Burger and $600,000 for Big Steak. The market prices of the stocks were $30 and $20, respectively, and their betas were 1.00 and 1.15. Financial information pertaining to prior years is not readily available to Maggie Washington. Assume that all notes payable are current liabilities and that all bonds payable are long-term liabilities.

Income Statements (in thousands)

	Quik Burger	Big Steak
Sales	$53,000	$86,000
Cost of Goods Sold (including restaurant operating expense)	37,000	61,000
Gross Margin from Sales	$16,000	$25,000
General Operating Expenses		
Selling Expenses	$ 7,000	$10,000
Administrative Expenses	4,000	5,000
Interest Expense	1,400	3,200
Income Taxes Expense	1,800	3,400
Total Operating Expenses	$14,200	$21,600
Net Income	$ 1,800	$ 3,400

Required

Conduct a comprehensive ratio analysis of Quik Burger and Big Steak and compare the results. The analysis should be performed using the following steps (round all ratios and percentages to one decimal point):

1. Prepare an analysis of liquidity.
2. Prepare an analysis of profitability.
3. Prepare an analysis of long-term solvency.
4. Prepare an analysis of market tests.
5. Compare the two companies by inserting the ratio calculations from the preceding four steps into a table with the following column headings: Ratio Name, Quik Burger, Big Steak, and Company with More Favorable Ratio. Indicate in the last column the company that apparently had the more favorable ratio in each case. (Consider differences of .1 or less to be indeterminate.)
6. In what ways would having access to prior years' information aid this analysis?

Balance Sheets (in thousands)		
	Quik Burger	Big Steak
Assets		
Cash	$ 2,000	$ 4,500
Accounts Receivable (net)	2,000	6,500
Inventory	2,000	5,000
Property, Plant, and Equipment (net)	20,000	35,000
Other Assets	4,000	5,000
Total Assets	$30,000	$56,000
Liabilities and Stockholders' Equity		
Accounts Payable	$ 2,500	$ 3,000
Notes Payable	1,500	4,000
Bonds Payable	10,000	30,000
Common Stock ($1 par value)	1,000	3,000
Paid-in Capital in Excess of Par Value, Common	9,000	9,000
Retained Earnings	6,000	7,000
Total Liabilities and Stockholders' Equity	$30,000	$56,000

Answer to Review Problem

Ratio Name	Quik Burger	Big Steak
1. Liquidity analysis		
a. Current ratio	$\frac{\$2,000 + \$2,000 + \$2,000}{\$2,500 + \$1,500}$	$\frac{\$4,500 + \$6,500 + \$5,000}{\$3,000 + \$4,000}$
	$= \frac{\$6,000}{\$4,000} = 1.5$	$= \frac{\$16,000}{\$7,000} = 2.3$
b. Quick ratio	$\frac{\$2,000 + \$2,000}{\$2,500 + \$1,500}$	$\frac{\$4,500 + \$6,500}{\$3,000 + \$4,000}$
	$= \frac{\$4,000}{\$4,000} = 1.0$	$= \frac{\$11,000}{\$7,000} = 1.6$
c. Receivable turnover	$\frac{\$53,000}{\$2,000} = 26.5$ times	$\frac{\$86,000}{\$6,500} = 13.2$ times
d. Average days' sales uncollected	$\frac{365}{26.5} = 13.8$ days	$\frac{365}{13.2} = 27.7$ days
e. Inventory turnover	$\frac{\$37,000}{\$2,000} = 18.5$ times	$\frac{\$61,000}{\$5,000} = 12.2$ times

Ratio Name	Quik Burger	Big Steak
2. Profitability analysis		
a. Profit margin	$\frac{\$1,800}{\$53,000} = 3.4\%$	$\frac{\$3,400}{\$86,000} = 4.0\%$
b. Asset turnover	$\frac{\$53,000}{\$30,000} = 1.8$ times	$\frac{\$86,000}{\$56,000} = 1.5$ times
c. Return on assets	$\frac{\$1,800}{\$30,000} = 6.0\%$	$\frac{\$3,400}{\$56,000} = 6.1\%$
d. Return on equity	$\frac{\$1,800}{\$1,000 + \$9,000 + \$6,000}$ $= \frac{\$1,800}{\$16,000}$ $= 11.3\%$	$\frac{\$3,400}{\$3,000 + \$9,000 + \$7,000}$ $= \frac{\$3,400}{\$19,000}$ $= 17.9\%$
e. Earnings per share	$\frac{\$1,800}{1,000} = \$1.80$	$\frac{\$3,400}{3,000} = \$1.13$
3. Long-term solvency analysis		
a. Debt to equity ratio	$\frac{\$2,500 + \$1,500 + \$10,000}{\$1,000 + \$9,000 + \$6,000}$ $= \frac{\$14,000}{\$16,000}$ $= 0.9$	$\frac{\$3,000 + \$4,000 + \$30,000}{\$3,000 + \$9,000 + \$7,000}$ $= \frac{\$37,000}{\$19,000}$ $= 1.9$
b. Interest coverage ratio	$\frac{\$1,800 + \$1,800 + \$1,400}{\$1,400}$ $= \frac{\$5,000}{\$1,400}$ $= 3.6$ times	$\frac{\$3,400 + \$3,400 + \$3,200}{\$3,200}$ $= \frac{\$10,000}{\$3,200}$ $= 3.1$ times
4. Market test analysis		
a. Price/earnings ratio	$\frac{\$30}{\$1.80} = 16.7$ times	$\frac{\$20}{\$1.13} = 17.7$ times
b. Dividends yield	$\frac{\$500,000 \div 1,000,000}{\$30} = 1.7\%$	$\frac{\$600,000 \div 3,000,000}{\$20} = 1.0\%$
c. Market risk	1.00	1.15

5. Comparative analysis

Ratio Name	Quik Burger	Big Steak	Company with More Favorable Ratio*
1. Liquidity analysis			
a. Current ratio	1.5	2.3	Big Steak
b. Quick ratio	1.0	1.6	Big Steak
c. Receivable turnover	26.5 times	13.2 times	Quik Burger
d. Average days' sales uncollected	13.8 days	27.7 days	Quik Burger
e. Inventory turnover	18.5 times	12.2 times	Quik Burger
2. Profitability analysis			
a. Profit margin	3.4%	4.0%	Big Steak
b. Asset turnover	1.8 times	1.5 times	Quik Burger
c. Return on assets	6.0%	6.1%	Neutral
d. Return on equity	11.3%	17.9%	Big Steak
e. Earnings per share	$1.80	$1.13	Noncomparable†
3. Long-term solvency analysis			
a. Debt to equity ratio	0.9	1.9	Quik Burger
b. Interest coverage ratio	3.6 times	3.1 times	Quik Burger
4. Market test analysis			
a. Price/earnings ratio	16.7 times	17.7 times	Big Steak
b. Dividends yield	1.7%	1.0%	Quik Burger
c. Market risk	1.00	1.15	Quik Burger is less risky

* This analysis indicates the company with the apparently more favorable ratio. Class discussion may focus on conditions under which different conclusions may be drawn.

† Earnings per share are noncomparable because of the considerable difference in the number of common stockholders of the two firms. If information for prior years were available, it would be helpful in determining the earnings trend of each company.

6. Usefulness of prior years' information

Prior years' information would be helpful in two ways. First, turnover and return ratios could be based on average amounts. Second, a trend analysis could be performed for each company.

Chapter Assignments

Discussion Questions

1. What differences and similarities exist between the objectives of investors and those of creditors in using financial statement analysis?
2. What role does risk play in making loans and investments?
3. What standards are commonly used to evaluate financial statements, and what are their relative merits?
4. Why would a financial analyst compare the ratios of Steelco, a steel company, to the ratios of other companies in the steel industry? What might invalidate such a comparison?
5. Where may an investor look to find information about a company in which he or she is thinking of investing?

6. What is the basis of the statement "Accounting income is a useless measurement because it is based on so many arbitrary decisions"? Is the statement true?
7. Why would an investor want to see both horizontal and trend analyses of a company's financial statements?
8. What does the following sentence mean: "Based on 1967 equaling 100, net income increased from 240 in 1983 to 260 in 1984"?
9. What is the difference between horizontal and vertical analysis?
10. What is the purpose of ratio analysis?
11. Under what circumstances would a current ratio of 3:1 be good? Under what circumstances would it be bad?
12. In a period of high interest rates, why are receivable and inventory turnover especially important?
13. The following statements were made on page 35 of the November 6, 1978 issue of *Fortune* magazine: "Supermarket executives are beginning to look back with some nostalgia on the days when the standard profit margin was 1 percent of sales. Last year the industry overall margin came to a thin 0.72 percent." How could a supermarket earn a satisfactory return on assets with such a small profit margin?
14. Company A and Company B both have net incomes of $1,000,000. Is it possible to say that these companies are equally successful? Why or why not?
15. Circo Company has a return on assets of 12 percent and a debt to equity ratio of .5. Would you expect return on equity to be more or less than 12 percent?
16. The market price of Company J's stock is the same as that of Company Q's. How might one determine whether investors are equally confident about the future of these companies?
17. Why is it riskier to own a stock whose market price is more changeable than the market price of other stocks? Why might it be beneficial to own such a stock?

Communication Skills Exercises

Communication 15-1. Standards for Financial Analysis *(L.O. 2)*

Helene Curtis is a well-known, publicly owned corporation. "By almost any standard, Chicago-based Helene Curtis rates as one of America's worst-managed personal care companies. In recent years its return on equity has hovered between 10% and 13%, well below the industry average of 18% to 19%. Net profit margins of 2% to 3% are half that of competitors. . . . As a result, while leading names like Revlon and Avon are trading at three and four times book value, Curtis's trades at less than two-thirds book value."[12] Considering that many companies are happy with a return on equity (owners' investment) of 10 percent to 13 percent, why is this analysis so critical of Curtis's performance? Assuming that Curtis could double its profit margin, what other information would you need to project the resulting return on owners' investment? Why are Revlon's and Avon's stocks trading for more than Curtis's?

Communication 15-2. Quality of Earnings[13] *(L.O. 4)*

International Business Machines Corporation (IBM), the world's largest computer manufacturer, on Tuesday, January 19, 1988, reported greatly increased earnings for the fourth quarter of 1987. In spite of this reported gain in earn-

12. *Forbes* (November 13, 1978), p. 154.
13. "Technology Firms Post Strong Earnings But Stock Prices Decline Sharply," *Wall Street Journal*, January 21, 1988; Donald R. Seace, "Industrials Plunge 57.2 Points—Technology Stocks' Woes Cited," *Wall Street Journal*, January 21, 1988.

ings, the price of IBM's stock on the New York Stock Exchange declined by $6 per share to $111.75. In sympathy with this move, most other technology stocks also declined.

Fourth-quarter net earnings rose from $1.39 billion, or $2.28 a share, to $2.08 billion, or $3.47 a share, an increase of 49.6 percent and 52.2 percent over the year-earlier period. Management declared that these results demonstrated the effectiveness of IBM's efforts to become more competitive, and that, in spite of the economic uncertainties of 1988, the company was planning for growth.

The stock price declined, however, apparently because the huge increase in income was the result of nonrecurring gains. Investment analysts pointed out that IBM's high earnings stemmed primarily from elements such as a lower tax rate. Despite most analysts' expectations of a tax rate between 40 and 42 percent, IBM's rate was down from the previous year's 45.3 percent to a low 36.4 percent.

In addition, analysts were disappointed in the revenue growth. Revenues within the United States were down, and much of the growth in revenues came through favorable currency translations, increases that may not be repeated. In fact, some estimates of the fourth-quarter earnings attributed $.50 per share to currency translations and another $.25 to tax rate changes.

Other factors contributing to the rise in earnings were one-time transactions such as the sale of Intel Corporation stock and bond redemptions, which, along with a corporate stock buyback program, reduced the amount of stock outstanding in the fourth quarter by 7.4 million shares.

The analysts are concerned about the quality of IBM's earnings. Identify four quality of earnings issues reported in the case and the analysts' concern about each. In percentage terms, what is the impact of the currency changes on fourth-quarter earnings? Comment on management's assessment of IBM's performance. Do you agree with management?

Communication 15-3. Financial Analysis and Interpretation[14] *(L.O. 5, 6)*

Motorola, Inc., a world leader in electronic equipment, systems, components, and services, including two-way radios, pagers, cellular telephones and systems, semiconductors, and other products, attempts to achieve superior financial results through applying the concept of Total Customer Satisfaction. In its 1990 Annual Report to stockholders and friends, the company summarized 1990 financial results as follows:

> While sales grew during 1990, earnings were the same as in 1989, as we continued to aggressively reduce prices and increase strategic investments, despite weaker economic conditions in some of our markets.
>
> Sales increased 13 percent to $10.88 billion from $9.62 billion in 1989. Earnings were $499 million, or $3.80 per share, compared with $498 million, or $3.83 per share, a year ago. Return on average invested capital was 9.4%, compared with 10.3% in 1989.
>
> We acknowledge the lower than desirable financial returns of 1990. Some stockholders and analysts believe we are over-investing in research and development and pursuing too many technologies in our strategic areas of interest. We respectfully disagree and believe that sustained, long-term investments in promising technologies provide the platform for solid, profitable growth.

14. Excerpts from Motorola's Annual Report reprinted courtesy of Motorola, Inc.

Motorola, Inc. and Consolidated Subsidiaries
Consolidated Balance Sheets
December 31, 1990 and 1989

(In millions, except per share amounts)	1990	1989
Assets		
Current assets:		
Cash and cash equivalents	$ 265	$ 231
Short-term investments, at cost (approximating market)	312	202
Accounts receivable, less allowance for doubtful accounts (1990, $68; 1989, $35)	1,857	1,683
Inventories	1,245	1,173
Future income tax benefits	419	337
Other current assets	354	289
Total current assets	4,452	3,915
Property, plant and equipment, net	3,778	3,337
Other assets	512	434
Total assets	$8,742	$7,686
Liabilities and Stockholders' Equity		
Current liabilities:		
Notes payable and current portion of long-term debt	$ 995	$ 787
Accounts payable	889	789
Accrued liabilities	1,164	1,078
Total current liabilities	3,048	2,654
Long-term debt	792	755
Deferred income taxes	203	183
Other liabilities	442	291
Stockholders' equity:		
Common stock, $3 par value		
Authorized shares: 1990, 300.0; 1989, 300.0		
Outstanding shares: 1990, 131.7; 1989, 130.4	395	391
Preferred stock, $100 par value issuable in series		
Authorized shares: 0.5 (none issued)	—	—
Additional paid-in capital	929	878
Retained earnings	2,933	2,534
Total stockholders' equity	4,257	3,803
Total liabilities and stockholders' equity	$8,742	$7,686

See accompanying notes to consolidated financial statements.

Motorola, Inc. and Consolidated Subsidiaries
Statements of Consolidated Earnings
Years ended December 31, 1990, 1989, and 1988

(In millions, except per share amounts)	1990	1989	1988
Net sales	$10,885	$9,620	$8,250
Costs and expenses			
Manufacturing and other costs of sales	6,882	5,905	5,040
Selling, general and administrative expenses	2,414	2,289	1,957
Depreciation expense	790	650	543
Interest expense, net	133	130	98
Total costs and expenses	10,219	8,974	7,638
Earnings before income taxes	666	646	612
Income taxes provided on earnings	167	148	167
Net earnings	$ 499	$ 498	$ 445
Net earnings per share	$ 3.80	$ 3.83	$ 3.43
Average shares outstanding	131.3	130.0	129.6

Comparative balance sheets for 1990 and 1989 are provided on page 786 and income statements for 1990, 1989, and 1988 are provided above. The total assets, stockholders' equity, net accounts receivable, and inventories for 1988 were $6,710,000,000; $3,375,000,000; $1,400,000,000; and $1,144,000,000, respectively. Conduct a financial analysis of liquidity, profitability, and long-term solvency for 1990 and 1989. Assess the profitability of Motorola in light of the letter to stockholders and comment on the effects, if any, of the change in profitability on the liquidity of the company.

Communication 15-4. Basic Research Skills *(L.O. 3)*

In your school library, find either *Moody's Investors Service, Standard and Poor's Industry Guide,* or *The Value Line Investment Survey.* Find the reports on three corporations. You may choose them at random or choose them from the same industry, if directed to do so by your instructor. (If you did a related exercise in a previous chapter, use the same three companies.) Write a summary of what you learn about each company from the reference works, and be prepared to discuss your findings in class.

Classroom Exercises

Exercise 15-1. Effect of Alternative Accounting Methods *(L.O. 4)*

At the end of its first year of operations, a company could calculate its ending merchandise inventory according to three different accounting methods, as follows: FIFO, $47,500; weighted-average, $45,000; LIFO, $43,000. If the weighted-average method is used by the company, net income for the year would be $17,000.

1. Determine net income if the FIFO method is used.
2. Determine net income if the LIFO method is used.

3. Which method is more conservative?
4. Will the consistency convention be violated if the company chooses to use the LIFO method?
5. Does the full-disclosure convention require disclosure of the inventory method selected by management in the financial statements?

Exercise 15-2. Effect of Alternative Accounting Methods *(L.O. 4, 6)*

Jeans F' All and Jeans 'R' Us are very similar companies in size and operation. Jeans F' All uses FIFO and straight-line depreciation methods, and Jeans 'R' Us uses LIFO and accelerated depreciation. Prices have been rising during the past several years. Each company has paid its taxes in full for the current year, and each uses the same method for figuring income taxes as for financial reporting. Identify which company will report the greater amount for each of the following ratios:

a. current ratio
b. inventory turnover
c. profit margin
d. return on assets

If you cannot tell which company will report the greater amount, explain why.

Exercise 15-3. Horizontal Analysis *(L.O. 5)*

Compute the amount and percentage changes for the following balance sheets, and comment on the changes from 19x1 to 19x2. (Round the percentage changes to one decimal point.)

Herrera Company
Comparative Balance Sheets
December 31, 19x2 and 19x1

	19x2	19x1
Assets		
Current Assets	$ 18,600	$ 12,800
Property, Plant, and Equipment (net)	109,464	97,200
Total Assets	$128,064	$110,000
Liabilities and Stockholders' Equity		
Current Liabilities	$ 11,200	$ 3,200
Long-Term Liabilities	35,000	40,000
Stockholders' Equity	81,864	66,800
Total Liabilities and Stockholders' Equity	$128,064	$110,000

Exercise 15-4. Trend Analysis *(L.O. 5)*

Prepare a trend analysis of the following data using 19x1 as the base year, and tell whether the situation shown by the trends is favorable or unfavorable. (Round your answers to one decimal point.)

	19x5	19x4	19x3	19x2	19x1
Sales	$12,760	$11,990	$12,100	$11,440	$11,000
Cost of Goods Sold	8,610	7,700	7,770	7,350	7,000
General and Administrative Expenses	2,640	2,592	2,544	2,448	2,400
Operating Income	1,510	1,698	1,786	1,642	1,600

Exercise 15-5. Vertical Analysis *(L.O. 5)*

Express the comparative income statements that follow as common-size statements, and comment on the changes from 19x1 to 19x2. (Round computations to one decimal point.)

Herrera Company
Comparative Income Statements
For the Years Ended December 31, 19x2 and 19x1

	19x2	19x1
Sales	$212,000	$184,000
Cost of Goods Sold	127,200	119,600
Gross Margin from Sales	$ 84,800	$ 64,400
Selling Expenses	$ 53,000	$ 36,800
General Expenses	25,440	18,400
Total Operating Expenses	$ 78,440	$ 55,200
Net Operating Income	$ 6,360	$ 9,200

Exercise 15-6. Liquidity Analysis *(L.O. 6)*

Partial comparative balance sheet and income statement information for Prange Company follows:

	19x2	19x1
Cash	$ 3,400	$ 2,600
Marketable Securities	1,800	4,300
Accounts Receivable (net)	11,200	8,900
Inventory	13,600	12,400
Total Current Assets	$30,000	$28,200
Current Liabilities	$10,000	$ 7,050
Sales	$80,640	$55,180
Cost of Goods Sold	54,400	50,840
Gross Margin from Sales	$26,240	$ 4,340

The year-end balances for Accounts Receivable and Inventory in 19x0 were $8,100 and $12,800, respectively. Compute the current ratio, quick ratio, receivable turnover, average days' sales uncollected, and inventory turnover for each year. (Round computations to one decimal point.) Comment on the change in the company's liquidity position from 19x1 to 19x2.

Exercise 15-7. Turnover Analysis *(L.O. 6)*

McEnroe's Men's Shop has been in business for four years. Because the company has recently had a cash flow problem, management wonders whether there is a problem with receivables or inventories. Here are selected figures from the company's financial statements (in thousands):

	19x4	19x3	19x2	19x1
Net Sales	$144	$112	$96	$80
Cost of Goods Sold	90	72	60	48
Accounts Receivable (net)	24	20	16	12
Merchandise Inventory	28	22	16	10

Compute receivable turnover and inventory turnover for each of the four years, and comment on the results relative to the cash flow problem that McEnroe's Men's Shop has been experiencing. Round computations to one decimal point.

Exercise 15-8. Profitability Analysis *(L.O. 6)*

At year end, Bodes Company had total assets of $320,000 in 19x0, $340,000 in 19x1, and $380,000 in 19x2. Its debt to equity ratio was .67 in all three years. In 19x1, the company made a net income of $38,556 on revenues of $612,000. In 19x2, the company made a net income of $49,476 on revenues of $798,000. Compute the profit margin, asset turnover, return on assets, and return on equity for 19x1 and 19x2. Comment on the apparent cause of the increase or decrease in profitability. (Round the percentages and other ratios to one decimal point.)

Exercise 15-9. Long-Term Solvency and Market Test Ratios *(L.O. 6)*

An investor is considering investing in the long-term bonds and common stock of Companies B and C. Both companies operate in the same industry, but Company B has a beta of 1.0 and Company C has a beta of 1.2. In addition, both companies pay a dividend per share of $2, and have a yield of 10 percent on their long-term bonds. Other data for the two companies follow.

	Company B	Company C
Total Assets	$1,200,000	$540,000
Total Liabilities	540,000	297,000
Net Income Before Taxes	144,000	64,800
Interest Expense	48,600	26,730
Earnings per Share	1.60	2.50
Market Price of Common Stock	20	23.75

Compute the debt to equity, interest coverage, price/earnings (P/E), and dividends yield ratios, and comment on the results. (Round computations to one decimal point.)

Exercise 15-10. Preparation of Statements from Ratios and Incomplete Data *(L.O. 6)*

Following are the income statement and balance sheet of Chang Corporation, with most of the amounts missing.

Chang Corporation
Income Statement
For the Year Ended December 31, 19x1
(in thousands of dollars)

Sales		$9,000
Cost of Goods Sold		?
Gross Margin from Sales		?
Operating Expenses		
Selling Expenses	$?	
Administrative Expenses	117	
Interest Expense	81	
Income Taxes Expense	310	
Total Operating Expenses		?
Net Income		$?

Chang Corporation
Balance Sheet
December 31, 19x1
(in thousands of dollars)

Assets

Cash	$?	
Accounts Receivable (net)	?	
Inventories	?	
Total Current Assets		$?
Property, Plant, and Equipment (net)		2,700
Total Assets		$?

Liabilities and Stockholders' Equity

Current Liabilities	$?	
Bond Payable, 9% interest	?	
Total Liabilities		$?
Common Stock—$10 par value	$1,500	
Paid-in Capital in Excess of Par Value, Common	1,300	
Retained Earnings	2,000	
Total Stockholders' Equity		4,800
Total Liabilities and Stockholders' Equity		$?

Chang's only interest expense is on long-term debt. Its debt to equity ratio is .5, its current ratio 3:1, its quick ratio 2:1, the receivable turnover 4.5, and its inventory turnover 4.0. The return on assets is 10 percent. All ratios are based on the current year's information. Complete the financial statements using the information presented. Show supporting computations.

Interpretation Cases from Business

ICB 15-1. The Walt Disney Company *(L.O. 4)*

The Walt Disney Company is, of course, a famous entertainment company that produces films and operates theme parks, among other things. The company is also well known as a profitable and well-managed business. On November 15, 1984, the *Wall Street Journal* ran the following article by Michael Cieply, under the title "Disney Reports Fiscal 4th-Period Loss After Taking $166 Million Write-Down."

> Walt Disney Productions reported a $64 million net loss for its fiscal fourth quarter ended Sept. 30, after writing down a record $166 million in movies and other properties.
>
> In the year-earlier quarter, Disney had net income of $24.5 million, or 70 cents a share. Fourth-quarter revenue this year rose 28% to $463.2 million from $363 million.
>
> In the fiscal year, the entertainment company's earnings rose 5% to $97.8 million, or $2.73 a share, from $93.2 million, or $2.70 a share, a year earlier. Revenue rose 27% to $1.66 billion from $1.31 billion.
>
> The company said it wrote down $112 million in motion picture and television properties. The write-down involves productions that already have been released as well as ones still under development, but Disney declined to identify the productions or projects involved.
>
> "This just reflects the judgment of new management about the ultimate value of projects we had under way," said Michael Bagnall, Disney's executive vice president for finance. . . ."
>
> The company also said it charged off $40 million to reflect the "abandonment" of a number of planned projects at its various theme parks. An additional $14 million was charged off as a reserve to cover possible legal obligations resulting from the company's fight to ward off a pair of successive takeover attempts last summer, Mr. Bagnall said.
>
> Disney said its full-year net included a $76 million gain from a change in its method of accounting for investment tax credits. The change was made retroactive to the fiscal first quarter ended Dec. 31, and will boost that quarter's reported net to $85 million, from $9 million.
>
> Mr. Bagnall said the $76 million credit stemmed largely from construction of Disney's Epcot Center theme park in Florida. By switching to flow-through from deferral accounting, the company was able to take the entire credit immediately instead of amortizing it over 18 years, as originally planned, Mr. Bagnall said. Flow-through accounting is usual in the entertainment industry.[15]

Required

1. What two categories of issues does the user of financial statements want to consider when evaluating the quality of a company's reported earnings? Does Disney have one or both types of items in fiscal 1984?

15. "Disney Reports Fiscal 4th-Period Loss After Taking $166 Million Write-Down," *The Wall Street Journal*, November 15, 1984. Reprinted by permission of *The Wall Street Journal*,

2. Compare the fourth-period earnings or losses for 1983 and 1984 and full fiscal 1983 and 1984 earnings or losses before and after adjusting for the item or items described in **1**. Which comparisons do you believe give the best picture of Disney's performance?

ICB 15-2. Ford Motor Company I[16] *(L.O. 6)*

Standard & Poor's Corporation (S & P) offers a wide range of financial information services to investors. One of its services is rating the quality of the bond issues of U.S. corporations. Its top bond rating is AAA, followed by AA, A, BBB, BB, B, and so forth. The lowest rating, C, is reserved for companies that are in or near bankruptcy. *Business Week* reported on February 2, 1981, that S & P had downgraded the bond rating for Ford Motor Company, a leading U.S. automobile maker, from AAA to AA. The cause of the downgrading was a deterioration of Ford's financial strength as indicated by certain ratios considered important by S & P. The ratios, S & P's guidelines, and Ford's performance are summarized in the following table.

Ratio	S & P Guidelines for AAA Rating	Ford's Performance 1980	1979	1978
Interest Coverage	15 times	Loss	6.5 times	15.3 times
Pretax Return on Assets	15% to 20%	Loss	6.6%	13.4%
Debt to Equity	50%	63.4%	37.8%	34%
Cash Flow as a Percentage of Total Debt*	100%	91%	118.5%	152.6%
Short-Term Debt as a Percentage of Total Debt	25%	52.5%	48.3%	43.1%

* Cash flow includes net income plus noncash charges to earnings

Required

1. Identify the objective (profitability, liquidity, long-term solvency) measured by each of the S & P ratios. Why is each ratio important to the rating of Ford's long-term bonds?
2. The *Business Week* article suggested several actions that Ford might take to regain its previous rating. Tell which of the ratios each of the following actions would improve: (a) "cutting operating costs"; (b) "scrapping at least part of its massive spending plans over the next several years"; (c) "eliminate cash dividends to stockholders"; (d) "sale of profitable nonautomobile-related operations such as its steelmaker, aerospace company, and electronic concerns."

ICB 15-3. Ford Motor Company II[17] *(L.O. 6)*

Part A: By 1983, S & P had dropped the rating on Ford's bond issues to BBB. Selected data for the years ended December 31, 1982 and 1983, from Ford Motor Company's 1983 annual report, follow (in millions):

16. Excerpts from the 1978, 1979, and 1980 annual reports used by permission of Ford Motor Company. Copyright © 1978, 1979, and 1980.
17. Excerpts from the 1983 and 1986 annual reports used by permission of Ford Motor Company. Copyright © 1983, 1986, and 1989.

	1983	1982
Balance Sheet Data		
Short-Term Debt	$10,315.9	$10,424.0
Long-Term Debt	2,712.9	2,353.3
Stockholders' Equity	7,545.3	6,077.5
Total Assets	23,868.9	21,961.7
Income Statement Data		
Income (Loss) Before Income Taxes	2,166.3	(407.9)
Interest Expense	567.2	745.5
Statement of Changes in Financial Position		
Funds (Cash Basis) Provided by Operations	5,001.5	2,632.0

Required

1. Compute for 1982 and 1983 the same ratios that were used by S & P in Ford Motor Company I.
2. If you were S & P, would you raise the rating on Ford's long-term bonds in 1984? Why or why not?

Part B: By the end of 1986, Ford's financial situation had improved enough to warrant an A rating from Standard & Poor's. Then, in 1990, as discussed in the decision point at the beginning of this chapter, Ford's rating was lowered by Moody's, another bond rating company. Selected data for the years ended December 31, 1986 and 1989, from Ford Motor Company's 1986 and 1989 annual reports follow (in millions):

	1989	1986
Balance Sheet Data		
Short-Term Debt	$20,180.6	$15,625.6
Long-Term Debt	1,137.0	2,137.1
Stockholders' Equity	22,727.8	14,859.5
Total Assets	45,819.2	37,993.0
Income Statement Data		
Income (Loss) Before Income Taxes	6,029.6	5,552.2
Interest Expense	321.1	482.9
Statement of Cash Flows		
Net Cash Flows from Operating Activities	5,623.6	7,624.4

Total assets were $31,603.6 million in 1985 and $43,127.7 million in 1988.

Required

1. Compute for 1986 and 1989 the same ratios that were used by Standard & Poor's in Ford Motor Company I.
2. Do you agree that Ford's performance had improved enough by 1986 (see Part A) to warrant an increase to an A rating?
3. Do the 1989 figures warrant a reduction in the bond rating? If not, how do you explain the downgrade described in the decision point at the beginning of the chapter?

Problem Set A

Problem 15A-1. Effect of Alternative Accounting Methods
(L.O. 4, 6)

Sarrafi Company began operations by purchasing $300,000 in equipment that had an estimated useful life of nine years and an estimated residual value of $30,000.

During the year, Sarrafi Company purchased inventory as presented in the chart below:

January	2,000 units at $25	$ 50,000
March	4,000 units at $24	96,000
May	1,000 units at $27	27,000
July	5,000 units at $27	135,000
September	6,000 units at $28	168,000
November	2,000 units at $29	58,000
December	3,000 units at $28	84,000
Total	23,000 units	$618,000

During the year the company sold 19,000 units for a total of $910,000 and incurred salary expenses of $170,000 and expenses other than depreciation of $120,000.

Sarrafi's management is anxious to present its income statement fairly in its first year of operation. It realizes that alternative accounting methods are available for accounting for inventory and equipment. Management wants to determine the effect of various alternatives on this year's income. Two sets of alternatives are required.

Required

1. Prepare two income statements for Sarrafi Company, one using a FIFO basis for inventory and the straight-line method for depreciation, and the other using a LIFO basis for inventory and the sum-of-the-years'-digits method for depreciation.
2. Prepare a schedule accounting for the difference in the two net income figures obtained in **1**.
3. What effect does the choice of accounting methods have on Sarrafi's inventory turnover? What conclusion can you draw?
4. What effect does the choice of accounting methods have on Sarrafi's return on assets?

Use year-end balances to compute ratios. Round all ratios and percentages to one decimal point. Assume that the only other asset in addition to plant assets and inventory is $30,000 cash. Is your evaluation of Sarrafi's profitability affected by the choice of accounting methods?

Problem 15A-2. Horizontal and Vertical Analysis *(L.O. 5)*

The condensed comparative balance sheets and income statements for Kelso Corporation are on page 796.

Required

(Round all ratios and percentages to one decimal point.)

1. Prepare a schedule showing the amount and percentage changes from 19x1 to 19x2 for the comparative income statements and the balance sheets.
2. Prepare common-size income statements and balance sheets for 19x1 and 19x2.
3. Comment on the results of **1** and **2** by identifying favorable and unfavorable changes in the components and composition of the statements.

Kelso Corporation
Comparative Balance Sheets
December 31, 19x2 and 19x1

	19x2	19x1
Assets		
Cash	$ 31,100	$ 27,200
Accounts Receivable (net)	72,500	42,700
Inventory	122,600	107,800
Property, Plant, and Equipment (net)	577,700	507,500
Total Assets	$803,900	$685,200
Liabilities and Stockholders' Equity		
Accounts Payable	$104,700	$ 72,300
Notes Payable	50,000	50,000
Bonds Payable	200,000	110,000
Common Stock—$10 par value	300,000	300,000
Retained Earnings	149,200	152,900
Total Liabilities and Stockholders' Equity	$803,900	$685,200

Kelso Corporation
Comparative Income Statements
For the Years Ended December 31, 19x2 and 19x1

	19x2	19x1
Sales	$800,400	$742,600
Cost of Goods Sold	454,100	396,200
Gross Margin from Sales	$346,300	$346,400
Operating Expenses		
Selling Expenses	$130,100	$104,600
Administrative Expenses	140,300	115,500
Interest Expense	25,000	20,000
Income Taxes Expense	14,000	35,000
Total Operating Expenses	$309,400	$275,100
Net Income	$ 36,900	$ 71,300

Problem 15A-3. Analyzing the Effects of Transactions on Ratios *(L.O. 6)*

Estevez Corporation engaged in the transactions listed in the first column of the following table. Opposite each transaction is a ratio and space to mark the effect of each transaction on the ratio.

Transaction	Ratio	Effect		
		Increase	Decrease	None
a. Issued common stock for cash.	Asset turnover			
b. Declared cash dividend.	Current ratio			
c. Sold treasury stock.	Return on equity			
d. Borrowed cash by issuing note payable.	Debt to equity ratio			
e. Paid salary expense.	Inventory turnover			
f. Purchased merchandise for cash.	Current ratio			
g. Sold equipment for cash.	Receivable turnover			
h. Sold merchandise on account.	Quick ratio			
i. Paid current portion of long-term debt.	Return on assets			
j. Gave sales discount.	Profit margin			
k. Purchased marketable securities for cash.	Quick ratio			
l. Declared 5% stock dividend.	Current ratio			

Required

Place an X in the appropriate column to show whether the transaction increased, decreased, or had no effect on the indicated ratio.

Problem 15A-4. Ratio Analysis *(L.O. 6)*

Additional data for Kelso Corporation in 19x1 and 19x2 follow. These data should be used in conjunction with the data in Problem 15A-2.

	19x2	19x1
Dividends Paid	$31,400	$35,000
Number of Common Shares	30,000	30,000
Market Price per Share	$40	$60
Beta	1.00	.90

Balances of selected accounts at the end of 19x0 were Accounts Receivable (net), $52,700; Inventory, $99,400; Total Assets, $647,800; and Stockholders' Equity, $376,600. All of Kelso's notes payable were current liabilities; all of the bonds payable were long-term liabilities.

Required

Note: Round all answers except earnings per share to one decimal point, and consider changes of .1 or less to be indeterminate.

1. Prepare a liquidity analysis by calculating for each year the: (a) current ratio, (b) quick ratio, (c) receivable turnover, (d) average days' sales uncollected, and (e) inventory turnover. Indicate whether each ratio improved or deteriorated from 19x1 to 19x2 by adding an F for favorable or a U for unfavorable.
2. Prepare a profitability analysis by calculating for each year the: (a) profit margin, (b) asset turnover, (c) return on assets, (d) return on equity, and (e) earnings per share. Indicate whether each ratio had a favorable (F) or unfavorable (U) change from 19x1 to 19x2.
3. Prepare a long-term solvency analysis by calculating for each year the: (a) debt to equity ratio and (b) interest coverage ratio. Indicate whether each ratio had a favorable (F) or unfavorable (U) change from 19x1 to 19x2.
4. Conduct a market test analysis by calculating for each year the: (a) price/earnings ratio, (b) dividends yield, and (c) market risk. Note the market risk measure, and indicate whether each ratio had a favorable (F) or unfavorable (U) change from 19x1 to 19x2.

Problem 15A-5. Comprehensive Ratio Analysis of Two Companies *(L.O. 6)*

Louise Brown has decided to invest some of her savings in common stock. She feels that the chemical industry has good growth prospects, and has narrowed her choice to two companies in that industry. As a final step in making the choice, she has decided to make a comprehensive ratio analysis of the two companies, Morton and Pound. Balance sheet and income statement data for the two companies appear below and at the top of the next page.

	Morton	Pound
Assets		
Cash	$ 126,100	$ 514,300
Marketable Securities (at cost)	117,500	1,200,000
Accounts Receivable (net)	456,700	2,600,000
Inventories	1,880,000	4,956,000
Prepaid Expenses	72,600	156,600
Property, Plant, and Equipment (net)	5,342,200	19,356,000
Intangibles and Other Assets	217,000	580,000
Total Assets	$8,212,100	$29,362,900
Liabilities and Stockholders' Equity		
Accounts Payable	$ 517,400	$ 2,342,000
Notes Payable	1,000,000	2,000,000
Income Taxes Payable	85,200	117,900
Bonds Payable	2,000,000	15,000,000
Common Stock—$1 par value	350,000	1,000,000
Paid-in Capital in Excess of Par Value, Common	1,747,300	5,433,300
Retained Earnings	2,512,200	3,469,700
Total Liabilities and Stockholders' Equity	$8,212,100	$29,362,900

	Morton	Pound
Sales	$9,486,200	$27,287,300
Cost of Goods Sold	5,812,200	18,372,400
Gross Margin from Sales	$3,674,000	$ 8,914,900
Operating Expenses		
Selling Expense	$1,194,000	$ 1,955,700
Administrative Expense	1,217,400	4,126,000
Interest Expense	270,000	1,360,000
Income Taxes Expense	450,000	600,000
Total Operating Expenses	$3,131,400	$ 8,041,700
Net Income	$ 542,600	$ 873,200

During the year, Morton paid a total of $140,000 in dividends, and its current market price per share is $20. Pound paid a total of $600,000 in dividends during the year, and the current market price per share is $9. An investment service reports that the beta associated with Morton's stock is 1.05, while that associated with Pound's is .8. Information pertaining to prior years is not readily available. Assume that all notes payable are current liabilities and that all bonds payable are long-term liabilities.

Required

Conduct a comprehensive ratio analysis of Morton and of Pound using the current end-of-year data. Compare the results. (Round all ratios and percentages except earnings per share to one decimal point.) This analysis should be done in the following steps:

1. Prepare an analysis of liquidity by calculating for each company the: (a) current ratio, (b) quick ratio, (c) receivable turnover, (d) average days' sales uncollected, and (e) inventory turnover.
2. Prepare an analysis of profitability by calculating for each company the: (a) profit margin, (b) asset turnover, (c) return on assets, (d) return on equity, and (e) earnings per share.
3. Prepare an analysis of long-term solvency by calculating for each company the: (a) debt to equity ratio and (b) interest coverage ratio.
4. Prepare an analysis of market tests by calculating for each company the: (a) price/earnings ratio, (b) dividends yield, and (c) market risk.
5. Compare the two companies by inserting the ratio calculations from **1** through **4** in a table with the following column heads: Ratio Name, Morton, Pound, and Company with More Favorable Ratio. Indicate in the right-hand column of the table which company had the more favorable ratio in each case.
6. How could the analysis be improved if prior years' information were available?

Problem Set B

Problem 15B-1. Effect of Alternative Accounting Methods
(L.O. 4, 6)

Jewell Company began operations this year. At the beginning of the year the company purchased plant assets of $385,000, with an estimated useful life of ten years and no salvage value. During the year, the company had sales of $650,000, salary expense of $100,000, and other expenses of $40,000, excluding depreciation. In addition, Jewell Company purchased inventory as follows:

January 15	400 units at $200	$ 80,000
March 20	200 units at $204	40,800
June 15	800 units at $208	166,400
September 18	600 units at $206	123,600
December 9	300 units at $210	63,000
Total	2,300 units	$473,800

At the end of the year, a physical inventory disclosed 500 units still on hand. The managers of Jewell Company know they have a choice of accounting methods, but are unsure how they will affect net income. They have heard of the FIFO and LIFO inventory methods and the straight-line and sum-of-the-years'-digits depreciation methods.

Required

1. Prepare two income statements for Jewell Company, one using a FIFO basis and the straight-line method, the other using a LIFO basis and the sum-of-the-years'-digits method.
2. Prepare a schedule accounting for the difference in the two net income figures obtained in **1**.
3. What effect does the choice of accounting method have on Jewell's inventory turnover? What conclusions can you draw?
4. What effect does the choice of accounting method have on Jewell's return on assets?

Use year-end balances to compute ratios. Assume that the only other asset in addition to plant assets and inventory is $40,000 cash. Is your evaluation of Jewell's profitability affected by the choice of accounting methods?

Problem 15B-2. Horizontal and Vertical Analysis
(L.O. 5)

The condensed comparative balance sheets and income statements of Jensen Corporation are presented on the next page. All figures are given in thousands of dollars.

Required

(Round percentages to one decimal point.)

1. Prepare schedules showing the amount and percentage changes from 19x1 to 19x2 for Jensen's income statements and balance sheets.
2. Prepare common-size income statements and balance sheets for 19x1 and 19x2.
3. Comment on the results in **1** and **2** by identifying favorable and unfavorable changes in the components and composition of the statements.

Jensen Corporation
Comparative Balance Sheets
December 31, 19x2 and 19x1

	19x2	19x1
Assets		
Cash	$ 40,600	$ 20,400
Accounts Receivable (net)	117,800	114,600
Inventory	287,400	297,400
Property, Plant, and Equipment (net)	375,000	360,000
Total Assets	$820,800	$792,400
Liabilities and Stockholders' Equity		
Accounts Payable	$133,800	$238,600
Notes Payable	100,000	200,000
Bonds Payable	200,000	—
Common Stock—$5 par value	200,000	200,000
Retained Earnings	187,000	153,800
Total Liabilities and Stockholders' Equity	$820,800	$792,400

Jensen Corporation
Comparative Income Statements
For the Years Ended December 31, 19x2 and 19x1

	19x2	19x1
Sales	$1,638,400	$1,573,200
Cost of Goods Sold	1,044,400	1,004,200
Gross Margin on Sales	$ 594,000	$ 569,000
Operating Expenses		
Selling Expenses	$ 238,400	$ 259,000
Administrative Expenses	223,600	211,600
Interest Expense	32,800	19,600
Income Taxes Expense	31,200	28,400
Total Operating Expenses	$ 526,000	$ 518,600
Net Income	$ 68,000	$ 50,400

Problem 15B-3. Analyzing the Effects of Transactions on Ratios *(L.O. 6)*

Rader Corporation engaged in the transactions listed in the first column of the following table. Opposite each transaction is a ratio and space to indicate the effect of each transaction on the ratio.

Transaction	Ratio	Effect		
		Increase	Decrease	None
a. Sold merchandise on account.	Current ratio			
b. Sold merchandise on account.	Inventory turnover			
c. Collected on accounts receivable.	Quick ratio			
d. Wrote off an uncollectible account.	Receivable turnover			
e. Paid on accounts payable.	Current ratio			
f. Declared cash dividend.	Return on equity			
g. Incurred advertising expense.	Profit margin			
h. Issued stock dividend.	Debt to equity ratio			
i. Issued bond payable.	Asset turnover			
j. Accrued interest expense.	Current ratio			
k. Paid previously declared cash dividend.	Dividends yield			
l. Purchased treasury stock.	Return on assets			

Required

Place an X in the appropriate column to show whether the transaction increased, decreased, or had no effect on the indicated ratio.

Problem 15B-4. Ratio Analysis *(L.O. 6)*

Additional data for Jensen Corporation in 19x1 and 19x2 follow. This information should be used together with the data in Problem 15B-2 to answer the requirements below.

	19x2	19x1
Dividends Paid	\$22,000,000	\$17,200,000
Number of Common Shares	40,000,000	40,000,000
Market Price per Share	\$9	\$15
Beta	1.40	1.25

Balances of selected accounts (in thousands) at the end of 19x0 were Accounts Receivable (net), \$103,400; Inventory, \$273,600; Total Assets, \$732,800; and Stockholders' Equity, \$320,600. All of Jensen's notes payable were current liabilities; all of the bonds payable were long-term liabilities.

Required

(Round percentages and ratios except earnings per share to one decimal point, and consider changes of .1 or less to be indeterminate.)

1. Conduct a liquidity analysis by calculating for each year the: (a) current ratio, (b) quick ratio, (c) receivable turnover, (d) average days' sales uncollected, and (e) inventory turnover. Indicate whether each ratio had a favorable (F) or unfavorable (U) change from 19x1 to 19x2.
2. Conduct a profitability analysis by calculating for each year the: (a) profit margin, (b) asset turnover, (c) return on assets, (d) return on equity, and (e) earnings per share. Indicate whether each ratio had a favorable (F) or unfavorable (U) change from 19x1 to 19x2.
3. Conduct a long-term solvency analysis by calculating for each year the: (a) debt to equity ratio and (b) interest coverage ratio. Indicate whether each ratio had a favorable (F) or unfavorable (U) change from 19x1 to 19x2.
4. Conduct a market test analysis by calculating for each year the: (a) price/earnings ratio, (b) dividends yield, and (c) market risk. Note the market beta measures, and indicate whether each ratio had a favorable (F) or unfavorable (U) change from 19x1 to 19x2.

Problem 15B-5. Comprehensive Ratio Analysis of Two Companies *(L.O. 6)*

Charles Tseng is considering an investment in the common stock of a chain of retail department stores. He has narrowed his choice to two retail companies, Kemp Corporation and Russo Corporation, whose balance sheets and income statements follow.

	Kemp Corporation	Russo Corporation
Assets		
Cash	$ 80,000	$ 192,400
Marketable Securities (at cost)	203,400	84,600
Accounts Receivable (net)	552,800	985,400
Inventory	629,800	1,253,400
Prepaid Expenses	54,400	114,000
Property, Plant, and Equipment (net)	2,913,600	6,552,000
Intangibles and Other Assets	553,200	144,800
Total Assets	$4,987,200	$9,326,600
Liabilities and Stockholders' Equity		
Accounts Payable	$ 344,000	$ 572,600
Notes Payable	150,000	400,000
Accrued Liabilities	50,200	73,400
Bonds Payable	2,000,000	2,000,000
Common Stock—$10 par value	1,000,000	600,000
Paid-in Capital in Excess of Par Value, Common	609,800	3,568,600
Retained Earnings	833,200	2,112,000
Total Liabilities and Stockholders' Equity	$4,987,200	$9,326,600

	Kemp Corporation	Russo Corporation
Sales	$12,560,000	$25,210,000
Cost of Goods Sold	6,142,000	14,834,000
Gross Margin from Sales	$ 6,418,000	$10,376,000
Operating Expenses		
Sales Expense	$ 4,822,600	$ 7,108,200
Administrative Expense	986,000	2,434,000
Interest Expense	194,000	228,000
Income Taxes Expense	200,000	300,000
Total Operating Expenses	$ 6,202,600	$10,070,200
Net Income	$ 215,400	$ 305,800

During the year, Kemp Corporation paid a total of $50,000 in dividends. The market price per share of its stock is currently $30. In comparison, Russo Corporation paid a total of $114,000 in dividends, and the current market price of its stock is $38 per share. An investment service has indicated that the beta associated with Kemp's stock is 1.20, while that associated with Russo's stock is .95. Information for prior years is not readily available. Assume that all notes payable are current liabilities and all bonds payable are long-term liabilities.

Required

Conduct a comprehensive ratio analysis for each company using the available information and compare the results. (Round percentages and ratios except earnings per share to one decimal point, and consider changes of .1 or less to be indeterminate.) This analysis should be done in the following steps:

1. Prepare an analysis of liquidity by calculating for each company the: (a) current ratio, (b) quick ratio, (c) receivable turnover, (d) average days' sales uncollected, and (e) inventory turnover.
2. Prepare an analysis of profitability by calculating for each company the: (a) profit margin, (b) asset turnover, (c) return on assets, (d) return on equity, and (e) earnings per share.
3. Prepare an analysis of long-term solvency by calculating for each company the: (a) debt to equity ratio and (b) interest coverage ratio.
4. Prepare an analysis of market tests by calculating for each company the: (a) price/earnings ratio, (b) dividends yield, and (c) market risk.
5. Compare the two companies by inserting the ratio calculations from **1** through **4** in a table with the following column heads: Ratio Name, Kemp Corporation, Russo Corporation, and Company with More Favorable Ratio. Indicate in the right-hand column which company had the more favorable ratio in each case.
6. In what ways could the analysis be improved if prior years' information were available?

Financial Decision Cases

15-1. Tedtronics Corporation *(L.O. 4)*

Ted Lazzerini retired at the beginning of 19x1 as president and principal stockholder in Tedtronics Corporation, a successful producer of word-processing equipment. As an incentive to the new management, Ted supported the board of directors' new executive compensation plan, which provides cash bonuses to key executives for years in which the company's earnings per share equal or exceed the current dividends per share of $2.00, plus a $.20 per share increase in dividends in each future year. Thus for management to receive the bonuses, the company must earn per share income of $2.00 the first year, $2.20 the second, $2.40 the third, and so forth. Since Ted owns 500,000 of the one million common shares outstanding, the dividend income will provide for his retirement years. He is also protected against inflation by the regular increase in dividends. Earnings and dividends per share for the first three years of operation under the new management were as follows:

	19x3	19x2	19x1
Earnings per share	$2.50	$2.50	$2.50
Dividends per share	2.40	2.20	2.00

During this time management earned bonuses totaling more than $1 million under the compensation plan. Ted, who had taken no active part on the board of directors, began to worry about the unchanging level of earnings and decided to study the company's annual report more carefully. The notes to the annual report revealed the following information:

a. Management changed from the LIFO inventory method to the FIFO method in 19x1. The effect of the change was to decrease cost of goods sold by $200,000 in 19x1, $300,000 in 19x2, and $400,000 in 19x3.
b. Management changed from the double-declining-balance accelerated depreciation method to the straight-line method in 19x2. The effect of this change was to decrease depreciation by $400,000 in 19x2 and by $500,000 in 19x3.
c. In 19x3, management increased the estimated useful life of intangible assets from five to ten years. The effect of this change was to decrease amortization expense by $100,000 in 19x3.

Required

1. Compute earnings per share for each year according to the accounting methods in use at the beginning of 19x1.
2. Have the executives earned their bonuses? What serious effect has the compensation package apparently had on the net assets of Tedtronics? How could Ted have protected himself from what has happened?

15-2. Great Lakes Seafood Restaurant, Inc. *(L.O. 2, 5)*

Sam Slaski is the owner of Great Lakes Seafood Restaurant, Inc., which operates a 100-seat seafood restaurant in a suburb of a large midwestern city. Teresa Kelly, Sam's CPA, is going over the recently prepared income statement for last year with Sam.

Sam is disturbed to see that the restaurant had a net loss for the year. "I honestly don't know what to do," Sam comments. "I think I run an efficient

Income Statements
For the Year Ended December 31, 19x7

	Great Lakes Seafood Restaurant, Inc.		Profitable Restaurants in the U.S.— Average Dollars per Seat	
Sales				
Food		$272,100		$3,935
Beverage		98,400		1,457
Total Sales		$370,500		$5,392
Cost of Goods Sold				
Food	$112,400		$1,608	
Beverage	29,300		377	
Total Cost of Goods Sold		141,700		1,985
Gross Margin from Sales		$228,800		$3,407
Operating Expenses				
Wages and Salaries Expense	$116,500		$1,410	
Employee Benefits Expense	19,900		237	
Direct Operating Expense	30,700		290	
Music and Entertainment Expense	3,800		40	
Advertising and Promotion Expense	8,300		97	
Utility Expense	11,900		128	
Administrative and General Expense	22,800		278	
Repairs and Maintenance Expense	6,200		89	
Rent, Property Taxes, and Insurance Expense	22,800		249	
Depreciation Expense	12,900		117	
Interest Expense	5,100		53	
Total Operating Expenses		260,900		2,988
Net Income (Loss) Before Other Items		$ (32,100)		$ 419
Other Income and Expenses				
Other Income	$ 2,400		$ 43	
Less Other Expenses	1,200		16	
Net Other Income		1,200		27
Net Income (Loss) Before Taxes		$ (30,900)		$ 446

operation, and people say I have a good restaurant. Do you think I should try to cut costs or try to get more business?" Teresa replies, "Maybe it would be helpful to compare your restaurant with other successful restaurants. I will try to see if any industry data are available."

One week later Teresa returns with the "Restaurant Industry Operations Report," published by the National Restaurant Association in cooperation with the international accounting firm of Laventhol & Horwath. "Sam, let's see how your restaurant compares. On page 23 is an income statement for restaurants in the United States that showed a profit last year. The amounts are on a per seat basis, so we can make a direct comparison with your restaurant." Data from the national survey (slightly rearranged) are shown in comparative form with Sam's income statement on page 806.

Required

1. Prepare comparative income statements on a per seat basis and common-size income statements for Great Lakes Seafood Restaurant, Inc., and the average profitable restaurant.
2. Identify and comment on the areas where Great Lakes is significantly different from the national average.
3. On the basis of your analysis, what would you say is Great Lakes' major problem? How would the items identified in **2** be affected if this problem were solved?

LEARNING OBJECTIVES

1. *Define* exchange rate and record transactions that are affected by changes in foreign exchange rates.
2. *Describe* the restatement of a foreign subsidiary's financial statements in U.S. dollars.
3. *Describe* progress toward international accounting standards.
4. *Apply* the cost method and the equity method to the appropriate situations in accounting for long-term investments.
5. *Explain* when to prepare consolidated financial statements, and describe their uses.
6. *Prepare* consolidated balance sheets at acquisition date for purchase at (a) book value and (b) other than book value.
7. *Prepare* consolidated income statements for intercompany transactions.

CHAPTER 16

International Accounting and Intercompany Investments

Perhaps nowhere is the complexity and power of the modern corporation better demonstrated than in the expansion of its activities through international trade and through investment in the securities of other corporations. By expanding beyond national boundaries and by exerting influence or control over other corporations through ownership of their stock, corporations have been able to grow to sizes never thought possible. This chapter explores the fundamental accounting impact of these two areas of expansion. After studying this chapter, you should be able to meet the learning objectives on the left.

DECISION POINT

Schneider S.A. and Square D Company (Part 1)[1]

Schneider S.A., a French company, is a $10 billion business whose sales are divided equally between electrical products and construction. On March 4, 1991, Schneider made a hostile takeover offer for Square D Company, a U.S. electrical products company. Schneider offered $78 per share, 55 percent above market price, or a total of $2 billion. Didier Pineau-Valencienne, chairman of Schneider and a tough negotiator, launched the attack after discussions of joint efforts between the two companies were unsuccessful. *Business Week* reports that "The French executive faces an equally

1. Based on information in Stewart Toy, "Schneider: 'Dr. Attila' Has Big Plans," *Business Week* (March 18, 1991), quotation on p. 36; Charles Storch, "Square D Co. Accepts $2.2 Billion for Merger with French Firm," *Chicago Tribune*, May 13, 1991; James P. Miller, "Square D Accepts Sweetened Bid of $2.23 Billion from Schneider," *Wall Street Journal*, May 13, 1991.

tough rival, however, in Square D's dug-in chairman, Jerre L. Stead. Stead blames an artificially cheap dollar for the 'unfair' French raid. Schneider's boss shrugs. 'When the dollar was strong, Americans came over and bought up French paintings,' says Pineau-Valencienne, an art collector. 'Now,' he says, 'it's our turn to buy." What role does a "cheap dollar" play in this takeover battle?

In transactions between U.S. firms or between French firms, the relative values of the currencies of the two countries do not play a part in the negotiations because both parties are dealing in the same currency. However, when companies that operate in different countries engage in transactions, the relative values of the two currencies play an important role in the negotiations. If the U.S. dollar is "cheap" relative to the French franc, French francs will "purchase" more dollars. Although the dollar purchase price of assets in the United States, such as the Square D Company, may be the same as it was before, their purchase costs Schneider less in terms of French francs. Stead considers this situation "unfair" because Schneider is taking advantage of the relatively low value of the dollar to attempt a bargain purchase in the United States. The low value of the U.S. dollar relative to other currencies has been behind many of the purchases of U.S. assets and companies by Japanese, British, German, and French companies over the past few years. The next section will increase your understanding of these international transactions. ■

International Accounting[2]

As businesses grow, they naturally look for new sources of supply and new markets in other countries. Today, it is common for businesses, called **multinational** or **transnational corporations**, to operate in more than one country, and many of them operate throughout the world. Table 16-1 shows the extent of foreign business in a few multinational corporations. IBM, for example, has operations in eighty countries and receives about half its sales and income from outside the United States. Unilever, the giant British/Dutch company, operates around the world and receives 75 percent of its revenues from outside its home countries. Together, the economies of such industrial countries as the United States, Japan, Great Britain, Germany, and France have given rise to numerous worldwide corporations. More than five hundred companies are listed on at least one stock exchange outside their home country.

In addition, sophisticated investors no longer restrict their investment activities to domestic securities markets. Many Americans invest in foreign securities markets, and non-Americans invest heavily in the stock

2. At the time this chapter was written, exchange rates were fluctuating rapidly. Thus, the examples, exercises, and problems in this book use exchange rates in the general range for the countries involved.

market in the United States. Figure 16-1 shows that from 1980 until 1989, the total value of securities traded on the world's stock markets has grown almost ten times, while the United States's share of the pie has declined from 58 to 29 percent.

Foreign business transactions have two major effects on accounting. First, most sales or purchases of goods and services in other countries involve different currencies. Thus, one currency needs to be translated into another, using exchange rates. An **exchange rate** is the value of one currency in terms of another. For example, a German person purchasing goods from a U.S. company and paying in U.S. dollars must exchange German marks for U.S. dollars before making payment. In effect, currencies are goods that can be bought and sold. Table 16-2 lists the exchange rates of several currencies in terms of dollars. It shows the exchange rate for the German mark as $.60 per mark on a particular date. Like the price of any good or service, these prices change daily according to supply and demand for the currencies. For example, only two months earlier the exchange rate for German marks was $.50, a difference of 20 percent. Accounting for these price changes in recording foreign transactions and preparing financial statements for foreign subsidiaries is the subject of the next two sections.

The second major effect of international business on accounting is that financial standards differ from country to country, which hampers comparisons among companies from different countries. Some of the obstacles to achieving comparability and some of the progress in solving the problem are discussed later in this chapter.

Table 16-1. Extent of Foreign Business for Selected Companies

Company	Home Country	1989 Total Sales (Billions)	Sales outside home country	Assets outside home country	Shares held outside home country
Michelin	France	9.4	78.0	NA	0.0
Hoechst	W. Germany	27.3	77.0	NA	42.0
Unilever	Britain/Neth.	35.3	75.0*	70.0*	27.0
Air Liquide	France	5.0	70.0	66.0	6.0
Canon	Japan	9.4	69.0	32.0	14.0
Northern Telecom	Canada	6.1	67.1	70.5	16.0
Sony	Japan	16.3	66.0	NA	13.6
Bayer	W. Germany	25.8	65.4	NA	48.0
BASF	W. Germany	13.3	65.0	NA	NA
Gillette	U.S.	3.8	65.0	63.0	10.0*
Colgate	U.S.	5.0	64.0	47.0	10.0*
Honda	Japan	26.4	63.0	35.7	6.9
Daimler Benz	W. Germany	45.5	61.0	NA	25.0*
IBM	U.S.	62.7	59.0	NA	NA

**Business Week* estimates.

Source: "The Stateless Corporation" © 1990. Reprinted by special permission of *Business Week*.

Figure 16-1. Value of Securities Traded on the World's Stock Markets

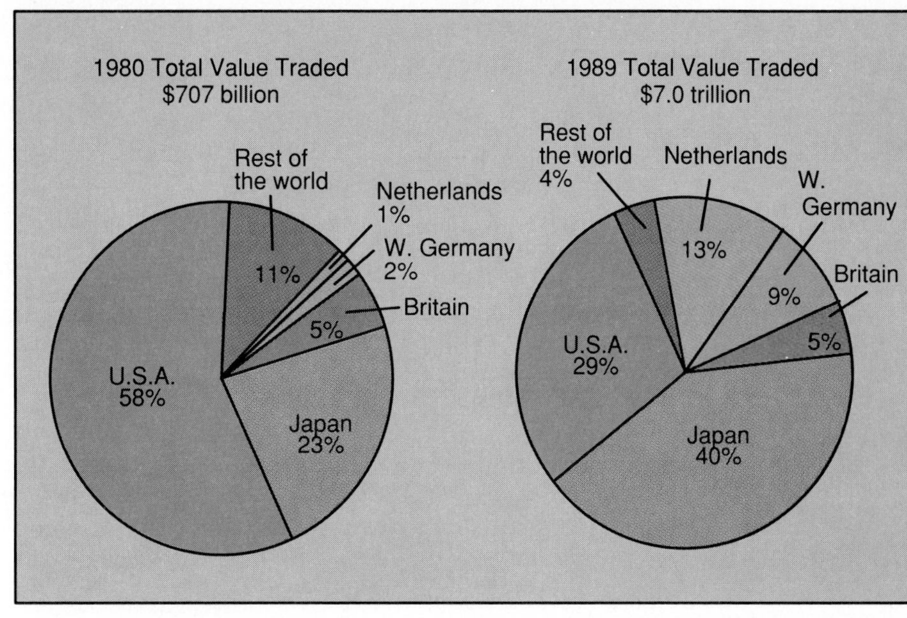

Source: From *Emerging Markets Factbook* (Washington, D.C.: International Finance Corporation, 1990). Reprinted by permission.

Accounting for Transactions in Foreign Currencies

OBJECTIVE 1
Define exchange rate *and record transactions that are affected by changes in foreign exchange rates*

Among the first activities of an expanding company in the international market are the buying and selling of goods and services. For example, a maker of precision tools may try to expand by selling its product to foreign customers. Or it might try to lower its product cost by buying a less expensive part from a source in another country. In previous chapters, all transactions were recorded in dollars, and it was assumed that the dollar is a uniform measure in the same way that inches and centimeters are. But in the international marketplace, a transaction may take place in Japanese yen, British pounds, or some other currency. The values of these currencies rise and fall daily in relation to the dollar.

Foreign Sales. When a domestic company sells merchandise abroad, it may bill either in its own country's currency or in the foreign currency. If the billing and the subsequent payment are both in the domestic currency, no accounting problem arises. For example, assume that the precision toolmaker sells $170,000 worth of tools to a British company and bills the British company in dollars. The entry to record the sale and payment is familiar:

Date of sale		
Accounts Receivable, British company	170,000	
Sales		170,000
Date of payment		
Cash	170,000	
Accounts Receivable, British company		170,000

Table 16-2. Partial Listing of Foreign Exchange Rates

Country	Prices in $ U.S.	Country	Prices in $ U.S.
Britain (pound)	1.79	Italy (lira)	.0008
Canada (dollar)	.87	Japan (yen)	.0073
France (franc)	.18	Mexico (peso)	.0003
Germany (mark)	.60	Philippines (peso)	.037
Hong Kong (dollar)	.13	Taiwan (dollar)	.037

Source: From "World Markets/Foreign Exchange," *The Wall Street Journal*, April 10, 1991. Reprinted by permission of *The Wall Street Journal*, © 1991 Dow Jones & Company, Inc. All Rights Reserved Worldwide.

However, if the U.S. company bills the British company in British pounds and accepts payment in pounds, the U.S. company may incur an **exchange gain or loss**. A gain or loss will occur if the exchange rate of dollars to pounds changes between the date of sale and the date of payment. Exchange gains or losses are reported on the income statement. For example, assume that the sale of $170,000 above was billed as £100,000, reflecting an exchange rate of 1.70 (that is, $1.70 per pound) on the sale date. Now assume that by the date of payment, the exchange rate has fallen to 1.65. The entries to record the transactions follow:

Date of sale		
Accounts Receivable, British company	170,000	
Sales		170,000
£100,000 × $1.70 = $170,000		
Date of payment		
Cash	165,000	
Exchange Gain or Loss	5,000	
Accounts Receivable, British company		170,000
£100,000 × $1.65 = $165,000		

The U.S. company has incurred an exchange loss of $5,000 because it agreed to accept a fixed number of British pounds in payment, and the value of each pound dropped before the payment was made. Had the value of the pound in relation to the dollar increased, the U.S. company would have made an exchange gain.

Foreign Purchases. Purchases are the opposite of sales. So the same logic applies to them, except that the relationship of exchange gains and losses to changes in exchange rates is reversed. For example, assume that the maker of precision tools purchases $15,000 of a certain part from a Japanese supplier. If the purchase and subsequent payment are made in U.S. dollars, no accounting problem arises.

Date of purchase		
Purchases	15,000	
Accounts Payable, Japanese company		15,000
Date of payment		
Accounts Payable, Japanese company	15,000	
Cash		15,000

However, the Japanese company may bill the U.S. company in yen and be paid in yen. If so, the U.S. company will incur an exchange gain or loss if the exchange rate changes between the dates of purchase and payment. For example, assume that the transaction is for 2,500,000 yen and the exchange rates on the dates of purchase and payment are $.0060 and $.0055 per yen, respectively. The entries follow.

Date of purchase		
Purchases	15,000	
Accounts Payable, Japanese company		15,000
¥2,500,000 × $.0060 = $15,000		
Date of payment		
Accounts Payable, Japanese company	15,000	
Exchange Gain or Loss		1,250
Cash		13,750
¥2,500,000 × $.0055 = $13,750		

In this case the U.S. company received an exchange gain of $1,250 because it agreed to pay a fixed ¥2,500,000, and between the dates of purchase and payment the exchange value of the yen decreased in relation to the dollar.

Realized Versus Unrealized Exchange Gain or Loss. The preceding illustration dealt with completed transactions (in the sense that payment was completed). In each case the exchange gain or loss was recognized on the date of payment. If financial statements are prepared between the sale or purchase and the subsequent receipt or payment, and exchange rates have changed, there will be unrealized gains or losses. The Financial Accounting Standards Board, in its *Statement No. 52,* requires that exchange gains and losses "shall be included in determining net income for the period in which the exchange rate changes."[3] The requirement includes interim (quarterly) statements, and applies whether or not a transaction is complete.

This ruling has caused much debate. Critics charge that it gives too much weight to fleeting changes in exchange rates, causing random changes in earnings that hide long-run trends. Others feel that the use of current exchange rates to value receivables and payables as of the balance sheet date is a major step toward economic reality (current values).

To illustrate, we will use the preceding case, in which a U.S. company buys parts from a Japanese supplier. We will assume that the transaction

3. *Statement of Financial Accounting Standards No. 52,* "Foreign Currency Translation" (Stamford, Conn.: Financial Accounting Standards Board, 1981), par. 15.

has not been completed by the balance sheet date, when the exchange rate is $.0051 per yen:

	Date	Exchange Rate ($ per Yen)
Date of purchase	Dec. 1	.0060
Balance sheet date	Dec. 31	.0051
Date of payment	Feb. 1	.0055

The accounting effects of the unrealized gain are as follows:

	Dec. 1	Dec. 31	Feb. 1
Purchase recorded in U.S. dollars (billed as ¥2,500,000)	$15,000	$15,000	$15,000
Dollars to be paid to equal ¥2,500,000 (¥2,500,000 × exchange rate)	15,000	12,750	13,750
Unrealized gain (or loss)	—	$ 2,250	
Realized gain (or loss)			$ 1,250

Date	Account	Debit	Credit
Dec. 1	Purchases	15,000	
	Accounts Payable, Japanese company		15,000
Dec. 31	Accounts Payable, Japanese company	2,250	
	Exchange Gain or Loss		2,250
Feb. 1	Accounts Payable, Japanese company	12,750	
	Exchange Gain or Loss	1,000	
	Cash		13,750

In this case, the original sale was billed in yen by the Japanese company. Following the rules of *Statement No. 52,* an exchange gain of $2,250 is recorded on December 31, and an exchange loss of $1,000 is recorded on February 1. Even though these large fluctuations do not affect the net exchange gain of $1,250 over the whole transaction, the effect on each year's income statements may be important.

Restatement of Foreign Subsidiary Financial Statements[4]

OBJECTIVE 2 *Describe the restatement of a foreign subsidiary's financial statements in U.S. dollars*

Growing companies often expand by setting up or buying foreign subsidiaries. If a foreign subsidiary is more than 50 percent owned and if the parent company exercises control, then the foreign subsidiary should be included in the consolidated financial statements. The consolidation procedure is the same as that for domestic subsidiaries (discussed later in this chapter), except that the statements of the foreign subsidiary must be re-

4. This section is based on the requirements of *Statement of Financial Accounting Standards No. 52,* "Foreign Currency Translation" (Stamford, Conn.: Financial Accounting Standards Board, 1981).

stated in the reporting currency before consolidation takes place. The **reporting currency** is the currency in which the consolidated financial statements are presented. Clearly, it makes no sense to combine the assets of a Mexican subsidiary stated in pesos with the assets of the U.S. parent company stated in dollars. Most U.S. companies present their financial statements in U.S. dollars, so the following discussion assumes that the U.S. dollar is the reporting currency.

Restatement is the stating of one currency in terms of another. The method of restatement depends on the foreign subsidiary's functional currency. The **functional currency** is the currency of the place where the subsidiary carries on most of its business. Generally, it is the currency in which a company earns and spends its cash. The functional currency to be used depends on the kind of foreign operation in which the subsidiary takes part. There are two broad types of foreign operation. Type I includes those that are fairly self-contained and integrated within a certain country or economy. Type II includes those that are mainly a direct and integral part or extension of the parent company's operations. As a general rule, Type I subsidiaries use the currency of the country in which they are located, and Type II subsidiaries use the currency of the parent company. If the parent company is a U.S. company, the functional currency of a Type I subsidiary will be the currency of the country where the subsidiary carries on its business, and the functional currency of a Type II subsidiary will be the U.S. dollar. *Statement No. 52* makes an exception when a Type I subsidiary operates in a country such as Brazil or Argentina, where there is hyperinflation (as a rule of thumb, more than 100 percent cumulative inflation over three years). In such a case, the subsidiary is treated as a Type II subsidiary, with the functional currency being the U.S. dollar.

The Search for Comparability of International Accounting Standards

OBJECTIVE 3
Describe progress toward international accounting standards

International investors need to compare the financial positions and results of operations of companies from different countries. At present, however, many accounting standards are not recognized worldwide. For example, the LIFO method of valuing inventory is the most popular in the United States, but it is not acceptable in most European countries. Another example is that whereas historical cost is strictly followed in Germany, replacement cost is used to prepare the financial statements of some companies in the Netherlands, and a mixed system, allowing lower of cost or market in some cases, is used in the United States and England. Even the formats of financial statements differ from country to country. In England and France, for example, the balance sheets are presented in almost reverse order to those in the United States. In these countries, property, plant, and equipment is the first asset listed.

A number of major problems stand in the way of setting international standards. One is that accountants and users of accounting have not been able to agree on the goals of financial statements. Some other problems are differences in the way in which the accounting profession has developed in various countries, differences in the laws regulating companies, and differences in government and other requirements. Further difficulties are the failure to deal with differences among countries in the basic economic factors affecting financial reporting, inconsistencies in practices recommended by the accounting profession in different countries, and the influence of tax laws on financial reporting.[5] In the last area, for example, a survey for a major accounting firm found widely differing requirements. In nine countries, strict adherence to tax accounting was required. In eleven countries, adherence to tax accounting was required in some areas. In four countries (including the United States), adherence to tax practice was mostly forbidden.[6]

Some efforts have been made to achieve greater international understanding and uniformity of accounting practice. The Accountants International Study Group, formed in 1966 and consisting of the AICPA and similar bodies in Canada, England and Wales, Ireland, and Scotland, has issued reports that survey and compare accounting practices in the member countries. Probably the best hopes for finding areas of agreement among all the different countries are the International Accounting Standards Committee (IASC) and the International Federation of Accountants (IFAC). The IASC was formed in 1973 as a result of an agreement by accountancy bodies in Australia, Canada, France, Germany, Japan, Mexico, the Netherlands, the United Kingdom and Ireland, and the United States. More than one hundred professional accountancy bodies from over seventy countries now support the IASC.

The role of the IASC is to contribute to the development and adoption of accounting principles that are relevant, balanced, and comparable throughout the world by formulating and publicizing accounting standards and encouraging their observance in the presentation of financial statements.[7] The standards issued by the IASC are generally followed by large multinational companies that are clients of international accounting firms. The IASC has been especially helpful to companies in developing economies that do not have the financial history or resources to develop accounting standards. The IASC is currently engaged in a major project to enhance the comparability of financial statements worldwide by reducing the number of acceptable accounting methods in twelve areas, including inventory and depreciation accounting and accounting for investments and business combinations.

The IFAC, which was formed in 1977 and also consists of most of the world's accountancy organizations, fully supports the work of the IASC and recognizes the IASC as the sole body having responsibility and authority to issue pronouncements on international accounting standards. The IFAC's objective is to develop international guidelines for auditing,

5. *Accounting Standards for Business Enterprises Throughout the World* (Chicago: Arthur Andersen, 1974), pp. 2–3.
6. *Accounting Principles and Reporting Practices: A Survey in 38 Countries* (New York: Price Waterhouse International, 1973), sec. 233.
7. "International Accounting Standards Committee Objectives and Procedures," *Professional Standards* (New York: American Institute of Certified Public Accountants, 1988), Volume B, Section 9000, par. 24–27.

ethics, education, and management accounting. Every five years an International Congress is held to judge the progress toward achieving these objectives. In Europe, attempts are also being made to harmonize accounting standards. The European Community has issued a directive (4th) requiring certain minimum and uniform reporting and disclosure standards for financial statements. Other directives deal with uniform rules for preparing consolidated financial statements (7th) and qualifications of auditors (8th). At present, the European Community is paying considerable attention to the comparability of financial reporting as the organization moves toward the goal of a single European market in 1992.[8]

The road to international harmony is a difficult one. However, there is reason for optimism because an increasing number of countries are recognizing the appropriateness of international accounting standards in international trade and commerce.

DECISION POINT

Schneider S.A. and Square D Company (Part 2)

Corporations often find it desirable to invest in the securities of other corporations with the intent of holding them for an indefinite period. There are many reasons for making such long-term investments. One reason, of course, is simple: the prospect of earning a return on the investment. Another might be to establish a more formal business relationship with a company with which the acquiring company has ties. As noted in the first decision point in this chapter, on March 4, 1991, Schneider, a French electrical and construction company, made a hostile takeover offer for Square D Company, a U.S. electrical products company, after negotiations for a friendly arrangement broke down. What reasons may Schneider's chairman, Didier Pineau-Valencienne, have had for persisting in this takeover attempt when the chief executive of Square D Company, Jerre L. Stead, clearly did not want to cooperate?

Takeovers are often attempted when one company wants another company's assets or other advantages, such as established customers, markets, products, expertise, or operations. According to *Business Week*, Pineau-Valencienne "covets the U.S. company for two reasons: to broaden the payoff from Schneider's $400 million research budget and to sell each other's products in the other's home market. Pineau-Valencienne assails Square D's business strategy as far too inward-looking. 'Their idea is small is beautiful,' says he, noting that only 10.4% of Square D's sales are in Europe."[9] Schneider finds it easier and less expensive to buy Square D, even when Square D does not want to be taken over, than to start a whole operation independently. Furthermore, legally and for tax

8. "Comparability of Financial Statements," *Exposure Draft No. 32* (New York: International Federation of Accountants, 1989).
9. Stewart Toy, "Schneider: 'Dr. Attila' Has Big Plans," *Business Week* (March 18, 1991), p. 36.

purposes, it is easier to buy or invest in a company than to start a new business.[10] There are significant accounting implications of takeovers like this and of other long-term investments of one corporation in another. The following sections explore these implications. ■

Long-Term Intercompany Investments

One corporation may invest in another corporation by purchasing bonds or stocks. These investments may be either short-term or long-term. In this section, we are concerned with long-term investments in stocks. Long-term investments in bonds are covered in an appendix.

All long-term investments in stocks are recorded at cost, in accordance with generally accepted accounting principles. The treatment of the investment in the accounting records after the initial purchase depends on the extent to which the investing company can exercise significant influence or control over the operating and financial policies of the other company.

OBJECTIVE 4
Apply the cost method and the equity method to the appropriate situations in accounting for long-term investments

The Accounting Principles Board defined the important terms *significant influence* and *control* in its *Opinion No. 18*. **Significant influence** is the ability to affect the operating and financial policies of the company whose shares are owned, even though the investor holds less than 50 percent of the voting stock. Ability to influence a company may be shown by representation on the board of directors, participation in policy making, material transactions between the companies, exchange of managerial personnel, and technological dependency. For the sake of uniformity, the APB decided that unless there is proof to the contrary, an investment in 20 percent or more of the voting stock should be presumed to confer significant influence. An investment of less than 20 percent of the voting stock would not confer significant influence.[11]

Control is defined as the ability of the investing company to decide the operating and financial policies of the other company. Control is said to exist when the investing company owns more than 50 percent of the voting stock of the company in which it has invested.

10. Schneider was successful in its attempt to take over Square D Company. Square D's board accepted an offer of $88 per share, or a total of $2.23 billion on May 12, 1991. (*Wall Street Journal*, May 13, 1991.)

11. The Financial Accounting Standards Board points out in its *Interpretation No. 35* (May 1981) that though the presumption of significant influence applies when 20 percent or more of the voting stock is held, the rule is not a rigid one. All relevant facts and circumstances should be examined in each case to find out whether or not significant influence exists. For example, the FASB notes five circumstances that may remove the element of significant influence: (1) The company files a lawsuit against the investor or complains to a government agency. (2) The investor tries and fails to become a director. (3) The investor agrees not to increase its holdings. (4) The company is operated by a small group that ignores the investor's wishes. (5) The investor tries and fails to obtain additional information from the company that is not available to other stockholders.

Thus, in the absence of information to the contrary, a noninfluential and noncontrolling investment would be less than 20 percent ownership. An influential but noncontrolling investment would be 20 to 50 percent ownership. And a controlling investment would be more than 50 percent ownership. The accounting treatment differs for each kind of investment.

Noninfluential and Noncontrolling Investment

The **cost method** of accounting for long-term investments applies when the investor owns less than 20 percent of the voting stock. Under the cost method, the investor records the investment at cost and recognizes income as dividends are received. The Financial Accounting Standards Board states that long-term investments in marketable equity securities accounted for under the cost method should be valued at the lower of cost or market after acquisition.[12] The lower-of-cost-or-market rule is used here for the same reason it was used in the valuation of inventories. It is a conservative approach that recognizes the impairment in the value of an asset when its market value is less than cost. Conversely, a rise in the market above cost is not recognized until the investment is sold.

At the end of each accounting period, the total cost and the total market value of these long-term stock investments must be determined. If the total market value is less than the total cost, the difference must be credited to a contra-asset account called Allowance to Reduce Long-Term Investments to Market. Because of the long-term nature of the investment, the debit part of the entry, which represents a decrease in value below cost, is treated as a temporary decrease and does not appear as a loss on the income statement. It is shown in a contra-owners' equity account called Unrealized Loss on Long-Term Investments. Thus both these accounts are balance sheet accounts. If at some later date the market value exceeds the valuation reported in the earlier period, the Long-Term Investment account is written up to the new market value, but not to more than the acquisition cost of the investments.[13]

When long-term investments in stock are sold, the difference between the sale price and what the stock cost is recorded and reported on the income statement as a realized gain or loss. Dividend income from such investments is recorded by a debit to Cash and a credit to Dividend Income in the amount received.

For example, assume the following facts about the long-term stock investments of Coleman Corporation:

June 1, 19x0 Paid cash for the following long-term investments: 10,000 shares Durbin Corporation common stock (representing 2 percent of outstanding stock) at $25 per share; 5,000 shares Kotes Corporation common stock (representing 3 percent of outstanding stock) at $15 per share.

12. *Statement of Financial Accounting Standards No. 12,* "Accounting for Certain Marketable Securities" (Stamford, Conn.: Financial Accounting Standards Board, 1975).

13. If the decrease in value is deemed permanent, a different procedure is followed to record the decline in market value of the long-term investment. A loss account that appears on the income statement is debited instead of the Unrealized Loss account.

Dec. 31, 19x0	Quoted market prices at year end: Durbin common stock, $21; Kotes common stock, $17.
Apr. 1, 19x1	Change in policy required sale of 2,000 shares of Durbin Corporation common stock at $23.
July 1, 19x1	Received cash dividend from Kotes Corporation equal to $.20 per share.
Dec. 31, 19x1	Quoted market prices at year end: Durbin common stock, $24; Kotes common stock, $13.

Entries to record these transactions follow:

Investment

19x0			
June 1	Long-Term Investments	325,000	
	Cash		325,000
	To record investments in Durbin common stock (10,000 shares × $25 = $250,000) and Kotes common stock (5,000 shares × $15 = $75,000)		

Year-End Adjustment

19x0			
Dec. 31	Unrealized Loss on Long-Term Investments	30,000	
	Allowance to Reduce Long-Term Investments to Market		30,000
	To record reduction of long-term investment portfolio to market		

Company	Shares	Market Prices	Total Market	Total Cost
Durbin	10,000	$21	$210,000	$250,000
Kotes	5,000	17	85,000	75,000
			$295,000	$325,000

Cost − market value = $325,000 − $295,000 = $30,000.

Sale

19x1			
Apr. 1	Cash	46,000	
	Loss on Sale of Investment	4,000	
	Long-Term Investments		50,000
	To record sale of 2,000 shares of Durbin		
	2,000 × $23= $46,000		
	2,000 × $25= $50,000		
	Loss $ 4,000		

Dividend Received

		Debit	Credit
July 1	Cash	1,000	
	Dividend Income		1,000
	To record receipt of cash dividends from Kotes stocks 5,000 × \$.20 = \$1,000		

Year-End Adjustment

		Debit	Credit
Dec. 31	Allowance to Reduce Long-Term Investments to Market	12,000	
	Unrealized Loss on Long-Term Investments		12,000
	To record the adjustment in long-term investment so it is reported at lower of cost or market		

The adjustment equals the previous balance (\$30,000 from the December 31, 19x0 entry) minus the new balance (\$18,000), or \$12,000. The new balance of \$18,000 is the difference at the present time between the total market value and the total cost of all investments. It is figured as follows:

Company	Shares	Market Prices	Total Market	Total Cost
Durbin	8,000	\$24	\$192,000	\$200,000
Kotes	5,000	13	65,000	75,000
			\$257,000	\$275,000

Cost − market value = \$275,000 − \$257,000 = \$18,000.

The Allowance to Reduce Long-Term Investments to Market and the Unrealized Loss on Long-Term Investments are reciprocal contra accounts, each with the same dollar balance, as can be shown by the effects of these transactions on the T accounts:

Contra-Asset Account

Allowance to Reduce Long-Term Investments to Market

Debit		Credit	
19x1	12,000	19x0	30,000
		Bal. 19x1	18,000

Contra-Owners' Equity Account

Unrealized Loss on Long-Term Investments

Debit		Credit	
19x0	30,000	19x1	12,000
Bal. 19x1	18,000		

The Allowance account reduces long-term investments by the amount by which cost exceeds market of the investments; the Unrealized Loss account reduces owners' equity by a similar amount.

Influential but Noncontrolling Investment

As we have seen, ownership of 20 percent or more of a company's voting stock is considered sufficient to influence the operations of another corporation. When this is the case, the investment in the stock of the influenced company should be accounted for using the **equity method**. The equity method presumes that an investment of more than 20 percent is more than a passive investment, and that therefore the investing company should share proportionately in the success or failure of the investee company. The three main features of this method are as follows:

1. The investor records the original purchase of the stock at cost.
2. The investor records its share of the investee's periodic net income as an increase in the Investment account, with a corresponding credit to an income account. Similarly, the investor records its share of the investee's periodic loss as a decrease in the Investment account, with a corresponding debit to a loss account.
3. When the investor receives a cash dividend, the asset account Cash is increased and the Investment account decreased.

To illustrate the equity method of accounting, we will assume the following facts about an investment by the Vassor Corporation. Vassor Corporation, on January 1 of the current year, acquired 40 percent of the voting common stock of the Block Corporation for $180,000. With this share of ownership, the Vassor Corporation can exert significant influence over the operations of the Block Corporation. During the year, the Block Corporation reported net income of $80,000 and paid cash dividends of $20,000. The entries to record these transactions by the Vassor Corporation are:

Investment

Investment in Block Corporation	180,000	
Cash		180,000
To record investment in Block Corporation common stock		

Recognition of Income

Investment in Block Corporation	32,000	
Income, Block Corporation Investment		32,000
To recognize 40% of income reported by Block Corporation 40% × $80,000 = $32,000		

Receipt of Cash Dividend

Cash	8,000	
Investment in Block Corporation		8,000
To record cash dividend from Block Corporation 40% × $20,000 = $8,000		

The balance of the investment in the Block Corporation account after these transactions is $204,000, as shown here:

Investment in Block Corporation

Investment	180,000	Dividends received	8,000
Share of income	32,000		
Balance	**204,000**		

Controlling Investment

In some cases, an investor who owns less than 50 percent of the voting stock of a company may exercise such powerful influence that for all practical purposes the investor controls the policies of the other company. Nevertheless, ownership of more than 50 percent of the voting stock is required for accounting recognition of control. When a controlling interest is owned, a parent-subsidiary relationship is said to exist. The investing company is known as the **parent company**, the other company as the **subsidiary**. Because both corporations are separate legal entities, each prepares separate financial statements. However, owing to their special relationship, they are viewed for public financial reporting purposes as a single economic entity. For this reason, they must combine their financial statements into a single set of statements called **consolidated financial statements**.

Accounting for consolidated financial statements is very complex. It is usually the subject of an advanced-level course in accounting. However, most large public corporations have subsidiaries and must prepare consolidated financial statements. It is therefore important to have some understanding of accounting for consolidations.

The proper accounting treatments for long-term investments in stock are summarized in Table 16-3.

Table 16-3. Accounting Treatments of Long-Term Investments in Stock

Level of Ownership	Percentage of Ownership	Accounting Treatment
Noninfluential and noncontrolling	Less than 20%	Cost method; investment valued subsequent to purchase at lower of cost or market.
Influential but noncontrolling	Between 20% and 50%	Equity method; investment valued subsequently at cost plus investor's share of income (or minus investor's loss) minus dividends received.
Controlling	More than 50%	Financial statements consolidated.

Consolidated Financial Statements

OBJECTIVE 5 *Explain when to prepare consolidated financial statements, and describe their uses*

Most major corporations find it convenient for economic, legal, tax, or other reasons to operate in parent-subsidiary relationships. When we speak of a large company such as Ford, IBM, or Texas Instruments, we generally think of the parent company, not of its many subsidiaries. When considering investment in one of these firms, however, the investor wants a clear financial picture of the total economic entity. The main purpose of consolidated financial statements is to give such a view of the parent and subsidiary firms by treating them as if they were one company. On a consolidated balance sheet, the Inventory account includes the inventory held by the parent and all its subsidiaries. Similarly, on the consolidated income statement, the Sales account is the total revenue from sales by the parent and all its subsidiaries. This overview is very useful to management and stockholders of the parent company in judging the company's progress in meeting its goals. Long-term creditors of the parent also find consolidated statements useful because of their interest in the long-range financial health of the company as an integrated economic unit.

It was acceptable in the past not to consolidate the statements of certain subsidiaries, even though the parent owned a controlling interest, when the business of the subsidiary was not homogeneous with that of the parent. For instance, a retail company or an automobile manufacturer might have had a wholly-owned finance subsidiary that was not consolidated. However, such practices were criticized because they tended to remove certain assets (accounts and notes receivable) and certain liabilities (borrowing by the finance subsidiary) from the consolidated financial statements. For example, in 1986, General Motors' financing subsidiary, GMAC, with assets of $90 billion and liabilities of $84 billion, was carried as a long-term investment of $6 billion on GM's balance sheet. It was also argued by those who favored consolidation that financing arrangements such as these are an integral part of the overall business. The Financial Accounting Standards Board has ruled that effective in 1988 all subsidiaries in which the parent owns a controlling interest (more than 50 percent) must be consolidated with the parent for financial reporting purposes.[14] As a result, with few exceptions, the financial statements of all majority-owned subsidiaries must now be consolidated with the parent company's financial statements for external reporting purposes.

Methods of Accounting for Business Combinations

Interests in subsidiary companies may be acquired by paying cash; issuing long-term bonds, other debt, or preferred stock; or working out some combination of these forms of payment, such as exchanging shares of the parent's own unissued capital stock for the outstanding shares of the subsidiary's capital stock. For parent-subsidiary relationships that arise when cash is paid or debt or preferred stock is issued, it is mandatory to use the purchase method, which is explained below. For simplicity,

14. *Statement of Financial Accounting Standards No. 94*, "Consolidation of All Majority-Owned Subsidiaries" (Stamford, Conn.: Financial Accounting Standards Board, 1987).

our illustrations assume payment in cash. In the special case of establishing a parent-subsidiary relationship through an exchange of common stock, the pooling of interests method may be appropriate. The pooling of interests method is the subject of more advanced courses.

Consolidated Balance Sheet

In preparing consolidated financial statements under the **purchase method**, similar accounts from the separate statements of the parent and the subsidiaries are combined. Some accounts result from transactions between the parent and subsidiary. Examples are debt owed by one of the entities to the other and sales and purchases between the two entities. From the point of view of the consolidated group of companies as a single business, it is not appropriate to include these accounts in the group financial statements; the purchases and sales are only transfers between different parts of the business, and the payables and receivables do not represent amounts due to or receivable from outside parties. For this reason, it is important that certain **eliminations** be made. These eliminations avoid duplication of accounts and reflect the financial position and operations from the standpoint of a single entity. Eliminations appear only on the work sheets used in preparing consolidated financial statements. They are never shown in the accounting records of either the parent or the subsidiary. There are no consolidated journals or ledgers.

Another good example of accounts that result from transactions between the two entities is the Investment in Subsidiary account in the parent's balance sheet and the stockholders' equity section of the subsidiary. When the balance sheets of the two companies are combined, these accounts must be eliminated to avoid duplicating these items in the consolidated financial statements.

To illustrate the preparation of a consolidated balance sheet under the purchase method, we will use the following balance sheets for Parent and Subsidiary companies:

Accounts	Parent Company	Subsidiary Company
Cash	$100,000	$25,000
Other Assets	760,000	60,000
Total Assets	$860,000	$85,000
Liabilities	$ 60,000	$10,000
Common Stock—$10 par value	600,000	55,000
Retained Earnings	200,000	20,000
Total Liabilities and Stockholders' Equity	$860,000	$85,000

100 Percent Purchase at Book Value. Suppose that Parent Company purchases 100 percent of the stock of Subsidiary Company for an amount

OBJECTIVE 6a
Prepare consolidated balance sheets at acquisition date for purchase at book value

exactly equal to the Subsidiary's book value. The book value of Subsidiary Company is $75,000 ($85,000 – $10,000). Parent Company would record the purchase as follows:

Investment in Subsidiary Company	75,000	
Cash		75,000
To record 100 percent purchase of Subsidiary Company at book value		

It is helpful to use a work sheet like the one shown in Exhibit 16-1 in preparing consolidated financial statements. Note that the balance of Parent Company's Cash account is now $25,000 and that the Investment in Subsidiary Company is shown as an asset in Parent Company's balance sheet, reflecting the purchase of the subsidiary. To prepare a consolidated balance sheet, it is necessary to eliminate the investment in the subsidiary. This procedure is shown by elimination entry **1** in Exhibit 16-1. This elimination entry does two things. First, it eliminates the double counting that would take place when the net assets of the two companies are combined. Second, it eliminates the stockholders' equity section of Subsidiary Company.

The theory underlying consolidated financial statements is that parent and subsidiary are a single entity. The stockholders' equity section of the consolidated balance sheet is the same as that of Parent Company. So after eliminating the Investment in Subsidiary Company against the stockhold-

Exhibit 16-1. Work Sheet for Preparation of Consolidated Balance Sheet

Parent and Subsidiary Companies
Work Sheet for Consolidated Balance Sheet
As of Acquisition Date

Accounts	Balance Sheet Parent Company	Balance Sheet Subsidiary Company	Eliminations		Consolidated Balance Sheet
			Debit	Credit	
Cash	25,000	25,000			50,000
Investment in Subsidiary Company	75,000			(1) 75,000	
Other Assets	760,000	60,000			820,000
Total Assets	860,000	85,000			870,000
Liabilities	60,000	10,000			70,000
Common Stock— $10 par value	600,000	55,000	(1) 55,000		600,000
Retained Earnings	200,000	20,000	(1) 20,000		200,000
Total Liabilities and Stockholders' Equity	860,000	85,000	75,000	75,000	870,000

(1) Elimination of intercompany investment.

ers' equity of the subsidiary, we can take the information from the right-hand column in Exhibit 16-1 and present it in the following form:

Parent and Subsidiary Companies
Consolidated Balance Sheet
As of Acquisition Date

Cash	$ 50,000	Liabilities	$ 70,000
Other Assets	820,000	Common Stock	600,000
		Retained Earnings	200,000
Total Assets	$870,000	Total Liabilities and Stockholders' Equity	$870,000

Less than 100 Percent Purchase at Book Value. A parent company does not have to purchase 100 percent of a subsidiary to control it. If it purchases more than 50 percent of the voting stock of the subsidiary company, it will have legal control. In the consolidated financial statements, therefore, the total assets and liabilities of the subsidiary are combined with the assets and liabilities of the parent. However, it is still necessary to account for the interests of those stockholders of the subsidiary company who own less than 50 percent of the voting stock. These are the minority stockholders, and their **minority interest** must appear on the consolidated balance sheet as an amount equal to their percentage of ownership times the net assets of the subsidiary.

Suppose that the same Parent Company buys, for $67,500, only 90 percent of Subsidiary Company's voting stock. In this case, the portion of the company purchased has a book value of $67,500 (90% × $75,000). The work sheet used for preparing the consolidated balance sheet appears in Exhibit 16-2. The elimination is made in the same way as in the case above, except that the minority interest must be accounted for. All of the Investment in Subsidiary Company ($67,500) is eliminated against all of Subsidiary Company's stockholders' equity ($75,000). The difference ($7,500, or 10% × $75,000) is set as minority interest.

There are two ways to classify minority interest on the consolidated balance sheet. One is to place it between long-term liabilities and stockholders' equity. The other is to consider the stockholders' equity section as consisting of (1) minority interest and (2) Parent Company's stockholders' equity, as shown here:

Minority Interest	$ 7,500
Common Stock	600,000
Retained Earnings	200,000
Total Stockholders' Equity	$807,500

Purchase at More than or Less than Book Value. The purchase price of a business depends on many factors, such as the current market price, the

Exhibit 16-2. Work Sheet Showing Elimination of Less than 100 Percent Ownership

Parent and Subsidiary Companies
Work Sheet for Consolidated Balance Sheet
As of Acquisition Date

Accounts	Balance Sheet Parent Company	Balance Sheet Subsidiary Company	Eliminations		Consolidated Balance Sheet
			Debit	Credit	
Cash	32,500	25,000			57,500
Investment in Subsidiary Company	67,500			(1) 67,500	
Other Assets	760,000	60,000			820,000
Total Assets	860,000	85,000			877,500
Liabilities	60,000	10,000			70,000
Common Stock—$10 par value	600,000	55,000	(1) 55,000		600,000
Retained Earnings	200,000	20,000	(1) 20,000		200,000
Minority Interest				(1) 7,500	7,500
Total Liabilities and Stockholders' Equity	860,000	85,000	75,000	75,000	877,500

(1) Elimination of intercompany investment. Minority interest equals 10 percent of Subsidiary's stockholders' equity.

OBJECTIVE 6b Prepare consolidated balance sheets at acquisition date for purchase at other than book value

relative strength of the buyer's and seller's bargaining positions, and the prospects for future earnings. Thus it is only by chance that the purchase price of a subsidiary will equal the book value of the subsidiary's equity. Usually, it will not. For example, a parent company may pay more than the book value of a subsidiary to purchase a controlling interest if the assets of the subsidiary are understated. In that case, the recorded historical cost less depreciation of the subsidiary's assets may not reflect current market values. The parent may also pay more than book value if the subsidiary has something that the parent wants, such as an important technical process, a new and different product, or a new market. On the other hand, the parent may pay less than book value for its share of the subsidiary's stock if the subsidiary's assets are worth less than their depreciated cost. Or the subsidiary may have suffered heavy losses, causing its stock to sell at rather low prices.

The Accounting Principles Board has provided the following guidelines for consolidating a purchased subsidiary and its parent:

> First, all identifiable assets acquired . . . and liabilities assumed in a business combination . . . should be assigned a portion of the cost of the acquired company, normally equal to their fair values at date of acquisition.

Exhibit 16-3. Work Sheet Showing Elimination Where Purchase Cost Is Greater than Book Value

Parent and Subsidiary Companies
Work Sheet for Consolidated Balance Sheet
As of Acquisition Date

Accounts	Balance Sheet Parent Company	Balance Sheet Subsidiary Company	Eliminations		Consolidated Balance Sheet
			Debit	Credit	
Cash	7,500	25,000			32,500
Investment in Subsidiary Company	92,500			(1) 92,500	
Other Long-Term Assets	760,000	60,000	(1) 10,000		830,000
Goodwill			(1) 7,500		7,500
Total Assets	860,000	85,000			870,000
Liabilities	60,000	10,000			70,000
Common Stock—$10 par value	600,000	55,000	(1) 55,000		600,000
Retained Earnings	200,000	20,000	(1) 20,000		200,000
Total Liabilities and Stockholders' Equity	860,000	85,000	92,500	92,500	870,000

(1) Elimination of intercompany investment. Excess of cost over book value ($92,500 – $75,000 = $17,500) allocated $10,000 to Other Long-Term Assets and $7,500 to Goodwill.

Second, the excess of the cost of the acquired company over the sum of the amounts assigned to identifiable assets acquired less liabilities assumed should be recorded as goodwill.[15]

To illustrate the application of these principles, we will assume that Parent Company purchases 100 percent of Subsidiary Company's voting stock for $92,500, or $17,500 more than book value. Parent Company considers $10,000 of the $17,500 to be due to the increased value of Subsidiary's other long-term assets and $7,500 of the $17,500 to be due to the overall strength that Subsidiary Company would add to Parent Company's organization. The work sheet used for preparing the consolidated balance sheet appears in Exhibit 16-3. All of the Investment in Subsidiary Company ($92,500) has been eliminated against all of the Subsidiary Company's stockholders' equity ($75,000). The excess of cost over book value ($17,500) has been debited in the amounts of $10,000 to Long-Term Assets and $7,500 to a new account called **Goodwill**, or **Goodwill from Consolidation**.

15. Accounting Principles Board, *Opinion No. 16,* "Business Combinations" (New York: Accounting Principles Board, 1970), par. 87.

The amount of goodwill is determined as follows:

Cost of investment in subsidiary	$92,500
Book value of subsidiary	75,000
Excess of cost over book value	$17,500
Portion of excess attributable to undervalued long-term assets of subsidiary	10,000
Portion of excess attributable to goodwill	$ 7,500

Goodwill appears on the consolidated balance sheet as an asset representing the excess of cost of the investment over book value that cannot be allocated to any specific asset. Long-Term Assets appears on the consolidated balance sheet as the combined total of $830,000 ($760,000 + $60,000 + $10,000).

When the parent pays less than book value for its investment in the subsidiary, Accounting Principles Board *Opinion No. 16,* paragraph 87, requires that the excess of book value over cost of the investment be used to lower the carrying value of the subsidiary's long-term assets. The belief is that market values of long-lived assets (other than marketable securities) are among the least reliable of estimates, since a ready market for such assets does not usually exist. In other words, the APB advises against using negative goodwill, except in very special cases.

Intercompany Receivables and Payables. If either the parent or the subsidiary company owes money to the other, there will be a receivable on the creditor company's individual balance sheet and a payable on the debtor company's individual balance sheet. When a consolidated balance sheet is prepared, both the receivable and the payable should be eliminated because, from the viewpoint of the consolidated entity, neither the asset nor the liability exists. In other words, it does not make sense for a company to owe money to itself. The eliminating entry would be made on the work sheet by debiting the payable and crediting the receivable for the amount of the intercompany loan.

Consolidated Income Statement

OBJECTIVE 7 *Prepare consolidated income statements for intercompany transactions*

The consolidated income statement is prepared for a consolidated entity by combining the revenues and expenses of the parent and subsidiary companies. The procedure is the same as in preparing a consolidated balance sheet. That is, intercompany transactions are eliminated to prevent double counting of revenues and expenses. Several intercompany transactions affect the consolidated income statement. They are (1) sales and purchases of goods and services between parent and subsidiary (purchases for the buying company and sales for the selling company); (2) income and expenses on loans, receivables, or bond indebtedness between parent and subsidiary; and (3) other income and expenses from intercompany transactions.

To illustrate the eliminating entries, we will assume the following transactions between a parent and its wholly-owned subsidiary. Parent Com-

Exhibit 16-4. Work Sheet Showing Eliminations for Preparing a Consolidated Income Statement

Parent and Subsidiary Companies
Work Sheet for Consolidated Income Statement
For the Year Ended December 31, 19xx

Accounts	Income Statement Parent Company	Income Statement Subsidiary Company	Eliminations		Consolidated Income Statement
			Debit	Credit	
Sales	430,000	200,000	(1) 120,000		510,000
Other Revenues	60,000	10,000	(2) 2,000		68,000
Total Revenues	490,000	210,000			578,000
Cost of Goods Sold	210,000	150,000		(1) 120,000	240,000
Other Expenses	140,000	50,000		(2) 2,000	188,000
Total Deductions	350,000	200,000			428,000
Net Income	140,000	10,000	122,000	122,000	150,000

(1) Elimination of intercompany sales and purchases.
(2) Elimination of intercompany interest income and interest expense.

pany made sales of $120,000 in goods to Subsidiary Company, which in turn sold all the goods to others. Subsidiary Company paid Parent Company $2,000 interest on a loan from the parent.

The work sheet in Exhibit 16-4 shows how to prepare a consolidated income statement. The purpose of the eliminating entries is to treat the two companies as a single entity. Thus it is important to include in Sales only those sales made to outsiders and to include in Cost of Goods Sold only those purchases made from outsiders. This goal is met with the first eliminating entry, which eliminates the $120,000 of intercompany sales and purchases by a debit of that amount to Sales and a credit of that amount to Cost of Goods Sold. As a result, only sales to outsiders ($510,000) and purchases from outsiders ($240,000) are included in the Consolidated Income Statement column. The intercompany interest income and expense are eliminated by a debit to Other Revenues and a credit to Other Expenses.

Other Consolidated Financial Statements

Public corporations also prepare consolidated statements of retained earnings and consolidated statements of cash flows. For examples of these statements, see the Toys "R" Us statements in the chapter on accounting concepts and classified financial statements.

Chapter Review

Review of Learning Objectives

1. **Define *exchange rate* and record transactions that are affected by changes in foreign exchange rates.**
An *exchange rate* is the value of one currency stated in terms of another. A domestic company may make sales or purchases abroad in either its own country's currency or the foreign currency. If a transaction (sale or purchase) and its resolution (receipt or payment) are made in the domestic currency, no accounting problem arises. However, if the transaction and its resolution are made in a foreign currency and the exchange rate changes between the time of the transaction and its resolution, an exchange gain or loss will occur and should be recorded.

2. **Describe the restatement of a foreign subsidiary's financial statements in U.S. dollars.**
Foreign financial statements are converted to U.S. dollars by multiplying the appropriate exchange rates by the amounts in the foreign financial statements. In general, the rates that apply depend on whether the subsidiary is separate and self-contained (Type I) or an integral part of the parent company (Type II).

3. **Describe progress toward international accounting standards.**
There has been some progress toward establishing international accounting standards, especially through the efforts of the International Accounting Standards Committee and the International Federation of Accountants. However, there still are serious inconsistencies in financial reporting among countries. These inconsistencies make the comparison of financial statements from different countries difficult.

4. **Apply the cost method and the equity method to the appropriate situations in accounting for long-term investments.**
Long-term stock investments fall into three categories. First are noninfluential and noncontrolling investments, representing less than 20 percent ownership. To account for these investments, use the cost method, adjusting the investment to the lower of cost or market for financial statement purposes. Second are influential but noncontrolling investments, representing 20 percent to 50 percent ownership. Use the equity method to account for these investments. Third are controlling interest investments, representing more than 50 percent ownership. Account for these investments using consolidated financial statements.

5. **Explain when to prepare consolidated financial statements, and describe their uses.**
The FASB requires that consolidated financial statements be prepared when an investing company has legal and effective control over another company. Control exists when the parent company owns more than 50 percent of the voting stock of the subsidiary company. Consolidated financial statements are useful to investors and others because they treat the parent company and its subsidiaries realistically, as an integrated economic unit.

6. **Prepare consolidated balance sheets at acquisition date for purchase at (a) book value and (b) other than book value.**
At the date of acquisition, a work sheet entry is made to eliminate the investment from the parent company's financial statements and the stock-

holders' equity section of the subsidiary's financial statements. The assets and liabilities of the two companies are combined. If the parent owns less than 100 percent of the subsidiary, minority interest equal to the percentage of the subsidiary not owned by the parent multiplied by the stockholders' equity in the subsidiary will appear on the consolidated balance sheet. If the cost of the parent's investment in the subsidiary is greater than the subsidiary's book value, an amount equal to the excess of cost over book value will be allocated on the consolidated balance sheet to undervalued subsidiary assets and to goodwill. If the cost of the parent's investment in the subsidiary is less than book value, the excess of book value over cost should be used to reduce the book value of the long-term assets (other than long-term marketable securities) of the subsidiary.

7. **Prepare consolidated income statements for intercompany transactions.** When consolidated income statements are prepared, intercompany sales, purchases, interest income, and interest expense must be eliminated to avoid double counting of these items.

Review of Concepts and Terminology

The following concepts and terms were introduced in this chapter:

(L.O. 4) **Consolidated financial statements:** Financial statements that reflect the combined operations of parent company and subsidiaries.

(L.O. 4) **Control:** The ability of the investing company to decide the operating and financial policies of another company through ownership of more than 50 percent of its voting stock.

(L.O. 4) **Cost method:** A method of accounting for long-term investments in which the investor records the investment at cost and recognizes income as dividends are received. Used when the investing company owns less than 20 percent of the voting stock of the other company.

(L.O. 5) **Eliminations:** Entries made on consolidated work sheets to eliminate transactions between parent and subsidiary companies.

(L.O. 4) **Equity method:** The method of accounting for long-term investments in which the investor records its share of the investee's periodic net income or loss as an increase or decrease in the Investment account. Used when the investing company exercises significant influence over the other company.

(L.O. 1) **Exchange gains or losses:** Changes due to exchange rate fluctuations that are reported on the consolidated income statement.

(L.O. 1) **Exchange rate:** The value of one currency in terms of another.

(L.O. 2) **Functional currency:** The currency of the place where a subsidiary carries on most of its business.

(L.O. 6b) **Goodwill (goodwill from consolidation):** The amount paid for a subsidiary that exceeds the fair value of the subsidiary's assets less its liabilities.

(L.O. 6a) **Minority interest:** The amount on a consolidated balance sheet that represents the holdings of stockholders who own less than 50 percent of the voting stock of a subsidiary.

(L.O. 1) **Multinational (transnational) corporation:** A company that operates in more than one country.

(L.O. 4) **Parent company:** An investing company that owns a controlling interest in another company.

(L.O. 5) **Purchase method:** A method of accounting for parent company/subsidiary relationships in which similar accounts from separate statements are combined. Used when the investing company owns more than 50 percent of a subsidiary.

(L.O. 2) **Reporting currency:** The currency in which consolidated financial statements are presented.

(L.O. 2) **Restatement:** The stating of one currency in terms of another.

(L.O. 4) **Significant influence:** The ability of an investing company to affect the operating and financial policies of another company, even though the investor holds less than 50 percent of the voting stock.

(L.O. 4) **Subsidiary:** An investee company in which a controlling interest is owned by another company.

Review Problem Consolidated Balance Sheet: Less than 100 Percent Ownership

(L.O. 6) In a cash transaction, Taylor Company purchased 90 percent of the outstanding stock of Schumacher Company for $763,200 on June 30, 19xx. Directly after the acquisition, separate balance sheets of the companies appeared as follows:

	Taylor Company	Schumacher Company
Assets		
Cash	$ 400,000	$ 48,000
Accounts Receivable	650,000	240,000
Inventory	1,000,000	520,000
Investment in Schumacher Company	763,200	—
Plant and Equipment (net)	1,500,000	880,000
Other Assets	50,000	160,000
Total Assets	$4,363,200	$1,848,000
Liabilities and Stockholders' Equity		
Accounts Payable	$ 800,000	$ 400,000
Long-Term Debt	1,000,000	600,000
Common Stock—$5 par value	2,000,000	800,000
Retained Earnings	563,200	48,000
Total Liabilities and Stockholders' Equity	$4,363,200	$1,848,000

Additional information: (a) Schumacher Company's other assets represent a long-term investment in Taylor Company's long-term debt. The debt was purchased for an amount equal to Taylor's carrying value of the debt. (b) Taylor Company owes Schumacher Company $100,000 for services rendered.

Required Prepare a work sheet as of the acquisition date for preparing a consolidated balance sheet.

Answer to Review Problem

Taylor and Schumacher Companies
Work Sheet for Consolidated Balance Sheet
June 30, 19xx

Accounts	Balance Sheet Taylor Company	Balance Sheet Schumacher Company	Eliminations		Consolidated Balance Sheet
			Debit	Credit	
Cash	400,000	48,000			448,000
Accounts Receivable	650,000	240,000		(3) 100,000	790,000
Inventory	1,000,000	520,000			1,520,000
Investment in Schumacher Company	763,200	—		(1) 763,200	
Plant and Equipment (net)	1,500,000	880,000			2,380,000
Other Assets	50,000	160,000		(2) 160,000	50,000
Total Assets	4,363,200	1,848,000			5,188,000
Accounts Payable	800,000	400,000	(3) 100,000		1,100,000
Long-Term Debt	1,000,000	600,000	(2) 160,000		1,440,000
Common Stock—$5 par value	2,000,000	800,000	(1) 800,000		2,000,000
Retained Earnings	563,200	48,000	(1) 48,000		563,200
Minority Interest				(1) 84,800	84,800
Total Liabilities and Stockholders' Equity	4,363,200	1,848,000	1,108,000	1,108,000	5,188,000

(1) Elimination of intercompany investment. Minority interest equals 10 percent of Schumacher Company Stockholders' Equity (10% × [$800,000 + $48,000] = $84,800).
(2) Elimination of intercompany long-term debt.
(3) Elimination of intercompany receivables and payables.

Chapter Assignments

Discussion Questions

1. What does it mean to say that the exchange rate for a French franc in terms of the U.S. dollar is .15? If a bottle of French perfume costs 200 francs, how much will it cost in dollars?

2. If an American firm does business with a German firm and all their transactions take place in German marks, which firm may incur an exchange gain or loss, and why?
3. What is the difference between a reporting currency and a functional currency?
4. If you as an investor were trying to evaluate the relative performance of General Motors, Volkswagen, and Toyota Motors from their published financial statements, what problem might you encounter (other than a language problem)?
5. What are some of the obstacles to uniform international accounting standards, and what efforts are being made to overcome them?
6. Why are the concepts of significant influence and control important in accounting for long-term investments?
7. For each of the following categories of long-term investments, briefly describe the applicable percentage of ownership and accounting treatment: (a) noninfluential and noncontrolling investment, (b) influential but noncontrolling investment, and (c) controlling investment.
8. What is meant by a parent-subsidiary relationship?
9. Would the stockholders of Paramount Communications, Inc. be more interested in the consolidated financial statements of Paramount Communications, Inc. than in the statements of its principal subsidiaries, such as Paramount Pictures, Madison Square Garden, or Simon & Schuster? Explain.
10. The 1987 annual report for Merchant Corporation included the following statement in its Summary of Principal Accounting Policies: "*Principles applied in consolidation.*—Majority-owned subsidiaries are consolidated, except for leasing and finance companies and those subsidiaries not considered to be material." How did this practice change in 1988, and why?
11. Also in Merchant's annual report, in the Summary of Principal Accounting Policies, was the following statement: "*Investments.*—Investments in companies, in which Merchant has significant influence in management and control, are on the equity basis." What is the equity basis of accounting for investments, and why did Merchant use it in this case?
12. Why should intercompany receivables, payables, sales, and purchases be eliminated in the preparation of consolidated financial statements?
13. The following item appears on Merchant's consolidated balance sheet: "Minority Interest—$50,000." Explain how this item arose and where you would expect to find it on the consolidated balance sheet.
14. Why may the price paid to acquire a controlling interest in a subsidiary company exceed the subsidiary's book value?
15. The following item also appears on Merchant's consolidated balance sheet: "Goodwill from Consolidation—$70,000." Explain how this item arose and where you would expect to find it on the consolidated balance sheet.
16. Subsidiary Corporation has a book value of $100,000, of which Parent Corporation purchases 100 percent for $115,000. None of the excess of cost over book value is attributed to tangible assets. What is the amount of goodwill from consolidation?
17. Subsidiary Corporation, a wholly-owned subsidiary, has total sales of $500,000, $100,000 of which were made to Parent Corporation. Parent Corporation has total sales of $1,000,000, including sales of all items purchased from Subsidiary Corporation. What is the amount of sales on the consolidated income statement?

Communication Skills Exercises

Communication 16-1. Effect of Change in Exchange Rate *(L.O. 1)*

Compagnie Générale des Etablissements Michelin, the famous French maker of Michelin tires, became the world's largest tiremaker when it purchased the U.S. tiremaker Uniroyal Goodrich Tire Company in 1990. The *Wall Street Journal* reported that excluding Uniroyal Goodrich sales, sales revenue in fiscal 1990 decreased 4.4 percent to 52.74 billion francs. The decrease was due mainly to the weak dollar in 1990. Michelin executives said, the article reported, that about 25 percent of Michelin's sales, not counting those of Uniroyal Goodrich, were exports to the United States. Without the dollar's drop, revenue expressed in francs would have increased instead of decreased.[16] Explain why a weak dollar would lead to a decrease in Michelin's sales. Why are sales of Uniroyal Goodrich excluded from this discussion?

Communication 16-2. Effects of Changes in Exchange Rates *(L.O. 1)*

Japan Air Lines, one of the world's top-ranking airlines, has an extensive global network of passenger and cargo services. The company engages in sales and purchase transactions throughout the world. At the end of the year, it will have receivables and payables in many currencies that must be translated into yen for preparation of its consolidated financial statements. The company's 1990 annual report notes that these receivables and payables are translated at the applicable year-end rates.[17] What will be the financial effects (exchange gain or loss) under each of the following independent assumptions about changes in the exchange rates since the transactions that gave rise to the receivables or payables occurred? (1) Receivables exceed payables, and on average the yen has risen relative to other currencies. (2) Receivables exceed payables, and on average the yen has fallen relative to other currencies. (3) Payables exceed receivables, and on average the yen has risen relative to other currencies. (4) Payables exceed receivables, and on average the yen has fallen relative to other currencies. Suggest some ways in which Japan Air Lines can minimize the effects of the fluctuations in exchange rates as they relate to receivables and payables.

Communication 16-3. Effects of Accounting Treatments of Long-Term Investments *(L.O. 4, 5)*

Masco Corporation is a Michigan-based home furnishings company with revenues in excess of $2 billion. According to *Forbes*, the company has several affiliates, including a 40 percent ownership in Masco Industries, an industrial products business; from a practical standpoint, Masco Corporation controls Masco Industries. The two firms have the same chairman and operate out of the same headquarters. When Masco Industries was formed, it assumed a substantial debt on its balance sheet. If the two entities were in fact consolidated for financial reporting, Masco Corporation, according to *Forbes*, "would look a lot less financially healthy than it does now."[18] Should Masco Industries be consolidated with Masco Corporation under FASB *Statement No. 94*? According to current practice, how should Masco Corporation's investment in Masco Industries be accounted for? How does carrying the debt on Masco Industries' books improve the financial picture of Masco Corporation? Do you

16. E. S. Browning, "Michelin Sees Heavy Net Loss for the Year," *Wall Street Journal* (October 19, 1990).
17. Annual Report, Japan Air Lines (1990), p. 33.
18. Penelope Wany, "What's Off, What's On?" *Forbes* (February 20, 1989), p. 110.

think a case could be made for consolidating Masco Industries with Masco Corporation for financial reporting purposes?

Communication 16-4. Basic Research Skills *(L.O. 1)*

Go to the section of the library where recent issues of the *Wall Street Journal* are located. From the index on the front page of Section C, "Money & Investing," find the page number of world markets. In the "Currency Trading" portion of that page, find a table entitled "Exchange Rates." This table shows the exchange rates of the currencies of about fifty countries with the U.S. dollar. Choose the currency of any country in which you are interested. Write down the value of that currency in U.S. dollar equivalents for one day in the first week of each month for the past six months, as reported in the *Wall Street Journal*. Prepare a chart that shows the variation in exchange rate for this currency over this time period. Assuming that you run a company that exports goods to the country you chose, would you find the change in exchange rate over the past six months favorable or unfavorable? Assuming that you run a company that imports goods from the country you chose, would you find the change in exchange rate over the past six months favorable or unfavorable? Explain your answers and tell what business practices you would follow to offset any adverse effects of exchange rate fluctuations. Be prepared to discuss your results in class.

Classroom Exercises

Exercise 16-1. Recording International Transactions: Fluctuating Exchange Rate *(L.O. 1)*

States Corporation purchased a special-purpose machine from Hamburg Corporation on credit for 50,000 DM (marks). At the date of purchase, the exchange rate was $.55 per mark. On the date of the payment, which was made in marks, the value of the mark had increased to $.60.

Prepare journal entries to record the purchase and payment in States Corporation's accounting records.

Exercise 16-2. Recording International Transactions *(L.O. 1)*

U.S. Corporation made a sale on account to U.K. Company on November 15 in the amount of £300,000. Payment was to be made in British pounds on February 15. U.S. Corporation's fiscal year is the same as the calendar year. The British pound was worth $1.70 on November 15, $1.58 on December 31, and $1.78 on February 15.

Prepare journal entries to record the sale, year-end adjustment, and collection on U.S. Corporation's books.

Exercise 16-3. Methods of Accounting for Long-Term Investments *(L.O. 4, 5)*

Diversified Corporation has the following long-term investments:

1. 60 percent of the common stock of Calcor Corporation
2. 13 percent of the common stock of Virginia, Inc.
3. 50 percent of the nonvoting preferred stock of Camrad Corporation
4. 100 percent of the common stock of its financing subsidiary, DCF, Inc.
5. 35 percent of the common stock of the French company Maison de Boutaine
6. 70 percent of the common stock of the Canadian company Alberta Mining Company

For each of these investments, tell which of the following methods should be used for external financial reporting.

a. Cost method
b. Equity method
c. Consolidation of parent and subsidiary financial statements

Exercise 16-4. Long-Term Investments: Cost Method *(L.O. 4)*

Heard Corporation has the following portfolio of investments at year end:

Company	Percentage of Voting Stock Held	Cost	Year-End Market Value
N Corporation	4	$160,000	$190,000
O Corporation	12	750,000	550,000
P Corporation	5	60,000	110,000
Total		$970,000	$850,000

The Unrealized Loss on Long-Term Investments account and the Allowance to Reduce Long-Term Investments to Market account both currently have a balance of $80,000 from the last accounting period. Prepare the year-end adjustment to reflect the above information.

Exercise 16-5. Long-Term Investments: Cost and Equity Methods *(L.O. 4)*

On January 1, Terry Corporation purchased, as long-term investments, 8 percent of the voting stock of Holmes Corporation for $250,000 and 45 percent of the voting stock of Miles Corporation for $1 million. During the year, Holmes Corporation had earnings of $100,000 and paid dividends of $40,000. Miles Corporation had earnings of $300,000 and paid dividends of $200,000. The market value of neither investment declined during the year. Which of these investments should be accounted for using the cost method? Which with the equity method? At what amount should each investment be carried on the balance sheet at year end? Give a reason for each choice.

Exercise 16-6. Long-Term Investments: Equity Method *(L.O. 4)*

On January 1, 19xx, Romano Corporation acquired 40 percent of the voting stock of Burke Corporation for $2,400,000 in cash, an amount sufficient to exercise significant influence over Burke Corporation's activities. On December 31, Romano determined that Burke paid dividends of $400,000 but incurred a net loss of $200,000 for 19xx. Prepare journal entries in Romano Corporation's records to reflect this information.

Exercise 16-7. Elimination Entry for a Purchase at Book Value *(L.O. 6)*

The Maki Manufacturing Company purchased 100 percent of the common stock of the Burleson Manufacturing Company for $150,000. Burleson's stockholders' equity included common stock of $100,000 and retained earnings of $50,000. Prepare the eliminating entry in general journal form that would appear on the work sheet for consolidating the balance sheets of these two entities as of the acquisition date.

Exercise 16-8. Elimination Entry and Minority Interest
(L.O. 6)

The stockholders' equity section of the Sher Corporation's balance sheet appeared as follows on December 31:

Common Stock—$5 par value, 40,000 shares authorized and issued	$200,000
Retained Earnings	24,000
Total Stockholders' Equity	$224,000

Assume that Edmunds Manufacturing Company owns 80 percent of the voting stock of Sher Corporation and paid $5.60 for each share. In general journal form, prepare the entry (including minority interest) to eliminate Edmunds's investment and Sher's stockholders' equity that would appear on the work sheet used in preparing the consolidated balance sheet for the two firms.

Exercise 16-9. Consolidated Balance Sheet with Goodwill
(L.O. 6)

On September 1, Y Company purchased 100 percent of the voting stock of Z Company for $960,000 in cash. The separate condensed balance sheets immediately after the purchase follow:

	Y Company	Z Company
Other Assets	$2,206,000	$1,089,000
Investment in Z Company	960,000	—
	$3,166,000	$1,089,000
Liabilities	$ 871,000	$ 189,000
Common Stock—$1 par value	1,000,000	300,000
Retained Earnings	1,295,000	600,000
	$3,166,000	$1,089,000

Prepare a work sheet for preparing the consolidated balance sheet immediately after Y Company acquired control of Z Company. Assume that any excess cost of the investment in the subsidiary over book value is attributable to goodwill from consolidation.

Exercise 16-10. Analyzing the Effects of Elimination Entries
(L.O. 6)

Some of the separate accounts from the balance sheets for F Company and G Company, just after F Company purchased 85 percent of G Company's voting stock for $765,000 in cash, follow:

	F Company	G Company
Accounts Receivable	$1,300,000	$400,000
Interest Receivable, Bonds of G Company	7,200	—
Investment in G Company	765,000	—
Investment in G Company Bonds	180,000	—
Accounts Payable	530,000	190,000
Interest Payable, Bonds	32,000	20,000
Bonds Payable	800,000	500,000
Common Stock	1,000,000	600,000
Retained Earnings	560,000	300,000

Accounts Receivable and Accounts Payable included the following: G Company owed F Company $50,000 for services rendered, and F Company owed G Company $66,000 for purchases of merchandise. F bought G Company's bonds for an amount equal to G's carrying value of the bonds. Determine the amount, including minority interest, that would appear on the consolidated balance sheet for each of the accounts listed.

Exercise 16-11. Preparation of Consolidated Income Statement *(L.O. 7)*

Marcus Company has owned 100 percent of Green Company since 19x0. The income statements of these two companies for the year ended December 31, 19x1 follow.

	Marcus Company	Green Company
Sales	$1,500,000	$600,000
Cost of Goods Sold	750,000	400,000
Gross Margin from Sales	$ 750,000	$200,000
Less: Selling Expenses	$ 250,000	$ 50,000
General and Administrative Expenses	300,000	100,000
Total Operating Expenses	$ 550,000	$150,000
Net Income from Operations	$ 200,000	$ 50,000
Other Income	60,000	—
Net Income	$ 260,000	$ 50,000

Additional information: (a) Green Company purchased $280,000 of inventory from Marcus Company, which had been sold to Green Company customers by the end of the year. (b) Green Company leased its building from Marcus Company for $60,000 per year. Prepare a consolidated income statement work sheet for the two companies for the year ended December 31, 19x1.

Interpretation Cases from Business

ICB 16-1. Maxwell Communication Corporation plc[19] *(L.O. 3)*

In reading and analyzing the financial statements of non-U.S. companies, the analyst is often faced with financial statements that do not follow the same format as statements of U.S. companies. The 1990 Group Balance Sheet and Group Profit and Loss Account (income statement) shown on pages 842 and 843 for Maxwell Communication Corporation plc, a British firm and a world leader in publishing, present such a situation. In these statements, the word *Group* is used in the same way that the word *Consolidated* is used in U.S. financial statements. It means that the company's financial statements are combined with those of a number of subsidiary companies.

19. Excerpts from the 1990 Financial Statements of Maxwell Communication Corporation plc used with permission.

Maxwell Communication Corporation plc
Group Balance Sheet
At 31st March

	1990 £ million
Fixed Assets	
Intangible assets	2,162.7
Tangible assets	337.3
Investments in convertible loan notes	—
Partnerships and associated companies	582.5
Investments	188.1
	3,270.6
Current Assets	
Stocks	108.4
Debtors	757.6
Investments	1.3
Cash at bank and in hand	65.3
	932.6
Creditors—amounts falling due within one year	(1,024.5)
Net Current Assets / (Liabilities)	(91.9)
Total Assets Less Current Liabilities	3,178.7
Creditors—amounts falling due after more than one year	(1,679.7)
Provisions for liabilities and charges	(55.1)
Accruals and deferred income	(140.4)
	1,303.5
Capital and Reserves	
Called up ordinary share capital	161.5
Share premium account	60.3
Special reserve	566.7
Capital reserve	59.2
Revaluation reserve	2.7
Profit and loss account	155.9
	1,006.3
Minority shareholders' interests	297.2
	1,303.5

Required

1. Show that you can read these British financial statements by computing as many of the following ratios as you can: (a) current ratio, (b) receivable turnover, (c) inventory turnover, (d) profit margin, (e) asset turnover, (f) return on assets, (g) return on equity, and (h) debt to equity. Use year-end figures to compute ratios that normally require averages. Indicate what data are missing for any ratio you are not able to compute.

Maxwell Communication Corporation plc
Group Profit and Loss Account
For The Year Ended 31st March 1990

	Year 1990 £ million
Sales	1,242.1
Operating costs	(1,006.1)
Share of profits of partnership and associated companies	25.2
Operating Profit Before Exceptional Item	261.2
Exceptional item	19.2
Total Operating Profit	280.4
Net interest and investment income	(108.1)
Profit Before Taxation	172.3
Taxation on profit on ordinary activities	(34.5)
Profit on Ordinary Activities After Taxation	137.8
Minority shareholders' interests	(11.0)
Extraordinary items less taxation	(25.7)
Profit Attributable to Shareholders	101.1
Dividends paid and proposed	(95.8)
Retained Profit for the Period	5.3
Retained Profits at Beginning of Period	173.3
Transfer of depreciation from revaluation reserve	—
Exchange translation differences	(22.7)
Retained Profits at End of Period	155.9
Earnings per Share	20.0p

2. What terms or accounts did you have trouble interpreting? How do you evaluate the usefulness of the formats of the British financial statements relative to those of U.S. financial statements?

ICB 16-2. General Electric Company and RCA[20]
(L.O. 6)

One of the major corporate buyouts in 1986 was General Electric Company's purchase of RCA Corporation. This transaction is described in a note to GE's financial statements in its 1986 annual report as follows:

On June 9, 1986, GE acquired RCA Corporation and its subsidiaries (RCA) in a transaction for which the total consideration to former RCA shareholders was $6.406 billion in cash. RCA businesses include the manufacture and sale of a wide

20. Excerpts from the 1986 Annual Report used by permission of General Electric. Copyright © 1986.

range of electronic products and related research and services for consumer, commercial, military and space applications; the National Broadcasting Company's (NBC) radio and television stations and network broadcasting services; and domestic and international message and data communications services.

The acquisition was accounted for as a purchase, and the operating results of RCA have been consolidated with those of GE since June 1, 1986. In preparing 1986 financial information, the purchase price ($6.426 billion, including an estimated $20 million of related costs) has been allocated to the assets and liabilities of RCA based on estimates of fair market values. The excess of purchase price over the estimate of fair values of net assets acquired (goodwill) was $2.7 billion, which is being amortized on a straight-line basis over 40 years.

Required

1. Show the entry in GE's records to record the purchase of RCA.
2. Did GE pay more or less than book value for RCA?
3. Show the year-end adjusting entry on GE's records related to goodwill. (GE's year end is December 31.)

ICB 16-3. USX and Marathon Oil[21] *(L.O. 6)*

In 1981 USX Corporation fought Mobil Oil Corporation for control of Marathon Oil Company. USX won this battle of the giants by reaching an agreement to purchase all of Marathon's stock. The *Chicago Tribune* reported on March 12, 1982 that the $6 billion merger, as approved by the stockholders of Marathon, was the second largest in history and created the twelfth largest industrial corporation in the United States.

In a note to USX's 1981 annual report, the details of the purchase were revealed. USX "purchased 30 million common shares of Marathon Oil Company for $125 per share . . . as the first step in its planned acquisition of the entire equity of Marathon." Additional Marathon shares would be purchased by issuing $100 principal amount of 12½ percent notes due in 1994 for each share of stock. These notes were estimated by the financial press to have a fair market value of $80 per note. The total number of Marathon shares prior to these two transactions was 59.0 million. On December 31, 1981, just before the merger, the condensed balance sheets of USX and Marathon Oil appeared as shown at the top of the next page (in millions).

Further information in USX's annual report indicated that when consolidated financial statements were prepared using the purchase method, management would adjust Marathon's assets and liabilities in the following manner. It would (a) increase inventory by $1,244 million; (b) increase current liabilities by $392 million; and (c) decrease deferred income taxes by $588 million. After these adjustments, any remaining excess of the purchase price over book value of Marathon's shares would be attributed to property, plant, and equipment.

Required

1. Prepare the entry in USX's journals to record the purchase of Marathon Oil.
2. Prepare the eliminating entry, including the adjustments indicated, that would be made to consolidate USX and Marathon.
3. Prepare a consolidated balance sheet for the merged companies.
4. Did USX pay more or less than book value for Marathon? Why would USX take this action? Did the purchase raise or lower USX's book value per share?

21. Excerpts from the 1981 Annual Report used by permission of USX Corporation. Copyright © 1981.

	USX	Marathon Oil
Assets		
Current Assets, Excluding Inventories	$ 4,214	$ 907
Inventories	1,198	576
Property, Plant, and Equipment (net)	6,676	4,233
Other Assets	1,228	278
Total Assets	$13,316	$5,994
Liabilities and Stockholders' Equity		
Current Liabilities	$ 2,823	$1,475
Long-Term Debt	2,340	1,368
Deferred Income Taxes	732	588
Other Liabilities	1,161	501
Total Liabilities	$ 7,056	$3,932
Stockholders' Equity	6,260	2,062
Total Liabilities and Stockholders' Equity	$13,316	$5,994

Problem Set A

Since foreign exchange rates can fluctuate widely, a variety of rates have been used in Problem Sets A and B.

Problem 16A-1. Recording International Transactions *(L.O. 1)*

Tsin Import/Export Company, whose year end is December 31, engaged in the following transactions (exchange rates in parentheses):

Oct. 14 Sold goods to a Mexican firm for $20,000; terms n/30 in U.S. dollars (peso = $.0004).
26 Purchased goods from a Japanese firm for $40,000; terms n/20 in yen (yen = $.0040).
Nov. 4 Sold goods to a British firm for $39,000; terms n/30 in pounds (pound = $1.30).
14 Received payment in full for October 14 sale (peso = $.0003).
15 Paid for the goods purchased on October 26 (yen = $.0044).
23 Purchased goods from an Italian firm for $28,000; terms n/10 in U.S. dollars (lira = $.0008).
30 Purchased goods from a Japanese firm for $35,200; terms n/60 in yen (yen = $.0044).
Dec. 2 Paid for the goods purchased on November 23 (lira = $.0007).
3 Received payment in full for the goods sold on November 4 (pound = $1.20).
8 Sold goods to a French firm for $66,000; terms n/30 in francs (franc = $.11).

Dec. 17 Purchased goods from a Mexican firm for $37,000; terms n/30 in U.S. dollars (peso = $.0004).
18 Sold goods to a German firm for $90,000; terms n/30 in marks (mark = $.30).
31 Made year-end adjusting entries for incomplete foreign exchange transactions (franc = $.09; peso = $.0003; pound = $1.10; mark = $.35; lira = $.0008; yen = $.0050).
Jan. 7 Received payment for the goods sold on December 8 (franc = $.10).
16 Paid for the goods purchased on December 17 (peso = $.0002).
17 Received payment for the goods sold on December 18 (mark = $.40).
28 Paid for the goods purchased on November 30 (yen = $.0045).

Required Prepare general journal entries for these transactions.

Problem 16A-2. Long-Term Investment Transactions *(L.O. 4)*

On January 2, 19x0, the Durham Company made several long-term investments in the voting stock of various companies. It purchased 10,000 shares of Kang at $2.00 a share, 15,000 shares of Pearl at $3.00 a share, and 6,000 shares of Calderone at $4.50 a share. Each investment represents less than 20 percent of the voting stock of the company. The remaining transactions of Durham in securities during 19x0 were as follows:

May 15 Purchased with cash 6,000 shares of Ross stock for $3.00 per share. This investment comprises less than 20 percent of the Ross voting stock.
July 16 Sold the 10,000 shares of Kang stock for $1.80 per share.
Sept. 30 Purchased with cash 5,000 additional shares of Pearl for $3.20 per share.
Dec. 31 The market values per share of the stock in the Long-Term Investments account were as follows: Pearl, $3.25; Calderone, $4.00; and Ross, $2.00.

Durham's transactions in securities during 19x1 were as follows:

Feb. 1 Received a cash dividend from Pearl of $.10 per share.
July 15 Sold the 6,000 Calderone shares for $4.00 per share.
Aug. 1 Received a cash dividend from Pearl of $.10 per share.
Sept. 10 Purchased 3,000 shares of Jolley for $7.00 per share.
Dec. 31 The market values per share of the stock in the Long-Term Investments account were as follows: Pearl, $3.25; Ross, $2.50; and Jolley, $6.50.

Required Prepare the journal entries to record all of Durham Company's transactions in long-term investments during 19x0 and 19x1.

Problem 16A-3. Long-Term Investments: Equity Method *(L.O. 4)*

Mathis Corporation owns 35 percent of the voting stock of Albers Corporation. The Investment account on the books of Mathis Corporation as of January 1, 19xx was $360,000. During 19xx, Albers Corporation reported the following quarterly earnings and dividends:

Quarter	Earnings	Dividends Paid
1	$ 80,000	$ 50,000
2	120,000	50,000
3	60,000	50,000
4	(40,000)	50,000
	$220,000	$200,000

Because of the percentage of voting shares Mathis owns, it can exercise significant influence over the operations of Albers Corporation. Under these conditions, Mathis Corporation must account for the investment using the equity method.

Required

1. Prepare the journal entries that Mathis Corporation must make each quarter to record its share of earnings and dividends.
2. Prepare a ledger account for Mathis Corporation's investment in Albers, enter the beginning balance, and post the relevant entries from **1**.

Problem 16A-4. Consolidated Balance Sheet: Less than 100 Percent Ownership *(L.O. 6)*

The Lobos Corporation purchased 80 percent of the outstanding voting stock of the Yost Corporation for $820,800 in cash. The balance sheets of the two companies immediately after acquisition were as follows:

	Lobos Corporation	Yost Corporation
Assets		
Cash	$ 150,000	$ 60,000
Accounts Receivable	360,000	200,000
Inventory	1,600,000	700,000
Investment in Yost	820,800	—
Property, Plant, and Equipment (net)	2,500,000	1,000,000
Other Assets	100,000	40,000
Total Assets	$5,530,800	$2,000,000
Liabilities and Stockholders' Equity		
Accounts Payable	$ 400,000	$ 150,000
Salaries Payable	50,000	20,000
Taxes Payable	20,000	4,000
Bonds Payable	1,300,000	800,000
Common Stock	2,500,000	900,000
Retained Earnings	1,260,800	126,000
Total Liabilities and Stockholders' Equity	$5,530,800	$2,000,000

Additional information: (a) The Other Assets account on the Yost balance sheet represents an investment in Lobos's Bonds Payable. The investment in Lobos was made at an amount equal to Lobos's carrying value of the bonds. (b) $50,000 of the Accounts Receivable of Lobos Corporation represents receivables due from Yost.

Required

Prepare a work sheet as of the acquisition date for the preparation of a consolidated balance sheet.

Problem 16A-5. Consolidated Balance Sheet: Cost Exceeding Book Value *(L.O. 5)*

The balance sheets of Cheever and Ham Corporations as of December 31, 19xx are shown as follows.

	Cheever Corporation	Ham Corporation
Assets		
Cash	$ 600,000	$ 120,000
Accounts Receivable	700,000	600,000
Inventory	250,000	600,000
Investment in Ham Corporation	800,000	—
Property, Plant, and Equipment	1,350,000	850,000
Other Assets	20,000	50,000
Total Assets	$3,720,000	$2,220,000
Liabilities and Stockholders' Equity		
Accounts Payable	$ 750,000	$ 500,000
Salaries Payable	300,000	270,000
Bonds Payable	350,000	800,000
Common Stock	1,500,000	500,000
Retained Earnings	820,000	150,000
Total Liabilities and Stockholders' Equity	$3,720,000	$2,220,000

Required

Prepare a consolidated balance sheet work sheet for the two companies, assuming that Cheever purchased 100 percent of the common stock of Ham for $800,000 immediately prior to December 31, 19xx, and that $70,000 of the excess of cost over book value is attributable to the increased value of Ham Corporation's inventory. The rest of the excess is considered goodwill.

Problem Set B

Problem 16B-1. Recording International Transactions *(L.O. 1)*

Mountain States Company, whose year end is June 30, engaged in the following international transactions (exchange rates in parentheses):

May 15 Purchased goods from a Japanese firm for $110,000; terms n/10 in U.S. dollars (yen = $.0080).

17 Sold goods to a German company for $165,000; terms n/30 in marks (mark = $.55).

May 21 Purchased goods from a Mexican company for $120,000; terms n/30 in pesos (peso = $.0004).
25 Paid for the goods purchased on May 15 (yen = $.0085).
31 Sold goods to an Italian firm for $200,000; terms n/60 in lire (lira = $.0005).
June 5 Sold goods to a British firm for $56,000; terms n/10 in U.S. dollars (pound = $1.30).
7 Purchased goods from a Japanese firm for $221,000; terms n/30 in yen (yen = $.0085).
15 Received payment for the sale made on June 5 (pound = $1.80).
16 Received payment for the sale made on May 17 (mark = $.60).
17 Purchased goods from a French firm for $66,000; terms n/30 in U.S. dollars (franc = $.16).
20 Paid for the goods purchased on May 21 (peso = $.0003).
22 Sold goods to a British firm for $108,000; terms n/30 in pounds (pound = $1.80).
30 Made year-end adjustment for incomplete foreign exchange transactions (franc = $.17; peso = $.0003; mark = $.60; lira = $.0003; pound = $1.70; yen = $.0090).
July 7 Paid for the goods purchased on June 7 (yen = $.0085).
19 Paid for the goods purchased on June 17 (franc = $.15).
22 Received payment for the goods sold on June 22 (pound = $1.60).
30 Received payment for the goods sold on May 31 (lira = $.0004).

Required Prepare general journal entries for these transactions.

Problem 16B-2. Long-Term Investments Transactions *(L.O. 4)*

Herbst Corporation made the following transactions in its Long-Term Investments account over a two-year period:

19x0
Apr. 1 Purchased with cash 20,000 shares of Babbitt Company stock for $76 per share.
June 1 Purchased with cash 15,000 shares of Kanter Corporation stock for $36 per share.
Sept. 1 Received a $.50 per share dividend from Babbitt Company.
Nov. 1 Purchased with cash 25,000 shares of Moran Corporation stock for $55 per share.
Dec. 31 Market values per share of shares held in the Long-Term Investments account were as follows: Babbitt Company, $70; Kanter Corporation, $16; and Moran Corporation, $61.

19x1
Feb. 1 Because of unfavorable prospects for Kanter Corporation, Kanter stock was sold for cash at $20 per share.
May 1 Purchased with cash 10,000 shares of Gayle Corporation for $112 per share.
Sept. 1 Received $1 per share dividend from Babbitt Company.
Dec. 31 Market values per share of shares held in the Long-Term Investments account were as follows: Babbitt Company, $80; Moran Corporation, $70; and Gayle Corporation, $100.

Required Prepare entries to record these transactions in the Herbst Corporation records. Assume that all investments represent less than 20 percent of the voting stock of the company whose stock was acquired.

Problem 16B-3. Long-Term Investment: Equity Method
(L.O. 4)

The Yu Company owns 40 percent of the voting stock of the Sargent Company. The Investment account for this company on the Yu Company's balance sheet had a balance of $300,000 on January 1, 19xx. During 19xx, the Sargent Company reported the following quarterly earnings and dividends paid:

Quarter	Earnings	Dividends Paid
1	$ 40,000	$20,000
2	30,000	20,000
3	80,000	20,000
4	(20,000)	20,000
	$130,000	$80,000

The Yu Company exercises a significant influence over the operations of the Sargent Company and therefore uses the equity method to account for its investment.

Required

1. Prepare the journal entries that the Yu Company must make each quarter in accounting for its investment in the Sargent Company.
2. Prepare a ledger account for the investment in common stock of the Sargent Company. Enter the beginning balance and post relevant portions of the entries made in **1**.

Problem 16B-4. Consolidated Balance Sheet: Less than 100 Percent Ownership
(L.O. 6)

In a cash transaction, Alter Company purchased 70 percent of the outstanding stock of Damon Company for $296,800 cash on June 30, 19xx. Immediately after the acquisition, the separate balance sheets of the companies appeared as follows.

	Alter Company	Damon Company
Assets		
Cash	$ 160,000	$ 24,000
Accounts Receivable	260,000	120,000
Inventory	400,000	260,000
Investment in Damon Company	296,800	—
Plant and Equipment (net)	600,000	440,000
Other Assets	20,000	80,000
Total Assets	$1,736,800	$924,000
Liabilities and Stockholders' Equity		
Accounts Payable	$ 320,000	$200,000
Long-Term Debt	400,000	300,000
Common Stock—$5 par value	800,000	400,000
Retained Earnings	216,800	24,000
Total Liabilities and Stockholders' Equity	$1,736,800	$924,000

Additional information: (a) Damon Company's other assets represent a long-term investment in Alter Company's long-term debt. The debt was purchased for an amount equal to Alter's carrying value of the debt. (b) Alter Company owes Damon Company $40,000 for services rendered.

Required

Prepare a work sheet for preparing a consolidated balance sheet as of the acquisition date.

Problem 16B-5. Consolidated Balance Sheet: Cost Exceeding Book Value
(L.O. 6)

The balance sheets of Perez and Lloyd Companies as of December 31, 19xx follow.

	Perez Company	Lloyd Company
Assets		
Cash	$ 60,000	$ 40,000
Accounts Receivable	100,000	30,000
Investment in Lloyd Company	350,000	—
Other Assets	100,000	180,000
Total Assets	$610,000	$250,000
Liabilities and Stockholders' Equity		
Liabilities	$110,000	$ 30,000
Common Stock—$10 par value	400,000	200,000
Retained Earnings	100,000	20,000
Total Liabilities and Stockholders' Equity	$610,000	$250,000

Required

Prepare a consolidated balance sheet work sheet for the Perez and Lloyd Companies. Assume that the Perez Company purchased 100 percent of Lloyd's common stock for $350,000 immediately before the above balance sheet date. Also assume that $65,000 of the excess of cost over book value is attributable to the increased value of Lloyd Company's other assets. The rest of the excess is considered by the Perez Company to be goodwill.

Financial Decision Cases

16-1. San Antonio Corporation
(L.O. 4)

San Antonio Corporation is a successful oil and gas exploration business in the southwestern part of the United States. At the beginning of 19xx, the company made investments in three companies that perform services in the oil and gas industry. The details of each of these investments are presented in the next three paragraphs.

San Antonio purchased 100,000 shares in Levelland Service Corporation at a cost of $4 per share. Levelland has 1.5 million shares outstanding, and during 19xx paid dividends of $.20 per share on earnings of $.40 per share. At the end of the year, Levelland's shares were selling for $6 per share.

San Antonio also purchased 2 million shares of Plainview Drilling Company at $2 per share. Plainview has 10 million shares outstanding. In 19xx Plainview paid a dividend of $.10 per share on earnings of $.20 per share. During the current year the president of San Antonio was appointed to the board of directors of Plainview. At the end of the year Plainview's stock was selling for $3 per share.

In another action, San Antonio purchased 1 million of Brownfield Oil Field Supplies Company's 5 million outstanding shares at $3 per share. The president of San Antonio sought membership on the board of directors of Brownfield but was rebuffed by Brownfield's board when shareholders representing a majority of Brownfield's outstanding stock stated that they did not want to be associated with San Antonio. Brownfield paid a dividend of $.20 per share and reported a net income of only $.10 per share for the year. By the end of the year, the price of its stock had dropped to $1 per share.

Required

1. What principal factors must you consider in order to determine how to account for San Antonio's investments? Should they be shown on the balance sheet as short-term or long-term investments? What factors affect this decision?
2. For each of the three investments, make general journal entries for each of the following: (a) initial investment, (b) receipt of cash dividend, and (c) recognition of income (if appropriate).
3. What adjusting entry (if any) is required at the end of the year?
4. Assuming that San Antonio's investment in Brownfield is sold after the first of the year for $1.50 per share, what general journal entry would be made? Assuming that the market value of the remaining investments held by San Antonio is above cost at the end of the second year, what adjusting entry (if any) would be required?

16-2.
Metropolitan Stores Corporation
(L.O. 5, 6)

Metropolitan Stores Corporation is one of the largest owners of discount appliance stores in the United States. It owns Highway Superstores among several other discount chains. The company has a wholly owned finance subsidiary to finance its accounts receivable. Condensed 1991 financial statements for Metropolitan Stores and its finance subsidiary appear on page 853 (in millions). The fiscal year ends January 31.

Total sales to customers were $4 billion. The Financial Accounting Standards Board's 1987 statement (FASB *Statement No. 94*) requires all majority-owned subsidiaries to be consolidated in the parent company's financial statements. Metropolitan's management believes that it is misleading to consolidate the finance subsidiary because it distorts the real operations of the company. You are asked to assess the effects of the statement on Metropolitan Stores' financial position.

Required

1. Prepare a consolidated balance sheet for Metropolitan Stores and its finance subsidiary.
2. Demonstrate the effects of FASB *Statement No. 94* by computing the following ratios for Metropolitan Stores before and after the consolidation in **1**: receivable turnover, average days' sales uncollected, and debt to equity (use year-end balances).

	Metropolitan Stores Corporation	Finance Subsidiary
Assets		
Current Assets (except Accounts Receivable)	$ 866	$ 1
Accounts Receivable (net)	293	869
Property, Equipment, and Other Assets	933	—
Investment in Finance Subsidiary	143	—
Total Assets	$2,235	$870
Liabilities and Stockholders' Equity		
Current Liabilities	$ 717	$ 10
Long-Term Liabilities	859	717
Stockholders' Equity	659	143
Total Liabilities and Stockholders' Equity	$2,235	$870

3. What other ratios will be affected by the implementation of FASB *Statement No. 94*? Does consolidation assist investors and creditors in assessing the risk of investing in Metropolitan Stores securities or loaning the company money? Relate your answer to your calculations in **2**. What do you think of management's position?

APPENDIX A

Accounting for Unincorporated Businesses

LEARNING OBJECTIVES

1. *Record the basic transactions affecting the owner's equity of a sole proprietorship.*
2. *Identify the major characteristics of a partnership.*
3. *Identify the advantages and disadvantages of a partnership, and compare it to other forms of business.*
4. *Record investments of cash and of other assets by the partners in forming a partnership.*
5. *Compute the profit or loss that partners share, based on a stated ratio, a capital investment ratio, and salaries and interest to partners.*
6. *Record the admission of a new partner.*
7. *Describe the implications of the withdrawal or death of a partner and of the liquidation of a partnership.*

Accountants need to understand the three major forms of business organization: sole proprietorships, partnerships, and corporations. Accountants recognize each form as an economic unit separate from its owners, though legally only the corporation is considered separate from its owners. The main focus of this book has been on corporations. In this appendix, however, the focus is on sole proprietorships and partnerships. After studying this appendix, you should be able to meet the learning objectives listed on the left.

Accounting for Sole Proprietorships

A **sole proprietorship** is a business owned by one person. This business form gives the individual a means of controlling the business apart from his or her personal interests. Legally, however, the proprietorship is the same economic unit as the individual. The individual business owner receives all the profits or losses and is liable for all the obligations of the proprietorship. Proprietorships represent the largest number of businesses in the United States, but typically they are the smallest in size. The life of a proprietorship ends when the owner wishes it to or at the owner's death or incapacity.

When someone invests in his or her own company, the amount of the investment is recorded in a capital account. For example, the entry to record the initial investment of $10,000 by Clara Hooper in her new mail-order business would be:

Cash	10,000	
Clara Hooper, Capital		10,000
To record initial investment in sole proprietorship		

OBJECTIVE 1
Record the basic transactions affecting the owner's equity of a sole proprietorship

During the period, Clara will likely withdraw assets from the business for personal living expenses. Since legally there is no separation between the owner and the sole proprietorship, it is not necessary to make a formal declaration of a withdrawal, as would be required in the case of corporate dividends. The withdrawal of $500 by Clara is recorded as follows:

Clara Hooper, Withdrawals	500	
Cash		500
To record withdrawal of $500 for personal use		

Revenue and expense accounts are closed out to Income Summary in the same way for sole proprietorships as they are for corporations. Income Summary, however, is closed to the Capital account instead of to Retained Earnings. For example, the closing entry, assuming a net income of $1,000, is as follows:

Income Summary	1,000	
Clara Hooper, Capital		1,000
To close Income Summary in a sole proprietorship		

Further, the Withdrawals account is closed to the Capital account as follows:

Clara Hooper, Capital	500	
Clara Hooper, Withdrawals		500
To close Withdrawals		

Accounting for Partnerships

The Uniform Partnership Act, which has been adopted by a majority of the states, defines a **partnership** as "an association of two or more persons to carry on as co-owners of a business for profit." Normally, partnerships are formed when owners of small businesses wish to combine capital or managerial talents for some common business purpose.

Characteristics of a Partnership

OBJECTIVE 2
Identify the major characteristics of a partnership

Partnerships differ in many ways from other forms of business. The next few paragraphs describe some of the important characteristics of a partnership.

Voluntary Association. A partnership is a voluntary association of individuals rather than a legal entity in itself. Therefore, a partner is responsible under the law for his or her partners' business actions within the scope of the partnership. A partner also has unlimited liability for the debts of the partnership. Because of these potential liabilities, an individual must be allowed to choose the people who will join the partnership. A person should select as partners individuals who share his or her business objectives.

Partnership Agreement. A partnership is easy to form. Two or more competent people simply agree to be partners in some common business purpose. This agreement is known as the **partnership agreement** and does not have to be in writing. However, good business practice calls for a written document that clearly states the details of the partnership. The contract should include the name, location, and purpose of the business; the partners and their respective duties; the investments of each partner; the methods for distributing profits and losses; the procedures for admission or withdrawal of partners; the withdrawals of assets allowed each partner; and procedures for dissolving, or ending, the business.

Limited Life. Because a partnership is formed by a contract between partners, it has **limited life**; anything that ends the contract dissolves the partnership. A partnership is dissolved when (1) a partner withdraws, (2) a partner goes bankrupt, (3) a partner is incapacitated (as when a partner becomes ill), (4) a partner dies, (5) a new partner is admitted, (6) a partner retires, or (7) the partnership ends according to the partnership agreement (as when a major project is completed).

Mutual Agency. Each partner is an agent of the partnership within the scope of the business. Because of this **mutual agency** feature, any partner can bind the partnership to a business agreement as long as he or she acts within the scope of normal operations of the business. For example, a partner in a used-car business can bind the partnership through the purchase or sale of used cars. However, this partner cannot bind the partnership to a contract for buying men's clothing or any other goods unrelated to the used-car business. Because of this mutual agency characteristic, it is very important for an individual to choose business partners who have integrity and business objectives similar to his or her own.

Unlimited Liability. Each partner is personally liable for all the debts of the partnership. If a partnership is in poor financial condition and cannot pay its debts, the creditors must first satisfy their claims from the assets of the partnership. When the assets of the business are not enough to pay all debts, the creditors may seek payment from the personal assets of each partner. If a partner's personal assets are used up before the debts are paid, the creditors may claim additional assets from the remaining partners who are able to pay the debts. Each partner could conceivably be required by law to pay all the debts of the partnership; therefore, all the partners have **unlimited liability** for their company's debt.

An exception to the unlimited liability rule is the **limited partnership**, which is a partnership formed for a specific purpose such as the development of a shopping center or an apartment complex. In a limited partnership, there is a general partner who runs the partnership business and has generally unlimited liability, and there are limited partners who are investors in the project whose liability is generally limited to their investment in the partnership.

Co-ownership of Partnership Property. When individuals invest property in a partnership, they give up the right to their separate use of the property. The property becomes an asset of the partnership and is owned jointly by all the partners.

Participation in Partnership Income. Each partner has the right to share in the company's profits and the responsibility to share in its losses. The partnership agreement should state the method of distributing profits and losses to each partner. If the agreement describes how profits are to be shared but does not mention losses, the losses are distributed in the same way as profits. If the partners fail to describe the method of profit and loss distribution in the partnership agreement, the law states that profits and losses must be shared equally.

Advantages and Disadvantages of a Partnership

OBJECTIVE 3 *Identify the advantages and disadvantages of a partnership, and compare it to other forms of business*

Partnerships have both advantages and disadvantages. Several of the advantages are that the partnership is easy to form and to dissolve; it is able to pool capital resources and individual talents; it has no corporate tax burden (because the partnership is not a legal entity, it does not have to pay an income tax but must file an informational return); and it gives freedom and flexibility to its partners' actions.

Several of the disadvantages of a partnership are that its life is limited; one partner can bind the partnership to a contract (mutual agency); the partners have unlimited personal liability; and it is hard in a partnership to raise large amounts of capital and to transfer ownership interest.

The partnership form of business is compared with the sole proprietorship and the corporation in Table A-1.

Accounting for Partners' Equity

OBJECTIVE 4 *Record investments of cash and of other assets by the partners in forming a partnership*

Accounting for a partnership is very similar to accounting for a sole proprietorship. A major difference is that the owners' equity of a partnership is called **partners' equity**. In accounting for partners' equity, it is necessary to maintain separate capital and withdrawal accounts for each partner and to divide the profits and losses of the company among the partners. The differences in the capital accounts of a sole proprietorship and a partnership are illustrated at the top of the next page.

Sole Proprietorship		Partnership			
Blake, Capital		**Desmond, Capital**		**Frank, Capital**	
	50,000		30,000		40,000
Blake, Withdrawals		**Desmond, Withdrawals**		**Frank, Withdrawals**	
12,000		5,000		6,000	

In the partners' equity section of the balance sheet, the balance of each partner's Capital account is listed separately, as shown in the partial balance sheet below.

Liabilities and Partners' Equity

Total Liabilities		$28,000
Partners' Equity		
Desmond, Capital	$25,000	
Frank, Capital	34,000	
Total Partners' Equity		59,000
Total Liabilities and Partners' Equity		$87,000

Each partner invests cash, other assets, or a combination of both in the partnership according to the agreement. When other assets are invested, the partners must agree on their value. The value of noncash assets should

Table A-1. Comparative Features of the Forms of Business Organization

	Sole Proprietorship	Partnership	Corporation
1. Legal status	Not a separate legal entity	Not a separate legal entity	Separate legal entity
2. Risk of ownership	Owner's personal resources at stake	Partners' personal resources at stake	Limited to investment in corporation
3. Duration or life	Limited by desire or death of owner	Limited by desire or death of any partner	Indefinite, possibly unlimited
4. Transferability of ownership	Sale by owner establishes new company	Changes in any partner's interest require new partnership	Transferable by sale of stock
5. Accounting treatment	Separate economic unit	Separate economic unit	Separate economic unit

be their fair market value on the date they are transferred to the partnership. The assets invested by a partner are debited to the proper account, and the total amount is credited to the partner's Capital account.

To illustrate the recording of partners' investments, we shall assume that on July 1 Jerry Adcock and Rose Villa agree to combine their capital and equipment in a partnership for the purpose of operating a jewelry store. Adcock will invest $28,000 cash and $37,000 of furniture and displays, and Villa will invest $40,000 cash and $20,000 of equipment, according to the partnership agreement. The general journal entries that record the initial investments of Adcock and Villa are as follows:

July	1	Cash	28,000	
		Furniture and Displays	37,000	
		Jerry Adcock, Capital		65,000
		To record the initial investment of Jerry Adcock in Adcock and Villa		
	1	Cash	40,000	
		Equipment	20,000	
		Rose Villa, Capital		60,000
		To record the initial investment of Rose Villa in Adcock and Villa		

Distribution of Profits and Losses

OBJECTIVE 5
Compute the profit or loss that partners share, based on a stated ratio, a capital investment ratio, and salaries and interest to partners

A partnership's profits and losses can be distributed according to any method that the partners specify in the partnership agreement. The agreement should be specific and clear to avoid disputes among partners over later distributions of profits and losses. However, if the partnership agreement does not mention the distribution of profits and losses, the law requires that they be shared equally by all partners. Also, if the partnership agreement mentions only the distribution of profits, the law requires that losses be distributed in the same ratio.

The profits of a partnership normally have three components: (1) return to the partners for the use of their capital, (2) compensation for services that the partners have rendered, and (3) further economic income for the business risks the partners have taken. The breakdown of total profit into its three components helps to clarify how much each partner has contributed to the firm.

If all partners are spending the same amount of time, are contributing equal capital, and have similar managerial talents, then an equal sharing of profits and losses would be fair. However, if one partner works full time in the firm whereas another partner devotes only one-fourth of his or her time, then the distribution of profits or losses should reflect this difference. This arrangement would apply to any situation in which the partners contribute unequally to the business.

Several ways for partners to share profits are (1) by stated ratio, (2) by capital investment ratio, and (3) by salaries to the partners and interest on partners' capital, with the remainder according to a stated ratio.

Stated Ratio. One method of distributing profits and losses is to give each partner a stated ratio of the total. If each partner is making an equal contribution to the firm, each may receive the same share of the profits and losses. The equal contribution of the partners may take many forms. For example, each partner may have made an equal investment in the firm. On the other hand, one partner may be devoting more time and talent to the firm, whereas the second partner may make a larger capital investment. Also, if the partners contribute unequally to the firm, unequal stated ratios can be appropriate, such as 60 percent and 40 percent. To illustrate this method, we shall assume that Adcock and Villa made a profit last year of $140,000. The partnership agreement states that the percentages of profits and losses distributed to Adcock and Villa will be 60 and 40, respectively. The computation of each partner's share of the profit and the journal entry to show the distribution are as follows:

Adcock ($140,000 × 60%)	$ 84,000
Villa ($140,000 × 40%)	56,000
Total profits	$140,000

June 30	Income Summary	140,000	
	Jerry Adcock, Capital		84,000
	Rose Villa, Capital		56,000
	To distribute the profits for the year to the partners' capital accounts		

Capital Investment Ratio. If the invested capital produces the most income for the partnership business, then profits and losses may be distributed according to capital investment. One way of distributing profits and losses in this case is to use the ratio of capital balances of each partner at the beginning of the year. To show how this method works, we shall assume that the beginning capital balances for Adcock and Villa were as follows:

	Capital	Capital Ratio
Jerry Adcock	$ 65,000	65/125
Rose Villa	60,000	60/125
Total capital	$125,000	

The profit that each partner will receive when distribution is based on beginning capital investment ratios is figured by multiplying the total profit by each partner's capital ratio.

Jerry Adcock	$140,000 × 65/125 =	$ 72,800
Rose Villa	$140,000 × 60/125 =	67,200
Total profit		$140,000

The entry showing distribution of profit is as follows:

June 30	Income Summary	140,000	
	Jerry Adcock, Capital		72,800
	Rose Villa, Capital		67,200
	To distribute the profits for the year to the partners' capital accounts		

Another way of using the capital investment ratio approach would be to use the average capital balance of each partner during the year instead of the beginning balance.

Salaries, Interest, and Stated Ratio. Partners generally do not contribute equally to a firm. To make up for these unequal contributions, some partnership agreements will allow for partners' salaries, interest on partners' capital balances, or a combination of both in the distribution of profits. Salaries and interest of this kind are not deducted as expenses before the partnership profit is determined. They represent a method of arriving at an equitable distribution of the profit or loss.

To illustrate an allowance for partners' salaries, we shall assume that Adcock and Villa agree to the following salaries: $8,000 for Adcock and $7,000 for Villa. Any remaining profits will be divided equally. Each salary is charged to the appropriate partners' withdrawal account. If we assume the same $140,000 profit for the first year, the calculations and journal entry for Adcock and Villa are shown below.

	Income of Partners		Income
	Adcock	**Villa**	**Distributed**
Total Income for Distribution			$140,000
Distribution of Salaries			
Adcock	$ 8,000		
Villa		$ 7,000	15,000
Remaining Income After Salaries			$125,000
Equal Distribution of Remaining Income			
Adcock	62,500		
Villa		62,500	125,000
Remaining Income			—
Income of Partners	$70,500	$69,500	

June 30	Income Summary	140,000	
	Jerry Adcock, Capital		70,500
	Rose Villa, Capital		69,500
	To distribute the profits for the year to the partners' capital accounts		

Salaries allow for differences in the services that partners provide to the business. However, they do not consider differences in invested capital. To allow for capital differences, each partner may receive, in addition to salary, a stated interest on his or her invested capital. To illustrate, we shall assume that Adcock and Villa agree to receive 10 percent interest on their beginning capital balances as well as annual salaries of $8,000 for Adcock and $7,000 for Villa. They will share any remaining income equally. The calculations and journal entry for Adcock and Villa, if we assume $140,000 profits, are as follows:

	Income of Partners		Income
	Adcock	Villa	Distributed
Total Income for Distribution			$140,000
Distribution of Salaries			
Adcock	$ 8,000		
Villa		$ 7,000	15,000
Remaining Income After Salaries			$125,000
Distribution of Interest			
Adcock ($65,000 × 10%)	6,500		
Villa ($60,000 × 10%)		6,000	12,500
Remaining Income After Salaries and Interest			$112,500
Equal Distribution of Remaining Income			
Adcock	56,250		
Villa		56,250	112,500
Remaining Income			—
Income of Partners	$70,750	$69,250	

June 30	Income Summary	140,000	
	Jerry Adcock, Capital		70,750
	Rose Villa, Capital		69,250
	To distribute the profits for the year to the partners' capital accounts		

If the partnership agreement allows for paying salaries or interest or both, the partners must receive these amounts even if the profits are not enough to cover the salaries and interest. This would result in the partners' sharing a negative amount after salaries and interest are paid. The negative amount after payment of salaries and interest must be distributed according to the stated ratio in the partnership agreement, or equally, if the agreement does not mention a ratio.

The distribution of income for Adcock and Villa under the previous example, assuming profits of $20,000, would be as follows:

	Income of Partners		Income
	Adcock	Villa	Distributed
Total Income for Distribution			$20,000
Distribution of Salaries			
Adcock	$ 8,000		
Villa		$7,000	15,000
Remaining Income After Salaries			$ 5,000
Distribution of Interest			
Adcock ($65,000 × 10%)	6,500		
Villa ($60,000 × 10%)		6,000	12,500
Negative Balance After Salary and Interest			($ 7,500)
Equal Distribution			
Adcock	(3,750)		
Villa		(3,750)	7,500
Remaining Income			—
Income of Partners	$10,750	$9,250	

Dissolution of a Partnership

Dissolution of a partnership occurs when there is a change in the original association of the partners. When a partnership is dissolved, the partners lose their authority to continue the business as a going concern. This does not mean that the business operation is necessarily ended or interrupted. The remaining partners can act for the partnership in finishing the affairs of the business or in forming a new partnership. The dissolution of a partnership through admission of a new partner, withdrawal of a partner, and death of a partner is discussed next.

OBJECTIVE 6 *Record the admission of a new partner*

Admission of a New Partner. Admission of a new partner will dissolve the old partnership because a new association has been formed. However, the firm cannot admit a new partner without the consent of all the old partners. When a new partner is admitted, a new partnership agreement should describe the new arrangement in detail.

An individual may be admitted into a firm in one of two ways: (1) by purchasing an interest in the partnership from one or more of the original partners, or (2) by investing assets in the partnership.

In the first case, when an individual is admitted to a firm by purchasing an interest from an old partner, each partner must agree to the change. The interest purchased must be transferred from the Capital account of the selling partner to the Capital account of the new partner.

For example, assume that Jerry Adcock of Adcock and Villa decides to sell his interest in the business, represented by his Capital account balance of $70,000, to Richard Davis for $100,000 on August 31, 19x3. Rose Villa agrees to the sale. The entry that records the sale would be:

Aug. 31	Jerry Adcock, Capital	70,000	
	Richard Davis, Capital		70,000
	To record the transfer of Jerry Adcock's equity to Richard Davis		

Note that this entry records the book value of the equity and not the amount paid by Davis. The amount that Davis paid is a personal matter between him and Adcock. Because the amount paid did not affect the assets or liabilities of the firm, it should not be entered into the records.

In the second case, when a new partner is admitted by an investment in the partnership, both the assets and the owners' equity of the firm are increased. This is so because, in contrast to the case of buying a partner out, the assets that the new partner invests become partnership assets, and this increase in assets creates a corresponding increase in owners' equity. For example, assume that Richard Davis wished to invest $75,000 for a one-third interest in the partnership of Adcock and Villa. The Capital accounts of Adcock and Villa are $70,000 and $80,000, respectively. The assets of the firm are correctly valued. Thus, the partners agree to admit Davis to a one-third interest in the firm for a $75,000 investment. Davis's $75,000 investment will equal a one-third interest in the firm after the investment is added to the previously existing capital, as shown below:

Adcock, Capital	$ 70,000
Villa, Capital	80,000
Davis's investment	75,000
Total capital after Davis's investment	$225,000

$$\text{One-third interest} = \frac{\$225{,}000}{3} = \$\ 75{,}000$$

The entry to record this investment would be a debit to Cash for $75,000 and a credit to Richard Davis, Capital, for the same amount.

Sometimes a partnership is so profitable or otherwise advantageous that a new investor will be willing to pay more than the actual dollar interest that he or she receives in the partnership. An individual may have to pay $100,000 for an $80,000 interest in a partnership. The $20,000 excess of the payment over the interest purchased is considered a bonus to the original partners. The bonus should be distributed to the original partners according to their agreement concerning distribution of profits and losses.

As an illustration of the bonus method, assume that the Adcock and Villa Company has operated for several years and that the partners' capital balances and the new profit and loss ratio are as follows.

Partners	Capital Balances	Profit and Loss Ratio
Adcock	$160,000	55%
Villa	140,000	45%
	$300,000	100%

Richard Davis wishes to join the firm, and he offers to invest $100,000 for a one-fifth interest in the business and profits. The original partners agree to the offer. The computation of the bonus to the original partners is as follows:

Partners' equity in the original partnership		$300,000
Cash investment by Richard Davis		100,000
Partners' equity in the new partnership		$400,000
Partners' equity assigned to Richard Davis ($400,000 × 1/5)		$ 80,000
Bonus to the original partners		
Investment by Richard Davis	$100,000	
Less equity assigned to Richard Davis	80,000	$ 20,000
Distribution of bonus to original partners		
Jerry Adcock ($20,000 × 55%)	$ 11,000	
Rose Villa ($20,000 × 45%)	9,000	$ 20,000

The journal entry that records the admission of Davis to the partnership, on December 1, is as follows:

Dec. 1	Cash	100,000	
	Jerry Adcock, Capital		11,000
	Rose Villa, Capital		9,000
	Richard Davis, Capital		80,000
	To record the investment of Richard Davis for a one-fifth interest and a bonus to the original partners		

In addition, there are several reasons why a partnership might seek a new partner. For example, a firm in financial trouble might seek additional cash from a new partner. Or the original partners, wishing to expand the firm's markets, might require more capital than they can provide. Also, the partners might know a person who would add a unique talent to the firm. Under these conditions, a new partner may be admitted to the partnership with the understanding that part of the original partners' capital will be transferred (credited) in their profit and loss ratio to the new partner's capital as a bonus.

OBJECTIVE 7
Describe the implications of the withdrawal or death of a partner and of the liquidation of the partnership

Withdrawal of a Partner. A partner has the right to withdraw from a partnership whenever he or she chooses. To avoid any disputes when a partner does decide to withdraw or retire from the firm, the partnership agreement should describe the appropriate actions to be taken. The agreement may specify (1) whether or not an audit will be performed by CPAs, (2) how the assets will be reappraised, (3) how a bonus is to be determined, and (4) by what method the withdrawing partner will be paid.

There are several ways in which a partner may withdraw from a partnership. A partner may (1) sell his or her interest to an outsider with the consent of the remaining partners, (2) sell his or her interest to another partner with the consent of the remaining partners, (3) withdraw assets that are equal to his or her capital balance, (4) withdraw assets that are greater than his or her capital balance (in this case the withdrawing partner must receive a bonus), or (5) withdraw assets that are less than his or her capital balance (in this case the remaining partners must receive a bonus). These alternatives are illustrated in Figure A-1.

Death of a Partner. When a partner dies, the partnership is dissolved because the original association has changed. The partnership agreement should state the action to be taken upon the death of a partner. Normally the books will be closed and financial statements will be prepared. These actions are necessary to determine the capital balance of each of the part-

Figure A-1. Alternative Ways for a Partner to Withdraw

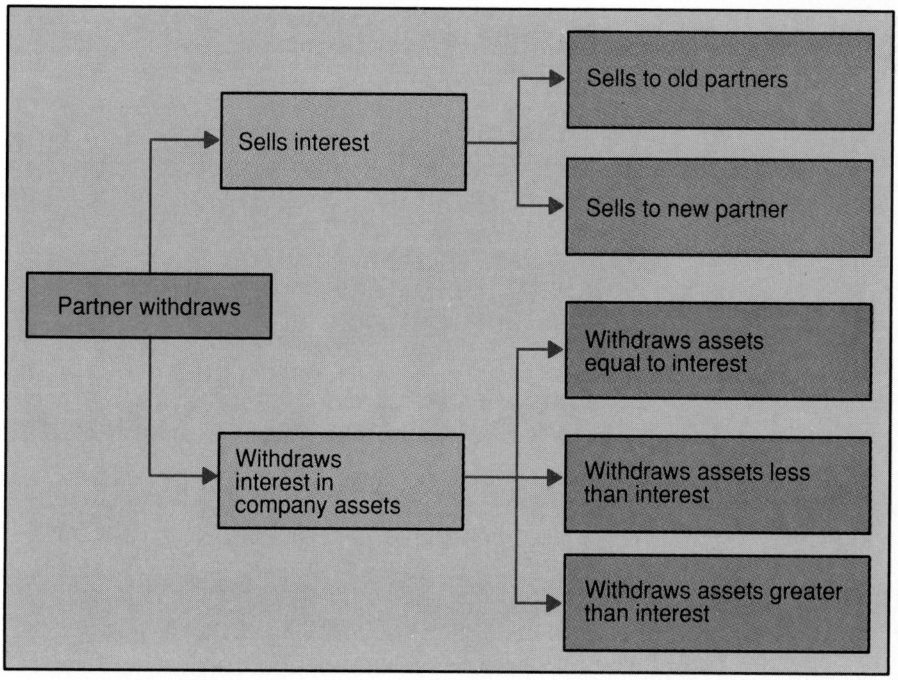

ners at the date of the death. The agreement may also indicate whether or not an audit should be conducted, assets appraised, and a bonus recorded, as well as the procedures for settling with the heirs of the deceased partner. The conditions for settling with the heirs may be that the remaining partners purchase the deceased's equity, sell it to outsiders, or deliver certain business assets to the estate. If the firm intends to continue, a new partnership must be formed.

Liquidation of a Partnership

Liquidation of a partnership is the process of ending a business, which entails selling enough assets to pay the liabilities and distributing any remaining assets among the partners. Unlike the case of mere dissolution, if a partnership is liquidated, the business will not continue.

The partnership agreement should indicate the procedures to be followed in the case of liquidation. Normally, the books should be adjusted and closed, with the income or loss being distributed to the partners. As the assets of the business are sold, any gain or loss should be distributed among the partners according to the established profit and loss ratio. As cash becomes available, it must be applied first to outside creditors, then to partners' loans, and finally to the partners' capital balances.

Questions

1. In what ways is accounting for withdrawals by sole proprietorships similar to and different from accounting for dividends by corporations?
2. Briefly define a partnership, and list several major characteristics of the partnership form of business.
3. What is the meaning of unlimited liability when applied to a partnership? What exception exists to this characteristic?
4. Abe and Bill are partners in a drilling operation. Abe purchased a drilling rig to be used in the partnership's operations. Is this purchase binding on Bill even though he was not involved in it?
5. The partnership agreement for Karla and Jean's partnership does not disclose how they will share income and losses. How would the income and losses be shared in this partnership?
6. What are several major advantages of a partnership? What are some possible disadvantages?
7. What characteristics of a partnership differ from those of a sole proprietorship and a corporation?
8. In the liquidation of a partnership, Robert's Capital account showed a $5,000 deficit balance after all the creditors were paid. What obligation does Robert have to the partnership?
9. Describe how a dissolution of a partnership may differ from a liquidation of a partnership.
10. Tom Howard and Sharon Thomas are forming a partnership. What are some of the factors they should consider in deciding how income might be divided?

Exercises

Exercise A-1. Proprietorship Transactions *(L.O. 1)*

Perceiving a need for a message service to serve downtown businesses, Clare Alvarez established Alvarez Message Delivery on July 1. Prepare general journal entries to record the following transactions that affect the company's proprietorship accounts.

July	1	Alvarez invested $5,000 in cash and an automobile valued at $6,000 in the business.	
	15	Withdrew $750 in cash from the business for living expenses.	
	31	Closed the following revenue and expense accounts:	
		Service Revenue	$1,000
		Rent Expense	300
		Telephone Expense	50
		Utility Expense	200
		Depreciation Expense, Automobile	100
	31	Closed Income Summary account	
	31	Closed Withdrawals account	

Exercise A-2. Partnership Formation *(L.O. 4)*

Beau Buckner and Rudy Alvaro are watch repairmen who wish to form a partnership and open a jewelry store. They have their attorney prepare their partnership agreement, which indicates that assets invested in the partnership will be recorded at their fair market value and liabilities will be assumed at book value. The assets contributed by each partner, the liabilities assumed, and their fair market and book values are as follows.

Assets	Beau Buckner	Rudy Alvaro	Total
Cash	$20,000	$15,000	$35,000
Accounts Receivable	26,000	10,000	36,000
Allowance for Uncollectible Accounts	2,000	1,500	3,500
Supplies	500	250	750
Equipment	10,000	5,000	15,000
Liabilities			
Accounts Payable	$16,000	$ 4,500	$20,500

Prepare the journal entry necessary to record the original investments of Buckner and Alvaro in the partnership.

Exercise A-3. Distribution of Income and Losses *(L.O. 5)*

Elmore Davis and Jan Johnson agreed to form a partnership. Davis contributed $100,000 in cash, and Johnson contributed assets with a fair market value of $200,000. The partnership, in its initial year, reported income of $60,000.

Determine how the partners would share the first year's income, and prepare the journal entry to distribute the income to the partners under each of the following conditions: (1) Davis and Johnson failed to include stated ratios in the partnership agreement. (2) Davis and Johnson agreed to share the income and losses in a 3:2 ratio. (3) Davis and Johnson agreed to share the income and losses in the ratio of original investments. (4) Davis and Johnson agreed to share the income and losses by allowing 10 percent interest on original investments and sharing any remainder equally.

Exercise A-4. Distribution of Income: Salary and Interest *(L.O. 5)*

Assume that the partnership agreement of Davis and Johnson in Exercise A-3 states that Davis and Johnson are to receive salaries of $10,000 and $12,000, respectively; that Davis is to receive 6 percent interest on his capital balance at the beginning of the year; and that the remainder of income and losses are to be shared equally.

Prepare the journal entries for distributing the income under the following conditions: (1) Income totaled $60,000 before deductions for salaries and interest. (2) Income totaled $24,000 before deductions for salaries and interest. (3) There was a loss of $1,000. (4) There was a loss of $20,000.

Exercise A-5. Admission of New Partner: Bonus to Old and New Partners *(L.O. 6)*

Ted, Dave, and Reg have equities in a partnership of $20,000, $20,000, and $30,000, respectively, and they share income and losses in a ratio of 1:1:3. The partners have agreed to admit Chet to the partnership.

Prepare journal entries to record the admission of Chet to the partnership under the following assumptions: (1) Chet invests $30,000 for a one-fifth interest in the partnership, and a bonus is recorded for the original partners. (2) Chet invests $30,000 for a 40 percent interest in the partnership, and a bonus is recorded for Chet.

Problems

Problem A-1. Partnership Formation and Distribution of Income *(L.O. 4, 5)*

Lew Sanders and Irwin Thau agreed in January 19x1 to produce and sell printed T-shirts. Lew contributed $120,000 in cash to the business. Irwin contributed a building and equipment with values of $110,000 and $70,000, respectively. The partnership had an income of $42,000 during 19x1 but was less successful during 19x2, when the income was only $20,000.

Required

1. Prepare the journal entry to record the investment of both partners in the partnership.
2. Determine the share of income for each partner in 19x1 and 19x2 under each of the following conditions: (a) The partners agreed to share income equally. (b) The partners failed to agree on an income-sharing arrangement. (c) The partners agreed to share income according to the ratio of their original investments. (d) The partners agreed to share income by allowing interest of 10 percent on original investments and dividing the remainder equally. (e) The partners agreed to share income by allowing salaries of $20,000 to Sanders and $14,000 to Thau, and dividing the remainder equally. (f) The partners agreed to share income by allowing interest of 9 percent on original investments, paying salaries of $20,000 to Sanders and $14,000 to Thau, and dividing the remainder equally.

Problem A-2. Distribution of Income: Salaries and Interest
(L.O. 5)

Gloria and Dennis are partners in a tennis shop. They have agreed that Gloria will operate the store and receive a salary of $52,000 per year. Dennis will receive 10 percent interest on his average capital balance during the year of $250,000. The remaining income or losses are to be shared by Gloria and Dennis in a 2:3 ratio.

Required

Determine each partner's share of income and losses under each of the following conditions. In each case, the income or loss is stated before distribution of salary and interest.

1. The income was $84,000.
2. The income was $44,000.
3. The loss was $12,800.

Problem A-3. Admission and Withdrawal of a Partner
(L.O. 6, 7)

Renee, Esther, and Jane are partners in Seabury Woodwork Company. Their capital balances as of July 31, 19x4 are as follows:

Renee, Capital		Esther, Capital		Jane, Capital	
	90,000		30,000		60,000

Each partner has agreed to admit Maureen to the partnership.

Required

Prepare the journal entries to record Maureen's admission to or Renee's withdrawal from the partnership under each of the following conditions: (a) Maureen pays Renee $25,000 for one-fifth of her interest. (b) Maureen invests $40,000 cash in the partnership. (c) Maureen invests $60,000 cash in the partnership for a 20 percent interest in the business. A bonus is to be recorded for the original partners on the basis of their capital balances. (d) Maureen invests $60,000 cash in the partnership for a 40 percent interest in the business. The original partners give Maureen a bonus according to the ratio of their capital balances on July 31, 19x4. (e) Renee withdraws from the partnership, taking $105,000. The excess of assets over the partnership interest are distributed according to the balances of the capital accounts. (f) Renee withdraws by selling her interest directly to Maureen for $120,000.

LEARNING OBJECTIVES

1. *Explain and differentiate some basic concepts related to governmental and not-for-profit accounting.*
2. *Describe the types of funds used in governmental accounting.*
3. *Explain the modified accrual basis of accounting used by state and local governments.*
4. *Describe the financial reporting system used in governmental accounting.*
5. *Provide a brief introduction to other types of not-for-profit accounting.*

APPENDIX B

Overview of Governmental and Not-for-Profit Accounting

State and local governments and not-for-profit organizations account for a significant share of all spending in the American economy. Courses in accounting, however, have devoted relatively little time to discussing the accounting and reporting issues unique to these organizations. This appendix provides a brief introduction to accounting for several categories of governmental and not-for-profit groups. They include state and local governments, colleges and universities, hospitals, and voluntary health and welfare organizations. After studying this appendix, you should be able to meet the learning objectives listed on the left.

Governmental, Not-for-Profit, and Business Accounting

Businesses in the United States are organized to produce profits for their owners or shareholders. This fact requires that the accounting system provide shareholders, creditors, and other interested parties with information that will help them evaluate the firm's success in making a profit. The rules and practices of business accounting are referred to as generally accepted accounting principles (GAAP), which are established by the Financial Accounting Standards Board (FASB). Historically, governmental GAAP have been the responsibility of the National Council on Governmental Accounting (NCGA). In 1984 the Financial Accounting Foundation founded the Governmental Accounting Standards Board (GASB). The GASB has the power to establish accounting rules and practices for governmental units. Its responsibilities parallel those of the FASB in that it defines generally accepted accounting principles for governmental units. Standards set by the GASB do not apply to nongovernmental not-for-profit organizations like private universities and hospitals. Accounting practices for these nongovernmental not-for-profit organizations fall under the pronouncements of the FASB.

Financial Reporting Objectives of Governmental Units

OBJECTIVE 1
Explain and differentiate some basic concepts related to governmental and not-for-profit accounting

State and local governments have different objectives from those of businesses, and thus they have traditionally had different GAAP. Governmental units chiefly provide services to citizens, with expenditures for these services limited to the amounts legally available. Governmental units need not be profitable in the business sense; however, they do need to limit their spending to the funds made available for specific purposes. For these reasons, the GASB has established the following financial reporting objectives for governmental units:

1. Financial reporting should assist in fulfilling government's duty to be publicly accountable and should enable users to assess that accountability.
2. Financial reporting should assist users in evaluating the operating results of the governmental entity for the year.
3. Financial reporting should assist users in assessing the level of services that can be provided by the entity and its ability to meet its obligations when due.[1]

The primary objective of governmental GAAP is, therefore, not profit measurement, but the assessment of and accountability for the funds available for governmental activities. To help satisfy this objective, governmental GAAP have several unique accounting features, the most important of which are the use of funds to account for various activities and the use of modified accrual accounting. A **fund** is defined as a fiscal and accounting entity. **Modified accrual accounting** attempts to provide an accurate measure of increases and decreases in resources available (especially in cash) to fulfill governmental obligations.

The operations of state and local governments are recorded in a variety of funds, each of which is designated for a specific purpose. This means that each fund simultaneously shows (1) the financial position and results of operations during the period and (2) compliance with legal requirements of the state or local government. State and local governments rely on the following types of funds:

OBJECTIVE 2
Describe the types of funds used in governmental accounting

General fund To account for all financial resources not accounted for in any other fund. This fund accounts for most of the current operating activities of the governmental unit (administration, police, fire, health, and sanitation, for example).

Special revenue funds To account for revenues legally restricted to specific purposes.

1. *Concept Statement No. 1,* "Objectives of Financial Reporting" (Stamford, Conn.: Governmental Accounting Standards Board, 1987).

Capital projects funds To account for the acquisition and construction of major capital projects.

Debt service fund To account for resources accumulated to pay the interest and principal of general obligation long-term debt.

Enterprise funds To account for activities that are financed and operated in a manner similar to private business activities. These funds are most appropriate for activities that charge the public for goods or services, such as municipal golf courses or utilities.

Internal service funds To account for the financing of goods or services provided by one department or agency of a governmental unit to other departments or agencies of governmental units.

Trust and agency funds To account for assets held by a governmental unit acting as a trustee or agent for individuals, private organizations, or other funds.

The first four funds are called **governmental funds**. The enterprise and internal service funds are **proprietary funds**. Trust and agency funds are **fiduciary funds**. A political unit may properly have only one general fund. There is no limit, however, on the number of other funds used. There is also no requirement that a state or local government have all of these funds; individual needs govern the type and number of funds used.

In addition to the above funds, state and local governments use two unique entities called **account groups** to record certain fixed assets and long-term liabilities.

General fixed assets account group To account for all long-term assets of a governmental unit except long-term assets related to specific proprietary or trust funds. This account group does not record depreciation.

General long-term debt group To account for all long-term liabilities of a governmental unit except for long-term liabilities related to specific proprietary or trust funds. This account group records the principal amounts of long-term debt as well as the amounts available in the debt service fund and the amounts to be provided in the future for the retirement of the debt.

Long-term assets and long-term liabilities related to proprietary and trust funds are accounted for in essentially the same manner as in business accounting.

Modified Accrual Accounting

OBJECTIVE 3
Explain the modified accrual basis of accounting used by state and local governments

Governmental funds, as well as certain types of trust funds, use the modified accrual method of accounting. Proprietary funds, as well as certain types of trust funds, use the familiar full accrual accounting common to business organizations. This section will concentrate on the less familiar modified accrual basis of accounting.

Modified accrual accounting has several features that distinguish it from accrual accounting used in business. The measurement and recognition of revenues and expenditures, the incorporation of the budget into the formal accounting system, and the use of encumbrances to account for purchase commitments will each be described briefly.

In governmental accounting, **revenues** are defined as increases in fund resources from sources other than interfund transactions or proceeds of long-term debt. They are recognized in the accounts when "measurable and available." In most cases these conditions are met when cash is received. **Expenditures** are defined as decreases in fund resources caused by transactions other than interfund transfers. These concepts of revenues and expenditures result in some unusual situations, as the following examples illustrate.

1. Assume that a city sells a used police car for $2,500 cash. This transaction would be recorded in the general fund as follows:

Cash	2,500	
Revenues		2,500
Sale of used police car		

2. When a city purchases a new police car for $12,000 cash, the transaction would be recorded in the general fund as follows:

Expenditures	12,000	
Cash		12,000
Purchase of new police car		

The transactions are recorded in this way because they satisfy the definitions of revenues and expenditures.

To further illustrate the contrast between governmental and business-type accrual accounting, we can examine the way in which a business would record the above transactions:

1. Assume that a firm sells a used car for $2,500 cash and that the car has a carrying value of $2,000 (cost of $7,500 less accumulated depreciation of $5,500):

Cash	2,500	
Accumulated Depreciation, Car	5,500	
Car		7,500
Gain on disposal		500
Sale of used car		

Unlike governmental accounting, accrual accounting recognizes revenues only to the extent that cash received exceeds carrying value.

2. If a firm purchases a new car for $12,000 cash, the transaction would be recorded as follows:

Car	12,000	
Cash		12,000
Purchase of new car		

The car would be shown as an asset on the firm's balance sheet. No expense would be recorded until depreciation is recognized in subsequent years. As discussed throughout this book, business accounting focuses on the matching of revenues and expenses to compute net income or loss for the period. Governmental accounting, in contrast, concentrates on inflows and outflows of fund resources.

Another unique feature of governmental accounting is the formal incorporation of the budget into the accounts of the particular fund. This approach is required for the general fund and the special revenue fund and is optional for the other governmental funds. The general fund, for example, would record its budget as follows:

Estimated Revenues	1,000,000	
Appropriations		950,000
Fund Balance		50,000
To record budget for fiscal year		

This example assumes that the governmental unit expects revenues to exceed legally mandated expenditures (or appropriations). The use of budgetary accounts enables the governmental unit to have a continuous check or control on whether actual revenues and expenditures correspond to original estimates. In addition, the various funds' financial statements will show both the budgeted and actual amounts of major revenue and expenditure categories. At the end of the accounting period, the budget entry would be reversed, since its control function is no longer needed. A new budget would then be recorded in the subsequent period to control revenues and expenditures in that period. Businesses also use budgets, but they do not integrate those budgets formally into the regular accounting system.

A third unique feature of governmental accounting is the use of **encumbrance accounting**. Since governments cannot legally spend more than the amounts appropriated for specific purposes, it is necessary to keep track of anticipated, as well as actual, expenditures. Whenever a significant lapse of time is expected between a commitment to spend and the actual expenditure, governmental GAAP require the use of encumbrance accounting.

For example, a city orders $10,000 of supplies on July 1, but does not expect to receive the supplies until September 1. The bill received on September 1 amounts to $10,200. The general fund would record this transaction as follows:

July 1	Encumbrances	10,000	
	Reserve for Encumbrances		10,000
	Order of supplies		
Sept. 1	Reserve for Encumbrances	10,000	
	Encumbrances		10,000
	Reverse encumbrance upon receipt of bill for supplies		
1	Expenditures	10,200	
	Cash (or Vouchers Payable)		10,200
	Payment for supplies		

The purpose of an encumbrance system is to ensure that the governmental unit does not exceed its spending authority. This is accomplished by recording not only actual expenditures but also anticipated expenditures under the current period's appropriations. In addition to normal expenditures, the Reserve for Encumbrances account represents that portion of the fund balance already committed to future expenditures. Regardless of the original estimated encumbrance amounts, on September 1, the encumbrance is eliminated by reversing the original entry of July 1, and Expenditures is debited for the actual amount spent.

Financial Reporting System

OBJECTIVE 4 *Describe the financial reporting system used in governmental accounting*

The accounting system we have described is designed to produce periodic financial statements. The financial statements recommended by the NCGA in its Government Accounting Standard No. 1 include the following:

Combined balance sheet This statement is prepared for all fund types and account groups. Each fund type and account group lists major categories of assets, liabilities, and either fund balances or owners' equity accounts.

Combined statement of revenues, expenditures, and changes in fund balances—all governmental funds This statement is prepared for all governmental fund types. Since only governmental funds are reported in this statement, all revenues and expenditures would be measured according to the principles of modified accrual accounting.

Combined statement of revenues, expenditures, and changes in fund balances—budget and actual—general and special revenue funds This statement presents budget and actual amounts for general and special revenue fund types. The statement includes the budgetary data described earlier and directly compares actual revenues and expenditures to budgeted revenues and expenditures. It indicates, for each type of revenue and expenditure, the amount by which actual amounts differ from budgeted amounts.

Combined statement of revenues, expenses, and changes in retained earnings (or equity) This statement is prepared for all proprietary fund types. It is prepared on the full accrual basis and resembles the financial statements prepared by businesses.

Combined statement of changes in financial position This statement is prepared for all proprietary fund types.

Not-for-Profit Organizations

OBJECTIVE 5 *Provide a brief introduction to other types of not-for-profit accounting*

This section provides a very brief view of accounting for certain types of not-for-profit organizations. Colleges and universities, hospitals, and voluntary health and welfare organizations, among others, share characteristics of both governments and business entities. Like governments, they are not intended to make a profit; however, they lack the taxing ability of a government. Because the lack of taxing ability requires that the revenues of not-for-profit organizations at least equal expenses over the long run, these organizations rely on accrual accounting for most of their activities. These organizations also use funds to account for different types of resources and activities. The use of funds is necessary because of the legal restrictions imposed on many of the resources available to these groups.

Colleges and Universities

Colleges and universities, with a few exceptions, use full accrual accounting. Until recently one notable exception was that depreciation on fixed assets did not have to be recorded. However, the FASB issued Statement No. 93 to eliminate this exception. Because of the controversial nature of the issue, FASB No. 93 was not implemented until 1990. Another is that revenues from restricted sources can be recognized only when expenditures are made for the purposes specified by the revenue source. Several types of funds are employed:

Unrestricted current fund Accounts for general operating activities.

Restricted current fund Accounts for funds available for a specific purpose, as designated by groups or individuals outside the school.

Loan funds Accounts for funds available for loans to students, faculty, and staff.

Endowment funds Accounts for gifts or bequests, the principal of which usually cannot be spent.

Annuity and life income funds Are similar to endowment funds, except that the donor receives some form of financial support from the school.

Plant funds Accounts for funds available for acquisition and replacement of plant assets, as well as retirement of debt. These funds also account for all plant assets of the school, except any that may be part of an endowment fund.

Agency funds Are similar to those used by state and local governments.

Financial statements used by colleges and universities include the following: (a) statement of current revenues, expenditures, and other changes; (b) combined balance sheet; and (c) statement of changes in fund balances.

Hospitals

Accounting for not-for-profit hospitals closely resembles the accrual accounting methods used by businesses. Funds used include the following:

Unrestricted fund Accounts for the normal operating activities of the hospital. This is the only fund that records revenues and expenses. It accounts for all assets and liabilities not included in other funds, including plant assets and long-term debt.

Specific purpose fund To account for resources that are restricted by someone outside of the hospital for specific operating purposes.

Endowment funds Are similar to those used by colleges and universities. (Example: annuity and life income funds.)

Plant replacement and expansion fund Accounts for resources that are restricted by someone outside of the hospital for capital outlay purposes.

Not-for-profit hospitals prepare a statement of revenues and expenses for the unrestricted fund, as well as a statement of cash flows. They also prepare balance sheets and statements of changes in fund balances for all funds.

An important aspect of hospital accounting is the classification of revenues and expenses. Revenues must be separated by *source,* including patient service and other operating and nonoperating revenues. Expenses must be classified by *function,* including nursing services, other professional services, administrative services, and so forth. Unlike other organizations described in this appendix, hospitals recognize depreciation on plant assets.

Voluntary Health and Welfare Organizations

Voluntary health and welfare organizations encompass a wide variety of groups, such as the Sierra Club, the American Cancer Society, and the National Rifle Association. Although accounting practices vary considerably, these organizations usually follow the full accrual basis of accounting. Their fund structure is as follows: current unrestricted fund; current restricted fund; land, building, and equipment fund; endowment funds; custodial (similar to agency) funds; and loan and annuity funds.

Three financial statements are prepared: (a) statement of support, revenues and expenses, and changes in fund balances, (b) balance sheets, and (c) statement of functional expenses. These organizations must strictly classify revenues and expenses. Revenues must be separated into public support revenues, for which the donor expects nothing in return, and revenues from charges for goods and services. Expenses must be separated by *program* (those activities for which the organization has been established) and *supporting services* (overhead). These classifications are useful in evaluating the relative efficiency of the groups' activities.

Summary

Governmental and not-for-profit accounting, as we have seen, shares some of the characteristics of business accounting but has its own unique features. Primary among these is the use of funds to organize transactions. Table B-1 summarizes the types of funds used by various organizations and reviews some of the important details of their accounting systems.

Questions

1. How do the objectives of governmental accounting differ from the objectives of business accounting?
2. What is the purpose of a *fund,* as that term is used in governmental accounting?

Table B-1. Overview of Governmental and Not-for-Profit Accounting

	Type of Organization			
	Governmental Units	Colleges and Universities	Hospitals	Voluntary Health and Welfare
Funds and Account Groups	General	Unrestricted current	Unrestricted	Unrestricted current
	Special revenue	Restricted current	Specific purpose	Restricted current
	Capital projects	Plant	Plant replacement and expansion	Land, building, and equipment
	Debt service	Plant		
	Enterprise			
	Internal service			
	Trust and agency	Loan Endowment Annuity and life income Agency	Endowment Annuity and life income	Endowment Custodian
	General long-term assets	Plant		Land, building, and equipment
	General long-term debt			
Special Characteristics	1. Only one general fund	1. Revenues recognized in restricted funds only as specified expenditures made	1. Depreciation may be computed on a replacement cost basis	1. Revenues segregated between voluntary contributions and charges for goods or services
	2. Proprietary funds (enterprise, internal service) use full accrual accounting	2. Depreciation recorded as an expense, after implementation of FASB No. 93	2. Only unrestricted fund shows revenues and expenses	2. Expenses segregated by program services and supporting (overhead) services
	3. Number of funds used depends on needs and complexity of governmental unit			

(continued)

Table B-1. (continued)

	Type of Organization			
	Governmental Units	**Colleges and Universities**	**Hospitals**	**Voluntary Health and Welfare**
	Basis of Accounting			
	Modified Accrual	Accrual	Accrual	Accrual
Financial Statements	Combined balance sheet—all fund types and account groups	Combined balance sheet	Balance sheet	Balance sheet
	Combined statement of revenues, expenditures, and changes in fund balances—all governmental fund types	Statement of current funds, revenues, expenditures, and other changes	Statement of revenues and expenses	Statement of support, revenues and expenses, and changes in fund balances
	Combined statement of revenues, expenditures, and changes in fund balances—budget and actual—general and special revenue fund types	Statement of changes in fund balances	Statement of changes in fund balances	Statement of functional expenses
	Combined statement of revenues, expenses, and changes in retained earnings—all proprietary fund types			
	Combined statement of changes in financial position—all proprietary fund types		Statement of cash flows	

3. Contrast the measurement of revenues and expenditures in governmental accounting with the measurement of revenues and expenses in business accounting.
4. What is a proprietary fund in governmental accounting? Why do such funds use accrual accounting?
5. What is the purpose of budgetary accounts in governmental accounting?
6. What are the major characteristics of modified accrual accounting as used in governmental accounting?

7. What are the purposes of recording encumbrances?
8. In what ways does accounting for colleges and universities resemble business accounting? How does it differ from business accounting?
9. Describe how revenues and expenses are classified in hospital accounting.
10. Describe and contrast the two types of revenues recognized in the accounts of voluntary health and welfare organizations.

Exercises

Exercise B-1. Basic Concepts and Funds
(L.O. 2, 3, 5)

Select the most appropriate answer for the following questions.

1. The fund that accounts for the day-to-day operating activities of a local government is the
   a. enterprise fund.
   b. general fund.
   c. operating fund.
   d. special revenue fund.
2. Accrual accounting is recommended for which of the following funds?
   a. Debt service fund
   b. General fund
   c. Internal service fund
   d. Capital projects fund
3. A debt service fund of a municipality is an example of what type of fund?
   a. Internal service fund
   b. Governmental fund
   c. Proprietary fund
   d. Fiduciary fund
4. What basis of accounting would a not-for-profit hospital use?
   a. Cash basis for all funds
   b. Modified accrual basis for all funds
   c. Accrual basis for all funds
   d. Accrual basis for some funds and modified accrual basis for other funds
5. After the implementation of FASB No. 93, which of the following types of organizations would be least likely to record depreciation expense on property, plant, and equipment?
   a. State and local governments
   b. Colleges and universities
   c. Hospitals
   d. Businesses

Exercise B-2. Recording the Budget in the General Fund
(L.O. 3)

The Village of Glencoe has adopted the following budget items for 19x4:

Estimated Revenues	$10,000,000
Appropriations	9,800,000

a. Prepare the journal entry to record the budget in the general fund for Glencoe on January 1, 19x4.
b. What entry, if any, would be required at the end of Glencoe's accounting year, December 31, 19x4?

Problem

Problem B-1. Journal Entries for the General Fund
(L.O. 3)

The following transactions occurred in North Shore City during 19x1. Record the journal entries necessary to account for these transactions in North Shore's general fund.

19x1	
Jan. 1	The budget was adopted. Estimated revenues are $4,000,000; appropriations are $4,100,000.
Feb. 11	Supplies with an estimated cost of $22,000 were ordered.
Mar. 1	Property taxes totaling $3,500,000 were levied. North Shore expects 2 percent of this amount to be uncollectible.
Apr. 10	The supplies ordered on February 11 were received. The actual bill for these supplies amounted to $21,750.
June 1	Property tax collections totaled $3,450,000. The rest were classified as delinquent.
Aug. 10	Equipment costing $11,300 was purchased for cash.
Dec. 31	Actual revenues for 19x1 totaled $4,050,000. Actual expenditures totaled $3,975,000.

LEARNING OBJECTIVES

1. *Explain the objectives and uses of special-purpose journals.*
2. *Construct and use the following types of special-purpose journals: sales journal, purchases journal, cash receipts journal, cash payments journal, and others as needed.*
3. *Explain the purposes and relationships of controlling accounts and subsidiary ledgers.*

APPENDIX C

Special-Purpose Journals

Companies that are faced with larger numbers of transactions, perhaps hundreds or thousands every week or every day, must have a more efficient and economical way of recording transactions in the journal and posting entries to the ledger. The easiest approach is to group the company's typical transactions into common categories and use an input device, called a **special-purpose journal**, for each category. The objectives of special-purpose journals are efficiency, economy, and control. In addition, although manual special-purpose journals are used by companies that have not yet computerized their systems, the concepts underlying special-purpose journals are found in computer systems. After studying this appendix, you should be able to meet the learning objectives listed on the left.

Types of Special-Purpose Journals

Most business transactions, usually 90 to 95 percent, fall into one of four categories. Each kind of transaction may be recorded in a special-purpose journal as shown below.

Transaction	Special-Purpose Journal	Posting Abbreviation
Sales of merchandise on credit	Sales journal	S
Purchases on credit	Purchases journal	P
Receipts of cash	Cash receipts journal	CR
Disbursements of cash	Cash payments journal	CP

OBJECTIVE 1 *Explain the objectives and uses of special-purpose journals*

The general journal is used for recording transactions that do not fall into any of the special categories. For example, purchases returns, sales returns, and adjusting and closing entries are recorded in the general journal. (When transactions are posted from the general journal to the ledger accounts, the posting abbreviation used is J.)

It is important to note that use of these four journals reduces the amount of detail work. For example, the amount of posting is greatly reduced because, instead of posting every debit and credit for each transaction, in most cases only column totals, which represent many transactions, are posted. In addition, the labor can be divided, assigning each journal to a different employee. This divi-

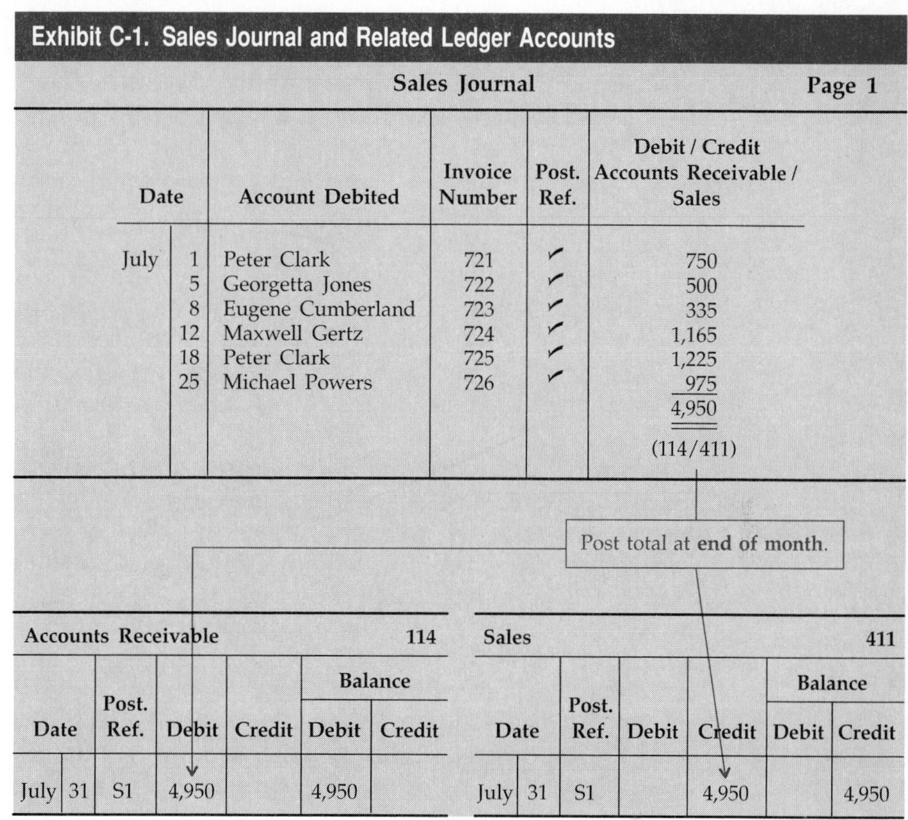

Exhibit C-1. Sales Journal and Related Ledger Accounts

Sales Journal — Page 1

Date		Account Debited	Invoice Number	Post. Ref.	Debit / Credit Accounts Receivable / Sales
July	1	Peter Clark	721	✓	750
	5	Georgetta Jones	722	✓	500
	8	Eugene Cumberland	723	✓	335
	12	Maxwell Gertz	724	✓	1,165
	18	Peter Clark	725	✓	1,225
	25	Michael Powers	726	✓	975
					4,950
					(114/411)

Post total at end of month.

Accounts Receivable — 114

Date		Post. Ref.	Debit	Credit	Balance Debit	Balance Credit
July	31	S1	4,950		4,950	

Sales — 411

Date		Post. Ref.	Debit	Credit	Balance Debit	Balance Credit
July	31	S1		4,950		4,950

sion of labor is important in establishing good internal control, as shown in the chapter on accounting for merchandising operations.

Sales Journal

Special-purpose journals are designed to record particular kinds of transactions. Thus all transactions in a special-purpose journal result in debits and credits to the same accounts. The **sales journal**, for example, is designed to handle all credit sales, and only credit sales. Cash sales are recorded in the cash receipts journal, which is explained later.

OBJECTIVE 2
Construct and use the following types of special-purpose journals: sales journal, purchases journal, cash receipts journal, cash payments journal, and others as needed

Exhibit C-1 illustrates a typical sales journal. Six sales transactions involving five customers are recorded in this sales journal. As each sale takes place, several copies of the sales invoice are made. The accounting department of the seller uses one copy to make the entry in the sales journal. The date, the customer's name, the invoice number, the amount of the sale, and possibly the credit terms are copied from the invoice. These data correspond to the columns of the sales journal.

Note the following time-saving features of the sales journal:

1. Only one line is needed to record each transaction. Each entry consists of a debit to each customer in Accounts Receivable. The corresponding credit to Sales is understood.

2. Account names do not have to be written out because account names occurring most frequently are used as column headings. Thus entry in a column has the effect of debiting or crediting the account.
3. No explanations are necessary, because the function of the special-purpose journal is to record just one type of transaction. Only credit sales are recorded in the sales journal. Sales for cash must be recorded in the cash receipts journal, which is described in detail later in this appendix.
4. Only one amount—the total credit sales for the month—needs to be posted. It is posted twice: once as a debit to Accounts Receivable and once as a credit to Sales. Instead of the six sales entries in the example, there might be hundreds of actual sales transactions in a more realistic situation. Thus one can see the saving in posting time.

OBJECTIVE 3
Explain the purposes and relationships of controlling accounts and subsidiary ledgers

Controlling Accounts and Subsidiary Ledgers. Every entry in the sales journal represents a debit to a customer's account in Accounts Receivable. In previous chapters, all such transactions have been posted to Accounts Receivable. However, this single Accounts Receivable entry does not readily tell how much each customer bought and paid for or how much each customer still owes. In practice, almost all companies that sell to customers on credit keep an individual accounts receivable record for each customer. If the company has 6,000 credit customers, there are 6,000 accounts receivable. To include all these accounts in the ledger with the other assets, liabilities, and owner's equity accounts would make it very bulky. Consequently, most companies take the individual customers' accounts out of the general ledger, which contains the financial statement accounts, and place them in a separate ledger called a **subsidiary ledger**. The customers' accounts are either filed alphabetically in this accounts receivable ledger or filed numerically if account numbers are used.

When a company puts its individual customers' accounts in an accounts receivable ledger, there is still a need for an Accounts Receivable account in the general ledger to maintain its balance. This Accounts Receivable account in the general ledger is said to control the subsidiary ledger and is called a **controlling** or **control account**. It is a controlling account in the sense that its balance should equal the total of the individual account balances in the subsidiary ledger. This is true because in transactions involving accounts receivable, such as credit sales, there must be postings to the individual customer accounts every day. Postings to the controlling account in the general ledger in total should be made at least each month. If a wrong amount has been posted, the sum of all customer account balances in the subsidiary accounts receivable ledger will not equal the balance of the Accounts Receivable controlling account in the general ledger. When these amounts do not match, the accountant knows that there is an error to find and correct.

The concept of controlling accounts is shown in Exhibit C-2, where boxes used for the accounts receivable ledger and the general ledger are presented. The principle involved is that the single controlling account in the general ledger summarizes all the individual accounts in the subsid-

Exhibit C-2. Relationship of Sales Journal, General Ledger, and Accounts Receivable Ledger and the Posting Procedure

Sales Journal **Page 1**

Date		Account Debited	Invoice Number	Post. Ref.	Debit / Credit Accounts Receivable / Sales
July	1	Peter Clark	721	✓	750
	5	Georgetta Jones	722	✓	500
	8	Eugene Cumberland	723	✓	335
	12	Maxwell Gertz	724	✓	1,165
	18	Peter Clark	725	✓	1,225
	25	Michael Powers	726	✓	975
					4,950
					(114/411)

Post individual amounts **daily** to subsidiary ledger accounts.

Post total at **end of month** to general ledger accounts.

Accounts Receivable Ledger

Peter Clark

Date		Post. Ref.	Debit	Credit	Balance
July	1	S1	750		750
	18	S1	1,225		1,975

Eugene Cumberland

Date		Post. Ref.	Debit	Credit	Balance
July	8	S1	335		335

Continue posting to Maxwell Gertz, Georgetta Jones, and Michael Powers.

General Ledger

Accounts Receivable **114**

Date		Post. Ref.	Debit	Credit	Balance Debit	Balance Credit
July	31	S1	4,950		4,950	

Sales **411**

Date		Post. Ref.	Debit	Credit	Balance Debit	Balance Credit
July	31	S1		4,950		4,950

iary ledger. Note that since the individual accounts are recorded daily and the controlling account is posted monthly, the total of the individual accounts in the accounts receivable ledger will equal the controlling account only after the monthly posting. The monthly trial balance is prepared using only the general ledger accounts.

Most companies, as you will see, use an accounts payable subsidiary ledger as well. It is also possible to use a subsidiary ledger for almost any account in the general ledger where management wants a specific account for individual items, such as Merchandise Inventory, Notes Receivable, Temporary Investments, and Equipment.

Summary of the Sales Journal Procedure. Observe from Exhibit C-2 that the procedures for using a sales journal are as follows:

1. Enter each sales invoice in the sales journal on a single line, recording date, customer's name, invoice number, and amount.
2. At the end of each day, post each individual sale to the customer's account in the accounts receivable ledger. As each sale is posted, place a check mark in the Post. Ref. (posting reference) column of the sales journal (or customer account number, if used) to indicate that it has been posted. In the Post. Ref. column of each customer account, place an S1 (representing Sales Journal—Page 1) to indicate the source of the entry.
3. At the end of the month, sum the Debit/Credit column in the sales journal to determine the total credit sales, and post the total to the general ledger accounts (debit Accounts Receivable and credit Sales). Place the numbers of the accounts debited and credited beneath the total in the sales journal to indicate that this step has been completed, and in the general ledger place an S1 in the Post. Ref. column of each account to indicate the source of the entry.
4. Verify the accuracy of the posting by adding the account balances of the accounts receivable ledger and by matching the total with the Accounts Receivable controlling account balance in the general ledger. This step can be accomplished by listing the accounts in a schedule of accounts receivable, as shown in Exhibit C-3.

Sales Taxes. Other columns, such as a column for credit terms, can be added to the sales journal. The nature of the company's business will determine whether they are needed.

Exhibit C-3. Schedule of Accounts Receivable

Mitchell's Used Car Sales
Schedule of Accounts Receivable
July 31, 19xx

Peter Clark	$1,975
Eugene Cumberland	335
Maxwell Gertz	1,165
Georgetta Jones	500
Michael Powers	975
Total Accounts Receivable	$4,950

Exhibit C-4. Section of a Sales Journal with a Column for Sales Taxes

Sales Journal							Page 7
					Debit	Credits	
Date		Account Debited	Invoice Number	Post. Ref.	Accounts Receivable	Sales Taxes Payable	Sales
Sept.	1	Ralph P. Hake	727	✓	206	6	200

Many cities and states require retailers to collect a sales tax from their customers and periodically remit the total amount of the tax to the state or city. In this case, an additional column is needed in the sales journal to record the necessary credit to Sales Taxes Payable. The required entry is illustrated in Exhibit C-4. The procedure for posting to the ledger is exactly the same as that previously described except that the total of the Sales Taxes Payable column must be posted as a credit to the Sales Taxes Payable account at the end of the month.

Most companies also make cash sales. Cash sales are usually recorded in a column of the cash receipts journal. This procedure is discussed later in the appendix.

Purchases Journal

The techniques associated with the sales journal are very similar to those of the purchases journal. The **purchases journal** is used to record all purchases on credit and may take the form of either a single-column journal or a multicolumn journal. In the single-column journal, shown in Exhibit C-5, only credit purchases of merchandise for resale to customers are recorded. This kind of transaction is recorded with a debit to Purchases and a credit to Accounts Payable. When the single-column purchases journal is used, credit purchases of things other than merchandise are recorded in the general journal. Also, cash purchases are not recorded in the purchases journal but in the cash payments journal, which is explained later.

As with Accounts Receivable, the Accounts Payable account in the general ledger is used by most companies as a controlling account. So that the company will know how much it owes each supplier, it keeps a separate account for each supplier in an accounts payable subsidiary ledger. The ideas and techniques described above for the accounts receivable subsidiary ledger and general ledger account apply also to the accounts payable subsidiary ledger and general ledger account. Thus the total of the separate accounts in the accounts payable subsidiary ledger will equal the balance of the Accounts Payable controlling account in the general ledger. The reason is that the monthly total of the credit purchases posted to the individual accounts each day is equal to the total credit purchases posted to the controlling account each month.

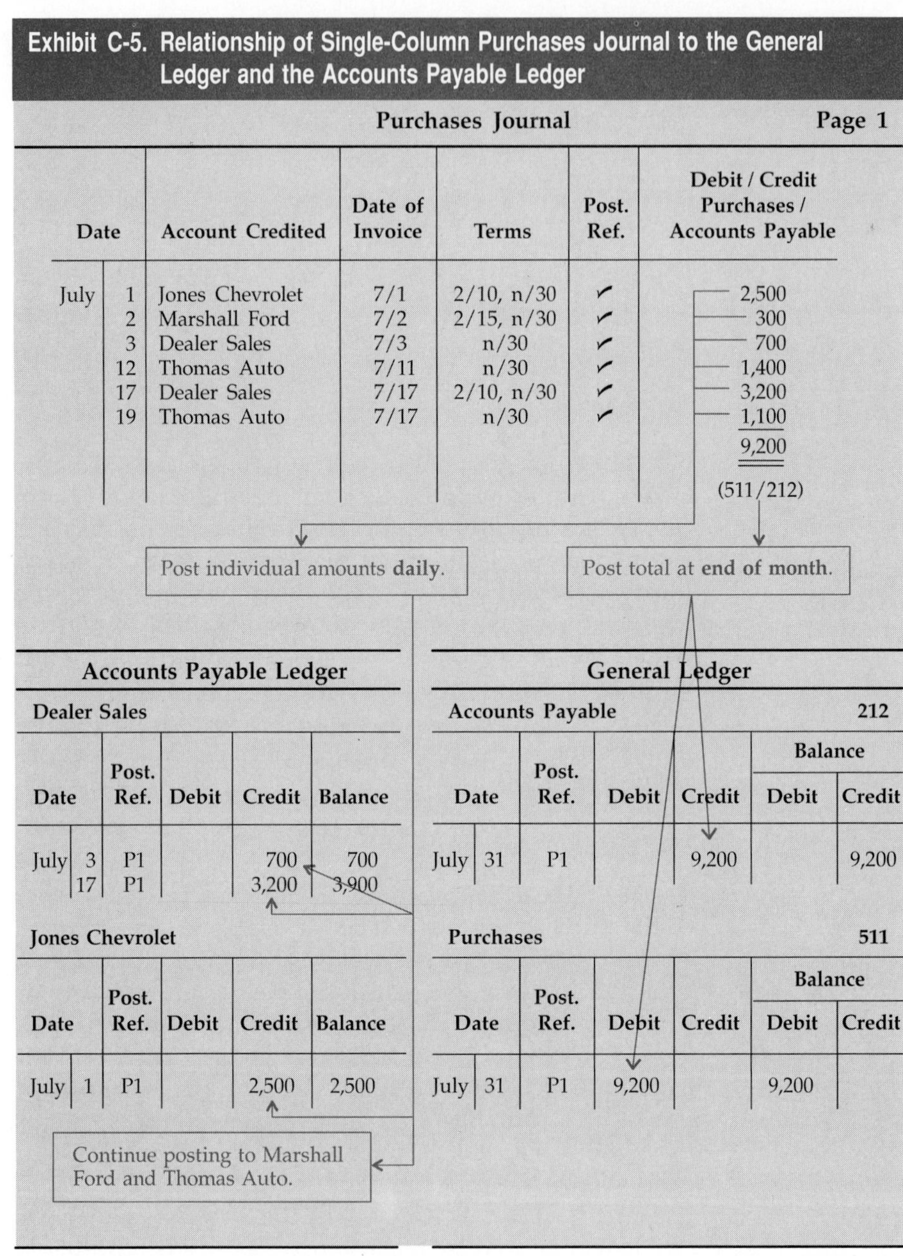

Exhibit C-5. Relationship of Single-Column Purchases Journal to the General Ledger and the Accounts Payable Ledger

Purchases Journal — Page 1

Date		Account Credited	Date of Invoice	Terms	Post. Ref.	Debit / Credit Purchases / Accounts Payable
July	1	Jones Chevrolet	7/1	2/10, n/30	✓	2,500
	2	Marshall Ford	7/2	2/15, n/30	✓	300
	3	Dealer Sales	7/3	n/30	✓	700
	12	Thomas Auto	7/11	n/30	✓	1,400
	17	Dealer Sales	7/17	2/10, n/30	✓	3,200
	19	Thomas Auto	7/17	n/30	✓	1,100
						9,200
						(511/212)

Accounts Payable Ledger

Dealer Sales

Date		Post. Ref.	Debit	Credit	Balance
July	3	P1		700	700
	17	P1		3,200	3,900

Jones Chevrolet

Date		Post. Ref.	Debit	Credit	Balance
July	1	P1		2,500	2,500

General Ledger

Accounts Payable — 212

Date		Post. Ref.	Debit	Credit	Balance Debit	Balance Credit
July	31	P1		9,200		9,200

Purchases — 511

Date		Post. Ref.	Debit	Credit	Balance Debit	Balance Credit
July	31	P1	9,200		9,200	

The steps for using a purchases journal, as shown in Exhibit C-5, are as follows:

1. Enter each purchase invoice in the purchases journal on a single line, recording date, supplier's name, invoice date, terms if given, and amount.
2. At the end of each day, post each individual purchase to the supplier's account in the accounts payable subsidiary ledger. As each purchase is posted, place a check in the Post. Ref. column of the purchases journal

to show that it has been posted. Also place a P1 (representing Purchases Journal—Page 1) in the Post. Ref. column of each supplier's account to show the source of the entry.

3. At the end of the month, sum the credit purchases, and post the amount in the general ledger accounts (Accounts Payable and Purchases). Place the numbers of the accounts debited and credited beneath the totals in the purchases journal to show that this step has been carried out.
4. Check the accuracy of the posting by adding the balances of the accounts payable ledger accounts and matching the total with the Accounts Payable controlling account balance in the general ledger. This step may be carried out by preparing a schedule of accounts payable.

The single-column purchases journal may be expanded to record credit purchases of things other than merchandise by adding a separate column for other debit accounts that are often used. For example, the multicolumn purchases journal in Exhibit C-6 has columns for Freight In, Store Supplies, Office Supplies, and Other. Here the total credits to Accounts Payable ($9,437) equal the total debits to Purchases, Freight In, Store Supplies, and Office Supplies ($9,200 + $50 + $145 + $42 = $9,437). As in the procedure already described, the individual transactions in the Accounts Payable column are posted regularly to the accounts payable subsidiary ledger, and the totals of each column in the journal are posted monthly to the correct general ledger accounts. Some credit purchases call for a debit to an account that has no special column (that is, no place to record the debit) in the purchases journal. These transactions are recorded in the Other Accounts column with an indication of the account to which the debit is to be made.

Exhibit C-6. A Multicolumn Purchases Journal

Purchases Journal **Page 1**

						Credit	Debits						
											Other Accounts		
Date		Account Credited	Date of Invoice	Terms	Post. Ref.	Accounts Payable	Purchases	Freight In	Store Supplies	Office Supplies	Account	Post. Ref.	Amount
July	2	Jones Chevrolet	7/1	2/10, n/30	✓	2,500	2,500						
	2	Marshall Ford	7/2	2/15, n/30	✓	300	300						
	2	Shelby Car Delivery	7/2	n/30	✓	50		50					
	3	Dealer Sales	7/3	n/30	✓	700	700						
	12	Thomas Auto	7/11	n/30	✓	1,400	1,400						
	17	Dealer Sales	7/17	2/10, n/30	✓	3,200	3,200						
	19	Thomas Auto	7/17	n/30	✓	1,100	1,100						
	25	Osborne Supply	7/21	n/10	✓	187			145	42			
						9,437	9,200	50	145	42			
						(212)	(511)	(514)	(132)	(133)			

Cash Receipts Journal

All transactions involving receipts of cash are recorded in the **cash receipts journal**. Examples of such transactions are cash from cash sales, cash from credit customers in payment of their accounts, and cash from other sources. To be most efficient, the cash receipts journal must be multicolumn. Several columns are necessary because, although all cash receipts are alike in that they require a debit to Cash, they are different in that they require a variety of credit entries. Thus you should be alert to several important differences between the cash receipts journal and the journals previously presented. Among these differences are an Other Accounts column, use of account numbers in the Post. Ref. column, and daily posting of the credits to Other Accounts.

The cash receipts journal illustrated in Exhibit C-7 is based on the following selected transactions for July:

July 1 Henry Mitchell invested $20,000 in a used-car business.
5 Sold a used car for $1,200 cash.
8 Collected $500 from Georgetta Jones, less 2 percent sales discount.
13 Sold a used car for $1,400 cash.
16 Collected $750 from Peter Clark.
19 Sold a used car for $1,000 cash.
20 Sold some equipment not used in the business for $500 cash. The carrying value of the equipment was $500.
24 Signed a note at the bank for a loan of $5,000.
26 Sold a used car for $1,600 cash.
28 Collected $600 from Peter Clark, less 2 percent sales discount.

The cash receipts journal, as illustrated in Exhibit C-7, has three debit columns and three credit columns. The three debit columns record Cash, Sales Discounts, and Other Accounts.

1. *Cash* Each entry must have an amount in this column because each transaction must be a receipt of cash.
2. *Sales Discounts* The company in the illustration allows a 2 percent discount for prompt payment. Therefore, it is useful to have a column for sales discounts. Note that in the transactions of July 8 and 28, the debits to Cash and Sales Discounts are equal to the credit to Accounts Receivable.
3. *Other Accounts* The Other Accounts column, sometimes called Sundry Accounts, is used in the case of transactions that involve both a debit to Cash and a debit to some other account besides Sales Discounts.

The credit columns are the following:

1. *Accounts Receivable* This column is used to record collections on account from customers. The customer's name is written in the space entitled Account Credited so that the payment can be entered in his or her account in the accounts receivable subsidiary ledger. The postings to the individual accounts receivable accounts are usually done daily so that the customer's account balance will be known in case of an inquiry.

Exhibit C-7. Relationship of the Cash Receipts Journal to the General Ledger and the Accounts Receivable Ledger

Cash Receipts Journal Page 1

Date		Account Debited / Credited	Post. Ref.	Debits: Cash	Debits: Sales Discounts	Debits: Other Accounts	Credits: Accounts Receivable	Credits: Sales	Credits: Other Accounts
July	1	Henry Mitchell, Capital	311	20,000					20,000
	5	Sales		1,200				1,200	
	8	Georgetta Jones	✓	490	10		500		
	13	Sales		1,400				1,400	
	16	Peter Clark	✓	750			750		
	19	Sales		1,000				1,000	
	20	Equipment	151	500					500
	24	Notes Payable	213	5,000					5,000
	26	Sales		1,600				1,600	
	28	Peter Clark	✓	588	12		600		
				32,528	22		1,850	5,200	25,500
				(111)	(412)		(114)	(411)	(✓)

Post individual amounts in Accounts Receivable credit columns **daily**.

Post totals at **end of month**.

Total not posted.

Post individual amounts in Other Accounts column **daily**.

General Ledger

Cash 111

Date		Post. Ref.	Debit	Credit	Balance Debit	Balance Credit
July	31	CR1	32,528		32,528	

Accounts Receivable 114

Date		Post. Ref.	Debit	Credit	Balance Debit	Balance Credit
July	31	S1	4,950		4,950	
	31	CR1		1,850	3,100	

Equipment 151

Date		Post. Ref.	Debit	Credit	Balance Debit	Balance Credit
					500	
July	20	CR1		500	—	

Accounts Receivable Ledger

Peter Clark

Date		Post. Ref.	Debit	Credit	Balance
July	1	S1	750		750
	16	CR1		750	—
	18	S1	1,225		1,225
	28	CR1		600	625

Georgetta Jones

Date		Post. Ref.	Debit	Credit	Balance
July	5	S1	500		500
	8	CR1		500	—

Continue posting to Notes Payable and Henry Mitchell, Capital.

Continue posting to Sales and Sales Discounts.

2. *Sales* This column is used to record all cash sales during the month. Retail firms that normally use cash registers would make an entry at the end of each day for the total sales from each cash register for that day. The debit, of course, is in the Cash debit column.
3. *Other Accounts* This column is used for the credit portion of any entry that is neither a cash collection from accounts receivable nor a cash sale. The name of the account to be credited is indicated in the Account Credited column. For example, the transactions of July 1, 20, and 24 involved credits to accounts other than Accounts Receivable or Sales. These individual postings should be done daily (or weekly if there are few of them). If a company finds that it is consistently crediting a certain account in the Other Accounts column, it may be appropriate to add another credit column to the cash receipts journal for that particular account.

The posting of the cash receipts journal, as illustrated in Exhibit C-7, can be summarized as follows:

1. Post the Accounts Receivable column daily to each individual account in the accounts receivable subsidiary ledger. A check mark in the Post. Ref. column of the cash receipts journal indicates that the amount has been posted, and a CR1 (representing Cash Receipts Journal—Page 1) in the Post. Ref. column of each ledger account indicates the source of the entry.
2. Post the debits and credits in the Other Accounts columns to the general ledger accounts daily or at convenient short intervals during the month. Write the account number in the Post. Ref. column of the cash receipts journal as the individual items are posted to indicate that the posting has been done, and write CR1 in the Post. Ref. column of each ledger account to indicate the source of the entry.
3. At the end of the month, total the columns in the cash receipts journal. The sum of the debit column totals must equal the sum of the credit column totals, as follows:

Debit Column Totals		**Credit Column Totals**	
Cash	$32,528	Accounts Receivable	$ 1,850
Sales Discounts	22	Sales	5,200
Other Accounts	0	Other Accounts	25,500
Total Debits	$32,550	Total Credits	$32,550

This step is called crossfooting—a procedure we encountered earlier.

4. Post the column totals as follows:
   a. Cash debit column—posted as a debit to the Cash account.
   b. Sales Discounts debit column—posted as a debit to the Sales Discounts account.
   c. Accounts Receivable credit column—posted as a credit to the Accounts Receivable controlling account.
   d. Sales credit column—posted as a credit to the Sales account.

e. The account numbers are written below each column in the cash receipts journal as they are posted to indicate that this step has been completed. A CR1 is written in the Post. Ref. column of each account to indicate the source of the entry.
f. Note that the Other Accounts column totals are not posted because each entry was posted separately when the transaction occurred. The individual accounts were posted in step **2** above. Accountants place a check mark at the bottom of the column to show that appropriate postings in that column have been made and that the total is not posted.

Cash Payments Journal

All transactions involving payments of cash are recorded in the **cash payments journal** (also called the cash disbursements journal). Examples of such transactions are cash purchases, payments of obligations resulting from earlier purchases on credit, and other cash payments. As with the cash receipts journal, the cash payments journal must be multicolumn. It is similar in design to the cash receipts journal.

The cash payments journal illustrated in Exhibit C-8 is based on the following selected transactions of Mitchell's Used Car Sales for July:

July 2 Purchased merchandise (a used car) from Sondra Tidmore for cash, $400.
6 Paid for newspaper advertising in the *Daily Journal,* $200.
8 Paid one month's land and building rent to Siviglia Agency, $250.
11 Paid Jones Chevrolet for July 1 invoice (previously recorded in purchases journal in Exhibit C-5), $2,500, less 2 percent purchase discount earned for payment in ten days or less.
16 Paid Charles Kuntz, a salesperson, his salary, $600.
17 Paid Marshall Ford invoice of July 2 (previously recorded in purchases journal in Exhibit C-5), $300, less 2 percent discount earned for payment in fifteen days or less.
24 Paid Grabow & Company for two-year insurance policy, $480.
27 Paid Dealer Sales invoice of July 17 (previously recorded in purchases journal in Exhibit C-5), $3,200, less 2 percent purchase discount for payment in ten days or less.
30 Purchased office equipment for $400 and service equipment for $500 from A&B Equipment Company. Issued one check for the total amount.
31 Purchased land for $15,000 from Burns Real Estate. Issued check for $5,000 and note payable for $10,000.

The cash payments journal, as illustrated in Exhibit C-8, has three credit columns and two debit columns. The credit columns for the cash payments journal are as follows:

1. *Cash* Each entry must have an amount in this column because each transaction must involve a payment of cash.

Exhibit C-8. Cash Payments Journal

Cash Payments Journal **Page 1**

Date		Ck. No.	Payee	Account Credited / Debited	Post. Ref.	Credits: Cash	Credits: Purchases Discounts	Credits: Other Accounts	Debits: Accounts Payable	Debits: Other Accounts
July	2	101	Sondra Tidmore	Purchases	511	400				400
	6	102	Daily Journal	Advertising Exp.	612	200				200
	8	103	Siviglia Agency	Rent Expense	631	250				250
	11	104	Jones Chevrolet		✓	2,450	50		2,500	
	16	105	Charles Kuntz	Salary Expense	611	600				600
	17	106	Marshall Ford		✓	294	6		300	
	24	107	Grabow & Company	Prepaid Insurance	119	480				480
	27	108	Dealer Sales		✓	3,136	64		3,200	
	30	109	A&B Equipment Company	Office Equipment	144					400
				Service Equipment	146	900				500
	31	110	Burns Real Estate	Notes Payable	213	5,000		10,000		
				Land	141					15,000
						13,710	120	10,000	6,000	17,830
						(111)	(512)	(✓)	(212)	(✓)

Post individual amounts in Other Accounts column **daily**.

Post individual amounts in Accounts Payable column **daily**.

Post totals at **end of month**.

Totals not posted.

General Ledger

Cash **111**

Date		Post. Ref.	Debit	Credit	Balance: Debit	Balance: Credit
July	31	CR1	32,528		32,528	
	31	CP1		13,710	18,818	

Prepaid Insurance **119**

Date		Post. Ref.	Debit	Credit	Balance: Debit	Balance: Credit
July	24	CP1	480		480	

Continue posting to Land, Office Equipment, Service Equipment, Notes Payable, Purchases, Salary Expense, Advertising Expense, and Rent Expense.

Continue posting to Purchases Discounts and Accounts Payable.

Accounts Payable Ledger

Jones Chevrolet

Date		Post. Ref.	Debit	Credit	Balance
July	1	P1		2,500	2,500
	11	CP1	2,500		—

Marshall Ford

Date		Post. Ref.	Debit	Credit	Balance
July	2	P1		300	300
	17	CP1	300		—

Dealer Sales

Date		Post. Ref.	Debit	Credit	Balance
July	3	P1		700	700
	17	P1		3,200	3,900
	27	CP1	3,200		700

2. *Purchases Discounts* When purchases discounts are taken, they are recorded in this column.
3. *Other Accounts* This column is used to record credits other than Cash or Purchases Discounts. Note that the July 31 transaction shows a purchase of Land for $15,000 through the issuance of a check for $5,000 and a Note Payable for $10,000.

The debit columns are as follows:

1. *Accounts Payable* This column total is used to record payments to suppliers that have extended credit to the company. The supplier's name is written in the space entitled Payee so that the payment can be entered in his or her account in the accounts payable ledger.
2. *Other Accounts* Cash can be expended for many reasons. Thus an Other Accounts or Sundry Accounts column is needed in the cash payments journal. The title of the account to be debited is written in the Account Debited column, and the amount is entered in the Other Accounts debit column. If a company finds that a particular account occurs often in the Other Accounts column, it may be desirable to add another debit column to the cash payments journal.

The posting of the cash payments journal, as illustrated in Exhibit C-8, can be summarized as follows:

1. The Accounts Payable column should be posted daily to each individual account in the accounts payable subsidiary ledger. A check mark is placed in the Post. Ref. column of the cash payments journal to indicate that the posting is accomplished.
2. The debits and credits in the Other Accounts debit and credit columns should be posted to the general ledger daily or at convenient short intervals during the month. The account number is written in the Post. Ref. column of the cash payments journal as the individual items are posted in order to indicate that the posting has been completed, and a CP1 (representing Cash Payments Journal—Page 1) is written in the Post. Ref. column of each ledger account.
3. At the end of the month, the columns are totaled and crossfooted. That is, the sum of the credit column totals must equal the sum of the debit column totals, as follows:

Credit Column Totals		Debit Column Totals	
Cash	$13,710	Accounts Payable	$ 6,000
Purchases Discounts	120	Other Accounts	17,830
Other Accounts	10,000	Total Debits	$23,830
Total Credits	$23,830		

4. The column totals for Cash, Purchases Discounts, and Accounts Payable are posted to their respective accounts in the general ledger at the end of the month. The account numbers are written below each column in the cash payments journal as they are posted to indicate that this

step has been completed, and a CP1 is written in the Post. Ref. column of each ledger account. A check mark is placed under the total of each Other Accounts column in the cash payments journal to indicate that appropriate postings in the column have been made and that the total is not posted.

General Journal

Transactions that do not involve sales, purchases, cash receipts, or cash payments should be recorded in the general journal. Usually there are only a few such transactions. The two examples that follow are entries that do not fit in a special-purpose journal: a return of merchandise, and an allowance from a supplier for credit. Adjusting and closing entries are also recorded in the general journal.

July 25 Returned one of the two used cars purchased on credit from Thomas Auto for $700 on July 11. Each car cost $700.

26 Agreed to give Maxwell Gertz a $35 allowance on his account because a tire blew out on the car he purchased.

These entries are shown in Exhibit C-9. The entries on July 25 and 26 include a debit or a credit to a controlling account (Accounts Payable or Accounts Receivable). The name of the customer or supplier is also given here. When such a debit or credit is made to a controlling account in the general journal, the entry must be posted twice: once in the controlling account and once in the individual account in the subsidiary ledger. This procedure keeps the subsidiary ledger equal to the controlling account. Note that the July 26 transaction is posted by a debit to Sales Returns and Allowances in the general ledger (shown by the account number 413), by a credit to the Accounts Receivable controlling account in the general ledger (shown by the account number 114), and by a credit to the Maxwell

Exhibit C-9. Transactions Recorded in the General Journal

General Journal — Page 1

Date		Description	Post. Ref.	Debit	Credit
July	25	Accounts Payable, Thomas Auto	212/✓	700	
		Purchases Returns and Allowances	513		700
		Returned used car for credit; invoice date: 7/11			
	26	Sales Returns and Allowances	413	35	
		Accounts Receivable, Maxwell Gertz	114/✓		35
		Allowance given because of faulty tire			

Gertz account in the accounts receivable subsidiary ledger (shown by the check mark).

Flexibility of Special-Purpose Journals

The functions of special-purpose journals are to reduce and simplify the work in accounting and to allow for the division of labor. These journals should be designed to fit the business in which they are used. As noted earlier, if certain accounts show up often in the Other Accounts column of a journal, it may be wise to add a column for those accounts when a new page of a special-purpose journal is prepared.

Also, if certain transactions appear over and over again in the general journal, it may be a good idea to set up a new special-purpose journal. For example, if Mitchell's Used Car Sales finds that it must often give allowances to customers, it may want to set up a sales returns and allowances journal specifically for these transactions. Sometimes, a purchases returns and allowances journal may be in order. In short, special-purpose journals should be designed to take care of the kinds of transactions a company commonly encounters.

Questions

1. How do special-purpose journals save time in entering and posting transactions?
2. Long Transit had 1,700 sales on credit during the current month.
   a. If the company uses a two-column general journal to record sales, how many times will the word *Sales* be written?
   b. How many postings to the Sales account will have to be made?
   c. If the company uses a sales journal, how many times will the word *Sales* be written?
   d. How many postings to the Sales account will have to be made?
3. What is the purpose of the Accounts Receivable controlling account? What is its relationship to the accounts receivable subsidiary ledger?
4. Why are the cash receipts journal and cash payments journal crossfooted? When is this step performed?
5. A company has the following numbers of accounts with balances: 18 asset accounts, including the Accounts Receivable account but not the individual customer accounts; 200 customer accounts; 8 liability accounts, including the Accounts Payable account but not the individual creditor accounts; 100 creditor accounts; 35 owners' equity accounts, including income statement accounts. The total is 361 accounts. How many accounts in total would appear in the general ledger?

Exercises

Exercise C-1. Matching Transactions to Special-Purpose Journals *(L.O. 1)*

A company uses a one-column sales journal, a one-column purchases journal, a cash receipts journal, a cash payments journal, and a general journal.

Indicate in which journal each of the following transactions would be recorded: (1) sold merchandise on credit; (2) sold merchandise for cash; (3) gave a customer credit for merchandise purchased on credit and returned; (4) paid a creditor; (5) paid office salaries; (6) customer paid for merchandise previously purchased on credit; (7) recorded adjusting and closing entries; (8) purchased merchandise on credit; (9) purchased sales department supplies on credit; (10) purchased office equipment for cash; (11) returned merchandise purchased on credit; (12) paid taxes.

Exercise C-2. Characteristics of Special-Purpose Journals *(L.O. 1)*

Sanchez Corporation uses a single-column sales journal, a single-column purchases journal, a cash receipts journal, a cash payments journal, and a general journal.

1. In which of the journals listed above would you expect to find the fewest transactions recorded?
2. At the end of the accounting period, to which account or accounts should the total of the purchases journal be posted as a debit and/or credit?
3. At the end of the accounting period, to which account or accounts should the total of the sales journal be posted as a debit and/or credit?
4. What two subsidiary ledgers would probably be associated with the journals listed above? From which journals would postings normally be made to each of the two subsidiary ledgers?
5. In which of the journals are adjusting and closing entries made?

Exercise C-3. Identifying the Content of a Special-Purpose Journal *(L.O. 2)*

Shown below is a page from a special journal.

1. What kind of journal is this?
2. Give an explanation for each of the following transactions: (a) August 27, (b) August 28, (c) August 29, (d) August 30.
3. Explain the following: (a) the numbers under the bottom lines, (b) the checks entered in the Post. Ref. column, (c) the numbers 115 and 715 in the Post. Ref. column, and (d) the check below the Other Accounts column.

Date		Account Credited	Post. Ref.	Debits		Credits		
				Cash	Sales Discount	Other Accounts	Accounts Receivable	Sales
		Balance Forward		39,799	787	26,100	10,204	4,282
Aug.	27	Betsy McCray	✓	490	10		500	
	28	Notes Receivable	115			1,000		
		Interest Income	715	1,120		120		
	29	Cash Sale		960				960
	30	Michael Harper	✓	200			200	
				42,569	797	27,220	10,904	5,242
				(111)	(412)	(✓)	(114)	(411)

Exercise C-4. Finding Errors in Special-Purpose Journals
(L.O. 2, 3)

A company records purchases in a one-column purchases journal and records purchases returns in its general journal. During the past month an accounting clerk made each of the errors described below. Explain how each error might be discovered.

1. Correctly recorded an $86 purchase in the purchases journal but posted it to the creditor's account as a $68 purchase.
2. Made an additional error in totaling the Amount column of the purchases journal.
3. Posted a purchases return recorded in the general journal to the Purchases Returns and Allowances account and to the Accounts Payable account but did not post it to the creditor's account.
4. Made an error in determining the balance of a creditor's account.
5. Posted a purchases return to the Accounts Payable account but did not post it to the Purchases Returns and Allowances account.

Exercise C-5. Posting from a Sales Journal
(L.O. 2, 3)

Grammas Corporation began business on September 1. The company maintained a sales journal, which appeared at the end of the month as presented below.

Sales Journal — **Page 1**

Date		Account Debited	Invoice Number	Post. Ref.	Amount
Sept.	4	Yung Moon	1001		172
	10	Stacy Kravitz	1002		317
	15	Arthur Hillman	1003		214
	17	Yung Moon	1004		97
	25	Juan Robles	1005		433
					1,233

1. On a sheet of paper, open general ledger accounts for Accounts Receivable (account number 112) and Sales (account number 411) and an accounts receivable subsidiary ledger with an account for each customer. Make the appropriate postings from the sales journal. State the posting references that you would place in the sales journal above.
2. Prove the accounts receivable subsidiary ledger by preparing a schedule of accounts receivable.

Exercise C-6. Multicolumn Purchases Journal
(L.O. 3)

Jablouski Company uses a multicolumn purchases journal similar to the one illustrated in Exhibit C-6.

During the month of October, Jablouski made the following purchases:

Oct. 1 Purchased merchandise from Cowen Company on account for $2,700, invoice dated October 1, terms 2/10, n/30.

Oct. 2 Received freight bill dated October 1 from Riker Freight for above merchandise, $175, terms n/30.
23 Purchased supplies from Zimmer, Inc. for $120; allocated one-half each to store and office; invoice dated October 20, terms n/30.
27 Purchased merchandise from Fleming Company on account for $987; total included freight in of $87; invoice dated October 25, terms n/30, FOB shipping point.
30 Purchased office supplies from Zimmer, Inc. for $48, invoice dated October 30, terms n/30.
31 Purchased a one-year insurance policy from Greenspan Agency, $240, terms n/30.

1. Draw a multicolumn purchases journal similar to the one in Exhibit C-6.
2. Enter the above transactions in the purchases journal. Then foot and cross-foot the columns.

Problems

Problem C-1. Identification of Transactions *(L.O. 2, 3)*

Chin Company uses a general journal, a purchases journal, a sales journal, a cash receipts journal, and a cash payments journal similar to those illustrated in the text. On September 30, the P. Quaid account in the accounts receivable subsidiary ledger appeared as shown below:

P. Quaid

Date		Item	Post. Ref.	Debit	Credit	Balance
Aug.	31		S4	816		816
Sept.	4		J7		64	752
	10		CR5		200	552
	15		S6	228		780

On September 30, the account of Diaz Company in the accounts payable subsidiary ledger appeared as follows:

Diaz Company

Date		Item	Post. Ref.	Debit	Credit	Balance
Sept.	16		P7		2,026	2,026
	21		J9	212		1,814
	28		CP8	1,814		—

Required

1. Write an explanation of each entry affecting the P. Quaid account receivable, including the journal from which the entry was posted.
2. Write an explanation of each entry affecting the Diaz Company account payable, including the journal from which the entry was posted.

Problem C-2. Cash Receipts and Cash Payments Journals *(L.O. 3)*

The items below detail all cash transactions by Baylor Company for the month of July. The company uses multicolumn cash receipts and cash payments journals similar to those illustrated in this appendix.

July 1 The owner, Eugene Baylor, invested $50,000 cash and $24,000 in equipment in the business.
2 Paid rent to Leonard Agency, $600, with check no. 75.
3 Cash sales, $2,200.
6 Purchased store equipment for $5,000 from Gilmore Company, with check no. 76.
7 Purchased merchandise for cash, $6,500, from Pascual Company, with check no. 77.
8 Paid Audretti Company invoice, $1,800, less 2 percent with check no. 78.
9 Paid advertising bill, $350, to WOSU, with check no. 79.
10 Cash sales, $3,910.
12 Received $800 on account from B. Erring.
13 Purchased used truck for cash, $3,520, from Pettit Company, with check no. 80.
19 Received $4,180 from Monroe Company, in settlement of a $4,000 note plus interest.
20 Received $1,078 ($1,100 less $22 cash discount) from Young Lee.
21 Paid Baylor $2,000 to reimburse travel expense undertaken for business purposes by issuing check no. 81.
23 Paid Dautley Company invoice, $2,500, less 2 percent discount, with check no. 82.
26 Paid Haywood Company for freight on merchandise received, $60, with check no. 83.
27 Cash sales, $4,800.
28 Paid C. Murphy for monthly salary, $1,400, with check no. 84.
31 Purchased land from N. Archibald for $20,000, paying $5,000 with check no. 85 and signing a note payable for $15,000.

Required

1. Enter the preceding transactions in the cash receipts and cash payments journals.
2. Foot, crossfoot, and rule the journals.

Problem C-3. Purchases and General Journals *(L.O. 2, 3)*

The following items represent the credit transactions for McGarry Company during the month of August. The company uses a multicolumn purchases journal and a general journal similar to those illustrated in the text.

Aug. 2 Purchased merchandise from Alvarez Company, $1,400.
5 Purchased van from Meriweather Company, $8,000.
8 Purchased office supplies from Daudridge Company, $400.
12 Purchased filing cabinets from Daudridge Company, $550.
14 Purchased merchandise, $1,400, and store supplies, $200, from Petrie Company.
17 Purchased store supplies from Alvarez Company, $100, and office supplies from Hollins Company, $50.
20 Purchased merchandise from Petrie Company, $1,472.
24 Purchased merchandise from Alvarez Company, $2,452; the $2,452 invoice total included shipping charges, $232.

Aug. 26 Purchased office supplies from Daudridge Company, $150.
30 Purchased merchandise from Petrie Company, $290.
31 Returned defective merchandise purchased from Petrie Company on August 20 for full credit, $432.

Required

1. Enter the preceding transactions in the purchases journal and the general journal. Assume that all terms are n/30 and that invoice dates are the same as the transaction dates.
2. Foot, crossfoot, and rule the purchases journal.
3. Open the following general ledger accounts: Store Supplies (116); Office Supplies (117); Trucks (142); Office Equipment (144); Accounts Payable (211); Purchases (611); Purchases Returns and Allowances (612); and Freight In (613). Open accounts payable subsidiary ledger accounts as needed. Post from the journals to the ledger accounts.

Problem C-4. Comprehensive Use of Special-Purpose Journals
(L.O. 2, 3)

Chung Refrigerating Company completed the following transactions:

May 1 Received merchandise from Costello Company, $2,500, invoice dated April 29, terms 2/10, n/30, FOB shipping point.
2 Issued check no. 230 to Roundfield Agency for May rent, $2,000.
3 Received merchandise from Vranes Manufacturing, $5,400, invoice dated May 1, terms 2/10, n/30, FOB shipping point.
5 Issued check no. 231 to Dukes Company for repairs, $560.
6 Received $400 credit memorandum pertaining to May 3 shipment from Vranes Manufacturing for unsatisfactory merchandise returned to Vranes Manufacturing.
7 Issued check no. 232 to Orta Company for freight charges on May 1 and May 3 shipments, $184.
8 Sold merchandise to C. Share, $1,000, terms 1/10, n/30, invoice no. 725.
9 Issued check no. 233 to Costello Company in full payment less discount.
10 Sold merchandise to R. Bell for $1,250, terms 1/10, n/30, invoice no. 726.
11 Issued check no. 234 to Vranes Manufacturing for balance of account less discount.
12 Purchased advertising on credit from WXYR, $450, terms n/20.
14 Issued credit memorandum to R. Bell for $50 for merchandise returned.
15 Cash sales for the first half of the month, $9,670. (To shorten this problem, cash sales are recorded only twice a month instead of daily, as they would be in actual practice.)
16 Sold merchandise to L. Stokes, $700, terms 1/10, n/30, invoice no. 727.
17 Received check from C. Share for May 8 sale less discount.
19 Received check from R. Bell for balance of account less discount.
20 Received merchandise from Costello Company, $2,800, invoice dated May 19, terms 2/10, n/30, FOB shipping point.
21 Received freight bill on merchandise purchased from Noh Company, $570, terms n/5.
22 Issued check no. 235 for advertising purchase of May 12.

May 23 Received merchandise from Vranes Manufacturing, $3,600, invoice dated May 22, terms 2/10, n/30, FOB shipping point.
24 Issued check no. 236 for freight charge of May 21.
26 Sold merchandise to C. Share, $800, terms 1/10, n/30, invoice no. 728.
27 Received credit memorandum from Vranes Manufacturing for defective merchandise received May 23, $300.
28 Issued check no. 237 to Espinoza Company for purchase of office equipment, $350.
29 Issued check no. 238 to Costello Company for one-half of May 20 purchase less discount.
30 Received check in full from L. Stokes, discount not allowed.
31 Cash sales for the last half of month, $11,560.
31 Issued check no. 239, payable to Payroll Account for monthly sales salaries, $4,300.

Required

1. Prepare a sales journal, a multicolumn purchases journal, a cash receipts journal, a cash payments journal, and a general journal for Chung Refrigerating Company similar to the ones illustrated in this appendix. Use 1 as the page number for each journal.
2. Open the following general ledger accounts: Cash (111); Accounts Receivable (112); Office Equipment (141); Accounts Payable (211); Sales (411); Sales Discounts (412); Sales Returns and Allowances (413); Purchases (511); Purchases Discounts (512); Purchases Returns and Allowances (513); Freight In (514); Sales Salaries Expense (521); Advertising Expense (522); Rent Expense (531); and Repairs Expense (532).
3. Open the following accounts receivable subsidiary ledger accounts: R. Bell, C. Share, and L. Stokes.
4. Open the following accounts payable subsidiary ledger accounts: Costello Company, Noh Company, Vranes Manufacturing, and WXYR.
5. Enter the transactions in the journals and post as appropriate.
6. Foot and crossfoot the journals, and make end-of-month postings.
7. Prepare a trial balance of the general ledger and prove the control balances of Accounts Receivable and Accounts Payable by preparing schedules of accounts receivable and accounts payable.

LEARNING OBJECTIVES

1. *Identify and compute the liabilities associated with payroll accounting.*
2. *Record transactions associated with payroll accounting.*

APPENDIX D

Introduction to Payroll Accounting

A major expense of most companies is the cost of labor and related payroll taxes. In some industries, such as banking and airlines, payroll costs represent more than half the operating costs. Payroll accounting is important because of the amounts of money involved and because the employer must conform to many complex laws governing taxes on payrolls. The employer is liable for meeting reporting requirements and for the money withheld from employees' salaries and for payroll taxes. After completing this appendix, you should be able to meet the learning objectives listed on the left.

Also, the payroll accounting system is subject to complaints and to possible fraud. Every employee must be paid on time and receive a detailed explanation of the amount of his or her pay. The payroll system calls for strong internal control and efficient processing and distribution of checks, as well as accurate reporting to government agencies.

This section will focus on the liabilities, the records, and the control requirements of payroll accounting. Although the illustrations in the following sections are shown in manual format to demonstrate the concepts, most businesses (including small businesses) use a computer to process payroll. The three general kinds of liabilities associated with payroll accounting are (1) liabilities for employee compensation, (2) liabilities for employee payroll withholdings, and (3) liabilities for employer payroll taxes.

It is important to distinguish between employees and independent contractors. Payroll accounting applies only to employees of the company. Employees are paid a wage or salary by the company and are under its direct supervision and control. Independent contractors are not employees of the company, so they are not accounted for under the payroll system. They offer services to the firm for a fee, but are not under its direct control or supervision. Some examples of independent contractors are certified public accountants, advertising agencies, and lawyers.

Liabilities for Employee Compensation

The employer is liable to employees for wages and salaries. The term **wages** refers to payment for the services of employees at an hourly rate or on a piecework basis. The term **salaries** refers to the compensation for employees who are paid at a monthly or yearly rate. Generally, these employees are administrators or managers.

OBJECTIVE 1
Identify and compute the liabilities associated with payroll accounting

Besides setting minimum wage levels, the federal Fair Labor Standards Act (also called the Wages and Hours Law) regulates overtime pay. Employers who take part in interstate commerce must pay overtime for hours worked beyond forty hours a week or more than eight hours a day. This overtime pay must be at least one and one-half times the regular rate. Work on Saturdays, Sundays, or holidays may also call for overtime pay under separate wage agreements. Overtime pay under union or other employment contracts may exceed these minimums.

For example, suppose that the employment contract of Robert Jones calls for a regular wage of $8 an hour, one and one-half times the regular rate for work over eight hours in any weekday, and twice the regular rate for work on Saturdays, Sundays, or holidays. He works the following days and hours during the week of January 18, 19xx:

Day	Total Hours Worked	Regular Time	Overtime
Monday	10	8	2
Tuesday	8	8	0
Wednesday	8	8	0
Thursday	9	8	1
Friday	10	8	2
Saturday	2	0	2
	47	40	7

Jones's wages would be figured as follows:

Regular time	40 hours × $8	$320.00
Overtime, weekdays	5 hours × $8 × 1.5	60.00
Overtime, weekend	2 hours × $8 × 2	32.00
Total wages		$412.00

Liabilities for Employee Payroll Withholdings

The amount paid to employees is generally less than the wages they earned because the employer is required by law to withhold certain amounts from the employees' wages and send them directly to government agencies to pay taxes owed by the employees. In this group are FICA taxes, federal income taxes, and state income taxes. Also, certain withholdings are made for the employees' benefit, often at their request. These include pension payments, medical insurance premiums, life insurance premiums, union dues, and charitable contributions. No matter what the reason for the withholding from employees' wages, the employer is liable for payment to the proper agency, fund, or organization.

FICA Tax

With the passage of the United States social security program in the 1930s, the federal government began to take more responsibility for the well-being of its citizens. The social security program offers retirement and disability benefits, survivor's benefits, and hospitalization and other medical benefits. One of the major extensions of the program provides hospitalization and medical insurance for persons over sixty-five.

The social security program is financed by taxes on employees, employers, and the self-employed. About 90 percent of the people working in the United States fall under the provisions of this program.

The Federal Insurance Contributions Act (FICA) set up the tax to pay for this program. The 1991 FICA tax rate is 7.65 percent. A two-step maximum wage has been enacted by Congress for 1991. The full 7.65 percent tax applies to the first $53,400, at which point the rate drops to 1.45 percent, which applies to a maximum of $125,000. The tax is paid by *both* employee and employer. This current schedule is subject to frequent amendments by Congress. We will use these figures throughout the appendix.

The FICA tax applies to the pay of each employee up to the levels indicated. Since the employee and the employer must each pay the tax, each pays an equal amount. The employer deducts the employee's tax from his or her wages and sends the amount, along with other employees' withholdings of FICA taxes and the employer's FICA taxes, to the government. Because of inflation and rising benefits under the social security system, these provisions are under constant study by Congress. They are subject to change and should be verified each year.

As an example of the FICA tax, suppose that Robert Jones will earn less than $53,400 this year and that the FICA withholding for taxes on his paycheck this week is $31.52 ($412.00 × .0765). The employer must pay an equal tax of $31.52 and remit a total of $63.04.

Federal Income Tax

The largest deduction from many employees' earnings is their estimated liability for federal income taxes. The system of tax collection for federal income taxes is to "pay as you go." The employer is required to withhold the amount of the taxes from employees' paychecks and turn it over to the Internal Revenue Service.

The amount to be withheld depends in part on the amount of each employee's earnings and on the number of the employee's exemptions. All employees are required by law to indicate exemptions by filing a Form W-4 (Employee's Withholding Exemption Certificate). Each employee is entitled to one exemption for himself or herself and one for each dependent.

The Internal Revenue Service provides employers with tables to aid them in computing the amount of withholdings. For example, Figure D-1 is a withholding table for married employees who are paid weekly. The withholding from Robert Jones's $412.00 weekly earnings is $31.00. The amount is shown in the intersection of columns for four withholding allowances (one for Robert and each of his three dependents) and the $410–420 wage bracket. (This table is presented for illustrative purposes only. Actual withholding tables change periodically as changes occur in tax rates and laws.)

State Income Tax

Most states have income taxes, and in most cases the procedures for withholding are similar to those for federal income taxes.

Other Withholdings

Some of the other withholdings, such as for a retirement or pension plan, are required of each employee. Others, such as withholdings for insurance premiums or savings plans, may be requested by the employee. The payroll system must allow for treating each employee separately with regard to withholdings and the records of those withholdings. The employer is liable to account for all withholdings and to make proper remittances.

Figure D-1. Wage Bracket Table

Weekly Payroll Period–Employee Married												
		And the number of withholding allowances claimed is–										
And the wages are–		0	1	2	3	4	5	6	7	8	9	10 or more
At least	But less than	The amount of income tax to be withheld shall be–										
$300	$310	$37	$31	$26	$20	$14	$ 9	$ 3	$ 0	$ 0	$ 0	$ 0
310	320	38	33	27	22	16	10	5	0	0	0	0
320	330	40	34	29	23	17	12	6	1	0	0	0
330	340	41	36	30	25	19	13	8	2	0	0	0
340	350	43	37	32	26	20	15	9	4	0	0	0
350	360	44	39	33	28	22	16	11	5	0	0	0
360	370	46	40	35	29	23	18	12	7	1	0	0
370	380	47	42	36	31	25	19	14	8	2	0	0
380	390	49	43	38	32	26	21	15	10	4	0	0
390	400	50	45	39	34	28	22	17	11	5	0	0
400	410	52	46	41	35	29	24	18	13	7	1	0
410	420	53	48	42	37	31	25	20	14	8	3	0
420	430	55	49	44	38	32	27	21	16	10	4	0

Computation of an Employee's Take-Home Pay: An Illustration

OBJECTIVE 2
Record transactions associated with payroll accounting

To continue with the example of Robert Jones, let us now compute his take-home pay. We know that his total earnings for the week of January 18 are $412.00, that his FICA tax at 7.65 percent is $31.52 (he has not earned over $53,400), and that his federal income tax withholding is $31.00. Assume also that his union dues are $2.00, his medical insurance premiums are $7.60, his life insurance premium is $6.00, he places $15.00 per week in savings bonds, and he contributes $1.00 per week to United Charities. His net (take-home) pay is computed as follows:

Gross earnings		$412.00
Deductions		
FICA tax	$31.52	
Federal income tax withheld	31.00	
Union dues	2.00	
Medical insurance	7.60	
Life insurance	6.00	
Savings bonds	15.00	
United Charities contribution	1.00	
Total deductions		94.12
Net (take-home) pay		$317.88

Employee Earnings Record

Each employer must keep a record of earnings and withholdings for each employee. Many companies today use computers to maintain these records, but small companies may still use manual records. The manual form of **employee earnings record** used for Robert Jones is shown in Exhibit D-1. This form is designed to help the employer meet legal reporting re-

Exhibit D-1. Employee Earnings Record

Employee Earnings Record

Employee's Name Robert Jones	**Social Security Number** 444-66-9999	
Address 777 20th Street	**Sex** Male	**Employee No.** 705
Marshall, Michigan 52603	**Single** **Married** X	**Weekly Pay Rate**
Date of Birth September 20, 1962	**Exemptions (W-4)** 4	**Hourly Rate** $8
Position Sales Assistant	**Date of Employment** July 15, 1988	**Date Employment Ended**

19xx		Earnings			Deductions							Payment		
Period Ended	Total Hours	Regular	Overtime	Gross	FICA Tax	Federal Income Tax	Union Dues	Medical Insurance	Life Insurance	Savings Bonds	Other: A—United Charities	Net Earnings	Check No.	Cumulative Gross Earnings
Jan. 4	40	320.00	0	320.00	24.48	17.00	2.00	7.60	6.00	15.00	A 1.00	246.92	717	320.00
11	44	320.00	48.00	368.00	28.15	23.00	2.00	7.60	6.00	15.00	A 1.00	285.25	822	688.00
18	47	320.00	92.00	412.00	31.52	31.00	2.00	7.60	6.00	15.00	A 1.00	317.88	926	1,100.00

Exhibit D-2. Payroll Register

Payroll Register **Pay Period: Week ended January 18**

		Earnings			Deductions							Payment		Distribution	
Employee	Total Hours	Regular	Overtime	Gross	FICA Tax	Federal Income Tax	Union Dues	Medical Insurance	Life Insurance	Savings Bonds	Other: A—United Charities	Net Earnings	Check No.	Sales Wages Expense	Office Wages Expense
Linda Duval	40	160.00		160.00	12.24	11.00		5.80				130.96	923		160.00
John Franks	44	160.00	24.00	184.00	14.08	14.00	2.00	7.60			A 10.00	136.32	924	184.00	
Samuel Goetz	40	400.00		400.00	30.60	53.00		10.40	14.00		A 3.00	289.00	925	400.00	
Robert Jones	**47**	**320.00**	**92.00**	**412.00**	**31.52**	**31.00**	**2.00**	**7.60**	**6.00**	**15.00**	**A 1.00**	**317.88**	**926**	**412.00**	
Billie Matthews	40	160.00		160.00	12.24	14.00		5.80				127.96	927		160.00
Rosaire O'Brian	42	200.00	20.00	220.00	16.83	22.00	2.00	5.80				173.37	928	220.00	
James Van Dyke	40	200.00		200.00	15.30	20.00		5.80				158.90	929		200.00
		1,600.00	136.00	1,736.00	132.81	165.00	6.00	48.80	20.00	15.00	14.00	1,334.39		1,216.00	520.00

quirements. Each deduction must be shown to have been paid to the proper agency, and the employee must receive a report of the deductions made each year. Most columns are self-explanatory. Note, however, the column on the far right, where cumulative earnings (earnings to date) are recorded. This record helps the employer comply with the rule of applying FICA taxes only up to the maximum wage level. At the end of the year, the employer reports to the employee on Form W-2, the Wage and Tax Statement, the totals of earnings and tax deductions for the year, so that the employee can complete his or her individual tax return. The employer sends a copy of the W-2 to the Internal Revenue Service. Thus the IRS can check on whether the employee has reported all income earned from that employer.

Payroll Register

The **payroll register** is a detailed listing of the firm's total payroll that is prepared each payday. A payroll register is presented in Exhibit D-2. Note that the name, hours, earnings, deductions, and net pay of each employee are listed. Compare the January 18 entry in the employee earnings record of Robert Jones (Exhibit D-1) with the entry for Robert Jones in the payroll register. Except for the first column, which lists the employee names, and the last column, which shows the wage or salary as either sales or office expense, the columns are the same. The columns help employers to record the payroll in the accounting records and to meet legal reporting requirements as noted above. The last two columns are needed to divide the expenses on the income statement into selling and administrative categories.

Recording the Payroll

The journal entry for recording the payroll is based on the total of the columns from the payroll register. The journal entry to record the payroll of January 18 follows. Note that each account debited or credited is a total from the payroll register. If the payroll register is considered a special-purpose journal, the column can be entered directly in the ledger accounts with the correct account numbers shown at the bottom of each column.

Jan. 18	Sales Wages Expense	1,216.00	
	Office Wages Expense	520.00	
	FICA Tax Payable		132.81
	Employees' Federal Income Tax Payable		165.00
	Union Dues Payable		6.00
	Medical Insurance Premiums Payable		48.80
	Life Insurance Premiums Payable		20.00
	Savings Bonds Payable		15.00
	United Charities Payable		14.00
	Wages Payable		1,334.39
	To record weekly payroll		

Liabilities for Employer Payroll Taxes

The payroll taxes discussed so far were deducted from the employee's gross earnings, to be remitted by the employer. There are three major taxes on salaries that the employer must pay in addition to gross wages: the FICA tax, the federal unemployment insurance tax, and state unemployment insurance tax. These taxes are considered operating expenses.

FICA Tax. The employer must pay FICA tax equal to the amount paid by the employees. That is, from the payroll register in Exhibit D-2, the employer would have to pay FICA tax of $132.81, equal to that paid by the employees.

Federal Unemployment Insurance Tax. The Federal Unemployment Tax Act (FUTA) is another part of the U.S. social security system. It is intended to fund programs to help unemployed workers. In this way, it is different from FICA taxes and state unemployment taxes. The dollars paid through FUTA provide for unemployment compensation. Unlike the FICA tax, which is levied on both employees and employers, the FUTA is assessed only against employers.

The amount of tax can vary. Recently it has been 6.2 percent of the first $7,000 earned by each employee. The employer, however, is allowed a credit against this federal tax for unemployment taxes paid to the state. The maximum credit is 5.4 percent of the first $7,000 of each employee's earnings. Most states set their rate at this maximum. Thus, the FUTA paid would be 0.8 percent (6.2 percent – 5.4 percent) of the taxable wages.

State Unemployment Insurance Tax. All state unemployment plans provide for unemployment compensation to be paid to eligible unemployed workers. This compensation is paid out of the fund provided by the 5.4 percent of the first $7,000 earned by each employee. In some states, employers with favorable employment records may be entitled to pay less than the 5.4 percent.

Recording Payroll Taxes

According to Exhibit D-2, the gross payroll for the week ended January 18 was $1,736.00. Because it was the first month of the year, all employees had accumulated less than the $53,400 and $7,000 maximum taxable salaries. Therefore, the total FICA tax was $132.81 (equal to the tax on employees); the total FUTA was $13.89 (.008 × $1,736.00); and the total state unemployment tax was $93.74 (.054 × $1,736.00). The entry to record this expense and the related liability in the general journal is as follows:

Jan. 18	Payroll Tax Expense	240.44	
	FICA Tax Payable		132.81
	Federal Unemployment Tax Payable		13.89
	State Unemployment Tax Payable		93.74
	To record weekly payroll taxes expense		

Payment of Payroll and Payroll Taxes

After the weekly payroll is recorded, as illustrated earlier, a liability of $1,334.39 exists for wages payable. How this liability will be paid depends on the system used by the company. Many companies use a special payroll account against which payroll checks are drawn. Under this system, a check must first be drawn on the regular checking account for total net earnings for this payroll, or $1,334.39, and deposited in the special payroll account before the payroll checks are issued to the employees.

The combined FICA taxes (both employees' and employer's share) and the federal income taxes must be paid to the Internal Revenue Service at least quarterly. Monthly payments are necessary if more than a certain amount of money is involved. The federal unemployment insurance taxes are paid yearly if the amount is less than $100. If it is more than $100, quarterly payments are necessary. Payment dates vary among the states. Other payroll deductions must be paid according to the particular contracts or agreements involved.

Questions

1. Why is payroll accounting important?
2. How does an employee differ from an independent contractor?
3. Who pays the FICA tax?
4. What role does the W-4 form play in determining the withholding for estimated federal income taxes?
5. What withholdings might an employee voluntarily request?
6. Why is an employee earnings record necessary, and how does it relate to the W-2 form?
7. How can the payroll register be used as a special-purpose journal?
8. What are three types of employer-related payroll liabilities?

Exercises

Exercise D-1. FICA and Unemployment Taxes *(L.O. 1)*

Ultra Company is subject to a 5.4 percent state unemployment insurance tax and a 0.8 percent federal unemployment insurance tax after credits. Currently, both federal and state unemployment taxes apply to the first $7,000 earned by each employee. FICA taxes in effect at this time are 7.65 percent for both employee and employer on the first $53,400 earned by each employee during this year and 1.45 percent from this amount to a maximum of $125,000. During the current year, the cumulative earnings for each employee of the company are as follows:

Employee	Cumulative Earnings	Employee	Cumulative Earnings
Brown, E.	$28,620	Lavey, M.	$16,760
Caffey, B.	5,260	Lehman, L.	6,420
Evett, C.	32,820	Massie, M.	51,650
Harris, D.	30,130	Neal, M.	32,100
Hester, J.	52,250	Pruesch, R.	36,645
Jordan, M.	5,120	Widmer, J.	5,176

1. Prepare and complete a schedule with the following columns: Employee Name, Cumulative Earnings, Earnings Subject to FICA Taxes, and Earnings Subject to Unemployment Taxes. Total the columns.
2. Compute the FICA taxes and the federal and state unemployment taxes for Ultra Company.

Exercise D-2. Net Pay Calculation and Payroll Entries *(L.O. 1, 2)*

Lynn Karas is an employee whose overtime pay is regulated by the Fair Labor Standards Act. Her hourly rate is $8, and during the week ended July 11, she worked forty-two hours. Lynn claims two exemptions, which include one for herself, on her W-4 form. So far this year she has earned $8,650. Each week $12 is deducted from her paycheck for medical insurance.

1. Compute the following items related to the pay for Lynn Karas for the week of July 11: (a) gross pay, (b) FICA taxes (assume a rate of 7.65 percent), (c) federal income tax withholding (use Figure D-1), and (d) net pay.
2. Prepare a general journal entry to record the wages expense and related liabilities for Lynn Karas for the week ended July 11.

Exercise D-3. Payroll Transactions *(L.O. 1, 2)*

Monroe Howard earns a salary of $60,000 per year. FICA taxes are 7.65 percent up to $53,400 and 1.45 percent from this amount to a maximum of $125,000. Federal unemployment insurance taxes are 6.2 percent of the first $7,000; however, a credit is allowed equal to the state unemployment insurance taxes of 5.4 percent on the $7,000. During the year, $15,000 was withheld for federal income taxes.

1. Prepare a general journal entry summarizing the payment of $60,000 to Howard during the year.
2. Prepare a general journal entry summarizing the employer payroll taxes on Howard's salary for the year.
3. Determine the total cost paid by Monroe Howard's employer to employ Howard for the year.

Problems

Problem D-1. Payroll Entries *(L.O. 1, 2)*

At the end of October, the payroll register for Mejias Corporation contained the following totals: sales salaries, $88,110; office salaries, $40,440; administrative salaries, $57,120; FICA taxes withheld, $14,108; federal income taxes withheld, $47,442; state income taxes withheld, $7,818; medical insurance deductions, $6,435; life insurance deductions, $5,856; union dues deductions, $684; and salaries subject to unemployment taxes, $28,620.

Required

Prepare general journal entries to record the following: (1) accrual of the monthly payroll, (2) payment of the net payroll, (3) accrual of employer's payroll taxes (assuming FICA tax equal to the amount for employees, a federal unemployment insurance tax of 0.8 percent, and a state unemployment tax of 5.4 percent), and (4) payment of all liabilities related to the payroll (assuming that all are settled at the same time).

Problem D-2. Payroll Register and Related Entries *(L.O. 1, 2)*

Huff Manufacturing Company employs seven people in the Drilling Division. All employees are paid an hourly wage except the foreman, who receives a monthly salary. Hourly employees are paid once a week and receive a set hourly rate for regular hours plus time-and-a-half for overtime. The employees and employer are subject to a 7.65 percent FICA tax on the first $53,400 earned by each employee and 1.45 percent thereafter up to a maximum of $125,000. The unemployment insurance tax rates are 5.4 percent for the state and 0.8 percent for the federal government. The unemployment insurance tax applies to the first $7,000 earned by each employee and is levied only on the employer.

Each employee qualifies for the Huff Manufacturing Profit Sharing Plan. Under this plan, each employee may contribute up to 10 percent of his or her gross income as a payroll withholding, and Huff Manufacturing Company matches this amount. The data for the last payday of October are presented below:

Employee	Hours: Regular	Hours: Overtime	Pay Rate	Cumulative Gross Pay Excluding Current Pay Period	Percentage Contribution to Profit Sharing Plan	Income Tax to Be Withheld
Branch, W.	40	4	$ 9.00	$14,350.00	2	$ 40.00
Choy, T.	40	2	8.50	6,275.00	5	48.00
Duran, P.	40	5	12.70	16,510.00	7	35.00
Finnegan, M.*	Salary	—	5,500.00	49,500.00	9	760.00
Patel, B.	40	—	12.50	15,275.00	3	60.00
Sammuals, J.	40	7	9.00	11,925.00	—	23.00
Tobin, R.	40	3	7.50	10,218.00	—	20.00

*Supervisory.

Required

1. Prepare a payroll register for the pay period ended October 31. The payroll register should have the following columns:

Employee	Deductions
Total Hours	FICA Tax
Earnings	Federal Income Tax
Regular	Profit Sharing Plan
Overtime	Net Pay
Gross	Distribution
Cumulative	Drilling Wages Expense
	Supervisory Salaries Expense

2. Prepare a general journal entry to record the payroll and related liabilities for deductions for the period ended October 31.
3. Prepare general journal entries to record the expenses and related liabilities for the employer's payroll taxes (FICA, federal and state unemployment) and contribution to the profit sharing plan.
4. Prepare the October 31 entries for the transfer of sufficient cash from the company's regular checking account to a special Payroll Disbursement account and for the subsequent payment of employees.

Problem D-3. Payroll Entries *(L.O. 1, 2)*

The following payroll totals for the month of April were taken from the payroll register of Tobias Corporation: sales salaries, $58,200; office salaries, $28,500; general salaries, $24,840; FICA taxes withheld, $8,533; income taxes withheld, $15,720; medical insurance deductions, $3,290; life insurance deductions, $1,880; and salaries subject to unemployment taxes, $78,300.

Required

Prepare general journal entries to record the following: (1) accrual of the monthly payroll, (2) payment of the net payroll, (3) accrual of employer's payroll taxes (assuming FICA tax equal to the amount for employees, a federal unemployment insurance tax of 0.8 percent, and a state unemployment tax of 5.4 percent), and (4) payment of all liabilities related to the payroll (assuming that all are settled at the same time).

Problem D-4. Payroll Register and Related Entries *(L.O. 1, 2)*

DiGregorio Pasta Company has seven employees. The salaried employees are paid on the last biweekly payday of each month. Employees paid hourly receive a set rate for regular hours plus one and one-half times their hourly rate for overtime hours. They are paid every two weeks. The employees and company are subject to 7.65 percent FICA taxes on the first $53,400 earned by each employee and 1.45 percent thereafter up to a maximum of $125,000. The unemployment insurance tax rates are 5.4 percent for the state and 0.8 percent for the federal government. The unemployment insurance tax applies to the first $7,000 earned by each employee and is levied only on the employer.

The company maintains a supplemental benefits plan that includes medical insurance, life insurance, and additional retirement funds for employees. Under the plan, each employee contributes 4 percent of his or her gross income as a payroll withholding, and the company matches the amount. Data for the November 30 payroll, the last payday of November, follow:

Employee	Hours: Regular	Hours: Overtime	Pay Rate	Cumulative Gross Pay Excluding Current Pay Period	Federal Income Tax to Be Withheld
Antonelli, J.	80	5	$ 8.00	$ 4,867.00	$ 71.00
Bertelli, A.	80	4	6.50	3,954.00	76.00
DiGregorio, G.*	Salary	—	5,000.00	50,000.00	985.00
Falcone, P.	80	—	5.00	8,250.00	32.00
Greco, B.*	Salary	—	2,000.00	20,000.00	294.00
Parilli, T.	80	20	10.00	12,000.00	103.00
Rosario, A.*	Salary	—	1,500.00	15,000.00	210.00

*Denotes administrative; the rest are sales.

Required

1. Prepare a payroll register for the pay period ended November 30. The payroll register should have the following columns:

   Employee
   Total Hours
   Earnings
     Regular
     Overtime
     Gross
     Cumulative
   Deductions
     FICA Tax
     Federal Income Tax
     Supplemental Benefits Plan
   Net Pay
   Distribution
     Sales Expense
     Administrative Expense

2. Prepare a general journal entry to record the payroll and related liabilities for deductions for the period ended November 30.
3. Prepare general journal entries to record the expenses and related liabilities for the employer's payroll taxes and contribution to the supplemental benefits plan.
4. Prepare the entries on November 30 to transfer sufficient cash from the company's regular checking account to a special Payroll Disbursement account and for the subsequent payment of the employees.

LEARNING OBJECTIVES

1. *Account for the purchase of bonds between interest dates.*
2. *Amortize the premium or discount of a bond.*
3. *Account for the sale of bonds.*

APPENDIX E

Accounting for Bond Investments

In the chapter on long-term liabilities, bond transactions and disclosures were discussed from the issuing corporation's viewpoint. Here, similar transactions will be presented from the investor's point of view. The focus is on transactions involving the purchase of the bonds, amortization of premium and discount, recording of receipt of interest, and sale of the bonds. In each case, there are small differences in accounting treatment from that used for the same transactions by the issuer. After studying this appendix, you should be able to meet the learning objectives listed at the left.

Purchase of Bonds Between Interest Dates

OBJECTIVE 1
Account for the purchase of bonds between interest dates

The purchase price of bonds includes the price of the bonds plus the broker's commission. When the bonds are purchased between interest dates, the purchaser must also pay the interest that has accrued on the bonds since the last interest payment date. On the next payment date, the purchaser will receive a payment of the interest for the whole period. The payment for accrued interest should be recorded as a debit to Interest Income, to be offset later by a credit to Interest Income when the semiannual interest is received.

Suppose that on May 1 Vason Corporation purchases twenty $1,000 MGR Corporation bonds that carry a face interest rate of 9 percent at 88 plus accrued interest and a broker's commission of $400. The interest payment dates are January 1 and July 1. The following entry records this purchase transaction:

May 1	Investment in Bonds	18,000	
	Interest Income	600	
	Cash		18,600
	To record purchase of MGR Corporation bonds at 88 plus $400 commission and accrued interest $20,000 × 9% × 1/3 = $600		

Note that the purchase is recorded at cost, as are all purchases of assets. The debit to Investment in Bonds of $18,000 equals the purchase price of $17,600 ($20,000 × .88) plus the commission of $400. Because in managing its investments, Vason Corporation will buy and sell as seems necessary and will probably not hold the bonds to maturity, the $20,000 face value of the bonds is not recorded. This case is very different from that of the issuing corporation, which must repay the bonds at the maturity date to anyone who holds them.

The debit to Interest Income of $600 represents four months' interest (one-third year from January 1 to May 1) that was paid to the seller of the bonds.

Amortization of Premium or Discount

OBJECTIVE 2 *Amortize the premium or discount of a bond*

Accounting Principles Board *Opinion No. 21* requires companies making long-term investments in bonds to amortize the difference between the cost of the investment and its maturity value over the life of the bond. The effective interest method, which results in a constant rate of return over the life of the investment, should be used.[1]

Because the investing company does not use separate accounts for the face value and any related discount or premium, the entry to amortize the premium or discount is made directly to the investment account. The amortization of a premium calls for a credit to the investment account to reduce the carrying value gradually to face value. The amortization of a discount calls for a debit to the investment account to increase the carrying value gradually to face value.

Returning to the case of Vason Corporation's purchase of bonds at a discount, we assume that the effective interest rate is 10½ percent. Remember that the amount of amortization of a premium or discount is the difference between (1) the face interest rate times the face value and (2) the effective interest rate times the carrying value. On July 1, the first interest date after the purchase, two months will have passed. The amount of discount to be amortized is as follows:

Two months' effective interest:	
$18,000 × 10½% × ⅙	$315
Two months' face interest:	
$20,000 × 9% × ⅙	300
Discount to be amortized	$ 15

The entry to record the receipt of an interest check on July 1 would be as follows:

1. Accounting Principles Board, *Opinion No. 21,* "Interest on Receivables and Payables" (New York: American Institute of Certified Public Accountants, 1971), par. 15.

July 1	Cash	900	
	Investment in Bonds	15	
	Interest Income		915
	To record receipt of semiannual interest, some of which was previously accrued, and to amortize discount		

In this entry, Cash is debited for the semiannual interest payment ($20,000 × 9% × ½ = $900), Investment in Bonds is debited for the amortization of discount, or $15, and Interest Income is credited for the sum of the two debits, or $915. Note that the net interest earned is $315, which is the net amount of the $600 debit on May 1 and the $915 credit on July 1 to Interest Income. This amount is equal to the two months' effective interest just computed.

To continue the example, assume that Vason Corporation's fiscal year corresponds to the calendar year. Although the interest payment will not be received until January, it is necessary to accrue the interest and amortize the discount for the six months since July 1 in accordance with the matching concept. The entry to record the accrual of interest on December 31 is as follows:

Dec. 31	Interest Receivable	900.00	
	Investment in Bonds	45.79	
	Interest Income		945.79
	To accrue interest income and amortize discount on bond investment		

The period covered by this entry is six months. Therefore, the amounts to be debited and credited are as follows:

Six months' effective interest:	
$18,015 × 10½% × ½	$945.79
Six months' face interest:	
$20,000 × 9% × ½	900.00
Discount to be amortized	$ 45.79

Note that the effective interest rate is applied to the new carrying value of $18,015. The next time the effective interest is calculated, the effective rate will be applied to $18,060.79 ($18,015 + $45.79). The entry to record receipt of the interest payment check on January 1 is as follows:[2]

Jan. 1	Cash	900	
	Interest Receivable		900
	To record receipt of interest on bonds		

Similar calculations are made when a company purchases bonds at a premium. The only difference is that Investment in Bonds is credited

2. This entry assumes that reversing entries are not made. Some companies may prefer to use reversing entries.

rather than debited to reduce the carrying value, and the interest earned is less than the face interest.

Sale of Bonds

OBJECTIVE 3
Account for the sale of bonds

The sale of a bond investment is recorded by debiting Cash for the amount received and crediting Investment in Bonds for the carrying value of the investment. Any difference in the proceeds from the sale and the carrying value of the bonds is debited or credited to Loss or Gain on Sale of Investments. If the sale is made between interest payment dates, the company is entitled to the accrued interest from the last interest date, just as it had to pay the accrued interest when the bonds were purchased.

If we assume that Vason Corporation sells the bonds in our continuing example at 94 less commission of $400 on March 1, two entries are required. The first entry is necessary to amortize the discount for two months:

Mar. 1	Investment in Bonds	16.06	
	Interest Income		16.06
	To amortize 2 months' bond discount		
	Effective interest:		
	$18,060.79 × 10½% × ⅙	= $316.06	
	Face interest:		
	$20,000 × 9% × ⅙	= 300.00	
	Discount to be amortized	$ 16.06	

The second entry is to record the sale:

Mar. 1	Cash	18,700.00	
	Gain on Sale of Investments		323.15
	Investment in Bonds		18,076.85
	Interest Income		300.00
	To record sale of bonds at 94 less $400 commission plus accrued interest		

The cash received is the selling price of $18,800 ($20,000 × .94) less commission of $400 plus the accrued interest for two months of $300 ($20,000 × 9% × ⅙). The gain on the sale of investments is the difference between the selling price less commission ($18,400) and the carrying value of $18,076.85. The carrying value represents the assigned purchase price plus all amortization of discount:

May 1 purchase	$18,000.00
July 1 amortization	15.00
Dec. 31 amortization	45.79
Mar. 1 amortization	16.06
Carrying value of bond investment	$18,076.85

Questions

1. Why does the buying company record a bond investment at cost when the issuing company will record the same issue at face value and adjust a separate account for any discount or premium?
2. What special accounting problem arises when bonds are purchased between interest dates, even if the purchase is made at face value?

Exercise

Exercise E-1. Bond Investment Transactions *(L.O. 1, 2, 3)*

On November 1, Halpern Corporation purchased as a long-term investment one thousand $1,000 bonds for $1,050,000 plus accrued interest. The bonds carried a face interest rate of 10 ½ percent paid semiannually on July 1 and January 1. Because of a change in investment plans, management decided to sell the bonds on January 1 for $1,070,000. Prepare journal entries to record the purchase on November 1, the receipt of interest and amortization of premium on January 1, assuming an effective interest rate of 9 ½ percent, and the sale of the bonds on January 1.

Problems

Problem E-1. Bond Investment Transactions *(L.O. 1, 2, 3)*

Transactions involving long-term bond investments made by Drury Corporation follow. Drury has a June 30 year end.

19x1

July 1 Purchased $500,000 of Stellos Corporation's 12½ percent bonds at 104, a price that yields an effective interest rate of 11½ percent. These bonds have semiannual interest payment dates of June 30 and December 31.

Nov. 1 Purchased $300,000 of Taft Company's 9 percent bonds, dated August 1, at face value plus accrued interest.

Dec. 31 Received a check from Stellos for semiannual interest and amortized the premium using the effective interest method.

19x2

Feb. 1 Received a check from Taft for the semiannual interest.

June 30 Received a check from Stellos for the semiannual interest and amortized the premium using the effective interest method.

30 Made a year-end adjusting entry to accrue the interest on the Taft bonds.

Aug. 1 Received a check from Taft for the semiannual interest (reversing entries were not used).

Nov. 1 Sold the Taft bonds at 98 plus accrued interest.

Dec. 31 Received a check from Stellos for the semiannual interest and amortized the premium using the effective interest method.

19x3

Jan. 1 Sold one-half of the Stellos bonds at 101.

Required

Prepare general journal entries to record these transactions.

Problem E-2. Bond Investment Transactions
(L.O. 1, 2, 3)

Lao Corporation purchases bonds as long-term investments. Lao's long-term bond investment transactions for 19x1 and 19x2 follow. Lao's year end is December 31.

19x1

Jan. 1	Purchased on the semiannual interest payment date $400,000 of Wilks Company 10 percent bonds at 91, a price yielding an effective interest rate of 12 percent.
Apr. 1	Purchased $200,000 of Simon Corporation 12 percent, twenty-year bonds dated March 1 at face value plus accrued interest.
July 1	Received a check from Wilks Company for semiannual interest and amortized the discount using the effective interest method.
Sept. 1	Received a check from Simon for semiannual interest.
Dec. 31	Made year-end adjusting entries to accrue interest on the Wilks and Simon bonds and to amortize the discount on the Wilks bonds using the effective interest method.

19x2

Jan. 1	Received a check from Wilks for semiannual interest (reversing entries were not made).
Mar. 1	Received a check from Simon Corporation for semiannual interest.
July 1	Received a check from Wilks for semiannual interest and amortized the discount using the effective interest method.
1	Sold one-half of the Wilks bonds at 96.
Sept. 1	Received a check from Simon for semiannual interest.
Nov. 1	Sold the Simon bonds at 98 plus accrued interest.
Dec. 31	Made year-end adjusting entry to accrue interest on the remaining Wilks bonds and to amortize the discount using the effective interest method.

Required

Prepare general journal entries to record these transactions.

APPENDIX F

Future Value and Present Value Tables

Table F-1 provides the multipliers necessary to compute the future value of a *single* cash deposit made at the *beginning* of year 1. Three factors must be known before the future value can be computed: (1) the time period in years, (2) the stated annual rate of interest to be earned, and (3) the dollar amount invested or deposited.

Example. Determine the future value of \$5,000 deposited now that will earn 9 percent interest compounded annually for five years. From Table F-1, the necessary multiplier for five years at 9 percent is 1.539, and the answer is:

$$\$5{,}000(1.539) = \underline{\underline{\$7{,}695}}$$

Situations requiring the use of Table F-2 are similar to those requiring Table F-1 except that Table F-2 is used to compute the future value of a *series* of *equal* annual deposits.

Example. What will be the future value at the end of thirty years if \$1,000 is deposited each year on January 1, beginning in one year, assuming 12 percent interest compounded annually? The required multiplier from Table F-2 is 241.3, and the answer is:

$$\$1{,}000(241.3) = \underline{\underline{\$241{,}300}}$$

Table F-1. Future Value of $1 After a Given Number of Time Periods

Periods	1%	2%	3%	4%	5%	6%	7%	8%	9%	10%	12%	14%	15%
1	1.010	1.020	1.030	1.040	1.050	1.060	1.070	1.080	1.090	1.100	1.120	1.140	1.150
2	1.020	1.040	1.061	1.082	1.103	1.124	1.145	1.166	1.188	1.210	1.254	1.300	1.323
3	1.030	1.061	1.093	1.125	1.158	1.191	1.225	1.260	1.295	1.331	1.405	1.482	1.521
4	1.041	1.082	1.126	1.170	1.216	1.262	1.311	1.360	1.412	1.464	1.574	1.689	1.749
5	1.051	1.104	1.159	1.217	1.276	1.338	1.403	1.469	1.539	1.611	1.762	1.925	2.011
6	1.062	1.126	1.194	1.265	1.340	1.419	1.501	1.587	1.677	1.772	1.974	2.195	2.313
7	1.072	1.149	1.230	1.316	1.407	1.504	1.606	1.714	1.828	1.949	2.211	2.502	2.660
8	1.083	1.172	1.267	1.369	1.477	1.594	1.718	1.851	1.993	2.144	2.476	2.853	3.059
9	1.094	1.195	1.305	1.423	1.551	1.689	1.838	1.999	2.172	2.358	2.773	3.252	3.518
10	1.105	1.219	1.344	1.480	1.629	1.791	1.967	2.159	2.367	2.594	3.106	3.707	4.046
11	1.116	1.243	1.384	1.539	1.710	1.898	2.105	2.332	2.580	2.853	3.479	4.226	4.652
12	1.127	1.268	1.426	1.601	1.796	2.012	2.252	2.518	2.813	3.138	3.896	4.818	5.350
13	1.138	1.294	1.469	1.665	1.886	2.133	2.410	2.720	3.066	3.452	4.363	5.492	6.153
14	1.149	1.319	1.513	1.732	1.980	2.261	2.579	2.937	3.342	3.798	4.887	6.261	7.076
15	1.161	1.346	1.558	1.801	2.079	2.397	2.759	3.172	3.642	4.177	5.474	7.138	8.137
16	1.173	1.373	1.605	1.873	2.183	2.540	2.952	3.426	3.970	4.595	6.130	8.137	9.358
17	1.184	1.400	1.653	1.948	2.292	2.693	3.159	3.700	4.328	5.054	6.866	9.276	10.76
18	1.196	1.428	1.702	2.026	2.407	2.854	3.380	3.996	4.717	5.560	7.690	10.58	12.38
19	1.208	1.457	1.754	2.107	2.527	3.026	3.617	4.316	5.142	6.116	8.613	12.06	14.23
20	1.220	1.486	1.806	2.191	2.653	3.207	3.870	4.661	5.604	6.728	9.646	13.74	16.37
21	1.232	1.516	1.860	2.279	2.786	3.400	4.141	5.034	6.109	7.400	10.80	15.67	18.82
22	1.245	1.546	1.916	2.370	2.925	3.604	4.430	5.437	6.659	8.140	12.10	17.86	21.64
23	1.257	1.577	1.974	2.465	3.072	3.820	4.741	5.871	7.258	8.954	13.55	20.36	24.89
24	1.270	1.608	2.033	2.563	3.225	4.049	5.072	6.341	7.911	9.850	15.18	23.21	28.63
25	1.282	1.641	2.094	2.666	3.386	4.292	5.427	6.848	8.623	10.83	17.00	26.46	32.92
26	1.295	1.673	2.157	2.772	3.556	4.549	5.807	7.396	9.399	11.92	19.04	30.17	37.86
27	1.308	1.707	2.221	2.883	3.733	4.822	6.214	7.988	10.25	13.11	21.32	34.39	43.54
28	1.321	1.741	2.288	2.999	3.920	5.112	6.649	8.627	11.17	14.42	23.88	39.20	50.07
29	1.335	1.776	2.357	3.119	4.116	5.418	7.114	9.317	12.17	15.86	26.75	44.69	57.58
30	1.348	1.811	2.427	3.243	4.322	5.743	7.612	10.06	13.27	17.45	29.96	50.95	66.21
40	1.489	2.208	3.262	4.801	7.040	10.29	14.97	21.72	31.41	45.26	93.05	188.9	267.9
50	1.645	2.692	4.384	7.107	11.47	18.42	29.46	46.90	74.36	117.4	289.0	700.2	1,084

Table F-2. Future Value of $1 Paid in Each Period for a Given Number of Time Periods

Periods	1%	2%	3%	4%	5%	6%	7%	8%	9%	10%	12%	14%	15%
1	1.000	1.000	1.000	1.000	1.000	1.000	1.000	1.000	1.000	1.000	1.000	1.000	1.000
2	2.010	2.020	2.030	2.040	2.050	2.060	2.070	2.080	2.090	2.100	2.120	2.140	2.150
3	3.030	3.060	3.091	3.122	3.153	3.184	3.215	3.246	3.278	3.310	3.374	3.440	3.473
4	4.060	4.122	4.184	4.246	4.310	4.375	4.440	4.506	4.573	4.641	4.779	4.921	4.993
5	5.101	5.204	5.309	5.416	5.526	5.637	5.751	5.867	5.985	6.105	6.353	6.610	6.742
6	6.152	6.308	6.468	6.633	6.802	6.975	7.153	7.336	7.523	7.716	8.115	8.536	8.754
7	7.214	7.434	7.662	7.898	8.142	8.394	8.654	8.923	9.200	9.487	10.09	10.73	11.07
8	8.286	8.583	8.892	9.214	9.549	9.897	10.26	10.64	11.03	11.44	12.30	13.23	13.73
9	9.369	9.755	10.16	10.58	11.03	11.49	11.98	12.49	13.02	13.58	14.78	16.09	16.79
10	10.46	10.95	11.46	12.01	12.58	13.18	13.82	14.49	15.19	15.94	17.55	19.34	20.30
11	11.57	12.17	12.81	13.49	14.21	14.97	15.78	16.65	17.56	18.53	20.65	23.04	24.35
12	12.68	13.41	14.19	15.03	15.92	16.87	17.89	18.98	20.14	21.38	24.13	27.27	29.00
13	13.81	14.68	15.62	16.63	17.71	18.88	20.14	21.50	22.95	24.52	28.03	32.09	34.35
14	14.95	15.97	17.09	18.29	19.60	21.02	22.55	24.21	26.02	27.98	32.39	37.58	40.50
15	16.10	17.29	18.60	20.02	21.58	23.28	25.13	27.15	29.36	31.77	37.28	43.84	47.58
16	17.26	18.64	20.16	21.82	23.66	25.67	27.89	30.32	33.00	35.95	42.75	50.98	55.72
17	18.43	20.01	21.76	23.70	25.84	28.21	30.84	33.75	36.97	40.54	48.88	59.12	65.08
18	19.61	21.41	23.41	25.65	28.13	30.91	34.00	37.45	41.30	45.60	55.75	68.39	75.84
19	20.81	22.84	25.12	27.67	30.54	33.76	37.38	41.45	46.02	51.16	63.44	78.97	88.21
20	22.02	24.30	26.87	29.78	33.07	36.79	41.00	45.76	51.16	57.28	72.05	91.02	102.4
21	23.24	25.78	28.68	31.97	35.72	39.99	44.87	50.42	56.76	64.00	81.70	104.8	118.8
22	24.47	27.30	30.54	34.25	38.51	43.39	49.01	55.46	62.87	71.40	92.50	120.4	137.6
23	25.72	28.85	32.45	36.62	41.43	47.00	53.44	60.89	69.53	79.54	104.6	138.3	159.3
24	26.97	30.42	34.43	39.08	44.50	50.82	58.18	66.76	76.79	88.50	118.2	158.7	184.2
25	28.24	32.03	36.46	41.65	47.73	54.86	63.25	73.11	84.70	98.35	133.3	181.9	212.8
26	29.53	33.67	38.55	44.31	51.11	59.16	68.68	79.95	93.32	109.2	150.3	208.3	245.7
27	30.82	35.34	40.71	47.08	54.67	63.71	74.48	87.35	102.7	121.1	169.4	238.5	283.6
28	32.13	37.05	42.93	49.97	58.40	68.53	80.70	95.34	113.0	134.2	190.7	272.9	327.1
29	33.45	38.79	45.22	52.97	62.32	73.64	87.35	104.0	124.1	148.6	214.6	312.1	377.2
30	34.78	40.57	47.58	56.08	66.44	79.06	94.46	113.3	136.3	164.5	241.3	356.8	434.7
40	48.89	60.40	75.40	95.03	120.8	154.8	199.6	259.1	337.9	442.6	767.1	1,342	1,779
50	64.46	84.58	112.8	152.7	209.3	290.3	406.5	573.8	815.1	1,164	2,400	4,995	7,218

Table F-3 is used to compute the value today of a *single* amount of cash to be received sometime in the future. To use Table F-3, you must first know: (1) the time period in years until funds will be received, (2) the annual rate of interest, and (3) the dollar amount to be received at the end of the time period.

Example. What is the present value of \$30,000 to be received twenty-five years from now, assuming a 14 percent interest rate? From Table F-3, the required multiplier is 0.038, and the answer is:

$$\$30{,}000(0.038) = \underline{\underline{\$1{,}140}}$$

Table F-4 is used to compute the present value of a *series* of *equal* annual cash flows:

Example. Arthur Howard won a contest on January 1, 1989, in which the prize was \$30,000, payable in fifteen annual installments of \$2,000 every December 31, beginning in 1989. Assuming a 9 percent interest rate, what is the present value of Mr. Howard's prize on January 1, 1989? From Table F-4, the required multiplier is 8.061, and the answer is:

$$\$2{,}000(8.061) = \underline{\underline{\$16{,}122}}$$

Table F-4 applies to *ordinary annuities,* in which the first cash flow occurs one time period beyond the date for which the present value is to be computed. An *annuity due* is a series of equal cash flows for N time periods, but the first payment occurs immediately. The present value of the first payment equals the face value of the cash flow; Table F-4 then is used to measure the present value of $N - 1$ remaining cash flows.

Example. Determine the present value on January 1, 1989, of twenty lease payments; each payment of \$10,000 is due on January 1, beginning in 1989. Assume an interest rate of 8 percent:

$$\text{Present value} = \text{immediate payment} + \begin{cases} \text{present value of 19} \\ \text{subsequent payments at 8\%} \end{cases}$$

$$= \$10{,}000 + [10{,}000(9.604)] = \underline{\underline{\$106{,}040}}$$

Table F-3. Present Value of $1 to Be Received at the End of a Given Number of Time Periods

Periods	1%	2%	3%	4%	5%	6%	7%	8%	9%	10%	12%
1	0.990	0.980	0.971	0.962	0.952	0.943	0.935	0.926	0.917	0.909	0.893
2	0.980	0.961	0.943	0.925	0.907	0.890	0.873	0.857	0.842	0.826	0.797
3	0.971	0.942	0.915	0.889	0.864	0.840	0.816	0.794	0.772	0.751	0.712
4	0.961	0.924	0.888	0.855	0.823	0.792	0.763	0.735	0.708	0.683	0.636
5	0.951	0.906	0.883	0.822	0.784	0.747	0.713	0.681	0.650	0.621	0.567
6	0.942	0.888	0.837	0.790	0.746	0.705	0.666	0.630	0.596	0.564	0.507
7	0.933	0.871	0.813	0.760	0.711	0.665	0.623	0.583	0.547	0.513	0.452
8	0.923	0.853	0.789	0.731	0.677	0.627	0.582	0.540	0.502	0.467	0.404
9	0.914	0.837	0.766	0.703	0.645	0.592	0.544	0.500	0.460	0.424	0.361
10	0.905	0.820	0.744	0.676	0.614	0.558	0.508	0.463	0.422	0.386	0.322
11	0.896	0.804	0.722	0.650	0.585	0.527	0.475	0.429	0.388	0.350	0.287
12	0.887	0.788	0.701	0.625	0.557	0.497	0.444	0.397	0.356	0.319	0.257
13	0.879	0.773	0.681	0.601	0.530	0.469	0.415	0.368	0.326	0.290	0.229
14	0.870	0.758	0.661	0.577	0.505	0.442	0.388	0.340	0.299	0.263	0.205
15	0.861	0.743	0.642	0.555	0.481	0.417	0.362	0.315	0.275	0.239	0.183
16	0.853	0.728	0.623	0.534	0.458	0.394	0.339	0.292	0.252	0.218	0.163
17	0.844	0.714	0.605	0.513	0.436	0.371	0.317	0.270	0.231	0.198	0.146
18	0.836	0.700	0.587	0.494	0.416	0.350	0.296	0.250	0.212	0.180	0.130
19	0.828	0.686	0.570	0.475	0.396	0.331	0.277	0.232	0.194	0.164	0.116
20	0.820	0.673	0.554	0.456	0.377	0.312	0.258	0.215	0.178	0.149	0.104
21	0.811	0.660	0.538	0.439	0.359	0.294	0.242	0.199	0.164	0.135	0.093
22	0.803	0.647	0.522	0.422	0.342	0.278	0.226	0.184	0.150	0.123	0.083
23	0.795	0.634	0.507	0.406	0.326	0.262	0.211	0.170	0.138	0.112	0.074
24	0.788	0.622	0.492	0.390	0.310	0.247	0.197	0.158	0.126	0.102	0.066
25	0.780	0.610	0.478	0.375	0.295	0.233	0.184	0.146	0.116	0.092	0.059
26	0.772	0.598	0.464	0.361	0.281	0.220	0.172	0.135	0.106	0.084	0.053
27	0.764	0.586	0.450	0.347	0.268	0.207	0.161	0.125	0.098	0.076	0.047
28	0.757	0.574	0.437	0.333	0.255	0.196	0.150	0.116	0.090	0.069	0.042
29	0.749	0.563	0.424	0.321	0.243	0.185	0.141	0.107	0.082	0.063	0.037
30	0.742	0.552	0.412	0.308	0.231	0.174	0.131	0.099	0.075	0.057	0.033
40	0.672	0.453	0.307	0.208	0.142	0.097	0.067	0.046	0.032	0.022	0.011
50	0.608	0.372	0.228	0.141	0.087	0.054	0.034	0.021	0.013	0.009	0.003

Table F-3. *(continued)*

14%	15%	16%	18%	20%	25%	30%	35%	40%	45%	50%	Periods
0.877	0.870	0.862	0.847	0.833	0.800	0.769	0.741	0.714	0.690	0.667	1
0.769	0.756	0.743	0.718	0.694	0.640	0.592	0.549	0.510	0.476	0.444	2
0.675	0.658	0.641	0.609	0.579	0.512	0.455	0.406	0.364	0.328	0.296	3
0.592	0.572	0.552	0.516	0.482	0.410	0.350	0.301	0.260	0.226	0.198	4
0.519	0.497	0.476	0.437	0.402	0.328	0.269	0.223	0.186	0.156	0.132	5
0.456	0.432	0.410	0.370	0.335	0.262	0.207	0.165	0.133	0.108	0.088	6
0.400	0.376	0.354	0.314	0.279	0.210	0.159	0.122	0.095	0.074	0.059	7
0.351	0.327	0.305	0.266	0.233	0.168	0.123	0.091	0.068	0.051	0.039	8
0.308	0.284	0.263	0.225	0.194	0.134	0.094	0.067	0.048	0.035	0.026	9
0.270	0.247	0.227	0.191	0.162	0.107	0.073	0.050	0.035	0.024	0.017	10
0.237	0.215	0.195	0.162	0.135	0.086	0.056	0.037	0.025	0.017	0.012	11
0.208	0.187	0.168	0.137	0.112	0.069	0.043	0.027	0.018	0.012	0.008	12
0.182	0.163	0.145	0.116	0.093	0.055	0.033	0.020	0.013	0.008	0.005	13
0.160	0.141	0.125	0.099	0.078	0.044	0.025	0.015	0.009	0.006	0.003	14
0.140	0.123	0.108	0.084	0.065	0.035	0.020	0.011	0.006	0.004	0.002	15
0.123	0.107	0.093	0.071	0.054	0.028	0.015	0.008	0.005	0.003	0.002	16
0.108	0.093	0.080	0.060	0.045	0.023	0.012	0.006	0.003	0.002	0.001	17
0.095	0.081	0.069	0.051	0.038	0.018	0.009	0.005	0.002	0.001	0.001	18
0.083	0.070	0.060	0.043	0.031	0.014	0.007	0.003	0.002	0.001		19
0.073	0.061	0.051	0.037	0.026	0.012	0.005	0.002	0.001	0.001		20
0.064	0.053	0.044	0.031	0.022	0.009	0.004	0.002	0.001			21
0.056	0.046	0.038	0.026	0.018	0.007	0.003	0.001	0.001			22
0.049	0.040	0.033	0.022	0.015	0.006	0.002	0.001				23
0.043	0.035	0.028	0.019	0.013	0.005	0.002	0.001				24
0.038	0.030	0.024	0.016	0.010	0.004	0.001	0.001				25
0.033	0.026	0.021	0.014	0.009	0.003	0.001					26
0.029	0.023	0.018	0.011	0.007	0.002	0.001					27
0.026	0.020	0.016	0.010	0.006	0.002	0.001					28
0.022	0.017	0.014	0.008	0.005	0.002						29
0.020	0.015	0.012	0.007	0.004	0.001						30
0.005	0.004	0.003	0.001	0.001							40
0.001	0.001	0.001									50

Table F-4. Present Value of $1 Received Each Period for a Given Number of Time Periods

Periods	1%	2%	3%	4%	5%	6%	7%	8%	9%	10%	12%
1	0.990	0.980	0.971	0.962	0.952	0.943	0.935	0.926	0.917	0.909	0.893
2	1.970	1.942	1.913	1.886	1.859	1.833	1.808	1.783	1.759	1.736	1.690
3	2.941	2.884	2.829	2.775	2.723	2.673	2.624	2.577	2.531	2.487	2.402
4	3.902	3.808	3.717	3.630	3.546	3.465	3.387	3.312	3.240	3.170	3.037
5	4.853	4.713	4.580	4.452	4.329	4.212	4.100	3.993	3.890	3.791	3.605
6	5.795	5.601	5.417	5.242	5.076	4.917	4.767	4.623	4.486	4.355	4.111
7	6.728	6.472	6.230	6.002	5.786	5.582	5.389	5.206	5.033	4.868	4.564
8	7.652	7.325	7.020	6.733	6.463	6.210	5.971	5.747	5.535	5.335	4.968
9	8.566	8.162	7.786	7.435	7.108	6.802	6.515	6.247	5.995	5.759	5.328
10	9.471	8.983	8.530	8.111	7.722	7.360	7.024	6.710	6.418	6.145	5.650
11	10.368	9.787	9.253	8.760	8.306	7.887	7.499	7.139	6.805	6.495	5.938
12	11.255	10.575	9.954	9.385	8.863	8.384	7.943	7.536	7.161	6.814	6.194
13	12.134	11.348	10.635	9.986	9.394	8.853	8.358	7.904	7.487	7.103	6.424
14	13.004	12.106	11.296	10.563	9.899	9.295	8.745	8.244	7.786	7.367	6.628
15	13.865	12.849	11.938	11.118	10.380	9.712	9.108	8.559	8.061	7.606	6.811
16	14.718	13.578	12.561	11.652	10.838	10.106	9.447	8.851	8.313	7.824	6.974
17	15.562	14.292	13.166	12.166	11.274	10.477	9.763	9.122	8.544	8.022	7.120
18	16.398	14.992	13.754	12.659	11.690	10.828	10.059	9.372	8.756	8.201	7.250
19	17.226	15.678	14.324	13.134	12.085	11.158	10.336	9.604	8.950	8.365	7.366
20	18.046	16.351	14.878	13.590	12.462	11.470	10.594	9.818	9.129	8.514	7.469
21	18.857	17.011	15.415	14.029	12.821	11.764	10.836	10.017	9.292	8.649	7.562
22	19.660	17.658	15.937	14.451	13.163	12.042	11.061	10.201	9.442	8.772	7.645
23	20.456	18.292	16.444	14.857	13.489	12.303	11.272	10.371	9.580	8.883	7.718
24	21.243	18.914	16.936	15.247	13.799	12.550	11.469	10.529	9.707	8.985	7.784
25	22.023	19.523	17.413	15.622	14.094	12.783	11.654	10.675	9.823	9.077	7.843
26	22.795	20.121	17.877	15.983	14.375	13.003	11.826	10.810	9.929	9.161	7.896
27	23.560	20.707	18.327	16.330	14.643	13.211	11.987	10.935	10.027	9.237	7.943
28	24.316	21.281	18.764	16.663	14.898	13.406	12.137	11.051	10.116	9.307	7.984
29	25.066	21.844	19.189	16.984	15.141	13.591	12.278	11.158	10.198	9.370	8.022
30	25.808	22.396	19.600	17.292	15.373	13.765	12.409	11.258	10.274	9.427	8.055
40	32.835	27.355	23.115	19.793	17.159	15.046	13.332	11.925	10.757	9.779	8.244
50	39.196	31.424	25.730	21.482	18.256	15.762	13.801	12.234	10.962	9.915	8.305

Table F-4. *(continued)*

14%	15%	16%	18%	20%	25%	30%	35%	40%	45%	50%	Periods
0.877	0.870	0.862	0.847	0.833	0.800	0.769	0.741	0.714	0.690	0.667	1
1.647	1.626	1.605	1.566	1.528	1.440	1.361	1.289	1.224	1.165	1.111	2
2.322	2.283	2.246	2.174	2.106	1.952	1.816	1.696	1.589	1.493	1.407	3
2.914	2.855	2.798	2.690	2.589	2.362	2.166	1.997	1.849	1.720	1.605	4
3.433	3.352	3.274	3.127	2.991	2.689	2.436	2.220	2.035	1.876	1.737	5
3.889	3.784	3.685	3.498	3.326	2.951	2.643	2.385	2.168	1.983	1.824	6
4.288	4.160	4.039	3.812	3.605	3.161	2.802	2.508	2.263	2.057	1.883	7
4.639	4.487	4.344	4.078	3.837	3.329	2.925	2.598	2.331	2.109	1.922	8
4.946	4.772	4.607	4.303	4.031	3.463	3.019	2.665	2.379	2.144	1.948	9
5.216	5.019	4.833	4.494	4.192	3.571	3.092	2.715	2.414	2.168	1.965	10
5.453	5.234	5.029	4.656	4.327	3.656	3.147	2.752	2.438	2.185	1.977	11
5.660	5.421	5.197	4.793	4.439	3.725	3.190	2.779	2.456	2.197	1.985	12
5.842	5.583	5.342	4.910	4.533	3.780	3.223	2.799	2.469	2.204	1.990	13
6.002	5.724	5.468	5.008	4.611	3.824	3.249	2.814	2.478	2.210	1.993	14
6.142	5.847	5.575	5.092	4.675	3.859	3.268	2.825	2.484	2.214	1.995	15
6.265	5.954	5.669	5.162	4.730	3.887	3.283	2.834	2.489	2.216	1.997	16
6.373	6.047	5.749	5.222	4.775	3.910	3.295	2.840	2.492	2.218	1.998	17
6.467	6.128	5.818	5.273	4.812	3.928	3.304	2.844	2.494	2.219	1.999	18
6.550	6.198	5.877	5.316	4.844	3.942	3.311	2.848	2.496	2.220	1.999	19
6.623	6.259	5.929	5.353	4.870	3.954	3.316	2.850	2.497	2.221	1.999	20
6.687	6.312	5.973	5.384	4.891	3.963	3.320	2.852	2.498	2.221	2.000	21
6.743	6.359	6.011	5.410	4.909	3.970	3.323	2.853	2.498	2.222	2.000	22
6.792	6.399	6.044	5.432	4.925	3.976	3.325	2.854	2.499	2.222	2.000	23
6.835	6.434	6.073	5.451	4.937	3.981	3.327	2.855	2.499	2.222	2.000	24
6.873	6.464	6.097	5.467	4.948	3.985	3.329	2.856	2.499	2.222	2.000	25
6.906	6.491	6.118	5.480	4.956	3.988	3.330	2.856	2.500	2.222	2.000	26
6.935	6.514	6.136	5.492	4.964	3.990	3.331	2.856	2.500	2.222	2.000	27
6.961	6.534	6.152	5.502	4.970	3.992	3.331	2.857	2.500	2.222	2.000	28
6.983	6.551	6.166	5.510	4.975	3.994	3.332	2.857	2.500	2.222	2.000	29
7.003	6.566	6.177	5.517	4.979	3.995	3.332	2.857	2.500	2.222	2.000	30
7.105	6.642	6.234	5.548	4.997	3.999	3.333	2.857	2.500	2.222	2.000	40
7.133	6.661	6.246	5.554	4.999	4.000	3.333	2.857	2.500	2.222	2.000	50

Index of Company Names

Note: Boldface type denotes real companies.

Subject Index

Note: Boldface type denotes key terms.

Accounting Format Guide

Headings identify
1. Name of company
2. Name of statement
3. Date or time period

Joan Miller Advertising Agency, Inc.
Income Statement
For the Month Ended January 31, 19xx

Components are indented

Totals are aligned with items to which they apply

Revenues		
Advertising Fees Earned	$4,400	
Art Fees Earned	400	
Total Revenues		$4,800
Expenses		
Office Wages Expense	$1,380	
Utility Expense	100	
Telephone Expense	70	
Rent Expense	400	
Insurance Expense	40	
Art Supplies Expense	500	
Office Supplies Expense	200	
Depreciation Expense, Art Equipment	70	
Depreciation Expense, Office Equipment	50	
Income Taxes Expense	400	
Total Expenses		3,210
Net Income		**$1,590**

Joan Miller Advertising Agency, Inc.
Statement of Retained Earnings
For the Month Ended January 31, 19xx

Retained Earnings, January 1, 19xx	$ 0
Net Income	$1,590
Subtotal	$1,590
Less Dividends	1,400
Retained Earnings, January 31, 19xx	$ 190

Commonly Used Formats